P9-CLE-401

ENCYCLOPEDIA OF AMERICAN LIVES
CSS

The SCRIBNER ENCYCLOPEDIA *of*

AMERICAN LIVES

The SCRIBNER ENCYCLOPEDIA *of*

AMERICAN LIVES

SPORTS FIGURES

VOLUME TWO

L–Z

ARNOLD MARKOE
VOLUME EDITOR

KENNETH T. JACKSON
SERIES EDITOR IN CHIEF

CHARLES SCRIBNER'S SONS

GALE GROUP

THOMSON LEARNING

New York • Detroit • San Diego • San Francisco
Boston • New Haven, Conn. • Waterville, Maine
London • Munich

Charles Scribner's Sons
An imprint of The Gale Group
300 Park Avenue South, 9th floor
New York, NY 10010

Library of Congress Cataloging-in-Publication Data

The Scribner encyclopedia of American lives. Sports figures / edited by Arnold Markoe.
p. cm.
Includes bibliographical references and index.
ISBN 0-684-80665-7 (set : alk. paper)—ISBN 0-684-31224-7 (vol. 1)—ISBN 0-684-31225-5 (vol. 2)
1. Athletes—United States—Biography—Dictionaries. 2. Sports—United States—Encyclopedias. I. Markoe, Arnie.
GV697.A1 S.42 2002
796'.092'2—dc21 201049603
CIP

1 3 5 7 9 11 13 15 17 19 20 18 16 14 12 10 8 6 4 2
PRINTED IN THE UNITED STATES OF AMERICA

The paper in this publication meets the minimum requirements of the American National Standard for Information Services—Permanence of Paper for Printed Library Materials, ANSI Z39.48–1992.

CONTENTS

VOLUME 1

VOLUME 2

The SCRIBNER ENCYCLOPEDIA *of*
AMERICAN LIVES

L

LAJOIE, Nap(oleon) (*b.* 5 September 1874 in Woonsocket, Rhode Island; *d.* 7 February 1959 in Daytona Beach, Florida), baseball player and manager who, as a second baseman for the Cleveland Blues (since 1915, the Indians), established several American League batting records; he was the sixth player elected to the National Baseball Hall of Fame.

Lajoie was the youngest of eleven children born to Jean Baptiste Lajoie, a laborer, and Celina (Guertin) Lajoie, natives of Quebec. After briefly attending grammar school, Lajoie went to work at the age of ten as a sweeper in a textile mill in Woonsocket, Rhode Island; later, he drove horse-drawn delivery wagons and hacks. He also discovered sandlot baseball and began to play with semiprofessional teams in Rhode Island. His professional career was launched on 30 April 1896 when he joined the Fall River, Massachusetts, team in the New England League, playing various positions. Three months after joining—and with a batting average of over .400—his contract was purchased by the Philadelphia Phillies of the National League (NL).

Standing six feet, one inch tall and weighing a muscular 195 pounds, Lajoie batted and threw right-handed. In the five years he played with the Phillies he set a cumulative batting average of .345; he played both infield and outfield positions but was usually found at second base. In 1901 Byron Bancroft ("Ban") Johnson formed the rival American League (AL). Attracted by better pay than the NL offered, Lajoie signed on with the Philadelphia Athletics, managed by Connie Mack. In his debut year with the new team, the second baseman won the AL batting championship with an average of .422 based on 229 hits—setting a record for highest league batting average for a single season, a record that stood for the rest of the twentieth century. Because the number of hits was later incorrectly printed in the record books, Lajoie's average was reduced to .405, and Ty Cobb and George Sisler were jointly credited as league seasonal batting champions. The error was not discovered until 1954, upon which Lajoie's rightful title was restored.

In 1902, sued for going over to the Athletics, Lajoie was subjected to an injunction against playing baseball in Pennsylvania with any team other than the Phillies and was transferred to the new AL team in Cleveland. In 1903, his first full season there, he established a record of .355 and became so popular with Cleveland fans that, as the result of a newspaper contest, the team was renamed the Naps in his honor. In 1904 his batting average stood at .381. In the fall of 1906 Lajoie married Myrtle E. Smith; they had no children. Meanwhile, from 1905 to 1909 he served as Cleveland's player-manager. A bitter career disappointment occurred in 1908, when his team came within a half game of clinching the pennant. Two years later—after he had gratefully relinquished his managing duties—he was able to concentrate on what became a legendary competition with Cobb for the AL batting championship. The easygoing, affable Lajoie was a great favorite with fans and fellow players alike; Cobb, on the other hand, was despised.

Nap Lajoie, 1912. ASSOCIATED PRESS AP

In a game between Cleveland and the St. Louis Browns at the end of the 1910 season, the Browns allowed Lajoie several bunts in an effort to make sure he would win out over Cobb. AL president Ban Johnson refused to countenance this and awarded the championship to Cobb; the totals stand in the records as .385 for Cobb and .384 for Lajoie.

Over the next three years Lajoie continued to field as magnificently as ever and to hit powerfully, but in 1914 his batting average slumped to .258, and Cleveland finished the season in last place. In 1915 Lajoie was traded back to the Athletics but was released the next year. He ended his twenty-one-year career in the majors with a game at Shibe Park, Philadelphia, on 22 August 1916. Acting as player-manager of the Toronto Maple Leafs in 1917, he led them to the International League pennant and turned in a .380 batting average of his own—his first pennant victory. In 1918 he moved on to an American Association team in Indianapolis, but at midseason the league folded and he left baseball. "I guess I could have played a few more years," the forty-four-year-old veteran acknowledged. "But all of a sudden I got so sick of trains, of bats, of fences . . . that I quit." He had played in 2,479 major league games and accrued a lifetime batting average of .338. His total of 3,244 hits ranks him tenth among all-time power hitters, and he hit eighty-three career home runs (a figure that might have been even greater in the modern era of the "lively ball").

Lajoie went from the playing field into business as a rubber company salesman. Unlike many ballplayers, he had saved and invested his earnings wisely and was able to live comfortably after retirement. In 1943 he and his wife moved from Mentor-on-the-Lake, Ohio (near Cleveland), to Holly Hill, Florida, north of Daytona Beach. He died of pneumonia at the age of eighty-four in Halifax Hospital in Daytona Beach, and is buried in Cedar Hill Cemetery. He had always been close to his large family and was survived by many relatives.

Lajoie, one of the few top-ranking French-Canadian major league ballplayers, was the sixth player chosen to enter the National Baseball Hall of Fame. He was elected in the 1937 voting, two years before the museum's official opening. His bronze plaque in Cooperstown, New York, echoes the opinion of baseball fans and writers that Lajoie, with his long reach and lightning speed, was "the most graceful" fielder of all time. Modest and retiring, he was assured and decisive on the diamond and played with intensity and bravery despite many illnesses and injuries (including a severe spiking that kept him sidelined much of the 1905 season). His devotion to the game continued throughout his life. At his death he was honorary president of the Daytona Beach Little League baseball teams. According to an editorial in the *Cleveland Plain Dealer* two days after his death, "as much as anyone else in the early 1900s, Napoleon Lajoie was responsible for making this a big league city."

★

The National Baseball Library in Cooperstown, New York, maintains files on Lajoie's career. Background information on Lajoie's place in baseball history can be found in Franklin Lewis, *The Cleveland Indians* (1949), and Lee Allen, *The American League Story* (1962). A short sketch of his career is included in Bob Broeg, *Super Stars of Baseball* (1971). Statistics quoted above are taken from *The Official Baseball Encyclopedia: The Complete and Definitive Record of Major League Baseball,* 10th ed. (1996). J. M. Murphy, "Napoleon Lajoie: Modern Baseball's First Superstar," *The National Pastime: A Review of Baseball History* 7, no. 1 (spring 1988), provides a brief but full biography of Lajoie. An obituary is in the *New York Times* (8 Feb. 1959).

ELEANOR F. WEDGE

LALAS, Alexi (*b.* 1 June 1970 in Royal Oak, Michigan), professional soccer player who, as a defender, was voted the U.S. Player of the Year in 1995 and is the only American ever to play in an Italian soccer league.

Born as Panaytois Alexander Lalas to Demetrius Peter Lalas, a mechanical engineer and meteorologist, and Anne

Alexi Lalas. AP/WIDE WORLD PHOTOS

Woodworth, a poet and publisher, Lalas grew up in Birmingham, Michigan, with his younger brother. At the age of six, after his parents divorced, he moved with his father to Athens, Greece, and learned the sport of soccer. Four years later, he returned to Michigan to live with his mother and started playing soccer in school. In high school he played ice hockey as well as soccer, and in 1987 he captained both the Michigan state ice hockey team and the soccer team at Cranbrook Kingswood High School in Bloomfield Hills, Michigan. That same year he received the Michigan Soccer Player of the Year Award.

Upon his graduation from Cranbrook Kingswood in 1987, Lalas was accepted at Rutgers University in New Jersey with a full athletic scholarship for hockey, and initially planned to study agriculture. He arrived at Rutgers with his guitar and the ambition to try out for the soccer team. The soccer coach Bob Reasso accepted him for the team and Lalas soon transferred out of the agriculture department. Initially playing both hockey and soccer, in 1988 he was the leading scorer on the men's varsity ice hockey team, but gave up hockey in his second year to devote himself to soccer. His decision paid off when he was named to the Atlantic Ten All-Conference team in 1989. That same year at the Olympic Festival he captained the West squad to a gold-medal finish. He then went on to lead the Rutgers Scarlet Knights to final-four appearances in 1989 and 1990 at the National Collegiate Athletic Association (NCAA) tournament. In 1991, as a senior, he won both the Hermann Trophy as the country's best college soccer player and the Missouri Athletic Club Award as National Player of the Year. Lalas was also named the Atlantic Ten Conference Eastern Division Player of the Year.

Lalas's style of play was described as fierce, bone crunching, and no-holds-barred. In 1991 he dropped out of college to join the Olympic team, and was a member of the gold-medal-winning U.S. team at the Pan America games in Cuba, but broke his left foot before the games began. Following his recovery, he caught the attention of the U.S. national soccer team coach Bora Milutinovic, who asked him to join the team on one condition—that he cut his hair. Lalas later told the *Detroit Free Press,* "For me to cut my hair was a big deal. I was really mad, but I wanted to play so badly. I would have run through L.A. naked if that's what it took." As part of the U.S. Olympic team in 1992 he scored three goals, and in the 1994 World Cup he scored one of the two goals that defeated England 2–0. In 1995 he received the U.S. Soccer Athlete of the Year Award. He was then chosen as one of three wild-card players to represent the United States in the 1996 Atlanta Olympics. In the same year he was named to the All-Copa America Team and scored a goal in the 3–0 win over Argentina.

Lalas is the only American to have played in a professional Italian league team, Serie A, after signing with Padova (Padua) at the end of 1994. He became known there, because of his wild appearance and natural flamboyance, as "Buffalo Bill" and learned to speak fluent Italian. He returned to the United States in 1996 and, with the start-up of Major League Soccer (MLS), joined the New England Revolutions and became a U.S. professional. He played the 1996 and 1997 seasons and was selected to the Eastern Conference All-Star team. In one day he played two games: seventy-eight minutes in the U.S. national team World Cup qualifying tie (2–2) against Mexico, followed by a three-minute cameo appearance in the 2–1 Revolutions win over Tampa Bay.

Although he made appearances for the national team in 1998, including starting six of the first nine U.S. games, he was traded to the New York/New Jersey Metro Stars. With this team, he scored game-winning goals in consecutive matches against Chicago and San Jose. The following year he moved to the Kansas City Wizards. He finished the 1999 season having scored four goals and one assist, making him the seventh-best scorer on the team. The Wizards were named the *Soccer America* team of the week four times in the season, and Lalas was elected by the team's fans as a starter for the 1999 All-Star game. He became the only MLS player to be a member of the winning team every year. He scored his MLS personal-high third goal with a chip shot in the thirty-ninth minute versus Tampa Bay and a diving header goal in the eighty-sixth minute versus Dallas. These goals gave him a career high in points in an MLS season.

As Lalas's professional career developed he gained a controversial reputation as a player who was better known for his looks than for his skill at the game. He was six feet, three inches tall, which made him powerful in the air, and 195 pounds with long-flowing, hippie-length red hair and a billy goat beard. He became known as the Big Red One. Lalas's instant recognizability as a soccer player propelled his career, which he acknowledged in 1997 by saying, "There are many, many soccer players who have more pure soccer skill in their pinky toes than I have in my entire body."

Capitalizing first on his visibility and second on his talent, Lalas was astute in parlaying himself to celebrity as a successful, driven player. Inevitably this celebrity gained him endorsements, from companies such as 7-Eleven, Dunkin' Donuts, Adidas, All Sport, Gargoyles, and British Petroleum, and he rose to the top of the MLS salary scale. Lalas appeared on popular late-night television talk shows and on MTV, and presented the "All-Hair Team" trophy at an MLS awards dinner. A high-income sports star, he also made considerable advisory contributions to the development of soccer in the United States and was a member of the advisory board of the Abdul Conteh Children's Fund (ACCF), which provides humanitarian relief to Sierra Leone.

While pursuing his soccer career, Lalas also promoted his classic rock music interests as an acoustic guitar player and a singer with the Gypsies, who released the compact discs *Woodland* and *Jet Lag* on the Alexi Lalas label. He went solo in 1998, releasing *Ginger* through the BMG/Sanctuary Records Group. Over Memorial Day weekend in 1999 Lalas made appearances in three rock concerts with his band Nectar Drop and sang the national anthem at a Kansas City Royals baseball game.

On 10 October 1999 Lalas announced his retirement from professional soccer following the final Wizards game for the year, planning to devote his time to performing with Nectar Drop and working as a sports commentator. He began this new career with the ABC television coverage of the MLS Cup. He also was the voice of the U.S. women's national team Toys 'R' Us Victory Tour game on CBS following their 1999 World Cup victory. Lalas handled NBC's coverage of the 2000 Olympic soccer games, increased his broadcasting scope with Fox Sports by covering the 2000 MLS season of the San Jose Earthquakes, and helped to launch ESPN2's weekly soccer highlights show *MLS Extra Time.* On 7 April 2001 Lalas returned to soccer, playing as a defender for the Los Angeles Galaxy. He had short hair and was clean shaven.

Lalas began playing during the emerging period of American professional soccer. With charisma and a forceful style of play, he attracted press coverage and brought widespread visibility to the game.

★

The soccer press coverage of Lalas's career has been immense, including articles in the *New Brunswick Underground Magazine* (winter 1998), *Sporting News* (15 May 1999), and *Soccer America* (30 June 2001). A player profile appears at http://www.samsarmy.com/men/players/lalas.html.

ROBERT POLLOCK

LAMBEAU, Earl Louis ("Curly") (*b.* 9 April 1898 in Green Bay, Wisconsin; *d.* 1 June 1965 in Sturgeon Bay, Wisconsin), founder and quarterback of the Green Bay Packers and Pro Football Hall of Famer who pioneered the passing offense during the earliest years of the National Football League (NFL).

Lambeau was one of two children of Belgian immigrants Marcel Lambeau, a successful building contractor, and Mary Lambeau. Nicknamed "Curly" because of his curly hair, Lambeau developed a natural flair for assuming command of situations from his youth. He attended Green Bay's East High School, where in his fervor for the gridiron he honed his natural athletic talents and developed a passing game that was singularly impressive for those times.

After graduating from high school in 1917, Lambeau

Curly Lambeau. AP/Wide World Photos

attended the University of Wisconsin, where his main interest lay in playing college football. Thus it was with little regret that he scrapped his college plans when the school suspended its football program at the onset of World War I. He returned to academia on a full football scholarship at the University of Notre Dame in the fall of 1918, playing for the famed coach Knute Rockne. Although Lambeau was still a freshman, he earned one of only thirteen athletic letters awarded by the school that year for football.

In August 1919 Lambeau married Marguerite Van Kessel; the couple later had one child. Also that year he abandoned his scholarship and his education after a single season of play at Notre Dame in order to accept a $250-per-month position with the Indian Packing Company in his hometown of Green Bay. This decision to work for the packing company set the stage for Lambeau to found a football team that evolved into the Green Bay Packers.

In the autumn of 1919, Lambeau approached his boss Frank Peck with a suggestion that the packing company sponsor an employee football team that might be dubbed the Packers. When Peck agreed to provide $500 for uniforms and other expenses, Lambeau picked up the proverbial ball and hit the ground running. One particularly brutal game, dominated by a primitive running offense against the team from Ishpeming, Michigan, left three of the Packers with broken bones and led the enterprising coach-quarterback to devise his trademark passing game—the rushing game produced too many injuries. On the strength of this passing game during a time when rushing was the general rule, Lambeau captained, coached, and quarterbacked the Packers through ten straight wins that year, garnering support from the local citizenry and earning $16.75 for each player during the first season of operation. Though a very small amount—the first professional football player earned $500 for one game—that the players pocketed any money at all was surprising. The fledgling Packers were unable to charge admission to their home games because their stadium was not enclosed by a fence, and funding was limited as a result.

In 1921 Lambeau brought the Packers into the American Professional Football Association (APFA)—the immediate precursor to the NFL. Although the Packers finished in a respectable fourth place, the NFL (the name APFA changed to NFL during the 1921 season) dropped the Green Bay franchise after the season when it was discovered that Lambeau committed an infringement of the rules by hiring amateur college players using aliases. After winning reinstatement in 1922, Lambeau's Packers strung together consecutive winning seasons through 1928. With the recruitment of future Hall of Famers Mike Michalske, Cal Hubbard, and Johnny Blood as new team members in 1929, Lambeau steered the Packers through three championship seasons from 1929 through 1931. After hiring Hall of Fame receiver Don Hutson in 1935, Lambeau led the Packers to additional championships in 1936, 1939, and 1944.

In the midst of the Packers championship years, Lambeau retired from active play in 1930. He remained with the Packers as head coach until 1950, when an ongoing series of management disputes led to his discharge. When Lambeau left the Packers after thirty-one years, he had a record of twenty-eight winning seasons. He spent the 1951 and 1952 seasons as head coach of the Chicago Cardinals and coached the Washington Redskins through a single season in 1953, posting his resignation during the preseason of 1954. After resigning from the Redskins, he retired to a ranch in California, which he had purchased during his years with Green Bay. In 1963 he was named among the seventeen charter members of the Pro Football Hall of Fame in Canton, Ohio. Lambeau's career accomplishments included 229 victories, 212 with Green Bay.

Lambeau had less success in marriage than he did in football. He and Marguerite divorced in 1934; he was married to his second wife, Sue, from 1935 until their divorce in 1940. Lambeau married Grace Nichols on 16 July 1945; they divorced in 1955. Lambeau was with a girlfriend, Mary Jane Sorgel, when he died after suffering a heart attack while mowing the lawn.

Lambeau held a reputation as a rigorous disciplinarian and was known as the "Bellicose Belgian," a reference to his parents' country of origin. He anticipated a level of intensity from his players that was rarely achieved by competing teams. Under Lambeau's coaching standard, Packers players received stiff fines for missing daily practice and for insubordination. Although his aggressive tactics backfired on occasion, he was a knowledgeable coach, having played halfback and fullback with the Fighting Irish under Knute Rockne. Lambeau prudently drew from lessons learned from Rockne, adopting innovative attack formations and leading the Packers to six league championships. Likewise, Lambeau tempered his trademark pass offense with equally effective power plays, an approach that brought to bear the solid strategy of his coaching style. He was one of the earliest coaches to review game film with his players as a method of improving play, and he was perhaps the first coach to observe a game from the vantage of the press box in order to obtain a better perspective of the field.

★

A biography of Lambeau is in George Sullivan, *Pro Football's All-Time Greats: The Immortals in Pro Football's Hall of Fame* (1968). Arthur Daley, *Pro Football's Hall of Fame: The Official Book*, (1963), includes individual articles on the seventeen charter members of the Pro Football Hall of Fame. Further biographical information is in Jeff Savage, *Top 10 Professional Football Coaches* (1998). An obituary is in the *New York Times* (2 Jun. 1965).

GLORIA COOKSEY

LAMBERT, John Harold ("Jack") (*b.* 8 July 1952 in Mantua, Ohio), outstanding linebacker for the Pittsburgh Steelers during their reign as perennial National Football League champions during the 1970s.

Born in Mantua, Ohio, Lambert attended Crestwood High School in that city, where he was a star quarterback on the football team. He also excelled in basketball and baseball. When Lambert, at six feet, four inches tall and 220 pounds, matriculated at Kent State University in 1970, he was made a defensive end. The next year he switched to middle linebacker. In his third year he was named Player of the Year by the Mid-America Conference, a rare honor for a defensive star. He repeated as an All-Conference player in his final season, when he was tri-captain of the squad. Lambert was also voted Most Valuable Player in the Tangerine Bowl in 1972. He graduated from Kent State in 1974.

Picked by the Pittsburgh Steelers in the second round of the 1974 National Football League (NFL) draft, Lambert performed outstandingly at the team's training camp that summer, drawing attention on a team that was loaded with experienced linebackers. When he reported to training camp, defensive line coach George Perles reportedly said, "We've got a rookie who's so mean he doesn't even like himself."

Jack Lambert, 1975. AP/WIDE WORLD PHOTOS

Because a number of veterans, including middle linebacker Henry Davis, reported to camp late, Lambert got extra work. In August, Davis suffered a concussion, and a later neck injury put him out for the season, opening the middle linebacker position to Lambert. Facing Pittsburgh's two outstanding veteran linebackers, Jack Ham and Andy Russell, many of the Steelers' opponents hoped to find a weakness with a rookie in the center; this forced Lambert to develop quickly.

Lambert played in all fourteen games of his first season for a Pittsburgh team that was built around defense. In his first playoff game the Steelers broke the game open in the second quarter. The defense gave up only two touchdowns in beating the Buffalo Bills, 32–14. In the conference title game the defense improved by holding the Oakland Raiders to a single touchdown in the Steelers' 24–13 victory. The team continued to show its talent in a defensive struggle against the Minnesota Vikings, whom they downed, 16–6, in Super Bowl IX. Lambert was the only rookie on that Steelers squad. He was named NFL Defensive Rookie of the Year.

In his second season, 1975–1976, Lambert continued to improve. Recognition came when he was voted to the Pro Bowl (the first of his nine straight selections, a record for linebackers). In the playoffs that year Pittsburgh hosted the Raiders on their ice-covered home field. Both defenses stood out as the Steelers gave up a single touchdown in a winning 16–10 effort.

The American Conference championship game that season may be the best Lambert ever played. He recovered three fumbles (a record for a linebacker) as the defensive-minded Steelers gave up just one touchdown in downing Baltimore, 28–10.

In Super Bowl X, Lambert rose to the heights as an inspirational leader. The Steelers trailed the Dallas Cowboys in the final quarter when Steelers' kicker Roy Gerela, who had cracked some ribs making a tackle on the opening kickoff, pulled a field goal wide for the second time. Dallas safety Cliff Harris taunted Gerela and hit him on the side of the helmet. Lambert, irritated, knocked Harris to the ground, and the aroused Steelers went on to score two fourth-quarter touchdowns to pull off a 21–17 victory for their second consecutive league championship.

The next season, after beating the Baltimore Colts 40–14 with a record-setting offensive performance, in 1976 the Steelers fell to their archrival, the Raiders, in the conference title game, 24–7. However, Lambert himself had such an outstanding season that he was named Defensive Player of the Year by the league. The year 1977 was a down year for both Lambert and the Steelers. Lambert missed three games, the first of his career, with a knee injury; Pittsburgh dropped its first playoff game to the Denver Broncos, 34–21.

The team rebounded in 1978 as they recovered their defensive form. In the playoffs they held Denver to a single touchdown (winning 33–6) and gave the Houston Oilers only a field goal and a safety (the final score was 34–5). In Super Bowl XIII they edged out Dallas, 35–31. In 1979 Lambert again earned honors as the league's outstanding defensive player. The Steelers stormed past the Miami Dolphins, 34–14, and Houston, 27–13. In Super Bowl XIV, Pittsburgh was clinging to a slim 24–19 lead in the fourth quarter against the Los Angeles Rams. As Los Angeles drove deep into Steelers' territory, Lambert intercepted a pass at the Steelers' fourteen-yard line. Pittsburgh went on to win their fourth Super Bowl, 31–19.

Because of the manner in which statistics were kept in the 1970s, it is difficult to compare offensive linemen and defensive players in general with players of later eras. Outstanding individual plays such as tackles, sacks, knockdowns, hurries, and passes batted down or deflected were all statistics of the future. However, Lambert's impact is evident by his nine-time selection to the Pro Bowl and his selection by the league as outstanding defensive player in both 1976 and 1979. In 1981 the Steelers chose him as their Most Valuable Player.

In 1984 Lambert injured a toe, then tried to return to action too quickly, which aggravated the injury. The problem was compounded by playing on the artificial surface of Pittsburgh's home field in Three Rivers Stadium. Lambert missed half of the regular season games that year and retired at the end of the season.

Lambert played his entire eleven seasons (including that shortened by the player strike in 1982) with the Pittsburgh Steelers. He earned the right to wear the victors' ring from four Super Bowls. In all, he played in 146 regular-season games. In that time he intercepted twenty-eight passes, returning them for over 240 yards. In each of two seasons, 1979 and 1981, he had six interceptions for the year.

Lambert, who has not married, always loved the outdoors. Following his retirement he moved to an eighty-five-acre farm in rural Armstrong County, Pennsylvania, to enjoy hunting and fishing.

Perhaps because of Perles's remark in his rookie season, Lambert gained a reputation as a player with an overly aggressive nature and a chip on his shoulder. The media played this up at every opportunity. When the league instituted new rules to protect quarterbacks, Lambert was quoted as saying that "they should wear skirts." Yet both teammates and opponents were aware that he was not a cheap-shot artist, and he was quick to speak out against those who played outside the rules of sportsmanship.

★

The archives of the Pro Football Hall of Fame in Canton, Ohio, have plenty of information about Lambert. Other useful sources include David L. Porter, ed., *Biographical Dictionary of American Sport: Football* (1987), and Bob Carroll et al., *Total Football: The Official Encyclopedia of the National Football League* (1997). Also see R. F. Jones, "Living Legend Called Mean Smilin' Jack," *Sports Illustrated* (12 July 1976).

ART BARBEAU

LAMOTTA, Jake (*b.* 10 July 1921 in New York City), middleweight boxing champion from 1949 to 1951, portrayed by Robert DeNiro in the 1980 film *Raging Bull,* who is best known for his six bouts with Sugar Ray Robinson.

The eldest of five children of the Italian immigrant Giuseppe LaMotta, an impoverished peddler, and his Italian-American wife, Elizabeth, Giacobe LaMotta was born on New York's Lower East Side but spent most of his troubled childhood on the mean streets of the Bronx, New York. As a young boy, LaMotta once came home crying after having been beaten up by some bullies. His father, a violent man who often abused his wife and children, slapped LaMotta across the face and thrust an ice pick into his hand, admonishing him to learn to defend himself with the advice, "Hit 'em first, and hit 'em hard." It was, LaMotta later said, the only good thing he ever got from his father. Soon an accomplished street fighter, LaMotta quit high school

Jake LaMotta. AP/WIDE WORLD PHOTOS

and drifted into delinquency. At the age of fifteen, he was convicted of attempted burglary and sentenced to three years at the state reform school at Coxsackie, New York, where he began boxing.

Upon his release he trained at the Teasdale Athletic Club in the Bronx and launched a successful amateur career, winning the light-heavyweight championship in the 1940 New York State Diamond Belt competition. LaMotta made his professional debut at age nineteen in 1941, winning seventeen and losing three. In 1942 LaMotta won eleven of fourteen bouts, one loss being to the incomparable Sugar Ray Robinson, who would become LaMotta's arch rival. "I fought Sugar Ray so many times," LaMotta later quipped, "it's a wonder I don't have diabetes." On 5 February 1943, in Detroit, a more confident LaMotta fought in typical bullying style, sending Robinson sprawling through the ropes in the eighth round. He won a unanimous decision and handed Robinson his first defeat in forty-one professional fights. In a third dustup, LaMotta again dropped Robinson but lost a close decision.

Nicknamed the "Bronx Bull" for his headlong charges, the stocky LaMotta fought out of a low crouch, constantly bending and weaving as he bulled his way forward while unleashing barrages of punches. In 1943–1944 he fought the former welterweight champion Fritzie Zivic in four sensational battles, of which he won three. In 1945 he resumed his rivalry with Robinson, losing two hotly contested decisions. LaMotta, however, remained a brooding loner plagued by personal and professional problems. Distrustful of everyone, he fired his manager, Mike Cipriano, and assumed control of his career. He also divorced his first wife, Ida, with whom he had one child, and on 9 November 1946 married Vikki, whom he often beat during fits of jealous rage. Although he was rated the top middleweight contender by 1947, LaMotta was denied a shot at the championship because he refused to cooperate with the mobsters who controlled boxing. Out of desperation, he agreed to throw a fight in exchange for a title bout. On 14 November 1947 he took a dive against Billy Fox in New York City. Barely defending himself and refusing to go down despite a dreadful beating, LaMotta suffered a technical knockout in the fourth round as the crowd jeered. He was fined $1,000 by the New York State Boxing Commission and suspended for seven months. As a result of this incident, LaMotta was to become one of boxing's most unpopular champions. The sportswriter Jimmy Cannon reflected popular opinion in calling him "the most detested man in sports."

LaMotta received his title shot against the Frenchman Marcel Cerdan on 16 June 1949 in Detroit's Briggs Stadium. In the first round Cerdan fell into a clinch, and as the fighters tussled, he was thrown to the canvas, injuring his right shoulder. LaMotta won the middleweight championship when Cerdan was unable to answer the bell for the tenth round. A rematch was precluded by Cerdan's death in a plane crash. Instead, in 1950 LaMotta successfully defended his title on 12 July against the Italian Tiberio Mitri and on 13 September against another tough Frenchman, Laurent Dauthuille, who had decisioned LaMotta the previous year. In the rematch, LaMotta absorbed a brutal beating and was behind on points, playing possum along the ropes, when he unleashed a crippling left hook that knocked out Dauthuille with only thirteen seconds remaining in the fight. LaMotta's final defense was against his old nemesis, Sugar Ray Robinson, in Chicago Stadium on 14 February 1951, a bout known as the "Saint Valentine's Day Massacre."

The fight followed the pattern of their earlier encounters, with LaMotta forcing the fight, tramping forward and flailing from a low crouch while Robinson, eluding the most punishing blows, landed explosive jabs and counterpunches. The fight was even after ten rounds, but in the eleventh a tiring LaMotta took his last best shot. Springing off the ropes, he cornered Robinson and unleashed a blistering two-fisted attack. Robinson outlasted the barrage and took control of the fight, punishing a defenseless LaMotta with savage combinations. Bloodied and battered in the thirteenth, the defiant LaMotta wrapped his arms around the top ropes to ensure he would not go down and endured a terrible beating before the referee mercifully stopped the slaughter. LaMotta continued fighting but rapidly declined. As a newspaper headline exclaimed, "LaMotta NoGotta!" In 1952 Danny Nardico became the first man to topple LaMotta to the canvas; two years later LaMotta hung up his gloves after losing to unheralded Billy Kilgore.

LaMotta moved with his wife and their three children to Miami Beach, Florida, where he opened a saloon, "Jake LaMotta's." There his life spun out of control as he succumbed to boozing and philandering, prompting Vikki to file for divorce in 1956. In March 1957 LaMotta was convicted of aiding and abetting prostitution when a fifteen-year-old girl was found soliciting in his bar. He was fined $500 and sentenced to six months in the Dade County Stockade. Following his release he married the model Sally Carlton, with whom he had two children before the marriage ended in divorce, as would LaMotta's three subsequent marriages. Returning to New York City in 1958, LaMotta worked haphazardly as an actor and launched a marginally successful career as a stand-up comic, lampooning the boxing racket and his marital woes. Soon broke and drinking heavily again, LaMotta worked as a trash collector in Central Park and a bouncer at Robbie's Mardi Gras, a topless go-go bar on Broadway. LaMotta's autobiography, *Raging Bull,* was published in 1970 and later turned into the critically acclaimed film of the same name starring Robert DeNiro as the loutish anti-hero. The film's success rekindled LaMotta's celebrity. He remains in demand as an after-dinner speaker, continues to perform his stand-up routine, and frequently attends sports and boxing memorabilia shows, signing autographs for a fee.

LaMotta was one of the most controversial champions in boxing history. Roundly despised for throwing the Fox fight, he was nevertheless a colorful fighter who drew large crowds because his nonstop swarming style made for action-packed bouts. Had not the popularity of the film *Raging Bull* rescued him from obscurity, he might be best remembered for that infamous fight and for his rivalry with Sugar Ray Robinson, arguably the best boxer in history. Instead, the film creates a disturbing yet compelling portrait of LaMotta as a deeply troubled loner who sought relief from his own feelings of worthlessness through punishment absorbed in the ring. As LaMotta told the writer Peter Heller, "I fought like I didn't deserve to live." LaMotta's official record stands at 106 bouts, 83 wins, 19 losses, and 4 draws with 30 knockouts. He was inducted into the World Boxing Hall of Fame in 1986 and into the International Boxing Hall of Fame in 1990.

★

LaMotta's autobiography *Raging Bull: My Story* (1970), written with Joseph Carter and Peter Savage, covers his life up to his release from jail and contains vivid descriptions of his major bouts, including his final fight with Sugar Ray Robinson. *Raging Bull II* (1986), by Chris Anderson and Sharon McGehee with LaMotta, continues LaMotta's story through the mid-1980s. Peter Heller, *"In This Corner . . . !": Forty-two World Champions Tell Their Stories* (1994), contains an informative profile. See also the film *Raging Bull* (1980), directed by Martin Scorsese.

MICHAEL MCLEAN

LANDIS, Kenesaw Mountain (*b.* 20 November 1866 in Millville, Ohio; *d.* 25 November 1944 in Chicago, Illinois), lawyer, federal judge, and first and most powerful Commissioner of Baseball who is credited with earning the public's respect for the integrity of professional baseball.

Landis was one of seven children of Abraham Landis and Mary Kumler Landis, a homemaker. Abraham Landis, a physician who had been a Union soldier during the Civil War, had a leg injured during a battle at Kennesaw (with two *n*'s) Mountain in Georgia on 27 June 1864. When his son was born, he named him after the place of the battle, misspelling Kenesaw with one *n*. Young Landis was a roustabout, a high school dropout whose ambition to work the railroads ended when Vandalia and Southern Railroad rejected his application to become a brakeman. He then

Kenesaw Mountain Landis *(right)* with Joe DiMaggio and Yankee owner Jacob Ruppert, 1937. ASSOCIATED PRESS AP

became a bicycle racer at fairs, earning some fame in the Midwest. For a time he seemed to have found his calling as a journalist, working for the Logansport *Journal* in Indiana from 1889–1891.

While working as a reporter, Landis became interested in the legal proceedings he covered, and he enrolled in the Young Men's Christian Association (YMCA) Law School of Cincinnati. He transferred to the Union Law School (later the law school of Northwestern University) in Chicago, graduating in 1891. After practicing law in Chicago for a few years he joined President Grover Cleveland's administration as secretary to the Secretary of State. Landis married Winifred Reed on 25 July 1896. The couple had two children.

Landis's work was highly esteemed, and in 1905 President Theodore Roosevelt appointed him a U.S. District Court Judge for the district of northern Illinois. He became well known for his antitrust rulings, especially those enforcing the Sherman Antitrust Act, but his rulings were often overturned by higher courts. Landis came to the attention of Major League Baseball team owners in 1915, when he presided over the lawsuit filed against the National League (NL) and the American League (AL) by the Federal League (FL), which was trying to establish itself as a major league and had raided major league ballplayers. NL and AL teams had been forced to increase the salaries of their ballplayers in order to keep them from jumping to the Federal League; thus the owners were unhappy and anxious about the FL's potential for success. The Federal League sued to have the major leagues declared a monopoly that violated the Sherman Antitrust Act, and trustbuster Landis was probably the last judge the major league owners wanted to have preside over the case. However, Landis confused everybody by delaying the case, insisting that the leagues negotiate. "Both sides must understand that any blows at this thing called baseball would be regarded by this court as a blow to a national institution," he said. The Federal League caved in, settled out of court, then folded. Landis was seen as the savior of "Organized Baseball," that is the major and minor professional leagues, for having prevented their breakup as monopolies.

In 1917 Landis garnered more national attention when he presided over several treason cases. America was fighting in World War I, and those who hindered the war effort were charged with sedition. In one case Landis sentenced labor leader William D. Haywood to twenty years in prison, only to have the U.S. Supreme Court overturn his ruling. Later he sentenced seven socialist antiwar activists, including Congressman Victor Berger, to prison for trying to harm the war effort. He jailed more than ninety people for impeding America's war mobilization. Even in cases in which Landis's rulings were overturned, most of the public thought he was morally right.

During the World Series of 1919 between the Cincinnati Reds of the NL and the Chicago White Sox of the AL, eight players for the White Sox conspired with gangsters to rig games. The White Sox lost the series to a Reds club that was good but not their equal. There were hints from the start of the series that something criminal was going on, and all through 1920 news reporters were finding evidence of a fix. By the final month of the season the evidence was overwhelming, and the owner of the White Sox suspended the offending players. Shaken by the sudden loss of public faith in professional baseball that resulted from the bribes, team owners tried to find a way to restore confidence in their game. The three-man board of governors that oversaw league operations had become ineffective. A new leader was wanted, and out of several possibilities arose the name of Kenesaw Mountain Landis, savior of the major leagues in 1915. Landis insisted that he be given sole and absolute authority over organized baseball and that no team owner be allowed to publicly criticize any of his decisions. His terms were agreed to on 12 November 1920 and formally ratified on 12 January 1921.

The White Sox conspirators were tried for taking bribes and found not guilty. A fire had been deliberately set in the prosecution's evidence room, destroying all the evidence against the White Sox, including confessions from three conspirators. The fire was almost certainly set by cronies of one of the gangsters who had bribed them. After the acquittal the players celebrated with the jurors, raising suspicions about the jurors' impartiality. Despite the acquittal, there was and is ample reason to believe the players were guilty, including public confessions by conspirators such as pitcher Eddie Cicotte. Landis banned all the conspirators from baseball for life, including Hall of Fame possibilities Cicotte and Joe Jackson. On 4 August 1921, two days after the trial, Landis declared, "Regardless of the verdict of juries, no player who throws a ball game, no player that undertakes or promises to throw a ball game, no player that sits in conference with a bunch of crooked players and gamblers where the ways and means of throwing a game are discussed and does not promptly tell his club about it, will ever play professional baseball." The standards Landis outlined in his statement in August 1921 have been gospel for the commissioners who succeeded him.

The decision to ban the players was Landis's most controversial decision, but he had other severe problems with which to contend. He found that Major League Baseball was rife with bribery, cheating, and thrown games, and in a few years he banned fifteen ballplayers and suspended more than fifty, including the game's greatest star, Babe Ruth. Ruth and teammates Bob Meusel and Bill Piercy were suspended on 16 October 1921 until 20 May 1922 for playing exhibition games against Negro League teams

(Landis wanted to avoid the embarrassment of major leaguers losing to African Americans).

During the 1920s and 1930s Landis became a popular folk figure, a symbol of rectitude and a comfort to those who wanted baseball to be more than a business. He said: "Baseball is something more than a game to an American boy. It is his training field for life work. Destroy his faith in its squareness and honesty and you have destroyed something more; you have planted suspicion of all things in his heart." Landis gained a reputation for looking out for the well-being of players, often declaring minor leaguers to be free agents because their teams were unfairly keeping them buried in farm clubs. In 1938 he freed more than ninety Cardinals minor leaguers from their contracts, including Pete Reiser, who signed with the Brooklyn Dodgers for a big bonus and would become the National League's batting champion in 1941. In 1940 Landis did the same for Detroit Tigers farmhands. He always opposed major league teams' having farm systems, asserting that independent minor league teams would be driven out of business and that major league–quality players were unfairly denied a chance to play in the majors.

Although Landis did much good by restoring public confidence in professional baseball and should be forgiven for grandstanding and enjoying being commissioner of baseball, he had a dark side. He was often arbitrary, and his decisions did not always make sense. Worse, he was racist. In 1942 he said to a reporter for the New York *Daily Worker*, "There is no rule, formal or informal, against the hiring of Negro players." In 1943 he declared to Paul Robeson at the annual meeting of Major League team owners, "There is no rule, formal or informal, or any understanding—unwritten, subterranean or sub-anything—against the hiring of Negro players by the teams of organized baseball. Negroes are not barred from organized baseball—never have been in the twenty-one years I have served." In both instances, he lied. In private, he had vowed from the start that African Americans would not be allowed to play in the major leagues while he was in charge.

Efforts by New York Giants manager John McGraw to play African Americans were squelched. In 1935, when Clark Griffith tried to sign Satchel Paige and Josh Gibson to his Washington Senators, he was threatened with financial ruin by other club owners, a majority of whom had throughout Landis's service opposed allowing African Americans into their leagues. In 1940 eccentric baseball man Bill Veeck led a group of investors that tried to buy the Philadelphia Phillies; when word got out that he would include African Americans on his club, Veeck's offer was discarded in favor of a lesser one from William D. Cox (whom Landis later banned from baseball for gambling). Veeck blamed Landis's prejudice against African Americans for his group's failure to buy the Phillies.

Landis's term as commissioner had been extended to 1953, but he died of a coronary thrombosis in 1944. He is buried in Oakwoods Cemetery in Chicago. Landis had always been a fervent supporter of the National Baseball Hall of Fame, and in 1944 he was voted in by the Hall's veterans committee.

★

For many years *Judge Landis and Twenty-Five Years of Baseball* (1947), by *Sporting News* reporter J. G. Taylor Spink was the best account of Landis's life, although it had errors and obscured some of the darker side of his character. A better account is David Pietrusza, *Judge and Jury: The Life and Times of Judge Kenesaw Mountain Landis* (1998), which is rich in baseball history and its depiction of Landis. Leonard Koppett, *The New Thinking Fan's Guide to Baseball* (1991), offers an historical perspective on Landis's contributions to baseball. Jerome Holtzman, *The Commissioners: Baseball's Midlife Crisis* (1998), places Landis in the context of the lives of the other commissioners, showing how Landis's often arbitrary conduct actually weakened the powers of his successors. An obituary is in the *New York Times* (26 Nov. 1944).

KIRK H. BEETZ

LANDRY, Thomas Wade ("Tom") (*b.* 11 September 1924 in Mission, Texas; *d.* 12 February 2000 in Dallas, Texas), Hall of Fame coach who guided the National Football League (NFL) Dallas Cowboys to five Super Bowls and two championships, winning 270 games in 29 years.

Landry was one of two children born to Ray Landry, an auto mechanic and volunteer fire chief, and Ruth Coffman, a homemaker. As a child, Landry overcame both a speech impediment and a near-fatal car accident, and was a high achiever in both scholastics and sports. Landry was class president and a member of the National Honor Society at Mission High School and played several positions on the football team, which went undefeated and unscored upon during his senior year of 1941. He entered the University of Texas at Austin in 1942, shortly before his older brother Robert was killed during World War II. Interrupting his studies, Landry enlisted in the U.S. Army, and flew thirty missions over Europe in three years, including one in which his plane ran out of fuel and crash-landed, fortunately without injuring Landry.

Following Landry's discharge in 1945 at the rank of first lieutenant, he returned to the University of Texas. In 1947 he was introduced to freshman Alicia Wiggs, a model whose picture had appeared in *Seventeen* magazine. As a junior at Texas, Landry was a star defensive back for the Longhorns when they beat the University of Alabama in the 1948 Sugar Bowl. That same year he made the all-Southwestern Conference second team. A Longhorn co-

Tom Landry, 1980. © BETTMANN/CORBIS

captain his senior year of 1948, Landry led Texas past the University of Georgia in the Orange Bowl in January 1949 by a score of 41–28, rushing for 117 yards while substituting at fullback in addition to his defensive duties. At the height of this triumph, he married Wiggs on 28 January 1949; they later had three children. Landry graduated with a Bachelor's degree in business in the spring of 1949, and joined professional football by signing with the New York Yankees of the All-America Conference.

When that league folded a year later, Landry joined the NFL's New York Giants, where he would become an All-Pro defensive back in 1954, and a player-coach. He retired as a player after the 1955 season to devote all his time to coaching the Giants defense from 1956 to 1959 under coach Jim Lee Howell. Landry introduced the 4–3 defensive alignment to football—featuring four linemen, three linebackers, and four defensive backs. He also began wearing his infamous fedora during games at this time to cover his balding head. In 1956 the New York Giants won the NFL championship, beating the Chicago Bears. The Giants again advanced to league title games in 1958 and 1959, losing each time to the Baltimore Colts. Landry committed himself to Christianity in 1958, and between seasons lived in Dallas, Texas, with his wife and three children.

Although Landry had never planned on a career coaching football, his work with the Giants was impressive enough that he had a choice of where to coach for the 1960 season. Although he could have been promoted to head coach for the New York Giants, or with the American Football League (AFL) Houston Oilers, Landry signed a five-year contract on 27 December 1959 to become the first head coach of the Dallas Cowboys, an NFL expansion team. "I decided to give it a shot for a while and just see how things worked out," Landry once said. It would "work out" for twenty-nine years. Winless in 1960, and just 13–38–3 after four seasons, Landry was nonetheless given a ten-year contract extension by Cowboys owner Clint Murchison, Jr. on 5 February 1964. He went on to post twenty consecutive winning seasons from 1966 to 1985, including eighteen playoff appearances, and thirteen division titles. Dallas reached its first Super Bowl following the 1970 season, but suffered a 16–13 loss to the Baltimore Colts on 17 January 1971 in Super Bowl V.

Combined with earlier post-season losses to the Cleveland Browns and Vince Lombardi's Green Bay Packers, the Cowboys had by then developed a reputation as a team unable to win big games, but that changed after Landry made Roger Staubach his number one quarterback midway through the 1971 season. With help from the "Doomsday" defense, the Staubach-piloted Cowboys defeated the Miami Dolphins in Super Bowl VI on 16 January 1972, by a score of 24–3. "Everyone felt a great sense of relief along with the satisfaction," noted Landry of the win. Although he rarely showed outward emotion, that day he wore a big smile.

Landry led the Cowboys to three more Super Bowls in the 1970s, losing twice to the Pittsburgh Steelers, but beating the Denver Broncos in Super Bowl XII on 15 January 1978 by a score of 27–10. The Cowboys became so popular nationwide they were dubbed "America's Team." However, after Staubach retired in 1980, Dallas began a slow decline that ended with Landry's dismissal on 25 February 1989, following a 3–13 season. The Cowboys new owner Jerry Jones replaced Landry with Jimmy Johnson, and two days later, the former coach gave a tearful farewell speech to his players.

During his tenure with the Cowboys, Landry was credited for inventing the multiple offense and the "flex" defense. He also reintroduced the "shotgun" formation to football, where the quarterback lines up several yards behind center to provide better protection in passing situations. Landry called all the offensive plays, relaying them either by hand signals or by shuttling players in and out of the game. The Cowboys were the first to rely heavily on computerized scouting. In addition, several of Landry's assistants became NFL head coaches, most notably Mike Ditka, who coached the Chicago Bears to a Super Bowl victory, and Dan Reeves, who took both the Denver Broncos and the Atlanta Falcons to Super Bowls.

Aside from his trademark fedora and stoic demeanor, Landry was also recognized for his deep religious beliefs, as he worked with the Fellowship of Christian Athletes and the Billy Graham Crusades. After his career, Landry maintained little connection with football. Despite all his success, the sport had never been top priority in his life. Nevertheless, Landry entered the Pro Football Hall of Fame in 1990, and was inducted into the Cowboys Ring of Honor in 1993, where his name is displayed beside a replica of his hat. He died on 12 February 2000 at the Baylor University Medical Center several months after being diagnosed with acute myelogenous leukemia, and is buried at Sparkman-Hillcrest Cemetery in Dallas (the same cemetery as Murchison).

★

Landry's autobiography, *Tom Landry: An Autobiography,* written with Gregg Lewis, was published in 1990, and a comprehensive biography entitled *Landry: Legend and the Legacy*, written by Bob St. John and Roger Staubach, was published shortly after his death in 2000. *The Book of Landry: Words of Wisdom from and Testimonials to Tom Landry, Former Coach of America's Team* (2000), compiled by Jennifer Briggs Kashi; and *I Remember Tom Landry* by Denne Freeman and Jaime Aron (2001), are also of interest. Obituaries are in the *Dallas Morning News* (13 Feb. 2000), and the *New York Times* (14 Feb. 2000).

JACK STYCZYNSKI

Richard Lane, 1964. © BETTMANN/CORBIS

LANE, Richard ("Night Train") (*b.* 16 April 1927 in Austin, Texas), football player who developed from an unlikely and unheralded walk-on to the acknowledged author of the book on playing cornerback in the National Football League (NFL).

Lane was abandoned by his mother shortly after his birth and was placed in the care of foster parents. With the foster parents, Lane was reared in a humble but loving atmosphere. One day when Lane ripped a pair of pants, which he later described as "the best pair of pants I ever owned," while playing football, his football career almost was sidetracked. Seeing the pants split up the back, his foster mother, whom he always called "Mom," said: "Richard, I'll tell you what. If you give up football, I'll buy you a horn or saxophone or anything you want." Lane was not about to give up sports though. At Austin's Anderson High School, he lettered in both football and basketball. Because his foster mother suffered a serious illness, Lane was forced to move to Scottsbluff, Nebraska, where his biological mother was living. While there he gained his only formal football experience past the high school level before turning pro by enrolling at Scottsbluff Junior College. Lane played just one season at Scottsbluff, in 1947, but in that season, he received Junior College All-America mention. He left Scottsbluff to join the U.S. Army and played three seasons for the Fort Ord (California) football team. He also got married while in the army. During the 1951 football season, he caught eighteen touchdown passes and attracted the attention of the nearby San Francisco 49ers of the National Football League (NFL). However, the 49ers offered no tryout or contract.

Following his discharge from the army, Lane found work in Los Angeles in one of the many aircraft plants in that city. He stacked large, oil-coated aluminum sheets in a bin, and he hated it. By his own count, he "ruined fifteen pairs of khakis messin' with that darned aluminum." Riding the bus to work one day in 1952, he noticed the Los Angeles Rams football office at 7813 Beverly Boulevard. Shortly thereafter he visited the office with a tattered scrapbook containing his high school, junior college, and service football clippings. He announced to the receptionist that he was a football player "looking for a job." When he met with the coaches Joe Stydahar and Red Hickey and the scout Eddie Kotal, they were impressed with his height, six feet two inches, but not his weight. Hickey asked how much he weighed. Lane responded, "'Bout one eighty-five." Hickey came back with, "Where you hidin' it?" Though they enjoyed a laugh, the Rams offered Lane a contract for $4,500. With a pregnant wife and a job he detested, Lane jumped at the chance.

The Rams first tried Lane at offensive end, the position in which he had made those eighteen touchdown catches at Fort Ord. But Lane, with so little formal experience, had trouble with the Rams' sophisticated system of plays. Compounding the situation, the Rams starting offensive ends were Elroy "Crazylegs" Hirsch and Tom Fears, who eventually were elected into the Hall of Fame. Lane visited Fears's room in training camp to get pointers on playing end in the Rams system. Fears had a 45 rpm record player and liked the current Buddy Morrow big band rendition of Jimmy Forrest's tune "Night Train," a slow, bluesy number. So did Lane. He began coming to Fears's room as much to hear "Night Train," which Fears played constantly, as he did to get tips on playing end from Fears. Ben Sheets, a rookie who was eventually cut from the Rams, roomed with Fears. Once as Lane entered the Fears-Sheets room, Sheets looked up and declared, "Look, here comes Night Train." The moniker stuck as one of pro football's most colorful and well-known nicknames.

The Rams coaching staff liked Lane's athleticism and switched his position to the defensive side of the ball, cornerback. They felt Lane had instincts "you couldn't teach." When the regular NFL rolled around in September 1952, Lane was tested by the best quarterbacks in the league, including Otto Graham, Sammy Baugh, Bobby Layne, and Y. A. Tittle, all future inductees into the Hall of Fame. Lane responded with a record fourteen interceptions, two of which he returned for touchdowns. He once said, "I coulda had more—I dropped another half-dozen or so." Lane enjoyed playing for Stydahar. But Hampton Pool became head coach, and he wanted Lane to cut down on his freelancing and play a more disciplined game. This approach hampered Lane's creativity and natural gambling instinct. He complained, was labeled a "malcontent," and was traded to the Chicago (now Arizona) Cardinals for the 1954 season. Things went well for Lane in Chicago. He continued to make passers and receivers wary, and his bone-rattling, necktie tackles caused ball carriers to look for him as they came into his territory. His interception total continued to climb in the Windy City also. Used as a receiver in clutch situations, Lane and an obscure quarterback named Ogden Compton teamed up on 13 November 1955 for a ninety-eight-yard touchdown pass, the second-longest distance in NFL history to that date. In his career as a receiver, Lane caught 8 passes for 253 yards, an astounding 31.6-yard average.

Always popular with his teammates, Lane ran afoul of another coach, Frank "Pop" Ivy, who did not appreciate Lane taking calculated risks in the secondary. Lane was traded to Detroit for the 1960 season, and for the first time he seemed to be fully appreciated by his team and his coaches. From 1960 to 1963 Lane made the Pro Bowl, and he earned All-Pro honors several times. After Lane and his first wife separated, Lane married the blues singer Dinah Washington (born Ruth Lee Jones) in Las Vegas, Nevada, on 2 July 1963. They were quite a high-profile couple, and their marriage was reported in *Time* magazine. Washington, known as "the Queen of the Blues," was famous for such songs as "What a Diff'rence a Day Makes," "I Don't Hurt Anymore," and "Dream." She died of an apparently accidental prescription drug overdose in the early hours of 14 December 1963.

The Detroit Lions could not get past the Green Bay Packers to play in championship games, but their defensive unit was accorded great respect by the Packers coach Vince Lombardi. The legendary coach told his quarterback Bart Starr, another Hall of Fame inductee: "Don't throw anywhere near him [Lane]. He's the best there is." Hickey, a Rams assistant who became the 49ers head coach, once switched his talented receiver R. C. Owens from the right side of the offensive formation to the left side to avoid Lane. Hickey said, "People go broke and lose their jobs throwing into Lane's territory." Lane, who played his man closely, is credited with starting the now-illegal "bump and run" tactic made popular by defensive backs of the 1960s and 1970s. He acknowledged freely that he was a gambler on the field, but his Lions Hall of Fame teammate Joe Schmidt said: "Yeah, 'Train' gambled, but he usually guessed right. He finished well ahead of the game."

In his six seasons with the Lions, Lane, now fully matured into 210 pounds, received accolades as the NFL's best. He retired after the last game of the 1965 season, on December 19. During his career he returned his 68 interceptions for 1,207 yards and 5 touchdowns. He was inducted into the Pro Football Hall of Fame in 1974.

After his playing career, Lane worked at the pro and college levels coaching and scouting. He also worked with youngsters in Detroit's Police Athletic League (PAL). He retired and moved into an assisted living facility in Del Valle, Texas, in 2001.

Even though seasons stretched to sixteen games rather than the mostly twelve games per season that Lane played, he retained the single-season interception record of fourteen at the beginning of the twenty-first century. His career total reached sixty-eight interceptions, bested only by Paul Krause (81) and Emlen Tunnell (79) at that time. Lane was the prototypical "cover" corner, the yardstick by which such stars as Herb Adderley, Mel Blount, Willie Brown, and Deion Sanders are measured.

★

Lane's life and career are discussed in Joe Falls, *The Specialist in Pro Football* (1966); Murray Olderman, *The Defenders* (1973); George Allen with Ben Olan, *Pro Football's 100 Greatest Players* (1982); and Rick Korch, *The Truly Great* (1993).

Jim Campbell

LANIER, Willie E. (*b.* 21 August 1945 in Clover, Virginia), football linebacker famed for the ferocity of his tackles and his team leadership; a member of the Pro Football Hall of Fame.

Lanier's ambition as a young man was to become a businessman. He began developing his athletic skills at the Randolph Center in Richmond, Virginia, and he played football for Maggie L. Walker High School, but he did not see his future in the National Football League (NFL). Although athletic scholarships were available to him, he wanted to go to a college that offered a business degree, and he wanted to go somewhere that racism was not as pressing a problem as it was in Richmond.

He decided on Morgan State University, a historically African-American college in Baltimore. When Lanier called Earl Banks, head coach for Morgan State, the coach was skeptical. Morgan had academic standards, and told Lanier that he would have to pass an entrance examination. Lanier made the journey to Baltimore, took the exam, and scored in the top 10 percent. Banks had said that no athletic scholarships were available, but Lanier wanted to attend Morgan State anyway. Eventually, after much effort, Banks was able to persuade the university to give Lanier a scholarship.

To Lanier, the purpose of college was to earn a degree, which he did, in business, in 1967. During his years at Morgan State, Lanier was cocaptain of the Bears football team for two years and the sole captain his last year. He played every down of defense and occasionally played on the offensive line, where he was outstanding as a blocker on running plays. In 1965 Lanier's defensive team allowed the opposition only 732 yards in total offense for the entire season. The Bears also launched a thirty-two-game winning streak. Morgan State went to two bowl games, in 1965 and 1966, with Lanier's play on offense being as notable as his hard-hitting play as linebacker was on defense.

Willie Lanier, 1973. AP/Wide World Photos

In 1967 the Kansas City Chiefs (then in the American Football League) drafted Lanier in the second round, the fiftieth overall pick. He almost immediately enrolled in the graduate business program at the University of Missouri Kansas City. When asked why, Lanier said that all the other business graduates from Morgan State were going on to graduate school, so he thought he would too. Even when entering professional football, Lanier's deep interest in business did not waver, and he eventually earned his M.B.A.

The Chiefs head coach in 1967 was Hank Stram, and he was mixing in rookies with veterans while building a team to beat Kansas City's league rivals, the Oakland Raiders. Lanier provided Stram with the final element he needed to create one of the finest linebacking corps ever, with veterans Bobby Bell and Jim Lynch. To Lanier, the name of the game was hitting, and he was given the nickname "Contact" because of how he pursued and hit opposing runners. He was also called "Honey Bear" because of his gentle manners off the field, and "Honey Bear" became the more popular nickname, perhaps because it captured the contrasts within Lanier—gentle and affable off the field, ferocious like an angry bear on the field.

Ferocity, intelligence, and a great physique all contributed to making Lanier immediately recognizable and fearsome. He carried 245 pounds on a six-foot, one-inch frame, with a twenty-inch neck and broad shoulders and a fifty-inch chest that tapered down to a thirty-four-inch waist. The sight of him created dismay among opposing fans, while inspiring hope in the Chiefs' faithful. He was also notable after his second season for his outsized helmet. During his first two seasons he played with more abandon than was wise, and he suffered several concussions—injuries that taken all together could have ended his career. He took to wearing a helmet with extra padding and he admitted, as a linebacker, "You must learn to control your aggression." Still, those who saw Lanier in his first seasons are likely to remember how his presence on the field was felt in each game from the very first Kansas City defensive play.

In 1969 Lanier helped the Chiefs achieve one of their greatest moments of glory. During the season, the Raiders had defeated the Chiefs twice in close, hard-fought games, among the most memorable in their long, angry rivalry. Under a convoluted playoff system invented by the American Football League (AFL) president for what would be the AFL's last season, the second-place team in each division would face the winners; the victors would then play for the right to appear in the Super Bowl. Both the Chiefs and Raiders won their games, thus pitting second-place Kansas City versus first-place Oakland; Kansas City won. This meant the Chiefs would meet the Minnesota Vikings in Super Bowl IV. The Vikings were led by their agile and inventive quarterback Fran Tarkenton and had a powerful running game; they were heavily favored to win. The game was a tough one, but Lanier made his mark by stuffing one running play after another, and he helped the Chiefs win their only Super Bowl championship.

During his years in the AFL Lanier was named All-AFL twice; after the AFL and NFL merged he was named All-American Football Conference nine times and played in six Pro Bowls. Although Lanier was always tough on running plays, he was also a fine defender against passes, with twenty-seven interceptions in his career at middle linebacker. Still, it may be his tackling that was most memorable. Raider fullback Hewritt Dixon said that when Lanier tackled him, "Part of me landed one place and the rest of me someplace else."

Lanier retired from the NFL in 1977 and entered the corporate business world. He became the senior vice president, capital markets liaison for Wheat First Union Bank and Brokerage Firm in Virginia. His business savvy was valued, and he became in demand as a speaker for business conventions. He was inducted into the Pro Football Hall of Fame in 1986. That year, he used his profits from banquets held in his honor to found the Willie E. Lanier Scholarship and Development Fund, which helps high school students enroll in historically African-American colleges.

★

Walton, Thompson, Lanier, Collins (1977), is a gathering of short biographies by longtime sports writer Bill Gutman. Its section on Lanier may be supplemented by Gutman's *Gamebreakers of the NFL* (1973). Charles Livingstone Allen and Ben Olan, *Pro Football's One Hundred Greatest Players* (1985), indicates why Lanier is regarded as a great player, as does Ron Smith et al., *The Sporting News Selects Football's 100 Greatest Players* (1999).

KIRK H. BEETZ

LAPCHICK, Joseph Bohomiel ("Joe") (*b.* 12 April 1900 in Yonkers, New York; *d.* 10 August 1970 in Monticello, New York), basketball player and coach of both college and professional teams who was elected to the James Naismith Memorial Basketball Hall of Fame in 1966.

Joe Lapchick, 1930s. HULTON ARCHIVE

Lapchick was the son of devout Catholics Frances Kassick, a homemaker, and Joseph B. Lapchick, a Czech immigrant who was a policeman in Yonkers, the town Lapchick always considered home. Lapchick was active in sports early on and by age twelve was over six feet tall. He began playing basketball at that time for a church team called the Trinity Midgets, and although he was awkward and gangly, he worked hard at the game. As the oldest of seven children, Lapchick was forced to go to work at an early age to help support the family. After finishing grade school, he worked in a factory as a machinist's apprentice and played basketball at night and on weekends. By age fifteen he was playing on a local semiprofessional team for $5 per game, and in 1917 he began playing on professional teams, negotiating his pay of $7 to $10 on a per game basis, while still working at the factory for $15 per week.

In 1919 Lapchick quit his machinist's job to play center for Holyoke in the old Western Massachusetts League and for Schenectady in the New York State League, two of the many professional leagues in the Northeast at that time. Over the next three years, Lapchick played on the New York Wanderers, Mount Vernon in the Interborough League, Troy in the New York State League, the Visitations in the Metropolitan League, and the Armory Big Five, establishing himself as one of the top centers in the region. He had grown to six feet, five inches tall, and was now both agile and fast for a big man.

In 1923 Lapchick signed a contract with New York's Original Celtics, the finest team of the era, and was a stalwart on this amazing team until 1928, when they disbanded after the 1927–1928 season. During that time the Celtics created modern basketball as it was played at the end of the twentieth century, with their switching man-to-man defense and their great passing and footwork on offense. In the years that Lapchick was a member of the Celtics, they were the acknowledged champions of basketball, as they traveled throughout the country playing the best U.S. teams. In the 1926–1927 and 1927–1928 seasons, the Celtics were members of the newly formed American Basketball League (ABL), which was the first truly national, as opposed to regional, professional league. The Celtics dominated the ABL, winning championships both years; the team was disbanded before their dominance created financial hardship for the league.

Lapchick and a number of the former Celtics ended up on the Cleveland Rosenblums, whom Lapchick led to two more ABL championships before the league succumbed to the financial exigencies of the Great Depression. Lapchick ended his ABL career in the 1930–1931 season, the league's last year, on the Toledo Redman squad. Following the demise of the ABL, Lapchick reconstituted the New York Celtics with financing from the singer Kate Smith, retaining a few of the old players, and the team returned to "barnstorming," or travelling from town to town playing either local teams or a team that accompanied them, with payment usually guaranteed or a percentage of the gate receipts. From 1930 to 1936, Lapchick served as both a player and the coach for the new Celtics. They often played the New York Renaissance, the top African-American professional team, and the two teams sometimes toured together.

On 14 May 1931 Lapchick married Elizabeth Sarubbi; they had three children. Having a family made constant touring more tedious and he readily accepted an offer in 1936 to coach Saint John's University, then located in Brooklyn, New York, even though he had never gone to high school or college, nor had he actually been formally coached at all. Nevertheless, Lapchick was an outstanding coach and extremely popular with the players, administrators, fans, and media. Lapchick coached the Saint John's basketball team from 1937 to 1947, and then again from 1957 (when it was located in Jamaica in Queens, New York) until his mandatory retirement in 1965. As a college coach Lapchick and his teams had a record of 334–130 and won the National Invitational Tournament (NIT) four times (1943, 1944, 1959, 1965). This was at a time when the National Collegiate Athletic Association (NCAA) tournament took no more than sixteen teams, and the NIT was considered just as prestigious.

In 1947 Lapchick accepted an offer to coach the New York Knickerbockers of the National Basketball Association (NBA), and he did so until February 1955, when he resigned. During that time his Knicks teams won 326 games, lost 247, and had the best record in the Eastern Division in both the 1952–1953 and 1953–1954 seasons. The Knicks were defeated, however, in the NBA Finals for three straight years, once by the Rochester Royals and twice by the Minneapolis Lakers, led by George Mikan. Throughout his coaching career, Lapchick suffered from a variety of ailments brought about by stress at work; his stomach was often "tied up in knots"(in his words), he slept poorly, and he had two heart attacks.

After his retirement from Saint John's in 1965, Lapchick served as the sports coordinator for Kutscher's Country Club in Monticello, New York, and continued his longtime association with the G. R. Kinney Shoe Company as an athletic footwear consultant. In 1966 he was elected to the James Naismith Memorial Basketball Hall of Fame. In August 1970 he suffered a third heart attack while playing golf at Kutscher's and, after a brief hospitalization, died on 10 August 1970. He is buried in Yonkers.

Lapchick was one of the first great "big men" in basketball and was certainly the most agile. He was the missing link who extended the greatness of the Original Celtics after their regular center became ineffective in 1923. Despite a lack of formal education, he displayed a keen mind that allowed him to learn Celtics basketball quickly as a player, and to coach successfully at both the college and professional levels.

★

The best account of Lapchick's life is in his autobiographical *Fifty Years of Basketball* (1968). His scrapbooks and memorabilia are at the James Naismith Memorial Basketball Hall of Fame in Springfield, Massachusetts, and at Saint John's University in Jamaica, New York. Lapchick's son Richard, the founder and director of the Center for the Study of Sport in Society at Northeastern University, details his father's playing career in the 1930s in *Five Minutes to Midnight: Race and Sport in the 1990s* (1991). Also see Al Hirshberg, *Basketball's Greatest Teams* (1966); Leonard Koppett, *Twenty-four Seconds to Shoot* (1968); Sandy Padwe, *Basketball's Hall of Fame* (1970); Leonard Koppett, *The Essence of the Game Is Deception* (1973); Neil D. Isaacs, *All the Moves* (1975); and Murry Nelson, *The Originals: The New York Celtics Invent Modern Basketball* (1999). An obituary is in the *New York Times* (11 Aug. 1970).

MURRY R. NELSON

LARDNER, Ringgold Wilmer ("Ring") (*b.* 6 March 1885 in Niles, Michigan; *d.* 25 September 1933 in East Hampton, New York), sportswriter and master of the short story who covered Chicago baseball and created the memorable character of pitcher "Jack Keefe," a "busher" with a large ego and a small brain.

Lardner was the youngest child of five in an economically comfortable, solidly Episcopal, conservative Republican family headed by Henry Lardner, a farmer and mortgage broker. Born in a mansion on the St. Joseph's River, surgery helped him overcome the handicap of a deformed left foot. Lardner received his early education from his mother, Lena Bogardus Phillips Lardner, a poet, and later graduated from Niles High School in 1901. At the Armour Institute of Technology in Chicago (now the Armour College of Engineering at Illinois Institute of Technology) from 1901 to 1902, Lardner briefly attempted to become the mechanical engineer his parents desired, but found he had "no more desire to be an engineer than a sheep herder." He held various odd jobs, finally leaving his position as bookkeeper for the Niles gas company to join the *South Bend Times* in South Bend, Indiana, as a reporter from 1905 to 1907. Hardly an athlete, although he "liked to watch tennis and play golf" according to his son, Lardner had found his métier almost by accident; sportswriting fulfilled his lifetime ambition to see "enough" baseball games. Reporting in succession for the newspapers *Chicago Inter Ocean, Chicago Examiner,* and *Chicago Tribune,* Lardner became managing editor of the *Sporting News* in St. Louis from 1910 to 1911, but left after arguing with owner Charles Spink. After he married Ellis Abbott on 28 June 1911, the couple moved to Boston, where Lardner wrote for the *Boston American* until he was fired for attending the World Series on his own. He remembered later that "Of all big cities one,/Is easy to get lost in,/I hardly need to tell you,/The one I mean is Boston."

Ring Lardner. LIBRARY OF CONGRESS

Lardner became a serious writer during his years with the *Chicago Tribune* from 1913 to 1919, while he and his wife raised their four sons. His column "In the Wake of the News" appeared daily, enlivened with baseball player argot. One comic invention of Lardner's was southpaw pitcher "Jack Keefe," and he sold several of the "busher's" (bush-leaguer's) letters home to the *Saturday Evening Post.* The first six of twenty-six Keefe stories appeared as *You Know Me, Al* (1916), the book that made Lardner's reputation as a humorist. *Gullible's Travel's, Etc.* (1917); *My Four Weeks in France* (1918), *Treat 'Em Rough* (1918), and *The Real Dope* (1919), quickly followed, and won Lardner a growing following.

Tall, dark, and fastidious, Lardner was always something of a puritan—his son considered him a "strait-laced prude"—who paradoxically reveled in traveling with both Chicago baseball teams. He was a fan as well as a commentator, a hard drinker who enjoyed an easy relationship with often-ignorant players basking in public adoration; Lardner's writing humanized them. As a reporter he lauded the artistry of the Chicago White Sox, who easily won the American League pennant in 1919, respecting players like star pitcher Eddie Cicotte far more than the club's penurious owner Charles Comiskey. Yet by the end of game two of the "World Serious," Lardner concluded that rumors of a "fix" were true and, as the train returned to Chicago, he drunkenly mocked the Sox for "blowing ball games." Lardner personally confronted Cicotte, and never forgave his denial. Nevertheless Lardner sat on the "Black Sox" story as unproved; even after the scandal broke and eight players admitted to a grand jury that they had thrown the series in return for a bribe, he never wrote about it. "Disenchanted" by sports, Lardner stopped going to ball games and permitted his other writing to become progressively more ironical and disillusioned.

By 1920 Lardner was well established as a humorist, but his apprehensions regarding orderly, middle-class life were apparent in *Own Your Own Home* (1919). He agreed to cover major sports for the Bell Syndicate, and moved his family east to Great Neck, New York; his automobile trip with his wife and child became the subject for *The Young Immigrunts* (1920). Lardner's song, "Prohibition Blues" (1920), demonstrated both his lifelong interest in music and his forlorn hope that the Nineteenth Amendment to the Constitution might stop his drinking. But with Long Island, New York, neighbors like Herbert Swopes, a war correspondent and the managing editor of the *New York*

World, and friends like F. Scott Fitzgerald, partying intensified. His literary output did increase, including *The Big Town* (1920), *Symptoms of Being 35* (1921), *How to Write Short Stories—With Examples* (1924), and *The Love Nest and Other Stories by Ring W. Lardner* (1926). With Fitzgerald as his advocate, Lardner's writing became more satirical. Critics praised his mocking of pretension, his insight into characters, and his ear for vernacular language; H. L. Mencken found his writing a "mine of authentic Americana." Lardner's stories like "Haircut" (1926), "Love Nest" (1926), "Alibi Ike" (1924), and "Champion" (1924), often appear in "best" short story anthologies.

A diagnosis of tuberculosis in 1926 hardly affected Lardner's drinking, his wit, or his deep cynicism regarding sports; he believed that the 1926 Dempsey-Tunney fight was fixed. Lardner's characters included not only flawed athletes but also stenographers, brokers, actresses, and social climbers "too ignorant to know how dull they are." Critics cited Lardner's "misanthropic nature," with one concluding he "just doesn't like people," but self-mockery was also apparent in his autobiography, *The Story of a Wonder Man* (1927). An abiding Lardner ambition was to write for Broadway, and in 1922 Will Rogers performed his baseball skit in the Ziegfeld Follies. In 1928 Lardner collaborated with George M. Cohan on *Elmer the Great,* the saga of a thickheaded pitcher; *June Moon* with George M. Kaufman in 1929 was an even bigger hit that parodied songwriters. Lardner's last important collection of stories, *Round-Up,* appeared the same year. After the Lardners moved to East Hampton, New York, in May 1928, Lardner was often hospitalized. He wrote a weekly radio commentary for *The New Yorker* from 1932 to 1933, and launched an "odd little campaign" against pornographic songs. Poor health made him more of a reader, Russian novels and Civil War history were his favorites, but his decline was rapid. Heart disease and alcoholism caused Lardner's death at the age of forty-eight, and after private burial services in East Hampton, New York, his remains were cremated.

★

Lardner's papers are deposited in the Newberry Library in Chicago; Matthew J. Bruccoli published a complete listing of his works in 1976, *Ring Lardner: A Descriptive Bibliography.* Excellent biographies have been written by Donald Elder, *Ring Lardner: A Biography* (1956); Walton R. Patrick, *Ring Lardner* (1963); Otto Friedrich, *Ring Lardner* (1965); Maxwell Geismar, *Ring Lardner and the Portrait of Folly* (1972); and Jonathan Yardley, *Ring: A Biography of Ring Lardner* (1977). Ring Lardner, Jr., *The Lardners: My Family Revisited* (1976), is often insightful; and Clifford M. Caruthers, ed., *Letters from Ring* (1979), provides a sense of the private man. Al Capp's introduction to *Ring Lardner's You Know Me Al: The Comic Strip Adventures of Jack Keefe* (1975), ought to be read, along with critical assessments compiled in Elizabeth Evans, *Ring Lardner* (1979). An obituary is in the *New York Times* (26 Sept. 1933), and F. Scott Fitzgerald, "Ring," *New Republic* (11 Oct. 1933), gives a contemporary's tribute.

GEORGE J. LANKEVICH

LARGENT, Steve (*b.* 28 September 1954 in Tulsa, Oklahoma), college and professional football player, U.S. representative, and member of the Professional Football Hall of Fame who at his retirement in 1989 held the National Football League (NFL) records for most receptions, yards, and touchdowns.

Largent was the eldest of three sons of Sue Stewart and Jim Largent, a salesman. Largent's father, whom he only saw twice in his childhood, abandoned the family when Largent was six. The rest of the family moved from Tulsa to Oklahoma City. When Largent was nine, his mother married John Cargill, a Federal Aviation Administration electrician. The marriage suffered because of Cargill's alcohol abuse, and Largent was often the target of his stepfather's violent alcoholic rages. In 1969 Largent entered Putnam City High School in Oklahoma City. Encouraged by his mother, he tried out for and made the football team. He also lettered in baseball during his high school years. In 1972 he enrolled in the University of Tulsa on a football scholarship. Given his stature, five feet, eleven inches and 191 pounds, and his lack of speed, conventional college football wisdom dictated that Largent would be a middling wide receiver. However, he was nothing less than spectacular for the Golden Hurricanes.

In the 1974 and 1975 seasons Largent lead the nation in touchdown receptions with fourteen, and he was Tulsa's scoring leader for each of those years with eighty-four points. Largent made the second team Associated Press (AP) All-America in 1975 and earned All-Missouri Valley Conference honors twice. In a 1974 game against Drake University, he scored five touchdowns. The achievement tied him with the College Football Hall of Fame receiver Howard Twilley in the Tulsa athletics record book for most touchdowns scored in a game. Along with Twilley and Michael Gunter, a member of the Golden Hurricane teams from 1980 to 1983, Largent ended his college career tied for the Tulsa career touchdown record with thirty-two. On 4 January 1975 Largent married Terry Bullock in Oklahoma City. They had four children. In 1976 he graduated from Tulsa with a B.S. in biology.

The Houston Oilers selected Largent in the fourth round of the 1976 National Football League (NFL) draft; he was 117th overall. Given his size and perceived want of

Steve Largent (*with ball*), 1987. ASSOCIATED PRESS AP

speed, many around the Oilers predicted taxi squad status at best. Largent nabbed only two passes in preseason play and was cut after the fourth preseason game. He told Mathew Robinson of *Investor's Business Daily* (30 July 1997): "I remember crying all the way home from Houston, dragging my little five-by-seven U-Haul trailer. I was preparing to move on to the next phase of my life. I had a Plan B." Largent thought he would enter the teaching field. After Houston dumped Largent, Jerry Rhome, an assistant coach with the Seattle Seahawks, saw his name on the waiver wire. Rhome, a former Tulsa quarterback and an assistant coach when Largent played there, went to the Seattle head coach Jack Patera with a recommendation. Seattle gave Houston its 1977 eighth-round draft selection for the unwanted wide receiver.

Largent's playing performance on his initial day in the Seahawks camp was abysmal. However, Rhome assured Largent he would not be cut. In the interview with Robinson, Largent said Rhome told him, "You do what I've seen you do for three years at the University of Tulsa and you'll be fine." Largent related: "Confidence has a lot to do with achieving success, I've seen a lot of guys who were more gifted than I was physically that had absolutely no confidence in themselves. That was reflected in their performance. Confidence only comes through experience."

The 1976 expansion Seattle Seahawks were a mix of NFL retreads and untested draft picks. The quarterback was the southpaw Jim Zorn, who like Largent was cut from a Texas NFL franchise, the Dallas Cowboys. In the season opener against the St. Louis Cardinals, Largent made five receptions, and Seattle's Zorn-Largent era began. Zorn garnered the National Football Conference (NFC) Offensive Rookie of the Year award. Largent racked up 54 receptions and 705 yards, good for third among NFC receivers.

Largent played fourteen seasons with Seattle. In 1978 he became the first Seahawk named to the Pro Bowl, and he played in the Pro Bowl seven times during his career. In 1983 Chuck Knox assumed the Seahawk coaching helm and lifted Zorn for Dave Kreig. Largent continued to be the primary receiver for the Seahawks and was a consistent, able, tough, performer. The Raiders cornerback, Lester Hayes remarked, "I call him the Albert Einstein of pass receivers because he's always coming up with some kind of new space age route I've never seen before." In eight out of nine seasons, from 1978 to 1986, Largent exceeded 1,000 yards. He also began a consecutive game reception stretch that capped at 177, an NFL record until broken by Jerry Rice.

The Seahawks general manager Mike McCormick was among some gridiron pundits who felt Largent cleverly promoted the lack of speed myth to deceive opposing players. Largent opined: "There's a difference between being fast and being quick and there is such a thing as football speed. Track guys run like crazy. But put a guy who holds the world record in the 100 on a football field, get a defensive back to jump in front of him, and he'll probably break his ankles trying to stop or change direction. The way you run on a track—with body leaning in on the balls of your feet—is different from how you run pass routes. To run routes you have to have more body control."

On 10 December 1989, against the Cincinnati Bengals, Largent broke the touchdown reception record of the Green Bay legend Don Hutson. At the time of his retirement in 1989, Largent had amassed 819 receptions, 13,089 yards, and 100 touchdowns. In 1999 *Sporting News* named Largent one of the 100 greatest football players of the century.

Largent returned to Oklahoma and started an advertising and marketing company. A devout Christian active in community service, he participated with such groups as Fellowship of Christian Athletes, Pro Athletes Outreach, United Way, and the Tulsa Police Department forensics laboratory. In 1994 U.S. representative James Inhofe vacated his seat to pursue a position in the U.S. Senate. Prompted by family and friends, among them Senator Don Nickles, Largent ran in the special election for representative and won with 63 percent of the vote. He became only the fifth player in NFL history to serve in the U.S. House of Representatives.

★

On 29 July 1995 Largent was inducted into the Professional Football Hall of Fame in Canton, Ohio. Easily reelected to his House seat in 1996, 1998, and 2000, he served on the House Energy Committee. Largent's football and political careers are discussed in David L. Porter, ed., *Professional Sports Team Histories: Football* (1987); *Superstars of Autumn: 75 Years of the NFL's Greatest Players* (1994); Ron Smith, *NFL Football: The Official Fan's Guide* (1995); Michael Barone and Grant Ujifusa, *Almanac of American Politics 2000* (1999); and *1999 Current Biography Yearbook* (1999). See also Don Smith, "Steve Largent," *Coffin Corner* (1995); Matthew Robinson, "Steve Largent: Channeling the Drive That Made Him a Gridiron Great," *Investor's Business Daily* (30 July 1997); Melinda Henneberger, "Putting a Christian Stamp on Congress," *New York Times* (13 Nov. 1997); Matthew Rees, "Looming Largent," *Weekly Standard* (24 Nov. 1997); Chris Elsberry, "The Distinguished Gentleman," *Connecticut Post* (11 Feb. 1998); and Paul Arnett, "Tulsa's Past Brighter Than Its Present," *Honolulu Star-Bulletin* (20 Oct. 1999). Informative Internet sites are www.house.gov/largent/biography; and www.tulsahurrican.fansonly.com.

JOHN VORPERIAN

LAYNE, Robert Lawrence, Sr. ("Bobby") (*b.* 19 December 1926 in Santa Anna, Texas; *d.* 1 December 1986 in Lubbock, Texas), professional football quarterback, who—by sheer force of will—drove teams to championships, and who is remembered as the first and leading proponent of the "two-minute drill."

Layne began life in Texas in the hardscrabble days of the Great Depression. Things worsened when his father, Sherman Cecil Layne, a farmer, died in 1935. Layne's mother, Beatrice Lowe, known as Bea, was not able to keep her four children together as a family. Layne went to live with his father's sister "Mimi" and her husband Wade Hampton in Fort Worth, Texas. They later moved to the Highland Park section of Dallas.

Bobby Layne, 1956. AP/WIDE WORLD PHOTOS

The move to Dallas was a fortuitous one for the tow-headed youngster. Layne's life took on a certain stability, and he blossomed as an athlete. He was a star passer in football, star pitcher in baseball, and a more than adequate basketball player. At Highland Park High School, Layne met and became friends with another talented athlete, Doak Walker. The pair formed a mutual admiration society that lasted until Layne's death. More than just friends, the lives of Layne and Walker are intertwined with each other and with football history. Except when they chose different colleges, Layne and Walker were in the same backfield from high school through championship seasons in the National Football League (NFL).

Layne was actually a year ahead of Walker in school, and went off to the University of Texas at Austin (UT) in 1944, where he had a successful freshman season. It was assumed that Walker would follow. However, World War II intervened, and in January 1945 Layne and Walker entered the U.S. Maritime Service or "merchant marine." Discharged after a year of service together, Layne and Walker were in New Orleans before both were to head to

UT, when they met Rusty Russell, who had coached the boys at Highland Park High. Russell was now an assistant coach for the Southern Methodist University (SMU) football team, and somehow Walker never made it to UT, attending SMU instead. The close friends would become rivals for the next three seasons, as both teams were members of the exciting Southwestern Conference (SWC).

Layne's team, the Longhorns, won two of the three head-to-head encounters, and Layne established himself as one of the SWC's all-time greats. He was a consensus All-American and set school career records for pass completions (210), passing yards (3,145), touchdown passes (35), and total yardage. He also became an outstanding pitcher, throwing two no-hitters in 1946, and never lost an SWC game (28–0) in a career that included a college championship and an overall pitching record of 39–7. While at the University of Texas, Layne and the former Carol Ann Krueger married on 17 August 1946; they later had two sons.

In spite of his success at baseball, football was the swashbuckling Layne's sport. The six-foot, one-inch, 201-pounder was drafted by, and signed with, the Chicago Bears for the 1948 season. The Bears quarterback position was crowded. Sid Luckman, a future Pro Football Hall of Famer, was winding down a stellar career, but Notre Dame Heisman Trophy–winner Johnny Lujack was also on the roster. Layne played little, completing only sixteen passes as a rookie, but three of them were for touchdowns. Before the 1949 season, Layne was traded to the New York Bulldogs where he became the starting quarterback. The team was owned by Ted Collins, the agent of popular singer Kate Smith. Layne once remarked, "Every time Kate got a sore throat we worried about getting paid."

Layne thought about retirement after being battered while directing the hapless Bulldogs, but he was traded to the Detroit Lions before the 1950 season, and reunited with Walker. By 1952 Layne had the Lions in the NFL Championship game. The Lions won, giving Detroit its first NFL championship since 1935. In 1953 he led his team—and there were no doubts that it was "his team"—to a thrillingly late come-from-behind win over the Cleveland Browns with a score of 17–16. In 1954 the Lions made another appearance in the championship game, although the Cleveland Browns won the rematch.

By now Layne had a reputation as a fiery leader with a genius for strategy on the field. He famously instilled confidence in tight spots by simply saying to his offensive line, "Y'all block an' ol' Bobby'll get us six points." They would block, and Layne often would come through a touchdown. He was a fierce competitor, who once said, "If it doesn't matter who wins or loses, why do they keep score?" One of the last players to play the game unprotected by a facemask, Layne also wore only skimpy shoulder pads—no flak jacket, no hip pads, no thigh pads, no knee pads. Off the field, Layne loved music, and it was nothing for him to get on stage and start jamming on a saxophone at a late-night jazz club. Layne rationalized his party-boy image by saying, "I'm no different from a lot of other pro athletes and celebrities, except I always go in the front door. Some use the back door or side door." Fellow Texan and teammate Harley Sewell summed up Layne's attitude by saying, "Bobby and I went out for toothpaste Thursday evening and never got back until game-time Sunday."

When Detroit Lions coach Buddy Parker quit in disgust right before the start of the 1958 season, he was hired by the Pittsburgh Steelers. At the time, the Steelers were the dregs of the NFL, but Parker improved the team immediately by bringing in Layne. Together they cajoled the team into respectability for a few years. After the 1962 season Layne retired to Lubbock, Texas, with his family. When he did hang up his cleats for the last time, he held NFL career records for passing attempts (3,700), pass completions (1,814), touchdown passes (196), and passing yards (26,768). Layne was inducted into the Pro Football Hall of Fame in 1967, and the College Football Hall of Fame in the following year.

Layne turned his attention to his real estate holdings in Lubbock, but there was always a welcome sign hung out for friends, old and new. Layne advised them, "Bring a clean shirt and a five-dollar bill, and I guarantee you won't change either one." Layne was a notorious check-grabber and big tipper. A friend once mused, "If there's reincarnation, I want to come back as Bobby's taxi driver." Layne's personal philosophy was "to run out of money and breath at the same time."

The high times caught up with Layne in 1986. A heavy smoker, he developed throat cancer and chronic liver disease that eventually caused a cardiac arrest. His well-attended funeral was held in Lubbock, where he is buried at Lubbock Memorial Cemetery.

Layne was a dashing figure on and off the field. His teammates would follow him to hell and back. He never quit trying. Doak Walker summed up Layne best in *Sporting News*, "Bobby never lost a game—sometimes time just ran out on him." If for nothing else, Layne will be remembered for the efficient way he used the clock late in each half of a football game. He was the first to really manage time on the field. As the *Los Angeles Times* sportswriter Jim Murray wrote at the time of Layne's death, "For Bobby, life was all fast Layne."

★

Layne, with Bob Drum, wrote an excellent autobiography, *Always on Sunday* (1963). A full-length biography of Layne is Bob St. John, *Heart of a Lion* (1991). Layne's life and career are discussed in Don Smith, *The Quarterbacks* (1963); George Sullivan,

Pro Football's All-Time Greats (1968), and *Gamemakers* (1971); Lou Duroska, ed., *Great Pro Quarterbacks* (1972); and George Allen, *Pro Football's 100 Greatest Players* (1982), written with Ben Olan. Obituaries are in the *Chicago Tribune*, *New York Times*, and *Washington Post* (all 2 Dec. 1986).

JIM CAMPBELL

LEAHY, Francis William ("Frank") (*b.* 22 or 27 August 1908 in O'Neill, Nebraska; *d.* 21 June 1973 in Lake Oswego, Oregon), successful football coach at Notre Dame who replaced a legend, Knute Rockne, and became a legend himself.

Leahy was one of eight children of Francis Leahy, a rancher and farmer, and Mary Winifred Kane. Shortly after Leahy's birth his father moved the family to Winner, South Dakota. Given Leahy's coaching success, much was later made of his hometown's name. Like many youths on the plains, Leahy began work early. At six years of age he rode a hay rake from sunup to sundown for a dollar a day. He also helped his father round up and herd horses, sometimes riding many miles into Montana. He talked his way onto the Winner High School football team as an eighth grader, once convincing an official to eject a player so he could play the final few minutes of a 108–0 loss.

Underaged and undersized, young Leahy boxed grown men in fairgrounds exhibition prizefights. He once stayed on his feet all three rounds with Ace Hudkins, who narrowly lost a middleweight championship bout during his professional career.

Frank Leahy *(right)* with University of Oklahoma coach Bud Wilkinson, 1950. ASSOCIATED PRESS AP

Leahy's father, though not formally educated, supplied the family with plenty of books. He challenged his offspring to find a word in the dictionary that he could not define. Reportedly they never could. Leahy also enhanced his considerable vocabulary by consulting the dictionary daily during much of his adult life. He is also said to have developed a stilted, Victorian way of speaking as a result of his voracious reading of popular pulp fiction in his youth.

As he progressed through high school, Leahy became a more than adequate halfback. Feeling he needed additional credits after his graduation from Winner High in 1926, he moved to Omaha, Nebraska, to live with his brother Gene Leahy, who had played football at Creighton University. Leahy enrolled at Omaha Central High School that fall and played another year of football, legally or illegally. Because of his size, now 180 pounds, he was made a tackle. He did so well it was eventually revealed that he was a "post graduate" player.

In 1927 Leahy arrived at Notre Dame as an unrecruited player. He had modest success as a college football player, and he was elected class president. During his sophomore and junior years Leahy was switched between center and tackle. He was not a starter but did play enough as a junior to earn a monogram (letter). His senior season ended before it began when he injured a knee in preseason practice. Leahy was free to move about the practice field, and he observed all coaches, especially Knute Rockne. When the 1930 season was over, Rockne needed to go to the Mayo Clinic in Rochester, Minnesota, for treatment. He asked Leahy to go along to have his knee repaired. The invitation may have changed the face of college football.

Leahy and "Rock" shared a room, and they spent hour after hour discussing football. Leahy lamented to Rockne that he wanted to be a college coach but that his brief career, only one season of much action, probably precluded that. Rockne, who would be killed in a plane crash before he could coach another season, flipped a dozen letters on Leahy's hospital bed and said, "Take your pick." All were seeking assistant coaches. Leahy chose Georgetown.

That fall, 1931, the Hoyas played Michigan State, coached by the former Notre Dame star Jim Crowley. Crowley was so impressed with the play of Georgetown's line that he asked Leahy to join his staff at Michigan State. Leahy accepted. In 1934, when Crowley took the coaching job at Fordham, Leahy followed. Leahy enhanced his reputation by developing the famed "seven blocks of granite" line. Included in that storied unit was the future coaching legend Vince Lombardi.

In July 1935 Leahy married Florence V. "Floss" Reilly. They eventually had eight children. In February 1939

Leahy was offered and accepted the head coaching post at Boston College (BC). At BC, Leahy's fabled pessimism surfaced in the media. A game was scheduled in New Orleans, Louisiana, against Tulane, and Leahy bemoaned the trip, saying, "We'll be stiff and sore from all that inactivity on the long train ride, while Tulane will have been sharpening up practicing." BC won 27–7. Later, when an Idaho team traveled east to play BC, Leahy lamented: "We won't have much of a chance. Idaho will be well-rested from their leisurely train ride." BC won 60–0. Before the existence of "spin doctors," Leahy could "spin" with the best of them. After two seasons and two bowl games with BC, Leahy was called back to Notre Dame in 1941.

In his first year at his alma mater, only a 0–0 tie with Army marred a perfect season. It was the first unbeaten season since Rockne's last, 1930. Leahy shocked Fighting Irish traditionalists in 1942, when he scrapped Rockne's oft-imitated box offense for the more modern and open T-formation. The Irish record of 7–2–2 only gave critics more cause to call for his job. The next season Leahy's lads went 9–1, losing the last game, 19–14, to a powerful service team, Great Lakes Naval Training State. Still the Irish were voted national champions. Leahy then enlisted and saw service in the Pacific with the U.S. Navy during World War II.

When Leahy and a group of mature players returned from service for the 1946 season, the Irish embarked on a thirty-nine-game winning streak and added three more national championships. When Purdue snapped the streak in the second game of 1950, it was a harbinger of Leahy's worst season, a record of 4–4–1. The 1951, 1952, and 1953 teams compiled 7–2–1, 7–2–1, and 9–0–1 records respectively, but Leahy was accumulating critics if not outright enemies—some right in South Bend. The coach's eternal pessimism—"We'll be lucky to get a first down this year"—in the face of great results alienated many, but nothing compared to the firestorm surrounding the 1953 14–14 tie with Iowa. Twice Notre Dame used fake injuries to gain timeouts to allow them to score as the first and second halves were about to expire. Fake injuries were part of every coach's repertoire, but because it was Notre Dame and Leahy, a furor arose.

On 31 January 1954 Leahy announced his resignation for "health reasons." True, he had collapsed and was administered the church's last rites during the 24 October 1953 Georgia Tech game, but "coaches' burnout" was only part of the story. Notre Dame and its new president Father Theodore Hesburgh were concerned about tarnishing Notre Dame's image with a win-at-all-costs approach. While Leahy was advised by his doctor to resign, evidence later showed the physician was pressured by university officials to make the recommendation. Consumed by arguably the most high-profile position in sports, Leahy stepped away from the game at age 45 with an enviable record of 107–13–9.

Leahy tried several business ventures and was even named general manager of the Los Angeles Chargers in 1960, the first year of the American Football League (AFL). But he never came close to the glory that was once Notre Dame football. Leahy spent his last years in the Portland, Oregon, area, where he died of leukemia. He is buried in Mount Calvary Cemetery in Portland.

Leahy, the man from Winner, wanted to win too much to suit some. But he was perhaps second only to his mentor Rockne as the keeper of the Fighting Irish football tradition of excellence. His winning percentage of .887 ranked second to Rockne's .897 among all who coached college football. Leahy was inducted into the College Football Hall of Fame in 1970. He is believed to be the first person from the field of athletics named a Knight of Malta by a Roman Catholic pope.

★

Leahy wrote a technical football book, *Notre Dame Football* (1949). Wells Twombly wrote a biography of Leahy, *Shake Down the Thunder* (1974). Leahy's life and career are discussed in Edwin Pope, *Football's Greatest Coaches* (1955); Francis Wallace, *Notre Dame: From Rockne to Parseghian* (1966); William Gildea and Christopher Jennison, *The Fighting Irish* (1976); and Jack Connor, *Leahy's Lads* (1994). An obituary is in the *New York Times* (23 June 1973).

JIM CAMPBELL

LEETCH, Brian (*b.* 3 March 1968 in Corpus Christi, Texas), hockey player who is a two-time Norris Trophy winner, the first U.S.-born player to win the Conn Smythe Trophy, and one of most skilled offensive defensemen in National Hockey League (NHL) history.

Leetch was the first of three children born to Jack Leetch, a pilot turned executive who was an All-American hockey player for Boston College in the 1960s, and Jan Leetch, a homemaker. After Leetch was born, the family moved to Oregon and then to California before settling down in Cheshire, Connecticut, where the elder Leetch began managing the town's ice skating rink in 1973. Before learning to skate at around the age of five, Leetch practiced stick handling with a cut-off hockey stick and tennis ball in the family's driveway. Once on skates, he quickly began to distinguish himself from his peers and often played against older players.

Leetch enrolled at Cheshire High School in 1982 and soon emerged as a two-sport star. At the age of sixteen he threw a ninety-mile-per-hour fastball and led Cheshire High's baseball team to the Connecticut State Championship in 1984. That same year he scored fifty-three goals and had fifty assists in twenty-two games for the school's

Brian Leetch, 2001. ASSOCIATED PRESS AP

hockey team. The summer after his sophomore year Leetch traveled to Europe as a member of the United States Junior National Team, of which he was a member through 1986.

Leetch then transferred to Avon Old Farms—a Connecticut prep school known for its outstanding hockey program—to increase his chances of earning a college scholarship. In baseball, he struck out nineteen hitters in one game, but as overpowering as he was on the pitching mound, Leetch was even better on the ice, scoring seventy goals and accumulating ninety assists in fifty-four games over two years. As a senior he was named New England Prep School Player of the Year, leading Avon Old Farms to a 24–0–1 regular-season record. His team's only loss came in the finals of the New England Championships to Thayer Academy, whose team included future NHL stars Tony Amonte and Jeremy Roenick. Following the season, the New York Rangers drafted Leetch with the ninth overall pick in the 1986 NHL Entry Draft.

In the fall of 1986 Leetch followed in his father's footsteps by enrolling at Boston College, where he left his mark despite playing only one season. He was named a first-team All-American, was the Hockey East Rookie of the Year and Player of the Year, and was the first freshman finalist for the Hobey Baker Memorial Award, given to the best college player in the nation. He left Boston College after his freshman year to play for the U.S. National Team, where he notched seventy-four points in sixty games. He was named captain of the 1988 U.S. Olympic Hockey Team, which finished seventh at the Calgary Games.

Leetch joined the Rangers following the Olympics toward the end of the 1987–1988 season, collecting fourteen points in seventeen games. In the 1988–1989 season he scored twenty-three goals, an NHL record for a rookie defenseman. He finished the year with seventy-one points and was awarded the Calder Trophy as the NHL Rookie of the Year.

Leetch was an All-Star the next two years but did not reach his full potential until 1991–1992. Before that season, the Rangers traded for Mark Messier and made him team captain. Messier told Leetch, "I've seen the best, played with the best—and you're the best." Inspired by Messier's focus, determination, and leadership, Leetch blossomed. He had a career-high 80 assists and became the fifth defenseman in NHL history to score 100 points in a season, with 102. Leetch won the Norris Trophy as the league's top defenseman, and the Rangers won the President's Trophy as the league's best regular-season team. However, after jumping out to a 2–1 series lead in the Eastern Conference Semifinals, the Rangers blew a two-goal lead in game four and were upset by the Pittsburgh Penguins in six games.

Despite missing most of the 1992–1993 season with injuries, Leetch signed a seven-year, $19-million contract in the spring of 1993. But when the Rangers struggled early in the 1993–1994 season, the lucrative deal did not preclude the new head coach, Mike Keenan, from benching him—the first time a coach had ever done so. Keenan felt Leetch was too offensive-minded, and the defenseman responded to his coach's disciplinary tactics by significantly improving his defensive game. Leetch began to attract comparisons to Hall of Famer Bobby Orr. During the 1994 Stanley Cup Finals, the Vancouver Canucks head coach Pat Quinn said that Leetch actually did some things even better than the Boston Bruin legend. Leetch proved that the comparisons were not too far-fetched, scoring the first goal and making two key defensive plays late in game seven as the Rangers beat Vancouver to win their first Stanley Cup in fifty-four years. He had five goals and six assists for a team-high eleven points in the finals, thus becoming the first U.S.-born player to win the Conn Smythe Trophy as the finals Most Valuable Player (MVP). He also led the Rangers in playoff scoring with eleven goals and twenty-three assists.

The Rangers did not get beyond the second round of the playoffs the next two years, but Leetch enjoyed success as captain of Team USA in 1996, winning the World Cup of Hockey. Before the 1996–1997 season the Rangers signed Wayne Gretzky and, as he did after the addition of Messier, Leetch responded with a terrific season, capturing his second Norris Trophy. The Rangers lost to the Florida Panthers in the Eastern Conference Finals and then, following the season, lost Mark Messier to Vancouver due to a contract dispute. Leetch was named captain, but he struggled to fill the void left by Messier. He endured sub-par seasons as the Rangers failed to qualify for the playoffs for three straight years. He was the alternate captain for the U.S. team in its disappointing showing at the 1998 Nagano Olympic Games. The 1999–2000 season was Leetch's worst as a professional. His defensive game slipped, and he missed thirty-two games with a fractured forearm, ending the year with only twenty-six points. On the plus side, Leetch was married in June 1999 to Mary Beth O'Neill.

In July 2000 the Rangers brought Messier back to New York. At a news conference announcing the signing, Leetch voluntarily returned the team captaincy, bringing Messier to tears. Leetch regained All-Star form in 2000–2001, leading the NHL's defensemen in goals, assists, and points, and leading the entire league in ice time. Leetch's son was born during the season.

Combining tremendous strength and conditioning with extraordinary stick handling and vision, Leetch brings offensive skills to hockey rarely seen in a defenseman. Though his soft-spoken and humble demeanor did not translate to success as team captain, his athletic ability is world class. Coaches often say that having Leetch on the ice is like playing a fourth forward. He makes crisp, precise passes out of his own zone and is the best in the game at jumping into the play when he sees an opening. Leetch's brilliant, often daring, rushes up ice turn defensive plays into offensive ones; they have become the trademark of one of the best offensive defensemen in NHL history.

★

Joe Gergen, "Leetch's Son Is Shining," *Newsday* (17 Dec. 1987), is a look back at Leetch's development through the eyes of his father. Laura Price, "Leetch Unleashed His Drive to Succeed," *Newsday* (15 May 1994), is an informative biographical source. Gergen, "Leetch's Moves Draw Raves," *Newsday* (8 June 1994), relates how Mike Keenan transformed Leetch's defensive game. For details on Pat Quinn's comparison of Leetch and Bobby Orr, see "Not a Conn Job, Believe It: NY's Leetch Is Best Bet to Win Smythe Trophy," *St. Louis Post-Dispatch* (9 June 1994). "Leetch's Best Is Standard Now," *Boston Globe* (28 Feb. 1996), includes details on the role Mark Messier played in Leetch's rise to stardom. The most comprehensive biographical article on Leetch is David Heuschkel, "Leetch's Home-Ice Advantage Future in Hockey Was Settled Early," *Hartford Courant* (24 Dec. 1999).

DANIEL MASSEY

LEMIEUX, Mario (*b.* 5 October 1965 in Montreal, Quebec, Canada), Hall of Fame hockey player and team owner of the Pittsburgh Penguins, the first player in the National Hockey League to score seventy goals in a season, and one of the first professional athletes to own a team for which he had played.

Born in the suburb of Ville Emard, Montreal, Lemieux was the youngest of three sons born to Jean-Guy, a construction worker, and Pierrette Lemieux. He began skating at about the age of two and was playing hockey by age five. By the time he was twelve years old, Lemieux was already cognizant of his budding strength and skills on the ice. As with many dedicated athletes before him, his sport took a central place in his life. He dropped out of school at sixteen, having completed tenth grade, to devote himself full-time to hockey. Two years later, while playing in the Quebec Major Junior Hockey League for the Laval Voisins, Lemieux scored a record-setting 282 points. The next year, 1984, Lemieux was selected as the number-one first-round draft pick in the National Hockey League (NHL) draft by the Pittsburgh Penguins, whose dismal record in the previous year gave them draft priority. Viewed as the top prospect by the Pittsburgh coaches and management, the talented

Mario Lemieux. AP/WIDE WORLD PHOTOS

young Lemieux, a six-foot, four-inch, 220-pound left-handed shooter, appeared on the ice for the Penguins just days after his nineteenth birthday. Wearing the number 66, Lemieux skated out on his first shift in the first period of his first game and shot the first of his hundreds of goals with his very first attempt.

Lemieux's career-long relationship with the Penguins began with a team that was dispirited by its previous record. Despite its lackluster history, the franchise began to turn around after Lemieux's appearance. Lemieux won the Calder Trophy as Rookie of the Year with 43 goals and 57 assists, becoming only the third rookie to score 100 points. In the following year he was selected for the Lester B. Pearson Award, voted by the NHL players themselves for Most Valuable Player (MVP). That year he had 141 points on 48 goals and 93 assists. The next season saw an even more spectacular performance, with Lemieux earning 168 points (70 goals, 98 assists) and winning both the Hart Memorial Trophy as the NHL's MVP and the Art Ross Trophy for his scoring abilities. In the 1988–1989 season, Lemieux had his best year ever, concluding the regular season with an amazing 199 points on 85 goals and 114 assists. He again earned the Art Ross Trophy.

The 1989–1990 season also began what was to become a lengthy battle against injury resulting from a herniated disk in Lemieux's back; he played in fifty-nine games that season and only twenty-six in the following year. Ironically, in the 1990–1991 season the Penguins succeeded in returning to the Stanley Cup playoffs and finally captured their elusive first Stanley Cup. Despite his prolonged injury, Lemieux was the recipient of that year's Conn Smythe Trophy as the MVP in the playoffs. With 131 points by the end of the 1991–1992 season, Lemieux had again earned the Art Ross Trophy, and with the team playing better than ever, he went on to earn a second Stanley Cup and a second Conn Smythe Trophy.

In the 1992–1993 season Lemieux once again won the Hart Trophy and was selected for the Lester B. Pearson Award. On 26 June 1993 Lemieux married Nathalie Asselin; they have four children. The future appeared grim despite these glowing achievements, for Lemieux soon was diagnosed with nodular lymphocytic Hodgkin disease, a form of cancer. He underwent radiation treatment and played in only twenty-two games in the 1993–1994 season; he sat out the following year to allow time to recover from his back pain as well as from the effects of his battle with cancer. During this time, Lemieux was the recipient of the Masterton Trophy for "perseverance, sportsmanship and dedication to hockey."

That Lemieux is an extremely dedicated athlete is evidenced by his performance when he returned to the Penguins in the 1995–1996 season; he scored 161 points (69 goals, 92 assists) and once again captured both the Hart Trophy and the Art Ross Trophy. Winning the Art Ross again the following year also placed Lemieux as one of the few in the sport to have had ten consecutive years at or above 100 points in the regular season. At the end of that season, in 1997, Lemieux left the Penguins, retiring because he felt at the time that hockey had degenerated into a fighting game. During these years as a Pittsburgh Penguin, Lemieux won a berth on the NHL First All-Star team a total of five times. Lemieux was inducted into the Hockey Hall of Fame in 1997.

Lemieux's role in the history of hockey and of the Penguins franchise was by no means finished with the athlete's retirement from play. Soon, as the franchise's fortunes dwindled, it appeared that the team would be sold and probably moved away from Pittsburgh. Ultimately, Lemieux himself purchased the organization from the owning partnership, vowing to keep the team in its hometown. Then the sports world was even more astounded when Lemieux announced after a three-and-a-half-year absence that he would return to the ice, again as center for the Penguins. The much-publicized return took place in December 2000. Lemieux's number, 66, and jersey, which had been retired and hung in the rafters, were brought back into play as he resumed his position as the team's leading athlete. In 43 games played before the end of the season, Lemieux earned 76 points on 35 goals and 41 assists, proving him a major asset once again to the Penguins. The team made it to the playoffs but lost the Eastern Conference finals to the New Jersey Devils. At the end of the 2000–2001 season, Lemieux had amassed 1,570 regular season points (in 788 games on 648 goals and 922 assists) and 172 career points in postseason play (107 games on 76 goals and 96 assists). Lemieux is the only player-owner in the league.

Throughout his career Lemieux's play has been characterized by the use of his formidable physical presence, his quick and skilled stick handling, and an impressive ability to predict the path of the puck during intense action, especially near the net. Over the years his style of play has developed from relying on strength and speed to incorporating these elements with steadiness and flashes of artistry on the ice. Lemieux also is admired for his stoic approach to a series of very serious health threats, all of which he appears to have conquered.

★

Lemieux's career timeline and statistics are cited in "Mario: A Tribute," *Pittsburgh Post-Gazette,* http://www.post-gazette.com/mario/, and in "Mario Lemieux," Pittsburgh Penguins, http://www.pittsburghpenguins.com/team/bio-Lemieux.asp. For more detailed information see Chrys Goyens and Frank Orr, *Mario*

Lemieux: Over Time (2001), and Tim O'Shei, *Mario Lemieux* (2001).

JAMES J. SULLIVAN

LEMON, Meadow George ("Meadowlark") (*b.* 25 April 1932 in Wilmington, North Carolina), professional basketball player for the Harlem Globetrotters, who also became an actor, musician, speaker, and minister.

Lemon was interested in athletics from a young age. At age eleven he viewed a newsreel about the Harlem Globetrotters. Inspired, Lemon dreamed of joining the squad and began foraging for materials to practice his craft. He found a coat hanger and bent it into a circle to create a homemade basketball rim. Cutting the bottom from an onion sack, he formed his net, and made a basketball out of a condensed milk can. Using rope and nails he made a goal and began practicing. Once introduced to regulation equipment, Lemon excelled in both basketball and football at Wilmington High School, earning All-State honors, and he attended Florida A&M University.

Lemon was invited to try out with the Globetrotters in 1952 after writing the front office to request an opportunity. "Goose" Tatum encouraged the young player and predicted he would become a great addition to the team. The Globetrotter "Clown Prince" of basketball directs comedy routines and manages the pace of the game, almost like a director on the floor. Lemon was ideal for the role, and his distinctive voice could be heard from almost any seat in a gym or arena. After a stint in the U.S. Army between 1952 and 1954, Lemon signed a contract and was assigned to the Globetrotters developmental team, the Kansas City Stars. He served as an understudy to "Rookie" Brown on a southern tour, and his name was changed to "Meadowlark."

Meadowlark Lemon. © BETTMANN/CORBIS

When Tatum left the team in the mid-1950s, Lemon was given a tryout to fulfill the role of Clown Prince. He was assigned to the position permanently in 1958 and served the team in that capacity for twenty years. His on-court antics included half-court hook shots and no-look, wraparound passes leading to slam dunks. Lemon adroitly managed passes generated behind his back, off his head, and off the back of one leg. His ability to turn a referee into a foil for his wit was unsurpassed. Sometimes Lemon would hide basketballs under his jersey or douse referees with water. When he threatened spectators with water, he would instead shower them with buckets of confetti. Lemon also enjoyed maneuvering a basketball attached to the end of a long elastic band and shooting a ball that wobbled in the air.

Globetrotter travel expanded shortly after Lemon joined the team, and the squad became a symbol of U.S. patriotic entertainment. In 1957 the Globetrotters began annual performances at Air Force bases and on naval aircraft carriers, in addition to gymnasiums around the world. The players even performed on Christmas day. In 1960 the Globetrotters performed a series of shows in the Soviet Union during the Cold War. U.S. diplomats and government officials worked with team officials to plan these events. Lemon's children recall Henry Kissinger calling Meadowlark at home to discuss upcoming journeys.

Lemon's popularity merged with growing television coverage. He starred in most of the Globetrotter appearances on the American Broadcasting Companies' (ABC) *Wide World of Sports* during the 1970s. He was also portrayed in the Saturday morning animated show *The Harlem Globetrotters* in 1970 and 1971. In 1972 he starred in *The Harlem Globetrotters Popcorn Machine,* a one-hour musical-variety TV series. During the 1971 season he became the team's player-coach and began acting as a spokesman for the organization. Lemon and his teammates gathered at the White House on 6 December 1974, when President Gerald R. Ford gave the Globetrotters a special Presidential Citation for giving millions of people "the priceless gifts of love and laughter" in addition to basketball. In 1978 a nationwide poll named Lemon the fourth most popular personality in the United States (after John Wayne, Alan Alda, and Bob Hope). That same year Lemon left the Globetrotters to pursue a career in Hollywood.

Lemon appeared in the television series *Alice* (1982–1983 season), *Diff'rent Strokes* (1979), and *Hello, Larry* (1979 and 1980), as well as the movies *The Fish that Saved Pittsburgh* (1979), and *Modern Romance* (1981). Shortly after these productions, Lemon formed his own basketball team, the Bucketeers, and continued to make television appearances. He also recorded an album titled *My Kids* in 1979 and began traveling around the United States, delivering inspirational talks and hosting camps. Lemon stressed the importance of drug awareness and the urgency of problems gripping at-risk youth. An ordained minister of a Christian nondenominational church, Lemon helped found Athletes International Ministries and started working with professional athletes seeking to provide social and economic assistance to their local communities. Music also became a passion for Lemon in the 1970s and 1980s. He recorded music on RMB and Casablanca records. Lemon was married to Willie Maultsby for several years (they later divorced), and he has five children.

In 1993 Lemon was coaxed from retirement and rejoined the Globetrotters on a domestic tour for fifty games. When added to his career with the team from 1954 to 1978 and his service with the Bucketeers, Lemon estimated he had played in nearly 8,000 games. More than 7,500 of these contests were consecutive games during the 1950s, 1960s, and 1970s. He entertained popes, kings, queens, and presidents, and played in more than 100 countries and more than 1,500 North American cities. Lemon's tour with the Globetrotters included participation with luminaries like Wilt "The Stilt" Chamberlain, "Curly" Neal, Bobby Joe Mason, "Geese" Ausbie, and "Sweet" Lou Dunbar.

Los Angeles Times sports writer Jim Murray described Meadowlark Lemon as "an American Institution whose uniform should hang alongside the Spirit of St. Louis and the Gemini Space Capsule in the halls of the Smithsonian Institute." Perhaps the highest compliment Lemon ever received was generated when longtime Philadelphia sports anchor Al Melzer interviewed Wilt Chamberlain in 2000, shortly before his death. Chamberlain, perhaps the most dominating player ever to play the game of basketball, called Lemon the greatest player of all time. "Meadowlark was the most sensational, awesome, incredible basketball player I've ever seen," Chamberlain said. On 13 October 2000 Lemon was awarded the John Bunn Award from the Basketball Hall of Fame in recognition of outstanding lifetime achievement.

★

Lemon's biography, *Meadowlark Lemon* (1987), describes his philosophy and includes anecdotes. Several other books describe elements of Lemon's career and events that occurred during his playing era, including George Vecsey, *Harlem Globetrotters* (1973), and Josh Wilker, *The Harlem Globetrotters* (1996). Nelson George, *Elevating the Game: Black Men and Basketball* (1992), outlines the impact of African-American participation in basketball in the United States, and serves as a good overview of the subject.

R. JAKE SUDDERTH

LEMOND, Greg(ory) James (*b.* 26 June 1961 in Lakewood, California), professional cyclist who stands as the first cyclist from the United States to win the Tour de France and the World Road Race Championship.

Greg LeMond is one of three children of Robert LeMond, a real-estate broker, and Bertha LeMond. In December 1968 the LeMond family moved from Lakewood to Lake Tahoe, California. It was there, at the age of seven, that LeMond discovered snow skiing. His interest in skiing got more serious when the LeMonds moved two years later to Washoe County in northwestern Nevada, where LeMond's father intended to start a real-estate business.

LeMond's passion for skiing continued to develop over

Greg LeMond in the 1990 Tour de France. ASSOCIATED PRESS AP

the next few years, and his involvement with cycling began mainly as training for the rigors of freestyle ski competitions. However, the 1975 Nevada state cycling championship happened to take place on the road that ran past the LeMond home, and Greg was intrigued by what he saw. LeMond began to devote more and more of himself to cycling, and skiing soon fell by the wayside.

With commitment to cycling came immediate success, as LeMond won his first four races, competing in the twelve-to-fifteen-year-old category. His competitive fires ignited, LeMond soon found himself wanting more competition. Permission was granted for LeMond to race with the juniors.

In 1977, only fifteen and not officially old enough to race as a junior, LeMond went to the U.S. Junior World Cycling team trials and won two out of three races. His age, however, kept him from being selected for the world championship team. Later that year he won the national Junior Road Race Championship, and the following year, 1978, saw LeMond finish ninth in the World Junior Road Race Championship. Busy making his mark in the cycling world, LeMond earned his high school diploma by taking correspondence courses.

A significant milestone in LeMond's career was the 1979 world championship meet held in Buenos Aires, Argentina. Competing in both road and track events, LeMond won the gold medal in the road race, silver in the individual pursuit, and bronze in the team time trial. LeMond was the first rider of any age to win three medals in one world meet.

His ever-increasing success bolstered by his status as reigning junior world champion, LeMond looked next to the 1980 Olympics. Although Olympic gold would seem to be the next logical step for the budding young champion, it was not to be, as the United States boycotted the Summer Games in Moscow in protest of the Soviet invasion of Afghanistan. With the possibility of Olympic competition removed, LeMond had to decide whether to continue competing as an amateur and wait for the 1984 Olympics, or to turn professional at the tender age of nineteen. For LeMond, the decision was plain; he had learned the ropes of amateur cycling and was ready for greater competition.

After winning the Circuit de la Sarthe, a grueling, 346-mile pro-am race in France, LeMond was paid a visit by Cyrille Guimard, a French cycling coach known for his ability to identify and develop champions. Guimard offered the cyclist a professional contract with the Renault team, captained by the great Bernard Hinault, for the 1981 season. LeMond, believing this to be the best choice for his development as a cyclist, signed on with Guimard. He then capped the year by marrying Kathy Morris on 21 December 1980. The couple has three children.

LeMond characterized his first year as a professional as "not an easy one." In typical fashion, though, LeMond began winning races and made his mark on the European circuit with a third-place finish in the Dauphiné Libéré, a weeklong stage race held on some of the same roads as the Tour de France. This performance showed that LeMond had the ability to win the top European stage races. Returning to the United States, LeMond won the Coors Classic, a victory made particularly sweet in that he defeated the Olympic champion, Sergei Soukhorouchenkov, whom he would have had to beat in Moscow for the Olympic gold medal.

The 1982 season saw LeMond return to Europe with greater confidence than ever, and he won the twelve-day Tour de l'Avenir by a record-setting margin of ten minutes. At the World Road Race Championship of that year held in Goodwood, England, he placed second.

In May of 1983, LeMond's third professional season, he took first place in the Dauphiné Libéré stage race, and then followed with a fourth-place finish in the Tour of Switzerland. His greatest victory to date came, however, at the 1983 World Road Race Championship, becoming the first cyclist from the United States to win this race. In recognition of his 1983 accomplishments, LeMond was awarded the Super Prestige Pernod Trophy, marking him as the best cyclist of the year.

In 1984, LeMond's fourth year as a professional cyclist, he made his debut in the world's most prestigious and difficult race, the Tour de France. Although he got off to a shaky start in the 23-day, 2,500-mile race, he finished third, becoming the first non-European to mount the winner's podium.

Bernard Hinault, LeMond's teammate of 1983, had spent the 1984 season racing for a new team, the French-based La Vie Claire. As the 1985 season approached, Hinault asked LeMond if he would join La Vie Claire and ride as cocaptain. LeMond accepted the offer, and in the Tour de France of that year put his personal ambitions aside and helped Hinault to win his fifth Tour while LeMond took second place. The 1986 edition of the Tour de France began with the expectation that LeMond would be the favorite to win, seconded by Hinault, the defending champion. It soon became clear that this was not entirely the case. Rather than working with LeMond, Hinault "attacked" his teammate again and again. It was only through immense force of will in the face of an apparent betrayal and a partisan French crowd that LeMond took the overall victory.

Coming into the 1987 season in preparation for his Tour de France title defense, LeMond was sidelined by a broken wrist received in a racing crash. Towards the end of his rehabilitation period on 20 April, LeMond was accidentally shot by his brother-in-law while turkey hunting outside Sacramento, California. Recovery was slow and painful, and his return to the race circuit was interrupted, first by an emergency appendectomy, and then by an infection in his shin, which eventually required surgery.

Having missed the 1987 and 1988 Tours de France, LeMond arrived in 1989 given little chance of returning to his former glory. Riding now for the Belgium-based ADR team, LeMond was not surrounded by the strong teammates he had worked with at La Vie Claire. Nonetheless, LeMond rode strongly and was in the yellow jersey of the leader by the end of the first week. The following two weeks bore witness to an epic duel between LeMond and two-time Tour winner Laurent Fignon, who had been LeMond's teammate at Renault.

LeMond trailed Fignon by fifty seconds coming into the final day of the tour. On that day LeMond rode the stage at an average speed of thirty-four miles per hour, the fastest ever for a time trial in the Tour de France. LeMond won the 1989 Tour de France by a margin of eight seconds, the closest in the history of the race. His seemingly miraculous comeback from the near-fatal shooting was completed just weeks later when he won his second World Road Race Championship at Chambéry, France, making him one of only five men to win the Tour de France and the World Road Race Championship in the same year. The close of the year found LeMond's photo on the cover of *Sports Illustrated,* as he was named Sportsman of the Year.

His comeback complete, LeMond signed a multimillion-dollar contract with the French-based Z team. Riding with the backing of a strong team, LeMond successfully defended his Tour de France title in 1990, firmly cementing his name among those of cycling's all-time greats with his third Tour victory.

Although LeMond received many endorsement deals and rode under lucrative racing contracts, the years following his 1990 Tour de France victory did not see him meeting with continued great success on the cycling front. Beset with health problems and faced with new, younger competition, LeMond struggled in subsequent Tours de France, finishing seventh in 1991, and his final major victory came in the 1992 Tour DuPont, a stage race in the United States. As 1994 came to a close, it was revealed that LeMond was suffering from mitochondrial myopathy, an impairment of muscle proteins that prevents the intense power delivery needed by a world-class cyclist. The disease signaled the end of LeMond's career as a professional cyclist.

No longer a competitor, LeMond continued to be deeply involved in the cycling world through the founding of a successful bicycle company that bore his name, as well as through significant relationships with other companies in the cycling industry. After giving up bicycle racing, LeMond turned to racing automobiles.

LeMond's significance in the world of cycling is immense. He was the first cyclist to wear a hard-shell helmet while competing in the Tour de France. His record of three Tour de France titles and two World Road Race Championships places him among the legends of cycling. LeMond will forever stand as the pioneer U.S. cyclist, the one who opened doors in what previously had been a sport only of European champions and who paved the way for future generations of U.S. cyclists to test themselves at the sport's highest level.

★

Greg LeMond's Complete Book of Bicycling (1987), which LeMond cowrote with Kent Gordis, offers insight into his life and development as a cyclist in addition to practical information on the sport. Cycling journalist Samuel Abt has written two works on LeMond, *LeMond: The Incredible Comeback of an American Hero* (1990), and *A Season in Turmoil* (1995). Lively accounts of LeMond's exploits in the Tour de France and World Road Race Championships can be found in *Bicycle Racing in the Modern Era* (1997), edited by the staff of *VeloNews,* and *John Wilcockson's World of Cycling* (1998), by John Wilcockson.

CHRISTOPHER T. GOZICK

LEONARD, Benny (*b.* 7 April 1896 in New York City; *d.* 18 April 1947 in New York City), world lightweight boxing champion between 1917 and 1925, who is universally regarded as among the best professional boxers in any weight division in the twentieth century.

Leonard was one of four children of Gershon Leiner, a tailor, and Minnie Leiner, a homemaker. Leonard's parents, Jewish immigrants from Russia, named him Benjamin Leiner, but because the values in Jewish families did not accept boxing as a respectable activity worthy of being pursued, he appropriated the name Benny Leonard at the age of fifteen to conceal his participation in professional boxing from his parents.

The Leiners lived in an apartment close to a public bathhouse on the Lower East Side of Manhattan, at the intersection of Eighth Street and Avenue C, bordering Greenwich Village. The working-class neighborhood was an ethnic amalgam of Italians, Irish, and Jews. Leonard's introduction to boxing was through street fights between people of various ethnic groups going to use the public baths.

Leonard began boxing for small purses at local informal athletic clubs in 1911. His pseudonym was soon disclosed when he returned from one of his encounters with a black eye and confessed its origin to his parents. However, his confession was accompanied by twenty dollars, which he placed on the kitchen table. His mother, opposed to his choice of profession, wept inconsolably, but Leonard's surprised father said: "All right, Benny, keep on fighting. It's worth getting a black eye for twenty dollars."

Benny Leonard, 1932. © BETTMANN/CORBIS

Though sources differ by several months as to date, it appears that Leonard's first professional fight was in September 1911 against Mickey Finnegan. All sources, however, are clear on the outcome: Leonard, not quite fifteen years old, was knocked out in only the third round. It was not an auspicious beginning. In his next twelve fights in 1911 and in 1912, Leonard won seven by knockouts, three were no-decision bouts, and he himself was knocked out twice. The no-decision designation was mandated by the state Frawley Act of 1911 for any fight that did not end in a knockout. Under the Walker Law of 1920, decisions by ringside judges and the referee as to the winner of a boxing bout replaced the no-decision fights specified by the Frawley Act.

Many of Leonard's early fights—and perhaps even some later ones—depended on promoters generating spectator participation and enthusiasm by exploiting the ethnic differences between the contestants or the religious prejudices held by their supporters—a reflection of the lamentable polarization that first directed Leonard into boxing. These differences and prejudices also resulted in Benny Leonard folktales—some true. On 3 September 1912 Leonard fought in New York City's Chinatown before a large crowd cheering loudly for his adversary, Ah Chung, who had been introduced as the lightweight champion of all China, just come to America. Though some observers suspected the Asian authenticity of Ah Chung, accessible records indicate a six-round knockout victory by Leonard over Ah Chung without mention of the latter's real name—Greenberg.

Leonard's career took a significant upward turn in 1914 when Billy Gibson, who owned an athletic club and was marginally active in Bronx politics, became his manager. Gibson hired a capable trainer, George Engel, who taught his intelligent and receptive student the finer points of both defensive and offensive scientific boxing. Under Engel's tutelage and Gibson's matchmaking, Leonard fought frequently and rapidly developed into a formidable lightweight contender. At five feet, five inches tall, and weighing between 130 and 133 pounds, he was an extremely hard puncher with both hands. Although not particularly robust for a world-class fighter, Leonard had a remarkable gift for avoiding and countering the attack of stronger opponents.

Leonard's direct road to the championship began with a nontitle ten-round fight against the world lightweight champion, Englishman Freddy Welsh, on 31 March 1916. Though a no-decision bout under the Frawley Act, it was clear to the boxing writers that Leonard had dominated the champion. A rematch on 28 July 1916 also led to a no-decision result, but this time Welsh had somewhat the better of their encounter. An ever-improving Leonard won five consecutive bouts by knockout between 22 March 1917 and 10 May 1917, then met Welsh for the third time at the Manhattan Casino in New York City on 28 May 1917, challenging him for the championship. A brave but totally overwhelmed Welsh was knocked down three times in the ninth round but refused to be counted out, struggling to his feet each time. The referee, after examining Welsh in his corner, wisely refused a resumption of the bout, and Leonard was the new lightweight world champion.

Leonard became an idol of the boxing world because of his willingness to fight often and against any adversary. His famous contemporary, the heavyweight champion Jack Dempsey, refused to fight men of color. In contrast, Leonard fought two capable African-American boxers in one week in 1917; he knocked out Leo Johnson in the first round on 21 September in New York City and Eddie Dorsey in the second round on 27 September in Buffalo, New York. Leonard was champion for seven years, longer than any lightweight in history. Subsequent to winning the championship, he fought eighty-three times, including eight defenses of his title.

Many of Leonard's bouts displayed his offensive and defensive skills. Among fights of great interest were two title fights with Lew Tendler of Philadelphia. On 27 July 1922 Tendler challenged Leonard for his title at Boyle's Thirty Acres in Jersey City, New Jersey, before a crowd of

60,000 customers. Under New Jersey rules, Leonard retained his championship with a no-decision result by going the twelve-round distance without being knocked out. The exciting fight led to public demand for a rematch, which was held on 24 July 1923 in New York City's Yankee Stadium. It was a superb contest between two splendid boxers, but Leonard had absorbed the lessons of the first encounter and defeated Tendler decisively in a fifteen-round contest to retain the championship.

At the peak of his fame and having become sufficiently wealthy to move his parents to a new home in Harlem, Leonard perceived that his great abilities were beginning to diminish. He had his last bout at this stage of his career on 1 August 1924 in Cleveland—a ten-round, no-decision fight against Pal Moran. Two weeks later, the twenty-eight-year-old Leonard asked his grateful and relieved mother to announce his retirement as the undefeated lightweight champion.

Leonard did not fight again for seven years. However, with advent of the Great Depression, he attempted a futile comeback as a welterweight beginning in October 1931. His opponents were of mediocre caliber, largely through his manager's selection, and Leonard prevailed in eighteen of nineteen bouts before encountering Jimmy McLarnin, a rising contender and future welterweight champion, on 7 October 1932 in Madison Square Garden. McLarnin charitably carried the thirty-six-year-old Leonard for five inept rounds before knocking him out in the sixth, ending one of the most illustrious careers in boxing history. Leonard's final record was 85 victories (69 by knockout), 5 defeats (including the 3 knockouts he experienced when he was 16 or younger), 1 draw, and 114 no-decisions. For the majority of the no-decisions, Leonard certainly would have been judged the winner if decisions had been rendered.

Though Leonard's personal character and conduct were exemplary in all respects and he was regarded as an exceptional role model for youth of the period, one of his losses in the ring indicates that he was not immune from the darker elements frequently afflicting the boxing profession. On 26 June 1922 Leonard, the lightweight champion at the zenith of his powers, stepped up to the next weight class, the 147-pound welterweight division, to challenge the welterweight champion Jack Britton for Britton's title. Before a capacity crowd in Madison Square Garden, Leonard floored Britton in the thirteenth round with a monstrous left hook to the body. As the referee began his count, the welterweight champion was unable to get up. The about-to-be triumphant Leonard inexplicably crossed quickly from a neutral corner and when the count reached nine swatted the floored Britton on the head, an obviously indefensible foul. The amazed referee waved Leonard away and immediately declared Leonard disqualified and Britton the winner.

According to Mannie Seamon, Leonard's trainer between 1917 and 1922, in an account given more than a quarter of a century later in 1948, a year after Leonard's death, Billy Gibson, Leonard's manager, had told the lightweight champion at the weigh-in just before the fight: "I'm sorry I've got to say this, but you can't win this fight tonight." According to Seamon, what prompted Gibson's remark to Leonard that amounted to an order was never made known to the fighter or his trainer.

Other than this single incredible incident, Leonard's long record both in and outside the boxing ring was one of consistent honor, civic decency, fairness, and good citizenship. During World War I, Leonard trained thousands of men as a U.S. Army lieutenant boxing instructor, encouraged enlistments, participated in war bond drives, and fought exhibition bouts to secure recreational equipment. His fame even enabled him to act in several motion pictures in 1924, though he did not achieve distinction as an actor. Leonard joined the Merchant Marine during World War II, where he rose to the rank of lieutenant commander and again made use of his athletic and public relations skills. After the conflict, he taught boxing at the City College of New York and refereed professional fights.

On 1 January 1936 Leonard married Jacqueline Stern, who had been his devoted secretary for ten years. They had no children.

On 18 April 1947, while refereeing the final six-round bout between Mario Ramon of Los Angeles and Bobby Williams of Harlem at St. Nicholas Arena in New York City, Leonard suffered a cerebral hemorrhage and died in the ring. He is buried at Mt. Carmel Cemetery in Queens, New York. Leonard was inducted into the International Boxing Hall of Fame in Canastota, New York, at its opening in 1954. In 1978 he was inducted into the International Jewish Sports Hall of Fame in the Orde Wingate Institute for Physical Education in Israel.

Leonard must have welcomed the Zionist tribute paid him after his 1924 retirement by a Jewish newspaper, *New Warheit,* which perceived him as greater than Albert Einstein. It observed, "It is said that only twelve people or at the most twelve times twelve the world over understands Einstein, but Benny is being understood by tens of millions in America and just as we [the Jewish people] need a country [a Jewish homeland] so as to be the equal of other people, so we must have a fist to become their peers." More concisely, the Hearst editor Arthur Brisbane said, "Benny Leonard has done more to conquer anti-Semitism than a thousand textbooks."

★

Nat Fleischer, *Leonard the Magnificent; Life Story of the Man Who Made Himself "King of Lightweights"* (1947) is the only full-length biography of Leonard. Written the same year as his death, the book was hurriedly put together and inadequately edited. What makes this out-of-print and inaccessible work worthwhile is the large number of interesting photographs not available elsewhere. In *The One Hundred Greatest Boxers of All Time* (1984), Bert Randolph Sugar rated Leonard fifth, between Jack Dempsey and Joe Louis. For a discussion of Leonard's disqualification in his welterweight championship fight with Jack Britton, see Ronald K. Fried, *Corner Men: Great Boxing Trainers* (1991). Several books present material on Leonard as a Jewish athlete. Although it contains several errors, Harold U. Ribalow and Meir Z. Ribalow, *The Jew in American Sports* (1985), offers an admiring description of Leonard's career. See also Robert Slater, *Great Jews in Sports* (1992); Allen Bodner, *When Boxing Was a Jewish Sport* (1997); and Steven A. Reiss, ed., *Sports and the American Jew* (1998). An obituary is in the *New York Times* (19 Apr. 1947).

LEONARD R. SOLON

LEONARD, Ray Charles ("Sugar Ray") (*b.* 17 May 1956 in Wilmington, North Carolina), boxing champion who held world titles in the welterweight, middleweight, super middleweight, and light heavyweight classes.

Leonard was the fifth of seven children of Cicero Leonard and Getha Leonard. If his mother had had her way, Leonard would have become a singer, like the legendary Ray Charles for whom he was named, but fate had other plans for him. Leonard and his family moved to suburban Washington, D.C., when he was a young boy. He grew up in Palmer Park, Maryland, a community once described by *Sports Illustrated* as "a poor, mixed neighborhood with more than enough trouble to go around." A quiet kid who avoided trouble, Leonard behaved himself in school and sang with his sisters in the church choir. He attended and graduated from Palmer Park High School. His father, in a *Washington Post* interview, described his son as "a funny sort of kid" who "always hung back." His son's apparent lack of interest in much of anything worried the elder Leonard. "All my other boys were always into something, but Ray . . . not until boxing."

Leonard discovered boxing when he was fourteen. At Palmer Park's Oakcrest Community Center, he was tutored by volunteer boxing coaches Dave Jacobs and Janks Morton, both of whom demanded strict discipline from their pupil both in and out of the ring. Their efforts paid off, for Leonard compiled an impressive amateur record of 145 wins and only 5 defeats. He won gold medals at both the 1975 Pan American Games in Mexico City and the 1976 Montreal Olympics.

Shortly after winning the Olympic gold by defeating Andres Aldama of Cuba, Leonard stunned the boxing world with an announcement that his gold medal match would be his last. Explaining that he wanted to return to the Washington area to study at the University of Maryland, he said, "My decision is final. My journey is ended, my dream fulfilled." This was but the first of a number of retirement decisions by Leonard that eventually were reversed. When product endorsements failed to materialize after he was married on 19 January 1980 to Juanita Wilkinson, the mother of a son he fathered out of wedlock (the couple later had another son), Leonard decided that he would go into professional boxing after all. Instead of seeking a boxing promoter, he put his fledgling professional career in the hands of attorney Mike Trainer.

Trainer, together with a group of several investors, incorporated Leonard and turned all shares in the newly formed corporation over to Leonard himself. Working hard to promote the boxer's best interests, Trainer brought in Angelo Dundee, Muhammad Ali's former trainer, to work with Leonard. Drawing on the wave of publicity unleashed in the wake of his gold medal win in the Olympics, Leonard kept himself in the public spotlight, adopting the nickname "Sugar Ray" after former boxing great Sugar Ray Robinson. Slowly but surely Leonard began to accumulate an impressive record of wins, most by technical knockout (TKO), the termination of a fight when a boxer is either unable or is declared unable to continue by a referee. With the guidance of Trainer and Dundee, Leonard faced a se-

Sugar Ray Leonard. AP/WIDE WORLD PHOTOS

ries of opponents who were good enough to challenge, but not to turn the tables on him.

Leonard's road to the top was not without potholes. He experienced severe pain in his hands for several days after most fights, and Dundee's training program was grueling. However, only two years after turning professional, Leonard faced Wilfredo Benitez on 30 November 1979 in the World Boxing Council (WBC) welterweight title fight in Las Vegas, the first fight ever in this weight class to pay each participant more than $1 million. Leonard took the title by TKO in the fifteenth round. Two fights later, defending his WBC title, Leonard suffered a defeat at the hands of the Panamanian Roberto Duran and surrendered the welterweight crown. However, he was well prepared to counter Duran's battering style when the two met again in a rematch in November 1980. Duran fled the ring during the eighth round, saying "no mas, no mas" (no more, no more) and claiming he was suffering stomach pains. In 1981 Leonard defeated the World Boxing Association welterweight champion Thomas Hearns to become the undisputed world champion in the welterweight class.

While training in 1982 Leonard experienced a sharp pain in his left eye that turned out to be a detached retina, an injury that could have cost him his vision in that eye. Surgery repaired the retina, but Leonard decided once again to abandon boxing after doctors warned that punches to the head could easily cause a recurrence. Explaining the reasons for his retirement, Leonard told *Sports Illustrated*, "There isn't enough money in the world for me to risk my eyesight. You can't put a price tag on that." Leonard got a job with HBO as a color commentator at boxing matches covered by the cable network, and the product endorsements he had hoped for after his Olympics win finally began to come his way.

Leonard made a brief return to boxing in 1984, when he met unranked Kevin Howard in what was supposed to be a warmup for an eventual faceoff with middleweight champion Marvin Hagler, high on Leonard's list of targets. Howard was no pushover, knocking Leonard to the canvas in the fourth round. Although Leonard won the fight on a TKO in the ninth round, he realized he was not yet ready for bigger challenges. He retired again and was out of the ring for just over two years. In the fall of 1986 Leonard returned to training with a vengeance and soon challenged Hagler to a match. Although most critics doubted he could pull it off, Leonard easily bested the older Hagler in a twelve-round match in the spring of 1987. In November 1988 Leonard picked up two more WBC titles by defeating Donny Lalonde, who was champion of both super middleweight and light heavyweight classes.

Leonard's June 1989 rematch with Hearns ended in a disappointing draw. He stayed away from the ring for more than a year before announcing plans to challenge the WBC junior middleweight champ Terry Norris for the title. The much younger Norris handily defeated Leonard in February 1991, prompting another retirement announcement.

This time it looked as though the retirement would stick. Leonard put his career in the hands of Los Angeles–based talent agency International Creative Management, released an exercise video, and settled down in an expensive new home in exclusive Pacific Palisades, California. Having divorced his first wife in 1990, Leonard married model Bernadette Robi on 20 August 1993.

Just a few months before his induction into the Boxing Hall of Fame on 15 June 1997, Leonard once again returned to the ring to fight Hector "Macho" Camacho in Atlantic City, New Jersey. Camacho easily defeated the aging Leonard with a TKO in the fifth round, prompting yet another retirement announcement. Although he hinted that he might fight again, Leonard has since limited his involvement in boxing to matters outside the ring. He works widely as a commentator, having appeared on the American Broadcasting System (ABC), the National Broadcasting System (NBC), ESPN, and HBO, and in mid-2001 announced the formation of Sugar Ray Leonard Boxing, Inc., a boxing promotional company. In a joint venture with ESPN, the company, of which Leonard is chairman, produces boxing events that air on the cable network. Leonard has served for many years as the international chairman of the Juvenile Diabetes Research Foundation's Walk for a Cure. He also actively participates in a number of national and international causes benefiting needy children.

Leonard's love of boxing is so great that time and again he has found himself pulled back into the ring, sometimes against the counsel of his closest advisers. Others may question his motives, but Leonard's reasons are clear: "Some people look down on boxing as barbaric, but it's a wonderful sport. It has enabled me to have an incredible life, not just materialistically, but because I've been exposed to so much and I've been able to give back. The gratitude I get back from helping people, kids in particular, is worth more than everything I've done. I'm truly happy."

★

James S. Haskins, *Sugar Ray Leonard* (1982), provides an excellent overview of Leonard's life and early amateur and professional career. Younger readers may enjoy the brief biography *Sugar Ray Leonard: The Baby-Faced Boxer* (1982), by Bert Rosenthal. Other books covering Leonard's life and career include Sue H. Burchard, *Sports Star: Sugar Ray Leonard* (1983), which focuses on Leonard's Olympic triumph; and Sam Toperoff, *Sugar Ray Leonard and Other Noble Warriors* (1986). To learn more about Leonard and his career, see Jack Friedman, "Jocks: Can Sugar Ray Leonard Make a Comeback," *People*, and Rick Reilly, "Bonus Piece: One Will Be Made Whole," *Sports Illustrated* (both 30 Mar.

1987). See also Pat Putnam, "Sugar Ray Leonard Demanded Only One Thing: Let Him Choose the Date," *Sports Illustrated* (18 Feb. 1991).

DON AMERMAN

LEONARD, Walter Fenner ("Buck") (*b.* 8 September 1907 in Rocky Mount, North Carolina; *d.* 27 November 1997 in Rocky Mount), Negro Leagues first baseman and member of the National Baseball Hall of Fame, who was compared to Lou Gehrig for his hard hitting and superb fielding.

Leonard was one of six children of John Leonard, a railroad fireman, and Emma Sesson Leonard, a homemaker. When his father died from influenza during the major 1919 outbreak, Leonard's formal education ended at the eighth grade. At the age of eleven, he helped to support the family by shining shoes. By the age of sixteen, he was working in the Atlantic Coastline railroad shop.

In 1921 Leonard, a left-handed batter and thrower, joined the semiprofessional Rocky Mount Elks, playing first base and managing the team. After Leonard lost his railroad job, he left home in 1933 to play baseball for Daughtry's Black Revels in Portsmouth, Virginia, earning $15 per week plus room and board. He also played with the Baltimore Stars, a barnstorming African-American team, and finished the season with the Brooklyn Royal Giants.

In 1934 Leonard joined the Homestead Grays, a club located in a blue-collar community across from Pittsburgh on the Monongahela River. The Grays, who joined the Negro National Leagues in 1935, were a dominant team in the league, and Leonard was the key to their success.

At five feet, eleven inches, and 185 pounds, Leonard, the league's finest defensive first baseman, hit for both average and power. Scorekeeping in the Negro Leagues was incomplete, and the many exhibition games made it difficult to compare statistics. The *Baseball Encyclopedia* and the National Baseball Hall of Fame record Leonard's career batting average as .324, while James A. Riley, a historian of the Negro Leagues, lists Leonard as a .341 career hitter. Leonard hit .410, the second highest average in the leagues in 1947, and in 1948 he led the league at .395 and tied for most home runs at forty-two. The Homestead Grays won nine straight pennants from 1937 to 1945.

After Jackie Robinson broke the color bar in Major League Baseball in 1947, the Negro Leagues declined, and the Negro National League failed after 1948. The Grays disbanded in 1950, ending Leonard's career in the Negro Leagues. From 1951 through 1955, he played in the Mexican League, including stints with Torreon (1951–1953), and Durango (1954–1955). He also played Mexican winter

Buck Leonard, 1972. ASSOCIATED PRESS FILE

ball at Obregon (1951), and Xalapa (1952–1953). In 1953 he played a brief stint with the Portsmouth Merrimacs. Leonard retired from baseball at age forty-eight in 1955.

Life in the Negro Leagues was hard. Official league games usually numbered less than 50, but exhibition play stretched the season to about 200 games. Players often slept and ate on the team bus, as few hotels and restaurants served African Americans at that time. Although many players spent their leisure time on the road gambling, Leonard worked crossword puzzles and read the Bible. During the Great Depression, Leonard earned $125 per month for the four-and-a-half-month season, an income insufficient for himself and Sarah Wooten, the first-grade teacher he married on 31 December 1937. Thirteen times Leonard supplemented his Negro Leagues salary by playing winter ball in Latin America, the Caribbean, or barnstorming with other Negro Leagues stars. During World War II, Leonard's salary jumped from $425 per month to $1,100, surpassed only by the salaries of pitcher Satchel Paige and teammate Josh Gibson. Leonard and Gibson were a powerful duo known as the "Thunder Twins" and were hailed as the "[Babe] Ruth and [Lou] Gehrig of black baseball." In 1948 Leonard's earnings reached $10,000 for the regular season and Cuban winter ball.

Although racial segregation was the rule, African-American teams often played exhibition games against white semiprofessional and, on occasion, All-Star teams of major leaguers. Leonard batted .382 against major league pitchers, including .500 in eight games with Satchel Paige's All-Stars in 1943. Clark Griffith, the Washington Senators' owner, approached Leonard and Gibson about playing for his team in 1938, but Leonard received his first real opportunity to join the major leagues in 1952, six years after Jackie Robinson broke the color bar. Bill Veeck, the St. Louis Browns owner, invited the forty-five-year-old Leonard to spring training, but he declined, believing his time was past.

After retiring from baseball in 1955, Leonard returned to Rocky Mount, working as a truant officer and athletic assistant for the Rocky Mount school district until 1970, and later as a real estate broker. He earned a high school diploma in 1959. Leonard's wife, Sarah, died in February 1966; they had no children. On 7 July 1986 Leonard married his second wife, Lugenia. From 1962 to 1975 Leonard served as vice president for the Rocky Mount Leafs baseball team in the Class-A Carolina League. On 7 August 1972 Leonard was inducted into the National Baseball Hall of Fame, one year after Satchel Paige became the first player from the Negro Leagues to be inducted. Leonard died in 1997 of complications related to a stroke he suffered in April 1986, and is buried at Gardens of Gethsemane in Rocky Mount.

Leonard, a member of the last generation of African-American players barred from Major League Baseball, played seventeen seasons in the Negro Leagues (1934–1950) with the Homestead Grays, contributing to the club's ten Negro National Leagues pennants (1937–1945, and 1948) and three Negro Leagues World Series championships (1943, 1944, and 1948). The hard-hitting, superb fielding first baseman played on twelve All-Star teams. Ironically, the racial integration of Major League Baseball in 1947 destroyed African-American professional baseball, which had been a significant cultural institution in black communities.

★

The National Baseball Hall of Fame Library in Cooperstown, New York, has a file on Leonard. His autobiography, *Buck Leonard, The Black Lou Gehrig: The Hall of Famer's Story in His Own Words* (1995), written with James A. Riley, describes life in the Negro Leagues. James A. Riley, *The Biographical Encyclopedia of the Negro Baseball Leagues* (1994), includes an article on Leonard. Obituaries are in the *New York Times* (29 Nov. 1997), and the *Washington Post* (30 Nov. 1997). Incomplete statistics and the paucity of press coverage make oral history important to the study of Negro Leagues ballplayers. Three of the best conversations with Leonard are John Holway, *Voices from the Great Black Baseball Leagues* (1975), and *Black Stars: Negro League Pioneers* (1988); also Brent Kelley, *Voices from the Negro Leagues: Conversations with 52 Baseball Standouts of the Period 1924–1960* (1998).

PAUL A. FRISCH

LESLIE, Lisa DeShaun (*b.* 7 July 1972 in Hawthorne, California), college, Olympic, and professional basketball player and professional model known for her grace, skill, and generosity.

Leslie was one of three girls born to Walter Leslie, a semiprofessional basketball player, and Christine Leslie, a postal worker. Leslie's father left the family in 1976 when she was four years old. In 1982, after learning her postal carrier job might be terminated, Leslie's mother, Christine, sold her house and bought an eighteen-wheel truck. Leslie and her sisters—one older, one younger—spent summers traveling with their mother and the school year with relatives. Despite these separations, the family was close-knit and mutually supportive. In school Leslie was embarrassed by her height and teased by other children. Her mother, herself six foot, three inches tall, encouraged Lisa to be proud of her stature and enrolled her in charm school and paid for

Lisa Leslie. AP/WIDE WORLD PHOTOS

modeling lessons. Leslie grew more comfortable with her height but still was irritated by the constant question, "Why don't you play basketball?"

Leslie's basketball career began at Whaley Junior High in Compton, California. Convinced to play by a friend, Leslie figured if she gave the game a try people would stop asking her why she did not play. To her surprise, she liked the game and expressed her interest to her cousin, Craig Simpson, who agreed to work with her over the summer. Simpson worked on basketball fundamentals and did a good deal of strength training. They did sit-ups, push-ups, and basketball drills.

By the time Leslie arrived at Morningside High School in Inglewood, California, she was ready to join Morningside's Lady Monarchs, who were rated among the top 10 girls' basketball teams in the United States. As a six-foot, three-inch freshman, Leslie made the varsity team and started every game. The Lady Monarchs coach Frank Scott said she needed work, but was impressed by Leslie's work ethic and daily improvement.

By her senior year Leslie usually played only the first half of the game so that her teammates could get playing time. She averaged more than twenty-seven points and fifteen rebounds per game. In her last game at Morningside, the Lady Monarchs tried to help Leslie break the school's single-game scoring record. By halftime Leslie had accumulated an incredible 101 points, which beat the school record and was only five points shy of breaking the single-game high school record set by Cheryl Miller. The opposing team declined to play the second half.

In addition to leading her team to two state championships, Leslie won a number of individual awards. A solid student, she maintained a 3.5 average, was class president three consecutive years, played volleyball, and was a champion high jumper. In 1989 Leslie earned the Dial Award as the best scholar-athlete in the nation (female), and in 1990 *USA Today* and Gatorade named her Prep Player of the Year. Leslie also received the prestigious Naismith Prep Player of the Year in 1990 and earned All-America honors in 1994, 1993, and 1992.

Leslie earned international attention for her basketball performance in the 1989 Junior World Championship. This experience, combined with her high school record, meant that she was fiercely recruited by colleges in her last year of high school (1989 to 1990). The decision was easy; she wanted to play where her mother could come to games. Accepting an offer from the University of Southern California (USC), a Pacific Ten (Pac-10) school, Leslie stayed in Los Angeles.

Leslie settled in to the demanding schedule of practice, games, and study. During her first game she accumulated thirty points, twenty rebounds, and four steals, and quickly earned the starting center position. By the end of her freshman season, Leslie averaged twenty points and ten rebounds per game, making her the leading freshman scorer and rebounder at USC. Leslie became the first freshman named to the Women's College Basketball All-Pac-10. Her other individual honors include National and Pac-10 Freshman of the Year awards, and Pac-10 Player of the Week honors three times—all as a freshman.

Overall Leslie averaged 20.1 points, 10.1 rebounds, and 2.7 blocked shots per game in her college career. She also totaled 2,414 points, 1,214 rebounds, and 321 blocked shots—all Pac-10 records. She became the only Pac-10 player to be named All-Pac-10 four times. During Leslie's time at USC, the team went to the NCAA tournament every year and made it to the quarterfinals Leslie's senior year. Leslie graduated from USC in 1994 with a Bachelor's degree in broadcasting.

Leslie's subsequent international experience included playing on the women's U.S. national team, which went to the world championships in 1994, and one season as a professional with team Sicilgesso in Alcamo, Italy, in the 1994–1995 season. In 1995 she made the U.S. Olympic Team. Leslie shone on the court no matter where she played. During the 1996 Olympic Games, the U.S. women's basketball team won every game, with Leslie as the team's leading scorer.

After the Olympics, Leslie took time to pursue her second dream career, modeling. She signed with Wilhelmina Models and appeared on the cover of *Vogue* and on a few television shows. She felt it important that people see a tough, driven woman athlete who was also feminine.

With the formation of the Women's National Basketball Association (WNBA) in June 1997, Leslie was again drawn to the courts. She signed with the Los Angeles Sparks in 1997 and became one of the league's three key spokespeople. While with the Sparks, Leslie was named to the All-WNBA first team in 1997, was one of the finalists for the 1997 Women's Pro Basketball ESPY award. In 1998 she was named USA Basketball's Female Athlete of the Year for the second time (the first was in 1993); and in 1999 and 2000 was the WNBA All-Star Most Valuable Player (MVP). In 2001 Leslie was named All-Star MVP for the second time and was the first woman to be named regular-season and All-Star MVP in the same season. She was named 2001 Women's Sports Foundation Sportswoman of the Year (co-recipient with pole-vaulter Stacy Dragila), as well as 2001 League MVP, Championship Series MVP, and All-Star MVP—the first player to be awarded all three. In addition, the Sparks won the WNBA championship in 2001. Leslie continued to play with the USA basketball team during the off-season, and the team won the gold medal in the 1996 and 2000 Olympic Games.

Having spent her whole life in Los Angeles, Leslie gives generously to her community. Her many projects include

"Taking It Inside with Lisa Leslie," a program that teaches young girls how to improve their self-esteem and how to set goals. She works with the Big Brother, Big Sister foster-care program, and is a spokesperson for Sears WNBA Breast Cancer Awareness. She donates money and equipment to her former high school and to her church, and owns her own company Lisa Leslie Enterprises. In 1999 Leslie was awarded the Young Heroes Award by the Big Sisters Guild of Los Angeles for her commitment to foster children.

Throughout her career Leslie has tried to do right. She knows she is a role model for children, both girls and boys, as well as one of the WNBA's most visible and best-loved players. Leslie's skill and talent speak volumes, and she brings depth and grace to the game. She is quick to point out that her height helps, but it nevertheless took a great deal of hard work to achieve her many successes. Leslie's role in women's basketball is matched only by her dedication to her community and her willingness to share her life with those around her.

★

Leslie's story appears in a number of books for young readers; the most complete is Brent Kelley, *Women Who Win: Lisa Leslie* (2001). She is also featured in Marlene Targ Brill, *Sport Success: Winning Women in Basketball* (2000).

LISA ENNIS

Carl Lewis at the 1992 Summer Olympics in Barcelona. AP/WIDE WORLD PHOTOS

LEWIS, Frederick Carlton ("Carl") (*b.* 1 July 1961 in Birmingham, Alabama), track-and-field competitor and nine-time Olympic gold medalist in short distance running events and the long jump, who is considered by many experts to be one of the greatest athletes of all time.

Carl Lewis was born to a family of athletes. His parents, William McKinley Lewis and Evelyn Lawler Lewis, were both track stars at the Tuskegee Institute in Birmingham, Alabama, during the late 1940s. The couple married after graduation and went on to careers as schoolteachers and civil rights activists while raising four children. In 1963 when Carl was still an infant, they moved the family to Willingboro, New Jersey, a suburb near Philadelphia, where both parents taught at local public schools. In his autobiography, *Inside Track*, Lewis paints a picture of an idyllic childhood: "We settled in a four-bedroom house with a large backyard. We were another middle-class American family, going to church, playing Little League, getting to know the neighbors, talking and laughing around the dinner table."

Lewis's parents, however, were unhappy with the limited opportunities that the schools district afforded young runners—the schools had no girls' track teams—and in 1969 they founded the coeducational Willingboro Track Club, which they developed into a regional power in novice competition. Consequently, Lewis quite literally grew up on a running track, calling the long-jump sawdust pit his "baby-sitter." Lewis attended Willingboro High School, graduating in 1979.

By the age of sixteen Lewis already showed evidence of world-class potential. He frequently made long jumps of more than 25 feet, less than 5 feet short of a world record, and he ran the 100-yard dash in under 9.3 seconds. He was widely sought after by collegiate track powers, including Villanova in nearby Philadelphia, but chose the University of Houston, principally to work with Cougars coach Tom Tellez, whom he admired for his scientifically based approach to training.

As a student at Houston, Lewis became a national track figure. In his sophomore year, he logged a string of impressive victories. These included two titles at the 1981 Southwest Conference Indoor Championships: the long jump, where he registered 27 feet, 10.75 inches, the fourth best jump in history; and the 60-yard dash at a time of 6.06 seconds, just .02 seconds short of the standing world record. In recognition of his achievements, he received the James E. Sullivan Award as Best Amateur Athlete and was named the Associated Press Athlete of the Year.

Given what he had already accomplished, and his family's credentials in the track world, Lewis seemed all but a prince heading toward his coronation as a national champion and hero. However, he began to assert himself publicly in ways that upset the conservative and often hypocritical establishment of what used to be called, often with a grain of salt, "amateur athletics." Although he would continue to work with Coach Tellez throughout his career, Lewis refused to keep up the pretense that he was simply a student member of a college track team, which was the preferred way of maintaining one's "amateur" standing at the time. He stopped attending classes in 1981 at the end of his sophomore year and began to compete in international track meets, openly accepting the backing of commercial sponsors. *Texas Monthly* reported that the twenty-year-old began receiving endorsement fees of up to $65,000 from Nike just for wearing the company's shoes. Although this kind of arrangement has since become commonplace for rising young Olympic superstars, it provoked much resentment from Lewis's contemporaries.

From this point on, Lewis's career can be followed by a trail of controversial actions, decisions, and words that run parallel to his remarkable achievements. His first Olympic competition, the 1984 Los Angeles Games, is a good example of this. The young athlete stunned the world with a series of remarkable performances, winning four gold medals in track-and-field events (long jump, 100- and 200-meter races, and 4 × 100 relay), thus equaling the record set by Jesse Owens in 1936. Yet even while making sports history, Lewis managed to alienate many of the 80,000 fans at the Los Angeles Coliseum for the long-jump competition.

In the finals of the event, Lewis made a first jump of 28 feet, .25 inches, a distance so much greater than any of the other competitors had ever recorded that he decided to pass on his next four attempts in order to conserve himself for the sprints. Even though Lewis won the medal easily on the strength of that jump, the crowd wanted to see him attempt to break the world record, and they let him know it by booing him roundly. According to sportswriter Skip Hollandsworth, "By the time the Olympics were over, he was being called arrogant and greedy, the Maria Callas of the Cinders."

Rumors about Lewis's sexuality have dogged him for much of his career. Whispers concerning homosexuality have been so widespread that the athlete felt the need to address the issue in his 1990 autobiography. He claims no prejudice against homosexuals, but denies being homosexual himself, attributing much of the rumor mongering to "a woman who had been in bed with me enough times to know I was not gay." According to Lewis's account, he refused to marry her and broke off their relationship, leading her to seek revenge. He also believes the falsehood was perpetuated as revenge by athletes who resented or feared his public denunciations of anabolic steroid use and his advocacy of effective drug testing.

Regarding the latter, in his personal campaign to rid the sport of performance-enhancing drugs, he even went so far as to publicly "name names" of athletes as users. Among those he charged was one of the most respected figures in U.S. track, sprinter Florence Griffith Joyner. These accusations put Lewis in the midst of another swirl of controversy and recrimination. Given his stance on the issue, it is no small irony that one of his nine Olympic gold medals was awarded to him after Canadian Ben Johnson, who had actually beaten him in 1988 in the 100-meter sprint, tested positive for steroids.

Poised, articulate, and strikingly handsome, Lewis made no secret of his desire to use sports as a stepping-stone toward a career in entertainment. In 1986 he recorded *Break It Up,* his debut as a singer. Although the album failed to catch on in the United States, it was a bestseller in the Scandinavian countries, where the African American athlete, sporting his distinctive buzz cut hairstyle, briefly achieved the status of a pop idol. In general, though, Lewis has had little success as a singer or actor. At the height of his celebrity in the late 1980s he could only manage several bit parts in feature films; later he appeared as a guest panelist on television game shows, including *Hollywood Squares* and *Sports Geniuses.*

Controversies and dubious forays into the entertainment world aside, Lewis emerged from the 1984 Olympics as one the world's premier athletes. He was voted into the Olympic Hall of Fame less than a year later. At the 1988 Games in Seoul, Lewis once again took gold in the long jump and 100 meters, as well as a silver medal in the 200 meters. *Track and Field News* declared Lewis its "World Athlete of the Decade" for the 1980s.

In 1991, at the ripe old sprinter's age of thirty, Lewis showed the track world that he was still at the height of his powers by breaking the world record in the 100-meter dash with a time of 9.86 seconds. This is just one of many world records Lewis holds in his various events. Sometimes overshadowed by his reputation as a "hot dog" out for individual glory is the fact that Lewis broke world records in the anchor leg of the 4 × 100-meter relay five times between 1981 and 1991. One record, however, eluded him. Even during his many years as the undisputed king of the long jump, he was never able to equal Bob Beamon's 1968 outdoor record jump of 29 feet, 2.5 inches. Perhaps Lewis's most impressive mark, especially given the circumstances under which he achieved it, is his total of nine lifetime Olympic gold medals in track and field, a record he shares with the 1920 Olympics star Paavo Nurmi of Norway.

Lewis went into the 1996 Olympics at thirty-five years of age with eight gold medals, but he just barely made the team. Although his string of sixty-five straight world-class competition long-jump victories had ended back in 1991, Lewis still believed he could win the event. Working with his coaches Tom Tellez and Joe Douglass at the Santa Monica Track Club, he took up an intense program of weight training, which had not been necessary in his younger days, while adhering to a strict vegetarian diet. Much to the unambiguous delight of the Atlanta crowd, Lewis took his ninth gold on his final attempt with a jump of just under twenty-eight feet. Even some of his harshest critics could not resist cheering. "Things have a way of coming back around. Don't they?" Lewis told a reporter with undisguised relish.

Lewis officially retired as a competitor in 1997. He chose a Berlin appearance for his last competition, probably as a thank-you to European track fans, with whom he has always been particularly popular. He thrilled the crowd with a winning effort in the anchor leg of the 4 × 100 relay. In an interview with the *Washington Post* following the meet, Lewis remained true to form, using the opportunity to castigate Primo Nebiolo, head of the International Track and Field Federation, as well as other officials, for their dictatorial style and for "losing the public's trust." Noting a recent public opinion survey that identified the five most popular athletes in the sport (a list that included himself), Lewis said, "Not one of us is under thirty years of age. If the public does not care much for the younger stars, that in itself should tell you that the future of track and field is in serious trouble." Lewis was voted into the National Track and Field Hall of Fame on 30 November 2001.

Lewis lives in Los Angeles. In 1999 he launched a clothing line of up-market sportswear, and he continues to make commercial endorsements and pursue possibilities in the entertainment field.

★

Lewis has written two books with collaborator Jeffrey Marx: *Inside Track* (1990), an autobiography that includes the Olympic star's views on many of the controversies that have surrounded him, and *One More Victory Lap* (1996), a "personal diary" in which he recorded his preparations for, and competition in, the Atlanta Games. A rich profile of Lewis, "Athlete of the Century: Carl Lewis," written by Skip Hollandsworth, appears in *Texas Monthly* (Dec. 1999).

DAVID MARC

LIEBERMAN-CLINE, Nancy (*b.* 1 July 1958 in Brooklyn, New York), pioneer and trailblazer in women's amateur and professional basketball who was the youngest basketball player, male or female, to win an Olympic medal and the first woman to play in a men's professional basketball league.

Lieberman-Cline was one of two children born to Jerry Lieberman, a building contractor, and Renee Lieberman. Lieberman-Cline's parents separated shortly after she was born and divorced when she was twelve. She rarely saw her father and claims that she never developed a strong relationship with her mother. Lieberman-Cline credits team sports for giving her the values necessary for success.

As a child growing up in Far Rockaway, New York, Lieberman-Cline played sports with the neighborhood boys and was known as a tomboy. At age nine, she tried out for the Police Athletic League (PAL) baseball team and learned about sex discrimination. Although she made the team, she was told girls were not eligible to play. Undaunted, she later joined a boys' YMCA basketball team (for ten- to thirteen-year-olds), and basketball became her sport.

At age thirteen Lieberman-Cline was recruited by Coach Lavoiser Lemar to play for the Harlem Chuckles boys' team, one of the best Amateur Athletic Union (AAU) teams in New York City. Because of her feisty attitude, she got the nickname "Fire." Playing against boys and later men, Lieberman-Cline developed the physically aggressive style for which she is famous.

As a seventeen-year-old student at Far Rockaway High School, Lieberman-Cline tried out and was selected as a forward for the U.S. national teams that won a gold medal at the 1975 Pan American Games and placed eighth in the 1975 World Championships. In 1976 she became the youngest member of the U.S. Olympic women's basketball team that won the gold medal.

Lieberman-Cline graduated from high school in 1976. Heavily recruited by college coaches, she decided to play basketball at Old Dominion University (ODU) in Norfolk, Virginia. During 1979 and 1980, her junior and senior years, Lieberman-Cline led the Lady Monarchs to two Association for Intercollegiate Athletics for Women (AIAW) national championships and to a 72–2 record. In both years she was awarded the Wade Trophy as the best women's collegiate basketball player and the Broderick Cup for top female college athlete. In her sophomore, junior, and senior years Lieberman-Cline was a Kodak All-American. Over her four years as a guard, she scored 2,430 points, made 961 assists, and grabbed 1,167 rebounds. During that time, attendance at ODU's women's basketball games increased from around 350 to 10,000 spectators per game.

While at ODU, Lieberman-Cline was selected for U.S. national teams that won a silver medal at the 1979 Pan American Games and a gold medal at the 1979 World Championships. She was also selected for the 1980 Olympic team that never played because the United States boycotted the Olympics to protest the Soviet Union's invasion of Afghanistan.

After graduating from ODU in 1980, Lieberman-Cline

Nancy Lieberman-Cline, 1997. Associated Press AP

spent the summer playing for the Gailyn Packers of the New York Pro Summer League, a men's semiprofessional league. That same year she signed a three-year contract for $100,000 with the Dallas Diamonds, a team in the recently formed Women's Basketball League (WBL). Lieberman-Cline led the Diamonds to the championship finals, and was named All-Pro and Rookie of the Year. Unfortunately, the WBL declared bankruptcy in 1981, and Lieberman-Cline became tennis star Martina Navratilova's trainer, personal manager, and confidante. In 1983 Lieberman-Cline and sports promoter Steve Corey organized a Ladies Over America All-Star Basketball tour featuring WBL players (including Lieberman-Cline). The Women's American Basketball Association (WABA) was formed in 1984, and Lieberman-Cline signed a three-year $250,000 contract to play for the new Dallas Diamonds. She was named Most Valuable Player of the All-Star Game and led the Diamonds to the WABA championship. Unfortunately, the WABA also folded after the championship playoffs in December 1984, and Lieberman-Cline again found herself out of a job.

Called "Lady Magic" (after Earvin "Magic" Johnson) for her ball-handling skills and great passes, Lieberman-Cline became the first woman to play in a men's professional basketball league in 1986, when she played for the Springfield Fame of the United States Basketball League (USBL). During the 1987–1988 season, she passed another milestone when she became the first white woman to play for the Harlem Globetrotters Organization. She played for the Washington Generals against the Harlem Globetrotters on their world tour, and married Tim Cline, a player for the Generals, on 18 May 1988. The couple has one son.

In 1997 the Women's National Basketball Association (WNBA) was formed, and Lieberman-Cline at age thirty-eight signed with the Phoenix Mercury. She played for one season before retiring and becoming head coach and general manager of the WNBA's Detroit Shock, a position she held until 2000. Lieberman-Cline earned a degree in interdisciplinary studies at Old Dominion University on May 6, 2000.

Lieberman-Cline is one of the first women basketball players to play an active role in sports media. Her broadcasting career with ESPN, the American Broadcasting System (ABC), ESPN2, Fox Sports Network, and the National Broadcasting System (NBC) covers two decades, including stints as an NBC color commentator for women's basketball at the 1988 Seoul Olympics and the 1992 Barcelona Olympics. She continues to be a broadcaster/commentator/analyst for ESPN for the Women's NCAA Championships and for WNBA games. Lieberman-Cline is a contributing editor to the *Dallas Morning News, USA Today,* and *New York Times,* and has written several books, including *Bas-*

ketball My Way (1982), with Myrna and Harvey Frommer, and *Basketball for Women: Becoming a Complete Player* (paperback, 1992), with ESPN/ABC Sports anchor Robin Roberts. Lieberman-Cline and her husband live in Dallas.

Lieberman-Cline's many honors include being the first woman to be inducted into the New York City Basketball Hall of Fame in 1993. She was also inducted into the Naismith Memorial Basketball Hall of Fame in 1996 and the Women's Basketball Hall of Fame in 1999. A longtime member of the Women's Sport Foundation, she served as president in 1999–2000. Lieberman-Cline continues to be active in the promotion of women's sports.

In an era when there were few opportunities for women to play amateur and professional basketball, Lieberman-Cline was a trailblazer. She successfully carved out a career in women's amateur and professional basketball, sports broadcasting, and sports marketing. She is the CEO of Nancy Lieberman Enterprises, a company that oversees her girls' basketball camps and her other marketing and business interests. Lieberman-Cline helped create many of the opportunities that women basketball players have today.

★

Lieberman-Cline's autobiography, written with Debby Jennings, is *Lady Magic: The Autobiography of Nancy Lieberman-Cline* (1992). A biography is Doreen and Nancy Greenberg, *A Drive to Win: The Story of Nancy Lieberman-Cline* (2000). A profile of Lieberman-Cline is "Nancy Lieberman-Cline," *The Women's Basketball Hall of Fame, Inaugural Weekend Celebration, Program and Yearbook* (1999). Another profile is in Richard Deitsch, "100 Greatest Women Athletes, 44. Nancy Lieberman-Cline, Basketball," *Sports Illustrated for Women* (winter 1999–2000).

GAI INGHAM BERLAGE

LILLARD, Joseph ("Joe") (*b.* 15 June 1905 in Tulsa, Oklahoma; *d.* September 1978 in Long Island City, New York), African-American athlete whose career playing football, basketball, and baseball was shortened due to racial prejudice.

Lillard's father shoveled coal into furnaces for a living; his mother was a homemaker. Orphaned at age ten, he grew up with his brother in Mason City, Iowa. Lillard first showed his athletic prowess at Mason City High School, where he was All-State twice in both basketball and football; a state track champion; and an imposing pitcher, outfielder, and switch hitter in baseball. As a football player Lillard was the classic "triple threat." He was a great passer, runner, and kicker, both punting and kicking (the latter a real art, as dropkicking, not placekicking, was the rule of the day). Lillard reportedly once drop-kicked a fifty-yard field goal. As was typical in that era, Lillard also played defense, where he was a standout defensive back known especially for his hard tackling.

In 1926 Lillard played basketball in Chicago for a new team formed by Abe Saperstein, first called the Savoy Big Five. This was the original squad that in 1930 renamed itself the Harlem Globetrotters. Lillard was thus one of the original Globetrotters.

Lillard, who graduated from high school in 1927, wanted to play for the University of Minnesota football team. At the end of the summer of 1930 the Minnesota coach Clarence ("Doc") Spears took a new job at the University of Oregon and invited Lillard to move with him. The West Coast had fewer entrenched barriers against African Americans than did other areas of the country, especially the South, where African Americans were still banned from major campuses. Lillard quickly proved a standout on the 1930 Oregon freshman team.

Prior to the opening of the 1931 Pacific Coast Conference (PCC) season, little was expected of Oregon. West Coast sportswriters predicted a championship for the University of Southern California (USC). Then in the first weeks of the 1931 season, Oregon surprised everyone by winning its first three games. Lillard was their star. Owing to the open prejudice of the day, fans dubbed Lillard "Shufflin' Joe" and "Midnight Express." But the Oregon fans meant it with affection; Lillard was a popular athlete on campus.

The following week, on 20 October, Oregon was slated to face USC. First considered an easy spot on the fall schedule for USC, Oregon and Lillard were now causes for great worry. The USC coach hired an African-American player to pose as Lillard in practice so the team could get used to keying on someone who looked like him. Behind the scenes, USC officials pulled other strings. A week before the game it came to light that in the previous summer Lillard had played semiprofessional baseball. Lillard maintained his innocence, claiming he had been paid only to drive the team's bus. Even if he was guilty, hundreds of other college football players had also played semiprofessional ball, including the USC quarterback, and other USC players had been given convenient work as extras on Hollywood sets. USC manipulated the PCC officials into banning Lillard. Oregon officials protested and at first won a reprieve. Then the conference commissioner threatened to resign unless Lillard was suspended, and the majority yielded to him. No other PCC player that season was banned, disciplined, or even reprimanded for playing semiprofessional baseball. USC went on to beat Oregon 53–0. Off the Oregon football team, Lillard dropped out of school. Oregon lost the rest of its games, and USC went to the Rose Bowl.

After leaving Oregon, Lillard moved to Chicago and played more exhibition football. In 1932 he tried out with the NFL Chicago Cardinals. He easily made the club, one of only two African Americans to make any team in the league that year or the next. (The other was Ray Kemp, who played sporadically for Pittsburgh.) The Cardinals were a poor team, but Lillard was their star. In 1932 and 1933 he led the team in passing and running, handled the punting and dropkicking, was their best defensive back, and ran back punts and kickoffs.

The Cardinals were the "second" team in Chicago, with the Bears dominating the local fans and press. When the two teams squared off, as they did twice a year, the game was a big event for the city. In the second 1933 Cards-Bears game, Lillard starred in an upset, running a punt back for the winning touchdown. A photograph showing Lillard's punt return as he eluded the grasp of the Bears great Harold "Red" Grange prompted shock and consternation in the white press (and celebration in the African-American *Chicago Defender*). After the Cardinals defeated Boston in 1933, a reporter proclaimed Lillard was "one of the greatest all-around players that has ever displayed his wares on any gridiron."

Typical of a star player on a weak team, Lillard was the focus of every opponent. Lillard's race added to the mix. One of his coaches, Paul Schlissler, admitted, "he was a marked man. [Opponents] would give Joe the works." As a result of the foul play, Lillard sustained numerous injuries. He missed several games and practices, and his teammates accused him of loafing and breaking rules. Lillard responded by generally keeping his distance from the rest of the team. In subsequent decades, Lillard's personality and style would have engendered labels like "brooding" and "intense." But in the 1930s an African-American man who showed such harsh tone and pride was in trouble. In 1932 his head coach suspended Lillard for several games for his attitude and behavior. Even reporters for the *Chicago Defender,* keenly aware that the end of African Americans in the NFL might be near, counseled Lillard to tone himself down, "to play upon the vanity of whites." This Lillard would not, and most likely could not, do. He had to be himself.

Whether or not Lillard's personality was a factor, between the 1933 and 1934 seasons the NFL team owners, led by the Boston (subsequently Washington) Redskins' George Preston Marshall, struck a "gentleman's agreement" excluding any remaining African-American players from the league and barring any in the future. Despite the obvious quality of such talented players as Lillard and several other college stars in the 1930s, this notorious ban held for thirteen years. As at Oregon, Lillard had played superbly but was caught in the snares of a racism that was impossible to disentangle. He was out of the NFL, and there was nothing he could do about it.

Lillard played more professional baseball, basketball, and football. He played in the baseball Negro Leagues. He formed his own professional basketball team, the Chicago Hottentotts. In 1936–1937, amidst an unsuccessful attempt at a football Negro League, Lillard played for Fritz Pollard and the New York Brown Bombers. In all his efforts he was never able to play on any teams that would avail him the national attention his talent merited. In 1938 a group of African-American athletes formed an all-star squad and staged a game with the Chicago Bears in which Lillard participated. But he was a bit past his peak, and the team, hastily organized and lightly practiced, lost 51–0.

The NFL ban on African-American football players continued through the World War II years, in spite of the shortage of players. When the color bar finally fell in 1946, Lillard was too old to take advantage of the opportunity. Like the great Josh Gibson in baseball, he had simply come along too soon. Every indication of his play with Oregon, the Globetrotters, and the Cardinals showed him to have had the makings of a true star, equal to any players of the time. But like so many African-American athletes of a time when laws enforced racial segregation in the South, the true extent of his talents will forever remain unknown.

Lillard spent most of his remaining years in New York. He served two years as a policeman, worked in a department store, and ran a community gymnasium, serving as a community social investigator and cultural director to help juvenile delinquents. He died of heart failure in Long Island City, New York, in September 1978. He is buried in Queens, New York.

Lillard was one of the truly outstanding athletes of the 1930s. His saga illustrates to how great a degree African Americans were the victims of the racial prejudice that was so pronounced in that era.

★

Lillard's football career is covered in Charles Kenyatta Ross, *Outside the Lines: African Americans and the Integration of the National Football League* (1999).

ALAN H. LEVY

LILLY, Kristine Marie (*b.* 27 July 1971 in Wilton, Connecticut), soccer player who became a member of the Women's U.S. National soccer team at the age of sixteen and has since appeared in more international matches than any player in the history of the sport, male or female.

Lilly was born and raised in Wilton, an upper-middle-class suburb northeast of New York City. She was by all accounts a natural athlete, playing not only soccer, but every other sport available, including the usually all-male tackle football games in her neighborhood. Lilly's older brother Scott recalls that none of the boys held back on her because she could catch a football on the run as well as any of them and was capable of giving as good as she got. Lilly refused to accept the sexual barriers of organized sport, playing

Kristine Lilly, 2001. AP PHOTO/ELISE AMENDOLA

second base in Little League and joining a boys' soccer team in the absence of a girls' league. As evidence of the respect she commanded from teammates, her father, Steven Lilly, points out that when a regional soccer tournament in Niagara Falls, New York, banned her, the entire team walked off the field rather than play without her.

Unperturbed by the hostility often directed against her by opposing players—and by their coaches and parents—Lilly thrived in an atmosphere that might have broken the spirit of others her age. She described her childhood experiences as an athlete this way: "I was surrounded by guys. It made me tough. It made me know there was nothing I couldn't do. My parents never said I couldn't do anything *because* I was a girl. My brother used to bring me along. I was a girl, but I was one of the guys."

In the summer of 1987, not yet a high school junior, the fifteen-year-old Lilly traveled to Chicago to try out for the U.S. Women's National soccer team. She became the national team's youngest player ever, and at five feet, four inches, she was also its shortest. Less than a month after her sixteenth birthday the left-footed Lilly started at left forward and scored a goal in a milestone 2–0 victory over the Chinese team in Tianjin. Back home, she captained her high school team, leading Wilton to three state titles in four years.

While Lilly was achieving these spectacular early successes, her family was breaking apart. Her parents divorced shortly before she left home in 1989 to accept an athletic scholarship to attend the University of North Carolina (UNC) at Chapel Hill. There, rather than let personal adversity distract her, she turned emotional distress into an opportunity to intensify her focus on the game. "The only place I expressed my feelings was in the game," she told writer Marla Miller. "I had this pain inside that spilled out on the field."

Lilly, along with another soccer great, Mia Hamm, led the UNC Tar Heels to four straight National Collegiate Athletic Association (NCAA) titles under Coach Tony DeCicco. Lilly's tenacious play earned her virtually every accolade that women's college soccer had to offer: the Hermann Trophy (1991); UNC's Athlete of the Year award (1993); and the designation as All-America, All-South, and All-Atlantic Coast Conference each of her four years at UNC. She finished her NCAA career with seventy-eight goals and forty-one assists, and her jersey number 15 was retired. Despite the extracurricular time and travel, she received her bachelor's degree in communication right on schedule in 1993.

Lilly is best known to the public as a member of the U.S. National team. Dubbed by *Soccer Times* the "iron woman" of the sport, she has been a member of the team every year since her teenage debut in 1987, appearing in over 215 international matches, the most by far of any player in the world. In a 1999 review of her career to date, *Soccer Times* found that she had played in 88 percent of the matches in the history of the U.S. National team, started in 186 of her 191 appearances, and, most remarkable of all, played a full 90 minutes in 157 games. Some of the memorable victories of the team during these years include the winning of the very first Women's World Cup competition in 1991, the 1996 Olympic gold medal in Atlanta, the 1998 gold medal at the Goodwill Games, and a second World Cup in 1999. Although known for her passing and defensive play, Lilly is the team's third all-time scoring leader.

Women's Sports and Fitness called Lilly one of the "foremothers of women's soccer" in the United States. In a country where soccer has always taken a backseat to other major sports and where women's sports have taken a backseat to men's, the achievement of these athletes in gaining nationwide and worldwide respect for their team is among the remarkable stories of U.S. sports. "With no professional league of their own," David Hirshey writes, "these women are forced for the most part to train alone in weight rooms, racquetball courts and empty stadiums . . . until they are summoned to international matches."

Lilly's role in all of this has been crucial, and her teammates on the foremothers' list are quick to acknowledge it. "Lilly is my favorite player," Michelle Ayers told an interviewer, "because she does the grunt work." Julie Foudy, in a characteristically blunt remark, called her "a total stud who has never had a bad game." Mia Hamm, who has been playing alongside Lilly since college, and whose movie-star good looks have gained her a disproportionate share of media attention, said that when people tell her they think she is the best player in the world, she replies that Lilly is. Lilly's tough, consistent, and unselfish play, as well as her team leadership, have helped make the United States a credible force in world competition.

Lilly has participated in sporadic attempts over the years to establish a professional women's soccer league, including a season spent with the Washington Warthogs of the ill-fated Continental Indoor Soccer League in 1995. However, with the general rise in acceptance and popularity of female athletes, she has gained a number of product endorsements. She teaches soccer and runs the Kristine Lilly Soccer Academy each summer in her hometown of Wilton, where pride in her achievements is in no short supply. High school students play their soccer matches at Kristine Lilly Field and a sign at the town line trumpets, "Welcome to Wilton, Hometown of Olympic Gold Medalist Kristine Lilly."

★

Almost any book written about U.S. women's soccer includes material on Lilly. Recommended are Jonathan Littman, *The Beautiful Game* (1999), Marla Miller, *All-American Girls* (1999), and Jere Longman, *The Girls of Summer* (2000). A profile of Lilly's career, including a complete statistical rundown, is available at <http://www.soccertimes.com>.

DAVID MARC

LILLY, Robert Lewis ("Bob") (*b.* 26 July 1939 in Olney, Texas), football player acknowledged by many as the greatest defensive tackle in National Football League (NFL) history, and the first member of the Dallas Cowboys to be inducted into the Pro Football Hall of Fame.

Bob Lilly, 1973. AP/WIDE WORLD PHOTOS

Lilly's father, John Earnest Lilly (known as Buster), was badly injured in a motorcycle accident as a teenager but was a huge influence on Lilly's life and athletic career. "He worked every day when I was growing up. And after work, even though he couldn't run, he'd throw me that football and teach me the game—more importantly, taught me values and life." Lilly's father worked as a farmer and heavy equipment operator and later as an independent contractor. His mother, the former Margaret Louise Redwine, was a homemaker who cared for Lilly and his two siblings.

Between eighth and tenth grade, Lilly shot up from five feet, eight inches to six feet, four inches tall. Although he was thin, Lilly was a starter for the Throckmorton High School football team and an excellent basketball player and volleyball player. In basketball he averaged twenty-seven points a game as a sophomore. As a junior he was the state high school javelin champion. Prior to his senior year, a prolonged drought forced the Lilly family to leave Texas for Pendleton, Oregon, where Lilly's father found employment as a bulldozer operator clearing land for developers.

Lilly earned All-State honors in both football and basketball at Pendleton High School, from which he graduated in 1957, and he attracted attention from college scouts in the Northwest. Some offers were quite lucrative—in Lilly's words, "cash, cars, jobs for my dad." But Lilly's heart was in Texas. When a postcard arrived in Pendleton from Texas Christian University (TCU) line coach Allie White, who remembered Lilly from a sophomore-season volleyball game at Throckmorton (he later said, "I never saw a big boy so quick"), Lilly accepted TCU's scholarship offer. His mother "packed about sixty ham sandwiches and a few gallons of lemonade," and Lilly and a buddy drove the 1,600 miles from Pendleton to Fort Worth nonstop in thirty-five hours—in Lilly's 1947 Studebaker. TCU Horned Frogs head coach Abe Martin remembered the rawboned recruit as "the longest drink of water I ever saw."

A physical education major at TCU, Lilly became enchanted by a course in water skiing. In fact, he spent so much time on it that other courses suffered. But Lilly found himself academically and remained in school and eligible after one rocky semester. He was named All-Southwest Conference (SWC) twice by a majority of those who voted, and in his senior year he was a unanimous All-American. One of the football honors teams Lilly was chosen for in 1960 was the Kodak All-America, and the team made an appearance on Ed Sullivan's television show. Each member of the team received a Kodak camera. Lilly was hooked and immediately began taking snapshots of nearly everything. In 1983 he published *Bob Lilly: Reflections*, a book almost exclusively made up of photographs Lilly took during his days with the Cowboys—mostly candid shots of his fellow players taken during training camp and while preparing for games.

Lilly's strength and ability became a legend at TCU. Finding a Volkswagen in his assigned parking space one day, he simply picked up the small car and placed it on the sidewalk. Lest he be compared to Superman, Lilly pointed out, "I picked up the front end and moved it and then picked up the back end and did the same thing—at no time did I have all four wheels off the ground at once." To amuse friends, Lilly, by his own count, "moved about a dozen cars this way" while on the Fort Worth campus. This feat became known as the "Lilly Test," and no one else passed it. In college Lilly grew to six feet, five inches tall, and 260 pounds, but lost neither his quickness nor his desire. He graduated from TCU in 1961 with a B.S. in education.

The fledgling Dallas Cowboys coveted Lilly's services, and worked a deal with the Cleveland Browns (who were in a position to draft Lilly) to sign him as the team's first-ever draft choice in 1961. (As an expansion team, the Cowboys were not eligible to participate in the 1960 draft, their first year in the National Football League.) It was a good choice; Lilly was the NFL's Defensive Rookie of the Year in 1961. Lilly continued to play defensive end for the Cowboys until he was switched to defensive tackle midway through the 1963 season. This conversion allowed Lilly to become what many observers call "the best ever at his position." Cowboys coach Tom Landry, recalling the success he had as an assistant coach for the New York Giants when he gave defensive tackle Roosevelt "Rosey" Grier the freedom to disrupt the opposing offense, did the same with Lilly by moving him inside to tackle.

Lilly became the cornerstone of the famed Dallas "Doomsday" flex defense. In the flex, Lilly crowded the line of scrimmage—hit, read, and reacted with lightning quickness. Both Landry and defensive line coach and coordinator Ernie Stautner said that after watching numerous game films of Lilly, they had never seen him neutralized by the first block. "He always broke through the initial contact. Teams tried to double-team and triple-team him, but nothing worked." Lilly was a consensus All-Pro choice eight times between 1964 and 1972, missing only in 1970. Because of Lilly's amazing ability to pursue, some teams tried to run plays directly at him, but his strength made this tactic only marginally successful. Coach George Allen of the rival Washington Redskins said, "He's the greatest defensive tackle ever! He was the smartest, the coolest. We tried everything against him, but could never confuse or contain him." Coach Marion Campbell of the Atlanta Falcons said, "His instincts were unreal. He knew where the ball was going before it was snapped."

Called "Next Year's Champions" by the media, the Cowboys and Lilly endured much frustration before finally winning Super Bowl VI in 1972. With the monkey off his back—Lilly felt somewhat personally responsible for the Cowboys "not being able to win the big one"—Lilly smoked a Texas-size victory cigar after the victory over the Miami Dolphins. This celebration was in stark contrast to the previous year, Super Bowl V, in which the Cowboys lost to the Baltimore (now Indianapolis) Colts in the final seconds. At the final gun, Lilly ripped off his helmet and hurled it fifty feet into the air. When it came down, he kicked it even farther. Lilly claimed he was unaware of what he had done "until a Colt came up and gave me back my helmet."

Lilly retired after the 1974 season when he could not shake a persistent back injury. Despite this ongoing back problem, Lilly missed only one game in his 14-year, 292-game career. On 23 November 1975, the Cowboys retired his number 74 jersey in appropriate Bob Lilly Day ceremonies. Lilly's name was the first in Texas Stadium's Ring of Honor (similar to a Hall of Fame). Lilly was inducted into the Pro Football Hall of Fame in 1980, after the mandatory five-year wait.

Lilly and Margaret Ann Threlkeld married on 22 June

1973. They have four children. They live in Georgetown, Texas, where Lilly heads his own promotions company, Pro Imaging.

Called the "Paul Bunyan of the West" by former Cowboys publicist Doug Todd, Lilly is known better as "Mr. Cowboy." Coach Ernie Stautner, also a Hall of Fame defensive tackle, said, "Bob Lilly simply was the best." Landry paid Lilly an even higher compliment, "A player like Bob Lilly comes along once in a generation."

★

No biography of Lilly has been published, but his career and life are discussed in Joe Falls, *The Specialist in Pro Football* (1966); Berry Stainback, *How the Pros Play Football* (1970); Murray Olderman, *The Defenders* (1973); Jeff Meyer, *Great Teams, Great Years—Dallas Cowboys* (1974); and Peter Golenbock, *Cowboys Have Always Been My Heroes* (1997).

JIM CAMPBELL

LINDSAY, Robert Blake Theodore ("Ted") (*b.* 29 July 1925 in Renfrew, Ontario, Canada), professional hockey player who helped lead the Detroit Red Wings to four Stanley Cup championships in the 1950s and was inducted into the Hockey Hall of Fame in 1966.

Ted Lindsay. HOCKEY HALL OF FAME

Unlike most of his contemporaries in the National Hockey League (NHL), Lindsay inherited his ice hockey credentials. His father, Bert Lindsay, played goalie at Montreal's McGill University from 1902 to 1905 before embarking upon an itinerant professional career. Forty years later Bert's son emerged as a star in junior hockey; Lindsay was a member of the Toronto Saint Michael's College team that lost to the Oshawa (Ontario) Generals in the 1943–1944 junior finals. Oshawa then added Lindsay to its roster in a successful bid for the Memorial Cup in 1944. That September, at the age of nineteen, Lindsay joined the Detroit Red Wings.

An assassin with the face of an altar boy, "Terrible Ted" cut a swath of mayhem and destruction through the NHL of the 1940s, 1950s, and 1960s. Diminutive even by the standards of the time, the five foot, eight inch, 163-pound Lindsay used his fists and his stick, which he called the "great equalizer," to cut opponents down to size. He paid for his contentious deportment, spending 1,808 minutes in the penalty box during a seventeen-year career and accumulating at least 400 stitches (and the nickname "Scarface"), after which he stopped counting.

During the 1946–1947 season the Red Wings coach Tommy Ivan assembled the acclaimed Production Line of Lindsay, Sid Abel, and Gordie Howe. The following year Lindsay tallied thirty-three goals and added nineteen assists, finishing ninth in the league in scoring and earning the first of nine All-Star selections at left wing. Lindsay remained a perennial All-Star for the better part of a decade, failing to make the squad only once between 1948 and 1957 when, in 1954–1955, injuries limited him to forty-nine games.

From 1949 until 1955 Lindsay and Howe paced the Red Wings to seven consecutive Prince of Wales Trophies, awarded to the team that compiled the best record during the regular season. Along with Abel, the duo also hoisted the Stanley Cup in 1950 and 1952. After the Red Wings prevailed in a grueling final series against the New York Rangers in 1950, Lindsay originated the tradition of parading the Stanley Cup around the rink and passing it from teammate to teammate. When Detroit traded Abel to the Chicago Blackhawks, Lindsay succeeded him as the captain and led the Wings to two more championships in 1954 and 1955.

Before the start of the 1955–1956 season, Jack Adams, Detroit's general manager, began to dismantle the club through a series of calamitous trades with Boston and Chicago. Detroit was still good enough to finish second to the powerful Montreal Canadiens and to open the playoffs against the Toronto Maple Leafs. Prior to game three at Maple Leaf Gardens, an anonymous caller telephoned the

Toronto Sun to warn that he would shoot Lindsay and Howe if they dared to skate. Contemptuous of the threat, Lindsay played his usually aggressive style and scored both the tying and winning goals in a 5–4 overtime victory. Once the game ended, he circled the rink and, aiming his stick like a machine gun, peppered the spectators with imaginary bullets.

Although he enjoyed one of his finest seasons, Lindsay sensed that his relations with Adams had been damaged beyond repair and that his days as a Red Wing were numbered. In 1956–1957 Detroit again finished atop the six-team NHL, with Lindsay registering eighty-five points on thirty goals and a league-leading fifty-five assists. Always brusque, outspoken, and independent, Lindsay incurred the wrath of management by starting an automobile parts company with his teammate Marty Pavelich in 1955. Whether it was business, marriage, or family, Adams wanted nothing to distract his players from hockey. "My first ten years in the league," Lindsay said with typical candor, "I could've kicked Jack in the ass and he would've hugged and kissed me. When Marty and I went into business he became a different person."

Along with the Montreal defenseman Doug Harvey, Lindsay served as a players' representative on the five-member board of the NHL Pension Society. When Lindsay and Harvey could not obtain basic information about the pension fund, which the league president Clarence Campbell administered personally, they rightly suspected that the team owners were making robust profits and concealing them from the players. The financial agreement that the Major League Baseball Players Association had recently negotiated—which, among other benefits, granted players a share of the proceeds from a lucrative television contract—induced Lindsay to challenge the rampant exploitation that the NHL players unwittingly suffered.

Violating Campbell's edict against fraternization among players on different teams, Lindsay and Harvey began in 1957 to recruit members for an NHL Players Association (NHLPA). With Lindsay serving as the president, the NHLPA filed a $3 million lawsuit against the NHL in an attempt to secure increased pension benefits and a larger percentage of television revenues. Within a year of its formation, however, the NHLPA was dissolved. Potentially influential players, such as Lindsay's teammates Gordie Howe and Leonard "Red" Kelly, succumbed to intimidation, abandoned the union, and accepted the marginal concessions that the owners offered.

Adams blamed Lindsay and goaltender Glenn Hall for an early exit from the 1957 playoffs, and in July he traded both players to the Blackhawks for Hank Bassen, Forbes Kennedy, Bill Preston, and Johnny Wilson. Lindsay never doubted that the real motive behind the trade was to punish him for his business dealings and unionizing efforts. "The trade to Chicago—that was because of the players association," Lindsay insisted. "See, Jack was losing control of his players, and like everybody else in management then, he couldn't stand the thought of that."

Following his banishment to Chicago, Lindsay toiled for three seasons with the Blackhawks, helping to revitalize the woeful franchise before retiring in 1960. Coaxed back onto the ice by his former linemate Abel, then the coach of the Red Wings, Lindsay made an extraordinary return to the NHL in 1964 at age 39. Scoring 28 points on 14 goals and 14 assists, while amassing 173 penalty minutes, Lindsay inspired the Wings to a record of 40–23–7, their best showing in 8 seasons. For Lindsay, the comeback had a more personal significance. "It's certainly not the money," he explained. "I'm well off. . . . I wanted to leave the game the way I started it: as a member of the Detroit Red Wings."

Lindsay left hockey for good at the end of the 1964–1965 season, retiring to the Detroit suburb of Rochester Hills with his second wife, Joanne. More than thirty years after leaving professional sports, he still rose daily at 5 A.M., exercised for an hour, and then went to the office to manage the auto-parts business he had started with Pavelich. "I'll never retire," he once said, "as long as the good Lord gives me my health." Lindsay also remained close to the Red Wings organization, serving as the general manager between 1976 and 1980 and as the coach for twenty-nine games during the 1979–1980 and 1980–1981 seasons. In attendance at all the Red Wings home games, Lindsay declared with pride, "I buy my own season tickets. That team doesn't owe me anything."

Lindsay finished his playing career with 379 goals, 472 assists, and 851 points in 1,068 regular-season games, adding 96 points on 47 goals and 49 assists in 133 play-off contests. In 1949–1950 he won the Art Ross Trophy as the leading scorer in the NHL, and was selected to the All-Star team nine times. Elected to the Hockey Hall of Fame in 1966, Lindsay stayed close to hockey, serving an analyst for the National Broadcasting Company (NBC) hockey telecasts during the 1972–1973 season. In a ceremony on 10 November 1991, the Red Wings organization retired Lindsay's number 7 to the rafters of the Joe Louis Arena. As the acknowledged leader of the magnificent Red Wings clubs of the 1950s, Lindsay was characteristically humble about his contributions and accomplishments. "Anything to help us win," he explained. "There was never anyone who liked to win more than I did."

★

Useful books on Lindsay and the Red Wings include Stan Fischler, *Motor City Muscle: Gordie Howe, Terry Sawchuk, and the Championship Detroit Red Wings* (1996); Richard Bak, *Detroit Red Wings: The Illustrated History* (1997); Paul R. Greenland, *Wings of Fire: The History of the Detroit Red Wings* (1997); and Brian

McFarlane, *Detroit Red Wings* (1998). Helpful articles include Roy MacSkimming, "Gordie Takes a Pass," *Saturday Night* (Nov. 1994); Kelley King, "Ted Lindsay, Hero of Hockey: March 18, 1957," *Sports Illustrated* (28 Feb. 2000); Ted Lindsay, "Facing the Rocket," *Hockey News* (30 June 2000); and Ted Lindsay and Chuck O'Donnell, "The Game I'll Never Forget," *Hockey Digest* (Dec. 2000). See also the official website of the Detroit Red Wings Alumni Association at http://www.redwingalumni.com.

MARK G. MALVASI

LIQUORI, Martin William, Jr., ("Marty") (*b.* 11 September 1949 in Cedar Grove, New Jersey), one of the best runners in the world at the high school, college, and post collegiate levels, who won the "Dream Mile" in 1971.

Liquori grew up in northern New Jersey with his father, Martin Liquori, who owned a service station, his mother, Sara Tosone Liquori, a homemaker, and three younger siblings. He entered Essex Catholic High School in Newark, New Jersey, in 1963. When he decided to try out for basketball, the coach suggested that he could build his strength by running cross-country, and, as they say, the rest is history.

Liquori's running was impressive, and coach Fred Dwyer, who had been an outstanding runner at Villanova University, devoted extra attention to his training. Their efforts culminated when, as a high school senior, Liquori ran a mile in 3:59.8, and became only the third high school student at that time to achieve a sub-four minute mile. At the Penn Relays that year (an undefeated year in which he broke four meet records for the mile), Liquori anchored the winning distance-medley relay team by running a 4:04 mile, which was the fastest any competitor at those Relays had run a mile, and was voted the outstanding high school performer. Villanova University's legendary coach "Jumbo" Elliott was at the Penn Relays with his team, and it was no surprise when Liquori accepted a track scholarship to that school. His high school classmates voted him the Foremost Essex Senior in 1967.

Marty Liquori, 1971. AP/WIDE WORLD PHOTOS

Arriving at Villanova University in the fall of 1967 as a finance major, Liquori set his sights on the 1968 Olympics in Mexico City. Not only did he make the team, he was the youngest person in the 1,500-meter finals. However, he suffered a hairline fracture in his left leg during the semifinals, and although Liquori decided to compete in the finals he finished twelfth. Ironically, this would be his only Olympics as a competitor.

Upon his return to Villanova in 1967, Liquori proceeded to blaze an outstanding collegiate career. During the indoor season in early 1969, he won the Wanamaker Mile at the Millrose Games held in Madison Square Garden in New York City, beginning a streak of thirteen consecutive races in which he was unbeaten. After several other meets in which he won races at 1,000 meters, 1,500 meters, and 2 miles, as well as being a member of two winning 2-mile relay teams, Liquori won the Inter-Collegiate Association of Amateur Athletes of America (IC4A) championship mile.

When the outdoor season came, after Liquori won the one-mile run in a dual meet, he went back to the Penn Relays and was part of three winning teams: the distance, two-mile, and four-mile relays. After another winning two-mile relay, Liquori won the 1,500 meters at the inaugural Martin Luther King Games, and then won the mile at the IC4A championships. He culminated the collegiate season by winning his first National Collegiate Athletic Association (NCAA) mile title in the time of 3:57.7, defeating the then world-record holder Jim Ryun. Liquori also defeated Ryun one week later, winning the national Amateur Athletic Union (AAU) mile in 3:59.5. He then won the 1,500-meter race in both the USA-USSR-British Commonwealth meet and the Americas versus Europe meet, running 3:37.2 in the latter—the fastest in the world that year. Accordingly, Liquori earned the number one ranking in the 1,500-meter and the mile for 1969.

In the indoor season of early 1970, Liquori again won the Wanamaker Mile, the AAU mile, and the IC4A mile. In the outdoor season, after a win in the three-mile relay in a dual meet and wins at the two- and four-mile relays, Liquori once again was part of three Penn Relay winning teams, anchoring the distance, two-mile, and four-mile relays. After winning the same three relays in the following week, he again won the 1,500-meter at the Martin Luther King Games, defeating Kip Keino, the Kenyan distance runner who won four gold Olympic medals, and was voted the outstanding male performer. After a four-mile relay win the next week, Liquori again won the IC4A mile in 3:58.5, and was on the winning mile relay team. He finished the collegiate season by winning another NCAA mile in 3:59.9.

In fall 1970 Liquori was named to President Richard M. Nixon's Council on Physical Fitness, and was part of Villanova's NCAA-winning cross-country team. In the indoor season of early 1971, Liquori won his third straight Wanamaker Mile, and after a 1,500-meters win at the U.S. Olympic meet, he won his third straight IC4A mile, and was the anchor of the winning two-mile relay team—in fact, Villanova won the team title all three years Liquori participated. Then, in impressive fashion, Liquori won both the one- and two-mile events at the NCAA races, resulting in the awarding to Villanova of the team title.

When the outdoor season came, after winning the one-mile run in a dual meet, Liquori again won three more races at the Penn Relays—the distance, two-mile, and four-mile relays—again anchoring all three teams. Then came his most famous moment: the "Dream Mile" against Jim Ryun at the Martin Luther King Games in 1971. In one of those sporting events moments that lived up to its "hype," Liquori won in 3:54.6, .2 of a second faster than Ryun. He then went on to win his third-straight IC4A mile (giving Villanova its second-straight team title), and his third straight NCAA mile in 3:57.6, breaking his two-year-old meet record. He then won the AAU mile in 3:56.5, ran the fastest 1,500 meters in the world that year (in 3:36), won the Pan American Games 1,500 meters, and was once more named the world's number one 1,500-meter and mile runner. The Philadelphia Sportswriters Association also named Liquori the Amateur Athlete of the Year for 1971.

Staying an extra year at Villanova University to complete his studies, Liquori married his high school sweetheart Carol Jones on 16 October 1971. That same month, however, he tore ligaments in his left heel, an injury that kept him from making the 1972 Olympic team. He did win both a one-mile and a three-mile race early that year, but when the Olympics began in Munich he was broadcasting the games for the American Broadcasting Companies (ABC) television. Liquori graduated from Villanova with a B.S. in finance in 1972, and attended the University of Florida's Graduate School of Journalism from 1973 to 1975 with the help of an NCAA Postgraduate Scholarship. Continuing to run, Liquori won the Philadelphia Track Classic indoor mile in 3:55.8 in 1975, and the mile event at Jamaica in 3:52.2—his best ever. He was aiming for the 5,000-meter event to make the 1976 Olympic team, but a torn hamstring again ended his Olympic bid. Nevertheless, Liquori won a 1,500 meters in Japan in 1977, then set the U.S. record for the 5,000 meters. He retired from running in 1980.

Liquori and his wife and son have lived in Gainesville, Florida, since 1973. He has had a career in broadcasting for both ABC and the Entertainment and Sports Programming Network (ESPN), covering the Olympics and hosting the show *Running and Racing* from 1986 to 1989. He has also written four books, *On the Run: In Search of the Perfect Race* (1977), with Skip Myslenski; *Playboy's Elite Runner's Manual* (1980), and *Playboy's Book of Real Running* (1980), with John L. Parker, Jr.; and *Marty Liquori's Home Gym Workout* (1987), with Gerald Secor Couzens. In addition, because of the interest in running and the fact that running shoes were not readily available to the public, Liquori and a partner rented a room above a women's shoe store in Gainesville to sell running shoes, calling it the Athletic Attic. It did so well that he expanded into hundreds of stores in the United States and overseas, finally selling the company in 1998. He is the president of Marty Liquori Sportswear, Inc., and vice-president of Athletic Lady.

Liquori is the national spokesperson for the "Team in Training" program of the Leukemia Society of America, which raises money for research by sponsoring people who want to compete in a marathon. Shortly after accepting the position in 1991, he was diagnosed with a mild case of chronic lymphocytic leukemia (CCL). Among Liquori's many honors are the Vitalis Cup for Sports Excellence in 1983, the Penn Relays Hall of Fame, the New York City Athletic Club Hall of Fame, the Villanova Athletic Hall of Fame in 1987, the Italian American Hall of Fame in 1991, the National Track Hall of Fame in 1995, and the NCAA Silver Anniversary Award in 1996. All these honors were well deserved by the physically and psychologically tough runner who believed not only in competing against another person, but in going the distance to triumph over himself.

★

Much material about Marty Liquori can be found in the Villanova University Sports Information Office and in the Alumni Office. Articles about Liquori and his career include "The Pressure Cooker," *Sports Illustrated* (7 July 1969); "Revenge Can Be Sour," *Sports Illustrated* (25 May 1970), and "A Dream Comes True," *Sports Illustrated* (24 May 1971). Other articles of interest are "Interview: Marty Liquori," *Sports Philadelphia* (spring 1976); "Life Doesn't Always Work That Way," *Track and Field News* (May 1978); and "Metre Minutes," *Metro Sports* (Dec. 1995).

ROBERT W. LANGRAN

LISTON, Charles ("Sonny") (*b.* 8 May 1932 in Saint Francis County, Arkansas; *d.* 30 December 1970 in Las Vegas, Nevada), boxing heavyweight champion from 1962 to 1964.

The ninth of ten children of the tenant farmer Tobe Liston and his second wife, Helen Baskin, Liston was born in a

Sonny Liston, 1962. © BETTMANN/CORBIS

dilapidated shack on the Morledge Plantation in Arkansas, where he endured a brutal and impoverished childhood. There is some debate concerning the exact date of his birth; records are sketchy, and some sources suggest that he was born in 1927 or 1928. Liston was a troubled youth who received no formal education and never learned to read or write. His father beat him regularly and had him working full-time in the cotton fields by age eight. In 1946 Liston's mother moved to St. Louis. The thirteen-year-old Liston soon followed and lived with her in an apartment at 1017 O'Fallon Street. He grew up in the streets, an incorrigible thug who took part in a string of muggings and holdups that led to his arrest in 1950. Convicted on several counts of first-degree robbery and larceny, he was sentenced to the Missouri State Penitentiary at Jefferson City for five years. There he was encouraged to begin boxing by the prison chaplain Father Alois Stevens. Standing six feet, one inch tall and weighing 210 pounds, with broad shoulders and a powerful build, Liston possessed devastating power and a killer's instinct. Nicknamed "Sonny" by his prison trainer, he quickly fought his way to the top of the prison's boxing program. While Liston was still behind bars, Father Stevens helped secure Frank W. Mitchell, the publisher of the *St. Louis Argus,* as Liston's manager.

Following his parole on 30 October 1952, Liston embarked on a successful amateur career culminating in the National Golden Gloves Heavyweight Championship. He turned professional on 2 September 1953, crushing Don Smith in one round in St. Louis. Liston lost just one of his first fifteen fights, an eight-round decision to Marty Marshall, who broke Liston's jaw, on 7 September 1954 in Detroit. Liston twice avenged this loss, once in 1955 and again in March 1956. During this time Liston's career fell partially under the control of John Vitale, a labor racketeer with ties to organized crime who employed Liston as a strong-arm man and strikebreaking goon. Liston was in frequent trouble with the police, a pattern that persisted throughout his life. On the night of 5 May 1956 he began arguing with a police officer over a friend's illegally parked taxi and ended up breaking the officer's leg and absconding with his gun. He pleaded guilty to assault and was sentenced to the St. Louis Workhouse for nine months.

After his release Liston married Geraldine Chambers, a single mother of one, on 3 September 1957. He resumed his career, winning eight bouts in 1958 and drawing the attention of the underworld boxing czar Frank Carbo and his minion Frank ("Blinky") Palermo, who assumed control of Liston. In 1959, after being warned by a St. Louis police captain to leave town before he was found dead in an alley, Liston moved to Philadelphia, Pennsylvania. There he began pounding his way through the heavyweight ranks despite a lack of any real ring refinement. Liston, who was known for his intimidating scowl, destroyed most opponents with brute strength and a left hand from hell. In 1959 he knocked out all four of his opponents, including the tough Cleveland Williams and Nino Valdez, in three rounds each. In 1960 he stopped the highly regarded Roy Harris after toppling him three times in the first round and then knocked out Zora Folley before having to settle for a decision over the crafty Eddie Machen.

By 1961 Liston was the top contender for the heavyweight crown held by Floyd Patterson. Patterson's wily manager, Cus D'Amato, however, forestalled any encounter with the dangerous Liston by claiming a mobbed-up ex-con was unfit to fight for the championship. Many Americans who viewed Liston as an unrepentant thug agreed. Under mounting pressure, however, the two eventually met on 25 September 1962 at Chicago's Comiskey Park, where Liston knocked Patterson out with a crippling left hook to the head in two minutes and six seconds to win the championship. On the return flight to Philadelphia, Liston felt confident that Americans would forgive his unsavory past. He fully expected a hero's welcome, but when the plane landed, the airport was empty. Liston was crushed. "It was one of the saddest things I've ever seen," said the boxing writer Jack McKinney, Liston's friend. "He never really recovered from that moment." Liston realized that no matter what he accomplished, he always would be considered a sinister beast and remain the champ nobody wanted.

In a rematch on 22 July 1963 in Las Vegas, Liston again knocked out Patterson in one round. These stunning victories reinforced Liston's reputation as an invincible ring predator. Outside the ring he maintained his menacing aura. Despite numerous arrests he continued drinking heavily, driving recklessly, and allegedly assaulting a number of women, mostly prostitutes. Liston seemingly reveled in the notoriety and once observed, "A prizefight is like a cowboy movie. There has to be a good guy and a bad guy. Only in my cowboy movies, the bad guy always wins."

The brash young boxer Cassius Clay (later Muhammad Ali) baited Liston as the "ugly old bear" for months and finally taunted him into a bout on 25 February 1964 in Miami Beach, Florida. The quicksilver Clay deftly outboxed the plodding Liston, peppering him with explosive jabs. The fight ended in controversy and a new champion when a bloodied Liston refused to answer the bell for the seventh round, complaining of a shoulder injury. Liston and Ali fought again in Lewiston, Maine, on 25 May 1965. The rematch ended as abruptly and mysteriously as the first fight when Liston succumbed in the first round to Ali's infamous "phantom punch," a blow unseen by many viewers or deemed not powerful enough to knock out the hulking Liston. Rumors of a fix quickly ensued, and Liston's reputation was ruined.

He nevertheless resumed boxing, knocking out four opponents in 1966 and 1967 in Sweden (where he and Geraldine adopted a son) and winning his next ten fights, nine by knockout, before being stopped by a former sparring partner, Leotis Martin, in the ninth round of a grueling battle in 1969. Liston's last fight was a tenth-round technical knockout of "Bayonne Bleeder" Chuck Wepner in a smoke-filled armory in Jersey City, New Jersey, on 29 June 1970. Back in Las Vegas, where he had settled in 1966, Liston was rumored to be involved in peddling narcotics and possibly loan-sharking. On 5 January 1971 Geraldine returned from an extended visit with her mother to discover Liston dead in their bedroom, where he had lain for approximately a week. Although his death was ascribed to pulmonary congestion and heart failure, traces of heroin were found in his body and needle marks on his arm. The police also discovered heroin and marijuana in the house. Whether Liston died of natural causes, an accidental overdose, or an intentional overdose administered by mobsters remains a mystery. He is buried in Paradise Memorial Gardens in Las Vegas.

Despite his fearsome reputation and criminal background, Liston was as much a figure of tragedy as of mayhem. An illiterate and uneducated man, he was never able to free himself from the grip of organized crime that guided his career and perhaps led to his ignominious defeats and eventual demise. Because his career flourished during the emerging civil rights movement of the early 1960s, Liston was despised and feared by many whites and denounced by many African Americans as an embarrassment to the cause. There was, however, another side to Liston, a brooding loner who loved children and maintained an easy empathy with the downtrodden. The brevity of his reign notwithstanding, some boxing experts consider Liston a great champion who may have squandered an even more considerable talent through a life of dissipation and petty crime. Perhaps the enigma was best summed up by the late publicist Harold Conrad, who observed that Liston "died the day he was born." His official record was fifty-four bouts, fifty won, four lost, with thirty-nine knockouts. He was inducted into the International Boxing Hall of Fame in 1991.

★

The most thorough biography of Liston is Nick Tosches, *The Devil and Sonny Liston* (2000), a brutally honest yet sympathetic account of the boxer's troubled life. Other biographies of note are A. S. ("Doc") Young, *Sonny Liston: The Champ Nobody Wanted* (1963), which chronicles Liston's life up to his winning the championship, and Rob Steen, *Sonny Boy: The Life and Strife of Sonny Liston* (1993). John D. McCallum, *The Encyclopedia of World Boxing Champions Since 1882* (1975), contains a biographical profile and accounts of Liston's major fights, while Nigel Collins, *Boxing Babylon* (1990), emphasizes the scandalous events that plagued the embattled champion. An obituary is in the *New York Times* (7 Jan. 1971).

MICHAEL MCLEAN

LLOYD, Christine Marie ("Chris") Evert. *See* Evert, Christine Marie ("Chris").

LLOYD, John Henry ("Pop") (*b.* 25 April 1884 in Palatka, Florida; *d.* 19 March 1965 in Atlantic City, New Jersey), baseball player who was a superstar shortstop in African-American baseball during the era of racial separation.

Lloyd was reared by his grandmother after his father died and his mother remarried. He left school with only an elementary education to work as a delivery boy to help support the family. He gravitated toward baseball and, in his spare time, played with an amateur local team. When he was a teenager, Lloyd traveled to Jacksonville, Florida, to work as a porter for the Southern Express Company and to play with a semiprofessional team called the Young Receivers. While playing on the sandlots of Jacksonville he was discovered by a trio of players that included Rube Foster, the man who later was known as the father of the Negro Leagues. A year later, in 1906, after having advanced another level in the semiprofessional ranks to the Macon (Georgia) Acmes, Lloyd was signed to play in Philadelphia,

Pennsylvania, with the Cuban X-Giants, a team considered to be among the best African-American ball clubs of the time. From that point on he dominated the professional ranks, quickly earning recognition as a star player.

Lloyd was a complete player who could run, field, throw, and hit with power. He was a consistent .300 hitter and often exceeded .400. He was called the Black Wagner, and the Pittsburgh Pirates superstar shortstop Honus Wagner said that he was honored by the comparison. Acknowledged as the best African-American player during the so-called dead-ball era (usually considered the first two decades of the twentieth century, when an almost soft ball was used for play), Lloyd was always in demand by the top ball clubs. This permitted him to play wherever it was most financially advantageous and, wherever he went, championships usually followed.

He played for Sol White's champion Philadelphia Giants (1907–1909), Rube Foster's champion Chicago Leland Giants (1910), Jess McMahon's champion New York Lincoln Giants (1911–1913), and Foster's champion Chicago American Giants (1914–1915, 1917). While he was with the Lincoln Giants, Lloyd was the playing manager and, in 1918, he was given the reins of Nat Strong's Brooklyn (New York) Royal Giants. From that point on he was usually at the helm of a ball club in addition to being a star player.

The Negro National League (the first African-American league) was organized in 1920. A year later Lloyd left the Royals to become the playing manager for the league's Columbus (Ohio) Buckeyes franchise. In 1923, when the rival Eastern Colored League was founded, Lloyd took the helm of the Hilldale (Pennsylvania) franchise and guided the team to the league's inaugural pennant. Despite winning the championship, Lloyd was not in good graces with the owner and, after the season, was dismissed for alleged dissension on the team. Subsequently he was the playing manager of the Bacharach Giants of Atlantic City before returning to the Lincoln Giants in 1926 to serve in the same capacity until the franchise folded after the 1930 season. In that final season the Lincolns dropped a hard-fought eastern championship series to the Homestead (Pennsylvania) Grays, who featured a rookie slugger named Josh Gibson. After the demise of the Lincolns, Lloyd continued to play professionally through 1932. He also played twelve intermittent winter seasons in Cuba between 1908 and 1930. In one memorable Cuban series in 1910 against Ty Cobb's Detroit Tigers, Lloyd led all hitters with a batting average of .500.

As a player, Lloyd was an aggressive competitor, in contrast to his genial demeanor off the field. He generally refrained from using alcohol, tobacco, and profane language. As a manager Lloyd was a master at building confidence and motivating young players. The respect he earned, both

John "Pop" Lloyd. AP/Wide World Photos

as a person and a manager, was reflected in his selection as the manager of the East squad in the inaugural East-West game in 1933. This was the Negro Leagues' All-Star game, which became the biggest African-American sports attraction in the country.

After ending his professional baseball career Lloyd settled in Atlantic City, where he worked as a custodian, first for the post office and then for the public school system, while still continuing his role as a baseball ambassador. Lloyd and his wife, Nan, had no children, but he devoted a large part of his life to working with the youth of Atlantic City, projecting a fatherly image and instilling in them good values and a solid work ethic. In his latter years he was affectionately known as "Pop" and was beloved by the youngsters he nourished. Lloyd was a playing manager on the sandlots with the Johnson Stars and the Farley Stars until the age of fifty-eight; he continued as a nonplaying manager for several more years. Later he served as the Atlantic City Little League commissioner.

On 1 October 1949 the Atlantic City government dedicated the John Henry Lloyd Park. In his speech at the ceremonies Lloyd said, "I do not consider that I was born at the wrong time. I felt it was the right time, for I had a chance to prove the ability of our race in this sport . . .

and . . . we have given the Negro a greater opportunity now to be accepted into the major leagues with other Americans." After a two-year illness Lloyd died from arteriosclerosis in Atlantic City, just one month before his eightieth birthday. He is buried in the Atlantic City Cemetery in Pleasantville, New Jersey.

The beloved elder statesman of African-American baseball posthumously received baseball's highest honor in 1977, when he was inducted into the National Baseball Hall of Fame in Cooperstown, New York. By his superlative performance on the baseball diamond and his personal dignity and righteous living, Lloyd demonstrated to a prejudiced society the worthiness of African Americans to participate in the American national pastime, and created a greater awareness of the need for racial equality.

★

Two excellent sources of information on Lloyd are "The Black Wagner," in Bob Peterson, *Only the Ball Was White* (1970), and James A. Riley, *The Biographical Encyclopedia of the Negro Baseball Leagues* (1994). Other useful sources include David Porter, ed., *The Biographical Dictionary of American Sports: Baseball* (1987); John Holway, *Blackball Stars* (1988); and Mike Shatzkin, ed., *The Ballplayers* (1990).

JAMES A. RILEY

LOBO, Rebecca Rose (*b.* 6 October 1973 in Hartford, Connecticut), collegiate basketball player who led the University of Connecticut to a perfect season and the National Collegiate Athletic Association (NCAA) title in 1995; professional basketball player and member of the 1996 U.S. Olympic gold medal team.

Lobo is the youngest of the three children of Dennis Lobo, a high school history teacher, and RuthAnn Hardy Lobo, a middle school guidance counselor. Lobo and her family moved from Connecticut to Southwick, Massachusetts, when she was two, but the children attended elementary school in Granby, Connecticut. Lobo inherited her height, six feet, four inches, from her parents. RuthAnn, who played basketball in college, is five feet, eleven inches tall, and Dennis is six feet, five inches tall.

In her early years Lobo showed her talent in sports and a love for basketball, which she began playing in the driveway of her home at age five. In the third grade when Lobo learned that her grandmother was going to a Boston Celtics game, she wrote a note and asked Granny Hardy to give it to Celtics president and general manager Red Auerbach. The note said, "I really like watching the Celtics play. You do a really good job. I want you to know that I am going to be the first girl to play for the Boston Celtics." Basketball meant more than sport to Lobo, as she described in *The Home Team* (1996), the mother-daughter autobiography written by Rebecca and RuthAnn Lobo. Most people need a way to handle pain or anxiety, and as Lobo wrote, "basketball became my way." At age ten, with no girls' basketball team available, Lobo joined a community boys' squad and earned a starting position on the traveling team.

Lobo became a star in basketball, track, softball, and field hockey at Southwick-Tolland Regional High School. She scored thirty-two points in her basketball debut as a freshman. Lobo's final average in her high school career was 29.8 points per game, and she eventually became the top scorer, male or female, in Massachusetts high school basketball history with a total of 2,710 points. Her single-game high was 62 points, which she described as an "embarrassment. I mean, it's a team game." Lobo was an excellent student. She was salutatorian of her graduating class in 1991, named a *Parade* high school All-American and Player of the Year in Massachusetts, and received offers from more than 100 colleges. Lobo decided to attend the University of Connecticut at Storrs, a decision based not only on the school's closeness to her home (Storrs is about forty miles from Southwick) but also because of the rising status of the UConn women's basketball team. The Lady Huskies, under the direction of coach Geno Auriemma, had reached the final four of the NCAA tournament in 1991, the year Lobo entered.

However, Lobo's debut with UConn was not impressive. She scored ten points on three of twelve attempts and fouled out after twenty-six minutes. Coach Auriemma was not satisfied by Lobo's early performances, but he believed in her potential. Lobo improved her skills season after season. She had game averages of 14.3 points and 7.9 rebounds in her freshman year, and by her junior year those figures jumped to 19.2 points and 11.2 rebounds. By the end of the 1993–1994 season Lobo improved her shooting statistics to career highs of 54.6 percent of field goals and 73.8 percent of free throws. Lobo was named Player of the Year in the Big East Conference and was selected as a Kodak All-American in 1994. The road had not been smooth. In December 1993 Lobo learned that her mother had breast cancer. "The best thing you can do for me is to continue to work hard," RuthAnn said to her daughter. "I don't want to have to worry about you too. You do what you have to do, and I'll do what I have to do." Inspired by her mother's fighting spirit, Lobo did her best and so did her mother. When Lobo was named Big East Player of the Year for 1993–1994 she dedicated the award to her mother, whose cancer has been in remission since then.

Lobo and the Lady Huskies enjoyed a dream season in 1994–1995. They earned number-one ranking by beating then top-seeded University of Tennessee in the regular season. They continued winning through the NCAA tournament, and defeated Tennessee again in the title game. UConn's record of 35–0 was the most victories ever posted

Rebecca Lobo. AP/Wide World Photos

by an undefeated NCAA Division I basketball team, men's or women's. Lobo was named Final Four Most Valuable Player. Lobo was a two-time basketball and academic All-American (1994 and 1995), only the second player, after Lynette Woodard of Kansas, to achieve this rare double honor. She finished her college career as UConn's all-time rebounder (1,286) and shot blocker (396) and second in scoring (2,133 points). Although it was not the Celtics, one men's professional basketball team (Jersey Turnpikes) did draft Lobo at the end of her senior year. Even though she regarded it as "just a publicity stunt," she was flattered.

Majoring in political science at UConn with a 3.63 grade-point average, Lobo earned Phi Beta Kappa honors. In 1995 Lobo's numerous awards included the Honda-Broderick Cup and the Wade Trophy; in the same year she was also the Naismith National Player of the Year, Associated Press Female Athlete, and Women's Sports Foundation Sportswoman of the Year.

Lobo and her teammates also helped sports fans develop an interest in and appreciation for women's basketball. When Lobo first saw the Lady Huskies play in 1990, only some of the bleachers were used. But the situation changed dramatically during Lobo's college years. Gampel Pavilion at UConn, with a capacity of 8,241, sold 6,541 season tickets for women's basketball in 1994–1995 and averaged crowds of about 7,900—up 485 percent from 1991—generating nearly $700,000 in revenue. In fact, the Lady Huskies championship game against Tennessee had a higher television rating in Connecticut than did the Super Bowl.

After graduating with a B.A. in political science, Lobo was selected by the U.S. Olympic team. She was the youngest player on the U.S. women's basketball team, which swept to the gold medal in the 1996 Atlanta Summer Olympics and kept Lobo's personal winning streak uninterrupted.

In 1997 the Women's National Basketball Association (WNBA) was created in response to the increasing popularity of women's basketball. Being in the first generation of women's professional basketball players, Lobo became the focus of the marketing campaign for the new venture. She might not be the best player in the new league, "but if you want to talk across-the-board popularity and box office draw or a surefire familiar face for a commercial," wrote Sally Jenkins of *Women's Sports and Fitness*, "Lobo remains the most in-demand star in the league."

Lobo joined the WNBA's New York Liberty and had a good start again. The Liberty won their first seven games before losing to Phoenix Mercury on 7 July 1997. For Lobo the loss ended her personal winning streak of 102 games in more than 3 years, a combined college (35–0), pre-Olympic (52–0), Olympic (8–0), and professional (7–0). Lobo finished the WNBA's inaugural season as the Liberty's second-highest scorer and was named to the all-WNBA second team. In 1999 Lobo was honored, along with Sheryl Swoopes, with a locker at the Basketball Hall of Fame.

On 10 June 1999 Lobo suffered a torn anterior cruciate ligament in her left knee during the first minute of play against the Cleveland Rockers in the season opener. The injury benched her through the rest of the season and the following one. She played for the Liberty in 2001, but was injured again and only played sixteen games for the season.

Lobo has been active in numerous organizations that support breast cancer research and awareness. She also supported the Children's Miracle Network and Pediatric AIDS Foundation. In 1997 *USA Today* named Lobo one of its Most Caring Athletes.

Lobo has been credited for boosting interest in women's collegiate and professional sports. She was regarded as a complete player and a complete person who excelled in both sports and academics. "I try to live my life the right way, like my parents taught me," Lobo said. "If a kid wants to make you a role model, you're a role model."

★

The dual autobiography, Rebecca and RuthAnn Lobo, *The Home Team: Of Mothers, Daughters, and American Champions* (1996), is a fascinating and inspiring story. Important articles on

Lobo include Malcolm Moran, "Lobo's Impact Resonates Far Beyond the Court," *New York Times* (6 Mar. 1995); Rick Telander, "The Post with the Most," *Sports Illustrated* (20 Mar. 1995); Andrew Abrahams, "The Enforcer," *People Weekly* (20 Mar. 1995); Mary Duffy, Heather Bernard, and Erin Kuniholm, "Center of Attention: Rebecca Lobo Has Become the Poster Girl for Women's Basketball and the Sport Couldn't Ask for a Better Role Model," *Women's Sports and Fitness* (1 Mar. 1996); and Sally Jenkins, "She's Got Fame," *Women's Sports and Fitness* (1 Jul. 1999).

DI SU

LOMBARDI, Vincent Thomas ("Vince") (*b.* 11 June 1913 in Brooklyn, New York; *d.* 3 September 1970 in Washington, D.C.), Hall of Fame football coach who built the Green Bay Packers into a dynasty in the 1960s and whose name adorns the Super Bowl trophy awarded annually to the National Football League (NFL) champion.

Lombardi was the oldest of five children born in Brooklyn, New York, to Harry Lombardi, a butcher and meat wholesaler, and Matilda Izzo, a homemaker. Lombardi attended Saint Francis Preparatory School in Brooklyn, and his early inclination was to become a priest. An All-City runningback at Saint Francis, Lombardi earned a football scholarship to Fordham University in 1933. Coached by Jim Crowley, who achieved fame for being one of the University of Notre Dame's legendary "Four Horsemen," and his assistant, the future Fighting Irish coach Frank Leahy, Lombardi played guard on the Fordham Rams' offensive and defensive units. Lombardi gained national notoriety his senior season when the Rams' defensive front was immortalized as the "Seven Blocks of Granite" by Fordham's sports information director, Tim Cohane.

Lombardi graduated magna cum laude from Fordham on 16 June 1937 with a B.S. degree and then played semiprofessional football. He worked for one year as an assistant manager at a New York finance company and in September 1938 enrolled at Fordham Law School. He withdrew on 1 February 1939, however, having completed just one semester. He subsequently worked as a chemist at the DuPont Chemical Company in Wilmington, Delaware, and then was asked by a former college classmate, Andy Palau, to accept a position as a teacher, head basketball coach, and assistant football coach at St. Cecilia High School, a small Catholic school in Englewood, New Jersey. He coached the Saints' basketball team to a 111–51 record and a State Parochial School Tournament title in 1945. He became head football coach at St. Cecilia's in 1942 and in 1943 coached the team to an unbeaten record. From 1943 to 1945 the Saints won twenty-five straight games and were unbeaten in thirty-two straight games.

Lombardi taught chemistry, Latin, and physics at St. Cecilia's and during his eight years at the school became a family man. On 31 August 1940 he married Marie Planitz, with whom he had two children. Lombardi left St. Cecilia's

Vince Lombardi. ARCHIVE PHOTOS, INC.

in 1947 to return to Fordham as head coach of the freshman football team and varsity assistant. His goal was to become Fordham's head football coach, but after he failed to gain the job, he began looking for other coaching opportunities. In 1949 he was hired as an assistant coach at West Point, where his coaching philosophies were influenced heavily by the head coach Earl ("Red") Blaik. Lombardi coached the offensive line, but the program was rocked by a cribbing scandal in 1951. West Point rebounded to win an Eastern championship in 1953 with a 7–1 record.

Lombardi made his move to the National Football League (NFL) in December 1953 when he was hired by the New York Giants as offensive coach. From 1953 to 1958, Lombardi joined with the defensive coordinator Tom Landry and the head coach Jim Lee Howell to build the Giants into a championship contender. New York won the NFL title in 1956 with a 47–7 victory over the Chicago Bears. The Giants returned to the NFL championship game in 1958, losing a classic overtime contest to the Baltimore Colts, 23–17, at Yankee Stadium. After rejecting an offer from the Philadelphia Eagles to become their head coach before the 1958 season, Lombardi was named head coach and general manager of the Green Bay Packers on 28 January 1958. One of the NFL's original small-town teams, the Packers had fallen from their glorious past and won just one game in 1957.

Lombardi and his assistant coaches drilled the Packers endlessly in football fundamentals. His number-one offensive play, the "power sweep," was based on the single-wing off-tackle play run by Jock Sutherland's University of Pittsburgh teams in the 1930s. Lombardi turned the Green Bay defense over to the assistant head coach Phil Bengston, and the two men became one of the greatest coaching tandems in NFL history. Proving himself a master motivator, Lombardi instilled in his young team a strong self-confidence and will to win. A devout Catholic and daily communicant, Lombardi preached to his team constantly, declaring the three most important things in their life to be God, family, and the Green Bay Packers. Standing five feet, nine inches tall and weighing 210 pounds, he presented a picture of strength and intelligence with his stocky, powerful build and thick glasses. He supplemented the grueling hours of daily practice and meticulous film study with such inspirational phrases as "Winning is not a sometime thing; it is an all-the-time thing," "Fatigue makes cowards of us all," and "The harder you work, the harder it is to surrender."

The Packers improved to end the 1959 season with a record of 7–5 and then went on to win the Western Conference championship in 1960 with a record of 8–4. On 26 December, Green Bay played a veteran Eagles team closely in the NFL championship game before losing in Philadelphia, by a score of 17–13. Led by Lombardi, Bengston and a talented corps of players that included ten future Hall of Famers—quarterback Bart Starr, halfback Paul Hornung, fullback Jim Taylor, offensive tackle Forrest Gregg, center Jim Ringo, middle linebacker Ray Nitschke, defensive end Willie Davis, defensive tackle Henry Jordan, cornerback Herb Adderley, and free safety Willie Wood—went 11–3 in 1961 to repeat as Western Conference champions. On New Year's Eve in 1961, Green Bay defeated Lombardi's former team, the New York Giants, 37–0 in City Stadium (now named Lambeau Field) to capture the NFL title.

In 1962 Lombardi fielded one of the greatest teams in NFL history. The Packers dominated the league, going 13–1 to win the Western Conference for the third straight year. Along with their list of future Hall of Famers, Green Bay's roster was filled with All-Pro performers in the guards Jerry Kramer and Fred ("Fuzzy") Thurston, the tight end Ron Kramer and the linebackers Dan Currie and Bill Forrester. The Packers led the league in most points scored and fewest allowed. On 30 December 1962 the Packers defeated the Giants for the NFL title for the second straight year, a 16–7 decision at frigid, windswept Yankee Stadium. The game stands as one of the most brutally contested postseason contests in NFL history.

The Packers finished second in both 1963 and 1964 and returned to the postseason in 1965. Green Bay defeated the Baltimore Colts in overtime 13–10, to win the Western Conference championship, and then beat the defending league champion Cleveland Browns, 23–12, in snowy Lambeau Field on 2 January 1966 to reclaim the NFL title. Bengston, Nitschke, and the Packer defense held the Cleveland fullback Jim Brown, the league's leading rusher, to fifty yards on the ground. Green Bay repeated as Western Conference champions in 1966 with a 12–2 record and then defeated the Dallas Cowboys in the Cotton Bowl on 1 January 1967 to win their fourth NFL championship. On 15 January, Lombardi's Packers beat the American Football League (AFL) champion Kansas City Chiefs, 35–10, in the historic first AFL-NFL World Championship Game. The Packer quarterback Bart Starr was named the Most Valuable Player (MVP) of this first Super Bowl after throwing for two touchdowns and completing sixteen passes for 250 yards.

The NFL realigned in 1967 to accommodate expansion, and the Packers joined traditional rivals Chicago, Detroit, and Minnesota in the Central Division. Lombardi, who had contemplated retirement following the 1966 season, guided the injury-riddled Packers to a 9–4–1 record and the Central Division crown. On 23 December, Green Bay defeated the favored Los Angeles Rams, 28–7, in Milwaukee's (Wisconsin) County Stadium to win a third straight Western Conference championship. On 31 December, Lombardi's Packers rematched with Coach Landry's Dallas Cowboys in the NFL championship game. Game-day temperatures of minus thirteen degrees and a windchill of minus fifty-eight made for treacherous conditions at Lambeau Field. In a classic game that has since become immortalized as the "Ice Bowl," Green Bay rallied to defeat Dallas 21–17, on Starr's quarterback sneak from one yard out with thirteen seconds remaining in the game.

The historic victory allowed the Packers to become the only team in the NFL's modern era to win three straight league championships. It also marked Green Bay's fifth title in seven years. Two weeks later, on 14 January 1968, Lombardi and the Packers earned a second straight victory over the AFL, a 33–14 victory over the Oakland Raiders. Starr was named Super Bowl MVP for the second straight year after throwing for one touchdown and completing thirteen passes for 202 yards. Lombardi stepped down as head coach of the Packers on 1 February 1968 but maintained his general manager's duties. In his nine years as Green Bay's head coach, the Packers had become a sports dynasty and a national symbol of excellence. Lombardi's coaching record during that time was 98–30–4, and 9–1 in the postseason. Rising to near mythic proportions, Lombardi was much in demand as a motivational speaker. A friend of the Kennedy family, Lombardi was touted as a possible candidate for national and local politics.

Lombardi resigned from the Packers on 5 February 1969 and moved to Washington, D.C., to become head coach, general manager, and part owner of the Washington Redskins. Just as he had ten years earlier with the Packers, Lombardi turned the Redskins around immediately, guiding them to a 7–5–2 record in 1969, a mark that virtually mirrored Green Bay's record his first year as head coach of the team. He was diagnosed with colon cancer on 25 June 1970 and treated at Georgetown University Hospital. On 13 August 1970, Lombardi was honored by the United States House of Representatives as "one of the great Americans." Lombardi succumbed to cancer on 3 September 1970 and is buried at Mount Olivett Cemetery in Middletown, New Jersey. He was inducted posthumously into the Pro Football Hall of Fame in 1971.

Lombardi is remembered as one of the greatest winners in sports history and the patron saint of NFL head coaches. He remains a symbol of excellence for people in sports and business. While his most famous quote—"Winning isn't everything; it's the only thing"—has too often been taken out of context, his desire for fair play, drive for perfection, and willingness to work hard to achieve worthy goals remain integral parts of the Lombardi legend.

★

Lombardi's autobiographical works are *Run to Daylight* (1968), written with W. C. Heinz, and the posthumously published *Vince Lombardi on Football* (1973). Lombardi has been the topic of numerous books, including several biographies. The Green Bay guard and author Jerry Kramer, who started for Lombardi during the Packers' glory years, has written several books about the Lombardi Packers, including *Lombardi* (1970), while his days with the Washington Redskins are remembered by Tom Dowling in *Coach: A Season with Lombardi* (1970). Other biographies include Robert W. Wells, *Lombardi: His Life and Times* (1971); John Wiebusch, ed., *Lombardi* (1971); Michael O'Brien, *Vince: A Personal Biography of Vince Lombardi* (1988); *Lombardi: A Dynasty Remembered* (1994), a collection of stories edited by Mike Bynum; *Winning Is a Habit: Vince Lombardi on Winning, Success, and the Pursuit of Excellence* (1997), edited by Gary R. George; David Maraniss, *When Pride Still Mattered* (1999); and Vince Lombardi, Jr., *What It Takes to Be Number One: Vince Lombardi on Leadership* (2000). Obituaries are in the *New York Times* (4 Sept. 1970), *Time* (14 Sept. 1970), and *National Review* (22 Sept. 1970).

EDWARD GRUVER

LONGDEN, John Eric ("Johnny") (*b.* 14 February 1907 in Wakefield, England), Thoroughbred jockey and trainer who founded the Jockeys' Guild and is the only person to have both ridden and trained Kentucky Derby winners.

Longden's father, Herb Longden, a coal miner, and his mother, Mary Longden, raised eight children. When the the Longdens' daughter Elsie was gravely ill, Mormons gave great spiritual support to the family. After Elsie recovered, the family adopted this faith and emigrated from England to Taber, a predominantly Mormon community in Alberta, Canada. Fortunately, train delays prevented the family from embarking on their booked passage on the *Titanic.*

Longden's childhood in Canada prepared him to become an able jockey. Long walks to his sister's farm to ride her horses strengthened his legs, and at age ten he began herding milk cows for a number of neighbors in his open range community. Riding a variety of horses, he was struck by their individuality and treated each one differently in order to obtain their best performance. At thirteen he began working in the coal mines, driving mules and digging coal, which he claimed built his strong upper body.

At sixteen Longden began riding half-mile races on the county fair circuit in western Canada and Montana. Longden found this experience invaluable. "You have to be more versatile in the saddle, think a lot quicker, and have more skill in being able to neck-rein in and out of traffic than you do on mile or more tracks." He also ran in sprint races and won sixteen consecutive Roman races (standing on the backs of two horses), which he later claimed improved his sense of balance. His height (four feet, eleven inches) and weight (114 pounds) were ideal for a jockey.

With the help of mine superintendent John Carmichael,

Johnny Longden, c. 1959. © BETTMANN/CORBIS

Longden in 1925 traveled to Calgary, Alberta, Canada, where he learned the finer points of racing. He won his first official Thoroughbred race on Hugo K. Asher on 4 October 1927 in Salt Lake City, Utah. He returned to Canada to attend school and signed a contract to ride for Fred Johnson in 1928. While in Calgary, he met Helen McDonald, a grocer's daughter; they were married in April 1929. Their son was born in 1930. That year Longden exercised horses for "Checks" Sloan in Tijuana, Mexico; returned to Calgary, where he met his lifelong friend Al Tarn, Thoroughbred owner and trainer; and led British Columbian jockeys in wins. During the winter, he traveled to Cuba and was second in winning mounts at Oriental Park. Longden used his earnings to buy the horse Reddy Fox from Tarn, traded it to Johnson for his contract, and became an independent rider. On 2 September 1931 he won his first stakes race, the Winnipeg Futurity, on Mad Somers.

In 1935 Longden met the great trainer Jim Fitzsimmons and began to ride Wheatley Stable horses. This change resulted in his riding more in the United States and, for the first time, earning over $100,000 in a year. In 1936 he was second in the United States in wins. As he traveled more and raced on better mounts, Longden enjoyed more success at the racetrack, but his home life suffered. Divorced in 1939, he married Hazel Tarn, Al Tarn's daughter, on 31 August 1941. They had two children. Longden attained U.S. citizenship on 1 March 1944.

Longden's notable riding accomplishments include winning the American Triple Crown on Count Fleet in 1943; winning the Illinois and Latonia Derbies on successive days, 22 and 23 May 1936, on Al Tarn's Rushaway; riding six winners on one day (5 December 1945) at Bay Meadows; and defeating Citation on Noor, the 1950 Handicap Champion, in the San Juan Capistrano and the Santa Anita Handicap. His other famous mounts included Busher (the 1945 Horse of the Year), Swaps, Silver Spoon, Whirlaway, and St. Vincent (the 1955 Turf Horse of the Year). He led the United States in wins in 1938, 1947, and 1948 and was in the top ten in 1936, 1938–1943, 1945–1953, and 1956. He also led the United States in earnings in 1943 and 1945 and was in the top ten from 1936 to 1957 and in 1961. In 32,413 races, Longden's mounts finished first 6,032 times (932 of these wins were at Santa Anita), second 4,914, and third 4,272. Longden became the world's winningest jockey on 3 September 1957 when he broke Sir Gordon Richard's record of 4,870 wins. Longden raised this record to 6,032, which was later broken by his friend Willie Shoemaker in 1970. (Laffit Pincay set a new record for wins in 1999.)

Longden was noted for his durability. He rode his last winner, George Royal, in the 1966 San Juan Capistrano at age fifty-nine. During his career, he broke both arms and collarbones, legs (one five times), both feet, his back, and numerous ribs and teeth. He suffered concussions and was troubled by arthritis. Injuries such as these were relatively common in horse racing. After Sammy Renick was injured in 1941 at Jamaica Racetrack, New York, Renick, Eddie Arcaro, and Longden formed the Jockeys' Guild. The guild negotiated insurance policies for jockeys, fought to require tracks to have first aid rooms and ambulances, and sponsored the development of improved safety helmets, flak jackets, and track safety rails.

Longden was also a successful trainer, just missing the Triple Crown with Majestic Prince in 1969. Other famous horses he trained included Jungle Savage, Money Lender, and Baffle. From 1965 to 1990 he sent 3,330 horses to the post: 443 won, 391 placed, and 397 showed. These horses won purses totaling $6,038,871. In 1990, following the death of his wife, Hazel, from cancer, he retired from training and moved to Banning, California.

Longden received the 1952 George Woolf Memorial Award and a Special Eclipse Award in 1994. He was inducted into Pimlico's National Jockeys Hall of Fame in 1956 and the National Museum of Racing's Hall of Fame in 1958. He is also a member of the Canadian Racing Hall of Fame. Longden, nicknamed the "Pumper" for his aggressive riding style down the stretch, was a tough, gritty rider who overcame many obstacles to achieve great success.

★

Brainerd Beckwith, *The Longden Legend* (1973), covers Longden's life through his early training days. Henry Mahan, "Longden Saga Unparalleled in Sports," *Daily Racing Forum* (12 Mar. 1966), provides a concise but relatively complete story of Longden's career as a jockey. Stephanie Diaz, "Johnny Longden: A Rider's Reverie," *Backstretch* (Apr. 1993), looks at Longden in retirement and relates his reminiscences. Longden can be seen in "Lucy and the Loving Cup," an episode of *I Love Lucy* (first aired 7 Jan. 1957).

STEVEN P. SAVAGE

LOPEZ, Nancy Marie (*b.* 6 January 1957 in Torrance, California), golfer best known as three-time winner of the Ladies Professional Golf Association (LPGA) Championship and four-time LPGA Player of the Year; the only golfer to have received the Vare Trophy, Rookie of the Year, and Player of the Year awards in the same season (1978).

Lopez was the second daughter of Domingo Lopez, an auto body shop owner and three-handicap golfer at local public courses, and Marina Griego Lopez, a homemaker. Although she was born in California where her parents had been visiting friends, Lopez grew up in Roswell, New Mexico. By the time Lopez was seven, her mother had become ill with a lung disorder. To lessen the severity of her health problem, Marina took up golf.

Without the funds to afford a babysitter, the Lopez family had to take Nancy with them when they practiced their game. As a result, Lopez was exposed to discrimination at an early age. She and her parents had to travel almost 200 miles to Albuquerque because Mexican Americans were not allowed to play golf at the nearby Roswell Country Club. At the age of eight, when her parents realized that she had talent, Nancy was given her first set of golf clubs, Patty Berg four-woods that were cut down to size. With her father acting as coach and teaching her how to cope with the game on an emotional level, Lopez won the Pee Wee tournament at the age of nine, and at ten, the Girls' State Championship. At age twelve, Lopez surpassed all other competitors at the New Mexico Women's Amateur title on her third try, the youngest person ever to do so. In 1972 and 1974 Lopez was victorious at the U.S. Golf Association Junior Girls' Championship. She also won the Western Junior Girls' Championship three times.

While attending Goddard High School in Roswell, Lopez played several sports including gymnastics, basketball, flag football, track, and swimming. She became the first female member on an all-male golf team at the high school. However, Lopez was not able to join local golf clubs because they were too expensive and did not permit Mexican Americans to join. Even without the benefit of club membership, Lopez earned $7,040 for winning second place at the Women's Open during her last year of high school. She also represented the United States on victorious 1976 Curtis Cup and World Amateur teams, and was the best amateur woman golfer in the world.

Lopez intended to major in engineering at the University of Tulsa in Tulsa, Oklahoma, and was offered an athletic scholarship. The school's first and only female coach, Dale McNamara, immediately noticed that Lopez played well enough to turn professional and encouraged her to do

Nancy Lopez. AP/WIDE WORLD PHOTOS

so. Soon after, Lopez's hectic golfing schedule interfered with her studies, so she quit school after her sophomore year in 1977, but not before becoming the women's intercollegiate champion. She placed second in her first three professional tournaments, breaking rookie earnings records for both men and women in that year.

On 29 September that same year, however, Lopez was faced with a devastating setback when her beloved mother unexpectedly died of a heart attack. Although her game suffered for a short while afterward, Lopez began to see her mother's death as an inspiration for her to work harder.

In 1978, her second year as a professional golfer, Lopez surpassed the previous earnings record of $150,000 and won an unprecedented number of tournaments in a row—five—including the LPGA Championship at King Island, Ohio, with a total score of 275. She was victorious in nine events that year and was the recipient of the Vare Trophy for the lowest average on the professional tour. In 1979 Lopez married Tim Melton, a television sportscaster, and limited her participation on the tour.

After divorcing her first husband in 1981, Lopez married Ray Knight, a broadcaster for the Entertainment and Sports Programming Network (ESPN) and former Cincinnati Reds player and manager, on 29 October 1982. The couple has three daughters. When Lopez became pregnant in 1983, she took part in only twelve tournaments, but still exceeded the $1 million mark in tour earnings.

In 1985 Lopez was in top form, winning five events including the Ladies Professional Golf Association (LPGA) Championship. In addition, she won the 1985 Henredon Classic with the lowest seventy-two–hole score ever recorded—268. By the time she turned thirty in 1987, Lopez had thirty-five tour wins, qualifying her for induction into the LPGA Hall of Fame. The following year she won the LPGA Championship and was LPGA Player of the Year for the fourth time. By 1989 Lopez was in second place in career earnings on the LPGA tour with more than $2.5 million, and in November of that year she was inducted into the Professional Golf Association (PGA) World Golf Hall of Fame.

After not winning any title for more than three years, Lopez won her forty-eighth career title in 1997 at the Chick-fil-A Charity Championship, the only LPGA Tour event in Georgia. This win was after Lopez lost forty pounds, worked out for two hours a day, and spent even more time practicing her swing. She then finished second at the U.S. Women's Open after firing four rounds in the sixties. To date, Lopez is the only woman to do this, yet she finished fourth and became runner-up in the Open—a title she has never won.

The LPGA Chick-fil-A Charity Championship, which Lopez won in 1997, was renamed in her honor the "Chick-fil-A Charity Championship Hosted by Nancy Lopez" in 1998. In 2000 Lopez established an annual award in her name, "The Nancy Lopez Award," for the best female amateur golfer in the world. Also in 2000, Lopez became spokesperson and a member of the Board of Directors of The First Tee chapter at Albany, Georgia. The First Tee is a World Golf Foundation initiative dedicated to providing affordable golf access to everyone who otherwise might not have an opportunity to play the game, with a special emphasis on young people. In 2001 Lopez made a hole-in-one during the third round of the AFLAC Championships presented by *Southern Living*.

Lopez is playing editor for *Golf for Women* magazine and founder of the Nancy Lopez Golf Company. She has received numerous accolades, including the Golfer of the Decade tribute for 1978–1987 by the Centennial of Golf in America celebration (1988), the Flo Hyman Award (1992), the Bob Jones Award (1998), the Richardson Award of the Golf Writers Association of America (2000), and the Old Tom Morris Award by the Golf Course Superintendents Association of America (2000). The Flora Vista elementary School that Lopez attended as a child was renamed the Nancy Lopez Elementary School in her honor in 1991. In 2000 Lopez was named one of the LPGA's top fifty players and teachers in honor of the organization's fiftieth anniversary.

Lopez overcame prejudice and fulfilled her childhood dream of becoming a Hall of Fame golfer. Her determination and the support of her close-knit family helped to build the character necessary for Lopez to become one of the greatest golfers ever.

★

Lopez's autobiography is *The Education of a Woman Golfer* (1979), written with Peter Schwed. A collection of true golf stories, Don Wade, *And Then the Shark Told Justin* (2000), includes a section on Lopez, and the book's foreword was written by her. Articles on Lopez appear in *People* (12 June 1978, 25 Apr. 1983); the *New York Times* (2 July 1978, 31 Mar. 1985, 19 May 1988); *Sports Illustrated* (3 Apr. 1995, 20 May 1996, 5 May 1997, 21 July 1997); and *USA Today* (16 Mar. 1994, 28 Mar. 1995, 13 Nov. 1996, 14 May 1977). Biographical sketches of Lopez can be found on the official website of the Ladies Professional Golf Association at http://www.lpga.com, as well as on the *Golf Journal* website at http://www.golfjournal.org/.

ADRIANA C. TOMASINO

LOTT, Ronald Mandel ("Ronnie") (*b.* 8 May 1959 in Albuquerque, New Mexico), All-Pro football player at three different positions, considered by many the finest defensive back in National Football League history.

Lott's father, Roy D. Lott, was a career noncommissioned officer stationed at Sandia (now Kirtland) Air Force Base

Ronnie Lott, 1990. ASSOCIATED PRESS AP

in New Mexico when his son was born. Lott's mother, the former Mary Carroll, was a stay-at-home mother. Fortunately, Roy Lott was stationed in the continental United States throughout his career. Lott, his brother, and his sister were always together. When he was four, the family moved to the Washington, D.C., area when the senior Lott was assigned to Bolling Air Force Base in Virginia. Young Lott quickly became a Washington Redskins fan. He fantasized that he was the Redskins' star receiver, Charley Taylor, and wore Taylor's jersey number (42) throughout high school, college, and with three National Football League (NFL) teams.

When Lott was nine, his father, by this time an Air Force recruiter, was transferred to San Bernardino, California. The family settled in nearby Rialto. At age eleven Lott was the star quarterback of the San Bernardino Jets Pee Wee League team, which was undefeated in ten games and outscored the opposition 377–22. Lott became immersed in sports, reading all he could and watching everything from archery to water skiing on television. He remarked that "had ESPN existed then, I probably would never have made it out of junior high."

Lott developed his fierce tackling style in junior high. He wasn't satisfied with just knocking an opponent off his feet. He said, "I had to drive my helmet into him, keep my feet moving, and lift him into the air before dumping him on his butt." This is the way every defensive coach teaches tackling, but few master the technique as well as Lott did. At Rialto's Eisenhower High School, Lott lettered all three years in football, basketball, and baseball. He earned honors in each of the sports—perhaps the most significant being a *Parade* magazine High School All-America selection in football. He graduated from Eisenhower High School in 1977.

The University of Southern California (USC) promised Lott jersey No. 42, which contributed to his choice of the Trojans as his college team. His career at USC was storied. He started some games as a freshman and was never out of the starting lineup thereafter. While a Trojan, Lott built his reputation as a hard-hitting, ball-hawking defensive back. He earned All-America mention as a sophomore and junior and was a unanimous choice as a senior in 1980, when he was also voted the team's Most Valuable Player (MVP) and most inspirational player. He graduated from USC in 1981 with a B.S. in public administration.

Lott was the San Francisco 49ers' first draft choice—the eighth player chosen overall. After a brief holdout he reported to camp and made an immediate impression. Not much was expected of the 49ers in 1981—they had been 6–10 the year before. But with the maturing of the quarterback Joe Montana and Lott and two other rookies in an inexperienced secondary, the 49ers won their first-ever Super Bowl, defeating the Cincinnati Bengals 26–21. Lott collected the first of his four Super Bowl rings that year. After the game coach Bill Walsh hailed him as "the best athlete this club has had at this point in time." Lott quickly became the unquestioned leader of the 49ers' defense, if not the entire team. He was simply awesome as a rookie. Although he missed out on Defensive Rookie of the Year honors (they went to Lawrence Taylor of the New York Giants), he tied a rookie record by returning three of his seven interceptions for touchdowns. He made All-Pro and received the first of an eventual ten Pro Bowl invitations.

Opponents soon recognized—and felt firsthand—the obstreperous Lott's warrior-like temperament. He studied martial arts, specializing in Tae Kwon Do. In his autobiography, *Total Impact*, Lott said of his style of play, "If you think you want to play in the NFL, and if you want to find out if you can handle being hit by Ronnie Lott, here's what you do: Grab a football and throw it in the air, and before you catch it, have a friend belt you with a baseball bat. No shoulder pads. No helmet. Just you, your friend, and the biggest Louisville Slugger you can find. Wham!"

In Super Bowl XXIII, a rematch with Cincinnati that the 49ers won, the Bengals' Ickey Woods was ripping off big gains early in the game. Lott said, "Don't worry about Ickey. I'm gonna put his fire out." Ray Rhodes, the 49ers' secondary coach, described the results of a savage Lott lick: "It just knocked the spark out of [Woods]. The game turned right there. Ickey just didn't run with the same authority after that."

Unselfishly, Lott moved from cornerback to free safety in 1985. Dallas coach Tom Landry, whose Cowboys were often pitted against the 49ers in postseason play, said, "[Lott] is a middle linebacker playing safety." It was a testament to Lott's physical style of play. Lott, though, was more than just a heavy hitter. He twice led the NFL in interceptions and finished his career with sixty-three steals—a total that was fifth best in NFL history as of 2001.

Lott also lost a little something in 1985. He dislocated and tore the tip of his little finger on his left hand. It didn't respond to treatment. In order to minimize lost playing time, Lott had part of his pinky amputated.

After moving across the San Francisco Bay to the Oakland Raiders in 1991, Lott returned to his college position of strong safety. It was with the Raiders that year that he rung up his second league-leading interception total (8). On 2 March of that year, Lott and Karen Collmer were married.

Lott moved on again after two years with the Raiders, the victim of salary cap considerations, and played the 1993 and 1994 seasons with the New York Jets. In his final season he was presented the Dennis Byrd Award as the team's most inspirational player. That same year Lott was named to the NFL's 75th Anniversary All-Time team. Former NFL coach Bill Parcells said of Lott at the time, "That guy's going to Canton on roller skates," a reference to Lott's surefire qualifications for the Pro Football Hall of Fame. In 2000, the first year he was eligible, Lott was taken into the Canton, Ohio, gridiron shrine. Always at his best in money games, Lott made nine interceptions, returning two for touchdowns, in twenty postseason games.

Since retiring as an active player, Lott can be seen on Fox Sports Net during football season. He, his wife, and three children live in Cupertino, California, where he is involved in an automobile agency and a venture capital organization.

Lott's accolades—the NFL's 75th Anniversary All-Time team and the Pro Football Hall of Fame induction—are prima facie evidence of his greatness. Giants' assistant coach Zev Yaralian summed up Lott's career, saying, "He intimidated receivers and could play the nasty role. He seemed to say, 'You come through my area and I'll knock your head off.' He moved to safety because of his ability as a hard hitter. He may have been a better safety than a cornerback—but he was about the best at either position." Pound for pound, the NFL may never see a more intimidating player. The six-foot, 203-pound Lott once said, "To analyze a player, you have to watch him in slow motion." He always seemed to be playing at fast forward himself.

★

Lott's autobiography, written with Jill Lieber, is entitled *Total Impact* (1991). His life and career are also discussed in Michael W. Tuckman and Jeff Schultz, *Team of the Decade* (1989); Dennis Pottenger, *Great Expectations* (1991); and Ron Smith, *Football's 100 Greatest Players* (1999).

JIM CAMPBELL

LOUGANIS, Greg(ory) Efthimios (*b.* 29 January 1960 in San Diego, California), one of the all-time dominant divers, admired as much for his aesthetic choreography and graceful execution as for his powerful athleticism, and the first competitor to capture Olympic gold medals in both springboard and platform events.

Louganis was adopted by Peter and Frances (Scott) Louganis when he was a baby. Little was known of his biological parents, except that his father was of Samoan ancestry, his mother was northern European, and both were teenagers when Louganis was born. He grew up in El Cajon, California, a middle-class suburb of San Diego. Louganis's adoptive father was a bookkeeper and later worked as a fishing boat dispatcher; his mother was a homemaker. When Louganis was just a preschooler, he began attending dance classes with his older sister. The instructor taught him to visualize dance routines from start to finish, a skill he later perfected when practicing various diving maneuvers.

Louganis attended public schools, and at an early age he began to suffer from two significant childhood maladies: dyslexia and asthma. To make matters worse, he stuttered badly, and his relatively dark skin made him the victim of racism at school. "I was called 'sissy,' 'nigger,' and 'retard,'" he told Barbara Walters in a televised interview. In his autobiography he wrote of childhood depression and suicidal feelings as a result of internalizing his social isolation. "I played negative messages over and over again in my head. My natural parents didn't want me; my adoptive parents don't love me; I'm retarded; I'm ugly."

However, these problems led him toward therapeutic activities that shaped a successful future. Louganis's mother encouraged him to continue with dance classes, hoping that he might learn poise and self-respect and also, as he told *Sports Illustrated,* because "Mom didn't want any klutzes." His doctor prescribed gymnastics classes, believing that in-

Greg Louganis, 1997. AP/WIDE WORLD PHOTOS

tense exercise might expand his lung capacity as a preventive measure against asthma attacks. Both activities helped Louganis to sharpen his concentration, learn discipline, develop his imagination, and gain the sense of competence that he was denied at school. At age nine he took a diving class at a public recreation center in nearby La Mesa. Within two years Louganis emerged as an accomplished competitive diver, qualifying for the 1971 Amateur Athletic Union (AAU) Junior Olympics and scoring a perfect "10" in the springboard diving competition.

Sammy Lee, a two-time Olympic diving champion, saw Louganis in that premier national performance and was particularly impressed by the height that the young diver achieved off the springboard. "He was the greatest talent I'd ever seen," Lee recalled, " . . . years ahead of his age group." Lee kept in touch with the Louganis family and several years later agreed to coach the teen for the trials for the 1976 Olympics in Montreal, Canada, refusing to accept any payment for his work. Lee took Louganis under his wing, moving him into his home for several months while drilling him in the fine points of the compulsory dives and encouraging him to experiment with new ideas. Louganis made the Olympic team, placing sixth in the springboard competition and winning his first Olympic medal, a silver, as a runner-up in the platform event to one of his idols, Klaus Dibiasi of Italy.

After the 1976 Olympics, Louganis felt a tremendous letdown from the attention and excitement of the world stage as he returned to life as a student at Valhalla High School in El Cajon. He then contracted mononucleosis. After a two-year recovery period, Louganis was ready, both mentally and physically, to compete again. He emerged as a serious contender, taking titles in springboard and platform events at the AAU Indoor Nationals, the World Aquatic Championships, and a host of other prestigious national and international meets.

Following his graduation from Valhalla in 1978, Louganis accepted an athletic scholarship from the University of Miami. In Florida he was forced to focus on his springboard work, which had lagged behind his platform performance, because the U.S. collegiate diving competition did not include platform events. He got immediate results, winning the National Collegiate Athletic Association (NCAA) three-meter springboard national title, and going on to win virtually every indoor and outdoor title in college diving. He was a heavy favorite for a gold medal at the 1980 Olympics in Moscow, Russia, when President Jimmy Carter mandated a boycott of the event in response to the Soviet Union's invasion of Afghanistan.

Although he was disappointed, Louganis took advantage of the unexpected downtime to concentrate on his studies, transferring in late 1980 to the University of California at Irvine, where he majored in drama and minored in dance. While at Irvine he continued to train, now at the Mission Viejo Nadadores Swim Club under the guidance of the coach Ron O'Brien. Following his college graduation in 1983, in which he earned a B.A. in drama, he accelerated his training for the 1984 Olympic Games.

Now in his early twenties, Louganis had reached full physical maturity at five feet, nine inches tall and 160 pounds, with a body-fat ratio of less than 7 percent. It was evident that he had truly come into his own as an athlete and artist, thrilling crowds and beating all comers with a dazzling repertoire of difficult dives that included a mind-boggling reverse three-and-a-half somersault tuck, which became his trademark. Louganis established his indisputable dominance of the sport at the 1984 Los Angeles Games as the first athlete ever to win gold medals in both the springboard and platform events. Moreover, he won with a total point score of 710.91, becoming the first diver in history to garner more than 700 points. He followed these achievements by winning a four-year string of championship titles at meets around the world, and then repeated his double-gold performances at the 1988 Olympic Games in Seoul, South Korea.

"There's nobody who combines all the elements like Greg does—power, grace, and that catlike awareness of his body that enable him to stay almost always straight up and down. He's the state of the art in diving," the former Olympic champion Phil Boggs told the *New York Times.* The diving expert Todd Smith added that Louganis's "greatest art . . . is his unique ability to make those difficult dives look easy."

Before retiring in 1988, Louganis compiled a staggering record: five Olympic medals, four of them gold; five world championships; and forty-seven U.S. national diving titles. He was also a three-time NCAA champion and earned scores of wins in dual meets and other events. In 1985 Louganis received the Sullivan Award as the outstanding amateur athlete in the United States. He won the Jesse Owens Award in 1987, received the Olympic Spirit Award at the close of the 1988 Seoul Games, and was inducted into both the Olympic Hall of Fame (1985) and the International Swimming Hall of Fame (1993).

Less than a year before the 1988 Olympics, Louganis learned that he had tested positive for the human immunodeficiency (HIV) virus, but was dissuaded from revealing his condition to the public by his coach, Ron O'Brien. To complicate matters, during the qualifying dives in Seoul he hit his head on the springboard and opened up a gash. Louganis remembered being "paralyzed by fear . . . I heard this big hollow thud, and then I found myself in the water." Remarkably he went on to win both diving competitions. However, his decision not to reveal his condition, even to the doctor who treated the wound, remained controversial.

In 1995, following the examples of the basketball star Magic Johnson and the tennis great Arthur Ashe, Louganis announced to the public that he was HIV-positive and had been formally diagnosed with acquired immunodeficiency syndrome (AIDS). Appearing on ABC's *20/20* television program, Louganis told Barbara Walters that he had been on antiviral drug therapy since 1987 and discussed his homosexuality, about which he had been open to his family and friends since he was a teenager. "I was lucky to find one person on the 1976 Olympic team who would room with me," he recalled.

Following his retirement from competitive diving, Louganis pursued an acting career sporadically, playing minor roles in several films, including *Touch Me* (1997) and *Mighty Ducks 2* (1994), as well as a part in the off-Broadway play *Jeffrey* (1993). In 1995 Louganis published his autobiography, *Breaking the Surface,* followed by *For the Life of Your Dog* (1999), which grew out of his personal interest in animals and the training of Great Danes. He also volunteered with PAWS/LA, helping AIDS patients to care for their animals.

Louganis's decade-long dominance of international diving will long be remembered in the sports world, and young divers will no doubt continue to strive for the aesthetic standards he defined for the sport. Arguably, however, his greatest contribution to society will remain the example of his perseverance of excellence in the face of the extraordinary series of personal difficulties that he faced throughout his life.

★

Louganis wrote an autobiography with Eric Marcus, *Breaking the Surface* (1995), and published a collaboration with Betsy Sikora Siino, *For the Life of Your Dog* (1999). Ron O'Brien, a longtime coach for the U.S. Olympic diving team, wrote *Diving for Gold* (1992), which outlines his coaching techniques, including those he used in training Louganis, his prize pupil. A useful article on the diver's early life and career appears in the *1984 Current Biography Yearbook.* Louganis's announcement of his AIDS diagnosis and homosexuality is reported in Richard Sandomir, *New York Times* (23 Feb. 1995).

DAVID MARC

LOUIS, Joseph ("Joe") (*b.* 13 May 1914 in Chambers County, Alabama; *d.* 12 April 1981 in Las Vegas, Nevada), boxer who defined the heavyweight boxing division and become a national and international hero.

Louis was born Joseph Louis Barrow, one of eight children of Munroe "Mun" Barrow and Lillie Reese Barrow, sharecroppers. Nothing in Louis's early life indicated future greatness. Louis knew only the customary "hard times" of growing up in the segregated rural South before the boom times of the 1920s. The nation's prosperity did not filter down into the Buckalew Mountains area of Alabama. To complicate matters, Louis's father was committed to a state hospital, suffering from epilepsy or mental illness—it was never determined which. Lillie Barrow took pride in raising her family and doing "a man's work," plowing fields, picking cotton, and chopping wood. Later, when the family received word that Munroe Barrow had died, Lillie Barrow married Pat Brooks, who had five children of his own from a previous marriage.

Louis's schooling in Alabama was informal at best, and he often played hooky to roam the woods and fields. Because he stuttered, Louis was reluctant to attend school regularly and expose himself to the taunts of other students. In 1926 some Brooks family relatives came to visit from Detroit, Michigan, where they had moved to work in the booming automobile industry. They were part of a mass migration of southern African Americans in the 1920s to industrialized northern cities. The Barrow-Brooks family soon moved to Detroit.

Louis and a friend, Freddie Guinyard, did odd jobs at the Eastern Market in the Motor City, moving crates of produce and making deliveries. As the Great Depression swept the land, hard times returned to Louis's family. De-

Joe Louis, 1940. AP/WIDE WORLD PHOTOS

spite this Louis's mother scraped together fifty cents a week for Louis's violin lessons. Another friend, Thurston McKinney, persuaded Louis to skip the music lessons and go with him to Brewster's East Side Gym to box. Louis showed an immediate aptitude in the ring, almost knocking out his more experienced friend. Louis was soon using his violin money to pay for a locker and boxing instruction at Brewster's, and dropped the use of his last name, Barrow. In late 1932 Louis entered the local Golden Gloves tournament for amateurs, where he lost to a fighter who had boxed in the 1932 Olympics. Although he lost the bout, Louis received a $7 merchandise certificate, which was welcomed by the family. When his mother learned of Louis's boxing, she said, "If that's what you want, I'll work for you to get it."

Louis's next fight in January 1933 produced results more readily associated with the future heavyweight champion of the world—a two-punch, first-round knockout. During the rest of 1933 and in 1934 Louis continued to fight, eventually winning the Golden Gloves light heavyweight championship of Detroit. As an amateur Louis compiled a 50–4 record. Of his fifty victories, forty-three were by knockouts. After winning the Golden Gloves title, Louis was introduced to John Roxborough, a local numbers kingpin, who took over the management of the young fighter. On 12 June 1934 Louis had his last amateur fight, a first-round knockout (KO) victory over Joe Bauer.

Under Roxborough's care Louis moved to Chicago, where Julian Black also assumed managerial duties and Jack Blackburn, a former fighter, took over Louis's training. Blackburn and Louis immediately connected, calling each other "Chappie." Blackburn became a true father figure to Louis.

Because the former heavyweight champion Jack Johnson, an African American, was perceived as arrogant, flamboyant, "uppity," and worse, "Roxy," as Roxborough was called by nearly everyone in the fight business, and Black, both African Americans, gave Louis at the start of his professional career certain rules to live by, both in and out of the ring. Louis was never to be photographed alone with a white woman, never to go in a nightclub alone, never to gloat over a fallen opponent, and always to keep a "deadpan" expression in front of the cameras. Louis adhered to these rules in public.

On 4 July 1934 Louis fought and won his first pro fight, and his managers let him keep the entire purse, $52. He was also a quick KO winner in his next three fights. Louis was making it look so easy, his managers paired him with a tougher, more experienced fighter. The opponent, Stanley Poreda, was just another first-round, knockout victim. Louis continued to fight and win. He also met Marva Trotter, whom he married just hours before knocking out Max Baer, an ex-champion, on 24 September 1935. Louis's managers knew that to get a shot at the title he needed a fight in New York, an important media center and home of the boxing mecca Madison Square Garden. They brought the renowned promoter Mike Jacobs into the picture. After a series of six fights (five KOs), Louis was matched with a former heavyweight champ, the giant 6-foot 6-inch, 260-pound Primo Carnera, in New York, outdoors at Yankee Stadium. In the 25 July 1935 bout Louis was a knockout winner in six rounds. The young fighter had arrived as a contender. He followed the Carnera bout with a pair of first-round and a pair of fourth-round knockout victories. One of the victories, over Paolino Uzcudun, was on 13 December 1935 in Madison Square Garden.

Louis's next fight, set for 19 June 1936, was with still another boxer who had held the heavyweight championship, Max Schmeling of Germany. About this time the oppressive Nazi regime of Adolf Hitler was in full power in Germany and already was effecting a considerable portion of Europe. Louis, who had been named *Ring* magazine's Number One Boxer of the Year in 1935, had been to Hollywood to make a quick, low-budget film about a poor boy who started out as a dishwasher and ended up a world champion. Louis set up training camp in Lakewood, New Jersey, but never really trained hard. He was complacent, and it did not help when oddsmakers installed him as a ten-to-one favorite to defeat Schmeling. While watching Louis beat Uzcudun, Schmeling said, "I noticed something—a flaw in Louis's defense." In the twelfth round, much later than most thought the fight would last, Schmeling, exploiting the flaw, used powerful right-hand punches to knockout Louis. While Louis was humiliated, Nazi Germany touted the victory as proof of their "master race." African Americans took the defeat feeling as much a sense of personal loss as they felt of personal elation when Louis won. To them Joe Louis was a symbol of hope, someone who could not be held down.

Rehabilitation for Louis began by fighting still another ex-champ, Jack Sharkey, and knocking him out in three rounds on 17 August 1936. Louis closed out 1936 with three more early KOs, one in twenty-six seconds, and four exhibition victories, all by knockout. Louis had three more victories in early 1937, two knockout victories and a ten-round decision over a retreating Bob Pastor. Despite the loss to Schmeling, the well-connected Jacobs, by now called "Uncle Mike" by Louis, was able to get a title fight versus the current champ Jim Braddock. Still stinging from the Schmeling defeat, Louis willingly let Chappie Blackburn put him through a tough training grind. When fight time arrived on 22 June 1937, Blackburn sent Louis into the ring, saying: "This is it, Chappie. You come home a champ tonight." Although Braddock knocked Louis down, one of the few fighters who could ever make the claim, the younger fighter was too much for the game-but-aging champion. In the eighth round Louis became the new world heavyweight champion when Braddock was counted out at 1:10 in the round. At twenty-three Louis became the youngest man to hold the most important title in all of boxing. He kept the championship belt for twelve years, longer than any other heavyweight champion before him.

On 30 August 1937 Louis staged the first of his twenty-five title defenses, more defenses than any previous fighter, when he won a fifteen-round decision from England's Tommy Farr in New York. Louis knocked out two others in title defenses before a rematch with Schmeling set for 22 June 1938. The political implications that had surrounded the first Louis-Schmeling bout were even thicker for the rematch. Nazi Germany had become more aggressive in the intervening two years, and Hitler was looking for an even bigger propaganda coup. President Franklin D. Roosevelt invited Louis to the White House before the fight, and while he did not ask Louis for a victory in so many words, he did say, as he felt Louis's bulging right biceps, "Joe, we need muscles like yours to beat Germany." At the time the United States was four years away from war with the Axis Powers.

Usually truly concerned about hurting an opponent, Louis was bent on revenge in the rematch with Schmeling. He trained diligently and was ready when he climbed into the ring. Schmeling threw the first punch, missing with a right. Louis countered with a left jab that made the German drop his guard. Louis followed with a hard right to the jaw. Schmeling's knees buckled. Louis kept up a steady pounding. As Louis continued hammering him, Schmeling turned while Louis launched a right hand that the referee Arthur Donovan said "could have dented concrete." It caught Schmeling in the area of his kidneys. Schmeling let out an agonizing gasp, and the long-awaited fight was over in two minutes. In Germany, where the Schmeling victory had been hailed as proof of Aryan supremacy, the national broadcast of Schmeling's defeat was cut off the air, and the Third Reich propaganda machine called it "a disappointment, but not a national disaster."

After the fight Louis took off the rest of 1938. The huge purse, $135,000, allowed him to continue to help others, including those close, such as his family, and those not so close, such as charitable organizations. Louis and his wife bought a horse farm in Utica, Michigan. His popularity, however, especially with women, was a strain on his marriage.

Louis defended his title against all comers in the next three years before an 18 June 1941 fight with Billy Conn, a popular light heavyweight. Conn, a quick boxer as opposed to a plodding slugger, had Louis in trouble. Though ahead on points, Conn carelessly went for the knockout. Louis caught up to him and KOed him in the thirteenth round. Louis had one more title defense before the United States was drawn into World War II. On 9 January 1942 Louis took a tremendous risk. He fought Buddy Baer with his title on the line. Louis received no purse upon his victory; the proceeds of the fight were donated to the Naval Relief Fund. "The Brown Bomber," as he was now widely known, enlisted in the U.S. Army the next day.

On 27 March 1942 Louis again risked his title with little to gain. The purse this time was donated to the Army Relief Fund, and if he lost, Louis was no longer heavyweight champion of the world. Louis retained his title.

Most unwittingly, Louis was getting himself into a financial bind. While serving Uncle Sam, he was without income other than his meager army pay. Uncle Mike Jacobs was advancing him money against future earnings, and the tax code at the time did not allow Louis to claim his donated purses as charitable deductions. The fighting he did in 1944 and 1945 consisted mostly of exhibitions to entertain the troops—no income. In the end Louis owed the government nearly $1 million in back taxes and penalties. Eventually the account was squared, but Louis never again experienced financial stability.

While in the service Louis did much in a subtle way to advance civil rights and racial equality. He found it incredible that the army wanted to give him, an eighth-grade dropout, a commission while denying other blacks, who were college graduates, a chance to go to Officer Candidate School (OCS). A group of nineteen blacks at Fort Riley, including the baseball color-line breaker Jackie Robinson, eventually became commissioned officers as a result of Louis's insistence. He also refused to box exhibitions in segregated theaters in England, resulting in integrated audiences.

Louis and his wife had a baby daughter, named Jacqueline in honor of Jack "Chappie" Blackburn, while Louis was stationed at Fort Riley. The couple, driven apart by Louis's military service and absentee lifestyle, divorced in 1945 but remarried in 1946. They had a son in 1947.

Louis won a rematch with Conn in 1946, and he also defended his title successfully versus Tami Mauriello. In late 1946 and in 1947 he fought exhibitions, mostly in South and Central America. On 5 December 1947 he defended his title against Jersey Joe Walcott, who had once been a Louis sparring partner. Louis was given a controversial fifteen-round decision. In a 1948 rematch Louis knocked out Walcott in the eleventh round, Louis's last fight. He retired as the first undefeated heavyweight champion (the Schmeling loss was before he was champ) in boxing history.

Louis fought meaningless exhibitions in 1950, when, because of tax troubles and failed business ventures, he came out of retirement and fought Ezzard Charles, who had won the tournament for Louis's vacated crown. Charles won a fifteen-round decision. Louis fought other "real" fights but against inferior opponents, winning eight straight until the young Rocky Marciano ingloriously ended his until then glorious career on 26 October 1951 with an eight-round KO. Louis was a sad figure at the end of his pugilistic career. Even the victorious Marciano felt a certain sadness in ending the career of the legendary champion and idol to millions.

Louis tried pro wrestling, refereeing boxing, and more dubious business deals after boxing, but nothing worked. His remarriage to Marva ended and was followed by several other unsuccessful marriages. By the 1960s drugs and paranoia ravaged the once invincible champion. He spent his final years as a greeter at a Las Vegas casino. Some felt "the Champ" was exploited. Louis, however, did not think so and wanted no sympathy. In 1977 he suffered a heart attack complicated by a stroke and was confined to a wheelchair. He enjoyed one last hurrah on 11 April 1981, when he received a long, standing ovation at a Larry Holmes–Trevor Berbick heavyweight title fight at Caesars Palace in Las Vegas. The next morning he died at his home from a massive heart attack. Louis was buried at Arlington National Cemetery in Arlington, Virginia, with full military honors.

Louis was arguably the world's greatest heavyweight champion. Unlike champions before and after him, he was a fighting champion, not content to capitalize on the title without risking it or seldom risking it. He was a beloved figure to millions, regardless of their race. Louis at the peak of his career always was introduced by ring announcers as "the heavyweight champion of the world and a credit to his race." The condescension of that statement eventually got to the New York columnist Jimmy Cannon, who wrote, "Yeah, Joe Louis is a credit to his race—the *human race.*" Millions worldwide agreed with Cannon.

Louis was memorialized when Detroit named its sports facility the Joe Louis Arena in 1979. In 1993 the U.S. Postal Service issued a commemorative stamp featuring a likeness of Louis at the pinnacle of his illustrious career.

★

Louis wrote an autobiography, with Edna Rust and Art Rust, Jr., *Joe Louis: My Life* (1978). The several biographies of Louis include Barney Nagler, *Brown Bomber: The Pilgrimage of Joe Louis* (1972); Chris Mead, *Champion: Joe Louis, Black Hero in White America* (1985); Robert Lipsyte, *Joe Louis, a Champion for All America* (1987); Jim Campbell, *The Importance of Joe Louis* (1997); and Richard Bak, *Joe Louis, the Great Black Hope* (1998). A front-page obituary is in the *New York Times* (13 Apr. 1981).

JIM CAMPBELL

LUCKMAN, Sid(ney) (*b.* 21 November 1916 in Brooklyn, New York; *d.* 5 July 1998 in North Miami Beach, Florida), college All-American and Pro Football Hall of Fame inductee, often considered to be the creator of the modern quarterback position and pioneer in the development of the T-formation.

Luckman was one of two sons of Meyer Luckman, owner of a small family trucking business, and Ethel Drukman, a homemaker. Luckman's father gave him a football when he was eight years old, sparking his interest in the sport. By the time he graduated from Brooklyn's Erasmus Hall High School in 1935, Luckman was a polished single-wing tailback, equally skilled at passing, running, and kicking.

Luckman received many enticing scholarship offers to play college football. After meeting Columbia University's coach Lou Little, though, Luckman decided to enroll at that Ivy League institution, even though the school did not offer athletic aid. Luckman spent four years painting walls and washing dishes at one of Columbia's fraternity houses to pay his way through school. On the football field he again excelled as a triple-threat tailback. During his senior season in 1938, Luckman was chosen as an All-American and was third in the voting for the Heisman Trophy. His accomplishments were made more impressive by the fact that he was not surrounded by a strong team. Without scholarships, Columbia attracted few good athletes and had a losing record during Luckman's tenure.

Sid Luckman, 1940. © BETTMANN/CORBIS

Following his graduation in 1939, Luckman played in the College All-Star game in Chicago. He also married Estelle Margolin, his high school sweetheart. They had three children.

At six feet, 197 pounds, Luckman believed he was too small to play professional football. George Halas, owner of the Chicago Bears in the National Football League (NFL), drafted him in the first round anyway and spent several weeks convincing Luckman to sign. Halas and Stanford University coach Clark Shaugnessy were in the process of developing a new offense, based on the old T-formation. Where the original formation had emphasized power and running, Halas and Shaugnessy were designing a system based on speed, deception, and the forward pass. Halas believed Luckman was the ideal candidate to play quarterback in this new scheme.

Luckman's transition from single-wing tailback to T-formation was not easy. Just receiving the ball directly from the center, instead of standing four yards behind the line, took adjustment. At the start of his rookie season, Luckman played halfback and defensive back while he practiced the new offense. By 1940 he was ready.

The Bears enjoyed immediate success with Luckman and the T-formation, winning the NFL championship in 1940, 1941, and 1943, and playing in the championship game, but losing, in 1942. The 1940 championship was particularly impressive. The Bears beat the Washington Redskins 73–0 in what is still the most lopsided victory in league history. Games like these, and the Bears 56–7 victory over the New York Giants in 1943, convinced many coaches that the T-formation was the future of football and that Luckman was its master.

In the off-seasons Luckman began to visit colleges across the United States, helping their coaching staffs implement the T-formation. The United States Military Academy, Notre Dame, Holy Cross, and Columbia are just a few of the schools that requested Luckman's help. Luckman also wrote two books, *Passing for Touchdowns* (1948), and *Luckman at Quarterback: Football as a Sport and Career* (1949), and wrote numerous articles for boys' magazines. Outside of football, Luckman worked for Cellu-Craft Products, a food product packaging company.

Luckman spent 1943 and 1944 as an officer in the U.S. Merchant Marine, working on tankers and transports. He was able to get leave during football season weekends, though, and continued to play for the Bears. Apparently, missing practices all week was not a problem—Luckman won the NFL's Most Valuable Player award in 1943. After World War II, Luckman returned to the Bears full time, leading them to another championship in 1946. Retiring after the 1950 season, Luckman left the Bears with 14,686 career yards passing and 137 touchdown passes, both team records. He set the still-standing NFL record for most touchdown passes in a single game—seven, against the New York Giants in 1943.

Luckman believed the key to the Bears' success was the

unselfishness of his teammates. Each player knew his role, and did not complain if he did not get the ball as often as he would have liked. Halas gave Luckman a greater share of the credit; he once said his quarterback had not called a bad play in twelve years. Luckman was like a playing coach. Knowing what to do, as well as having the physical skill to carry it out, was Luckman's main strength.

After he retired from professional football, Luckman continued to tutor college programs in the T-formation. Until 1964 he was also an unofficial assistant coach for the Bears, working regularly, but refusing to draw a salary. Luckman also continued his association with Cellu-Craft Products, eventually becoming the owner. The business made him a multimillionaire and allowed him to earn a reputation for gracious entertaining. Luckman was elected to the College Football Hall of Fame (1960), the Pro Football Hall of Fame (1965), and the New York Jewish Sports Hall of Fame (1975–1976).

Luckman retired to North Miami Beach, Florida, where he died of undisclosed causes. He is buried in Memorial Park Cemetery in Wilmette, Illinois.

Luckman's career changed the NFL more than any other player's. When he was drafted by the Chicago Bears in 1939, every team except Chicago and the New York Giants was running the single-wing formation. Today every team runs some variation of the T-formation. Luckman's success and ability to run the new offense made that change possible. Had the Bears failed in the 1940s, the T-formation and much of modern football might have failed as well. The T-formation opened up the game of football by encouraging passing instead of power running. More points were scored, making the game more exciting, especially for television audiences. The heightened excitement helped increase football's popularity relative to baseball and other slower-moving games. Luckman's role as a Jewish athlete was also important in a United States trying to overcome a legacy of ethnic and religious intolerance.

★

Luckman wrote two books about football and his career: *Passing for Touchdowns* (1948), and *Luckman at Quarterback: Football as a Sport and a Career* (1949). He was also interviewed extensively for two oral histories: Bob Curran, *Pro Football's Rag Days* (1969), and Richard Whittingham, *What a Game They Played* (1984). An obituary is in the *New York Times* (6 July 1998).

HAROLD W. AURAND, JR.

LUISETTI, Angelo Enrico ("Hank") (*b.* 16 June 1916 in San Francisco, California), basketball player who is credited with popularizing the one-handed jump shot.

Luisetti was the only child of Italian immigrants, Stefan and Amalia (Grossi) Luisetti. His father worked as a laborer and chef but eventually owned a restaurant in San Francisco. Luisetti's neighborhood produced a number of noted Italian-American athletes including Joe DiMaggio, Tony Lazzeri, and Frank Crosetti, all of whom played for the New York Yankees in the period from 1925 to 1950. Young Luisetti began playing basketball before he was nine, but he had trouble getting the ball to the basket and developed a one-handed push shot, instead of the more accepted two-handed set shot. By the time Luisetti entered Galileo High School in 1930, he was such an accurate shooter that his coach accepted his unorthodox shooting style, and Luisetti continued to perfect it. In his senior year in high school he was surprised to learn he might be eligible for a college basketball scholarship, and indeed he was.

Hank Luisetti, 1940. ASSOCIATED PRESS/STANFORD UNIVERSITY

In the fall of 1934 Luisetti, who had given himself the nickname "Hank" because he thought Angelo sounded too "goody-goody," enrolled at Stanford University. He augmented his scholarship by waiting on tables or working security at football games. Luisetti played on the freshman team, required of players in the Pacific Coast Conference (PCC) at that time. His team went undefeated in eighteen games, and he averaged just under seventeen points per game for the season. As he moved up to the varsity, there were great expectations for the hard-driving young Luisetti, and he did not disappoint. The Stanford Indians, who had won only one conference championship before (in 1920), won the PCC crown three straight years with Luisetti. In the 1935–1936 season the team went 22–7, led by Luisetti's 14.3 points per game and highlighted by his 32 points against the University of Washington.

In both the 1936–1937 and 1937–1938 seasons Luisetti was voted the Helms Athletic Foundation Player of the Year and was an All-America selection. In his junior year Stanford was 25–2, and he averaged seventeen points per game. The next year Stanford went 21–3, and Luisetti scored 465 points for a 17.2 average.

Probably the most important game that Luisetti played was in December 1936, his junior year, when Stanford made a seven-game eastern swing. On 30 December they played before more than 17,000 fans in New York City's Madison Square Garden against a Long Island University (LIU) squad coached by future Hall of Famer Clair Bee. The LIU team had won forty-three consecutive games and was highly favored over Stanford. Instead Stanford overwhelmed LIU 45–31, with the six-foot, three-inch, 175-pound Luisetti scoring fifteen points on both strong drives to the basket and one-handed jump shots. For many New York fans, this was the first time they had seen a one-handed shooter, a style that had aroused great skepticism. The fans and the New York media were lavish in their praise of Luisetti and the Stanford style of play. After the Stanford-LIU game, youngsters and some college coaches around the United States began to accept and, in some cases, embrace, the one-handed shot.

In a game against Duquesne played in Public Auditorium in Cleveland in January 1938, Luisetti became the first college player to score fifty points in one game. Stanford won 92–27, and at some point during the game it became obvious to Luisetti that his teammates had conspired (with coach John Bunn, as it turned out) to funnel him the ball so he could score a record number of points. Because his teammates would not shoot, Luisetti was forced to take open shots. After the record-setting game Luisetti was upset, explaining to the coach that he did not want to be known as a ball hog but rather as the team player he was. When Luisetti ended his playing career at Stanford, he was the all-time leading scorer in college basketball with 1,291 points and had been voted an All-American player three times. Luisetti graduated from Stanford in 1938 with a B.S. in social sciences.

Following his college career, Luisetti chose not to pursue professional basketball in the fledgling National Basketball League, hoping to maintain his amateur status and be eligible for the London Olympics of 1940, which ultimately were cancelled because of World War II. Instead he played Amateur Athletic Union (AAU) basketball, although he lost his eligibility for a year because he was paid to play basketball in a Betty Grable movie. He worked for Standard Oil of California from 1938 to 1941 and played for the San Francisco Olympic Club in the 1940–1941 season and the Phillips 66 Oilers in 1941–1942. The next year he enlisted in the U.S. Navy and was assigned to preflight school in Saint Mary's, California, where he was able to play on the Saint Mary's AAU team in the 1943–1944 season. Luisetti married Jane Rossiter on 18 April 1941; they had two children. He remarried after her death.

In 1944 Luisetti was scheduled for deployment overseas when he was hospitalized with life-threatening spinal meningitis. Despite his eventual recovery, Luisetti was severely weakened by the disease, and his playing career came to an end. After the war Luisetti worked for John Hancock Life from 1946 to 1948, and for Stewart Chevrolet from 1948 to 1959.

Despite interest from a number of colleges, Luisetti was not sure he wanted to coach. He did relent briefly in 1949, when he agreed to coach Stewart Chevrolet's AAU team in San Francisco. The team won the AAU championship in 1951 with George Yardley (another Stanford graduate and later the first to score 2,000 points in an NBA season) on the squad. After 1951 Luisetti left organized coaching, although he ran successful basketball clinics for a number of years in the Bay Area. He worked as an executive in the travel industry for many years before retiring. In a 1950 Associated Press poll to select the best basketball player of the first half of the twentieth century, Luisetti finished second, and he was elected to the James Naismith Memorial Hall of Fame in its inaugural class of 1959.

Luisetti changed the game of basketball profoundly by popularizing the one-handed shot and displaying brilliant all-around play. Had illness not interceded and forced him to terminate his playing career, he would have been far more widely known in the second half of the twentieth century. His sportsmanship and intensity were, along with his outstanding play, models for basketball players throughout the United States.

★

The Hank Luisetti file at the James Naismith Memorial Basketball Hall of Fame has letters, clippings, and photos from Luisetti's career. There is no biography of Luisetti and few articles of note that examine his life and career. He is highlighted in a chapter in Sandy Padwe, *Basketball's Hall of Fame* (1970).

MURRY NELSON

LUJACK, John Christopher, Jr. ("Johnny") (*b.* 4 January 1925 in Connellsville, Pennsylvania), Heisman Trophy winner and National Football League All-Pro on offense and defense who never lost to a college foe while quarterbacking the University of Notre Dame to national championships in 1943, 1946, and 1947.

Lujack was the fourth of six children born to John Lujack, a hardworking Polish boilermaker on the Pittsburgh and Lake Erie Railroad, and his wife, Alice. The youngest of four boys, Lujack was exposed early in life to baseball, football, basketball, and track and field through his highly competitive and skilled brothers—Val, Allie, and Stan. As a ten year old, Lujack hid in the trunk of the family car when his brothers drove off to play semiprofessional football games on Sunday afternoons in small towns across western Pennsylvania. His mother "didn't want them taking me so far from home," but his brothers, particularly Allie, who later played end at Georgetown University, made sure Lujack played and "knew what I was doing out there."

At age thirteen Lujack weighed only 120 pounds, but he showed a strong and surprisingly accurate arm as a quarterback for Cameron Junior High. On defense, he was even more impressive, assaulting the opposition with an aggression learned in the Lujack backyard. He became an outstanding two-way player on Connellsville High's varsity team beginning as a sophomore in 1939. He lettered in basketball and track and so impressed Pittsburgh Pirates scouts with his play at shortstop in a local amateur league that he was offered a contract, which he decided to turn down.

Lujack had listened to Notre Dame games on the radio and longed to play for the Fighting Irish, whose fame had been cemented by former coach Knute Rockne. Lujack's reputation as one of the outstanding high school players in the country grew when he intercepted two passes against Mount Pleasant High and returned each seventy yards for touchdowns. Thirty-five colleges were interested, and many offered scholarships. At the Connellsville graduation in 1942, Congressman J. Buell Snyder told class president Lujack that he was the first Connellsville boy ever appointed to the U.S. Military Academy at West Point. Lujack turned down the appointment and went to Notre Dame instead.

Johnny Lujack, 1946. AP/WIDE WORLD PHOTOS

Lujack's ambition as a 165-pound freshman had been "to make Notre Dame's traveling squad my junior or senior year." On the first day of fall practice, however, his tenacity as a hard-hitting safety caught the attention of Coach Frank Leahy in a freshman scrimmage against the varsity. He joined the varsity a year later, becoming the starting halfback behind All-America quarterback Angelo Bertelli. Six games into the 1943 schedule, Notre Dame was battling for a national championship when Bertelli was called into the U.S. Marines. Five days later, 78,000 fans in Yankee Stadium saw Lujack throw for 237 yards and two touchdowns and run for another, leading the Irish to a 26–0 upset over Army. On defense he three times tackled Army backs to keep them out of the end zone. With Lujack calling the plays, Notre Dame went on to win the national championship. Lujack lettered in football, baseball, basketball, and track, becoming Notre Dame's first four-letter winner in thirty-one years.

When Lujack completed Midshipmen's School in December 1944, he received his commission as navy ensign. For eleven months he served as executive officer on a submarine chaser, which patrolled the English Channel for four months. He returned to Notre Dame in 1946, when he quarterbacked Notre Dame to an undefeated national championship, was a unanimous All American, and finished third in the Heisman voting. At six feet, 180 pounds, Lujack played a sixty-minute game, dominating Illinois speedster Claude "Buddy" Young in the season opener and later in the year stopping Army's Doc Blanchard in the open field to preserve a scoreless tie. Red Smith of the *New York Herald-Tribune* reported that Lujack "ran the ball with speed and malevolence, and tackled with hideous violence."

Notre Dame's 27–7 thumping of Army highlighted their 1947 national championship season. Again, the team was undefeated with Lujack at quarterback. The "perfect" T-formation quarterback threw for 791 yards and nine touchdowns, becoming Leahy's "coach on the field" while winning the Heisman Trophy. Leahy predicted, "He can make a million dollars if he wants to. He has everything it takes for success—brains, character, and personality." The easy-going, pleasant-sounding star appeared in *The Adventures of Johnny Lujack*, a 1948 summer replacement show on the Jack Armstrong radio network. That same year, on 26 June,

Lujack married his college sweetheart, Patricia Ann Schierbrock; they had three children. Lujack was a first-round draft choice of the National Football League's (NFL) Chicago Bears, and he signed a lucrative $18,000 contract to play for the usually tightfisted George Halas.

Lujack backed up All-Pro Sid Luckman at quarterback his rookie season, throwing six touchdowns to earn a quarterback rating of 97.5. He ran for over seven yards a carry, kicked extra points, and starred on defense, intercepting three Green Bay passes in the first half of his first start on 26 September 1948 and finishing the season with eight interceptions. He was named defensive All-Pro. When Luckman was sidelined with a thyroid condition in 1949, Lujack took over as starting quarterback. He led the Bears on a six-game winning streak that included a record-setting season finale against their crosstown rival the Chicago Cardinals, in which Lujack threw for 458 yards and six touchdowns. His season totals of 162 completions, 2,658 yards passing, and 23 touchdowns led the NFL.

Lujack was an All-Pro on offense in 1950, passing for 1,731 yards and running for 397 more, but his years as a two-way star were taking their toll. A torn back muscle in his rookie season was followed by cartilage damage in one knee and a chipped anklebone in the other leg the next. Two shoulder separations had taken the zip out of his passing. Luckman retired and Halas had sold backup Bobby Layne, leaving Lujack to gut out 1951 by relying on a short passing game and seven rushing touchdowns. At this point Lujack's four-year contract was up, his throwing shoulder was ruined, and he was forced to retire.

Lujack was Notre Dame's backfield coach for two years before becoming a radio and television sports broadcaster with the New York Giants. In 1956 he became the first former professional football player to do color commentary on nationwide football broadcasts for the Columbia Broadcasting System (CBS). Lujack and his wife moved to Davenport, Iowa, her home, in 1954, and Lujack opened a successful car dealership. Lujack eventually retired from broadcasting to devote more time to his golf game. He served as toastmaster of the Heisman Trophy award dinners, and most Saturdays he made the eight-hour drive to South Bend to see his Fighting Irish play. When arthritis made travel difficult, he listened to the games on the radio, much as he had sixty years before, when as a boy he dreamed of one day "playing with pride" at a school that would forever "have a hold of my imagination."

★

Lujack's own view of the college and professional games appears in "Pro Football Is Better to Watch," an article he wrote for the *New York Times Magazine* (2 Dec. 1956). He was on the cover of *Life* magazine in 1947 (29 Sept.) and was the subject of an article in *Current Biography 1947* (1948). Lujack wrote the introduction to *The Glory of Notre Dame* (1971) and is the subject of a biographical chapter in that volume, "Glamour? Spell It L-U-J-A-C-K," written by Ed Fitzgerald. Lujack's career at Notre Dame is also chronicled in John T. Brady, *The Heisman: A Symbol of Excellence* (1984). Bernie McCarty's biographical article on Lujack appears in David L. Porter, ed., *Biographical Dictionary of American Sports* (1987).

BRUCE J. EVENSEN

M

McCARTHY, Joseph Vincent ("Joe") (*b.* 21 April 1887 in Philadelphia; *d.* 13 January 1978 in Buffalo, New York), the greatest manager in baseball history, he managed in two leagues and three teams (including the New York Yankees) for twenty-four years, during which his teams won 2,125 games for a winning percentage on .615; no team of his finished out of the first four in any league.

Joe McCarthy was born in the Germantown section of Philadelphia. His father died when he was three years old. As a teenager McCarthy worked in a silk mill for $6.50 a week. He broke a kneecap playing sandlot ball, but he was a good enough student and athlete to gain a scholarship to Niagara University, a Catholic college in Lewiston, New York. He left in 1906 after two years to join the Wilmington, Delaware, minor-league baseball team, the start of a twenty-year career in the high minors.

After playing for teams around the country, including Wilmington, Delaware; Franklin, Pennsylvania; and Indianapolis, Indiana; by 1913 McCarthy had become a player-manager for the Wilkes-Barre, Pennsylvania, team in the International League, the highest of the minor leagues. He hit .325 that year to tie for the batting championship and led the league in doubles with 36. From Wilkes-Barre, McCarthy moved on to Toledo, Ohio, and then to Buffalo, New York, where he signed a contract to play with Brooklyn in the ill-fated Federal League which soon collapsed. Minor leaguers who had signed to play in the Federal League were prohibited from playing in the International League, so McCarthy went to the American Association team of Louisville, Kentucky.

Several years later, while working as a player-manager for Louisville, McCarthy had an epiphany of sorts when he criticized shortstop Jay Kirke for a high throw on a double play. Kirke took offense and questioned McCarthy's right to tell a .380 hitter how to play ball. Evidently recognizing his ability to correct and improve other players, McCarthy became the team's nonplaying manager. Under McCarthy's leadership, Louisville won two pennants and finished out of the first division only once. During this time he codified his ten baseball rules, which included: Don't argue with umpires since they aren't as perfect as you. Keep your head up and you won't have to let it hang. Don't ever quit.

While in Buffalo, McCarthy met the woman who would become his wife, Elizabeth ("Babe") Lakeman. She followed him to Louisville, where they married on 14 February 1921; they had no children.

In 1926 McCarthy was chosen by William Wrigley, the owner of the Chicago Cubs, as the new pilot for his team of comfortable last-place veterans. McCarthy could see that changes were needed, but the veterans were disdainful of the bush-league manager and resisted his authority. The Cubs had a quality pitcher named Grover Cleveland ("Pete") Alexander, whose talents were tempered by an oversized ego and a passion for alcohol. Despite Alexander's pitching brilliance, McCarthy put him on waivers and

Joe McCarthy *(left)* with rival manager Casey Stengel of the New York Yankees, 1949. ASSOCIATED PRESS

sent him to St. Louis since, as he saw it, Alex obeyed "Alex's rules" and not McCarthy's. This authoritarian streak earned McCarthy the derisive nickname "Marse Joe," likening him to a plantation overseer. McCarthy then brought in a little-known player by the name of Hack Wilson, a short, stocky, bearlike man with an unusual ability to hit a baseball often and far.

Like Alexander, Wilson had a weakness for alcohol. Fortunately, McCarthy had great empathy for players who drank, for he himself was a devotee of White Horse Scotch whiskey. He was always aware, however, of players who imbibed too generously or too often. Legend has it that McCarthy took Wilson aside and showed him two glasses, one with water and one with whiskey. He put a worm in the water glass and it wriggled vigorously. He then put the worm in the whiskey glass and it died quickly. He asked Wilson what that told him. Wilson replied that if he drank whiskey he would not get worms.

Alcohol counseling aside, McCarthy put together a solid team with great pitching, defense, and power hitting. In 1929 the Cubs won the National League pennant and faced Connie Mack's Philadelphia Athletics in the World Series. The Cubs lost four games to one, losing the final game in spite of an 8–0 lead in the late innings.

The loss made Cubs owner Wrigley, who desperately wanted a World Series championship, disenchanted and unforgiving. He had already been upset by McCarthy's refusal to field Frank "Lefty" O'Doul, whom Wrigley had purchased in 1926 for $15,000. McCarthy did not feel the need to bring O'Doul to the Cubs after spring training, and he went to the Phillies. Far from floundering, O'Doul hit .398 in 1929 and .383 the following year. Adding insult to injury, he then hit two home runs at the close of the season, denying the Cubs a pennant in 1930. Smarting over the loss of O'Doul, Wrigley hired William Veeck as general manager. Veeck engineered a deal to bring Rogers Hornsby, a hard-nosed, brash, demanding player with tremendous physical ability, to the Cubs in 1929. Hornsby had managed St. Louis to a championship, and McCarthy, who despised him, could see that his days as manager were numbered. The two took the Cubs to the World Series in 1929, but with four games left in the 1930 season, McCarthy resigned. Predictably, he was quickly replaced by Hornsby.

McCarthy's abilities as a manager may best be illustrated by one player's performance after he left the team. Hack Wilson had his greatest year in 1930, with 56 home runs, 191 runs batted in (RBI), and a slugging percentage of .723. Baseball writers named Wilson the National League's Most Valuable Player that year, and his 191 RBI still stand as the all-time record. But Wilson was never the same after 1930, the year McCarthy left. Wilson had great rapport with McCarthy, who understood his hitting technique and was always willing to "turn him loose"; under Hornsby, however, he was ordered to take pitches he felt he could hit. In Wilson's defense, the league had also introduced a less lively ball after 1930, which may have also contributed to his declining production.

The sports reporter Warren Brown, who covered the

Cubs and liked McCarthy, let him know that Colonel Jake Ruppert, owner of the New York Yankees, was looking for a new manager. McCarthy, hired in 1931, spent the next fifteen years improving the record he began with Chicago. He became the most successful manager in baseball history, with a winning percentage of .615. McCarthy led the Yankees to seven World Series, including four straight from 1936 to 1939, finished second seven times, and never finished out of the first division.

Where Wrigley had publicly doubted McCarthy's ability to bring a championship to Chicago, Ruppert made no secret of his confidence that McCarthy would take the Yankees to World Series glory. This did not sit well with Babe Ruth, who wanted the manager's job and cared little for an upstart from the National League. Always pragmatic, however, McCarthy was able to work with Ruth, whom he also disliked, and even used Ruth to get retribution against the Cubs in the 1932 World Series, which the Yankees swept in four games.

The Yankees won their last World Series under McCarthy in 1943, beating the Cardinals four games to one. In that series, McCarthy relied on a hunch that an ailing, journeyman pitcher Marius Russo might be useful. Russo pitched a brilliant victory in the fourth game to give the Yankees a three-games-to-one advantage. This intuitive choice of pitchers in a critical game would come back to haunt McCarthy when, as manager of the Boston Red Sox in 1948, he passed over his ace pitchers for the first playoff for the American League pennant in baseball history, and chose another journeyman, Denny Galehouse, to face Lou Boudreau's Cleveland Indians. The Indians won the playoff due to the efforts of player-manager Boudreau, who went four for four, and Cleveland went on to win the series.

Ruppert died in 1939, and the team changed hands. McCarthy did not get along with the new Yankees owner Larry MacPhail, and was let go in midseason of 1946 after finishing third and fourth in 1944 and 1945. After a hiatus in 1947, the Boston Red Sox hired McCarthy, perhaps to cast off the "curse of the Bambino," which held that Boston's sale of Babe Ruth to the Yankees doomed the Red Sox to perpetual frustration in pursuit of a World Series win. Their devastating loss in the 1946 series had left Red Sox management and fans in poor spirits. McCarthy took the team to the playoffs in 1948, but lost to Cleveland. The Red Sox finished second again in 1949 in a tense down-to-the-wire race with the Yankees. In 1950 McCarthy was replaced in midseason once again; this time he chose to return to Buffalo, New York, and his sixty-one-acre homestead that he called "Yankee Farm."

Joe McCarthy was a man born to the game of baseball, even though he never played a major league game himself, one of the greatest managers in the long history of the great American game. He changed the way teams were developed, using utility players to supplement regular position players. McCarthy believed in using virtually his entire pitching staff as starters and staying with his starter as long as his team had a chance to come back. He exploited the use of relief pitchers to great advantage. McCarthy had an uncanny belief that there were ball players who could be nurtured into major leaguers, and showed it by developing talent in players who were not regulars on their former teams. A disciplinarian who never lost touch with his players, McCarthy nevertheless held biases against players who dared criticize his judgment or take any loss lightly.

McCarthy was held in high regard even by players who did not like him. The great relief pitcher Joe Page despised him, but called McCarthy the best manager he had ever played for. Joe DiMaggio said he had learned something from McCarthy every day. Gabby Hartnett, his catcher with the Cubs, saw him as a baseball genius. McCarthy's coach and good friend "Birdie" Tebbetts never ceased to admire his talent. For his own part, McCarthy was more than capable of caustic and witty remarks, including an observation he made when a player was stealing home with one out: "It is proof of reincarnation. No one could get that stupid in one lifetime." When asked by reporters whether he would be able to get along with the tempestuous Ted Williams, McCarthy replied, "a manager that can't get along with a .400 hitter is a fool."

In 1957 the veterans committee of the National Baseball Hall of Fame elected McCarthy to join the greats of the game, many of whom he had managed while with the Cubs, the Yankees, and the Red Sox. The Yankees granted him a standing invitation to come to Florida during spring training, but McCarthy lived in contented retirement on his farm until his death from pneumonia on 13 January 1978. (He had broken a hip the previous summer and had been hospitalized since November.) McCarthy is buried next to his wife in Mt. Olivet Cemetery in Tonawanda, New York, a suburb of Buffalo.

★

There is no full-length biography of McCarthy, though the reading "around" his career both enlightens and provides the perspective of his time. Ed Hurley, *Managing To Win* (1976), is a study of seven managers. David Halberstam, *Summer of '49* (1989), is a fine telling of the McCarthy years with the Boston Red Sox and their intense rivalry with the Yankees. An internal view of that rivalry and the McCarthy years can be found in Dom DiMaggio with Bill Gilbert, *Real Grass, Real Heroes: Baseball's Historic 1941 Season* (1990). Peter Golenbock, *Wrigleyville: A Magical History Tour of the Chicago Cubs* (1996), is a valuable study of the Cubs McCarthy years and the personalities associated with that team. Bill James, *The Bill James Guide to Baseball Managers: From 1870 to Today* (1997), is an invaluable source for contrasting and comparing baseball managers and for its statistical information and editorial assessments. Howard Siner, *Sweet Seasons: Baseball's Top Teams Since 1920* (1988), and David Anderson, *Pennant*

Races: Baseball at Its Best (1997), provide much personal material relating to pennant races in which McCarthy was involved, including the tense races in 1948 between the Red Sox and the Cleveland Indians, and the McCarthy Red Sox versus the Stengel Yankees in 1949. Obituaries are in the *New York Times* (14 Jan. 1978), and the *Buffalo Evening News* (15 and 17 Jan. 1978).

JACK J. CARDOSO

McCORMICK, Pat(ricia) Joan (*b.* 12 May 1930 in Seal Beach, California), first Olympic diver to win four gold medals and first woman named to the International Swimming Hall of Fame.

McCormick was one of three children born to Robert Keller and Harriet Keller. Although a decorated World War I soldier, Robert Keller was an alcoholic who was in and out of the home, leaving Harriet to raise and support the children on her own. She sometimes "read tea leaves"—predicted the future by interpreting the meaning of tea leaves left in the bottom of the cup—to get trolley money for McCormick so she could get to training and competitions.

Olympic high divers Pat McCormick *(center)*, Juno Irwin *(left)*, and Paula Myers *(right)*, who swept all three medals in the 1956 event. ASSOCIATED PRESS GOPA

Born on the second floor above a grocery store, McCormick spent her childhood hanging out along California's coastlines. McCormick and her siblings spent their days at Muscle Beach, becoming friends with the weightlifters who gathered there and performed shows. "Muscle Beach really helped me later as a diver because I became physically strong," McCormick said. "My mother tried to get me to be more ladylike, but I was a tomboy." McCormick spent her free time entering swimming and diving competitions. She honed her skills at the local Young Women's Christian Association (YWCA), mowing lawns, cleaning houses, and ironing to earn money for the bus fare. She attended Long Beach City College, where, after thirteen years, she finally earned a degree.

McCormick trained on her own until Aileen Allen, a coach from the Los Angeles Athletic Club, recognized her potential and invited her to train professionally in 1947. From that moment on, McCormick never looked back. She dedicated herself to diving and became one of the most skilled and daring divers of her day. Her resolve for perfection changed the sport and took it to a new level. Her grace and daring in her dives, combined with her intense dedication to perfection and training, upped the standard for all women. Before McCormick, female divers got by more on appearance than ability. McCormick changed that. She only did dives with a great degree of difficulty. She was the first athlete to perform a "double-double"—a double somersault with a double twist. She did dives only male competitors at the time were doing. In order to compete, other female athletes had to work harder, learn harder dives and train harder to reach her level of perfection.

In McCormick's day, training techniques were in their early stages, and there were no gymnastic harnesses of the type that aid today's divers. McCormick had to learn her dives over the open water. When learning new dives, she wore extra T-shirts over her swimsuit so she would not get so many welts from smacking the water at awkward angles.

At seventeen, McCormick missed making the 1948 Olympic team by less than a point. The blow both devastated and motivated her. Now, not only did she want to make the team, but she also wanted to win a gold medal. McCormick dedicated herself to making that dream come true. She made 80 to 100 dives a day, 6 days a week, 12 months a year. McCormick's coach once remarked that other divers may have had more talent, but McCormick had more determination.

On 1 June 1949 she married Glenn "Mick" McCormick, a college wrestler and gymnast who became her coach. As she continued to practice relentlessly, the five-foot, four-inch, 120-pound McCormick became a sturdy and practically unbeatable competitor. At the 1950 Amateur Athletic Union (AAU) national championships in High Point, North Carolina, McCormick swept all three championship titles, including the one- and three-meter springboard and the platform.

Though McCormick was happy with her titles, she was really working toward the Olympics. Just before the 1952 Olympic trials, McCormick cracked her head open on the bottom of the pool and doctors discouraged her from trying out. McCormick, however, was stubbornly determined. She attached a sponge to her head to protect her stitched-up skull and easily made the team, which that year competed in Helsinki, Finland. McCormick brought home a gold medal in both the platform and the springboard events.

McCormick competed again in the 1956 Olympics held in Melbourne, Australia, even though she had missed months of training because of her pregnancy and delivery of her son. For McCormick, the 1956 Olympics still stand out. She recalled the moments before her final dive, which she knew needed to be close to perfect: "I remember walking up those steps—there were 33, I counted every one of them. And all I could think was, 'You can live a lifetime in a moment.'" She knew this was her moment. McCormick again won the gold in both the platform and springboard events, becoming the first Olympic diver to win four gold medals. Since then, only two other divers—the U.S. diver Greg Louganis and Chinese diver Fu Mingxia—have won four gold medals.

Following the 1956 games and the birth of her daughter in 1960, McCormick's marriage began to crumble. Her fame took its toll on the relationship, and the couple grew apart, divorcing in 1973.

Over the duration of her career, McCormick won twenty-seven national championships, and three gold and two silver medals at the Pan American Games. She also won the 1956 Associated Press Female Athlete of the Year Award and the 1956 James E. Sullivan Amateur Athlete of the Year Award.

Although McCormick was a fierce competitor, she was also compassionate. During a competition in 1950 McCormick was diving against Mary Francis Cunningham. After Cunningham surfaced from her final dive, she erupted into tears. McCormick reassured her "that she had done a fine job." The problem was that Cunningham did not perform the dive she was supposed to do. She should have received a zero for the dive, but the judges did not seem to notice what had happened, and McCormick could not bring herself to tell them. McCormick lost the championship. When McCormick's coach admonished her, she said she could not speak up because Cunningham was her friend.

McCormick retired following the 1956 Olympics, saying that the fourth gold was a "sign to proceed with her life." Since retiring, McCormick has become a popular motivational speaker. She still lives in Seal Beach and enjoys volunteering in the local schools. In 1984 she established the Pat McCormick Education Foundation, which raises money to fund programs for at-risk students.

Diving remains a part of McCormick's life. Her daughter Kelly followed her example, winning a silver medal at the 1984 Los Angeles Olympics and a bronze at the 1988 Seoul Olympics.

While there are many talented divers competing today, McCormick's "double-double"—two gold medals won in two consecutive Olympics—may never be matched. In 1956 McCormick was the first woman to be inducted into the International Swimming Hall of Fame. The goal of the Hall of Fame is to immortalize the achievements and contributions of those who have distinguished themselves in the sport—especially on an international level. To be honored, you have to do more than just win medals. You have to "give back" to the sport. McCormick did that by opening up a diving camp to help train others.

★

There is no biography of McCormick, but in 1999 the Amateur Athletic Foundation of Los Angeles published a fifteen-page interview with her that can be viewed at http://www.aafla.org. Several books, including Al J. Stump, *Champions Against Odds* (1952); Siobhan Drummond and Elizabeth Rathburn, eds., *Grace & Glory: A Century of Women in the Olympics* (1998); and Janet Woolum, *Outstanding Women Athletes: Who They Are and How They Influenced Sports in America* (1998); include information on McCormick's life and career. See also Jerry Hicks, "McCormick Has the Gold-Medal Touch As a Speaker Too," *Los Angeles Times* (19 Sep. 1996), and Bill Dwyre, "McCormick Was As Gold As It Gets; Now It's Fu's Turn," *Los Angeles Times* (24 Sep. 2000).

LISA FRICK

McCOVEY, Willie Lee (*b.* 10 January 1938 in Mobile, Alabama), one of the greatest power hitters in Major League Baseball history; one of only 17 players to hit 500 home runs over the course of a career.

McCovey was one of ten children of Frank McCovey and Ester Jones McCovey. McCovey's father, a laborer, died in 1963, four years after his son's major league debut. Like Hank Aaron, McCovey played for the Mobile Black Bears, a semiprofessional, African-American team, while still in high school. McCovey did not play baseball at Mobile's Central High School because it did not have a team. Upon graduating from high school in 1955, however, McCovey was signed by the New York Giants of the National League (NL) and sent to Sandersville, a farm team for the Giants within the Georgia State League.

McCovey quickly moved through the Giants minor league system, playing for Danville (Carolina League) in 1956, Dallas (Texas League) in 1957, and Phoenix (Pacific

Willie McCovey, 1987. ASSOCIATED PRESS AP

Coast League) in 1958 and 1959. With the Phoenix Giants in 1959, he had a tremendous season, hitting twenty-nine home runs and driving in ninety-two runs through late July. On 30 July McCovey was recalled to the Giants, who were now in San Francisco, but still won the home run title and a share of the runs batted in (RBI) lead for the Pacific Coast League that season.

On 30 July 1959 McCovey made his major league debut for the Giants against the future Hall of Famer Robin Roberts of the Philadelphia Phillies. McCovey went 4 for 4, with 2 triples and 2 singles in the Giants 7–2 victory. McCovey had an excellent rookie season, hitting 13 home runs and driving in 38 runs while batting .354 in only 52 games. Despite playing just over one-third of the season, the twenty-one-year-old McCovey was the unanimous choice for 1959 NL Rookie of the Year, succeeding teammate Orlando Cepeda.

In 1960 McCovey dropped off greatly, as he batted only .238 while hitting the same number of homers as he did in 1959 in twice as many games. He was sent to the Tacoma Giants of the Pacific Coast League to hone his skills and played with them for seventeen games. McCovey turned his career around in 1961 and regained his position in San Francisco. While he competed directly with Cepeda for the first base position, the two players remained close during the period and were roommates when the team went on the road. In 1962 McCovey continued to improve with 20 home runs and a .293 batting average in only 91 games for the Giants, who won the NL pennant that year. In the 1962 World Series, played against the New York Yankees, McCovey played 4 games and batted .200 with a home run. However, his performance in game seven almost made him a hero. In the bottom of the ninth inning with two outs, Willie Mays on second, Matty Alou on third, and the Yankees holding a 1–0 lead, McCovey ripped a screaming line drive towards right field. The Yankees second baseman Bobby Richardson leaped into the air and caught the game-winning hit to end the game and the series. An exhibit of the greatest moments in baseball history by the National Baseball Hall of Fame calls that moment "just an inch higher." The 1962 World Series was McCovey's only opportunity to play in that contest.

Nicknamed "Stretch" because of his ability to get errant throws from infielders while playing first base, McCovey had some of his best seasons starting in 1963. That year he tied with Hank Aaron for the NL lead in home runs with forty-four. While his production dipped in 1964, he hit more than thirty-one homers every year from 1965 to 1970, and he led the NL in both home runs and RBI for both 1968 and 1969.

During the 1969 season, when he batted .320 with 45 home runs and 126 RBI, McCovey almost single-handedly kept the Giants in contention for the NL West title, which was eventually won by the Atlanta Braves. McCovey was elected Most Valuable Player of the National League, edging out the Mets Tom Seaver in a very close vote by baseball writers.

Throughout his career McCovey was plagued with injuries, primarily to his knees. His success on the field for the Giants began to wane in 1971 when he hit only 18 home runs and drove in 70 runs. While he had a slightly better season in 1973 with a batting average of .266, 29 home runs, and 75 RBI, McCovey was traded to the San Diego Padres at the end of the season. San Francisco fans were disappointed with the trade, although it appeared that the move, by pure baseball standards, was not bad for the team.

McCovey played with the Padres for two years, during which time his performance was mediocre in comparison to earlier seasons. In 1976 he had his worst year ever, batting .203 with only 7 home runs in 82 games. During that season, he was sold to the Oakland Athletics and became a free agent at the end of the season. McCovey signed with the Giants for the 1977 season and returned to a standing ovation in his first game. He repaid fan loyalty by playing one of his finest seasons ever in 1977, batting .280 with 28 home runs and 86 RBI, making him the clear choice for the Comeback Player of the Year award. McCovey played three more seasons with the Giants before retiring in 1980.

McCovey concluded his career in Major League Baseball with 521 home runs, tied with Ted Williams for ninth place on the all-time list of home run superstars at the time of his retirement. His lifetime statistics also included a batting average of .270, 1,555 RBI, and 2,211 hits. Moreover, McCovey at the time of his retirement was the foremost left-handed home-run batter in the history of the National League. McCovey is also the first player in baseball history to hit two home runs in the same inning twice in his career, and his eighteen grand slams place him first in the National League and second in the history of the major leagues in this category.

McCovey moved to the Giants front office as an instructor of major and minor league players and as the Community Fund Director. As his knees weakened in his later years, he became a senior advisor, working primarily with community groups. Since 1980 McCovey has presented the Willie Mac award, named in his honor, to the Giants player who "best exemplifies the spirit and leadership" shown by McCovey during his time with the Giants. In 1995, however, McCovey and fellow Hall of Famer Duke Snider were charged by the Internal Revenue Service with tax fraud for failure to report income associated with autograph shows. All told, McCovey was charged with failing to report $41,000 in income, a charge to which he pled guilty. This affair temporarily cooled McCovey's relationship with the Giants, and the team minimized his role for a few years.

In 1986, McCovey was the sixteenth player to be elected to the National Baseball Hall of Fame in the first year of eligibility. In his induction speech, he thanked his family, including his daughter Allison, then acknowledged his relationship with the baseball fans of San Francisco, saying, "I've been adopted, too, by all the thousands of great Giants fans everywhere and by the city of San Francisco, where I've always been welcome and, like the Golden Gate Bridge and the cable cars, I've been made to feel like a landmark, too." Although Willie Mays is often recognized as the greatest player in Giants history, McCovey has a special place in the hearts of San Francisco fans. He started as a rookie shortly after the Giants moved west from New York City and remained with the team for most of his career. To acknowledge this association, the Giants named the water in the China Basin Channel just beyond the right field wall of the Pacific Bell Park, their home stadium built in 2000, in his honor. Long home runs hit over the seats beyond right field end up in McCovey's Cove, a fitting tribute to San Francisco's favorite home run hitter.

★

Information on McCovey is available in his player's file at the National Baseball Hall of Fame Library in Cooperstown, New York. McCovey is the coauthor of *Hall of Fame Giants: In Commemoration of Willie McCovey's Induction* (1986). Information about McCovey can also be found in Jacob Jordan, *Six Seasons: A History of the Tacoma Giants, 1960–1965* (1996); Tom Schott and Nick Peters, *The Giants Encyclopedia* (1999); and other general interest histories of the San Francisco Giants, including Russ Hodges and Al Hirshberg, *My Giants* (1963), and Bruce Chadwick, *The Giants: Memories and Memorabilia from a Century of Baseball* (1993).

COREY SEEMAN

McELHENNY, Hugh Edward, Jr. (*b.* 31 December 1928 in Los Angeles, California), football player considered to be one of the greatest broken field running backs, who was inducted into the Pro Football Hall of Fame and the National Football Foundation College Football Hall of Fame, and who was among the first offensive backfields in professional football history with all members enshrined in the Hall of Fame.

McElhenny is the son of Hugh McElhenny, a businessman, and Pearl McElhenny, a homemaker. McElhenny played childhood sports as a young boy, and two incidents from his youth had impacts on his ensuing career. In one incident, while McElhenny was playing football in a carrot patch, the irate garden owner appeared and fired off a shotgun, and buckshot pellets lodged in McElhenny's backside. Years later McElhenny remarked that on a football field he always ran scared. In the other incident, McElhenny was playing football in a vacant lot when he stepped on the jagged neck of a broken milk bottle, severing tendons and nerves in his left foot. After surgery and months of bed rest, the foot was placed in a cast, and doctors warned that it might never grow normally. But McElhenny strengthened the foot through exercises and became an outstanding school athlete in both football and track and field. At

Hugh McElhenny, wearing number 39 for the San Francisco 49ers, 1955. ASSOCIATED PRESS AP

George Washington High School in Los Angeles, he set national scholastic records in high and low hurdles and received over fifty scholarship offers after his senior year.

After graduating from George Washington mid year, McElhenny entered the University of Southern California in January 1948 but left school when his pay for a campus job was late. After several months of traveling around the country with a high school friend and working at part-time jobs, he became homesick and returned to California, where he enrolled in Compton Junior College. In 1948 he led Compton to an undefeated season and a victory in the Junior Rose Bowl. He scored 23 touchdowns, including a punt return of 105 yards, over the course of the season. Also that year he married his childhood sweetheart, Peggy Ogston. The couple had two children. In the fall of 1949 McElhenny entered the University of Washington.

McElhenny's legend was created over time, starting with his high school and junior college exploits and continuing during his career at the University of Washington. At six feet, one inches tall and 198 pounds, he had craggy good looks, and his arrival on the Seattle campus was heralded by the local press. McElhenny and his wife lived in financial comfort, benefiting from the largesse of team boosters. (During the 1940s and 1950s, the Greater Washington Advertising Club provided illegal payments and other perks to the University of Washington's athletes; penalizations of the university's athletic program began after McElhenny had moved on to professional football, and the specifics of his case were not investigated.) Between 1949 and 1951 McElhenny rushed for 2,499 yards, including a team record 296 yards against Washington State University in 1950. His 233 points became a long-standing team mark. While in college, he developed a reputation for being temperamental, hard to handle, and something of a free spirit.

In 1952 McElhenny was selected in the first round of the National Football League (NFL) draft by the San Francisco 49ers. The team quarterback Frankie Albert influenced that decision with an early morning telephone call to Coach Buck Shaw. Albert had witnessed McElhenny's remarkable performance in the Hula Bowl All-Star game in Honolulu, Hawaii, against a team of professionals, including Albert. In his first professional play in an exhibition game against the Chicago Cardinals, McElhenny made a forty-two-yard touchdown run. It was the beginning of a brilliant rookie season that included rushing touchdowns of 89 and 82 yards and a 94-yard punt return touchdown. After McElhenny's performance on 19 October 1952 against the Chicago Bears, Albert presented him with the game ball and anointed him with the title "King of the Halfbacks," and McElhenny came to be known as simply, "The King." Throughout his career McElhenny retained the designation, which was universally recognized by his peers, the press, and football fans. Playing for San Francisco (1952–1960), the Minnesota Vikings (1961–1962), the New York Giants (1963), and the Detroit Lions (1964), his greatness was based not so much on his statistical attainments, although those are impressive, as on his distinctive running style. He uncannily navigated a broken field, used blockers expertly, and stopped, started, feinted, and accelerated with an intuitive ability to sense unseen defenders and avoid their tackles.

In 1952 McElhenny was named the NFL Rookie of the

Year, was chosen for the first of six Pro Bowl appearances, and was named by *Sport* magazine as the NFL Player of the Year. With the 49ers, McElhenny was part of an exciting team that often fell just short of championship caliber. From 1954 to 1956 he played in the same offensive backfield with the quarterback Yelberton Abraham "Y. A." Tittle, the fullback Joe "the Jet" Perry, and the halfback John Henry Johnson, who comprised the first professional football backfield to be selected to the Pro Football Hall of Fame. Despite their scoring capacity, the 49ers never played for a championship during McElhenny's time with them, instead fading after strong starts in 1952, 1954, and 1959. In 1954 McElhenny missed the final half of the season with a separated shoulder after running for 515 yards with an average of 8 yards per carry. His best season statistically with the 49ers was in 1956, when he ran for 916 yards and scored 8 touchdowns. Although foot injuries hampered McElhenny throughout his career, he was chosen Most Valuable Player of the 1958 Pro Bowl game.

The arrival of Coach Red Hickey in 1959 led to the break-up of the 49ers offensive nucleus, and McElhenny, who had his differences with the caustic Hickey, began playing less. In 1961 the expansion Minnesota Vikings acquired McElhenny, and he had his last good season, gaining 1,067 yards in rushing, pass receiving, and kick returns. Included in that total was a thirty-nine-yard touchdown run against his old team that the Viking coach Norm Van Brocklin called the greatest run he had even seen. After one more year with the Vikings, McElhenny underwent a knee operation in January 1963 and was traded to the New York Giants, where he was reunited with Tittle and played in the 1963 NFL championship game. McElhenny spent his final season with the Detroit Lions in 1964. At the time of his retirement McElhenny was one of three players with over 10,000 all-purpose yards (yards gained rushing, pass receiving, and returning kicks), with 11,369 yards. In addition he scored sixty-three touchdowns. In 1970 he was elected to the Pro Football Hall of Fame, and in 1981 he was elected to the National Football Foundation College Hall of Fame.

McElhenny began working for a potato chip manufacturing company in the offseason of his rookie year. He drove a delivery truck and opened new accounts with grocery stores and supermarkets, learning public relations and merchandising, and within five years he was a department head. In 1959, McElhenny opened his own food markets in California, but financial problems led to bankruptcy after only a few years. McElhenny then worked as a management trainee for the Burns Detective Agency in New York before moving back to the West Coast, where he worked in advertising and was associated with a group seeking an NFL franchise in Seattle in the early 1970s. After another failed business venture, he became a director with Pepsi-Cola in 1981, and retired from that position in 1995. In October 1996 he was stricken with Guillain-Barré syndrome, a virus that attacks the motor nerve system. Despite several months of incapacitation, he recovered.

McElhenny's football legacy is multifaceted. As a collegian his skills helped establish attendance records at Compton Junior College and the University of Washington, and he received All-America recognition in 1951. His emergence as the most exciting halfback in the NFL in 1952 brought more fans to 49ers games, and he became, in the words of the 49ers general manager Lou Spadia, a "franchise saver." The team owners Tony Morabito and Vic Morabito had considered selling the franchise, but they reconsidered after McElhenny's arrival. In a time before professional football effectively exploited television coverage and press coverage to seize national attention, McElhenny's heroics helped popularize the professional game. Through it all he remained popular with his teammates as a low-key, unassuming team leader who played without displays of ego or false bravado. Yet he was a believable, flawed hero who struggled with marital problems, a fiery temper, altercations with police, and conflicts with coaches. He was described by one writer as "among the last of a species, the open-field runners who lived on guile, their instincts, on reserves of the matador's art." At its finest, McElhenny's ability to run with the football approached an art form, a heightened level of self-expression combining athletic talent, grace, and intuitive brilliance.

★

An informative, insightful look at McElhenny and his Hall of Fame backfield mates is Dave Newhouse, *The Million Dollar Backfield: The San Francisco 49ers in the 1950s* (2000). McElhenny is profiled in Phil Berger, *Great Running Backs in Pro Football* (1970); and Mickey Herskowitz, *The Golden Age of Pro Football: A Remembrance of Pro Football in the 1950s* (1974). A perspective sketch of McElhenny with the Minnesota Vikings that waxes lyrical in describing his unique running style and rugged, elemental personality is in Jim Klobuchar, *Tarkenton* (1976). Reminiscences and statistics of McElhenny's college career are in John D. McCallum, *PAC-10 Football: The Rose Bowl Conference* (1982). His professional statistics are in David S. Neft, Roland T. Johnson, Richard M. Cohen, and Jordan Deutsch, *The Sports Encyclopedia: Football* (1976); and Bob Carroll, Michael Gershman, David S. Neft, and John Thorn, *Total Football: The Official Encyclopedia of the National Football League* (1999). Team histories of the 49ers are plentiful. Among the most useful in regard to McElhenny's career are Dan McGuire, *The San Francisco 49ers* (1960); Glenn Dickey, *The San Francisco 49ers: The First Fifty Years* (1995); and Joseph Hession, *Forty Niners: 49th Anniversary Collectors Edition* (1995). A somber, forthright look at McElhenny nearing the end of his career is Steve Gelman, "The King and the Turk," in Irving T. Marsh and Edward Ehre, eds., *Best Sports Stories* (1965).

Among the many magazine articles that profile McElhenny during his heyday is Melvin Durslag, "Takes Two to Touchdown," *Collier's* (3 Sept. 1954).

EDWARD J. TASSINARI

McENROE, John Patrick, Jr. (*b.* 16 February 1959 in Wiesbaden, Germany), world-class tennis player who helped to make tennis a popular sport in the United States.

McEnroe, one of the greatest U.S. tennis players of all time and a quintessential New Yorker, was actually born abroad, in West Germany at a U.S. Air Force base hospital. His father, John Patrick McEnroe, Sr., served in the military and his mother, Katherine C. (Kellaghan) McEnroe, was a surgical nurse. Shortly after McEnroe's birth, the family moved back to Queens, New York, and John, Sr., became a successful lawyer at one of New York City's top law firms. McEnroe and his two younger brothers grew up in the small, close-knit community of Douglaston on New York's Long Island. One of his brothers, Patrick, later forged a successful professional tennis career.

John McEnroe, 1984. ASSOCIATED PRESS AP

The young McEnroe attended the Buckley Country Day School and played many sports at school and in his neighborhood. When his parents joined the nearby Douglaston Club, McEnroe began playing tennis almost every day during his summer school breaks, and the club's members soon recognized his talent. Like many gifted tennis players from the New York area, McEnroe attended the Port Washington (Long Island) Tennis Academy, one of the most successful stables for developing young talent. Port Washington was run by a pair of former professional tennis players turned teachers; the Australian Harry Hopman was world famous as the coach of Rod Laver and Ken Rosewall, and Tony Palafox was a former Davis Cup player. With his father's connections, McEnroe was granted an interview at Port Washington, and Palafox instantly recognized the eleven year old's raw talent and rare ability to hit all the angles on the court at such a young age.

McEnroe hated Hopman's training regime, which required intense effort and hours of repetitious drills and workouts. He did not seem to need to work as hard as his classmates and practiced only when necessary, developing a unique style at an early age. He sought out coaching only when serious problems arose with his game. McEnroe simply wanted to play—his preferred method of practice was to play matches in both singles and doubles.

As a teenager McEnroe began attending the Trinity School, a prestigious college preparatory school in Manhattan. Trinity had a rigorous academic program that kept McEnroe very busy, and he excelled in his studies. He exhibited an independent streak and was mature for his age, traveling confidently every day through the streets of New York City. In 1976 McEnroe was suspended from Port Washington after a childish prank. He followed Palafox to the Cove Racket Club and continued playing junior tournaments (under-eighteen amateur events). Although he had obvious gifts, he was not one of the dominant junior players in the United States. At age sixteen he was named to the U.S. Junior Davis Cup Team. After graduating from Trinity in the spring of 1977, he began attending Stanford University in California that autumn. He led the Stanford tennis team to the National Collegiate Athletic Association title and also won the U.S. intercollegiate singles before leaving college in 1978 to become a professional player.

Anyone who saw McEnroe in his prime recognized both his natural talent and his unorthodox look. Tennis was a straitlaced sport, with aristocratic origins. McEnroe, with his long, unruly locks held under an unsightly bandanna or sweatband, stood out. His game was also unorthodox. The left-hander had a strange serve, in which he stood sideways and bent down so his hands almost touched his sneakers. His strokes were loose, and he often did not get his feet into the classic textbook position. Yet he was able to hit all the shots. He was extremely fast on the court and unsurpassed at the net. His relentless serve and volley attack allowed him to end points quickly. At five feet, eleven inches tall and 170 pounds, McEnroe was a bit chubby and looked sloppy on the court, yet he dominated the game.

In the summer of 1977, before entering Stanford, McEnroe qualified for Wimbledon at age eighteen and went on to reach the semifinals. That year he also announced his presence at the French Open, winning the mixed doubles with his childhood friend Mary Carillo. McEnroe became known as one of the finest doubles players in the world, winning five doubles titles at Wimbledon and four at the U.S. Open. With his longtime partner Peter Fleming, another Port Washington student, he eventually won a record-setting fifty-seven doubles titles. When Fleming retired, McEnroe continued to play with a series of other partners, bringing his career total to seventy-seven doubles titles.

In 1978 McEnroe began his longtime association with the Davis Cup (1978–1984, 1987–1989, 1991, 1992). Unlike other players of his generation, McEnroe made time to play for his country's national team, seeing it as a patriotic duty. He worked Davis Cup matches into his busy schedule, sometimes missing other tournaments and, as a consequence, losing money. He was a great booster for the team, pushing his fellow U.S. stars to play and thereby attracting corporate sponsors. McEnroe often was credited with saving Davis Cup tennis.

By the late 1970s McEnroe had earned the nickname "Superbrat" because of his courtside behavior. He questioned calls, shouted, and cursed. He recognized that tennis was 90 percent mental and often played with his opponents' heads. His 1979 match against fellow "bad boy" Ilie Nastase in the quarterfinals of the U.S. Open remains notorious. The match was halted as both questioned calls and cursed and taunted each other. The tournament officials were mortified, but the crowd was captivated by the spectacle. This controversial match made tennis more like other U.S. spectator sports, and McEnroe went on to win his first U.S. Open singles title.

McEnroe won more than seventy-seven career singles titles, including three at Wimbledon and four at the U.S. Open. But he was best known for his marathon matches against Bjorn Borg. The quiet Swede, with his looping topspin and inhumanly steady baseline game, was the perfect foil for McEnroe's aggressive net-rushing game. Their Wimbledon finals were unforgettable, so well matched were these opponents.

Perhaps the most memorable match was their meeting at the 1980 Wimbledon final. After McEnroe won the first set 6–1, Borg fought back and took the second set in a tiebreaker 7–5 and the third set 6–3. McEnroe pulled out the fourth set in another tiebreaker 7–6, throwing the match into a fifth set. Wimbledon did not allow a tiebreaker in the fifth set, so after the players carried it to 6–6, Borg took the next two games to finally win the fifth set, and the 1980 Wimbledon title. In 1981 McEnroe met Borg in the final of both Wimbledon and the U.S. Open. At Wimbledon that year, after losing the first set, McEnroe fought back to win the next two in tiebreakers and the final set 6–4. It was only a little easier at the U.S. Open. These matches brought tennis to a new level of popularity.

Following the most dominant years of his playing career, McEnroe married the actress Tatum O'Neal in 1986; the couple had three children. They divorced in 1992, and in April 1997 he married the singer Patty Smyth, with whom he had two daughters.

Although he retired from playing professional tennis in 1992, McEnroe remained active at the major tennis events as a television sports commentator. He also formed a senior tour, traveling around the United States with Borg, Jimmy Connors, and other retired tennis stars. He was a bit older and slower, but he still retained his passion and talent. He formed a rock band named the "Johnny Smith Band," and opened an art gallery in New York's Soho district. McEnroe also actively supported several charities, especially the Arthur Ashe Foundation for AIDS research.

In 1999 McEnroe was inducted into the International Tennis Hall of Fame and was named as the captain of the Davis Cup team. More than any other U.S. player, McEnroe served as the transitional figure between the older, country-club tennis fan and the modern tennis fan. He brought excitement and fireworks to tennis and he made it a popular U.S. sport. Together with his close friend Vitas Gerulaitis, and later alone, McEnroe visited parks and clubs across America to raise the public's awareness of tennis, encouraging youth to pick up a racket and play. As a player, sportscaster, and visible advocate, McEnroe truly became the tennis ambassador of the United States.

★

For details about McEnroe's life and career see Richard Evans, *McEnroe: A Rage for Perfection* (1982); Richard Evans, *McEnroe: Taming the Talent* (1990); and Richard Evans and John McEnroe, *The Davis Cup* (1999). An early magazine profile is in Pete Axthelm, "McEnroe: The Champ You Love to Hate," *Newsweek* (7 Sept. 1981), while a post-career profile is in Richard Sandomir, "You're Kidding, McEnroe Is Blunt?" *New York Times* (6 June 1995).

RICHARD A. GREENWALD

McGILLICUDDY, Cornelius. *See* Mack, Connie.

McGRAW, John Joseph (*b.* 7 April 1873 in Truxton, New York; *d.* 25 February 1934 in New Rochelle, New York), one of the most famous and successful baseball managers of all time who managed the New York Giants from 1902 to 1932; winning ten pennants and three World Series, he is second in games managed (4,845) and games won (2,816).

McGraw was the oldest of eight children (he also had an older half-sister) of John McGraw, an Irish immigrant railroad worker, and Ellen Comerfort. McGraw's mother and four of his brothers and sisters died in a diphtheria epidemic during the winter of 1884–1885 when he was eleven. His father became abusive, particularly disliking McGraw's penchant for playing baseball instead of doing chores. After one especially violent incident, McGraw, at age twelve, moved in with neighbors and thereafter saw little of his father. He spent his time in school, doing odd jobs around town (including selling snacks on the rail line from Truxton to Elmira), and playing baseball.

By age sixteen he was the best player on the town team, even though he was only five feet, six-and-a-half inches tall, and about 115 pounds. He talked his way onto his first professional team, Olean, of the newly formed New York-Pennsylvania League, signing a contract for $40 per month six days before his seventeenth birthday. His debut was a disaster; he made eight errors at third base and was quickly shifted to the outfield. He was released after a few more days.

McGraw migrated deeper into the minor league bushes to Wellsville of the Western New York League, along with five other Olean rejects. There he batted .365 in 107 trips to the plate and attracted the attention of Alfred Lawson, a journeyman pitcher and adventurous promoter who asked McGraw to play for his American All-Stars and tour Cuba that winter. At the end of the tour the team played Cleveland, then of the National League (NL), in a spring training exhibition game in Gainesville, Florida. McGraw clubbed three doubles and played errorless ball at shortstop. Within a week he had offers from many minor league clubs, and he signed contracts with at least five teams before ending up with the Cedar Rapids Canaries of the Three I League for the start of the 1891 season.

The Baltimore Orioles of the American Association, then a major league, called him up in August for the balance of the season after he hit .275 in 85 games and fielded well at shortstop. The 121-pounder was decidedly mediocre, hitting .245 and making 18 errors in 86 chances for a dismal .842 fielding average, but he was nonetheless signed by the Orioles for the following season.

The American Association collapsed after the 1891 season, and the Orioles were absorbed into the expanded twelve-team National League, then the only major league. The Orioles were abysmal, finishing in the cellar of the NL in 1892 with a 46–101 record as McGraw batted .267 in a utility role. He was kept home on some road trips to save the club money and collected tickets at turnstiles in full uniform to help pay his way.

Ned Hanlon, who would build the Orioles into a dynasty, became manager two weeks into the 1892 season. In 1893 McGraw had a breakthrough year and hit .321 while becoming the regular shortstop. In 1894 he shifted to third base and hit .340, as the Orioles, bolstered by Wee Willie Keeler, Dan Brouthers, Joe Kelley, Wilbert Robinson, and Hughey Jennings, won the first of three consecutive pennants and narrowly missed a fourth in 1897. McGraw bat-

John McGraw, 1904. AP/WIDE WORLD PHOTOS

ted over .325 each year, although he missed some of 1895 and most of 1896 with recurring bouts of malaria that brought him close to death. In the off-seasons he attended St. Bonaventure University near Olean, New York, with teammate Jennings. Together they coached the school's baseball team in the spring term.

The Orioles were known for their win-at-any-cost play (one umpire called them "a vile lot of blackguards"), and McGraw certainly helped earn the reputation. In the field he shoved, blocked, or held base runners, often hooking their belt as they rounded third. He abused umpires, brawled with opposing players, and was accused of being the dirtiest player in the league. Although he was an effective lead-off hitter, he remained somewhat of a liability in the field, even by the lower fielding standards of the day.

McGraw's leadership skills were evident early, for he was named to succeed Hanlon as manager of the Orioles before the 1899 season, a month before his twenty-sixth birthday. Hanlon had purchased an interest in the Brooklyn Trolley Dodgers and transferred many of the Orioles best players there. Nonetheless, McGraw led his leftover players to a surprising fourth-place finish. In late August, his wife Minnie Doyle, whom he had married two years earlier on 3 February 1897, died of acute appendicitis. She was only twenty-two years old. McGraw married Blanche Sindall of Baltimore on 8 January 1902. Married for thirty-two years, they remained childless.

The National League contracted to eight franchises for 1900, lopping off Baltimore and three other cities. McGraw ended up playing for St. Louis, along with old teammate Wilbert Robinson. In 1901 he joined forces with Ban Johnson in forming the American League (AL) and became player-manager of the new Baltimore franchise. In spring training in Hot Springs, Arkansas, McGraw flirted with signing Charley Grant, an accomplished African-American ballplayer, and passing him off as a full-blooded Cherokee called Chief Tokahoma. Charles Comiskey, owner of the Chicago White Sox, blew his cover; baseball was not integrated for another forty-six years. However, McGraw should not be characterized as a civil rights pioneer. He was probably just on the lookout for good baseball talent in his zeal to win.

McGraw quickly came into conflict with Johnson, generally over his own abuse of umpires. Their clashes escalated once the 1902 season began, and on 8 July he abandoned the American League and signed a four-year contract to manage the New York Giants of the National League for an annual salary of $11,000, the highest in baseball up to that time. McGraw was not yet thirty years old. He managed the Giants for thirty-one years and became one of the most dominant figures in baseball.

McGraw's Giants won their first pennant in 1904 but refused to play the AL champions, the Boston Pilgrims, in a World Series because of his continuing enmity against the AL founder Ban Johnson. Led by the great Christy Mathewson, the Giants won again in 1905 and defeated the Philadelphia Athletics four games to one in a World Series in which every game featured a shutout, three by Mathewson. The Giants lost a pennant in 1908 due to 19-year-old Fred Merkle's failure to touch second base in a late season game. Although McGraw could be very harsh with his players, he steadfastly defended his young player against all criticism. McGraw was an innovator, calling pitches from the bench and using relief pitchers, such as Doc Crandall, effectively. As combative and difficult as McGraw was, he had staying power, winning three consecutive pennants from 1911 to 1913, one in 1917, and four straight from 1921 to 1924.

After 1924 McGraw could not cajole his team into another pennant, although his Giants usually finished second or third. Although he was said to have passed on a young Tris Speaker, he was generally an outstanding identifier of baseball talent. After his first wave of success with Mathewson, Roger Bresnahan, "Turkey Mike" Donlin, and "Iron Man" Joe McGinnity, he brought in future Hall of Famers such as Ross Youngs, Fred Lindstrom, Travis Jackson, Carl Hubbell, Mel Ott, and Bill Terry. McGraw lamented the coming of the lively ball and the popularity of the home run brought on by the emergence of Babe Ruth, however, and, bothered by chronic sinus trouble and other ailments, finally stepped down as manager of the Giants on 3 June 1932. One year later McGraw came back to manage the National League in the first All-Star game in Chicago. He died of cancer only eight months later at the age of sixty and is buried in New Cathedral Cemetery in Baltimore. Known as "Little Napoleon" because of his strategic skill as a manager, McGraw was elected to the National Baseball Hall of Fame in 1937.

★

The National Baseball Library's collection on McGraw in Cooperstown, New York, is substantial. His memoirs were published as *My Thirty Years in Baseball* (1923). Biographies include the excellent Charles C. Alexander, *John McGraw* (1988); and several very good works such as Frank Graham, *McGraw of the Giants* (1944); Blanche Sindall McGraw, *The Real McGraw* (1953), edited by Arthur Mann; and Joseph Durso, *The Days of Mr. McGraw* (1969). *Pitching in a Pinch, or Baseball from the Inside* (reprint edition 1977), by Christy Mathewson, gives excellent insight into McGraw's "inside baseball" style of play. Other useful references include Frank Graham, *The New York Giants: An Informal History* (1952), and Neil Hynd, *The Giants of the Polo Grounds: The Glorious Times of Baseball's New York Giants* (1988). Frederick George Lieb, *The Baltimore Orioles: The History of a Colorful Team in Baltimore and St. Louis* (1955), and Burt Solomon, *Where They Ain't: The Fabled Life and Untimely Death of the*

Original Baltimore Orioles, the Team That Gave Birth to Modern Baseball (1999), detail McGraw's years with the Baltimore Orioles.

C. PAUL ROGERS III

McGWIRE, Mark David (*b.* 1 October 1963 in Pomona, California), first baseman who set a rookie record of forty-nine home runs in 1987 and a single-season home run record of seventy in 1998, eclipsing Roger Maris's celebrated 1961 record by nine.

McGwire is one of five sons of John, a dentist, and Ginger McGwire. When he graduated from Damien High School in Claremont, California, in 1981, he rejected a Major League Baseball contract to accept an athletic scholarship at the University of Southern California (USC). While at USC, McGwire set several school records. He received national recognition in 1984 as an All-American and was named to the 1984 Olympic team, which he led in doubles with thirteen. He also met and married his wife, Kathy, at USC. The marriage ended after three years; the couple had one son, Matthew, who would eventually work as a ball boy for the St. Louis Cardinals during McGwire's tenure with the team.

McGwire signed with the Oakland Athletics after the 1984 season, and the Athletics management saw him as the team's future starting first baseman. In 1987 he was given the first baseman's job and proved worthy of his team's faith in him. Because he played little in 1986, the year 1987 was considered his rookie year, and he set a rookie-year record of forty-nine home runs.

Mark McGwire. AP/WIDE WORLD PHOTOS

McGwire followed with seasons of thirty-two, thirty-three, and thirty-nine home runs, and he proved himself an outstanding fielder as well as a potent hitter, yet was not considered the best player on his team; right fielder Jose Canseco was. Canseco and McGwire became famous as the "Bash Brothers" for banging their forearms on each other after either hit a home run.

Still, McGwire became a favorite of fans, who loved watching his tremendous home runs, which soared farther than seemed humanly possible, and nearly everyone liked his quiet, understated style of play. At six feet, five inches in height and 220 pounds, he might have been expected to be awkward, but he was dazzling at first base, making quick grabs of line drives and diving his full body length to nab ground balls.

In 1991 McGwire's career seemed to be coming unglued. Injuries to his feet and back hampered him, and although he managed to play in 154 games, his play suffered and he hit only twenty-two home runs. Worse, he had only seventy-five runs batted in (RBI). Even so, perceptions of his status were actually improving. Canseco began behaving bizarrely in public and was in several scandals involving illegal guns, car wrecks, and confrontations with his estranged wife. By 1992 the quiet giant, McGwire, was becoming his team's emotional anchor, and in that year he rebounded with forty-two home runs and 104 RBI.

The next two years were miserable ones for McGwire. He had fractured and compressed vertebrae that required extensive surgery, and he hurt a foot very badly. He played only twenty-seven games in 1993 and forty-seven in 1994. In 1994 he began to show signs of returning to his old form, but major league ballplayers went on strike, prematurely ending the season and souring many fans of baseball. Especially disappointing was the sense that 1994 had been potentially one of the most entertaining seasons in history, with third baseman Matt Williams having an excellent chance of breaking Roger Maris's single-season record of sixty-one home runs. During this period, however, an extensive weight-training regimen increased his weight to 250 pounds while reducing his body fat.

In 1995 McGwire hit thirty-nine home runs in 104 games, and in 1996 he hit fifty-two home runs in only 130 games. This began talk of his potential for breaking Maris's home run record; McGwire's career home runs per at bat was higher than anyone else's in the history of the major leagues. This left the Athletics with a difficult problem in 1997, when his home run total rose to fifty-eight. McGwire became a free agent at the end of the season, and the Athletics had great trouble meeting his salary demands, which made trading him seem prudent; however, McGwire was plainly chasing Maris's record. Trading him meant the Athletics would lose the chance of having a player hit sixty-two home runs. Nevertheless, they traded him to the St. Louis Cardinals on 1 July 1997.

McGwire began the 1998 season by hitting home runs in the first four games his team played, including a grand slam in the first game. By June he was well on his way to setting a new home run record; the only player close to him was Ken Griffey, Jr., of the Seattle Mariners. For the Chicago Cubs, Sammy Sosa had a slow start. By mid-July, Griffey was fading; his home run total was impressive but lagged behind McGwire's. However, Sosa had a magnificent June and gained ground on McGwire. The race between Sosa and McGwire to break Maris's record was thrilling, and Sosa was all smiles and jokes, telling anyone who listened about how much fun he was having. McGwire had always been quiet and reserved, and he kept his private life to himself, but he followed Sosa's example and spoke cordially with reporters. Both players insisted that their rivalry was friendly and that it actually helped them deal with the pressures they were under.

In September the men were virtually tied in home runs, with Sosa actually edging ahead for a little while, but McGwire had a great month. On 8 September he hit his sixty-second home run of the season, breaking Maris's record, which had stood for twenty-seven years. In his last eleven at-bats of the season he hit five more home runs for a total of seventy home runs and 147 RBI.

At the end of the season Sammy Sosa received the National League Most Valuable Player award, something many observers thought McGwire should have won. Yet, Sosa's team went to the play-offs whereas McGwire's did not. Sosa also exceeded Maris's record with sixty-six home runs, and he was responsible for setting the friendly tone that seemed to heal the wounds caused by the 1994 strike.

During the 1998 season much of McGwire's personal life became public, especially his charitable work. He devoted time and money to helping children in need and gave $1 million per year to the Mark McGwire Foundation for Children, which helps treat victims of child abuse. This enlarged his reputation from great baseball player to great man.

In 1999 Sosa and McGwire had another thrilling home run chase, with McGwire ending up with sixty-five. In 2000 and 2001 he was beset by injuries, especially to his back, and his playing time was reduced considerably; his home run output was reduced to twenty-nine and thirty-two, respectively, for those years. On 5 October 2001 Barry Bonds of the San Francisco Giants broke McGwire's single-season home record and, two days later, extended the new record to seventy-three home runs. On 11 November 2001 McGwire announced his retirement from baseball, saying that he no longer was capable of performing at a level to match his enormous salary. His place in baseball history, however, seems clear. He hit home runs at a pace unmatched by any other player. His fielding was also good enough to win him a Gold Glove for first base in 1991. His dignity and humanity have endeared him to fans.

★

The single-season home run record is one of the most hallowed in baseball, held in turn by the charismatic Babe Ruth, the shy Roger Maris, and then by McGwire, whose 1998 record precipitated numerous books and other writings about him and his fabulous season. Among these are two fairly serious studies: Jonathan Hall, *Mark McGwire: A Biography* (1998), and Daniel Paisner, *The Ball: Mark McGwire's 70th Home Run Ball and the Marketing of the American Dream* (1999). A good comparative study is William F. McNeill, *Ruth, Maris, McGwire, and Sosa: Baseball's Single-Season Home Run Champions* (1999). The competition between McGwire and Sosa in 1998 is recounted by Lee R. Schreiber in *Race for the Record: The Great Home Run Chase of 1998* (1998), and by Mike Lupica in *Summer of '98: When Homers Flew, Records Fell, and Baseball Reclaimed America* (1999).

KIRK H. BEETZ

MACK, Connie (*b.* 22 December 1862 in East Brookfield, Massachusetts; *d.* 8 February 1956 in Philadelphia, Pennsylvania), baseball manager whose exceptional knowledge of the game, impeccable professional disposition, and extraordinary coaching abilities helped him capture nine pennants and five World Series and build two championship dynasties during his fifty years as the colorful manager of the Philadelphia Athletics.

Mack, born Cornelius McGillicuddy, was the third of seven children of the Irish immigrants Michael McGillicuddy, a wagon factory worker, and Mary McKillop, a homemaker. At age thirteen he left school to work in a Brookfield shoe factory and played baseball for the local team until 1886 when, at age twenty-four, he entered professional baseball as a catcher. Changing his name to Connie Mack so the sportswriters could "fit it into the box scores," he began his career at a time when baseball players were considered less prestigious than vaudeville actors.

As a player Mack embodied the more colorful nature of the game. Never a great hitter, he compiled a batting average of .249 during an eleven-year career with several teams of different leagues. In 1884 he played for Meriden in the Connecticut State League, and the following two years he played for Hartford in the Eastern League. Mack was better known for his excellent skills as a catcher. Often the six-foot one-inch, 160-pound backstop would rag an opposing hitter or call for a quick pitch, and he was even known to "tip the bat" on occasion.

From 1886 to 1889 he played for Washington in the National League, and then for Pittsburgh, also in the Na-

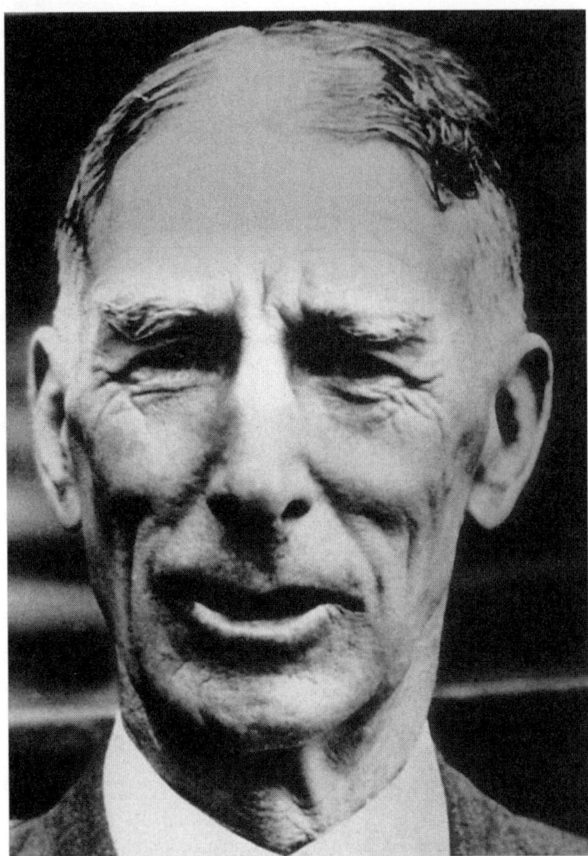

Connie Mack. ARCHIVES PHOTOS, INC.

tional League. On 2 November 1887 Mack married Margaret Hogan, with whom he had two children; she died in 1892. He began managing in 1896 with the Pittsburgh club but quickly fell into controversy with the ownership over the administration of the franchise. Three years later a disgruntled Mack left to establish a new league on the condition that he be given absolute freedom in running his own team. Together with two enterprising businessmen, Ban Johnson and Charles Comiskey, Mack organized the Western League, which became the American League and the rival to the National League, which was struggling for economic survival. In 1897 he played for the Milwaukee team of this new league. Mack was awarded the new Philadelphia franchise, the Athletics (A's), in 1901.

Almost from the moment he set foot in the City of Brotherly Love, Mack created controversy. By offering sizable pay increases, he attracted some National League stars to his team. His biggest catch was Napoleon Lajoie, second baseman of the rival league's Philadelphia Phillies. When the Phillies president John Rogers discovered the conspiracy, he obtained injunctions against his former player, forcing Lajoie to move to another team after the 1901 season.

Enraged by Mack's effort, John McGraw, the feisty manager of the National League's champion New York Giants, mocked the A's, predicting they would turn out to be a money loser, the "white elephants" of the new league. Mack found the remark amusing and adopted an elephant as the team's mascot. Not only did a likeness of the creature adorn the A's uniform, but Mack actually purchased an elephant for the enjoyment of the fans. Four years later Mack, with elephant in tow, met McGraw's Giants at Philadelphia's Shibe Park for the 1905 World Series. Though he did not capture the championship that year, the "Tall Tactician" got the last laugh when the A's defeated the Giants twice, first in 1911 and again in 1913.

Those titles were part of a championship dynasty built around a collection of a colorful personalities, including collegians like Eddie Collins, Jack Barry, Eddie Plank, and Albert "Chief" Bender, as well as dim-witted roustabouts like "Shoeless" Joe Jackson and Rube Waddell. Those A's teams captured the American League pennant four times in five seasons and won the World Series three times (1910, 1911, and 1913) in four seasons.

Mack's championship dynasty came in 1929, when he was the seasoned age of sixty-six and his managerial skills were being called into question by sportswriters. By that time baseball had changed dramatically from the earlier "dead ball era," when the game emphasized pitching, bunting, the hit-and-run, and stealing bases. Now the home run captured the imaginations of the fans, and power hitters reigned during this new "lively ball era." But Mack vindicated himself behind the pitching of Robert "Lefty" Grove and the power hitting of the first baseman Jimmie Foxx, the right fielder Al Simmons, and the catcher Mickey Cochrane. The A's won three straight pennants (1929, 1930, and 1931) and back-to-back World Series in 1929 and 1930, unseating the powerful New York Yankees, then widely considered the greatest team in the history of the game.

But Mack's managerial career was not a string of unbroken successes. In fact he piloted only two kinds of teams—unbeatable and lousy. His nine pennants were balanced with seventeen last-place finishes. His 3,776 victories were only exceeded by the 4,025 defeats his teams suffered, which set a record for most losses by a single manager. And his careful nurturing of two championship dynasties was only matched by his exceptional skill in dismantling two of the greatest teams of all time, in 1915 and between 1932 and 1935.

Still, over the course of his fifty-year managerial career, the Tall Tactician became a symbol of the enduring values of the national pastime, emphasizing team commitment, fair play, and clean living among his players. Rarely did Mack display anger or profanity, but he let his feelings be known with a stare or a question that would stifle the most unruly player. He even dressed the part of a gentleman. Believing that uniforms were meant for players only, Mack preferred to dress in a three-piece business suit, necktie, detachable collar, and derby or straw skimmer. Thus the congenial Irishman cut quite a dashing figure as he waved his trademark scorecard from the edge of the dugout, positioning outfielders with the skill of the unmistakable baseball genius he was.

Mack was also an enterprising businessman who anticipated many of the game's market trends as well as the fiscal practices of contemporary owners. In general he ran a tight payroll, more concerned about balancing his books than about taking the risks that would otherwise be necessary to purchase a championship. At the same time, however, he was capable of offering top dollar for a prospect if the player, in Mack's estimation, was worth it.

When attendance began to drop, Mack realized a correlation existed between a budding contender and fan appeal, or as he put it: "Once you win the championship the fans lose interest. Expenses increase and attendance decreases. I can make more money then, if the team finishes in second place because Philadelphians love to follow a contender."

As gate receipts declined, Mack did the only logical thing a businessman could do, sell his commodity while it still retained value and wait for the higher demand on the market before producing another winner. This he did twice, first in 1915, when he broke up his first championship dynasty whole scale, and again, more gradually, between 1932 and 1935. In 1940 Mack married a second time, to Katherine A. Hallahan, and they had five children.

The waning years of Mack's career were bittersweet. Elected to the Baseball Hall of Fame in 1937, his glory days were clearly behind him. His teams performed more like a "gentle comedy" than a legitimate contender. Outfielders ran into walls or, worse, into each other in pursuit of fly balls; quality players were constantly traded away for unknowns; and the team continued to lose and nobody seemed to mind. Faced with a weak and unprofitable team, a deteriorating, inaccessible stadium, and poor health, Mack in 1950 turned the ownership of the Athletics over to his sons. Four years later the A's left Philadelphia, first for Kansas City and later for Oakland, California. Mack died of old age on 8 February 1956.

★

Mack discussed his career in his autobiographical *My 66 Years in Baseball* (1950). He is the subject of William C. Kashatus, *Connie Mack's '29 Triumph* (1999), and Frederick G. Lieb, *Connie Mack: Grand Old Man of-Baseball* (1945). See also Ben Yagoda, "The Legend of Connie Mack," *Philly Sport* (Aug. 1989).

WILLIAM C. KASHATUS

McKAY, James McManus ("Jim") (*b.* 24 September 1921, in Philadelphia, Pennsylvania), network television sportscaster and commentator best known as anchorman for the American Broadcasting System (ABC) Sports television coverage of seven Olympic Games and as host of the network's long-running sports anthology showcase, *ABC's Wide World of Sports.*

James McManus is the birth name—and remains the legal name—of the man known to millions of U.S. sports fans for almost half a century as Jim McKay. McKay moved to Baltimore at age fifteen with his mother, Florence Gallagher and father, Joseph F. McManus, when his father gave up his real estate business for a job as a mortgage officer at a Maryland bank. The future sportscaster was so shy and timid as a boy that he depended on his sister to collect fees from delinquent customers on his paper route.

McKay had a Catholic education, attending St. Joseph's Prep in Philadelphia, then Loyola College in Maryland, where he earned his B.A. in 1943. Upon graduation he entered the U.S. Navy at the rank of lieutenant and commanded a wartime minesweeper in the South Atlantic. Following his discharge McKay returned home and took a job as a city reporter with the *Baltimore Sun* in 1946. While at the *Sun* he met Margaret Dempsey, a fellow reporter. The couple married on 2 October 1948, and later adopted a son and a daughter.

As did many newspapers during this period, the *Sun* started its own television station, WMAR, which went on air in 1948. McKay (still known as McManus) was transferred to the television operation, a move based largely on his college experiences as president of the drama club and a member of the debating society. His first assignment was to host a live three-hour, Monday-through-Friday afternoon program, *The Sports Parade.* Among his duties on the primitive television show were interviewing sports figures, announcing the horse racing results from Pimlico, and singing an occasional song. In 1950 McKay accepted an offer to do a similar show at WCBS in New York. A Columbia Broadcasting System (CBS) executive decided to name the program *The Real McKay,* requiring the host to change his professional name accordingly.

While at the CBS flagship station, other opportunities came McKay's way, including network jobs. But sports assignments, including the annual Master's Golf Tournament and the 1960 Olympic Games in Rome, proved the most important to his future. Roone Arledge, a former National Broadcasting Company (NBC) executive who had recently joined ABC Sports, admired McKay's compelling style of description and offered him a contract in 1961. "Some people . . . can make something dramatic by the inflections of their voices, without shouting," Arledge said of the decision. "Jim's not just somebody yelling at you. He has a sense of words, a sense of the drama of the moment." Arledge put McKay at the center of plans to build ABC Sports into an organization comparable to those of its two network rivals, CBS and NBC.

On Saturday, 29 April 1961, *ABC's Wide World of Sports* premiered with McKay as host and chief commentator. The opening of each show featured a montage of sports clips underscored by McKay's stirring narration: "Spanning the globe to bring you the constant variety of sports . . . the thrill of victory and the agony of defeat. . . . This is *ABC's Wide World of Sports*!" The series showcased different events each week, including unreported and underreported events in track and field, soccer, weightlifting, amateur wrestling, European grand prix racing, and skiing. Gymnastics, figure skating, and competitive swimming, to name a few prominent examples, owe much of their subsequent rise in popularity as U.S. spectator sports to the exposure afforded them by the show. McKay's name was synonymous with *Wide World of Sports* for a quarter of a century.

Over the years, as Arledge accomplished his goal of bringing ABC Sports first to parity and then to leadership among television sports organizations, part of his strategy was building a stable of recognizable personalities that was almost like a cast of characters. Among such figures as the boisterous, outspoken Howard Cosell and the glamorous all-American athlete Frank Gifford, McKay emerged as a steady, knowledgeable figure. He was prepared to keep fans informed on whatever came his way, whether it was the history of Grand Prix auto racing at LeMans, the meaning of the "Black Power" salute of track medalists John Carlos and Tommy Smith at the Mexico City Olympics, or the last twenty winners of the Kentucky Derby.

In 1972, as in 1968, McKay was passed over by ABC for the Olympic anchor position. But when the 1972 Munich Games were suddenly disrupted by terrorist violence—eleven Israeli athletes, coaches, and referees were taken hostage and subsequently killed by Palestinian terrorists—Arledge knew who to turn to for continuing coverage. McKay took the helm and guided viewers through the unfolding tragedy. He is particularly remembered for the poise, sensitivity, and journalistic skill he displayed when suddenly thrust into a position more appropriate for a seasoned network news anchor.

"All I could think of was the parents of David Berger [a U.S.-born Israeli weightlifter] sitting at home in Shaker Heights, Ohio, and that I was going to have to be the one to tell them whether their son was alive or dead," McKay told *Sports Illustrated.* At the closing ceremonies, as well-traveled news reporters and sportscasters alike struggled to find something appropriate to say, McKay touched the hearts of millions of viewers by reading "On the Death of a Young Athlete," a poem by A. E. Housman, which includes these lines: " . . .[on] the road all runners come, / Shoulder-high we bring you home, / And set you at your threshold down, / Townsman of a stiller town."

McKay's outstanding work at Munich won plaudits around the world, including two of his twelve career Emmy Awards (one each for news and sports), the George Polk Memorial Award for Journalism, and the Officer's Cross of the Legion of Merit from the West German Federal Republic. Other honors afforded McKay include the Peabody Award (1989) and membership in the Olympic Order (1998), the highest honor given by the International Olympic Committee. He was inducted into the Television Academy Hall of Fame in 1995. In all, McKay worked as either correspondent or anchor at twelve Olympiads.

Though McKay greatly reduced his responsibilities in the late 1980s after leaving the anchor spot at *Wide World of Sports,* he has never really retired. He continues to participate in ABC coverage of selected major events, including the British Open Golf Championship and all three legs of Thoroughbred racing's Triple Crown. In 1993 McKay and his wife bought a minority share of the Baltimore Orioles baseball team. They live in Monkton, Maryland, and maintain a winter home in Key Largo, Florida.

★

McKay is the author of two autobiographies, *My Wide World* (1973), and *The Real McKay: My Wide World of Sports* (1998). For an intricately detailed profile, see William Taaffe, "You Can't Keep Him Down on the Farm: ABC's Jim McKay," *Sports Illustrated* (18 July 1984). For a focused look at the Munich tragedy, see Richard Sandomir, "McKay Revisits Nightmare of the 1972 Olympics," *New York Times* (5 Sept. 1997).

DAVID MARC

McLAIN, Dennis Dale ("Denny") (*b.* 29 March 1944 in Markham, Illinois), American League (AL) pitcher, two-time Cy Young Award winner, and the last thirty-game winner in Major League Baseball.

McLain and his younger brother were raised in a far-south suburb of Chicago. His father Tom McClain, who died when his rambunctious son was fifteen years old, was an insurance adjuster who had played semiprofessional baseball as a shortstop. His strict, spare-not-the-rod approach to child rearing had little effect, perhaps because of his early death. McLain's mother, Betty McClain, was forced by her husband's death into the workforce as a cashier. McLain's athleticism gained him admission to the prestigious Catholic Mt. Carmel High School in Chicago, where he played basketball and football and excelled in baseball. The right-hander's 38–7 record earned him a $17,000 signing bonus with the Chicago White Sox upon graduation in 1962.

Although McLain started his professional career with a

Denny McLain after winning his thirtieth game of the season, 1968. AP/ WIDE WORLD PHOTOS

no-hit, no-run game, his high living, frequent absences and scorn for the "hick" towns of Harlan, Kentucky, and Clinton, Iowa, caused the White Sox to put him on waivers for a paltry $8,000. He was quickly picked up by the Detroit Tigers in the spring of 1963 but was not permanently brought up to the parent club until 1965, when he went 16–6 and recorded 192 strikeouts, the third-best tally in the league. In 1966 McLain compiled a 20–14 record and pitched three perfect innings in the All-Star game as the starter for the American League. But the man who taught McLain how to throw a curveball to complement his smoking fastball, manager Charley Dressen, died in August 1966, and McLain temporarily lost his confidence. His dismal record of 17–16 in 1967 was worsened by his failure to pitch six scheduled starts in September, causing the Tigers to lose the AL pennant by one game. The Detroit fans and media were skeptical of McLain's story that he had been startled by raccoons and had accidentally stubbed his toes. Years later, McLain alternately confirmed and denied that an unpaid gambling debt resulted in an enforcement visit during which his foot was stomped.

In 1968 McLain added a slider to his repertoire, which helped him earn an amazing 31–6 record, including 6 shutouts, the most since Lefty Grove won the same number in 1931. Dizzy Dean won thirty in 1934; no one has won thirty since. With the advent of the specialized relief pitcher and the current five-starter rotation system, it is unlikely that McLain's record will be surpassed. His dominant pitching in 1968 carried the Tigers to their first World Championship since 1945. McLain completed 28 games, had 280 strikeouts, and compiled a 1.96 earned run average (ERA). For this he simultaneously and unanimously won the Cy Young Award and most valuable player (MVP) honors—a rare occurrence, as MVP status is traditionally reserved for nonpitchers. Plagued by a sore right shoulder, McLain lost both showdowns with the National League ace Bob Gibson in the World Series, but, aided by cortisone, he won crucial game six. Mickey Lolich won game seven and the championship for the Tigers.

McLain's success continued in 1969. He garnered the team's first $100,000 contract by winning his second Cy Young Award (shared with Baltimore's Mike Cuellar) and again attained All-Star status with a 24–9 record, including a team record of 9 shutouts. McLain missed the first three months of the 1970 season when the baseball commissioner, Bowie Kuhn, suspended him for 1967 bookmaking transactions. His loss of income and his many failed business ventures caused McLain to file for bankruptcy later that summer. His second suspension of the season was for dumping a bucket of ice water over the heads of two sportswriters, his third was for gun possession. Fed up with McClain's misbehavior and his miserable 3–5 record, the Tigers traded him to the Washington Senators at the end of the season. In 1971 his frequent clashes with no-nonsense manager Ted Williams and his 10–22 record resulted in a trade to the Oakland Athletics. McLain's fastball was gone, and he finished the 1972 season in Atlanta after tallying a meager four victories for the year.

McLain self-destructed. On a certain path to the National Baseball Hall of Fame, his wanton disregard for the rules and his health cut short his career at age twenty-eight. Nevertheless, his career statistics remain impressive. Over the span of 10 years, McLain won 131 games and lost 91 for a winning percentage of .590. He started 264 games and completed 105. He had 1,282 strikeouts and a lifetime ERA of 3.39.

McLain proclaimed that music was actually his first love and that he had played the organ since childhood. He recorded two albums in 1968. His celebrity status enabled him to appear on several television shows, including the *Ed Sullivan Show* in 1968, and he also appeared on the *Steve Allen, Bob Hope, Joey Bishop, Glenn Campbell,* and *Smothers Brothers* shows. He spent time on the nightclub circuit, including Las Vegas, but this was never enough to pay for his high-flying lifestyle. His poor business sense and his eagerness to get rich quick resulted in many business failures.

In 1985 McLain was convicted of loan-sharking, bookmaking, extortion, and cocaine possession, but was released from prison after twenty-nine months because of prosecutorial errors. He regained his celebrity status quickly by becoming a popular radio talk-show host in the early 1990s on Detroit's WXYT. Sports was only a minor topic for the surprisingly well-informed liberal commentator. Few lessons were learned, however, as McLain loved to boast about his prison escapades, and past failures did not staunch his appetite for business deals. In 1994 McLain and two business partners purchased the ailing Peet Packing Company in tiny Chesaning, Michigan. The meat-products company had been the town's largest employer for over a century, and McLain was viewed as a savior. However, the new owners siphoned $3 million dollars from the $12 million-dollar pension fund for their personal expenses, and the company declared bankruptcy in 1995. McLain was convicted of conspiracy, mail fraud, theft of pensions, and money laundering in 1996 and sentenced to ninety-seven months at a minimum-security federal prison in Bradford, Pennsylvania. McLain is scheduled for release in 2004.

Married on 5 October 1963, McLain and Sharyn Boudreau, daughter of the Hall of Fame shortstop and manager Lou Boudreau, divorced in 1998. They had two sons and one daughter; another daughter died in a truck accident in 1992. There are four grandchildren. Although he is about six feet tall, McLain's prison weight is reportedly over 300 pounds, up from his playing weight of 190.

★

McLain has two autobiographies, *Nobody's Perfect* (1975), written with Dave Diles; and *Strikeout: The Story of Denny McLain* (1988), written with Mike Nahrstedt. The first book focuses on his baseball exploits and gambling problems; the second is a McLain-style apologia attempting to explain away his criminal misdeeds. For a straightforward account of McLain's career, see the "Dennis McLain" chapter in Bill Libby, *Star Pitchers of the Major Leagues* (1971). Steve Rushin, in the cover story for *Sports Illustrated* on the 1968 baseball season, "The Season of High Heat," (19 Jul. 1993), captures the personalities and the tumult of the times. Fred Goodman offers an analytical portrait of McLain in "Denny McLain Isn't Sorry," *Gentleman's Quarterly* (Mar. 1998).

FRANCIS R. MCBRIDE

McNALLY, John Victor ("Johnny Blood") (*b.* 27 November 1903 in New Richmond, Wisconsin; *d.* 28 November 1985 in Palm Springs, California), charter member of the Pro Football Hall of Fame (1963), and one of the sport's most remarkable characters.

McNally was one of six children and grew up a privileged youth in northern Wisconsin. His father, John McNally, was from a family that owned newspapers and flour mills. McNally's mother, Mary C. Murphy McNally, tried to instill fine tastes in her son by means of violin lessons and the like but, as he later said, "I had a definite resistance to culture." McNally graduated from New Richmond High School at the age of fourteen.

McNally's slender build precluded success in sports in his youth. He did what today would be called independent study and worked on a North Dakota farm for two years before enrolling at River Falls State Normal School in Wisconsin in 1920. After two years there he enrolled at St. John's, a small Benedictine university in Minnesota, where he blossomed as an athlete. He was skilled in football and baseball, and when pressed into service as a pitcher threw a one-hitter in his first and only attempt on the mound. McNally was a persuasive debater and filled leading roles in college theatricals. He also penned a poem (which he was fond of quoting), "Dear God, how sweet it is in spring to be a boy." McNally transferred to Notre Dame in 1923 after his junior year at St. John's. Now six feet, two inches tall, and 160 pounds, McNally was told by the Fighting Irish football staff that he was a tackle. When he protested, he was told to "play tackle or else." McNally elected the "else," which for him was buying a motorcycle, acquiring a female traveling companion, and taking off on a tour of New England. McNally said, "My only real contribution to Notre Dame football was doing Harry Stuhldreher's poetry assignments for him." Stuhldreher was the All-America quarterback of the famed Four Horsemen backfield.

In 1925 McNally was working as a stereotyper for the *Minneapolis Tribune* (owned by a family member) when he and a former St. John's teammate, Ralph Hanson, tried out with the East 26th Street Liberties, a semiprofessional football team. Knowing he had a year of college eligibility left—if he ever returned to school—McNally, following the common practice of the time for many college athletes who illegally earned money for playing on the side, knew he should not play under his given name. While speeding to the Liberties practice site, again on a motorcycle, the pair passed a theater marquee announcing a Rudolph Valentino bullfighting film entitled *Blood and Sand*. The ever-creative McNally elbowed Hanson and said, "That's it! I'll be Blood, you be Sand." Thus the legend of Johnny Blood was born. Some football historians, taking a more formal approach, list him as John ("Blood") McNally, making "Blood" seem like a nickname. However, Johnny Blood was an alias, not a sobriquet. To validate this, McNally signed his professional contracts—which were legal documents—with the name Johnny Blood. Not until much later did anyone know his given name. For a season's effort with the Liberties, McNally received $16.50.

McNally next played for an Ironwood, Michigan, team

in a tougher, more respected league, and then for the Milwaukee Badgers of the National Football League (NFL), but made a really big step in 1926 when he joined the Duluth, Minnesota, Eskimos, an NFL team fronted by the immortal Ernie Nevers. The team barnstormed the country, playing twenty-nine games—all but one on the road—but folded after the 1927 season. McNally spent 1928 with the Pottsville, Pennsylvania, Maroons. Official NFL statistics did not come into being until 1932, but anecdotal information shows that McNally, now a lithe 195 pounds, was not only a fast and elusive runner but also a threat as a pass receiver, even though NFL teams used the pass sparingly.

Although the Pottsville fire companies served beer twenty-four hours a day even during Prohibition, McNally felt that the small coal town offered little in off-field diversions. He was as pleased as Green Bay coach Earl ("Curly") Lambeau when the Packers and Maroons swung a deal that sent him to the Wisconsin town that was about to enjoy its first incarnation as "Titletown, USA." The Packers, with the eccentric but brilliant McNally calling signals, won three consecutive NFL titles—1929, 1930, and 1931. One pre-1932 statistic that does survive is the 14 touchdowns McNally scored in 1931. In an era when the leading pass receivers logged catches in the low teens for an entire season, McNally's reception total for 1935 was twenty-five.

McNally added to his own growing legend. Low on funds, he once hopped a freight train and rode the rails to the Packers training camp. A writer was going to refer to him in print as "the Hobo Halfback" but, being image-conscious, changed the phrase to "the Vagabond Halfback."

During the time that the Packers were an early NFL dynasty, McNally drove Green Bay coach Lambeau to distraction. Once, during contract negotiations, Lambeau offered McNally $110 a game if he stopped drinking after Tuesday each week. McNally countered, "Make it Wednesday and I'll take an even hundred." Once McNally, who always spent money as soon as—if not before—he had it, wanted an advance from Lambeau, who locked himself in his hotel room to avoid McNally. In a driving rainstorm McNally scaled a fire escape, leaped across a six-foot-wide air shaft onto Lambeau's narrow eighth-floor window ledge, regained his balance, and came through the coach's window. A shaken Lambeau gave him the money and said, "Just go, Johnny Blood. Go anywhere—just go."

Lambeau finally had enough in 1934 and traded McNally to Pittsburgh. McNally returned to the Packers in 1935 and 1936, but Lambeau traded him back. In Pittsburgh, McNally found a fellow Irish American in team owner Art Rooney. McNally was a player-coach in 1937 and 1938. As if to set an example for his players, he took back the opening kickoff of the first 1937 preseason game for a 100-yard touchdown. He was strictly a coach in 1939. McNally and Rooney convinced University of Colorado All-America "Whizzer" White to postpone his Rhodes Scholar studies in England and play for Pittsburgh at an unprecedented $15,800 annual salary—this in an era when the average professional player earned $100 – $150 a game and was paid only if he played. White, who later became better known as U.S. Supreme Court Associate Justice Byron R. White, responded by leading the NFL in rushing as a rookie in 1938. When President John F. Kennedy appointed White to the Supreme Court in 1962, McNally was at the swearing-in ceremony. Kennedy told him, "Your name is a household word in our house."

Rooney attempted, unsuccessfully, to get McNally to be a little more religiously devout. McNally's words on the subject were "I was a roamin' Catholic." When he retired from football in 1939, McNally held NFL career records for most seasons played (15), most touchdowns scored (37—only those after 1932 were officially counted), and most points scored (224—again, only those tallied after 1932 were counted). Once when asked about what it was like to be a professional football pioneer, McNally said, "If you don't like neckties, you can't beat it."

McNally drifted out of football. On 8 December 1941, a day after the Japanese attack on Pearl Harbor, he enlisted in the U.S. Army Air Corps. He served with distinction as a cryptographer in the China-Burma theater. Those who knew "the magnificent screwball," as writer Arthur Daley tagged him, most often expressed surprise that they had not read about McNally commandeering a plane and bombing Tokyo or some such strategic target.

In 1948 McNally married for the first time, to Marguerite Streater, and finally earned his B.A. from St. John's. He later coached there and was on the faculty for a few years. In 1958 he ran for sheriff of St. Croix County in Wisconsin. Perhaps all chance of victory faded when the semiserious McNally, asked to identify the main plank of his platform, replied, "a return to honest wrestling."

McNally's first marriage "didn't take," in his words, and the couple divorced in 1956. After living the bachelor's life for several years, he married Catherine Irene Kopp, a successful businesswoman, in 1966. McNally came to think of her three sons as his own. The couple lived in St. Paul, Minnesota, before moving to Palm Springs, California, where McNally died from the complications of a stroke—not having missed much, if anything, of what life has to offer. He is buried in Desert Memorial Park in Cathedral City, California.

The writer Jim Klobuchar wrote of McNally shortly before he died: "He is the kind of man who impels non-psychic types into rambling incantations about reincarnation. Nobody, the theory goes, could possibly pack that much living into one lifetime without some prior experience."

★

Ralph Hickock, a writer from New Bedford, Massachusetts, worked with McNally on a biography, but McNally declined to have it finished and published. No other full-scale biography has been written. McNally's life and career are discussed in Arthur Daley, *Pro Football's Hall of Fame* (1963); George Sullivan, *Pro Football's All-Time Greats* (1968); Murray Olderman, *The Running Backs* (1969); and Myron Cope, *The Game That Was* (1970). An obituary is in the *New York Times* (30 Nov. 1985).

JIM CAMPBELL

McNAMEE, Graham (*b.* 10 July 1888 in Washington, D.C.; *d.* 9 May 1942 in New York City), radio's first significant sports broadcaster and an all-purpose program announcer; generally considered the father of sportscasting.

McNamee was the only child of John Bernard McNamee, a lawyer, and Anne Liebold McNamee, a homemaker. Moving to St. Paul, Minnesota, in 1894, McNamee attended school there. At an early age it was noticed that he had an excellent voice and enjoyed singing. His mother, who sang in a church choir, encouraged him in piano and voice lessons for years, and as a teenager he began performing at local social events.

After graduation from high school, McNamee worked briefly as a freight clerk for the Great Northern Railroad but soon became a traveling salesman for the Armour Meat Packing Company. At that time salespeople traveled through their rural territories by horse-drawn buggy, and after McNamee wrecked a series of carriages during his first year he was dismissed.

After his father passed away in 1912, McNamee and his mother moved to New York City so he could continue his voice training with more prominent teachers. McNamee, a baritone, became a singer with various church and opera groups and made his solo debut on 22 November 1920 at New York's Aeolian Hall. He married Josephine Garrett, a professional singer, on 3 May 1921, and for the next few years struggled financially while continuing his musical career.

In April 1923, while serving jury duty in Manhattan, McNamee applied for a job at radio station WEAF, located in the AT&T Building. After a short audition he was hired as an all-purpose worker, with occasional singing and announcing duties, for $50 per week. On 23 August 1923 McNamee broadcast his first sporting event—the middleweight championship fight in New York between Harry Greb and Johnny Wilson. Station KDKA in Pittsburgh had been broadcasting the occasional sports event since 1921, but commitment to such programming was nonexistent, as were designated sportscasters. McNamee was made lead

Graham McNamee interviewing Babe Ruth. © BETTMANN/CORBIS

announcer midway through WEAF's live coverage of the 1923 World Series over a four-station network on the East Coast, and at the conclusion of the Series he received 1,700 letters.

That same fall McNamee broadcast his first football game and, while continuing to handle his announcing duties for studio shows, began to cover an increasing number of sporting events. By 1924 there were an estimated 3 million radios and over 200 broadcasting stations in the United States, and station managers were coming to realize that sports events were the hottest programming they offered at the time. However, it was a nonsporting event that launched McNamee to national renown.

In the summer of 1924 he was assigned to broadcast the Republican and Democratic National Conventions over a sixteen-station network—the first time the conventions had been broadcast. The Republican Convention was routine, but at New York's Madison Square Garden the Democrats became hopelessly deadlocked. For fifteen days, broadcasting sixteen hours a day and living on sandwiches and soda, McNamee covered the convention through over 100 ballots before John W. Davis was selected. These broadcasts made McNamee a nationally known celebrity. His status was solidified when he received 50,000 letters after his coverage of the 1925 World Series. He eventually broadcast the World Series for twelve years—through 1934.

McNamee possessed a superb speaking voice that soon was recognizable to listeners around the country, along with his trademark sign-on: "Good evening, ladies and gentlemen of the radio audience." Announcing sports with a vibrant and energetic style, he conveyed an obvious enthusiasm for the events. Although often criticized by newspaper reporters for his lack of technical knowledge in some sports, McNamee's informal, freewheeling, and chatty style of broadcasting conveyed a sense of on-site presence to listening sports fans. His game accounts were filled with asides about things happening in the grandstands, clouds in the sky, the scenery around the stadium, and celebrities in attendance. McNamee believed that this was an essential aspect of sports broadcasting, yet his announcing of championship boxing always conveyed incredible intensity and drama for the listeners.

When the National Broadcasting Company (NBC) was formed in 1926, the company's first president called McNamee "radio's greatest asset," and he was considered the most popular radio announcer on the air. McNamee joined NBC, and his fame continued to grow in 1927 as he broadcast the 1927 Rose Bowl football game and the World Series live over the network's first coast-to-coast hookup. McNamee also covered the 1927 return of Charles Lindbergh from Paris—considered the biggest assignment of his career.

By 1929 radio was significantly expanding the programming of variety shows, and McNamee was always busy announcing for many such programs through the remainder of his career. Among the more notable variety shows he announced were the *Fleischmann's Yeast Hour, Texaco Fire Chief, Major Bowes and His Original Amateur Hour, Atwater Kent Auditions,* and *Behind the Mike.*

McNamee covered events in ten sports for NBC as well as unusual events such as the National Marbles Tournament and the National Soapbox Derby. He always covered the most important sporting events. Among his favorites were the Jack Dempsey – Gene Tunney "long count" fight of 1927, Babe Ruth's "called" home run in the 1932 World Series, Glenn Cunningham's record-breaking mile run in 1934, and the golfer Ralph Guldahl's victory in the 1939 Masters.

By the 1930s radio was turning to sportscasting specialists, and McNamee's sports assignments were scaled back—he was considered too valuable to be removed from the commercial side of radio—although he never completely left sportscasting. In February 1932 McNamee was divorced from his first wife, and on 20 January 1934 he married Ann Lee Sims. His last broadcast appearance was on 24 April 1942. Soon afterward he died from a stroke at age fifty-three. He is buried at Calvary Cemetery in Columbus, Ohio.

In recognition of his many contributions to broadcasting history, McNamee was inducted into the National Association of Broadcasters Radio Hall of Fame in 1977 and the American Sportscasters Association Hall of Fame in 1984.

McNamee was a pioneer in a medium for which there were few ground rules when he began. His distinctive announcing style quickly swept radio audiences into the excitement of the events and provided a shared experience for listeners around the country. Shaping the outlines of sports broadcasting into an art form, McNamee was described by Red Barber as "the greatest sports announcer we ever had." McNamee played a major role in the expansion of radio's popularity, and sports announcers still emulate his technique.

★

McNamee coauthored a memoir, *You're On the Air* (1926), with Robert G. Anderson; the book provides some useful information but is limited by its early publication date. A valuable source of information on McNamee's personality and nonsports broadcasting is Sam J. Slate and Joe Cook, *It Sounds Impossible* (1963). Other useful sources include Red Barber, *The Broadcasters* (1970); Geoffrey T. Hellman, "Profiles," *New Yorker* (9 Aug. 1930); and T. R. Kennedy, Jr., "A Voice to Remember," *New York Times* (17 May 1942). An obituary is in the *New York Times* (10 May 1942).

RAYMOND SCHMIDT

MACPHAIL, Leland Stanford, Sr. ("Larry") (*b.* 3 February 1890 in Cass City, Michigan; *d.* 1 October 1975 in Miami, Florida), Major League Baseball executive whose creativity and inventiveness led to many changes in the game.

MacPhail was one of three children of Curtis McPhail, a Cass City banker, and Catherine MacMurtrie, a homemaker. (MacPhail later changed the spelling of his last name to call attention to his Scottish ancestry.) After graduating from Staunton Military Academy in Virginia in 1906, MacPhail enrolled at Beloit College in Wisconsin. Following his freshman year, he transferred to the University of Michigan Law School, but eye trouble forced him to withdraw after the first semester. He entered George Washington University as a junior and received his LL.B. in 1910 at age twenty. Following graduation, he married Inez Thompson; they had three children.

MacPhail practiced law, then rose to the rank of captain in the U.S. Army during World War I. Settling in Columbus, Ohio, after the war, he owned automobile distributorships, among many other business ventures. MacPhail and Thompson divorced in 1939, and on 16 May 1945 MacPhail married Jean Bennett Wanamaker, who had been his secretary while he was president of the Brooklyn Dodgers; they had one child.

Larry MacPhail *(left)* with Yankee manager Bucky Harris, 1947. ASSOCIATED PRESS AP

In 1931 the Columbus Triple-A club became a financial victim of the depression. Local businessmen rallied to keep the team operating, and because MacPhail was out of work due to the depression, they chose him to be team president. MacPhail convinced the St. Louis Cardinals to add Columbus to their well-established farm system. That negotiation brought him in contact with Branch Rickey, a prominent baseball executive, with whom he developed a long-term love-hate relationship. MacPhail's success in drawing fans to a new modern ballpark with lights bothered Rickey, and his resistance to providing Columbus players to help the parent club angered Rickey. During the 1933 season, Rickey unceremoniously fired MacPhail.

By the end of 1933 MacPhail had been hired as general manager of the Cincinnati Reds, a weak second-division team in the National League (NL). He raised fan interest through player acquisitions, promotions, and regular radio broadcasts with Walter "Red" Barber, the "Voice of the Reds." He also inaugurated airplane flights in the majors to replace tedious train travel. Night baseball had been played in the minors, but it was prohibited in the majors. MacPhail persuaded the NL to permit the Reds to play one night game with each team in the league. On 24 May 1935 President Franklin Delano Roosevelt, in Washington, D.C., flicked the switch to turn on the lights in Cincinnati's Crosley Field, and the majors' first-ever night game was played. In September 1936 the Reds' president Powell Crosley, Jr., fired MacPhail after he slugged a police sergeant in a hotel elevator. The Reds were a much-improved team after MacPhail left, and in 1939 the rejuvenated Cincinnati won the NL pennant.

MacPhail took on another challenge in 1938, becoming executive vice president of the downtrodden Brooklyn Dodgers. The slightly over six-foot, 195-pound entrepreneur with bright red hair, watery blue eyes, and a freckled face initiated the triumvirate of renovation, promotion, and acquisitions that was his prescription for breathing life into an unsuccessful franchise. He had new sod laid on the field and gave Ebbets Field a coat of paint—mostly orange. MacPhail created a festive atmosphere by having the newly organized Dodger Symphony Band produce a loud cacophony of raucous sound. His well-trained ushers were attired in flashy green-and-gold uniforms.

MacPhail had to completely revamp the Dodgers, a team known more for its comedic ineptness than its ability. He accomplished this through conniving, trades, and purchases. In 1938 commissioner Kenesaw Mountain Landis, who believed the depth of the Cardinals farm system prevented youngsters from a fair shot at reaching the majors, declared Pete Reiser and seventy-two other St. Louis minor leaguers to be free agents. MacPhail signed Reiser for $100. Branch Rickey thought Landis had agreed to hide Reiser for him in the Brooklyn farm system and later give him back to the St. Louis system. When Rickey asked to have Reiser back, MacPhail responded with a resounding "No."

The Cardinals Leo Durocher signed to play shortstop for the Dodgers in 1938, bringing an intensity that endeared him to MacPhail. One year later MacPhail, who had become the president of the club, appointed the thirty-three-year-old Durocher to be Brooklyn's player-manager. At times, the two men worked together well as they rebuilt the franchise. At other times, their relationship included fits of blind rage and anger, often precipitated and fueled by MacPhail's use of alcohol. During Durocher's four years as manager, the "Roaring Redhead" fired Leo "The Lip" at least four times, including the night in 1941 when Brooklyn clinched the pennant. After each firing, Durocher went right on managing and MacPhail looked the other way.

During his time as president of the Dodgers, which ended in 1942, MacPhail brought lights to Ebbets Field, had batting helmets manufactured for his players, scheduled special events to entertain fans before games, and brought Brooklyn to the airwaves with Red Barber at the microphone, ending a long-standing agreement by the three New York teams not to broadcast their games. MacPhail also arranged for a Brooklyn game to be televised. His inventive plan to use yellow baseballs failed to catch on in Brooklyn.

MacPhail, a staunch patriot, returned to military service on 1 October 1942 during World War II. Lieutenant Colonel MacPhail served as an aide to Undersecretary of War Robert Patterson. Following the war, MacPhail, Del Webb, and Dan Topping became owners of the New York Yankees. MacPhail was the club's president and helped build the foundation for a dynasty. His Yankees farm system, which numbered over twenty-five clubs, provided outstanding talent for many years.

MacPhail had lights installed in Yankee Stadium, was instrumental in bringing televised games to the New York area, set up a pension plan for Yankees players and front-office personnel, initiated a Stadium Club to cater to season-ticket holders and others, and organized Old Timers' Days, when retired players were honored before the start of a game and sometimes played shortened games themselves. MacPhail resigned as Yankees president at the Biltmore Hotel following the Yankees victory over the Dodgers in the 1947 World Series. At the celebration, MacPhail punched out general manager George Weiss and Dan Topping in a mêlée later known as the "Battle of the Biltmore." He retired to his Glenangus Farm in Bel Air, Maryland, with his wife and daughter to breed and run racehorses. Illness forced MacPhail to live his last few years in a Miami nursing home, where he died. He is buried in Cass City.

The dynamic, creative, charismatic, combative, heavy-drinking MacPhail worked in major league baseball for only eleven years, but he won world championships in both leagues and was responsible for many of the game's advances. MacPhail was elected posthumously to the National Baseball Hall of Fame in 1978. One of his sons, Leland S., Jr. ("Lee"), and a grandson, Andrew B. ("Andy"), also became successful major league executives. His son joined him as a member of the Hall of Fame in 1998.

★

Don Warfield, *The Roaring Redhead: Larry MacPhail, Baseball's Great Innovator* (1987), offers an account of MacPhail's life and accomplishments. G. Richard McKelvey, *The MacPhails: Baseball's First Family of the Front Office* (2000), presents an account of MacPhail's career, using the remembrances of his son Lee, his grandson Andy, and other baseball personnel as primary sources. A three-part series, "The Great MacPhail," by Gerald Holland, appeared in *Sports Illustrated* (17, 24, and 31 Aug. 1959). Obituaries are in the *New York Times* (2 Oct. 1975) and *Sporting News* (18 Oct. 1975).

G. RICHARD MCKELVEY

MADDEN, John Earl (*b.* 10 April 1936 in Austin, Minnesota), head coach of Oakland Raiders from 1969 to 1978, winning over a hundred games in ten seasons and a Super Bowl championship; also an Emmy-winning sports commentator.

Madden was the eldest of three children born to Earl Madden, an auto mechanic, and Mary O'Flaherty Madden. The family moved to Daly City, California, when Madden was six, and he began playing football and baseball behind the family's house in a vacant lot and working as a batboy at the Sarto Athletic Club. He befriended John Robinson, who would later serve as head coach to the Los Angeles Rams, in the fifth grade at Our Lady of Perpetual Help School in Downey, California, and considered him as close as a brother. Madden later fondly recalled the two friends hitching rides on trolley cars to San Francisco, where they would sneak into Seals Stadium and Kezar Stadium to watch baseball and football games. Madden played several sports at Jefferson Union High School, but excelled at baseball. In his senior year, the New York Yankees and Boston Red Sox approached him to play in the minor leagues.

Madden hesitated. While working as a caddy at the San Francisco Golf and Country Club, he noticed one thing that most successful people had in common—a college education. In 1954 Madden enrolled at the University of Oregon on a football scholarship, but after a knee injury he returned to California to attend the College of San Mateo. He attended Grays Harbor College in Aberdeen, Washington, for a semester and then enrolled at California Polytechnic State University where in 1957 and 1958 he played baseball (catcher) and made all-conference tackle.

John Madden *(left)* with fellow broadcaster Pat Summerall. ASSOCIATED PRESS FOX

Madden received a B.S. in education from Cal Poly in 1959. While at Cal Poly, Madden had met Virginia Fields; they married in 1960 and eventually had two sons.

In 1959 the Philadelphia Eagles recruited Madden as a guard in a twenty-first draft pick. After injuring his left leg in a scrimmage game, Madden began to think seriously about a career in coaching. While recovering, he learned the ins and outs of football by watching game films and listening to analysis from quarterback Norman Van Brocklin. Madden returned to California Polytechnic, received an M.A. in education in 1961, and started his first coaching job at Allan Hancock Junior College in Santa Maria, California.

Madden served as Hancock's line coach from 1960 to 1962, then as head coach from 1962 to 1964. After working as a defensive coordinator at California State University from 1964 to 1966, Madden was recruited by the Oakland Raiders as linebacker coach under John Rauch in 1967. The Raiders compiled the best American Football League (AFL) record (13–1) in the 1967 season, leading to a matchup against the Green Bay Packers in Super Bowl II, which Oakland lost 33–14. When Rauch suddenly departed to the Buffalo Bills in 1969 because of conflicts with team owner Al Davis, Madden became one of the youngest head coaches in the league.

Madden may have considered himself only a coach in training, but the Raiders chalked up an impressive 12–1–1 season in 1969, winning the AFL's Western division. He began the practice of holding preseason training camps for the benefit of rookies, but also as a method to learn more about coaching. As Oakland became successful, Madden received several offers from teams like the New York Jets, but he turned them down, preferring to work with Oakland owner and friend Al Davis. The Raiders won their division championship five out of six times between 1970 and 1975, but the American Football Conference title escaped them. In 1972, for instance, the Pittsburgh Steelers beat the Raiders with a deflected pass, later called the "immaculate reception," in the last twenty-two seconds of the game to capture the title. A furious Madden argued that a Steeler had illegally tipped the pass before it was caught, but a television replay proved inconclusive. This may have been the first time instant replay was used to review referees' calls.

Madden and Oakland's luck changed in 1976. Their 13–1 record placed them at the head of their division, and they defeated New England 24–21 in the first-round playoff game. Many expected a difficult challenge in the follow-up game against the Steelers, the defending champions, but the Raiders won a decisive 24–7 victory. On 9 January 1977 eighty-one million television fans watched the matchup between Oakland and the Minnesota Vikings at Super Bowl XI in the Rose Bowl in Pasadena. The Raiders came out strong, scoring on three successive drives and leading Minnesota 16–0 by halftime. Although the Vikings scored a touchdown in the third quarter, two fourth-quarter touchdowns by Oakland gave the team a 32–14 victory in their first Super Bowl title. It would be four more years before the Raiders returned to the Super Bowl.

On 5 November 1978 Madden won his 100th coaching victory and had done so within 10 years. His win percentage of .790 was the highest of any National Football League (NFL) coach who had won 50 or more games. Despite these successes, several incidents left Madden demoralized and feeling burned out. On 12 August 1978 during an exhibition game against the Raiders, New England Patriot Darryl Stingley's neck was broken, leaving him paralyzed. Madden visited Stingley daily, but he was disappointed that more people did not seem to care. Madden was also troubled by a conversation with his wife about the age of his son: she had to correct his assumption that his son was twelve when he was really sixteen. With a stomach ulcer and a less than glamorous 1978 season, Madden announced on 4 January 1979 that he would retire.

Madden quickly found activities to occupy his time during retirement including teaching, writing a newspaper column, and acting in commercials. He became widely known, more so than in his days as a coach, from his appearances in Miller Lite beer commercials. He continued to love football and follow the season, eventually joining

Columbia Broadcasting System's CBS-TV as an analyst in 1979. Madden's ability to balance technical information and colorful, entertaining reporting made him a popular commentator. By 1981 and 1982 he had won television Emmys for his work as a sports analyst and was covering the Super Bowl alongside broadcast veteran Pat Summerall. Madden is well known for his fear of flying and use of his private bus (called the Madden Cruiser) to travel to games. In 1998 Madden received a $40 million contract with Fox to continue as a lead football analyst. Madden's achievements as a coach, his books, and his continued involvement as a commentator, have left an unforgettable mark on the sport of football.

★

Madden's *Hey, Wait a Minute (I Wrote a Book!)* (1984), *One Knee Equals Two Feet* (1986), and *Hey, I'm Talking Pro Football!* (1996), offer anecdotes and reflections on the sport of football. For a lengthy account of Madden's career, see *Current Biography* (Aug. 1985). For a brief overview, see David L. Porter, ed., *Biographical Dictionary of American Sports: Football* (1987).

RONNIE D. LANKFORD, JR.

MADDUX, Greg(ory) Alan (*b.* 14 April 1966 in San Angelo, Texas), National League baseball pitcher who won four straight Cy Young awards.

As a child, Maddux frequently moved with his family because his father, Dave, served in the U.S. Air Force. He played Little League in Spain. When his family moved to Las Vegas, Nevada, Maddux starred at Valley High School, was twice named All-State, and graduated in 1984. His older brother, Michael, had already signed a professional baseball contract with the Philadelphia Phillies. Maddux was chosen in the second round of the 1984 draft by the Chicago Cubs. He distinguished himself at every level of minor league ball during his three years in the Cubs organization. He won thirty-six games and compiled a 2.86 earned run average (ERA).

Maddux was called up to the major leagues in September 1986 and the next year became a fixture in the Cubs rotation. He played with the Cubs for the next six years, establishing himself as one of the premier pitchers in the National League. He won 90 games, lost 75, and had three years of above 15 wins. In 1989 he led the Cubs to the playoffs against the San Francisco Giants. The Giants defeated the Cubs, and Maddux suffered one loss in his first postseason series.

During the 1992 season Maddux claimed a spot among the elite pitchers of the major leagues. He not only won twenty games for the Cubs but also hurled four shutouts, had a 2.18 ERA, and won his third straight Golden Glove as a fielding pitcher. He was rewarded with his first Cy Young Award as the best pitcher in the National League and was picked as an All-Star. Following the season Maddux tested the free agent market and eventually signed with the defending National League champion Atlanta Braves. From 1992 until 2001 the Braves and Maddux appeared in

Greg Maddux. ARCHIVE PHOTOS, INC.

the postseason every year except the strike-shortened 1994 season.

John Smoltz, Tom Glavine, and Maddux formed one of the most effective pitching staffs in modern baseball history. Maddux won three more Cy Young Awards (1993–1995) as a Brave, Glavine won two, and Smoltz one. No other pitcher in major league history had won four consecutive Cy Young awards. During that four-year period Maddux won 75 games, had an ERA of 1.97, and pitched 11 shutouts and 37 complete games. Considering that both the 1994 and 1995 seasons were shorter because of labor disputes, the achievement is even more remarkable. In addition, he allowed only thirty-three home runs during those four seasons.

As of the end of the 2001 season, Maddux had won fifteen or more games each year in fourteen consecutive years. Only two other pitchers in major league history, Cy Young and Gaylord Perry, achieved that feat. Maddux had accumulated 257 wins in his career by the end of the 2001 season. As an example of his consistency with the Atlanta Braves, from 1993 through 2001 he walked only 278 batters in 1,876 innings. He is famous for pitching in games that last less than two hours, and he has numerous complete games in which he threw fewer than ninety pitches.

Maddux has had remarkable streaks. During 2000 he pitched 30.33 consecutive scoreless innings and went thirty-two straight innings without issuing a walk. Twice in 1997 he went over thirty consecutive innings without issuing a walk. In 2001 he set a National League record by exceeding sixty-eight walkless innings. As a fielder he won ten straight Golden Glove Awards and has made more putouts than any pitcher in major league history. He also holds the record for consecutive victories on the road, pitching eighteen from late 1994 through the end of 1995. During the years 1994 and 1995 he won 35 games, lost 8, and had 10 complete games and 3 shutouts each year. In 1994 his ERA, at 1.56, was 1.09 below the second-place finisher, Steve Ontiveros of the Oakland A's. That set a major league record for the greatest spread in a single season. From 1992 to 1997 he had the lowest ERA, 2.14, for a six-year span of any pitcher since World War II. Maddux pitched over 200 innings for thirteen straight years, which is the most among active pitchers. His average ERA for 1994 and 1995 was 1.60, the lowest in modern baseball history for successive years. Another amazing Maddux statistic is that by the end of the 2001 season, he had not yet been placed on the disabled list during his major league career.

The Braves were in the postseason repeatedly, although they won the World Series only in 1995. As of 2001 Maddux had made twenty-nine appearances in the Division, League, and World Championship series, posting ten wins and thirteen losses. His World Series record is two wins and three losses, with a 2.09 ERA. His two-hit complete-game victory in game one of the 1995 World Series was his best postseason outing. The Braves won 3–2, and both runs against Maddux were unearned. The next year Maddux defeated the Yankees 4–0 in game two of the World Series, when he pitched a six-hitter for eight innings, but he lost game six 3–2.

In eight of his seasons Maddux has been selected as an All-Star for the summer classic. His first selection came as a Chicago Cub when he was only twenty-two years old. He has never been involved in an All-Star decision.

Maddux's career statistics put him on a direct route to the National Baseball Hall of Fame. His win-loss percentage, four straight Cy Young Awards, ten Golden Gloves, postseason play, and career ERA all make him worthy of induction. In all probability he will attain the 300-victory milestone as well. His durability and consistency also give him top consideration.

In addition, Maddux has earned the admiration of his peers. Tony Gwynn of the San Diego Padres said of him, "He's like a meticulous surgeon out there. . . . He puts the ball where he wants to. You see a pitch inside and wonder, 'Is it the fastball or the cutter?' That's where he's got you." Maddux's pitching coach, Leo Mazzone, said, "He drives himself tremendously when he does his work on the side. If he is off target just a couple of inches, he gets very angry. It's something he takes a great deal of pride in." The Hall of Fame player and announcer Joe Morgan added, "I coined the phrase, Greg Maddux could put a baseball through a Lifesaver if you asked him!"

Maddux and his wife, Kathy, direct the Maddux Foundation, which supports numerous charitable activities, especially programs designed to create opportunities for youngsters. They have a son and a daughter.

★

Useful books about Maddux include Tom Glavine, *None but the Braves: A Pitcher, a Team, a Champion* (1996); Norman L. Macht, *Greg Maddux* (1997); and Matt Christopher, *On the Mound with Greg Maddux* (1997).

F. Ross Peterson

MAHRE, Phil(lip) (*b.* 10 May 1957 in Yakima, Washington), the most successful U.S. male Alpine skier in history.

Mahre is one of nine children born to David Mahre and Mary Ellen Chotl Mahre, a homemaker. He was born four minutes before his fraternal twin, Steven. In 1962 the Mahre family moved fifty-three miles from Yakima to the tiny Cascade Mountain town of White Pass, where Mahre's father became a manager of the local ski area. Living within walking distance of the ski lift, the Mahre twins spent much of their childhood on skis. At the age of eleven they began entering and winning regional ski competitions.

Phil Mahre, 1976. ASSOCIATED PRESS AP

As a teenager Mahre commuted down the mountain with his twin to Naches Valley High School. There he played running back for the football team, taking handoffs from Steve, the quarterback. Both boys were good students. Mahre graduated as valedictorian, and Steve placed fifth out of a class of eighty-four students. The twins' parents sought to raise them in an environment that included academics and religion, in addition to sports and recreation. The Mahres were Roman Catholic and brought a priest to White Pass each week to celebrate mass. Parental enforcement of academic diligence helped the children to excel in school. Yet by the end of their high school careers, the twins' athletic talent was already too remarkable not to become a top priority. Instead of going to college, both young men chose to enter the World Cup skiing circuit.

Of the three events in World Cup competition at the time, the Mahres specialized in the slalom and giant slalom (GS) races, with less focus on the downhill. Throughout his career, Mahre was consistently a faster skier than his brother, but his first World Cup season ended early due to a broken leg. However, Mahre placed fifth in the Olympic GS the following year. In 1978 a second-place finish in the overall World Cup standings made him the highest-placing American ever. A broken ankle in 1979 destroyed his chances of winning the Cup and required the implant of a metal plate and three steel screws. Mahre's marriage to a high school sweetheart ended badly in the same year; they had been married just over a year when they divorced in October.

The 1980 winter games in Lake Placid, New York, brought Mahre his first Olympic medal—a silver in the slalom. He also placed tenth in the giant slalom and fourteenth in the downhill. Mahre was back on the World Cup circuit in 1981, striving to become the first American to win an overall title. Toward the end of the season at an event in Borovetz, Bulgaria, Mahre needed to place second in the slalom in order to secure the title, but his brother finished ahead of him, bumping him down to third. Mahre won the overall World Cup title the following week in Laax, Switzerland, with a second-place finish in giant slalom. After the race he credited his victory to his brother, and to the competition and comradeship between them. "That's what got me where I am today," Mahre told the *New York Times.* "Maybe I would have gotten there, but maybe I wouldn't have. It probably would have been a lot slower coming without him."

Mahre repeated his World Cup victory in 1981 and again in 1982. Years later in an interview with *Ski Magazine,* he described the 1982 victory as his career's crowning moment. Prior to that season, critics predicted that Mahre could not win the overall title without competing in the super G event—a new, controversial blend of downhill racing and giant slalom that he boycotted. He proved his critics wrong, however. "It came down to the last race of the season. It was [Ingemar] Stenmark, Max Julen and myself—whoever won the last GS would win the GS World Cup title." In fact, with this World Cup win, Mahre became the first man since Jean-Claude Killy to win four Alpine skiing titles in a single season.

Mahre won his first Olympic gold medal at the 1984 Olympics in Sarajevo, Yugoslavia. His principal rival, Stenmark, had been disqualified from competition for violating a 1980 regulation banning direct payments to skiers from commercial sponsors. The Mahre brothers had legally complied with the regulation by channeling endorsements through the U.S. ski team. Mahre's slalom victory in Sarajevo was made sweeter by his brother's silver medal win in the slalom. Mahre's second wife, Holly, gave birth to their second child (of three) on the same day.

The Mahre brothers retired after the 1984 season, but returned to skiing in 1988 when $300,000–$500,000 in annual endorsements lured them to compete in the North American Pro Racing Tour. They had not been away from competition for long. In the previous year, both brothers had become race car drivers, alternately piloting the same Pontiac GTO. Their Reno team was the 1990 champion of the American Cities Racing League, the professional autoracing series started in 1988 with teams from twelve western U.S. cities, and Mahre earned the league's individual title.

Mahre was a pioneer for the United States in the world of Alpine skiing. In a sport historically dominated by Europeans, he was the first skier from the United States to win an overall World Cup title, which he did three times, in 1981, 1982, and 1983. With his slalom victory at the 1984 Winter Games, Mahre became the only American man ever to win an Olympic Gold medal in this event, and one of only three to win a gold medal in any Alpine skiing event. Mahre received attention not only for his consistent ability to win, but also for his competitive yet loving relationship with his brother. Today the twins teach skiers of all abilities at the Mahre Training Center in Keystone, Colorado.

★

"Skiing Double" and "Alpine Skiing: A Pair of Mahres" in the *Washington Post Magazine* (10 Feb. 1980 and 5 Feb. 1984), and "Sportspeople: Mahre Makes a Comeback" in the *New York Times* (1990), provide a great deal of factual and personal information on the Mahre brothers. See also "U.S. Chances Ride with the Mahres" in *Newsweek* (13 Feb. 1984), and "Going Out In Style" (27 Feb. 1984), which gives details on U.S. victories in the Sarajevo Olympics. "Ski Life: Gold-Medal Roundtable" in *Ski Magazine* (Jan. 2000) includes a recent but brief interview. "It's All Uphill from Here" and "Motorsports Almanac: 1990 Year in Review" in *Autoweek* (7 Mar. 1988 and 17 Dec. 1990) cover the Mahres' auto racing activities.

VALERIE LINET

MALONE, Karl Anthony (*b.* 24 July 1963 in Summerfield, Louisiana), professional basketball player who remains one of the most prolific scorers and rebounders in the history of the game.

Malone is the eighth of nine children of A. P. and Shirley Malone. The family lived in Summerfield, a tiny community of 600 people in north-central Louisiana. Malone's father left the family when Karl was just four and eventually died of cancer. In 1975 his mother married Ed Turner. Malone credits his mother as the biggest influence in his early life. As part of a large family in a subsistence situation, he learned to work hard, and his brothers taught him to play sports, especially basketball. He led Summerfield High School to three consecutive class C state titles in Louisiana, and many colleges began to recruit him.

Closely attached to home, Malone chose to attend Louisiana Tech, only forty miles away. His high school grades and SAT scores prevented him from playing during his freshman year, but he eventually helped Louisiana Tech to a 74–19 record during his three years of participation in the early 1980s. Twice they made it to the National Collegiate

Karl Malone. AP/WIDE WORLD PHOTOS

Athletic Association tournament, and in Malone's senior year the team made it to the round of sixteen. A local sportswriter wrote that the "Mailman" always delivers, and the nickname has continued to describe his play. In all of Malone's seasons at Louisiana Tech, he was named First Team All-Southland Conference. After his sophomore season, 1984, he was invited to the Olympic trials and almost made the team. At the tryouts he met another player who also failed to make the squad, John Stockton of Gonzaga University, who would eventually be Malone's teammate with the Utah Jazz. Although bitterly disappointed, Malone realized that he could play with anyone, including professional stars such as Michael Jordan, Patrick Ewing, Charles Barkley, and others who attended the tryouts.

At six feet, nine inches tall and 256 pounds, Malone considered himself physically ready to assume a professional career. He hoped the Dallas Mavericks, the team closest to his home in Louisiana, would select him in the National Basketball Association (NBA) draft, but they passed, and the Utah Jazz drafted him with the thirteenth pick in 1985. Frank Layden, the Jazz head coach, called Malone's selection "one of the greatest steals in NBA draft history." The synergy of Malone, Stockton, and Jerry Sloan, who succeeded Layden, has been impressive and long-lasting. Another stabilizing factor in the team's success is its long-term ownership by Larry Miller, who bought the franchise in the same year Malone signed.

Malone's consistent improvement and dedication are hallmarks of his career. A fitness fanatic, he is a dedicated athlete who lifts weights, runs, and works out year-round. The success of this regimen is evident in that Malone has played in all but seven of a possible 1,280 regular-season and 163 playoff games. Of the seven missed, only three were due to injuries. At one point he played in 541 consecutive games. This phenomenal record is unparalleled.

Through sixteen seasons, Malone's Jazz have made the playoffs every year. Malone's records include an all-time fourth in minutes played and ninth in games played. Most significantly, he is second to Kareem Abdul-Jabbar in points scored in a career and second in free throws attempted. He is also second in defensive rebounds and in the top ten in total rebounds gathered in a career. Ralph Wiley of *Sports Illustrated* wrote, "Now the question isn't whether Malone belongs in the NBA paint—the question is who belongs in there with him."

As of 2001 Malone had averaged more than twenty points per season for fifteen consecutive years. He holds the NBA record for most consecutive seasons (11) of over 2,000 points and most seasons (12) with that amount. Between December 1991 and March 1999 he scored in double figures in 575 straight games. He also led the league a record seven times in number of free throws made. Free throw shooting is another example of Malone's work ethic. In his first two seasons he shot 55 percent from the charity stripe. Since then he has made over 75 percent of his free throws. At the conclusion of the 2000–2001 season Malone ranked high in many NBA statistical career categories. In addition to the statistics noted above, Malone is third in field goals attempted and is second to Stockton in most games played with one franchise and consecutive trips to the playoffs with one team.

Malone's honors are many and well deserved. He has been recognized as one of the fifty greatest players in NBA history. Twice, in 1997 and 1999, Malone received the coveted Most Valuable Player (MVP) award for the entire league. In 1989 and 1993 his play at the NBA All-Star game garnered him the MVP title. In the latter year he shared the award with his longtime teammate, Stockton. He is the only player in NBA history to be named All-NBA First Team in eleven straight years (1989–1999). Three times he has been elected to the All-NBA Defensive Team. Malone and Stockton were selected for the U.S. Olympic team in 1992 and 1996 and won gold medals in both the Barcelona and Atlanta games.

Malone, still physically durable, has a chance to set numerous career playoff records as well. He is first in defensive rebounds, third in free throws made and attempted, and fourth in points and field goals made. He has played in 163 career playoff games and in 2001 was fifth all-time in total rebounds and field goals attempted in the playoffs and seventh in scoring average. However, as of 2001 an NBA title still eluded the Jazz, who played the Chicago Bulls in 1997 and 1998 for the championship. They lost both series in six games to the Michael Jordan–led Bulls.

Malone is generous, community oriented, and compassionate. His charity work through the Karl Malone Foundation for Kids, coupled with donations to Utah Special Olympics, Native Americans, homeless schools, and western firefighters earned him recognition by *Sporting News* as one of "99 Good Guys in Sports," as well as the Henry B. Iba Citizen Athlete Award. Malone maintains strong family ties as well. He and his wife, Kay, have three daughters and one son. His love and concern for his mother is visible and heartfelt. His brother helps him operate a cattle ranch in Arkansas. Other business enterprises include car dealerships in Albuquerque, New Mexico, and Salt Lake City, Utah. At one time Malone owned a small fleet of eighteen-wheelers.

Malone's great deeds are sometimes overshadowed in unexpected ways. On 27 July 1998, under the aegis of the World Championship Wrestling Federation (WCW), he wrestled against Dennis Rodman. His attempt to get Salt Lake City–based sports talk show hosts, also Jazz employees, terminated after they criticized his playoff performance caused waves. In addition, his support of National Rifle Association positions on gun control has upset some fans. Malone briefly attempted his own career as a talk show host during the 1998 lockout. He toys with the idea of acting as a career beyond basketball and has taken numerous cameo roles. His video, "Karl Malone's Body Shop," demonstrates his style of workout.

Malone is fiercely loyal, dedicated, and passionate. He is the epitome of an athlete constantly striving to improve. He always speaks his mind and prepares to succeed, and he expects the same from teammates. Every year he tries to inspire young players, free agents, and others to join with him and the Jazz in their last remaining quest: the NBA Championship.

★

Useful books on Malone include Bob Schnakenberg and Robert E. Schnakenberg, *Teammates: Karl Malone and John Stockton* (1998); Roland Lazenby, *Stockton to Malone: The Rise of the Utah Jazz* (1998); and Clay Latimer, *Special Delivery: The Amazing Basketball Career of Karl Malone* (1999).

F. ROSS PETERSON

MALONE, Moses Eugene (*b.* 23 March 1955, in Chesterfield County, Virginia), professional All-Star basketball player known for his fierce rebounding and high-scoring games.

Malone was an only child and was raised primarily by his mother, Mary Hudgins Malone, a nurses' aide and meatpacker. Malone and his mother moved to Petersburg, Virginia, after her separation from his alcoholic father. Malone embraced the game of basketball early and practiced incessantly. By age twelve he was already six feet, three inches tall, and a local youth league required that he play guard and stay out of the key area. That injunction, designed to keep taller players from dominating the area around the basket, only improved his dribbling and shooting. A personal prediction placed in the family Bible forecast that Malone would be the best player on the local high school team; a second, placed slightly later, predicted that he would go immediately into professional leagues. Malone's basketball statistics at Petersburg High School, from which he graduated in 1974, were 31 points, an astounding 26 rebounds, and 10 blocked shots per game.

Not surprisingly, in spite of Malone's poor grades more than 300 colleges offered him scholarships. Malone signed a letter of intent to play for the University of Maryland, then changed his mind and signed a six-year, $3 million contract with the Utah Stars of the American Basketball Association (ABA), thereby becoming the first modern player to go directly into professional basketball from high school.

Malone explained that his reason for the jump to the professional league in 1974 was not strictly financial. He had watched both collegiate and professional games and judged the undergraduate matches to be "too soft." Malone

Moses Malone, 1983. AP/WIDE WORLD PHOTOS

immediately established his toughness in his rookie year with the Stars, averaging almost nineteen points and fifteen rebounds per game and making the Western Division All-Star team of the ABA. He led the league in offensive rebounds, one of the most important statistics in the game. Observers were impressed by Malone's incessant drive at either end of the court, his quickness, and his leaping ability. Less impressive were his shooting and pass-catching.

Malone was injured the first half of the 1975–1976 campaign and the Utah franchise folded at midseason. The St. Louis Spirits picked up his contract and he averaged 14.6 points a game for them. When the entire ABA disbanded after the season, Malone bounced among several teams in the National Basketball Association (NBA). Finally, he went to the Houston Rockets, coached by Tom Nissalke, his mentor at Utah; Nissalke built the Rockets around Malone's talents. Malone reached his playing height of six feet, ten inches, and developed into a 255-pound powerhouse. He prospered with Houston and Nissalke. He was a five-time All-Star and was NBA Most Valuable Player (MVP) in 1979 and 1982. At the age of only twenty-one, Malone set a new season record for offensive rebounds with 437. He led the Rockets into the playoffs, taking them as far as a losing effort to the Boston Celtics in the 1981–1982 season. He perennially led the league in offensive rebounds and total average rebounds and was among the leaders in scoring. While Kareem Abdul-Jabbar was the era's most famous center, Malone perfected the offensive rebound and was as dominant in the overall game. Jabbar's elegant skyhook recalled the earlier days of the game, Malone's pound-it-inside methods foretold the tough, defensive wrestling that characterized basketball for the rest of the century.

Despite his lack of a college education, Malone was astute in contract sessions. Already making more than $1 million a year in 1979, he signed a six-year, $13.2 million contract with the Philadelphia 76ers in 1982. In his first year he earned (with bonuses) almost $3 million, the highest salary in professional basketball. He invented a number of bonus clauses. If Malone seems mercenary, consider that during his career he was sold once, selected twice in dispersal drafts, traded four times, and signed four free-agent contracts.

Malone's greatest year was 1982, in his first season with Philadelphia. Teaming up with the legendary forward Julius Erving and All-Star guards Maurice Cheeks and Andrew Toney, Malone and the 76ers won sixty-five games during the regular season then roared through the playoffs, losing only one game and winning the championship easily from the Los Angeles Lakers. In 1983 Malone was voted MVP of the regular season and the playoffs. He led the NBA in rebounding, a feat he repeated the next two years, although the 76ers lost key players to injuries and could not defend their crown. Malone was a highly consistent player who mapped the area around the basket in an unceasing struggle for rebounds and dunks. Anticipating the rebounding exploits of Dennis Rodman, Malone often tipped the ball to himself when boxed out. Other players remarked that his hands were like flypaper. A cagey defender, Malone holds the record of 1,027 games without fouling out.

In the summer of 1986, following the curious logic that because Malone had skipped college his career was four years older than his chronological age, 76ers owner Harold Katz traded Malone to the Washington Bullets. Although he accepted the trade placidly, Malone later forecast that he would never lose to his old team. The deal was a disaster for Philadelphia. Jeff Ruland, Malone's replacement, had an injury-prone career, while Malone terrorized the 76ers every time the teams met. He averaged more than twenty-nine points and fourteen rebounds against his former teammates and led Washington to four straight victories until an overtime defeat late in the season. In fact, Malone had forced the trade to Washington when he demanded an extension of his earlier contract.

Malone played well with the Bullets, averaging more than twenty points per game, but the team did not win and allowed him to sign a contract worth at least $4.6 million a year with the Atlanta Hawks in 1988. He earned his twelfth straight All-Star berth in 1988 and led the Hawks into the playoffs. In 1990 Malone signed with the Milwaukee Bucks. In 1993 he returned to Philadelphia to help the 76ers with their seven-foot, six-inch center, Shawn Bradley, although in spite of Malone's teaching Bradley never developed into an outstanding player. Malone spent his final year playing for the San Antonio Spurs. He ruptured a tendon at midseason, an injury that forced him into retirement.

Malone spends his retirement at his home in Sugar Land, Texas, raising his two sons. His former wife, Alfreda Gill, from whom he was divorced in 1992, lives in a nearby town. Malone closed out his career with more than 27,000 points, fourth best in the history of the NBA, and 16,212 rebounds, also among historic leaders. During his career Malone was a mentor and role model for such stars as Hakeem Olajuwon and Charles Barkley. His credo for his career was, "Playing hard is not about the money, it's all pride." Malone was inducted into the Basketball Hall of Fame in 2001.

★

Biographical material on Malone can be found in *Current Biography Yearbook* (1986). Malone is featured in Jack McCollum, "Back to Haunt the Sixers," *Sports Illustrated* (15 Mar. 1987), and John O'Keefe, "Catching Up with Moses Malone, NBA All-Star Center," *Sports Illustrated* (12 Apr. 1999).

GRAHAM RUSSELL HODGES

MANTLE, Mickey Charles (*b.* 20 October 1931 in Spavinaw, Oklahoma; *d.* 13 August 1995 in Dallas, Texas), New York Yankees switch-hitting center fielder ranked among the greatest baseball legends along with Babe Ruth and Joe DiMaggio.

Born the first of five children in a poor family in rural Oklahoma, Mantle's father Elvin ("Mutt") Mantle dreamed that his son would be the player he had tried to become. Mantle's father held a variety of blue-collar jobs before, during, and after the Great Depression, and gave substance to his baseball dream by naming his son after his hero, the great Hall of Fame catcher Gordon ("Mickey") Cochrane. Elvin taught the game to his son, focusing especially on the art of switch-hitting. Mantle's ability to swing a baseball bat from either side of the plate would later prove to be his most enduring and vital skill. Mantle's mother, Lovell Richardson Mantle, was a homemaker. She made Mantle's first baseball uniform in 1934, when he was just three years old.

Through high school Mantle was a superb athlete, play-

Mickey Mantle. ARCHIVE PHOTOS, INC.

ing both football and baseball. Baseball, however, was his first love. Mantle started playing semiprofessional ball for the Baxter Springs Whiz Kids in 1948, while still attending Commerce (Oklahoma) High School, and continued to play for them until graduation. During practice for a high school football game, Mantle was injured when he was accidentally kicked in the left shin. The wound developed into the chronic bone infection osteomyelitis. Doctors wanted to amputate his leg, but his mother pushed for treatment by a new "wonder drug" called penicillin. The drug helped save his leg, but Mantle still required a series of five operations to control the damage. These operations were completed before he left high school, but Mantle lived with their debilitating effects his whole life. Over the years, the aftereffects of the osteomyelitis and surgeries slowly eroded Mantle's speed and leg strength, critical in achieving great hits. Clem Labine, pitcher for the Brooklyn Dodgers in the 1950s, played against Mantle in Triple-A ball and recalled that Mantle's speed early in his career was the most dominating feature of his game. Labine stated that by the time Mantle reached the majors he was already slowing down. Mantle underwent seven operations as a Yankee, including six on his knees.

On the day of his high school graduation in spring 1949, Mantle was signed by the Yankees scout Tom Greenwade, who had seen him play for the Whiz Kids and was impressed by his power from both sides of the plate. Mantle received the then-astronomical sum of $400 to play for the summer, and a signing bonus of $1,100. He started his career in 1949 as a shortstop, playing for the Yankees Class D minor league affiliate in Independence, Missouri. He played in 89 games his first summer, batting .313 but committing 47 errors. Despite the errors, his batting and his superior speed earned him a promotion in 1950 to Class C. Playing for the Missouri Miners, he batted .383, and had 199 hits and 326 total bases. His fielding and, more notably, his throwing, was less than stellar; in 137 games, Mantle committed 55 errors. Nonetheless, the annual late season call-ups of promising minor league players led to Mantle's being elevated to the Yankees in November 1950, not to play, but merely to observe and learn from the Yankees greats. Mantle did not take a single at bat. He sat and watched, and by his own account of those earliest days, spent most of the time in sheer wonderment, dressing and sitting on the bench with so many Yankees he had idolized in his youth. Mantle could not even look at Joe DiMaggio; he was so awed by his presence. Some speculated that Mantle would one day replace Phil Rizzuto at shortstop.

However, Yankee management had something else in mind. Mantle was placed in right field beginning with spring training in 1951, playing alongside DiMaggio who roamed the broad expanse of center field. The news accounts regarding the Yankees new addition generated enormous expectations and understandable pressure on the nineteen-year-old kid from Oklahoma. Mantle's father is reported to have chastened his son, saying, "[Y]ou've made all the headlines, now make the team!"

Mantle made his game debut for the Yankees on opening day in 1951, playing right field in New York. Vic Rashi was pitching, Rizzuto was at short, and DiMaggio was in center. Mantle was quoted as saying he felt nervous playing with all these brilliant players, but opined he must be pretty good himself to be playing with all of them. His first season in the "bigs" was interrupted by a spate of strikeouts. Perhaps trying a bit too hard, Mantle was sent down to the Triple-A farm club in Kansas City. There he played center field in anticipation of DiMaggio's retirement, and focused on his hitting. Forty games later, having demolished Triple-A pitching, Mantle was back with the Yankees, this time for good. He finished his rookie season batting .267, and hit 13 home runs in the 96 games he played.

The Mantle era began in earnest in 1952, when Mantle became the regular center fielder. He had a brilliant season, earning a spot on the American League (AL) All-Star team, a position he would retain for fourteen consecutive seasons, and in sixteen of his eighteen total seasons in Major League Baseball. Fans and friends soon began calling Mantle "the

Mick," a term they used affectionately, but exactly how and when use of the nickname began remains a mystery. He fielded well, ran the bases with abandon, batted .311, and hit 23 home runs. In a city that boasted three great teams, each with its own certifiable superstar (Duke Snider for the Dodgers and Willie Mays for the Giants), Mantle's star blazed brightest. By 1955 Mantle led the league in home runs (37). The following year, he led the league in batting average (.353), runs batted in (130), and home runs (52). He was named the AL Most Valuable Player, receiving the honor again in 1957 and 1962. He led the league in home runs in four seasons: 1955, 1956, 1958, and 1960. And he finished second in 1961, sharing the incredible pressure and attention that fell on him and his teammate Roger Maris during the historic chase of Babe Ruth's single season home run record. Maris hit sixty-one, Mantle "only" fifty-four.

Mantle's performance propelled the Yankees of the 1950s and early 1960s to the AL pennant on a regular basis. Mantle's Yankees played in the World Series in twelve of his first fourteen seasons, and won seven of those series. Mantle holds the following World Series records: home runs (18), runs scored (42), bases on balls (43), total bases (123), and runs batted in (40). During the last of the World Series the Yankees won during the Mantle era, Mantle was experiencing the decline in production expected after twelve seasons and the recurring leg problems linked to his osteomyelitis. The 1962 World Series against the San Francisco Giants went seven games. Mantle suffered a particularly frustrating afternoon in the fourth game, striking out twice against Juan Marichal. Asked afterward why he had so much trouble hitting Marichal, Mantle told the reporters "at first all you see is his glove in your face, then all you see is his leg in your face. By the time you see the ball, it's too late." Despite the frustration, Mantle and Marichal became good friends and remained close after retirement, which for Mantle was in 1969. He was elected to the National Baseball Hall of Fame in 1974.

Even with the new statistical measures of performance that link batting averages with on-base percentages, slugging percentages, stolen base percentages, total bases, runs scored, and runs batted in, Mantle's career and single season statistics stand the test of time. He led the AL in runs scored six times, home runs four times, bases on balls five times, on-base percentage three times, slugging percentage four times, player production eight times, and in the Total Player Rating scale eight times. His career statistics are equally impressive. Although Mantle ranks only at 100th on the number of career at bats (8,102), consider what he accomplished—runs scored (1,677), ranked 24th; runs per game in his era (1942 to 1960), 5th; home runs (536), 9th overall; home run percentage, 10th overall; total bases (4,511), 29th; runs batted in (1,509), 36th overall and 4th during his era; 6th overall in number of walks (1,733); and 9th overall in number of strikeouts (1,710). His on-base percentage (.413) ranks 14th overall, and his slugging average (.557) ranks 16th overall. Total career production (.979) ranks 8th overall; Mantle ranks 16th overall in runs created (2,069), and finished his career with a lifetime batting average of .298.

For all of his superior play on the field, his play off the field was less than stellar. His friends, and there were many, remember him as a prankster, especially when in the company of his pals Whitey Ford and Billy Martin. His country roots never left him, despite the glitter and sophistication of New York. But the prankster had a darker side, and he became addicted to alcohol. He harbored a belief that he would die early in life of Hodgkin's disease as his father had. Though Mantle remained free of the disease, it would claim one of the four sons he had with Merlyn Louise Johnson, whom he had married on 23 December 1951. Mantle and Johnson separated in 1988.

Mantle remained active during retirement. He did television commercials, appeared in golf tournaments, and opened a restaurant in Manhattan. He died in 1995 after a prolonged battle with alcoholism and the resulting complications of cirrhosis and ultimately liver cancer, and is buried at Sparkman-Hillcrest cemetery in Dallas. Toward the end of his life he recognized how foolish he had been wasting so much of his career and remainder of his life on alcohol. He commented to Roger Kahn, the fabled baseball writer, "If I knew I was going to live this long, I would have taken better care of myself." Reacting to a controversy that arose regarding his being authorized to receive a liver transplant, Mantle established a foundation to encourage organ donation and was instrumental in promoting the program among minorities through the State University of New York's Downstate Medical Center in Brooklyn.

★

Mantle cowrote *My Favorite Summer, 1956* (1991), with Philip Pepe. Further information about Mantle's life and career is in David Falkner, *The Last Hero: The Life of Mickey Mantle* (1995), and in *Total Baseball: The Official Encyclopedia of Major League Baseball,* 6th ed. (1999), John Thorn, Peter Palmer, and Michael Gershman, eds.

ROBERT L. KING

MARAVICH, Peter Press ("Pete") (*b.* 22 June 1947 in Aliquippa, Pennsylvania; *d.* 5 January 1988 in Pasadena, California), professional basketball player who revitalized the game in the 1970s with his fancy dribbling, precise passing, and improbable shots.

Maravich was the son of Peter Maravich, a college basketball coach, and Helen Maravich, a homemaker. His father, nicknamed "Press" because, like the *Pittsburgh Press,* he was never at a loss for words, came from a family of Aliquippa steelworkers. After the war Press played professional basketball for the Youngstown Bears, and in June 1946 he married Helen Gravor Montini, a one-time Aliquippa high school cheerleader whose husband had been killed in the D-Day invasion. The couple moved to different college towns where Press found coaching work.

Maravich gained a love of basketball from his father, who was consumed by the game. He often accompanied his father into the team's locker room, where the sights and sounds of the game became ingrained in the young boy. During the summer vacation Maravich was on the court from 8 A.M. until after dark. He practiced dribbling blindfolded; he dribbled while riding his bicycle; he went to sleep with a basketball.

Because Maravich was so talented, the small, frail seventh grader played on the junior varsity of Daniel High School in Clemson, South Carolina, where his father coached Clemson College (now Clemson University). By the ninth grade in 1962, he had earned the nickname "Pistol Pete" because of his off-the-hip style in firing up a one-hand push shot. Maravich spent six to eight hours a day in the gym practicing, and he was averaging twenty points a game.

In 1963 Press Maravich became the coach at North Carolina State, and Maravich attended Broughton High School in Raleigh, where he immediately became a varsity starter. By 1965, his senior year, the six-foot, three-inch, 160-pound star was averaging thirty-two points per game. Beginning in high school, Maravich was distinguished by the floppy gray socks he wore, which often slid to the bottom of his spindly legs, and his brown shaggy hair. Following Maravich's graduation, his father sent him to Edwards Military Academy in Salemsburg, North Carolina, for a year of prep school to increase his strength. Because of his low Scholastic Aptitude Test (SAT) scores, Maravich could not get into North Carolina State, so his father took a job coaching varsity basketball at Louisiana State University so he could coach him there. At this time Maravich's mother, Helen, depressed from living the life of a basketball coach's wife with its frequent relocations, began to drink heavily.

In his first game on the freshman team of LSU in 1966, Maravich scored fifty points, grabbed fourteen rebounds, and earned eleven assists. By the end of the season, he had averaged 43.6 points. A varsity player in the following year, Maravich scored fifty-eight points against Mississippi State, leading LSU to its first winning season since 1961. He became the nation's leading scorer, averaging 43.8 points per game, and was named to the All-America team.

In his junior year Maravich became LSU's all-time leading scorer and was featured in national magazines like *Sports Illustrated* and *Life.* By his senior year in 1970, Maravich, who had always enjoyed partying, began to drink before games. He was expelled from college in April 1970 for prolonged absences from class. Nevertheless, by the end of his senior year, he led the nation in scoring for the third straight year and was named College Basketball Player of the Year. During his time at LSU, Maravich scored a total of 3,667 points, and averaged 44.2 points per game, the highest ever recorded. In 1971 LSU named its $11.5 million, 14,000-seat sports arena after Maravich.

Pete Maravich, 1979. ASSOCIATED PRESS AP

In 1970 Maravich was drafted into the National Basketball Association (NBA) by the Atlanta Hawks. His five-year contract, worth $1.5 million, made him the highest paid athlete in the history of sports; and other Hawks players resented the high-priced rookie who was the only player interviewed by the media after games. Maravich kept on drinking, partying, and scoring. In 81 games he scored 1,880 points, a 23.2 per game average. He was named to the NBA All-Rookie team.

Maravich missed part of the 1971–1972 season due to mononucleosis. The 1972–1973 season was Maravich's only winning season in the NBA. His 26.1 points-per-game average earned him a spot in his first All-Star game in 1973. In 1973–1974 Atlanta had a losing season, and Maravich was suspended indefinitely by Lowell "Cotton" Fitzsimmons for drinking. By the end of the season he was traded to a new NBA team, the New Orleans Jazz, signing a three-year $1.2 million contract.

The 1974–1975 season was a tragic one for Maravich. His father was fired as coach of Appalachian State in North Carolina, the Jazz finished a 23–59 season, worst in the league, and in October his mother, Helen, shot herself. Somehow Maravich recovered. On 11 January 1976 he married Jackie Elliser, his college sweetheart. He began to lift weights for strength. The Jazz hired a new coach, Elgin Baylor, the legendary former basketball player, and Maravich was voted to the All-NBA team for the first time. In 1977 Maravich led the league in scoring. On 25 February 1977, against the New York Knicks, guarded by Walt Frazier, one of the all-time best defensive players, Maravich scored sixty-eight points, the most ever scored by a guard in a single game to that time.

Then disaster struck again. In a game against the Buffalo Braves on 31 January 1978, Maravich tore the cartilage in his knee after delivering a nearly impossible between-the-legs pass. The injury resulted in surgery, a cumbersome brace, and a loss of most of his playing time for the next two seasons. By 1979, when the Jazz had moved to Utah, Maravich had an infant son but was drinking more and more. He stopped working out, and his new coach, Tom Nissalke, benched him for hogging the ball. Maravich was waived by the Jazz, and in January 1980 the Boston Celtics, who were having a great year thanks to rookie Larry Bird, picked him up. Maravich played only twenty-six games with Boston and retired on 20 September 1980, even though Boston had offered to renew his contract.

Maravich disappeared from public view for the next two years. While he looked after his small construction business in Covington, Louisiana, he contemplated suicide and continued to drink heavily. Although Maravich and his wife now had another son, he began to dabble in astrology and mysticism. One night in November 1982, he thought God spoke to him. After this experience Maravich became a born-again Christian, touring schools and prisons and preaching the gospel. On 5 January 1988 Maravich died of a heart attack after playing a three-on-three pickup game in the First Church of the Nazarene gym in Pasadena, California. An autopsy revealed that he had been born without one of the two arterial systems that carry blood to the heart. He is buried at Resthaven Cemetery in Baton Rouge, Louisiana.

Although Maravich was often accused of refusing to share the ball with his teammates, his achievements on the basketball court are undeniable. At LSU he set NCAA records that are still unbroken. He scored 43.8, 44.2, and 44.5 points per game in his 1968–1970 varsity seasons, leading the nation in scoring each year. He scored fifty-plus points in twenty-eight games. He owns NCAA records for most points in a season (1,381), most points in a career (3,667), highest career scoring average (44.2 points per game), most field goals made in a career (1,387), and most field goals attempted (3,166). As a professional basketball player, Maravich was named an All-Star five times and led the league in scoring in 1977 with a 31.1 points-per-game average; he had a career average of 24.2 points per game. Maravich was elected to the Basketball Hall of Fame on 1 May 1987, and in 1997 he was honored for being among the NBA's fifty greatest players of all time.

★

Maravich's autobiography, *Heir to a Dream* (1987), written with Daniel Campbell, reveals the player's love-hate relationship with his father and his personal disappointment at the public perception that he was a loser. Phil Berger, *Forever Showtime: The Checkered Life of Pistol Pete Maravich* (1999), traces Maravich's life and career in an unsentimental, realistic manner. Obituaries are in the *Los Angeles Times, New York Times, San Diego Union Tribune,* and *Washington Post* (all 6 Jan. 1988). The *Union Tribune* obituary contains a lengthy summary of Maravich's college and professional statistics. The television drama *The Pistol: Birth of a Legend* (1990) explores the early life of Maravich, showing how the thirteen-year-old introverted boy not only made the high school varsity team while still in the eighth grade but also led it to the state championship.

JOHN J. BYRNE

MARBLE, Alice (*b.* 28 September 1913 in Beckwith, California; *d.* 13 December 1990 in Palm Springs, California), world champion of women's tennis in the 1930s and a woman of extraordinary courage, resourcefulness, and spirit.

Marble was to the fourth of five children of Harry Briggs Marble, a high climber lumberjack, and Jessie Wood, a former nurse. When Marble was five, her family moved from the Sierra Nevada town of Beckwith to San Francisco. Sadly, her father died two years later on Christmas Eve, plunging the family into poverty and causing her two older brothers to leave school to help support the family.

Marble was blessed with a photographic memory, extraordinary athletic ability, and a keen love of sports. At thirteen her baseball skills earned her the title "Little Queen of Swat" as an unpaid warm-up player and official mascot of the San Francisco Seals, a feeder team for the New York Yankees. Alice loved baseball, but when she was fifteen her brother Dan bought her a tennis racket, encouraging her to pick a more ladylike sport. In spite of her initial disappointment, within a week she was hooked on tennis, and soon was playing and winning local and then statewide tournaments.

Three years later Marble represented California in the Eastern Tournaments and the U.S. Nationals. Her excellent hand-eye coordination, natural athletic ability, quick foot speed, and years of practice pitching had given her an aggressive game and a powerful serve. At first her ground strokes were terribly performed, but she improved as she watched others play. Coming from a family with few economic resources, Alice at first felt uncomfortable, as if she didn't belong in the rarefied atmosphere of tennis. By 1932 she knew she belonged. That year, as an unknown, Marble beat a seeded player in the first round at Forest Hills, where she earned a national ranking in singles and in doubles.

In 1932 a famous tennis coach, Eleanor "Teach" Tennent, discovered Marble, and would guide her career and her life for the next thirteen years. By 1933, with Tennent's help, Marble had sharpened her game with a change in grip, improved ground strokes, and a winning attack game at the net, and improved her singles national ranking to third. Because of her ability to get to every shot, and her ferocious net game, she was also a great doubles player. It was said that Marble, both a golden blond beauty and a bold and free powerhouse on the tennis court, could play like a man. This was because unlike other women players of her time, she used her powerful serve and attack and volley game to dominate her opponents. She pioneered an aggressive style of power tennis for women, a strategy followed by later champions, such as Billie Jean King and Martina Navratilova.

There was no questioning Marble's tennis skills. One day in 1933, in a final qualifying tournament on Long Island, Marble showed the world that she also had great spirit, fortitude, and courage. Tournament officials decreed that she play five matches on a scorchingly hot day of over 100 degrees. She played a total of 108 games and was on the court without much rest from ten o'clock in the morning to seven in the evening. Losing twelve pounds, she managed to finish out the day. Later that evening she collapsed from sunstroke and anemia. Although she would play the following season, she could not recover her health. At the French Open in 1934, she played in pain until she collapsed and had to be carried off the court and rushed to a hospital. Suffering from anemia and pleurisy, she was misdiagnosed with tuberculosis, and doctors said she would never play competitive tennis again. Marble returned to her family to recuperate, but soon realized that her care was an added burden to her overworked and economically precarious family. She asked her coach for help, and Tennent responded by taking over responsibility for Marble's care, including the costs of a stay in a tuberculosis sanitarium. Later, at Marble's insistence, Tennent smuggled her out of the facility against the director's orders. Together, the two engineered Marble's return to competitive tennis. Tennent worked to provide for them financially, while Marble worked to recover her health and her tennis skills.

Alice Marble, 1937. AP/WIDE WORLD PHOTOS

Two years later, in 1936, Forest Hills tournament officials had to be convinced of Marble's readiness to return to tennis competition. They made her play a demonstration match against a male player, who faded under her relentless power and stamina. When finally given permission to enter, she proved them wrong again when she beat Helen Jacobs to win the U.S. Singles Championship and the mixed doubles title (with Gene Mako) as well. She had made her way back and became the top woman player in the United States. For the next four years, her tennis skills, determination, and winning spirit would win her three more U.S. Singles Championships, three doubles championships (with Sarah Palfrey Fabyan), and three mixed doubles championships (with Donald Budge [1938]; Harry Hopman [1939]; and Bobby Riggs [1940]). In 1937 she won the mixed doubles at Wimbledon (with Budge); in 1938 she won both the doubles and mixed doubles there (with Fabyan and Budge); and in 1939 she reached her ultimate goal, winning Wimbledon Championships in singles, doubles (with Fabyan), and mixed doubles (with Riggs).

In the years from 1936 to 1940, Marble dominated women's tennis. She was ranked number one in the world, and the Associated Press named her Female Athlete of the Year in 1939 and 1940. Then, at the height of her career, Marble's personal financial obligations and her desire to contribute to the war effort caused her to sign a professional contract. She toured the country in exhibition matches, promoted physical fitness for the Office of Civilian Defense, entertained servicemen and -women with tennis exhibitions, visited military hospitals, helped sell war bonds, and tried to enlist, always being turned down because of her continual health problems.

In 1941 Marble met and fell in love with Captain Joseph Crowley, an army intelligence officer. They were secretly married during one of Joe's brief military leaves. The couple was deeply in love, but had only brief interludes of marital happiness. Marble was thrilled when she learned she was pregnant, but suffered a miscarriage. This tragedy was compounded in 1944 when she learned that her husband had been killed in action. When she learned of his death, she unsuccessfully attempted suicide and plunged into despair.

As Marble was slowly emerging from her depression, Army Intelligence recruited her as a spy. She went to Switzerland on a tennis tour, and while there courageously gathered information about German financial accounts. She was shot in the back while escaping a counteragent, was rescued, and then went on with her life. Always needing to earn a living and to repay Tennent, this multitalented woman sang in New York City nightclubs, debuting at New York's Waldorf Hotel in 1938; served as a sports announcer for WNEW in New York in 1940; and designed a line of tennis wear. She had a long-standing affair with television writer Rod Serling, and made a cameo appearance in the movie *Pat and Mike* with Katharine Hepburn and Spencer Tracy. She coached future champions Billie Jean King, Darlene Hard, and Maureen Connolly. In 1950 her editorial in *American Lawn Tennis Magazine* shamed the tennis establishment into breaking its whites-only policy to allow Althea Gibson, a woman Marble had mentored, to play in the U.S. Lawn Tennis Association tennis tournaments.

Throughout her busy and productive life, Marble suffered from health problems, but nothing seemed to stop her, including colon cancer and the loss of a lung to pneumonia. In 1964 she was inducted into the International Tennis Hall of Fame. By 1965 she was happily settled at the Palm Desert Country Club in Palm Desert, California, where she taught tennis and continued to follow and visit with the young champions of the day until her death there in 1990.

★

Marble wrote two autobiographical works, *The Road to Wimbledon* (1946) and, with Dale Leatherman, *Courting Danger* (1991). Her place in tennis history and her powerful style of play is covered in Owen Davidson and C. M. Jones, *Great Women Tennis Players* (1971); Virginia Wade's and Jean Rafferty, *Ladies of the Court: A Century of Women at Wimbledon* (1984); and Janet Woolum, *Outstanding Women Athletes, Who They Are and How They Influenced Sports in America* (1998). An obituary is in the *New York Times* (14 Dec. 1990). There is a discrepancy in her birthdate, most sources giving it as 28 September rather than 13 September 1913.

JULIANNE CICARELLI

MARCHETTI, Gino John (*b.* 2 January 1926 in Smithers, West Virginia), one of the greatest defensive ends in professional football and a member of the Pro Football Hall of Fame.

Marchetti's parents, Ernest Marchetti and Maria Dalporto, emigrated from Lucca, Italy—the town that was, coincidentally, the birthplace of another Pro Football Hall of Famer, Leo Nomellini—to the United States shortly before he was born. The family then moved from West Virginia across the country to Antioch, California, an industrial town about fifty miles east of San Francisco. Marchetti was not particularly interested in sports as a youngster. He did not play much football until 1943, his senior year at Antioch High School. With World War II raging, Marchetti enlisted in the U.S. Army on his eighteenth birthday, quitting high school to do so. By December of that year he was a member of the much-decorated "Fighting 69th" Infantry Division, taking an active part in the fierce combat in Belgium that would become known as the Battle of the Bulge.

Gino Marchetti, 1959. ASSOCIATED PRESS HO

When he returned to Antioch after the war, Marchetti tended bar in his father's tavern for a couple of years, at the same time forming a semiprofessional football team known as the Antioch Hornets. Marchetti's brother Angelo, known as Itzy, was a good enough player to gain the attention of college recruiters. Stan Pavko, an assistant at Modesto (California) Junior College, was reportedly signing Itzy to play for his team when he looked at Gino and said, "Hey, kid, you look big enough to play football. Wanna go along?" Marchetti did, but he left Modesto soon after the season. In 1948 Brad Lynn, the assistant football coach at the University of San Francisco (USF), walked into the family tavern and asked the six-foot, four-inch, 220-pound Marchetti if he wanted to try out for the USF team. When Marchetti showed up at USF, he made a less than favorable impression on the Dons head coach, Joe Kuharich. As Marchetti tells it, "I roared up on a big motorcycle, wearing heavy boots and a black leather jacket with fifteen zippers." But Marchetti stayed and, with the help of eleven teammates who would eventually play in the National Football League (NFL), gave Kuharich an undefeated season in 1951.

Marchetti, who played tackle at USF, was drafted by the New York Yanks, who became the Dallas Texans before the 1952 season began. The Texans folded, but in 1953 Marchetti and a nucleus of Texans emerged as the Baltimore Colts. Their coach Keith Molesworth still played Marchetti at tackle, on offense. Marchetti, by this time a 245-pounder, did not like the position and thought about quitting the NFL for the Canadian Football League (CFL). But Weeb Ewbank took over as coach and said, presciently, "I think your future is as a defensive end." Not only did Marchetti become a defensive end, he became *the* defensive end. He perfected his craft—rushing the passer and stopping runners in their tracks—so well that he was regarded as more of an artist than artisan. He quickly earned a reputation as "the best at his position in the NFL."

With an influx of new talent—Johnny Unitas, Raymond Berry, Alan Ameche, Jim Parker, and others—the Colts were soon contending for NFL honors. An example of Marchetti's toughness and dedication occurred in a 1955 game in which he suffered a dislocated shoulder in the first half. The battle-hardened combat war veteran simply asked the team physician, "Can you get me ready for the second half, Doc?"

After getting close in 1957, in a watershed game the following year the Colts won it all—the NFL championship. The 1958 Colts–New York Giants sudden-death overtime game has been called the greatest game ever played. It was not, from an artistic standpoint. But what it did—to raise the nation's awareness of professional football through a coast-to-coast telecast—cannot be overestimated. The broadcast game was the first shot in football's war to replace baseball as the national pastime. It was the signal for the professional football explosion that followed and continued into the next century. Marchetti played a key role late in the game—the first his father ever saw him play. The Giants, ahead 17–14, were driving for a clinching touchdown when Marchetti's clutch tackle stopped Frank Gifford a yard shy of a drive-sustaining first down. As the play was ending, 288-pound Eugene "Big Daddy" Lipscomb fell across Marchetti's leg, breaking his ankle. After Marchetti was carried off the field, the Giants punted, and Unitas drove the Colts seventy-nine yards in the waning moments to set up the tying field goal. This sent the game, for the first time in NFL championship play, into sudden-death overtime, meaning the first team to score would be the victor.

In the overtime period the Colts began their historic drive to the championship. Fearing Marchetti would be further injured if the Colts scored and the triumphant Colts fans surged onto the field, he was moved toward the locker room. At a crucial moment in the game Marchetti ordered the stretcher put down while he watched the play. An alert photographer recorded the epic moment: a classic photo of Marchetti, ignoring his pain and intently watching the action, survives today. Marchetti was in the Colts locker room before Ameche's short touchdown run ended the game, but the hoots and hollers of his jubilant teammates told him the Colts were the champions. The team defeated the Giants again in 1959.

It was at this time that Marchetti and teammates Ameche and Joe Campanella opened a few fifteen-cent hamburger restaurants. Ameche already had a restaurant, so the new fast food outlets were named "Gino's." Business took off in those heady days, when McDonald's was still primarily a West Coast operation. Marchetti, dubbed the East Coast Hamburger King, eventually saw his name in neon above more than 500 locations along the eastern seaboard.

Marchetti's on-field performance remained stellar through the early 1960s. His quickness, the best on the team, amazed even his own teammates in film sessions. The linebacker who played behind him, Bill Pellington, said, "Game after game we'd watch film, and game after game Gino would make plays that seemed impossible—he was just unreal!" At age thirty-eight, Marchetti retired after the 1964 season. But when Colts owner Carroll Rosenbloom—the man who gave Marchetti and many teammates their start in off-field businesses—asked him to come back in 1966, the ever-loyal, ever-grateful Marchetti suited up for four more games.

Marchetti played in every Pro Bowl from 1955 to 1965, except 1959, which he missed with the aforementioned broken ankle. He was also All-Pro nine consecutive years, from 1956 to 1964. When the NFL picked an All-Time team in

1969, the fiftieth anniversary of the league, Marchetti represented the defensive end position on the eleven-man team. He was inducted into the Pro Football Hall of Fame in 1972. Marchetti and his second wife, the former Joan Placenik, live in West Chester, Pennsylvania.

Marchetti still defines the defensive end position in the NFL, as shown by his selection for the league's seventy-fifth anniversary team. His friend and partner Alan Ameche once said, "Marchetti was the best defensive end of his time, and today, and if there's pro football a hundred years from now, he'll still be the best damned defensive end in the world."

★

No full-length biography of Marchetti has been published, but his life and career are discussed in John F. Steadman, *Football's Miracle Men: The Baltimore Colts' Story* (1959); Murray Olderman, *The Defenders* (1973); George Allen and Ben Olan, *Pro Football's 100 Greatest Players: Rating the Stars of Past and Present* (1982); and Rick Korch, *The Truly Great: The 200 Best Football Players of All Time* (1993).

JIM CAMPBELL

MARCIANO, Rocky (*b.* 1 September 1923 in Brockton, Massachusetts; *d.* 31 August 1969 near Newton, Iowa), boxer who is best remembered for his heavyweight record of forty-nine professional wins and no losses.

Born Rocco Francis Marchegiano, Marciano entered the world weighing twelve pounds, the first of six children of Italian immigrants Pierino Marchegiano, a machinist at a shoe factory, and Pasqualena Picciuto Marchegiano, a homemaker. "Marciano" became his stage name when a ring announcer had trouble pronouncing Marchegiano. Marciano was not pleased, but at least satisfied that it remained an Italian name. Despite a serious bout with pneumonia at eighteen months of age, Marciano enjoyed a vigorous youth on the streets of Brockton. He regularly brought lunch to his father at the shoe factory, and dismayed at the prospect of such drudgery, Marciano began to dream that sports could help him escape the poverty and hard work of his parents.

As a youth Marciano spent most days at the James Edgar Playground, one of the few places in ethnically segregated Brockton where working-class Irish and Italians congregated. He played baseball and dreamed of becoming a major leaguer. He also developed a reputation as a fighter who was unafraid to engage other kids on and off the field. Still, by the time he was fourteen, his notoriety as a baseball slugger eclipsed his reputation as a pugilist. He would later declare that baseball was always his first love.

In 1938 Marciano entered Brockton High School and within a year won the position of linebacker on the varsity football team. In the spring of 1940 he became the starting catcher on the school's varsity baseball team. At the same time he played in a local church baseball league, violating a school rule that prohibited students from playing for more than one team. Though school officials warned him repeatedly that he would have to leave the St. Patrick's team, Marciano refused and was cut from the team at high school. Displaying characteristic defiance, he decided not to return to Brockton High the following fall.

Without the prospect of a higher education, Marciano turned to a number of odd jobs, trying his luck as a gardener, a delivery boy, a laborer for the gas company, and a leather tanner at the shoe factory where his father worked. In 1943 he was inducted into the U.S. Army and shipped overseas to England. He did not see combat in Europe during World War II and was soon flown back to Fort Lewis, Washington, where he represented his army unit in a series of amateur fights. After scoring several successes in the ring and acquiring some serious hand injuries, Marciano realized that a successful boxing career would require more training and more experience than he had believed.

Following an honorable discharge from the army, Marciano returned to Brockton in 1946 to pursue his dream of success on the baseball diamond. He played on local teams and even tried out for a Chicago Cubs farm team the following year, but he learned he just was not good enough to be a professional baseball player. Legend has it, ironically, that he was told he did not have a strong enough right arm.

Determined to avoid the menial jobs that his father had endured, Marciano focused his energies on becoming a champion boxer. With the help of a family friend, Allie Colombo, he trained on Brockton's streets and began to work seriously to optimize his physical condition. At five feet, ten inches tall, and 185 pounds, Marciano was smaller and slower than most heavyweights. Tradition holds that since his mother was opposed to boxing, he and Colombo tossed a football back and forth when she was around to fool her into thinking he was training for the gridiron. Within a few months the "Brockton Blockbuster" was trimmed down and ready to fight professionally. He was signed by New York manager Al Weill, and groomed for greatness by experienced trainer Charley Goldman.

Marciano's career is the stuff of Hollywood legends. His first professional bout, held in Massachusetts on 17 March 1947, was a third-round knockout over Lee Epperson. He became nationally known in 1950 after a 24 March bout in which he fought Roland LaStarza to a decision and won. Like Marciano, LaStarza had been an undefeated newcomer. Experienced fighters such as Don Mogard, Ted Lowry, and even Joe Louis soon fell victim in Marciano's battle for the championship. Marciano and Barbara Cous-

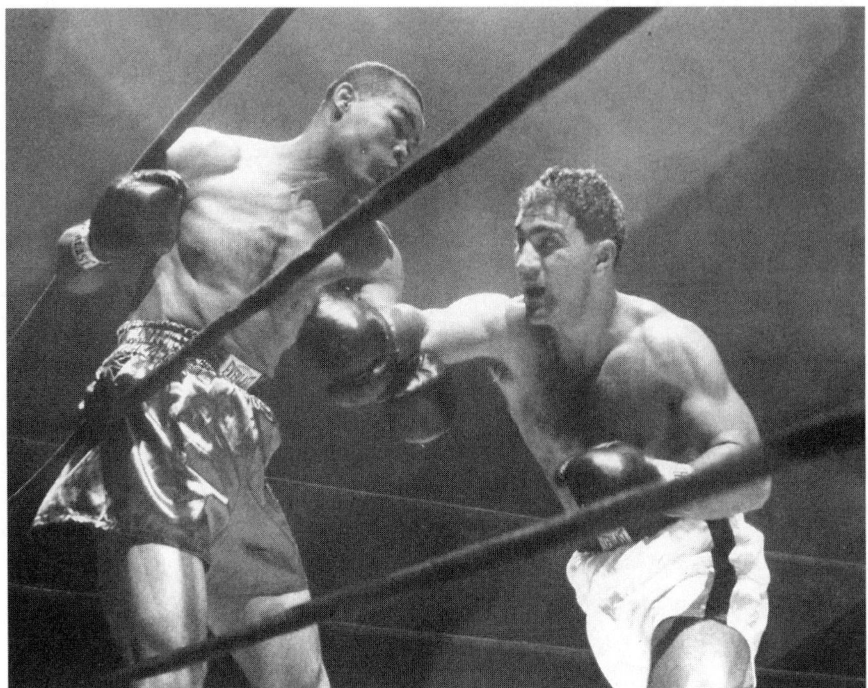

Rocky Marciano *(right)* throwing a punch at Joe Louis. AP/WIDE WORLD PHOTOS

ins married on 31 December 1950. They had one daughter and adopted a son.

After winning thirty-seven fights by knockouts, Marciano finally achieved his goal on 23 September 1952, when he fought Jersey Joe Walcott for the World Heavyweight Championship. Although he was knocked down in the first round—and was behind in the scoring for the first seven rounds—Marciano finally won in the thirteenth by knocking out Walcott with a desperately powerful—and accurate—right punch. He dubbed this crashing right "Suzie Q."

Marciano defended his title six times, winning five by knockout. "The Rock" was undefeated in forty-nine professional fights, forty-three of which were won with knockouts. In addition to those he fought on the road to championship, Marciano successfully defended his title against Archie Moore, Don Cockell, and Ezzard Charles. He was named *Ring Magazine*'s Fighter of the Year in 1952, 1954, and 1955. Marciano said it was personal determination that pushed him past his rivals. Still, he took none of his success for granted. "I'm heavyweight champion of the world, but is there some young fighter somewhere who wants it as much as I did?" As it turned out, there was not. Marciano would later leave the ring with a record of forty-nine wins, a champion who completed his career undefeated.

Marciano said his most challenging fight was his encounter with the boxer he had idolized as a youth, Joe Louis. In his dressing room before the match, Marciano is reported to have said, "This is the last guy on Earth I want to fight." It was a tough match, since the aging Louis was still a formidable opponent. But in the eighth round, Marciano landed several punches from which Louis could not recover. "When he defeated me, I think it hurt him more than it hurt me," Louis later said. It was Louis's last fight. By age thirty-two, Marciano himself was ready to retire. He told family and friends that "he didn't want to go out broke or beaten." With an eye toward his legacy, he founded a boxing foundation that aided and gave security to boxers later in their lives.

On 31 August 1969, one day before his forty-sixth birthday, Marciano died in a plane crash near Newton, Iowa, en route to a birthday party. He is buried in Forest Lawn Memorial Cemetery in Fort Lauderdale, Florida.

The likelihood that Marciano would succeed in boxing seemed about the same as his chance of reaching baseball's major leagues. He was a street brawler with a short reach, a heavyweight who was considered too short and too light. What he did have, however, was the instinct to win and the refusal to fall. He might get cut (he was known for a slash above his eye), but he would not be beaten. According to the Pulitzer Prize–winner Red Smith "He was the toughest, strongest, most completely dedicated fighter who ever wore gloves."

★

Biographies of Marciano include Robert Arthur Cutter, *The Rocky Marciano Story* (1954); Bill Libby, *Rocky: The Story of a*

Champion (1971); Everett Skehan, *Rocky Marciano: Biography of a First Son* (1977); and Michael N. Varveris, *Rocky Marciano: The 13th Candle—The True Story of an American Legend* (2000).

MOLLY BOYLE

MARICHAL, Juan Antonio (*b.* 24 October 1937 in Laguna Verde, Montecristi, Dominican Republic), Hall of Fame National League (NL) pitcher, known for his high-kick delivery and impeccable control, who won twenty games in each of six different seasons during the 1960s with a blazing fastball and a baffling variety of breaking pitches.

As a child in the fishing village of Laguna Verde, right-handed Marichal threw rocks at oranges and pineapples until he could hit the fruit with few misses. At the age of nine he made his first baseball out of rubber bands, stocking thread, and tape. Soon he was playing for his school team. Marichal began as a shortstop but blossomed into a rifle-armed pitcher. He credits his brother Gonzolo, a former semiprofessional player, with teaching him the curveball. He also studied baseball books that contained pictures of famous pitchers.

By the time he was sixteen, Marichal was paid $18 a week by the United Fruit Company to play for its semiprofessional club at the nearby port of Manzanillo. After pitching a 2–0 shutout of the powerful Dominican Air Force team, run by the son of the dictator Rafael Trujillo, Trujillo was so impressed that Marichal was drafted into the Air Force so his services as a baseball player could be secured. He pitched for the Air Force in the Pan-American World Series in Mexico City and left the team a highly polished pitcher.

On 20 October 1957 the San Francisco Giants scout Alex Pompez signed Marichal to a $500 bonus contract. When the Giants farm director Carl Hubbell saw the new recruit in spring training, he gave instructions not to tamper with Marichal's catapult delivery. What Hubbell saw was a style that was eye-catching, graceful, and pure. Marichal delivered the ball from a high kick in which he reared back on his right foot and kicked the left skyward. It looked, said one observer, "like he had one continuous leg, with a spiked shoe on either end." Sometimes Marichal's kick was so high that his pitching hand nearly grazed the dirt on the pitching mound. Not since the debut of the Cleveland Indians Bob Feller in 1936 had anyone seen such a form.

Of medium build, standing only five feet, eleven inches tall, and weighing less than 190 pounds, Marichal was able to generate overpowering speed from his high kicking motion. He threw overhand, three-quarters, and sidearm. In addition to his fastball, Marichal presented an effective array of curves, sliders, screwballs, and change-ups, and possessed pinpoint control of all of them. This stylish delivery and high leg kick earned him the nickname the "Dominican Dandy." Marichal eventually struck out more than 200 batters in each of 6 major-league seasons and never allowed more than 90 walks per season. The home run king, Hank Aaron, remarked that Marichal could "throw all day within a two-inch space, in and out, up or down. I've never seen anyone as good as Juan."

In 1958, with Michigan City of the Class D Midwest League, Marichal was spectacular, winning 21 games while losing just 8. He led the league with a 1.87 earned run average (ERA) and struck out 246 batters. At Class A Springfield in 1959, Marichal dominated the Eastern League with 18 wins, a 2.39 ERA, and 208 strikeouts. By the 1960 season he was at Tacoma in the Pacific Coast League, where he won 11 games before being called up to San Francisco in midseason to play for the Giants.

Marichal's major-league debut is legendary. On 19 July 1960 he held the Phillies hitless for 7 ⅔ innings and struck out 12 batters in a one-hit, 2–0 victory. He finished the season with 5 more wins and won 13 more in 1961.

Marichal emerged as a star in 1962 with 18 wins as he helped pitch the Giants into the World Series. In 1963 he began the first of six 20-win seasons with a 25–8 record and a 2.41 ERA. The next three years he had records of 21–8, 22–13, and 25–6 (leading the league with 10 shutouts in 1965). Injured in 1967, he won 14 games, but returned to form in 1968 with a 26–9 record and 21–11 in 1969.

Marichal pitched the best game of his career on 15 June

Juan Marichal, 1971. ASSOCIATED PRESS AP

1963—an 89-pitch no-hitter against the Houston Colt .45s—in front of the home crowd in Candlestick Park. That season also saw one of the greatest pitching duels of all time, in which Marichal defeated Warren Spahn and the Milwaukee Braves 1–0 in 16 innings, during which he allowed only 8 hits.

For Marichal, 1965 was a fateful season. After a shutout performance, he was named the Most Valuable Player (MVP) in the All-Star game. The Giants were in a tight pennant fight with the rival Los Angeles Dodgers, when on 22 August Marichal faced Sandy Koufax in a game at Candlestick Park. Responding to earlier provocations, Marichal brushed back Dodgers hitters Maury Wills and Ron Fairly. When Marichal came to the plate, he expected Koufax to retaliate. Instead, catcher John Roseboro fired his return throw past Marichal's ear, and words ensued. Roseboro ripped off his mask and stood up, and Marichal hit Roseboro squarely over the head with his bat, sparking a fourteen-minute brawl. It was one of the most brutal moments in baseball history. Marichal was fined $1,750 and suspended for eight days. Roseboro sued Marichal, agreeing to a $7,500 cash settlement in 1970. The two combatants later became friends. For Marichal, who was normally mild mannered, the incident cast a shadow over the rest of his baseball career.

During the 1960s Marichal was as good a pitcher as there was in baseball, with 191 wins in the decade. By 1969 he had set a NL record for highest lifetime winning percentage. Marichal was the first NL right-hander since Grover Cleveland Alexander to win twenty-five or more games three times. However, he was denied a Cy Young award due to the preeminence of Sandy Koufax, his Dodgers mound rival. Phillies slugger Richie Allen said that "even when Koufax was around, I thought Marichal was the best. Koufax was a thrower. Marichal is a pitcher. With Marichal, he's got five pitches, and he can bring them all in." The pitching-rich decade also pitted Marichal against Cardinals great Bob Gibson, who won the Cy Young award in 1968 on the strength of his 1.12 ERA, and the Mets Tom Seaver, who won 25 games in 1969, the year Marichal won the ERA title at 2.10.

Chronic arthritis and a back injury hampered Marichal in 1970, limiting him to a 12–10 record. He rebounded in 1971 to win eighteen games, including the division title clincher on the last night of the season. The back problems, however, limited his effectiveness for the next two seasons. In 1974 he was traded to the Boston Red Sox and won five games as a spot starter. Signing with the Dodgers in 1975, Marichal was ineffective in two starts and retired. That same year, the Giants retired his number 27.

Elected to the Hall of Fame in 1983, Marichal was named to nine All-Star teams, compiling a 2–0 record and an 0.50 ERA. His lifetime ERA is 2.89, with 244 complete games and 52 career shutouts. Marichal's record of 243 career wins stood as most victories by a Latin American pitcher until broken by Dennis Martinez of the Atlanta Braves in 1998. He was also the first Latin American pitcher to record a no-hitter. Marichal ranks with Christy Mathewson and Carl Hubbell in the pantheon of Giants pitching immortals.

Marichal returned to the Dominican Republic immediately upon retirement. A revered figure in his homeland, he is minister of sports. He married Alma Rosa Carnaval in March 1962. They have six children.

★

Biographies of Marichal include his own *A Pitcher's Story* (1967), written with Charles Einstein, and John Devaney, *Juan Marichal, Mister Strike* (1970). Chapters on Marichal may be found in Maury Allen, *Baseball 100: A Personal Ranking of the Best Players in Baseball History* (1981), and Donald Honig, *The Greatest Pitchers of All Time* (1988). A detailed portrait of Marichal is in Al Stump, "Juan Marichal: Behind His Success," *Sport* (Sept. 1964). Robert H. Boyle, "The Latin Storm Las Grandes Ligas," *Sports Illustrated* (9 Aug. 1965), contains an excellent analysis of the impact of Latin American ball players. Nine top hitters discuss Marichal in Jack Zanger, "From 9 Top Batters: A Unique View of Juan Marichal," *Sport* (Sept. 1967).

DOUGLAS E. COLLAR

MARINO, Daniel Constantine, Jr. ("Dan") (*b.* 15 September 1961 in Pittsburgh, Pennsylvania), quarterback who, after an outstanding college career at the University of Pittsburgh and seventeen years with the Miami Dolphins, held every major passing record in the National Football League (NFL) at the close of the twentieth century.

Marino was the first of three children and the only son born to Daniel Constantine Marino, Sr., a delivery-truck driver, and Veronica Kolczynski Marino, a homemaker. He was raised in South Oakland, a neighborhood near the University of Pittsburgh whose population was primarily Irish-American, Italian-American, and Roman Catholic. He entered his parish school, Saint Regis, where his father coached the football team. Marino took to sports, especially football and baseball. He entered Central Catholic High School in 1976, attracted by its sports programs, and began receiving inquiries from the University of Pittsburgh (Pitt) football recruiters as a sophomore. He passed for more than 1,000 yards in both his junior and senior seasons, gaining *Parade* magazine All-America recognition in 1979, his final year. Baseball scouts were also impressed with Marino, who pitched to a 25–1 record his senior year; he was a fourth-round amateur draft pick by the Kansas City Royals in 1979. After serious consideration he opted for the football

Dan Marino *(left)*. AP/Wide World Photos

grant-in-aid from Pitt, beginning college in autumn 1979 only four blocks from his boyhood home.

Pitt's winning football tradition had been revived in the 1970s by Coach Johnny Majors with a legendary national championship in 1976, and Marino kept the Panthers at their renewed high level. Replacing the injured starting quarterback in the middle of his freshman year, Marino led Pitt to five consecutive wins and an 11–1 record, and remained the starter for the rest of his college days. Pitt again finished 11–1 in both his sophomore and junior years, then fell to 9–3 in 1982. Marino's best year in college was 1981 when, as a junior, he set school records for touchdown passes (37), passing yards (2,876), and completed passes (226); was named an All-American; and finished fourth in the voting for the Heisman Trophy. In addition, he was named the Most Valuable Player (MVP) in the Sugar Bowl, where he passed for three touchdowns, including the winner, with thirty-five seconds left in the game (Pitt defeated the University of Georgia 24–20). By the time he received his B.A. in communications in 1983, Marino was Pitt's all-time offensive leader, with 8,290 yards gained, 693 pass completions, and 79 career touchdown passes, and he became the fourth Pitt player to have his number retired. Pitt's overall record was 42–6 in the Marino years, and the team twice was rated number two in the final national polls.

The 1983 NFL draft was legendary for its quarterbacks. John Elway of Stanford University was the number-one choice in the draft, while Marino was taken as the next-to-last pick in the first round, twenty-seventh choice overall, by the Miami Dolphins. Marino and the head coach Don Shula got along well from the start. Shula, who quickly fell in love with his new six-foot, four-inch, 227-pound field leader, soon was adjusting his team and his offensive scheme to fit Marino's obvious talents, focusing on a strong offensive line to protect his quarterback. In the middle of his rookie season Marino got his first start, against Buffalo, and made his mark, completing nineteen of 29 passes for 322 yards and 3 touchdowns in a 38–35 overtime loss. Marino finished the year as the leading passer of the American Football Conference (AFC), set a record for lowest percentage interceptions in a rookie year (2.03), and highest completion percentage for a rookie (58.45), became the first rookie quarterback to start the Pro Bowl, and was chosen as the Rookie of the Year. The NFL Marino legend was born.

Following this auspicious start to his professional career, Marino made 1984 even greater, leading the Dolphins to a 14–2 record and the Super Bowl. Marino's passing was phenomenal even by his standards, as he set records for touchdown passes (48, which exceeded the old record by 12) and passing yards (5,084) that stood for the rest of the century. The Dolphins scored 28 or more points in 14 of their 16 games. A pure, drop-back passer, Marino piled up the numbers with his quick release, downfield vision, self-confidence, and poise. Protected by a strong line, he threw often and successfully to the "Marks Brothers," the receivers Mark Clayton and Mark "Super" Duper. He had 4 games with more than 400 yards each, 12 games with 3 or more touchdown passes, and was an obvious choice as the NFL's MVP. Marino played in what was fated to be his only (and Shula's last) Super Bowl against the quarterback Joe Montana and the San Francisco Forty-niners. Marino completed 29 of 50 passes for 318 yards, but was sacked 4 times, a high for the season, and threw 2 interceptions as San Francisco defeated the Dolphins in Super Bowl XIX. Ten days later, on 30 January 1985, Marino married Claire Veazey in his parish church in Pittsburgh; they raised five children together.

Given his 1984 performance, Marino's desire to renegotiate his contract was understandable, but the Dolphins held out, and Marino eventually caved in after holding out for thirty-seven days. Despite missing training camp, he still wound up leading the league in touchdown passes (30), passing yards (4,137), and completions (336), while the Dolphins (12–4) again made it to the AFC title game, losing 31–14 to the New England Patriots. Marino's September 1986 agreement with the Dolphins was then the top package in NFL history (six years, $9 million, plus incentives). His 1986 season made the Dolphins look like wise investors as he again led the AFC in yards completed and touchdown passes, his high being six versus the New York Jets on 21 September.

Marino continued to pile up impressive numbers even as the Dolphins defense declined in the late 1980s. In 1990 he passed the 30,000 passing yards mark in his 114th game, the fastest pace ever, and in 1993 the 40,000 milestone, also the fastest (153rd career game). He suffered his first serious injury, a torn Achilles tendon, on 10 October 1993. After rehabilitation and serious training, in his next regular-season game, on 4 September 1994 against New England, Marino passed for 473 yards and 5 touchdowns in a comeback 39–35 win that he termed his most memorable game. He led the AFC in passing efficiency and touchdown passes and was named the Comeback Player of the Year. During the 1995 season he broke Fran Tarkenton's career passing records. Marino retired after the 1999 season, his seventeenth with the Dolphins, with a gracious statement full of praise and thanks for others that he delivered on 13 March 2000.

Marino was a confident, likable, fun-to-watch quarterback whose comebacks, long gains, and touchdown bombs were familiar to football fans of the 1980s and 1990s. He was a strong team leader, respected by his teammates as well as by fans. His career totals included 61,361 passing yards and 420 touchdowns, both records, 9 seasons of more than 3,000 yards gained in the air, and 6 of more than 4,000. His number "13" jersey was retired by the Dolphins. Fans mourned that he never won a Super Bowl.

★

Marino has produced two autobiographies: with Steve Delsohn, *Marino!* (1986), and with Marc Serota and Mark Vancil, *Marino: On the Record* (1996). He is also featured in Peter King, *Greatest Quarterbacks* (1999), and Beckett Publications, *Dan Marino: The Making of a Legend* (1999).

LAWSON BOWLING

MARIS, Roger Eugene (*b.* 10 September 1934 in Hibbing, Minnesota; *d.* 14 December 1985 in Houston), one of the most talented baseball players of his era who held the major league record for home runs in a season from 1961 to 1998.

Maris was the younger of two sons of Rudy Maris, a railroad engineer, and Connie Sturbitz Maris, a homemaker. An outstanding high-school athlete in basketball, track, and football, he attended Bishop Shanley High School in Fargo, North Dakota, and played American Legion baseball. In 1953, after his graduation, he declined a football scholarship from the University of Oklahoma and instead signed a professional baseball contract with the Cleveland Indians that included a $5,000 signing bonus. A left-handed batter, he became the Rookie of the Year for 1953 in the Class C Northern League. He played for four pennant-winning teams in his first four years of professional ball in Fargo and Moorhead, Minnesota (1953); Keokuk, Iowa (1954);

Roger Maris, 1962. © BETTMANN/CORBIS

Reading, Pennsylvania (1955); and Indianapolis, Indiana (1956).

In 1957 Maris was promoted to the Cleveland club and batted a respectable .235 with 14 homers during his first major league season. On 15 June 1958 he was traded to the Kansas City Athletics and on 11 December 1959 to the New York Yankees, where he soon blossomed into a star. Although Maris stood six feet tall and weighed about 190 pounds for most of his career, he was hardly as large or as strong as most power hitters, and depended on his ability to pull pitches into right field. In 1960 he was selected as the Most Valuable Player (MVP) in the American League (edging out his teammate Mickey Mantle by a vote of 225 to 222), hitting 39 home runs (second in the league to Mantle), batting .283, and receiving a Golden Glove for his outfield play. As Casey Stengel, who managed Maris that year, later remarked, he "had the greatest first half of the season for us [in 1960] that you ever saw. In spite of getting hurt during the second half, he led the league for the year in runs batted in with 112. . . . And Maris could throw and make sensational catches in right field."

However, the 1960 season was a mere prelude to one of the most incredible summers in baseball history. For most of the 1961 season, Maris and Mantle chased the ghost of Babe Ruth as they stalked the major league single-season home run record of sixty, set by Ruth in 1927. Usually batting third in the Yankee lineup, Maris did not receive an intentional walk all year because Mantle batted behind him in the order. Midway through the season, the Commissioner of Baseball Ford Frick ignited a controversy when he announced that, given the lengthened season of 162 games in 1961 compared to 154 games in 1927, Ruth's record had to be broken during the first 154 games of the season. Any home run record set after 154 games would be given a "distinctive mark" (the so-called asterisk) to distinguish it from Ruth's record. Maris hit 59 home runs in the first 154 games of the 1961 season—more than any other player except Ruth—and hit his 61st home run on the last day of the season, 1 October 1961. Although the press reported often on the ostensible "feud" between Maris and Mantle as they chased the home run record, the players in fact shared an apartment during the 1961 season. As Mantle later recalled, "There might have been better players [than Maris], but no one was a better man. . . . When Roger hit his sixty-first home run, I was the second happiest person in the world."

In addition to setting a single-season home run record in 1961, Maris scored 142 runs, knocked in 132 to lead the American League (AL), and batted .269. He was voted the AL MVP for the second consecutive year; was named the *Sporting News* Player of the Year, *Sports Illustrated* Sportsman of the Year, *Sport* magazine Man of the Year, and Associated Press Professional Athlete of the Year; and was awarded the Hickok Belt as the top professional athlete of the year. Maris and Mantle, known as the home-run twins "M and M," hit a combined 115 home runs, the highest total in baseball history for two players on the same team, surpassing the 107 home runs that Ruth and Lou Gehrig stroked for the 1927 Yankees. As Maris reminisced after the 1961 season, "Even if I never do another thing in baseball, at least I have had one year that put me in good company."

Although often described as sullen and taciturn, Maris was, according to those who knew him best, a shy and intensely private man with an inclination to speak his mind. "I have always tried to be completely frank and honest about everything, even if sometimes it might be easier to be the other way," he reflected in his autobiography. He earned about $40,000 for the 1961 season and, despite his successful year, his salary negotiations with the Yankees in the spring of 1962 were contentious; he went to spring training without a contract and finally settled for $72,500 to play the 1962 season. Yet he also became a marked man. As his teammate Ralph Terry remembered, "The trouble around Roger really started in the 1962 season, when a couple of bad articles were written about him. . . . The players didn't believe any of that stuff for one minute. To us Roger was a great guy, a real hero." Jimmy Cannon of the *New York Journal-American* complained that Maris's "whining" was undermining the team and insisted that "Maris violates all the laws of protocol established by Joe DiMaggio and Babe Ruth." For the rest of his life, according to his biographer Maury Allen, Maris "never fully trusted any reporter."

As a result, Maris's career with the image-conscious Yankees began to suffer. He broke a bone in his hand during the 1965 season that prevented him from playing for most of the year and robbed him of much of his power for the rest of his career. He also believed the Yankees mishandled his injury by failing to inform him of its severity in the hopes that he would simply return to the lineup. He was traded by New York to St. Louis on 8 December 1966, and played with the Cardinals in 1967 and 1968. In all, during his twelve-year major league career, Maris batted .260 with 275 home runs, scored 826 runs, and batted in 851. He played in seven All-Star games (1959–1962), and seven World Series, including five straight with the Yankees (1960–1964), and two with St. Louis (1967–1968).

After his retirement from baseball following the 1968 season, Maris lived in Gainesville, Florida, with his wife, the former Patricia Carville, who he had married on 13 October 1956, and their six children. In partnership with his older brother Rudy Maris, Jr., he owned and managed a beer distributorship. Maris finally reconciled with the Yankees after the team was sold to George Steinbrenner in 1973, and returned to Yankee Stadium to be honored in April 1978. His number 9 was retired at Old Timers' Day there in 1984. Maris died of lymphatic cancer and is buried in Holy Cross Cemetery in Fargo, North Dakota.

Although Maris enjoyed only a few stellar seasons as a player, his pursuit of the single-season home-run record in 1961 was one of the most memorable events in Major League Baseball history. He is the only two-time MVP in either league eligible for, but not elected to, the National Baseball Hall of Fame.

★

After his remarkable 1961 season, Maris collaborated with Jim Ogle on a near-daily account of the year, *Roger Maris at Bat* (1962). See also Maury Allen, *Roger Maris: A Man for All Seasons* (1986), and Harvey Rosenfeld, *Roger Maris: A Title to Fame* (1991). Tony Kubek and Terry Pluto, *Sixty-one: The Team, the Record, the Men* (1987), devote more than fifty pages to Maris. Ralph Houk and Robert W. Creamer, *Season of Glory: The Amazing Saga of the 1961 New York Yankees* (1988), and David Halberstam, *October 1964* (1994), are less sympathetic to Maris and discuss his personality and aloofness in public. An obituary is in the *New York Times* (15 Dec. 1985).

GARY SCHARNHORST

MARSHALL, George Preston (*b.* 11 October 1896 in Grafton, West Virginia; *d.* 9 August 1969 in Washington, D.C.), flamboyant businessman and professional sports entrepreneur who originated many of the ideas that made the National Football League a popular and commercial success.

Marshall was the only child of T. Hill Marshall, the publisher of West Virginia's *Grafton Leader* and the owner of a Washington, D.C., laundry, and Blanche Preston (Sebrell) Marshall, a homemaker. After graduating from Friends Select School in Washington, D.C., Marshall briefly attended Randolph-Macon College in Ashland, Virginia, before beginning a theater apprenticeship as a stock company player. Although he lacked great acting skills, Marshall enjoyed performing before an audience and learned the importance of publicity and showmanship.

Marshall considered a career in theater management, but he was drafted into the military during World War I in 1918. By the time of his discharge in 1919, he had inherited his father's laundry business. Launching an aggressive advertising campaign under the motto "Long Live Linen," Marshall expanded the company into a chain of fifty-seven stores.

During this business success, Marshall retained some ties to his theatrical past. In 1920 he married Elizabeth Mortensen, a former Ziegfeld Follies dancer; they had two children. Marshall associated with other show-business personalities and occasionally produced local theater. He also became interested in sports promotion. In 1925 he founded the Washington Palace Five of the short-lived American Basketball League. Marshall also promoted automobile racing at New York's Roosevelt Raceway.

In 1932 Marshall and three partners purchased a National Football League (NFL) franchise in Boston. They named the team the Braves because they shared a stadium with the baseball team of that name. Marshall hoped to use the Native American imagery associated with the team's name and his own sense of showmanship to create interest in the Braves. The team members occasionally played in war paint and had publicity photos taken in feathered headdresses. Still, the public remained cool. The Braves lost $46,000 the first year. Marshall bought out his partners before the start of the 1933 season, moved the team across town to Fenway Park, and renamed them the Redskins. The team continued to lose money.

Although the Redskins were not a financial success in Boston, Marshall immediately became a leader of the NFL. He believed the key to football's success was to score points and generate excitement. To do this he suggested moving the goalposts from the back of the end zone to the goal line to make field-goal kicking easier. Marshall proposed legalizing the forward pass from anywhere behind the line of scrimmage, as well as moving the ball out from the sidelines to hash marks nearer the middle of the field at the end of each play. Finally, Marshall suggested splitting the league into two divisions and having the winners meet in a postseason championship game. All of these suggestions were implemented.

Marshall's influence on professional football may have been felt in one other area as well. Since the founding of the NFL in 1920, African-American players, although rare, had been an accepted part of the game. Following the 1933 season, the league became segregated. This change apparently was enforced through a gentleman's agreement. No formal rule barring African-American players was ever passed or even discussed at league meetings. Most football historians believe Marshall was the leader in segregating the NFL.

In 1935 Marshall divorced Mortensen, and on 20 June 1936 he married the silent film star Corinne Griffith, a woman whose theatrical sense matched his own. Griffith brought two adopted children into the marriage, and she played a large role in changing the Redskins' fortunes. They later divorced in 1957.

The 1936 Redskins were the first of Marshall's teams to reach the championship game. Despite their high quality of play, fans in Boston continued to be few. Griffith urged Marshall to move the championship game to New York, where the Redskins lost to Wisconsin's Green Bay Packers 21–6, and then to permanently relocate the team to Washington, D.C., in 1937. Marshall had a lot of contacts in Washington because of his laundry. He was known to support congressional representation for the District of Columbia, and he had been involved in the arts community. Marshall's wife helped to create a volunteer Redskins marching

George Marshall, 1935. AP/Wide World Photos

band, with a team fight song, and to choreograph elaborate halftime shows, including an annual arrival of Santa Claus. Marshall's Redskins played in an almost collegiate atmosphere. For many Washington politicians, bureaucrats, and military personnel, the Redskins became a substitute alma mater, linking the transient community together. Soon tickets were hard to find, and trainloads of fans appeared at away games.

Another reason for the Redskins' success was the 1937 drafting of Sammy Baugh from Texas Christian University. Marshall dressed up the urbanized Baugh as a Texas cowboy for the media. Baugh was one of the greatest players of all time. With his passing and punting and the running of backs like Cliff Battles, the Redskins became consistent winners. During their first nine years in Washington, Marshall's team played in five championship games, winning two. Marshall basked in the limelight of his winning team. He came to games dressed in a full-length raccoon coat and berated officials, coaches, and players. Even though he had little football experience, he tried to make on-the-field decisions for his team, hiring and firing coaches, signing players, and making trades almost on a whim. Marshall sold off his laundry business in 1945 so he could focus exclusively on football.

With the end of World War II, the Redskins' fortunes began to decline. In 1946 the Los Angeles Rams and Cleveland Browns broke the gentleman's agreement and reintegrated professional football. Marshall refused to go along. For years he would not even give tryouts to African-American players. From an economic standpoint, this policy may have made sense. Marshall was one of the first NFL owners to recognize the potential for television revenue. Because they were the only team south of the Mason-Dixon Line, the Redskins were able to create a network of southern stations to carry their games. Teaching the marching band to play "Dixie," drafting primarily southern players, and keeping the team all-white helped to sell Marshall's team to the South. But cutting the Redskins off from the African-American talent that other teams were using hurt the team on the field. After appearing in six championship games in ten years, the Redskins did not appear in any during the last twenty-three years of Marshall's life. In fact, they only had three winning seasons.

In 1962, under pressure from President John F. Kennedy's administration, Marshall finally signed his first African-American players. It was one of his last football decisions. In 1963 a stroke left Marshall unable to manage the Redskins. Three court-appointed conservators ran the team until his death from hemiphlagia, a heart ailment that in Marshall's case was compounded by diabetes.

Marshall was one of seventeen charter members of the Pro Football Hall of Fame in 1963. He also originated the Pro Bowl, an annual showcase for the game's All-Stars.

Marshall's impact on professional football was unique. He was the first team owner to see football more as a form of entertainment than a sport. Generating excitement, filling seats, and building interest were as important to him as wins and losses. Viewers of the televised pageantry of Super Bowls at the end of the twentieth century saw football the way Marshall wanted it played. In fact, he advocated a warm-weather championship game held at a neutral site years before it became a reality. At the same time, Marshall's bigotry overshadowed his positive contributions to the game.

★

Memorabilia and newspaper clippings about Marshall's career are in the Pro Football Hall of Fame in Canton, Ohio. For the best account of how Marshall ran the Redskins and his role in the NFL, see the reflections of his second wife, Corinne Griffith, *My Life with the Redskins* (1947). Additional information about Marshall is in George Sullivan, *Pro Football's All Time Greats* (1968); Thom Loverro, *The Washington Redskins: The Authorized History* (1996); and Richard Whittingham, *Hail Redskins: A Celebration of the Greatest Players, Teams, and Coaches* (2001). Obituaries are in the *Washington Post* and *New York Times* (both 10 Aug. 1969).

HAROLD W. AURAND, JR.

MARTINEZ, Pedro Jaime (*b.* 25 October 1971 in Santo Domingo, Dominican Republic), baseball pitcher who won the Cy Young Award in both the American and National Leagues and who set the major league record for the most strikeouts per nine innings pitched in one season.

Martinez grew up with three brothers and two sisters in the impoverished, rural Dominican town of Manoguayabo. A sensitive child who kept a diary and did homework in the branches of a mango tree, Martinez played stickball every day using makeshift equipment. He and two of his brothers, Ramon and Jesus, regularly threw rocks across a ravine behind their home to see whose landed the farthest; all three eventually became baseball pitchers in the United States. Their father, Paulino Jaime Abreu, a school janitor, was a former amateur baseball player. Martinez's parents divorced when he was nine, and the children were raised by their mother, Leopoldina Martinez, a homemaker.

When Martinez was thirteen, his brother Ramon signed with the Los Angeles Dodgers organization. Martinez often tagged along and carried equipment bags when Ramon pitched in the Dominican Summer League. Three years later the Dodgers signed Martinez for $6,000.

Eleodoro Arias, the Dominican Dodgers pitching instructor, was concerned about Martinez's wispy 137-pound build, but felt he had a big heart. Throughout every stage of Martinez's career his durability was questioned. The coaching staff at Single-A Great Falls (Montana) threatened to fine him if he ran laps around the stadium. When Martinez was with the Dodgers, the manager Tommy Lasorda assigned him to the bullpen because he did not feel he had the size to be a starter. In his late twenties, Martinez made midseason trips to the disabled list, sparking baseball experts to question how long he could maintain his edge as a flame thrower.

In 1991 *Sporting News* named Martinez the Minor League Player of the Year. The Dodgers called him up from Triple-A Albuquerque (New Mexico) late in the 1992 sea-

Pedro Martinez. AP/WIDE WORLD PHOTOS

son, and he made his major league debut against the Cincinnati Reds, throwing two scoreless innings in relief. Martinez thrived in the Dodgers bullpen in 1993, winning ten games in sixty-five appearances. During the off-season the Dodgers, who were looking to shore up their infield, traded Martinez to the National League's Montreal Expos for the second baseman Delino Deshields.

Under the Dominican Expos manager Felipe Alou, Martinez sharpened his curveball, adding to his arsenal of pitches. He notched fifty-five wins in four seasons as a starter. Martinez pitched a perfect nine innings in June 1995 against the San Diego Padres, but Montreal could not score and lost the game in the tenth. In his fourth year he went 17–8, with a razor-sharp 1.90 earned run average (ERA). In 1997 he became the first Dominican to win a Cy Young Award for the outstanding pitcher in the National League.

The Expos had a history of trading emerging superstars before paying them top dollar. One week after winning the Cy Young award, Martinez was traded to the Boston Red Sox for two pitching prospects. Martinez signed a $75 million, six-year contract with the Red Sox, which at the time made him the highest-paid player in baseball.

In Boston, Martinez's signing sparked excitement and an influx of Latino baseball fans. Dominican-American fans brought *tamburos* (Dominican-style drums), *guiras* (metal scrapers), and accordions and proudly waved Dominican flags, creating a World Cup atmosphere at the traditionally staid Fenway Park. In 1998 Martinez finished his first season in the American League with nineteen wins and 251 strikeouts. The following season the still 170-pound ace pitched what many journalists characterized as the best season ever by a pitcher. His record was 23–4 with a 2.07 ERA, which was 1.37 better than the next best in the American League and the greatest winning margin in the twentieth century. His strikeout average of 13.2 per nine innings set a major-league record.

In September 1999 Martinez and his brother Ramon were reunited on the same team. Ramon had an impressive career as a starter with the Dodgers, but after he underwent rotator cuff surgery in 1998, the Dodgers declined to pick up the option year on his contract. After a fourteen-month recovery Ramon returned to the mound, pitching well enough to help the Red Sox nail down a play-off spot.

Martinez reserved his finest performance for the decisive game of the 1999 division series. He left game one after the fourth inning with a pulled muscle behind his shoulder and came in as a reliever in game five, hoping he could contribute one inning. With a stabbing sensation in his back after every pitch, Martinez delivered cut fastballs at various angles and held the Cleveland Indians hitless for six innings. (The Indians were the most prolific scoring team in more than fifty years.) Boston won the game 12–8 and took the series. For his 1999 performance Martinez won his second Cy Young Award, this time with the American League.

In 2000 Martinez lowered his ERA to 1.74. He fashioned an 18–6 record with little run support and gave up a total of only seven runs over the six losses. That same year he received the Cy Young Award for a third time, becoming one of only two pitchers in the American League to twice earn unanimous selection for the award.

In the dugout Martinez's creative antics, jokes, and zany catcalls to opposing players earned him the nickname "Pedro Zawacki" (a borrowed surname from Rich Zawacki, the team's physical trainer). Outside the ballpark, he was soft-spoken, read the Bible, listened to music, and tended to a flower garden on his balcony. He also was an eloquent, charismatic spokesperson for the impoverished people of the Dominican Republic. After signing his long-term contract with the Red Sox, he financed the building of a church, an elementary school, a playground, and three houses for homeless families in Manoguayabo. In his twenties, Martinez was the father of three children.

On the mound Martinez was fiercely competitive, with a studying stare known to unnerve hitters. When he delivered the ball, he grimaced like a bulldog sucking a lemon. His remarkable pitching repertoire, control, and ability to change speeds kept hitters guessing. He had a straight fastball that clocked consistently in the mid-nineties (miles per hour), a change-up that kept hitters off-balance, and a knee-buckling curveball. Martinez was also known to pitch inside, in an era when pitchers preferred to paint the outside corner. Opposing teams accused Martinez of being a beanball pitcher, a charge he denied. His longtime pitching coach and manager, Joe Kerrigan, credited Martinez's high-torque legs with a good part of his success. Martinez also acknowledged his long, crooked fingers, which bent back to add extra spin. Many baseball watchers noted his ability to read a hitter's body language.

At the turn of the century Martinez was the leader among active starting pitchers in career winning percentage, ERA, strikeout-walk ratio, hits per nine innings, and opponents' batting average. Baseball pundits enjoyed comparing Martinez's best years to Sandy Koufax's (1961–1966), when Koufax won three Cy Young Awards with a 2.19 ERA and a .733 winning percentage. Koufax often pitched on three days' rest without the pitch count. Martinez maintained a low ERA in an era of bulked-up hitters, lower pitcher mounds, and smaller ballparks. The debate itself is a tribute to the place Martinez holds in baseball history.

★

A file on Martinez is maintained at the National Baseball Hall of Fame Library, Cooperstown, New York. Jim Gallagher, *Pedro Martinez* (1999), is a children's book that provides details of his life. Dan Shaughnessy, "The Man at Ease: A Conversation with

Pedro Martinez," *Boston Globe* (3 Oct. 1999), and Tom Verducci, "The Power of Pedro," *Sports Illustrated* (27 Mar. 2000), are excellent profiles. Seth Livingstone, "Dominican Dreaming: Martinez and Lima—Two Dominating Dominicans," *USA Today Baseball Weekly* (8 Mar. 2000), offers more insight into Martinez's childhood. Mat Olkin, "Pedro Martinez' Season Was One for the Ages," *USA Today Baseball Weekly* (17 Nov. 1999), and Tom Verducci, "Duel Exhaust," *Sports Illustrated* (11 June 2001), offer interesting comparisons of Martinez and pitchers from earlier eras.

DAN GORDON

MATHEWSON, Christopher ("Christy") (*b.* 12 August 1880 in Factoryville, Pennsylvania; *d.* 7 October 1925 in Saranac Lake, New York), baseball pitcher who was, in the days before radio, television, and other mass media, one of America's first national sports heroes.

Growing up in northeastern Pennsylvania, Mathewson was better off than most boys in rural areas. He was the third of five children of Gilbert Bailey Mathewson, a landowner and developer who isolated his family from the heavy anthracite coal industry that flourished in and around the not-too-distant city of Scranton, and Minerva J. Capwell.

Christy Mathewson, 1905. AP/WIDE WORLD PHOTOS

From the time he was four, Mathewson pleaded with his older brothers to be included in their games. With guidance from an older cousin, Mathewson became adept at making tossed stones change their trajectory by manipulating his grip on them. When he was about eight, he declared that one day he would be a major league pitcher—an unusual ambition in that, at the time, professional baseball was only about a decade old.

After completing grammar school, Mathewson entered nearby Keystone Academy in 1894, where he had a chance to do with a baseball what his cousin had taught him to do with stones. Mathewson could make a ball dart in several different directions by use of a different grip. His two most baffling pitches were his "fade away," or curve, and a "drop," which broke down from a batter as it approached home plate. In his mid-teens, "Husk," as he was also called, was offered a dollar a game to pitch for Mill City, a neighboring town, after the Factoryville team folded in mid-season.

In June 1898 Mathewson graduated from Keystone. On a trip to Scranton, he attended a game between a local YMCA team and the Pittston Reds. The start of the game was delayed, and Mathewson was told that the "Y" team's manager wanted to see him. Mathewson was asked to pitch. He related that the request hit him "like a bomb." "All I could manage to say was 'Yes.'" Mathewson pitched several games for Scranton, but his real "summer job" was throwing for the Honesdale Eagles in a town thirty miles away. He earned $25 a month, plus room and board at a local hotel. Mathewson won three straight games: his first, a 16–7 victory; his second, a rare—for the time—shutout; and his third, an even rarer no-hitter.

That fall, Mathewson used some of his pitching money toward tuition on enrolling at Bucknell University. Mathewson's family, staunch Baptists, approved of his matriculation at the small, church-related school. Having played football, basketball, and baseball at Keystone, Mathewson made the Bucknell varsity football team. He was a hard-charging fullback and accurate drop-kicker. He was also nearly fully matured, at six feet, one inch and 195 pounds. College football at that time was described as "eleven prize-fights going on at once." Nevertheless, the fair-minded Mathewson excelled.

In 1899 Bucknell University football coach George Hoskins offered a new raincoat to the first Bucknell player to score against the University of Pennsylvania, and a pair of shoes to the second player to score. Although Bucknell lost to Penn, 47–10, Mathewson's two five-point field goals allowed him to augment his collegiate wardrobe. In fact, at Bucknell, Mathewson's football skills actually overshadowed his pitching. A true student-athlete, he was also freshman class historian, a member of the band and glee club, cast in class plays, a member of the Latin and philosophy clubs, and a member of Phi Gamma Delta fraternity.

In 1899, during the summer after his freshman year, Mathewson returned to play again for Honesdale and met Dave Williams, a left-handed pitcher, who worked on a pitch he called his "freak ball." Williams never had the control to use the pitch in a game, but he showed Mathewson the grip and technique. The pitch broke toward a right-handed batter, a fine complement to Mathewson's curve that broke away from the hitter.

Before reporting to the Taunton, Massachusetts, team, which offered him better pay, Mathewson stopped off in Boston to see his first major league game, in which two of the prime pitchers of the day, future Hall of Famers Cy Young and Kid Nichols, opposed each other. It is doubtful that young Mathewson could have imagined that within two years he would occupy the same Boston pitcher's mound, throwing against Nichols.

In spite of Taunton's success in garnering a 5–2 record, its team members were seldom paid the promised wage of $90 a month, and the team disbanded by late summer. Mathewson had, however, impressed a manager of another New England League team, who signed him to play the 1900 season at Norfolk, Virginia. In the spring of that year, a nervous nineteen-year-old Mathewson took the mound in Norfolk. The pinpoint control that he would be famous for later had not yet developed. However, Mathewson settled down to win the first game and compiled a 20–2 record that included a no-hitter. This earned him a promotion to the New York Giants, where, not ready for the majors, Mathewson recorded an 0–3 mark and was returned to Norfolk. Mathewson played a final season of football for Bucknell—eligibility rules were not enforced or were nonexistent—and was elected class president before his early departure from the university to pursue baseball. He was also drafted by the Cincinnati Reds, but quickly dealt to the Giants again.

While the Giants were not the dynasty they would become under manager John McGraw, Mathewson did have a respectable first year as a fulltime pitcher, scoring 20–17. His religious convictions prevented him from pitching on Sundays, something he observed all during his storied career.

Mathewson was becoming the toast of New York. In the rough-and-tumble sport of professional baseball, Mathewson stood apart. He had attended college and projected a clean-cut "Christian gentleman" image, in marked contrast to that of most of his teammates and other major league players of his time. His outstanding character set him even further apart from the average players who were not held up as role models and some of whom were referred to as "rounders," the term of the day used to describe crude characters.

At about this time Mathewson picked up the nickname "Big Six." There are several versions of its origin. One has to do with his height—a six-footer was not a common sight in those days, when the average player was a half-foot shorter than Mathewson. Another credits the No. 6 Fire Company. A new, sleek fire-fighting apparatus was in use, and Mathewson as a pitcher could surely "put out the fire." So popular was "Matty," or "Big Six," that it was reported that a large "6" cut out of a newspaper headline by a Chicago man, who had affixed it with the proper postage to an envelope and deposited it in a mailbox, had been delivered directly to Mathewson.

In 1902 Mathewson had a 14–17 record for the last-place Giants, despite throwing eight shutouts. It would be his last sub-.500 season until 1915, his last full year as a pitcher. Mathewson followed the advice of an early manager, George Davis, and pitched economically. He seldom threw more than 100 pitches in a complete, nine-inning game, and once completed a game throwing only sixty-seven pitches. He got a raise to $3,000 and two new suits in 1903. In that year the Giants got a new manager, John "Muggsy" McGraw, a hard-bitten, rough-edged man. As Norman Macht wrote, "Most baseball men thought Matty and McGraw would go together like ketchup and corn flakes." But the two divergent personalities meshed, and Mathewson flourished. From 1903 to 1905, Mathewson had a record of 94–33, winning at least thirty games each year. On 4 March 1903 Mathewson married Jane Stoughton; the couple had a son, John Christopher, known as Christy, Jr.

It was the 1905 World Series versus Connie Mack's seemingly invincible Philadelphia Athletics that sealed Mathewson's reputation. In a five-game series (the Giants won, 4–1) every game was a shutout. Mathewson authored three of them. Mathewson was a twenty-plus game-winner for the next nine seasons after his three-year run of thirty-win seasons. He truly dominated major league pitching in this period, peaking with thirty-seven victories in 1908. While Mathewson continued to set high standards personally, enabling the Giants to win numerous National League pennants, he would never again match the success he had in 1905. Mathewson suffered a shoulder injury in 1914 and was essentially finished as an effective pitcher.

In the middle of the 1916 season, Mathewson persuaded McGraw to let him join the Cincinnati Reds as its manager. The Reds finished in last place, but jumped to fourth in 1917, and third in 1918—Mathewson's last season before he joined the Army's Chemical Warfare Service at the advanced age of thirty-eight, as World War I was winding down. Captain Mathewson was assigned to a "gas and flame division." While training young doughboys near the Belgian border, Mathewson was exposed to chlorine gas, and later the residue of German mustard gas. When he then contracted tuberculosis, its cause was wrongly attributed to the "gassing," according to biographer Ray Robinson. Mathewson spent much of the next three years at a sanatorium in Saranac Lake, New York, being treated for tuberculosis. He won the battle, it seemed, and returned to New York for the 1922 World Series, in which his old Giants team defeated the Yankees. In December, he again returned to New York to kick off the annual Christmas Seal campaign to fight tuberculosis. He was held up as the "Saranac Miracle." Sadly, the miracle was not enduring. Mathewson was named president of the Boston Braves in 1925, becoming one of the few to rise from player to team executive, but he succumbed to tuberculosis in the fall of that year. He was buried with full military honors in the Lewisburg Cemetery in Lewisburg, Pennsylvania. In 1936, when the Baseball Hall of Fame was conceived, Mathewson was one of five members of the charter class, and he continues to be regarded by some as the best righthander to have ever played the game.

So revered was Matty by organized baseball that funds were raised for the construction and dedication in 1927 of the Christy Mathewson Memorial Gateway on the Bucknell University campus, which stands as an entrance to the Bison athletic fields. The top award given to a graduating Bucknell senior student-athlete, the Christy Mathewson Award, was established in the 1960s. In 1989 a renovated Memorial Stadium at Bucknell (a football and track and field facility) was rededicated as the Christy Mathewson Memorial Stadium, in a tribute to Mathewson's former prowess on the gridiron.

Through a combination of his outstanding record—(378–188); an earned run average of 2.13; 2,502 strikeouts; and 80 shutouts—and his gentlemanly example, Mathewson did as much as anyone to move baseball from a sport of ruffians and toughs to America's national pastime.

★

With John N. Wheeler, Mathewson wrote *Pitching in a Pinch* (1912), which was well received. Ray Robinson's full-length biography is *Matty: An American Hero* (1993). Mathewson's life and career are discussed in Donald Honig, *Baseball America* (1985); Milton Shapiro, *Baseball's Greatest Pitchers* (1969); Gene Schoor, *Christy Mathewson, Baseball's Greatest Pitcher* (1953); and John J. McGraw, *My Thirty Years in Baseball* (1923). Since 1985, Actor Eddie Frierson has performed *Matty, An Evening with Christy Mathewson*, a one-man show in which he assumes the persona of Mathewson.

JIM CAMPBELL

MATHIAS, Robert Bruce ("Bob") (*b.* 17 November 1930 in Tulare, California), track and field athlete who was the first to win two Olympic gold medals in the decathlon and, at the turn of the century, remained history's youngest male Olympic track and field champion.

Mathias was the second of four children of Charlie Milfred Mathias, a physician, and Lillian Harris Mathias, a homemaker. He was born a few months after the family relocated from Oklahoma to Tulare, a small town in California's farming-rich San Joaquin Valley. His father had been a tackle at the University of Oklahoma in the 1920s, and all of the Mathias children exhibited athletic prowess. Mathias suffered from anemia in early childhood, so his father prescribed large doses of iron pills and built a minitrack in the family backyard, complete with jumping pits and throwing circles. By the time Mathias was twelve years old he was able to high-jump five feet, six inches. "We knew we had an athlete on our hands," remarked his mother.

At Tulare Union High School, Mathias starred at basketball (averaging eighteen points per game his senior year), football (as a running back), and track and field (as a hurdler, sprinter, and thrower). On Mathias's seventeenth birthday, the track coach Virgil Jackson suggested that he begin working on additional events like the javelin and pole vault. After Mathias's senior track season (1948), Jackson

Bob Mathias. AP/WIDE WORLD PHOTOS

suggested that his versatile star try the decathlon. Neither knew all ten decathlon events. "Work hard at it, and I bet you make the Olympic team . . . in 1952," Jackson said. The two-day, ten-event decathlon is designed to determine track and field's most versatile athlete; its champion is universally known as the world's greatest all-around athlete. Each athlete must compete in the 100-meter sprint, long jump, shot put, high jump, and 400-meter race on day one. On the following day the athlete contests the 110-meter hurdles (42-inch barriers), discus, pole vault, javelin, and 1,500-meter race.

Surprisingly the six-foot, two-inch, 190-pound Mathias won the Southern Pacific Amateur Athletic Union (AAU) decathlon in early June 1948, qualifying him for the Olympic trials in Bloomfield, New Jersey. His high school and the local Elks club raised funds to send him to the trials, where he again won, sending him to the Olympic Games in London, England. Three months shy of his eighteenth birthday, the unflappable Mathias, under cold and rainy conditions, totaled 7,139 points (under the 1934 International Association of Athletics Federations [IAAF] tables) to become the youngest male ever to win an Olympic track and field gold medal. He was awarded the 1948 Sullivan Award as the nation's top amateur athlete. When asked what he would do for an encore, Mathias reportedly replied, "I'll start shaving, I guess."

That autumn Mathias enrolled at the Kiski(minetas) School, a preparatory school in Saltsburg, Pennsylvania, to enhance his grades; in autumn 1949 he enrolled at Stanford University in California, where he pursued both football and track. Mathias dispelled any notion that his London performance was an aberration by annexing the 1949 and 1950 national AAU decathlon titles—the latter in front of hometown fans, with a world-record score of 8,042 points. On the gridiron his ninety-six-yard kickoff return for a touchdown led Stanford to a 1951 win over the University of Southern California and into the 1952 Rose Bowl. At age twenty-one, now six feet, three inches tall and 204 pounds, he went back to Tulare in July 1952 and rewarded an enthusiastic home crowd by winning the combined AAU nationals/Olympic trials with a second world decathlon record. So vast was his improvement that he posted new lifetime bests in eight of the ten events.

Twenty-four days later at the Helsinki Olympics in Finland, Mathias overcame a leg injury to record his second Olympic victory and his third world record (7,887 points on a new set of IAAF scoring tables). He became the first athlete to play in the Rose Bowl and win an Olympic gold medal in the same year. He then retired from the decathlon undefeated, a four-time national champion, three-time world record holder, and two-time Olympic champion, all by age twenty-one.

Mathias graduated from Stanford with a B.A. in education in June 1953, and enlisted in the U.S. Marine Corps. In 1954, when Allied Artists decided to produce a movie about his life, they cast about for someone to portray him. The studio searched for someone bright, with matinee-idol good looks, who was also a good athlete—they selected Mathias himself, and the role cost him his amateur standing. During his two-and-a-half-year stint in the marines he served as a goodwill ambassador to numerous Third World nations. On one U.S. State Department tour of the Far East, Mathias presented a javelin to an unheralded Formosan teenager named C. K. Yang, who went on to break the decathlon world record in 1963. After three seasons without competition or training, Mathias won the 1956 interservice decathlon, scoring 7,193 points (without running the 1,500 meters) and illustrating that he would have been a contender, had he been allowed, for the 1956 Olympic title.

Mathias married Melba Wiser in June 1953; they had four children. He subsequently had a movie and television career and established the successful Bob Mathias Sierra Boys Camp. He then served four terms (1967–1975) in the U.S. House of Representatives for California's Eighteenth Congressional District. A Republican, he lost his seat in the Democratic sweep of the post-Watergate era. President Gerald R. Ford, who was the Republican leader of the House of Representatives in 1966 when Mathias came to Washington, D.C., said of him, "You were initially attracted by his name, his presence, and appearance, but once you got to know him, it was his sound judgment that was very impressive." Many of Mathias's final-term legislative efforts focused on solving the amateur sports dispute between the AAU and the National Collegiate Athletic Association (NCAA). His efforts resulted in the Amateur Sports Act of 1978, passed after he left Washington. From 1977 to 1983 Mathias served as the director of the U.S. Olympic Training Center in Colorado Springs, Colorado, and subsequently as the executive director of the National Fitness Foundation. Mathias and Wiser divorced in 1977; he married Gwen Haven on 31 December 1977.

Mathias's place in sporting history would have been secure had he done nothing but win the 1948 Olympic decathlon. Of that experience Paul Helms of the Helms Athletic Foundation said it best: "We sent a boy over to do a man's job, and he did it far better than any man ever could." During Mathias's decathlon career he was acknowledged as the world's greatest all-around athlete. He was honored by a dozen halls of fame, including the U.S. Olympic Hall of Fame and the U.S. National Track and Field Hall of Fame. A half-century after his Olympic triumphs, his name remained one of the most recognizable in sport.

★

Mathias's candid memoir, *A Twentieth-Century Odyssey: The Bob Mathias Story* (2001), was written with Bob Mendes. Mathias's decathlon career is chronicled in two books by Frank Zarnowski, *The Decathlon: A Colorful History of Track and Field's Most Challenging Event* (1989), and *American Decathletes: A Twentieth-Century Who's Who* (2001). Chris Terrence, *Bob Mathias: Across the Fields of Gold* (2000), offers numerous family photos and quotes from peers. Dwight Chapin, "Before There Was Dan and Dave There Was Bob," *Los Angeles Times* (5 July 1992), is a clever newspaper piece. The film *The Bob Mathias Story* (1954), produced by Allied Artists and starring Mathias, emphasizes his Olympic success and ends with his enlistment into the U.S. Marine Corps.

FRANK ZARNOWSKI

MATSON, James Randel ("Randy") (*b.* 5 March 1945 in Kilgore, Texas), phenomenal track-and-field athlete who won Olympic medals in the shot put, including a gold medal in 1968, set many shot and discus records, and was first to throw the sixteen-pound shot over seventy feet.

Matson was the second of three children born to Charles Wesley Matson, an oil company employee, and Ellen Erezeal Cole, a homemaker. In September 1945 the family moved from Kilgore to Borger, Texas, then in 1951 to West Browning Street in Pampa, Texas. With his parents' support, Pampa was the base from which Matson's athletic career was lofted.

Randy Matson, 1966. ASSOCIATED PRESS AP

Matson's first sporting love was baseball, and he spent many childhood summers playing and dreaming about the game. Matson's father led Little League practice sessions, and Matson was encouraged at Pampa's Sam Houston Grade School by teacher Beverley Ross. However, in Pony League baseball, nearsightedness interfered with Matson's judgment of the ball, so he became active and successful in junior high football, basketball, and track. When knee problems prevented his participation in football, coaches made Matson team manager assistant to keep him involved in sports. This was somewhat of a turning point, because one of his duties was tossing the shot put back to athletes practicing the event, a boring activity Matson found increasingly easy. He joined junior high track and won several shot and discus awards, which his mother kept in a dresser-top box. Eventually, Dwaine Lyon, the Pampa High School football and track coach, noticed Matson's potential and coached him extra hours to develop it.

In high school, foot injuries temporarily interfered with some athletic pursuits, but Matson eventually excelled in football, basketball, and track. Starting in his junior year, he set new shot and discus records in nineteen consecutive high school track meets. In April 1962 he officially surpassed 60 feet when he tossed the 12-pound shot 60 feet, 10 inches, to take first place in a meet. The dresser-top box continued to fill. As a junior Matson experimented with the 16-pound college shot—a rusty one Coach Lyon gave him but which Matson cleaned and continued to use during college—and threw it 55 feet. Given that the Southwest Conference record was 57 feet, Lyon told him, "You could make the Olympic team one day."

Although he never forgot this remark, Matson's greatest source of motivation was his desire to throw the shot farther than anyone ever had to set a world record. He was state shot and discus champion in his junior and senior years. As a senior he was All-District defensive end in football and All-State in basketball. For two years he was All-State and All-America in track and continued to set shot and discus records. Not long after his high school graduation in 1963, Matson threw the 16-pound shot 60 feet, 6 inches, becoming the first Texan to surpass 60 feet. He was named Texas High School Athlete of the Year in 1963.

Even before graduation, about 200 colleges recruited Matson. He enrolled in Texas A&M University in College Station, Texas, in the fall of 1963. One reason that he chose Texas A&M was trainer Emil Mamaliga's weight-training program and the philosophy behind it: "You can't fire a 16-inch shell from a PT boat. You have to have a big, heavy ship." When he entered Texas A&M, Matson weighed 215 pounds and stood nearly six feet, seven inches, but under Mamaliga he reached 267 pounds and attained longer shot and discus throws. On 30 July 1966 Matson married Margaret Louise Burns, whom he had met in grade school. They had three children. Matson graduated from Texas A&M in 1967 with a bachelor's degree in marketing.

Matson's athletic achievements and awards during and after college packed a 16-pound wallop. In 1964 he won the shot put silver medal at the Tokyo Olympics with a throw of 66 feet, 3.5 inches. After his gold-medal throw of 66 feet, 8.5 inches, Dallas Long—Matson's idol—said of Matson, "This guy was fantastic out there today. Two more years and he'll be throwing the thing out of sight. He has everything—strength, timing, poise, and a great competitive spirit. I'm glad I got my gold medal this time because it's going to be his to win four years from now."

Matson was the Amateur Athletic Union (AAU) national shot-put champion in 1964, 1966, 1967, 1968, 1970, and 1972. In 1965 he broke the shot world record three times. On 8 May 1965, at Texas A&M, Matson became the first person to throw the shot over 70 feet, with a toss of 70 feet, 7 inches. In 1965, 1966, and 1967 he was Southwest Conference shot and discus champion. He was National Collegiate Athletic Association (NCAA) shot and discus champion in 1966 and 1967. Matson's best discus performance was 213 feet, 9 inches, on 8 April 1967. Fourteen days later, again at Texas A&M and on Randy Matson Day, he lofted the shot 71 feet, 5.5 inches for his best shot performance. Both performances were NCAA and U.S. records. Later that year Matson won the AAU's Sullivan Award as best amateur athlete.

At the 1968 Mexico City Olympics, as Long had predicted, Matson won the gold medal with a throw of 67 feet, 4.5 inches, a new Olympic record; he had wanted to avoid the stigma of holding the world record but never having won Olympic gold. Only later in life did he fully appreciate this medal as an achievement—unlike records—that he would keep forever. In 1970 Matson was *Track and Field News* Athlete of the World. He has been inducted into several sports halls of fame, including the Texas A&M Hall of Fame (1972), the United States National Track and Field Hall of Fame (1984), and the National High School Sports Hall of Fame (1988). During his athletic career Matson was drafted by professional football and basketball teams, but chose to remain in track and field, retiring in 1972.

Upon his retirement Matson began working at Texas A&M's Association of Former Students and served as its executive director from 1980 until the end of 1999. He has been active in several civic and charitable affairs, including the Bryan/College Station Chamber of Commerce and the Brazos Valley Rehabilitation Center. He has also been a member of the Texas A&M Church of Christ since 1972 and has lived in the same home near the Texas A&M campus since 1974.

The old saying that everything is bigger in Texas fits Matson's physical size, character, competitive drive, and lasting reputation. Although momentous, there is more to Matson's legacy than the first seventy-foot shot put. Before Matson, most athletes who put the shot did so because they were inadequate at other sports. Matson, on the other hand, was a great all-around athlete who chose the shot over other sports. He was an intense, yet modest competitor, who always tried to throw as far as he could and enjoyed solitary training. He converted competition's pressures into long, frequently record-setting throws. He felt blessed when fans honored him or made personal sacrifices to see him compete and expressed his appreciation with spectacular performances. On one occasion in 1967, in a Swedish village above the Arctic Circle, all 1,500 inhabitants withstood the weather to see Matson put the shot. There were no bleachers, and they had to clear snow from around the shot-put ring. Matson's put was 68 feet, his longest ever in Europe. Because of his popularity, he continued to receive autograph requests from youngsters in Europe and the United States for over thirty years and was a great role model for young people. Although he threw the shot over seventy feet for brief moments on particular days, his reputation has traveled worldwide for decades.

★

Carlton Stowers describes Matson's life in *The Randy Matson Story: The Life and Athletic Career of History's Greatest Shot-Putter* (1971). This biography contains several black-and-white photographs of Matson and many of his shot-put statistics. Additional statistics can be found in *Encyclopaedia of Athletics* (1977), compiled by Mel Watman. An article about Matson is P. Putnam, "No Practice Makes Almost Perfect," *Sports Illustrated* (8 Feb. 1971).

GARY MASON CHURCH

MATSON, Oliver Genoa, II ("Ollie") (*b.* 1 May 1930 in Trinity, Texas), Olympic medalist in track and field and one of the greatest running backs in football history who was traded by the Chicago Cardinals to the Los Angeles Rams in 1959 for nine players, and who was inducted into the Pro Football Hall of Fame and the National Football Foundation College Football Hall of Fame.

Matson is the son of Oliver Matson, a railroad brakeman, and Gertrude Matson, a school teacher. Matson's parents separated and divorced when he was very young. He and his twin sister moved with their mother from Trinity to Houston, Texas, when Matson was in junior high school. After two years in Houston, Matson's mother married again, and the family moved to San Francisco, California.

Ollie Matson, 1954. AP/Wide World Photos

Matson became interested in sports through an uncle who played semiprofessional football. At George Washington High School in San Francisco, Matson demonstrated great speed and potential as an end and halfback despite suffering a broken ankle early in his first season in 1945. His high school football coach suggested he participate in track to stay in condition for football. Initially indifferent, Matson became obsessed with the sport and developed into a nationally recognized scholastic sprinter and quarter-miler. He set a scholastic record for the quarter mile in 1948 and barely failed to qualify for the U.S. Olympic team that year. He also starred in football as an all-city running back, scoring 102 points in 7 games in 1947 to set a city record.

In 1948, after graduating from George Washington, Matson attended San Francisco City College, where he scored nineteen touchdowns for an undefeated team, setting a national junior college record, and was named All-America Junior College halfback. Disdaining many scholarship offers from much larger schools, he entered the University of San Francisco, a Jesuit institution that, he later said, had made him feel at home. In 1951 Matson led the nation in rushing with 1,566 yards in 245 attempts, and averaged 6.39 yards per attempt and 174 yards per game. The team, which finished with a 9–0 record, included eight players who later played professional football, three of whom were chosen for the professional Hall of Fame. Matson led the nation in scoring with 126 points and received All-American recognition as a defensive back. In the team's lone eastern appearance on 20 October 1951 against Fordham University, Matson returned two kickoffs for touchdowns (94 and 90 yards) and scored a third touchdown. Totaling 302 yards in a 32–26 victory, he made a powerful impression on such influential sportswriters as Grantland Rice.

Matson was drafted in the first round of the 1952 National Football League (NFL) draft by the downtrodden Chicago Cardinals, but before he began his professional football career, his old passion for track reemerged. After several years of not competing seriously, Matson began to train for the 1952 U.S. Olympic team. Defying the predictions of the track team coach Dink Templeton that he would never make the squad, Matson qualified at the Olympic trials. He won a bronze medal in the 400-meter run and a silver medal in the 1,600-meter relay at the Helsinki Olympics. After the Olympics, Matson participated in the College All-Star Game, then reported to the Cardinals training camp. In his second regular season game he scored twice, including a 100-yard kick return, in a victory against the Chicago Bears. Despite a broken wrist, he starred as a defensive back, running back, pass receiver, and kick returner. At six feet, two inches and 210 pounds, Matson was the fastest running back of his time, a rare combination of size, speed, power, and elusiveness. He was the one bright spot on generally losing Cardinal teams in 1952 and from 1954 through 1958. In 1956, playing on a contending team, Matson had his best season for the Cardinals, rushing for 924 yards and scoring 8 touchdowns, including a 105-yard kick return. Matson served in the U.S. Army in 1953 and part of 1954, playing service football at Fort Ord, California. Matson had met Mary L. Paige at a Baptist Church social in San Francisco when he was fifteen. They married on 22 August 1954 and had five children.

Matson was an all-pro selection four times and played in five Pro Bowl games, winning the Most Valuable Player award in the 1956 game. Despite his individual brilliance, his inability to turn the Cardinals into a contender prompted the team to trade him to the Los Angeles Rams on 28 February 1959 for nine players, including four starting linemen. Many believed the trade would make the Rams a championship team, but despite another strong season from Matson in 1959, the team finished last in the Western Division. In his four years with the Rams, Matson never found his niche and was shifted from halfback to fullback, to tight end, to slotback, and to defensive back. On 21 August 1963 he was traded to the Detroit Lions, and he finished his career with the Philadelphia Eagles from 1964 to 1966. In a fourteen-year career Matson gained 12,884 combined yards and scored 73 touchdowns. He was particularly dangerous returning kickoffs and punts with nine return touchdowns, including two kick return touchdowns in both 1952 and 1958. In 1972, his first year of eligibility, he was elected to the Pro Football Hall of Fame.

In 1976 he was elected to the National Football Foundation College Football Hall of Fame.

When his playing career ended, Matson scouted for the Eagles from 1966 to 1968, and he later taught and coached in the Los Angeles, California, school system. Starting in 1971 he was for a time head football coach at Los Angeles High School. Later he served as the backfield coach at San Diego State University. In January 1989 Matson retired after ten years as event supervisor for the Los Angeles Coliseum.

A quietly confident family man who eschewed controversy, worked hard to remain in condition throughout his career, and was one of the most durable players of his time, Matson was a world-class athlete in both track and field and football. His football accomplishments are particularly notable as he played on only two winning teams in his professional football career. An all-NFL selection on both defense and offense, he was arguably the most versatile player of his time and one of the finest players of all time. In his prime he was among the most highly paid players in professional football. He often drew the attention of multiple defenders and special defenses, which created opportunities for his teammates. At the time of his retirement his total yardage numbers were second only to Jim Brown's. As a man of color, Matson encountered prejudice throughout his career, perhaps most notably when the integrated and undefeated University of San Francisco team of 1951 was bypassed as a bowl selection for a team with no black players that San Francisco had defeated. Hailed as a messiah who would lead the Cardinals from mediocrity to respectability, Matson never quite accomplished that objective. With the disappointing Rams, he became the scapegoat after four losing seasons. In the final stages of his career, his statistical achievements were less substantial than during the 1950s. Yet he remained a valuable and reliable performer and a steadying force for every team he joined.

★

Matson is profiled in Jack Drees and James C. Mullen, *Where Is He Now?* (1973). An informative biographical sketch by John E. Evers is in *The Biographical Dictionary of American Sports: Football,* edited by David L. Porter (1987). His exploits are recounted in several league and team histories, including Steve Bischoff, *The Los Angeles Rams* (1973); Joseph Hession, *Rams: Five Decades of Football* (1987); and Mike Rathet and Don R. Smith, *Their Deeds and Dogged Faith* (1987). His professional statistics are in David S. Neft, Roland T. Johnson, Richard M. Cohen, and Jordan Deutsch, *The Sports Encyclopedia: Football* (1976); and Bob Carroll, Michael Gershman, David S. Neft, and John Thorn, *Total Football: The Official Encyclopedia of the National Football League* (1999). Of the countless magazine articles that cover Matson at various stages of his career, the most informative are A. S. "Doc" Young, "Speed Is Matson's Trademark," *Sport* (Jan. 1953); Tex Maule, "Run for the Money," *Sports Illustrated* (7 Oct. 1957); Bill Furlong, "Is Ollie Matson Worth It?" *Sport* (Oct. 1959); and Larry L. King, "They Couldn't Cut Old Ollie, Could They?" *Saturday Evening Post* (22 Oct. 1966). A nostalgic overview of the undefeated University of San Francisco team of 1951 is Ron Fimrite, "Yesterday: Best Team You Never Heard Of," *Sports Illustrated* (12 Nov. 1990).

EDWARD J. TASSINARI

MAYNARD, Don(ald) Rogers (*b.* 25 January 1935 in Crosbyton, Texas), receiver for the New York Jets from 1963 to 1972.

Born in West Texas to a cotton-gin manager, Maynard's family moved thirteen times, and Maynard had little chance to make friends. He attended five high schools in Texas and New Mexico, and it was not until his junior year at Colorado High School in Colorado City, Texas, that he finally joined the football team as a halfback. At a small college called Rice and Texas Western (now the University of Texas El Paso), Maynard excelled as a hurdler on the track team and played safety and running back on the foot-

Don Maynard, 1968. ASSOCIATED PRESS

ball team. In 1957, while still a junior, he was drafted in the ninth round as a future player for the New York Giants of the National Football League (NFL).

Maynard made quite an impression in 1958 when he arrived at Yankee Stadium (where the Giants played from 1956 through 1973) wearing a cowboy hat, boots, and long sideburns, a style of dress that struck many as odd since most players at the time sported crew cuts. He printed the number 13 on his boots and asked for a uniform with the same number. When asked years later what might have happened if management had refused his request, Maynard speculated that he would have played for another team. While some perceived the six-foot, one-inch, 173-pound player to be contentious, friends found Maynard easygoing, noting that even during the most trying times he seldom lost his temper.

During Maynard's first season with the Giants, he returned punts and kickoffs and substituted for star running backs. A fumble during a crucial game, however, left Maynard with the stigma of having "bad hands," and he was cut from the team. He played a year with the Hamilton Tiger-Cats in the Canadian Football League before being offered the first position on a new American Football League (AFL) team, the New York Titans, in 1960.

Titans coach Sammy Baugh decided to try Maynard out as a receiver, and he never regretted it. Maynard developed a reputation for ignoring pre-arranged pass patterns, but while this may have frustrated management, his ability to outrun the defense made him a valuable receiver. During the 1960 season he caught 72 passes (most of them from quarterback Al Dorow) for 1,265 yards and 6 touchdowns. In 1963 Sonny Werblin and several associates bought the New York Giants franchise for $1 million and renamed the team the Jets. After the team drafted a young quarterback from Alabama named Joe Namath in 1965, Maynard's career really took off. In 1965 he caught 68 passes for 1,218 yards; in 1967 he completed 71 passes for a career high of 1,434 yards.

The Jets had their greatest season in 1968. An 11–3 record matched them against Oakland for the American Football Conference title, a game Maynard would later call the most memorable of his life. On the day of the game, the cold wind created poor conditions for passing. Namath persevered nonetheless, throwing a touchdown pass to Maynard in the first four minutes of the game. The Jets led at halftime, but Oakland pulled ahead in the third quarter, threatening to defeat New York as they had earlier that season in the "Heidi" game, when television viewers missed the last few minutes of the game because the network, thinking the game was over, switched to the children's movie. In the fourth quarter the Jets made their move—Namath completed a fifty-two-yard pass to Maynard, placing the team within scoring distance. Several plays later a six-yard pass hit Maynard in the end zone, giving New York the victory.

Although the Jets victory against Oakland allowed them to play Baltimore in Super Bowl III, most sportswriters expected them to lose. But on 12 January 1969 everything went well for the Jets. Namath completed 17 passes for 206 yards, Jim Turner kicked 3 field goals, and the defense intercepted 3 of Oakland quarterback Earl Morrall's passes. The victory proved to be one of the biggest upsets in NFL history. "We didn't think it was an upset," Maynard told the Associated Press. "We thought we were going to win all along."

During his years with the Jets, Maynard gained a reputation for outlandish behavior. He drove a butane-powered Ford coupe that teammates nicknamed the "El Paso Flame Thrower." Once, several teammates bet Maynard $75 that he would not jump into an icy hotel swimming pool fully clothed. He jumped, reasoning that it would cost only a few dollars to have his suit cleaned. Maynard was also known for trying to make extra money on the side, as when he was hired to promote a solvent called Swipe. To prove that it was safe, Maynard drank a glass of it before a Lions Club meeting. The solvent caused no serious injury, but he complained that the liquid drew so much moisture out of his mouth that he had to keep a bucket of ice beside him during practice the next day.

In 1972, during the thirteenth game of his thirteenth season, Maynard caught his 632nd pass, breaking Baltimore Colts receiver Raymond Berry's career record. "[A]s I lay on the ground with the ball," he said to Gwilym S. Brown of *Sports Illustrated,* "it sort of jumped into my head about how many things had had to go right . . . to make . . . one catch possible." This triumph was somewhat tempered by Maynard's dwindling yards per season since 1970.

In 1973 the Jets coach Weeb Ewbank asked Maynard to retire, but the receiver refused, he believed he still had a couple of good years left. The Jets traded Maynard to the St. Louis Cardinals, where he played only three games before being released to the Los Angeles Rams, where he spent the remainder of the season on the bench. Maynard considered playing for the New York Stars of the World Football League but instead decided to hang up his cleats in 1973.

During Maynard's 13 years as a receiver, he caught 633 passes for a total of 11,834 yards. He caught 50 or more passes for 1,000 yards or better in 5 seasons and was the first receiver to exceed the 10,000- and then the 11,000-yard mark. He played in three AFL All-Star games and one Super Bowl, and was added to the All-Time AFL team in 1969. In 1987 Maynard was elected into the Pro Football Hall of Fame. Since retirement he has worked as an independent business consultant.

★

A brief overview of Maynard's career can be found in David L. Porter, ed., *Biographical Dictionary of American Sports: Football* (1987). Maynard's career is also covered in Howard Coan, *Great Pass Catchers in Pro Football* (1971), and John Devaney, *Star Pass Receivers of the NFL* (1972). A lengthy portrait is in Gwilym S. Brown, "Oh How Gently Flows This Don," *Sports Illustrated* (23 Jul. 1973).

RONNIE D. LANKFORD, JR.

MAYS, Willie Howard (*b.* 6 May 1931 in Westfield, Alabama), baseball player generally regarded as one of the most exciting athletes of the twentieth century and one of the best all-around players in baseball history.

Mays was the only child of William Howard Mays, a steel mill worker and railway porter who may once have played for the Birmingham, Alabama, Black Barons of the Negro National League, and Ann Sattlewhite, a high school track and field athlete. His parents divorced soon after his birth, and his mother remarried. She and her second husband had ten children; Mays has two half brothers and eight half sisters. Mays continued to live with his father, who, aided by a young woman called Aunt Sarah, raised Mays and taught him the fundamentals of baseball. By age ten, Mays was playing in sandlot games with boys several years older. He entered Fairfield Industrial High School in 1946, where he excelled in football and basketball and trained to work in a laundry. The school had no baseball team, so Mays pitched and played the outfield for his father's mill team and a local semiprofessional team, earning about $100 a month.

Willie Mays. TRANSCENDENTAL GRAPHICS

Mays's father arranged a tryout with the Black Barons in 1948, and the team manager, Lorenzo "Piper" Davis, signed the seventeen-year-old to play during his summer vacation with the proviso that he complete high school. Mays broke in by starting the second game of a doubleheader, much to the dismay of his older teammates, and got two hits against a veteran pitcher. He moved into the starting lineup after the regular centerfielder broke his leg and, over the course of three seasons, profited from Davis's careful instruction to become a promising young player. After Mays graduated from high school on 20 June 1950, the New York Giants paid the Barons $10,000 for the right to sign him to a contract. Still underage, Mays needed his father's consent to accept a signing bonus of $5,000 and a salary of $250 a month.

The Giants assigned Mays to their Trenton, New Jersey, club in the Class B Interstate League, where he batted .353 in eighty-one games and led the league's outfielders in assists. Advanced to the Giants top farm club, the Minneapolis Millers in the American Association, in 1951, Mays hit an astounding .477 before being promoted to the parent club after just thirty-five games. Manager Leo Durocher inserted him into the lineup on 25 May, but Mays had no hits in his first twelve times at bat. After getting his first major league hit, a home run off Warren Spahn, he went hitless again in thirteen at bats and began to doubt the level of his skills. Durocher, a belligerent, profane man, nevertheless consoled his insecure rookie, reassuring him that he was in the major leagues to stay. Mays responded by batting .274 for the year with twenty home runs. Both the Baseball Writers' Association of America and *The Sporting News* named Mays National League (NL) Rookie of the Year. When Giant Bobby Thomson hit his legendary home run, the "Shot Heard Round the World," in the decisive playoff game that deprived the favored Brooklyn Dodgers of the NL pennant, Mays waited in the on-deck circle, a threat all the same.

Mays was served with a draft notice immediately after the 1951 World Series, which the Giants lost to the New York Yankees, and played only thirty-four games in 1952 before being inducted into the U.S. Army. He spent the bulk of the two years at Fort Eustis, Virginia, playing ball until he was able to rejoin his team during spring training of 1954. That season, Mays came into his own as one of baseball's young stars. He led the league in batting with a .345 average, hit 41 home runs, drove in 110 runs, and won the NL's Most Valuable Player (MVP) award. The Giants won the pennant and upset the Cleveland Indians in the World Series. Mays hit only .286, but in game one he made what quickly became, and has remained, the most famous catch in baseball history. Cleveland's Vic Wertz hit a towering drive to deep centerfield. Mays turned his back to the plate and ran at full speed to the deepest recesses of the Polo Grounds. He glanced back over his left shoulder, and the ball settled into his glove, more than 450 feet from home plate. He wheeled and threw to second baseman Davey Williams, who relayed the ball home, preventing Larry Doby from scoring from second base. Mays later claimed that he made several better catches, and maybe he did, but this one, coming in a World Series, has been immortalized.

Over the next few seasons, Mays cemented his reputation as a superstar and a gifted "five-tool" player. He could hit, hit with power, run, throw, and field. Casual observers often described Mays as a natural athlete, but in truth he honed his craft with hard work and intense dedication. Moreover, in the competitive cauldron that was New York baseball in the post–World War II era, he more than held his own in the debate over who was the better centerfielder: Edwin "Duke" Snider of the Dodgers, Mickey Mantle of the Yankees, or Mays. All three were sluggers, but Mays and Mantle augmented their power with unusual speed, both in the field and on the base paths. Mantle hit several prodigious home runs, legendary for their length, but his achievements and career statistics were truncated by frequent injuries that caused him to retire prematurely. As a result, baseball historians have often placed Mays higher in the ranks of the game's all-time greats.

Mays endeared himself to fans by the flair with which he played and the childlike joy he seemed to exude. One of baseball's first African-American stars, he also was one of the first sluggers to possess exceptional speed and utilize it with abandon. He wore a cap too large for his head just so it would fly off as he rounded first base or dashed across the Giants' vast Polo Grounds outfield to snare fly balls. He played stickball with kids in the streets of Harlem and greeted people with a cheery "Say hey." Whereas most outfielders caught flies with their hands positioned above their shoulders, he perfected the basket catch, holding his hands below his waist and allowing the ball to drop into his glove. The celebrated entertainer and Giants fan Tallulah Bankhead captured his greatness this way: "There have been only two authentic geniuses in the world, Willie Mays and Willie Shakespeare."

Mays married Marghuerite Wendell Kennedy Chapman in February 1956. They adopted an infant boy, but were divorced after five years of marriage. In November 1971 Mays married Mae Allen. He continued to play with the Giants through their move to San Francisco after the 1957 season, was traded in May 1972 to the New York Mets, and retired after the 1973 World Series. He batted over .300 ten times, scored over 100 runs in 12 consecutive seasons, and drove in over 100 runs 10 times. He led the National League in stolen bases 4 times and home runs 4 times, including 51 in 1955 and 52 in 1965, when he was again named the league's MVP. In 1955 he became the first player to hit at least fifty homers and steal at least twenty bases in the same season. On 30 April 1960 he became the ninth player to hit four home runs in one game, and on 18 July 1970 he collected his 3,000th hit. He set league records for putouts and chances and won eleven straight Gold Glove awards, emblematic of fielding excellence. Mays played in four World Series and in every All-Star game between 1954 and 1973, often making this contest his personal showcase. The *Sporting News* named him Major League Player of the Decade for the 1960s.

Over a 22-year career, Mays batted .302, stole 338 bases, drove in 1,903 runs, and hit 660 home runs, third on the all-time list. He was elected nearly unanimously to the National Baseball Hall of Fame in 1979, his first year of eligibility. Just three months after his induction, though, Commissioner Bowie Kuhn forced Mays to end his association with baseball after he signed a contract to represent the Bally Manufacturing Corporation, a company with gambling interests. Kuhn's successor, Peter Ueberroth, lifted this ban in 1985. In 2000 Mays received three crowning honors. Major League Baseball chose him for its All-Century team, ESPN ranked him as the eighth best athlete of the century, and the *Sporting News* named him the second-best player of all time, behind only Babe Ruth.

Mays's decision to appear at autograph shows across the country, but not to interact with fans in a friendly manner, dimmed some of his luster in his retirement, but his status as a player remained secure. "Willie Mays's glove," Dodgers executive L. Fresco Thompson said once, is "the place where triples go to die," and sportswriter Walter "Red" Smith, who reported on New York baseball during the "Willie, Mickey, and the Duke" years, wrote, "You could get a fat lip in any saloon by starting an argument as to which was best. One point was beyond argument, though. Willie was by all odds the most exciting."

★

Mays worked with two sportswriters to produce three autobiographies: *Born to Play Ball,* as told to Charles Einstein (1955); *Willie Mays: My Life In and Out of Baseball,* as told to Charles Einstein (1966); and *Say Hey: The Autobiography of Willie Mays,* with Lou Sahadi (1988). Other fine portraits of Mays are included in Donald Honig, *Mays, Mantle, Snider* (1987); and Bob Broeg, "Willie Mays," in *Superstars of Baseball: Their Lives, Their Loves, Their Laughs, Their Laments* (1994).

STEVEN P. GIETSCHIER

MEOLA, Tony (*b.* 21 February 1969 in Belleville, New Jersey), professional soccer player who was the World Cup goaltender in 1990 and 1994 and the Major League Soccer Most Valuable Player (MVP) in 2000.

Meola's parents were Maria Meola, a homemaker, and Vincent Meola, a professional soccer player and barber. They came to the United States from Avellino, Italy, where Meola's father had played for a second division soccer club. Meola and his older brother grew up in Kearny, New Jersey, alongside immigrants from Italy, Scotland, Ireland, and other European countries. Soccer was the favorite sport in the area and as soon as Meola could stand up, he began kicking a soccer ball.

Meola's first coach did not consider him to be a good player. "He just stuck me in goal because he thought I was fat and couldn't run," Meola said. "None of the kids ever wanted to go in goal because they wouldn't get to run around. But I liked being the team's last defense." By the time Meola was a senior at Kearny High School, he had developed into an accomplished athlete. At six feet, one inch tall, and 205 pounds, he played both baseball and soccer. He played briefly in the New York Yankees minor league system in the early 1980s, but his prime ambition was to be a soccer player. In 1987 Meola got his first experience playing in a World Cup environment, when he starred for the United States in the U-20 Junior World Cup in Chile.

His success in high school earned him a soccer/baseball scholarship to the University of Virginia (UVA) in Charlottesville, and he entered the university in the fall of 1987. In 1989 he won the Missouri Athletic Club Player of the Year award for leading the UVA Cavaliers to their first National Collegiate Athletic Association (NCAA) soccer championship. In 1988 and 1989 he had 17 shutouts in 33 college games and allowed only 11 goals in 2,922 minutes. He was awarded the Hermann Trophy in 1988 and was named as a first-team All-American in both 1988 and 1989. In the same period he was also a two-year letter winner in baseball.

The offer of a spot on the 1990 World Cup team prompted Meola to drop out of UVA in his sophomore year. He started in four World Cup qualifying games, including a 1–0 victory in Trinidad and Tobago. The result was that the U.S. team qualified for their first World Cup selection in forty years. Meola played every minute of all three World Cup games in Italy. In the interim Meola played for two professional teams in England. He started with the Brighton Football Club, gaining the attention of the pop star Elton John, who owned a competing professional soccer

Tony Meola, 2000. ASSOCIATED PRESS AP

team. John bought his contract, and Meola began playing for the Watford team.

In the United States, Meola had practiced with Team USA since 1992 and had eighty-five caps in international competition. In 1993 he married Colleen Silvers, his high school sweetheart; the couple had two children. In the 1994 World Cup, Meola was again selected as the U.S. goalie. By then he had more than ninety-eight caps in international competition, more than any other goalie in U.S. history, and he was the logical choice to be honored as the team captain. The United States tied Switzerland in their first game, and then went on to a 2–1 victory over Colombia when Colombia's star player Andres Escobar accidentally kicked the ball into his own net. The United States advanced to the second round after beating Colombia, but lost in the quarterfinal to Brazil, the eventual world champions, 1–0 in the seventy-fourth minute of play. For an inexperienced team, the U.S. players made a respectable showing.

Off-season and off-Broadway, Meola costarred in the 1995 show *Tony 'n' Tina's Wedding* for eight weeks. He also played drums in the band Mushmouth. In 1996 Meola received the Thurman Munson Award for his efforts in helping children's charities. That same year he signed with Major League Soccer (MLS) and joined the New York / New Jersey MetroStars. He was named the MetroStars Bic Tough Defender of the Year and led the league with nine shutouts. He finished the season as *Soccer America*'s top-rated goalkeeper. By 1998 Meola was recognized as one of the top MLS goalkeepers and became a three-time MLS All-Star. He finished the 1998 season first in both minutes played (2,790) and goals saved (164).

In 1998 Meola moved to the Kansas City Wizards and became one of the most recognizable U.S. soccer players, acting as a spokesperson for such companies as Buick, Adidas, Champs Sport, and The Wiz. His formidable statistics as an MLS player from 1996 to 2001 included: four-time All-Star; first in all-time shutouts (37); leader in goalkeeper charts for minutes played (11,675), games played (130), saves (620), and catch/punches (431); tied for third all-time in wins (56) and fourth all-time in save percentage (.737); played the most consecutive minutes in MLS history (8,083); most saves in one game (15); and longest shutout streak (681 minutes). Because of his achievements, Meola has become one of the most recognizable faces in U.S. soccer history.

★

An authorized biography of Meola is Mark Stewart, *Tony Meola* (1996). For biographical profiles, see Meola's official website at http://www.tonymeola.com.

ROBERT POLLOCK

METCALFE, Ralph Horace (*b.* 30 May 1910 in Atlanta Georgia; *d.* 10 October 1978 in Chicago Illinois), sprinter who set or tied eight world records, won four Olympic medals, became the first African-American Illinois state athletic commissioner, and served as a congressional representative.

Metcalfe was one of three children born to Clarence Metcalfe, who worked in the stockyards, and Maria Attaway Metcalfe, a dressmaker. During World War I, while he was still in elementary school, Metcalfe's family moved from Atlanta to Chicago. He attended Tilden Technical High School, where he was advised by his coach to concentrate on track and forget football if he wanted to earn a college scholarship. His coach also told him that "as a black person he'd have to put daylight between himself and his nearest competitor if he expected to be declared the winner in a race."

As a result of hard training, Metcalfe emerged as a world-class sprinter in 1928. That year, as a high school junior, he placed second in the 100- and 220-yard dashes at the National Interscholastic Meet held at the University of Chicago. The following year he won both events in record times at the National Interscholastic Meet and the Uni-

Ralph Metcalfe *(right)* with Jesse Owens. AP/WIDE WORLD PHOTOS

versity of Michigan Interscholastic Meet. In August 1930, running for the Chase Park Athletic Club, he won the Amateur Athletic Union (AAU) junior championships in both sprint events and placed fourth in the national senior AAU 220-yard dash; the next year he placed second in the 220 at the senior championships. In 1932 he set a world record in the 100-yard dash at the National Collegiate Athletic Association (NCAA) championships, and won both dash events at the AAU championships.

Metcalfe paid his way to the 1932 Olympic trials by working in dining cars on the Santa Fe railroad. He secured a place on the team at the Los Angeles games, and managed to tie the world record in the 100-meter dash. Unfortunately, this was not fast enough to win the race, and he placed second to Eddie Tolan in a photo finish. He finished behind Tolan again in the 200-meter dash, but because his lane was mismeasured, he ran nearly 4 feet farther than his opponents and had to content himself with a bronze medal, even though he had probably earned the silver.

Metcalfe dominated sprinting for the next four years, until Jesse Owens emerged on the scene. In 1936 Metcalfe graduated from Marquette University in 1936 with a Ph.B., and again qualified for the U.S. Olympic team. At the Berlin Olympics that year he became the unofficial spokesperson for the African-American trackmen. He won a silver medal behind Jesse Owens in the 100-meter dash, and shared a team gold in the 4 x 100 relay. The Olympic games had a profound impact on Metcalfe's life, a sentiment also expressed by Jesse Owens, who noted, "Without athletics, neither one of us would have attained our positions in life."

After the Olympics, Metcalfe taught political science and coached track at Xavier University, a small African-American college in New Orleans, from 1936 to 1942. In 1939 he took a leave of absence from Xavier to earn an M.A. in physical education from the University of Southern California in 1940. He joined the U.S. Army in 1942, reaching the rank of first lieutenant. After the war he returned to Chicago where he became director of the civil rights department of the Chicago Commission on Human Rights (1945), a cause for which he maintained a lifelong commitment. In 1947 he married Madalynne Fay; they had one child.

From 1949 to 1952 Metcalfe served as the Illinois state athletic commissioner; he continued to pursue an active interest in track and field, sometimes officiating at the *Chicago Daily News* relays. He became the Democratic committee member for Chicago's Third Ward in 1952 and held that powerful position until 1972. He served as an alderman from 1955 to 1970, and in 1968 became the first African American to be elected president pro tempore of the Chicago City Council. He was elected to the U.S. House of Representatives in 1970, representing the First Congressional District, and remained a representative until his death in 1978. Although he was originally a political insider in the Richard Daley organization, he broke with Daley in 1972 over issues involving police brutality toward African Americans. In 1976 he aligned himself with Jesse Jackson and Renault Robinson, and won reelection to Congress despite Daley's opposition.

Metcalfe was a member of the Presidential Commission on Olympic Sports (1975), the National Association for the Advancement of Colored People (NAACP), the Urban League, the Corpus Christi Roman Catholic Church of Chicago, the Wisconsin Hall of Fame, and the National Track and Field Hall of Fame. He also sponsored the Ralph H. Metcalfe Youth Foundation, which provided athletic and educational programs for young people. Metcalfe, who had a long history of diabetes, emphysema, and high blood pressure, suffered his first heart attack in 1967. He died of a second heart attack eleven years later at age sixty-eight.

★

There is no formal biography of Metcalfe, but newspaper articles provide much information: *Chicago Tribune* (3 June 1928, 2 June 1929, 13 Oct. 1978); *Atlantic Daily World* (3 Apr. 1952); *Detroit Times* (12 May 1929, 5 July 1931); and the *Milwaukee Journal* (12 June 1932, 2 Aug. 1932). Metcalfe is discussed in *Spaulding's Official Athletic Almanac* (1931); Lewis H. Carlson and John J. Fogarty, eds., *Tales of Gold* (1987); and David Wallechinsky, *The Complete Book of the Olympics* (1996). An obituary is in the *New York Times* (11 Oct. 1978).

KEITH MCCLELLAN

MEYERS, Ann Elizabeth (*b.* 26 March 1955 in San Diego, California), pioneer in women's basketball, sports announcer, and the first female basketball player to sign a contract with a professional men's team.

Meyers was the sixth of eleven children born to Bob Meyers, an athlete, and Patricia Meyers, a homemaker, and the fourth member of her family to play organized basketball. Her father played for Marquette University in Wisconsin and for the Milwaukee Shooting Stars, and her older sister and brother played college basketball.

Although Meyers was originally most interested in track and field, she played basketball on the boys' team in the fifth and sixth grades. Because her junior high school did not have coed teams, she did not play organized basketball again until she entered high school where she played on the girls' team. She earned Most Valuable Player (MVP) honors in her freshman year at Sonora High in La Habra, California, in 1971. In her sophomore year she transferred

Ann Meyers. AP/WIDE WORLD PHOTOS

to Connelly High School in Anaheim, where she earned MVP again. As a junior she transferred back to Sonora, where she was the team captain and MVP for the third consecutive year. In 1974, during her senior year, girls became eligible to play on the boys' team. Meyers wanted desperately to try out but was discouraged from doing so by her family and friends—a decision she said she would regret for the rest of her life. In her senior year Meyers was selected to the U.S. National girls' team, the first high school player ever to be so honored.

Meyers's record-setting basketball career continued when she entered the University of California at Los Angeles (UCLA) in the fall of 1974. She was the first woman to receive a full basketball scholarship from UCLA, and UCLA's support of Meyers made an important and powerful statement. For a high-profile basketball program like that at UCLA to show enough confidence and respect to award a full scholarship to a woman made national news.

UCLA's confidence in Meyers was not misplaced. During her freshman year she led the Bruins in scoring, rebounds, and assists. Meyers made the All-America team in each of her four college years; she was the only freshman on the team in 1975. She led the Bruins to postseason tournaments each year, finally winning the national championship in 1978 as a senior. More than just an outstanding player, Meyers proved herself an inspirational leader as well. She set an example with a hard-work ethic that motivated her teammates.

At the end of her college career Meyers was the third leading all-time scorer at UCLA. The record was quite an accomplishment at a school whose men's team produced National Basketball Association (NBA) superstars and dominated college basketball through the 1960s and 1970s. In 1978 Meyers won the Broderick Cup, which honors the outstanding women's college basketball player of the year, and the National Association for Girls and Women in Sports recognized her as the Collegiate Woman Athlete of the Year. Her number 15 jersey was retired and placed in the Naismith Memorial Basketball Hall of Fame in 1978.

Meyers's college career also included international play. She won gold medals in the 1975 and 1979 Pan-American Games. As a member of the 1976 U.S. Olympic team, Meyers, joined by Nancy Lieberman-Cline and Patricia Summitt, won a silver medal. Meyers also competed in the 1977 World University Games, where her team placed second.

Her college basketball career over, Meyers remained at UCLA to finish her degree, graduating with a bachelor's degree in sociology in 1979. She also competed on the track team in the high jump and on the volleyball team. Then in 1979, Sam Nassi, owner of the NBA's Indiana Pacers, announced the team was signing Meyers to a free agent's contract. She is the only woman ever to try out for an NBA team. Many people criticized Meyers's signing as a publicity stunt, and the owner of the New York Knicks called the contract "disgraceful" and a "travesty."

Meyers had her share of supporters as well, including Pacer teammates Johnny Davis and Billy Knight, but despite the support she was released from her contract. Pacers coach Bob Leonard stated she had the skills but not the size (she was five feet, nine inches, and 135 pounds). According to Leonard, if she had been six inches taller and forty pounds heavier, "it would have been a different story." Meyers remained with the Pacers as a color analyst for their broadcasts.

With the formation of the Women's Basketball League (WBL) in 1978, Meyers became the top overall draft pick. She signed her second basketball contract with the New Jersey Gems in 1979. During her first year with the Gems she averaged 22.2 points per game and was voted co-MVP. In 1981 Meyers left the Gems over a contract dispute and enrolled in broadcasting school.

Meyers's broadcasting career took off during the 1984 Los Angeles Olympics and grew to include the American Broadcasting System (ABC), the Central Broadcasting System (CBS), the National Broadcasting System (NBC), and ESPN and ESPN2. The exposure she received in the Women's Superstars Competition, sponsored by *Ladies Home Journal* and *WomenSports* magazine, also furthered her career in television. This competition of well-known women athletes, which included softball throwing, cycling, rowing, swimming, and running events, aired on ABC during the early 1980s. Meyers won three years in a row until she was forced to retire from the competition.

In 1999 Meyers was a member of the inaugural class inducted into the new Women's Basketball Hall of Fame in Knoxville, Tennessee, rounding out her previous elections to the International Women's Sports Hall of Fame (1985), and the Naismith Memorial Basketball Hall of Fame (1993). Given her love for sport, it was no surprise that she married another Hall of Famer, Don Drysdale, a baseball player with the Los Angeles Dodgers and a fellow broadcaster. The couple married in November 1986, becoming the first husband-and-wife Hall of Famers. They had three children before Drysdale died suddenly of a heart attack in 1993.

Meyers's contribution to basketball and women's sports has proved long-lasting and significant. The exposure she brought to the game through college, international, and professional play greatly increased public awareness of women athletes. Her string of basketball firsts paved the way for countless young female players. Her success in the male-dominated world of sports broadcasting opened that door for other women as well.

★

A brief biography of Meyers is in J. Kelly, *Superstars of Women's Basketball* (1997). There is also an entry on Meyers in Janet Woolum, *Outstanding Women Athletes* (1998). A number of basketball websites include data about Meyers; one of the best is the Naismith Memorial Basketball Hall of Fame website at http://www.hoophall.com. Other sources that address Meyers's accomplishments as an athlete and a sportscaster include Mary Anne Hudson, "A Sporty Family; If Don Drysdale Jr. Takes After His Mom and Dad, He Figures To Be Natural in Basketball or Baseball," *Los Angeles Times* (25 Dec. 1988); and Donna Carter, "Q and A with Ann Meyers; Woman of Many Firsts Hopes Her Sports Endeavors Will Last," *Los Angeles Times* (20 Aug. 1989).

LISA A. ENNIS

MIKAN, George Lawrence, Jr. (*b.* 18 June 1924 in Joliet, Illinois), professional basketball player and executive considered to be the top player of the first half of the twentieth century.

Mikan was one of four children born to Joseph L. Mikan and Minnie (Blinstrup) Mikan, who owned a restaurant in Joliet. Mikan attended Joliet Catholic High School in 1936–1937, but then transferred to Quigley Prep in Chicago with the intention of becoming a priest. Mikan played center on the high school's basketball team but was a big, awkward teenager whose only real asset at the time was his height; he was six feet, six inches tall at age fourteen. He also wore glasses and was told that it was impossible for a basketball player with glasses to be successful at the game. He was a good student and considered attending the University of Notre Dame in Indiana, where he hoped to join the basketball team, but he played poorly during a tryout. Notre Dame's coach suggested that Mikan enroll at a smaller

George Mikan, 1952. © BETTMANN/CORBIS

school where he might get to play more and develop his game.

In 1941 Mikan, who was not a candidate for military service because he exceeded the height restrictions, enrolled at De Paul University in Chicago, making the eighty-mile round-trip commute from Joliet each day. Mikan did not play basketball as a freshman, but in 1942 he became the protégé of the newly appointed coach Ray Meyer, who led the De Paul squad to success during Mikan's four years on the team. Meyer was a demanding coach, keeping Mikan behind for extra practice each day. Meyer made Mikan jump rope daily and take dancing lessons to help with his footwork. Mikan worked diligently at all of this, with the characteristic endurance that he displayed throughout his professional life.

In the 1942–1943 season De Paul went 19–5, losing in the National Collegiate Athletic Association (NCAA) semifinals, but Mikan proved to be a fine player, averaging just over eleven points per game for the year. During the next three years, Mikan averaged 18.6, 23.3, and 23.1 points per game and was voted an All-American at center all three years. For the last two years, he led the nation's major colleges in scoring and was voted the Player of the Year in college basketball in 1946. De Paul went to the National Invitational Tournament (NIT) twice, winning it in 1945. At that time the NIT was considered as prestigious as the NCAA tournament and, for many schools, was more lucrative. De Paul was 81–17 in the "Mikan era." He completed his collegiate career with 1,868 points, an average of over nineteen per game, at a time when team scores were routinely in the forties. In the 1945 NIT, Mikan scored 120 points in three games, including 53 in the semifinals.

Shortly after the De Paul basketball season ended in February 1946, Mikan signed a contract with the Chicago American Gears of the National Basketball League (NBL) on 16 March 1946. He received $60,000 over five years as well as bonuses for baskets and free throws made. He also was allowed to pursue a law degree at De Paul during the off-season, a degree he eventually earned in 1957. He began to play almost immediately in two exhibition games that preceded the World Professional Tournament, which was held each year in Chicago. Led by Mikan, the Gears finished third in the tournament and their prospects were high for the next season. Unfortunately, a contract dispute limited Mikan to playing just twenty-five of Chicago's forty-four league games. Still, he was voted first team, all-league, averaging 16.5 points per game, which led the league. The Gears won the NBL play-offs, defeating Rochester, New York, in the finals.

In May 1947 Mikan married Patricia Lu Devaney. Also in 1947, the Gears owner Maurice White decided to form his own league, the Professional Basketball League of America (PBL), with sixteen teams. The league folded in less than one month and so did the Gears. The league assigned Mikan's contract to the new NBL franchise in Minneapolis, and he led the Lakers to the NBL championship in 1948. Mikan averaged 21.3 points per game and scored 1,195 points, both top marks in the NBL. During the summer of 1948 four NBL teams, including the Lakers, were convinced to join the rival Basketball Association of America (BAA) and the Lakers, led again by Mikan and his 28.3 points per game, were BAA league champions, again defeating Rochester in the finals.

During the 1949 – 1950 season the BAA merged with the NBL to form the National Basketball Association (NBA). The Lakers won the first NBA championship, and Mikan led the league in scoring. The Lakers won the NBA championships in 1952, 1953, and 1954, with Mikan consistently finishing in the top four in the league in scoring (1950–1954), leading the league twice. In 1954 Mikan announced his retirement and became the Lakers general manager. Without Mikan playing, the Lakers were bound to regress, but in the 1955–1956 season the team slipped considerably, losing more games than it won, and Mikan agreed to return midway through the season. He was able to average only 10.5 points and 8.3 rebounds per game and played just twenty-six minutes per game. Mikan retired for good in the spring of 1956. In 1957 he became the Lakers coach, but the team's record (9–30) was miserable, and he resigned as the coach halfway through the season. Mikan also wished to spend more time with his wife, Patricia, and their six children.

From 1958 until 1967 Mikan devoted his energy to his legal career, practicing corporate and real-estate law in the Minneapolis area while buying and renovating buildings in the region. He also owned a successful travel agency. In 1967 he was part of the group that created the American Basketball Association (ABA), an NBA rival until 1976, when the NBA absorbed four ABA teams and the newer league folded. Mikan became the first ABA commissioner, serving until 1969. In the mid-1980s he worked to get NBA basketball back to the Twin Cities area, resulting in the award of the Minnesota Timberwolves franchise in 1989.

Mikan was voted the outstanding college basketball player of the first half of the twentieth century by the Associated Press in 1950. He was one of the inaugural class elected to the Naismith Memorial Basketball Hall of Fame in 1959. In 1996 he was named a member of the NBA Fiftieth Anniversary All-Time team. He was the dominant player of his era, always among the league leaders in scoring, rebounding, free throws, and fouls. His six-foot, ten-inch, 245-pound frame absorbed tremendous beatings in games, but Mikan's heart and will to win resulted almost annually in league championships. As the first truly great "big man" in basketball, Mikan set the standard for future centers.

★

The George Mikan file in the James Naismith Memorial Basketball Hall of Fame has clippings, photos, and programs from Mikan's career. Mikan published an autobiography, *Mr. Basketball* (1951), and also wrote, with Joseph Oberle, *Unstoppable: The Story of George Mikan* (1997). His De Paul years are discussed in Ray Meyer and Ray Sons, *Coach* (1987). The best account of his Chicago Gears play is in Richard Triptow, *The Dynasty That Never Was* (1996).

MURRY R. NELSON

MIKITA, Stan (*b.* 20 May 1940 in Sokolce, Czechoslovakia), center for the Chicago Blackhawks hockey team, one of the best all-time assist leaders, and the first person to win the Hart, Ross, and Byng trophies in the same year.

Mikita was born in a rural area of Nazi-occupied eastern Czechoslovakia, one of three children of a textile factory maintenance worker, Juraj Gvoth, and his wife, Emilia Mikita, who worked the family's small farming plots. After World War II, Emilia's brother Joe journeyed from Canada

Stan Mikita, 1964. AP/Wide World Photos

to visit the family, and soon he and young Mikita left Prague to move to Canada. They settled in St. Catharines, Ontario, where Joe was a housing contractor.

In the 1956–1957 season, Mikita played on the St. Catharines Junior A team, the Teepees. Bobby Hull was also on that team, and Rudy Pilous coached the Blackhawks affiliate. Hull and Pilous soon went to the Chicago major league team, and Mikita was called up briefly in November 1958 to replace Glenn Skov; he immediately centered for "Terrible Ted" Lindsay and Ken Wharram. Mikita had a right-hand shot, stood five feet, nine inches tall, and weighed 170 pounds; he soon became known as *le petit diable* (the little devil) for his run-ins with players. Once he even accidentally charged the referee. Vern Buffey, the referee (the only one in that era) and an experienced official, called a penalty. Mikita accidentally bumped him and was given a game misconduct penalty, the most severe penalty an on-ice official can give. A few days later, Mikita had to appear before league President Clarence Campbell. Campbell let Mikita off relatively mildly, but Mikita felt he never had Campbell's respect as a player afterward, even with all his achievements. In the 1960–1961 season he was placed on the "scooter line," a line of players that accelerate rapidly as they approach the opposing goal, with Ab McDonald and Ken Wharram. In the 1961 semifinals Mikita scored the winning goal in the third overtime despite being hit with a seventeen-minute penalty at the end of regulation. Mikita's twenty-one points paced all scorers to lead the Hawks to their first Stanley Cup since 1938.

During the 1962–1963 season Pilous was replaced by Billy Rey. In the following season Chicago missed the Cup finals despite having five players on the All-Star team—Mikita, Hull, Pierre Pilote, Wharram, and Moose Vasko. In the 1964–1965 season Mikita drew 154 minutes in penalties, the record for a center in one season. His targets were Henri Richard, the feisty brother of the all-time great Maurice Richard; Toronto's Bob Pulford; and Lew Fontinato; who switched from entertaining Rangers fans with his fisticuffs to enforcing for the far more skillful Montreal Canadiens. About this time Mikita's young son asked his father why he was always in the penalty box.

In the 1966–1967 season Mikita said he became tired of sitting in the penalty box when he could be scoring. When he went without a penalty in the first five games of the season, he was on his way to winning the first of two Lady Byng trophies for sportsmanship. He had begun to find his own style. He started to use a slap shot with his full body—most players had previously used only their arms. He also tried curving the stick in various ways, which caused the puck to rise more quickly off the ice when shot. This was soon adopted with astonishing success by teammate Bobby Hull and New York's Rod Gilbert. Mikita thus developed a very distinctive style of play—he could skate strongly through a crowd and then use his whole body to get off a powerful shot toward the goal. Or he could pass off quickly just inside the offensive zone to Hull, who arguably had the most blistering shot of all time. Mikita also became one of the first players to wear a helmet, which he started to do after getting hit by Kent Douglas's stick in the 1965–1966 season. After Bat Masterson died of head injuries sustained on the ice, Mikita argued for mandatory helmets for all National Hockey League (NHL) players.

The 1966–1967 season saw the Chicago team transformed. Ed Van Impe, Lou Angotti, Dennis Hull (Bobby's brother), Wally Boyer, and Ken Hodge joined Mikita. Although Hull and Mikita remained the indisputable stars of the Hawks, most of the new players were great puck handlers and made good shots, which resulted in a great offense. The team set an all-time Chicago record, 41–17–12, and scored 264 goals. Mikita became the first player ever to win the Hart, Ross, and Byng trophies in the same season. The Hawks won the regular season championship, but in hockey the emotional goal is winning the Stanley Cup. That year the Hawks ran into a Toronto team not nearly as flashy but extremely tight defensively, when Toronto beat Chicago in the semifinal series and then went on to win the Stanley Cup.

Amazingly, Mikita repeated the triple trophy feat the next year. He claimed that he paid little attention to his records until the last three weeks of the season because many things could happen before then to take him out of contention for a title. Chicago faced Detroit in the spring of 1968, and Mikita was leading a three-way race with forty-year-old Gordie Howe and Phil Esposito in a race of generations. Howe was the most durable player of all time; Esposito, the upcoming scoring champion; and Mikita, then the best center in North American hockey. Howe trailed by five points, but he was on ice against Chicago for the final game. Esposito had emotional incentive, since the Blackhawks had traded him the season before. But Mikita scored forty goals in the Detroit game and beat out Howe and Esposito for the scoring championship. The next season, however, he would yield the All-Star game nomination to Esposito.

In the 1970s Hull defected to the newly formed World Hockey Association, but Mikita remained to play 1,394 NHL games—all with the Blackhawks. He scored 541 goals and amassed 1,467 points. Mikita played on nine All-Star teams, the last being in 1975. He won four Art Ross scoring trophies, and in 1983 he was inducted into the Hockey Hall of Fame.

On 27 April 1963 Mikita married Jill Cerny, the secretary of an Illinois congressman. The couple had three children. Mikita lived in Elmhurst, Illinois, throughout his career. During the off-season he served as vice president of a hockey equipment company. He founded the Stan Mikita Hockey School for the Hearing-Impaired, a weeklong youth camp for deaf children inspired by the son of a friend of Mikita's.

★

I Play to Win is Mikita's 1969 autobiography. It is well written and contains many stories of Mikita's contemporaries, but it is now dated since it was written at the height of his career. He later wrote *Inside Hockey* (1971), with George Vass, a how-to-play manual for high school players that has many useful suggestions, although the training chapter seems quaint by contemporary standards. Articles are also in *Sports Illustrated* (30 Apr. 1962 and 31 Jan. 1966), and *Sport* magazine (Feb. 1968).

JOHN DAVID HEALY

MILLER, Cheryl DeAnn (*b.* 3 January 1964 in Riverside, California), basketball player whose athletic prowess and captivating style helped to increase the pace and popularity of women's basketball during the 1980s.

Miller learned to play basketball at home. Her father, Saul, a musician and computer professional, had played basketball in high school and college, and taught Miller the basics of the game on a concrete half-court in their backyard. Her mother, Carrie, a nurse, had also played basketball earlier in life. Miller's three brothers also had a huge impact on her athletic development. As Miller recounted in an interview, "When I was five years old, my older brothers used to play with their friends, and every time the ball went out in the bushes or out in the lawn, it was my job to run over there and grab it and dribble it. They used to get a kick out of it, and I used to enjoy it because I got to hang out with my brothers. So it started from there just playing against their friends, to playing against Reggie, to playing on a boy's team, to where I am today." Reggie, her younger brother, later became an All-Star player for the Indiana Pacers of the National Basketball Association (NBA); the Millers are considered the best sister-brother duo in basketball history.

Cheryl Miller. AP/WIDE WORLD PHOTOS

By the time Miller was in high school, she already was a basketball powerhouse. During her four years as a six-foot, three-inch forward at Riverside Polytechnic High School (1978–1982), the team won 132 games and lost only 4. Miller averaged 32.8 points and 15 rebounds per game. In one game she scored 105 points. Miller was the first high-school athlete, male or female, chosen as a Parade All-American four years in a row. Her phenomenal playing did not go unnoticed: more than 250 colleges offered her scholarships.

Miller chose to attend the University of Southern California (USC) in Los Angeles. During her first year she led the Women of Troy to a national title. In the championship game Miller scored twenty-seven points as USC came back from a halftime deficit to beat the defending champions, Louisiana Tech, by two points. Miller was named the tournament's Most Valuable Player (MVP). During the summer of 1983, Miller traveled to Brazil and Venezuela as part of the U.S. national team that won the silver at the World Championships and the gold at the Pan-American Games. Back at USC for her sophomore year, Miller and the Women of Troy were again national champions with Miller again named as the MVP.

Over the summer, Miller led the United States to its first gold medal in women's basketball at the 1984 Olympics in Los Angeles. Miller led the team in scoring, rebounds, assists, and steals. USC went 21–9 in Miller's junior season, but despite her producing college career-high numbers in points (26.8) and rebounds (15.8) per game, the team lost in an early round of the National Collegiate Athletic Association (NCAA) tournament. During her senior year, USC entered its third NCAA championship game in four years, losing to the University of Texas. Miller finished her stellar college career with a record of 112–20, two national titles, 3,018 points, and her name in the USC record book in categories including points scored, rebounds, steals, blocked shots, and games played. Miller's jersey number 31 was the first basketball jersey retired at USC.

Miller also attracted national honors. She won the Naismith Award three times as the nation's top player. A four-time All-American, she also won the Wade Trophy (1986) and the Broderick Cup (1985, 1986). ESPN named her the Woman Athlete of the Year in 1985, and *Sports Illustrated* put her on its cover that same year, naming her the number-one basketball player in the country. Miller was the first female basketball player ever nominated for the Amateur Athletic Union's Sullivan Award, the sports equivalent of an Oscar. She also enjoyed celebrity status, appearing on magazine covers, making cameo appearances at the Grammy Awards and on the television show *Cagney and Lacey,* meeting heads of state, being interviewed by Barbara Walters, and having a "Cheryl Miller Day" declared by the mayor of Los Angeles.

After graduating from USC in 1986, Miller continued to play for the United States in international competitions. Miller led gold-medal teams at both the World Championships and Goodwill Games in 1986. A severe knee injury kept Miller out of the 1988 Olympics. She retired from basketball in 1988 with a 29–2 record in international play, four gold medals and a silver, and her name in the record book as the lead U.S. scorer in all five international competitions in which she played.

Miller channeled her passion for basketball into sports broadcasting and coaching. Although she was on record as saying, "No coaching, definitely no coaching," she served as the assistant women's basketball coach at USC for five seasons (1987–1991) and became the head coach in 1993. During her two years as the head coach, USC compiled a 44–14 record, won the Pacific Ten conference title, and made it into the NCAA tournament both years. When Miller left coaching at USC in 1995, she joined Turner Sports as a television analyst and reporter covering NBA games. The following year Miller made history by becoming the first woman to provide play-by-play commentary for a nationally televised NBA game.

When the Women's National Basketball Association (WNBA) was formed in 1997, Miller was the first coach hired. During her four seasons as the head coach and general manager of the Phoenix Mercury, the team posted a 70–52 record and made it into the play-offs three years, including playing in the championship game in 1998. The team also led the league in attendance during its first season, averaging 13,703 spectators per game. Miller was a favorite with the Phoenix fans, receiving loud cheers when she entered the arena. It wasn't unusual for Miller to dance with the team's hip-hop squad on the court after home games. She occasionally stood on the scorer's table, grabbed a microphone, and addressed the fans. To their disappointment, Miller resigned as the Mercury coach in 2000, choosing to focus her energy on her sports broadcasting career.

Miller brought new dimensions to the game of women's basketball. She helped to usher in a faster, quicker, more exciting brand of play with her athleticism and intensity. Her engaging and flamboyant personality as a player and a coach helped to promote and popularize women's basketball. Miller was elected to the International Women's Sports Hall of Fame (1991), the Naismith Memorial Basketball Hall of Fame (1995), and the Women's Basketball Hall of Fame (1999).

★

For details about Miller's college career, see Curry Kirkpatrick, "Lights! Camera! Cheryl!" *Sports Illustrated* (20 Nov. 1985).

Miller's statistics in international competition can be found on the website http://www.usabasketball.com. Several photographs of and anecdotes about Miller are in Kelly Whiteside, *WNBA: A Celebration: Commemorating the Birth of a League* (1998).

KELLY NELSON

MILLER, Marvin Julian (*b.* 14 April 1917 in New York City), labor economist and former head of the Major League Baseball Players' Association (MLBPA) who built the organization into one of the strongest labor unions in the United States and established the modern concept of free agency.

Born in the Bronx, the northernmost borough of New York City, and raised in Brooklyn, Miller was one of two children born to Alexander Miller, a salesman in a women's shoe store, and Gertrude Wald Miller, a schoolteacher. Both of his parents were the children of immigrants from Eastern Europe. Miller attended elementary school at P.S. 153 in Brooklyn, graduating in 1929. He then went to James Madison High School in Brooklyn, where he credits "a good economics teacher" with awakening within him an interest in the subject. After high school, Miller majored in education at Ohio's Miami University, planning eventually to become an economics teacher himself. After his junior year at Miami, he transferred to New York University, from which he graduated in 1938 with a B.S. in economics.

Marvin Miller, 1972. AP/WIDE WORLD PHOTOS

Fresh out of college, Miller worked first as a clerk for the U.S. Department of the Treasury in Washington, D.C. In 1940 he returned to New York City and a job as an investigator for the city's Department of Welfare. He next worked as a labor economist and disputes hearing officer, serving for three years during World War II with the National War Labor Relations Board. Leaving government employment behind, Miller worked first for the International Association of Machinists and then the United Auto Workers. In 1950 Miller accepted a position as staff economist for the United Steelworkers of America, and by 1966 he was the chief economist and assistant to the president, as well as the union's leading negotiator.

When a committee of ballplayers approached Miller in 1966 offering him a job as the MLBPA's first full-time executive, he found it impossible to resist. Raised by a father who was a staunch New York Giants fans (although as a boy Miller had always rooted for the hometown Brooklyn Dodgers), he was a lifelong baseball enthusiast. Miller was the players' third choice for the position, as they had been turned down by their first two candidates, but this turned out to be an incredibly fortuitous turn of events that put Miller in the driver's seat at the loosely organized union. With a union treasury of $5,400, he began to put together an extremely powerful labor union, one that in time would serve as a model for others.

An accomplished bargainer, Miller drew on all the lessons he had learned while working for the steelworkers, autoworkers, and machinists. One of his first goals was to renegotiate the standard players' contract, which he branded "one of the worst labor documents." When team owners threw up roadblocks, refusing to provide accurate information on players' salaries, Miller selected a few union members from each team to find out and anonymously report the salary of all the other players on that team. Only two years into his job with the MLBPA, Miller managed to raise the minimum salary for players from $6,000 to $10,000, the first such increase negotiated in more than twenty years. But Miller was only getting started.

When management balked at the union's request to conduct union business in the locker rooms, Miller on one occasion held a union meeting in the outfield of a ballpark. In 1973 he won for players the right to arbitration to resolve grievances. He also managed to negotiate a pension plan for players that is considered one of the best such benefit packages in the United States.

Miller's most enduring contribution to the game undoubtedly is free agency. In 1975 he managed to wrest from management an agreement giving players the right to sign with other teams once their contracts with their old teams were up. But Miller was careful not to push too hard. Well aware that unlimited free agency would overburden the market and hold down players' salaries, he offered owners this "compromise"—players would win the right to free agency only after playing for six years in the majors. In one fell swoop, Miller had managed to mold a labor system that ended forever the owners' career control over players, regulated the pool of talent, and provided established major leaguers with a degree of security they had never before enjoyed.

In Miller's view, the key to free agency was a flaw in the language of the standard player contract. Players were bound to their teams through the reserve clause, allowing a team to renew a player's contract in perpetuity. Section 10A of the contract, which spelled out the reserve clause, read in part, "the Club may tender to the Player a contract for the term of that year by mailing the same to the Player. If prior to the March 1 next succeeding said January 15, the Player and the Club have not agreed upon the terms of such contract, then on or before 10 days after said March 1, the Club shall have the right . . . to renew this contract for the period of one year." Miller's reading of the contract language convinced him that it amounted to only a one-year option for the club. If a player did not sign a contract, the club, according to 10A, could renew him "for the period of one year." But after that year, the contractual obligation between player and team would be satisfied.

Miller desperately needed a player to test his interpretation of 10A. He found such a test case in pitcher Andy Messersmith of the Los Angeles Dodgers, who became the first true free agent after an arbitrator's ruling on 23 December 1975 confirmed Miller's interpretation of Section 10A. Also declared a free agent in the arbitrator's ruling was pitcher Dave McNally, who actually had retired from the game in June 1975 rather than sign a one-year contract with the Montreal Expos. In an earlier challenge to the legality of the reserve clause, St. Louis Cardinals player Curt Flood had gone to court after he was traded without his knowledge to the Philadelphia Phillies. The case went all the way to the Supreme Court, which ruled against Flood 5 to 3. However, the Flood case paved the way for a system of arbitration to settle such disputes between players and club owners. Other areas in which Miller fought hard for the interests of ballplayers include the division of revenues from licensing and broadcasting and steps taken to make the game safer. The master negotiator successfully bargained for padded outfield walls, better-defined warning tracks, and safer locker rooms.

Veteran sports broadcaster Red Barber once called Miller "one of the two or three most important men in baseball history." What could this mild-mannered labor leader from the Bronx have done to warrant such reverence from fans and players alike? After all, he never hit a home run, nor led his team to victory in a pennant race or World Series. In fact, he never played professional baseball, but his crowning achievement has transformed the game forever and will live on long after Miller himself is laid to rest. As head of the baseball players' union from 1966 through 1983, Miller was responsible for establishing the concept of free agency. In the spring of 1972, he led players out on a 13-day strike, eventually winning from owners an agreement to contribute about $1 million more each year to the players' pension fund. A tough negotiator, Miller in 1975 managed to win from club owners recognition of each player's right to sign employment agreements with other teams once his contractual obligations with the old team concluded.

As a tribute to Miller and his contributions to professional baseball as we know it today, sportswriters, players, and many fans have long called for his induction into the National Baseball Hall of Fame. Of Miller, National Broadcasting Company (NBC) sportscaster Bob Costas said, "There is no nonplayer more deserving of the Hall of Fame," with the possible exception of Branch Rickey, who was inducted into the Hall of Fame in 1967.

★

Perhaps the best insight into Miller's years as executive director of the MLBPA can be found in Miller's own *Whole Different Ball Game: The Sport and Business of Baseball* (1991). In it, Miller details how he helped to shape the MLBPA into a strong and powerful union and also covers the negotiations that led to the establishment of free agency. Miller also wrote the foreword to *Man on Spikes* (1998), an excellent novel tracking the triumphs and tragedies of a single baseball player. An outsider's view of Miller's years as head of the players' union is John Helyar, *Lords of the Realm: The Real History of Baseball* (1994).

DON AMERMAN

MILLER, Reginald Wayne ("Reggie") (*b.* 24 August 1965 in Riverside, California), basketball sharpshooter who became the first player in National Basketball Association (NBA) history to make 2,000 three-point shots.

When Miller was born, doctors doubted he would ever have the skills to walk, much less become a three-point wizard on the basketball court. The fourth of five children born to Saul and Carrie Miller, Miller had a hip deformity that caused his legs and ankles to turn in. As a youngster he wore leg braces and could get around only with the help of crutches or a wheelchair.

Miller overcame his troubles by learning discipline from his father, a chief master sergeant in the Air Force, and optimism from his mother, a nurse. He remembers being trapped inside the house while his siblings played outside. In his book, *I Love Being the Enemy,* Miller said his mother's encouragement made all the difference. "My mom would see me looking out the window and say, 'Don't

Reggie Miller. ARCHIVE PHOTOS, INC.

worry, honey. You'll be out there soon. Your legs just got to get stronger, that's all.'"

When Miller turned four, the braces came off and he made up for lost time. However, he spent most of his days being smacked around the basketball court by his sister Cheryl. Older, taller, and more skilled, Cheryl easily blocked his shots. Day after day, she kept beating him. His life's goal became "Beat Cheryl."

Eventually, Miller found a way to score against his sister. He moved back—back beyond the confines of his family's basketball court and into his mother's rose garden, twenty-five feet from the basket. When his mother wasn't watching, he worked on that shot. He practiced relentlessly, taking 500 to 700 shots a day.

Once Miller could nail shots from the back of the court, it did not matter how tall his opponents were, whether his sister or the neighborhood boys. Instead of driving toward the basket, Miller backed up and drilled his loopy launchers right over their heads. The shot he mastered in his youth with the goal of beating his sister turned him into an NBA three-point standout.

Although Miller played basketball as a child, his first love was baseball. He tore up the Little League. He wanted to be a professional baseball player like his older brother Darrell, a catcher for the California Angels. All that changed during Miller's freshman year at Riverside Polytechnic High School. Standing in the outfield one day, Miller decided baseball was too quiet and slow for him. He turned to basketball and began fighting the shadow of his sister, who also played basketball for Polytechnic High. Miller returned home one evening bragging that he had scored 39 points, only to find that his sister had scored 105 in her game. Cheryl Miller later led the 1984 women's U.S. basketball team to an Olympic gold medal and became a highly successful coach at the University of Southern California. She was also the first head coach of the Phoenix Mercury of the Women's National Basketball Association (WNBA).

As a junior, Miller led his team to the state high school championship. In his senior year he averaged thirty points a game and helped his team to another state title. He graduated from Riverside Polytechnic in 1983.

That fall Miller entered the University of California at Los Angeles (UCLA). During the 1984–1985 season he led UCLA to the National Invitation Tournament (NIT) championship and was named the tournament's Most Valuable Player (MVP). In his junior year he averaged twenty-six points per game, the fourth-highest tally in the nation. When he graduated in 1987 Miller had scored 2,095 career college points, at the time making him UCLA's second-leading scorer in history, behind Kareem Abdul-Jabbar.

Miller entered the 1987 NBA draft and was picked eleventh by the Indiana Pacers. At six feet, seven inches tall, and 185 pounds, Miller was gangly by NBA standards, and no one paid him much attention. He averaged only ten points per game his first season. During his third season, however, Miller began to stand out, proving himself one of the most dangerous scorers in the game, able to drill three-pointers from the outside or drive to the hoop. In that season, 1989 – 1990, he averaged 24.6 points per game and made the All-Star team. In 1992–1993 he led the NBA with 167 three-pointers. He also scored 57 points in one game.

Miller's enormous potential and talents have often been overshadowed by his on-court antics—his trash talking. When he is on the road, he plays the role of the outlaw, the rebel. He ridicules other players and the crowd until they boo him. Then he eggs the crowd on more, cocking his head to the side and placing his hand to his ear, pretending he cannot hear them. Then he nails a killer three-pointer.

Miller says his trash talking is all in fun. He says it builds him up, gives him security. "I don't think my messing with a player, talking a little trash, demeans the game. I don't go after a player's race, religion, or family. Those things are off limits. Hell, half the time when I'm talking on the court, I'm talking to myself. I'm trying to get myself pumped up, to get a mental edge. But people see it and say, 'Oh, there he is again, talking trash.' But that's not always what I'm doing."

Those who know Miller say he has spent a career on the court cultivating an image of himself that is far removed from his actual personality. They say he's the nicest guy you'll ever meet.

While Miller talks the talk, he has also proved he can walk the walk. While facing the New York Knicks during the 1994 playoffs, Miller scored twenty-five points in the final period. His feat is considered one of the greatest shooting performances in NBA playoff history. Also in 1994, as cocaptain of the U.S. "Dream Team II," he led the United States to a gold medal in the World Basketball Championships in Toronto, Canada.

On 29 August 1992 Miller married Marita Stavrou, an actress and model, whom he met at a benefit dinner in Los Angeles. They separated in August 2000 and later divorced.

On the court Miller continues to stack up records. During the 2000–2001 season he became the 21st player in NBA history to score 21,000 points. What he wants most, however, is to win an NBA championship, and he plans to play until he does. As he notes in his book, "No matter how many points you score, none of it's worth fifty cents unless you get that ring."

★

Miller's *I Love Being the Enemy: A Season on the Court with the NBA's Best Shooter and Sharpest Tongue* (1995), written with Gene Wojciechowski, details his 1994–1995 NBA season, although throughout he talks passionately about his upbringing and his love for his family and the game. Among the more informative short biographies are Ted Cox, *Reggie Miller: Basketball Sharpshooter* (1995), and Barry Wilner, *Reggie Miller* (1997). Also see Jack McCallum, "Heroic Measures: Having Bulked Up His Body (Well, a Little) and Embellished His Game, Reggie Miller Is Trying to Carry the Pacers to Their First Finals Appearance," *Sports Illustrated* (22 May 2000).

LISA FRICK

MILLER, Shannon Lee (*b.* 10 March 1977 in Rolla, Missouri), America's most decorated gymnast, male or female, in the history of the sport, and the first American to win three individual gold medals in gymnastics at a world or Olympic competition.

Shannon Miller was the second of three children born to Ron Miller, a physics professor, and Claudia Ann Miller, a bank vice president. The family moved to Edmond, Oklahoma, when Shannon was six months old, and she grew up there. She wore a corrective shoe bar to correct severely turned legs, yet learned to crawl and walk on schedule, demonstrating the tenacity and determination that dominated her career in gymnastics. These qualities, as well as her faith as a Christian Scientist, have had a major role in her success.

Shannon Miller, 1996. © MIKE KING/CORBIS

A Christmas gift of a trampoline at age five sparked Miller's interest in tumbling. Gymnastics lessons at a local center, Adventures in Gymnastics, soon followed. At age nine Miller joined Dynamo Gymnastics in Oklahoma City, where she trained with Steve Nunno and his assistant and choreographer Peggy Liddick. Miller's organizational skills enabled her to balance school and stringent athletic training and competition, and she graduated from Edmond North High School with a 4.0 GPA on 18 May 1995.

Miller placed in her first national competition in 1987 at the U.S. Association of Independent Gymnastics Clubs (USAIGC) National Gymnastics Championship held at the University of Delaware. Her first major, elite-level meet was the 1988 U.S. Classic, where she won the vault, balance beam, and all-around competitions. Other performances of note were at the 1990 Catania Cup, with first place finishes in the vault, balance beam, floor exercise, and all-around; the all-around title at the 1991 Swiss Cup in St. Gallen, Switzerland, and the gold medal in the balance beam at the 1991 U.S. Gymnastics Championship.

Shortly before her first Olympic competition Miller suffered a dislocated elbow and bone chip. She elected for surgical repair and, and with her usual determination, returned to training in one month. In spite of this setback, she competed with great success at the 1992 Barcelona Olympics. Miller won silver medals in the all-around and balance beam; and bronze medals in the uneven bars, floor exercise, and the team competition—more medals than any other U.S. athlete that year.

Miller's winning ways continued in 1993, as she captured three gold medals in the World Championships in Birmingham, England, set or tied seven gymnastics records at the Olympic Sports Festival in San Antonio, Texas, swept the American Cup, and became the all-around victor at the U.S. Championships. The latter victory was her first national title. She overcame burnout and continued training with increased vigor. In fact, Miller won her second consecutive World Gymnastics all-around title in 1994, becoming the only U.S. gymnast ever to accomplish this feat. The fifteen-year-old Miller was only four feet, seven inches, and seventy-five pounds for her first Olympic competition in 1992. Many critics felt that the nineteen-year-old Miller, at five feet and ninety-seven pounds, was past her prime in 1996; however, she proved her detractors wrong. She went on to win an individual gold medal on the balance beam and was a member of the "Magnificent Seven" that captured the team Olympic gold in Atlanta.

After winning fifty-eight international and forty-nine national competitions, Miller retired from amateur gymnastics and continued her studies in marketing at the University of Oklahoma. Miller married physician Chris Phillips on 12 June 1999 and moved to Houston. At age 23, Miller attempted a comeback for the 2000 Sydney Olympics. She trained intensively for ten months, but withdrew from the U.S. trials in Boston after jamming a knee on her first vault of the evening. With competition behind her, Miller stated: "Hopefully, I'll be remembered as someone who enjoyed the sport, someone who put in the effort and worked hard." She continues to write, makes personal appearances, is a motivational speaker, and works with many charitable organizations. Miller's book, *Winning Every Day: Gold Medal Advice for a Happy, Healthy Life* (1998), consists of inspirational, autobiographical essays to encourage aspiring athletes.

A sign erected at the outskirts of Edmond praises Miller's achievements by proclaiming the city as "Home of Shannon Miller, winner of 5 medals, 1992 Olympics." Edmond further honored her in 1998 with her own street—Shannon Miller Parkway—and construction of a bronze statue of Miller in Shannon Miller Park began in 2001.

★

Biographies of Miller include Septima Green, *Going for the Gold: Shannon Miller* (1996); Krista Quiner, *Shannon Miller: America's Most Decorated Gymnast* (1997); and Claudia Ann Miller (Miller's mother) with Gayle White, *Shannon Miller: My Child, My Hero* (1999). Miller is also profiled in Nancy A. Kleinbaum, *The Magnificent Seven: The Authorized Story of American Gold* (1996), which features each member of the first U.S. gymnastics team to win Olympic gold. Also of interest is Selena Roberts, "The Road to Sidney, Miller Out but Dawes and Chow Make the Team," *New York Times* (21 Aug. 2000).

JEANNIE P. MILLER

MITCHELL, Robert Cornelius, Sr. ("Bobby") (*b.* 6 June 1935 in Hot Springs, Arkansas), Hall of Fame football player who amassed impressive statistics as a leading running back, pass receiver, and kick returner; the first African American to play for the Washington Redskins.

Mitchell was born to the Reverend Albert James Mitchell, an ordained minister, and Avis Mary Warthon Mitchell, a homemaker. He was one of nine children—six boys and three girls. Mitchell attended Langston High School in Hot Springs, Arkansas, where he earned a reputation in football, basketball, and baseball. The blazing speed that would serve him so well in football also enabled him to set records in track and field. He was such a fine baseball prospect that the St. Louis Cardinals offered him a contract after his graduation from high school in 1954. Mitchell was re-

Bobby Mitchell *(receiving)*, 1962. ASSOCIATED PRESS AP

cruited by several big-time football schools. He chose the University of Illinois and enrolled there in the fall of 1954. On one of his first days on campus he met Gwen Ezelle Morrow. They later married on 2 May 1958—the spring before Mitchell reported to his first professional football training camp.

As a sophomore Mitchell was an immediate football sensation. He gained 466 yards, a modest total, but he did it at an 8.8-yards-per-carry average. The Fighting Illini, which had finished 1–8 the previous year, rocketed to a 5–3–1 record. Mitchell was named to the All–Big Ten team. That year he was also outstanding in track and field, setting a world record of 7.7 seconds in the indoor 70-yard low hurdles. He also ran a 9.6-second 100-yard dash and broad jumped 24 feet, 3 inches (this competition is now called the long jump). His 13 individual points propelled Illinois to the Big Ten championship.

Unfortunately, Illinois's improvement in football was short-lived. When Mitchell was a junior his team's record was just 2–5 – 2; in his senior year, 4–5. While the team was going nowhere, however, Mitchell was going somewhere—usually in a hurry. He established a reputation as a runner and pass catcher at Illinois. He also was a world-class sprinter. Mitchell graduated from Illinois with a B.S. in physical education.

Mitchell was selected by the Cleveland Browns in the seventh round of the 1958 National Football League (NFL) draft. At six feet tall and 185 pounds, he was considered only average in size for professional football, and thus was projected as a receiver rather than as a heavy-duty runner. He agreed with this assessment of his talents and looked forward to missing out on the pounding he would have taken as a running back. His relatively low position in the draft was attributable to his reputation as a fumbler. Another factor was the thought that he was seriously considering pursuing a spot on the 1960 U.S. Olympic team as a sprinter. But Mitchell and Gwen had just married, and he was committed to football.

Mitchell was also selected to play in the Chicago College All-Star game against the NFL defending champions, the Detroit Lions. In that game he quickly established what became a lasting reputation as a "big play guy." First he got behind the Lions All-Pro defensive back Jimmy David, and scored on an eighty-four-yard touchdown bomb. Then he scored again on an eighteen-yard pass. Mitchell received Most Valuable Player (MVP) honors after the game—a 35–19 upset victory for the collegians.

As a rookie with the Browns, Mitchell started in the backfield with Hall of Famer Jim Brown because of the team's shortage of runners. Brown, 1957's Rookie of the Year and the NFL's rushing leader, did the bulk of the ball-carrying, but Mitchell got his share of attempts and gained an even 500 yards on 80 rushes for a lofty 6.3-yard average. He also scored on a 98-yard kickoff return. Mitchell and the larger Brown were like thunder and lightning. Early in his career Mitchell showed that he really could hang onto the football and that his fumbler reputation was undeserved. When someone asked Browns coaching legend Paul Brown how he managed to cure Mitchell of "fumble-itis," Brown said, "Simple. We told him not to fumble."

The next year Mitchell turned in one of the NFL's best-ever single-game rushing marks—232 yards on just fourteen carries—on 15 November 1959. Only Jim Brown surpassed this yardage, and then by a scant five yards as the still-standing Browns all-time single-game high. In addition to running the football, Mitchell also averaged thirty-two catches in each of his four Cleveland seasons.

Despite Mitchell's stellar performance, the Browns were looking to team another power back with Jim Brown. The player they coveted was the 1961 Heisman Trophy winner, Ernie Davis, like Brown a Syracuse running back. The Washington Redskins held the rights to the ill-fated Davis, who died of leukemia before playing in the NFL. Cleveland traded Mitchell to Washington, along with Leroy Jackson, for Davis's rights. It was a significant trade because Mitchell and Jackson became the first African Americans to play for Washington. Other NFL teams had integrated as early as 1946, but the Redskins owner George Preston Marshall contended that his team's large southern following made it nearly impossible for him to integrate. However, because the Redskins were about to play in a government-funded stadium—D.C. Stadium, later named Robert F. Kennedy Memorial Stadium—Marshall was the object of considerable political pressure. He knew what Mitchell could do, having seen him burn the Redskins in the past. Mitchell looked at the trade optimistically, saying, "When Jim Brown and I would come to Washington to play we talked about the first black who would play here. We both agreed he'd be a big man—there was such a large black fan base here. I just never thought I'd be the guy, but it worked out fine."

Mitchell, at last, became exclusively a pass receiver in 1962. He carried the ball only once from scrimmage—a 5-yard gain. He led the NFL in catches (72) and yards (1,384) and scored 11 touchdowns. In 1963 he caught 69 passes and led the league in yards with 1,436. For the next four years Mitchell averaged over 59 catches a season. He worked hard—perhaps too hard—in the 1968–1969 off-season in preparing for his new coach, Vince Lombardi. He experienced hamstring problems in training camp and announced his retirement before the start of the 1969 season. Mitchell left behind amazing numbers—521 receptions for 7,954 yards and 65 touchdowns, 2,735 rushing yards and 18 touchdowns, a kickoff return average of 26.4 yards and 5 touchdowns, and a 10.1-yard punt return average and 3 touchdowns. In 1963 Mitchell scored on a 99-

yard pass play from quarterback George Izo against his old Cleveland teammates.

Mitchell moved right into the Redskins front office after retiring as an active player and has been there ever since. He worked first as a scout and later as assistant general manager. He was inducted into the Pro Football Hall of Fame in 1983. He lives in Washington, D.C., with his wife, who is a law school graduate and a federal government administrator. They have a son and a daughter.

Mitchell is active in charity golf tournaments, Redskins community outreach programs, and does much behind-the-scenes work in D.C. racial relations. He is a member of the Metropolitan Washington (D.C.) Area Leadership Council and is on the board of the American Lung Association of D.C. One of the most respected and best-liked executives in the NFL, Mitchell is a role model and father figure to young Redskins players. As a player, the pioneering Mitchell was one of the most versatile and electrifying performers in NFL history. His philosophy was simple but effective. "You have to play with confidence—make him worry about you, not you worry about him."

★

There is no biography of Mitchell, but his life and career are discussed in Jack Clary, *Great Teams, Great Years—Washington Redskins* (1974), one of a series of books written in the early 1970s featuring NFL teams; Don Smith, *All-Time Greats* (1988); and Richard Whittingham, *The Washington Redskins* (1990).

JIM CAMPBELL

MONROE, Earl Vernon, Jr. (*b.* 21 November 1944 in Philadelphia, Pennsylvania), member of the Naismith Memorial Basketball Hall of Fame who is considered one of the top fifty players in National Basketball Association (NBA) history.

Earl Monroe *(left)*. AP/WIDE WORLD PHOTOS

Monroe was the first of three children born to Earl Vernon, a touring dancer and a night watchman, and Rose Smith Monroe Vernon, a grocery store manager, who divorced when he was five. Monroe graciously credits his family with helping him reach his dreams. As a child, Monroe's athletic interests favored soccer and baseball, but a leg break and reaching his full adult height of six feet, three inches by the age of fourteen, directed his life to the world of hoops. As a center on the John Bartram High School court in Philadelphia from 1959 to 1963, Monroe invented many clever and flamboyant basketball moves, earning the nickname "Thomas Edison." Monroe claims that he needed to invent these trick shots and fancy moves because other centers were taller than he was and had more experience on the court. Monroe finished his senior year in high school in 1963 with 21.7 points per game, earning him a spot on the Philadelphia All-City team.

Attending North Carolina's Winston-Salem State College (now University) from 1963 to 1967 as an elementary education major, Monroe played guard on its basketball team, the Rams. He was influenced and guided by one of the most successful coaches in college basketball, Hall of Famer Clarence ("Big House") Gaines. During his senior year in the 1966–1967 season, Monroe averaged an amazing 41.5 points per game. As the leading scorer in both the National Collegiate Athletic Association (NCAA) College Division and the National Association of Intercollegiate Athletics (NAIA), he led the Rams to an NCAA Division II championship. That season he earned a most valuable player award as the most outstanding player in an NCAA college division tournament. Monroe scored 1,329 points that year, the most ever scored by a Division II player in a single season. During his college career, Monroe tallied 2,935 points in 110 games, an average of 26.7 points per game. An All-American in 1966 and 1967, he was elected to the NAIA Basketball Hall of Fame in 1975. Monroe's other collegiate honors include the *Sporting News* First-Team All-American in 1966, the NCAA College Division All-Tournament Team in 1967, and the NAIA Golden Anniversary Team in 1986. In addition to these athletic honors, Monroe received a B.S. in education in 1967.

Monroe began his professional basketball career as the second choice in the 1967 NBA draft. Picked up by the Baltimore Bullets (now the Washington Wizards), he scored 1,991 points, an average of 24 points per game, playing guard in his first season. In a 13 February 1968 overtime game against the Los Angeles Lakers, Monroe scored a staggering fifty-six points, the third highest ever scored by a rookie and his own career scoring high. He was NBA Rookie of the Year in 1968.

Awesome scoring ability was not the only talent that drew attention to Monroe—his dazzling style infused fresh energy into the NBA, introducing new moves only seen before on urban playgrounds. Indeed, NBA great Bill Bradley described Monroe as the "ultimate playground player." Monroe could hang in the air before making one of his acrobatic shots. He called this mid-air state "la-la." Among his many "patented" moves were the wrap-around dribble, the super-quick spin move, the turn-around jump shot, and his fancy double-pump dribbling, often done between his legs. These jazzy moves led film director and avid Knicks fan Spike Lee to dub Monroe as "the Miles Davis of hoop." Monroe is also recognized as the master of the one-on-one, easily "juking" (faking out) opponents with head, shoulder, and body fakes. He was a deadly shot from outside, and although only six feet, three inches tall, he could also move easily from a shot that would score two points to one that could score three.

Monroe pioneered the "finesse, aggression, one-on-one play" that is now common in the NBA. Wes Unseld, Monroe's teammate and eventual Bullets general manager, acknowledged that Monroe "revolutionized this game." Many criticized Monroe's innovations, and he was called a flake, a "hot dog," and too flashy. The Bullets left him alone, however, perhaps because, as Monroe has said, "it's hard to knock 40 points a game." These critics "never understood that I was never overly big and I needed to use my guile." His guile and style earned the admiration of many fans and players alike.

Monroe finished the 1968–1969 season with a career high 2,065 points, an average of 25.8 points per game. In a 6 February 1970 double overtime game against the Detroit Pistons, Monroe scored thirteen points in one overtime, setting a record for that time. Monroe led his team to the NBA finals in 1971. Following that season, unhappy with management's contractual negotiations, he requested a trade to the New York Knickerbockers (Knicks).

Early in the 1971–1972 season, the Bullets honored Monroe's request, and he became a Knickerbocker. Many sportswriters and fans questioned whether Monroe could fit in with the team-oriented structure of the Knicks, particularly with its flamboyant Walt Frazier and other greats including Willis Reed, Dave DeBusschere, and Bill Bradley, plus coach Red Holzman—Hall of Famers all. Spike Lee observed that Monroe unselfishly sacrificed some of his flashy style of play to mesh with the Knicks offense. Not only did he fit in, he was named team captain during the 1976–1977 season.

Monroe missed much of his first season with the Knicks due to bone spurs in his left heel. In the following 1972–1973 season, Monroe helped New York win the NBA championship. That season, he averaged 15.5 points per game, and performed even better during playoffs, averaging 16.1 points per game. During his nine-year tenure with the Knicks, Monroe averaged 16.2 points per game and ranks as the team's eleventh all-time leading scorer.

Monroe retired in 1980 because of an arthritic knee condition. Within his thirteen-year NBA career, he racked up some remarkable statistics. As a guard, Monroe scored 17,454 points, averaging 18.8 points per game, which ranks 24th on the NBA all-time list. He is also credited with 3,594 assists, an average of 3.9 per game, and scored 1,000 points or more in 9 of his 13 years. He was a four-time member of the NBA's All-Star team, was named to the 1969 All-NBA First Team, and was selected for the NBA's Fiftieth Anniversary All-Time Team in 1996. In 1986 the Knicks retired his number 15 jersey. Monroe was bypassed for three years by the Naismith Memorial Basketball Hall of Fame but was eventually inducted in 1990.

Monroe remains interested in basketball. In March 1985 he was named the first commissioner of the fledgling United States Basketball League. He actively gives his time and one-on-one contact to inner-city kids playing basketball, and has been a radio commentator for the NBA All-Star game. Monroe has also been drawn to another passion, music. He founded an entertainment production and management firm called Pretty Pearl, Inc., and is its president and CEO. Appropriately coined from his basketball career, the company's two record labels are Pretty Pearl and In Your Face.

Throughout his successful career, Monroe earned several nicknames, including "Black Jesus" and "Magic." However, the one nickname that suited him best was "the Pearl." He sparkled on the court and bedazzled the game.

★

Monroe and former teammate Wes Unseld wrote *The Basketball Skill Book* (1973). Monroe himself has been the subject of a number of books, including Robert Blake Jackson, *Earl the Pearl: The Story of Earl Monroe* (1974), and Donald Goines, *Street Players* (2000). He has also graced the covers of a number of magazines including *Basketball Digest* (Mar. 1973), and *Sports Illustrated* (4 Nov. 1968), which contains an excellent article about his early career by Frank Deford, "The Doctor Works His Magic."

BENNET SUSSER

MONTANA, Joseph Clifford, Jr. ("Joe") (*b.* 11 June 1956 in New Eagle, Pennsylvania), quarterback for the San Francisco 49ers who led the team to four Super Bowl victories; known as one of the best quarterbacks in NFL history.

Montana was born to Theresa Montana, a homemaker, and Joseph C. Montana, Sr., a finance company officer who encouraged their only child to participate in all sports. Montana began playing pee wee football at age eight through his father's efforts, although the minimum age was nine. At Ringgold High School he was a fine all-around athlete—good enough in football to begin receiving recruiting letters from major colleges as a junior; good enough in basketball to seriously consider a scholarship offer from North Carolina State. Early indications were that Montana would go to Notre Dame to play football. However, his father once challenged him by saying, "You'll probably take the easy way out and take the basketball scholarship." Joe responded to the challenge by electing to play the more physically demanding football at the more academically challenging Notre Dame.

Joe Montana, 1980s. © BETTMANN/CORBIS

When Montana arrived at the South Bend, Indiana, campus, he found he was one of seven highly recruited, prized freshmen quarterbacks. As he did in high school, Montana had to prove himself to skeptical coaches (Notre Dame's Ara Parseghian and Dan Devine) before becoming a starter. Despite leading the Fighting Irish to several comeback victories early in his career, Montana was not a starter until 1977, his junior season, and then only because of injuries to other quarterbacks. When given the chance, Montana showed a penchant for performing late-game heroics, as he led the Irish to a national championship, including a 38–10 victory over the University of Texas at Austin in the Cotton Bowl on 2 January 1978. Firmly entrenched as the starter in 1978, Montana would not lead the Irish to a repeat of the national championship, but he earned a permanent place in Notre Dame gridiron lore with an incredible comeback victory over the University of Houston in the Cotton Bowl in Dallas on 1 January 1979.

In miserable weather—an ice storm with thirty-mile-per-hour winds, making the windchill minus-ten degrees—and battling the flu (Montana had to be taken out of the game and into the locker room, where he was covered with blankets and fed chicken soup), he led the Irish to victory. Trailing Houston 34–12 with 7:37 to play, Montana hit a 2-point conversion after a blocked-punt touchdown to make the score 34–20. Another quick score and 2-point conversion made it 34–28. As Notre Dame was driving toward a potentially winning touchdown, Montana was stripped of the ball. Houston had only delayed what seemed to be preordained. Notre Dame and Montana got the ball a final time with thirty-five seconds left to play. Two passes by Montana to Kris Haines produced the tying points. Joe Unis kicked the winning extra point, but not until a second try. The first attempt was nullified by an Irish penalty. Montana had led his team to victory in what became a classic game.

Given an extra year of eligibility because he missed 1976 with an injury, Montana graduated in December 1978 with a B.S. in marketing. He moved to Manhattan Beach, California, to await the 1979 NFL player draft. There is credible evidence that Montana was a hard sell to the San Francisco 49ers coach Bill Walsh. Walsh had previously coached at Stanford and was said to prefer Steve Dils, who played quarterback for Walsh there. On the third round, chosen after such nondescript college passers as Jack Thompson and Steve Fuller, the 49ers tapped Montana. He was brought along slowly in Walsh's soon-to-be-famous "West Coast" offense, but responded well in limited action during the 1979 and 1980 seasons. The 49ers were 8–24 during these seasons.

Surprisingly, the next year (1981) Montana led the team

to a 26–21 victory over Cincinnati in Super Bowl XVI. To get to the Super Bowl, though, Montana had to connect in the back of the endzone with receiver Dwight Clark in the final minutes of the NFC Championship game on a play simply known as "the catch." The miraculous play defeated Dallas 28–27. Montana again paced the 49ers in Super Bowl XIX over Miami (38–16); in Super Bowl XXIII over Cincinnati (20–16), with Montana leading a comeback that culminated with the winning touchdown to Jerry Rice in the final minute; and in Super Bowl XXIV over Denver (55–10). Montana was voted Most Valuable Player (MVP) in all but Super Bowl XIX.

After the victory in Super Bowl XVI, the mayor of Monongahela, Pennsylvania, was asked if the town was going to name a street after Montana. The mayor said, "A street? He's already got a state named for him." In a similar move in 1993, the hamlet of Ismay, Montana, voted to change its name to Joe for that NFL season.

The rigors of NFL competition caught up with the six-foot, two-inch, 195-pound Montana in the late 1980s. By then a future Super Bowl MVP, Steve Young, had produced well as a replacement for Montana when needed. The 49ers were faced with a dilemma, showing loyalty to the legendary Montana or going with Young, who was five years younger than Montana. In a move that many thought lacked grace, Montana was traded to the Kansas City Chiefs in 1993, where he played two more seasons.

Montana retired after the 1994 season with sure Hall of Fame statistics: a 63.2 career pass-completion percentage; 40,551 yards passing; and 273 touchdowns. But it is as a cool, unflappable leader and last-minute victor that Montana is most remembered. His fourth-quarter, final-moment comebacks numbered in the dozens. His Super Bowl records are many and seemingly unreachable: three MVP awards, highest passer rating (127.8), most completions (85), most consecutive completions (13), most yards gained passing (1,142), most touchdown passes (11), and lowest interception percentage (0).

Montana's former Chiefs coach Marty Schottenheimer spoke for much of the professional football world, saying, "If I had one game I absolutely had to win, I'd want Joe Montana at quarterback." Bill Walsh, not especially known for sharing the glory, said, "If the 49ers are the team of the decade for the eighties—and they are—then Joe Montana is the player of the decade."

Montana, whose marriage to his high school sweetheart while a freshman at Notre Dame failed, married model Jennifer Wallace in 1985. They have four children and live in Calistoga in Northern California's wine country. After a stint in television broadcasting, Montana is involved in several business ventures, including some with former 49ers teammate Ronnie Lott.

It is generally conceded that if Joe Montana has any competition for "the greatest quarterback ever" it is fellow Western Pennsylvanian Johnny Unitas. Certainly, Montana's consistently high level of accomplishment ranks him among the most elite to have played the game.

★

Montana wrote an autobiography with Bob Raissman, *Audibles* (1986). His life and career are also discussed in Michael W. Tuckman and Jeff Schultz, *Team of the Decade* (1989); Beau Riffenburgh and David Boss, *Great Ones* (1989); and Dennis Pottenger, *Great Expectations* (1991).

JIM CAMPBELL

MOODY, Helen Wills. *See* Wills (Moody), Helen Newington.

MOORE, Archibald Lee ("Archie") (*b.* 13 December 1913 in Benoit, Mississippi; *d.* 9 December 1998 in San Diego, California), light-heavyweight boxing champion from 1952 to 1962, during a career that spanned almost thirty years; elected to the Boxing Hall of Fame in 1966.

Moore, who was born Archibald Lee Wright, claimed a birth date of 13 December 1916, although other sources—

Archie Moore, 1955. © BETTMANN/CORBIS

including his mother, Lorena Wright—indicated the year was 1913. Characteristically, Moore quipped that his mother was probably the more reliable source with a better memory of the event and that he must have been three years old when he was born. Moore's mother separated from his father, a farm worker named Thomas Wright, when Moore was an infant. Sent to live with his aunt Willie Pearl Moore and her husband, Cleveland, young Archie adopted the surname Moore to prevent confusion among their St. Louis neighbors. The couple was devoted to Moore and his sister and eventually took in their two half-brothers as well.

During Moore's teenage years, his beloved sister tragically died in childbirth and his Uncle Cleveland suffered a fatal injury shortly thereafter. Stricken by the losses, Moore earned a reputation as a troublesome gang member and street fighter by the time he entered Lincoln High School in St. Louis. After his arrest for stealing fares from a streetcar, Moore was sentenced to a three-year term at the Missouri Training School, of which he served twenty-two months. His time in reform school turned out to be productive; there he decided to become a professional boxer, started to train in earnest, and soon became a well-known personality.

Joining the Civilian Conservation Corps after his release, Moore continued to practice his boxing skills and organized tournaments in his Poplar Bluff, Missouri, camp. He also boxed in a number of amateur matches before his professional debut in 1936. His first thirteen opponents went down for the count, and the five-foot, eleven-inch Moore established a reputation as a powerful fighter. In 1938 he relocated to San Diego, which was his home base for the rest of his life. He married Mattie Chapman in 1940—the first of five marriages for the athlete. That same year Moore went on his first international tour, appearing in a series of bouts in Australia. Although the experience taught him to take a more active role in managing his own career, his extended absence contributed to the breakup of his first marriage.

While Moore was well on his way to getting a chance at a title fight in the light-heavyweight division, a series of illnesses kept him sidelined for almost a year. Recovering from surgery for a perforated ulcer, Moore slipped a metal license plate inside his high-waisted foul cup to keep his opponents from aggravating the injury and reentered the ring in 1942. Despite an impressive string of victories, however, Moore did not get a chance at the title for another ten years. After a vigorous letter-writing campaign to sports editors across the country, Moore finally got his title fight with Joey Maxim on 17 December 1952 in St. Louis, which he won by a unanimous decision.

By then in his forties, Moore set his sights on the world heavyweight crown held by Rocky Marciano. A study in contrasts when they met for the bout in Yankee Stadium on 21 September 1955, Marciano's raw slugging outpowered Moore's more deliberate approach, which relied on quick punches and a cross-armed defensive posture that earned him the nickname "The Old Mongoose" after the fast-acting animal. Although Moore lost the fight by a knockout in the ninth round, he later claimed that Marciano benefited from a long count after being knocked down in the second round. After Marciano's retirement, Moore fought Floyd Patterson in Chicago for the title in 1956; Moore went down by a knockout in the fifth round.

Moore's most memorable bout came with his defense of the light-heavyweight title against Canadian Yvon Durelle in Montreal on 10 December 1958. Moore was knocked down three times in the first round and again in the fifth before slowly wearing down his opponent. In round seven, Moore flattened Durelle for a count of three; the Canadian went down again in the tenth round and twice more in the following round, when he went down for a knockout. As Moore's 127th career knockout, it set a record for the most knockout victories and earned him the honor of Fighter of the Year from the Boxing Writers Association. Moore knocked Durelle out again in their rematch the following year, and he held the light-heavyweight title until 1962, when it was taken away from him for staying out of the ring for a prolonged period. Moore was named to the Boxing Hall of Fame in 1966.

In 1955 Moore entered into his fifth marriage, to Joan Hardy. The couple had two daughters and three sons. The Moores also adopted a son, and Moore had two other children as well. With his appearance in the 1960 movie *The Adventures of Huckleberry Finn,* in which he played a leading role as Jim, the fugitive slave, and the publication of his autobiography the same year, Moore's public profile exceeded that of almost any other boxer. After his last fight in 1965 Moore devoted himself to philanthropic work with disadvantaged youth, using boxing as a method to teach them self-discipline and determination. For his efforts Moore received numerous philanthropic distinctions, and in 1981 he was appointed by President Ronald W. Reagan to the Project Build program to bring sports programs to public housing residents. Moore also continued to train boxers, most notably George Foreman, whom he accompanied on his legendary 1974 fight against Muhammad Ali in Zaire.

With an estimated 194 victories in 228 fights—141 wins by knockout—Moore's career span was one of the longest in professional boxing. Unlike many of his contemporaries, Moore thrived during his postprofessional career as a trainer and philanthropist, and he was respected for his wit and integrity as well as his dedication to the sport. Moore's death from heart failure in San Diego brought numerous tributes that hailed him as a one-of-a-kind personality with an unparalleled career. He is buried at Cypress View Memorial Gardens in San Diego.

★

Moore's autobiography, *The Archie Moore Story* (1960), recounts his active career as a boxer. He also wrote *Any Boy Can: The Archie Moore Story* (1971), with Leonard B. Pearl, which covers much of the same ground, with the addition of his work as a philanthropist. Marilyn Green Douroux, *Archie Moore—The Old Mongoose: The Authorized Biography of Archie Moore, Undefeated Light-Heavyweight Champion of the World* (1991), provides an account of Moore's life through various sketches and includes numerous personal photographs and documents. An interview with Moore is included in Peter Heller, *In This Corner: Forty-two World Champions Tell Their Stories* (expanded and updated, 1994). The numerous tributes to Moore upon his death include portraits by Michael Hirsley, *Chicago Tribune* (10 Dec. 1998); Michael Katz, *New York Daily News* (10 Dec. 1998); Bill Lyon, *Philadelphia Inquirer* (11 Dec. 1998); Dave Kindred, *Sporting News* (21 Dec. 1998); and George Plimpton, *Sports Illustrated* (21 Dec. 1998).

TIMOTHY BORDEN

MORGAN, Joe Leonard (*b.* 19 September 1943 in Bonham, Texas), baseball player who was the second baseman for Cincinnati's Big Red Machine in the 1970s, who later became a member of the National Baseball Hall of Fame and was a sports analyst.

Morgan was born in the segregated community of Bonham. When he was ten his family moved to Oakland, California. Morgan's father, Leonard Morgan, had served in the military and completed three years of college before joining Pacific Tire and Rubber to support his six children.

With his father's encouragement, Morgan became a star in Oakland's Little League. He idolized Jackie Robinson, the first player to integrate Major League Baseball, and he played Robinson's position of second base. While attending Castlemont High School in Oakland, Morgan made the varsity baseball squad his freshman year, when he was just fifteen years old. Because of his small size (five feet, seven inches tall and 155 pounds), Morgan was not initially recruited by the major league teams. Following his high-school graduation he enrolled at Oakland City College, where he continued to play baseball.

In 1963 the Houston Colt .45s (who changed their name to the Astros in 1965) took a chance and signed Morgan. From 1963 to 1964 he played for Houston farm teams in Modesto, California; Durham, North Carolina; and San Antonio, Texas, with brief stints in Houston at the end of each season. As a rookie second baseman in 1965, Morgan's defense improved under the tutelage of the Houston coach Nellie Fox. He batted .271, hit 14 home runs, drove in 40

Joe Morgan. ASSOCIATED PRESS AP

runs, and, developing the reputation for a careful eye, walked 97 times. In a *Sporting News* poll of National League (NL) players, he was voted the Rookie Player of the Year.

From 1966 to 1971 Morgan continued to start at second base for Houston, although he missed most of the 1968 season with a knee injury. He was selected for the All-Star game in 1966 but was unable to play due to injury; he was selected again in 1970 and was able to play in the game. In April 1967 Morgan married his high-school sweetheart, Gloria Stewart; they had two daughters. Following the 1971 season, Morgan was traded to the Cincinnati Reds as part of an eleven-player deal. Morgan was bitter about the trade, and in his 1993 autobiography he blamed the Houston manager Harry Walker for labeling him as a "troublemaker."

The trade to Cincinnati, nevertheless, proved to be a blessing, and Morgan enjoyed his best major league seasons with the Reds. He joined Tony Perez, Johnny Bench, and Pete Rose to create a dynasty known as the Big Red Machine. In 1972 the Reds won the NL pennant, but lost in the World Series to the Oakland Athletics (or A's). The

Reds attained a division championship in 1973, while in 1975 and 1976 Cincinnati won consecutive World Series titles. Morgan was the catalyst for these championship teams, earning the NL's Most Valuable Player honors in 1975 and 1976. During the 1975 campaign Morgan batted .327, hit 17 home runs, knocked in 94 runs, stole 67 bases, and walked 132 times. The following season, the slick-fielding second baseman hit .320 with 27 home runs, 111 runs batted in, and 60 stolen bases.

However, the Big Red Machine began to unravel during the late 1970s, and in 1978 Morgan batted only .236. After the 1979 season Morgan declared for free agency and rejoined the Houston Astros. Morgan was critical of the Reds' fiscal conservatism, blaming management for not pursuing free agents as salary figures increased with the abolishment of baseball's reserve clause. Morgan asserted that the Reds' front office failed to change with the times. Houston won a divisional title in 1980, but Morgan moved on to the San Francisco Giants for the 1981 and 1982 seasons. Batting .289 with fourteen home runs, Morgan kept the Giants in the 1982 divisional race and was selected by the *Sporting News* as the NL's Comeback Player of the Year.

In 1983 Morgan turned down an offer to manage in Houston, and signed with the Philadelphia (Pennsylvania) Phillies. He considered taking the Houston position to further African-American advancement in baseball management, but his desire to play was still too strong. While the Phillies reached the World Series, losing to the Baltimore Orioles, Morgan only batted .230 with sixteen home runs. He announced his retirement in 1984, but the Oakland A's president Roy Eisenhardt convinced him to sign for one more campaign. Morgan explained, "I happen to love Oakland. I grew up there. I got a great education there, and I feel a debt to the city." After a subpar season with the A's, hitting only .244 with six home runs, Morgan followed through with his retirement from the game of baseball. In twenty-two seasons, Morgan hit 268 home runs, drove in 1,133 runs, stole 689 bases, garnered 2,517 hits, walked 1,865 times, and attained a lifetime batting average of .271. Morgan was elected to NL All-Star teams nine times, won five Gold Glove Awards, and was inducted into the National Baseball Hall of Fame in 1990.

Morgan decided to go into business after his playing days, asserting, "You can't pass a baseball job along to your children and grandchildren." Keeping a promise to his mother, Morgan returned to college and in 1990 acquired a B.A. in physical education from California State University, Hayward. He acquired and ran three Wendy's hamburger franchises in Oakland from 1985 to 1988 and operated a Coors beer distributorship from 1987 to 1995. Following his retirement from playing baseball, Morgan divorced Stewart and married his second wife, Theresa.

Morgan also carved out a career in baseball broadcasting. From 1986 through 1993 he announced for the San Francisco Giants and served as a commentator for the NBC television network's *Game of the Week*. In 1994 he began working for ESPN, forming a lively and informative collaboration with the broadcaster Jon Miller. He won a Cable ACE Award for broadcasting in 1990 and an Emmy Award in 1998. In the 1990s Morgan continued to play golf, tennis, and billiards, and he remained an articulate voice for the inclusion of African Americans in baseball management.

Morgan's life and career proved that one need not be held back by a diminutive stature. He combined power and speed in a small frame, leading the Cincinnati Reds teams of the 1970s, one of the best teams in baseball history, to two world championships. The articulate Morgan is a successful businessman and remains an outstanding spokesman for Major League Baseball in his role as a television analyst.

★

A file on Morgan is available at the National Baseball Hall of Fame in Cooperstown, New York. Morgan's perspectives, although not necessarily the details of his life, are well developed in his book with David Falkner, *Joe Morgan: A Life in Baseball* (1993). For his years in Cincinnati, see Bob Hertzel, *The Big Red Machine* (1976), and Robert H. Walker, *Cincinnati and the Big Red Machine* (1988). For secondary accounts of Morgan's life, see Mark Mulvoy, "The Little Big Man," *Sports Illustrated* (12 Apr. 1976); Joel H. Cohen, *Joe Morgan: Great Little Big Man* (1978); and J. Armstrong, "Little Joe," *Sport* (Nov. 1997).

RON BRILEY

MOSBACHER, Emil, Jr. ("Bus") (*b.* 1 April 1922 in Mount Vernon, New York; *d.* 13 August 1997 in Greenwich, Connecticut), yachtsman who was a winner of One Design championships and the winning skipper in two America's Cup competitions; he was also a businessman and Chief of Protocol for President Richard M. Nixon.

Mosbacher was one of three children of Emil Mosbacher, Sr., a businessman and stockbroker, and Gertrude Schwartz Mosbacher, a homemaker. Mosbacher got his nickname early. When he was a newborn, a hospital nurse pronounced him a "Buster," a term for a good-sized infant. The term was contracted to "Bus," and it stuck. Mosbacher's career as a sailor began at age five when his father, a sailing enthusiast and member of the Knickerbocker Yacht Club, put him into a dinghy. He spent his summers sailing on Long Island Sound, initially in the family's small catboat. When Mosbacher was nine, he was given his own boat, a Star-Class. After a summer of professional coaching from his father's helmsman, Mosbacher won his first race, defeating the only other boat in the race. Over the summers,

Emil "Bus" Mosbacher, at the wheel of *Weatherly* in the 1962 America's Cup. ASSOCIATED PRESS AP

more races and victories followed. Sailing Stars, he won the Midget championship in 1935 and 1936. He moved up to the Juniors in 1937 and took that national title two years later.

Mosbacher's father was his harshest critic, and several family meals were spoiled because of the rehashing of a race. As Mosbacher remarked in a *Time* magazine article, "He was most sparing with his compliments." When Mosbacher made a serious mistake, such as taking the wrong tack, he would have dinner with a friend. Mosbacher Sr. was adamant against filing protests. He believed a race should be won on the racecourse, not in a protest meeting, and always stressed the importance of good sportsmanship. When Mosbacher was fifteen, he finished so close to another boat that he could not tell who won. The other skipper acted as if he were the winner, and Mosbacher, showing good sportsmanship, yelled to the other boat, "Nice race." Mosbacher's crew, the singer and actress Ethel Merman, shook her fist at the committee boat and screamed that they were blind if they thought the other boat won. Merman's Broadway-trained voice carried, and Mosbacher had, in fact, won the race.

Mosbacher attended Choate Preparatory School (now called Choate Rosemary Hall) in Wallingford, Connecticut, and graduated in 1939 with honors. He enrolled at Dartmouth College in Hanover, New Hampshire, majoring in economics. At Dartmouth he sailed with the varsity sailing club, and they won two intercollegiate championships. Mosbacher received his B.A. in 1943. He served in the U.S. Navy from 1942 to 1945, advancing in rank from apprentice seaman to lieutenant. His time spent on a minesweeper in the Pacific was a change in perspective for the Long Island Sound sailor.

Following the war, Mosbacher went to work in the family real estate, oil, and natural gas businesses and continued to sail for recreation. He returned to competitive sailing in 1949, skippering a thirty-three-foot International One Design sloop to victory in the Amorita Cup in Bermuda. The same year he won the British-American Cup at the Isle of Wight, sailing a six-meter. On 24 November 1949 Mosbacher married Patricia Ann Ryan; they had three sons.

Throughout the 1950s Mosbacher sailed his International Class sloop *Susan,* named after his grandmother, winning the class championship eight years in a row. His competitors were the elite of U.S. racing. Following his 1957 victory in *Susan,* he competed for the Prince of Wales Trophy, a match racing series, and won. Match racing pits one boat against one other, and the starts are critical. Each skipper looks for the other to make a mistake and then capitalizes on it. As Mosbacher said in a 1967 interview for *Time* magazine: "The idea is to find your opponent's Achilles' heel—and sink your teeth into it."

Mosbacher's success in racing International-class boats led to an opportunity to be helmsman on *Vim,* a twelve-meter, for the elimination trials to decide which yacht would defend the America's Cup. The America's Cup is the most prestigious award in sailing and had been successfully defended by U.S. yachts since 1851. *Vim* was not expected to do well in the elimination trials as she was older and slower than her competitors, but with Mosbacher at the helm, *Vim* became a serious contender. Mosbacher harassed his opponents into making errors and exhausted everyone with his tacking duels, but lost to *Columbia* by twelve seconds. In this defeat he won an enormous amount of respect for his aggressiveness and sailing acumen. *Columbia* easily beat the British challenger.

Impressed by Mosbacher's accomplishment with *Vim,* the sponsors of the America's Cup, the New York Yacht Club, invited Mosbacher to join and skipper the next contender. For the defense of the America's Cup in 1962 Mosbacher was sailing *Weatherly,* a boat he beat in the 1958 trials. Under Mosbacher's direction, modifications were made, chiefly in the distribution of weight. *Weatherly* had been refitted, but was not considered as fast as the Australian challenger *Gretel.* Although Mosbacher was a superb tactician, he knew that the best tactics do not always mean victory. Crew is critical, and Mosbacher picked his own crew, built around men with whom he had sailed when he campaigned *Vim.* From 15 September 1962 to 25 September 1962, off the coast of Rhode Island with a huge spectator fleet (including President John F. Kennedy in a destroyer) Mosbacher looked for "Jock" Sturrock, the skipper of the *Gretel,* to make mistakes. In a close series Mosbacher kept the Cup, winning four out of five races against a faster boat.

After the series concluded, Mosbacher, who had taken six months off from work, went back to running the family's businesses. Mosbacher announced his retirement from America's Cup competition, but changed his mind in 1967 when he had a chance to help design a new yacht *Intrepid,* described in *Time* as "the shortest (at sixty-four feet), homeliest, most radical, and most expensive twelve-meter yacht ever built." The competition was held between 12 and 18 September 1967. Sailing against the Australian yacht *Dame Pattie,* Mosbacher won all four races easily.

In 1969 Mosbacher was appointed as Chief of Protocol (1969 to 1972) during the administration of President Richard M. Nixon. Nixon offered him the opportunity to take time off to defend the America's Cup, but Mosbacher declined. Mosbacher was the chairman of the first Operation Sail, which brought the tall ships to New York Harbor in 1976. He also helped organized two other Operations Sail events in 1986 and 1992. Mosbacher died at his home of cancer, a disease he had been battling for years.

Mosbacher was voted Yachtsman of the Year in 1962 and 1967, chiefly because of his successful defense of the America's Cup. Sailing twelve-meters as if they were dinghies, Mosbacher showed fearlessness as well as his knowledge of how to get the most out of his boat and his crew.

★

Bob Bavier, *America's Cup Fever; an Inside Look at 50 Years of America's Cup Competition* (1980), includes a chapter on Mosbacher as well as background on the America's Cup. Periodical articles include: "Mosbacher: Yachting's Unassuming Magician," *New York Times* (26 Aug. 1962); "A Buster at the Helm: Emil Mosbacher, Jr.," *New York Times* (26 Sept. 1962); "The Intrepid Gentleman," *Time* (18 Aug. 1967); and Noel F. Busch, "The Savvy Skipper of Protocol," *Reader's Digest* 99 (Oct. 1971). An obituary is in the *New York Times* (14 Aug. 1997).

MARCIA B. DINNEEN

MOSES, Edwin Corley (*b.* 31 August 1955 in Dayton, Ohio), track-and-field star who won the gold medal in the 400-meter hurdles at the 1976 and 1984 Olympic Games and the bronze medal at the 1988 Olympics, and who was undefeated for 122 consecutive high-hurdle events.

The son of two educators, and one of three boys, Moses spent most of his childhood reading books and concentrating on his studies. He was reared in Dayton, Ohio, where his father, Irving S. Moses, worked as an elementary school principal, and his mother, Gladys H. Moses, worked as a high school curriculum supervisor. Education was stressed in the Moses household, and extracurricular activ-

Edwin Moses, 1984. ASSOCIATED PRESS AP

ities were only permitted if they did not interfere with academics. Moses showed a penchant for math and science at an early age and spent his spare time dissecting frogs and collecting fossils.

Moses attended Fairview High School, a predominantly white school, where he was one of twenty African-American students. He maintained a high grade-point average and had a reputation for being a "smart guy." While most kids spent their summer vacation enjoying the outdoors, Moses took math and science courses for extra credit. His studious qualities actually led him to his track career; he learned how to hurdle by reading a Boy Scout handbook on track and field. Moses's strong academic record earned him a scholarship as a National Merit Scholar to the historically African-American college, Morehouse, in Atlanta, where he majored in physics. Despite his grueling course work, Moses joined the school's track team and managed to maintain a 3.5 grade-point average.

Moses's body went through a metamorphosis during his years at Morehouse; he grew several inches and gained about 35 pounds. At six feet, two inches and 165 pounds, it took Moses only thirteen strides to go from one hurdle to the next, and he won his races with ease. His coach saw a great deal of promise in the young athlete and encouraged him to tryout for the 1976 Summer Olympic Games in Montreal, Canada.

Moses's opportunity to go to the Olympics came during the 1976 Florida Relays in Gainesville. Although he did not win any races, his hurdling technique caught the attention of Olympic track-and-field coach Leroy Walker. Walker believed Moses would be the future champion for the 400-meter intermediates, and took him under his wing. Under Walker's tutelage, Moses qualified to compete at the Olympics and headed to Montreal, where he took home the gold medal and set a new world record by completing the 400-meter hurdles in 47.63 seconds with a 1.05-second margin of victory—the longest margin of victory in the history of the Olympic event.

After winning the gold, Moses became an instant celebrity, but he had a love/hate relationship with the media. Journalists found Moses to be aloof and mistook his prescription sunglasses as a sign of antisocial behavior. However, Moses's winning streak continued, and he became more popular in both Europe and the United States. His public persona also changed with some help from his wife, artist Myrella Bordt, whom he married on 30 May 1982. During the height of his popularity, Moses used his celebrity status to change certain practices in track and field. He became a spokesperson for a litany of causes and spoke out against the use of anabolic steroids. He also chastised the practices of some sports promoters, whom he felt exploited the athletes financially, and challenged them to increase appearance fees and lobbied for the compensation of amateur athletes. Moses's popularity also won him endorsement deals from various companies and increased his income to an estimated $500,000 a year.

Despite his success and fame, Moses continued to focus on his studies. He went back to college and graduated from Morehouse College with a B.S. in physics in 1978. Four years after his first Olympic victory, Moses was still in the midst of a long winning streak and was believed to be a sure winner in the 1980 Summer Olympics in Moscow. However, when President Jimmy Carter boycotted the Olympic games that year, Moses had to wait another four years before he could again compete in the Olympics. Eight years after he took home the gold, Moses, because of his age, was seen as the underdog in the 1984 Summer Olympics in Los Angeles. Skeptics were doubtful that he would even make the U.S. Olympic team. Moses not only qualified for the team, but he also won a second gold medal, beating out his more youthful competitors. That year, *Sports Illustrated* named him the Sportsman of the Year.

In 1987 Moses's winning streak came to an end when, at the age of thirty-one, he lost to twenty-one-year-old Danny Harris. At the time of the loss, Moses had won 122 consecutive races in nearly 10 years, one of the longest winning streaks in track history. Moses recovered the same year when he defeated Harris in Rome to regain the world title.

At thirty-three, Moses was one of the oldest athletes to qualify on the U.S. Olympic track team for the 1988 Summer Olympics in Seoul, Korea. His attempt to win the gold came at a high price. He suffered back and knee injuries from excessive training and required physical therapy every day. Over a decade older than his opponents, Moses finished the 400-meter hurdles in third place and won the bronze medal. He made another attempt at winning a medal in the 1992 Winter Olympics, but this time on the U.S. bobsled team. He trained with the team in hopes of winning the berth position. But those dreams never came to fruition, and Moses retired from professional sports.

After retiring, Moses decided to pursue a graduate degree in business. In 1994 he graduated from Pepperdine University's M.B.A. program and became a financial consultant and partner for Salomon Smith Barney's Platinum Group. He was inducted into the National Track and Field Hall of Fame in St. Louis, Missouri, in 1994.

An accomplished athlete, Moses is revered for his performance on and off the track. His intelligence, dedication, and natural ability have brought him success as a track star and as a businessman. Moses is also a philanthropist and an active member of various charities and community organizations. He lives in Atlanta with his wife and son.

★

Biographical information about Moses can be found in *Current Biography Yearbook* (1986), and *Black Olympian Medallist* (1991).

He is also featured in *Ebony* (May 1984 and July 1992); *Jet* (26 Dec. 1994 and 22 July 1996); *People Weekly* (23 July 1984 and 19 Sept. 1988); *Sports Illustrated* (30 July 1984, 24 Dec. 1984, 9 June 1986, 15 June 1987); and the *Washington Post* (28 Apr. 1985).

SABINE LOUISSAINT

MOTLEY, Marion (*b.* 5 June 1920 in Leesburg, Georgia; *d.* 27 June 1999 in Cleveland, Ohio), professional football player considered to be one of the greatest running backs of all time.

Motley was one of three children born to Shakeful Motley, a mill worker, and Blanche Jones Motley, a homemaker. Born in rural Georgia, he moved with his family as a young boy to Canton, Ohio, where his father worked in a foundry. He was a three-sport standout at the perennial football powerhouse Canton McKinley High School, from which he graduated in 1939. He attended South Carolina State College in Orangeburg for one year and then in 1940 transferred to the University of Nevada (later the University of Nevada, Reno), where his former high-school coach Jim Aiken was the head coach.

Motley was a star football performer at Nevada for three seasons (1940–1942). A punishing linebacker on defense, he also excelled as a running back. His 105-yard return of a kickoff against San José State College (later San José State University) set a Wolf Pack record, and he received regional All-Star recognition. His career was imperiled during the 1940 season when, while driving back from a football game in San Francisco, he struck and killed a person in Fairfield, California. He spent several days in jail and was charged with involuntary manslaughter. He was supported by Nevada students and Reno boosters, who provided legal assistance and raised the funds to pay a $1,000 fine. Impressed with Motley's character and the strong community support evidenced on his behalf, the judge granted him probation. Two days after being released from jail, Motley repaid his supporters by scoring two first-quarter touchdowns in a 78–0 romp over Arkansas A&M College.

Marion Motley, 1956. © BETTMANN/CORBIS

With one year of eligibility remaining, Motley left Nevada without earning a degree for the U.S. Navy in 1943; he spent much of his wartime service at the Great Lakes Naval Station playing for the powerful teams coached by Paul Brown. Motley's high-school team had lost only three games, all to the Massillon High School Tigers coached by Brown. In 1945 Brown was selected by Mickey McBride, a Cleveland taxicab magnate who also operated the largest nationwide wire service for horse-race betting parlors, to coach his new professional team in the upstart All-America Football Conference (A-AFC). In assembling one of the greatest professional teams of all time, Brown defied the unwritten all-white rule then current in professional football by signing African-American players. In addition to Motley, Brown invited the star defensive lineman Bill Willis, a former Massillon player. Thus in 1946 Motley and Willis, along with Woody Strode and Kenny Washington of the Los Angeles Rams, reintegrated professional football for the first time since the 1930s.

At six feet, one inch, and 235 pounds, Motley was a bruising inside runner. His initial burst of speed often got him through the line, where he then ran over smaller defensive backs. "Don't get fancy when you pass the line of scrimmage," Brown instructed his talented fullback. "Just run right at them and over them." The innovative Brown created a special play ("Trap 34") to take advantage of Motley's explosive running, which was made effective by the deft ball handling of the quarterback Otto Graham and the crisp blocking by such lineman as Lou Groza and Chuck Noll. The Browns dominated the All-America Football Conference, winning its championship all four years of its existence with a 47–4–3 overall record. During those four seasons Motley gained 3,024 yards on 489 carries. He also caught forty-five passes for 644 yards, many coming on screen pass plays. He also played middle linebacker; his games were so memorable that in 1991 Brown said that he never had coached a more determined or effective linebacker than Motley.

In 1950 the Browns joined the National Football League (NFL) after the A-AFC folded. Most experts predicted that the Browns would get their comeuppance after playing in what they considered a lesser league. Instead, the Browns devastated the heavily favored Philadelphia (Pennsylvania) Eagles 35–10 in their inaugural league game and stormed on to win the conference title. Motley led the NFL with 810 rushing yards on 140 carries and was named to the All-League first team. In one memorable performance on 29 October 1950, he gained 188 yards on just eleven attempts against the Pittsburgh Steelers. Between 1950 and 1953 the Browns won forty games and lost eight; a late-season injury forced Motley to sit out the 1954 season, and in 1955 he ended his career as a substitute linebacker for the Steelers. He ended his entire career with 4,720 rushing yards and thirty-one touchdowns. He averaged an extraordinary 5.7 yards per carry. He always felt that he could have gained many more yards had Brown accepted his suggestion of running outside the ends on option plays.

After retirement Motley faced many frustrations. His highest salary as a Brown was just $15,000, and the league at the time lacked a retirement program. His efforts to obtain an assistant coaching position in the NFL proved fruitless; he blamed racism for his rejections. When he once asked a Browns official about possible employment, he was met with a caustic, "Have you tried the mills?" After leaving football Motley initially found work as a parking lot attendant and later worked for the U.S. Postal Service in Cleveland. During the 1980s he served as a spokesperson for the Ohio Lottery. He and his wife, Eula Coleman, who were married in 1943, had three children. He died in 1999 after a year-long battle with prostate cancer.

In 1968 Motley became the second African American to be named to the Pro Football Hall of Fame, which is located just a mile from his former home in Canton. Despite losing three prime playing years during World War II, Motley made a lasting impression after joining the Browns as a twenty-seven year old. Blanton Collier, an assistant coach with the Browns during Motley's tenure and later the team's head coach, once commented that Motley was "the greatest all-around football player I ever saw. He had no equal as a blocker. He could run with anybody for thirty yards. And this man was a great, great linebacker." Paul Brown, Jr., commented upon Motley's death, "My dad always felt Marion was the greatest back he ever had."

★

There is an interpretative segment on Motley's role as a racial pioneer in professional football in Richard O. Davies, *America's Obsession: Sports and Society Since 1945* (1994). See also George Sullivan, *Pro Football's All-Time Greats: The Immortals in Professional Football's Hall of Fame* (1968), and Jack Clary, *The Cleveland Browns: Great Teams' Great Years* (1973). An obituary is in the *New York Times* (28 June 1999).

RICHARD O. DAVIES

MOURNING, Alonzo Harding, Jr. (*b.* 8 February 1970 in Chesapeake, Virginia), professional basketball player; National Basketball Association (NBA) All-Star; member of the 1994 world champion "Dream Team II" and the U.S. basketball team that won the gold medal in the 2000 Summer Olympics in Australia.

Mourning was born to Alonzo Mourning, Sr., a machinist in the Portsmouth, Virginia, shipyards, and Julia Mourning. Mourning's parents separated in 1980, and he was later sent to live in a group home in Chesapeake. His parents reunited and had a second child, Tamara, in 1981. They divorced in September 1983. At the age of twelve Mourning moved in with family friend Fannie Threet, a retired teacher. Although Threet and her husband had two children of their own, they continually took in foster children. Mourning lived with up to nine children in the Threets' four-bedroom house in Chesapeake until he left for Georgetown University.

In the seventh grade Mourning was already six feet, three inches tall, and played football and basketball. It was

Alonzo Mourning, 2001. ASSOCIATED PRESS AP

then that he got his nickname "Zo." He was not serious about playing basketball until he saw the 1982 National Collegiate Athletic Association (NCAA) basketball championship game on television. He was impressed by Georgetown University's center Patrick Ewing, who would later become a close friend. In the summer of 1986 Mourning was invited to the prestigious Five Star basketball camp in Pittsburgh. Mourning's performance impressed not only the Five Star coach, Frank Marino, but also college recruiters. In his junior year of high school, Mourning led his team, under the direction of Coach Bill Lassiter, to an unbeaten season and the 1987 Virginia State Class AAA Championship. He was named Virginia High School Player of the Year (1987). Mourning finished his final year as the team's leading scorer and rebounder, and was named the National High School Player of the Year by both Gatorade and *USA Today* in 1988.

That same year Mourning entered Georgetown University, where Coach John Thompson ran a fine program and stressed education; more than 95 percent of his players earned their degrees. Mourning finished his first season with averages of 13.2 points, 7.3 rebounds, and 4.9 blocks per game. His eleven blocks in one game broke the previous school record of ten held by Ewing. In 1989 Mourning was named the Big East Defensive Player of the Year, and also named to the Big East All-Rookie Team and Second Team All-Big East.

The following two seasons were disappointing for Mourning, who played the power forward position, but he was nevertheless awarded Big East Co-Defensive Player of the Year (1990) and named First Team All-Big East (1990). Later in the season, Mourning was criticized for making an allegedly anti-Semitic remark to Nadav Henefeld, the University of Connecticut's Israeli forward, during a game. During Mourning's college years, a growing number of players dropped out of college early to enter the NBA draft. Mourning would have had a good chance in the draft, but he decided to stay in college to mature both as a basketball player and a person. The decision to stay at Georgetown was especially important to his foster mother, Fannie Threet.

Mourning went back to center in his senior year. He led Georgetown to the Big East Co-Championship with the season averages of 21.7 points, 10.7 rebounds, and 5 blocks per game. He became the second player after Ewing to have scored more than 2,000 points and grabbed more than 1,000 rebounds in Georgetown school history. He was named Most Valuable Player (MVP) of the Big East Tournament in 1992, and became the first Big East player ever to receive both Eastern Basketball Player of the Year and Big East Defensive Player of the Year awards in the same season. He was also named First Team All-America by the Associated Press and won the Henry Iba Defensive Player of the Year Award. In the spring of 1992, Mourning received his bachelor's degree in sociology.

In the 1992 NBA draft, as the first-round, second-pick behind Shaquille O'Neal, Mourning was selected by the Charlotte Hornets, an expansion team that had been struggling in its five-year existence as an NBA team. Mourning's arrival in Charlotte made an immediate impact. He and Larry Johnson, the 1991 NBA Rookie of the Year, led the Hornets to their first ever playoff with a 44–38 record. He was named the NBA Rookie of the Month for the last two months of the season and was a unanimous choice for the NBA All-Rookie First Team. People compared Mourning with Shaquille O'Neal, because the two great centers entered the NBA in the same year. In 1994 Mourning was chosen as a member of the U.S. basketball team, the "Dream Team II," that won the World Championship in Canada. During the 1993–1994 season, Mourning missed a number of games because of injuries. He was named to the Eastern Conference All-Star team in 1994, and in the summer of 1994, Mourning joined Dikembe Mutombo and Ewing to conduct basketball clinics for children in South Africa. In the 1994–1995 season, the Hornets compiled their best record, 50–32. Mourning was named to the NBA All-Star team in 1995.

In 1995 Mourning was traded to the Miami Heat, and led the Heat to the 1995–1996 playoffs with a 42–40 record. Mourning's second season with the Heat brought a team record of 61 wins and captured the Atlantic Division title.

On 24 August 1996 Mourning and longtime girlfriend Tracy Wilson had their first child. They married on 30 August 1997.

Mourning had to miss many games in the 1997–1998 season due to a knee injury and a broken cheekbone, but he came back strong in the 1998–1999 season, averaging 20.1 points, 11.0 rebounds, and 3.9 blocks per game. He was awarded Defensive Player of the Year and named to the All-NBA First Team and All-Defensive First Team. In the 1999–2000 season, Mourning played a career high of 79 games, averaging 21.7 points, 9.5 rebounds, and 3.7 blocks. He earned the Defensive Player of the Year again, and was named to the All-Defensive First Team and the All-NBA Second Team. He was also selected as a member of the U.S. basketball team that would compete in 2000 Summer Olympics in Australia. During the Olympics, Mourning flew halfway around the world back to Miami to be at his wife's side when she gave birth to their second child on 22 September 2000. Three days later, Mourning returned to Australia and helped the U.S. team win the gold medal.

On 16 October 2000 Coach Pat Riley announced that Mourning would miss the season to undergo treatment for the kidney disease focal glomerulosclerosis. The disease would be first treated with medication, but could eventually require dialysis or a transplant. Mourning's longtime friend Patrick Ewing, who was also the godfather of Mourning's daughter, announced that he would donate one of his kidneys to Mourning if he ever needed a transplant. Despite his illness, Mourning was selected as a member of the Eastern Conference team for the 2001 NBA All-Star Game. Since his disease was in remission, Mourning returned to the Miami Heat at the end of the regular season, but the Heat was eliminated before the conference semifinals.

Off the court, Mourning served as the NBA's national spokesperson for the prevention of child abuse, and was an active participant in the NBA's Healthy Families America program. He was a regular visitor and spokesperson for Thompson's Children's Home in Charlotte. He founded Zo's Summer Groove, an annual charity event, to benefit the Miami-based Children's Home Society and 100 Black Men of South Florida.

Mourning is regarded as one of the hardest working and toughest players in the NBA. A relatively short center at six feet, ten inches, Mourning is nevertheless intimidating. He always treats the game as serious business, and his relentless work ethic is praised by his coaches and teammates. His intense style brings his opponents to the foul line, but also has made him one of the league's best combined shot-blockers, rebounders, and scorers.

★

There are several book-length biographies of Mourning, including Neil Cohen, *Head to Head Basketball: Patrick Ewing/Alonzo Mourning* (1994); Frank Fortunato, *Sports Great Alonzo Mourning* (1997); Bill Gutman, *Alonzo Mourning: Center of Attention* (1997); Bert Rosenthal, *Alonzo Mourning* (1998); and Judith Mandell, *Super Sports Star Alonzo Mourning* (2001). Biographical essays can be found in *Newsmakers 1994; Sports Stars* (1994–1998); and *Contemporary Black Biography* (1998). Lengthy articles include Amy Shipley, "Alonzo Mourning's Hidden Side: Surly Star's Secret Life Is Just for Family," *Charlotte Observer* (12 Nov. 1996); S. L. Price, "The Man in the Iron Mask," *Sports Illustrated* (30 Mar. 1998); Ira Winderman, "The Other Side of Zo: The Heat's Star Has a Soft Side, But Rarely Shows It," *Fort Lauderdale (Florida) Sun-Sentinel* (30 Dec. 1997); D. L. Cummings, "Changed Man," *Miami Herald* (13 Feb. 2000); and David DuPree, "Keeping It in Perspective," *USA Today* (17 Oct. 2000).

DI SU

MULDOWNEY, Shirley Roque (*b.* 19 June 1940 in Burlington, Vermont), pioneering female drag racer who won an unprecedented three National Hot Rod Association Winston World Championships.

Muldowney was born Shirley Roque, the only child of Mae Roque and Belgium "Tex Rock" Benedict Roque. Her father was a professional boxer and drove a taxi, and her mother worked in a laundry service. The family moved from Burlington to Schenectady, New York, shortly after Muldowney's birth. Formal schooling held little interest for Muldowney, and by age thirteen she was skipping classes and hanging around with drag racing enthusiasts from a local car club. She kept these meetings and her passion for drag racing from her parents for fear they would disapprove. At the car club she met Jack Muldowney, her future husband, who taught her to drive and introduced her to drag racing.

Muldowney, a quick study, participated in street racing throughout the 1950s. When her father did find out about her racing, rather than punishing her, he encouraged her to continue. In 1956 she dropped out of school, married Jack, and began racing full time. A year later she gave birth to a son (who eventually became part of her racing team), but not even that slowed her down. Using various cars she competed locally in both amateur and semiprofessional races, earning the nickname "Cha Cha" (the phrase had been written in shoe polish on the side of her pink car) and making some money to help support her family.

In 1965 Muldowney became the first woman licensed by the National Hot Rod Association (NHRA) to race dragsters in their Top Gas (T/G) category. From 1965 to 1969 she competed in one-on-one duels in small towns with other drag racers. During this period of her racing career, the drag strip establishment tried to portray Muldowney as part feminist, part temptress. She allowed herself to be filmed dressed in go-go boots, hot pants, and a halter top, before donning an asbestos suit and slipping into her car of the time, Bounty Huntress. This was supposed to show that, even though she was a determined racer, there was still a pretty girl underneath. The image bothered Muldowney and she began to subtly alter that image. Meanwhile, her racing abilities were earning her increasing fame and prestige. As Muldowney's career began to take off, her marriage began to sour, and she and Jack divorced in 1972.

During the early 1970s the NHRA introduced the Top Fuel category of cars, in which the car's engine is behind the driver, which undercut the popularity of the more dangerous T/G class of cars, in which the engine is in front. In 1971 Muldowney moved to Armada, Michigan, and began working with the drag racer Conrad "Connie" Kalitta. Muldowney and Kalitta switched to the Funny Cars, those with fiberglass bodies and the engines in front of the driver like T/G cars, and began racing against each other. The collaboration turned into a tumultuous relationship that lasted seven years. Muldowney raced Funny Cars from 1971 until 1973, winning the International Hot Rod Association (IHRA) title in 1971. She suffered four engine fires during this period, including one at Indianapolis in 1973 that left her seriously burned. This injury convinced

Muldowney to switch to the less dangerous Top Fuel racers in 1973, with Kalitta as her crew chief. That year she raced in a car owned by another racer, but the next year Kalitta had a dragster built for her. In her first year as a Top Fuel racer, Muldowney posted the second-best speed at the U.S. nationals, and the following year she was the first female to enter the NHRA national event finals. In spite of her successes, Muldowney suffered indignities because she was a woman, including being excluded from several races for no real reason, and she gradually stopped using the name "Cha Cha."

In 1977 Muldowney became the first driver to win three consecutive NHRA Top Fuel races and the Winston World Championship. For this accomplishment, the U.S. House of Representatives recognized her with an outstanding achievement award on 14 October 1977, and *Car Craft* magazine named her their person of the year. Her success, however, put additional strain on her already volatile relationship with Kalitta. In 1978 she fired him, and he returned to racing. Muldowney took over as the team manager, with Rahn Tobler as her crew chief, and the late 1970s were a time of rebuilding as she and her crew sought to make up for Kalitta's departure.

By 1980 Muldowney returned to form, winning four NHRA national events and again winning the Winston World Championship. She won the American Hot Rod Association World Championship the following year, becoming the first and only woman to do so. Her 1982 season was virtually a repeat of the previous year, making her the first person to win the Winston World Championship three times. In 1983, *Heart Like a Wheel,* a film biography of her life starring Bonnie Bedelia and Beau Bridges, premiered and won critical praise, although Muldowney and Kalitta disputed the accuracy of the movie.

Muldowney's winning streak seemed unstoppable, but a crash on 29 June 1984 at the Grand Nationals at Sanair Raceway in Montreal, Canada, nearly killed her. The accident broke both her legs, her pelvis, and three fingers. She was hospitalized for almost two months and required five follow-up surgeries and eighteen months of rehabilitation. In 1986 Muldowney returned to racing, but from 1986 to 1989 did not win a single race. In 1988 she married her pit boss Rahn Tobler. In 1989, in order to help Muldowney get back into racing, Tobler asked Muldowney's longtime friendly rival and supporter "Big Daddy" Don Garlits to serve as her adviser. She reached the finals in several events that year and won the NHRA fall nationals held in Phoenix.

From 1989 until 1995 Muldowney focused her attention on match races, those where the challenger's cars are evenly matched. During this time, she achieved an elapsed time of 4.974, qualifying her for membership in the hallowed "four-second club." She also finished in the top ten in the Winston World Cup for the next several years. In 1996 she entered several IHRA competitions, earning honors as the fastest driver five times and winning three consecutive races. She set a new top speed record for the IHRA for that year, 294.98 miles per hour, and placed second in the IHRA nationals in both 1996 and 1997.

Muldowney continued to receive awards and honors throughout the 1990s, including being voted to the U.S. Sports Academy's distinguished list of Top Twenty-five Professional Female Athletes and being awarded the Mildred "Babe" Didrikson Zaharias Courage Award for her comeback to racing. In 1998 the New York Senate named Muldowney as one of thirty women of distinction during that state's women's history month exhibit. Although she continued to race in her signature pink dragster, Muldowney mostly participated in friendly match-racing duels with Don Garlits. She was one of the few drag racers to finance her own racing when she could not find sponsorship, but that handicap never slowed her down. At the end of the twentieth century, Muldowney continued to break records and maintained her position as the queen of drag racing.

★

For details about Muldowney's life and career see Tony Sakkis, *Drag Racing Legends* (1996). Useful articles include Al Harvin, "People in Sports," *New York Times* (1 Apr. 1976); Bruce Newman, "Cha Cha Waltzed Home," *Sports Illustrated* (18 July 1977); Sam Moses, "The Best Man for the Job Is a Woman," *Sports Illustrated* (22 June 1981); Sam Moses, "Fiery Return of a Leadfoot Lady," *Sports Illustrated* (10 Feb. 1986); "A Champion Comes Back," *Newsweek* (17 Feb. 1986); and J. E. Vader, "Two Foes Bury the Hatchet, But Not the Competition," *Sports Illustrated* (4 Sep. 1989). Muldowney's official website is at http://www.muldowney.com.

BRIAN B. CARPENTER

MULLEN, Joseph ("Joey") (*b.* 26 February 1957 in New York City), hockey player who overcame major obstacles to emerge as the all-time U.S. leading scorer with 502 goals and 1,063 points and was inducted into the Hockey Hall of Fame in 2000.

Mullen, the son of Tom and Marion Mullen, was raised in a tenement in the Hell's Kitchen area of New York City. Since the family could not afford expensive ice hockey equipment, his father, who worked at the old Madison Square Garden, brought home discarded hockey sticks for Mullen and his brother. Mullen learned to stickhandle, wearing clamp-on roller skates in a schoolyard on West Fiftieth Street, and finally received his first pair of ice skates at age ten.

Mullen played for four years in the New York Metro

Joey Mullen, 1997. AP PHOTO/KEITH SRAKOCIC

Junior Hockey League, earning recognition as the Most Valuable Player (MVP) of the 1974–1975 season. After graduating from the High School of Art and Design in 1975, he attended Boston College in Chestnut Hill, Massachusetts, where he became a standout goal scorer, earning Eastern College Athletic Conference (ECAC) First All-Star Team and National Collegiate Athletic Association (NCAA) First Team All-America honors in both his junior and senior years. As a junior Mullen helped lead the Eagles to the 1978 NCAA championship against Boston University. One of his more memorable performances came earlier that season against Rensselaer Polytechnic Institute in the first game of the ECAC tournament, when he scored the tying goal and then the winning goal in overtime.

Mullen graduated from Boston College in 1979, and the same year played on the U.S. team at the World Championships in Moscow, scoring eight points in eight games. While he was one of a handful of players highly coveted by Herb Brooks for the 1980 Olympic team, Mullen opted for professional hockey and its sizable paychecks in order to help his father, who was seriously ill. In August 1979 he signed with the St. Louis Blues. The Blues sent him to their Central Hockey League (CHL) Salt Lake City, Utah, affiliate, the Golden Eagles, where he played for two seasons, joining the big club mostly for postseason action. For his forty-goal performance at Salt Lake during the 1979–1980 season, Mullen earned the McKenzie Trophy as the CHL's top rookie and was thrown into play-off action with the Blues for one game. The next year he followed that performance with a league-leading 117-point season, which made him the clear choice for the Tommy Ivan Trophy as the league's MVP.

In the 1982–1983 season the tough little right winger began his long and prolific National Hockey League (NHL) career. Through four and one-half seasons in St. Louis, Mullen averaged better than one point per game. In February 1986 the Blues sent him to Calgary, Alberta, Canada, as part of a six-player blockbuster deal. It was with the Flames that he enjoyed his most productive years. His best season ever was 1988–1989 when, while helping the Flames to their first Stanley Cup triumph, Mullen led the league in plus-minus (plusses given for points scored at even-strength or short-handed in man power, minuses for goals-against at even strength or one man up), won the Lady Byng Trophy, was named to the NHL First All-Star Team, and led all play-off scorers with twelve goals.

In June 1990 the Flames surprisingly dealt him to the Pittsburgh Penguins for a second-round draft pick in the 1990 entry draft. The move to western Pennsylvania worked out well for the New York City native, who saw his name inscribed on Lord Stanley's cup after each of the next two seasons. On 7 February 1995 Mullen made hockey history by becoming the first American-born player to score 1,000 points in an NHL career, with an assist in a 7–3 victory over Florida, his 935th career game. Later in 1995 Mullen and his brother, Brian, a forward for the NHL New York Islanders, each won the Lester Patrick Trophy for outstanding contributions to U.S. hockey.

In September 1995 Mullen signed as a free agent with the Boston Bruins. After an injury-riddled year in Boston,

Mullen returned to Pittsburgh the following season to become the first American-born player to score five hundred goals. He retired at the season's end and was inducted into the Hockey Hall of Fame in 2000. With 502 goals and 1,063 points, Mullen stands alone as the most prolific American-born goal scorer and point producer in NHL history.

★

For further information on Mullen see Kevin Hubbard and Stan Fischler, *Hockey America* (1997). See also James Duplacey, Joseph Romain, Stan Fischler, Morgan Hughes, and Shirley Fischler, *Twentieth-Century Hockey Chronicle* (1999), and Dan Diamond, *Total Hockey: The Official Encyclopedia of the National Hockey League,* 2d ed. (2000).

STAN FISCHLER

MURPHY, Calvin Jerome (*b.* 9 May 1948 in Norwalk, Connecticut), Hall of Fame basketball player who was one of the greatest small guards and most proficient foul shooters in National Basketball Association (NBA) history.

Murphy was the only boy in a family of seven sisters. As a basketball player for Norwalk High School he was three times selected All-State and twice All-America. A five-foot, nine-inch dynamo, Murphy was the most valuable player (MVP) of the prestigious Dapper Dan Classic in 1966 with thirty-seven points and the Allentown Classic with sixty-six points. *The Basketball News* voted him the top high school player in the country in 1966, his senior year at Norwalk High School.

After an outstanding high school career, Murphy turned down over 230 scholarship offers to attend Niagara University in Lewiston, New York, just north of Buffalo. He made his mark immediately when he averaged 48.9 points per game as a member of the freshmen team. After a stellar freshman season, Murphy joined the varsity team for the next three years. He played under head coaches Frank Layden and Jim Maloney and led the Purple Eagles in scoring each year.

As a child he twirled the baton—as did many of his sisters—and during his first two years in college he was featured at many of the Buffalo Bills' American Football League (AFL) games.

A three-time consensus All-America (first team twice, 1968–1969 and 1969 – 1970; second team 1967–1968), Murphy finished his college career with 2,548 points. His 33.1 per-game average still ranks as fourth best in Division I history behind Pete Maravich of Louisiana State University (44.2), Austin Carr of Notre Dame (34.6), and Oscar Robertson of Cincinnati (33.8). Only five players in NCAA Division I history have averaged more points in one season than Murphy.

On 7 December 1968 Murphy scored 68 points against Syracuse—still the third-best mark against a Division I opponent. He scored 30 or more points in 42 of the 77 games he played for Niagara, 30–39 points 23 times, 40–49 points on 13 occasions, and 50 or more points 6 times. He also made 84.9 percent of his free throws.

In 1969 – 1970, his senior season, Murphy led the Purple Eagles to a 22–7 record and a berth in the NCAA tournament. Niagara lost in the second round to Villanova. Murphy earned his B.A. in 1970 and faced his professional career. Also in 1970 he married Vernetta Sykes; they eventually had seven children.

Murphy's tremendous scoring ability continued in the thirteen years he spent as a member of the San Diego/Houston Rockets. (He was also drafted by the Pittsburgh Condors of the American Basketball Association, but chose to play in the NBA.) Murphy was selected by the Rockets, then a San Diego team, in the second round (eighteenth pick overall) of the 1970 NBA draft, and averaged 15.8 points and 4.0 assists his first year. He was chosen for the All-Rookie team in 1971, joining Dave Cowens of the Boston Celtics, Pete Maravich of the Atlanta Hawks, Geoff Petrie of the Portland Trailblazers, and Bob Lanier of the Detroit Pistons. He finished fourth that year in Rookie of

Calvin Murphy, 1981. AP/WIDE WORLD PHOTOS

the Year balloting. After Murphy's first season, the Rocket franchise moved to Houston, where he spent the remaining twelve years of his career.

Murphy became recognized as the leader of the Rockets and arguably the most identified player with the young franchise. He scored more than 1,000 points in eleven straight seasons from 1970–1971 to 1980–1981. When he retired in 1983, Murphy's 17,949 career points ranked him first in Rocket history. (Hakeem Olajuwon has since passed him.) He was named to the All-Star game in 1979 and is one of four Rockets to have his number (23) retired. The other three are Rudy Tomjanovich (45), Moses Malone (24), and Clyde Drexler (22).

Aside from his scoring, Murphy made his mark with his proficient free-throw shooting. He held the NBA record for consecutive free throws made, with seventy-eight shot between 27 December 1980 and 28 February 1981, until Michael Williams of the Minnesota Timberwolves made eighty-four straight to end the 1992–1993 season. (Williams eventually extended his record to ninety-seven straight free throws at the beginning of the 1993–1994 season.) Murphy still holds the record for best free-throw percentage in a season (.958 in 1980–1981) and is third on the all-time NBA free-throw percentage list (.892). Murphy (in five seasons) and fellow Hall of Famer Rick Barry (in seven seasons) are the only two players in NBA history to have shot .900 or better from the foul line in five or more seasons. Murphy led the NBA in free-throw percentage in 1980–1981 (.958) and 1982–1983 (.920), and finished among the top five in nine other seasons. In a 1981 playoff series against San Antonio, Murphy made all twenty-three of his foul shot attempts.

Murphy ranks as a great playmaker as well, with 4,402 assists in 1,002 regular-season games and 213 assists in 51 playoff games. He is the Rockets' all-time assist leader. Murphy is one of only two Rockets (the other is Olajuwon) to rank among the NBA top ten in four statistical categories in one season. In the 1973–1974 season Murphy was second in assists (7.4) and free-throw percentage (.868), fourth in field-goal percentage (.522), ninth in steals (1.94 average), and twentieth in scoring (20.4 average).

In Rockets' history, Murphy is second in points (17,949), first in assists (4,402), second in games played (1,002), second in minutes played (30,607), second in steals (1,165), second in free-throw percentage (.892), and seventh in scoring average (17.9). In 1978 he received the J. Walter Kennedy Humanitarian Award from the Professional Basketball Writers' Association of America in recognition of his work with Houston-area youth.

Murphy retired from the Rockets in 1983 as a player, and in 1989 returned to the organization as the team's community service adviser and an analyst for Rocket TV. He also works for the Clutch City Foundation, handling charitable service activities and marketing. In addition, Murphy runs the Texas Youth Academy, an organization where youngsters can meet for sports, educational development, and counseling.

In 1993 Murphy was enshrined in the Naismith Memorial Basketball Hall of Fame. He is also a member of the City of Houston Hall of Fame and the Connecticut High School Coaches Association Hall of Fame, and is a recipient of the Connecticut Sportswriters' Gold Key Award.

★

For information about Murphy's career, see "Niagara's Hounding Won Calvin Murphy," *Philadelphia Evening Bulletin* (5 May 1977); Mickey Herskowitz, "Murphy's Contributions Make Him a Giant-sized Value," *Houston Post* (19 Mar. 1978); George White, "Calvin Can Hunt New Dragons Now," *Houston Chronicle* (28 Oct. 1983); Charlie Mitchell, "Calvin Won't Forget May 23," *The Hour* (Norwalk, CT) (24 May 1984); Mickey Herskowitz, "'Pocket Rocket' Still Flying High," *Houston Post* (20 Feb. 1986); Mike Weber, "Ten Years Later, Murphy Stands Tall Among NBA's Free-throw Shooters," *Star-Ledger* (6 Mar. 1991).

DOUGLAS A. STARK

MURRAY, James Patrick ("Jim") (*b.* 29 December 1919 in Hartford, Connecticut; *d.* 16 August 1998 in Los Angeles, California), *Los Angeles Times* columnist, founding staff member of *Sports Illustrated*, and Pulitzer Prize winner who is considered to have been one of the best sportswriters in American journalism.

Born into a prosperous family, Murray's young life was marked by two tumultuous events: the onset of the Great Depression and the rancorous divorce of his parents, James Murray and Molly O'Connell Murray. Although Murray's father had at one time owned a chain of drugstores, his business crashed along with the stock market in 1929. The Murray's marriage was in similar disarray, and their son was sent to live with his grandmother, who eventually obtained permanent custody. Murray and his sister were reunited when Murray's mother was forced to move back in with her own parents due to financial difficulties. Murray graduated from William H. Hall High School in 1938. Fortunately the family finances were sound enough for him to attend exclusive Trinity College in Hartford, where he gained a professional writing job with the *Hartford Times* as a campus correspondent in 1943, the year in which he completed his B.A.

After covering police and government stories for the *New Haven Register* for a year, Murray moved to the West Coast in 1944 to take a job as a reporter with the *Los Angeles Examiner*. Forever after, he was a true Californian, scorning

Jim Murray *(left)*, upon winning the Sports Writers Award for lifetime achievement, 1996. At right is Peter Vecsey of the *New York Post.* ASSOCIATED PRESS AP

the bad weather and provincialism of heartland America—an attitude that often caused an avalanche of letters to his editors protesting his not-so-gentle gibes.

Murray married Geraldine Brown in 1945. Their family soon included three sons and a daughter; eventually, they moved to the exclusive enclave of Malibu. Murray took a job as *Time* magazine's Los Angeles contributor in 1948, usually covering the movie industry. His down-to-earth sensibility gained him the friendship of several important show business figures. One archetypal story had Murray squiring Marilyn Monroe about town one evening during the early days of her romance with Joe DiMaggio. When Monroe asked shyly if Murray minded if DiMaggio escorted her home, Murray could only marvel at his good fortune in finally meeting the legendary Yankee, not bothering to notice his loss of the world's biggest movie star as a companion. Murray also befriended Humphrey Bogart and was a favorite drinking companion of the star during his final battle with lung cancer.

Although Murray's entertainment industry reporting first brought him notice as a sharp-eyed writer with a gift for epigrams—often directed at overinflated egos—his longtime love of sports got him drafted for *Time*'s effort to start a new national sports magazine, *Sports Illustrated,* in July 1953. Although Murray was hired as a reporter, the magazine's staff was so disorganized that Murray became a de facto assignment editor in its early days, sending reporters out on stories and handling many of the other details of the inaugural issue. He served as West Coast editor from 1959 to 1961. Although his initial recommendation to call the magazine *Fame* was a rare misstep, Murray's contributions made *Sports Illustrated* an outstanding success by the time of his departure in 1961. His coverage of the 1956 Rose Bowl set the tone for the magazine by presenting in-depth portraits of the coaches and teams, not just the details of the game itself. Although this kind of reporting is standard practice among contemporary sports journalists, it was an innovation that gained *Sports Illustrated* a reputation as the leading magazine in its field. Murray's achievements also brought an offer from the *Los Angeles Times* to join the paper as a columnist in 1961. He remained at the *Times* for the rest of his career, earning dozens of national awards in the process.

Intending to become a novelist or screenwriter, Murray insisted that becoming a sportswriter was the last thing on his mind when he began his career; indeed, the newspaper work that he did in Connecticut and Los Angeles helped broaden his frame of reference as a sports journalist. So too did his Connecticut youth as a fan of both Boston- and New York–based teams. Although he occasionally devoted column inches to his personal life—detailing his losing battle with failing eyesight in the late 1970s, for example—Murray's talent lay in creating insightful portraits of athletes that assured them their rightful place in sports history. He was no less capable in describing pivotal moments in sporting events with an economy of phrase that earned him honors as America's Best Sports Writer by the National Association of Sportscasters and Sportswriters for the first time in 1964; he received the award a total of fourteen times. Inducted into the association's Hall of Fame in 1977, Murray was also honored with an inclusion in the Writers' Wing of the Baseball Hall of Fame in 1988. In 1990 Murray was only the fourth sportswriter honored with a Pulitzer Prize for his body of work.

Murray was a prolific journalist well past the typical retirement age, taking comfort in his work to cope with a succession of challenges that beset him in the 1990s. Although a series of operations restored some of his eyesight, Murray endured a number of heart operations as well. However, the loss of his wife in 1984 and the death of his son from a drug and alcohol overdose in 1982 were harder to overcome. In 1996 Murray married a longtime family friend Lisa McCoy, and he continued to turn out columns on everything from horse racing to boxing to his own favorite pastime, golf. Stricken by cardiac arrest on the morning of 16 August 1998 in his Los Angeles home, Murray left behind a wife, a daughter, two sons, and a stepson in addition to three grandchildren.

Those who were stung by Murray's criticism sometimes indicted him as a booster of Southern California at the expense of the rest of the country; however, Murray's work—gibes and all—was acknowledged as the best sports commentary of his generation time and again by his colleagues. At his death, lengthy tributes appeared in several industry journals, and the *Los Angeles Times* posthumously published two volumes of his collected works.

★

Murray provided an overview of his life in *Jim Murray: An Autobiography of the Pulitzer Prize–Winning Sports Columnist* (1993), and published several collections of his work, including *The Best of Jim Murray* (1965), *The Sporting World of Jim Murray* (1963), and *The Jim Murray Collection* (1988). Another view of Murray's early career is recounted in Michael MacCambridge, *The Franchise: A History of* Sports Illustrated *Magazine* (1997). After his death, the *Los Angeles Times* published his collected works in *Jim Murray: The Last of the Best* (1998), and *The Great Ones* (1999). Murray's colleagues produced numerous tributes to the writer upon his passing, including notices in the *Los Angeles Times* (18 Aug. 1998); *American Journalism Review* (Oct. 1998); *Sports Illustrated* (24 Aug. 1998); and *Editor and Publisher* (22 Aug. 1998). An obituary is in the *Los Angeles Times* (18 Aug. 1998).

TIMOTHY BORDEN

MUSIAL, Stanley Frank ("Stan the Man") (*b.* 21 November 1920 in Donora, Pennsylvania), one of baseball's all-time greats who played for the St. Louis Cardinals of the National League and was inducted into the Baseball Hall of Fame.

Musial was the fifth of six children of Lukasz Musial, a Polish immigrant, and Mary Lancos, a homemaker and second-generation Slovak. Musial's father worked on the loading dock of the American Steel and Wire Company some twenty-nine miles south of Pittsburgh, Pennsylvania. Life was bleak by the time Musial reached adolescence. In early 1932 the Great Depression closed the mill, and most of the residents of Donora lost their regular jobs. The Musial family was particularly hard hit because of Lukasz Musial's unsteady employment. This forced Musial's mother and sisters into domestic labor. Musial overcame adversity in part because of his resourceful mother and local educators and businesspeople, especially Michael "Ki" Duda, his high school coach, and Frank Pizzica, an auto dealer who provided financial assistance and advice.

Despite his father's opposition, Musial signed a contract with the St. Louis Cardinals on 29 September 1937, nearly two years before he graduated from Donora High School. He began his professional baseball career in 1938 as a left-handed pitcher at Class D Williamson, West Virginia, where his wildness reduced him to mediocrity. In 1940 he improved under the tutelage of manager Richard Kerr at Class D Daytona Beach, Florida, where he finished with an 18–5 record.

Two events significantly affected Musial's life during

Stan Musial. ARCHIVE PHOTOS, INC.

that 1940 season. First, near the close of that campaign, playing center field, Musial snagged his cleats on the turf while attempting to make a shoestring catch. He tumbled onto his left shoulder and permanently damaged his ability to throw hard. Second, he married Lillian Labash, his high school sweetheart, on 25 May. That year Lil gave birth to Richard Stanley Musial (named after Kerr); they later had three daughters.

Unaware of the seriousness of his injury, the Cardinals elevated Musial to Class C ball in 1941 only to determine that he was "damaged goods." The manager Ollie Vanek of the Springfield, Missouri, Cardinals, however, gave him a chance as an outfielder. Musial developed into the league's top hitter, batting .379 with 26 homers by mid-July. The Cardinals promoted him to Rochester, New York, one of their top farm teams, where he hit .326. Consequently, he came up for the Cardinals' final twelve games amid a heated pennant race with the Brooklyn Dodgers. Musial nearly carried the ball club to a pennant by hitting an astounding .426, ending an extraordinary season that began on the brink of extinction.

In 1942, his rookie season, Musial reached six feet in height, and weighed 175 pounds. Called the "Donora Greyhound" by the press, he was quick afoot, particularly on the base paths, and he hit from a deep crouch, moving the bat and his hips in a hula-like wiggle with his body twisted away from the plate in a cobra-like fashion. A Brooklyn Dodgers coach commented that Musial "looks like a kid peeking around the corner to see if the cops are coming." Musial played left field on a young team dominated by outstanding pitching, team speed, and fielding. The Cardinals won the National League pennant and unexpectedly defeated the New York Yankees in the World Series. Musial played an integral part in the team's success by hitting .315.

Musial contributed mightily to the Cardinals in the following two seasons. In the midst of World War II, which drew top major league players into military service, the Cardinals' depth prevailed as the result of an outstanding farm system. St. Louis won the pennant in 1943 only to lose to the Yankees in the World Series. Musial won his first batting title in 1943 by hitting .357. He was named the National League Most Valuable Player, the first of three such awards. In 1944 the Cardinals became the world champions, and Musial batted a second-best .347. He spent 1945 in the U.S. Navy, where he played service ball, mostly at Pearl Harbor.

The 1946 campaign represented the last of the Cardinal teams of the Musial era to win the National League pennant. They went on to defeat the Boston Red Sox in the World Series. That season also clearly established Musial as one of the premier hitters of his time as he snared the league batting title with a .365 average, his second-best season ever. To address a team deficiency, he played first base for the first time. Because of his extraordinary hitting at Ebbets Field, Dodgers fans nicknamed him "Stan the Man," his most defining signature. Grossly underpaid by the skinflint owner Sam Breadon, Musial that June nearly bolted to the Mexican League, who promised him a big signing bonus and a guaranteed five-year contract of $25,000 annually at a time when Musial earned $13,500. He held out for a higher salary from the Cardinals the following spring, his last major salary dispute. By the 1950s he was the first National League player to earn $100,000 annually.

The 1947 season witnessed the integration of Major League Baseball, beginning with Jackie Robinson of the Brooklyn Dodgers. That event divided ball clubs, especially the Cardinals, with talk of a player strike being reported. Musial, who had played with blacks in Donora, quietly defended Robinson's right to play in the major leagues, earning the appreciation of Robinson and other black players who soon followed. Musial's unexpected health problems further made 1947 a troubling season. Acute appendicitis drained him before he rebounded to finish the year batting at .312, his lowest average until 1956. Following off-season surgery, Musial had a career year in 1948, leading the National League in virtually every hitting category, including batting average (.376), hits (230), doubles (46), triples (16), and slugging percentage (.702). His 39 home runs were his most ever and one shy of winning the triple crown, that is, finishing at the top of the league in batting average, home runs, and runs batted in.

Musial won four more batting titles and contended virtually every other year in the 1950s. In the process he surpassed 3,000 career hits in 1958 and set a National League mark for playing in 895 consecutive games. The latter took its toll as the aging Musial slipped to a .255 average in 1959. His comeback reached extraordinary heights in 1962, when he hit .330 at the age of 41 in his next to last season. He retired with a career batting average of .331 and several major league records, including total bases (6,124) and extra base hits (1,337). Among his many National League records were hits (3,630), runs scored (1,949), and runs batted in (1,951).

Following his baseball career Musial expanded his business activities beyond a popular steakhouse and a bowling alley in St. Louis to hotels in Florida and St. Louis. He became an inspiration to other players, who began to give more thought to their futures after sports. He also served as President Lyndon Johnson's physical fitness adviser from 1964 to 1967. Musial was the Cardinals' general manager for the 1967 season and was inducted into the Baseball Hall of Fame in 1969. Beginning in the 1980s his many public service activities included the introduction of baseball into Poland.

Of all the superstars of his era, none was more accommodating with the press and fans than Musial. Unlike Joe DiMaggio and Ted Williams, he rarely refused interviews, and he often went to great lengths to sign autographs. He was especially popular with opposing players because he was complimentary and learned the names of even the most marginal players. Never did he provoke an umpire enough to eject him from a game. Overall Musial elevated the standards of many performers who modeled themselves after him. His sunny disposition hid an intense competitive spirit, leading one observer to write, "[Ty] Cobb wore his fire on his sleeve and it was written all over his face; Musial concealed it in a facade of geniality and placidness, but it burned as deeply inside of him as it did in Cobb." Musial's fun-loving spirit and his competitive fire came together most clearly in his duels with Hall of Famer Warren Spahn of the Boston and Milwaukee Braves. Musial usually raised three fingers at Spahn as he entered his stance, meaning he intended to get three hits that day. Spahn usually laughed and said, "Yeah?" He then sent Musial on his back with a high tight pitch. In one matchup, after Spahn threw at him Musial said something and laughed. He then lined the next pitch into Spahn's stomach. As he ran to first base Musial made some comment and laughed again. Spahn then removed his hat and bowed.

★

Correspondence related to Musial is in the Lyndon Johnson Papers at the Lyndon Johnson Library and in the Branch Rickey Papers at the Library of Congress. Extensive clippings files on Musial are at the National Baseball Library in Cooperstown, New York, and the *Sporting News* archives in St. Louis, Missouri. See also Musial's autobiography, *Stan Musial: "The Man's" Own Story, as Told to Bob Broeg* (1964). It was republished in 1977 to include information of Musial's activities following his baseball retirement. The only full-scale biography is James N. Giglio, *Musial: From Stash to Stan the Man* (2001).

JAMES N. GIGLIO

N

NAGURSKI, Bronislau ("Bronko") (*b.* 4 November 1908 in Rainy River, Ontario, Canada; *d.* 7 January 1990 in International Falls, Minnesota), Pro Football Hall of Famer, unstoppable All-Pro fullback and defensive tackle for the Chicago Bears.

Nagurski's parents, Nykoleig and Michalina Nagurski, were from the Russian Ukraine; his father was a grocer. The family, which included four children, moved to International Falls, Minnesota, in 1912. A grade school teacher dubbed the boy "Bronko"; the name stuck and proved prophetic for Nagurski, who as a hard-hitting collegiate and professional football player in the 1920s and 1930s was renowned for dragging would-be tacklers into the end zone as he scored.

Nagurski enjoyed football as a child and played for two years at International Falls High School. As an upperclassman, he transferred to nearby Bemidji High School but was barred from participation in the football program for being an out-of-district student. An influential University of Minnesota alumnus, having seen Nagurski play earlier, recommended the young athlete to Gopher coach Clarence ("Doc") Spears, who in 1925 went to visit Nagurski. The story of their first meeting became a legendary testament to Nagurski's unusual strength. According to Spears, he was driving through the farm country near Nagurski's home when he came upon Nagurski plowing a field without a horse or mule. Nagurski lifted his hand to indicate a direction without dropping the plow. This unusual show of strength impressed Spears, and he recruited Nagurski to play for the University of Minnesota Gophers after he graduated from Bemidji in 1926.

The Gophers performed admirably during Nagurski's time with the team. By the end of his final season in 1929, the team had amassed a three-year record of 18–4–2. In 1928 Nagurski became the only collegiate player ever to be named All-America for two different positions (fullback and defensive tackle) in the same season. He received that honor for a second time in 1929.

By 1930 when he received his B.A., Nagurski was a hulking six-foot, two-inch bruiser and weighed 225 pounds. Coach George Halas personally signed Nagurski to play with the Chicago Bears of the National Football League (NFL) in 1930. In nine seasons with the Bears, Nagurski—wearing jersey number 3—distinguished himself as both fullback and offensive tackle; he also played as a defensive lineman. Nagurski made All-Pro fullback in 1932, 1933, and 1934, and received compensation at various rates of pay during his career, up to $5,000 per season. Among his more memorable plays was a fourth-quarter touchdown pass launched during the 1932 NFL championship playoff against the Portsmouth Spartans (now the Detroit Lions). Nagurski, in order to release the pass, leaped above the players on the line of scrimmage and connected successfully with teammate Harold ("Red") Grange. The play broke a scoreless tie and won the championship for the Bears. The team won a second title in 1933, and won three playoffs in all during the Nagurski years, leaving him with a collection of leviathan championship rings in size nineteen and one-half.

On 28 December 1936 Nagurski married Eileen Kane; the couple had six children. The following year Nagurski resigned from professional football after eight seasons of NFL play. Unable to serve in the military due to his athletic injuries, he rejoined the Bears for a single season as a defensive tackle during World War II, and for the third time in his career helped the team to a championship in 1943. According to the Pro Football Hall of Fame in Canton, Ohio, into which he was inducted in 1963, Nagurski's rushing total after nine years of play was 4,031 yards. He was named to the College Football Hall of Fame in 1951.

After the NFL years Nagurski pursued a career as a professional wrestler for more than a decade. He retired from wrestling in 1960 and opened a filling station in International Falls. In 1963 he was enshrined along with Grange, Jim Thorpe of the New York Giants, and fourteen others as a charter entrant to the new Pro Football Hall of Fame in Canton, Ohio.

Nagurski spent his later years in Rainy Falls, Minnesota, four miles from International Falls. A self-admitted recluse, he avoided the press but made a brief public appearance in 1984 in Tampa, Florida, as the honorary coin flipper at Super Bowl XVIII. After some months in a nursing home in the late 1980s, Nagurski died of undisclosed causes at Falls Memorial Hospital in International Falls. He is buried at Saint Thomas Cemetery.

Stories of Nagurski's unparalleled strength on the football field abound. As sportswriter Arthur Daley said, "He shook off secondary tacklers as a dog shakes off fleas." Nagurski summed up his paradigm of play: "If somebody got in my way, I ran through them." On one occasion eyewitnesses concurred that Nagurski collided with and knocked over a mounted policeman—along with his horse—who was stationed on the arena field to quell an unruly crowd. On another day, according to Nagurski's teammates, he leveled four opposing players on his way to the end zone. After scoring on that run and unable to slow down, he rebounded off the goalpost before slamming into the brick arena wall of Chicago's Wrigley Field. Still on his feet, Nagurski returned to the sideline and complained to the team, "That last guy hits hard!"

Solid, strong, agile, and easygoing by nature, Nagurski was the prototype of the NFL professional. He was twelve years old when the NFL was organized in 1921, and the league was only in its tenth year when he joined the Bears. The college draft was not yet established, and NFL franchises operated with meager crews of eighteen to twenty-two players. Football historians cite Grange and Thorpe as the greatest backfield players overall, but the impassable

Bronko Nagurski, 1943. ASSOCIATED PRESS FILE

Nagurski is revered by many as the greatest football player ever. Although others among his contemporaries were taller or faster, none were stronger than the square-shouldered, square-jawed Nagurski. On the gridiron he rushed a straightforward course, never to the sideline, even in the absence of teammates to run interference. In 1984 *New York Times* columnist Grantland Rice said, "Eleven Bronko Nagurskis could beat eleven Red Granges and eleven Jim Thorpes."

★

Arthur Daley, *Pro Football's Hall of Fame* (1963), includes a chapter on Nagurski. Articles on Nagurski appear in Andrew H. Malcolm, *New York Times Biographical Edition* (23 Apr. 1972), and Ira Berkow, *New York Times Biographical Service* (21 Jan. 1984). Nagurski is discussed in conjunction with Red Grange in Robert H. Shoemaker, *Famous Football Players* (1953). An obituary is in the *New York Times* (9 Jan. 1990).

GLORIA COOKSEY

NAGY, Steve (*b.* 10 April 1913 in Shoaf, Pennsylvania; *d.* 10 November 1966 in Cleveland, Ohio), professional bowler who rolled the first televised perfect game in history.

Nagy was one of the three sons of Hungarian immigrant parents. Always interested in athletics, Nagy had no opportunities to play sports professionally until after he became established as a cabinetmaker. Golf would remain a hobby throughout his life, but bowling would become his second career.

Nagy began bowling seriously at age twenty-six, starting in 1939 on a Booster division team in a league reserved for lower-level players. He quickly dominated his competition, however, and by 1941 he was bowling on the American Bowling Congress (ABC) professional circuit. He was competitive throughout the 1940s but stardom eluded him, and he never placed higher than third in the annual ABC All-Star competition.

Nagy became more well known during the 1950s, as bowling reached its zenith of popularity in North America. In 1951 Nagy posted an average of 208 for 10 consecutive tournaments. Then, in the ABC tournament on 8 April 1952, Nagy rolled a 698 series and his partner Johnny Klares scored 755 for a new record doubles total of 1,453 pins, beating the old record of 1,415 that had been set in 1933. Aided by a 705 series in the singles event, Nagy won the tournament's all-events category with a score of 2,065—only 5 pins short of the all-time record. Nagy was a prominent member of the Cleveland Radiarts team, which won the 1952 ABC all-events team championship. Also that year, he bowled a 299 during the ABC Masters tournament, missing a perfect game by one pin in the last frame. He was chosen ABC Bowler of the Year for 1952.

Steve Nagy, 1956. AP/Wide World Photos

After getting to the final field of sixteen bowlers seven times in thirteen seasons, Nagy finally won the ABC All-Star event in 1954. In 1955 Nagy again was chosen ABC Bowler of the Year after winning the Lakewood Holiday Classic tournament in Long Beach, California; the Struthers, Ohio, singles tournament, and the West Coast doubles crown at Los Angeles with Buzz Fazio.

A square-jawed, broad-shouldered man weighing 220 pounds, Nagy, always smiling and exuberant, with dark, slicked-back hair and thin mustache, resembled comedian Ernie Kovacs. He became known for his emotional displays during matches. With his huge arms, he would fling the ball down the lane, then run sideways until the ball hit the pins. Often he would run as far as three lanes to the side. If his ball did not do what he wanted it to do, he would sometimes take off his belt and whip the ball before rolling it again.

When the network television series *Championship Bowling* began filming in 1954, the producers offered $1,000 to anyone who could bowl a perfect game during its telecast. In 1955 Nagy came to Chicago's Faetz-Niesen Recreation Center, where he had never bowled, to face the reigning champion of the series, Chicago bowler Eddie Kawolics, who was a regular at Faetz. Nagy rolled a few practice games, smiled, and said to announcer Joe Wilson, "This place gives you your confidence back."

Nagy got off to a slow start, losing the first game of the match to Kowalics. In the second game, Nagy rolled nothing but strikes. In the ninth frame, he left a ten-pin, but it fell over just in time. Nagy's last roll was a strike, and he became the first player ever to roll a perfect game on television.

Also in 1955 Nagy moved from Cleveland to Detroit to join that city's Pfeiffers team. In 1956 and 1958 Nagy was named to *Bowling* magazine's All-America team. In 1957 Nagy moved to St. Louis to join Fazio on the Falstaffs team, which in 1958 won the ABC championship and the all-events team championship.

In 1959 Nagy became captain of the Falstaffs for two years. He next was named captain and general manager for the Los Angeles Toros in the short-lived National Bowling League. In 1960 Nagy finished second to Billy Golembiewski in the ABC Masters tournament, the closest he would ever come to winning bowling's most prestigious tournament. Nagy returned to Cleveland in 1961.

Throughout his career the good-natured Nagy was known for his approachability. He was outgoing with fans and competing players. For many years he was part of the promotional staff of Brunswick, a bowling manufacturer, and conducted hundreds of clinics and exhibitions across the United States and Canada.

In 1963 Nagy was elected to the ABC Hall of Fame. Though he was only in his early fifties, his health was failing. In 1964 he had a stroke and was hospitalized for six weeks. In the spring of 1965, although wheelchair-bound, he traveled to Brooklyn to see his friend Buddy Bomar inducted into the ABC Hall of Fame. Later that year he returned to bowling. In August, Nagy was getting ready to compete in a PBA (Professional Bowlers Association) tournament in Brockton, Massachusetts, when he suffered another stroke. He returned to Cleveland, where he lost more than half his weight while battling his ailments for more than a year, but this time he would not recover. After his death, his fellow bowlers held fund-raising benefits in Cleveland and Detroit, raising more than $18,000 for the Steve Nagy Trust Fund to aid his wife Helen and their daughter.

Nagy was a consistent high scorer and one of bowling's most visible and personable stars. He averaged 197 for 24 seasons in the ABC, and was credited with 6 sanctioned perfect games and 4 other games of 299. The demonstrative Nagy was a fan favorite who helped make the game popular. His televised perfect game drew national attention to professional bowling as a spectator sport.

★

The best place to find material on Nagy is in *Bowling* magazine, notably the May 1952 and December 1955 issues, and in the archives of the International Bowling Museum and Hall of Fame in St. Louis, Missouri. Obituaries are in the *National Bowlers Journal and Billiards Revue* and *Bowling Magazine* (both Dec. 1966).

MICHAEL BETZOLD

NAISMITH, James (*b.* 6 November 1861 near Almonte, Ontario, Canada; *d.* 28 November 1939 in Lawrence, Kansas), athlete and educator who invented the game of basketball.

Naismith was one of three children born to Scottish immigrants John Naismith and Margaret Young Naismith. In 1869 John Naismith moved his family to Grand Calumet Island, where he began work in a sawmill. A year later both of Naismith's parents died of typhoid fever. James and his siblings, Annie and Robert, lived with their maternal grandmother until her death in 1873 and then moved back to Almonte to stay with their uncle, Peter Young. Naismith began high school in Almonte in 1875, but dropped out during his second year to help support the family. Five years later at the age of twenty, he returned to Almonte High School, completing his studies in 1883.

Naismith received a scholarship to McGill University in Montreal, where he earned a B.A. in physical education and divinity in 1887. In addition to being one of the best students in his class, he was also one of the school's top all-around athletes, participating in rugby, soccer, lacrosse, and gymnastics. Intending to become a minister, Naismith enrolled in Presbyterian College in Montreal, a theological school affiliated with McGill. To finance his education, he took a position as physical education instructor at McGill's gymnasium.

James Naismith. ASSOCIATED PRESS AP

Naismith's involvement in athletics had a profound effect on the direction of his career. His professors at Presbyterian College viewed this involvement with dismay, and urged him to give up the "evils" of athletics and devote himself to his studies and Christian duties. Naismith believed that athletics could be good for the soul—that the clean living, discipline, and hard work of the dedicated athlete could help foster moral and spiritual growth. During a rugby game in his senior year, a player near Naismith unleashed an outburst of profanity, then turned to him and apologized, "I beg your pardon, Jim; I forgot you were there." Naismith recalled this brief exchange as a turning point. He decided he could do more good by ministering to people through athletics. With that in mind, he left Presbyterian College in 1890 as an unordained minister and enrolled at the Young Men's Christian Association (YMCA) Training School in Springfield, Massachusetts, becoming an instructor at the school in 1891.

In the autumn of 1891, the superintendent of the YMCA

gymnasium Luther Gulick assigned Naismith an unwelcome task—to develop a new indoor game that would hold the interest of a class of "incorrigibles," mostly men who were Naismith's age or older. Two previous instructors had already become frustrated by the class and had asked to be replaced. Naismith had two weeks to complete his assignment. Initially he tried adopting childhood games and outdoor sports to suit the indoor playing area, but these proved unsuccessful. He realized that because of the space limitations, running must be kept to a minimum; and because of the hard floor surface, tackling and other rough play must be eliminated.

With these parameters in mind, Naismith found inspiration from a game he had played in his childhood called "duck on a rock," in which they tried to knock a stone, or "duck," from atop a boulder by throwing a rock at it. One player was "it" and placed his rock on the boulder for the others to knock off. If a thrower successfully knocked the duck off, he had to run to retrieve his stone and return to his throwing base before the one who was "it" could pick up the duck and tag him with it. If the thrower missed, he still had to retrieve his stone, but the guard did not have to pick up the duck before attempting to tag him. The most successful players lobbed their stones in an arc—stones thrown in a hard, straight line often traveled so far that the thrower did not have time to retrieve it and return to base safely. Naismith adapted this idea of an arching shot to his new game. Players would pass the ball and score by throwing it into an elevated goal.

Using a soccer ball and two peach baskets nailed to the ten-foot high balcony that served as an elevated track at the gymnasium, Naismith introduced the new game to his students. It was an immediate success. Within a decade, most major Canadian and U.S. cities had basketball leagues. In 1936, basketball was introduced into the Olympic games in Berlin. Naismith was able to attend the first Olympics to include his game, thanks to a nationwide penny campaign. From 9 through 15 February 1936, the heart of basketball season, one penny from each ticket sold at high school, college, and professional basketball games in the United States and Canada went to the Naismith travel fund. The campaign caught the public's fancy. Soon groups such as the Boy Scouts and Girl Scouts were soliciting extra penny donations at games. At the Olympic games, Naismith was greeted by each of the twenty-one basketball teams, and tears came to his eyes when they dipped their flags to him.

After inventing basketball, Naismith continued to minister through athletics. In 1895 he became the physical education director at the Denver YMCA, and in 1898 he earned a medical degree at the Gross Medical College (later the University of Colorado Medical School) in Denver, Colorado. Before leaving Springfield, "Doc" Naismith married Maude E. Shermann on 20 June 1894. They had five children. Naismith was appointed as director of the chapel and director of physical education at the University of Kansas in 1898, where he remained until his retirement in 1937. In 1915 he was ordained as a Presbyterian minister. During World War I Naismith worked with the YMCA to oversee the recreational, educational, physical, and spiritual activities of U.S. soldiers overseas. From 1917 to 1919, he spent nineteen months in France lecturing on sex education and making recommendations for the recreation programs at army bases.

Although Naismith had a long, successful career as an educator and published two books related to his educational work, *A Modern College* (1911) and *The Basis of Clean Living* (1918), he is still best remembered for the invention of basketball. The game has evolved from his original conception, but his basic rules still apply and ten feet is still the regulation height of the basket. (Naismith suggested that there be nine players on each team, although he allowed for up to forty, and he did not conceive of the dribble.) He never sought fame or fortune from his invention, once turning down a lucrative sponsorship offer from a tobacco company shortly after his brief moment of fame at the Olympics because he believed tobacco was detrimental to the health of young people. His fame as basketball's inventor has been largely posthumous. His book about the sport that he invented, *Basketball, Its Origin and Development* (1941), was published two years after his death. The Naismith Memorial Basketball Hall of Fame is named in his honor.

Naismith's wife, Maude, died in March 1937, and Naismith married Florence Kincaid on 11 June 1939. He suffered a cerebral hemorrhage on 19 November 1939 and died at home of a second stroke nine days later. He is buried in Memorial Park Cemetery in Lawrence, Kansas, next to his first wife.

★

The best source of information on Naismith is Bernice Larson Webb, *The Basketball Man* (1973). See also "In Search of Naismith's Game," *Sports Illustrated* (6 Mar. 1967). The James Naismith Foundation maintains a website at http://collections.ic.gc.ca/.

J. CHRISTOPHER JOLLY

NAMATH, Joseph William ("Joe") (*b.* 31 May 1943 in Beaver Falls, Pennsylvania), Pro Football Hall of Fame quarterback seen as the embodiment of the 1960s counterculture in professional football.

Namath was born in a blue-collar town in Pennsylvania, the fourth child (all sons) of Hungarian-born steelworker John Andrew Namath and Rose Juhasz Namath. He lived

Joe Namath. AP/WIDE WORLD PHOTOS

in the racially mixed Lower End area of Beaver Falls, just northwest of Pittsburgh, and many of his childhood friends were African American. He quarterbacked Beaver Falls High School to an undefeated season in 1960, his senior year, and accepted an athletic scholarship to the University of Alabama.

Namath found Alabama difficult, from the school's racial segregation to the discipline imposed by legendary coach Paul "Bear" Bryant, but he persevered. In his sophomore year he led the team to a 17–0 victory over Oklahoma in the Orange Bowl. His junior season ended prematurely when Namath was reported for drinking before the last game of the season. He confessed and was suspended for the final game and the postseason.

In his senior year, 1964, Namath was off to an excellent start until the North Carolina State game. There, he rolled out on an option play and collapsed, untouched, with torn cartilage and ligaments in his right knee. He returned to action two weeks later and reinjured the knee, then injured it again during practice for the Orange Bowl. Namath was on the bench for the beginning of the Orange Bowl, but with Alabama trailing the University of Texas Longhorns by two touchdowns, Namath limped onto the field to lead a valiant but unsuccessful comeback effort.

The bidding war between the National Football League (NFL) and the upstart American Football League (AFL) was at its height in 1965. There were questions about Namath's knee despite successful surgery, but he was considered the prize of that year's draft. David "Sonny" Werblin had bought the failing AFL franchise in New York, changing its name from the Titans to the Jets. Realizing that his team needed star power, Werblin offered Namath an unprecedented $427,000 contract and won him away from the St. Louis Cardinals.

Namath immediately attracted attention, and more sportswriters covered his first exhibition game than had attended the previous year's AFC championship. He began his rookie season on the bench but was the starting quarterback by midseason. He was voted AFL Rookie of the Year and was selected to that year's AFL All-Star game, where he threw two touchdown passes. From then on Namath was an established star. In 1967 he became the first player to pass for over 4,000 yards (4,007) in a single season.

The United States was undergoing a generational and cultural rebellion in 1968, and Namath came to symbolize that battle in professional football. In retrospect, Namath's countercultural image seems to have been greatly exaggerated. Namath was not the first NFL player with a mustache, but he may have been the first white one, and he was noticed. He was by no means the first to enjoy a bit of alcohol and female companionship. In any case, his playboy image earned him the nickname "Broadway Joe."

The AFL-NFL competition that had led to a bidding war for Namath's services was settled in 1966, and the champions of the two leagues played at the end of each year. Namath led the Jets to the AFC Eastern Division title, then threw three touchdown passes in the AFC championship, giving the Jets the opportunity to meet the Baltimore Colts in the Super Bowl.

Few gave the Jets much chance of winning; in fact, the Colts were seventeen-point favorites. The older teams of the NFL were assumed to be superior, and indeed the NFL had won the first two Super Bowls by easy margins. In a speech to the Miami Touchdown Club the week before the game, Namath shocked the nation by saying, "We're going to win Sunday. I guarantee you."

Namath made good on his promise, when on 12 January 1969 the Jets beat the Colts 16–7. Namath's numbers were not outstanding, but he played flawlessly as the Jets ground out a victory with ball control. For that year he won the AFL Most Valuable Player award, the Hickok Belt, and the George Halas Award as most courageous football player of the year.

Namath considered quitting the game shortly thereafter. In June 1969 AFL Commissioner Pete Rozelle ordered Namath to divest himself of his interest in Bachelors III, a bar in New York frequented by alleged gamblers. In an emotional press conference, Namath announced that he had done nothing wrong and, as a matter of principle, would retire rather than give in. Eventually Rozelle and Namath reached an agreement whereby Namath would sell the New York Bachelors III but could run a national chain of bars with that name.

Namath remained at the top as an individual in 1969, though the team's performance slipped. In 1970, however, he suffered a broken wrist playing against the Colts, and missed most of the following year with a knee injury. He had his greatest single game in 1972, once again playing against the Colts, when he threw for 496 yards and six touchdowns, then missed much of the following season with a shoulder injury.

The damage was accumulating, and Namath was getting older. After the 1976 season the Jets released him, and he signed with the Los Angeles Rams. On 10 October 1977, before the national television audience of *Monday Night Football* on ABC, Namath threw four interceptions, then was knocked out of the game with yet another injury. That was his last game; he retired at the end of the year.

Namath had learned to profit from his image. In 1968 he received a substantial sum to shave off the famous mustache in a razor commercial. In 1974 some viewers were shocked by a commercial in which a pair of panty-hosed legs turned out to be his. He appeared in a few movies, with substantial roles in *Norwood* and *C.C. and Company* (both 1970), but these were not particularly successful. He has also done some sportscasting, including *Monday Night Football* in 1985 and 1986. On 7 November 1984 Namath surprised many by marrying. He and the former Deborah Lynn Mays, an actress, have two daughters.

Namath was elected to the Pro Football Hall of Fame in 1985. In his career he completed 1,886 out of 3,762 passes for 27,663 yards and 173 touchdowns. There are those who say that he was never the same after the damage to his knees in college, and his figures would have been much more impressive if he had stayed healthy. Nonetheless, in addition to being a memorable cultural figure, Namath was a key player in the transition from two leagues to one.

★

Namath, writing with sports journalist Dick Schaap, told a lighthearted version of his story in *I Can't Wait Until Tomorrow 'Cause I Get Better-Looking Every Day* (1969). Schaap recalled Namath and the pleasures of working with him in his memoir, *Flashing Before My Eyes* (2001). Namath's mother, Rose Namath Szolnoki, wrote *Namath, My Son Joe* (1975), with Bill Kushner.

ARTHUR D. HLAVATY

NAVRATILOVA, Martina (*b.* 18 October 1956 in Prague, Czechoslovakia), world-class tennis player who was number one in the world through most of the 1980s and whose devotion to physical fitness revolutionized the sport.

Navratilova was born Martina Subertova. Her mother, Jana, was a national tennis star in Czechoslovakia. Her father, Mirek, worked on the ski patrol in the Krkonoše Mountains and taught Navratilova to ski as soon as she could walk. In 1959 the couple divorced, and Navratilova went to live with her grandmother in a one-room apartment in Revnice. (Her father committed suicide some time after the divorce, when Navratilova was a teenager.) Navratilova's family had once lived an upper-middle-class lifestyle but now possessed little except a prized red-clay tennis court where young Navratilova learned to play tennis.

In 1961 Navratilova's mother married Mirek Navratil. (In Czechoslovakia women take the feminized form of a man's surname.) Mirek was the first to notice his stepdaughter's talent. While he was playing on the family's court one day, he heard the girl, age six at the time, hitting a ball against the wall. He recognized a promising force and consistency in her hitting and became her first coach.

Navratilova played her first tournament at age eight, where she won match after match. Mirek quickly realized the extent of her talent and took her to the Czech Tennis Federation, where George Parma was coach.

Parma, who would become a huge influence in Navra-

Martina Navratilova. AP/WIDE WORLD PHOTOS

tilova's life, taught her to play aggressively. Most women tennis players at this time played a baseline game. But Navratilova learned the serve and volley format, rushing the net at every opportunity. She hit the ball harder than most women did; her serve would eventually be clocked at ninety-five miles per hour. Under Parma's guidance she rose quickly in the Czech Federation.

The Soviet occupation of Czechoslovakia in 1968 changed the lives of many Czechs. Parma became one of the 120,000 Czech defectors. In 1969, coachless, Navratilova went to West Germany to play, where she "beat the West Germans like a drum." What really got her attention, though, was seeing the life that existed beyond the Iron Curtain.

In 1969 she captured the national fourteen-and-under title. In 1971, at age fifteen, she was placed on the premier national tennis team at the Sparta Club. Life at "Camp Sparta," as Navratilova called it, alleviated her loneliness. In 1973 she won the Czech National Championship, her first adult title, which recognized her as the best female tennis player in the nation—a status that she would maintain throughout 1974 and 1975.

During the winter months of 1973, Navratilova was granted permission to play in the United States. She arrived in Florida, chaperone in tow, to play eight tournaments. Navratilova immediately caught everyone's attention with her aggressive style and fierce strokes. But American fast food caused her to gain twenty pounds in six weeks, which appalled her self-conscious fellow athletes. Her handlers worried that she was embracing American excesses and capitalism. Amid all the speculation, Navratilova made it to the quarterfinals of the French Open.

Navratilova returned to the United States in 1974 and was reunited with her old coach George Parma, who connected her with an exiled Czech community. She found homes and friends in all the U.S. cities she played in. But the Czech Federation continued to exercise control over her life. That same year, she met Fred Barman, a movie agent whose daughter was also competing on the tennis circuit. Barman negotiated with the Czech Federation and got her an 80/20 split for all tournament winnings and endorsement deals, with Navratilova getting the 80 percent.

In 1974, while in Czechoslovakia, Navratilova decided to defect. Her reasons were not wholly political or professional. Navratilova realized that she could not imagine living as a lesbian in the Soviet bloc. Still, she wavered. But the Czech Federation made the decision for her when it hassled her regarding her travel plans.

Fred Barman helped Navratilova apply for political asylum while she was competing in the U.S. Open in 1974. She made it to the semifinals that year. Her application was approved in 1975 and she arrived for good on the professional women's tennis circuit.

Players such as Billie Jean King had pushed to increase the visibility of women's professional tennis. By 1975 there were a number of women's tennis tournaments. And the media played up the rivalry between Navratilova, an outsider, and U.S. favorite Chris Evert. Navratilova won a record nine Wimbledon singles titles, four U.S. Open singles titles, and dozens of others. She also excelled in doubles. By 1978 she was number one in the world and would dominate women's tennis until 1986, trading the number one spot with Evert ten times. During the 1970s and 1980s, at the height of her career, she had lengthy relationships with the author Rita Mae Brown and then with Judy Nelson, a socialite from Fort Worth, Texas, where Navratilova lived. The latter relationship ended badly, with Nelson suing Navratilova for financial support.

One of the reasons Navratilova stayed on top as long as she did was her dedication to physical training. Starting in 1981, the year she became a U.S. citizen, she put together what she called "Team Navratilova." Her team included a trainer, coach, and nutritionist. She practiced for hours each day, ran two to four miles, and worked out in a gym. She became stronger and was one of the fastest women on the court. After Navratilova, raw talent would no longer be enough to carry young players. Her training program became a standard in both men's and women's tennis in the 1990s.

Navratilova accumulated more titles than any other women playing professional tennis. While she officially retired in 1994, she still plays doubles at the major events. Since her retirement, she has become increasingly outspoken on the issue of gay rights. She has also written mystery novels, including *The Total Zone* (1994) and *Breaking Point* (1996).

Navratilova dominated professional tennis with her athleticism and unsurpassed serve and volley style, and she revolutionized the game with her devotion to physical fitness.

★

Navratilova cowrote two books: an autobiography, *Martina* (1985), and *Tennis My Way* (1983). Also see Gilda Zwerman, *Martina Navratilova* (1995).

RICHARD A. GREENWALD

NELSON, (John) Byron, Jr. (*b.* 4 February 1912 in Waxahachie, Texas), golfer who developed the modern golf swing and ranks with the greatest American players during the first half of the twentieth century.

Nelson was one of three children of John Nelson, a farmer and agricultural merchant, and Madge Nelson, a homemaker. The Nelson family lived in a modest house beside

Byron Nelson. AP/WIDE WORLD PHOTOS

the Glen Garden Country Club in Fort Worth, Texas. At age twelve Nelson joined his contemporary, Ben Hogan, as a caddy at the club. However, unlike Hogan, Nelson was a natural golfer who began to shoot low scores soon after taking up the game. He had the additional advantage of being singled out for instruction by the club professionals, Ted Longworth and his assistants, Dick and Jack Grout (the latter became Jack Nicklaus's lifelong coach and mentor).

Nelson turned professional in 1932 on the cusp of the Great Depression, at a time when the dominant figures of the 1920s—Bobby Jones, Walter Hagen and Gene Sarazen—were retired or past their apogees. "Golf without Jones," historian Herbert Warren Wind has written, "was like France without Paris—leaderless, lightless, and lonely." Nelson was the first of the 1912 triumvirate—Sam Snead and Hogan shared Nelson's birth year—to reach the pinnacle of golfing excellence, and the first to reinject excitement into the game.

During his relatively short career, Nelson won sixty-one tournaments, which included fifty-four events sanctioned by the Professional Golf Association (PGA), among them five majors: the Masters (1937 and 1942), the U.S. Open (1939), and the PGA Championship (1940 and 1945). He won his first notable tournament, the Southwest Amateur, in 1930. Strapped for funds, he turned professional, achieving moderate success but not enough (given the small purses of the day) to give up his "day job" as a golf professional at a club in Texarkana, on the border of Texas and Arkansas. In 1935 he moved to the Ridgewood Country Club in New Jersey as an assistant pro, where he began to adapt his swing to the new steel shafted clubs. By 1936 the change produced results when he won the Metropolitan Open, a PGA sectional (New York–New Jersey) in which he competed against well-known professionals Craig Wood and Tommy Armour.

The following year Nelson came to the attention of golfing fans with a dramatic performance in the 1937 Masters, where he made up a six-stroke deficit in two holes in the final round to win his first major. That year he won the Vardon Trophy for the lowest stroke average. He won the U.S. Open in 1939 in a grueling thirty-six-hole playoff in which he hit his one-iron into the fourth hole for an eagle two during the final eighteen. That year he also won the Western Open and the North and South.

In 1940 Nelson won three tournaments including his third major, the PGA Championship, beating Sam Snead one-up by birdying two of the final three holes. Nelson played on four U.S. Ryder Cup teams (1937, 1939, 1941, and 1947), and in 1965 he was the team's nonplaying captain.

In 1942 Nelson won the Masters again, this time by a single stroke in a memorable battle against Hogan. Rejected from military service because of hemophilia, Nelson continued to play during World War II. In 1944 he won thirteen of the twenty-three events he played, and he was the leading money winner with a record $37,000.

During 1945, the most remarkable year of his career, "Lord Byron," as Nelson was called, set a record that is not likely to ever be bettered. He won eleven consecutive PGA tournaments. (No one else has ever done better than six.) Moreover, he amassed a total of eighteen victories in the thirty-one tournaments he entered that year, and he was the runner-up in seven others.

Nelson's 1945 performance has produced a simmering debate among golf historians and fans. Did his records signify extraordinary talent or the lack of competition during the war? Perhaps the appropriate conclusion is "some of each," but as golf journalists and historians have pointed out, his two primary challengers, Snead and Hogan, played in several of those 1945 tournaments. Furthermore, all but one of the events was stroke play, in which it is the course rather than the other competitors against which the game is played. His stroke average for the year was a remarkable 68.33, another record that has never been broken.

At the end of the 1945 season Nelson was physically exhausted and mentally drained. He had always considered golf a means to an end, rather than an end in itself. Nelson and his wife, Louise, wanted more than anything else to spend the better part of their lives on a Texas cattle ranch and, as he tells it, "Each drive, each iron, each chip, each putt was aimed at the goal of getting that ranch." In 1946, at the age of thirty-four, Nelson retired from regular competition and moved to his newly acquired 750-acre Fairway Ranch in Roanoke, Texas.

But Nelson did not abandon golf. When television discovered the game, Nelson was among the original golf analysts on the American Broadcasting Companies' ABC-TV. He also hosted the annual Byron Nelson Classic, a PGA tournament in Irving, Texas, near Dallas. And with Gene Sarazen and Sam Snead, Nelson continued to appear annually at the Masters to hit one of the honorary opening tee shots.

The advancement of technology has had a significant impact on sports, and golf is no exception. The development of the golf ball and the golf club (as well as the course itself) have revolutionized how golf is played. Whippy hickory shafts were best controlled by bending the left elbow (for right-handed golfers) in the backswing, followed by a relatively flat downswing that emphasized fast hands and a quiet body. Bobby Jones was the first major golfer to modify this classic "Saint Andrews" swing by adopting a straight left arm in his backswing. But Jones's hands still led and controlled the downswing, and his lower body remained a platform rather than a piston.

Beginning with Jones's straight left arm, Nelson invented the modern golf swing to fit the firmer steel shafts that came into vogue during the 1930s. Over six feet tall, he began to experiment with harnessing the potential power of his long lower body by making it more active in his take-away and unleashing it in a more vertical downswing by driving forward hard with his legs. This made his arms and hands centrifugal extensions of his large body muscles, which he dipped as his club came in contact with the ball. The result was prodigious power and unprecedented accuracy, resulting in what some insist was the best golf swing on the planet. If Nelson had played in the television age, his supporter's argue, this view would be widely shared.

Nelson's swing was so fluid and close to perfection that the United States Golf Association (USGA) designed its automatic ball-testing machine to emulate it. The "Iron Byron," in use beginning in 1976, flight tested golf balls for conformity, distance, and accuracy. It was finally retired in 2001.

Nelson's achievements have been recognized over the decades. In 1944 and 1945 he was the Associated Press Athlete of the Year. In 1953 he was elected into the PGA Hall of Fame. In 1955 the Texas Sports Hall of Fame honored him, as did the World Golf Hall of Fame in 1974. In 1974 he also received the Bobby Jones Award for his contributions to golf.

In October 1985 his wife, Louise, died after a long illness. In 1986 Nelson met Peggy Simmons, forty years his junior, and married her after a brief courtship. A journalist, she helped Nelson compose his biography, *How I Played the Game.*

★

Nelson's autobiography is *How I Played the Game* (1993). The only full-length biography is Martin Davis, *Byron Nelson: The Story of Golf's Finest Gentleman and the Greatest Winning Streak in History* (1997).

MARTIN SHERWIN

NEVERS, Ernest Alonzo ("Ernie") (*b.* 11 June 1903 in Willow River, Minnesota; *d.* 3 May 1976 in San Rafael, California), talented and versatile athlete and a durable football player who in 1929 scored 40 points in a single game, a National Football League (NFL) record that still stands.

Nevers's parents, George Nevers and Mary Nevers, who emigrated from Nova Scotia, Canada, to northern Minnesota, owned a tavern until Prohibition dealt the business a severe blow. After that, the family moved to Superior, Wisconsin, where Nevers got his first taste of organized

Ernie Nevers, 1925. © BETTMANN/CORBIS

football. It is a wonder he stuck with the sport. Seeing Nevers's potential, his coach used him as a tackling dummy, literally, to toughen him up. Nevers said of standing motionless in a sawdust pit as he was continuously hit by his teammates, "The only difference between me and an actual tackling dummy was I could talk and I wasn't suspended from a rope."

Nevers excelled in all sports at Superior's Central High School until 1919, when the family moved to Santa Rosa, California, and his father took up farming. However, during his senior year he returned to Wisconsin and led the Central High team to the state basketball championship.

Nevers probably would have gone to the University of Wisconsin after graduation from high school in 1921, but the school did not offer him a scholarship. Instead, the six-foot, one-inch, 210-pound fullback went to Stanford in 1922, following a year at Santa Rosa Junior College to correct a foreign language deficiency. He continued to excel in football, basketball, and baseball at Stanford. He was a consensus football All-American and good enough in baseball and basketball to sign professional contracts. Nevers earned eleven varsity letters at Stanford.

Perhaps Nevers's most memorable game was the 1 January 1925 Rose Bowl after his junior season. Nevers had broken an ankle in preseason practice earlier that fall but recovered to play the last regular-season game—in which he broke his other ankle. The determined, rugged Nevers vowed to play in the Rose Bowl against the Notre Dame team that featured the fabled Four Horsemen backfield. With both ankles heavily taped, Nevers played the entire sixty minutes, but as one man he was no match for the Four Horsemen. Nevers, always a workhorse, gained almost as many yards (114) as the entire Notre Dame team. Depending on one's allegiance, Nevers did or did not cross the goal line on a crucial fourth-down play. If indeed he was stopped, it was one of the few times Notre Dame halted the "Blond Blockbuster," as Nevers was sometimes known. The score was 20–10 in favor of Notre Dame at the time of the still-disputed play. Nevers returned for his senior collegiate season and led Stanford to a 7–2 record as the consensus All-America fullback. A highlight of his senior year was a 27–14 victory over University of California, Berkeley, in "the Big Game." It was Stanford's first victory in eight tries against California.

Nevers signed contracts to play professional baseball with the St. Louis Browns, and basketball with a Chicago team in a professional league that predated the National Basketball Association (NBA), but it was football in which he gained the most fame and fortune. Nevers's gridiron reputation was second only to that of the Chicago Bears "Galloping Ghost," Red Grange. He signed a contract for a $10,000 bonus, plus a salary of $22,500 (unusually high for the time—and, again, second only to Grange) to play the 1926 season with an NFL team based in Duluth, Minnesota. The team was owned by a high school friend, Ole Haugsrud, and played as the Kelleys in 1925. To take full advantage of Nevers's fame, the team officially changed its name to Ernie Nevers's Eskimos, originally just for the 1926 season, although the team played another season in 1927. The squad always numbered in the low teens and, because the starting eleven players usually played the entire game, the press dubbed them "the Iron Men of the North."

The Eskimos were really a road team. After they left Duluth in late September, they did not return until January 1927; they traveled 17,000 miles and once played five games in eight days. The Eskimos played fourteen NFL games, finishing 6–5–3, and played fifteen exhibition games as well. The durable Nevers missed only twenty-seven minutes of those twenty-nine games—he was knocked cold in one game, missing all twenty-seven minutes at once. Nevers earned most of the money, but his mates—just eager to play with him—did not complain about the pay scale. They were paid $75 for a victory, $60 for a tie, and $50 for a loss. Nevers married Mary Elizabeth Haegerty in 1926; she died in 1943.

Once when the Eskimos were in New York to play the Giants, the host team's owner Tim Mara sent a sightseeing bus to show them the town. When just thirteen Eskimos showed up, Mara said, "Where's the rest of the team?" Haugsrud, too embarrassed to admit his entire team was present, said, "Oh, they must still be sleeping. Let's just go without them." The next day the outnumbered Eskimos lost to the Giants 14–13.

Playing baseball with the Browns in 1927, Nevers became part of American folklore, when as a pitcher, he served up two of Babe Ruth's record 60 home runs. Whenever anyone mentioned Nevers's place in the baseball record book, he was quick to point out, "But I hit .347 as a pinch hitter."

During the 1927 football season the Eskimos managed only a 1–8 record, but they did much better in their exhibition games, with Nevers again the star. He missed the entire 1928 season due to an injury, and the Eskimos were no longer in existence when he returned for the 1929 season as a player-coach, so Nevers accepted an offer to play for the Chicago Cardinals. Nevers etched his name in the NFL record book on Thanksgiving Day that year when he led his underdog Cardinals to a 40–6 victory over the crosstown rival Bears. Nevers scored all 40 points—6 touchdowns and 4 extra points. No one has scored more touchdowns in an NFL game, and only Dub Jones and Gale Sayers ever matched the half-dozen touchdowns, and Nevers earned his rushing. Knute Rockne, perhaps remembering the 1925 Rose Bowl, had his Notre Dame team in attendance that day. When Nevers finished his record-setting performance, Rockne turned to his team and said, "That, gentlemen, is the way to play this game."

Nevers continued as the Cardinals workhorse for the 1930 and 1931 seasons, but the team struggled to stay around the .500 mark. Once Nevers was knocked unconscious when an opponent landed on Nevers's back with both knees. As Nevers was brought to and led to the sidelines, he broke free, saying, "You're not taking me out." He ran the ball sixteen straight times until he scored a much-needed touchdown. In another game he threw a 62-yard pass in the final minute to win 7–0. Against Hartford (then in the NFL) he kicked five field goals to win 15–0. Playing against the Pottsville (Pennsylvania) Maroons, a team that claimed the 1925 NFL championship, Nevers completed seventeen consecutive passes.

Nevers organized a barnstorming team in 1931 called the Ernie Nevers All-Stars. His squad was comfortably ahead in a game against a local team from San Francisco when a teammate suggested he sit out the final few minutes. Nevers replied matter-of-factly, "The name of the team is the Ernie Nevers All-Stars; the fans paid their money and deserve to see Ernie Nevers." As usual, he played the entire sixty minutes.

Nevers's NFL career ended after the 1931 season, perhaps because business and coaching opportunities offered more security than depression-era professional football wages. He was All-Pro in each of his five seasons, the briefest career of anyone enshrined in the Pro Football Hall of Fame. After his active playing career was over, Nevers coached on the college and professional levels. He also served as a captain in the U.S. Marine Corps in World War II. He entered into several business ventures in the San Francisco Bay Area, and in 1947 married Margery Luxem. Nevers's two marriages produced a son and a daughter. He died of kidney disease and is buried in Mount Tamalpais Cemetery in San Rafael, California.

Nevers's greatness is attested to by his induction in both the College Football Hall of Fame and the Pro Football Hall of Fame. Coach Glenn Scobey ("Pop") Warner, who picked Nevers over Jim Thorpe as his greatest player, said of him, "No one ever gave more of himself than Ernie Nevers."

★

A biography of Nevers is Jim Scott, *Ernie Nevers* (1969). His life and career are discussed in Arthur Daley, *Pro Football Hall of Fame* (1963); George Sullivan, *Pro Football's All-Time Greats* (1968); Harold Rosenthal, *Fifty Faces of Football* (1981); and Joe Ziemba, *When Football Was Football* (1999). An obituary is in the *New York Times* (4 May 1976).

JIM CAMPBELL

NEWELL, Peter ("Pete") (*b.* 31 August 1915 in Vancouver, British Columbia, Canada), the first coach to win basketball's Triple Crown (the National Invitation Tournament [NIT] championship, the National Collegiate Athletic Association [NCAA] championship, and the Olympics); one of the finest teachers and tacticians the game has ever known.

Newell was the youngest of eight children born to Peter Newell, who worked for the Knights of Columbus, and Alice Heffron Newell, a homemaker. In 1916 or 1917 the Newells moved from Canada to California. Newell was a child actor when he was four years old, and was featured in several *Our Gang* movie comedies, which were about children simulating adult situations, and was a finalist for the title role in *The Kid,* one of Charlie Chaplin's greatest films. After the end of his brief acting career, Newell focused his attention on playing baseball and basketball.

Baseball was Newell's favorite sport as a child, and basketball was secondary. He switched mainly to basketball by

Pete Newell, 1998. ASSOCIATED PRESS AP

his high school years, when he played at Saint Agnes of Los Angeles under Coach Bill Lauremany. After graduating in 1933, he enrolled at Loyola University in Los Angeles, where he was a three-year player for the basketball team. His coach was Jimmy Needles, who coached the first U.S. Olympic basketball team in 1936. Newell graduated with a B.A. in political science in 1939 and immediately began his coaching career at Saint John's Military Academy in Los Angeles. He had two undefeated seasons at the school before enlisting in the U.S. Navy, where he served for four years (1942–1946).

In 1946 Newell was hired to coach baseball and basketball at the University of San Francisco (USF). In four years there he guided the basketball team to a 70–37 record and the 1949 NIT championship, defeating Loyola of Chicago 48–47 in the title game. USF All-America forward Don Lofgran was named the NIT most valuable player (MVP). The team's invitation to the tournament was the first ever for a West Coast school. With the conclusion of the 1949–1950 season, Newell left San Francisco to coach Michigan State. In four seasons he compiled a 45–42 record and led the Spartans to two Big Ten championships in 1953 and 1954.

Newell returned to California to coach at the University of California at Berkeley (Cal). In six seasons he guided his teams to a 119–44 record and four Pacific Eight (now Pacific Coast) Conference titles (1957–1960). In 1957 and 1958 he led the Golden Bears to the West Regional Finals of the NCAA tournament. In 1959 his team won the championship with a thrilling 71–70 victory over West Virginia, led by tournament MVP Jerry West. The next year Newell brought his team to the NCAA championship game, where they lost to Ohio State 75–55, due in large part to the efforts of tournament MVP Jerry Lucas. Newell was named the College Coach of the Year in 1960 after guiding Cal to a 28–1 record and the NCAA Finals.

In the summer of 1960 Newell coached one of the finest Olympic teams ever assembled. Led by future Hall of Famers Walt Bellamy, Jerry Lucas, Jerry West, and Oscar Robertson, the team also included future National Basketball Association (NBA) players Darrall Imhoff, Bob Boozer, and Terry Dischinger. The United States won all eight of its games by an average of 42.4 points per game and defeated Brazil 90–63 for the gold medal in Rome, Italy.

With the gold medal, which made him the first coach to win basketball's Triple Crown (the NIT, the NCAA, and the Olympics), Newell officially retired from coaching. In fourteen years he had compiled a 234–123 record, a .655 winning percentage. His success was based on his unsurpassed knowledge of the game's fundamentals. At Cal his teams initiated and popularized the use of pressure defense, and in 1959 and 1960 his teams led the nation in team defense points per game allowed. With John Bennington he cowrote *Basketball Methods* (1962), an instructional textbook that has become a basketball bible. He also wrote *Pete Newell's Defensive Basketball: Winning Techniques and Strategies* (2001).

In 1960 Newell became the athletic director at Cal, a position he held for the next eight years. He also was a member of the NCAA Basketball Tournament Committee and helped guide the tournament to the prestigious standing it has today. In 1968 he received the Metropolitan Award, given annually by NCAA coaches to the person who has contributed most to the game of basketball. From 1960 to 1968 Newell served on the U.S. Olympic Committee, and in 1964 and 1968 he chaired the Olympic Coach Selection Committee. He served on the U.S. Olympic Committee again from 1978 to 1990.

Newell's contribution to basketball extended beyond his coaching record. In 1957 he created the first basketball film used to develop intersectional officiating consistencies. From 1962 to 1973 he was an adviser to the Peace Corps' worldwide basketball program.

International basketball has been an integral part of Newell's life. He has given basketball seminars in Europe and in Central and South America for the U.S. State Department. During the 1950s he spoke at more basketball clinics in the United States and abroad than any other coach. Newell's interest in fostering the international game extended to his volunteer involvement in the Japanese Basketball Association and to his helping prepare the Japanese team for the 1964 and 1972 Olympics. In the mid-1970s he organized an annual trip by an NBA All-Star team to Japan. Newell's two-plus decades of contributions to Japanese basketball earned him the prestigious Order of the Sacred Treasure from the Japanese emperor in 1987.

After eight years as athletic director at Cal, Newell was named the general manager of the second-year San Diego Rockets of the National Basketball Association (NBA). When the Rockets moved to Houston in the 1971–1972 season, Newell remained with the organization in an advisory capacity until the Los Angeles Lakers hired him as general manager in 1972. While with the Rockets, Newell drafted Calvin Murphy from Niagara and Rudy Tomjanovich from Michigan.

Newell served with the Lakers until 1976, when he was hired as a talent consultant for the Golden State Warriors prior to the 1977–1978 NBA season. He also broadcast University of Southern California (USC) games and the Pac-10 Monday night Game of the Week. In 1976 Newell developed his highly regarded "Big Man's Camp," which focuses on improving the skills of NBA forwards and centers. Camp attendees have included Hakeem Olajuwon and Shaquille O'Neal. In 1984 Newell became the director of player personnel for the Warriors.

In 1991 Newell was hired by the Cleveland Cavaliers to scout the West Coast and to evaluate college player talent in preparation for the annual NBA draft. He held that position until the end of 1999–2000 season, when he retired. Newell married Florence J. O'Connor, and they eventually had four sons.

Newell was elected to the Naismith Memorial Basketball Hall of Fame in 1978. In 1987 he received the Naismith Outstanding Contribution to Basketball Award, given by the Atlanta Tipoff Club. In December of that year Cal honored Newell's accomplishments at the university by renaming its home court Harmon Arena/Newell Court; in 1990 the school endowed the Pete Newell Scholarship to further honor his service to the school. In December 1997 the first annual Pete Newell Basketball Challenge Tournament was held at the Oakland Coliseum.

Within the coaching fraternity, Newell has earned an impeccable reputation for his uncanny ability to teach the game of basketball. His aptitude in evaluating talent, combined with his innovative coaching techniques, has landed him high praise from every level of the coaching profession. A true "basketball educator," Newell established a system of tight, aggressive defense combined with a disciplined, pattern offense. Through his coaching seminars, film programs, and clinics, Newell has achieved acclaim as a world-renowned teacher.

★

Material about Newell's career is in his file at the Naismith Memorial Basketball Hall of Fame in Springfield, Massachusetts. A biography of Newell is Bruce Jenkins, *A Good Man: The Pete Newell Story* (1999). An account of Newell's life and philosophy at the pinnacle of his career is Robert H. Boyle, "We Don't Concede Anything," *Sports Illustrated* (18 Jan. 1960). Other articles of interest include Pam King, "Pete Newell: The Guru of the NBA," *NBA Today* (26 Mar. 1982), and Ron Thomas, "Pros Take Time Out to Learn Game," *USA Today* (23 Aug. 1983).

DOUGLAS A. STARK

NICKLAUS, Jack William (*b.* 21 January 1940 in Columbus, Ohio), golfer whose accomplishments include winning the most major championship victories in the history of golf; he received the "Golfer of the Century" award in 1988.

Jack Nicklaus. ARCHIVE PHOTOS, INC.

Nicklaus is the son of Louis Charles Nicklaus, Jr., a pharmacist and an enthusiastic golfer who sparked his son's interest in the game, and Helen Schoener. Nicklaus was a natural athlete with many athletic interests. At Upper Arlington High School he played center on the basketball team, catcher on the baseball team, and quarterback on the football team. But from the age of ten he also played golf. As the golfer Chi Chi Rodriquez said, Nicklaus became "a legend in his spare time."

But Nicklaus, the all-around teenage athlete, was able to focus on his goals, and his ambition was to become the world's best golfer. Along with an abundance of natural talent, he had two other advantages: a world-class home course, the Scioto Country Club, and one of the finest golf instructors in America, Jack Grout, who remained his lifelong teacher and mentor.

At the age of thirteen Nicklaus began a streak of amateur victories by winning the Ohio State Junior and Columbus Junior Match-Play Championships. During the next six years, he won fourteen tournaments, including the Trans-Mississippi Championship at age eighteen, and qualified for the second year in a row for the U.S. Open. In 1959 he won the U.S. Amateur, the North and South, and the Trans-Mississippi Championships. In 1960, still an amateur, Nicklaus came within two strokes of beating Arnold Palmer in the U.S. Open at Cherry Hills, Denver, with a record 282 for an amateur playing in an Open.

On 23 July 1960, having just completed his junior year at Ohio State University, Nicklaus married Barbara Bash. In between visits to Manhattan and Atlantic City during their honeymoon, Jack played golf at Winged Foot and then at Pine Valley, a men-only club that barred Barbara from the grounds.

In 1961 Nicklaus won the U.S. Amateur title for a second time, a victory that led him to abandon a career as an insurance salesman to join the Professional Golf Association (PGA) tour. In 1962 Nicklaus turned professional and also won the Rookie of the Year award. Nicklaus's first major victory, the U.S. Open at Oakmont Country Club in 1962, not only tested his golfing skills but his self-control and character. It was an unpopular triumph, perhaps the most unpopular in the history of golf. "Arnie's Army" (as Arnold Palmer's many golf fans proudly called themselves) did not want this overweight, country club–bred, deliberately playing upstart to beat their hero. But Nicklaus won the play-off decisively, 71 to 74. For accomplishing this feat he was considered a villain. He was verbally abused—"Fat Jack" and "Nick Louse" were among the gentler names shouted at him from the gallery. A man of lesser confidence and character might understandably have reacted with hostility to such treatment. But Nicklaus took the high road, never complained, continued to play superior golf, became good friends with Palmer, and won over U.S. golf fans by consistently setting an example of athletic excellence. His fans gave him the more flattering nickname "Golden Bear," because of his body shape and blond hair. Watching Nicklaus win the 1965 Masters by nine strokes with a record 271, the golf legend Bobby Jones remarked, "He plays a kind of golf with which I am not familiar."

In 1971, after winning the PGA Championship, Nicklaus became the first golfer ever to record a double grand slam, completing the cycle of major championship victories twice. Nicklaus not only holds the record for the most majors won, but through 1998 he had played in an amazing 154 consecutive majors, an accomplishment that can only be appreciated when set alongside that of the runner-up Nick Faldo, who played in forty-four straight major tournaments. Nicklaus's record is often called the greatest streak in sports history.

Nicklaus's U.S. Open victory in 1972 at Pebble Beach also produced a great one-iron shot onto the seventeenth green that hit the pin for a tap-in. At the 1975 Masters, he hit a one-iron 246 yards in the final round to the fifteenth green, which led to a one-shot victory over Johnny Miller and Tom Weiskopf. This is often spoken of as the most impressive shot of his career.

But his last tour win, the 1986 Masters, when he was forty-six years old, was his most dramatic victory. In the final round he eagled the fifteenth, and birdied the sixteenth and seventeenth to pass Greg Norman and Tom Kite by a stroke. It was a fitting achievement with which to cap the most successful playing career in golf.

Nicklaus was also competitive off the course. Once golf course architecture caught his interest, he committed to it thoroughly (perhaps to the detriment of his game). By the end of the century Nicklaus had designed nearly 200 courses in the United States and in more than twenty-four other countries. Over twelve of these courses are among the U.S. top 100, as selected by *Golf Digest.*

In business, Nicklaus has had some serious failures along with his many successes. His company, Golden Bear International Inc., almost failed around 1990 when Nicklaus made an admittedly "very, very big tactical error" by diversifying and going public. "I should have stayed with our core businesses and invested instead with money managers in the proper places," he told *Golf Digest.* "I'm still working because I think I have to."

Jack and Barbara had five children, and they make their home in North Palm Beach, Florida. His home golf club is Muirfield Village Golf Club, Dublin, Ohio.

Nicklaus won seventy tour victories, among them eighteen majors, twenty when his two National Amateur championships (1959 and 1961) are included. His career tour average was 71.0 strokes per round. He was the top money winner eight times and runner-up six times. He was the PGA Player of the Year five times and Athlete of the Decade for the 1970s. He was a member of the U.S. Ryder Cup Teams, compiling a record of 17–8–3, and was the nonplaying captain of the 1983 and 1987 teams. Nicklaus won every major at least three times, while no one else has even won every major twice.

Until Eldrick "Tiger" Woods came on the scene thirty-five years later, no golfer ever dominated the field as thoroughly as Nicklaus. He was the longest and the straightest off the tee, he hit his irons with Hoganesque accuracy, and his squat, hunched-over putting setup led to remarkable results, especially under pressure. Combined with this exceptional collection of physical skills, Nicklaus added a mental discipline that was equally impressive. He was a master of course strategy and self-control. Every important shot was calculated to balance success against failure. He played to be a winner, not a hero. Asked if his emotions might affect his game playing at his beloved Saint Andrews golf course in Scotland, Nicklaus responded, "That's kind of a silly question, don't you think?"

Lee Trevino once quipped that the best way to avoid being struck by lightning on a golf course is to hold a one-iron over your head because, "Even God can't hit a one-iron." But Nicklaus could. Asked in 2000 to recall the best golf shots of his life, he named three of his most memorable one-iron swings. In 1967 at the U.S. Open at Baltusrol he was 238 yards away from the pin on the last hole, and with his one-iron—and hitting into the wind—he put the ball close enough to putt it in. That shot earned him victory at 275, which beat Hogan's record 276 held since 1948. Because of hip problems, Nicklaus decided that 2000 would be the final year that he would play in all four major tournaments.

On 20 June 1988 Nicklaus received the "Golfer of the Century" award at the "Centennial of Golf in America Celebration." The panelists, composed of journalists and golf officials, had to pass over many of the century's greatest golfers, including the most popular golfer in America, Arnold Palmer. But their choice was a foregone conclusion. Jack Nicklaus's long career and his extraordinary record of accomplishments left them no option. As Bobby Jones once observed: "I think it is completely safe to say that there has not yet been a more effective golfer than Jack Nicklaus."

★

Nicklaus's autobiography, written with Ken Bowden, is *Jack Nicklaus: My Story* (1997). For perspective on Nicklaus's final tour of golf's major tournaments, see David S. Shedloski, *Golden Twilight* (2001).

MARTIN SHERWIN

NITSCHKE, Ray(mond) Ernest (*b.* 29 December 1936 in Elmwood Park, Illinois; *d.* 8 March 1998 in Venice, Florida), key defensive player for the Green Bay Packers whose aggressive on-field persona belied a sensitive and caring off-field personality. He overcame a troubled youth to become an inductee of the Pro Football Hall of Fame.

Nitschke was born in a working-class Chicago suburb to Robert Nitschke, a Chicago Surface Line employee, and Anna Petersen Nitschke, a homemaker and later a restaurant cook. Tragedy struck the family early in young Ray's life. His father, coming home from a union meeting, was killed in a car-trolley collision when Nitschke was three years old. To provide for her family of three boys—Ray and two older brothers—Anna Nitschke went to work at a restaurant-tavern owned by Nitschke's Uncle Pete. At an early age, Nitschke also worked at Pete's Place, peeling potatoes and doing other kitchen chores. Life was hard without a father, but Nitschke said, "We were never hungry, and we always had clean clothes."

The family suffered a second blow when Nitschke was thirteen. His mother, to whom he was very close, died from a blood clot resulting from untreated internal bleeding. Nitschke later recalled the devastating event, "All of a sudden, everything fell apart—I was an orphan at thirteen." By his own admission, Nitschke said, "I didn't have a chip on my shoulder, I had a two-by-eight plank on my shoulder. I wanted to fight everyone. I was a skinny runt, but I took on the world." He continued, "I was angry and hurting." Nitschke was always playing some kind of ball with the neighborhood kids, and when he was not, he played ball by himself. "I remember kicking a football, chasing it, and kicking it again," he said. "Sports was what kept me out of real trouble."

Although he weighed only 100 pounds as a freshman at Priviso East High School in Maywood, Illinois, Nitschke played football on a "C" team. Academic deficiencies prevented him from competing in sports as a sophomore, but by his junior year he weighed 170 pounds and played quarterback on the Priviso East varsity. A strong thrower, as a senior Nitschke led his team to the Chicago Suburban League championship. His coach Andy Puplis, who had been an All-America quarterback at Notre Dame, gave him much needed guidance, for which Nitschke later expressed appreciation.

Nitschke was good enough in high school baseball to warrant a $3,000 bonus offer from the St. Louis Browns. Nitschke wanted to sign, but Puplis steered him toward attending the University of Illinois on a football scholarship. Nitschke had earned honorable mention high school All-America selection in football. Nitschke still thought of himself as a quarterback, but the Fighting Illini coach Ray Eliot thought otherwise, saying, "Ray, what would you rather be—second-string quarterback or first-string fullback?" Nitschke replied, "First-string quarterback." Despite Nitschke's answer, he became the Illini fullback. In that single-platoon era, where the starting eleven played both offense and defense, he excelled as a linebacker on defense, but he was still impressive running with the ball. He averaged 6.2 yards per carry as a senior—the average was boosted by an 84-yard touchdown run against Northwestern. Nitschke did not make All-America, but he was selected to play in the Senior Bowl All-Star game and the 1958 College All-Star game in Chicago. As a College All-Star, he was instrumental in the collegians defeating the defending National Football League (NFL) champion Detroit Lions 35–19.

Shortly after the All-Star game, Nitschke reported to the Green Bay Packers training camp as a six-foot, three-inch, 235-pound, third-round draft choice. These were the pre-Lombardi Packers, a motley crew. In Nitschke's rookie season, the Packers won a game, tied a game, and lost ten others. But Nitschke was one of six future Hall of Famers awaiting the arrival of coach Vince Lombardi in 1959—the others were Forrest Gregg, Paul Hornung, Jim Ringo, Bart Starr, and Jim Taylor. Nitschke was a work-in-progress when Lombardi took over. With more money than he had ever seen (even though his early NFL salary was in the $7,500 range) and single, Nitschke was someone to avoid when he was cruising Green Bay's bars—something he did quite often. Nitschke said, "I didn't drink that much, but after just one or two, I started flexing my 'beer muscles.'

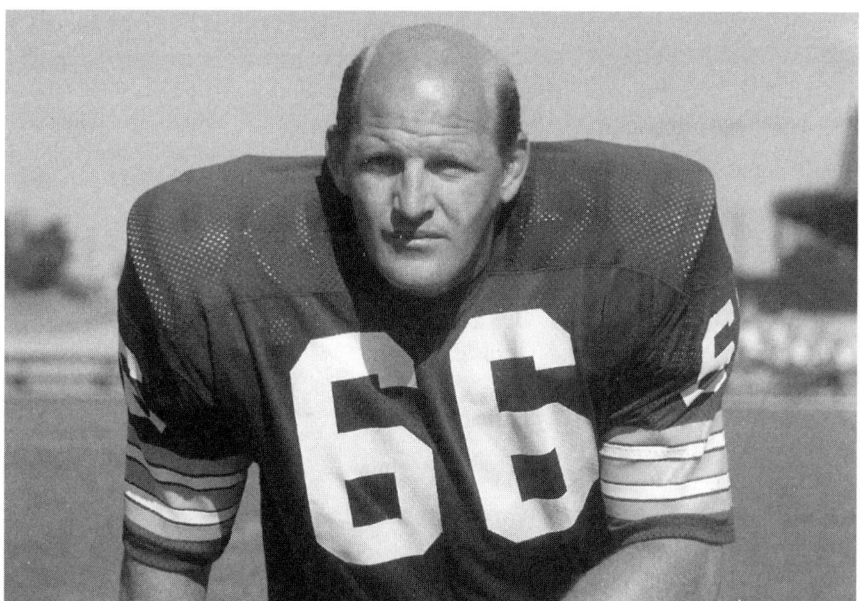

Ray Nitschke, 1973. ASSOCIATED PRESS AP

I was ready to fight anyone who looked at me sideways." That changed in early 1961, when Nitschke met Jackie Forchette. The couple married later that fall, and soon adopted three children. A stable home life settled Nitschke down. He not only appreciated his own children, but also devoted time to children's charities throughout the rest of his life. Nitschke was still "Mr. Hyde" on the field, knocking down opponents with authority. He established himself as the linchpin of the Packers defense, and as one of the NFL's most ferocious tacklers.

The Packers flourished under Lombardi, getting to the NFL title game in 1960 (losing to Philadelphia) and winning championships in 1961 and 1962. On a cold and blustery 30 December 1962 at New York's Yankee Stadium, the Packers defeated the Giants 16–7. Nitschke recovered two fumbles and deflected a pass, and was named the game's Most Valuable Player. Nitschke also stayed over in New York after the game to appear on the popular television show, *What's My Line?* Prematurely bald and wearing black horn-rim glasses and a three-button suit, Nitschke's professorial look easily stumped Bennett Cerf and his fellow panelists.

Nitschke continued to contribute to the Packers dynasty. The team won three consecutive NFL titles in 1965, 1966, and 1967, and the first two Super Bowls, Super Bowl I on 25 January 1967, and Super Bowl II on 14 January 1968. If anything, Nitschke's reputation as an intimidator grew, and he was acknowledged as the NFL's hardest hitter. Opponents had to account for him on every play, or pay the consequences. He retired after the 1972 season, having been a four-time All-Pro and having played in 190 games—second-most in Packers history. He had intercepted 25 passes and returned them 385 yards—2 for touchdowns. However, the thousands of thunderous, crunching tackles are what teammates and opponents remembered most.

Nitschke stayed in Green Bay after retiring, doing commercials, playing in football-centered movies such as *The Longest Yard* (1974), working with youngsters, and playing in charity golf tournaments. He was also involved as a publisher and columnist with the *Packers Report*, a team newspaper. Nitschke was inducted into the Pro Football Hall of Fame in 1978, and is also a member of the Wisconsin and Packers Halls of Fame.

Nitschke and his family wintered in Naples, Florida, where he suffered a heart attack and died while going to visit a friend in nearby Venice. His remains were cremated.

When Nitschke came into the NFL in 1958, he was an unlikely candidate to play fifteen seasons and establish himself as one of the game's greats. Though inexplicably selected for only one Pro Bowl, he had the respect of all connected with professional football. His Pro Football Hall of Fame induction should allay any doubts about his greatness. So, too, should the fact that he was chosen for the NFL's All-Time teams when the league celebrated its fiftieth (1969) and seventy-fifth (1994) anniversaries. Opposing coach George Allen said of him, "Nitschke was one of those few players who did things others couldn't do. When I was with the [Chicago] Bears we named one of our defenses '47 Nitschke,' because it copied the way Ray played a certain situation. Naming a defense after a player, especially an opponent, is a pretty high compliment in my book."

★

Nitschke wrote an autobiography with Robert W. Wells, *Mean On Sundays* (1973). His life and career are also discussed in Chuck Johnson, *The Greatest Packers of Them All* (1968); Phil Bengtson and Todd Hunt, *Packer Dynasty* (1969); and Murray Olderman, *The Defenders* (1973).

JIM CAMPBELL

NOLL, Charles Henry ("Chuck") (*b.* 5 January 1932 in Cleveland, Ohio), the first coach in the National Football League (NFL) to win four Super Bowls.

Noll was the son of William Noll, a butcher and occasional truck driver, and Katherine Steigerwald, a florist. Noll attended the Benedictine High School in Cleveland. Although he only played football during the final two years of high school, he earned a scholarship to the University of Dayton. Entering Dayton in 1949, he played on the offensive line of the football team. He graduated with a B.S. in education in 1953 and was taken by the Cleveland Browns in the twenty-first round of the professional football draft that year.

Cleveland coach Paul Brown used offensive linemen to carry plays to the quarterback. At six feet, one inch tall and 218 pounds, Noll was one of the messenger guards used for that purpose. When injuries created a problem on defense, he was switched to linebacker. Noll played seventy-seven games in seven years with the Browns. He was part of five Eastern Conference championships and played in two NFL title games.

It was difficult for a lineman and, in those days, for a defensive player to demonstrate his ability statistically. On defense Noll had a career total of eight interceptions for ninety-two yards and one touchdown. He had a fumble recovery for another touchdown. He also had one tackle for a safety. On two kick returns, he gained twenty-two yards.

Following his career as a player, Noll joined Coach Sid Gillman of the Los Angeles (later San Diego) Chargers of the new American Football League (AFL). During Noll's six years under Gillman, the Chargers won four Western Conference championships and two AFL titles. In 1966 Noll joined Coach Don Shula of the Baltimore Colts as defensive backs coach. In his three years with the Colts, the team lost only three games. Winning the NFL title in 1968, the Colts lost Super Bowl III to the New York Jets, led by Joe Namath.

In 1969, at the age of thirty-seven, Noll took over as the head coach of the Pittsburgh Steelers. Although one of the original members of the NFL, the hapless Steelers had never appeared in a league championship game. Noll won his first game as a Steeler, but the team reverted to its expected form and lost the next thirteen. They started the 1970 season with three more losses but ended with five wins and nine losses. In his third season Noll improved marginally to 6–8.

Fortunately, Noll was working for Art Rooney, Sr., an owner noted for his patience and loyalty. He endorsed Noll's strategy for bringing success to Pittsburgh, a policy that became impossible once free agency and salary caps became the norm. Noll believed that a winning team could

Chuck Noll, 1971. ASSOCIATED PRESS AP

be built through the annual player draft and that players needed to be developed slowly; his predecessors had traditionally traded away their draft picks for established players generally past their prime. In his first sixteen years as head coach of the Steelers, Noll traded for only ten players.

In his use of draft choices, Noll felt that he should take the best player available regardless of the position. At the same time, he was convinced that a successful team should be built on a solid defense. By early in the 1970s the mettle of the Steelers defensive squad earned it the nickname the "Steel Curtain." Noll depended on fast, aggressive linebackers to back the solid front line.

Despite this concentration on defense, the Steelers slowly developed an adequate offense. Some experts considered Noll out of date because he believed in allowing his quarterbacks to call their own plays. He allowed Terry Bradshaw, an early draft pick, five years to develop as a competent play caller. For the backfield Noll acquired Franco Harris of Penn State, although he was not highly ranked. The blocking back was "Rocky" Bleier, who took several years to recover from leg wounds suffered in Vietnam. In front of the runners Noll anchored his line on outstanding centers and mobile guards who could pull to lead a sweep. Lynn Swann and John Stallworth became Bradshaw's prime receivers.

Noll's patience began to pay off in 1972, when the Steelers posted a winning record of eleven wins and three losses. For the first time in their history the team won the American Football Conference (AFC) Central Division title. It was the Steelers' misfortune to lose 21 – 17 to the undefeated Miami Dolphins in the AFC championship game.

In 1974 the Steelers won divisional and conference titles to advance to Super Bowl IX and then, behind their outstanding defense, defeated the Minnesota Vikings 16–6. The Vikings were able to gain only seventeen yards on the ground. The following year the Steelers returned to Super Bowl X against Dallas. Pittsburgh won 21 – 17 in a game highlighted by the stalwart Steelers' defense and a sixty-four-yard touchdown pass from Bradshaw to an acrobatic Swann.

Between 1972 and 1984 the Steelers had thirteen winning seasons; their victory in the division championship in 1974 was the first of six consecutive Central Division titles. The Steelers returned to the top in 1978 when they edged the Dallas Cowboys 35–31 in Super Bowl XIII. After this win Noll became the first professional football coach to win three Super Bowls. Not resting on their laurels, the Steelers returned the next year, becoming the first four-time winners by drubbing the Los Angeles Rams 31–19, and Noll became the first coach to win four Super Bowls. Despite his 12 – 30 record in his first three years, Noll had an overall record of 209 wins, 156 losses, and 1 tie in 23 years. He was elected to the Pro Football Hall of Fame in 1993.

Noll and his wife, Marianne, have one son. Noll enjoys fine wine and is considered a gourmet cook. A lover of classical music, he has a regular seat at the performances of the Pittsburgh Symphony. He also enjoys literature. Out of doors, Noll is a gardener and a proficient scuba diver. When he decided to become a pilot, his confidence was such that he bought a plane before he started taking lessons.

One of Noll's outstanding linebackers, Andy Russell, described him as a "very stern, very strict" taskmaster, but one who was quite realistic about what the players could or could not do. He was a players' coach. Despite his high profile, Noll tried to keep in the background. He made only one product endorsement, feeling that these were better left to the players. Perhaps the highest compliment to Noll's philosophy as a person and a coach is that twenty-one Steelers earned four Super Bowl rings.

★

Material on Noll's career is in the archives of the Pro Football Hall of Fame in Canton, Ohio. For more information, see David L. Porter, ed., *Biographical Dictionary of American Sports: Football* (1987), and Bob Carroll et al., *Total Football* (1997). Also see articles by Roy Blount, Jr. (24 July 1974) and Paul Zimmerman (21 July 1980) in *Sports Illustrated.*

ART BARBEAU

NYAD, Diana (*b.* 22 August 1949 in New York City), world-record marathon swimmer, Women's Sports Foundation International Sports Hall of Fame inductee, television correspondent, and radio producer.

Born Diana Sneed, Nyad is the daughter of William Sneed, a stockbroker, and Lucy Curtis. She was raised in Fort Lauderdale, Florida, and began swimming at the age of six months. At age eleven she started training seriously under Olympic coach Jack Nelson and became a nationally ranked backstroker. After a bout of endocarditis at age sixteen kept Nyad from trying out for the 1968 Olympics, her conditioning suffered greatly and her dream of being an Olympic athlete faded quickly.

Nyad was introduced to the sport of marathon swimming in 1968. Her first marathon held in 1970 in Hamilton, Ontario, was ten miles long. Nyad recounted that Judith de Nijs, the best marathon swimmer in the world throughout the 1960s, told her before the race that she would beat Nyad, and if not, she would retire. Nyad beat her by fifteen minutes in a record-breaking four hours and twenty-three minutes; de Nijs did indeed retire. In 1975 Nyad swam the twenty-eight-mile circuit around the island of Manhattan and set another record: seven hours and fifty-seven minutes.

For marathon swimmers, great perseverance is the

Diana Nyad, 1975. AP/WIDE WORLD PHOTOS

norm. Nyad has written about the psychology of a marathoner and how sensory deprivation leads to an altered state of consciousness. In 1978 Nyad attempted to swim 103 miles from Cuba to Florida, a feat that had never been accomplished. Unfortunately, a storm curtailed her swim, but not until she had completed seventy-nine miles in forty-one hours and forty-nine minutes. She wanted to try again in 1979, but the politics of obtaining a visa were difficult. On 22 August 1979 Nyad set a world record by swimming eighty-nine miles from Bimini Island to Jupiter, Florida, in twenty-seven hours and thirty-eight minutes. Nyad also holds the record for men and women for the north-to-south crossing of Lake Ontario.

Nyad attained the women's world record for a twenty-six-mile race in the Parana River in Argentina. In addition, she swam twenty-two miles from Capri to Naples, Italy, and fifty miles from the Great Barrier Reef to the Australian Coast. Nyad was named the top marathon swimmer from 1969 to 1977.

Nyad attended Emory University and Université de Dijon, and graduated with honors and was Phi Beta Kappa from Lake Forest College in Lake Forest, Illinois, in 1973. She received an M.A. in comparative literature from New York University in 1975. Nyad coached the Barnard College swim team between 1975 and 1977.

Throughout her life, Nyad has been a spokesperson for justice, advocating on behalf of gays and lesbians as well as women in sport. She was named *Ms.* magazine's Woman of the Year in 1975, and she was inducted into the Women's Sports Foundation International Hall of Fame in 1986. She was also inducted into the halls of fame of her college, Lake Forest, and her high school, Pine Crest Preparatory.

Beginning in 1980 Nyad worked as a television correspondent, eventually holding positions at ABC, CNBC, and Fox Sports Net. In 1998 she joined the latter network as a senior correspondent on the weekly sports magazine show *Goin' Deep.* In addition, she is a radio producer and host of *The Savvy Traveler,* a National Public Radio show.

★

For details on the intricate aspects of a marathon swimmer, see Diana Nyad, *Other Shores* (1978). Nyad also contributed "Mind over Water" to Laurel Blossom, ed., *Splash! Great Writing About Swimming* (1986). Many encyclopedias of women in sport highlight Nyad's accomplishments, the best being C. Oglesby et al., eds., *Encyclopedia of Women and Sport in America* (1998).

SHAWN LADDA

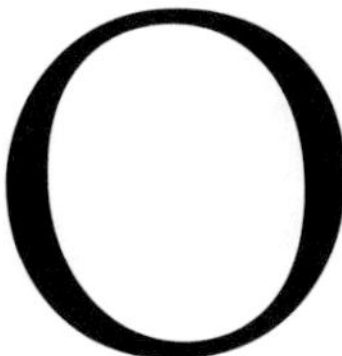

O'BRIEN, (William) Parry, Jr. (*b.* 28 January 1932 in Santa Monica, California), world record-setting shot-putter, Olympic champion, and inventor of a revolutionary technique for throwing the shot.

O'Brien became interested in shot-putting during a family trip to Canada when he was fourteen. While playing in a riverbed, he picked up huge, rounded stones and amused himself by seeing how far he could hurl them.

O'Brien's personality was uniquely suited to his solitary sport. After graduating from Santa Monica High School, he entered the University of Southern California (USC) in Los Angeles on a football scholarship, but was soon steered into track and field by the football coach Jess Hill, who saw his potential in the other sport. This was a startling decision, since O'Brien was six feet, three inches tall, weighed 220 pounds, and could run 100 yards in fewer than 10 seconds. However, he found that he loved shot-putting because winning or losing was solely under his control and not dependent on the actions of other team members. "I gave up football because I wanted to be able to take the credit or the blame for what I did in sports. I always wanted to be the soloist."

Thickly built and powerfully muscled, O'Brien had the perfect physique for his sport, but he added determination, long hours of training, and a great deal of thought to his physical ability. In 1951, his sophomore year at USC, O'Brien came in second at a meet in Fresno, California, with a throw almost two feet short of his best mark, and even shorter than the national freshman record of 53 feet, 1.5 inches he had set the year before. Disappointed, he was determined to find out what he was doing wrong, and stayed in the shot-putter's circle long after the event, practicing and analyzing his throws. He was so absorbed in the practice that he almost missed his airplane home. At 3:30 the next morning, his father found him behind their house, shot-putting in the glare of a streetlight. After each throw, O'Brien had to use a flashlight to search for the shot in a nearby vacant lot before throwing it again. "I think I've discovered something," he told his father, and kept practicing until four in the morning. His father commented, "He has more determination than four mules." Later in life, O'Brien told a reporter that he threw the sixteen-pound shot 150 times per day, and remarked, "I don't quit until my hands are bleeding. And that's the God's truth."

Despite his determination, he lost by one inch at the National Collegiate Athletic Association (NCAA) meet in Seattle later in 1951, and shortly afterward lost again. Again he continued to practice for several hours after the meet, and this time, it paid off. At his first national Amateur Athletic Union (AAU) meet in 1951, the nineteen-year-old sophomore put the shot 55 feet, 9.25 inches for a victory, ending the shot-putter Jim Fuchs's string of 88 consecutive victories. Eventually O'Brien set his own streak of 116 victories in a row.

During a series of European meets in 1951, O'Brien

Parry O'Brien, 1956. © BETTMANN/CORBIS

began to experiment, turning his right foot farther and farther toward the back of the circle, and turning his whole body so his back faced the direction of the throw before executing a 180-degree spin. Coaches and others criticized O'Brien for this unusual stance, but he was convinced that the new move would eventually allow him to throw from fifty-nine to sixty feet. He drew a chalk circle on the asphalt behind his fraternity house at college and practiced shot-putting into a parking lot, working long hours every day. He wanted to be alone, so that he could concentrate on his technique and work out any flaws himself, without input from a coach. During this time, O'Brien often threw his shot put over the fence of the Los Angeles Coliseum, climbed over after it, and practiced there in the field for hours, under the light of the huge Olympic flame tower that remained from the 1932 Games. The flame intensified his determination to participate in the 1952 Olympics in Helsinki, Finland.

In addition to his intense practice sessions, O'Brien studied yoga, believing it would give him mental discipline and increase his ability to visualize and concentrate on a throw. He also listened to African tribal chants before competitions, using the music to pump up his energy. He believed in the value of "psyching out" his opponents, and often ostentatiously drank a mysterious fluid from a white plastic jar before events. If competitors asked what it was, he said, "It's an energy-giving substance." It was clover honey mixed with water, but his opponents always believed he had a high-powered secret and were effectively demoralized.

Some observers made fun of O'Brien's unusual throwing style, but they were no longer laughing when he won the gold medal at the 1952 Summer Olympics. He also set an Olympic record with his throw of 57 feet, 1.5 inches. Before his innovation, shot-putters shuffled across the ring, facing the direction they were going to throw. After he changed the sport, athletes used a rotational technique in which they whirled their bodies before throwing in order to achieve greater force and drive.

In 1953, using his new style, he set a world record with a throw of 59 feet, 0.75 inches. At the time, 60 feet was deemed an almost insurmountable barrier, just as the 4-minute mile and 7-foot high jump had been, but O'Brien surpassed it in 1954 at the Los Angeles Coliseum with a throw of 60 feet, 5.5 inches. In a following meet, he made four 60-foot throws within 5 minutes, proving that his feat was not a fluke. O'Brien was also a champion discus thrower, winning two U.S. collegiate titles. O'Brien appeared on the cover of *Sports Illustrated* twice, on 21 March 1955 and 31 August 1959, and on the cover of *Time* on 3 December 1956. In 1959 he won the Sullivan Award as the nation's best amateur athlete.

In the 1956 Olympics in Melbourne, Australia, O'Brien won the gold medal and set another record with 60 feet, 11.008 inches. At the 1960 Olympics in Rome, Italy, he threw 62 feet, 8.25 inches, but was beaten by Bill Nieder, who threw 64 feet, 6.75 inches. At the 1964 Olympics in Tokyo, Japan, O'Brien improved again and set a mark of 63 feet, 0.25 inches, but only came in fourth. Other, younger athletes had adopted his innovative throwing style and were putting the shot farther than ever before. Despite his fourth-place finish in Tokyo, O'Brien's drive to compete was strong, and he continued to practice and improve. In 1966, his nineteenth season, he set a personal best with a throw of 64 feet, 7.5 inches.

After retiring from competition, O'Brien worked in banking and real estate in southern California. No other shot-putter has earned as many number-one world rankings as O'Brien, and he will forever be remembered in his sport for his longevity, determination and drive, and revolutionary throwing technique. He once said, "It's gratifying to know that I have contributed something to the sport that has done so much for me." O'Brien was elected to the U.S. Olympic Hall of Fame in 1984.

★

O'Brien tells his story in his own words in Lewis H. Carlson and John J. Fogarty, eds., *Tales of Gold* (1987). There are excellent chapters on O'Brien in Cordner Nelson, *Track and Field: The*

Great Ones (1970), and the *Lincoln Library of Sports Champions,* 6th ed. (1993).

KELLY WINTERS

OERTER, Al(fred) Adolph, Jr. (*b.* 19 August 1936, in Astoria, New York), track and field athlete who specialized in the discus throw, set four world records, and won four consecutive Olympic gold medals from 1956 to 1968, becoming the first Olympic athlete to do so in the same track and field event.

Oerter, the son of Alfred and Mary Strup Oerter, grew up playing stickball, baseball, and football on the streets of Long Island in the 1940s. "It was a great training ground for becoming an athlete," Oerter later recalled, noting that he "certainly loved sports as a kid." When he was sixteen, his mother died of cancer, and so, temporarily, did his love of sports. After quitting the Sewanhaka High School football team that fall, Oerter went out for the track team in the spring, first trying the sprints and then the mile before discovering his talent as a discus thrower. One day while practicing for the mile, he picked up a stray discus and threw it back to his teammates, lofting the implement high above their heads. His coach Jim Faley, a former New York Giants fullback, switched Oerter immediately from the mile to the discus. In 1954 he set a national high school record of 184 feet, 2 inches in the discus throw.

After graduating from high school in 1954, Oerter enrolled in the University of Kansas. He attributes his success there as a discus thrower to having an academic, rather than an athletic, scholarship. Oerter believes that if he had had an athletic scholarship, the Athletics Department probably would have forced him to play football because of his size.

Having established a national freshman class record of 171 feet, 6 inches in the discus throw in 1955, Oerter won the Big Seven (later Big Eight) Conference championship in 1956. Fourth place and sixth place finishes in the National Collegiate Athletic Association (NCAA) and the Amateur Athletic Union (AAU) notwithstanding, Oerter qualified for the U.S. Olympic Team in 1956. After watching the favorites, Adolfo Consolini of Italy and Fortune Gordien of the United States, take their first throws, the unheralded Oerter, felt "inspired" and hurled the discus 184 feet, 10.5 inches, then the longest throw of his career and an Olympic record. "I don't know how I did it," he later remarked. "Somehow or other everything just went right and this throw came out." Oerter's first throw remained the best of the day, and secured him an Olympic gold medal.

Back at Kansas, Oerter won Big Seven Conference titles in both the discus and the shot put in 1957 and 1958 (out-

Al Oerter. AP/WIDE WORLD PHOTOS

doors) and the shot put in 1957 and 1958 (indoors). Despite winning both the NCAA and AAU titles in the discus throw in 1957, he was tied by Rink Babka of the University of Southern California for the 1958 NCAA title and finished second to Babka in the AAU championship. In 1958 Oerter married Corinne Benedetto; the couple divorced in 1975. After graduating from Kansas in 1959, he returned to New York, going to work for Grumman Aircraft Company as a data processor. That year he won the discus throw in both the AAU national championships and the Pan American Games.

At the 1960 Olympic Trials, Oerter suffered his first loss in two years to Babka, who had equaled the world record of 196 feet, 6.5 inches. He trailed Babka through the first four rounds of Olympic competition until Babka advised Oerter to shift the position of his left arm while throwing. Following this advice, Oerter unleashed the discus 194 feet, 2 inches, establishing a new Olympic record and securing the gold medal. "That's what sports should be about," commented Oerter, looking back upon that time, "one teammate helping another teammate in the best of competition."

In 1962 Oerter established a world record of 200 feet, 5.5 inches, for the first official throw over 200 feet. Seventeen days later, however, Vladimir Trusenyov of the Soviet Union erased this record with a toss of 202 feet, 2.5 inches. Despite falling short of Trusenyov's standard by half an inch in winning the 1962 AAU title, Oerter exceeded it at the USA-USSR dual meet that year with a performance of 204 feet, 10.5 inches. He raised the world record to 205 feet, 5.5 inches in 1963 and to 206 feet, 4 inches in 1964. Suffering from a chronic cervical disc injury throughout much of 1964, Oerter competed wearing a neck brace fashioned from a belt and several towels. Although he won the AAU championship that year, he finished second to Jay Silvester in the Olympic Trials. In the 1964 Olympic Games, Oerter opened the competition with an Olympic record of 198 feet, 8 inches in the qualifying rounds. In the finals he trailed Ludvik Danek of Czechoslovakia until hurling the discus 200 feet, 1.5 inches in the fifth round to establish another Olympic record and win a third gold medal.

Oerter did not compete in 1965 but returned in 1966 to win the AAU title. In 1967 he finished fourth in the AAU, and in 1968 third in the Olympic Trials behind Silvester and Gary Carlsen. In the 1968 Olympic final, Oerter trailed his competitors until the third round when he threw 212 feet, 6 inches, for yet another Olympic record and gold medal. For good measure, Oerter's next throw reached 212 feet, 5 inches, and his final throw of the day measured 210 feet, 1 inch. In comparison, Lothar Milde of the former German Democratic Republic threw only 206 feet, 11 inches for second place.

After an eight-year retirement Oerter returned to competition in 1977, winning the discus throw at the Kansas Relays. In 1978 he improved his personal best to 221 feet, 4 inches, and in 1980 to 227 feet, 11 inches; the 1980 distance remained the world record for 40–44-year-olds in 2001. In 1980 Oerter, then aged 43, finished fourth in the Olympic Trials. In 1982 he established a world record of 216 feet, 11 inches for 45–49-year-olds, and in 1989, a U.S. record of 205 feet, 10 inches for 50–54-year-olds. In 1983 Oerter married Cathy Jo Carroll.

One of the greatest Olympic athletes in history, Oerter became the first track and field performer to win four consecutive gold medals in the same event, the discus, in 1968. His feat remained unequaled until 1996, when Carl Lewis won a fourth consecutive Olympic gold medal in the long jump. Ranked by *Track and Field News* among the world's top ten best discus throwers every year from 1956 to 1969 (excluding 1965, because he did not compete that year), Oerter earned the number one ranking six times, more than any other discus thrower since 1947, when the journal started ranking athletes. *Track and Field News* also recognized Oerter as the number one discus thrower of the 1960s and as the twentieth century's best performer.

★

For information about Oerter's life and career, see Frank G. Menke, *The Encyclopedia of Sports,* 4th rev. ed. (1969); Cordner Nelson, *Track's Greatest Champions* (1986); Roberto L. Quercetani, *Athletics: A History of Modern Track and Field Athletics (1860–1990), Men and Women* (1990); and David Wallechinsky, *The Complete Book of the Summer Olympics: Sydney 2000 Edition* (2000).

ADAM R. HORNBUCKLE

OLAJUWON, Hakeem Abdul (*b.* 21 January 1963 in Lagos, Nigeria), basketball player who starred on the University of Houston team and the professional Houston Rockets, whom he led to consecutive National Basketball Association (NBA) titles in 1994 and 1995.

Olajuwon was the third of six children born to Salam and Abike Olajuwon, middle-class Muslims who owned a thriving cement business in Lagos, Nigeria. A gifted athlete, he was a soccer goalkeeper from an early age before learning to play team handball as a junior at Muslim Teachers College, a high school in Lagos. Olajuwon did not play basketball until late 1978 when, at the age of fifteen, he joined the school's basketball team coached by Ganiyu Otenigbade, who taught him to play the center position.

Richard Mills, a U.S. coach who was head of the Nigerian National Sports Coaching Institute, spotted Olajuwon playing in a pick-up game in Lagos and invited him to play with the Nigerian National Team. The other players were older, bigger, and stronger than Olajuwon, who was still in high school, and he saw limited action. Mills

Hakeem Olajuwon. AP/WIDE WORLD PHOTOS

then selected the seventeen-year-old Olajuwon for the Nigerian Junior National Team and, just two years after he began playing basketball, Olajuwon starred in the All-Africa games in Luanda, Angola. The Nigerians lost in the semifinals to the Central African Republic, but Olajuwon, the tournament's Most Valuable Player (MVP), impressed the opposing team's U.S.-born coach, Chris Pond, with his size and quickness. Pond called various basketball contacts in the United States and arranged for Olajuwon to visit six schools, including St. John's University and the University of Houston.

Olajuwon arrived in New York City in October 1980. Shocked by the hustle and bustle of the airport and New York's cold weather, he cancelled his trip to St. John's and flew straight to Houston, where he asked a taxi driver to take him to the "University of Austin." The driver figured that Olajuwon meant the University of Houston, and when Olajuwon arrived on campus, the coaching staff immediately knew that they had struck gold. The six-foot, eleven-inch Nigerian was offered a full scholarship.

At the suggestion of head coach Guy Lewis, Olajuwon, who weighed barely 190 pounds in 1980, "red-shirted," or sat out, his first year to mature physically and learn the fundamentals of basketball. Olajuwon spent the summer after his freshman year playing basketball at Houston's Fonde Recreation Center, where he gained toughness in frequent match-ups against the bruising Moses Malone, who was then playing for the Houston Rockets.

In his first year of college basketball, Olajuwon played a minimal role in the Houston Cougars run to the 1982 Final Four, where they lost to the University of North Carolina. That summer, he began a seven-year relationship with Lita Spencer, a student at Rice University. The two never married, but they had a daughter together in 1988. In 1983 Olajuwon blossomed as a player, leading Houston on a twenty-two-game winning streak while averaging over twenty points and twenty rebounds per game. Olajuwon became known as "The Dream," and the Cougars, who also had Clyde Drexler, Larry Micheaux, and Michael Young, were nicknamed "Phi Slama Jama" for their high-flying, dunking style of play. Olajuwon led Houston to victory over a potent Louisville team in the national semifinals, but the heavily favored Cougars lost to North Carolina State in the title game. Olajuwon was named the MVP of the Final Four.

In 1984, with Drexler gone to the NBA's Portland Trailblazers, Olajuwon became the focal point of the Houston team, leading the nation in rebounding, averaging 13.5 per game, and field-goal accuracy with 67.5 percent, while earning Player of the Year honors. He led the Cougars to the National Collegiate Athletic Association (NCAA) championship game, but Houston lost again, this time to the Georgetown Hoyas, led by Patrick Ewing. After the 1984 season, Olajuwon opted to turn professional.

By winning a coin toss against Portland, the Houston Rockets were awarded the first pick in the 1984 NBA draft and selected Olajuwon ahead of such players as Michael Jordan and Charles Barkley. Though Jordan beat out Olajuwon for Rookie of the Year honors in 1985, Olajuwon teamed with seven-foot, four-inch center Ralph Sampson to form a "twin towers" front line that transformed the previously porous Rockets defense into a championship caliber unit. The Rockets reached the NBA Finals in 1986, where they lost to the Boston Celtics in six games. The next year, Sampson injured his knee and the Rockets lost to the Seattle Supersonics in the second round of the playoffs. In December 1987 the Rockets traded Sampson, leaving Olajuwon with little interior support and dooming the team to three straight first-round playoff defeats. Despite the Rockets' mediocre play, Olajuwon excelled, becoming the first player in NBA history to record 200 blocks and 200 steals in the same season in 1988–1989. In 1990, he recorded the third "quadruple double" (when a player records 10 or more in four personal statistical categories in one game: Olajuwon scored 18 points, had 16 rebounds, 10 assists, and 11 blocked shots) in NBA history.

During 1988 Olajuwon began regular visits to a Houston mosque and started to study the Muslin holy book, the Qur'an, intensively. In March 1991 he changed the spelling of his name from "Akeem" to "Hakeem" to reflect the proper Arabic spelling. That summer, he made a pilgrimage to Mecca and returned with a determination to integrate Islam into his everyday life. This new commitment led Olajuwon to fast each year during the month of Ramadan, despite the rigors of the NBA schedule. In 1992 Olajuwon became embroiled in a bitter dispute with Rockets management when his request for a new contract led them to claim that he faked a hamstring injury as a negotiating ploy. The Rockets missed the playoffs for the first time in Olajuwon's career. He nearly left the team before the 1992–1993 season, but eventually ended his dispute with the Rockets management and signed a four-year extension worth $25.4 million. In the 1992–1993 season, under new head coach Rudy Tomjanovich, Olajuwon was the runner-up to league MVP Charles Barkley, but the Rockets lost to the Supersonics in the Western Conference semifinals. On 2 April 1993 Olajuwon was sworn in as a United States citizen.

In game six of the 1994 NBA Finals against the New York Knicks, Olajuwon blocked John Starks's potential series-winning three-point shot at the buzzer. The Rockets won game seven, and Olajuwon became the first player in NBA history to win MVP, Defensive Player of the Year, and NBA Finals MVP honors in the same season. In 1994–1995 Olajuwon was reunited with college teammate Clyde Drexler and, after suffering through a below-average season due to anemia, he excelled in the playoffs, helping Houston overcome a 3–1 deficit to the Phoenix Suns in the Western Conference semifinals. The Rockets then beat the San Antonio Spurs, and Olajuwon was the Finals MVP again in a four-game sweep of the Orlando Magic.

In 1996 Olajuwon won an Olympic gold medal playing for the U.S. "Dream Team" in Atlanta. The next year he was named one of the fifty greatest players in NBA history. In 2000 he married Dalia Asafi; they have two children.

Olajuwon's career appeared to be in jeopardy toward the end of the 2000–2001 season when he underwent treatment for blood clotting that might have sidelined him for a year, but he quickly returned to the lineup. His seventeen-year career as a Rocket ended in August 2001, when he was traded to the Toronto Raptors for two draft picks. The twelve-time All-Star left Houston as the Rockets all-time leader in points, rebounds, steals, and blocks, and as the city's most popular athlete of all time.

Olajuwon brought a rare combination of size and grace to the NBA, using speed and quickness more than strength to outmaneuver defenders. He developed incredible footwork playing soccer and team handball in Nigeria that enabled him to make basketball moves seldom seen in players his size. His fast feet and great sense of timing also made him an intimidating defender; he is the NBA's all-time leader in blocked shots. Olajuwon's best offensive move came to be known as the "Dream Shake," a move adapted from his days playing soccer, where he faked to the middle of the court, then spun to the baseline to shoot a fade-away turnaround jumper. Like Kareem Abdul-Jabbar's "Sky Hook" and Wilt Chamberlain's "Dipper Dunk," the "Dream Shake" is one of the unstoppable shots in NBA history.

★

The most comprehensive source of information on Olajuwon is his autobiography, *Living the Dream: My Life and Basketball* (1996), written with Peter Knobler. Jerry Briggs, "Phi Slama Jama—Houston's Most Famous (and Tallest) Fraternity," *San Antonio Express-News* (18 Jan. 1996), is a look back at Olajuwon's talented Houston Cougar team. Bob Ryan, "American Dream," *Boston Globe* (7 July 1996), traces the events that led to Olajuwon's selection to the 1996 U.S. Olympic team. Robert Marquand, "Hakeem Olajuwon: An Athlete and a Gentleman," *Christian Science Monitor* (5 Feb. 1997), examines the impact of Islam on Olajuwon's life and career. Michael Murphy, "End of Dream? From Raw Talent to Icon, Olajuwon Does It All Here," *Houston Chronicle* (14 Mar. 2001), looks back on Olajuwon's Rockets career and his place in Houston sports history.

DANIEL MASSEY

OLDFIELD, Berna Eli ("Barney") (*b.* 29 January 1878 in Wauseon, Ohio; *d.* 4 October 1946 in Beverly Hills, California), race driver who is best known for his record set at the Indianapolis Fairgrounds on 20 June 1903 as the first person to drive a car at the speed of one mile a minute; he epitomized U.S. car racing more than any other driver, before or since.

Oldfield was born to Clay Oldfield, a farmer, and Sarah Yarnell Oldfield, who lived in a log cabin in rural Ohio. In 1889, the family, including Oldfield's sister, moved to Toledo, Ohio, where his father had a job as caretaker at a mental institution, the Toledo State Hospital. Nicknamed "Barney" during his teens, Oldfield left school in 1893 to work as a kitchen helper at the hospital where his father was employed. He later worked as a bell porter and as an elevator operator.

Oldfield's first bicycle race took place in Toledo on 30 May 1894—he placed second riding a Royal Flush—and he was eventually successful enough to be known as "The Champion of Ohio." His introduction to motor racing came about with Henry Ford's famous "999" car, and it was with this cumbersome machine that Oldfield started his climb to fame in 1903. When Alexander Winton designed a faster car, Oldfield shifted allegiance away from Ford and became just as famous driving Winton "Bullet

Barney Oldfield, 1927. AP/WIDE WORLD PHOTOS

Number 2." It was a curious move, as Oldfield had won for Ford its first National Championship in 1902, and his defeat of a Winton product had facilitated Henry Ford's efforts to raise capital for what eventually developed into the Ford Motor Company. It is said that many years later, Henry Ford told Oldfield, "You made me and I made you." To which Oldfield replied, "I did a damn lot more for you than you did for me."

Other famous automobiles driven by Oldfield included the Green Dragon, a Peerless machine, and the phenomenal Blitzen, a gray Benz-powered car that took Oldfield to a legitimate world speed record when he drove it at 131 miles per hour at Daytona Beach, Florida, in 1910. Oldfield was also quite successful with Maxwells, winning the 300 Miler road race at Venice, California, on 17 March 1915, and at Tucson, Arizona, on 20 March the same year, in their automobile. Driving a Stutz, he came in fifth at the 1914 Indianapolis 500-mile race (Indy 500), making it the best U.S. car in a race dominated by European entries. The following year saw his last appearance at Indianapolis, when he again placed fifth in a Delage. Another interesting machine driven by Oldfield was the Golden Submarine, an enclosed cockpit automobile designed by Harry Miller. And, as proof of his versatility, he also raced the tricky front-wheel-drive vehicle designed by Walter Christie.

Oldfield had a running feud with the Contest Board of the American Automobile Association (AAA), as two chairmen of the contest board saw fit to suspend him for life in 1910. The first was Sam Butler, who took exception to the promotion of a match race at the Sheepshead Bay track between Oldfield and Jack Johnson, the heavyweight world boxing champion at the time. Butler prohibited Oldfield from racing based upon the fact that Johnson, no matter how skilled as a boxer, was no race driver, and, furthermore, had no license. But when Oldfield's shady manager Bill Pickings obtained a racing license for Johnson, the race was held on 25 October 1910, over Butler's objections. Of course the race was a charade, and the result was that both Oldfield and Pickings were suspended for life.

On 30 April 1912 the new AAA chairman, William Schimpf, revoked Oldfield's suspension, claiming, "A successful merchant doesn't hide his best goods beneath the counter." But Oldfield could not stand prosperity. While under the influence of alcohol, he challenged the next chairman, Richard Kennerdell, to a fistfight. Kennerdell prudently beat a hasty retreat, and from the sanctuary of his office fined Oldfield $250 for "unbecoming conduct." That was not to be the end of it, however, for when Oldfield joined Ernie Moross and some other outlawed racers in non-AAA sanctioned events, Kennerdell once more banned him for life.

The ban did little to deter Oldfield from his lucrative appearances. As he aptly announced, he would race "[w]ith or without official sanction, wherever I get the sugar." The incomparable Oldfield was almost continuously rolling across the country in a carefully orchestrated show. He would parade before the gaping crowd, cigar in mouth. His car would arrive and be pushed to the side of the track, near the fence. After a little tinkering with the engine to give the locals the impression of fine-tuning, a demonstration lap or two would be run, followed by the announcer's call of an incredible time. Later, the race was on. Not surprisingly, Oldfield almost always won. Sometimes, they would set up three heats, in which the "Speed King of the World" would easily take the first, lose the second by a close margin, and then run away in the third and final. Other variations of this show included one-mile record attempts. Oldfield was well paid for these exhibitions, which more often than not resulted in a new "unofficial" world record. Furthermore, these arranged runs were a lot safer than any other race, staged or not.

All told, it is estimated that Oldfield drove in more than 2,000 races and exhibitions. He drove his last race in 1918, after almost twenty years of showing his skill and determination in tracks, road races, and record attempts. Following retirement, Oldfield started the Oldfield Tire and Rubber Company, which eventually was purchased by the Firestone Tire Company. He remained in touch with the automobile industry, mostly as a consultant in engineering. The financial crash of 1929 hit him hard, however, and he saw his accumulated fortune, estimated at more than $1 million, evaporate.

Oldfield was married and divorced several times. His first marriage was to Beatrice Loretta Oatis on 12 August 1896. They separated in September 1901, and divorced on 16 November 1906. His second marriage was to a widow, Rebecca ("Bess") Gooby Holland in January 1907. They separated in July 1923, and divorced in 1924. The third time around, Oldfield married Hulda R. Braden in December 1925; they divorced in 1945. His fourth marriage, in late 1945 or early 1946, to his former wife Bess, lasted until his death.

In 1946 the automobile manufacturers based in Detroit staged an extravaganza to celebrate the first fifty years of the motorcar. Appropriately named the Automobile Golden Jubilee, it was the setting for the recognition of Oldfield as one of the pioneers of car racing. Some four months later, he died of a cerebral hemorrhage at his home in Beverly Hills, California. He is buried in the Holy Cross Cemetery in Culver City, California.

Oldfield's contribution to the acceptance and tremendous popularity of automobile racing was unsurpassed. There were certainly better drivers, and perhaps more skillful promoters, but no one came close to Oldfield when it came to charisma and adoration by the crowds. The image of this daredevil racing car driver, sliding through the treacherous dirt tracks of the United States with a big cigar clenched firmly between his teeth and wearing a red jersey, remained indelibly fixed in the eyes of all who saw him perform. Never mind that many of the races were previously arranged, that other drivers were on his payroll, or that timekeepers were on the take—Oldfield and his circus gave the crowds what they wanted to see and hear. His fame and personal appeal was such that during the last century it was common for a traffic cop to say to a speeding motorist: "Who do you think you are? Barney Oldfield?" Aptly, though perhaps belatedly, he was inducted to the International Motorsports Hall of Fame in 1990.

★

While Oldfield did not write a full-length autobiography, he did pen *Barney Oldfield's Book for the Motorist* (1919). The most complete source of information on Oldfield is provided by *Toledo's Attic: The Oldfield File*, an Internet resource located at http://www.attic/utoledo.edu/att01/bo/preface.html. The website contains a listing of track records, newspaper archives, photos, and biographical accounts. Other resources include Brock W. Yates, *Racers and Drivers: The Fastest Men and Cars from Barney Oldfield to Craig Breedlove* (1968), and Ralph Hickok, *A Who's Who of Sports Champions* (1995). Obituaries are in the *New York Times* and *Toledo Blade* (both 5 Oct. 1946).

HORACE A. LAFFAYE

OLSEN, Merlin Jay (*b.* 15 September 1940 in Logan, Utah), professional football defensive lineman who made fourteen Pro Bowl appearances; after retiring from football he had a successful broadcasting and acting career.

Born and raised in Logan, Olsen was one of six children born to Lynn Olsen, a government worker, and Merle Barrus Olsen, a homemaker. Early in his career at Logan High School, Olsen struggled as a football player. He recalled once being asked by his high school coach if he might consider trying out for the band rather than playing football. Nevertheless, he eventually achieved both athletic and scholarly success in high school. Upon graduation from Logan High School, he enrolled at Utah State University. He chose the school, which was located in his hometown of Logan, so his parents would be able to see him play.

At Utah State he quickly established himself as a leader and distinguished himself as a football player. In his junior and senior seasons the team went 18–3–1, made two bowl appearances, and won two Skyline Conference Championships. Olsen was named first-team All-America in each of his college years and received the Outland Trophy in 1961 as the outstanding college lineman in America. During his years as a student he developed a very close relationship with his line coach, Tony Knap, who also coached future National Football League (NFL) stars Len Rhode, Clark Miller, Lionel Alridge, and Clyde Brock, all of whom played with Olsen.

At the university Olsen served two years in student government, was named the school's outstanding Reserve Of-

Merlin Olsen. AP/WIDE WORLD PHOTOS

ficers' Training Corps (ROTC) cadet, and won a national award from the Sigma Chi fraternity as the nation's top undergraduate. He graduated from the College of Business in 1962 with a degree in finance and is a member of many academic fraternities. While still playing in the NFL, he returned to Utah State and received a master's degree in economics in 1970. On 30 March 1962 he married Susan Wakley, a Utah State graduate in education; they have three children.

Olsen was selected by the Los Angeles Rams, the team with whom he would play his entire career, in the first round of the 1962 NFL draft. He was regarded as a premier defensive lineman almost immediately, was named a starter before the season began, and was named Defensive Rookie of the Year in 1962. Along with Lamar Lundy, Roosevelt Grier, and Deacon Jones, he formed the fabled "Fearsome Foursome," a defensive unit legendary for both its size and skill.

At six-feet, five-inches tall and 275 pounds, Olsen was a feared pass-rusher who, despite his size, had the speed and agility to chase down both running backs and quarterbacks. During his NFL career he was named to the Pro Bowl fourteen times, a league record. In twenty-two seasons of high school, college, and professional football—208 games in total—he missed only two games, both in his first year in high school. He played the following 198 games consecutively.

One of his coaches, George Allen, said, "We've never had a bad game from Merlin Olsen. You always got a good game from him, and more often than not, you got a great game." Tony Knap added, "He always had a tendency to do things . . . with finesse, rather than just blowing them off the line . . . he was never satisfied with his performance. He'd walk off the field and say, 'Coach don't even look at the film.' " Olsen said, "We were innovators. . . . It was fun knowing every time we went on the field we were the guys who were going to make something happen."

Olsen received numerous accolades when he retired after the 1976 season. He was elected into the Pro Football Hall of Fame in 1982, his first year of eligibility. The National Football foundation, the GTE Academic Hall of Fame, and the National College Football Hall of Fame chose Olsen as a member. He was also selected as a member of college football's team of the century and the *Sports Illustrated* all-time NFL team for the sport's seventy-fifth anniversary.

Before he completed his football career, he began acting in movies and on television. His most famous roles were on *Little House on the Prairie* and as the title character in *Father Murphy*. He also had a very successful stint as a lead commentator for NBC telecasts of NFL games, covering five Super Bowls and numerous college bowl games with Dick Enberg. Olsen's articulate analysis became a standard for television commentators.

In athletics, business, and entertainment, Olsen has been extremely successful. However, he is also committed to helping others by working with numerous charities. He has been associated with Child Help, which assists abused children in California, the Primary Children's Hospital in Salt Lake City, Utah, and other charitable agencies. He has hosted the Children's Miracle Network telethon and was named National Outstanding Multiple Sclerosis Volunteer in 1981. Olsen also is a national spokesman for the FTD Florist group and General Motors automobiles.

Throughout his career, Olsen has also remained loyal to Utah State and his hometown. He has served the school in fund-raising and academic searches and has also established numerous student scholarships. Olsen and his wife reside in Park City, Utah, and Fish Haven, Idaho, on Bear Lake.

★

A biography of Olsen is Michael Gershman, *Merlin Olsen: Gentlemanly Giant* (2001). Information about Olsen's decision to retire as a football commentator is in Steve Woodward, "Search for Different Roles Prompts Olsen to Retire," *USA Today* (27 Dec. 1991). An analysis of Olsen's relationship with his son Nathan, a football player at Stanford University, is the focus of "Cardinal Sons," *Sports Illustrated* (10 Oct. 1994).

F. ROSS PETERSON

O'NEAL, Shaq(uille) Rashaun (*b.* 6 March 1972 in Newark, New Jersey), one of the top players in the National Basketball Association (NBA) at the end of the twentieth century who capitalized on his sports celebrity to pursue projects in the music and entertainment industries.

O'Neal, whose first names mean "little warrior," was one of two sons and two daughters of Philip Harrison, a career serviceman in the military, and Lucille O'Neal, a municipal employee. His biological father, Joe Taney, abandoned the family shortly after O'Neal's birth. During O'Neal's childhood, Harrison was transferred to several different army bases, and the boy had difficulty making friends. He also was teased about his height; by age thirteen, O'Neal was six feet, five inches tall.

As an adolescent O'Neal found he could get attention by pulling the school's fire alarms, and he was almost expelled for his displays of bad temper. Concerned about his poor behavior, his parents encouraged him to play basketball, baseball, and football, although O'Neal showed little natural athletic talent. When he was twelve the family was stationed in West Germany, where O'Neal attended a basketball clinic given by Dale Brown, the head coach at Louisiana State University (LSU). Brown could not believe that O'Neal was only thirteen years old and already wore a size seventeen shoe. Brown urged Harrison to eventually enroll his son at LSU in Baton Rouge. Ironically, O'Neal was cut from his ninth-grade basketball team; the coach told him that his feet were too big and his movements too clumsy.

In 1987 Harrison was stationed at Fort Sam Houston, Texas, and moved the family to San Antonio, where O'Neal attended Robert G. Cole Senior High School and played center for the basketball team. At six feet, ten inches tall and 250 pounds, he was bigger and stronger than the other centers in the league and helped his team win the state championship. During his two years at Cole he averaged 32 points, 22 rebounds, and 8 blocked shots per game, and his team achieved a 68–1 record. O'Neal set numerous scoring and rebounding records. He also grew to his adult height of seven feet, one inch. Following his senior year he was invited to play in the McDonald's High School All-America game, in which he scored eighteen points and grabbed sixteen rebounds. Upon graduation in 1989, O'Neal was one of the top college recruits, but he had already decided to attend LSU.

Shaquille O'Neal *(left)*. AP/WIDE WORLD PHOTOS

O'Neal enrolled at LSU in 1990, and truly began to blossom, even though he found it difficult being away from home for the first time. The big freshman had a solid season in the tough Southeastern Conference. In 1990 he averaged a respectable 13.9 points per game, but he received more attention for his ability to rebound and block shots. As a first-year player O'Neal averaged more than twelve rebounds per game, an impressive total for one so young and so new to big-time college basketball. He also established a conference record of 115 blocked shots. During his first season he found that opponents would double and triple team him. In response, O'Neal learned to shoot a jump shot and a hook shot, quickly gaining a reputation as one of the best centers in college basketball. He played with incredible strength and agility, achieving first-team All-America honors.

In his second varsity season at LSU, O'Neal made a great leap forward. He doubled his scoring average and increased his rebounding average to 14.6 per game, leading the nation in that category. After his sophomore season he was named the Player of the Year by *Sports Illustrated,* the Associated Press, and United Press International. Because of the beating O'Neal was taking each night in the pivot and concern over his family's modest means, he decided to turn professional. Although he left LSU in 1992 without earning a degree, he later received a B.A. in general studies with a minor in political science in December 2000, through LSU's independent study program.

On 24 June 1992 O'Neal was selected in the first round by the Orlando (Florida) Magic, an expansion team. The Magic signed him to a seven-year, $40 million contract, making him professional basketball's highest-paid rookie. Even before O'Neal decided to leave LSU and become eligible for the NBA draft, he was deemed one of the most marketable young players ever. This was somewhat surprising, given that he had not led his college team to a National Collegiate Athletic Association championship, and it was uncertain that he would develop into a dominating player of the caliber of Kareem Abdul-Jabbar, Patrick Ewing, or Michael Jordan. However, in addition to his contract, O'Neal signed lucrative endorsements and became an instant multimillionaire.

O'Neal had a great first year in the NBA. He was voted the Rookie of the Year and was selected to start in the All-Star game, the first rookie to do so since Jordan in 1985. Basketball fans in NBA cities flocked to see the new young superstar and the rapidly improving Magic. O'Neal was perhaps the strongest player in the league, even as a rookie, and fans loved to watch his thunderous dunks, which occasionally pulled the basket down off its support stand.

In O'Neal's second season with the Magic (1993–1994), the team made it to the NBA finals for the first time, and O'Neal was named the Player of the Week. Off the court he endorsed Pepsi and Reebok, recorded a song with the Brooklyn rap trio Fu-Schnickens, and released his successful first album, *Shaq Diesel* (1993). He also appeared on Fu-Schnickens's 1994 top-forty single "What's Up Doc? (Can We Rock)." Thanks to a slew of guest stars, O'Neal's second album, *Shaq-Fu Da Return* (1994), established him as a gold-certified rap artist. His first single, "Biological Didn't Bother," quickly rose to the top twenty, and led to a collaboration with the singer Michael Jackson on the album *MJ's HIStory* (1995).

O'Neal realized after the 1995 season that he would need to mature both physically and mentally before he could win a championship ring. The Magic suffered from player injuries for the next two seasons, including O'Neal's; he had plantar fascitis (inflammation of a ligament) in his right foot that limited his movement and made pushoffs difficult. Some sportswriters noted his pathetic free-throw shooting (53.3 percent in 1994–1995) and said that, with his busy music career, he was spreading himself too thin to ever fulfill his enormous basketball potential. O'Neal also had started a movie career, playing his first leading role as a rapping genie in Disney's *Kazaam* (1996). He next starred in *Steel* (1997), as a larger-than-life DC Comics superhero.

Despite his off-court commitments, in 1995 O'Neal led Orlando to an Eastern Conference crown and the NBA finals, where they were swept by the Houston Rockets. In 1996, after being swept again in the play-offs (this time by the Chicago Bulls), O'Neal signed a seven-year, $120 million contract with the Los Angeles Lakers. His first year with the Lakers was a learning experience, and the team lost to the Utah Jazz in the conference semifinals. However, by the 2000 season O'Neal had developed in both strength and agility, and he helped lead the Lakers to their first NBA championship. This outstanding feat was repeated in the 2001 season.

In 2001 O'Neal was seven feet, one inch tall, weighed 310 pounds, and wore a size 22 shoe. With best-selling rap recordings and Hollywood movies to his credit, the charismatic player had emerged as a multifaceted pop-culture icon, promoted by the NBA and his upmarket corporate sponsors as a young superstar equipped to carry the league's message to a new, global generation of fans.

★

O'Neal has written two autobiographies, *Shaq Attaq!: My Rookie Years* (1993), with Jack McCallum; and *Shaq Talks Back* (2001). He also has written a children's book, *Shaq and the Beanstalk and Other Very Tall Tales* (1999), and *Shaq Talks Back: The Uncensored Word on My Life and Winning in the NBA* (2001). Books by other authors about O'Neal's career are Barry Cooper, *The Magic Shaq: A Season Inside the Orlando Magic* (1993), and Dennis Eichhorn, *Shaq* (1995). Further information can be found in Phil Taylor, "Unstoppable," *Sports Illustrated* (4 June 2001).

REED B. MARKHAM

ORR, Robert Gordon ("Bobby") (*b.* 20 March 1948 in Parry Sound, Ontario, Canada), hockey player whose offensive skills led the Boston Bruins to two Stanley Cup championships in 1970 and 1972, in the process altering the role of the defenseman and revolutionizing professional hockey.

Orr was the third child born to Doug Orr, an explosives packer, and Arva Orr. He started skating at the age of four when a family friend bought him a pair of skates. They were too large, but his father filled the toes with paper to make them fit. While still in kindergarten Orr began playing in the Parry Sound Minor Squirt Hockey League, which he dominated by the time he was nine years old. Although shorter and thinner than many of the older boys against whom he competed, Orr exhibited a singular resolve to improve his strength, conditioning, and skill, practicing alone every day after school until dark. His work ethic, combined with his natural ability, gave Orr a critical advantage over his rivals. The Boston Bruins scouts discovered Orr in 1960 when he was playing midget hockey for the Parry Sound Bantam All-Stars. When he was thirteen he signed a junior amateur contract with Boston, agreeing to play for the Oshawa Generals of the Ontario Hockey Association. He never graduated from high school.

Orr played thirty-four games for the Generals in 1962, scoring twenty-one points on six goals and fifteen assists. Against older, more experienced, and more physically mature players (Orr weighed only 125 pounds when he joined the team), he still managed to control the pace and action of the game every time he skated onto the ice. During his three years with Oshawa, Orr averaged nearly thirty-four goals per season—excellent totals for a forward, extraordinary for a defenseman. In 1966 Bruins officials thought Orr ready to make his NHL debut. They signed him to a

Bobby Orr. ARCHIVE PHOTOS, INC.

two-year, $50,000 contract with a $25,000 signing bonus, at the time the largest sum a rookie had ever commanded. It was the best investment in the history of the franchise.

Contrary to prevailing assumptions, Orr did not revolutionize hockey during his rookie season in which he tallied thirteen goals and twenty-eight assists in sixty-one games. He could not even propel the Bruins into the playoffs; the team finished in last place for the sixth time in seven seasons. Yet as the Rookie of the Year and a Second-Team All-Star, Orr's exploits hinted at future glory. Among defensemen, only Pierre Pilote of the Chicago Blackhawks (six goals, forty-six assists) had scored more points than Orr. Bruins coach Harry Sinden pronounced Orr "a star from the moment they played the National Anthem in his first NHL game." No one refuted Sinden's judgment.

Regrettably, Orr's rookie season was not auspicious in all respects. Toward the end of the campaign he sustained the first in a series of knee injuries that ultimately shortened his career. Rehabilitation was long, slow, and painful, limiting Orr to only forty-six of seventy-four regular season games in 1967–1968. He nonetheless earned a berth as a First-Team All-Star, won the Norris Trophy, and led the Bruins to the playoffs for the first time since 1959. The following season Orr scored sixty-four points (twenty-one goals, forty-three assists) in sixty-seven games, establishing a new NHL record for scoring by a defensemen.

Orr nearly doubled his output in the 1969–1970 season, netting 33 goals and registering 87 assists for an incredible 120 points. He became the first defenseman and only the fourth player in NHL history, along with Phil Esposito, Gordie Howe, and Bobby Hull, to accumulate 100 points in a season. But Orr was only beginning. Between 1969 and 1975 he averaged more than 30 goals and 122 points, becoming the only defenseman ever to lead the NHL in scoring, a feat he accomplished in 1970 and again in 1975.

Statistically, Orr's finest season was 1970–1971 when, finishing second to Esposito in the scoring race, he amassed 139 points on 37 goals and 102 assists. No defenseman has ever exceeded Orr's point total, and only two other players, Wayne Gretzky and Mario Lemieux, have recorded more than 100 assists in a single season. Orr's incomparable displays of offensive prowess struck fear into the hearts of Bruins opponents. "Well, the first thing [I did] when I saw Orr coming down on me," confessed Hall of Fame goalie Johnny Bower of the Toronto Maple Leafs, "was to say a little prayer, if I had time."

Orr's offensive wizardry never compromised his defensive play. During the years in which he was rewriting the record books and transforming the nature of hockey, Orr averaged 101 penalty minutes per season and earned accolades for his rugged performance in the defensive zone. He excelled at intercepting passes, blocking shots, and stripping onrushing players of the puck. At times he could be a one-man penalty-killing unit by taking control of the puck and refusing to surrender it. Nor was Orr timid about dropping the gloves, especially early in his career. As a rookie, for instance, he twice felled veteran scrapper Ted Harris of the Montreal Canadiens in the same fight. Harry Sinden insisted that this unique combination of skill and toughness made Orr the best player in the history of the NHL. "Howe could do everything," Sinden said, "but not at top speed. Hull went at top speed but couldn't do everything. The physical aspect was absent from Gretzky's game. Orr would do everything, and do it at top speed. He's the perfect hockey player."

Orr may have saved his best for last. In the 1974–1975 season he coaxed his fragile, aching knees onto the ice for all eighty regular-season games, finishing with forty-six goals and eighty-nine assists. It was, however, the beginning of the end. Five knee operations had begun to take their toll. Orr played in only thirty-six more NHL games, ten for Boston and twenty-six over three seasons for the Chicago Blackhawks, with whom he signed a five-year, $3-million contract on 24 June 1976. Orr might never have left the Bruins had his agent Alan Eagleson informed him that club officials were offering part ownership of the franchise as an incentive to remain in Boston.

Determined to honor his contract with the Blackhawks, Orr underwent surgery for the sixth time on 19 April 1977 in an effort to repair his damaged knees. He missed the entire 1977–1978 season attempting to recuperate, but to no avail. Orr played only six more games for the Hawks before retiring. "My knees can't handle playing any more," he explained to reporters at a tearful news conference on 8 November 1978. He was thirty years old.

Orr won the Norris Trophy as the best defenseman in the National Hockey League (NHL) for eight consecutive years from 1968 to 1975. During that remarkable period he also twice won the Art Ross Trophy as the leading scorer in the NHL (1970 and 1975), and was runner-up to teammate Phil Esposito three times (1971, 1972, and 1974). After winning the Calder Memorial Trophy as Rookie of the Year in 1967, Orr took home the Hart Memorial Trophy for most valuable player (MVP) during the regular season for three straight years (1970 – 1972). He also won the Conn Smythe Trophy for MVP in the 1970 and 1972 playoffs, when he led the Boston Bruins to Stanley Cup championships after a drought of nearly three decades.

Orr finished his career with 270 goals, 645 assists, and 915 points in only 657 games. Later generations of players have emulated his style, but few have matched the rare blend of finesse, courage, toughness, and skill that he displayed. To magnify his already legendary fame, Orr scored what is arguably the most celebrated goal in NHL history. Forty seconds into overtime in game four of the 1970 Stanley Cup Finals, Orr took a centering pass from Derek Sanderson and fired the puck by St. Louis Blues goaltender Glenn Hall. Attempting to prevent the goal, Blues defenseman Noel Picard hooked Orr's skate and sent him sprawling headlong to the ice. The photograph of Orr in flight, arms outstretched, his stick raised in triumph, has become for many the defining image of the modern NHL.

Off the ice Orr's impact was equally great. Although his earnings were modest by contemporary standards, he was the first NHL player to employ an agent to represent him during contract negotiations, thus initiating the rise in salaries that has benefited so many current players.

In his prime Orr stood six feet tall and weighed approximately 197 pounds. With his blond hair, winning smile, and youthful appearance, he was the epitome of the boy next door. Invariably self-effacing, humble, polite, and accommodating with both fans and the media, Orr's popularity and appeal have not diminished in the years since his retirement. Such companies as General Motors, Nabisco, Mastercard, Nynex, Baybank, Callnet Software, and Doubletree Suite Hotels have courted Orr as a spokesperson, desiring to associate their products and services with his wholesome image. Orr also continues to promote the NHL and assist the younger generation of players as a sports agent for Woolf Associates in Boston.

When Orr announced that he was retiring, the Board of Governors of the Hockey Hall of Fame suspended the customary waiting period of three years and made him eligible for immediate induction. Inducted in 1979, Orr became at thirty-one the youngest player ever elected. It was a fitting tribute to the man who, as former teammate Phil Esposito said, changed "the face of hockey all by himself."

★

Orr's book, *Bobby Orr: My Game* (1974), written with Mark Mulvoy, details his early life and career. For more information, see Clark Booth, *The Boston Bruins: Celebrating 75 Years* (1998); Stan Fischler, "Franchise Histories: The Boston Bruins," in Dan Diamond et al., *Total Hockey: The Official Encyclopedia of the National Hockey League* (1998); Stan Fischler, *The Greatest Players and Moments of the Boston Bruins* (1999); Craig MacInnis, ed., *Remembering Bobby Orr: A Celebration* (1999); and Brian McFarlane, *The Bruins* (1999).

MARK G. MALVASI

OSBORNE, Thomas William ("Tom") (*b.* 23 February 1937 in Hastings, Nebraska), professional football player and head coach of the University of Nebraska Cornhuskers from 1973 to 1998, during which time his teams won three National Collegiate Athletic Association (NCAA) national championship titles.

Osborne was the elder of two children born to Charles Osborne, a traveling car salesman and later owner of an irrigation business, and Erma Welsh Osborne, a teacher. During World War II, Charles Osborne served in the mili-

Tom Osborne, 1993. AP/WIDE WORLD PHOTOS

tary and the family moved to St. Paul, Nebraska, where they lived with Erma Osborne's parents. After the war, the family returned to Hastings.

In his junior high years Osborne enjoyed playing all sports. At Hastings High School he made his mark in football and basketball. Osborne was the starting quarterback in his junior and senior seasons and made the second-team All-State squad his senior year. In 1955, as a senior on the basketball squad, Osborne was selected to the All-State team. For his senior year athletic achievements he was named Nebraska's High School Athlete of the Year.

Both Osborne's father and paternal grandfather had played football at Hastings College, so after graduating from high school in 1955, Osborne passed up scholarships in football and basketball from the University of Nebraska in Lincoln and enrolled in Hastings in the fall to major in history. He played football, basketball, and track for the small liberal arts college, quarterbacking the football team during his sophomore year and in 1957, his junior year, leading Hastings to an undefeated season. Osborne's efforts on the field earned him All-Conference recognition in his sophomore, junior, and senior years. The *Lincoln Journal Star* named him the State College Athlete of the Year in 1958 and 1959 for his outstanding performances.

Osborne graduated from Hastings College in 1959 with a B.A. in history. He entered the National Football League (NFL) draft and was picked in the eighteenth round by the San Francisco 49ers. He made the team as a member of the practice squad, but in 1960 at the beginning of his second year with the 49ers he was released and picked up by the Washington Redskins, where he assumed the position of flanker. Osborne played a few games and returned for 1961–1962, but a persistent hamstring injury forced him to retire at the end of the season.

In 1962 Osborne returned to Nebraska, where he enrolled at the University of Nebraska and pursued a master's degree in educational psychology. He also worked as a graduate assistant football coach. Shortly after enrolling for the spring semester he met Nancy Tederman; the couple married on 4 August 1962. Osborne finished his M.A. in 1963 and earned a Ph.D. in educational psychology in 1965. A few months before Osborne completed the Ph.D., the first of his three children was born.

Osborne struggled to decide whether to teach educational psychology or to coach football full time. In 1967 he accepted the full-time receivers coach position under the Nebraska Cornhuskers head coach Bob Devaney. When on 17 January 1972 Devaney announced he would not return, he named Osborne as his replacement. Osborne became head coach in January 1973, and he was immediately under considerable pressure to win. Under Devaney, the Cornhuskers had won two national championships in the last three years.

Throughout Osborne's twenty-five year coaching career with the Cornhuskers, the team developed intense rivalries with their Big Eight conference opponents, and in the 1980s came close to winning two national championships. In 1982 the Huskers were defeated by Penn State and prevented from claiming the national title. The team had another chance at a national title when they played Miami in the Orange Bowl following the 1983 season. The Nebraska team, led by Mike Rozier, recipient of that year's Heisman Trophy, mounted a drive late in the game that produced a touchdown. An extra point attempt would have tied the game, but with forty-six seconds left Osborne decided to go for the win with a two-point conversion. Unfortunately, the conversion attempt fell short, and Osborne's hope of capturing his first national championship died.

From 1985 to 1993 the national championship title eluded Osborne. The teams he coached during this period played exceptionally well and all made postseason bowl appearances, but at the end of the season the Huskers were never number one. For the 1993 season Osborne changed Nebraska's defensive scheme from a 5–2 to a 4–3, which placed more emphasis on speed and allowed Nebraska's defense to equally defend the rush and the pass. The move was designed to make the Cornhuskers more competitive against pass-oriented offenses.

In the 1994 season, with the new defensive scheme in

place and the exceptional leadership of quarterback Tommie Frazier, the Cornhuskers finished the regular season undefeated and beat the University of Miami in the Orange Bowl for Osborne's first national championship. The American Football Coaches Association voted Osborne National Coach of the Year in 1995. The following year the team repeated its national championship success by defeating Florida in the Fiesta Bowl. The 1995 season was marred by a series of off-the-field incidents involving members of the team. In September 1995 Osborne suspended running back Lawrence Phillips for assaulting his girlfriend, but later reinstated him, a decision that drew fire from the media.

The Cornhuskers returned as co-national champions (the Associated Press poll voted Michigan number one and Nebraska number two; the ESPN Coaches Poll voted the Huskers number one) in 1997, defeating Tennessee in the Orange Bowl. The victory was bittersweet for Osborne because on 10 December 1997 he announced the Orange Bowl game would be his last. The Orange Bowl victory marked his 255th career win and brought to a close a 25-year career that included twelve Big Eight Conference Titles, one Big Twelve Crown, and three national championship titles. In 1998 Osborne was inducted into the National Football Foundation and the College Football Hall of Fame.

In retirement, Osborne and his wife established the Osborne Endowment for Youth's Husker Teammates, a mentoring program that matched Husker football players and area business leaders with junior high school students. The couple also established an endowment fund at Hastings College. In November 2000 Osborne, a Republican, was elected to serve as a U.S. representative from Nebraska's third Congressional District.

Osborne, an outstanding Nebraska athlete and former professional football player, is most recognized for his successful tenure as head coach of the Nebraska Cornhuskers. Although he coached excellent teams, Osborne struggled to win a national championship in the first half of his career, epitomized in the games played between the University of Nebraska and the University of Oklahoma, and in the close Orange Bowl losses of the 1970s and 1980s. By the end of the 1990s Osborne found success and captured three national titles, but they came with controversy, as off-the-field problems with players and questions about the Nebraska program flooded the press. Osborne, always calm on and off the football field, took the praise and criticism in stride and relied on his faith to weather these victories and storms.

★

Biographical information can be found in Osborne's own books, including *More than Winning: The Story of Nebraska's Tom Osborne* (1985), written with John E. Roberts; *On Solid Ground* (1996); and *Faith in the Game* (1999). Additional biographical data is in Julie Koch, ed., *A Salute to Nebraska's Tom Osborne: A 25-Year History* (1998). Information regarding specific games Osborne coached can be found in Tom Shatel, *Red Zone: The Greatest Victories in the History of Nebraska Football* (1998).

JON E. TAYLOR

OTT, Mel(vin) Thomas (*b.* 2 March 1909 in Gretna, Louisiana; *d.* 21 November 1958 in New Orleans, Louisiana), baseball Hall of Famer who, when he retired as a power-hitting right fielder for the New York Giants (1926–1947), held the National League (NL) record for career home runs with 511.

Ott's father, Charles Ott, toiled as an oil refinery worker in the Mississippi River town of Gretna, and was himself a former semiprofessional baseball player; Ott's mother, Catherine Miller Ott, was a homemaker. Ott was the firstborn son; he had an older sister and a younger brother. A precocious athlete, Ott was a three-sport star at McDonoghville-Jefferson (later renamed Gretna) High School, excelling in football, in basketball, and as the star catcher and hitter for the school's baseball team, as well as the local semiprofessional Patterson Grays. The Grays were owned by the wealthy local lumber magnate Harry Williams, a close friend of legendary New York Giants manager John McGraw, and Williams recommended his sixteen-year-old star to McGraw.

Arriving late for his major league tryout in spring 1926, the diminutive Ott—five feet, eight inches, and 165 pounds—greatly impressed McGraw. Ott's unorthodox swing was described by baseball historian Fred Stein as being "preceded by a quick raising and lowering of his front leg just before his upper body moved into the pitch." McGraw said, "I don't give a damn about that crazy kick . . . that's the best natural swing I've seen in years," and added, "Ott is the most natural hitter I ever saw. His style at the plate is perfect." Ott explained, "I found that when I tossed my right leg up, it threw all my weight on the left leg. In this way I got my full strength into my swing." Fearing that minor league managers would try to correct Ott's unique style, the fire-breathing McGraw refused all requests to send him down to the minors for more seasoning. Even Casey Stengel, then the skipper of the Giants Double-A affiliate, Toledo, was rebuffed. "The kid stays with me!" McGraw gruffly barked.

The sixteen-year-old Ott became McGraw's personal development project, and McGraw practically adopted "Master Melvin" (as the New York sportswriters dubbed the young natural) as a surrogate son. Ott, who never had played an inning of minor league ball, was forbidden to fraternize with "the men" on the club, no cards, no drink-

Mel Ott, 1933. ASSOCIATED PRESS AP

ing or carousing, and no sitting next to the "rough and tumble" bunch in the dugout. Playing sparingly his initial two seasons, Ott did hit .383 in 35 games as a rookie (mainly as a pinch hitter). McGraw shifted the catcher to right field, aware that his stocky slugger's career would be shortened if he remained behind the plate.

The Giants Polo Ground's short (257 feet) right-field corner was ideal for a left-handed power hitter and soon became known as "Ottville." Ott hit 18 home runs in his third season in 1928, but the "Boy Wonder" exploded during his second full-time season in 1929. He hit 42 home runs and drove in 152. On the last day of the season, he was tied with the Philadelphia Phillies Chuck Klein for the NL home run lead. The Giants played the Phillies in a historic doubleheader that afternoon. Ott's best friend and longtime roommate, pitching great Carl Hubbell, gave up home run number forty-three to Klein in the opener. The Phillies pitching staff issued Ott five intentional walks in the nightcap, number five coming with the bases loaded, thus depriving Ott of the chance to tie Klein for the NL home run title. Ironically, Ott, who led the league in homers six times, hit his greatest number the year he finished second.

Ott possessed a sharp eye for the strike zone and an uncommon discipline at the plate; he walked 113 times in 1929. He earned 90 or more walks in a dozen seasons and led the league in bases on balls 6 times, and his 1,708 free passes (an NL record) were eclipsed by Joe Morgan (then playing for the San Francisco Giants) in 1982. Ott, who would become an All-Star eleven times, was not only an offensive threat. Rated for most of his twenty-two-year career as the premier defensive right fielder, despite a lack of foot speed, Ott possessed a superb right-handed throwing arm, averaging 17 outfield assists per (154-game) season.

In October 1930 Ott married New Orleans native Mildred ("Mickey") Wattigny; the couple had two daughters. In the thrilling 1933 World Series against the AL pennant–winning Washington Senators, Ott provided dramatic game-winning heroics. With the Giants leading three games to one and the score tied 3–3 in the top of the tenth inning, Ott hit a long drive toward the center field bleachers at the old Griffith Stadium. The Senators outfielder Fred Schulte made a valiant effort to snare the long ball, but it bounced off his glove, disappearing over the fence to give Ott his only World Series victory.

Ott's finest single season came in 1936 when as the heart of the team he belted 33 homers, hit for a .328 average, drove in 135 runs, scored 120, and walked 111 times. The easygoing Ott, a fan favorite, was also the consummate team player. He obligingly switched position to third base during both the 1937 and 1938 seasons for the good of the club.

In 1942 Bill Terry was promoted by Giants owner Horace Stoneham to the general manager's office, and Ott became field manager. Ott's record at the helm was mediocre. During his six and one-half year tenure he compiled a 464–530 record, a winning percentage of only .467. In contrast to the combative McGraw, Ott was quiet and deliberative. In an out-of-character performance in 1946, he was the first major league manager ejected from both games of a doubleheader for vociferously arguing an umpire's calls. Ott, who retired from active playing in 1947 due to chronic leg problems, was probably able to extend his career due to the lack of quality major league talent available during the later years of World War II.

During this historic postwar year of 1947, a well-known American expression was coined regarding Ott and his genial manner. With the Giants mired in the NL cellar, rival manager Leo "the Lip" Durocher of the Brooklyn Dodgers mused prior to a game, "Do you know a nicer guy than Mel Ott? Or any of the other Giants? Yet those guys are in last place." His words became mangled in the press and evolved into the sharply tinged quip, "Nice guys finish last." In an ironic twist of fate, Ott was relieved of his managerial duties the following season, and the intensely disliked, but more aggressive, Durocher took over in July 1948.

Ott remained employed by the Giants, running their farm system along with Carl Hubbell until 1950. In 1951 he began a two-year stint managing the Oakland Oaks of the Pacific Coast League, leaving them to join the Mutual Broadcasting System as a baseball announcer. This was followed by several years as the radio voice of the Detroit Tigers in the late 1950s.

In 1951, at the relatively young age of forty-two, Ott was inducted into the National Baseball Hall of Fame in Cooperstown, New York. His career numbers are staggering, considering his lack of size and his years playing in the pre-expansion 154-game seasons: a .533 career slugging percentage, a .304 lifetime batting average, driving in more than 100 runs 9 times, leading the Giants in homers 18 times, and batting over .300 eleven times. He played 2,730 games and stroked 2,876 hits. As the first National Leaguer to hit 500 home runs, Ott retired with 511 (then third all-time to Babe Ruth and Jimmie Foxx). Baseball historians debate the validity of Ott's 511 home runs, noting the inordinate number (311) he blasted in the friendly confines of the Polo Grounds with its short right field porch. Away from the Coogan's Bluff stadium, Ott was a much less prolific slugger, connecting for only 187. At his retirement he also held NL career records (all subsequently broken) for runs batted in (1,860), runs scored (1,859), and walks (1,708).

Ott's untimely death at age forty-nine came after his car was hit in a head-on collision with a car driven by a drunk driver. He is buried in Metairie Cemetery in Metairie, Louisiana. Rival manger Leo Durocher said of Ott, "I never knew a player who was so universally loved. Why even when he was playing against the Dodgers at Ebbets Field he would be cheered . . . and there are no more rabid fans than in Brooklyn."

★

Fred Stein, *Mel Ott: The Little Giant of Baseball* (1999), is an in-depth, well-researched full-length biography containing a number of personal recollections by Ott's contemporaries, detailed career statistics, and an excellent list of related books, articles, periodicals, and newspapers. A short chapter in Donald Honig, *The Power Hitters* (1989), places Ott in perspective and includes biographical detail. Henry F. Graff, *Dictionary of American Biography, Supplement 6: 1956-1960* (1980), contains a detailed and insightful biography of Ott. An excellent account of the baseball glory years of the 1930s with several Ott stories is Peter Williams, *When the Giants Were Giants: Bill Terry and the Golden Age of New York Baseball* (1994). Liz Scott, "Giant Steps: Gretna's Mel Ott," *New Orleans* (July 1988), includes local flavor on Ott's childhood, family life, and popularity. An obituary is in the *New York Times* (22 Nov. 1958).

JEFFREY S. ROSEN

OUIMET, Francis DeSales (*b.* 8 May 1893 in Brookline, Massachusetts; *d.* 2 September 1967 in Newton, Massachusetts), amateur golfer whose stunning victory in the U.S. Open Championship of 1913 made him the first American hero in his sport.

Ouimet (pronounced wee-MET) was the fourth of five children of Arthur Ouimet and Mary Ellen Burke. His father, a Canadian immigrant, worked as a coachman and gardener, while his mother, a Brookline, Massachusetts, native of Irish descent, was a homemaker. Ouimet grew up in Brookline across the street from The Country Club, the first country club in the United States. His first encounter with the game that made him famous came when he cut across Country Club fairways on his way to grade school and found golf balls in the rough. He and his older brother Wilfred exchanged the balls for a few clubs at a local sporting goods store and learned to play on a three-hole "course" Wilfred had set up in a cow pasture. After the likable Ouimet turned eleven and became a caddie, he accumulated more golf equipment from kindly club members. He also got the opportunity to observe the techniques of some of the finest amateur and professional golfers as they played in tournaments at The Country Club. Although club members sometimes allowed Ouimet to join them for a round, he more often slipped onto the private course to hone his game out of the sight of greenskeepers early in the morning and on rainy days, or took the trolley into neighboring Boston to play with friends at the Franklin Park public links.

Francis Ouimet, 1923. © HULTON-DEUTSCH COLLECTION/CORBIS

At Brookline High School, Ouimet chose to play golf rather than baseball. He helped organize the school's golf team and won the individual match-play competition in the Greater Boston Interscholastic Golf Championship in 1909. Ouimet left school shortly thereafter, he wrote, because he had "devoted too much time to golf."

After his failure to qualify for match play by one stroke at the U.S. Amateur Championships of 1910, 1911, and 1912, Ouimet blossomed as a competitive golfer in 1913. In June he captured the first of his six Massachusetts State Amateur titles. Then, after qualifying for the U.S. Amateur at Garden City, New York, in September, the cool New Englander with the fluid swing impressed observers with his fine play in a narrow second-round loss to Jerry Travers, who was considered the best match player of his day. Travers went on to win his fourth Amateur.

Having exhausted his vacation time from his job at Wright and Ditson, a Boston sporting goods firm, Ouimet initially declined to participate in the U.S. Open Championship two weeks after the Amateur. But Robert G. Watson, the president of the United States Golf Association (USGA), convinced him to enter, and his employer allowed him to play.

Ouimet and the rest of the Americans in the 1913 U.S. Open field were considered supporting players in what was expected to be a showcase for two highly acclaimed British professionals. Harry Vardon, a five-time British Open champion and winner of the 1900 U.S. Open, and Ted Ray, the long-hitting 1912 British Open titlist, were playing exhibition matches on a U.S. tour sponsored by Lord Northcliffe, the publisher of the *Times* of London. Their presence at The Country Club lent prestige to an event that had up to that time attracted scant attention.

Brimming with confidence after his strong showing at the Amateur, Ouimet managed the difficult Open course and wet conditions well enough to surpass all other challengers and tie the heavily favored Vardon and Ray at eight over par 304 for 72 holes. After his game seemed to fall apart in the cold, steady rain that plagued the fourth round, the twenty-year-old rebounded remarkably, playing two-under-par golf on the last six holes to catch his British rivals, who had finished long before. The key stroke during this brilliant run was a slippery downhill putt of some twenty feet for a three on the par-four seventeenth hole. So great was his concentration that Ouimet did not hear the honking and yelling of motorists in a traffic jam on an adjacent street when he rammed home his birdie.

In the ensuing eighteen-hole playoff, the youthful amateur was composed and on top of his game, while the seasoned professionals seemed nervous and out of sync. Hitting accurate iron shots and putting superbly, Ouimet grabbed the lead from his more erratic opponents on the back nine and held it. When Vardon made a late run to move within a shot of Ouimet, the latter holed another crucial birdie putt on the seventeenth to virtually close out the tournament. Ouimet's round of 72 (two under par) easily outdistanced Vardon's 77 and Ray's 78. According to Bernard Darwin, the correspondent of the *Times* of London, the American "slowly but surely . . . wore his men down and finally he battered and trampled them."

The story of the young Bay State David's defeat of golf's reigning Goliaths spread across the country, headlined the *New York Times*, and evoked national pride, sparking new interest in a game heretofore scorned as "foreign" or the province of the social elite. In the humble, clean-cut Ouimet, an immigrant's son, a former caddy, and a workingman of modest means, America found a genuine hero. In the ten years that followed his Open heroics, the number of golfers in the United States exploded from less than 350,000 to 2 million. The 1913 U.S. Open also marked the beginning of golf as a popular spectator sport in the United States. While previous tournaments attracted small crowds in the hundreds, between 3,000 and 5,000 tramped around The Country Club in foul conditions following Ouimet in the dramatic final round, and over 10,000 watched the next day's playoff contest. In addition, the galleries in Brookline proved more demonstrative and vocal than the usually reserved audiences of the past.

Although Ouimet gained lasting fame for his 1913 victory, he played in only five more U.S. Opens and only seriously contended in 1925 at the Worcester, Massachusetts, Country Club, finishing one stroke out of another playoff. Ouimet preferred to leave medal-play events like the Open, in which golfers had to play cautiously to protect their scores, to the professionals, and participate in mostly amateur match-play events where he could take more risks. Consequently, he came to regard his relatively obscure 1914 U.S. Amateur victory at the Ekwanok Country Club in Manchester, Vermont, which was accomplished with a 6 and 5 trouncing of Jerry Travers in the final, as a greater milestone in his career than his celebrated Open win. The Open win, gratifying though it was, had been something Ouimet never dreamed of accomplishing. The Amateur, on the other hand, had been his objective since boyhood.

When Ouimet and his friend and fellow golfer Jack Sullivan opened a sporting goods store in Boston in 1915, the USGA took away their amateur status. The controversial declaration that the selling of golf equipment made a player a professional was widely decried as unfair, but Ouimet accepted it. With his induction into the U.S. Army in 1918, the USGA quietly reinstated the popular Ouimet as an amateur. He married Stella Mary Sullivan, Jack Sullivan's sister, on 11 September 1918; they had two daughters.

Ouimet was discharged in 1919 with the rank of second lieutenant in the Quartermaster Corps. After returning to form on the links, he reached the final of the 1920 U.S.

Amateur but lost to Chick Evans, an ex-caddy from Chicago who had been a major rival in the 1910s. And although he remained in the top rank of U.S. players during the 1920s, Ouimet never got beyond the Amateur semifinals in that decade. All in all, he reached the semifinals six times between 1923 and 1932. Three of his defeats came at the hands of golf's new superstar, Bobby Jones. In 1931, the year after Jones retired from competitive golf, Ouimet won his second Amateur title, beating Jack Westland 6 and 5 in the final at the Beverly Country Club in Chicago.

Chosen as a member of the first U.S. Walker Cup team in 1922, Ouimet became a mainstay of the eight-man U.S. aggregation that periodically competed in a series of matches against the best amateurs from Great Britain. He played in eight matches from 1922 to 1934, compiling an overall record of nine wins, five defeats, and two halves. As Walker Cup captain Ouimet led the U.S. team to victories in 1932, 1934, 1936, 1947, and 1949. His only defeat at the helm, in 1938, was the first ever suffered by the Americans.

The gentlemanly Ouimet, who left competitive golf in 1949, became a genuine golf icon in retirement. He was enshrined as a charter member of the PGA Golf Hall of Fame in 1949, and became the first American elected captain of the Royal and Ancient Golf Club of Saint Andrews, Scotland, in 1951. Ouimet also lent his name to a highly successful caddie scholarship fund founded by the Massachusetts Golf Association in 1949 that continues to this day. For most of his adult life, Ouimet worked in the investment field. He headed the stock department of White, Weld and Company in the 1930s and 1940s, and was a broker with Brown Brothers, Harriman from 1954 until his death. A celebrated sportsman in his native New England, Ouimet also served as president of the Boston Bruins hockey team, vice president of the Boston Braves baseball team, and chairman of the Boston Arena Authority. He died of a heart attack and is buried in Holyhood Cemetery in Brookline.

Although overshadowed by players of succeeding generations, Ouimet remains a historic figure in golf. His astonishing performance in the 1913 U.S. Open inspired the great American golfers of the 1920s and 1930s, notably Walter Hagen, Bobby Jones, and Gene Sarazen. Bernard Darwin, who became the greatest British golf writer, noted that Ouimet's playoff triumph over Vardon and Ray "founded the American Golfing Empire."

★

The Ouimet Museum in Weston, Massachusetts, and the Ouimet Room at the USGA Museum and Library in Far Hills, New Jersey, have memorabilia on display relating to Ouimet's golf career. His books *Golf Facts for Young People* (1921), and *A Game of Golf—A Book of Reminiscence* (1932), contain important autobiographical information. For contemporary coverage, see the *Boston Globe,* the *Boston Herald,* the *Boston Post,* the *New York Times* (all 16–21 Sept. 1913), and the *Times* of London (16–20, 22 Sept. 1913). Historical assessments of Ouimet and the 1913 Open are included in H. B. Martin, *Fifty Years of American Golf* (1936); Herbert Warren Wind, *The Story of American Golf—Its Champions and Its Championships* (1948); Elmer Osgood Cappers, *Centennial History of The Country Club, 1882–1982* (1981); Stephen Hardy, *How Boston Played: Sports, Recreation, and Community, 1865–1915* (1982); and Robert Sommers, *The U.S. Open: Golf's Ultimate Challenge* (1987). Useful articles are Lawrence Robinson, "Francis Ouimet: The Miracle 50 Years Later," *Golf Magazine* (June 1963), and Glenn Stout, "The Amateur," *Boston Magazine* (June 1988). Obituaries are in the *Boston Globe, Boston Herald Traveler,* and *New York Times* (all 3 Sept. 1967).

RICHARD H. GENTILE

OWENS, James Cleveland ("Jesse") (*b.* 12 September 1913 in Oakville, Alabama; *d.* 31 March 1980 in Tucson, Arizona), track and field athlete who set world records in sprints, hurdles, and long jump events and won four gold medals at 1936 Olympics in Berlin.

Owens was the last of ten surviving children of Henry Cleveland Owens and Mary Emma Fitzgerald Owens, who were sharecroppers. Located in the played-out soil of northern Alabama not far from Huntsville, his hometown of Oakville was typical of many small country towns in the South where tenant farming and limited opportunity were a way of life for generations after the Civil War. Henry Owens considered the season a success if his family was sufficiently fed and decently clothed. With racial restrictions and outright violence holding sway, striving for anything more seemed foolhardy, if not dangerous.

Although life as a sharecropper took its toll on Henry Owens, Mary Owens was determined to seek a better life for the family. After daughter Lillie went to Cleveland and wrote letters back home with descriptions of ready jobs, high wages, and more freedom than they ever could have dreamed of in Alabama, her mother insisted on moving the family to the North. Although Henry objected at first, he took their two oldest sons to Cleveland to work for a while and save enough for the rest of the family to join them. Around 1922 the entire Owens family was reunited in Cleveland.

Like thousands of other African-American families taking part in the Great Migration northward during and after World War I, the Owenses were both delighted and disappointed in what they found. Henry Owens and his older sons quickly found work in Cleveland's steel mills, but it was months before Mary Owens could bring herself to open the drapes out of fear that strangers could look in on the family's apartment. Eventually, the family adjusted to its

Jesse Owens. AP/WIDE WORLD PHOTOS

new surroundings. Owens—called "J.C." by his family but soon rechristened "Jesse" after a teacher misunderstood his southern drawl—quickly adapted to the multicultural environment in which immigrants from Eastern Europe were the majority at his new grade school. With an outgoing and optimistic personality, Owens was immediately popular with his classmates. Although he was several years older than his fellow pupils and would always struggle with academic work, Owens's smile seemed to belie any struggles he encountered.

Recognized as a sprinter of enormous potential during his days at Cleveland's Fairmount Junior High, Owens's most important early mentor was track coach Charles Riley. Under Riley's tutelage, Owens streamlined his sprinting style, a fleet form that commentators likened to floating around the track. In 1928 Owens set his first two world records at the junior high level with a 6-foot high jump and long jump of 22 feet, 11.75 inches. Entering East Technical High School in the fall of 1930, Owens continued his achievements in the long jump, 100-yard dash, and 200-yard dash, setting records at the high school level in each event. In June 1933 Owens led the East Tech team to a National Interscholastic Championship when he scored a majority of the team's points in the competition. He also set a new record in the 200-yard dash in 20.7 seconds and 100-yard dash record of 9.4 seconds. Upon his return to Cleveland, Owens was greeted as a conquering hero with a parade through the city and addresses from the mayor and city councilmen. During his high school career, Owens, who was five feet, ten inches tall, and weighed 165 pounds, won 75 of the 79 races he entered.

With such an impressive string of victories, Owens was offered admittance to a number of colleges with the promise of an easy job to cover his expenses; in an era when athletic scholarships were rare in track and field, such arrangements were commonplace. Owens accepted an offer from Ohio State University (OSU) that included a job as a page in the Ohio State House. He also earned a significant amount of money from weekly appearances at local business and civic groups, where he began to learn the public-speaking skills that would become invaluable later in his life. The young athlete sent much of his earnings back to Cleveland, since his father had become disabled after he was hit by a car. Owens also had his own family to support, as his relationship with former Fairmount classmate Minnie Ruth Solomon had resulted in the birth of their daughter in 1932. The two married on 5 July 1935, although Owens would later insist in deference to the morals of the day that they had secretly eloped years before. The Owens family eventually included three daughters.

Owens's achievements as a collegiate athlete were astounding. Building on his work with Charles Riley, Owens refined his sprinting and jumping techniques with OSU Coach Larry Snyder and set numerous state, intercollegiate, and American Amateur Union (AAU) records. The highlight of his college career occurred on 25 May 1935 at the Big Ten Track and Field Championship in Ann Arbor, Michigan. Arriving at the meet with a sore back,

Owens barely made it through the qualifying heats. The day of the finals, however, Owens turned in record-breaking performances in the 220-yard dash, broad jump, 220-yard hurdles, 200-meter dash, and 200-meter low hurdles. He also tied the existing record in the 100-yard dash with a time of 9.4 seconds. In recognition of his astonishing accomplishment, Owens was elected captain of the OSU track team, the first African American to receive such an honor in the Big Ten.

By now a national celebrity, Owens faced the first of many controversies when the AAU threatened to exclude him from further competition. Upon learning that the Ohio State House had reimbursed his travel expenses under the guise of paying him for his job as a page, the AAU launched an investigation that threatened to keep Owens from going to the trials for the 1936 Olympics in Berlin. The AAU eventually deemed Owens a victim of circumstance, but not before it had removed him from consideration for the 1935 Sullivan Award for the outstanding amateur athlete of the year. The controversy behind him, Owens prepared to take part as one of nineteen African-American athletes on the U.S. track and field squad headed for Berlin. Their sheer presence signified that a new generation of African-American athletes had come of age; although four African Americans had taken part in the Olympic track and field events in 1932, none had done so in 1928.

Owens was the undisputed star of the delegation, and the press detailed the well-dressed athlete's every move and utterance. Always calm in competition, Owens remained affable and accessible throughout the games, and was careful to sidestep the enormous political outcry against holding the Olympics in Hitler's Berlin. In the finals of the 100-meter dash on 3 August 1936, Owens took the gold medal with a time of 10.3 seconds that tied the world record. He followed that victory with a new Olympic record in the long jump of 26 feet, 5.25 inches. Two days later, Owens earned his third gold medal of the games with an Olympic-record time of 20.7 seconds in the 200-meter finals. Capping off his historic Olympic run, Owens then received a fourth gold medal as part of the U.S. relay team in the 400-meter race.

Hailed in the United States in direct repudiation of Hitler's beliefs in Aryan superiority, Owens joined boxer Joe Louis as one of the nation's first African-American sports heroes. In the aftermath of such acclaim, however, Owens struggled for several years to capitalize on his success. Leaving OSU to take up a series of promotional appearances—including a campaign for 1936 Republican presidential nominee Alf Landon for which he earned $10,000—Owens was banned by the AAU from further amateur competition. With his career on the track effectively over, Owens attempted to start his own dry-cleaning business in Cleveland. After a year of mounting debts and extravagant spending on new cars and homes, Owens had to close his business. The former Olympian also faced tax evasion charges for earnings that he had failed to declare. Returning to OSU to finish his undergraduate degree, Owens did not pass enough of his classes and left the university for good in 1941.

After a stint as assistant personnel manager for African-American employees at the Ford Motor Company from 1943 to 1945, Owens moved his family to Chicago, where he opened a public relations firm. As a motivational speaker with his own story of triumph over poverty and racism, Owens was much sought after by business and civic clubs, and his work finally brought him success off the track. For his efforts on behalf of the Republican Party, Owens was also rewarded with a patronage job with the Illinois State Athletics Commission in 1953, a job that allowed him to reshape the myths that became part of the Jesse Owens story. One of the athlete's favorite anecdotes related to a supposed snubbing that Hitler delivered after Owens won the first of his gold medals. Although Hitler had stopped meeting with any gold medal winners after the first day of competition and had not singled Owens out, the story nevertheless became part of Owens's stock of Olympic tales.

Although Owens enjoyed a comfortable income from corporate sponsorships, his conviction on tax evasion charges in 1965 tarnished his image as a successful businessman. His legacy as an Olympic hero also came under attack for his opposition to black power supporters at the 1968 Olympic games in Mexico City. After sprinters Tommie Smith and John Carlos raised their fists on the medals stand, Owens was furious at what he perceived as their lack of patriotism. With cowriter Paul Niemark, Owens published a critique of militant activists, *Blackthink: My Life as a Black Man and White Man* (1970). He later softened his rhetoric in the 1972 work *I Have Changed,* but the gulf between Owens's outlook and the younger generation remained stark.

Although he maintained a heavy schedule of public appearances, Owens retired to Scottsdale, Arizona in the 1970s. After a stressful period in their marriage brought about by his innumerable extramarital affairs, Jesse and Ruth Owens remained together and shared in the glory as Owens was hailed as an elder statesman among U.S. Olympic champions. Among the many honors, OSU awarded Owens an honorary doctorate in 1972; Owens also received the Medal of Freedom Award from President Gerald R. Ford four years later. After decades of heavy smoking, Owens was diagnosed with lung cancer in 1979; the following year the illness took his life. He is buried in Oak Woods Cemetery in Chicago. Ruth Owens became the chairperson of the Jesse Owens Foundation, which provided scholarships to students active in their communities; she died in June 2001.

★

Jesse Owens published a number of autobiographical and inspirational works during his lifetime in collaboration with Paul Niemark, *Blackthink: My Life as a Black Man and White Man* (1970); *The Jesse Owens Story* (1970); *I Have Changed* (1972); *Jesse: A Spiritual Autobiography* (1978); and *Jesse, the Man Who Outran Hitler* (1978). There are numerous biographies of Owens, perhaps the leading work is William J. Baker, *Jesse Owens: An American Life* (1986). Owens's story as part of the 1936 Olympics is recounted in Duff Hart-Davis, *Hitler's Games: The 1936 Olympics* (1986); Allen Guttmann, *The Olympics: A History of the Modern Games* (1992); and Alfred E. Senn, *Power, Politics, and the Olympic Games: A History of the Power Brokers, Events, and Controversies That Shaped the Games* (1999). The Owens story is regularly invoked in any discussion of the Olympics and the history of African Americans in sports—often reviving the myths popularized by Owens himself—including essays by Lerone Bennett, Jr., "Jesse Owens's Olympic Tribute Over Time and Hitlerism," *Ebony* (Apr. 1996); Gloria Owens Hemphill, "Humiliating Hitler," *Newsweek* (25 Oct. 1999); Phil Taylor, "Flying in the Face of the Fuhrer," *Sports Illustrated* (29 Nov. 1999); and Timothy Kelley, "Stealing Hitler's Show," *New York Times Upfront* (4 Sep. 2000). An obituary is in the *New York Times* (1 Apr. 1980). Footage from Owens's 1936 Olympic triumph is included in the film *Olympia* (1940), directed by the German filmmaker Leni Riefenstahl. A fictionalized account of Owens's life appeared as *The Jesse Owens Story* (1984); a television documentary of his life, *Jesse Owens: Champion Athlete* (1994), is included in the Black Americans of Achievement Video Collection and is available on videocassette.

TIMOTHY G. BORDEN

P

PAGE, Alan Cedric (*b.* 7 August 1945 in Canton, Ohio), football player who changed the nature of defense in the National Football League (NFL) and subsequently won a seat on the Minnesota Supreme Court.

Page's father was a bartender whose education did not extend beyond high school, and Page's mother raised four children. Page attended Central Catholic High School in Canton, Ohio, but did not play football until the ninth grade, when his older brother Howard Page encouraged him to join the team. Alan Page excelled in high school football and in academics, and he earned a scholarship to Notre Dame. There he studied political science and played defensive end for the football team from 1964 to 1966. A member of the 1966 national championship team, Page was an All-American.

In 1967 Page graduated with a B.A. in political science, and the Minnesota Vikings of the National Football League (NFL) acquired him as the fifteenth pick in the first round of the draft. During his second year in the NFL, Page attended three weeks of night school at the William Mitchell College of Law in St. Paul, Minnesota. He said it was "over my head" and took another three weeks to figure out how to drop out. Page remembered, "It was a sink or swim situation, and I decided to get out of the pool." In 1973 he married Diane Sims, with whom he had four children. In the 1970s he played defensive tackle on the original Vikings "purple people eaters," the front four consisting of Page, Carl Eller, Jim Marshall, and Gary Larsen. The name derived from a popular song by Sheb Wooley and from the fact that the Vikings' uniform colors were purple and white. Page wore number 88. The Viking defense was so dominant that the team usually chose to kick off when it won the coin toss prior to the beginning of a game rather than take the ball on offense first.

The Vikings won the Central Division title of the National Football Conference (NFC), which along with the American Conference comprises the NFL, in all but two of the twelve years Page played with the team. Page led the Vikings in quarterback sacks and in forced fumbles for six of those twelve years and scored two safeties in 1971. He was the team leader in blocked kicks for seven seasons and started 160 straight games.

During the 1970s the team played but lost four Super Bowls (IV, VIII, IX, XI) in eight years under coach Harry "Bud" Grant, a stern, unemotional figure once described as looking like "the town marshal." After Super Bowl XI, which Oakland won 32–14 in January 1977, somebody said that instead of going to the dressing rooms at halftime the teams should have gone to Appomattox.

The intimidating Page was named the NFL Most Valuable Player in 1971, his fifth year with the Vikings. He was the first defensive player in NFL history to win this award, although it did not lead to lucrative product endorsements. Page was the National Football League Players' Association representative between 1970 and 1974 and again be-

Alan Page, 1973. ASSOCIATED PRESS AP

tween 1976 and 1977. Most of that time he argued that NFL contracts exploited players by denying them free agency. He felt Commissioner Pete Rozelle was not neutral in player-management disputes but favored the owners. Page served on the association's executive committee between 1972 and 1975.

Page ordinarily lost twenty to forty pounds jogging during the off-season, and Grant felt he could not continue as an all-pro at 230 pounds. In October 1978, when Page played poorly against the Bears, Grant removed him from the game, then told him to return after another player was hurt. Page initially refused. When he was released the next day, Chicago picked him up on waivers for $100, and Page played with the Bears until 1981. He led Chicago in sacks in 1978 and 1979.

Page was known for his speed getting into opponents' backfields and for his one-handed tackles. The Viking quarterback Fran Tarkenton said Page was the fastest defensive lineman off the ball he had ever seen. Page, who always played as if he had something to prove, moved both forward and backward with great agility and could keep up with ball carriers moving laterally. He played in nine Pro Bowls and was named the NFC Defensive Player of the Year four times. Page's career totals included 1,398 tackles, 148.5 quarterback sacks, and 30 forced fumbles. A six-time NFL All-Pro selection, Page was inducted into the Professional Football Hall of Fame on 30 July 1988, in his second year of eligibility. He was inducted into the College Football Hall of Fame in 1993.

During the off-seasons Page worked with a vending-machine company, sold cars for a year, and was a college recruiter for Control Data. By the mid-1970s he decided to give law school another try. He spent thirteen weeks in a summer preparatory program in Texas and entered the University of Minnesota Law School in 1975. He read law books in the Viking locker room and on the team bus. He loved law because he was stimulated by the subject. He no longer had to play football if he chose not to, and the money gave him power and freedom.

After graduating in June 1978, Page practiced law for seven years (1979–1984) with the firm of Lindquist and Vennum before joining the state attorney general's office. He was a special assistant to the Minnesota attorney general in the employment law division between 1985 and 1987 and was an assistant attorney general between 1987 and 1993. He ran for a seat on the Minnesota Supreme Court and won easily in November 1992, becoming the first African-American supreme court justice in Minnesota.

Page was a member of the Board of Directors of the Minneapolis Urban League between 1987 and 1990 and a member of the Board of Regents of the University of Minnesota between 1989 and 1992. He joined the advisory board of the Mixed Blood Theater in Minneapolis in 1984. In 1988 he established the Page Education Foundation to help minority students attend colleges in Minnesota. Each scholarship winner agrees to return to his or her community to work with children in kindergarten to eighth grade.

Among other accolades, Page was named one of America's Ten Outstanding Young Men in 1981, he won the Aetna Voice of Conscience Arthur Ashe, Jr., Achiever Award in 1994, and in 2001 he received the Dick Enberg Award. Page holds honorary doctorates from the University of Notre Dame (1993); St. John's University (1994); Westfield State College (1994); Luther College (1995); the University of New Haven (1999); and Winston-Salem State University (2000).

★

Page gave a speech, "Violence in Sports," about student athletes and education rather than violence in sports at Westminster Town Hall, Minneapolis, Minnesota, on 25 Feb. 1982; the tape is available at the Minneapolis Public Library. He is discussed in

Jim Klobuchar with Jeff Siemon, *Will the Vikings Ever Win the Superbowl?* (1977); Klobuchar and Fran Tarkenton, *Tarkenton* (1977); Klobuchar, *Purple Hearts and Golden Memories: 35 Years with the Minnesota Vikings* (1995); and Sid Hartman with Patrick Reusse, *Sid! The Sports Legend, the Inside Scoops, and the Close Personal Friends* (1997). See also Steve Rusdhin, "Thanks, Your Honor," *Sports Illustrated* (31 July 2000).

JOHN L. SCHERER

PAIGE, Leroy Robert ("Satchel") (*b.* 7 July 1906 in Mobile, Alabama; *d.* 8 June 1982 in Kansas City, Missouri), baseball pitcher from the 1920s to 1967 who is considered to be one of the greatest players of the Negro Leagues.

Paige's parents were John Paige, a gardener, and Lulu Paige, a washerwoman. He and his ten siblings grew up poor. When Paige was twelve he was caught stealing, so from 1918 to 1924 he attended the Industrial School for Negro Children in Mount Meiss, Alabama, where he developed an interest in baseball. His nickname might be derived from his attempt to steal a suitcase, which was one of several brushes he had with the law at a young age.

Satchel Paige. ASSOCIATED PRESS AP

After leaving school, Paige pitched for the semiprofessional Mobile Tigers before he signed a contract with the Chattanooga Black Lookouts in 1925. Between 1926 and his entry into the major leagues in 1948 (he was only the seventh black player recruited), Paige played for ten Negro National League teams and also played in the Dominican Republic and Mexico. In 1935 he pitched for a white semiprofessional team in Bismarck, North Dakota, and in 1939 for a team he formed called "Satchel Paige's All Stars." When the regular season ended, Paige made barnstorm tours, playing irregularly for many teams.

Paige's frequent career moves stemmed from his dealings with exceedingly frugal club owners who outdid major league team owners in their zest for frugality. Although these frequent moves may make it seem as if Paige was obsessed with money, in the context of Negro League economics, he did what he had to do to capitalize on his talent and popularity. Paige had no agent or players association to rely on; he had to make his own deals.

From 1927 to 1934 Satchel compiled 101 wins versus only 30 losses in Negro League season play. Just as spectacular was his pitching in the annual East-West All-Star games, which sold out stadiums like Comiskey Park in Chicago. During this period his most memorable performance was a 1–1 ten-inning tie, pitching against Slim Jones in Yankee Stadium. Paige's flamboyant personality enhanced his popularity. He gave his unique pitches names like the "bee ball," "jump ball," "trouble ball," and "long ball." In 1934 he married Janet Howard. They divorced two years later.

In 1939 Paige joined the Kansas City Monarchs, a team that he would play for off and on until 1955. At the time Kansas City was a mecca of opportunity for African Americans. It boasted both a professional class of doctors, lawyers, dentists, and journalists and a growing group of entrepreneurs, including the first African-American automobile dealer in the United States. With no white major league team to compete with, the Monarchs consistently drew large crowds. From 1939 to 1942 it dominated Negro League play, winning four straight Negro League World Series titles, including a sweep of the Homestead Grays in the 1942 competition. In 1943 many key Monarchs, not including Paige, were drafted into service in World War II, and the team did not experience its former glory again until 1946, when it returned to the Negro League World Series. In 1947 Paige married Lahoma Jean Brown. They had four children.

Black sportswriters, who were passionate advocates for the integration of Major League Baseball, frequently criticized Paige, believing that he preferred to retain his high-salaried position in the Negro League rather than risk an attempt to pitch in the major leagues. Negro league players tended to be more interested in their own careers than in larger social issues. Paige was not optimistic that integration of Major League Baseball could be achieved, and speculated whether any major league team would pay him the $31,000 a year he claimed to be making in the Negro League. The endless salary disputes Paige engaged in with owners also drew the wrath of black sportswriters. They believed ballplayers needed to be ambassadors to white Americans and refrain from any selfish or disruptive conduct. Paige was criticized for forming his All-Star team in 1939 and for threatening to boycott the East-West All-Star game in 1944 unless the proceeds were donated to charity, a move that one African-American sportswriter believed revealed Paige to be little more than a pawn of the Jewish owner of one of the Negro League teams.

Coverage of Paige in the white press was more positive, although it relied on racial stereotypes. In a 1941 *Life* magazine article, Paige comes across as a happy-go-lucky, talented but undisciplined athlete who is much more interested in showmanship than in wins and losses. There is no mention of the Negro League or any other black ballplayer, although Dizzy Dean and Joe DiMaggio pay tribute to Paige. One picture stands out. It shows Paige striding down a street with several worshipful youngsters following him and a caption noting that Paige ranked with Joe Louis and "Bojangles" Bill Robinson as a role model for black youth.

Paige's career statistics remain elusive. Negro League game scores made only sporadic appearances in print. Seasons were punctuated by frequent barnstorming tours against semiprofessional teams. Paige's stints in foreign competition, winter leagues, and the 160 games he reportedly pitched for a semiprofessional team in North Dakota are a nightmare for statisticians.

Paige's reputation is mostly a result of his performances during exhibition games against teams composed of white major league players. He got to pitch against all-time greats like Dizzy Dean and Bob Feller, and Hall of Fame hitters like Joe DiMaggio. DiMaggio claimed that Paige was the greatest pitcher he ever saw, and Dizzy Dean was equally generous with his praise. Unfortunately for Paige, his chance to compete regularly in the major leagues did not arrive until the late 1940s, when he was far past his pitching prime. But despite his age, Paige turned in some remarkable performances for the Cleveland Indians and the Saint Louis Browns from 1948 to 1953. He returned to pitch for the Kansas City Athletics in 1965 when he was fifty-nine years old and ended his playing days with the Indianapolis Clowns in 1967.

Stories about Paige abound. Paige relished his showdowns with Josh Gibson, who was a feared Negro League hitter. Paige would tell Gibson what pitch he planned to throw and would still strike Gibson out. During exhibition games, Paige would walk the bases, call his outfielders to the infield, and then proceed to strike out the next three batters. When a rookie catcher did not show Paige the respect he demanded, Paige threw a warm-up pitch so hard that it knocked off both mitt and mask.

In 1971 Paige was inducted into the Baseball Hall of Fame in Cooperstown, New York. Eleven years later, he died of a heart attack while at home in Kansas City and was buried in Forest Hills Cemetery. Paige claimed to have pitched over 2,000 games during his five-decade career and gave himself credit for 300 shutouts and 55 no-hitters. Unfortunately, there is no way to verify or deny his claims. He endures as a legend, though the man behind the legend remains as difficult to pin down as his pitches were to hit.

★

Paige's two autobiographies are titled *Pitchin' Man: Satchel Paige's Own Story* (1948) and *Maybe I'll Pitch Forever: A Great Baseball Player Tells the Hilarious Story Behind the Legend* (1962). For information on Paige's life and career with the Negro Leagues, see Mark Ribowsky, *Don't Look Back: Satchel Paige in the Shadows of Baseball* (1994). Obituaries are in the *New York Times* (9 June 1982), *Ebony* (spring 1982), and *Sports Illustrated* (21 June 1982).

MICHAEL POLLEY

PALMER, Arnold Daniel ("Arnie") (*b.* 10 September 1929 in Latrobe, Pennsylvania), indomitable golf professional and sports hero who ranks among the twentieth century's most successful golfers.

Palmer was born in a small steel town fifty miles east of Pittsburgh to Milfred ("Deacon") Palmer, the golf professional and greenskeeper at Latrobe Country Club, and Doris Morrison Palmer, a homemaker. His father taught him to play golf at age five, and remained his only teacher. Attending Latrobe High School, Palmer was the star of its golf team, losing only one match in four years, and winning three Western Pennsylvania junior championships and three Western Pennsylvania Amateur titles.

From 1947 to 1950 Palmer attended Wake Forest College (now Wake Forest University) in North Carolina, where he became a golf star, winning twenty-four amateur titles, including the 1954 U.S. Amateur Championship, before turning professional. His studies were interrupted by service in the U.S. Coast Guard from 1950 to 1953, but he then returned to Wake Forest. Golf interfered with school, however, and he did not receive his degree until 1970, when Wake Forest gave him an honorary LL.D. In September 1954, shortly after winning the National Amateur, Palmer met his future wife, Winifred ("Winnie") Walzer of Allen-

Arnold Palmer, 2000. ASSOCIATED PRESS AP

town, Pennsylvania. They were married on 20 December 1954; the couple eventually had two daughters.

Palmer won his first tour tournament as a professional in 1955, the Canadian Open, with a 265, the second-lowest score recorded in the tournament's forty-six-year history. From 1955 to 1973 he won sixty Professional Golfers Association (PGA) tournaments, including seven majors: four Masters championships (1958, 1960, 1962, and 1964), two British Opens (1961 and 1962), and one U.S. Open (1960). Between 1980 and 1988 he won ten tournaments on the Senior PGA Tour. He played on six Ryder Cup teams (1961, 1963, 1965, 1967, 1971, and 1973), accumulating a 22–8–2 record, and captained the team in 1973 and 1975. He was the PGA Player of the Year in 1960 and 1962, and won the Vardon Trophy for lowest score average in 1961, 1962, 1964, and 1967.

In 1960, having won the Masters and the U.S. Open, Palmer became the first top American player since Hogan to play in the British Open. It was a self-conscious (and ultimately successful) effort to restore that tournament to its status as a major, and the Old Course at Saint Andrews, in Scotland, as golf's premier arena. "I always felt this was a championship you had to play to be the complete professional," Palmer said of his decision. In honor of these achievements, he was proclaimed Hickok Athlete of the Year, and *Sports Illustrated* Sportsman of the Year.

Palmer, a man of many interests and hobbies, was one of the first postwar professionals to become seriously involved with golf course architecture, and worked as a design consultant with golf architect Frank Duane from 1969 to 1974. In 1975, with architect Edwin Seay, he established the Florida-based Palmer Course Design Company. Palmer's company built courses throughout the United States as well as in Italy, Australia, Ireland, Japan, Korea, Malaysia, and, in 1984, the first golf course in the People's Republic of China.

Palmer ranks among the twentieth century's most successful golfers. Long off the tee and a great putter, his charisma and dramatic playing style made him one of America's most popular sports heroes. Some insist that he saved the game while others say that he merely changed it for the better. But all agree that by playing golf as he did, he altered its character, its reputation, and its economics. Millions became fans because they liked to watch this handsome, likeable five-foot, eleven-inch, 175-pound man attack a golf ball. Palmer was the "King," an athlete who came closer than any other to approaching a "fleshy apotheosis," as one sports columnist wrote in 1962. At the end of the century, Tiger Woods emulated Palmer's role as golf-superhero, but the second coming was not as important to the sport as the first.

Before Palmer arrived on the scene, golf fans generally viewed tournaments as aficionados of the game. Of course, everyone had a favorite player, and quite naturally, the most favored were the best. But as Palmer rose to prominence his personality, charm, and his aggressive style of play turned mobs of golf fans into irrational Palmer partisans, a horde that at times proved nearly uncontrollable in their enthusiasms. They were "Arnie's Army," cheering his every move, screaming "Charge!" as he drove to overtake a leader in the final round of a tournament. He did that gloriously and unforgettably in the 1960 U.S. Open at Cherry Hills in Denver, when he began the final round by driving the 346-yard first green, and then charging from seven shots down to beat Ben Hogan and Jack Nicklaus. "He gave birth to excitement in the game," Nicklaus remarked.

Palmer's golf swing was unique, combining the violence of a hockey player's slap shot with a power batter's follow-through. The club head was not swung through the ball so much as smashed through it. It was not pretty to watch, but the results were awesome to witness. That so many of those drives landed well outside the fairway simply increased the excitement. More often than not, certainly during his peak years from 1958 to 1964, Palmer blasted his way through weeds and woods onto the green. Once there, he was home. "If I ever had an eight-foot putt, and everything I owned depended upon it," the legendary Bobby Jones once quipped, "I'd want Arnold Palmer to take it for me." Palmer's concentration was total, his desire to win was palpable, and his disappoints were agonizing. He shared all his emotions with his fans, and they gave him their love. He was the charismatic hero incarnate. Palmer's fans loved to see him win, and they hated anyone who made him lose, especially Jack Nicklaus, who in beating Palmer in an eighteen-hole playoff to win the 1961 U.S. Open at Oakmont, began his steady climb to edge the "King" off his throne.

Palmer's personal presence, and the business acumen of his manager Mark McCormack, CEO of International Management Group (eventually the most powerful agency in sports), helped to lay the economic and cultural foundation for professional golf as it is played today. Palmer was the first millionaire PGA tour player and the first golf professional wealthy enough to own (and pilot) an airplane. However, his tournament earnings were small compared to the income he made from endorsements, exhibitions, corporate associations, and numerous business ventures. A prolific writer, Palmer wrote numerous books on the game of golf, including *Arnold Palmer's Golf Book: Hit It Hard!* (1961); *My Game and Yours* (1965, rev. 1983); *Situation Golf* (1970); *Go for Broke* (1973), with William Barry Furlong; *Arnold Palmer's Best 54 Golf Holes* (1977); *Arnold Palmer's Complete Book of Putting* (1986) with Peter Dobereiner; and *Play Great Golf* (1987).

In the sociology of mass hero worship, whether in sports or politics, the hero must find a means of communicating with his followers. President Franklin D. Roosevelt turned to radio fireside chats to assure Americans that the Great Depression would be conquered, and Arnold Palmer played golf under the watchful lenses of television cameras. No other sports figure of the 1960s was as photogenic, attractive, and as approachable as Palmer. That his play and his personality could be projected visually to millions, and that he knew how to capitalize on his popularity, changed how golf was viewed, and how golfers (and in years to come other athletes) were paid. "Palmer is a legend," former President George H. W. Bush said in 1996. "If you compared him to politicians, he'd be a Winston Churchill."

★

Autobiographies of Palmer include *Portrait of a Professional Golfer* (1964); *Arnold Palmer: A Personal Journey* (1994), with Thomas Hauser; and *A Golfer's Life* (1999), with James Dodson. Biographies include M. H. McCormack, *Arnie* (1967), and F. Bisher, *The Birth of a Legend: Arnold Palmer's Golden Year* (1972). Palmer's career is covered in Nick Seitz, *Superstars of Golf* (1978); Will Grimsley, ed., *The Sports Immortals* (1972); and Robert J. Condon, *The Fifty Finest Athletes of the 20th Century* (1990). Articles with information about Palmer are Rick Reilly, "Arnold Palmer," *Sports Illustrated* (19 Sept. 1994); and Larry Dorman, "An Army Bids Palmer One Last Cheerio at Open," *New York Times Biographical Service* (July 1995).

MARTIN SHERWIN

PALMER, James Alvin ("Jim") (*b.* 15 October 1945 in New York City), baseball player for the Baltimore Orioles, three-time Cy Young Award winner, and one of the dominant pitchers of the 1970s.

Palmer was placed up for adoption at birth and never knew his natural parents; he was adopted two days later by Moe Wiesen, a Jewish dress manufacturer, and his Roman Catholic wife, Polly Kiger, the owner of a boutique. Palmer had one sister, who was also adopted. As Jim Wiesen, he lived first in a Park Avenue apartment in Manhattan and then in Westchester County, where he attended schools in Rye and White Plains, New York, and learned to pitch with a family butler as his catcher. But his life changed when his father died of a heart attack in 1954.

The family moved to California where, after a brief period in Whittier, they settled in Beverly Hills, where Polly Wiesen married Max Palmer, a television actor who also managed the bars at the Hollywood Park and Santa Anita racetracks. In 1959 the family moved to Scottsdale, Arizona, where Palmer attended Scottsdale High School and was All-State in baseball, football, and basketball. He was so good at basketball that the University of California at Los Angeles offered him a scholarship, but his first love was baseball. He played several infield and outfield positions in

Jim Palmer, 1970. ASSOCIATED PRESS AP

addition to pitching and was an outstanding hitter until his senior year, 1963, when he developed an astigmatism in his left eye, a problem that made his decision to become a full-time pitcher much easier.

Palmer was playing in the amateur Basin League in Winner, South Dakota, when Harry Dalton, the personnel director of the Baltimore Orioles, signed him to a contract with an estimated bonus of $50,000 in August 1963. He attended Arizona State University in Tempe in the fall of 1963, and then studied briefly at Towson State College in Maryland in early 1964, but in the spring of that year he joined the Aberdeen (South Dakota) Pheasants, an Orioles farm team, where he finished the season with an 11–3 record. On 25 February 1964 he married his high-school sweetheart, Susan Ryan; they later had two daughters.

In 1965 Palmer joined the Orioles, appearing in twenty-seven games in relief, and in 1966, as a starter, Palmer led the team with fifteen wins. He proved his dominance in important games by winning the pennant-clinching games in Baltimore's first four post-1900 World Series appearances. In the 1966 World Series, he became the youngest player, at age twenty, to pitch a complete game shutout—his first in major league competition—against Sandy Koufax of the Los Angeles Dodgers, leading the Orioles to their first world championship. Overall he was 8–3 in postseason play and, in 1983, became the only pitcher to win a World Series game in three different decades.

A sore arm and back forced Palmer back to the minors for most of 1967 and all of 1968 until doctors diagnosed the problem: Palmer was vulnerable to back problems because his left leg was noticeably shorter than his right. With a specially padded shoe, he returned to form in 1969, winning sixteen games and pitching in his second World Series. In 1968 Palmer began a contentious battle with the new Orioles manager Earl Weaver. Palmer, who also had a reputation for combativeness with umpires, feuded openly with Weaver when he felt the manager did not take his injuries seriously or tried too specifically to tell him how to pitch. Yet, they were able to work together.

Between 1970 and 1978 Palmer won at least twenty games each year, excluding 1974, when a pinched nerve in his elbow handicapped him for most of the season. He was selected to the American League All-Star team six times (1970–1972, 1975, 1977, 1978). Incredibly, he was not selected for the team in 1976, even though he had the best record in the league. The Baseball Writers of America awarded him the Cy Young Award as the outstanding pitcher in 1973, 1975, and 1976, the same years that the *Sporting News* named him the American League Pitcher of the Year.

Injuries limited Palmer to just twenty-two starts and ten wins in 1979 and sixteen wins in 1980. He bounced back in 1982 with a 15–5 record, eleven of them coming in a row, but by May 1983 he realized that his career was coming to an end. He relieved in the third game of the 1983 World Series and won his last postseason game. After a 0–3 start in 1984, he pitched his last professional game on 12 May. There was talk of an attempted comeback in 1991, but it never materialized.

Handsome and urbane, Palmer began a second career, even while he was playing, as a corporate spokesman for the Money Store and as a model for Jockey Shorts. By the late 1990s he was hosting his own regional talk show and providing color commentary on radio and television for Baltimore Orioles games. After his retirement as a professional player Palmer also gave motivational speeches and served as a spokesman and the national sports chairman for the Cystic Fibrosis Research Foundation.

From his early days as one of the "baby birds" of the Orioles staff until the end of his career, Palmer proved to be one of the most reliable pitchers in the majors. He was one of only 18 pitchers to win 20 games or more in each of 8 seasons and finished his career in the top 30 pitchers of all time in wins, winning percentage, games started, and shutouts. From 1961 to 1980 his lifetime earned run average of 2.86 placed him second only to Koufax. The fourth edition of the official encyclopedia of Major League Baseball, *Total Baseball,* named him as one of the top one hundred players in the game, and his career concluded with his election to the Baseball Hall of Fame in 1990.

★

There are numerous sources covering Palmer's life and career, starting with two books written by Palmer with Joel H. Cohen, *Pitching* (1975), a how-to book, and *Jim Palmer: Great Comeback Competitor* (1978). Also see Palmer and Jim Dale, *Together We Were Eleven Foot Nine: The Twenty-year Friendship of Hall of Fame Pitcher Jim Palmer and Orioles Manager Earl Weaver* (1996). There is a chapter on Palmer in Hal Butler, *Baseball's Champion Pitchers* (1974), as well as entries about him in *Who's Who in Baseball* (1978), *Who's Who in America* (1978–1979), *Current Biography* (1980), and *Total Baseball* (1995).

PATRICK A. TRIMBLE

PARCELLS, Duane Charles ("Bill") (*b.* 22 August 1941 in Englewood, New Jersey), highly successful professional football coach who led both the New York Giants and the New England Patriots to the Super Bowl.

Son of labor negotiator and former FBI agent Charles Parcells and homemaker Ida Naclerio Parcells, Parcells was born in Englewood but grew up in nearby Hasbrouck Heights and Oradell. He came by the nickname "Bill" quite by accident. Repeatedly mistaken for a look-alike named Bill, he came to prefer to prefer that moniker to

Duane and soon asked that all his friends call him Bill. A star in baseball, basketball, and football, he was a member of the first graduating class at Oradell's River Dell High School in 1959. Attending college, Parcells played football first at Colgate University and later at Wichita State University, from which he graduated in 1963. Although he played quarterback during his high school football career, he switched to linebacker while in college.

Parcells kicked off his coaching career in 1964 when he took a job as assistant defensive coach at Hastings College, but a year later he returned to his alma mater—Wichita State—as a defensive line coach. In 1966 he headed back to the East Coast for a coaching job at West Point. Before landing his first head coach job at the Air Force Academy in 1978, Parcells had also put in time on the coaching staffs at Florida State University, Vanderbilt, and Texas Tech.

Only a year after winning the head coach job at the Air Force Academy, Parcells made it to the big time when he joined the New York Giants organization as an assistant to head coach Ray Perkins. A year later he left the Giants for a season as linebacker coach for the New England Patriots, but soon was back with the Giants as defensive coordinator and linebacker coach. In 1983 he took over as head coach of the Giants. In his first year as coach, Parcells concentrated on reorganizing the team and building a powerful defensive force centered on linebacker Lawrence Taylor. His preoccupation with building for the future was reflected in the team's miserable record for the year—three wins, twelve losses, and one draw.

The following season the Giants won nine games, and it got better from there. Over the next six years Parcells coached the Giants to three division titles and two Super Bowl victories. Shortly after the Giants 20–19 victory over the Buffalo Bills in Super Bowl XXV in 1991, Parcells began seriously considering job offers from other teams. In the end, however, concerns about his health took him away from football for a couple of years. After undergoing cardiac bypass surgery, he worked for two years as a sports analyst for the National Broadcasting System (NBC).

Once he got the green light from his doctors, Parcells headed back to coaching, hiring on in 1993 as head coach of the New England Patriots, who in the previous season had turned in a disastrous record of 2–14. In no time at all Parcells had turned things around, coaching the team into the playoffs two years after taking over. In his fourth season as coach the Patriots played in Super Bowl XXXI, where they lost to the Green Bay Packers 35–21. Only Don Shula before him had managed to lead two separate National Football League (NFL) teams to the Super Bowl. Parcells was clearly at the top of his game but unhappy with his boss, Robert Kraft, owner of the Patriots. By the summer of 1997 Parcells had been offered the position of head coach and general manager with the New York Jets, but Kraft

Bill Parcells, 1997. ASSOCIATED PRESS AP

and the Patriots were not prepared to let him go without a fight. Claiming breach of contract, they fought to block Parcells from joining the Jets, but eventually a compromise agreement was hammered out, allowing Parcells to take the job and giving the Patriots several draft picks.

For Parcells the job with the Jets represented a homecoming. Home field for the Jets was the Meadowlands in New Jersey, only a stone's throw from where Parcells had grown up. In taking the job, Parcells told the press, "There is something special about doing your job where you grew up, where you're comfortable, and where you have great support." He quickly transformed the Jets—who had records of 3–13 and 1–15 in their two previous seasons—into winners again. In 1997, his first year as coach, he turned in a record of 9–7. In 1998 the Jets advanced to the American Football Conference (AFC) championship game on a record of 12–4, adding further luster to Parcells's reputation as a first-rate coach.

In January 2000 Parcells decided to bow out of coaching while still at the top of his game. He agreed, however, to stay on as the Jets director of football operations. Some observers expressed doubt that Parcells would be able to remain away from football. Of the game's powerful hold on him, Parcells surely explained it best when he told *Sporting News:* "It's like a narcotic. It's hard to get it out of your system sometimes. But I've been at it a long time, and I feel there's a chance I'll get it out of my system."

Parcells and his wife, Judith, live in New Jersey with their three daughters. In addition to his duties with the Jets, Parcells has signed on with Joe Montana, former quarterback of the San Francisco 49ers, to coach a heart health campaign developed jointly by the NFL and Merck and Company. The NFL Cholesterol Screen Team will educate fans about the dangers of high cholesterol and encourage them to get tested regularly.

Parcells was one of the most influential forces in professional football during the final decades of the twentieth century. The philosophy by which he lived—and instilled in the players he coached—is simple, as he told *Sports Illustrated:* "You are what you are. You get exactly what you deserve in this game."

Noted for an uncanny ability to coax the very best from the players he coached, Parcells proved his effectiveness by taking two of the three NFL teams he coached to the Super Bowl. And he came breathtakingly close to making it three when he led the New York Jets to the AFC title game in 1998.

★

In *Parcells: Autobiography of the Biggest Giant of Them All* (1987), written with sportswriter Mike Lupica, the coach recounts his life in football from his school days through the New York Giants triumph in Super Bowl XXI. Parcells updates his life story, taking readers through his years as coach of the New York Jets, in *The Final Season: My Last Year as Head Coach in the NFL* (2000), written with Will McDonough. Another view of Parcells's contribution to professional football can be found in *Parcells: A Biography* (2000), written by Bill Gutman and Bill Pronzini. See also Bob Glauber, "Draft Gaffes Put Strain on Parcells-Grier Alliance," *Sporting News* (26 Aug. 1996); Bill Plashke, "Getting It Done—His Way," *Sporting News* (27 Oct. 1997); and Jack MacCallum, "A Hard Man for a Hard Job," *Sporting News* (14 Dec. 1998).

DON AMERMAN

PARENT, Bernard Marcel ("Bernie") (*b.* 3 April 1945 in Long Pointe, Quebec, near Montreal, Canada), one of the best goaltenders in the history of the National Hockey League (NHL) and inductee of the Hockey Hall of Fame.

It would have been impossible for the Philadelphia Flyers to attain one Stanley Cup, let alone two straight championships, without Bernie Parent. If he was not the greatest goaltender in NHL history, Parent certainly was the very best in the early and mid-1970s, when Philadelphia's Broad Street, a main thoroughfare, was the hub of a pair of championship parades. While the team's captain, Bobby Clarke, supplied the heart, and the center Rick MacLeish furnished the pivotal goals, neither of those meaningful assets could have produced a title without the virtually airtight goaltending of Parent. A disciple of the immortal Canadian goalie Jacques Plante, Parent was an original Flyer. Drafted from the Boston Bruins organization in 1967, he already had been touted as a future star and became the first player to join Philadelphia in the NHL's first expansion year. (The NHL expanded several times, beginning with the 1967–1968 season, when it doubled from the "original six" to twelve teams.) The Flyers were fortunate, because Boston had two fine goaltenders to choose between: Parent and the veteran Gerry Cheevers. When the Bruins opted for Cheevers, Parent was left unprotected in the draft, and Philadelphia snatched him.

When Parent reported to training camp in 1967, he competed for the top goaltending job with the equally young Doug Favell, whose acrobatic style starkly contrasted with Parent's classic standup puck stopping. The Favell-Parent duo paced the Flyers to first place in the NHL's expansion division, while Parent turned in an impressive record of 2.48 goals against average and 4 shutouts. Reaching the top was not easy. Parent was a worrier, but with the encouragement of a fellow teammate, the veteran Larry Zeidel, he overcame his jitters. After a 4–1 win against the Montreal Canadiens early in the first season, Parent came away with a new outlook on life. That game was a turning point for his career. Slowly but relentlessly he established himself as Philadelphia's premier goalie. During the 1969–1970 season, Parent posted 2.79 goals against average in sixty-two games, but the Flyers had trouble scoring goals in those early years. To remedy the problem, they traded Parent midway through the 1970–1971 season to the Toronto Maple Leafs for center Mike Walton and goaltender Bruce Gamble.

Parent was shocked and disappointed. He had established firm roots in Philadelphia and was a favorite with the fans. That was the bad news. The good news was that Parent ended up playing alongside his boyhood idol, Jacques Plante. It was the best thing that could have happened to Parent. He honed his goaltending style to sharpness under the tutelage of Plante and, in the 1971–1972 season, lowered his goals against average to 2.56. In 1972 a rival major league, the World Hockey Association (WHA), was launched, and a team in Miami known as the Screaming Eagles was awarded a franchise. The Eagles persuaded Parent to sign for the inaugural 1972–1973 season, but before the first puck was dropped the Florida franchise dissolved. Parent found himself playing for the WHA's Philadelphia Blazers. That season he played fifty-seven consecutive games out of a total of sixty-three nonconsecutive games, and chalked up thirty-three victories, the most in the WHA. After just one season, however, it

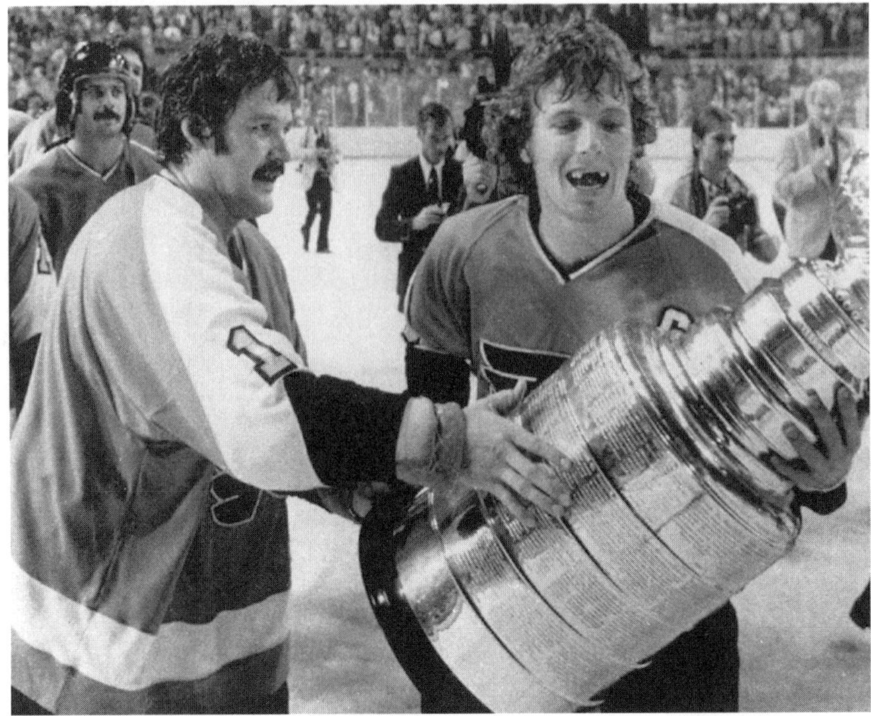

Bernie Parent *(left)* and Bobby Clark of the Philadelphia Flyers after winning the Stanley Cup, 1975. Associated Press AP

was apparent that the Blazers were a second-rate operation, and they were dissolved as a Philadelphia WHA team. When the Flyers' owner Ed Snider suggested that Parent return, he was quick to agree.

"I never wanted to leave in the first place," said Parent as he signed a multiyear contract with the Flyers on 22 June 1973. "Now that I'm back, I couldn't be happier. I've always considered myself a Flyer." Parent was welcomed by his teammates. "Bernie," said the Flyers' Bobby Clarke, "is the most valuable player in all of hockey." Parent certainly bolstered his reputation during the 1973–1974 season. Playing in 73 of 78 games—more than any other NHL goalie that season—Parent produced a dazzling 1.89 goals against average, the best score in the NHL. Up to that time an expansion team had never won a Stanley Cup, but the Flyers were driven by Coach Fred Shero, by Clarke at center, and by Parent's goaltending. This winning combination took them to the finals against the Bruins, who had won championships in 1970 and 1972 and were led by the superstars Bobby Orr and Phil Esposito. Philadelphia took a lead of 3 games to 2 going into the sixth game of the series, whereupon Parent blanked the Bruins, 1–0. The Flyers had their first Stanley Cup, and Parent won the Conn Smythe Trophy as the Most Valuable Player in the playoffs.

Perhaps Parent's most decisive moment in his bid to win over the demanding Flyers fans occurred on opening night in 1973. Philadelphia was facing the Toronto Maple Leafs, Parent's former team. Parent shut them out, allowing the Flyers to win by a score of 2–0. He had a total of twelve shutouts that season, just three shy of a league record. Parent was looking more and more like a vintage Plante every night. Whenever he would slump, he would recall the advice of the old master. "We had pretty much the same styles," said Parent. "I watched everything he did, how he handled himself on shots, and whatever he was doing, I tried to do."

Parent's finest hour was reserved for 19 May 1974, when the Flyers beat Boston for the Stanley Cup, a feat duplicated the following year against the Buffalo Sabres. Unfortunately for Parent, his 1975 Stanley Cup–winning experience would be his last. He missed most of the 1975–1976 season because of back surgery and was never quite as sharp afterward, although he performed brilliantly in the 1978 playoffs. In 1979 his career came to a sudden end. During a game against the New York Rangers on 17 February 1979, the Flyers defenseman Jimmy Watson was attempting to clear an opponent away from the net. Watson's stick blade pierced Parent's mask, permanently damaging the goaltender's right eye. Parent's career ended after just thirty-six games of the season. In 1982 Parent became the Flyers' goaltending coach, a position he held until 1994. Parent had two sons and a daughter with his wife, Carol. In 1994, Parent became vice president for Rassanaio-Baillet-Talamo, a marketing firm in Cherry Hill, New Jersey.

Parent's credentials were more impressive than those of

any goaltender who wore the Flyers' orange and black. He finished his ten-year Philadelphia career with a goals against average of 2.42 and an overall record of 232 wins, 141 losses, and 103 ties, including an amazing 50 shutouts. His playoff numbers were equally impressive: a 35–28 record of wins and losses, supported by 2.38 goals against average and 6 shutouts. The Flyers retired Parent's goaltender jersey number in 1979. Parent was a classic, from style to performance. In 1984, he was inducted into the Hockey Hall of Fame.

★

Parent's autobiography, written with Bill Fleischman and Sonny Schwartz, is *Bernie!* (1975). See also Jay Greenberg, *Free Spectrum: The Complete History of the Philadelphia Flyers Hockey Club* (1996), and Stan Fischler, *The Greatest Players and Moments of the Philadelphia Flyers* (1998). For further information on Parent see James Duplacey, Joseph Romain, Stan Fischler, Morgan Hughes, and Shirley Fischler, *Twentieth-Century Hockey Chronicle* (1999), and Dan Diamond, *Total Hockey: The Official Encyclopedia of the National Hockey League,* 2d ed. (2000).

STAN FISCHLER

Jim Parker, 1959. ASSOCIATED PRESS FILES

PARKER, James Thomas ("Jim") (*b.* 3 April 1934 in Macon, Georgia), football player who was the prototype of the modern offensive lineman and who was All-Pro at both offensive tackle and offensive guard, becoming the first exclusively offensive lineman to be elected to the Pro Football Hall of Fame (1973).

Parker was a good high school football player, but he was not regarded as a great one. He played for three years in Macon, but played his senior year at Scott High School in Toledo, Ohio. The move was fortuitous, because in Ohio he caught the eye of Woody Hayes, the fabled coach for Ohio State University. Parker remembered being very surprised when he was offered a scholarship to attend Ohio State in Columbus. Hayes saw something special in Parker and made a point of helping the young man. During Parker's freshman year, he lived in Hayes's home.

In college Parker played on both the offensive line and the defensive line. He came to national attention in 1955, when his ferocious blocking opened big lanes for his team's running backs in a 17–0 victory over the heavily favored University of Michigan. Already 250 pounds, Parker added speed and high intelligence to his play, overwhelming the defensive linemen who faced him. In 1956 journalists paid attention to him, and he became an All-American at offensive guard. That year he won the Outland Trophy, an award given to the nation's outstanding college football lineman.

In 1957 he was drafted in the first round, the eighth pick overall, by the Baltimore Colts of the National Football League (NFL). Hayes told the Colts that he thought Parker was stronger on defense than offense, but the Colts' head coach Weeb Ewbank put Parker in as offensive tackle from the start. At 275 pounds and six feet, three inches tall, Parker was a big lineman for his era, presaging the big, agile linemen who came to be preferred in modern football. In his first exhibition game, playing against the Chicago Bears, he faced the veteran Doug Atkins, who at 275 pounds and six feet, eight inches tall was every bit as intimidating as Parker. Atkins swatted Parker around that day, beginning a hard-fought rivalry that lasted for the next eleven seasons. For Parker, that first exhibition game was a lesson in the standard he had to meet in order to succeed in the NFL.

During the regular season, placing Parker at left offensive tackle began paying off for the Colts right away. The position was crucial for the Colts, to protect their great right-handed quarterback, Johnny Unitas. For a right-handed passer, the area to his left is a blind spot, which means a defender can approach him from the left side, hitting him while he is entirely unaware of what is happening. Parker was told that a sure way to have everyone in his clubhouse hate him was to let a defender hit Unitas from that blind side. It was a sign of Ewbank's confidence in him that Parker was stationed at left tackle.

Both Hayes and Ewbank were sticklers for good technique, and with their help Parker mastered the footwork required to move in front of opposing defensive ends. The defensive ends tended to be smaller than Parker, as did most players, but they were quick footed; as a big man, Parker found it challenging to keep up with such men, but he did because of his mastery of footwork and blocking technique. Parker's skills began to reshape coaches' ideas of the sort of athlete best suited to being an offensive lineman. Parker was a big slab of determined muscle, quickly meeting the moves of pass rushers. Even more innovatively, he was aggressive; sometimes he did not just get in the way of rushers, he knocked them down.

It is no wonder Hayes thought Parker might fit into the NFL as a defensive lineman; by the techniques of the day, he played offense as if he were on defense when running plays were called. Blockers in the 1950s typically were expected to shove opposing linemen to one side or the other, depending on where the runner was supposed to go, but Parker charged his opponents, often blasting them back several feet and taking out a linebacker or two for good measure. When in 1958 the Colts came back from a 27–7 halftime deficit to defeat the San Francisco 49ers, 35–27, Parker's explosive blocking, as well as Unitas's passing, helped to wear out San Francisco's defense and open the way for victory. Veterans of that Colts team insisted that the game against the 49ers was greater than the championship game they then played at Yankee Stadium against the New York Giants, even though the later game has been called the greatest game in professional football history. In that game Parker shone, first protecting Unitas as the quarterback passed for two late scores, and then opening holes for the running backs who finished off the Giants in the NFL's first overtime game, 23–17.

Parker was an All-Pro tackle, playing in the Pro Bowl from 1958 to 1961. In the middle of the 1962 season, he was switched from left offensive tackle to left offensive guard. He liked that position, although it wore out his legs because of all the pulling off the line. The defensive tackles he faced were bigger and slower than defensive ends, making them good targets for his aggressive style of play. Alertness and quickness were essential at offensive guard, and Parker had both. Instead of waiting for the defensive tackle to make his move, Parker would hammer chest-to-chest into him, driving him backward and off balance. From 1962 to 1965 Parker was an All-Pro guard, playing in the Pro Bowl. From 1957 to 1966 he did not miss a game. Then in 1967 he was injured, and by midseason he was not playing up to his own standards. Even though the Colts were undefeated at the time, Parker retired in December 1967, saying he believed he would hurt his team's chances if he continued to play.

In 1973, in his first year of eligibility, "Big Jim" Parker became the first full-time offensive lineman to be enshrined in the Pro Football Hall of Fame. He was praised at the time as a selfless player and a compassionate man, and he is remembered for his legacy, having set the pattern for numerous offensive tackles and guards to follow.

★

It is hard to find good studies of Parker's football career, but one good place to start is Vince Bagli and Norman L. Macht, *Sundays at 2:00 with the Baltimore Colts* (1995); they devote a chapter to Parker's remarkable effect on his team's performance. George Allen with Ben Olan, *Pro Football's 100 Greatest Players: Rating the Stars of Past and Present* (1982), and Ron Smith, *The Sporting News Selects Football's 100 Greatest Players: A Celebration of the Twentieth Century's Best,* ed. Carl Moritz and John Rawlings (1999), offer perspectives on how Parker helped to shape modern football.

KIRK H. BEETZ

PATERNO, Joseph Vincent ("Joe") (*b.* 21 December 1926 in Brooklyn, New York), football coach who as of 2001 led college coaches in the number of career wins and who is perhaps best known for his belief that athletics should play a secondary role to academics in college life.

Paterno was the oldest of three surviving children of Angelo Lafayette Paterno, a law clerk, and Florence de la Salle Cafiero Paterno, a homemaker. After serving in the U.S. Army, then marrying, Angelo had taken night classes in order to earn his high school, college, and law degrees. From watching his father, Paterno learned the value of education.

Joe Paterno, 1999. ASSOCIATED PRESS AP

Paterno became an avid student at the prestigious Brooklyn Prep School, where he was president of the student council and belonged to a book discussion group. He volunteered to do extra work outside of class, most notably translating Virgil's *Aeneid* from the Latin. He also began his athletic career playing basketball and football. On Brooklyn Prep's football team he was a heady leader, entrusted with calling plays for Coach Zev Graham's no-huddle offense. During his senior season, Brooklyn Prep lost only one game. Paterno and his younger brother George were the team's stars.

Paterno graduated from high school second in his class in 1945, and was immediately drafted into the military. He served as a radio operator with the U.S. Army of Occupation in Korea. Discharged in 1946, he enrolled at Brown University, where he majored in English literature with a specialization in the Romantic Period.

Charles A. ("Rip") Engle, one of the originators of the complex wing-T formation, was Brown's football coach. Although Paterno was only five feet, eleven inches tall, and 170 pounds, and did not throw the ball well, he soon mastered the quarterback position and became adept at calling plays. When Brown was on defense, Paterno played in the secondary and set records for pass interceptions that stood over fifty years. He also returned kicks and punts. During his senior year Paterno led the team to an 8–1 record, one of the best in the school's history, and was considered one of the best signal callers in the East.

Following his graduation in 1950 Paterno planned to enroll in Boston University's law school. Engle, however, had just accepted the position of head coach at Penn State College, now Penn State University, and invited Paterno to join his staff. Engle needed help. Penn State had run the single-wing formation, but the other coaches were not experienced with the wing-T. Together, Engle and Paterno had to teach the other coaches the new offense, then help them instruct the players.

Paterno believed he would coach for only a few years in order to earn money for law school. Having grown up in New York City, he was initially unimpressed with Penn State's rural location. Soon, though, he began to enjoy his work. Penn State had an enlightened attitude toward intercollegiate athletics. Coaches were considered to be members of the faculty and socialized with them freely. National Collegiate Athletic Association (NCAA) rules on player eligibility were tightly enforced. Paterno began to find the university conducive to his intellectual and athletic interests and decided to make coaching there his permanent career.

Furthermore, the school's football team, the Nittany Lions, enjoyed success on the field. Victories over schools like Ohio State and the University of Illinois brought the team national attention. During Engle's sixteen years as head coach, Penn State won the 1959 and 1960 Liberty Bowls and 1961 Gator Bowl, and three Lambert Trophies for being the best team in the East. Paterno, whose duties expanded from just coaching the quarterbacks to being responsible for the entire offense, received much of the credit. By the early 1960s he had received and turned down several offers to coach in the National Football League.

In 1962 Paterno married Suzanne Pohland of Latrobe, Pennsylvania. They had five children, including one, Joseph Vincent (Jay) Paterno, Jr., who would later serve on his father's coaching staff.

In 1963 Yale University offered Paterno the position of head coach. Paterno was interested in the offer, but Engle told him he would soon be retiring. Paterno decided to stay at Penn State, where was promoted to the position of associate coach. Following the 1965 season, Engle stepped down and Paterno became Penn State's head coach. In his first season, the Nittany Lions finished with a 5–5 record. In the spring of 1967 Paterno created a new, complicated defense, and in 1967 season the team lost only twice and was invited to the Gator Bowl. In 1968 and 1969 the Nittany Lions finished undefeated, winning the Orange Bowl at the end of each season. This long winning streak earned Paterno the first of his four Kodak Coach of the Year Awards. It also gave him the status to speak out on intercollegiate athletics. Paterno called his approach "The Grand Experiment." Penn State, he said, would recruit only the players who could excel in the classroom. They would be expected to interact with nonathletes and to treat football as just another extracurricular activity.

Although in many ways this attitude reflected Penn State's traditional approach to athletics, Paterno's success drew more attention to the idea. He began to be considered an idealist and reformer. His rejection of a big job offer in 1973 furthered this image. Billy Sullivan, owner of the New England Patriots, wanted Paterno to be the coach of his team. He offered him a contract that would make Paterno a millionaire, and included part ownership of the franchise. Paterno initially accepted the offer but changed his mind the following morning. In explaining his decision, he said that he thought there were more important goals than winning football games and earning money. At Penn State, he had the opportunity to affect the lives of young people and to be an educator as well as a coach. Newspapers across the country wrote articles about Paterno, the coach who would turn down $1 million as a matter of principle. Paterno's stance led Penn State's seniors to choose him as their commencement speaker in 1973.

Throughout the 1970s Paterno's team continued to win. In 1973 the Nittany Lions went undefeated, and running back John Cappelletti won the Heisman Trophy (awarded annually by the Downtown Athletic Club of New York City to the player voted the best in college football), but the team finished fifth in the national polls. In 1978, after another undefeated season, Penn State lost a national championship showdown to the University of Alabama in the Sugar Bowl.

In 1980 Paterno's position within the university changed. In addition to being the head football college, he was named athletic director, a job he would hold for three years. In 1982 Penn State overcame an early season loss to win the school's first national championship in football. Following the clinching victory over the University of Georgia in the national championship game held at the Sugar Bowl, Paterno was invited to address the university's board of trustees. Most expected that he would strike a celebratory tone. Instead Paterno chastised the trustees, telling them they were not doing enough to raise outside money for the university. The football team was the nation's best, but the library and academic programs needed improvement.

Paterno's speech encouraged Penn State to undertake a major fundraising campaign, with Paterno as the vice chairman of the effort. Paterno continued with this involvement in university fundraising. In 1984 he started the Paterno Libraries Endowment. In 1997, after he donated $250,000 and campaigned for further contributions, ground was broken for the Paterno Library. In 1998 Paterno donated $3.5 million to endow faculty positions, scholarships, and building projects.

Paterno also became involved in NCAA issues. He was a major proponent of Proposition 48, a rule requiring high school athletes to achieve designated grade-point averages and scores on standardized tests before receiving scholarships, which was passed in 1983. Paterno believed that in order to win games, colleges had been admitting students who had no chance of earning degrees.

In 1986 Paterno's team won a second national championship, finishing an undefeated season by beating the University of Miami Hurricanes 14–10 in the Fiesta Bowl. In 1993 the Nittany Lions joined the Big Ten Conference. The next year Paterno's team again went undefeated and won the Rose Bowl. He is the only football coach to lead his team to perfect seasons in 1968, 1969, 1973, 1986, and 1994. On 20 October 2001, with a win over the Northwestern Wildcats, Paterno tied Paul "Bear" Bryant in career victories among major college coaches with 323. He has subsequently surpassed Bryant's record.

Paterno's record as a football coach is exemplary. He has won more major college games at a single school than any other coach. He has the record for bowl victories and has won twenty-one Lambert Trophies. His peers have voted him Coach of the Year four times, and in 1995 a coaches' poll voted his program the best in the country. At the same time, Paterno's outspoken position on academic integrity and philanthropy has brought him respect from outside the athletic community. *Sports Illustrated* named him Sportsman of the Year in 1986. In 1991 he won the National Football Foundation and College Football Hall of Fame Distinguished American Award. He holds three honorary degrees: an LL.D. from Brown University, an H.L.D. from Gettysburg College, and an LL.D. from Allegheny College. Bill Lyon, a writer for the *Philadelphia Inquirer,* wrote "even though he is enormously successful at it, from the perspective of meaningful contributions to society, the least important thing Paterno does is coach football."

★

Paterno is the subject of five biographies, Mervin D. Hyman and Gordon S. White, Jr., *Joe Paterno: Football My Way* (1971), and Joe Paterno (with Bernard Asbell), *Paterno: By the Book* (1989) are traditional sports biographies. Gene Collier, et al., *The Paterno Legacy: An Authorized Biography* (1997), is a coffee table book. George Paterno, *Joe Paterno: The Coach from Byzantium* (1997), provides the best insight into Paterno's character and personality. Michael O'Brien, *No Ordinary Joe: The Biography of Joe Paterno* (1998), is well documented, with footnotes and a full bibliography. See also William Johnson, "Not Such an Ordinary Joe," *Sports Illustrated* (Nov. 1973), and Rick Reilly, "Not an Ordinary Joe," *Sports Illustrated* (22–29 Dec. 1986).

HAROLD W. AURAND, JR.

PATRICK, (Curtis) Lester (*b.* 30 December 1883 in Drummondville, Quebec, Canada; *d.* 1 June 1960 in Victoria, British Columbia, Canada), ice hockey player, coach, manager, and team owner credited with introducing many innovations to the sport and popularizing hockey in the northeastern United States.

Of Irish descent, Patrick was the eldest of eight children of Grace Nelson, a schoolteacher, and Joe Patrick, a successful lumberman who settled in the predominantly French-speaking area of Drummondville, Quebec. Patrick's first ice skates had metal runners that attached to his shoes with a clamp. He was not exposed to ice hockey until 1893, when his family moved to Point Saint Charles, a Montreal suburb, where Patrick and friends made crude sticks out of tree branches and played on the nearby Saint Lawrence River.

A natural athlete who grew to over six feet in height, Patrick attended McGill University in Montreal for one year in 1901 to 1902 while playing varsity basketball and hockey. His hockey prowess later led to an offer of $25 per month in expenses to play for Brandon, Manitoba, in a 1903–1904 challenge for the Stanley Cup. Afterward he played for Westmount of the Canadian Amateur Hockey Association alongside the future hockey great Art Ross before joining the Montreal Wanderers in 1906; the team won two consecutive Stanley Cup championships with Patrick.

Lester Patrick. HOCKEY HALL OF FAME

In spring 1907 the Patrick family moved to Nelson, British Columbia, to establish a lumber company. Putting the family business ahead of his burgeoning hockey career, Patrick played hockey locally and joined an Edmonton team in an unsuccessful challenge for the Stanley Cup in 1908. Despite his obligations, Patrick, later known as "The Silver Fox," was lured back to eastern Canada to play for the Renfrew Millionaires for the 1909–1910 hockey season at a salary of $3,000. Following the season he returned to western Canada and married Grace Linn on 7 March 1911.

However, Patrick's goal was not to simply be a star player; he, his brother Frank, and his father entertained the idea of bringing high-caliber hockey to western Canada. In Patrick's words, "The idea was firmly planted to move to the West Coast, start a new hockey league, and pioneer Canada's first artificial ice rinks." Arenas were built in Vancouver and Victoria with proceeds from the Patrick Lumber Company, which was sold in January 1911, to host the newly formed Pacific Coast Hockey Association (PCHA). The showpiece of the Patricks' league was the 10,500-seat Denman arena in Vancouver, which featured luxury seating, a swimming pool, and fourteen sheets of ice for curling. Frank played for and operated the Vancouver team, while Patrick became the captain, coach, manager, and owner of the Victoria franchise. Players were acquired from the eastern Canadian leagues, and a coup occurred when Vancouver persuaded "Cyclone" Taylor, considered the most exciting player of that period, to join them. Both Frank and Patrick had enlisted in World War I, but were told by the Canadian government to continue operating the PCHA to provide an entertainment diversion on the home front.

During the thirteen-year existence of the PCHA, Patrick and his brother were credited with a number of important rule changes and innovations that improved the sport of hockey, including having players substitute during the course of play. They created blue lines that divided the rink into three areas, and allowed players to pass forward in the neutral area of the ice at a time when forward passing was forbidden in the sport. In addition, rule changes such as allowing goalies to leave their feet to make a save and players to kick the puck with their skates were instituted. The Patricks also introduced the modern playoff format, began awarding assists on goals to recognize playmakers on teams, and implemented one of the most exciting features of a hockey game—the penalty shot.

Even with the PCHA's innovations and its merger with the Western Canada Hockey League in 1924–1925, the smaller western markets could not compete with the East for player salaries. In the spring of 1926, the Patricks masterminded a scheme to sell player rights to the National Hockey League (NHL), where a number of new U.S.-based franchises were in need of players. In a large-scale transaction, the players' rights were sold for a total of $377,000, which was split among the western teams.

Despite the limited financial success of the PCHA, hockey magnates in the East recognized Patrick's hockey acumen, and he joined the New York Rangers as a coach on 27 October 1926. In 1928 the team reached the Stanley Cup finals against the Montreal Maroons, a series in which Patrick was involved in one of hockey's most memorable moments. The Rangers had lost the first game of the series 2–0, and in the second period of the second game the Rangers goalie, Lorne Chabot, was injured. At the time, teams did not carry extra goaltenders on their rosters. Relying on a common tactic, Patrick asked the opposing coach, Eddie Gerrard, if he could replace Chabot with a player from another team (Alex Connell of the Ottawa Senators) who happened to be in the rink. Gerrard refused, and the Rangers were in danger of losing the game by forfeit until it was suggested that the forty-four-year-old Patrick play goal himself. Despite his inexperience at the position, Patrick agreed, and the Rangers rallied around their coach, controlling much of the play through overtime. The Rangers prevailed, winning the game and eventually the cup championship, as Patrick added to his already considerable hockey resume.

The Rangers won the Stanley Cup again in 1933 and 1940. Patrick was named a first-team All-Star coach seven times between 1930 and 1938. He also coached his two sons, Lynn and Muzz, both of whom later coached the Rangers. In 1939 Patrick left coaching to become the general manager of the Rangers and the vice president of Madison Square Garden (MSG), but resigned on 22 February 1946 after seeing the team's performance slip. On 3 December 1947 Lester Patrick Night was held at MSG to honor Patrick's service to the Rangers and his induction that year into the Hockey Hall of Fame.

Patrick's involvement in the sport continued. In spring 1948 he moved to Victoria, where he operated a local hockey club. He remained in western Canada for the rest of his life. He was diagnosed with lung cancer in 1960 and died in June of that year with his sons at his bedside. He is buried in the Royal Oak Burial Park Cemetery in Victoria.

In 1966 the NHL introduced the Lester Patrick Trophy, given annually to players, officials, coaches, executives, or referees "for outstanding service to hockey in the United States." Lynn Patrick joined his father in the Hockey Hall of Fame, as did Patrick's grandson Craig, who played in the NHL and went on to a successful management career with the Rangers and the Pittsburgh Penguins. It would be difficult to overestimate the impact that Patrick had on hockey in general and on the growth of the sport in the United States.

★

A detailed review of Patrick and his life is in Eric Whitehead, *The Patricks: Hockey's Royal Family* (1980). Patrick's playing days with the Renfrew Millionaires are covered in Frank Cosentino, *The Renfrew Millionaires: Valley Boys of 1910* (1990). The *Boston Globe* featured a seven-part series on Frank and Lester Patrick that appeared in autumn 1935.

DANIEL S. MASON

PATTERSON, Floyd (*b.* 4 January 1935 in Waco, North Carolina), the first boxer in history to hold the heavyweight title twice, he later served as athletic commissioner for the state of New York.

Patterson was the third of eleven children born to Thomas Patterson, a laborer, and Annabelle Johnson. The family moved from North Carolina to Brooklyn, New York, in 1936 to allow Patterson's father to find work (which he did; in construction, as a longshoreman, in sanitation, and in a fish market). Patterson became involved in gangs, and after a series of arrests for petty thievery was sent at age ten to the Wiltwyck School for Boys in Esopus, New York, a school for emotionally disturbed youths, where he learned to read and box. After Wiltwyck, he attended P.S. 614, a vocational elementary school. Here he got the idea that he could use boxing to earn money for his family.

In 1949 he began working at Gramercy Gym with

Floyd Patterson, 1966. ARCHIVE PHOTOS, INC.

trainer Cus D'Amato (later Mike Tyson's trainer and manager), who gave him boxing equipment and taught him the fundamentals of the sport. In January 1950 Patterson entered and won his first Amateur Athletic Union (AAU) tournament in the 147-pound weight class. In the next year he won his weight class as a 160-pound fighter and went to Chicago to box in the national AAU Championships. In 1951 he won the Golden Gloves middleweight championship. Patterson, now sixteen, wanted to turn professional that year, but D'Amato would not let him, perhaps with the idea of saving him for the 1952 Olympics. The next year Patterson won the New York Golden Gloves light heavyweight title. On 2 August 1952, fighting as a middleweight, Patterson knocked out Vasial Tita one minute into the first round to win an Olympic gold medal in Helsinki, Finland. Patterson fought forty-four bouts as an amateur, winning forty, thirty-seven by knockout.

Patterson made his professional debut on 12 September 1952 as a light heavyweight, defeating Eddie Godbold by knockout in the fourth round. Over the next two years, he bested twelve more opponents, knocking out nine. On 7 June 1954 he lost a contested decision to former champion Joey Maxim, but went on to win sixteen consecutive bouts over the next twenty-four months.

In 1956 Rocky Marciano retired from the ring, leaving his title vacant. To win the championship, Patterson first defeated Tommy Jackson by decision in twelve rounds. On 30 November 1956 he knocked out Archie Moore in five rounds, becoming, at twenty-one years, five months old, the youngest man ever to win the heavyweight title. That same year Patterson married Sandra Hicks on 11 February in a civil ceremony. After Patterson converted to Catholicism later that year, the two were married again in a religious ceremony on 13 July. The couple later had had four children. They moved into an expensive home in Scarsdale, New York, until a racial incident forced them to relocate to Great Neck, Long Island.

Patterson became prominent during the heyday of New York boxing and was immensely popular with the crowd at Madison Square Garden. His troubled youth left him sensitive, introspective, and shy; his nickname was "Freudian Floyd." Admirers regarded Patterson as a perfect gentleman and noted that he had once stooped to pick up an opponent's mouthpiece in the middle of a round. Before bouts, Patterson prayed not for victory, but to avoid serious injury to his opponents or himself. His boxing method was unique. He held his gloves high in front of his face, then stunned opponents with lashing, unexpected hooks. At five feet, eleven inches tall, and usually weighing around 195 pounds, Patterson used speed, timing, and finesse to overcome his opponents. D'Amato carefully guided him through his career, but because of D'Amato's disputes with the boxing powers-that-be, top contenders such as Nino Valdes and Ezzard Charles would not fight Patterson.

Patterson successfully defended his championship four times in the two and a half years he held the title (November 1956–June 1959), starting with Tommy Jackson on 29 July 1957. He then beat two journeymen boxers and the English champion Brian London. In a stunning upset, however, Ingemar Johannson, the Swedish challenger and number-one contender for the title, knocked out Patterson in the third round on 28 June 1959. Deeply ashamed, Patterson wore disguises to avoid public criticism, a habit that by 1966 cost him $3,000 annually. Patterson made boxing history when he became the first to regain the heavyweight championship by knocking out Johannson in the fifth round of their rematch a year later on 20 June 1960. A second rematch followed on 13 March 1961, but Johannson survived only one round longer, losing by KO in the sixth round.

In the next two years Patterson defended his title only once, stopping the lightly regarded Tom McNeeley in the fourth round on 4 December 1961. He could not avoid a more serious challenger, however, and on 22 September 1962 Patterson lost his crown when the glowering Sonny Liston knocked him out in the first round and then repeated this humiliation in their rematch nine months later.

No longer champion, Patterson stayed in the ring. He beat five opponents, the best known of whom was George Chuvalo. When Cassius Clay (later Muhammad Ali) upset Liston for the championship and then proclaimed his victory was due to Allah, Patterson took offense. A devout Roman Catholic and staunch integrationist, Patterson vowed to take the crown away from Ali (who had proclaimed himself to be a Muslim, not an American), and give it back to America. He insisted on referring to his opponent as Clay, which Ali called his "slave name." Such prefight posturing became politicized in the ring. Ali taunted Patterson throughout the bout, yelling, "Come on White America," at the defenseless contender. Black Muslim spectators at ringside shouted, "Play with that Uncle Tom!" Although Ali said later that Patterson had taken his best punches and proclaimed him a good man, many observers, including Joe Louis, felt that Ali deliberately refrained from knocking Patterson out until the twelfth round.

Patterson's advisors encouraged him to retire, and his wife, Sandra, divorced him in August 1966 after he insisted on staying in boxing. Still a contender, Patterson won his next three bouts, then fought to a draw with Jerry Quarry, only to lose in the rematch. After Ali was stripped of his title for draft evasion in 1968, Patterson lost a unification bout for the championship to Jimmy Ellis on 14 September 1968.

Patterson announced his retirement after the match with Ellis. Then, after a two-year layover, he resumed his career in September 1970. He won seven fights against little-known boxers before winning an unimpressive decision against the rugged Oscar Bonavena on 11 February 1972. Patterson's father had died two days before, and he acknowledged later that he had not been at this best during the bout. After a six-round win, over Pedro Agosto on 14 July 1972, Patterson lost his last title match to Ali on 20 September 1972. He retired permanently after this defeat, with a professional record of fifty-five wins (forty by knockout), eight losses, and a draw.

Patterson, his second wife Janet, and their three children retired to their home in New Paltz, New York. In 1973 Patterson opened the Huguenot Boxing Club, a youth center intended to give youngsters an alternative to drugs; by 1988 the center had helped over 1,200 teenagers. Patterson was a member of the New York State Boxing Commission from 1977 to 1985, and used the position to push successfully for the adoption of a thumbless boxing glove for amateurs. In 1985 he was appointed head of the Off-Track Betting Commission in New York, and was named Boxing Commissioner for New York State ten years later. Patterson served until 1998 when he resigned after disclosing that he suffered from severe memory loss, probably caused by years of boxing. He was elected to the Boxing Hall of Fame in 1977 and to the Olympic Hall of Fame in 1987.

★

Patterson's autobiography, coauthored with Milton Gross, is *Victory over Myself* (1961). Another biography is Jack Newcombe, *Floyd Patterson: Heavyweight King* (1961). Magazine articles include Gay Talese, "Portrait of the Ascetic Champ," *New York Times Magazine* (5 Mar. 1961), and Pete Hamill, "Floyd's Fight to Save His Pride," *Saturday Evening Post* (27 June 1964). See also "Floyd Patterson: Still Making a Mark in the Ring," *Ebony* (Mar. 1987), and "Boxing's Last Gentleman," the *New Yorker* (31 July 1995).

GRAHAM RUSSELL HODGES

PAYTON, Walter Jerry (*b.* 25 July 1954 in Columbia, Mississippi; *d.* 1 November 1999 in Barrington, Illinois), one of the greatest running backs in the history of football, who as of 2001 still held several National Football League rushing and total offense records.

Payton was one of three children born to Peter Payton, a factory worker, and Alyne. As a youngster Payton was shy and inclined to the artistic. He loved music and playing the cymbals and he was a good dancer, earning a spot in the national finals of a contest organized by the television band show *Soul Train.* Although he became a star athlete in high school, academics were important to him and he earned good grades. This dedication to learning would pay off not only in his performances on the football field but in his business career after his retirement from the National Football League (NFL).

Walter Payton, 1981. © BETTMANN/CORBIS

Payton had scholarship offers from several prominent colleges, but he chose to attend Jackson State University in Jackson, Mississippi, because his older brother, Edward, played there. Edward later played in the Canadian Football League, as well as in the NFL. Payton's collegiate career was legendary, including feats that fans remembered for decades after they occurred. As a running back at Jackson State, Payton rushed for 3,563 career yards. His sixty-six touchdowns stood as a record until 2000. He also kicked five field goals and had fifty-four points after touchdowns, making for a total of 464 points scored for his career, then a National Collegiate Athletic Association record. In addition he averaged forty-three yards per kickoff return, and he was a punter who averaged thirty-nine yards per punt. In 1973 he led the nation in scoring with 160 points. There are several accounts of how he got the nickname "Sweetness," but the likeliest is that he received it as a college player, not for his amazing running in games, as some have supposed, but for his soft-spoken, affable demeanor off the field. Payton earned a degree in communications from Jackson State.

During the 1975 NFL draft of college players, the general manager and coach of the Chicago Bears sweated through the first three draft picks, worried that one of the teams picking before the Bears had seen Payton's unique skills. But the knock against Payton was that at five feet, eleven inches tall and 203 pounds he was too small to play in the NFL, a league populated by 300-pound defensive tackles. Thus he was picked fourth in the first round of the draft by the Bears.

Payton had the flu for his first game in the NFL, but he burst through the opposing line for twenty-nine yards on one of his carries. For the season, his numbers were good but not spectacular. He led the league in kickoff returns and showed the work ethic and running style that would make him a terror in future seasons. He ran almost stiff-legged, hardly bending his knees, putting most of the pressure on his hips and thighs, and he ran on his toes, often vaulting like a dancer over opponents—sometimes over ones who were standing up. He was selected to play in the Pro Bowl in 1976, as he would be for eight additional seasons (1976–1981, 1983–1986). He twice ran for more than 200 yards in a game in 1976. In 1977 he was spectacular, having one of the best seasons ever by any player. He gained 1,852 yards that season, and he rushed for 275 yards in one game against the Minnesota Vikings, a record that stood until 2000. He was voted the 1977 Most Valuable Player and NFL Player of the Year.

Payton was known for his small, understated kindnesses, and quickly became popular with the entire Bears organization, but he was also known for his brash pranks. He said that he played pranks to feel young, because life was too short. Setting off fireworks was a favorite pastime, and he would sneak into the coaches' offices, rearrange their desks, and plant dribble glasses, whoopee cushions, and other gags to lighten the mood of his teammates. Traditionally, NFL veterans do not talk to rookies until they prove themselves on the field of play, but Payton always welcomed new players, helping them orient themselves and encouraging them—something most remembered with gratitude, in spite of his alarming them with firecrackers on their first days. Payton also began his philanthropic work, to which he devoted the same all-out energy as he did to football, establishing the Walter Payton Foundation to provide funding for educating abused children.

Payton learned to face challenges both on and off the gridiron with every resource he had. In the NFL he followed a workout regime that exhausted even other professional football players, men in prime physical condition. Payton was again named the Most Valuable Player and NFL Player of the Year in 1985. He rushed for 1,551 yards and had another 483 yards receiving on forty-nine catches. He hammered into defenses; instead of taking the opportunity to run out of bounds he would charge full-body into tacklers. He tired out defenses, and as they grew weaker he seemed to grow stronger, running faster and with more energy as the game progressed. His obsessive conditioning program paid off. The Bears won fifteen and lost one that season, and in Super Bowl XX they defeated the New England Patriots, 46–10.

After his retirement in 1987 Payton began another career as an enterprising businessman of daunting savvy and skill. He owned the nightclubs Studebaker's and Thirty-four's, which he parlayed into a huge business complex. During the 1990s his Walter Payton Power Equipment company in Streamwood, Illinois, became the dominant supplier of power equipment in the Midwest and was expanding westward and eastward at the time of his death. His many enterprises also included the First Northwest Bank, which he helped to establish in Arlington Heights, Illinois, where he and his family lived. He served on the bank's board of directors; in 1999 First Northwest had assets of more than $125 million. By the late 1990s Payton had made arrangements to establish a team in the Arena Football League, a start toward eventually owning an NFL team.

But his plans for the future were not to be. By early 1999 he had been diagnosed with the rare liver disease primary sclerosing cholangitis, which is fatal without a liver transplant. Payton refused to use his celebrity to move himself up on the transplant waiting list of more than 12,000 people. Later he learned he had cancer of the bile duct which had spread beyond hope of treatment. Payton withered and lost weight, but even in his last week of life he was playing pranks on friends, persuading a Bears running back to sneak into a friend's garage and leave a milk shake and hamburger without explanation. When Payton died on 1 November 1999, there was a national outpouring of grief. His many good deeds were expressed in newspapers and magazines, as well as at a memorial service that drew more than 20,000 people and 50,000 toys, which Payton had asked mourners to donate for needy children. Payton was survived by his wife, Connie, and their two children.

While Payton was valued more as a good man than as a football player, his talents on the gridiron remain an inextricable part of his legacy. In 1993, his first year of eligibility, he was elected to the Pro Football Hall of Fame. Watching Payton carry a football filled opposing fans with dismay; his very presence on the field seemed to make the Chicago Bears an outstanding team. In addition to gaining a league-record 16,726 yards during his career, he was one of the best receivers of his era, with 492 receptions for a total of 4,538 yards gained for 9.2 yards per reception and fifteen touchdowns. He was a complete offensive threat who also passed for 34 receptions for a total of 331 yards and 8 touchdowns. In addition, he was a consummate blocker who took pride in protecting his quarterback and could throw devastating blocks, leading another runner through the line. Throughout his life Payton found success by following his father's advice: "My father always told me never to settle for second best, that you either try to do your best or don't try at all."

★

Walter Payton with Don Yaeger, *Never Die Easy: The Autobiography of Walter Payton* (2000), is of interest not only for its information about Payton's career but for its insights into his thinking. A good juvenile biography is Philip Koslow, *Walter Payton* (1995). Mike Towle, *I Remember Walter Payton: Personal Memories of Football's "Sweetest" Superstar by the People Who Knew Him Best* (2000), is a tribute to Payton, offering anecdotes about his conduct on and off the football field.

KIRK H. BEETZ

PENSKE, Roger S. (*b.* 20 February 1937 in Shaker Heights, Ohio), accomplished business executive whose auto-racing team won numerous championships and races, including the Indianapolis 500.

Penske was raised in Shaker Heights, the son of Martha and Jay Penske, a corporate executive who taught his son the value of hard work. Penske was a prize-winning news-

Roger Penske *(foreground)*, 2000. ASSOCIATED PRESS AP

paper carrier and, as a teenager, bought and fixed used cars to sell at a profit. In 1951 he attended his first Indianapolis 500. Not long after, he severely injured his ankle while riding a motorcycle and nearly had to have his foot amputated, but recovered to play high school football. Penske graduated from Lehigh University in 1959 with a business administration degree. Beginning his career in aluminum sales, he later used a loan from his father to purchase a Chevrolet dealership in Philadelphia that spawned various transportation businesses. But as successful as Penske became in the corporate world, auto racing would be his claim to fame.

Penske drove in his first sports car race in 1958 and won his first race a year later. By 1962 he had earned Driver of the Year honors from *Sports Illustrated* and the *New York Times*. But after winning races in several classifications and a road racing championship, Penske retired from driving in 1965, since it began to conflict with his business career. "I don't want to be known as a race driver," he reportedly said before quitting.

With Mark Donohue as his driver, Penske started running his own race team in 1966. The team quickly succeeded at several levels of racing and hit the jackpot when Donohue won the Indianapolis 500 in 1972. Donohue died in 1975 after crashing during a practice run for a Formula One race, and Team Penske soon began focusing almost entirely on Indianapolis-style "Champ Car" racing.

Nicknamed the "Captain," Penske developed a reputation as the unquestioned leader of his team. In 1975 he met and offered Tom Sneva a chance to drive his Norton-sponsored car. "Roger told me what he wanted, and I told him what I wanted," recalled Sneva in *The Norton Spirit* (1978). "The result was simple. We did what he wanted." In 1977 and 1978 the duo broke the 200-mile-per-hour barrier at the Indianapolis Motor Speedway and teamed for consecutive season championships. But Penske let Sneva go because he failed to win enough races. It wouldn't be the last time Penske parted with a successful driver.

One driver who did stay with Penske for the long haul was Rick Mears. Known as the "King of the Ovals," Mears won the Indianapolis 500 for Penske in 1979 and repeated the feat in 1984, 1988, and 1991. In all, he won twenty-nine races and three season championships for Penske before retiring from driving in 1992 to become a team consultant. "I couldn't have hoped for or dreamed of having a better career," said Mears. "And for that I have to thank Roger and the team."

Several drivers benefited from Penske's winning touch. Bobby Unser won the Indianapolis 500 in 1981, and his brother Al did likewise in 1987 with a year-old car that was being displayed in a hotel. Al Unser also captured the 1983 and 1985 season titles. Danny Sullivan took the 1985 Indianapolis 500 and 1988 season championship. Emerson Fittipaldi won at Indianapolis in 1993.

Undoubtedly, Penske Racing's greatest year was 1994. Following in the footsteps of his father and his Uncle Bobby, Al Unser, Jr., joined the team as a driver. Unser, Jr., Fittipaldi, and Paul Tracy combined to win twelve races, with Unser winning eight en route to the season title. Penske's trio of Marlboro-sponsored cars finished one-two-three in five separate races. Yet the year's top achievement was Unser's Indianapolis 500 triumph with a Mercedes push-rod engine that was secretly built and tested. "It was a whole team effort by Marlboro Team Penske that helped me win," said Unser. "That included the Mercedes-Benz engine which Roger himself saw in the rulebook would be an advantage." The motor was so dominant it was banned from competition after one race.

In 1995 Penske's cars did not even qualify at Indianapolis. The exclusive Penske chassis did not work well at many tracks. The team failed to win a race in 1996, and after Tracy won three straight races in the spring of 1997 to bring Penske's Champ Car victory total to ninety-nine, the team again went winless for the rest of that year and all of 1998 and 1999 as well. Making things worse was that the team was no longer racing at Indianapolis, as a split between Championship Auto Racing Teams (known as CART, which Penske cofounded in 1979) and the new Indy Racing League divided the sport.

After three years without a victory, Penske scrapped his own chassis in favor of a Reynard, and new driver Gil de Ferran finally gave him his 100th Champ Car win at Nazareth Speedway on 27 May 2000. The subsequent fall, de Ferran set the world closed-course speed record of 241.428 miles per hour at California Speedway and captured Penske's tenth season championship.

In May 2001 the team raced at Indianapolis for the first time in seven years, and Helio Castroneves won Penske Racing's eleventh Indianapolis 500. With de Ferran coming in second, the team achieved its first ever one-two finish at the Brickyard. "It kind of takes away the pain of 1995," said Penske afterward. Penske also won his eleventh season championship in 2001 when de Ferran clinched his second consecutive title. "I'm a very fortunate person to be driving for a guy like Roger and a team like we have," stated de Ferran. "To me, I've been living in a dream since I joined the team two years ago."

Penske was inducted into the International Motorsports Hall of Fame in 1998. Along with his Champ Car team, he has run a National Association of Stock Car Auto Racing (NASCAR) racing team and various speedways.

Penske and his wife, Kathryn, are the parents of two sons and a daughter. He has two sons from a previous marriage to Lissa Stouffer.

Away from the racetrack, Penske founded the Penske Corporation, including Penske Truck Leasing, Penske Auto Centers, and several other subsidiaries. Annual revenue has been estimated to be in the billions of dollars. Penske has also served as a director of the Detroit Diesel Corporation and General Electric Company.

★

A comprehensive profile of Penske appears in *Automotive News* (17 Jan. 2000). Some information can be found in *The Norton Spirit: 1978 Racing with the Champion* (1978). Other quotes and facts can be found in articles by Gordon Kirby, which are printed in various race day programs. Up-to-date information on Penske's career is available at http://www.penskeracing.com and http://www.cart.com.

JACK STYCZYNSKI

PEP, Willie (*b.* 19 September 1922 in Middletown, Connecticut), world featherweight boxing champion from 1942 to 1951, who was renowned for his agile fighting style and vibrant personality.

Born Gugliemo (William) Papaleo, Pep grew up on Middletown's tough east side as part of a large Italian family. The son of a construction worker, Pep began boxing before he was five years old. He retained vivid memories of the hard times his family faced during the Great Depression, when his father was chronically out of work. Eventually his father found employment with the Works Progress Administration, but money was still in short supply. When Pep first boxed as an amateur at age fifteen and brought home $50 in prize money, his father took most of the winnings and suggested that his son box more often.

Adopting the name "Willie Pep" as an Americanized version of his name that nicely reflected his boxing style, the amateur boxer won the Connecticut flyweight championship in 1938 and the bantamweight championship the following year. At five feet, five-and-a-half inches, and never more than 139 pounds, Pep astounded his opponents with his rapid and intricate footwork, which some compared to tap dancing while throwing punches. He began

Willie Pep *(left)* in a bout against Chalky Wright. AP/WIDE WORLD PHOTOS

to fight as a professional in 1940 and worked his way through dozens of fights, winning his first sixty-four matches on his way to earning a title match against Chalky Wright for the New York featherweight championship on 20 November 1942. In a fifteen-round decision, Pep took the title, which he defended against Sal Bartolo in Boston in another fight that went the distance on 8 June 1943. Pep met Wright for a return match in New York on 29 September 1944, a bout that was the first boxing event televised from Madison Square Garden, and one that Pep won. The televised *Friday Night Fights* that followed the Pep-Wright match became a sports institution through the 1960s.

On 19 February 1945 Pep met Phil Terranova in New York for another bout that he took in a fifteen-round decision. Pep's victory over the National Boxing Association featherweight champion meant that he was the sole holder of the title. In 1947, however, Pep was injured as a passenger on a chartered plane bound for Hartford; the accident killed three people, and Pep was left with a broken leg and two cracked vertebrae. He spent five months in a body cast, then defied his doctors' orders and began planning his comeback. After just a few weeks of training, he reentered the ring and beat Victor Flores in a ten-round win in Hartford on 17 June 1947. Pep later called the fight the biggest one of his career because it conquered doubts that he could ever fight again. On 27 August of that year he defended his featherweight title with a twelve-round technical knockout against Jock Leslie, a feat he repeated on 24 February 1948 with a ten-round technical knockout against Humberto Sierra.

Pep delighted boxing fans with his antics in the ring. In one legendary performance in Minneapolis on 25 July 1946 against Jackie Graves, Pep bet that he could win a round without throwing a single punch. Putting his fast footwork on display, Pep kept Graves off balance and on the defensive throughout the round. Even though he never threw a punch, Pep indeed won the round. Pep was also a favorite with sports columnists for his ready wit and a lifestyle that favored the nightlife. Although he cleared well over a million dollars during his career, Pep joked that he lost it to "fast women and slow horses." Married six times, Pep had two children from his first marriage, one son from his third marriage, and a daughter from his fifth marriage.

Between 1948 and 1951 Pep fought a series of fights against Sandy Saddler over the featherweight title. In the first match on 29 October 1948, Pep was betrayed by overconfidence and lost the title in a fourth-round knockout. The two had a rematch on 11 February of the following year, and Pep was determined to reclaim the title. Fighting aggressively in the early rounds, he eventually took the title by decision. In their third match, on 8 September 1950, Pep suffered a dislocated shoulder in the eighth round, and Saddler won on a technical knockout. The culmination of the series took place in New York at the Polo Grounds on 26 September 1951, in one of the wildest fights of the era. Both fighters committed numerous fouls, and at one point the referee got tangled up and fell while trying to separate them. Eventually Saddler landed enough blows to Pep's right eye that it closed up completely, and Pep failed to come out for the start of the ninth round. It was his last attempt to recapture the featherweight title. In all, he held the title from 1942 to 1948 and again from 1949 to 1950.

Pep continued to fight until 1959, when he retired from the ring; after a brief comeback in 1965–1966—during which he won another nine of ten matches—he retired for good. He compiled a record of 230 wins, 11 losses, 1 draw, and 65 knockouts over his 26-year career. He later wrote that he was disappointed in the direction that boxing had taken in the 1950s, as the lure of televised matches forced boxers to rush their development instead of training properly in neighborhood clubs. However, with his vast experience and wealth of anecdotes, Pep served as one of the sport's most notable ambassadors to the public at large. He was elected to the International Boxing Hall of Fame in 1990.

After his athletic career drew to a close, Pep secured a job with the boxing office of the State of Connecticut's Athletic Division, a position he held for almost twenty years. Although most of his boxing earnings were long gone, he enjoyed a modestly comfortable retirement with a small state pension that he supplemented with personal appearances as a popular speaker on the history of his sport.

★

Pep's anecdotal *Willie Pep Remembers . . . Friday's Heroes* (1973), written with Robert Sacchi, recounts many stories of boxers during the 1940s and 1950s. An interview with Pep was included in Peter Heller, *In This Corner!: Forty-Two World Champions Tell Their Stories,* 2nd ed. (1994). Profiles of Pep during his retirement appear in *Sports Illustrated* (16 July 1990), and the *Boston Globe* (26 Oct. 1999). John T. Kavanaugh published a brief reminiscence about Pep in *Yankee* (Aug. 1991). A full account of Pep's record as a professional fighter is in *The Boxing Register: International Hall of Fame Official Record Book,* 2nd ed. (1999).

TIMOTHY BORDEN

PETTIT, Robert E. Lee, Jr. ("Bob") (*b.* 12 December 1932 in Baton Rouge, Louisiana), professional basketball player who was the greatest forward of his era and the first ever to score 20,000 career regular-season points.

Pettit was the only son of Robert E. Lee Pettit, a county sheriff, and Margaret Pettit, a realtor. Pettit wanted to participate in sports, but was cut from the football, basketball, and baseball teams during his first two years at Baton

Bob Pettit after being named MVP in the 1958 NBA All-Star Game. AP/ WIDE WORLD PHOTOS

Rouge High School. He was tall, but gangly and lacking in the skills to compete effectively. Undaunted by his early failures and encouraged by his father, Pettit practiced shooting baskets in his back yard for hours at a time. His efforts were rewarded when he was chosen for the basketball team in his junior year. By his senior year, already six feet, seven inches tall, Pettit had developed into a formidable player. In 1950 he led the team to its first state championship in over twenty years and was named first team All-State center. Following graduation in 1950, Pettit accepted a scholarship to play basketball at Louisiana State University (LSU).

Pettit had received scholarship offers from fifteen schools, but selected LSU because he did not believe he could live up to the expectations of the "fancier" scholarships. His freshman team coach, former National Basketball Association (NBA) player John Chaney, verified these self-doubts. After his first practice, Pettit commented: "My reflexes were slow. I was lost on defense. I didn't know how to drive in for a shot, or fake and pass off the pivot. Much as I dislike this expression, I've got to admit I was a goon." In spite of this early negative evaluation, Pettit soon developed the moves that would make him a future star, and his many fans at LSU certainly never thought of him as anything but a great player.

By the time Pettit graduated from LSU in 1954 with a Bachelor's degree in business administration, he had scored 2,002 points and been named an All-American twice, in 1953 and 1954. He was also selected to the first-team All-Southeast Conference three times, and led the Tigers to conference titles in 1953 and 1954 and to the NCAA Final Four in 1953. In his three seasons at LSU, Pettit led the league in scoring with an average of 27.4 points per game. He also excelled at rebounding, and averaged 17.3, an LSU best, in 1954.

The Milwaukee Hawks (who moved to St. Louis a year later) selected Pettit in the first round of the 1954 National Basketball Association (NBA) draft. Considered by some to be too thin to play pivot—he stood six feet, nine inches tall, and weighed only 200 pounds—he became a forward, where he used his intelligence and finesse to beat bigger men to the ball. Pettit is credited with inventing the power forward position, which demands the size and strength of a pivot, the athleticism and shooting skills of a small forward, and the nastiness of a middle linebacker. Lenny Wilkens, who also played for the St. Louis Hawks, said of Pettit, "he was a power forward who could really score. You didn't find guys like that in those days." Pettit's power shot involved getting the ball near the basket, holding it high, then swinging around and shooting with one or both hands. His beautifully soft, but deadly, jump shot combined toughness with finesse and became a model for the league. Pettit was the first big man with an accurate outside shot.

Pettit was also known for his relentless drive. If he missed his first ten shots in the first half, he would take ten more in the second half, thinking that he would make those and would be ten-for-twenty. Bill Russell, a rival player and future Hall of Famer, said "Bob made 'second effort' a part of the sport's vocabulary. He kept coming at you more than any man in the game. He was always battling for position, fighting you off the boards." Pettit was the best scorer and rebounder on the team, but he would always give up the ball to a teammate who was in a better position.

In his debut season with the Hawks (1955–1956), Pettit was the Rookie of the Year, the NBA's Most Valuable Player (MVP), and the All-Star MVP. He also won the NBA's scoring championship twice (1955–1956; 1958–1959). The Hawks went to the finals four times during Pettit's tenure, but were successful only once, at the end of the 1957–1958 season. Pettit scored fifty points in game six of this series—one of only two games he remembers clearly (the other was his high school state championship title game in 1950). He earned a second MVP award in 1959, and made the all-NBA first team for ten consecutive seasons. In those ten seasons, Pettit never finished lower than fifth in scoring and rebounding, an accomplishment unmatched by any other player to date.

A true superstar who played for love of the game, Pettit

retired after the 1965 season. At that time, he was the highest scorer in the history of the NBA, averaging 26.4 points, and the game's leading rebounder, with 14 per game. He scored 20,880 career points in 792 games, the first player in the NBA to break the 20,000-point ceiling. He also posted a .436 field-goal percentage; 12,849 rebounds and a 16.2 rebound percentage; and 2,369 assists with a 3.0 assist percentage. Pettit was named All-Pro ten years in a row and the NBA's All-Star Game MVP four times.

After retiring from professional sports, Pettit returned to Baton Rouge, where he worked in insurance and banking. The city honored him by naming Bob Pettit Boulevard in his honor. Pettit was the first LSU player in any sport to have his jersey retired (number 50) in 1954; the St. Louis Hawks also retired his number 9 jersey. He was inducted into the Naismith Memorial Basketball Hall of Fame in 1970.

At the NBA's fiftieth anniversary in 1996, Pettit was selected as one of the fifty greatest players of all time by a panel of former players, coaches, general mangers, team executives, and media representatives. He was runner-up to Pete Maravich as Player of the Century, as selected by the Louisiana Association of Basketball Coaches in 1999. Pettit was also a member of the First Team All-Louisiana Team of the Century, 1999. He married Carole Crowell on 19 June 1965; they have three children. They now live in New Orleans, where Pettit is employed by Prudential Securities.

★

Pettit chronicled his NBA career with coauthor Bob Wolff in *Bob Pettit: The Drive Within Me* (1966). Pettit was a featured athlete in Phil Burger, *Heroes of Pro Basketball* (1968); Richard Rainbolt, *Basketball's Big Men* (1975); and Martin Taragano, *Basketball Biographies: 434 U.S. Players, Coaches, and Contributors to the Game, 1891–1990* (1991). "Powering Forward," the *Denver Post* (1 June 1997), describes the evolution of the position from Bob Pettit to Karl Malone. Other articles about Pettit's career include: Z. Hollander, "Big Shot Bob!," *Senior Scholastic* (8 Mar. 1954); "Golden Hawk," *Time* (3 Feb. 1958); and "Solid Man, Solid," *Senior Scholastic* (1 Feb. 1961).

JEANNIE P. MILLER

PETTY, Richard Lee (*b.* 2 July 1937 in Level Cross, North Carolina), professional race car driver who won seven Winston Cup championships, seven Daytona 500 races, and 200 National Association for Stock Car Automobile Racing (NASCAR) races between 1958 and 1992.

Petty was the elder of two sons born to Lee Petty, a pioneer of NASCAR and a three-time Grand National racing champion, and Elizabeth Toomes, a homemaker. Petty's childhood was filled with the normal activities of an upbringing in the rural South during the 1940s, racing bicycles, swimming in nearby creeks, and engaging in other childhood adventures with his younger brother. However, Petty learned the value of hard work at an early age. While still in grade school he earned spending money by picking cotton on Saturdays and during school holidays. He attended Randleman High School, where he was an average student and a good athlete, becoming an All-Conference guard on the football team. After graduating in 1955 he took a business course at Greensboro Junior College and began to work full-time in his father's racing company, Petty Enterprises. In 1958 Petty and Lynda Owens, who had been a cheerleader at Randleman High, were married. In addition to their son, Kyle, who followed his father into racing, the couple had three daughters.

Between the late 1940s and 1958 Petty worked as a mechanic for his father. As a member of Lee Petty's pit crew, he watched stock car racing evolve from a backcountry pastime into a major spectator sport. The coming of age of stock car racing was initiated by two major events: the creation of NASCAR in 1948 and the opening of a superspeedway stock car racing track at Darlington, South Carolina, in 1950. Petty's father became one of the first champions of NASCAR, winning three national championship titles and fifty-four Grand National races. While Lee Petty was earning his place in racing history, his son was learning everything he could about racing engines and suspensions. Though Petty readily admits that his younger brother Maurice was the mechanical genius of the Petty racing team, his own understanding of the technical aspects of racing greatly enhanced his skill as a driver. Throughout his career he possessed the ability to push his race cars up to, but not beyond, their breaking point.

In 1958, the day after his twenty-first birthday, Petty began racing cars instead of working on them. He finished sixth in his first contest, driving one of his father's older cars on a dirt track near Columbia, South Carolina. The rest of the year was less than spectacular. In his first nine races he managed to win only $760, but it was enough to maintain his interest in driving. During the following year Petty began to establish himself as a formidable competitor. He won NASCAR Rookie of the Year honors by posting nine top-ten finishes in twenty-two racing events and earned nearly $8,000 for the year.

During the 1960s Petty continued to be a force in stock car racing. In 1960 he won his first Grand National circuit race on the dirt track in Charlotte, North Carolina, and he finished just behind Rex White in the Grand National (later Winston Cup) year-end point standings. To accomplish this feat he posted sixteen top-five finishes in forty races. When injuries from a near-fatal crash forced Lee Petty to retire in 1962, Petty assumed all the driving duties

Richard Petty, 1999. ASSOCIATED PRESS AP

for Petty Enterprises, while his father went to work in the pits. The father-son combination proved a winner. Petty won fourteen races in 1963 and again finished second in the point standings for the national championship title. In 1964 Petty won his first Grand National championship. In what proved to be a record year, he won his first Daytona 500, eight other victories, and thirty-seven top-five finishes in sixty-one races, earning an astonishing $98,810 in prize money.

In 1965 NASCAR imposed limitations on the size of engines used in stock cars. These new rules essentially outlawed the powerful Chrysler 426-inch hemispherical head engine that Petty had used in his racing cars. As a result Chrysler temporarily withdrew their sponsorship from stock car racing and began to support drag racing. Petty made the move with Chrysler, but instead of finding glory at the drag strips, he met with tragedy. On 28 February 1965, on a strip in Dallas, Georgia, the left front suspension of Petty's car broke, causing the vehicle to careen out of control into a crowd of spectators. Six racing fans were injured, and an eight-year-old boy was killed. The event proved traumatic for Petty, and he vowed to never drive again in a drag racing event.

In 1966 Petty returned to NASCAR to win his second Daytona 500. In 1967 he passed his father's career record of fifty-four wins. That year he had thirty-eight top-five finishes out of forty-eight races and won his second Grand National championship.

The 1970s marked the high point in Petty's racing career. In 1971 he became the first stock-car driver to boost his career earnings to more than $1 million, and he won his third NASCAR Grand National title. Over the decade Petty won five Winston Cup championships (including those from the earlier Grand Nationals) and four Daytona 500 races.

In the early 1980s Petty still seemed to be at the top of his sport. He won his seventh Daytona 500 in 1981 and three years later, with President Ronald W. Reagan in attendance, he won the Firecracker 400, giving him his 200th career victory—95 more wins than the driver closest to him, David Pearson. However, Petty's 1984 victory at the Firecracker 400 was his last, even though he did not retire from the NASCAR circuit until 1992.

Petty underwent successful surgery for prostate cancer in 1995. A year later he ran an unsuccessful political campaign as the Republican candidate for Secretary of State in North Carolina. He was inducted into the National Motor Sports Hall of Fame in 1998. He remains active in NASCAR events, operating Petty Enterprises and serving as owner of the racing team his father originally built and his son, Kyle, continues to represent.

Few men have done more for their sport than Petty. Called "the King" because of his many successes, Petty's seven Daytona 500 wins, seven Winston Cup championships, and a remarkable 200 NASCAR wins placed him in the record books.

★

Petty has three autobiographies: *Grand National: The Autobiography of Richard Petty as Told to Bill Neely* (1971), written with William Neely; *"King Richard": The Richard Petty Story* (1977), written with Bill Libby; and *King Richard I: The Autobiography of America's Greatest Auto Racer* (1986), written with William Neely. These books are filled with valuable information about Petty's personal views and racing career. Two biographies are Marshall and Sue Burchard, *Sports Hero: Richard Petty* (1974), and Frank Vehorn, *A Farewell to the King: A Personal Look Back at the Career of Richard Petty, Stock Car Racing's Winningest and Most Popular Driver* (1992). The latter is the more comprehensive study. Periodical articles include Robert F. Jones, "Petty Blue, STP Red, and Blooey!," *Sports Illustrated* (9 Apr. 1973); M. H. Gregory, "20 Years in the Fast Lane: King Richard Celebrates an Anniversary," *Motor Trend* (Sept. 1978); and Sam Moses, "It's All in the Family—Again," *Sports Illustrated* (26 Nov. 1979).

KENNETH WAYNE HOWELL

PIAZZA, Michael Joseph ("Mike") (*b.* 4 September 1968 in Norristown, Pennsylvania), baseball player for the Los Angeles Dodgers and the New York Mets who is considered the best-hitting catcher in the history of the game.

Piazza, the second of five sons born to Vincent and Veronica Piazza, was raised in Phoenixville, near Philadelphia, Pennsylvania. His father, a high school dropout, worked in a tire plant at night and fixed used cars during the day until he earned enough money to buy a car dealership, which he parlayed into a multimillion-dollar business empire. His mother earned a nursing degree but opted to stay home to care for her sons. When Piazza was eleven, he and his father built a batting cage out of scrap wood in the family's backyard, where Piazza hit 200 to 300 balls each day. In cold weather Piazza would heat the balls on a gas stove and wrap pipe insulation around his bat to prevent his hands from taking a beating. His father owned box seats along the third base line at Veterans Stadium, where Piazza had an unencumbered view of the Philadelphia Phillies' third baseman Mike Schmidt, whom he idolized. When the Los Angeles Dodgers came to town, Piazza sat in an even better seat: his father's childhood friend and distant cousin, the Dodgers' manager Tommy Lasorda, arranged for him to be a batboy.

In the summer of 1984 Ted Williams, the former Boston Red Sox star who once hit over .400 in a season, met Vince Piazza through a mutual friend and found out that he had a son who could hit. He visited the Piazza home to watch the fifteen-year-old slugger in action. Williams said he had never seen a better hitter at such a young age. He recommended that Piazza get his book, *The Science of Hitting.* When Piazza, who had already read the book, returned from his room with his copy, Williams inscribed it "Don't forget me. One day, I'll be looking for you for tickets to get into the major leagues."

Mike Piazza, 2000. © REUTERS NEWMEDIA INC./CORBIS

But the major leagues were a long way off for Piazza. Despite batting over .400 and breaking the former Cleveland Indians' slugger Andre Thornton's all-time Phoenixville High School home-run record during his senior year (1986), Piazza attracted scant interest from scouts. With Lasorda's help, Piazza was given opportunities to play college ball at the University of Miami (1986 to 1987) and then at Miami-Dade Community College (1987 to 1988). After friends in five organizations scoffed when Lasorda asked them to draft the first baseman, the Dodgers' manager turned to his own team and said that after forty-four years of service, he was owed a favor. Los Angeles selected Piazza in the sixty-second round of the June 1988 draft. He was the 1,390th player taken, of 1,433 players selected overall. But Piazza was not signed until months after the draft, when he displayed awesome power during a workout at Dodger Stadium, repeatedly hammering balls into the seats. The exhibition of power piqued the interest of Dodgers' scouting director Ben Wade, but he remained skeptical of Piazza's speed and fielding ability. Lasorda recalled asking Wade, "If I brought in a catcher and he swung like that, what would you do?" When Wade said, "I'd try to sign him," Lasorda responded, "Well, then he's a catcher."

Wade offered Piazza a $15,000 signing bonus under the condition that he enroll in the Dodgers' Dominican Republic training academy to learn the catching position.

After a stint in spring training in March 1989, Piazza was sent to the rookie league Salem Dodgers in Oregon in June. Piazza was promoted to the Single-A Vero Beach (Florida) Dodgers in March 1990. In June he lost his starting spot to a more polished defensive catcher. Feeling he was being unfairly punished because of Lasorda's perceived favoritism, Piazza quit the team. Four days later he returned and apologized. After the season Dodgers' farm director Charlie Blaney proposed the catcher be released because of his poor attitude. Lasorda intervened, demanding Piazza be given a chance to play every day for a full season. In 1991 Piazza was sent to Class-A Bakersfield (California) and the next year to the Dodgers' Double-A team in San Antonio, Texas, before being promoted to the Triple-A team in Albuquerque, New Mexico. He was called up to the Dodgers in September 1992 and hit .232 in twenty-one games. In the off-season Mike Scioscia, the veteran Dodgers catcher, left Los Angeles as a free agent when the team refused to guarantee him a starting position. Piazza was invited to the Dodgers' spring training camp in March 1993. With the starting catching position up for grabs, he hit an astounding .478 and beat out four other players for the job. Piazza did more than just win the starting role; he became an immediate sensation, hitting .318 with 35 homers and 112 runs batted in (RBI) in 1993. He was only the sixth player unanimously selected as the National League Rookie of the Year. He went on to make 6 All-Star teams as a Dodger, capped by a remarkable 1997 season in which he hit .362 with 40 homers and 124 RBI—the best offensive year ever by a catcher.

In 1998, when contract talks between the Dodgers and Piazza broke off, Piazza was traded to the Florida Marlins in a blockbuster seven-player deal. After only five games he was traded to the New York Mets in exchange for three minor leaguers. With Piazza hitting .328, the Mets played their best baseball in years, but they lost their last five games as their catcher struggled, blowing what appeared to be a sure wild-card spot in the play-offs. In what was to become a familiar reprise, fans began to wonder whether the rigors of catching over a full season affected Piazza's hitting late in the year. Despite being roundly booed toward the end of the season, Piazza remained with the Mets, signing a seven-year, $91 million contract in October 1998, making him the highest paid player in baseball history at the time.

Piazza hit forty home runs in 1999 and collected 124 RBI, but he again struggled toward the end of the year. Unlike the previous campaign, the Mets rebounded in time to salvage their season, winning the last four games to force a one-game play-off against the Cincinnati Reds. The Mets beat the Reds 5–0 to qualify for the play-offs for the first time since 1988. They then upset the Arizona Diamondbacks three games to one to advance to the National League East play-offs, where they lost to the Atlanta Braves. In 2000 Piazza powered the Mets to the World Series, hitting thirty-eight home runs. However, his season was marked by confrontations with the New York Yankees' pitcher Roger Clemens. Piazza was struck in the head by a fastball thrown by Clemens during an 8 July game, resulting in a concussion. Piazza, who thought that he had been hit intentionally, had harsh words for Clemens after the contest. Later that year the Mets won an exciting play-off series against the San Francisco Giants. They then dominated the St. Louis Cardinals to win the National League pennant and set up a "subway series" match-up with the New York Yankees.

The second game of the subway series brought the much-anticipated rematch between Piazza and Clemens, the first time the two had faced off since the incident in July. In a bizarre set of events, Piazza broke his bat while connecting with a pitch thrown by Clemens. The barrel of the splintered bat shot toward Clemens, who inexplicably picked up the chunk of wood and fired it like a spear in the direction of Piazza. Stunned, Piazza simply stared at Clemens but did not charge at the Yankees pitcher. The umpires allowed Clemens to remain in the game, which the Yankees won, giving them a 2–0 lead in the series. They eventually captured the series four games to one, with Piazza making the last out on a fly ball to centerfield in game five.

Piazza is the best-hitting catcher in baseball history. Entering the 2001 season, he had hit at least 30 home runs in 6 consecutive years and batted over .300 for 8 straight years. The belief that he would be an even better hitter if he moved back to first base has prompted much debate about the catcher's future. Opponents frequently take advantage of his poor throwing arm, which has a lot to do with the prospective move. But the main reason is the belief that if he were relieved of the physical demands of the catching position, Piazza could become one of baseball's all-time best hitters.

★

The earliest and most comprehensive source on Piazza's development is Kelly Whiteside, "A Piazza with Everything," *Sports Illustrated* (5 July 1993). For insight into the relationship between Vince Piazza and Tommy Lasorda and the impact it had on Piazza's development, see Michael Goodman, "Pumped Up Dodger Catcher Building Confidence So He Can Ward Off the Dreaded Sophomore Jinx," *Los Angeles Times Magazine* (3 Apr. 1994). Jason Reid examines the reasons behind the trade of Piazza from the Dodgers to the Marlins in "This Trade Is History," *Los Angeles Times* (16 May 1998). Wayne Coffey writes of Piazza's years as a high school slugger in "Hometown Hero: Mets' Piazza Has

Become Favorite Son of Phoenixville, PA," *New York Daily News* (7 June 1998). Joe Gergen traces Piazza's rise to stardom in "Wanderin' Star: Piazza Finds His Home with the Mets," *Newsday* (5 July 1998).

DANIEL MASSEY

PINCAY, Laffit Alegando, Jr. (*b.* 29 December 1946 in Panama City, Panama), Thoroughbred jockey known for scoring the most career wins of all time.

Pincay's father, Laffit Alegando Pincay, Sr., was a jockey, and his mother, Rosario, was a newspaper distributor. When Pincay was still young, his father deserted the family and moved to Venezuela to ride horses. Pincay was an undisciplined youth who on several occasions very nearly got into serious trouble with the police. He was passionate about sports, however, and baseball gave his life a degree of structure. Eventually he became the second baseman for the Panamanian national baseball team. This was a considerable achievement, especially in view of his size—he was just five feet, one inch tall and weighed 117 pounds.

Pincay was described by the writer Michael Watchmaker as a rider "who can practically pick a tiring horse up and carry him across the finishing line." Like his fellow Panamanians Jorge Luis Velasquez and Braulio Baeza, Pincay was immersed in the horseracing subculture from an early age. He first took a job as a groom and a "hot walker," a person who helps a horse warm down after exercise. He worked for no pay, trying to find an opportunity to ride. Pincay began his racing career in 1964 in Panama, and by the end of his rookie season he was established as the leading apprentice in his country. A year later he was Panama's top jockey, and in 1966 he joined Velasquez and Baeza in the United States, signing a three-year contract with the owner Fred Hooper. In 1968 Pincay married Linda Radkovich; they had two children.

Pincay's extraordinary successes and his astonishing longevity were remarkable in light of the fact that his career was plagued by a never-ending battle with weight. During the 1970s his many wins took place against a background of diuretics, diet pills, jogging, fad diets, and injections of protein and vitamins. Pincay spent hours in the steam and sauna rooms at the track; he even had a private steam system set up in his home. By 1973 he was forcing himself to vomit after eating. The *New York Times* reporter Steven Crist wrote that for seven years Pincay "was setting records and winning titles even though he was dizzy, nauseated, and hostile most of the time."

In 1976 Pincay fired his agent Vince DeGregory because he felt DeGregory was pressuring him to race too often and had failed to be supportive when he finished out of the money. A critical turnaround for Pincay was a 1978 race at Del Mar, California. His horse lost by a nose, and Pincay saw the failure as the direct result of his lack of fitness. He hired the nutritionist Joyce Richards and embraced a Spartan diet of grains, nuts, and fruits totaling 850 calories per day. More than twenty years later, he still adhered to this diet. Pincay's ability to sustain a career of nearly four decades has been attributed to the caliber of the horses he has been invited to ride and to his phenomenal strength.

Laffit Pincay, 2000. ASSOCIATED PRESS BENOIT PHOTO

Pincay was elected to the National Museum of Racing Hall of Fame in 1975 at the relatively young age of twenty-nine. His precocious rise to prominence came from his daily eagerness to ride, love of travel, and amazing stamina in coping with numerous racing "starts" that would have overwhelmed a lesser jockey. He received the Eclipse Award as the nation's leading jockey six times and won three consecutive Belmont Stakes, triumphing aboard Conquistador Cielo in 1982, Caveat in 1983, and Swale in 1984. On 14 March 1987 he became the only jockey to ride seven winners on a single program, a feat he achieved at the Santa Anita racetrack in Arcadia, California. By the end of the 1992 racing season, Pincay had made 37,473 starts and recorded 7,888 first-place wins, 6,210 second-place finishes, and 5,174 third-place finishes. In virtually 50 percent of his starts, Pincay had placed. In his many successful years of racing, one race remained special for Pincay: his 1984 Kentucky Derby win riding Swale.

Pincay was a record setter as early as 1973. In that year he became the first jockey to go over the $4 million mark, with winnings of $4,093,492. A year later, on 13 December, he bested that figure with race purses that amounted to $4,094,560. Pincay's defining moment was his eclipse of Willie Shoemaker's career record of riding 8,833 winners, with $123.4 million in stakes money. On 10 December 1999, in the sixth race at Hollywood Park in Inglewood, California, Pincay was riding Irish Nip. He steered the horse to a two-length triumph and his 8,834th career win. For his victory Pincay received a white Porsche convertible, courtesy of the Hollywood Park racetrack. Shoemaker was on hand to say, "I can't think of anybody better to break the record than Laffit." Pincay's response highlighted an athletic credo buoyed by a passion for racing: "Many times I thought about giving up, but the reason I didn't . . . was the love of the game, the love of riding horses." Following this win, Pincay did not rest; he rode in the day's final two races.

In 1985 Pincay's wife of seventeen years committed suicide after undergoing painful surgery and suffering months of depression. Pincay married again in 1992. He and his second wife, Jeanine, had one child. The words on his 1975 Hall of Fame induction plaque understate yet encapsulate Pincay's genius, calling him a "strong rider who could keep unruly colts to their task." In a close race Pincay could "make the difference at the wire." His longevity was legendary. While in 2001 Pincay was no longer the stellar jockey of the 1970s and 1980s, he continued to be a competitive rider.

★

Contemporary Newsmakers 1986 (1987) has an early career profile of Pincay that makes excellent use of primary source materials. Shorter portraits are in Ralph Hickok, *Who's Who of Sports Champions: Their Stories and Records* (1995); David L. Porter, ed., *Biographical Dictionary of American Sports* (1995); and George B. Kirsch, Othello Harris, and Claire E. Nolte, eds., *Encyclopedia of Ethnicity and Sports in the United States* (2000). *Jockey News* has many valuable reports on Pincay's racing accomplishments. The National Museum of Racing and Hall of Fame in Saratoga Springs, New York, has archival material on Pincay's life. Andrew Beyers captures the magic of the day Pincay broke Shoemaker's record in "The Best in the Business Is Still Coming On Strong," *Washington Post* (11 Dec. 1999). For an excellent overview of Pincay's life-long battle to maintain his best riding weight, see Richard Hoffer, "It Takes a Hungry Man," *Sports Illustrated* (3 Sept. 2001).

SCOTT A. G. M. CRAWFORD

PIPPEN, Scottie (*b.* 25 September 1965 in Hamburg, Arkansas), professional basketball player who won six National Basketball Association (NBA) championships and two Olympic gold medals, and who was named to the NBA's Fiftieth Anniversary All-Time Team.

Pippen was the youngest of Preston and Ethel Pippen's twelve children, six sons and six daughters. He spent his childhood and early adulthood in Hamburg, a town with a population of 3,000. His father worked at a local paper mill, while his mother was a homemaker. The family had very little money and struggled to make ends meet. Pippen attended Hamburg High School. During his freshman year his father suffered a severe stroke and was confined to a wheelchair. Pippen joined the basketball team that year but spent most of his time on the bench. A late bloomer, the fifteen-year-old Pippen was still shorter than his mother. He was almost cut from the team his junior year. At the end of his senior year Pippen had not been recruited by any college, and his future seemed uncertain.

Pippen graduated from high school in 1983, but without a scholarship he had little chance of attaining a college education. However, his high school coach was determined to get him enrolled in college and called in a favor from a friend at the University of Central Arkansas in Conway. Pippen was admitted to the university, a member of the

Scottie Pippen *(right)*, 2001. ASSOCIATED PRESS AP

National Association of Intercollegiate Athletes, on a work-study program. By the time he entered college in autumn 1983, Pippen was six feet, three inches tall. He worked as the equipment manager of the basketball team during his freshman year. By his sophomore year he had grown another two inches and was playing on the team as a small forward. Pippen brought a great deal of versatility to the team; he could pass like a point guard and score like a shooting guard. His offensive and defensive skills improved over the next two years, and he became the team's Most Valuable Player (MVP). In 1987 Pippen graduated from the University of Central Arkansas with a B.A. in industrial education.

Pippen's all-around performance in college did little to impress the National Basketball Association (NBA) recruiters, however, who were mostly interested in players from Division One schools. His big break came at an all-star celebrity game in Virginia. His performance at the event caught the attention of NBA scouts, and he was recruited in 1987 by the Seattle Supersonics as their fifth draft pick. Shortly afterward the Sonics traded Pippen to the Chicago Bulls for the center Olden Polynice. Pippen headed to the Windy City with a six-year contract worth more than $5 million.

Pippen's first two years in the NBA were uneventful, and he spent most of his time on the bench. In 1988 he had spinal surgery to repair a herniated disk which kept him out of the entire preseason and the first eight games of 1988–1989. During his third season, Phil Jackson became the Bulls head coach. Jackson's new offensive strategy gave Pippen more freedom and movement with the ball, allowing him to use his skills as both a forward and a guard. Pippen's scoring average rose to 16.5 points, along with 6.7 rebounds and 5.4 assists per game. He also blocked 101 shots and was the third best in steals, with 101 total. His overall performance impressed basketball fans, who selected him to the NBA All-Star team.

The following season Pippen was involved in a bitter contract dispute with the Bulls management. He eventually signed a deal guaranteeing him $3.5 million per year until the 1997–1998 season. That year Pippen's overall game improved, with an average score of 17.8 points per game and with 595 rebounds, 511 assists, and 193 steals. He also stepped up during the postseason, averaging 21.6 points, 8.9 rebounds, and 5.8 assists per game. His performance helped the Bulls win the Eastern Conference finals against their arch-rivals, the Detroit Pistons, and head to the finals, where they faced the Los Angeles Lakers. The Bulls nearly swept the Lakers and won the championship. Sadly, Pippen's father died early in the season and never got to see his son's victory.

Pippen and his star teammate Michael Jordan continued to play well over the next two seasons and led the Bulls to two more championships. During the summer of 1992 Pippen was chosen to play for the U.S. Olympic team in Barcelona, Spain. The "Dream Team," as they were called by sports journalists, dominated all opponents and won the gold medal. Just before the start of the 1993–1994 season, Jordan announced his retirement from professional basketball. No longer in Jordan's shadow, Pippen was suddenly the leader of the team. He played well that season, averaging 22.0 points, 8.7 rebounds, and 2.93 steals per game. He also was named the MVP of the NBA All-Star game in Minneapolis.

During the 1994–1995 season Pippen's personal life became the focus of much public attention with the emergence of two scandals. He was arrested on two separate occasions for allegedly pushing and grabbing the arm of his fiancée, Yvette DeLeone, and for gun possession, although both charges were later dropped. He also was involved in a paternity suit after the model Sonya Roby claimed he had fathered her child. Although he denied the charge, Pippen was ordered by the courts to pay Roby $10,000 in maternity costs. Pippen has been married twice, first to Karen McCullom and later to DeLeone, and has fathered four children.

In spring 1995 Jordan returned to the Bulls after an unsuccessful stint at minor league baseball. The following season the Bulls won their fourth NBA title, with a record-setting 72–10 win-loss record during the regular season. Pippen also was selected to play with the U.S. Olympic Dream Team II at the 1996 Summer Games in Atlanta, where he won his second gold medal.

Over the next two years the Bulls reigned as the NBA champions and made their mark in basketball history as a dynasty, winning six NBA titles within eight years. Their reign ended in 1998 when Jordan retired from basketball for the second time and Pippen, unhappy with the Bulls management, signed a lucrative deal with the Houston Rockets. However, his days as a Rocket were short lived. His style did not mesh well with the team and he was traded to the Portland (Oregon) Trail Blazers the following year. The change was just what Pippen needed. He had a strong season with the Trail Blazers, leading them to the Western Conference finals before losing to the Los Angeles Lakers in game seven.

Although he will always be linked to Jordan, Pippen's versatility, agility, and quickness have made him one of basketball's most talented players, and he was named to the NBA's Fiftieth Anniversary All-Time Team. He has gained the respect of his peers and is considered a role model to many adolescents. His popularity has led to many endorsement deals, including one for a candy bar name after him. Despite his fame and success, Pippen has not forgotten his humble beginnings; he remains close to his family and supports many charities.

★

Pippen has written an autobiography, with Greg Brown, *Reach Higher* (1996). Information on his life and accomplishments can be found in *Current Biography* (Mar. 1994), and *Contemporary Black Biography* (1997). See also articles about Pippen in *Sports Illustrated* (30 Nov. 1987), *New York Times* (27 Oct. 1991), *People Weekly* (6 May 1996), *Sport* (June 1996), and *Sports Illustrated* (24 Nov. 1997).

SABINE LOUISSAINT

POLLARD, Frederick Douglass ("Fritz") (*b.* 27 January 1894 in Chicago, Illinois; *d.* 11 May 1986 in Silver Spring, Maryland), Hall of Fame football player and coach whose exploits in the collegiate and the professional game paved the way for other African-American athletes.

Pollard was the seventh of eight children from a middle-class African-American family. His father, John W. Pollard, was a barber and his mother, Amanda Hughes, a seamstress. Pollard attended Lane Technical High, a virtually all-white school in Chicago. He was a three-sport star, helping his school win the Cook County football championship in 1911, the Cook County track title in 1912 (with an individual 220-yard hurdles title), and the state track and field championship in 1912 (with an individual 440-yard title). He made the All-County teams in football (as halfback), track and field, and baseball (playing shortstop). Pollard graduated from high school in 1912.

After a year of playing semiprofessional football, Pollard moved east in spring 1913 to attend Brown University in Providence, Rhode Island, but he failed to meet a foreign language requirement and did not enroll as a regular student until 1915. In the interim Pollard built a dubious reputation as a tramp athlete, attending Brown (as a special student), Dartmouth, Harvard, and Bates. In June 1914 he married Ada Laing of Providence. Their first child, Frederick Douglass ("Fritz") Pollard, Jr., who would compete in the track and field competition at the 1936 Olympics, was born the following year; they later had three daughters.

Pollard earned his foreign language credit at Springfield High School in Massachusetts in the spring of 1915 and entered Brown in the fall. He was ostracized by his teammates at first, but his outstanding performance on the football field won their acceptance. A left halfback, Pollard displayed a speedy and adept running style that made Brown a leading eastern contender. Brown's 5–4–1 season included a surprise 3–0 upset victory over Yale. Pollard devastated the Yale team, the Elis, with his punt returns, while the New Haven crowd chanted racist epithets at him. Like other African Americans who played football at mostly white colleges, he was singled out for particularly nasty assaults by opposing players. To defend himself after being tackled, Pollard would roll over on his back and thrash his legs in a bicycle pumping motion to thwart attacks. In 1915 he became the first African American to play in the Rose Bowl; Brown lost to Washington, 14–0.

The following year Pollard led Brown to an 8–1 record, the most successful season in the school's history. What particularly caught the attention of sports writers were the school's two easy victories over Yale (21–6) and Harvard (21–0). Pollard was selected in the halfback position by Walter Camp for his famed All-America team, only the second African American up to that time so honored (the first was William Lewis of Harvard, in 1892 and 1893). Pollard also won New England intercollegiate track and field titles in the hurdles during 1916 and 1917.

Pollard became academically ineligible to play football in 1917, and he dropped out of school in spring 1918 to become physical director in the Army's Young Men's Christian Association unit at Camp Meade, Maryland. From the fall of 1918 through 1920 he served as head football coach at Lincoln University in Pennsylvania.

Pollard extended his football career by joining the emergent professional game, playing for the Akron Indians in 1919. The following year the Akron team, renamed the Pros, joined the newly formed American Professional Football Association, which became the National Football League (NFL) in 1922. Pollard's crucial runs helped his team win the league's first championship with a 6–0–3 record, and he was named to its first All-Star team. Pollard became the first African-American NFL coach—and the first in any major league sport—when he coached Akron in 1921, followed by stints with Milwaukee, Hammond, and Akron again. Because of a fear of public backlash, he was paired with a white coach at each of these franchises to disguise his responsibilities.

During 1924 Pollard played full-time for Gilberton in the Pennsylvania Anthracite League, but he returned to the NFL in 1925, playing on three different teams and coaching two of them. He retired after the 1926 season and went on to coach two African-American professional barnstorming teams, the Chicago Black Hawks (1928–1932) and the New York Bombers (1935–1937). Pollard was trying to advance achievement by African Americans in the sport and demonstrate that they were worthy of participating in the professional game, at a time when the NFL owners were keeping African Americans out of the league in a "gentleman's agreement" from 1934 to 1945.

Pollard entered the business world in 1922, founding an investment firm that served the African-American community. When his firm went bankrupt in 1931 he moved to New York, where he headed a coal company. Pollard founded the first African-American tabloid newspaper, the *New York Independent News* (1935–1942). He also entered the African-American entertainment world, as a casting agent for former Akron teammate Paul Robeson for the film

The Emperor Jones (1933). Pollard continued to book African-American talent in nightclubs, and in 1942 he began producing Soundies, musical film shorts for playing on jukebox-like movie machines in bars. In 1943 Pollard assumed control of Suntan Studios, a talent agency and rehearsal hall located in the Bronx. Pollard and his first wife divorced in the early 1940s, and in 1947 he married Mary Ella Austin.

After World War II, Pollard continued as a booking agent for nightclubs, radio, and television. In 1956 he produced an obscure film, *Rockin' the Blues,* which over the years has become an invaluable documentation of notable rhythm-and-blues acts. Pollard achieved most of his financial success as a tax consultant, working in that field from the early 1950s until his retirement in 1975. After his death from pneumonia he was cremated, and his ashes interred in Brentwood, Maryland. In 1954 Pollard was inducted into the National Collegiate Hall of Fame, the first African American so enshrined.

Pollard came from that generation of African Americans who emerged as pioneers in breaking down color barriers. His struggle to win acceptance on the football field led him in his post-playing years to a lifetime commitment toward African-American advancement in other areas—notably in business, entertainment, and journalism. At every level of endeavor in which Pollard triumphed, he became a target of hatred and abuse, but he persevered with dignity and strength and, like Jackie Robinson, became an elder statesman and symbol of the African-American movement for full equality in American society.

★

Papers relating to Pollard's football career are in the Brown University Archives. His biography is John M. Carroll, *Fritz Pollard: Pioneer in Racial Advancement* (1992). Also of value are Jay Barry, "Fritz," *Brown Alumni Monthly* (Oct. 1970): 30–33; and Carl Nesfield's two-part article, "Pride Against Prejudice: Fritz Pollard, Brown's All-American Pre–World War I Vintage," *Black Sports* (Nov. and Dec. 1971). An obituary is in the *New York Times* (31 May 1986).

ROBERT PRUTER

POLLARD, James Clifford ("Jim") (*b.* 9 July 1922 in Oakland, California; *d.* 22 January 1993 in Stockton, California), basketball player with the Minneapolis Lakers who became the first true small forward in National Basketball Association history.

Pollard was the youngest of four children of Henry Augustus Sherril Pollard, a carpenter, and Suzie Elora Pollard, a homemaker. As a child in Oakland his primary interest was baseball, but in the eighth grade he turned to basketball, a sport he learned to play from his older siblings. Pollard excelled at Oakland Technical High School and earned All-State honors in 1940, his senior year, when he led his team to its third conference title and an undefeated season. As a senior he broke the school's scoring record by tallying 139 points in seven games. Pollard was named All-City and All-County center for two years. He also broke every existing high-school scoring record in the Bay Area and was an honorary scholastic All-American in 1939. During his senior year he was recruited by the former Stanford University basketball star Angelo "Hank" Luisetti to attend Stanford University.

As a Stanford sophomore in 1942, Pollard led the Indians to the National Collegiate Athletic Association (NCAA) championship in a 53–38 victory over Dartmouth. Although the flu prevented him from playing in the championship game, he was the tournament's high scorer. As a sophomore sensation, Pollard teamed with Howie Dallmar, Ed Voss, Don Burness, and Bill Cowden to form one of the finest quintets in NCAA basketball history. He led the team to the Pacific Coast Championship, was selected as an All-American, was named to the All-Pacific Coast Conference team, and was the league's second-leading scorer.

Pollard's college career was cut short during World War II. From 1942 to 1946 he served in the U.S. Coast Guard and played service basketball, where he excelled. After his service ended, Pollard went to San Diego, where he played for the Dons of the American Amateur League. He had an outstanding season in 1946–1947 as the league's high scorer and was named the Most Valuable Player (MVP). In the 1947–1948 season Pollard returned to the Bay Area to play for the Oakland Bittners, a strong Amateur Athletic Union (AAU) team. His sixteen-point average led the league in scoring. During the season Pollard enrolled at San Francisco State University to continue his studies toward a degree in physical education. Prior to entering professional basketball, Pollard was named the MVP in the 1948 College All-Star game held in Chicago, sponsored by the *Chicago Herald.* In that game he scored nineteen points, breaking the individual scoring record set by George Mikan in 1946.

Beginning in the 1947–1948 season, Pollard joined the Minneapolis Lakers of the National Basketball League (NBL). For the next eight seasons he was a mainstay on the Lakers teams that won championships in three different professional leagues—the NBL, Basketball Association of America (BAA), and National Basketball Association (NBA). Pollard was the first multitalented and multiskilled forward in NBA history. His versatility served as the model for all future NBA small forwards. Known as the "Kangaroo Kid" for his jumping ability, Pollard became the NBA's first true small forward through his ability to score, rebound, and defend. In addition, he was one of the few players of his era who could dunk a basketball. During his

Jim Pollard *(number 17)* and the Stanford NCAA Final Four champions of 1942. ASSOCIATED PRESS STANFORD UNIVERSITY

career he was considered one of the cleanest players in basketball, and in one three-year period he committed only 194 personal fouls.

During his first season with the Lakers, Pollard averaged 12.9 points in fifty-nine games and helped the Lakers capture the NBL championship. He was named to the All-NBL First Team and to the NBL Rookie Team. He missed being the NBL Rookie of the Year by one vote to Sheboygan's Marko Torodorvich. Before the start of the 1948–1949 season, the Lakers left the NBL and moved their franchise to another league, the upstart and rival BAA. The Lakers continued to dominate and won the BAA championship, and Pollard continued to excel. He averaged 14.8 points and 2.7 assists per game and was named to the All-BAA First Team.

After the NBL and BAA merged to form the NBA in 1949–1950, Pollard played on championship teams with Minneapolis in 1950, 1952, 1953, and 1954. Along with the center George Mikan and the power forward Vern Mikkelsen, he helped to form perhaps the greatest frontline in NBA history. With a dominant center, rugged power forward, and versatile small forward, the Lakers were the NBA's first dynasty and the model for all other teams hoping to build a championship squad.

Pollard's greatness and value to the team rested not just with his statistical contributions but with his ability to do the little things to win games. The former scoring leader was willing to sacrifice his scoring to be on a winning team. Unconcerned with headlines, Pollard deferred attention to the better-known Mikan, the NBA's first superstar. Despite playing behind Mikan, Pollard enjoyed an exceptional career. A four-time NBA All-Star (1951, 1952, 1954, 1955), he scored in double figures each year to finish with a 13.4 average. He was an All-NBA First Team in 1950, an All-NBA Second Team in 1952 and 1954, and the first team captain in Laker history. In 1952 Pollard was selected as the top basketball player by a *Sporting News* poll of seven six-year BAA/NBA veterans, finishing ahead of Mikan.

In 1954 Pollard earned a B.S. degree from the University of Minnesota at Minneapolis Saint Paul, where he had studied since 1951. The following year he was chosen as the All-Time Pacific Coast Forward along with Hank Luisetti by sportswriters and sportscasters. After retiring from basketball in 1955–1956, Pollard began a coaching career at LaSalle University in Philadelphia, Pennsylvania, where his teams compiled a 48–28 record in three seasons. In 1959–1960 he briefly coached the Minneapolis Lakers, taking over for John Castellani and posting a 14–25 record in the regular season. In the 1961–1962 season Pollard was hired to coach the newly formed Chicago Packers of the NBA. During his single season in Chicago, the Packers compiled an 18–62 record and finished fifth in the Western Division.

In 1964 Pollard was selected by the Academy of Sports

as one of ten players for its All-Time NBA Team. After several years away from coaching, Pollard returned to coach the Minnesota Muskies of the American Basketball Association in 1967–1968. The Muskies finished with the second-best record in the league, 50–28. After the team moved to Miami and became the Floridians, he coached for two more years. From 1971 through 1973 he was the basketball coach and athletic director at Florida's Fort Lauderdale University.

In 1977 Pollard was inducted into the Naismith Memorial Basketball Hall of Fame. He was also inducted into the Helms Foundation Hall of Fame, National AAU Hall of Fame, Bay Area Hall of Fame, and Stanford Hall of Fame. In 1979 he moved to Lodi, California, with his wife, Arilee Hansen, whom he had married on 24 June 1944, and their three children. He served both the Lodi Unified School District and the California Youth Authority as a teacher, counselor, and coach, and also was a teacher at Senior Elementary School and Delta Sierra Middle School. Pollard died at age seventy due to complications from blockage of the bowels. His body was cremated and the remains interred at Lodi Memorial Cemetery in Lodi. A smooth shooter whose game was graced with finesse and class, Pollard enjoyed a stellar career with the Minneapolis Lakers. With his all-around ability to score, defend, rebound, and pass, Pollard became the NBA's prototypical small forward.

★

Material about Pollard is available from his Hall of Famer file at the Basketball Hall of Fame. For additional information on his career, see Bill Carlson, "Pollard Chosen No. 1 Pro by NBA's Six-Year Vets," *Minneapolis Star* (16 Dec. 1952), and Carl Underwood, "Jim Pollard an Innovative Basketball Pioneer," *Lodi News-Sentinel* (16 Feb. 1993). For information about the Minneapolis Lakers and the early days of the NBA, see Stew Thornley, *Basketball's Original Dynasty: A History of the Lakers* (1989); Jack Clary, *Basketball's Great Dynasties: The Lakers* (1992); and Roland Lazenby, *The Lakers: A Basketball Journey* (1993).

DOUGLAS A. STARK

POTVIN, Denis Charles (*b.* 29 October 1953 in Ottawa, Ontario, Canada), Hall of Fame hockey player who, as team captain, led the New York Islanders to four consecutive Stanley Cup championships between 1980 and 1983 and was the highest-scoring defenseman in the history of the National Hockey League (NHL) upon his retirement in 1988.

The youngest son of Armand Jean Potvin and Lucille St. Louis, Potvin learned to skate by the age of three. His father had constructed a makeshift ice rink in the backyard that flooded and froze over during the long Ottawa winters. A civil servant in the Department of Supply and Services, Armand Potvin had himself entertained hopes of playing in the NHL, but a broken back suffered in training camp with the Detroit Red Wings ended his dream.

Disappointed but undaunted, Armand Potvin passed his love of hockey, as well as his skates, on to his three sons. Potvin recalled that by the time he acquired the skates from his older brothers, they were "all broken down [and] had no insulation. . . . I had to sprinkle pepper into them to keep my feet warm."

Under the tutelage of his father and one of his older brothers, Jean, Potvin became an accomplished hockey player by the time he was ten years old. He later credited both his parents and his brothers, not only with enabling him to develop his hockey skills, but also with bracing him to endure the anxiety and disappointment that were a normal part of life in the NHL. "There was plenty of love and emotion in our family but very little pity," Potvin recounted in his autobiography.

At thirteen Potvin signed with the Ottawa 67s of the Ontario Hockey Association (OHA). Joining the team in 1968 reunited him with Jean, who knew from the outset that as a hockey player his younger brother "was special, a guy with no limits." Playing the aggressive, physical style he had learned in pick-up games against older boys, Potvin soon became one of the most intimidating defensemen in the OHA.

Although he accumulated 800 penalty minutes during his tenure in the OHA, Potvin's rugged play was hardly his only asset. In five seasons with the 67s (1968–1969 through 1972–1973), he totaled 329 points, scoring 95 goals and recording 234 assists in only 254 games. Voted a First-Team All-Star three times (1971, 1972, and 1973), Potvin's 123 points on 35 goals and 88 assists during the 1972–1973 campaign shattered Bobby Orr's league record of 94 (38 goals, 56 assists) for a defenseman—a record set in 1965–1966 when Orr was a member of the Oshawa Generals. Orr, however, had accomplished this feat in only 47 games; it took Potvin 61. Late in his career, Potvin reflected on the mixed blessing of being forever compared to Orr. "It was a heck of a compliment," he said, "but after a while you say, 'But I did it . . . *I* did it!'"

Trying to live up to his exalted reputation and his lucrative three-year $1.2 million contract, the nineteen-year-old Potvin put tremendous pressure on himself to succeed when he arrived in the NHL in 1973. As a result his play was unusually tentative and his behavior uncharacteristically erratic. On one occasion he overslept, missed the team bus, and failed to arrive at the arena in time for a game against the Philadelphia Flyers. The media immediately portrayed him as "spoiled," "immature," "overpaid," and "undermotivated." Stung by the criticism, Potvin goaded himself to excel with a relentless determination. Yet his

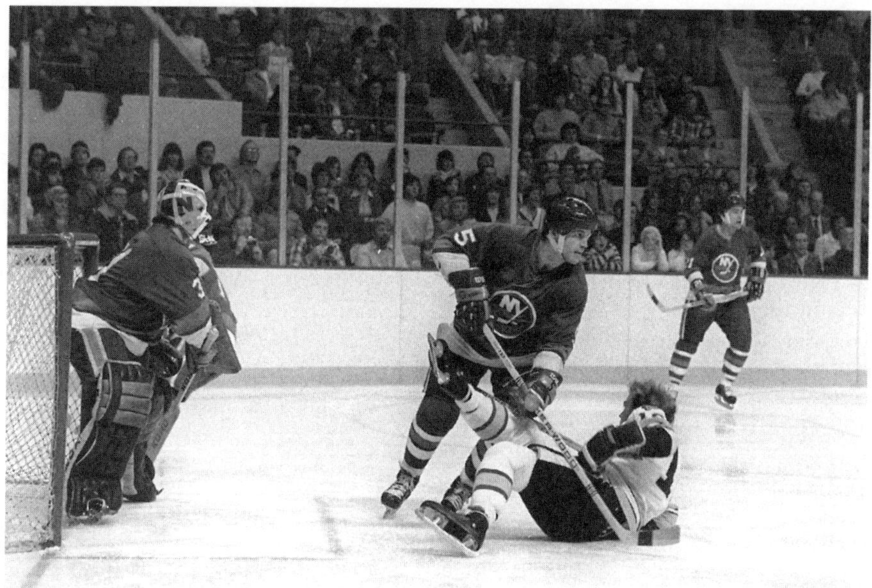

Denis Potvin *(number 5)*, 1977. ASSOCIATED PRESS AP

unyielding tenacity and voluble self-confidence only alienated his teammates. Potvin exacerbated this disaffection by criticizing their play once his own began to improve.

Controversies notwithstanding, Potvin's rookie season (1973–1974) was a triumph. Edging out Tom Lysiak of the Atlanta Flames and Borje Salming of the Toronto Maple Leafs, he became the first defenseman since Orr to win the Calder Memorial Trophy as NHL Rookie of the Year. With Potvin's arrival, the Islanders record also improved from 12 wins, 60 losses, and 6 ties in 1972–1973 to 19 wins, 41 losses, and 18 ties in 1973–1974. During the 1974–1975 season Potvin led the Islanders to the playoffs for the first time in franchise history, upsetting both the New York Rangers and the Pittsburgh Penguins before being eliminated by the eventual Stanley Cup champion Flyers.

Potvin garnered First-Team All-Star honors in 1975, and the following season received the first of three Norris Trophies as the best defenseman in the NHL, unseating Orr, who, between 1968 and 1975, had enjoyed a monopoly on the award. Potvin won the Norris twice more in 1978 and 1979 and was runner-up in 1975 and 1981. He was voted a First-Team All-Star four more times, in 1976, 1978, 1979, and 1981, and was a Second-Team All-Star in 1977 and 1984. Known as "The Navigator" for the smooth efficiency with which he directed the Islanders power play, Potvin, along with coach Al Arbour and teammates Mike Bossy, Clark Gillies, Bob Nystrom, Billy Smith, John Tonelli, and Bryan Trottier, guided the Islanders to four straight Stanley Cup championships between 1980 and 1983.

According to Arbour, Potvin was "like a monument" who provided the Islanders with "a bottomless well of poise." Writing in *The Sporting News,* Tim Moriarity described the six-foot, 205-pound defenseman as having "the look of eagles in his blue eyes. He has a square face, a strong chin, and shoulders that appear to be two ax handles wide." The pugnacity Potvin displayed on the ice, however, contrasted sharply with the reserved demeanor he tried to exhibit in public.

Maintaining such decorum was not always easy. In an editorial published on 25 October 1976, sportswriter Red Fisher of the *Montreal Star* called Potvin an "insufferable crybaby." A crescendo of boos greeted him in one arena after another, and more than once the intelligent, articulate, and brusque Potvin incurred the wrath of his teammates for his tactless critiques of their play. Only when he apologized to them in a locker-room meeting held during the 1976 season did Potvin at last gain a measure of acceptance and respect. "I think it was the beginning of putting our [championship] team together," Arbour declared. In an interview with the *New York Times* in 1985, when Potvin was in the twilight of his career, he explained that "there was a constant battle inside me to keep up the level of intensity I knew I needed to do what everyone expected of me. . . . It didn't mean I thought I was better than everyone else."

Potvin also endured his share of trouble off the ice. His father's prolonged battle with cancer and a bitter divorce from his first wife, Deborah, whom he had married in 1974, left him emotionally spent. His play became inconsistent, and in 1982–1983 he suffered through his worst season, netting only twelve goals in sixty-nine games. He performed splendidly in the playoffs, though, helping the Islanders secure their fourth and last Stanley Cup.

When he retired following the 1987–1988 season, Potvin was the highest-scoring defenseman in the history of the NHL, having totaled 1,052 points (310 goals, 742 assists) in 1,060 games. On 20 December 1985 he surpassed Orr, collecting his 916th career point. Although numerous defensemen have since eclipsed Potvin's mark, he was justifiably proud of the accomplishment. At the same time he showed a becoming modesty that had been absent earlier in his career. Noting that Orr, beset by injuries, had played only nine full seasons in the NHL, Potvin told reporters that the scoring record did not "mean that I'm better than Bobby Orr, just that I scored more points."

Elected to the Hockey Hall of Fame in 1991, Potvin has been a broadcaster for the Florida Panthers since the inception of the franchise in 1993. He married his second wife, former model Valerie Cates, with whom he resides in Lighthouse, Florida, with their son and two daughters. An avid traveler and sportsman, Potvin fishes, collects art and antiques, reads voraciously, and is addicted to working crossword puzzles.

The same careful preparation and hard work that distinguished Potvin's hockey career have also made him successful in business. He became a partner in People & Properties, an entertainment marketing company, at the age of twenty-two, and began selling commercial real estate and pursuing investment opportunities before his retirement.

Stan Fischler, who collaborated with Potvin on his autobiography, characterized him as "a marvelous, Renaissance man" who has a "grasp of the world around him and [a] genuine, insatiable interest in everything from the arts to the subway system of New York." Potvin, of course, was first and foremost a hockey player. At the height of his career from the late 1970s through the mid-1980s, he was the finest defenseman in the NHL. On an Islanders club that did not want for talent, Potvin remained the most important and indispensable man.

★

Potvin's autobiography, written with Stan Fischler, is *Power on Ice* (1977). Additional material on Potvin's career can be found in Mark Evenson, *New York Islanders* (1995). See also Stan Fischler, "Franchise Histories: New York Islanders," and Gary Mason, "NHL History: 99 and 66, 1979–80 to 1991–92," both in Dan Diamond, et al., *Total Hockey: The Official Encyclopedia of the National Hockey League* (1998).

MARK G. MALVASI

POVICH, Shirley Lewis (*b.* 15 July 1905 in Bar Harbor, Maine; *d.* 4 June 1998 in Washington), longtime sportswriter and editor for the *Washington Post*.

Povich was one of ten children born to Nathan Povich and Rosa Orlovich Povich, the only Orthodox Jewish family in Bar Harbor. The family moved to Bath, Maine, in 1920, and Povich graduated from Morse High School in 1922. A summer job as a teenager caddying for the newspaper mogul Edward McLean at the Kebo Valley Club, a Bar Harbor reserve for the wealthy and privileged, led Povich to employment at the *Washington Post* in 1922, when he was seventeen. McLean persuaded Povich to move to Washington, D.C., offering him $20 per week to caddy and another $12 per week to work as a copyboy. For the next seventy-five years, Povich drew a paycheck "every week, as caddy, copyboy, [war] correspondent, and columnist, finding joy in every category."

On his first morning in Washington, D.C., Povich found himself at the first tee of a private golf club with McLean and President Warren G. Harding. He heard McLean say, "Mr. President, this is Shirley Povich, the best caddy in the United States, and he's going to caddy for you today." Povich's life back in Bar Harbor had not been like that. At 74 Main Street, he had lived above the store where his father sold porch furniture to well-heeled summer visitors, like the Rockefellers and Vanderbilts. "We were never mistaken for either of those families," he later wrote. On his second day in Washington, Povich began his job as a copyboy at the *Washington Post*. McLean invited him to enroll in Georgetown University's law school and told the dean to send the tuition bills to him. Povich attended Georgetown from 1922 until 1924, when he left without earning a degree. In August 1924 Povich registered his first byline with a description of the Washington Senators taking over the American League by defeating the New York Yankees. After posting the story, Povich sneaked into the composing room and stole a galley proof of the column. Not until he ran his fingers across the metal and "fondled my name in type was I certain of this dream come true." Fittingly, his last column, published on the day he died, was on baseball, a game he loved.

In 1926 McLean made Povich a sports editor. At age twenty Povich was the youngest sports editor of any major U.S. newspaper. In August 1926 he began his long-running column, "This Morning with Shirley Povich," which was a standard in the *Washington Post* until his retirement in 1974. Povich met Ethyl Friedman on a blind date in 1930. They were married on 21 February 1932 and later had three children. One son, Maury, became a popular television talk show host.

Through the years Povich's column was one of the great chronicles of sports. He wrote about the baseball greats Babe Ruth, Joe DiMaggio, Ted Williams, Sandy Koufax, and Lou Gehrig; the golfers Bobby Jones and Sam Snead; the tennis star Bill Tilden; the fighter Rocky Marciano; and the jockey Earl Sande. He covered many uplifting moments in sports history, ranging from the first World Series win for the Washington Senators in 1924 to Cassius Clay's upset of Sonny Liston to win the heavyweight title in 1964, and on to the 2,131st consecutive game played by Cal Ripken of the Baltimore Orioles in 1995, which broke Lou Gehrig's record. Povich also took up controversial subjects, such as Gene Tunney's defeat of Jack Dempsey in a 1927 heavyweight bout, which was said to be the result of a "long count" that gave Tunney extra time to get up from the floor. Povich also reported on the terrifying events of the 1972 Munich Olympics, when eleven Israeli athletes were murdered by terrorists.

When asked what time of day he wrote his column, Povich responded, "When my head comes off the pillow." In 1969, after having written his column for more than forty years, he admitted that he still wrote "scared." He took that as a sign of maturity, not cowardice. "The easy writer is either the lazy one or the conceited one." By his own admission he was never an easy writer. Povich's son Maury said in an interview, "Long after the game had ended, long after the lights were out and everyone went home and the locker rooms were empty, my father and Red Smith were still in the press box writing and rewriting their stories." Povich once counseled a young reporter always to remember, "The story has never been written that couldn't be written better."

In addition to writing his daily column, Povich became a prolific freelance writer. In 1946, after the Brooklyn Dodgers signed a contract with Jackie Robinson, the first African American to play in the major leagues, Povich wrote an award-winning fifteen-part series called "No More Shutouts" on the impact of the color line in baseball. The first paragraph of the first installment set the tone for the rest of the series: "Four hundred and fifty-five years after Columbus eagerly discovered America, major league baseball reluctantly discovered the American Negro." Likewise, because the Washington Redskins football team had a long history of racial exclusion, Povich wrote, "The Redskins' colors are burgundy, gold and caucasian." After a game when the Redskins were clobbered by the Cleveland Browns in 1960, Povich wrote, "Jim Brown, born ineligible to play for the Redskins, integrated their end zone three times yesterday." Much of his writing was memorable. When Don Larsen pitched a perfect game in 1956, Povich had this to say: "The million-to-one shot came in. Hell froze over. A month of Sundays hit the calendar. Don Larsen today pitched a no-hit, no-run, no-man-reaches-first game in a World Series."

Povich did not care for basketball. Writing in *Sports Illustrated* in 1958, he argued that basketball "is for the birds." He went on to say, "The game lost this particular patron years ago . . . when it went vertical and put the accent on carnival freaks who achieved upper space by growing into it. They don't shoot baskets anymore, they stuff them, like taxidermists." Povich was proud that this column later was anthologized and widely used as an example of excellent writing.

After his formal retirement from the *Washington Post* in 1974, Povich continued writing for the newspaper, taught journalism and sportswriting at leading colleges and universities, and appeared as a guest speaker on television and on Ken Burns's award-winning history of baseball on the Public Broadcasting Service in 1994. Povich was awarded many honors; among the earliest was the Grantland Rice Award for sportswriting in 1964. He garnered the J. G. Taylor Spink Award from the Baseball Hall of Fame in 1976, and was thereby inducted to the writers wing of the Baseball Hall of Fame. He was a recipient of the Red Smith Award from the Associated Press Sports Editors in 1983 and was elected to the National Sportscasters and Sportswriters Hall of Fame in 1984. In 1995 he was given Lifetime Achievement Awards from the National Press Club and the Anti-Defamation League. Povich was the first sportswriter to receive the Fourth Estate Award presented by the National Press Club in 1997.

Povich was included in the 1962 edition of *Who's Who of American Women*. "I made it, right between Louise Pound and Hortense Powdermaker," he joked. When the publisher apologized for the mistake, Povich confessed that he enjoyed the experience. As he put it, "For years I've been hearing this is no longer a man's world and I am glad to be listed officially on the winning side." Povich died of a heart attack at age ninety-two and is buried in a simple wood coffin in Elevesgrad Cemetery in southeast Washington, D.C.

In his tribute to Povich, Ben Bradlee, the former executive editor of the *Washington Post,* stated, "Shirley Povich was why people bought the paper. . . . He was the sports section. For a lot of years, he carried the paper, and that's no exaggeration."

★

Povich's autobiography is *All These Mornings* (1969). His reminiscences and reflections on the golden age of sports—the time between the two world wars—are included in Jerome Holtzman, *No Cheering in the Press Box* (1995). Brief biographical sketches are in James C. Kaufman, "Shirley Povich," *Dictionary of Literary Biography,* vol. 171: *Twentieth-Century American Sportswriters* (1997), and *Who's Who in America* (1997). See also Mike Schatzkin, *Ballplayers: Baseball's Ultimate Biographical Reference* (1990). The *Washington Post* compiled an extensive biographical essay (15 Oct. 1997), and published many tributes to Povich, including those by Leonard Shapiro (5 June 1998), Doug Struck and Thomas Heath (8 June 1998), and Bill Gilbert (12 June 1998). An obituary is in the *New York Times* (7 June 1998).

JOHN KARES SMITH

PREFONTAINE, Steve Roland (*b.* 25 January 1951 in Coos Bay, Oregon; *d.* 30 May 1975 in Eugene, Oregon), popular long-distance runner who held every U.S. record between 2,000 and 10,000 meters and who campaigned for the reform of U.S. amateur athletics.

Born to Raymond Prefontaine, a carpenter, and Elfriede Senholz Prefontaine, a seamstress, Prefontaine and his two sisters were raised in a small coastal town in Oregon. A bench-warmer on his junior high school football team, Prefontaine turned to running during his sophomore year in high school, when he discovered that the longer the run, the closer he was to the lead. The five-foot, nine-inch, 152-pound athlete was far better suited to running, a sport that emphasized speed and agility. In 1967 he joined the Marshfield High School track team. Under the coaching of Walter McClure, a former track star at the University of Oregon, Prefontaine went undefeated his junior and senior years, setting the national high school record for the two-mile run. Prefontaine graduated from Marshfield in 1969. At the conclusion of his high school career, Prefontaine quickly entered international competition. He placed fourth at the Amateur Athletic Union (AAU) championships the summer after his senior year, earning a spot on the national team that competed at international events. He went on to race in four international meets that summer, placing as high as second in the 5,000 meters against world-class competition.

Steve Prefontaine in his last race, 1975. ASSOCIATED PRESS AP

Widely recruited by college track programs, Prefontaine chose the nearby University of Oregon. Oregon's legendary track coach Bill Bowerman had already trained several U.S. and world record holders, and he recognized that same potential in Prefontaine. In a letter to the Coos Bay community thanking them for their role in Prefontaine's success so far, Bowerman showed confidence that Prefontaine could become "the greatest runner in the world." In thanking Coos Bay, Bowerman touched upon a key aspect of Prefontaine's appeal—his connection with the community of fans that supported him throughout his career. The chants of "Go Pre!" at the University of Oregon's Hayward Field could become deafening. In thirty-eight races at Hayward, Prefontaine lost only three times, all at one mile, which was not his specialty. He openly admitted that he ran best in front of "his people."

In 1970 Prefontaine won the first of his unprecedented four National Collegiate Athletic Association (NCAA) three-mile track titles. That he won despite suffering a cut on his foot that required twelve stitches only three days before the race underscored the tough, go-for-broke style that characterized Prefontaine's running. Though at times considered arrogant, he ran for guts, not glory. Prefontaine became known for pushing the pace of a race early, running in front rather than hanging back to conserve his strength for a finishing kick, or sprint, at the end. This style usually worked well for him, and in his collegiate races he routinely broke his opponents with a fast, punishing pace.

Though Prefontaine's all-or-nothing approach to running made for exciting races, it did not serve him well in his biggest race on the international stage. Since his first successes as a high school junior, he had thought about competing in the 1972 Munich Olympic Games. He had dominated the 5,000 in the U.S. Olympic trials and considered himself well prepared. Though shaken by the terrorist attack on Israeli athletes at the games, Prefontaine looked good in the qualifying heats. The field of runners for the final was perhaps one of the best ever assembled, including Lasse Viren of Finland, who had won the 10,000 meters in world-record time earlier in the games, and Mohamed Gamoudi of Tunisia. At twenty-one, Prefontaine was the youngest in the field by two years.

The race began at a surprisingly slow pace that favored Viren, Gamoudi, and other strong kickers in the world-class field. Prefontaine wanted a fast race that came down to "who's toughest"—his kind of race. With four laps to go and the crowd on his side, he took control and dramatically increased the pace. After two more laps most of the field had dropped back, but Viren and Gamoudi stayed with him. Viren held a slight lead, and with 300 meters left Prefontaine started to pull away from the inside of the track to pass him, but Gamoudi, showing a veteran's tactical sense, moved to cut him off before he could pass. Prefontaine tried to pass Viren again on the last curve, and again Gamoudi quickly cut him off. His momentum gone and energy spent, Prefontaine staggered the last dozen meters and was passed by Ian Stewart of Great Britain for the bronze.

Prefontaine was deeply disappointed and upset that the race had been decided by tactical tricks rather than blood-and-guts running. Still, he was young, and long-distance runners typically reached their prime in their late twenties. Prefontaine rebounded after his loss to have an outstanding senior season at Oregon. At the end of his college career he had won seven NCAA titles, three in cross-country (he skipped the 1972 cross-country season to recover from the Olympics) and four in the three-mile. Prefontaine graduated from the University of Oregon in 1973 with a B.A. in communications. He spent the next two years running as an amateur for the Oregon Track Club. By the end of his career Prefontaine owned every U.S. record between 2,000 and 10,000 meters and between 2 and 6 miles. He was the best U.S. distance runner of his time.

There was much more to Prefontaine than races and records. He often held running clinics at high schools and at the Oregon State Prison. He was also an activist for the reform of amateur athletics. The AAU's restrictions on financial support for amateur athletes, as well as its sanctions on athletes for skipping AAU events to participate in European meets, made life difficult for many amateurs in the United States. Prefontaine was an outspoken and defiant critic of the system. Despite having little money, he refused to become a professional, although he was offered up to $200,000 a year to join the emerging professional circuit. Instead, he continued to push for a reorganization of amateur athletics.

Prefontaine was also the first athlete to sign with Nike, a company cofounded by his former track coach Bill Bowerman. He took the title of National Public Relations Manager and initiated the campaign to get top international athletes to wear Nike shoes. A statue of Prefontaine stands at the Nike corporate headquarters, and the Prefontaine Classic track meet, held annually at Hayward Field, has become one of the premier track events on U.S. soil.

Prefontaine ran his last race on 29 May 1975 at Hayward Field in front of his hometown crowd. It was the final meet of a tour of top Finnish athletes that he had organized. He won, extending his winning streak at distances over a mile at Hayward to twenty-five. Later that night, while driving home, Prefontaine died in a single-car accident. He is buried at Sunset Memorial Park in Coos Bay. His brief but extraordinary career was captured years later in a documentary and two feature films.

Prefontaine's brash, charismatic style, both on and off the track, helped to popularize the sport of running and gave him the stature to further the cause of athlete's rights. Donna De Verona, a 1964 Olympic medalist in swimming and television sports commentator, noted that Prefontaine's outspokenness and willingness to risk AAU sanctions made him a "lightning rod for the tensions between the AAU and amateur athletes," and that "he was instrumental in helping the cause of athletes' rights."

In 1978, three years after Prefontaine's death, Congress passed the Amateur Sports Act, which stripped the AAU of its authority over amateur athletes. The Prefontaine Classic continues to draw the top national and international track and field athletes and is one of the best attended meets in the U.S. Prefontaine was inducted into the USA Track and Field Hall of Fame in 1976.

★

Prefontaine's biography, *Pre!* (1977), was written by Tom Jordan. Obituaries are in the *New York Times* (31 May 1975), and in *Newsweek* and *Time* (both 9 Jun. 1975). A documentary film on his life, *Fire on the Track: The Steve Prefontaine Story* (1995), was narrated by Ken Kesey. Two feature films were produced about his life: *Prefontaine* (1996), and *Without Limits* (1998).

J. CHRISTOPHER JOLLY

R

RADBOURN, Charles Gardner ("Charley"; "Old Hoss") (*b.* 11 December 1854 in Rochester, New York; *d.* 5 February 1897 in Bloomington, Illinois), baseball pitcher who won 309 games over an 11-year career, and whose record 59 wins in 1884 earned him a reputation as one of the most durable pitchers of the nineteenth century.

Radbourn was the second of eight children of Charles Radbourn and Caroline Gardner, English immigrants who arrived in the United States in early 1854. In 1855 the Radbourn family joined the growing number of American immigrants migrating west. They settled in Bloomington, Illinois, where Radbourn's father found work as a meat cutter. Though Radbourn slaughtered livestock in his father's butcher shop for a time, he was soon drawn to baseball. By the time he was a teenager he was already honing his pitching skills by firing fastballs against barn doors. After a stint working as a railroad brakeman, in 1879 Radbourn signed on to pitch for Dubuque, of the Northwest League, for $75 per month.

The five-foot, nine-inch, 168-pound Radbourn quickly proved his skills, leading Dubuque to the pennant. After a shoulder injury cut short his 1880 season, he signed on with the Providence Grays of the National League prior to the 1881 campaign. Although the Grays' pitching already boasted one future Hall of Famer in John Ward, Radbourn soon established himself as the team's best pitcher. Over his first four seasons he improved each year in every major pitching category—wins, strikeouts, earned run average, and innings pitched. Radbourn set a major league record in 1883 with 48 victories while hurling 632 innings, figures that would be unthinkable in modern baseball.

But that year 632 innings did not even lead the league. With the pitcher's box just fifty feet from home plate, and with one ball typically lasting an entire game, home runs were rare and pitchers had the luxury of coasting for long stretches at a time. The rulebook also placed its share of restrictions on pitchers, and until 1884 they were barred from throwing overhand. Though many sought to circumvent this rule, Radbourn thrived under it. One writer singled out the right-hander's delivery for its "easy, frictionless underhand swing" through which the pitcher "would play with weak batters like a cat would with a mouse."

His easy manner in the box belied the personality of a man described as "ill-tempered" and "capricious." In many of the existing photographs of Radbourn he can be seen slyly making an obscene gesture with his middle finger. (Some sources suggest that an 1886 team picture in which Radbourn's middle finger is extended is the first known photographed image of the gesture.) However, his teammates respected him. In his first three seasons with Providence, Radbourn pitched the Grays to two second-place finishes. In 1884 he put them over the top, in a roller-coaster season that saw his integrity attacked in the press, his future in the profession placed in doubt, and then finally, shockingly, the defining accomplishment of his career.

Things started out well enough. During the first three

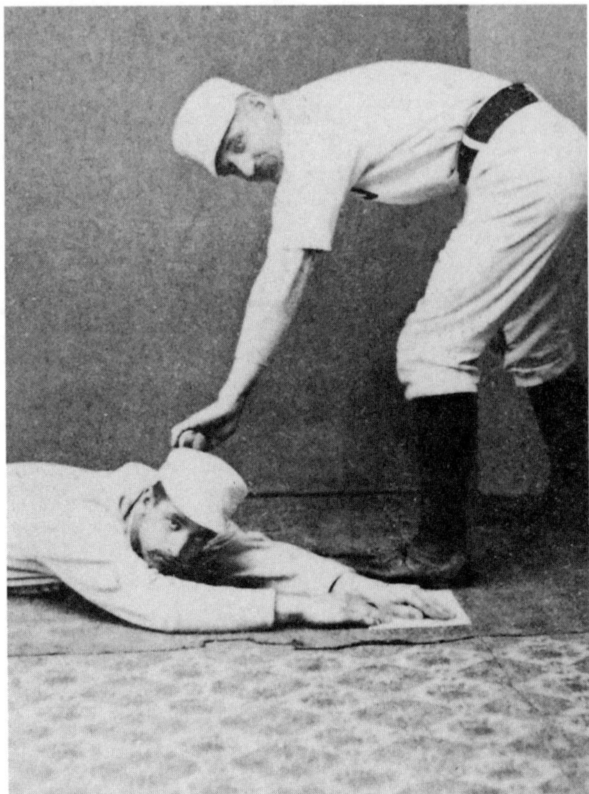

Charley "Old Hoss" Radbourn (standing), from a Goodwin & Co. baseball card, c. 1887–1890. BASEBALL CARDS FROM THE BENJAMIN K. EDWARDS COLLECTION/THE LIBRARY OF CONGRESS

months of the season, Radbourn accumulated twenty-four victories against just eight defeats, helping to bring the Grays to within two games of first-place Boston. But all was not well in the Providence clubhouse. In early July the Grays other pitcher Charlie Sweeney was sidelined with a lame arm, and when Radbourn was forced to pitch nearly every day to compensate, he demanded to be paid more money. The Providence management refused, and the pitcher's mood began to sour. On 16 July, he lost his temper in the late innings of a crucial game against Boston. With the score tied in the eighth inning, Radbourn reacted to an umpire's balk call by throwing several wild pitches, allowing three runs to score. Accused of throwing the game, Radbourn was suspended indefinitely by the club. The press charged him with "ugliness" on the mound, and some Providence fans even threatened to boycott games if Radbourn pitched again.

The suspension lasted only one week. On 22 July Sweeney was also expelled from the team for insubordination. Desperate for a pitcher, the club petitioned Radbourn to return, offering him the extra money he sought. He accepted, promising his manager, "I will win or pitch my right arm off." He would do both. Over the last three months of the season, Radbourn started nearly every game, winning thirty-five and losing only four. At one point he won eighteen consecutive games, transforming a tight pennant race into a blowout. When the season ended, the Grays held a commanding ten-game lead over their rivals. Of his startling performance, the *Boston Herald* wrote that Radbourn "threw into his work an amount of determination and energy that surprised his admirers and confounded his depreciators. 'His arm will give out,' was said on all sides, but it did not give out." Radbourn's season total of fifty-nine victories smashed the all-time record he had set just the previous year. He also led the league in complete games (73), earned run average (1.38), strikeouts (441), and innings pitched (678.7). In the wake of this overwhelming performance, the press took to calling him "Old Hoss," for his reliability and endurance.

But Radbourn had ruined his arm. Years later, his manager would recall how the pitcher often came to the park unable to lift his right arm high enough to comb his hair and required the assistance of teammates to dress himself. When he resumed pitching in 1885, the once great pitcher had become merely average. The Providence franchise folded following the 1885 season. Radbourn would pitch six more seasons for three teams in two leagues, but never win even half as many games as he had in 1884. When he managed to win a mere eleven games in 1891, he retired. Of his last years on the diamond, one writer commented that "[Radbourn's] uniform only was pitching . . . the physique of the original was there no more."

After leaving the game Radbourn returned to Bloomington, where he operated a billiard hall with his wife, Carrie Clarke Stanhope, whom he had married in 1887. For a time Radbourn contemplated returning to professional baseball, and in 1894 he contacted the St. Louis Browns about a tryout. However, any possibility of a comeback evaporated on 13 April of that year, when Radbourn lost the vision in his left eye in a hunting accident. Permanently disfigured, he lived the remaining years of his life as a recluse. At some point he had also contracted syphilis, and the resulting muscular weakness quickly eroded his health. He died at the age of forty-two, and is buried at Evergreen Memorial Cemetery in Bloomington.

Radbourn pitched under circumstances vastly different from those we know today, making historical comparison difficult, if not impossible. Among his contemporaries, his 309 career victories rank fourth, and his lifetime 2.68 earned-run average ranks tenth. But it was his remarkable stretch of pitching in 1884 that made, and ultimately cut short, his career, and it was on the basis of that feat that he was included among the first group of players to be inducted into the National Baseball Hall of Fame when the museum opened in 1939. Radbourn's record of 59 victories in a single season has now stood for more than 117 years. Barring drastic changes in the way the game is played, it is a record unlikely ever to be broken.

★

No full-length biography of Radbourn exists. The best single source of information on him is the collection of articles on file at the National Baseball Hall of Fame Library in Cooperstown, New York. Game accounts and box scores from the 1884 season published in the *Boston Herald* also provide valuable commentary. Radbourn is also discussed in David Nemec, *The Great Encyclopedia of Nineteenth Century Baseball* (1997). The definitive source for all baseball statistics is John Thorn, Pete Palmer, and Michael Gershman, eds., *Total Baseball: The Official Encyclopedia of Major League Baseball*, 7th ed. (2001).

DAVID JONES

REED, Willis, Jr. (*b.* 25 May 1942 in Hico, Louisiana), Hall of Fame center and power forward, coach and basketball executive, who scored two of the most memorable baskets in National Basketball Association (NBA) history.

Reed was the only child of Willis Reed, Sr., an industrial laborer, and Inell Ross Reed, a domestic worker. Born on his grandfather's farm, Reed grew up in Bernice, a tiny, segregated community in rural northern Louisiana, where he enjoyed fishing and hunting. Reed attended the local public schools. By eighth grade he was already over six feet tall, and by tenth grade in 1957, Reed was a starting center on the West Side High School basketball team. He also played football and baseball, and threw the shot put and the discus for the school's track team.

Willis Reed, 1970. ASSOCIATED PRESS AP

Reed later went on to lead West Side High School to state championships in both basketball and football. With encouragement from his high school basketball coach, Reed discovered that his height and athletic ability could be used to obtain a college education. Young Reed understood the attention he received as a star high school athlete was secondary to the academic and moral discipline provided by his parents and teachers. "That discipline helped me in college at Grambling, and it definitely helped me get into the pros," said Reed. This discipline pushed Reed to be the best at whatever he embarked on and it would become a lifelong lesson that would later be the driving force behind one of the greatest moments in athletic history.

In 1960 Eddie Robinson, the legendary football coach from Grambling State University, recruited Reed, and although Reed did attend Grambling, he chose to play for the noted basketball coach Fred C. Hobdy. He especially liked the Tigers NBA-like fast break running game. Reed was twice named an All-American at Grambling. Grambling won the National Association of Intercollegiate Athletics Championship (NAIA) in Reed's freshman year (1961), and with Reed's help as a dominating center, Grambling later won three Southwestern Athletic Conference Championships. In 1963, Reed's senior year, he won a gold medal at the Pan American Games in São Paulo, Brazil. He averaged 26.6 points and 21.3 rebounds as a senior, and ended his career at Grambling with a total of 2,280 points. Reed was elected to the NAIA Hall of Fame in 1970.

During the political and social upheaval of the 1960s, Reed shied away from political activism for fear of losing his athletic scholarship. Reed was well liked at Grambling, a small, historically African-American land grant college, and he and a few of his teammates even joined Phi Beta Sigma, a national fraternity. But Reed never really sought the limelight, a characteristic that defined his professional basketball career. Reed married his college sweetheart Geraldine Marie Oliver on 12 February 1963. They had two children but divorced in 1969. Reed graduated from Grambling in 1964 with a B.A. in physical education and a minor in biology. Although he had dreams of playing professional basketball, Reed worked to became a certified teacher and planned to be a physical education instructor and coach.

While teaching an eighth grade gym class, Reed learned that the New York Knicks had drafted him as the tenth overall pick in the second round of the March 1964 NBA draft. He was disappointed because he had expected a higher draft position and had wanted to play for the Detroit

Pistons, but he signed a contract with the Knicks for a salary just under $10,000. Reed moved to New York City, living in a hotel a few blocks from the famed Madison Square Garden. He often walked to practice during his rookie year.

During Reed's first season in the NBA, 1964–1965, he ranked seventh in scoring, averaging 19.5 points per game, and ranked fifth in rebounding, fielding 14.7 rebounds per game. That same year Reed made his first All-Star appearance, and he was the first Knicks player ever to be named NBA Rookie of the Year. Reed played in seven All-Star Games during his ten-year career in the NBA, and he quickly established himself as a reliable leader on the team. During the 1969–1970 season Reed was named NBA Most Valuable Player (MVP), NBA Finals MVP, and All-Star game MVP. Michael Jordan (while playing for the Chicago Bulls) is the only other player to have won all three in the same year (1995–1996).

Although Reed amassed an impressive statistical record as a professional basketball player, most fans remember him for his dramatic performance during the opening minutes of game seven of the 1970 NBA Finals against the Lakers at Madison Square Garden. Reed, the captain and backbone of the Knicks, was sidelined with a severe injury to his right thigh and hip and was not expected to play in the pivotal home game. When Reed walked onto the court with barely a limp to the thunderous applause of the home crowd, he recalled, "There we were knocking on the door of a National Championship. I was always taught to try my best, and after all the hours of practice and soreness, there was no way that I would not go for it." Reed had to leave at twenty-seven minutes into the game after making two baskets, but the Knicks were inspired and went on to capture their first national title, and Reed became a sports legend. Reed also helped the Knicks win their second NBA championship in 1973, and he was named NBA Finals MVP of that year, and MVP for 1973. Plagued with injuries, Reed retired at the end of the 1973–1974 season. He played 23,073 minutes as a New York Knick and was ranked among the team's top three scorers with 4,859 field goals; 12,183 total points; and 8,414 rebounds.

Reed served as head coach of the Knicks during 1977–1978 season. He then went on to coach at the collegiate level as an assistant coach at St. John's University in New York City during the 1980–1981 season, and then as head coach at Creighton University in Omaha, Nebraska, from 1981 to 1982, and from 1984 to 1985. He was elected to the Naismith Memorial Basketball Hall of Fame in 1981. On 20 August 1983 Reed married Gale I. Kennedy; they had two children. Reed served as an assistant coach for the Atlanta Hawks, the Sacramento Kings, and was the head coach of the New Jersey Nets from 1987 to 1989. Reed became the general manager of the Nets in 1993, and eventually became senior vice-president of the team.

In 1997 during the NBA's Fiftieth Anniversary, Reed was named one of the fifty greatest players in the league's history. Because he has often shunned the national spotlight, some may overlook his outstanding contributions, but Reed's impressive record stands out among the many basketball luminaries.

★

See Willis Reed with Phil Pepe, *A View from the Rim: Willis Reed on Basketball* (1971), for Reed's thoughts on the game. A biography chronicling Reed's Hall of Fame career in the NBA is George Kalinsky, *A Will To Win: The Comeback Year* (1973). Mark Vancil, *NBA at 50: The Colorful History of America's Number 1 Pro Sports League* (1997), provides a historical reference of Reed's achievements and his place in professional basketball history. Two insightful articles that capture the essence of Reed's role in winning the 1970 and 1973 NBA championships are Frank Deford, "In For Two Plus the Title," *Sports Illustrated* (18 May 1970), and Peter Carry, "Where There's a Willis," *Sports Illustrated* (21 May 1973).

F. ROMALL SMALLS

REESE, Harold Henry ("Pee Wee") (*b.* 23 July 1918 near Ekron, Kentucky; *d.* 14 August 1999 in Louisville, Kentucky), Baseball Hall of Fame shortstop who captained the "Boys of Summer"–era Brooklyn Dodgers and helped ease Jackie Robinson's integration in the major leagues.

Reese was born on a farm in Meade County, Kentucky, between the towns of Ekron and Brandenburg, to Carl and Emma Reese. When he was three years old, his father

Pee Wee Reese, 1940. © BETTMANN/CORBIS

moved the family forty miles northeast to Louisville, where Carl Reese took a job as a detective with the Louisville and Nashville Railroad.

Though just five feet, four inches and 110 pounds as a high school senior, Reese reportedly was nicknamed "Pee Wee" because of his skill at shooting marbles, a "pee wee" being a common type of marble.

As a senior at Louisville's Du Pont Manual High School, Reese did not appear to have much of a future in baseball, playing just five games at second base. After graduating in 1936 he took an $18-per-week job splicing cables for the Kentucky Telephone Company.

Reese continued to play baseball on weekends for a church league, from which he was signed as a shortstop to the Louisville Colonels, a minor league team, in 1938. In 1939, during his second season, he led the American Association in triples and stolen bases, swiping thirty-five bases in thirty-six attempts.

That year the American League's Boston Red Sox purchased the Colonels, and the following winter it sold Reese to the National League's Brooklyn Dodgers for a reported $150,000—a less famous variation of the team's 1919 sale of a young Babe Ruth to the New York Yankees. Reese would play shortstop for the Dodgers for the next eighteen years.

Called up to Brooklyn in 1940, Reese spent much of his rookie season injured. He became a regular the following season, playing 151 games at shortstop on a Brooklyn team that won its first pennant in twenty-one years.

Reese credited Brooklyn manager Leo Durocher with getting his career off to the right start, and Durocher, who also played shortstop, told of taking Reese aside in August 1941, when the young player was on his way to leading the league with forty-seven errors.

"He was down, and hoping I would take him out and play myself," Durocher recalled. "I said, 'Pee Wee. If you think I'm going in there to bail you out, you're nuts. You're playing even if you make twelve errors a day.' " In his 1984 Hall of Fame induction speech, Reese said, "If it wasn't for Leo, I doubt I would be up here today."

Reese also enjoyed a special relationship with Jackie Robinson, the African-American infielder the Dodgers signed after World War II to break baseball's color barrier. Reese, who had missed three seasons while serving in the U.S. Navy, was coming home from Guam on a transport ship when he heard the Dodgers had signed Robinson. Initially worried at possibly losing his job to an African American, Reese said he tried to place himself in Robinson's position.

"I mean, if they said to me, 'Reese, you got to go over and play in the colored guys' league,' how would I feel? Scared. The only white. Lonely. But I'm a good shortstop and that's what I'd want them to see. Not my color. Just that I can play the game," he told Roger Kahn for the book *The Boys of Summer* (1972). "And that's how I've got to look at Robinson. If he's man enough to take my job, I'm not going to like it, but damn it, black or white, he deserves it."

When the Dodgers prepared to bring Robinson to its big league team in the spring of 1947, Reese's fellow Southerner, Dixie Walker of Georgia, gathered signatures for a petition threatening a boycott. Reese refused to sign, and the petition failed.

During the Dodgers' first road trip, the players visited Cincinnati, just up the Ohio River from Reese's hometown. There, on the edge of the still-segregated South, Robinson took torrents of abuse from fans and Cincinnati players. Finally, Reese went to Robinson at first base and put his arm around his teammate. Dodger pitcher Rex Barney later described the gesture as one that said "This is my boy. This is the guy. We're gonna win with him." "After Pee Wee came over like that," Robinson recalled later, "I never felt alone on a baseball field again."

With Reese at shortstop, the Dodgers never finished lower than third in the National League. The team played in seven World Series. It was Reese who fielded the ground ball that was the final out of the 1955 World Series, in which the Dodgers defeated the hated Yankees and won what would be their only title in Brooklyn. Reese was the unchallenged leader of that era's Dodgers, the only member of the team with an armchair in front of his locker instead of a stool.

Reese went west with the team to Los Angeles in 1958, but played only fifty-nine games that season before retiring with 2,170 hits, a .269 career batting average, and 232 stolen bases. These were impressive totals in an era in which shortstops were valued more for their fielding than for offense. Reese's leadership of one of baseball's most storied teams helped secure his 1984 selection to the National Baseball Hall of Fame.

Reese married Dorothy "Dottie" Walton on 29 March 1942; they had a son and a daughter.

Reese worked as a coach for the Dodgers in 1959, then began a career as a broadcaster, first with CBS and NBC, and later with the Cincinnati Reds and Montreal Expos. (He broadcasted a few times with baseball great Jay "Dizzy" Dean.) In 1971 Reese joined the Louisville-based company Hillerich and Bradsby, maker of the Louisville Slugger baseball bat, working in sales and promotions. Reese also owned a Louisville bowling alley, Pee Wee Reese Lanes, for many years.

Reese was diagnosed with lung cancer in 1997. He had surgery to remove a malignant tumor, then underwent radiation treatment. He also suffered from cancer in his left leg and from prostate cancer. He died at his home in Louisville and was buried at Resthaven Memorial Park.

On Reese's Hall of Fame plaque, the first accomplishments listed are "Intangible qualities of subtle leadership on and off field, competitive fire and professional pride." It is for these qualities—even more than for his steady play in the field, his intelligent baserunning, and his timely hits—that Reese is remembered in baseball history.

★

Though there are no full-length biographies of Reese, he figures prominently in Roger Kahn's seminal memoir/history of the 1950s-era Dodgers, *The Boys of Summer* (1972), and in Peter Golenbock, *Bums: An Oral History of the Brooklyn Dodgers* (1984). A tribute to Reese, written by Kahn, appears in the *Los Angeles Times* (19 Aug. 1999). The friendship that developed between Reese and Robinson is the subject of *Teammates* (1990), a children's book written by Golenbock and illustrated by Paul Bacon. Obituaries of Reese are in the *New York Times* and the *Courier-Journal* (Louisville) (both 15 Aug. 1999). Reese was the subject of the documentary film *The Quiet Ambassador* (1993).

TIM WHITMIRE

RETTON, Mary Lou (*b.* 24 January 1968 in Fairmont, West Virginia), first U.S. female gymnast to win an Olympic gold medal in the all-around event, with a perfect score in the floor exercise and the final vault, at Los Angeles in 1984; her cumulative five medals were the most won by any Olympian that year.

Retton was the youngest of five children and the second daughter of Lois Retton, a homemaker, and Ronnie Retton, a security guard who later formed his own company repairing transportation cables for the coal-mining industry. Everyone in Retton's family was athletically inclined. Her father had been a sixth man for the West Virginia University basketball team, and later was signed to a minor league contract to play shortstop for the New York Yankees. Retton's three brothers were baseball players, and her sister was an All-America gymnast at West Virginia.

At age four Retton began taking dance classes with her sister at Monica's Dance Studio. The following year Lois found one-hour gymnastics classes for her daughters at West Virginia University, and later they began taking lessons at the Aerial-port, a small, newly opened gym in Fairmont. At age eight, Retton was inspired to achieve great heights in the sport of gymnastics while watching Nadia Comaneci amaze the world with her talent and three gold medals at the 1976 Olympics in Montreal, Canada. Retton took part in her first competition in 1976 at Parkersburg, a town on the Ohio border. Although she did not win, a short while later she was victorious in a tournament for beginners. In school she was a Pop Warner majorette and the Pee Wee football homecoming queen, as well as a top student. She was also a good sprinter, placing second in a Hershey's track and field competition at age eleven.

By age twelve Retton was serious about gymnastics, and her dedication and talent were evident. She had done so well at the beginners' level that she was permitted to skip the intermediates and move on to Class I competitions, including the nationals in Tulsa, Oklahoma. She entered her first international meet in Canada, where she won the all-around event. After achieving some success, but seeing little improvement in her style, Retton decided she needed to train with the best coach she could find; this was the Romanian Béla Karolyi, who had helped Nadia Comaneci achieve her dreams years earlier.

Mary Lou Retton at the 1984 Summer Olympics in Los Angeles. ARCHIVE PHOTOS, INC.

Retton was still a student at Fairmont Catholic School when she went to compete in the junior nationals in Salt Lake City, Utah, where she and her father spoke with the renowned coach. This was a difficult time for her family, since Karolyi's acceptance of Retton as a student meant that her training would take her to Houston. She had to leave high school and continue her classes through correspondence courses. Approximately two weeks after her move to Houston, Retton's decision paid off. She achieved her first perfect "10" in the vault in the qualifying meet for the U.S. championships. Victory after victory followed; Retton won the McDonald's American Cup in New York in 1982 and the Caesars Palace Invitational in Las Vegas in 1983, during which she became the first woman to do a new routine called the Tsukahara (SOOK-uh-harra) with a double twist.

Not everything was easy, however. Retton was constantly in pain from all the broken bones and other injuries sustained during her extensive training. In 1983 she was unable to compete in the World Championships after missing the trials due to a broken wrist. She made up for it, however, by becoming the first American to win the Chunichi Cup in Japan. From autumn 1983 to the Olympic Games in 1984, Retton was victorious in an amazing fourteen consecutive all-around competitions. Six weeks before the Los Angeles Olympics, however, Retton's right knee began to feel uncomfortable. Doctors warned her that she would not be able to compete in the long-awaited games because she had torn the cartilage in her knee and would require surgery. Retton had other plans and completed her three-month rehabilitation work in three weeks.

Retton defied the usual image of the wisp-thin female gymnast, with a solid, muscular build that gave her exceptional power. In 1984 she achieved what no other U.S. woman had ever been able to, she won the Olympic gold medal in the all-around in women's gymnastics. She was also a member of the silver medalist team from the United States, captured an individual silver medal in the vault, and earned bronze medals in the uneven bars and the floor exercise. As a result of winning five medals, she became the athlete with the most medals at the 1984 Olympics.

Retton was selected as the *Sports Illustrated* Sportswoman of the Year, with a 1984 cover exclaiming, "Only You Mary Lou!" That same year the Associated Press named her their Amateur Athlete of the Year. In 1985 she was inducted into the U.S. Olympic Hall of Fame and received the Flo Hyman Award from the Women's Sports Foundation. Retton became an official spokesperson for Wheaties cereal; the first woman featured on the front of a Wheaties box, she also appeared in several television commercials for the product.

After her Olympic successes, Retton retired as a competitive gymnast and worked as a sportscaster, which included providing commentary for the 1988 Olympics in Seoul, South Korea. She also worked as a motivational speaker, encouraging young people to reach for their goals, and saying, "You've got to give your dream everything you've got. When it gives you so much, you have to give back the pride, inspiration, and enthusiasm to others." Retton is also on the board of directors of the Children's Miracle Network and serves as its national chairperson.

Retton is married to Shannon Kelley, an investment broker, with whom she has three daughters. Her retirement from gymnastics competition has freed Retton to pursue other high-risk activities such as roller blading and skiing, which were off-limits during training. She has also appeared in movies, including *Scrooged* (1988) and *Naked Gun 33⅓* (1994), and as a guest on several television shows, such as *Guiding Light, Knot's Landing, Dream On,* and *Baywatch.*

Enthusiasm and exuberance combined with talent and dogged persistence have enabled Retton to become America's sweetheart. Nine years after achieving victory and earning the only U.S. individual gold medal in gymnastics at the 1984 Olympics, she was named the most popular athlete in America in a national survey conducted by the Associated Press. Since then, the image of the young woman with the radiant smile remains indelibly etched in the minds of Americans everywhere.

★

Retton has written an autobiography, with Bela Karolyi and John Powers, *Mary Lou: Creating an Olympic Champion* (1986). She also has written *Mary Lou Retton's Gateways to Happiness: Seven Ways to a More Peaceful, More Prosperous, More Satisfying Life* (2000), which includes stories from her personal life and career. Biographical sketches appear in Bob Schaller, Mary Lou Retton, Dan O'Brien, Mary Joe Fernandez, and Bela Karolyi, *The Olympic Dream and Spirit: Stories of Courage, Perseverance, and Dedication* (1999), and at the International Gymnastics Hall of Fame website, http://www.ighof.com.

ADRIANA C. TOMASINO

RICE, Grantland (*b.* 1 November 1880 in Murfreesboro, Tennessee; *d.* 13 July 1954 in New York City), sportswriter who was the most powerful and far-reaching voice in U.S. sports for nearly half a century, and who first said it mattered "not that you won or lost, but how you played the game."

Rice was born into a family whose roots in the U.S. South dated to the Revolutionary War. He grew up in Nashville, Tennessee, and graduated from Vanderbilt University in 1901. During his senior season at Vanderbilt he was the captain of the baseball team, and his slick fielding and power at the plate attracted the attention of scouts from the Nashville team of the Southern League. However, his fa-

Grantland Rice *(center),* with Army football coach Wallace Wade *(left)* and former Tennessee coach Robert Neyland, 1942. AP/WIDE WORLD PHOTOS

ther forbade him from signing a professional baseball contract. Rice turned to journalism, accepting a job at the *Nashville Daily News*. He moved quickly to the *Atlanta Journal*, where he wrote about the young baseball player Ty Cobb. In autumn 1905 he moved to the *Cleveland News* and stayed for a year and a half before returning to Nashville to join the staff of the *Nashville Tennessean* in 1907.

During this apprenticeship, Rice developed the singular style that would mark his career and influence so much of sportswriting. He sprinkled his prose with references from Greek and Roman mythology, and used metaphors of battles and crusades to describe golf matches and college football games. His articles were terribly overwritten by modern standards, but they were colorful and clear and enormously popular with readers. From the very beginning, Rice interspersed verse and rhyme with his prose; at the height of his career his reputation as a poet rivaled his reputation as a sportswriter. Rice published four books of verse during his lifetime and critics praised his work; one called it "a sturdy clarion of fellowship, humor, and work" and compared him to the popular U.S. poet James Whitcomb Riley.

Rice's most enduring phrase came from a poem entitled "Alumnus Football," first published in the *Nashville Tennessean* in 1908. It was an ode to football as a metaphor for life, and the phrase that immortalized Rice came in the penultimate stanza: "For when the One Great Scorer comes / To write against your name, / He marks not that you won or lost— / But how you played the Game." "Alumnus Football," slightly rearranged so that the famous couplet would stand at the poem's close, was reprinted in his column throughout Rice's life, and was included in two of his books of verse, *Only the Brave* (1941) and the posthumous *The Final Answer* (1955).

In 1906 Rice married Katherine Hollis of Americus, Georgia. They had one child, Florence, who gained considerable fame on her own as a Broadway and Hollywood actress in the 1930s and 1940s. Rice moved to New York City and syndication in 1911, writing first for the *Evening Mail* and then for the *New York Tribune* (later the *New York Herald Tribune*). When the United States entered World War I, he enlisted and served in France with the 115th Field Artillery. He reached the height of his popularity and influence following the war, in the 1920s and 1930s.

"Granny," as he was known to the athlete and reader alike, became a virtual one-man media conglomerate. His column was syndicated in more than 100 newspapers, with a combined daily readership in excess of 10 million. He wrote a weekly column in *Collier's* magazine; hosted a weekly radio program on the National Broadcasting Company (NBC); edited annual guidebooks for college football and Major League Baseball; edited *The American Golfer* magazine; and produced and hosted *Sportlight Films,* an Academy Award–winning series of one-reel films that concentrated largely on participatory sports such as golf, tennis, hunting, and fishing. Rice's newspaper readers also got game-day stories from big events such as the World Series, major golf championships, and football bowl games.

In those days of limited radio coverage, it is not unfair to say that U.S. fans saw sport largely through Rice's eyes. It was a gentle and kindly view, and Rice's mythmaking, celebratory style became known as the "gee whiz" school of sportswriting. The "aw nuts" school was best embodied by Rice's close friend Ring Lardner. Rice lauded the virtues of sportsmanship and fair play, and in many ways created the heroes of the golden age of sport. He christened the football player Red Grange as "The Galloping Ghost" and the backfield of Notre Dame University's football team "The Four Horsemen." The culture of athlete as celebrity began during the 1920s, and Rice played a significant role in making Babe Ruth, Jack Dempsey, and Bobby Jones household names. Along the way he became as well paid and as well known as any of the athletes he wrote about.

Following the end of World War II, Rice slowed notably. He traveled less and his columns became less topical as he reminisced frequently of games and athletes past. Still, he remained the nation's most widely syndicated sportswriter, and successors such as the Pulitzer Prize winners Red Smith and Jim Murray were quick to cite him as an influence throughout their careers.

Rice died of a heart attack at the age of seventy-three, and is buried in Woodlawn Cemetery in the Bronx, New York. He was eulogized on the front pages of newspapers across the country. His posthumous memoir, *The Tumult and the Shouting* (1954), outsold all previously published sports books. Jimmy Cannon of the *New York Post* summed up Rice's life and career by noting that the values he wished for sport were values that defined his own life and personality. "He cherished decency above all and searched for it in the characters of those he knew," wrote Cannon. "It was often hard to find but Granny didn't become discouraged. His dream remained pure and glowed with an obsolete splendor because of his faith in the goodness of men."

★

Rice's memoir is, *The Tumult and the Shouting: My Life in Sports* (1954). The first full-length biography of Rice was written by Charles Fountain, *Sportswriter: The Life and Times of Grantland Rice* (1993). See also Robert Downs and Jane Downs, *Journalists of the United States* (1991), and William Harper, *How You Played the Game: The Life of Grantland Rice* (1999). An obituary is in the *New York Times* (14 July 1954).

CHARLES FOUNTAIN

RICE, Jerry Lee (*b.* October 13, 1962 in Starkville, Mississippi), professional football player who holds the National Football League (NFL) record for most touchdown receptions in consecutive games, he was NFL Most Valuable Player (MVP) for 1987 and Super Bowl MVP in 1989.

Rice was one of six sons born to Joe Nathan, a bricklayer, and Eddie B. Rice, a homemaker. He was reared in a rural African-American community in Crawford, Mississippi. The family lived in a large house that his father built at the edge of a pasture, where Rice and his brothers would play sports and chase horses to ride. A strict disciplinarian, Rice's father instilled a strong work ethic in his sons; they had many chores and would sometimes help their father at work by carrying bricks and mixing mortar.

Rice attended Starkville High School, where he would often get into mischief. In fact, his football career got its start as a result of one his pranks. While trying to skip class one day, he was spotted by his vice principal and was ordered to return to the school. Afraid of the punishment he would face, Rice started running with the vice principal chasing after him. He was caught and whipped, but then encouraged to try out for the school's football team. Rice made the team and soon became its most valuable player. His quickness and versatility allowed him to play nearly every position from quarterback to tackle.

Despite Rice's outstanding high school career, few college recruiters were willing to make the trip to Crawford to watch him play. One person who did was Mississippi Valley State University coach Archie Cooley. Cooley was so impressed by Rice's performance that he offered him a football scholarship to the school in Itta Bene, Mississippi, and began devising new strategies that would best utilize Rice's talents as a wide receiver.

After graduating from high school in 1980, Rice made the transition to college easily and became one of the most popular athletes on campus. He caught over 100 passes during his last 2 years and had 28 touchdown receptions his senior year alone. Rice helped put Mississippi Valley State University on the map by leading the Delta Devils with a 24–6–1 record within their conference. His achievements caught the attention of many recruiters, including San Francisco 49ers coach Bill Walsh, who selected him as the sixteenth pick in the first round of the 1985 NFL draft.

Many sports journalists and fans second-guessed Walsh's decision because Rice had not attended a "Big Ten" college. Unfamiliar with the complex offenses found in top-level college and professional competitions, he had great difficulty his rookie year and dropped fifteen passes. However, he worked diligently at learning all the moves and practiced until he could play them without thinking. His dedication paid off and he ended the season with a record-setting 241 receiving yards in one game and was selected to the 1985–1986 National All-Rookie team.

Rice emerged as a premiere player his second season; he scored 15 touchdowns while averaging 18.1 yards per carry. His third season was one of the best in his professional career. He set NFL records for receiving 22 touchdown catches in 13 consecutive games, and led the league in scoring with 138 points. He was named MVP by the Pro Football Writers of America, the *Sporting News*, *Pro Football Weekly*, and the Maxwell Club. Yet despite the awards and accolades, Rice felt unaccomplished because he had not yet played on a team that won a Super Bowl.

Jerry Rice. AP/WIDE WORLD PHOTOS

He got his wish in 1989 when the 49ers faced the Cincinnati Bengals in Super Bowl XXIII. Rice played through a sprained ankle to lead his team to a 20–16 victory and was named MVP. His Super Bowl performance catapulted his reputation to new heights and he became one of the NFL's most feared receivers. Two years later after an outstanding season, Rice and the 49ers made it to the Super Bowl again, beating the Denver Broncos 55–10.

The 1992 regular season was memorable for the six-foot, two-inch Rice and for the 49ers. The team had the best record in the NFL with fourteen wins and only two losses. On 6 December 1992 Rice caught a twelve-yard reception during a game against the Miami Dolphins to raise his total number of touchdown catches to 101, an NFL record. By the end of the season, he had become the NFL's all-time leader in touchdown catches with 103. He set another record in 1994 when he opened the season with three touchdowns to bring his total to 127, breaking Jim Brown's record for most career touchdowns. The following year Rice became the NFL's reception leader with a total of 942 catches.

In 1996 Rice faced one of the biggest scares of his life when his wife, Jackie, nearly died after giving birth to the youngest of their three children. After experiencing complications she had to undergo two operations and spent ten days in intensive care. Rice held a vigil at his wife's side and stayed with her the entire time. Later that year, Rice made NFL history after catching the 1,000th pass of his career to make his mark as one of the best receivers ever to play in the NFL.

In June 2001, after sixteen seasons with the 49ers, Rice was released from his contract and offered a bonus of $1 million to retire. He declined the offer and later signed a four-year, $5 million deal with the Oakland Raiders. Rice is one of the oldest receivers in the NFL and competes with athletes half his age. His strong work ethic, discipline, and character have brought him success on the field as well as off the field. He is known for his pleasant demeanor and his willingness to share his time and knowledge of the game with younger players. When he is not trying to get to the end zone, Rice spends time with his family at their homes in California and Crawford, Mississippi. A philanthropist, Rice devotes his time and money to numerous charities, including the United Negro College Fund, March of Dimes, Packard Children's Hospital, and AIDS Research.

★

Rice is the subject of two full-length biographies detailing his life and career: Glenn Dickey, *Sports Great Jerry Rice* (1993), and Edward J. Evans, *Jerry Rice: Touchdown Talent* (1993). Entries on Rice can be found in *Current Biography* (1990), and *African American Sports Greats* (1995). Rice has also been featured in *Legends in their Own Time* (1994), *Sports People in the News* (1996), and *Athletes and Coaches of Winter* (2000); as well as in articles in *Sports Illustrated* (28 Sept. 1987), and *Jet* (12 Jan. 1998).

SABINE LOUISSAINT

RICHARDS, Robert Eugene ("Bob") (*b.* 20 February 1926 in Champaign, Illinois), versatile track and field athlete who was the only man to win two Olympic pole vault titles, and who used his ministry and celebrity status to motivate millions of Americans.

Richards was the third of five children of Leslie Richards, a telephone linesman, and Margaret Palfrey Richards, a homemaker. Even at a young age Richards was a prominent athlete in and around his hometown. For example, he was a finalist in the Illinois State Young Men's Christian Association (YMCA) junior diving championships; he won a city park tumbling contest; he starred on the junior high school basketball squad; and he quarterbacked the Champaign High School football team. But after he won a junior high school pole-vaulting contest (at six feet, nine inches), Richards became hooked on the event and practiced relentlessly in his back yard with a makeshift pit and crossbar perched between a telephone pole and a tree limb.

Apart from athletics, Richards had a difficult adolescence. At age fifteen he fell in with a gang of hooligans engaged in petty robbery, a number of whom eventually spent time in correctional facilities. When Richards was seventeen, his parents divorced. Fortunately, he came under the influence of the Reverend Merlin E. Garber, who both made his home available and steered the youngster toward religion and academics. Garber was a minister of the Church of the Brethren, a group originally nicknamed the "Dunkers" because of their rite of baptismal soaking. Richards graduated from high school in spring 1943, and in February 1944 Garber helped him enroll at Brethren-affiliated Bridgewater College in Virginia's Shenandoah Valley. At Bridgewater, where his track coach was a young biology instructor named Harry ("Doc") Jopson, Richards tore the Mason-Dixon Conference apart, winning six individual events, including the pole vault, at the 1945 league meet alone.

Bob Richards at the 1952 Olympics in Helsinki. ASSOCIATED PRESS AP

At age twenty, Richards became an ordained minister in the Church of the Brethren, and he received a scholarship enabling him to transfer to the main campus of the University of Illinois at Urbana-Champaign. At Illinois, where his track coach was Leo Johnson, Richards focused on the pole vault, reaching a best of 14 feet, 3.25 inches. In 1947 he finished in a seven-way tie for first at the National Collegiate Athletic Association (NCAA) Championships. A B.A. from Illinois followed in 1947, and with the help of a teaching fellowship, Richards also earned an M.A. in philosophy from Illinois in 1948. Richards studied for one year at Chicago's Bethany Biblical Seminary, then returned to the University of Illinois at Urbana-Champaign in 1949 to teach in the department of sociology.

Richards made the U.S. Olympic team that competed in London in 1948, winning the bronze medal. The pole vault had been dominated by Cornelius ("Dutch") Warmerdam, the first man to vault over 15 feet (in 1940). In 1950 Richards reached 14 feet, 11 inches, and a year later at the Millrose Games at Madison Square Garden in New York City, he became history's second 15-footer.

In 1951 Richards joined the faculty at Brethren-affiliated LaVerne College in Southern California as an associate professor of philosophy. He won both Amateur Athletic Union (AAU) indoor and outdoor vault titles, then turned his versatile talents to the decathlon. He followed a pair of early season wins with the national AAU decathlon championship, scoring 7,834 points (1950 tables). It was history's third highest total. For his efforts Richards was named the "outstanding athlete in North America" by the Helms Foundation and won the 1951 James E. Sullivan Memorial Award, emblematic of the nation's top amateur athlete.

At the 1952 Olympic Games in Helsinki, Finland, Richards set a new meet record of 14 feet, 11 inches, to win the gold medal. He repeated his Olympic triumph four years later in Melbourne, Australia, with 14 feet, 11.25 inches. Tied for first, he watched USA teammate Robert Gutkowski fail at the next height. On his own final attempt, Richards hit the crossbar on the way down, then lay in the sawdust pit for over thirty seconds as the crossbar wobbled, hanging on the edge of the standards. Olympic myth has it that the "Vaulting Vicar" lifted his hands in prayer, willing the bar to stay put. It did. Yet it was not quite that dramatic. "I did look up and point at the bar, but it wasn't a prayer," Richards said. "It was like, 'Oh Lordy, is that thing going to fall off?' " Richards said later, "I can see how people thought it was a prayer, but it wasn't." Thus Richards became the first (and remains the only) athlete to win two Olympic pole vault gold medals.

Few athletes ever dominated their sport the way Richards dominated his. He was world ranked in the pole vault for eleven consecutive seasons (1947–1957) and world ranked number one in eight. He claimed seventeen national pole vault championships (nine outdoor, eight indoor). By 1957, when few athletes could reach fifteen feet on bamboo, steel, or aluminum vaulting poles, Richards vaulted fifteen feet or better on more than 130 occasions, more times than all other worldwide athletes *combined.* As well as his three Olympic medals, Richards won a pair of gold medals at Pan American Games (1951 and 1955) and was victorious at the Millrose Games eleven times.

Less well known is Richards's record as a multievent athlete. As a decathlete he won twelve of twenty career meets, captured three AAU titles (1951, 1954, and 1955), and made the 1956 Olympic team (placed thirteenth in Melbourne). Richards also took on the all-around, a decathlonlike contest, setting a U.S. record in 1951 and winning the AAU title in 1953. Twice (1951 and 1954) Richards was the world's top-ranked decathlete.

In January 1957 the *DuPont Theatre* presented "Leap to Heaven," a half-hour dramatization of Richards's life, with Richards playing himself. Beginning in 1958 Richards became a spokesperson for Wheaties, appearing on their cereal box for a record thirteen years (1958–1970). His autobiography, *Heart of a Champion,* was released in 1959. Millions became familiar with his motivational speeches and inspiring sermons. When veterans' track and field became popular in the 1970s, Richards returned to the athletic arena competing in masters' events into the 1990s.

Married to Mary Leah Cline on 17 February 1946, Richards had five children, three of whom became prominent athletes. Richards lost his family vault record to son Bob, Jr., who went on to clear 17 feet, 6 inches. In 1990 another son, Brandon, went even higher (18 feet, 4.5 inches), and a third son, Tommy, was an outstanding collegiate decathlete. Richards was elected to the National Track and Field Hall of Fame in 1975 and to the U.S. Olympic Hall of Fame in 1983.

Richards was a shining example of the competitive and sportsmanlike person about whom he spent a lifetime preaching. An Olympian who neglected neither his mind nor his soul, Richards used his athletic status and the pulpit to challenge countless Americans to live like champions.

★

Richards's autobiography is *Heart of a Champion* (1959). His decathlon career is chronicled in Frank Zarnowski, *American Decathletes: A 20th Century Who's Who* (2001).

FRANK ZARNOWSKI

RICKARD, George Lewis ("Tex") (*b.* 2 January 1871 in Kansas City, Missouri; *d.* 6 January 1929 in Miami Beach, Florida), Jazz Age fight promoter who helped turn boxing into a major American spectator sport.

Rickard, known to his parents as "Dink," was the second child and first son born to Robert Woods Rickard, a chronically ill and unemployed millwright, and Lucretia Rickard, a homesteader with as much spirit as her son. She would later tell reporters that the supreme showman of ring violence had been born during a shootout between the James Gang, her nearest neighbor, and the Pinkertons. When Rickard was four the family crammed into a covered wagon and settled in Sherman, Texas. A year later their wagon wheeled into Cambridge, a two-year-old frontier town in the Texas panhandle at the edge of Comanche country. Five of the town's first nine businesses were saloons, and Rickard made his money outside one of them by shining cowboys' boots.

When Rickard was ten the six-member family moved to neighboring Henrietta, where they lived in a dirt shack, ate

Tex Rickard, 1929. AP/WIDE WORLD PHOTOS

corn pone, turnip greens, and sowbelly, and settled into what Rickard later described as "the somber melancholy of poverty." At eleven Rickard left home for good and became a hired hand at a grown man's wage of $10 a month. Within a year his father died, and the rancher who had taken him in was shot and killed in a saloon fight. While still a teen Rickard was a $30-a-month cowhand. At one point while on the trail to Honeywell, Kansas, a friend died, and Rickard sat guard all night fending off wolf attacks against the corpse.

By the age of nineteen Rickard was a six-foot, straight-backed, dark-eyed veteran trail driver making $50 a month. He returned to Henrietta and became town marshal. He married Leona Bittick, who died soon thereafter. In 1895 he left for the Klondike in northwest Canada, searching for gold, but instead found fifteen months of uninterrupted insolvency as a $20-a-day bartender, faro dealer, and front man in a variety of Dawson City saloons. In the fall of 1898 he opened a saloon of his own in Rampart at the edge of the Arctic Circle. Along with buddy Rex Beach, soon a best-selling author of Alaskan adventures, he promoted his first fight, which ended when one combatant was knocked out from a head butt.

Rickard had a half interest in Cape Nome's Great Northern Saloon, which opened in May 1900. The business made $100,000 its first year and $500,000 during Rickard's four years in Nome, Alaska, a period that saw more than $30 million in gold mined from the Seward Peninsula. Rickard served on the city council and put on fight cards at the Standard Theater in Nome. On one memorable night, veteran heavyweight Paddy Ryan took on a jilted bridegroom at the Standard, and they entertained miners by simultaneously knocking each other out. With the $65,000 Rickard made from his sale of the Great Northern, he sailed to South Africa in search of a secret diamond mine. A year later he returned to San Francisco, busted.

Rickard earned a modest salary as a faro dealer and married Edith Mae Myers, an eighteen-year-old who had played piano in the Great Northern. He opened a saloon in Seattle that failed when he refused to pay protection money to organized crime figures. In 1906 he took his wife and adopted daughter to the Nevada gold fields, thinking it his "last chance to make a fortune." He rebuilt his gambling business and became a one-man chamber of commerce in Goldfield, Nevada. He promoted a fight for the lightweight championship of the world between Battling Nelson and Joe Gans by placing the fight's $30,000 guarantee in $20 gold pieces in his saloon front. The Associated Press reported the publicity stunt. On 3 September 1906 Gans won and so did Rickard, pocketing $13,000 in fight profits.

In 1909 Rickard sold his saloon and began publicizing his $101,000 guarantee of a heavyweight championship bout between Jack Johnson and Jim Jeffries, set for Independence Day 1910 in San Francisco. A stadium was built and $300,000 in tickets sold for the long-awaited clash between the black champion and white challenger. When California governor James Gillett bowed to political pressure and blocked the bout, Rickard staged it in Reno, Nevada. Johnson's fifteen-round knockout of the previously unbeaten "surly bear of the Sierras" touched off street fighting and race riots nationwide. The film of the fight was banned in several states. Rickard left the country to raise cattle on a 5,000-acre ranch in Paraguay but returned to the United States in the summer of 1915, broke again, though eager to resume his ring career.

Rickard parlayed a $10,000 loan into a title fight between Jess Willard, who had defeated Johnson for the heavyweight crown, and Frank Moran in New York City's Madison Square Garden on 25 March 1916. The $152,000 gate was the largest in sports history for an indoor attraction. Backed by John Ringling's money, Rickard sought a white challenger he could promote into a "killer" contender. He found him in Jack Dempsey, a skinny-legged fighter from the West with a high-pitched voice and an unremarkable fight record. By the time Dempsey stepped into the ring against the aging Willard on Independence Day 1919, he looked and acted the part of the "Manassa Mauler." His brutal beating of the "Pottawatomie Giant" coincided with the close of World War I and the beginning of a decade of prosperity. Greatly aided by Grantland Rice, Damon Runyon, Ring Lardner, Paul Gallico, and other highly paid and widely read sports columnists, Rickard created a golden age in boxing that repositioned the sport as a civic spectacle. As head of a new and expanded Madison Square Garden, Rickard heralded many "battles of the century," some of which were too big to be staged in the building. Dempsey's four-round demolition of French war-hero Georges Carpentier at Boyle's Thirty Acres in Jersey City, New Jersey, on 2 July 1921 produced a record-shattering gate of $1,625,580. Eighty-eight thousand fight fans, including Hollywood stars and members of President Coolidge's cabinet, cheered Dempsey's second-round dispatch of Luis Firpo, the "Wild Bull of the Pampas," in September 1923 at the Polo Grounds in New York City. Dempsey's fights with Gene Tunney in 1926 and 1927 each earned over $2 million and were carried nationwide on the infant NBC and CBS radio networks. Even Rickard's nontitle fight between Dempsey and Jack Sharkey in July 1926 produced a $1 million gate.

Rickard's second wife died in 1925. He married Maxine Hodges in Lewisburg, West Virginia, in October 1926. In January 1929 they were living with their one-year-old daughter in Miami Beach, Florida, where Rickard was preparing to open a casino and resort, when he was stricken with appendicitis. He died from an acute infection and was buried in Woodlawn Memorial Cemetery in New York City.

A teary-eyed Dempsey told the tabloids that "boxing's lost the best friend it's ever had." Twenty thousand mourners filed past Rickard's casket in Madison Square Garden. The *New York Times* editorialized that Rickard's "name will long remain identified with an extraordinary social development in the United States." Writer Paul Gallico praised Rickard's "Midas touch" at promotion. Will Rogers thought Rickard would be remembered for his "gorgeous imagination." He considered Rickard "one of the very few outstanding personalities of our time" and spoke for many when he added, "I wouldn't a missed knowing him for anything."

★

Rickard's widow, Maxine Hodges, coauthored, with Arch Obeler, *Everything Happened to Him* (1936), a fanciful biography of Rickard's life and career. A more careful chronology of his life and achievements is Charles Samuels, *The Magnificent Rube: The Life and Gaudy Times of Tex Rickard* (1957). Rickard's role in cultivating sports writers and readers is the subject of Bruce J. Evensen, *When Dempsey Fought Tunney: Heroes, Hokum, and Storytelling in the Jazz Age* (1996). Rickard is remembered by one of the most perceptive writers of the Jazz Age in Paul Gallico, *The Golden People* (1965). His contribution to the world of sport and celebrity is captured in Jack Kofoed, "The Master of Ballyhoo," *North American Review* (Mar. 1929). Lengthy tributes to Rickard are in three issues of the *New York Times* following Rickard's death (8, 9, and 10 Jan. 1929). An obituary is in the *New York Times* (7 Jan. 1929).

BRUCE J. EVENSEN

RICKEY, Branch Wesley (*b.* 20 December 1881 near Stockdale, Ohio; *d.* 9 December 1965 in Columbia, Missouri), baseball executive who established a highly successful farm system for the development of major league prospects while with the St. Louis Cardinals in the 1920s and 1930s, and who brought about the racial integration of Major League Baseball in 1947 while with the Brooklyn Dodgers.

Rickey was one of six children of Jacob Franklin Rickey, a farmer, and Emily Brown Rickey, a homemaker. He was named for John Wesley, the founder of Methodism, and although Rickey dropped "Wesley" from his name at the age of twelve, his nearly impoverished parents instilled in him a deep and abiding religious faith, a strong work ethic, and a profound respect for learning. After attending a local school in Lucasville, Ohio, Rickey taught for two years in a nearby one-room country school. He then attended Ohio Wesleyan University in the town of Delaware, where he played and coached both baseball and football. He completed a five-year course of study in three years and received a Litt.B. from Ohio Wesleyan in 1904 and a B.A. in 1906. Rickey married Jane Moulton in 1906 and they eventually had six children, including Branch Rickey, Jr., who followed in his father's footsteps and became a Major League Baseball executive.

Branch Rickey. ARCHIVE PHOTOS, INC.

During his time at Ohio Wesleyan, Rickey launched a playing career in professional baseball. In 1903 and 1904 he played in the minor leagues before joining the St. Louis Browns in the American League as a catcher for the 1905 and 1906 seasons. Rickey's refusal to play on Sundays or drink and carouse with the other players was an early indication of his personal integrity and rigid moral principles. In the off-seasons he taught and coached at Allegheny College in Pennsylvania, Delaware College in Ohio, and Ohio Wesleyan. In 1907 the Browns traded him to the New York Highlanders (later the Yankees), but after one season the development of a sore arm, hitting a mere .182, and contracting tuberculosis ended his playing career. After recovering from tuberculosis, Rickey coached baseball and, beginning in 1909, attended law school at the University of Michigan in Ann Arbor. He obtained an LL.B. from Michigan in 1911 and set up a law practice in Boise, Idaho, the same year.

Rickey was less than successful as a practicing lawyer, and in 1913 he accepted a position with the St. Louis Browns as the de facto general manager. In September 1913 he also became the team's field manager, a post he held for the next two seasons. While failing to improve the Browns' record, Rickey, perhaps influenced by his own extensive formal education and the popular principles of scientific management, approached player training more systematically than had ever been done before. He lectured the players on both the fundamentals of the game and the importance of nurturing a strict personal morality, earning him the epithet "Professor of Baseball." The sportswriter who coined the nickname added that Rickey's "efficiency courses in sliding, baserunning, and batting mark a new departure in the game." Rickey later set up a preseason "baseball college" for instruction in fundamentals and introduced such new paraphernalia as sliding pits, batting cages, and batting tees.

In 1917 Rickey left the St. Louis Browns and joined their crosstown rivals, the Cardinals, in the National League. Initially he was employed as the general manager and president of the club, but from the 1919 through the 1925 seasons he also served—with indifferent success—as the team's field manager. Thereafter until 1943 he was officially the vice president and business manager of the Cardinals. In this capacity Rickey, along with the Cardinals' owner Sam Breadon, pioneered the construction of a farm system—a network of minor league clubs owned by a major league franchise.

Rickey's farm system represented a bold break from past practices. Earlier, the recruitment of raw talent had been left mainly in the hands of the lower-level, independently owned minor league franchises. A player who had proven his potential at that level of competition could either be purchased or drafted for a set price by a major league franchise. Without large financial resources to purchase players, franchises located in cities with smaller populations were put at a severe disadvantage. To offset this handicap, Rickey and Breadon decided to "grow" their own players. Rickey envisioned, as the baseball historian Jules Tygiel observed, "a vertically integrated network of teams owned by the parent club, ranging from the lowest to the highest level of organized baseball, through which players might be trained, sifted, and selected en route to the major leagues." Asserting his own version of the natural selection process described by Charles Darwin, Rickey said that "out of quantity comes quality." During the Great Depression of the 1930s he expanded the Cardinals scouting system and set up three-day tryout camps that attracted thousands of prospects. The most promising of these athletes were signed to contracts and then assigned to Cardinals' minor league franchises, where they had an opportunity to move up the hierarchy to the parent club. By 1936 the Cardinals' farm system had grown to twenty-eight minor league teams.

Rickey's farm system paid rich dividends. While located in the lowest population center in the National League (when the city's population was divided between the Cardinals and the Browns), the farm system furnished much of the personnel that from 1926 to 1946 produced nine league flags and six second-place finishes. The most famed of the Rickey teams was the "Gas House Gang" of the 1930s, a team Rickey believed was the best ever to play the game. The farm system also permitted the Cardinals to profit repeatedly by selling to other major league teams their surplus minor league talent and their established stars at the peak of their careers. By obtaining a percentage of each sale price, Rickey also profited. Although in the 1930s other teams began to copy the Cardinals' farm system, its heyday was actually short-lived. Kenesaw Mountain Landis, the commissioner of baseball, led a campaign against it, and after World War II new rules on player acquisition and the changing fortunes of the minor leagues brought about the demise of the Rickey-type farm systems.

After being fired by St. Louis in a dispute with Breadon in 1942, Rickey joined the Brooklyn Dodgers as the president, general manager, and eventually co-owner. With the Dodgers, Rickey again proved to be a daring innovator. In October 1945, by signing Jackie Robinson to a minor league contract with the Montreal Royals, a Dodgers' farm team, Rickey defied organized baseball's unwritten but firm ban against African-American players. In 1947 Robinson advanced from the Royals to the parent club. While in the wake of World War II the national climate of opinion and the growing political power of African Americans in New York State created conditions more favorable to the racial integration of baseball than ever before, Rickey's bold act arose from a combination of moral and practical considerations. Rickey believed that racial segregation was immoral, but he also acknowledged that the employment of African-American players could strengthen his team and increase attendance. Notoriously parsimonious in salary negotiations, he believed that opening up a new pool of player talent could also reduce his team's salary costs. With the aid of Robinson and other African-American players, Rickey brought pennants to Brooklyn in 1947 and again in 1949, but a year later he was forced to sell his share of the club to the co-owner Walter O'Malley.

In 1951 Rickey began a five-year stint as the general manager of the Pittsburgh Pirates. His talents for putting together winning teams did not bring a pennant to Pittsburgh until 1960, five years after he had been named as the chairman of the board, a position of nominal authority. In 1959 he accepted the presidency of the Continental League, a proposed third league that challenged baseball's major league monopoly. While the league never played a game, the threat it posed to the existing cartel led both the National and American Leagues to expand the number of their franchises. In 1962 Rickey returned to the Cardinals as an adviser and club president, but without the authority he had enjoyed earlier as the general manager of the Cardinals, Dodgers, and Pirates. In 1965, while delivering a speech accepting his induction into the Missouri Sports Hall of Fame, he suffered a heart attack; he died several weeks later.

Few executives left a more important legacy to the game of baseball than Rickey. His contribution was in part one of spectacular success in building winning baseball teams. Despite competing against franchises located in much larger cities, Rickey, by identifying early those players with major-league potential and building an elaborate farm system, made the St. Louis Cardinals franchise the most successful in baseball, with the possible exception of the New York Yankees. Rickey's role in breaching baseball's long-standing ban against African-American players was even more significant. It initiated not only what Tygiel aptly described as "baseball's great experiment," but helped to launch the civil rights movement of the 1950s and 1960s.

★

For Rickey's observations on baseball, see his *American Diamond* (1965), written with Robert Riger. Biographical details may be found in Arthur Mann, *Branch Rickey: American in Action* (1957), and David Lipman, *Mr. Baseball: The Story of Branch Rickey* (1966). For more recent and analytical examinations of aspects of Rickey's life in baseball, see especially John C. Chalberg, *Rickey and Robinson: The Preacher, the Player, and America's Game* (2000), and Jules Tygiel, *Past Time: Baseball as History* (2000). The Manuscripts Division of the Library of Congress holds the Branch Rickey Papers, while both the archives of the *Sporting News* in St. Louis, Missouri, and the National Baseball Library in Cooperstown, New York, contain extensive Rickey clipping files. An obituary is in the *New York Times* (12 Dec. 1965).

BENJAMIN G. RADER

RIGBY, Cathy (*b.* 12 December 1952 in Long Beach, California), two-time Olympic gymnast and the first American to win a medal in an international gymnastics competition, who later became known as a sports commentator, actress, singer, and motivational speaker.

Rigby, born to Paul Rigby, an aeronautical engineer, and Anita Peters Rigby, a materials analyst, was the third of five children. She was born prematurely, weighing four pounds, and with two collapsed lungs. Her early years were fraught with bouts of pneumonia and bronchitis. But Rigby was a fighter and a competitor from birth. She purportedly roller-skated at eighteen months and nearly always delivered the last punch in altercations with her older siblings.

By age ten Rigby knew gymnastics was her sport. Her tumbling coach referred the eleven-year-old Rigby and her father to Bud Marquette, the well-known coach of the Southern California Acro Team (SCAT). Marquette told *Sports Illustrated* that Rigby came to him "looking like a ragamuffin who could do only cartwheels." In two months she was better than girls who had been training for two years. Marquette also noted that Rigby was totally dedicated to gymnastics and completely fearless when she performed.

Cathy Rigby, 1972. ASSOCIATED PRESS FILES

Rigby's life during these years was not easy. She practiced eight hours each day, seven days a week, often leaving the gymnasium for two hours in the afternoon to prepare dinner for her family. Her mother had contracted poliomyelitis during her second pregnancy and could not walk for several years.

On occasion, tension developed between Marquette and Rigby's father about training tactics. Team travel both at home and abroad was frequent. As Rigby moved into puberty, her body matured and she gained weight. She became bulimic at approximately age fifteen and remained so for twelve years; she was hospitalized twice for serious complications. Nevertheless, she graduated from Los Alamitos High School in 1971 with a "B" average and attended California's Long Beach City College briefly until gymnastics commitments forced her to withdraw.

In 1967 Rigby took second place in her age group in the Midwest Open in Chicago, her first meet. In the 1968 World Cup she was a gold medalist and a World Cup champion. In the 1968 Olympic Games in Mexico City, Rigby, at four feet, eleven inches tall, looked more like the U.S. team's mascot than a serious contender. However, she placed sixteenth and emerged from the Olympic Games as a new star in gymnastics, an inspiration to all U.S. gymnasts, and a charmer to her public.

At the 1970 World Games in Ljubljana, Yugoslavia,

Rigby made gymnastics history as the first U.S. gymnast to win a medal in world championships. She received the silver medal for her performance on the balance beam. In 1971 Rigby won gold medals at the World Cup in Miami and the Riga Cup in Latvia. Also in 1971 she was the South African Cup champion and in the U.S.–U.S.S.R. Dual Meet was a champion in the floor exercise. At home and abroad Rigby won a total of twelve medals, eight of them gold.

Following the win at the 1970 World Games and her 1971 successes, Rigby entered the 1972 Olympics as the U.S. favorite to win gold in Munich, Germany. She was a marquee gymnast, appearing on many television shows, including *What's My Line, The Johnny Carson Show,* and *The Dick Cavett Show.* Even foreign newspapers featured her on their front pages. The 1972 Olympic trials started well for Rigby in March at Terre Haute, Indiana, when she won over the Olympic veteran Linda Metheny. However, on the second day of the May finals at Long Beach, Rigby fell on the dismount during compulsory bar exercises, the first such misstep for her and one that cost her the lead. On the third day she regained the lead, but as she executed an Arabian, she pulled the ligaments in her right ankle and could not compete on the final day. Nevertheless, the U.S. Olympic Gymnastics Committee decided to make Rigby an official member of the Olympic team.

In the 1972 Munich Games, Rigby was key to the U.S. team's fourth-place finish in the all-around competition. She finished tenth in the overall standings in the year when Olga Korbut was the star. But the U.S. star was still Rigby, who continued to capture her country's imagination. Rigby had decided, however, that at age nineteen the time had come for her to retire.

Rigby stated that when she left gymnastics, she never wanted to go back. Many of her accomplishments after 1972 took their impetus from her gymnastics discipline. In 1972 she married Tommy Mason, a former All-Pro running back for the Washington Redskins, and had two sons. However, bulimia remained a serious problem for Rigby until she finally sought medical help. In 1981 she and Mason divorced, and on 11 September 1982 she married Tom McCoy, with whom she had two daughters. Soon after her retirement she became a television commentator for ABC Sports, an association that continued for eighteen years and prompted ABC's *Wide World of Sports* to name her one of America's most influential women in sports.

During this period Rigby began studying acting and voice with the same diligence she had applied to the bars. She made her acting debut in 1981 in the role of Dorothy in *The Wizard of Oz; Variety* called her "a genuine theatrical talent." Her initial success was followed by roles in productions of *Meet Me in St. Louis* (touring production, 1982), *Peter Pan* (1990–1991, and Broadway production, 1998–1999), *Annie Get Your Gun* (touring production, 1993–1994), *South Pacific* (1994), *The Unsinkable Molly Brown* (touring production, 2000), and *Seussical* (Broadway production, 2001). She earned a Tony Award nomination for her performances in the 1998–1999 production of *Peter Pan.* She also appeared in the Arts and Entertainment television network's production of *Peter Pan* in October 2000. In Las Vegas she headlined and received the George M. Cohan Award for best specialty act in 1981. She was featured in a number of dramatic television movies, including *The Perfect Body* (1977), *The Great Wallendas* (1978), and *Challenge of a Lifetime* (1985). Rigby and her husband became executive producers at the La Mirada Theatre for the Performing Arts in La Mirada, California.

In addition to acting and singing, Rigby became a successful motivational speaker. Her efforts in this area were targeted to collegiate, corporate, and women's groups. Her subjects included conscientious nutrition, the practice and benefits of "balanced wellness," and the art of becoming a champion in any area of life.

In the United States, Rigby moved gymnastics from a backseat sport to a headline event. Her ability on the bars, her fearlessness as a performer, and her firm grip on America's heart brought pride and delight to her country. After retirement she offered award-winning entertainment in theater and television, and she provided a public service through the frank revelations of her twelve-year eating disorder.

★

The best source for a detailed account of Rigby's importance to U.S. gymnastics and her athletic career is Irvin Stambler, *Women in Sports* (1975). Anne Janette Johnson, *Great Women in Sports* (1996), outlines Rigby's personal life and career. See also a cover story about Rigby in *Life* (5 May 1972), and Anita Verschoth, "Sugar and Spice—and Iron," *Sports Illustrated* (21 Aug. 1972), which provides information about Rigby's family life, training, and career prior to the 1972 Olympics.

MARY BOYLES

RIGGS, Robert Larrimore ("Bobby") (*b.* 25 February 1918 in Los Angeles, California; *d.* 25 October 1995 in Leucadia, California), tennis player and promoter best known for his 1973 win over Margaret Court and defeat by Billie Jean King in the "Battle of the Sexes," one of the most widely watched sports events of the decade.

Riggs was the youngest of five brothers and one sister; he was tutored in many sports by his older siblings. When he was eleven Riggs caught the eye of Esther Bartosh, an anatomy professor and a top-ranked women's tennis player in Los Angeles. She bought Riggs his first racket and helped him obtain sponsorship and funding.

Riggs was a natural on the court. Despite an awkward, toes-out style of walking and his irrepressible clowning, he soon made a mark. At only five feet, eight inches tall and 130 pounds, Riggs was often underrated by opponents, who were beaten by his winning combination of speed, agility, and a relentless competitive spirit. A second woman, Eleanor Tennant, also was instrumental in Riggs's development as a player. She became his coach when he was eighteen, and a year later he was playing some of the best tennis of his life.

In 1938 men's tennis was ruled by Don Budge, the top U.S. and international player who that year won the Grand Slam of the British, French, U.S., and Australian championships. Budge turned professional in 1939, and Riggs quickly filled the number-one amateur spot. At the Wimbledon tournament in England in 1939, Riggs won the singles against his fellow American Elwood Cooke. He then teamed with Cooke to win the doubles and joined Alice Marble to win the mixed doubles. It was a remarkable achievement, worthy of Budge or "Big Bill" Tilden at their best. Yet Riggs was about six inches shorter than either Tilden or Budge, and never had the power to overwhelm his opponents. Instead he outthought them, outran them, and simply outplayed them.

Bobby Riggs with Billie Jean King in a publicity shot for the "Battle of the Sexes." ASSOCIATED PRESS

Both amateur and professional tennis suffered during World War II, with no championships held at Wimbledon between 1940 and 1945. Riggs turned professional in 1942 and played a long series of exhibition matches against Budge, Frank Kovacs, and the British great Fred Perry. Riggs continued to be underrated. Many thought the other professionals would eat him alive. Instead Riggs defeated Budge in exhibition matches in 1946, and then won a brilliant straight-set victory over Budge at the first U.S. national professional singles championship, held later that year in Forest Hills, New York. For spectators who thought Budge was unbeatable, Riggs's victories were incredible.

Riggs soon faced another keen competitor, Jack Kramer, who had the offensive skill and the size and power that Riggs lacked. Although Riggs won the opening match of their long exhibition tour, Kramer beat him 82–20 over the course of the year. Riggs continued to perform well on the tour, winning the national professional singles title in 1947 and 1949, but his best days as a player had passed.

Riggs joined Kramer's professional tour. He was known to make large bets on himself and to make fine money in the process. By 1950 Riggs was one of the older players on the tour, and he lacked the offensive punch to compete with players like Pancho Gonzales and Kramer. However, in his book *The Game* (1979), Kramer placed Riggs among the seven best players of all time, and declared that he was, beyond any doubt, the most underrated of the top rank.

In 1968 the new "open era" began in tennis, allowing both amateurs and professionals to compete in events like the U.S. National Championship at Forest Hills. Players like Riggs, Kramer, and Gonzales were sometimes bitter about the huge monetary awards given to the new young players, when the older greats had played for peanuts in their heyday. In the early 1970s Riggs drew attention back to his contemporaries by asserting that most of the older male players could defeat the best younger female players. The perennial boaster soon received an invitation to test his claim.

In 1973 the United States was in conflict over women's roles, men's prerogatives, and the relationship between the sexes. Promoters quickly came forward and arranged a Mother's Day tennis competition between Riggs and Margaret Court, the great Australian champion. The match seemed ridiculous: Court was taller than the fifty-five-year-old Riggs; she was in terrific condition; and she had proved herself to be consistently the best of the women players. Riggs beat her 6–2, 6–1.

Even the commentators were flabbergasted by Riggs's triumph. He had bet a great deal of money on himself and walked away richer, more famous than ever, and as the recipient of anger from feminists around the world. Riggs, the hustler, promoter, and self-made man, had done it again. Those who tried to analyze the match found that words failed them. How had Riggs's soft shots and moon lobs demoralized Court? How had he kept up with her, the ultimate woman athlete? When asked, Riggs kept to his story line, which was that men were naturally better than women, and that most good male club players could have done the same.

A second match was in order. It came on 20 September 1973, when Riggs met Billie Jean King in an indoor match at the Houston Astrodome. Millions of people around the world tuned in to watch the televised "Battle of the Sexes." King creamed Riggs, 6–4, 6–3, 6–3. He never had a chance to psych her out; she kept him running the whole time, and he was unable to pull off a repeat of his victory against Court. Instead Riggs admitted he had "underestimated Billie Jean and overestimated myself. But I think it helped give women's tennis credibility."

Riggs and King became good friends in the years that followed, and women's tennis not only gained credibility—it boomed. When the women received their own professional tour, the singer Elton John commemorated the new beginning with the hit song "Philadelphia Freedom!" (1975). Riggs remained one of the old men in tennis. He never became a commentator, a profession at which he might have excelled. Instead he played occasional exhibition matches and continued to bet, both for and against his own performances. He died at age seventy-seven after a battle with prostate cancer.

Few tennis enthusiasts appreciated Riggs's complex and multifaceted personality. In 1939 he was the great U.S. hope "after Budge," a role he fulfilled to perfection. As a player who owed much of his success to two female coaches, he later became known as a virulent male chauvinist. He excelled in the gentleman's game of the 1940s, and he lived to make it big in the 1970s world of televised tennis. In his life, career, and eccentricities, Riggs was one of the most visible symbols of tennis as a public sport.

★

For details about Riggs's life, see his autobiography, with Robert Larrimore, *Tennis Is My Racket* (1949). See also Jack Kramer with Frank Deford, *The Game: My Forty Years in Tennis* (1979), and Bud Collins, *My Life with the Pros* (1989). Articles about Riggs include "How Bobby Runs and Talks, Talks, Talks," *Time* (10 Sept. 1973), and "How King Rained on Riggs' Parade," *Time* (1 Oct. 1973). An obituary is in the *New York Times* (27 Oct. 1995).

SAMUEL WILLARD CROMPTON

RILEY, Pat(rick) James (*b.* 20 March 1945 in Rome, New York), professional basketball coach who led the Los Angeles Lakers to four National Basketball Association championships in the 1980s and went on to coach the New York Knicks and the Miami Heat.

Riley grew up on the streets of Schenectady, New York, and saw his life transformed by the game of basketball. He was the son of the minor league baseball coach Leon "Lee" Riley and Mary Riley. Lee Riley ordered Riley's older brothers to take him to tough neighborhoods to play baseball, to make sure that Riley grew up strong and unafraid. Riley counted his father among the three biggest influences in his life; the other two were his high-school and college basketball coaches. At Linton High School his coach Walt Przybylo opened every basketball practice session with words of wisdom about life and how the game related to it. After graduating from Linton in 1962, Riley entered the University of Kentucky in Lexington, where he played ball under the legendary coach Adolph Rupp, whose practice regimen of hard work and discipline served as a model for Riley as a coach.

Pat Riley, 1999. ASSOCIATED PRESS AP

At six feet, four inches tall, Riley was a member of the 1965–1966 Kentucky team known as Rupp's Runts, because no starter was taller than six feet, six inches. Playing center, Riley helped to lead the team, all of whose starters were white, to the National Collegiate Athletic Association title game, where they were defeated by Texas Western with its all-African-American starting team. In the 1967 National Basketball Association (NBA) draft, Riley was the first-round pick of the San Diego Rockets. A waterskiing accident left Riley with an injured disk that required surgery and made his rookie season with San Diego a painful nightmare, but one that he saw his way through with courage. Over nine seasons with the NBA, Riley played for the Rockets, Los Angeles Lakers, and Phoenix Suns, averaging 7.4 points per game. In 1970 Riley married Chris Rodstram, a family therapist; they had two children.

Riley's playing career ended in 1976 when the Phoenix Suns cut him from the team. His attempts to find a job coaching college ball were unsuccessful, and he was about to go into the athletic shoe business when he was offered a job as a color analyst with the Los Angeles Lakers' broadcasting team. For the next three years, Riley threw himself into broadcasting, learning all he could about video. This knowledge proved useful when he finally broke into the ranks of coaching. In 1979, when the Lakers coach Jack McKinney was injured seriously in a biking accident, Paul Westhead took over as the head coach and asked Riley to become his assistant. When Westhead lost out to the star player Magic Johnson in a battle of wills early in the 1981–1982 season, Riley moved into the head coach's job. His debut season as a coach started and ended with a bang: Riley coached the Lakers to victory in eleven of his first thirteen games, and the team took the NBA title for 1982. During the 1982–1983 season the Lakers won fifty-eight games but were stopped in the finals by the Philadelphia 76ers, triggering a crisis of confidence for Riley. Tempted at first to quit because of the loss, the coach eventually decided to tough it out, only to face a similar disappointment in the 1984 NBA finals, when the Lakers lost to the Boston Celtics.

Revenge is sweet, and Riley tasted it in 1985 when the Lakers bested the Celtics to take a second NBA title. The Lakers became the first team in two decades to win back-to-back NBA titles, in 1987 and 1988. Throughout this period, Riley developed a unique coaching style that inspired his players to work on improving their performances. Using his knowledge of video, Riley put together tapes of game action, adding sound tracks of rock music. Late each summer, well before the start of the season, he sent each player a letter detailing the goals he wanted the player to pursue individually. To help players focus on the team's goals, he created seasonal themes and snappy slogans, such as "the career-best year" and "no rebounds, no rings."

After nine seasons with the Lakers, Riley was forced out in June 1990, when his once-loyal players began to tire of his increasingly dogmatic lectures and coaching style. A year later he signed to coach the New York Knicks, a team marked as classic underachievers despite the presence of the star center Patrick Ewing. In fact, Ewing had become so disillusioned by the team's lackluster performance that he was trying to bolt the team as a free agent, a defection that Riley was able to prevent. For the next four years, he helped to shape the Knicks into a real team and not just a group of players wearing identical uniforms. Under Riley the Knicks twice fought their way into the NBA finals. In 1995 Riley became the head coach for the Miami Heat, a team he co-owned. Under his tutelage the team blossomed into a potent threat in the NBA's Eastern Conference.

By the late 1990s Riley's face was familiar to most Americans, flashing across the television screen frequently in countless commercials and talk-show appearances. A three-time recipient of the NBA's Coach of the Year award (1990, 1993, 1997), Riley holds the record as the coach with the most play-off wins (137 at the beginning of the 2001–2002 season). There is little doubt that Riley will be remembered as a gifted player, and as an even more brilliant coach who was able to coax the very best from his players. In a 1983 interview with the *Charlotte Observer,* Riley explained his drive and passion for the game that changed his life: "If you're really into winning, there's only two things: winning and misery. If there's complacency or acceptance, I don't think you're passionate about it."

★

Riley dissects the 1987 championship season of the Los Angeles Lakers in *Show Time: Inside the Lakers' Breakthrough Season* (1988). In his second book, *The Winner Within: A Life Plan for Team Players* (1993), Riley lays out his eleven-step plan "to glory in all of life's pursuits." The winning ways of Riley as a coach in the NBA, as well as some of his earlier incarnations, are explored in Mark Heisler, *The Lives of Riley* (1994).

DON AMERMAN

RINGO, James Stephen ("Jim") (*b.* 21 November 1931 in Orange, New Jersey), undersized overachiever who became a vital part of Vince Lombardi's Green Bay Packers dynasty and an inductee of the Pro Football Hall of Fame.

Ringo was one of three children of James S. Ringo, a professional dynamiter, and Vera Young Ringo, a homemaker. The family moved from Orange, New Jersey, when Ringo was a youngster, and he grew up in Phillipsburg, New Jersey, an industrial town in the Lehigh Valley across the Delaware River from Easton, Pennsylvania. His father left his job in an area quarry and became a power maintenance man at the crayon factory of Binney and Smith Company. Early on Ringo was schooled in the importance of football, a game for which his region of the Lehigh Valley is noted. "In the area where I grew up, you went out for football. . . . The other sports really hardly existed. . . . Football was a ticket for me to a college education, because our parents couldn't have afforded to send me to school." Ringo played for Phillipsburg High School as a fullback, but a suggestion from his line coach brought about a change in Ringo's plans and the direction of his career.

Coach Wiz Rinehart thought Ringo might have a better and longer career playing as a center. He was right. Ringo made the conversion to the line and later rewarded Rinehart for his advice and confidence by choosing him to be the presenter at his induction into the Pro Football Hall of Fame in 1981. When Ringo, an All-State selection, graduated from high school in 1949, Floyd ("Ben") Schwartzwalder recruited him to play for Syracuse University. Ringo was one of thirty-five freshmen recruited as Orangemen football players. When he matriculated, Syracuse was not considered a major college football university; the team played the likes of Lafayette College, Cornell University, and Holy Cross and closed each season with a game against nearby rival Colgate University. While he was attending Syracuse, Ringo met Elizabeth Martin. The couple married in July 1951; they had four children and later divorced.

Ringo had a solid, if not spectacular, career at Syracuse. He did not think much about a professional playing career, especially after his final college game—a lopsided 61–6 Orange Bowl loss to Alabama. However, he soon learned via a telegram that the Green Bay Packers of the National Football League (NFL) had taken him in the seventh round of the annual college player draft in December 1952. All Ringo had to do was find Green Bay, Wisconsin: "I had to look on a map to see exactly where it was." Ringo graduated in 1953 with a B.A. in sociology.

When he reported to the Packers' preseason training camp in the summer following graduation, Ringo stood six feet, one inch tall and weighed 211 pounds, a little light by pro standards for a center. His blocking assignment was to take the opposing middle guard. In the early 1950s that position usually was occupied by such men as the Detroit Lions' Les Bingaman, who tipped the scales at just over 349 pounds. Ringo was the smallest of the seven men vying for the center position. Discouraged, he left camp. When he arrived home, neither his wife nor his father was sympathetic. The elder Ringo could not comprehend where else a young man could earn $5,250 for four months' work. Sheepishly, Ringo called the assistant coach, Chuck Drulis, who asked him to return. He went and stayed for ten years. While the Packers were bad, Ringo was good. He played in the Pro Bowl All-Star game after the 1957 and 1958 seasons. In 1959 Vince Lombardi arrived as coach, and things changed drastically. Lombardi took a team that had been 1–10–1 a year earlier and converted them into 7–5 winners in his first season. The next year the Packers were in the NFL Championship game. Although they lost 17–13 to the Philadelphia Eagles, they began the Green Bay dynasty by winning in 1961 and 1962, defeating the New York Giants both times.

By that time Ringo was the leader of the Packers' offensive line. He made all the critical calls on blocking assignments once the team got to the line of scrimmage. Although he never weighed more than 232 pounds, he used his quickness and intelligence to become an All-Pro. Ringo credited his former teammate Dave ("Hawg") Hanner with teaching him to handle bigger players. The 260-pound Hanner told Ringo, "Anytime you get a chance, take a shot at me." Ringo did, saying, "I would fire off on him in practice. He taught me that I had to be quick and not block too high or too low. Dave Hanner helped me become an NFL player—I'll always be grateful."

Jim Ringo, 1964. AP/Wide World Photos

Before the 1964 season Ringo wanted a substantial pay raise; otherwise, he wanted to be traded. A myth grew up around the situation. The story goes that Ringo hired an agent to negotiate his contract—an NFL first at the time. Supposedly, Lombardi, who valued loyalty above all else, met with the agent for a few minutes and then excused himself. When he went back into his office to continue the meeting with Ringo's agent, he reportedly said, "I'm afraid you're in the wrong place. Mr. Ringo is now the property of the Philadelphia Eagles." It simply did not happen that way. Ringo never had an agent, but neither man denied the story. The trade to the Eagles was made. Lombardi liked looking tough in facing up to a player's demands, and Ringo welcomed a chance to close out a great career closer to home.

While he was with the Eagles, Ringo continued his Pro

Bowl caliber of play. In fact, the last game of football he played before he retired was the 1968 Pro Bowl. At the time Ringo was one of only a few players to make the Pro Bowl with two different teams—a total of ten times over fifteen years. After retiring as a player, he turned to coaching, working with the Chicago Bears, the Buffalo Bills, and the New England Patriots. Ringo married Judith Lischer on 4 June 1988 and lives in retirement in Chesapeake, Virginia.

Ringo was a tough and durable player. When he retired he held the record for the most consecutive games played—182 games over fifteen seasons. He habitually ignored injuries to continue in the starting lineup. Once, in 1955, Ringo played through a serious back injury that bothered him for the remainder of his career. He even got out of a hospital bed to play on several occasions, just to keep intact his consecutive games streak. Given his position as center—right in the thick of the violent collisions that take place in what the pros call "the pit"—Ringo was a true iron man and one of the most durable and best linemen ever to play the game.

★

There is no biography of Ringo. His career and life are discussed in Chuck Johnson, *The Greatest Packers of Them All* (1968); George Allen with Ben Olan, *Pro Football's 100 Greatest Players: Rating the Stars of Past and Present* (1982); Stuart Leuthner, *Iron Men: Bucko, Crazylegs, and the Boys Recall the Golden Days of Professional Football* (1988); and Don Smith, *All-Time Greats: Pro Football Hall of Fame* (1988).

JIM CAMPBELL

RIPKEN, Cal(vin) Edward, Jr. (*b.* 24 August 1960 in Havre de Grace, Maryland), baseball player, primarily at shortstop, who set a new record in 1998 for the most consecutive games played.

Ripken was the second of four children of Calvin Edward Ripken, Sr., a professional baseball player, coach, scout, and manager, and Violet Gross, a homemaker. The Ripkens made their family home in Aberdeen, Maryland, where Ripken pitched and played shortstop for the Aberdeen High School baseball team from 1974 to 1978. In his senior year Ripken helped lead the team to the Maryland Class A state baseball championship.

After graduation Ripken was drafted as the fifth pick in the second round of the June 1978 draft by the Baltimore Orioles. After three years in the minor leagues, Ripken was called up to the Orioles major league roster on 7 August 1981. The following season Ripken won the American League (AL) Rookie of the Year award, finishing the season with twenty-eight home runs and ninety-three runs batted

Cal Ripken, Jr. ARCHIVE PHOTOS, INC.

in (RBI); he had not missed a game since the second game of a doubleheader on 30 May 1982. Ripken followed his rookie season with a stellar year in 1983 in which he batted .318 with 27 home runs and 102 RBI. He was voted the AL Most Valuable Player (MVP), becoming the fourth Oriole to win the award. Ripken also became the first player in major league history to win a Rookie of the Year award in his first season and an MVP award in his second. Ripken's award was heightened by Baltimore's performance, as the team won the World Series for the first time since 1970.

Ripken played every inning of every game in the 1983 season, as well as in the 1984 and 1985 seasons, becoming the first player since 1905 to play every inning of every game for three consecutive years. Ripken's streaks of consecutive games and consecutive innings played continued through the 1986 season. Shortly after the conclusion of that season, on 6 October 1986, Ripken's father was named as the manager of the Baltimore Orioles. It marked the third time in major league history that a player was managed by his father. When Ripken's younger brother Billy was called up to the Orioles on 11 July 1987, the Ripkens became the first pair of brothers to be managed by their father on the same team.

On 14 September 1987 Ripken's consecutive innings-played streak ended at a record 8,243, although his consecutive games-played streak continued. On 13 November 1987 Ripken married Kelly Geer; they later had two children. The following season Ripken's father was fired as the manager after the Orioles lost their first six games of the season. On 25 June 1988 Ripken became the sixth man in major league history to play in 1,000 consecutive games.

On 28 July 1990 Ripken made an error for the first time in ninety-five games, establishing a new record for shortstops. The next season Ripken earned his first of two Gold Glove awards as the AL's best defensive shortstop. He was also named the AL MVP that season. After Maury Wills of the 1962 Los Angeles Dodgers, he was the second man in baseball history to win the MVP award, the All-Star game's MVP award, a Gold Glove award, and the Player of the Year awards of both *Sports Illustrated* and the Associated Press in the same season.

After playing every game during the 1992 and 1993 seasons, on 1 August 1994 Ripken played in his 2,000th consecutive game, making him only the second man to reach that milestone in baseball history, behind Lou Gehrig, who played in 2,130 consecutive games for the New York Yankees between 1925 and 1939. On 5 September 1995 Ripken tied Gehrig's record, and the following day he surpassed it. Ripken added more drama to the record-tying and record-breaking games by homering in each. Because of the timing of Ripken's record-breaking game, he was credited with helping to make baseball exciting again for many fans who had become disillusioned following the players' strike the previous season, which had caused the cancellation of the 1994 World Series.

Ripken's streak of consecutive games played lasted three more years until he finally sat out a game on 20 September 1998, establishing a mark of 2,632 games. Shortly after the 1999 season began, Ripken went onto the disabled list for the first time in his major league career. Ripken returned to hit his 400th career home run on 2 September of that year. He hit 345 of his home runs at shortstop, which set a record for the most home runs while playing that position. On 15 April 2000 Ripken became the twenty-fourth player in major league history to record 3,000 hits. In 2001 he was elected to his nineteenth consecutive All-Star game, tying a record for the most All-Star game berths, set by Ozzie Smith a few years earlier. Although some criticized Ripken's selection because of his subpar season, he homered in the All-Star game and was named the Most Valuable Player. Ripken retired at the end of the 2001 season. He had played in 3,001 games, and from a career total of 11,551 at bats, had accumulated 3,184 hits, 603 doubles, 1,647 runs, 1,695 RBI, and 431 home runs.

Ripken was credited with redefining the role of the shortstop in a major-league lineup. While a few exceptions provided powerful offensive statistics before Ripken, shortstops tended to be defensively skilled but unimpressive at the plate. After Ripken established himself as an offensive threat, shortstops increasingly added offensive production to their defensive ability. Ripken was more recognized, however, for his record of consecutive games played, as many believed Gehrig's record would never be broken. At various points when his statistics were below his normal average, Ripken received criticism for not taking a day off during what became known as "The Streak." Ripken maintained that he would rest if the situation called for it, and suggested that "The Streak" was more a byproduct of his desire to play than a reason for playing. That desire to play made Ripken the most durable "Iron Man" in baseball.

★

For a discussion of Ripken's personal life and career, see his autobiography with Mike Bryan, *The Only Way I Know* (1997). See also the biography by Harvey Rosenfeld, *Iron Man: The Cal Ripken, Jr., Story* (1995), which provides information about Ripken's personal life, but focuses more on his career. Also insightful are Ralph Wiley, "A Monumental Streak," *Sports Illustrated* (18 June 1990), and Steve Wulf, "Iron Bird," *Time* (11 Sept. 1995).

RAYMOND I. SCHUCK

ROBERTS, Robin Evan (*b.* 30 September 1926 in Springfield, Illinois), Hall of Fame baseball player who was the dominant pitcher in all of baseball from 1950 through 1955 and the top right-hander in the National League (NL) in the 1950s.

Roberts was the fifth of six children of Tom and Sarah Gatrick Roberts. His parents had emigrated from Wales in 1921 to the United States because his coal miner father sought work in the mines of central Illinois; his mother was a homemaker. Roberts attended a small, rural, two-room grade school where his love of sports was nurtured by his fifth grade teacher. He grew up listening to Chicago Cubs games on the radio, and he acted out the ball games as they were played.

Roberts played baseball, basketball, and football at Lanphier High School in Springfield. After graduating in 1944, he qualified for the U.S. Air Force Cadet Training Program and was sent to Michigan State University. There he starred for the Spartans basketball team and was named Michigan Collegiate Player of the Year for the 1945–1946 season by the *Detroit Free Press.* Roberts decided to try out for the baseball team that spring. When Spartans baseball coach John Kob asked what position he played, Roberts asked what position Kob needed. Kob said, "Pitchers." Roberts replied, "Then I'm a pitcher."

Roberts's first win for Michigan State was a no-hitter

Robin Roberts, 1966. ASSOCIATED PRESS AP

against the very good Great Lakes Training Station. During the summers of 1946 and 1947 he pitched in the semiprofessional Northern League for Montpelier, Vermont, under the tutelage of University of Michigan coach Ray Fisher. In the summer of 1947 he came into his own with an 18–3 record, attracting the attention of numerous major league scouts. Later that summer he worked out for the Philadelphia Phillies in Wrigley Field in Chicago and had invitations from the Yankees, the Tigers, the Red Sox, the Athletics, and the Braves. Phillies coach Cy Perkins, soon to become Roberts's mentor, was heard to say, "Don't let that kid get out of the park." The Phillies signed Roberts for the then hefty bonus of $25,000.

Roberts graduated from Michigan State University in 1948, earning a B.A. in physical education, and reported to spring training with the Phillies two weeks late. Although he had an outstanding spring, Roberts was sent to the Wilmington Blue Rocks of the Class B Interstate League to open the season. He was called up by the Phillies to stay in June, after compiling a 9–1 record and posting 121 strikeouts and a 2.06 earned run average in 96 innings.

Roberts posted a 7–9 record with the Phillies that year and in 1949, his first full season in Major League Baseball, won fifteen and lost fifteen. Then came the breakthrough year 1950, when he led the fabled "Whiz Kids" to the NL pennant, defeating the legendary Brooklyn Dodgers 4–1 in ten innings on the last day of the season to clinch the title and his first twenty-win season. The win saved the Phillies from blowing the 7½ game lead (nine games over the Dodgers) they had had ten days earlier. Beset by injuries, particularly to their pitching staff, and the loss of star southpaw Curt Simmons to the U.S. Army, Whiz Kids manager Eddie Sawyer started Roberts five times in the final eight days of the season.

Although the Phillies were not able to repeat their 1950 performance, Roberts went on to true stardom and dominance. He won twenty or more games in six consecutive seasons, missing a seventh straight twenty-win year on the last day of 1956. His best year was 1952 when he won twenty-eight games and had only seven losses, the first of four straight years he led the NL in wins. In 1952 the NL's next most winning pitcher had eighteen victories.

Roberts threw over 300 innings for 6 consecutive years. He led the NL in complete games 5 straight times and pitched an incredible 28 straight complete games during the 1952 and 1953 seasons. For the 1950s, he posted 192 wins, tops for a right-hander and trailing only Warren Spahn. He started in a record 5 All-Star games for the NL. Overall, his exceptional career spanned 18 seasons and 286 major league victories from 1948 to 1966. He was elected to the National Baseball Hall of Fame in 1976.

Roberts had particularly keen rivalries with the Brooklyn Dodgers and Jackie Robinson, whom he faced more than any other pitcher, and with Stan Musial of the St. Louis Cardinals. He generally refused to brush hitters back from the plate and holds the record for the most home runs allowed. The majority of the home runs he allowed came with no one on base because Roberts had a unique ability to bear down in tight situations.

After dominating the National League for much of 1950s, Roberts struggled with the bad Phillies teams of the late 1950s. His career reached rock bottom when he was sold to the New York Yankees before the 1962 season, then released by that club without ever appearing in a game. Roberts soon signed with the Baltimore Orioles, however, where he resurrected his career for a young team that would soon win championships, winning forty-two games over the next three and a half years. He joined the Houston Astros in the middle of 1965 and in 1966 pitched the first regular season major league game on the new artificial "grass" AstroTurf in Houston's Astrodome. He ended his active major league career that year as a playing pitching coach for Leo Durocher's Chicago Cubs.

Roberts's off-the-field influences on baseball are also significant. He was instrumental in the hiring of Marvin Miller to be the first executive director of the Major League Baseball Players' Association. As the head of the screening committee for the Association, Roberts convinced the players' representatives from the individual teams that Miller was the right choice.

Roberts had pushed within the association for a full-time executive director since 1960. When Miller was hired in 1966, Roberts's intent was for Miller to negotiate with the owners to improve the players' pension plan and secure their licensing rights. When Roberts offered Miller the job, he exacted a promise from him that the players' union would never strike. When the Players' Association, under the leadership of Miller, struck against Major League Baseball for the first time in 1972, Roberts, by then retired as an active player, immediately called Miller to remind him of his promise. Miller said, "Robin, I have been waiting for your call." Miller did not end the strike, however.

After retiring from baseball, Roberts worked as a stockbroker and served as baseball coach at the University of South Florida for eight years. Now retired, he lives in the Tampa, Florida, area with his wife, the former Mary Kalnes, whom he had married on 26 December 1949. They have four sons. Roberts remains active in baseball, serving on the Board of Directors of the Baseball Hall of Fame, into which he was inducted in 1976, and the Baseball Assistance Team (BAT).

★

There is no full-scale biography of Roberts, but the Library at the National Baseball Hall of Fame in Cooperstown, New York, houses material on his career. His book, *The Whiz Kids and the 1950 Pennant* (1996), coauthored with C. Paul Rogers III, contains a substantial amount of autobiographical material. Roberts was featured in "The Whole Story of Pitching," *Time* (28 May 1956), a cover story. Donald Honig devotes a chapter to Roberts in his oral history *Baseball Between the Lines: Baseball in the '40s and '50s as Told by the Men who Played It* (1976).

C. Paul Rogers III

ROBERTSON, Oscar Palmer (*b.* 24 November 1938 in Charlotte, Tennessee), one of the greatest basketball players of all time, the highest-scoring guard in National Basketball Association (NBA) history, and the only player ever to achieve "triple-double" averages for an entire season.

Robertson was the youngest of three sons born to Henry Bailey Robertson and Mazell Bell Robertson. When Robertson was very young his family moved to Indianapolis, where his father became a sanitation worker. His mother worked as a domestic, and later became a beautician. Growing up in abject poverty in a segregated housing project, Robertson was drawn to basketball because of its popularity in his neighborhood, and by his brothers who played at the local YMCA. The Robertson brothers also practiced by shooting a makeshift basketball—a rag-wrapped tennis ball bound with rubber bands—into a peach basket behind his family's home. The young Oscar improvised by shooting with tin cans and tennis balls, and at the age of eleven received his first basketball, which was almost thrown away by the family who employed his mother as a maid.

Mazell Robertson was determined to help her sons make lives for themselves beyond the projects. "People were doing all kinds of wrong things," she recalled, "I had to tell my children why they had to be different." She made sure they stayed out of trouble by keeping busy with schoolwork and sports. Her son Bailey, Oscar's older brother, went on to play for the Harlem Globetrotters.

Robertson attended Crispus Attucks High School, an African-American institution that was part of Indianapolis's segregated school system. The building had no gym, and white schools refused to play against its teams, but even under these circumstances Robertson's exceptional ability and sharp instincts emerged. His coach Ray Crowe polished and refined his raw talent with intensive fundamentals. The hard work paid off: Robertson led his team to two consecutive state championships (1955 and 1956), a state record of forty-five straight wins, and the first undefeated season in the history of the Indiana state high school system. In 1956, his senior year, Robertson was named Indiana's "Mr. Basketball."

Robertson was not only a basketball star, but also excelled in track and field as a high jumper and in baseball as a pitcher. In spring 1956 he graduated sixteenth in his class of 171 students, and was a Scholar-Athlete and member of the National Honor Society. He was also chosen for three All-America high school teams. More than thirty colleges recruited him, but Robertson chose to stay close to home and attend the University of Cincinnati because its flexible system enabled him to study part-time, work part-time at the Cincinnati Gas & Electric Company, and play full-time basketball for the Bearcats.

Robertson was the first African American to play basketball for Cincinnati at a time when the Jim Crow laws enforced racial segregation throughout the South. Even though he was brilliant on the basketball court, Robertson experienced off-court discrimination at both the university and on the road. Though initially barred from college locker rooms, he was allowed entrance once the other players saw his abilities. Robertson was frequently denied entry to whites-only establishments, such as theaters and restaurants, even in Cincinnati. Traveling through the Midwest and South as part of an integrated college sports team was also dangerous. Unable to stay in hotels with his team until his junior year, Robertson often was forced to stay alone in college dorms. Especially while in the South, Robertson coped with fears of the Ku Klux Klan, who had attacked and lynched individuals involved in the Civil Rights Movement; he nearly dropped out of college because of the emotional distress.

At six feet, five inches tall, and 215 pounds, Robertson

Oscar Robertson *(center)*, 1959. ASSOCIATED PRESS AP

excelled at all aspects of basketball. He set nineteen school and fourteen National Collegiate Athletic Association (NCAA) division scoring records. He led the Bearcats to a 79–9 record and two straight NCAA tournament third-place finishes in 1959 and 1960, tallying 62 points against North Texas State University his senior year. Robertson's scoring, which averaged 33.8 points per game and totaled 2,973 points, placed him seventh on the all-time NCAA scoring list. It was during his college days that Robertson earned his nickname "the Big O" for his relentless offense. He possessed not only a deadly outside shot, but also worked tirelessly to create scoring opportunities for himself and his teammates.

In 1960, after graduating with a degree in business administration, Robertson and future NBA Hall of Famer Jerry West led the 1960 U.S. Olympic basketball team to a gold medal, a team that many consider one of the most talented ever assembled. That same year he began his fourteen-year National Basketball Association (NBA) career with the Cincinnati Royals, earning $33,000 his first year. From 1960 to 1967, Robertson also served in the United States Army with the rank of Private first class.

In his first season, 1960–1961, Robertson finished third in the league in scoring with an average of 30.5 points per game. He also won NBA Rookie of the Year honors, and was named the All-Star Game Most Valuable Player (MVP) after scoring 23 points and making a record 14 assists. Robertson's second year was even more spectacular: he became the only player in NBA history to average a "triple-double"—double-digit averages in scoring (30.8), rebounds (12.5), and assists (11.4)—for an entire season.

The 1963–1964 season was another banner year for Robertson. He earned both regular-season and All-Star MVP honors, cementing his place as one of the NBA's dominant players. No other player excelled in as many categories as Robertson did. Sports fans marveled at his intense work ethic and hard-nosed play. New York Knicks guard Dick Barnett once said, "If you give him a twelve-foot shot, he'll work on you until he's got a ten-foot shot. Give him six, he wants four. Give him two feet and you know what he wants? That's right, man, a layup." Over his first five seasons (384 games), Robertson averaged a cumulative triple-double (30.3 points, 10.4 rebounds, and 10.6 assists), an amazing series of averages.

In 1970 Robertson, who was president of the players' union from 1963 to 1974, filed an antitrust suit against the league to stall the proposed merger of the NBA and the American Basketball Association. He challenged not only the legality of the merger, but also the legitimacy of the college draft and the NBA's prohibition against free agency. Six years elapsed before the NBA finally settled the case, and by then the leagues merged and the draft remained intact. Drafted players won the right, however, to ignore their prospective employers for a year and reenter the draft. In addition, teams were no longer required to provide compensation when signing a free agent. This allowed more players to negotiate as free agents and eventually led to higher salaries for all players.

In the 1970–1971 season, the Royals stunned the basketball world by trading Robertson to the Milwaukee Bucks. Rumors flew that the Royals coach Bob Cousy instigated the trade out of jealousy that Robertson had broken all of his records. A more likely reason, however, was Robertson's search for a championship.

The move to the Bucks was the right one. Robertson and teammate Kareem Abdul-Jabbar led the Bucks to the

NBA title in the 1970–1971 season. Robertson played three more years with the Bucks, but managed to get to the playoffs only in his last season. The classic contest, which pitted Milwaukee against Boston, stretched over seven games before Boston sealed its fifteen-point victory.

Robertson left the NBA in 1974 with 26,710 points, 9,887 assists, and 7,804 rebounds, which he collected in 1,040 games. He shot .485 from the field and .838 from the line. In 86 playoff games, Robertson averaged 22.2 points, 8.9 assists, and 6.7 rebounds. He made 12 consecutive trips to the All-Star game, and led the league in assists 6 times and in free-throw percentages twice. His team made the playoffs in 10 of his 14 years in the league. With superior offensive and defensive skills, he single-handedly redefined the role of the guard position and was considered the first "big guard" in the game.

Since Robertson's retirement from basketball he has worked as a broadcaster and served as president of the retired players association. He also served as national director of the Basketball Hall of Fame from 1987–1989. Married to Yvonne Crittenden Robertson since 25 June 1960, Robertson is the father of three daughters; in 1997 he donated a kidney to one daughter who was suffering from lupus to save her life. Robertson wrote *The Art of Basketball: A Guide to Self-Improvement in the Fundamentals of the Game* (1998), with Michael O'Daniel. In 2001, Robertson ran five companies, with interests in chemicals, packaging, media, and real estate.

Robertson has taught and mentored hundreds of youngsters through various organizations. He also became involved in numerous charitable and community activities, including the NBA Legends Foundation, National Association for the Advancement of Colored People (NAACP), American Red Cross, American Cancer Society, Housing Opportunities Made Equal (HOME), Boys and Girls Clubs of America, the National Lupus Foundation, and the National Kidney Foundation, for whom he acts as an advocate for organ donation.

Whenever basketball discussions turn to naming the greatest player in history, Robertson's name is always one of the first to be mentioned. *Sports Illustrated* and ESPN listed him as one of the greatest athletes of the twentieth century. Red Auerbach, former coach of the Boston Celtics, rated him as the most versatile player he had ever seen on a basketball court, and most basketball experts agree. In 1998 the United States Basketball Writers renamed their Player of the Year Award the Oscar Robertson Trophy in his honor.

★

Biographical information on Robertson can be found in David L. Porter, *African-American Sports Greats: A Biographical Dictionary* (1995); and Bert Randolph Sugar, *The 100 Greatest Athletes of All Time: A Sports Editor's Personal Ranking* (1995). A useful website is <http://global.nba.com/history/robertson_bio.html>. Biographies for young readers include Les Etter, *Basketball Superstars: Three Great Pros* (1974), and Joel H. Cohen, *Oscar Robertson* (2001).

JOHNNIEQUE B. LOVE

ROBINSON, Brooks Calbert, Jr. (*b.* 15 May 1937 in Little Rock, Arkansas), baseball Hall of Famer who was the greatest fielding third baseman of his era, winning sixteen American League gold gloves from 1960 through 1975, also known for his clutch hitting and outstanding play in the 1970 World Series.

Robinson spent his entire childhood in Little Rock with his younger brother and his parents, Brooks Calbert Robinson, Sr., and Ethel Mae Denker Robinson. He enjoyed all sports, but his favorite was always baseball. Robinson was raised a Methodist. He was humble, unassuming, and cool-headed. Ambidextrous, Robinson wrote and ate left-handed, but batted and threw right-handed in baseball

Brooks Robinson, 1963. © BETTMANN/CORBIS

and dribbled and shot primarily with his right hand in basketball.

Robinson gained his love for baseball from his father, who played semiprofessional ball and worked as a fireman. As a youngster, Robinson followed the exploits of Stan Musial and the St. Louis Cardinals. He starred as an All-State basketball player for Little Rock Central High and was offered a basketball scholarship at Little Rock University (later the University of Arkansas). Because his high school did not field a baseball team, he played American Legion ball. He played a major role in his team's success, mostly as a second baseman. George Haynie coached Robinson in high-school basketball and Legion baseball.

Various major league scouts watched Robinson closely while he played Legion ball. Lindsay Deal, a friend of Robinson's father and a former player for Paul Richards in Atlanta, praised his baseball skills in a 1955 letter to Richards, then the manager of the Baltimore Orioles. Upon Robinson's high-school graduation in 1955, two teams offered him major league contracts, the Cincinnati Reds and the Orioles. On 1 June 1955 Robinson signed a contract with the Orioles, who were only in their second season after being converted from the St. Louis Browns. They were the perennial last-place finisher in the standings and still thin on talent at most positions.

On the baseball field, Robinson was a manager's dream—always trying to play in every game, injured or not. At six feet, one inch tall and 190 pounds, he was an average base runner in terms of speed, but made few mistakes on the base paths. He had very fast reflexes in the field, a good throwing arm, and a very quick release of his throws to first. Robinson was especially adept at fielding bunts one-handed down the third-base line.

Robinson started his professional career in 1955 by playing for the minor league Orioles' club in York, Pennsylvania, where he batted .331 until being called up to the majors late in the season. He batted two for four against the Washington (D.C.) Senators in his major league debut on 17 September, then was hitless in his last eighteen at bats with the Orioles that season. In a fortuitous move, the York manager George Staller and Richards converted Robinson from a second baseman to a third baseman about midway through his minor league stint. Robinson split the 1956 and 1957 seasons between the Orioles and the San Antonio club. In 1958 he played the entire season for the Orioles; he was a flashy fielder but had only a mediocre batting average of .238 in 145 games. In 1959 he was sent to the Vancouver club of the Pacific Coast League and, after an early season injury to his forearm healed, batted .331 and seemed to gain confidence. After the All-Star break, he returned to the Orioles and hit well for the rest of the season, with a final batting average of .284.

Robinson met his future wife, Connie Louise Butcher, a flight attendant, on a United Airlines flight from Kansas City to Boston in July 1959. They were married on 8 October 1960; the couple had three sons and one daughter. In 1970 Robinson converted to Catholicism to be the same religion as his wife and children.

Robinson first starred for the Orioles in 1960. He batted .294 (175 for 595), slugged 14 home runs, and drove home 88 runs as the Orioles challenged the New York Yankees for first place until mid-September. He won the first of sixteen straight gold gloves in 1960 as the best-fielding third baseman in the American League (AL), and made the first of eighteen All-Star game appearances. Robinson cemented his reputation as a clutch batter and the major league's best-fielding third baseman from 1961 through 1963. He had his best season as a batter in 1964, hitting .317 (194 for 612), second in the AL to Tony Oliva's .323 mark. Robinson smacked twenty-eight home runs and led the league in runs batted in (RBI) with 118. He was selected as the league's Most Valuable Player (MVP) as the Orioles finished just two games behind the pennant-winning Yankees.

From 1965 through 1971 Robinson averaged about twenty home runs, eighty-five RBI, and a .270 batting average per season. He teamed up with Frank Robinson, Boog Powell, Jim Palmer, and Dave McNally, among others, to lead the Orioles to AL pennants in 1966, 1969, 1970, and 1971, and to World Series wins in 1966 over the Dodgers and in 1970 over the Reds. Robinson slammed a home run in his first at bat in the 1966 series and was the MVP of the 1970 series. A national television audience saw him rob Cincinnati's Lee May and Johnny Bench of several hits each. Robinson batted .429 (nine for twenty-one) with two home runs in the 1970 series.

Robinson retired in 1977. That year, the Orioles staged a "Thanks, Brooks" day on 18 September before a record regular-season crowd of 51,798 at Memorial Stadium. Robinson was inducted into the Baseball Hall of Fame on 31 July 1983, in front of 12,000 fans. Up to that time, it was the largest crowd at a Hall of Fame induction ceremony.

Robinson was the part owner in a restaurant and a sporting goods store during his playing career. After his retirement from playing baseball, he worked as a television commentator for the Orioles, a special assistant for Crown Central Petroleum Company, and for Personal Management Associates, a company providing athletes with counseling and support services.

Many fans and historians rank Robinson as the best-fielding third baseman of all time. He was the cornerstone of the Orioles from 1960 through 1975. His penchant for clutch hitting was especially evident in postseason play-offs and the World Series. In the 1970s Robinson was idolized by a future great player for the Orioles, Cal Ripken, Jr. During the era that the Orioles played at Memorial Stadium (1954–1991), Robinson was the team's franchise player, and eventually was succeeded by Ripken, Jr.

★

Robinson's autobiographies include, with Fred Bauer, *Putting It All Together* (1971), and, as told to Jack Tobin, *Third Base Is My Home* (1974). The *Baltimore Orioles 1984 Media Guide* contains extensive information on Robinson's playing career. Other books with significant information on Robinson include Gordon Beard, *Birds on the Wing: The Story of the Baltimore Orioles* (1967), and John Eisenberg, *From Thirty-third Street to Camden Yards: An Oral History of the Baltimore Orioles* (2001).

MARK R. MILLIKIN

ROBINSON, David Maurice (*b.* 6 August 1965 in Key West, Florida), professional basketball player best known as a dominant center for the San Antonio Spurs and as the only male basketball player in U.S. history to appear in three Olympic Games.

Robinson was one of two children of Ambrose Robinson, an engineer in the U.S. Navy, and Freda Robinson, a homemaker. When Robinson was a youngster, his father was transferred from Key West to Virginia Beach, Virginia.

David Robinson *(left)*. ASSOCIATED PRESS AP

Robinson excelled both academically and in most sports, with the notable exception of basketball. While he was in junior high school the family moved again because his father retired from the navy and took a job as a civilian engineer in Manassas, Virginia, just outside Washington, D.C.

A late bloomer in the world of basketball, Robinson did not become involved with the game until his senior year in high school. A brief flirtation with the sport while he was in junior high school ended almost as quickly as it began. The basketball coach at Osbourn Park High School in Manassas prevailed upon Robinson, who was six feet, seven inches tall (and later topped out at seven feet, one inch), to join the team in his senior year. Although Robinson earned All-District and All-Area honors, he attracted little interest from college basketball scouts.

Graduating from high school in 1983, Robinson's academic achievements opened the door to virtually any college he chose to attend. Given the family's strong connections to the navy, he decided to enroll at the U.S. Naval Academy in Annapolis, Maryland. After a slow start in college basketball, Robinson began to come into his own during his sophomore year. Still growing, he towered above most of his classmates and his added height made him a dominant force on the basketball court. As a sophomore Robinson led his team to a Colonial Conference title with a 26–6 record. The following year he led the Midshipmen to the Great Eight of the National Collegiate Athletic Association tournament and was named to the Associated Press 1986 All-America Team. As a senior he made the All-America team again and won the Naismith Award as the College Player of the Year.

Because of his impressive college record, Robinson was the first player selected in 1987 by the San Antonio (Texas) Spurs, despite the fact that his obligation to the navy would keep him from professional play until the 1989–1990 season. After his 1987 graduation from the U.S. Naval Academy with a B.S. in mathematics, Robinson reported to Kings Bay Naval Submarine Base at St. Mary's, Georgia, where he worked as an engineer. As a member of the U.S. national basketball team, he played in the Pan-American Games of 1987 and the 1988 Olympic Games in Seoul, South Korea.

After his discharge from the navy in May 1989, Robinson began playing for the Spurs, lifting the team from a dismal 21–61 record the previous year to an impressive 56–26. At the end of his first professional season, "Admiral" Robinson ranked tenth in National Basketball Association (NBA) scoring with an average of 24.3 points per game, second in rebounding with 12 per game, and third in blocked shots with an average of 3.89 per game. Led by Robinson, the Spurs won the Midwest Division title and advanced to the second round of the play-offs. Not surprisingly, he was unanimously voted NBA Rookie of the Year.

Robinson improved on his performance in the 1990–1991 season, averaging 25.6 points per game, 13 rebounds, and 3.9 blocks. The following season Robinson became only the third player in NBA history to land in the top ten in five separate categories. He was seventh in scoring with 23.2 points per game, fourth in rebounding with 12.2, first in blocks with 4.49, fifth in steals with 2.32, and seventh in percentage of field goals completed with 55.1 percent. He was also the first player in NBA history to rank in the top five in rebounding, blocks, and steals. That year he played in his third straight All-Star game and attended the 1992 Olympics in Barcelona, Spain, as part of the first U.S. "Dream Team."

Robinson married Valerie Hoggat in 1991; the couple later had three sons. In November 1992 Robinson and his wife created the David Robinson Foundation to support programs addressing the physical and spiritual needs of the family. During summer 1997 the Robinsons contributed $5 million to help create the Carver Academy, an independent school designed to serve elementary and middle-school students on the east side of San Antonio.

During the 1993–1994 season Robinson won the NBA scoring title with an average of 29.8 points per game. The following season Robinson's average of 27.6 points per game paced the Spurs to the NBA's best record of 62–20. San Antonio advanced to the conference finals, where they lost to the Houston Rockets. In 1995–1996 Robinson was tapped for both the All-NBA and All-Defensive First Team. He was named as an All-Star for the seventh consecutive time and played on the U.S. Dream Team at the 1996 Olympic Games in Atlanta. In 1996 the NBA named him as one of the fifty greatest players of all time.

Injuries sidelined Robinson for much of the 1996–1997 season, but he returned in 1997–1998 to play 73 games and teamed with the rookie Tim Duncan to lead the Spurs to 56 wins. Robinson averaged 21.6 points and 10.6 rebounds per game. During the 1998–1999 season Robinson tweaked his game a bit to maximize Duncan's strengths. They led the Spurs to the club's first NBA title. Robinson continued to demonstrate his strength in 1999–2000, when he averaged 17.8 points and 9.6 rebounds per game, and again in 2000–2001 with 14.4 points and 8.6 rebounds.

As one of the most dominant players in the NBA during the late twentieth century, Robinson surely will be remembered for his mastery of the game. Perhaps even more enduring will be his reputation as a decent human being. While still active in the sport, Robinson devoted his energies and millions of dollars toward bettering the lives of others.

★

Robinson's early years in the NBA are explored in detail in Dawn M. Miller, *David Robinson: Backboard Admiral* (1991). Additional details of Robinson's life and basketball career are covered in several magazines and periodicals. Some of the more insightful articles are Ben Kaplan, "San Antonio Spurs David Robinson and Tim Duncan Team Up to Wear Down NBA Opponents," *Sports Illustrated for Kids* (1 May 1998); Phil Taylor, "Here's to You, Mr. Robinson," *Sports Illustrated* (7 July 1999); and Ian Thomsen, "Three San Antonio Spurs: The Old Center Persuaded the Young Star Who Persuaded the New Guard to Play Here and Win," *Sports Illustrated* (30 Oct. 2000).

DON AMERMAN

ROBINSON, Edward Gay ("Eddie") (*b.* 13 February 1919 in Jackson, Louisiana), college football coach who won a record 408 games during his fifty-six years as head coach at Grambling University.

Robinson was the only son of Frank Robinson, a cotton sharecropper, and Lydia Stewart, a domestic worker. Be-

Eddie Robinson. AP/WIDE WORLD PHOTOS

cause few economic opportunities existed for African Americans living in the segregated South during the 1920s, Robinson's father sought employment in nearby Baton Rouge, Louisiana, while Robinson lived with his mother and grandparents on a farm in Jackson. The Robinsons reunited after Frank found work at an oil facility, but divorced when Robinson was ten years old. Robinson split the remainder of his childhood between his parent's homes, where he shined shoes, delivered newspapers, and picked strawberries to supplement their meager incomes.

In addition to developing the strong work ethic that later characterized his coaching career, Robinson also discovered a passion for football at an early age. He spent many afternoons watching the McKinley High School football team practice and was a star on the squad when he attended the Baton Rouge school. Robinson's athletic abilities earned him a football scholarship to Leland College, an African-American institution in Baker, Louisiana, where he played fullback, tailback, and once completed fifty-nine consecutive passes as quarterback. After he graduated from Leland, Robinson married Doris Mott on 24 June 1941 and worked at a Baton Rouge feed mill for twenty-five cents an hour to support his new family.

Later the same year, the twenty-two-year-old Robinson became football coach for the 320-student Louisiana Negro Normal and Industrial Institute in north central Louisiana's Lincoln Parish. Team facilities consisted of used equipment and a dirt field. Robinson had no assistants, worked as the school's night watchman, led the drill team at halftime, coached the baseball and basketball teams, and wrote game summaries for local newspapers for $63.75 a month. His first football team won three games and lost five, but the 1942 squad held all opponents scoreless and finished with a 9–0 record. Although the school fielded no team in 1943 or 1944 due to World War II, Robinson spent the period recruiting the best African-American high school athletes in Louisiana. He also coached high school football during this time.

In 1945 the Negro Normal and Industrial Institute, now named Grambling College, resumed its football program, and Robinson established it as an emerging power among African-American schools. From 1945 to 1948 the Tigers compiled a 35–11 record. The 1950s proved one of Grambling's most successful decades, as Robinson led his team to an undefeated 1955 season, achieved his 100th victory in 1957, and joined the Southwestern Athletic Conference (SWAC) in 1958. During the 1960s Robinson's stature grew to unprecedented heights as Grambling competed in venues across America and played opponents from Division I schools. In 1966 the Football Writers Association of America declared Robinson the person who most contributed to college football during the previous twenty-five years. Three years later the American Broadcasting Company (ABC) television network showcased Grambling in the first televised Division II football game. Robinson's success continued throughout the 1970s as his teams accumulated a 94–21 record over the period. In 1971 forty-three of Robinson's former players attended National Football League (NFL) training camps, and Grambling's stature as the most recognized African-American university in America continued to grow. By 1973 over 100 television stations across the nation broadcast Tiger football games as part of the Grambling Football Network. Although many ignored Grambling's accomplishments from the 1940s to the 1970s, Robinson surpassed several hallowed records during his last twenty-five years as a coach.

In 1982 Robinson joined Glenn "Pop" Warner, Amos Alonzo Stagg, and Paul "Bear" Bryant as the fourth coach to earn 300 victories. Three years later on 5 October 1985, Grambling defeated Prairie View A&M 27–7, and Robinson passed Bryant as the coach with the most wins in college football. On 14 October that year, *Sports Illustrated* made Robinson the only coach of a historically African-American college team to appear on the cover of a major sports publication. When Robinson achieved his 329th victory later in the 1985 season, he passed former Chicago Bears coach George Halas as the professional coach with the most wins in football history.

Robinson's career ended on a mixed note. In 1994 he led Grambling to a Southwestern Athletic Conference (SWAC) cochampionship and earned conference coach of the year honors, but it was his last winning season. In 1995 he earned his 400th victory, yet only one major daily newspaper, the *Atlanta Journal,* covered the story on the first page of its sports section. Amidst pressure to resign following his third straight season with a losing record, Eddie Robinson retired from coaching the sport he loved. He won 408 career games, a record many argue no collegiate coach will ever surpass.

Eddie Robinson also holds the record for most games coached (588) and the longest coaching career at one college (fifty-six years). Throughout his tenure at Grambling, Robinson missed no scheduled games, had forty-five winning seasons, no consecutive losing seasons until his last three, won seventeen SWAC championships and nine African-American college national championships, and earned four honorary doctorate degrees, including one from Yale University, which Robinson called his proudest achievement. Robinson's teams played the first collegiate football game in Tokyo, Japan, and appeared in prestigious venues such as the Orange Bowl, Rose Bowl, Superdome, Astrodome, Hoosier Dome, Meadowlands, and Yankee Stadium. NFL rosters have included over 200 of Robinson's former players, and four Grambling alumni are in the Pro

Football Hall of Fame. Robinson is also enshrined in numerous Halls of Fame, including those for the Sugar Bowl, Louisiana Sports, the SWAC, College Football, and the National Football Foundation. In 1998 he received the NFL Player's Lifetime Achievement Award, despite the fact that no professional team or Division I school offered him a head coaching position. Robinson often proclaimed that his lifelong affiliation with one school and his enduring marriage made him most proud. He and his wife had two children.

Robinson's winning record as coach established his illustrious career, but his role as a teacher and mentor to his players was equally important. His work also brought attention to African-American college athletics. During a period of strict social segregation in the South, Robinson produced a winning and nationally recognized program with inadequate facilities and meager funding while teaching his players that hard work, self-improvement, and respect for others would bring social equality. Robinson took pride in his players' 85 percent graduation rate and the fact that many were later successful in a variety of occupations. One of his most appreciated accolades came from former player Larry Scrubbs, who stated, "Robinson taught us as much about life as he did football." While Robinson's achievements alone ensure his legacy as one of the greatest coaches of all time, the challenging times in which he lived and worked guarantee his place in football history.

★

Robinson's autobiography written with noted sports writer Richard Lapchick, *Never Before, Never Again* (1999), traces his experiences from childhood through retirement. The book omits some important details concerning Robinson's early life and rise as a successful college football coach, but provides excellent insight into his motivations and personal philosophies. For more on Robinson's professional career see O. K. Davis, "Eddie Robinson: College Football's Winningest Coach," *Black Collegian* 21, no. 2 (Nov./Dec. 1990): 140; Eric Moskowitz, "Grambling's 'Coach Rob' Knocks on the Door of Win No. 400," *Christian Science Monitor* (21 Sept. 1995); Bob Stockard, "Eddie Robinson: A Living Legend," *Black Collegian* 26, no. 3 (Apr. 1996): 16; and Richard Hoffer, "Here's to You, Mr. Robinson," *Sports Illustrated* (1 Dec. 1997).

J. MICHAEL BUTLER

ROBINSON, Frank (*b.* 31 August 1935 in Beaumont, Texas), one of the greatest baseball players of the twentieth century, the first athlete named as the Most Valuable Player for both the National and American Leagues, and the first African American to manage a major league team.

Frank Robinson. ARCHIVE PHOTOS, INC.

Robinson was the youngest of ten children. His father, Frank Robinson, deserted the family when Robinson was young, leaving his mother, Ruth Shaw Robinson, to raise the children. When Robinson was four, the family moved to the San Francisco Bay area of California, where they eventually settled in Oakland. Robinson was an athletic child, and he blossomed under the coaching of George Powles, the local baseball coach who also worked with Curt Flood and other future professional baseball players. Robinson excelled for Powles's American Legion baseball club and at McClymonds High School. After graduating from high school in 1953, he signed with the Cincinnati Reds for a $3,500 bonus.

In his first year of minor league baseball, Robinson was sent to Ogden of the Pioneer League for the 1953 season. Although the team was based in Utah, Ogden still had many discriminatory regulations in place that Robinson had never seen growing up in Oakland. For the bulk of the next two seasons, Robinson played for Columbia of the Class A South Atlantic League and established his credentials as a major league prospect. In 1956 Robinson made the leap to the Cincinnati Reds and responded with an excellent season. He batted .290 with thirty-eight home runs, establishing a rookie National League (NL) record for home runs, and winning the Rookie of the Year award.

During the course of his career, Robinson mostly played

outfield and first base, although he did play third base on occasion. While he continued to hit well for the Reds, his finest year with that organization was in 1961, when the Reds won the NL pennant. Robinson won the league's Most Valuable Player (MVP) award with a .323 average, 37 home runs, and 124 runs batted in (RBI). On 28 October 1961 Robinson married Barbara Ann Cole; they had three children. After having an even better season in 1962, his offensive production began to wane. Even though he remained one of the best power hitters in the league, Robinson quickly fell out of favor with the Cincinnati management and despite being only thirty years old, Robinson was written off by the Reds and traded to the Baltimore Orioles in December 1965, in time for the 1966 season.

In Baltimore, Robinson rejuvenated his career, immediately leading the Orioles to the World Series in 1966. During the regular season Robinson batted .316 with 49 home runs and 122 RBI, winning the American League (AL) triple crown. He was a natural choice for the MVP as well, becoming the first player to win the award in both leagues. Although his batting average slipped over the following years, Robinson was a critical member of the pennant-winning Orioles teams in 1969 and 1971 and the World Series team in 1970. In December 1971 Robinson was traded to the Los Angeles Dodgers and played with them for one season. In November 1972 he was traded again, this time across town to the California Angels; he played with the Angels for the 1973 season and most of the 1974 season.

While Robinson was still contributing as a player in the 1970s, including hitting thirty home runs for California in 1973, he set his sights on maintaining an active role in baseball following his playing career. Robinson made numerous public comments about his desire to become the first African American to manage a major league team. While the African-American former players Larry Doby and Buck O'Neil served as coaches in the majors, the lack of management opportunities for African Americans was as real as in the years before 1947, when Jackie Robinson broke the color line for players.

To build his credentials and skills, Robinson succeeded Earl Weaver, the Orioles manager, as the manager of the Santurce Crabbers of the Puerto Rican Winter League for the 1968–1969 season. The Crabbers were the winter team of many Latin American major- and minor-league players as well as others that needed to continue work in the off-season. During Robinson's first year as the manager, the team included his Orioles teammates Paul Blair and Jim Palmer and qualified for the playoffs. He had a number of successful years, including the playoff championship in the 1972–1973 season, and managed the team through the 1974–1975 season. He also managed them in the 1979–1980 and 1980–1981 seasons (a total of nine seasons).

In September 1974 Robinson was traded to the Cleveland Indians and at the end of the season was named the player-manager for the upcoming 1975 season, becoming the first African American to manage a major league team. During his first game as a player-manager, he hit a home run in the Indians win over the Yankees at home in a game attended by Rachel Robinson (Jackie Robinson's widow) and the commissioner Bowie Kuhn. Cleveland improved slightly under Robinson as they finished 79–80 in 1975 and 81–78 in 1976. Some felt that Robinson, as one of the best players in baseball, had little tolerance for less-talented players. He played sparingly over those two seasons, putting a cap on a career that saw him hit 586 home runs (fourth on the all-time list) and 1,812 RBI.

Robinson gave up the player-manager title in 1977, focusing solely on his role as a manager. However, after the team started the 1977 season 26–31, he was fired, returning to the Orioles as a coach for his old manager Earl Weaver. He remained in Baltimore until he was named as the manager of the San Francisco Giants (1981–1984). His best season with the Giants was 1982, when they went 87–75. Also in 1982 Robinson was elected to the Baseball Hall of Fame. He was fired as the Giants manager during the 1984 season and was rehired as a coach with the Orioles.

In April 1987 Robinson was the most vocal critic of the Dodgers general manager Al Campanis and his remarks that African Americans "lacked the necessities" to manage in the major leagues. Robinson earned his third opportunity to manage a major league team shortly thereafter when the Baltimore manager Cal Ripken, Sr., was fired after starting the 1989 season 0–6. Robinson took over the team, but unfortunately they proceeded to lose the next fifteen games in a row, giving the 1983 World Series champions a 0–21 start. The Orioles bounced back the next season and finished only two games behind the Toronto Blue Jays, the AL East Division winners. The team's turnaround earned Robinson the AL Manager of the Year award.

In 1991, after a slow start, Robinson was moved from Baltimore's manager to the assistant to the general manager, where he evaluated players and other baseball-related decisions. In 2000 he moved to the Major League Baseball headquarters as the vice president of on-field operations, assuming a large number of the disciplinary tasks formerly maintained by the league presidents.

Robinson's baseball career is remarkable in that he made tremendous contributions both on and off the field. On the field Robinson was one of the game's best power hitters, ending his career tied for fourth on the all-time home run list. Off the field he was a respected manager who broke the color barrier and who served with distinction as an executive with the Baltimore Orioles and Major League Baseball.

★

Information about Robinson can be found in the National Baseball Hall of Fame Library in Cooperstown, New York. Robinson wrote three books about his life and career: with Al Silverman, *My Life in Baseball* (1968); with Dave Anderson, *Frank: The First Year* (1976); and with Berry Stainback, *Extra Innings* (1988). See also Russell J. Schneider, *Frank Robinson: The Making of a Manager* (1976), and Thomas Van Hyning, *The Santurce Crabbers: Sixty Seasons of Puerto Rican Winter League Baseball* (1999).

COREY SEEMAN

ROBINSON, Jack Roosevelt ("Jackie") (*b.* 31 January 1919 in Cairo, Georgia; *d.* 24 October 1972 in Stamford, Connecticut), legendary baseball player who broke the color barrier in modern Major League Baseball. He was the first player to be selected rookie of the year, the first African American to earn Most Valuable Player, and first African American elected to the Baseball Hall of Fame.

America's most celebrated black athlete, Robinson was the youngest of five children born to Mallie McGriff and Jerry Robinson. Jerry ran off with another woman, leaving Mallie to bring up the children alone. In 1920 she moved her family to Pasadena, California, at the suggestion of her brother Frank. There, Mallie worked as a domestic laborer, and the family purchased a house in an all-white neighborhood.

Jackie Robinson. AP/WIDE WORLD PHOTOS

To compete with his older siblings in street games, Jackie used speed and quickness against size and strength. As the neighborhood's best athlete, he succeeded at whatever sport he attempted, from Ping-Pong (he won the Pasadena championship in 1936) to baseball. He was later a star athlete at Pasadena Junior College (1937–1939), where he eclipsed the national junior college record in the broad (now long) jump set by his brother, Mack, with a leap of 25 feet, 5½ inches. This performance was followed by a spectacular athletic career at the University of California at Los Angeles (UCLA; 1939–1941), where he played football, basketball, baseball, and ran track. In the 1940 Pacific Coast Conference (PCC) football season, he finished second in total yards—440 running, 435 passing. As a basketball player he led the PCC in scoring. Arguably, he was the best all-round athlete in America since Jim Thorpe.

Robinson met his future wife Rachel Isum, a vivacious straight-A student, three years his junior in 1941. In that same year financial difficulties forced Robinson to leave UCLA before graduation. Drafted into the U.S. Army in 1942, he was involved in a series of racial confrontations. Robinson pursued an aggressive course of action to redress wrongs. He was rewarded with a court martial, found innocent, and discharged in 1944 for medical reasons.

Robinson joined the Kansas City Monarchs, a powerhouse in the Negro League, for the 1945 season. Despite a weak arm, he played shortstop. Soon after, Brooklyn Dodger General Manager Branch Rickey decided to sign "a Negro ball player," as he informed the broadcaster and Dodgers' announcer Walter "Red" Barber, the Dodger Board of Trustees, his wife, and family. Rickey sent out a flood of scouts seeking the right man. He received favorable reports on several players, but he fixed on Robinson for a number of reasons essential to his grand plan. He wanted the right man off as well as on the field. He wanted positive press and support from the African-American community. He wanted to win acceptance from Dodger teammates. As an officer and a gentleman, as a superior athlete and a solid family man, as an articulate individual who sprang from poverty, Robinson became the pioneer.

On 29 August 1945 Branch Rickey interviewed Robinson for three hours, during which he hectored, lectured, and tested the young athlete. He wanted Robinson to wear a "cloak of humility" as part of a long-term strategy designed to win acceptance. To a skeptical Robinson, he said: "I want a ball player with guts enough not to fight back! You've got to do this job with base hits and stolen bases and fielding ground balls, Jackie." On 23 October 1945 Robinson signed a contract with the Montreal Royals, the Dodgers' Triple AAA club in the International League.

He married Rachel on 16 February 1946. With Rachel

leading the chorus of 25,000 cheering fans, Robinson enjoyed a spectacular debut in April at Jersey City's Roosevelt Stadium. In five trips to the plate, he banged out four hits including a three-run homer, scored four runs, and stole two bases to lead the Royals to a 14–1 win. Despite frequent threats, Robinson enjoyed a dream season before record-shattering crowds: batting a league-best of .349 with 113 runs scored and fielding a team best of .985. The Royals won the pennant by 19½ games and the Little World Series over the Colonels of Louisville, four games to two. French Canadian fans serenaded Robinson at the conclusion of game six with a stirring rendition of "Il a gagné ses epaulettes." Fans hugged and kissed their hero. "It was probably the first time in history," observed reporter Sam Maltin, "that a black man ran from a white mob with love, instead of lynching, on its mind."

Robinson's elevation to baseball's major leagues stirred anxiety. Some of his own future teammates circulated a petition expressing their hostility to Rickey's brainstorm. Rickey and Dodger Manager Leo Durocher (soon to be banished for gambling) immediately squelched this move. In that first year—"when all hell broke loose" according to Dodgers' announcer Barber—Americans witnessed a milestone in race relations. Defying the odds, Robinson integrated professional baseball on 15 April 1947. Though hitless, he scored the winning run in a 5–3 victory over the Boston Braves. Robinson played under wraps. Containing his fury, he channeled his energies into batting and base running. A .297 average and excellent fielding at a new position, first base, earned rookie-of-the year laurels. He led the Dodgers to a National League pennant, the first of six during his ten-year career.

In the first nationally televised World Series, Robinson drove rookie Yankees catcher Yogi Berra crazy with his antics on the base paths. The Dodgers extended the highly favored Yankees to seven games until they succumbed to superior relief pitching and abler management, 5–2. Eddie Miksis, normally an infielder, was sent to left field instead of Al Gionfreddo, whose spectacular catch of Joe DiMaggio's towering drive in game six secured a Brooklyn victory. Miksis misplayed a fly ball in left field that led to a Yankees rally and World Series triumph.

During that first summer, Robinson endured verbal abuse, particularly from Phillies' manager Ben Chapman; physical intimidation from St. Louis Cardinals' player Enos "Country" Slaughter, who has vigorously denied it; and racists who rooted for Robinson to fail. As Robinson proved his worth on the field and at the turnstiles, he won friends and influenced people. African Americans felt ennobled by Robinson. In his first year he fielded expertly at a new position, showing wide range and an impressive .989 average, and "tore up" Red Barber's "pea patch" with a league-leading twenty-nine stolen bases while terrorizing opposing pitchers.

Robinson's style transformed the national pastime, bringing a distinctive Negro League synthesis of "Cool Papa" Bell's speed and science with the prevalent power of Josh Gibson. The twenty-eight-year-old rookie aroused the public imagination as no other athlete since the heavyweight boxer Joe Louis. His charismatic personality and exciting play evoked admiration from whites as well as blacks. To the latter, he arose as a savior. Fans flocked to the games; listened to the radio coverage; idolized their hero. Robinson inspired America not only by serving as trailblazer but also, according to Jules Tygiel, because he combined heroics, courage, and triumph—the stuff of Horatio Alger dreams. He validated our nation's quest for fair play coupled with social progress. Ultimately, he opened the doors for African Americans in other fields: education, public accommodations, business, broadcasting, banking, insurance, and construction. Dr. Martin King, Jr., acknowledged that "Jackie made my work much less difficult."

Shifted to second base in 1948 after Eddie Stanky was traded to the Boston Braves, Robinson grew in confidence and improved with experience. He hit .296, one point less than in his rookie year, but almost doubled his RBI output with eighty-five, and led all second basemen with only thirteen errors and a .980 fielding average. In the summer of 1948 the Dodgers brought up a second black ballplayer destined for glory: catcher Roy Campanella. The following year, pitcher Don Newcombe joined them. The trio would contribute to Dodger hegemony in the National League for the next seven years.

In 1949 Rickey's restraints on Robinson were removed, and the "Flatbush Flash" had a banner year with a league-leading and career-high .342 batting average, 16 homers, and 124 RBI. He also ranked first in stolen bases with thirty-seven. Voted the league's Most Valuable Player (MVP), Robinson crested as the Dodgers won an exciting pennant race on the season's final day. New York's other dominant team, the Yankees, thwarted a dream season with a four games to one triumph in the 1949 World Series.

After this superlative season, Robinson was summoned to Washington, D.C., to refute another black hero's stand on cold war politics. While traveling in Europe, the singer, actor, and activist Paul Robeson had asserted that American blacks would never take up arms against the Soviet Union. Before the House Un-American Activities Committee (HUAC), at the behest of Branch Rickey, Robinson testified: "I've got too much invested . . . in the future of this country . . . for any of us to throw it away for a siren song in bass. . . ." Although obviously scripted, this text endeared Robinson to the press corps bent on patriotism. While acknowledging the persistence of racism, the Dodgers' star reaffirmed the American success story, thereby enhancing his popularity. The anti-Communists achieved a great coup with his testimony. Realizing that he had been used as a pawn in a power game, Robinson would later express regret for the assault on Robeson, "who . . . sacrificed himself, his career, and the wealth and comfort he once enjoyed because, I believe, he was sincerely trying to help his people."

Playing himself, the National League's MVP starred in the *Jackie Robinson Story* (1950), opposite Ruby Dee as wife Rachel. Robinson earned rave reviews from *New York Times* film critic Bosley Crowther. The movie highlights the love, support, and calming influence of Rachel and their two children (they eventually had another child).

The joy of fatherhood was offset by the agony of defeat, which plagued Robinson and the Dodgers on the last day of the next two seasons. The Philadelphia Phillies avoided a certain loss in the ninth inning of the 1950 finale, as the plodding Cal Abrams was gunned down by the weak-armed centerfielder Richie Ashburn. The Phillies won the pennant in the tenth on Dick Sisler's three-run home run against Dodgers' pitcher Don Newcombe. History repeated in 1951 as Bobby Thomson's homer—"the shot heard round the world"—propelled the New York Giants to a dramatic comeback win over the Dodgers 5–4 in the ninth. In both of these heartbreak seasons, Robinson continued his superior hitting, .328 and .338, and sensational fielding, .986 and .992, the latter a league record.

Robinson led the Dodgers back to the top of the National League in 1952, 1953, 1955, and 1956, his final season. In his later years he adapted to team needs and demonstrated valuable versatility. To accommodate younger players like Jim "Junior" Gilliam, Robinson played third base and left field. He played a shallow third base in his final year to compensate for a weak throwing arm. He covered the hot corner with catlike agility and amazing grace. Playing three positions, he helped the Dodgers gain their only World Series victory, won in 1955 against the Yankees.

In the 1956 World Series, a loss to the Yankees, Robinson knocked in the winning run in the tenth inning of game six and made the final out in a 9–0 Yankees rout in game seven. It was the last hurrah of a magnificent athlete. Over a ten-year span, he led the Brooklyn Dodgers to six pennants and one—Brooklyn's only—World Series victory. During that decade he hit .311 with the Dodgers and .333 in All-Star games (1949–1954). He led the National League in stolen bases in 1947 and 1949. An excellent fielder, he paced all second basemen in double plays in 1949, 1950, 1951, and 1952. His on-base percentage of .410 ranks historically among the best twenty-five.

Refusing to be traded to the New York Giants in 1957 "for thirty pieces of silver" as wife Rachel remembered, Robinson retired from baseball and launched a new career as vice president of a restaurant chain, Chock Full O'Nuts. The qualities that he brought to baseball, indeed all sports, carried over into business, civil rights activism, and civic concerns. His crowning glory—election to the Baseball Hall of Fame in Cooperstown, New York—came in 1962, the first year of his eligibility. He was the first African American to be so honored.

Unfortunately, a long happy life eluded the "Lion at Dusk," as aptly described in Roger Kahn's poignant memoir *The Boys of Summer*. Robinson lost his oldest child and namesake first to drugs then to a high-speed car wreck. Racked by diabetes and its attendant miseries, Robinson suffered blindness and heart trouble. Undaunted, Robinson made his last public appearance at the 1972 World Series, where he was honored on 16 October, twenty-five years after his major league debut. To a television public in the millions, Robinson exhorted the baseball establishment to hire black managers and black coaches. Nine days later, Robinson died at the age of fifty-three.

On 28 October 1972 Robinson received a hero's funeral, as 2,500 people turned out to pay tribute. In Manhattan's Riverside Church, over a silver-blue coffin decorated with red roses, Jesse Jackson delivered the eulogy, saying "Today we must balance the tears of sorrow with the tears of joy. . . . When Jackie took the field, something reminded us of our birthright to be free." Robinson was, as Red Smith put it in a single word, "unconquerable."

★

Roger Kahn's brilliant tome, *The Boys of Summer* (1972), reawakened national interest in Jackie Robinson and the Brooklyn Dodgers. Robinson coauthored several autobiographies, the best of which is the last: *I Never Had It Made,* with Alfred Duckett (1995). Jules Tygiel, *Baseball's Great Experiment: Jackie Robinson and His Legacy* (1997), remains definitive, and his collection of essays, *The Jackie Robinson Reader* (1997), is useful. Arnold Rampersad, *Jackie Robinson: A Biography* (1997), offers the most comprehensive study of a heroic life. Maury Allen, *Jackie Robinson* (1987), is full of pertinent information and quotations. For an insider's view coupling love and illumination with a trove of photographic treasures, see Rachel Robinson, *Jackie Robinson: An Intimate Portrait* (1996). Though Sharon Robinson, *Stealing Home* (1996), provides fewer pictures of her famous dad, her book confronts the dilemma of a child living in the shadow of a giant Dodger. Joram Warmund and this writer, Joseph Dorinson, contribute new perspectives in *Jackie Robinson: Race, Sports and the American Dream* (1998).

JOSEPH DORINSON

ROBINSON, Walker Smith, Jr. ("Sugar Ray") (*b.* 3 May 1921 in Detroit, Michigan; *d.* 12 April 1989 in Culver City, California), welter- and middleweight boxer who was the only fighter to win the middleweight title five times.

Robinson was born Walker Smith, Jr., the youngest of three children born to Walker Smith, a construction worker, and Leila Hurst Smith, a chambermaid, in the Black Bottom section of Detroit. A mischievous kid who liked to fool around, Robinson learned the elements of boxing at the Brewster Center in Detroit. He grew up idolizing his neighbor, Joe Louis, and in his autobiography, *Sugar Ray* (1970), reminisced about the privilege of carrying Louis's training bag to the gym. Leila Smith separated from her husband in 1927, and in 1932 moved with her three children to 419 West Fifty-third Street in the Hell's Kitchen section of Manhattan; the family subsequently moved to Manhattan Avenue and 119th Street in Harlem.

While his mother worked as a laundress, Robinson combined an education at Cooper Junior High School with dance lessons at the Roy Scott Studios, shooting craps, and dancing for dimes on street corners. He also ran errands for a grocery store, sold driftwood, and shined shoes. He fathered a child with a teenage girl, Marjorie Joseph, and married her to make the child legitimate, but the union was annulled three months later. Robinson soon dropped out of DeWitt Clinton High School to pursue his boxing career.

At Police Athletic League contests, Robinson met George Gainford, who soon placed him into the bootleg boxing circuit in New England and upstate New York. Since Robinson was underage for his first fight, Gainford gave him the Amateur Athletics Union (AAU) card of another boxer, Ray Robinson. A *Watertown (New York) Daily Times* sportswriter named Jack Case dubbed the fledgling fighter "sweet as sugar." The name stuck, and "Sugar Ray" Robinson roared through the amateur ranks with a record of 85–0, winning the New York City Golden Gloves titles as a featherweight (1939) and a lightweight (1940). He turned professional in 1940 under Gainford's management.

Sugar Ray Robinson. ARCHIVE PHOTOS, INC.

Robinson quickly became famous for his speed, agility, and extraordinary repertoire of punches. Winning his first forty fights (twenty-nine by knockout), he was named outstanding fighter of 1942 by *Ring* magazine. In the first of their six battles, Robinson won over Jake LaMotta on points in 1942, though most sportswriters favored LaMotta, who was known as the "Raging Bull." In their rematch, LaMotta won over Robinson by a decision after nearly knocking him out in the eighth round. In a third match, Robinson won in twelve rounds. He continued to dominate LaMotta in three more fights, though LaMotta insisted in his autobiography *Raging Bull* that he won at least two of them. LaMotta also boasted that although Robinson padded his record by knocking out mediocre opponents, "he was never able to flatten me."

Robinson was drafted into the U.S. Army on 27 February 1943, and that March he was inducted as a sergeant in Joe Louis's boxing troupe. The boxers gave exhibition tours of boxing at military bases for fifteen months. On 29 May 1943 Robinson married a former showgirl named Edna Mae Holly, with whom he had a son. After his honorable discharge on 3 June 1944, Robinson returned to full-time boxing.

Robinson fought sixteen bouts in 1946, entering the ring at times every ten days. He capped the year by winning his first title on points over Tommy Bell for the World Welterweight Championship in New York on 20 December. Six months later, in his first defense of the title, Robinson beat Jimmy Doyle by a technical knockout in the ninth round. After Doyle died the next day from a brain injury, a grieving Robinson established a trust fund for Doyle's mother.

Robinson won forty-eight consecutive bouts between 1946 and 1950, but only five were title defenses. The others were income opportunities for Robinson, who shrewdly negotiated his own contracts, saying, "I don't see why I should take fifty cents when I have a dollar coming." Robinson backed up these words by canceling bouts if he was not satisfied with the financial arrangements. Before a fight with LaMotta in 1951, for example, Robinson forced the New York State Boxing Commission and the television networks to accept his terms. They did so because of his ability to attract huge crowds to his matches.

During the late 1940s, years after he had bragged to his Harlem playmates that he would own property "around here someday," Robinson was the proprietor of a top Harlem nightclub, a dry cleaning store, apartment buildings, a lingerie boutique, and a barbershop. More famously, he drove a pink Cadillac convertible.

In 1950 he took his title, car, and entourage to Paris. He won five bouts—four by knockout—while touring Europe in twenty-nine days. Adoring Frenchmen flocked around him and the pink convertible. As policemen cleared his way, droves of cyclists trailed behind like small fish after a cruise ship. Robinson, a sharp dresser and notorious ladies' man, charmed U.S. columnists Damon Runyon and Walter Winchell by denouncing Paul Robeson, who claimed to have signed Communist Party petitions as "simply autographs." Later he offered to fight Orval Faubus, the segregationist governor of Arkansas, "after I take care of [Carmen] Basilio."

On 14 February 1951 Robinson returned to business by beating LaMotta for the last time, winning the world middleweight title and vacating his welterweight crown. Flush with success, Robinson returned to Europe. On one occasion, he kept French notables waiting for an hour as he toured the town. As bejeweled ladies were pushed aside in the rush to meet "Monsieur Roban-sahn," he donated a large check to the Damon Runyon cancer fund and bussed Madame Vincent Ariole, the first lady of the nation, on each cheek.

Robinson's grand tour hit a pothole when the black English boxer Randy Turpin beat him by decision in fifteen rounds in London. Licking his wounds, Robinson returned to his adoring fans in New York, who included the mayor, the chief of police, and 3,500 people at city hall. Part of this adulation was due to the fact that columnist Walter Winchell had reported that Robinson had donated nearly $60,000 to the cancer fund. Robinson offered no excuses for his defeat and promised the next match would end differently. He regained his title on September 12 with a tenth round knockout of Turpin.

Robinson fought only three times in 1952; all were title defenses. He beat Bobo Olson in fifteen rounds on March 13; knocked out Rocky Graziano in the third round, then lost his challenge for the light heavyweight championship by knockout to the tough Joey Maxim in the fourteenth round in a sweltering Yankee Stadium. Six months later Robinson announced his retirement, citing a potential acting career, tap dance engagements, and an admission that he could "not [*sic*] longer give the public his best."

Robinson stayed in retirement in 1953 and most of 1954. He announced his comeback in October of that year, then fought an exhibition in Ontario the following month. Observers thought his thirty-four-year old reflexes were sluggish and his punching combinations "lacked their once deadly, almost blurry swiftness." On 19 January 1954 his return was marred by a loss in ten rounds to Tiger Jones. After four tune-ups, however, Robinson flattened Bobo Olson in two rounds to regain the middleweight championship, and repeated his domination of Olson by knocking him out in four rounds in their rematch.

In the next few years, while he restored his pattern of easy bouts against inferior opponents, Robinson also thrilled U.S. television audiences with a series of classic title matches against Gene Fullmer and Carmen Basilio. Robinson first lost to Fullmer in fifteen rounds in Los Angeles on 2 January 1957, then knocked him out in five rounds in Chicago on 2 May 1957. Three months later Basilio took away Robinson's crown in fifteen rounds in Madison Square Garden. Robinson won it back for the fifth time in Chicago on 25 March 1958. He fought only once in 1959 and lost his title for good to Paul Pender in a fifteen-round decision the following year. Two rematches with Fullmer that year also ended in defeat.

Although he never again fought for a title Robinson stayed in the ring, prompting his mother to comment, "The older he gets, the more he wants to prove he isn't." In 1962, with clearly declining skills, Robinson lost three of his six bouts. Undaunted, he entered the ring ten times in 1963 and 1964. Few of these matches were headliners; most were fought in smaller cities or in Europe. In 1965 he fought fourteen times; three bouts were with Young Joe Walcott. He lost five of the matches. After an embarrassing loss to Joey Archer, Robinson retired for good. He had achieved an extraordinary lifetime record of 175 wins, 19 losses, 6 draws, 2 no-contests, and 109 knockouts.

Robinson spent his retirement in Los Angeles. After his wife, Edna Mae, obtained a Mexican divorce in 1963, he married his longtime companion Mildred Wiggins Bruce on 25 May 1965; they had no children. His $4 million of ring earnings had largely vanished. In 1969 he established the Sugar Ray Robinson Youth Foundation, which seeks to build the self-esteem of underprivileged youth by giving them an opportunity to realize their potential through sports, fine arts, and performing arts activities. Robinson suffered from Alzheimer's disease in his last years before dying of heart ailments and is buried in Inglewood Cemetery in Los Angeles.

A generally accepted accolade is that, "pound for pound," Robinson was the best boxer ever. His influence on Muhammad Ali's boxing technique and flamboyant style, and the way in which his public persona created a role model for the African-American working class, will carry his name into future generations.

★

Robinson's autobiography, written with Dave Anderson, is *Sugar Ray: The Sugar Ray Robinson Story* (1971). LaMotta's comments can be found in Jake LaMotta, Joseph Carter, and Peter Savage, *Raging Bull* (1970). Further biographical information on Robinson can be found in Michael McLean, "Sugar Ray Robinson," *Scribners Encyclopedia of American Lives* (1999); and David A. Nathan, "Sugar Ray Robinson, the Sweet Science, and the Politics of Meaning," *Journal of Sport History* 26:1 (spring 1999): 163–172.

GRAHAM RUSSELL HODGES

ROBUSTELLI, Andrew ("Andy") (*b.* 6 December 1925 in Stamford, Connecticut), defensive line football player who propelled the New York Giants to the championships in 1956 and to the Eastern Division title every year between 1958 and 1963.

Robustelli's father, Louis, a barber, and mother, Katie Galasso, a seamstress, taught their six children to value diligent effort, family, and religion. At Stamford High School, Robustelli starred in football and baseball. After graduating in 1943, he attended La Salle Military Academy in Oakdale, Long Island, but only for three months. As soon as he reached eighteen, he enlisted in the U.S. Navy, serving in 1944 and 1945. After World War II ended, Robustelli matriculated at Arnold College in Milford, Connecticut, now part of the University of Bridgeport. There he excelled at baseball, batting .400 as a catcher and third baseman, and starring in football, playing sixty minutes a game as a two-way end. He also married Jeanne Dora on 17 July 1948.

Andy Robustelli, 1956. AP/WIDE WORLD PHOTOS

Robustelli graduated in 1951 with three choices: he had a physical education degree and offers to teach in high school; the New York Giants wanted him to play Class B baseball in Knoxville, Tennessee; and as a nineteenth-round draft pick of the Los Angeles Rams, he was offered one-way plane fare and $4,200 a year if he made the team.

Robustelli went to Los Angeles. One would have expected his chance of success to be minimal. Small by today's standards, at six feet tall and 220 pounds, he quickly made his presence felt. At his very first practice with the Rams, Robustelli's physical prowess was evident as he stampeded over linemen, harassed passers, and stopped runners in their tracks. It was immediately apparent that the "Iron Man," as he would later be nicknamed, was made of some very tough stuff. He made the team, and with Robustelli at defensive end, the Rams made it all the way to the 1951 championships, where they beat the Cleveland Browns, 24–17. Robustelli went on to spearhead the Rams defense for five seasons.

Then in 1956, with his wife, Jeanne, expecting their fourth child, Robustelli told head coach Sid Gillman that he would be a little late to training camp. Gillman said, "Get to camp or I'm going to trade you." Robustelli, thinking Gillman was bluffing, replied, "If you want to trade me, trade me." The next day, he became a New York Giant. Heading back east to his family, who lived in Stamford, was a welcome move.

If the Rams traded Robustelli because they thought that, at age thirty, he might be slowing down, they were wrong. With the Giants, a team that had always stressed defense, Robustelli starred in the New York spotlight. Tom Landry, the Giants genius defensive coach from 1956 to 1959, admired the way Robustelli combined his athletic skills with intelligence and enthusiasm on the field. For nine seasons, Robustelli anchored a defensive line that was respectfully referred to as the "Fearsome Foursome" (an accolade that also stuck with the Los Angeles Rams' defensive line). Alongside Rosie Grier, Dick Modzelewski, and Jim Katcavage, the Giants front four gave very little ground. Together with the rest of the defense, they earned praise previously reserved for the offense. Cheers of "De-fense! De-fense!" were heard for the first time from the Giants' fans.

In 1959, during a five-game stretch in which the Giants' offense fizzled, the defense gave up only two touchdowns. The Giants won all five games. Toward the end of that streak, with the defense trotting off the field after stopping their opponent repeatedly, a Giant defenseman yelled to his offense, "Hold 'em till we get back."

Jim Brown, the legendary Cleveland Browns running back, called Robustelli "one of the two toughest men I have ever met." (The other was eight-time all pro Gino Marchetti.) In 1960, during a win in Cleveland, the Giants defense held the Browns to an incredible total of four yards rushing. Fierce competitor Bobby Layne, the former Detroit Lions quarterback, said, "Andy hits you so hard your bones rattle."

Robustelli asserted that he performed in an era when players played with pride, dedication, integrity, and loyalty—all for the team. It was before free agency and the astronomical contracts that some say soften an athlete's commitment to the team. Robustelli played professional football for fourteen bruising years—and missed but a single game.

After a game in 1963, Robustelli's knee swelled so much that he couldn't bend it. Mid-week he went to the team doctor and asked him to aspirate the fluid from the knee. The doctor refused and recommended rest. Robustelli then went to the trainer. He too refused, saying, "You're not playing for three weeks." "You're crazy," Robustelli told him, "I can't sit out that long. I want to play this Sunday." The trainer said "No way!" So Robustelli went to his own doctor on Friday afternoon. The knee was aspirated. Robustelli played on Sunday.

In 1964, Robustelli's ninth and final Giants season, he played full-time as well as being the team's defensive coach. That year, his salary was $24,000. In those days, most football players had to work in the off-season. Robustelli built successful businesses in sports marketing and travel services that helped support his wife and their nine children.

In 1966 Robustelli returned to football as the head coach of the Continental Football League's Brooklyn Dodgers. Though the league lasted only one year, Robustelli loved the job and delighted in the fact that several of his players and coaches improved enough to go on to the National Football League (NFL).

A telephone call from New York Giants owner, Wellington Mara, in December 1973 lured Robustelli back to the team, where he served as director of operations from 1974 until the completion of the 1978 season.

Robustelli was a hard-nosed player, and the New York Giants squad that he captained elevated NFL defenses to prominence for the first time. Though his focus was on "the team," his personal accomplishments were extraordinary. During his fourteen-year career, he was named to the Pro Bowl and All-NFL teams seven times. He played in eight championship games. In 1962, at age thirty-seven, the Maxwell Club named him NFL Player of the Year. Robustelli received perhaps his greatest honor when he was enshrined in the National Football League Hall of Fame in 1971.

★

In *Once a Giant, Always . . .* (1987), Robustelli, with sports specialist Jack Clary, presents an in-the-trenches look at Robustelli's distinguished football career. The book touches on his five years with the Los Angeles Rams, but concentrates on his career with the New York Giants, from the Giants' dynasty of the mid-1950s and early 1960s to Robustelli's tenure as director of operations. In Gerald Eskenazi, *There Were Giants in Those Days* (1976), the excitement of the Giant teams from 1954 to 1963 is rekindled. Richard Whittingham, *Giants in Their Own Words* (1992), quotes Giants greats, including Robustelli.

HY ROSEN

ROCKNE, Knute Kenneth (*b.* 4 March 1888 in Voss, Norway; *d.* 31 March 1931 near Bazarr, Kansas), legendary football coach at the University of Notre Dame credited with three national championships, five undefeated seasons, a lifetime winning percentage of .881, and one of the initial members elected to the National Football Hall of Fame in 1951.

Rockne was the only son in a Norwegian family of five children. His father, Lars Knuson Rockne, was a stationary engineer and amateur inventor. Lars Rockne came to the United States in October 1891 to demonstrate a carriage he built for the Columbian Exhibition in Chicago. Eighteen months later, his wife, Martha Gjermo Rockne, and his children settled in Chicago. Rockne grew up in Chicago, where he attended Brentano Grammar School and North-

Knute Rockne. THE LIBRARY OF CONGRESS

west Division High School. However, academics were not important to him during his formative years, and he was dropped from the high school rolls for cutting classes.

At the age of twenty-two, after completing the necessary preparatory courses to qualify for admittance and saving money by working several jobs, Rockne was accepted to the University of Notre Dame in 1910. By then serious-minded in his academic pursuits, he graduated with distinction in 1914 with a B.S. in chemistry. At Notre Dame, Rockne distinguished himself in other ways as well. He was editor of the college literary annual in his senior year and captain of the 1913 football team that defeated a powerful Army squad.

Rockne was an all-around athlete, but his first effort with the football team ended in failure. He subsequently turned his attention to track. His speed, however, convinced football coach Frank Longman that Rockne's talents could be an asset to the team. Rockne's roommate, Wisconsin native Charles "Gus" Dorais, already had an excellent reputation as a baseball player. With Rockne's speed and Dorais's strong arm, the game of college football was about to change.

In early 1913 Jess Harper was named football coach and athletic director at Notre Dame. During that summer Dorais and Rockne worked and reworked passing combinations. Their efforts have been credited for the introduction of the buttonhook play in football. The buttonhook, based on the forward pass, was put into play during Notre Dame's 1913 game against Army.

Arranged to fill a vacant spot in Army's schedule, Notre Dame was considered a pushover for the West Point team. Notre Dame's name in football meant nothing in the East at that time. But with quarterback Dorais throwing to end Rockne and to back Joe Pliska, Notre Dame caught Army completely unprepared and scored an easy 35–13 victory over the Black Knights of the Hudson. Football historians agree that the work of Dorais and Rockne against Army opened the eyes of football coaches throughout the country to the possibilities of what was then termed the "open game."

On 15 July 1914 Rockne married Bonnie Gwendoline Skiles of Sandusky, Ohio. They had four children. After receiving his undergraduate degree, Rockne signed on as a chemistry instructor and assistant football coach at Notre Dame. Coaching seemed to suit his personality more than classroom instruction. When Harper retired in 1918, Rockne became the head coach. Under his leadership Notre Dame football became synonymous with national success. In thirteen seasons Rockne's teams won 105 games, while losing only twelve and tying five. Notre Dame was undefeated in five of those years, and was considered consensus national champion three times. Six times during his coaching tenure his teams were voted national champions by at least one organization. Rockne trained such famous players as George Gipp and the 1922–1924 backfield men known as the "Four Horsemen." Rockne prefigured the modern "platoon system" by substituting complete teams, which he called "shock troops," during games. His .881 winning percentage remains the highest in college football history.

Rockne and Notre Dame established their preeminence in intercollegiate football in 1924. That year's team featured the "Four Horsemen" and an offensive line known as the "Seven Mules." Loaded with talented athletes, Notre Dame went undefeated during the regular season, outscoring their opponents 258–44. The closest game was a 13–7 victory over Army at the Polo Grounds in New York. Their 1 November victory over Georgia Tech also marked the university's 200th win. Accepting an invitation to play Stanford in the Rose Bowl, the "Ramblers," as Rockne's teams were then called, defeated legendary coach Glenn "Pop" Warner and his star player, Ernie Nevers, 27–10. Perhaps the most astonishing aspect of the game, one revealing Rockne's flair for theatrics and guile, was his decision to start his second team to the complete surprise of all in attendance.

Rockne's promotional skills were also revealed in his advocacy of intersectional football. His teams traveled all over the country, "meeting strong opponents in the East, the West, and the South." Rockne's colorful and highly trained teams became favorites with the non-college public. The advent of the "subway alumni" began with Notre Dame's regular appearance in New York City against Army. His teams constantly attracted huge crowds. Over 112,000 fans witnessed the 16 November 1929 game between Notre Dame and the University of Southern California at Soldier Field in Chicago. Rockne possessed a magnetic personality and he knew how to motivate players. The most repeated story, immortalized in the 1940 movie *Knute Rockne—All-American,* took place during a game against the powerful Army team in 1928, when Rockne implored his players to "Win one for the Gipper." The veracity of Rockne's speech remains debatable, but Johnny O'Brien's winning touchdown catch and the so-called pep talk are forever embedded in Notre Dame folklore.

As a coach, Rockne knew best how to utilize players. He relied on a large pool of recruits to match his multiple offenses and defenses. The so-called "Rockne System" featured speed and deception and "provided a place for the lighter and faster man on the football field." This was a product of his own experience as a player. He also introduced the forward pass, another byproduct of his days as a player; the shift, "in which the backs moved just before the snap of the ball from their T-formation into a box alignment behind the left or right side of the line"; the spinner plays; and the "flexing-end play to a high type of perfection."

In spite of all these tactical innovations, Rockne and the university's football reputation rested largely in the hands of one person. In 1924 sportswriter Grantland Rice began his account of that year's Notre Dame–Army game with the following words, which would be forever etched in college football memory: "Outlined against the blue-gray October sky, the Four Horsemen rode again. In dramatic lore they were known as famine, pestilence, destruction and death. These are only aliases. Their real names are Stuhldreher, Miller, Crowley and Layden."

Rockne was not without detractors. Michigan head coach Fielding Yost despised him and the small Midwestern Catholic college he represented. Yost constantly blocked Notre Dame's efforts to join the Big Ten. Because of religion and success on the field, Big Ten schools were reluctant to provide any additional exposure to Notre Dame. Notre Dame's geographic location in northwestern Indiana, a pro–Klu Klux Klan state in the 1920s, also generated anti-Catholic sentiment. Ironically, Rockne himself did not become a Catholic until the mid-1920s.

At Notre Dame, moreover, a constant battle ensued between the academicians determined to improve the learning curve, and Rockne, who was even more determined "to manipulate the educational system for his own ends." It is true that most of his early recruits came from working-class backgrounds and "felt comfortable within Notre Dame's traditional 'masculine democracy.' " It is also true that his recruits were willing converts in Rockne's efforts to abuse the system in order to benefit the football program. If Rockne was unable to obtain athletic scholarships that included on-campus jobs for recruits, he had Notre Dame alumni sponsor them. He tolerated, or simply chose to ignore, his players' personal indiscretions, particularly drinking and gambling, for the sake of victory. Yet Rockne's successes on the field outweighed these shortcomings. As such, he knew how to negotiate his worth as a coach. He realized that Notre Dame was not about to lose its most valuable asset and instrument of recognition. His contract flirtations with other universities, including Iowa and Columbia, led the Reverend Matthew Walsh, in 1924, to ink Rockne to an agreement for "ten academic years of ten months" per annum at an annual salary of $10,000, a very high income in the 1920s.

The 1920s were the golden era of college football, and Rockne was the beneficiary of such exciting times. At the height of his earning power, Rockne's estimated income from coaching and his outside deals was close to $75,000 a year—a sum "not matched by anyone in his profession for another forty years."

On 31 March 1931, while traveling on a business trip to the West Coast, his plane crashed in a barren cornfield near Bazarr, Kansas. There were no survivors. He died at the age of forty-three and is buried in Notre Dame, Indiana. In 1988 the United States Postal Service issued a commemorative stamp celebrating the 100th anniversary of his birth. He became the first athletic coach in any sport to be so honored. Forever immortalized in the 1940 Warner Brothers film *Knute Rockne—All-American,* featuring actors Pat O'Brien, James Cagney, Spencer Tracy, Paul Muni, and future president of the United States Ronald Reagan, Rockne's success was as much a product of the "growth of Notre Dame's unique athletic culture" and religious ties to Catholicism as it was to his coaching greatness. He remains the most famous coach in college football history. He was inducted into the National Football Hall of Fame in the first year of its inception, 1951.

★

The best primary source is the Athletic Department Records and Presidential Records, University of Notre Dame Archives, Hesburgh Library. Of special importance are the presidential records of the Reverends John W. Cacanaugh, 1905–1919; James Burns, 1919–1922; Matthew Walsh, 1922–1928; and Charles L. O'Donnell, 1928–1934. *The Autobiography of Knute Rockne* (1931), was probably written by John B. Kennedy. Scholarly histories of the university are numerous but two stand out: Reverend David J. Arthur, "The University of Notre Dame, 1919–1933: An Administrative History" (Ph.D. dissertation, University of Michigan, 1973), and Thomas Schlereth, *The University of Notre Dame: A Portrait of Its History and Campus* (1976). By far the best scholarly work is Murray Sperber, *Shake Down the Thunder: The Creation of Notre Dame Football* (1993). Rockne's obituary is in the *New York Times* (1 Apr. 1931).

CHARLES F. HOWLETT

RODGERS, William Henry ("Bill") (*b.* 23 December 1947 in Hartford, Connecticut), long-distance runner who won both the Boston and New York Marathons four times, and whose accomplishments contributed to the popularization of recreational running in the United States during the 1970s and 1980s.

Rodgers was one of four children of Charles Andrew Rodgers, head of the mechanical engineering department at Hartford State Technical College, and Kathryn Malloy Rodgers, a nurse's aide. When Rodgers was two years old, the family moved from Hartford to suburban Newington, Connecticut. As a youth Rodgers was impatient in the classroom but loved the outdoors, so running suited his personality. As a senior at Newington High School, he was a state cross-country champion. In 1966 Rodgers enrolled at Wesleyan University in Middletown, Connecticut. There, he came under the influence of fellow runner Ambrose ("Amby") Burfoot, two years older than Rodgers. Burfoot, who as a college senior trained for and won the 1968 Boston Marathon, routinely ran 100 to 140 miles per week. Rodgers, who had never run more than twelve miles as a high

Bill Rodgers, 1980. ASSOCIATED PRESS AP

school athlete, increased his mileage when running with Burfoot.

In the spring of 1968 a particular training run proved significant. Rodgers, then a sophomore, accompanied Burfoot on a twenty-five-mile run during Burfoot's preparation for the approaching Boston Marathon. Despite the increasingly vigorous pace set by his mentor, Rodgers ran step for step until the final two miles, when Burfoot pushed himself all out. Rodgers had unwittingly provided Burfoot with the last necessary test before his Boston Marathon victory. More importantly, the performance foretold Rodgers's own enormous marathon talent.

From Burfoot, Rodgers learned to build training mileage slowly, increasing his endurance with long-distance runs and with moderate interval speed workouts. Moreover, Burfoot was an inspiration to Rodgers, who would later compare him to Abebe Bikila, the two-time Olympic marathon champion from Ethiopia.

Nevertheless, with Burfoot's graduation, Rodgers's training fell off precipitously. By the time he graduated from Wesleyan in 1970 with a B.A. in sociology, Rodgers had stopped running. He began to smoke and frequent bars. To avoid fighting in the Vietnam War, which he found unconscionable, Rodgers applied for and was granted conscientious objector status. Alternative service was mandated, which Rodgers met by working as a low-paid escort messenger at the Peter Bent Brigham Hospital in Boston. The job required him to transport mail, supplies, medical samples, and patients throughout the hospital. Rodgers found the work, which at times included taking bodies to the morgue, emotionally upsetting. The result was that by 1972, to raise his spirits, Rodgers returned to running and the accompanying sense of personal satisfaction. His running was spurred further by the thefts of his bicycle and motorcycle.

In September 1972 Frank Shorter won the gold medal in the marathon at the ill-fated Munich Olympic games, during which eleven Israeli athletes were murdered by Palestinian terrorists. Shorter was the first American to win the Olympic marathon in sixty-four years. Although the two men would later become fierce rivals, Rodgers drew inspiration from Shorter's victory and began to train for the 1973 Boston Marathon.

Unionizing activities caused Rodgers to be fired from his job at the hospital. Out of work for a year, he eventually found a part-time job at the Fernald School, a state institution for the mentally impaired and emotionally disturbed in Waltham, Massachusetts. Despite his training, Rodgers failed to complete the 1973 Boston Marathon, dropping out after twenty-one miles. Undeterred, Rodgers entered and won the 1973 Bay State Marathon in Framingham, Massachusetts. While his winning time of 2:28:12 was not extraordinary, the experience proved valuable. Rodgers placed fourteenth in the 1974 Boston Marathon in 2:19:34. He joined the Greater Boston Track Club (GBTC) and was coached by Bill Squires. His transcendence into the world running elite was complete when, on 16 March 1975, he placed third in the 12,000-meter World Cross-Country Championship in Rabat, Morocco, finishing ahead of Shorter.

Still, Rodgers was unknown to the public at large when on 21 April he stood at the starting line of the 1975 Boston Marathon. In an era before widespread corporate financial endorsement, Rodgers wore a hand-lettered tee shirt reading "BOSTON" and "GBTC." The shoes he wore had been sent to him by Olympian Steve Prefontaine. He sported a headband that had just been handed to him by a fellow marathon runner, Tom Fleming, to "keep the hair out of your eyes." He wore a pair of white gardening gloves because of the cool weather.

Rodgers was not expected to be a factor in the race. Ron Hill, from Great Britain, held the course record of 2:10:30.

Canadian Jerome Drayton had won the highly regarded Fukuoka Marathon in 1969, and had finished third at Boston the previous year.

Rodgers found himself next to Hill in the lead pack of runners for the first five miles. At six miles into the race, Drayton and another runner pulled away from the lead pack. Rodgers followed, and by nine miles was running alone with Drayton. When a spectator cheered Drayton with shouts of "Go Jerome! Go Canada!," Rodgers's competitive fires were stoked. He felt that a Boston crowd should support a Boston runner. Rodgers accelerated the pace and Drayton fell back. By the halfway point of the race, Rodgers was running by himself. Pushing his lead through the middle portion of the course, Rodgers became calm and composed, actually stopping twice to drink water, and a third time to tie a shoelace. He called out to a childhood friend he spotted on the sidelines. His insouciance belied the fact that he was setting a new record for the Boston course. Rodgers's winning time of 2:09:55 was the fastest marathon run by an American to that date.

While Rodgers's lighthearted nature at times masked a competitive spirit, it captured the public's attention. At five feet, nine inches tall and 128 pounds, with his long, reddish-blond hair and pale blue eyes, Rodgers appeared almost angelic while running, floating above the ground. Friendly by nature, he was known at times to actually slow his own training runs to accommodate joggers who recognized him on the street. Rodgers repeated his Boston Marathon victory in 1978, 1979, and 1980. He also won the New York Marathon four times from 1976 through 1979. His 1978 and 1979 New York wins were featured on the covers of *Sports Illustrated* magazine, the latter race chosen as the feature over the Pittsburgh Pirates' World Series victory. Along with Shorter and Jim Fixx, the author of *The Complete Book of Running* (1977), Rodgers is credited with the growth of recreational running.

"Being a runner is very ordinary, really," he has said. "I believe in living an active life—using your body and muscles. We're all meant to move. We're all meant to be athletes."

Rodgers won twenty-one marathons during his running career. He was ranked the top world marathon runner in 1975, 1977, and 1979. Rodgers subsequently set age group records while running in his forties and fifties. Despite his success, Rodgers was at times haunted by his rivalry with Shorter, noting, "Even though I've run the marathon faster than he has and twice broken his American records, even though Frank has never won Boston, people will always say 'Rodgers was good, but Shorter got a Gold Medal.' " Rodgers was inducted into the National Distance Running Hall of Fame in Utica, New York, in 1998, and into the National Track and Field Hall of Fame in Indianapolis, Indiana, in 1999.

Rodgers earned a master's degree in special education at Boston College in 1975. He is the owner of Bill Rodgers Running Center, a chain of running stores in the Boston area. A running apparel company, Bill Rodgers and Co., was lost to foreclosure in 1987, although Rodgers remained a spokesperson for a successor company, Bill Rodgers Sportswear. Rodgers's 13 September 1975 marriage to Ellen Lalone ended in divorce in 1981. On 8 September 1983 he married Gail Swain, with whom he has two daughters.

★

Rodgers has written an autobiography, *Marathoning* (1980), with Joe Concannon. In addition, he is the coauthor of *Bill Rodgers and Priscella Welch on Masters Running* (1991), with Priscella Welch and Joe Henderson; *Bill Rodgers' Lifetime Running Plan* (1996), with Scott Douglas; and *The Complete Idiot's Guide to Jogging and Running* (1998), with Scott Douglas. His Boston Marathon victories are extensively treated in Hal Higdon, *Boston: A Century of Running* (1995), and Tom Derderian, *Boston Marathon: The History of the World's Premier Running Event* (1994). See also Diane Shah, "Master of the Marathon," *Newsweek* (21 Apr. 1980).

DENNIS WATSON

RODRIGUEZ, Alex Emmanuel (*b.* 27 July 1975 in New York City), baseball player who earned the highest rookie batting average of all time, hit more home runs than any other shortstop, and signed the largest contract in the history of sports.

Rodriguez, popularly known by the nickname "A-Rod," is the third child of Victor and Lourdes Navarro Rodriguez. His parents emigrated from the Dominican Republic to New York City, where Rodriguez was born, in the hope of finding better work prospects. They settled in Washington Heights, a Dominican stronghold. His father ran a small shoe store in Manhattan and his mother worked the night shift at an automotive plant. By the time Rodriguez was four, his parents had saved enough money to retire in their homeland. They purchased a house in Santo Domingo, the Dominican capital, and returned home. Financial losses on bad investments, however, forced them to re-emigrate to the United States when Rodriguez was nine. This time they settled in Kendall, Florida, outside Miami.

When the family moved back to the United States, Rodriguez played Khoury League Baseball, sponsored by the Boys' Club in Coconut Grove (Miami), a league he still supports. From an early age, Rodriguez displayed exceptional baseball skills. His dream was to play in the major leagues. "He was very focused from the time he was a child—he was not interested in anything else," his mother recalled. His idol was Cal Ripken, Jr., the Baltimore Orioles shortstop, and Rodriguez kept a poster of Ripken in his room.

Alex Rodriguez. AP/Wide World Photos

Rodriguez was not yet ten when his father deserted the family. His mother provided for the family by working two jobs, as a secretary and as a waitress. Although two men became strong surrogate fathers—Eddie Rodriguez, who ran the Boys' Club in Miami, and J. D. Arteaga, Sr., the father of his best friend—it was from his mother that Rodriguez acquired a strong work ethic.

By the time he began high school, Rodriguez had become an all-around athlete. At Westminster Christian High School he played varsity basketball as a sophomore, was an All-State selection at quarterback, and led the baseball team to the state and national high school championships. As a senior he was touted as one of the best baseball prospects in the country, batting .505 with 9 home runs and 36 RBI in 33 games, and stealing 35 bases without being thrown out once. He was named high school All-American and USA Junior Baseball Player of the Year. He also was a good student and made the honor roll.

Rodriguez was the first pick in the 1993 draft, and was taken by the Seattle Mariners of the American League (AL). Negotiations between his agent Scott Boras and the Mariners did not go well, and Rodriguez prepared to start classes at the University of Miami. He planned to major in communications and become a sportscaster. Just hours before his first class at Miami, Rodriguez signed a three-year contract with the Mariners.

Rodriguez started his first season of professional ball at Appleton, Wisconsin, in the Midwest League. He started well, hitting .319 in 65 games before being promoted to Double-A Jacksonville (Florida), and just 17 games later promoted again, this time to the Mariners. At age eighteen, with less than a full year of professional ball, Rodriguez was in the big leagues. He finished out the season in Triple-A, where the organization thought he would get more playing time. Being sent back to the minor leagues, however, proved to be fortunate. In mid-August the major league players went out on strike, wiping out the rest of the season. Instead of being forced to join the walkout, he was able to continue playing in Triple-A, where he gained the preparation he needed to become a successful big league player.

That winter Rodriguez played in the Dominican Republic, and he slumped badly, hitting only .179. "It was the toughest experience of my life," he said. "I just got my tail kicked and learned how hard this game can be. It was brutal, but I recommend it to every young player." In 1995 he shuttled between the Triple-A Tacoma Rainiers and the Mariners. The third time he was demoted, and he was so discouraged that he briefly considered quitting and returning to Miami. He hit .232 for the Mariners, but a phenomenal .360 at Tacoma.

Rodriguez spent much of the off-season watching videotapes of hitters, particularly teammate Edgar Martinez, who had led the league in hitting in 1995. The following season, 1996, was Rodriguez's breakout season. He put up numbers no other shortstop in the history of the game had achieved, leading the league in hitting with a .358 average, the highest batting average ever by a rookie, and the highest average by a right-handed hitter in the American League in sixty-seven years. He was also among the league leaders with thirty-six home runs, 123 RBI, 141 runs scored, and fifty-four doubles. He was selected to the AL All-Star team, the youngest shortstop ever to play in an All-Star game. He narrowly missed being voted Most Valuable Player (MVP), finishing second to Juan Gonzalez by three votes. After slumping slightly in his sophomore year with a .300 batting average, twenty-three homers, and eighty-four RBI, Rodriguez has achieved All-Star numbers ever since. In his first seven seasons, from 1994 to 2000, he posted a .309 batting average, and he is only the third player ever to join the 40-40 club (40 home runs and 40 stolen bases in a single season).

In 2000 Rodriguez signed a ten-year contract with the American League's Texas Rangers for $252 million. It was the richest contract ever awarded to an athlete—twice the dollar amount of the previous record contract of National Basketball Association (NBA) star Kevin Garnett. It was more than Rangers owner Tom Hicks paid for his entire team plus the ballpark. The contract was negotiated by Boras, Rodriguez's hardball agent, who came armed with a glossy self-published seventy-page booklet, *Alex Rodriguez: Historical Performance.* With statistics from Rodriguez's first five years in the major leagues, Boras projected Rodriguez to break every offensive record in baseball and to be the greatest ballplayer of all time.

Boras got from the Rangers what he believed was fair value for a once-in-a-lifetime performer, but most baseball people were shocked. Some predicted the ruin of the game. While few disputed Rodriguez's ability, they questioned whether any player was worth that kind of money. His $25.2 million average annual salary was $1 million more than the total player payroll for the Minnesota Twins that year. And it translated into more than $155,000 per game. To help offset the cost of Rodriguez's contract, the Rangers raised prices at the ballpark by about $2 a ticket. (It was the fifth straight year with a price increase). Disenchanted fans around the league took to calling Rodriguez "Pay-Rod." Rodriguez handled the scrutiny and criticism as well as anyone could, sometimes saying he would play for nothing if he had to, such was his devotion to the game. However, he seemed to be earning his money. In his first season with the Rangers, Rodriguez hit 52 home runs, setting the franchise record and the all-time record for shortstops. Rodriguez also hit .318 and drove in 135 runs.

Rodriguez has a multiracial appearance—kinky dark hair, bright gray-green eyes, and light bronze skin—and a Spanish surname. (*People* magazine named him as one of the world's Fifty Most Beautiful People.) He says that most people do not perceive him as Dominican or Latino. "I want to be known as a Dominican, that is what I am, 100%. . . . I have a duty and responsibility to continue the legacy of Dominican baseball."

Rodriguez has a squeaky clean image. He is polite, humble, shows respect for his teammates and fans, and handles his success graciously. "He is Mr. Clean," said former teammate David Segui. "He is milk and cookies." Citing his belief that players are role models for youths, Rodriguez has affirmed that players "have a responsibility to be the best people we can."

Rodriguez likes to work with children. In Miami he developed Grand Slam for Kids, a program that encourages elementary school students to focus on reading, math, physical fitness, and citizenship; as part of the program he visits school and holds assemblies. Some sportswriters have described him as the anti-Rodman, a star athlete who cherishes the values of the past, notably a love for the game, hard work, and gratitude.

★

For information about Rodriguez and his career, see Stew Thornley, *Alex Rodriguez: Slugging Shortstop* (1998); and Jim Gallagher, *Latinos in Baseball: Alex Rodriguez* (2000).

GEORGE GMELCH

ROONEY, Arthur Joseph, Sr. ("Art") (*b.* 27 January 1901 in Coulterville, Pennsylvania; *d.* 25 August 1988 in Pittsburgh, Pennsylvania), owner of the Pittsburgh Steelers of the National Football League (NFL) and one of the most beloved figures in American sports who persevered long enough to see his team shed its "lovable losers" label and establish a Super Bowl dynasty in the 1970s.

Rooney, the oldest of the eight children of Daniel M. Rooney, a tavern owner, and Margaret Murray Rooney, a homemaker, grew up in Pittsburgh's Northside in a predominantly Irish ward. Rooney spent his childhood not far from where his Steelers eventually ruled the pro football world from Three Rivers Stadium. Rooney lived all his adult life in a sturdy but not ostentatious Victorian house, from which he walked to his Three Rivers office everyday, even in his seventies and eighties.

As youngsters Rooney and his brothers, especially Dan Rooney, were fine all-around athletes. They formed the core of a semipro football team, the Hope-Harveys, that was good enough to play Jim Thorpe and the Canton Bulldogs in the era before the National Football League (NFL). Art Rooney was a minor league baseball player and a skilled boxer, an Amateur Athletic Union welterweight and middleweight champion. He qualified for the 1920 U.S. Olympic boxing team, although he did not participate in the games. He played football at Duquesne Prep, Georgetown, Indiana State Normal School (now Indiana University of Pennsylvania), and Duquesne University but did not complete his degree work.

In his early twenties Rooney developed a fondness for horse racing and became an expert handicapper. He seldom had a losing day at the track. Racing and football legend has it that one unbelievable weekend allowed Rooney to buy the Pittsburgh franchise in 1933. The numbers are a little fuzzy, depending on who is telling the story, but it is generally accepted that the weekend at New York's Empire City and Saratoga Springs tracks netted him between $250,000 and $350,000 at the height of the Great Depression. Upon arriving home, Rooney told his wife, Kathleen McNulty, "We'll never have to worry about money again." After they married in 1925, he and his wife had five sons.

The NFL was founded in 1920, but "blue laws" that prohibited professional sports on Sundays in Pennsylvania prevented either Philadelphia or Pittsburgh from having a franchise in the league in the early years. In 1933 the po-

Art Rooney *(left)* and his son, Dan, 1970. ASSOCIATED PRESS AP

litical climate was such that the November election would surely see the repeal of the archaic laws. Knowing a good bet when he saw one, Rooney paid the $2,500 franchise fee and became an NFL team owner. The success he had at various racetracks eluded him with his football team. Known as the Pirates from 1933 to 1939 and the Steelers after that, the team was usually the league doormat, finishing last or close to it for forty years. Rooney was always popular with the press, and when the team got new uniforms at training camp, a writer mentioned how good the team looked. A realist, Rooney replied, "They look like the same old Steelers to me." When they started playing games, the results were the same. In Pittsburgh "S.O.S." took on a new meaning. As the team lost game after game, year after year, fans and the media voiced their feelings, "S.O.S.—same old Steelers."

Rooney, it was said, was "just too nice a guy" to ever be a winner in the NFL. For four decades that seemed a valid assessment. Rooney had a penchant for hiring coaches who shared his love of the racetrack. It was said he kept them employed as the only means of being repaid the money he lent them to play the horses (and mostly lose). Rooney said this about the constant losing: "They say losing never bothers me. That's foolishness. I keep a lot to myself when we lose, but you'd better believe I hurt inside every time. When we lose, I don't want to talk about it and I don't want to read about it." That was the rule in the Rooney household, that after a loss no one mentioned the Steelers for two days. The Rooney home experienced many silent Mondays and Tuesdays. Rooney was elected to the Professional Football Hall of Fame in 1964, its second year of existence.

The Steelers' fortunes began to change in 1969. Rooney, who had turned over much of the team's operation to his sons Dan Rooney and Art Rooney, Jr., told them, when hiring a new coach, "put friendship at the bottom of the list." Chuck Noll was known by reputation only, but it was a good reputation. He was hired, and the Steelers' fortunes, after a 1–13 start, began to soar. They won the Super Bowl in 1975, 1976, 1979, and 1980. No one was more pleased than the NFL commissioner Pete Rozelle when he handed "the Chief," as Rooney was affectionately known, his first Super Bowl trophy.

Though quietly proud of the Steelers' success, the Chief, unlike many other NFL owners, never wore it on his sleeve, and he declined media guide offers of cover photographs and biographical sketches. The only time Rooney's name appeared was as president on the quarter-page team directory. After the long-awaited first Super Bowl victory, Rooney placed a call to the Steelers' office from New Orleans, the site of the game, the next day. An enthusiastic receptionist answered, "Good morning, Pittsburgh Steelers, Super Bowl champions." The following day Rooney checked in again, and when he was greeted the same way he simply said, "That was OK yesterday, but we don't need to say that anymore."

Though he turned over the operations of the team, Rooney continued to go to his office everyday. He suffered a stroke at his stadium office in mid-August 1988 and passed away two weeks later from the stroke's complications with his family at his side. His beloved wife had died in 1982. Rooney is buried in Pittsburgh's Northside Catholic Cemetery. Public donations funded a statue of him that was moved from Three Rivers Stadium to the Steelers' new playing site in 2001. A street near the new stadium is named

Art Rooney Avenue. Commissioner Rozelle said at Rooney's passing: "It is questionable whether any sports figure was ever more universally loved and respected. His calm, selfless counsel made him a valuable contributor within the NFL, but he will better be remembered by all he touched for his innate warmth, gentleness, compassion, and charity."

Rooney was truly "a man of the people." His friends were industrial giants and Damon Runyon types. He always had coins (later bills) for kids he passed as he walked to work. He was what is known as a "soft touch." A writer once said of him: "What Art Rooney did for the NFL is well-documented. What he did anonymously for his fellow man may never be fully known."

★

Rooney's life and career are discussed in Myron Cope, *The Game That Was* (1970); Joe Tucker, *Steelers' Victory After Forty* (1973); Ray Didinger, *Great Teams, Great Years: The Pittsburgh Steelers* (1974); and Tucker, *Steelers Super Dynasty* (1980). An obituary is in the *New York Times* (26 Aug. 1988).

JIM CAMPBELL

ROSE, Peter Edward ("Pete") (*b.* 14 April 1941 in Cincinnati, Ohio), All-Star professional baseball player, manager, and holder of the all-time hit record who was barred from Major League Baseball in 1989 for gambling on games.

Rose was one of four children born to Harry Francis Rose, a bank teller and bookkeeper who played semiprofessional football, and LaVerne Bloebaum Rose, a homemaker. Rose grew up on the streets of a working-class neighborhood in western Cincinnati, where he was attracted to sports. He was a star in the city's "Knothole" summer youth baseball program, and graduated from Western Hills High School, where he evinced little interest in academics but was a standout running back on the football team. His baseball talents were less evident, and only the strong intervention of an uncle who was a "bird dog" scout for the Cincinnati Reds got him a minor league contract.

As a minor league player Rose evidenced a special zeal for the game, earning him the nickname "Charlie Hustle," coined by Mickey Mantle and Whitey Ford. He became a student of the game to compensate for his lack of size and speed, and in 1963 was promoted to the major league team as the Reds' second baseman. Rose batted .273 and scored 101 runs in his rookie season. Reds fans were taken with his high energy level and full-bore approach to the game.

On 25 January 1964 Rose married Karolyn Englehardt; they had two children and divorced in 1980, with Rose's frequent infidelities serving as a major factor in the divorce. Rose married Carol Woliung in 1984; they also had two children.

Pete Rose. ARCHIVE PHOTOS, INC.

As a local product, Rose became the favorite player of Cincinnati's fans. During the mid-1970s he was a key part of the "Big Red Machine," playing both left field and third base, always hitting for a good average, and playing with a ferocity few rivals could match. Rose was the classic "blue collar" player. "Pete doesn't have a lot of great physical abilities," Hall of Famer and former teammate Joe Morgan once said. "He made himself into a ballplayer." In the 1970 All-Star game he bowled over catcher Ray Fosse with a vicious body blow that stunned fans everywhere; such hell-for-leather tactics are seldom seen in an exhibition game. After the 1978 season he was traded to Philadelphia, where, as a first baseman, he helped lead the Phillies to a World Series championship in 1980. In 1984, as he was closing in on Ty Cobb's career hit record of 4,191, he returned to Cincinnati as a player-manager. He broke Cobb's record the following year, and an appreciative Cincinnati City Council renamed the street bordering Riverfront Stadium "Pete Rose Drive." He was unquestionably Cincinnati's most popular resident.

That popularity was soon to be tested. In 1986 baseball commissioner Peter Ueberroth ordered a secret probe of allegations that Rose was betting on baseball games. Strict antigambling rules had been in place ever since the 1919 Black Sox scandals. Rose was an enthusiastic gambler. He had learned to bet on horses with his father during his youth, and bookies had plied their trade in the bars and pool halls of the neighborhood where he grew up. He had never hidden his love of playing the horses at River Downs, a track near Cincinnati, and he often mentioned to friends and acquaintances his winning bets on football and basketball games. In the spring of 1989 the special investigator submitted a 225-page report with 2,000 pages of supporting documents to Commissioner Ueberroth detailing Rose's gambling addiction. The report detailed Rose's many connections with suspected drug dealers and bookmakers, revealing a personal life that cast considerable doubt upon Rose's character and judgment. The report by former FBI agent John Dowd concluded that Rose had not only bet for years on baseball games, but even on games in which he was the manager. The report was turned over to the incoming baseball commissioner, A. Bartlett Giamatti, who negotiated an agreement with Rose in which he agreed to be placed upon baseball's "permanently ineligible list" but would not admit to betting on games. He essentially pleaded *nolo contendere.* However, in his press conference Giamatti asserted, "I am confronted by the factual record . . . . On the basis of that, yes, I have concluded he bet on baseball."

Public sentiment, which had initially supported Rose, rapidly receded, even in his hometown of Cincinnati. The negative attitude of baseball's leadership toward Rose, who had violated organized baseball's most sacred rule, intensified when Giamatti died of a massive heart attack just ten days after announcing Rose's ban. Rose was thus faced with the fact that his dream of being elected to the Baseball Hall of Fame was in serious jeopardy. Throughout the ensuing years debate among sports fans as to whether or not Rose deserved to be enshrined in the Hall of Fame despite his gambling remained a hot topic. Although he has steadfastly denied betting on baseball, Rose was unable to explain why he had agreed to a lifetime ban. As James Reston, Jr., wrote, Rose "continued to deny the undeniable."

Rose's lifetime ban from baseball was not the greatest of his problems, however. For several years the Internal Revenue Service had been carefully monitoring his tax returns, and he was indicted for failure to report income over several years from the sale of memorabilia at sports shows, the sale of autographs, and even a six-figure "pic-six" horse race ticket he cashed at River Downs. He served five months in federal prison for income tax evasion. Although he denied the allegations, many suggested he had been forced to sell his memorabilia, such as gloves, World Series rings, uniforms, and even the bat with which he had broken Ty Cobb's record, to pay off bookies. It may be that Rose was not only a gambler, but a poor one at that.

In the years after his banishment Rose spent much of his time attempting to get his lifetime ban lifted. For a time he hosted a nationally syndicated sports radio talk show and made public appearances for a fee. Speculation remains that his ban may be lifted and that he could become eligible for admission to the Hall of Fame, assuming he publicly admits and apologizes for gambling on baseball.

★

For Rose's side of the story see Pete Rose and Roger Kahn, *Pete Rose: My Story* (1989). More reliable is James Reston, Jr., *Collision at Home Plate: The Lives of Pete Rose and Bart Giamatti* (1991), and Michael Y. Sokolove, *Hustle: The Myth, Life and Lies of Pete Rose* (1990). Periodical articles of interest include "Truly a Baseball Immortal," *Sports Illustrated* (23 Sept. 1985); Jill Lieber and Craig Neff, "An Idol Banned," *Sports Illustrated* (4 Sept. 1989); and Jill Lieber and Steven Wulf, "Sad Ending for a Hero," *Sports Illustrated* (30 July 1990).

RICHARD O. DAVIES

ROTE, Kyle, Jr. (*b.* 25 December 1950 in Dallas, Texas), soccer player, broadcaster, and leading sports agent who was the first rookie and first American to win the North American Soccer League scoring title with ten goals and ten assists for thirty points.

Rote was the son of Kyle Rote, a former All-Star, All-Pro wide receiver for the National Football League's New York Giants, and Betty Jamison Rote. His parents divorced when he was twelve. Rote was more than an award-winning soccer player, he was an accomplished athlete in football, swimming, tennis, golf, cycling, and baseball. In 1967 when Rote was sixteen and an All-State defensive safety in football at Highland Park High School in Dallas, he chose to play soccer as a conditioning exercise for football. He was also captain of the baseball and basketball teams. Graduating from high school in 1973, he was offered fifty football scholarships and decided to attend Oklahoma State University in Stillwater, Oklahoma.

After a year at Oklahoma State, Rote left to enroll at the University of the South in Sewanee, Tennessee, where he started to play soccer seriously. The day after his 4 June 1972 college commencement, Rote married Mary Lynne Lykins, his college sweetheart, in the chapel at Sewanee. The couple eventually had four children. Also in 1972 Rote was picked on the first round of the North American Soccer League draft by his hometown team, the Dallas Tornadoes.

Rote soon attracted national attention as a soccer player and became an immediate star. In 1973, his rookie year, he became the first U.S. player to win the scoring championship of the then-struggling North American Soccer League. He became the club's all-time leading goal scorer with forty-two goals and was named as the 1974 Rookie of the Year.

In 1974 he was invited to compete with forty-eight other

celebrity athletes in a mini-decathlon promoted by the American Broadcasting Companies (ABC) television network. He won the event and received the Fram Trophy as the Superstar of the Year. He proved this accomplishment was not a fluke by winning the trophy again in 1976 and 1977. At the end of the 1974 season Rote was selected to the national soccer team, which provided the opportunity to become one of the sixteen players to represent the United States in the 1978 World Cup.

U.S. soccer was in its developmental stage when Rote was playing. It was still adapting to a game that, on a national level, was foreign to most Americans. Many of the teams were made up of European players, and the great Brazilian player Pele, who was close to retirement, was signed by the New York Cosmos to boost U.S. interest in the game. Rote's visibility as a successful soccer player provided a tremendous boost to the sport's domestic profile. He later reflected, "It turns out that my best contribution to soccer was winning the Superstars."

Rote has written several books on soccer, including *Kyle Rote Junior's Complete Book of Soccer* (1978), with Basil Kane; and the *Wilson Guide to Soccer* (1994), with Donn Risolo. He also hosted national television shows, worked as a sports commentator, and gave motivational lectures to companies such as AT&T, Polaroid, IBM, and Pillsbury. President Gerald Ford invited him to speak at the White House.

Retiring as a player in 1980, Rote moved to Memphis in 1981 to develop an upstart soccer team. After a three-year stint as the general manager of the Memphis Americans, Rote and his associates sold the team and it was moved to Las Vegas, Nevada. Rote stayed in Memphis, and with Don Kessinger, a former star infielder for the Chicago Cubs, he started Athletic Resource Management (ARM), a company that manages star athletes in baseball, football, and basketball. Two years later Kessinger moved on and Jimmie Sexton became the company's vice president and then the president; Rote became the chief executive officer. In May 1995 ARM became a wholly owned subsidiary of the Memphis-based Morgan Keegan, Inc.

Rote also became a member of the National Basketball Association (NBA) agents committee. In a business known for shady deals, Rote's company became recognized not only for its size, but its integrity. Rote negotiated player contracts, handled the marketing deals, arranged product endorsements, and was a mentor to his clients, many of whom wanted money-management advice in addition to career advice.

He was also a mentor in other ways. A devout Christian since the age of sixteen, Rote seriously considered entering the ministry during his college years. At the end of the 1974 soccer season, the pressures of being a professional soccer player, plus personal health problems in his family, made him decide to channel his strong religious beliefs into other avenues. In 1980 he took a year off to work with Mother Teresa in a hunger relief mission in India and Southeast Asia. Back in Memphis in the 1980s, he became the chairperson of the Mile-O-Dimes Christmas fund drive. He and his wife also became deeply involved in the sponsorship of sports clubs and camps for underprivileged children.

★

The best source of information on Rote's playing career is his autobiography, with Ronald Patterson, *Beyond the Goal* (1975). A good article also appears at the *Decatur Sports Page* online at http://www.decatursports.com/articles/soc/kyle_rote_jr_interview.htm.

ROBERT POLLOCK

ROZELLE, Alvin Ray ("Pete") (*b.* 1 March 1926 in South Gate, near Los Angeles, California; *d.* 6 December 1996 in Rancho Santa Fe, California), National Football League commissioner who presided over the modern growth and development of the league and is considered by many to be the architect of the modern sports league.

Rozelle was the son of Raymond Foster Rozelle and Hazel Viola Healey; his uncle nicknamed him "Pete" when he was five. The family lived in Compton, California, a Los Angeles suburb, and Rozelle attended Compton High

Pete Rozelle. AP/WIDE WORLD PHOTOS

School, where he played basketball and tennis. After graduating from high school in 1944, he entered the U.S. Naval Reserve, serving on a coastal tanker that never ventured far from San Pedro, a Southern California port. While he was in the navy, he met Jane Coupe; they married in 1949 and had their only child, a daughter, in 1958. Upon completion of his two-year navy stint, Rozelle entered Compton Junior College. In 1947 he briefly worked as assistant to Maxwell Stiles, the public relations director of the Los Angeles Rams. After transferring to the University of San Francisco, Rozelle served as that school's athletic-news director from 1948 to 1950. He graduated with a B.A. in 1950 and became the school's assistant athletic director. In 1952 Rozelle joined the Rams as the team's publicity director. Three years later he left to work for the San Francisco–based public relations firm P. K. Macker and Company, and in 1957 he returned to the Rams as general manager.

After the respected National Football League (NFL) commissioner Bert Bell died suddenly while attending a Philadelphia Eagles game in October 1959, NFL owners gathered at the Kenilworth Hotel in Miami to select a new commissioner. Participants disagreed over the nomination of Marshall Leahy, an attorney for the San Francisco 49ers, and Rozelle emerged as a compromise candidate on the twenty-third ballot. The football league he inherited in 1960 was a fragmented collection of franchises operated as independent businesses. Five teams held individual television contracts; seven others had none. In 1951 the NFL received a reported $75,000 from the DuMont Network to televise its title game between the Cleveland Browns and the Los Angeles Rams. The national pastime was baseball, and the NFL faced significant competition for players and sponsorship from the newly formed American Football League (AFL), financed primarily by Lamar Hunt, one of the world's richest people. The NFL was more collegial than corporate, with headquarters located in a suburb of Philadelphia near a pharmacy where Bell liked to lunch. Two clerks and a temporary worker were the only employees.

Shrewd compromise, lobbying in Washington, D.C., a new corporate image, and Rozelle's understanding of the power of television helped launch the NFL into prominence. In the early 1960s Rozelle and the league moved to New York City and presented several petitions to Congress seeking the power to negotiate single-network contracts. A bill providing this exemption to the Sherman Anti-Trust Act passed the House of Representatives and the Senate and was signed into law by President John F. Kennedy. Rozelle persuaded NFL owners to reject individual deals for the benefit of the league. New contracts shared revenues, which strengthened league parity and, ultimately, equal access to capital for teams in small regional markets.

In 1966 Rozelle approached Congress again with a plan to merge the NFL and AFL without legal consequences. His lobbying of Senator Russell Long of Louisiana resulted in a second exemption to the Sherman Act that ensured the league would not have to address charges of stifling competition. Not surprisingly, New Orleans, in Senator Long's home state, received an expansion franchise from the NFL that year. After Rozelle negotiated the merger, he became the commissioner of the new conglomerate. Under their arrangement, the two leagues combined to form an expanded NFL, featuring two conferences (American and National) and twenty-five teams. Over the next seven years, three additional franchises were added. While maintaining separate schedules through 1969, the conferences agreed to play an annual World Championship Game beginning 15 January 1967. Rozelle oversaw this contest, a spectacle soon renamed the Super Bowl. There was no initial extravaganza—the top ticket price at the contest was only $12, and more than 32,000 empty seats graced the Los Angeles Coliseum as the Green Bay Packers crushed the Kansas City Chiefs in the inaugural game.

Rozelle began incorporating structure designed to promote licensed products, heritage, and community service conducted by the league. NFL Properties, NFL Films, and NFL Charities were created to manage this process. In 1967 Rozelle started lobbying network executives to televise live football in prime time on Monday evenings. After finally persuading executives at the American Broadcasting Companies (ABC), *Monday Night Football* premiered on 21 September 1970. The show evolved into the nation's longest-running sports series and one of the longest-running television programs in history. At Rozelle's retirement, nine of the ten most-watched television programs in history were Super Bowls, and several polls taken in the late 1970s and early to mid-1980s found pro football to be America's favorite sport by increasing margins over baseball.

Growing NFL power allowed the league to beat back challenges. Competition from the World Football League and the United States Football League was stifled during Rozelle's tenure, and the NFL emerged stronger from both these encounters. But there was nevertheless a successful internal challenge. Al Davis, the principal owner of the Oakland Raiders, filed a lawsuit for the right to move his team to Los Angeles in the early 1980s, after the NFL blocked the move. When a 1982 court decision superseded the NFL's prohibition, granting Davis the right to relocate, NFL officials portrayed Davis as a rogue owner.

In addition to legal battles, the league confronted drugs, gambling, and racism. Player strikes occurred in 1974, 1982, and 1987, and Rozelle was criticized during the latter two years for staying on the sidelines and leaving negotiations to the NFL Management Council. In 1982 the league played only a nine-game season, and in 1987 it used replacement players for three games. These conflicts wore on Rozelle over the years. At his retirement in 1989 he identified the constant struggle as commissioner as a reason for his resignation.

Rozelle was named Sportsman of the Year by *Sports Illustrated* in 1963 and received acclaim as one of *Time*'s 100 most influential people of the twentieth century when he was named to the list of twenty "Builders and Titans." His honors included election to the Pro Football Hall of Fame in 1985. In 1974 he married Carrie Cooke; they had no children. For a brief time in 1994, until illness forced him to leave, Rozelle worked on the board of NTN Communications, a company in Carlsbad launched by two men affiliated with the Houston Oilers football team; Rozelle's involvement symbolized his belief that technology and sports can work successfully in tandem to make money. Rozelle died in 1996 from complications related to brain cancer and is buried at El Camino Memorial Park in La Jolla, California.

Under Rozelle's leadership the NFL transformed from a national sporting organization into a worldwide marketing conglomerate. Tall, thin, and amiable, Rozelle navigated the league to expansion from twelve to twenty-eight teams during his tenure as commissioner from 1960 to 1989. His ability to negotiate lucrative television contracts and persuade owners to establish cooperative financial arrangements allowed the NFL to prosper.

★

Michael Lewis's short biography of Rozelle for a *Time* special issue, "Twentieth Century's 100 Most Influential Builders and Titans," focuses on Rozelle's foresight as a business manager and the leader of a large sports organization. In *Supertube: The Rise of Television Sports* (1984), Ron Powers describes the impact of pro football and Rozelle on modern television sports programming, advertisers, and the way in which sports leagues view television as a source of revenue. *Total Football II: The Official Encyclopedia of the National Football League* (1999), edited by Bob Carroll, Michael Gershman, and David Neft, is an excellent reference for facts, figures, and key events and players spanning Rozelle's career. Dave Kindred's "It Was Great—For Pete's Sake," *Sporting News* (16 Dec. 1996), is a thoughtful essay describing Rozelle's influence on modern sports. An obituary is in the *New York Times* (7 and 8 Dec. 1996)

R. JAKE SUDDERTH

RUDOLPH, Wilma Glodean (*b.* 23 June 1940 in St. Bethlehem, Tennessee; *d.* 12 November 1994 in Brentwood, Tennessee), world-class runner and the first woman from the United States to win three gold medals in one Olympiad.

Rudolph was the sixth of eight children of Eddie B. Rudolph, a railroad porter and handyman, and Blanche Pettus. Her father also had children from a previous marriage, although sources differ as to the exact number. At birth

Wilma Rudolph at the 1960 Summer Olympics in Rome. AP/WIDE WORLD PHOTOS

Rudolph weighed only four and a half pounds, and during her early childhood she contracted scarlet fever, double pneumonia, and polio. As a result, she was crippled and could walk only with a leg brace. For four years Rudolph's mother, who worked as a domestic, accompanied her daughter twice weekly on the 100-mile round-trip bus ride to Meharry Medical College in Nashville for treatments. During the rest of the week Rudolph's siblings massaged her leg and reported to their mother when Rudolph removed her brace, which she frequently did.

Rudolph was determined to be like other children. At age nine she decided that it was time to walk without the brace, so she unstrapped it and walked right down the center aisle of her church. She continued to wear the brace occasionally until age eleven, but by age twelve she was shooting hoops in the driveway with her brothers and sisters. Her goal was to make the school basketball team; by the seventh grade she did just that. Rudolph saw no action for three years, but she stuck with it. During that time her coach, Clinton Gray, started a girl's track team mostly to keep the girls in shape during the off-season. Rudolph joined the team and surprised everyone by winning every race she entered. But her first love was still basketball; she warmed the bench for one more year, giving her all during practices and pestering her coach about when she could start. Coach Gray nicknamed her "Skeeter," because she was skinny, had long limbs, and was constantly in motion. Finally, in her sophomore year at Burt High School, she made starting guard. By then she stood five feet, eleven inches, and weighed just over 100 pounds. She scored 32 points during one game that season and helped her team to a conference title.

During the state championship basketball tournament, Rudolph was spotted by Ed Temple, the women's track coach for the Tigerbells of Tennessee State University. Temple invited her to a running camp that summer in Nashville, during which he took the girls to an Amateur Athletic Union (AAU) meet in Philadelphia. He entered Rudolph in the 75-meter and 100-meter dashes and the 440-meter relay. She competed in nine races, including preliminary heats, and won them all. Through the following winter, she continued to work with Temple and on her own. (It was widely known and largely overlooked that she cut classes to practice.) One year later, in 1956, at the age of sixteen and just five years out of her leg brace, Rudolph went to the Olympic Games in Melbourne, Australia, and won a bronze medal in the women's relay.

The following year, her senior year of high school, Rudolph became pregnant and was unable to run that season. In September, Rudolph enrolled at Tennessee State University and set her sights on the Olympics. At the Nationals in July 1960, before the Rome Olympics, Rudolph set a woman's world record of 22.9 seconds in the 200-meter dash. The record stood for nearly eight years. Rudolph qualified for three Olympic events: the 100-meter and 200-meter dashes and the 400-meter relay. She headed off to Rome with her old friend and mentor Ed Temple as coach. In Rome, Rudolph won the 100-meter dash by a 3-yard margin in 11.0 seconds. She then set an Olympic record of 23.2 seconds in the opening heat of the 200-meter dash and ran the final in 24.0 seconds to win another gold medal. Rudolph also anchored the relay team—all women from Tennessee State—and ran her leg in 44.5 seconds to win a third gold medal, becoming the first U.S. woman to win three Olympic gold medals. (She also had set a world record of 44.4 seconds in the semifinals.) She was the only track-and-field athlete to win three gold medals at that Olympiad. Before returning home, Rudolph went to the British Empire Games in London and then to an invitational meet in Stuttgart featuring Olympic winners. She won every race she entered.

Clarksville, the town where Rudolph was raised, celebrated her homecoming with a victory parade and banquet, the first racially integrated event in the town's history. Rudolph went on a victory tour that covered nearly every state in the union. In 1960 she was named United Press Athlete of the Year and Associated Press Woman Athlete of the Year. She was honored again by the Associated Press in 1961. In 1961 Rudolph married William Ward, a fellow runner; they divorced in 1962. At that time Rudolph was starting to think about retiring. In 1962 she competed in a dual meet with the Soviet Union at Stanford University. As she sat on the bench, untying her shoes after winning the 100-meter dash and the relay, a young boy came up and asked for her autograph. She signed both shoes and handed them to him. Wanting to go out at the top of her game — "in style"—Rudolph had finished running.

In July 1963 Rudolph married Robert Eldridge, her high school sweetheart and the father of her first child; they had four children and were divorced in 1981. Also in 1963, Rudolph graduated from Tennessee State with a B.A. in elementary education and began teaching at Clarksville's Cobb Elementary School and coaching track at Burt High School. But she was restless. She accepted a job as director of a community center in Evansville, Indiana, and then worked for the Job Corps in Poland Spring, Maine, then in St. Louis, and at Pelham Junior High School in Detroit. In 1967 Vice President Hubert H. Humphrey invited her to work as a member of Operation Champion, a program that made professional training available to star athletes from the ghettos. After that, she worked for the Watts Community Action Committee in Los Angeles, California, and in Chicago for Mayor Richard Daley's Youth Foundation. Rudolph also founded her own foundation (the Wilma Rudoph Foundation), a not-for-profit, community-based amateur sports program that offered free coaching and academic assistance and support for underprivileged children. Wilma's advice to the youngsters was "[H]ave confidence in yourself. Triumph can't be had without a struggle."

In her later years Rudolph worked as a model, television commentator, talk show host, track coach at DePauw University, goodwill ambassador to French West Africa, lecturer, sports commentator, and the cohost of a network radio show. Nothing seemed to stick. She suffered from depression and was often in debt. She finally returned to Clarksville to be with her family. Rudolph died of a brain tumor at the age of fifty-four; she is buried at Edgefield Missionary Baptist Church in Clarksville.

Rudolph grew up with a disability in extreme poverty in a racially oppressive environment. However, she overcame all these obstacles to become the fastest woman runner in the world and an inspiration to many. After she broke two world records and won three gold medals at the 1960 Rome Olympics, teammate Bill Mulliken said of Randolph, "She was beautiful, she was nice, and she was the best."

★

Rudolph's autobiography, *Wilma: The Story of Wilma Rudolph* (1977), provides a very personal narrative on the early years of her life. There are three biographies: Tom Biracree, *Wilma Rudolph* (1988), Wayne Coffey, *Wilma Rudolph* (1993), and Victoria Sherrow, *Wilma Rudolph* (1995). For additional details on Rudolph's awards and accomplishments, see *Grace and Glory: A Century of Women in the Olympics* (1996), edited by Siobhan Drummond and Elizabeth Rathburn. There are several articles available at websites, including M. B. Roberts, "Rudolph Ran and the World Went Wild," and Larry Schwartz, "Her Roman Conquest," both at http://espn.go.com. An obituary is in the *Washington Post* (13 Nov. 1994).

KATHARINE F. BRITTON

RUNYON, Damon (*b.* 8 October 1880 in Manhattan, Kansas; *d.* 10 December 1946 in New York City), major sports reporter, columnist, and short story writer whose use of humor and "slanguage" created a unique style that earned him a wide and loyal readership.

Born Alfred Damon Runyan, Runyon was one of four children of Alfred Lee Runyan, a newspaper publisher, and Elizabeth Damon. After partnerships to establish newspapers in several towns failed, the family moved to Pueblo, Colorado, where on 3 March 1888 Runyon's mother died of consumption. While his three sisters went to live with relatives, Runyon stayed with his father, who was working as a printer on the *Pueblo Chieftain.*

Damon Runyon. THE LIBRARY OF CONGRESS

Runyon attended the Hinsdale School in Pueblo up to the sixth grade, but soon left to spend his days reading in the library, roaming the streets with a gang of friends, occasionally picking up odd jobs, and adopting his father's barroom habits of smoking and drinking. By the time he was fifteen, he was working for the *Pueblo Evening Press,* where an editor misspelled his name, changing it from Runyan to Runyon.

When the Spanish-American War began in 1898, Runyon tried to enlist. Rejected as too young and too small, he nevertheless got aboard the train moving the troops to San Francisco. Once there, he managed to get accepted as bugler to the Thirteenth Minnesota Volunteers, but sailed for Manila, in the Philippines, only after the fighting was over.

Discharged from the military in 1899, Runyon spent some time in San Francisco before returning to Pueblo and the *Pueblo Chieftain.* His problems with alcohol led to short-term employment at several newspapers, but in 1906 he landed a position at the *Rocky Mountain News* in Denver, where he remained for four years. In his off time, Runyon began to write poems and short stories, including "The Defense of Strikerville," which was published by a national magazine, *McClure's,* in February 1907. After a heavy bout of drinking sent him to the hospital in 1910, he made a vow to quit drinking, a vow that he upheld for the rest of his life. Writing to his son in his later years, Runyon explained that liquor "made me dull and stupid and quarrelsome. It made me dreadfully ill afterwards. . . . I quit because I saw that I was not going to get anywhere in the world if I didn't, and I wanted to go places."

In 1910 he was in San Francisco, covering the James J. Jeffries vs. Jack Johnson heavyweight championship bout, when his friend Charles Van Loan suggested that Runyon go to New York. There Van Loan helped him land a job as a sports reporter at William Randolph Hearst's *New York American,* where an editor shortened his name to Damon Runyon. By then sober, successful in selling his short stories and poetry, and with a promising future at the *American,* he proposed to Ellen Egan, society editor at the *Rocky Mountain News.* They were married on 6 May 1911. Their first child, a daughter, was born on 24 August 1914 while Runyon was covering a game between the New York Yankees and the Chicago White Sox. Their second child, a son, was born on 17 June 1918.

Writing for the *New York American,* Runyon developed the style that earned him a loyal readership. Setting up his portable typewriter in the press box, he went beyond simply reporting an event to include human-interest details about baseball players, fighters, and horses, as well as colorful descriptions of the spectators. At times his own personal interests were involved in promoting individual fighters, as in his biographical series on Jack Dempsey. At other times, following the adage "I never bite the hand that feeds me," he reflected the interests of Hearst and others important to his career. Some critics characterized Runyon's personal style as aloof and cold. Others, observing his generosity, saw a shy and sentimental side. With fellow journalists, he often helped newcomers, but turned competitive when his position was challenged.

Runyon was a keen observer of those around him. Frequenting the bars and, during Prohibition, the speakeasies, he gathered an eclectic group of acquaintances—politicians, entertainers, reporters, and gangsters. Many of these became models for the "guys and dolls" who peopled his short stories. As he downed cup after cup of coffee in a favorite bar or nightclub, sat in on gambling sessions, or roamed along Broadway, he listened and captured the rhythms and patterns of language used by his first person narrators.

The late hours and frequent out-of-town assignments created problems in Runyon's marriage, and he and his first wife separated in 1928. After Ellen Egan's death in 1931, Runyon married dancer Patrice Amati del Grande on 7 July 1932 in a ceremony performed by New York City Mayor Jimmy Walker. This marriage coincided with Runyon's most prolific period as an author, which saw the publication of several collections of his works including *Guys and Dolls* (1931), *Blue Plate Special* (1934), *Money from Home* (1935), *More Than Somewhat* (1937), *Take It Easy* (1938), *The Best of Damon Runyon* (1938), *My Old Man* (1939), and many others.

As his popularity soared, movie rights to several of Runyon's short stories were sold. *Lady for a Day* (1933), based on "Madame La Gimp," was nominated for three Academy Awards, and *Little Miss Marker* (1934), starred Shirley Temple. Trying his pen at drama, he collaborated with Howard Lindsay in writing the successful Broadway play *A Slight Case of Murder* in 1935. When the *New York American* suspended publication in 1937, Runyon's columns moved to Hearst's *New York Daily Mirror*. By then he had developed a hoarseness and pain in his throat. Continuing to ignore it, he worked as writer-producer for RKO Pictures and Twentieth Century-Fox from 1941 to 1943. Finally, in April 1944, he consulted a physician. The diagnosis was cancer. Several operations followed as the malignant growth recurred. Unable to talk, Runyon continued to write his columns and to converse with his friends through notes.

Runyon's separation from his second wife ended in divorce in 1946. On 6 December 1946, Runyon entered the hospital for the last time. He slipped into a coma and died on 10 December 1946. Following Runyon's request for no public display, his son and his friend, pilot Captain Eddie Rickenbacker, scattered his ashes over New York City from the air.

In his three and a half decades as a newspaperman, Runyon lived through the major changes in sports and society that accompanied World War I, the Prohibition era, the Great Depression, and the New Deal. He captured the human dimensions in reports from sports arenas across the country, from political events, and from courtroom trials such as that of Bruno Hauptmann for the Lindbergh baby kidnapping and Al Capone for income tax evasion. As a major sports reporter, Runyon drew on his remarkable knowledge of sports and sports figures to add humor, color, and breadth in writing about sporting events from boxing and baseball to horse racing. Collections of his columns include *Short Takes: Readers' Choice of the Best Columns of America's Favorite Newspaperman* (1946), *In Our Town* (1946), *Trials and Other Tribulations* (1948), and *The Turps* (1951).

Runyon was both prolific and versatile. During much of his career he turned in a daily column and a weekly feature, as well as writing short stories and poetry. In feature stories his use of humor and fictional narrators disguised his often critical view of the world. His short stories appeared regularly and were popular reading in the United States and abroad. The high regard of his readers and friends was evident when, at his death, they responded with millions in donations to the Damon Runyon Memorial Cancer Fund.

★

Collections of Runyon's letters are at the University of California, Berkeley, and Temple University in Philadelphia, Pennsylvania, and some of his manuscripts reside in the collection of the New York Public Library. A memoir by Damon Runyon, Jr., *Father's Footsteps* (1953), includes letters written by his father in the last years of his life. Biographies include Edwin P. Hoyt, *A Gentleman of Broadway* (1964), and Jimmy Breslin, *Damon Runyon: A Life* (1991). Tom Clark places Runyon within the context of the major sports events of his time in *The World of Damon Runyon* (1978). Patricia Ward D'Itri, *Damon Runyon* (1982), is a useful critical analysis. An obituary is in the *New York Times* (11 Dec. 1946).

LUCY A. LIGGETT

RUPP, Adolph Frederick (*b.* 2 September 1901 in Halstead, Kansas; *d.* 10 December 1977 in Lexington, Kentucky), basketball coach who led the University of Kentucky Wildcats for four decades, winning four National Collegiate Athletic Association (NCAA) championships, a National Invitational Tournament title, and a then-record 876 games.

Rupp was one of six children born to Heinrich Rupp, a farmer, and Anna Lichti Rupp, a homemaker. Both parents were Mennonites who had immigrated to the United States

Adolph Rupp, 1960. ASSOCIATED PRESS

in the latter years of the nineteenth century. Rupp's father died of pneumonia in 1910 and his oldest brother, Otto, quit school to run the farm with their mother. At Halstead High School, Rupp captained the basketball team and reportedly served as the de facto coach in his senior year, when he averaged more than nineteen points per game.

After graduating from high school in 1919, Rupp entered the University of Kansas in Lawrence, where he encountered James Naismith, the inventor of basketball and the university's director of physical education, and Forrest "Phog" Allen, Naismith's protégé and the Jayhawks' coach. Although Rupp was never more than a bench player at Kansas, he studied Allen closely. During his own coaching career, Rupp imitated many of Allen's habits and mannerisms and eventually surpassed Allen's records for most wins by a college coach. After earning a bachelor's degree, then spending additional time working toward a graduate degree, he left Lawrence in 1924 and spent several years teaching and coaching basketball and wrestling at high schools in Burr Oak, Kansas (1924); Marshalltown, Iowa (1924–1926); and Freeport, Illinois (1926–1930). While coaching in Freeport, Rupp spent summers studying at New York's Columbia University, earning an M.A. in educational administration and a college teacher's diploma in 1930.

In four seasons at Freeport High School in northern Illinois, Rupp's basketball teams scored 59–21, earning him an interview for the head coaching job at the University of Kentucky in Lexington in 1930. Asked why the job was given to Rupp, who was just twenty-eight years old at the time and one of seventy applicants, a school administrator said, "Because he told us he was the best damned basketball coach in the United States, and he convinced us he was." Like Allen at Kansas, Rupp ran his practices with military precision. Rupp and his assistants wore starched khaki, and players were silent as they ran through their drills: spot shooting, free throws, defense, and scrimmages. Players who failed to meet Rupp's expectations were subjected to his withering sarcasm. Rupp was intense about everything. He once said it felt like he had lye in his stomach before every game, and that he could not relax even when Kentucky was ahead. "Every time they score," he said of the opposition, "my heart bleeds. I don't care what the score is."

Rupp was also highly superstitious, always wearing a double-breasted brown suit as he sat on the bench during games. From his seat he ranted and raved, berating officials, the opposition, and even his own players. Rupp imported Allen's fast-break style of offense to Kentucky, and his first team went 15–3. On 29 August 1931 Rupp married Esther Schmidt, whom he had met and dated in Freeport; they had one child. Even though Rupp's teams were winners from the beginning, and basketball soon surpassed football as the top sport in Kentucky, the "Baron of the Bluegrass" came into his own as a coach only after the end of World War II. Kentucky dominated the national college basketball scene from 1946 through 1958, winning the National Invitational Tournament (NIT) title in 1946, four NCAA tournament titles (1948, 1949, 1951, 1958), and 302 of 340 games.

Rupp's Fabulous Five team of 1947–1948 won his first NCAA championship. Along with Rupp, the Kentucky starters went as part of the U.S. basketball team to the Olympic Games in London, England, in 1948, where they won a gold medal. Minus one starter, the Fabulous Four repeated as NCAA champions the following year, and the Wildcats made it three titles in four years in 1951. By then Rupp's arrogance had alienated coaches and rival fans throughout the South, Midwest, and East, and it was to the delight of many that several Kentucky players were caught in a federal probe of college basketball point shaving that became public in 1951. Three members of the 1948 and 1949 championship teams—Alex Groza, Ralph Beard, and Dale Barnstable—admitted shaving points in Kentucky's 67–56 loss to Loyola in the 1949 NIT. Bill Spivey, who was still playing on the team in 1951, also was implicated and lost a year of eligibility. Although the Southeastern Conference (SEC) and NCAA barred Kentucky from competition for the 1952–1953 season, Rupp kept his job and then rebuilt his program.

Kentucky won a then-record fourth NCAA title in 1958 with the Fiddlin' Five, a group notorious for "fiddlin' around and fiddlin' around and finally pulling it out at the end," explained the coach. It was Rupp's last great triumph. His final fourteen seasons were marked by a declining (although still robust) winning percentage, as a prideful Rupp struggled to adapt to the increasingly intense competition to recruit good players, particularly the African-American athletes who were remaking the college game. The Rupp's Runts of 1965–1966 reached the NCAA title game. The team, which was all white and rated number one in the country, lost the championship to Texas Western University and its all-African-American starting lineup, leaving a dubious legacy for their coach. Although that game's racial aspect was little remarked upon at the time, it later was viewed as a watershed, leading within a few years to the integration of college sports in the South and a new era in basketball.

In 1969 Rupp signed his first and only African-American player, the center Tom Payne. On racial issues Rupp appeared to be a product of his generation, a man comfortable coaching in the segregated SEC and in no hurry to push integration. Unlike many of his SEC colleagues, however, Rupp was willing to schedule games against integrated teams. In the 1966–1967 season Rupp's team finished with the worst record of any Kentucky team during his tenure (13–13). Rupp was forced to retire after the 1971–1972 season, when he reached the mandatory state-employee retirement age of seventy. He finished out his career with 876 career wins, a record that stood until North Carolina's Dean Smith surpassed it with 879 wins in 1997. He was inducted into the Naismith Memorial Basketball Hall of Fame in 1969.

Rupp suffered from diabetes as well as heart and kidney ailments for years before he showed signs of spinal cancer in 1976. Even though he was ill, he was in attendance on 30 November 1976 when the Wildcats played their first game at Rupp Arena in downtown Lexington. He died at the University of Kentucky Medical Center and is buried at Lexington Cemetery.

Driven by pride, perfectionism, and an intense desire to succeed, Rupp made the University of Kentucky a basketball powerhouse, rebuilding the team even after a gambling scandal nearly destroyed his program. It took time and the sweeping social change of integration to topple Rupp, but not before he compiled one of college basketball's greatest coaching records.

★

The former Kentucky sports information director Russell Rice used tapes of interviews with Rupp and his own experiences with the coach as the starting point for the biography *Adolph Rupp: Kentucky's Basketball Baron* (1994). Rupp figures prominently in an account of the 1966 NCAA title game by Frank Fitzpatrick, *And the Walls Came Tumbling Down: Kentucky, Texas Western, and the Game That Changed American Sports* (1999). The *Lexington Herald-Leader* has extensive coverage of Rupp's death and legacy (11 Dec. 1977). An obituary is in the *New York Times* (12 Dec. 1977). The longtime Kentucky sportswriter Dave Kindred wrote a remembrance of Rupp for the *Washington Post* (13 Dec. 1977).

TIM WHITMIRE

RUPPERT, Jacob (*b.* 5 August 1867 in New York City; *d.* 13 January 1939 in New York City), brewer, sportsman, and owner of the New York Yankees who was instrumental in bringing Babe Ruth to New York and starting baseball's outstanding dynasty of the 1920s and 1930s.

Ruppert was born in the German Catholic neighborhood of Yorkville in New York City to Jacob Ruppert, Sr., a brewer, and Anna Gillig Ruppert, a homemaker and mother of six. In 1851 his paternal grandfather Franz brought the brewing skills from Bavaria to the United States that became the basis of the family fortune when Jacob, Sr., founded the Jacob Ruppert Brewery in 1867. Ruppert attended Columbia Grammar School, graduating in 1885. He passed the entrance examination for the Columbia College School of Mines later that year, but never attended. In 1886 he entered the family business at his father's request.

Ruppert's apprenticeship at the brewery started at the bottom, but by 1890 he was the general superintendent and then, six years later, the acting head of the firm. Under Ruppert's management, the brewery's beer production rose from 350,000 barrels in 1892 to 1.3 million barrels in 1919. He became the president after his father's death in 1915. A major figure in the brewing industry, Ruppert was elected president of the U.S. Brewers Association sixteen times and in 1937 was the first chairman of the United Brewers Industrial Foundation.

Ruppert's interests outside the family business were extensive. In 1886 he joined the Seventh Regiment of the New York National Guard, the "silk-stocking" brigade, and became an aide-de-camp with the rank of colonel on the staff of the New York governor David B. Hill from 1889 to 1892, and then the senior aide to Governor Roswell Flower until 1895. Using his political influence, Ruppert ran as a Democrat in the largely Republican district of Yorkville, and was elected to the New York State Assembly for four consecutive terms (1898–1906). He was a powerful figure in Tammany Hall politics for the rest of his life.

Imperial and dignified, Ruppert was a model of the well-heeled socialite in New York City during the early twentieth century. He was a member of numerous social clubs,

Jacob Ruppert and Babe Ruth, shortly after Ruth left the Yankees for the Boston Braves, 1935. ASSOCIATED PRESS AP

including the Jockey Club, New York Athletic Club, National Democratic Club, Highland Golf Club, and two yachting clubs. A noted art collector, Ruppert also raced Thoroughbreds and showed pedigreed dogs. His 135-acre home, Eagle's Nest in Garrison, New York, contained a private zoo with one of the largest collections of monkeys in the world. He invested heavily in real estate, owning several Manhattan skyscrapers and serving on the board of directors for numerous corporations. In 1933 Ruppert donated $250,000 to support Admiral Richard Byrd's expedition to the South Pole; the donation inspired Byrd to name his flagship *Jacob Ruppert*.

Ruppert's most famous enterprise, after his brewery, was his ownership of the New York Yankees. The American League president Ban Johnson needed a strong team to compete with the New York Giants and Brooklyn Dodgers, but the New York Highlanders (later the Yankees) struggled under the ownership of the gambler Frank Farrell and the former police captain William Bevery, both of whom had Tammany Hall connections. Johnson asked Ruppert and his fellow sportsman Colonel Tillinghast L'Hommedieu Huston to purchase the Highlanders for $460,000, which they did late in 1914. Ruppert and Huston invested in better players and key personnel. In 1918 Ruppert used his political connections with the state senator Jimmy Walker and the newly elected governor Al Smith to get Sunday baseball approved in New York City. He also was instrumental in opposing Johnson's efforts to close down baseball during World War I, making Johnson a lifelong enemy. While Huston served in Europe during the war, Ruppert hired the former St. Louis Cardinals infielder Miller Huggins to manage the team, a move that eventually alienated Huston.

In 1919 there was a power struggle in baseball over the control of the major leagues. Their governing body, the national commission, was controlled by Johnson, who was now openly warring with Ruppert. The brewer joined with the Boston Red Sox owner Harry Frazee and the National League owners to vote the commission out of existence, replacing it with a single baseball commissioner, Judge Kenesaw Landis, who in turn replaced Johnson as the chief arbitrator of baseball. Also in 1919 Babe Ruth began dominating baseball with home runs, and Ruppert decided he wanted Ruth in New York. When the Red Sox floundered and Frazee's Broadway production folded that same year, Ruppert and Huston offered the Boston owner $100,000 for Ruth. Despite Johnson's attempt to block the deal, Frazee took the offer along with a personal loan from Ruppert for $350,000 against the mortgage of Boston's Fenway Park. Ruppert took over the mortgage when Frazee sold the team in 1923 and sold the stadium back to the Red Sox in 1931 at a substantial profit. When Ruth joined the team for spring training in 1920, the Yankee dynasty began; they won eleven pennants and eight world championships in Ruppert's lifetime.

The Yankees drew more than one million fans in 1920

while playing on a one-year lease in the Polo Grounds, the home of the Giants. Johnson tried to convince the Giants owner Charles Stoneham to cancel the lease, putting the Yankees out in the street and allowing Johnson to regain control of the team. Ruppert, in turn, sought to buy a half-interest in the Polo Grounds, but when that initiative failed began plans, against Huston's wishes, to build a new ballpark. On 5 February 1921 Ruppert announced his $650,000 purchase of land on the Astor family estate across the Harlem River from the Polo Grounds. "Yankee Stadium was a mistake," Ruppert exclaimed, "Not mine, but the Giants'." The structure, completed in 284 days at a cost of $2.5 million, held 62,000 seats and was situated 15 minutes by subway from Forty-second Street. While Huston lent his engineering expertise to building the stadium, he bridled at Ruppert's tactics and finally agreed to a buyout of $1.25 million; on 1 June 1923 Ruppert became the sole owner of the Yankees.

Ruppert spent most of the 1920s maintaining the team and especially its central star, Babe Ruth. When Ruth married Claire Hodgson in 1929, Ruppert broke with tradition by asking her to travel with the team to keep an eye on her husband. A fashion plate himself, Ruppert insisted the Yankees look the part of champions. He used pinstripes on the uniforms as early as 1915, and insisted on two sets of home and away uniforms so the team would always take the field looking fresh. In 1929 Ruppert was the first to add numbers to the backs of the uniforms so fans could identify the ballplayers. In the early 1930s he began building the Yankees farm system with teams throughout the eastern seaboard, recruiting talent that ensured the team's success for twenty-five years after his death.

Ruppert became ill with phlebitis in April 1938 and died in his New York penthouse on 13 January 1939. Babe Ruth was one of his last visitors. A lifelong bachelor, Ruppert left an estate estimated at between $40 and $45 million to the Ruppert family and to Helen Winthrope Weyant, a friend and former actress. He is buried in the family mausoleum at Kensico Cemetery in Valhalla, New York.

Ruppert epitomized dignity and instilled his values of confidence and style upon one of the roughest teams of his era, turning the Yankees into baseball's most successful dynasty. A shrewd businessman, he understood what attracted the fans and encouraged his players to look sharp, play hard, and treat the fans with respect. Under Ruppert's leadership, the New York Yankees became the aristocrats of baseball—proud, often arrogant, and driven to excellence. His team management set the standard for achievement in America's favorite game.

★

Details about Ruppert's life appear in the *National Cyclopedia of American Biography* (1940), *Who Was Who in America* (1942), *Biographical Directory of the American Congress* (1950), and *Dictionary of American Biography* (1958). There is also a great deal of information about his baseball career in Frank Graham, *The New York Yankees* (1943); John Durant, *The Yankees* (1950); and Marshall Smelser, *The Life that Ruth Built: A Biography* (1975). An obituary is in the *New York Times* (14 Jan. 1939).

PATRICK A. TRIMBLE

RUSSELL, William Felton ("Bill") (*b.* 12 February 1934 in Monroe, Louisiana), basketball player whose two NCAA titles, Olympic gold medal, and eleven National Basketball Association (NBA) championships qualify him as one of the greatest winners in American team sports history.

Russell is one of two sons of Charles Russell, a factory worker, and Katie Russell, a homemaker. The three most important influences on young Russell—his father "Mister Charlie," his mother Katie, and his grandfather, whom he knew as "the Old Man"—embodied strength and independence. In different ways each preserved an essential dignity despite living among the racial codes of Jim Crow Louisiana. When Russell was nine, his father left his factory job and moved his family to Oakland, California, for the opportunities in industry spurred by American involvement in World War II. Three years later Katie died unexpectedly. Shy and gangly, Russell retreated into books. He was a better student than athlete, and his basketball career at McClymonds High was thoroughly unremarkable. He barely made the team as a sophomore, and as a senior he did not even merit an honorable mention for all-league honors in a league with only six teams.

Fortune kissed him, however, in January 1952. He graduated from high school in the middle of the traditional scholastic year and joined the California All-Stars, a barnstorming squad of recent graduates. During their one-month tour through the Pacific Northwest, Russell's game blossomed. His team challenged basketball orthodoxy, which dictated that players should not leave their feet on offense or defense. The All-Stars took jump shots and leaped to block shots. This style, seen mostly on urban playgrounds, suited Russell's height, speed, and jumping ability. He also began approaching basketball as a scholarly endeavor, studying his teammates' moves. He developed so rapidly that he won a scholarship to the University of San Francisco for the next fall.

When Russell enrolled in 1952 the University of San Francisco was a small Jesuit school without its own basketball gymnasium. Under the tutelage of his freshman coach Ross Guidice and his teammate K. C. Jones, Russell learned not only basketball fundamentals but also strategies for defensive positioning and offensive ball movement. Russell excelled defensively, blocking shots and grabbing rebounds, and he attracted national attention his sophomore

Bill Russell *(right)*. ARCHIVE PHOTOS, INC.

year. During his junior year he and Jones led "the homeless Dons" to the National Collegiate Athletic Association (NCAA) championship, losing only one game. In Russell's senior year, 1955–1956, they went undefeated and again won the national title. Over these two seasons the team's record was 57–1.

The Boston Celtics selected Russell with the first pick in the National Basketball Association (NBA) draft in 1956. Before he joined them, Russell played in the Olympic Games in Melbourne, Australia. He led the United States to an undefeated record and the gold medal. Upon his return, he married Rose Swisier, with whom he would have three children. Russell then joined the Celtics two months into the season. Led by the master coach Red Auerbach, the Celtics featured such steady players as Frank Ramsey, Bill Sharman, Tom Heinsohn, and the extraordinary point guard Bob Cousy. Russell was the missing piece. His defense and rebounding proved crucial, especially in the playoffs. They beat the St. Louis Hawks in a deciding game seven in double overtime. In thirteen months Russell had won an NCAA championship, an Olympic gold medal, and an NBA title.

Winning defined the Celtics during Russell's tenure. In 1958 they reached the NBA finals again only to lose in six games to St. Louis after Russell sprained his ankle in game three and could not return. The next year the Celtics began a streak of eight consecutive NBA championships. Auerbach built a dynasty of self-motivated players who understood their roles. During Russell's thirteen-year career the Celtics made only one trade, and most of the key components, including Russell, Ramsey, Heinsohn, Sam Jones, K. C. Jones, and John Havlicek, played their entire careers for the franchise. The Celtics were also noteworthy for their interracial cooperation. The team rarely discussed race, but they exemplified the integrationist spirit of the early civil rights movement through their mutual professional and personal respect.

By the early 1960s Russell had presided over the African-American revolution in professional basketball, a change based on speed, athleticism, and spectacular performance. Although he had a fine array of offensive moves, Russell's hallmark was defense. Auerbach said in 1963, "Russell has had the biggest impact on the game of anyone in the last 10 years because he has instituted a new defensive weapon—that of the blocked shot. . . . He is by far the greatest center ever to play the game." The six-foot, ten-inch center had astounding leaping ability, a studied penchant for positioning, and the faculty to block shots toward his teammates, who would then key the Celtics' trademark fast break. He was also a master of psychology, using intimidation to plant doubt in opposing shooters. Especially after Cousy's 1963 retirement, the Celtics oriented themselves around a Russell-led defense.

Russell maintained his intellectual passion throughout

his career, and reporters frequently called upon him to make sense of the civil rights era. Many in the media liked to pigeonhole blacks with ideological labels, but Russell resisted simplistic characterizations. As he espoused the results of Martin Luther King, Jr.'s nonviolent protest, he challenged whites to understand the motivations of the Nation of Islam. He also traveled to Africa on a U.S. State Department trip and bought a rubber plantation in Liberia. It is a measure of Russell's status that, during the height of the delicate liberal consensus in the early 1960s, a *Sports Illustrated* reporter wrote that Russell "does not want the white man's sympathy or, indeed, his friendship. What he wants is recognition and acceptance as an individual, a black individual."

Because he refused to act conventionally or to speak in clichés, Russell also became a magnet for controversy. "I owe the public nothing," he told the *Saturday Evening Post.* He thought the practice of signing autographs was asinine, and in time he refused to sign them. He avoided false modesty or smiles. He spoke openly on taboo subjects, publicly complaining when he thought he deserved an award or believed the NBA had an unofficial quota for white players. His race magnified the animosity toward him. At a time when most black athletes mouthed colorblind platitudes, Russell conducted a basketball clinic in Mississippi shortly after the 1964 murder of Medgar Evers, defended Muhammad Ali's 1967 decision to avoid service in the Vietnam War, named his daughter after the Kenyan leader Jomo Kenyatta, wore a menacing goatee mustache, and dressed in lace-front shirts and long black capes.

In 1966 Russell broke an important barrier, becoming the first African American to coach a major professional sport. As a player-coach he replaced Auerbach, who moved on to the front office. Some feared that Russell's first season as coach signaled the demise of the Celtics dynasty. During that first season the Celtics lost the Eastern Conference finals in five games to the Philadelphia 76ers and Russell's great rival Wilt Chamberlain. Over the years reporters had made much of the contrast between Chamberlain's statistical superiority and Russell's championships. On this occasion, however, Chamberlain bested Russell and ultimately captured the NBA crown.

But Russell's dynasty continued. In the 1968 conference finals, the Celtics overcame a 3–1 deficit and downed Chamberlain's 76ers. The Celtics then won another title. In 1968–1969, after a fourth-place regular season finish, the Celtics pulled together for one final rally. They marched through the playoffs and in the finals met the heavily favored Los Angeles Lakers starring Jerry West, Elgin Baylor, and their new weapon, Chamberlain. This was a different Russell-Chamberlain rivalry. The Celtics leader was tired, aging, and privately certain he would retire, while Chamberlain no longer shouldered the entire scoring burden as in his Philadelphia days. They played to a game seven in Los Angeles. Solidifying their legacies, Chamberlain took himself out of the game with less than six minutes left due to an injury, and his coach refused to put him back in. Russell led the Celtics to another championship.

Russell retired with five Most Valuable Player (MVP) awards and eleven titles in thirteen seasons. He moved to Los Angeles for a short-lived career as a movie actor and talk show host before returning to basketball as a television announcer. In 1973 he became coach and general manager of the Seattle Supersonics and oversaw a revamping of a franchise that won the NBA championship two years after his departure. His second return to coaching, with the Sacramento Kings during the 1987–1988 season, was largely a failure. He had separated from Rose in 1969, and after a brief marriage to a former Miss USA, he married longtime friend Marilyn Nault in 1995. Without apologizing for his iconoclasm, he became more comfortable in his role as a basketball legend.

Russell's legacy is twofold. First, he deserves to be known as American team sports' consummate winner. His record lies not in individual statistics or awards but in championship rings. An appropriate measure of his achievement is that fourteen times Russell's season came down to one winner-take-all game, and fourteen times Russell's team prevailed. Second, Russell's leadership offers added significance because he was black. His was an unapologetic intellectual voice that challenged racial assumptions during a time of rapid social change. "Let them inscribe on my tombstone that I was not just an athlete, or a rich man, or a Negro," he wrote in 1966. "Let it be said simply: Russell. A man."

★

Russell wrote two autobiographies. *Go Up for Glory* (1966) with William McSweeney is a fine and unconventional memoir, and *Second Wind* (1979) with Taylor Branch is among the best works in its genre. Russell published a treatise on leadership with David Falkner, *Russell Rules* (2001). He also co-wrote articles, including with Bob Ottum, "The Psyche . . . and My Other Tricks," *Sports Illustrated* (25 Oct. 1965); and with Tex Maule, "I Am Not Worried About Ali," *Sports Illustrated* (19 June 1967). The best profiles of Russell are Gilbert Rogin, "We Are Grown Men Playing a Child's Game," *Sports Illustrated* (18 Nov. 1963); Edward Linn, "I Owe the Public Nothing," *Saturday Evening Post* (18 Jan. 1964); and Frank Deford, "The Ring Leader," *Sports Illustrated* (10 May 1999).

ARAM GOUDSOUZIAN

RUTH, George Herman ("Babe") (*b.* 6 February 1895 in Baltimore, Maryland; *d.* 16 August 1948 in New York City), baseball player who, with his home runs, free-swinging style of play, and media exposure, revolutionized the American national game.

Few athletes, past or present, have captured the public imagination like Babe Ruth. The child of a struggling working-class family in Baltimore, Ruth grew up over the saloon run by his father, George, Sr., where his mother, Kate Schamberger, also worked, despite a history of chronic illness. The Ruths had eight children but only George and a younger sister survived to adulthood. The parents, distracted by long working hours, left George to roam the streets, where he had several run-ins with the law. He was often truant. In spring 1902 the family committed him to the St. Mary's Industrial School for Boys, and Ruth spent the next twelve years learning shirt-making and playing baseball under the tutelage of a Xaverian brother named Matthias. Ruth later called him "the greatest man I've ever known." When his mother died of tuberculosis in 1912, Ruth became a permanent ward of the school.

In February 1914 Ruth's prowess at baseball brought him to the attention of Jack Dunn, owner of the minor league Baltimore Orioles. Dunn signed him for $600 and took him to spring training in Fayetteville, North Carolina, where Ruth acquired his nickname when a coach warned veterans to go easy on the rookie, "one of Jack Dunn's babes." So impressive were Ruth's pitching skills that Dunn sold him in July of that year to the Boston Red Sox. After his first win and several rocky starts, Ruth was sent down to Providence for seasoning, but he returned to Boston at the end of the season. There he courted a waitress, Helen Woodford, and they married on 17 October 1914. After the ceremony, Ruth and his bride returned to Baltimore to tend bar in his father's saloon.

Between 1915 and 1919 Ruth excelled as a premier left-handed pitcher, winning eighty-five games with an earned-run average of 2.02 when the entire league averaged over 2.66. He won three World Series games in 1916 and 1918 with an earned-run average of 0.87, including a record-setting streak of 29⅔ shutout innings. He also hit 49 home runs during that period; when Ruth was not pitching, the Boston Red Sox manager Ed Barrow had him play in the outfield and at first base.

Although the team did poorly in 1919, large crowds came to see the new slugger. Before Ruth, home runs were rare, and teams played for one run at a time, bunting and stealing bases, placing the ball rather than swinging away. Ruth swung from the heels, powering the ball out of ballparks faster and farther than anyone ever before. Crowds loved it and rooted for the long ball. Even when Ruth struck out, fans cheered his energy and enthusiasm. At an exhibition game in Baltimore before the 1919 season, he slammed four home runs in one game, and that year he topped the single season record of twenty-seven, set in 1884, by hitting twenty-nine.

Despite crowd-pleasing play, Ruth quarreled with the team's owner Harry Frazee. Ruth made $10,000 a year but saw the crowds going wild for him and wanted more. Frazee, a Broadway producer always short of money and wanting to keep salaries down, sold Ruth to the New York Yankees on 6 January 1920 for $100,000 plus a personal loan from the Yankees owner Jacob Ruppert. Ruth was reluctant to go, but the Yankees offered him $20,000 a year for the next two years, and Ruth signed.

Ruth became the darling of the New York City media when editors realized that he could sell papers and magazines as well as tickets. Writers dubbed him the "Sultan of Swat," the "Colossus of Clout," and the "Wizard of Wham"; sports pages were expanded to cover his feats. The news, in turn, swelled attendance, with the Yankees attracting record-breaking crowds in 1920. Fans watched Ruth club 54 home runs, hit a remarkable .376, and lead the league in runs batted in, walks, and runs scored.

Ruth found New York City to his taste off the field as well. In the spring of 1921 the Ruths bought a farm they named "Home Plate" in Sudbury, Massachusetts, where Helen lived during the season. This arrangement allowed Ruth to enjoy the New York City nightlife. Although his behavior led to conflicts with Yankee management, Ruth continued to produce on the field, hitting 59 home runs and driving in 170 runs, taking the Yankees to their first World Series. That same year, Ruth met Christy Walsh, an ex-sports cartoonist turned agent who began promoting Ruth's image everywhere, in advertising, magazines, movies, and barnstorming tours. Newspaper columns and articles, how-to baseball guides, even children's books were published under his name, ghost-written by the Christy Walsh Syndicate. That year Ruth made an extra $15,000 on newspaper income alone, and in 1922 his salary jumped to $52,000, making him the highest paid baseball player in the league.

But the 1922 season started poorly for Ruth; he ignored a ruling by the new commissioner of baseball, Judge Kenesaw Mountain Landis, that prohibited members of a World Series team from barnstorming after the season. Knowing a fine was useless, Landis suspended Ruth for the first thirty-nine days of the 1922 season. The nightlife also caught up with Ruth—his production that season fell to only 35 home runs and 96 runs batted in (RBI). On 13 November Walsh held a banquet for the New York City sportswriters and others who roasted Ruth for his disappointing season. The keynote speaker, state senator Jimmy Walker, condemned Ruth for letting down the "boys of America" in a speech that reduced Ruth to tears. In response Ruth vowed to spend the winter getting into shape. In fact, he had another reason for settling down; that summer, Helen and Ruth appeared in public with a new daughter, Dorothy. She was in fact the result of one of Ruth's many affairs, but to avoid scandal, Helen agreed to raise the child as her own.

Babe Ruth. THE LIBRARY OF CONGRESS

Yankee Stadium, dubbed "The House That Ruth Built," opened in 1923, and in the inaugural game Ruth christened it with a home run. He returned to form with 41 home runs, a .393 batting average, 170 walks (still a major league record in 2001), and an on-base percentage of .544, making him the unanimous choice for baseball's Most Valuable Player. His three home runs in the series over the Giants gave the Yankees their first World Championship. The Yankees failed to repeat as champions in 1924, but no one blamed Ruth, who had a sensational year.

The team's 1925 season was ruined early when Ruth collapsed before an exhibition game in Asheville, North Carolina. Newspapers as far away as London erroneously reported his death, but when it was revealed Ruth suffered from an intestinal disorder, the press called it "the bellyache heard round the world" and blamed Ruth's overeating. While some speculated that the illness was syphilis, medical records cited influenza combined with an intestinal abscess that required surgery. Ruth missed the first two months of the season and played below par for the rest of the year. He also struggled in his private life; he had met and fallen in love with an actress named Claire Hodgson two years earlier and was spending most of his free time with her. Helen wanted a divorce, but Ruth, a Catholic, would not agree, so the couple legally separated in June 1925.

The events of 1925 changed Babe Ruth, and for the first time he began to take spring training and his conditioning seriously. From 1926 to 1932 his success was unequaled in baseball; he averaged 49 home runs, 152 runs batted in, and a batting average of .353, leading the Yankees to a pennant and three World Series championships.

In 1927 Ruth's contract jumped to $70,000, and he celebrated by hitting sixty home runs, thus breaking his own record. In 1930 his $80,000 salary was double that of the next highest-paid player. An apocryphal story has a reporter asking Ruth if he thought it was right for the slugger to be paid more than President Herbert Hoover, to which Ruth replied, "Why not? I had a better year." Ruth's private life changed as well. Helen's death in a fire in January 1929 freed Ruth and Hodgson to marry on 17 April. The couple formally adopted Dorothy, and Ruth adopted Hodgson's daughter Julia.

The 1932 World Series produced Ruth's most famous home run, "the called shot." In the third game against Chicago, after heckling from the Cubs bench, Ruth supposedly held up two fingers (one for each strike against him) and pointed to the center field bleachers where he hit the next pitch for a home run. Only one paper, the *New York World-Telegram,* reported the called shot, and Ruth himself denied it after the game, but later, as word spread, Ruth, always the showman, changed his story. Despite denials from Cubs players and a film discovered in 1997 showing Ruth gesturing towards the Cubs bench and then pointing two fingers at the pitcher, the debate continues.

Whether or not he called it, this was Ruth's last home run in series play. As early as 1929, with the sudden death of the Yankees manager Miller Huggins, Ruth asked Ruppert for a chance to manage the Yankees, but Ruppert refused, noting that a man who could not control himself could not control a ball team. A disgruntled Ruth saw his numbers and salary drop in 1933, and again in 1934, his worst year in the majors. Ruth wanted to stay in baseball, but when Ruppert suggested he take the minor league manager's post in Newark, he refused. After the season Ruth toured Japan and vacationed in Europe but returned to a new contract for $1 a year. Ruppert wanted him to retire. When the Boston Braves offered Ruth the position of player/assistant manager for 1935, Ruth took the offer, believing that he would eventually become the manager, but as the season wore on he discovered they only wanted him as a gate attraction. After a spectacular day in Pittsburgh when he hit the last three home runs of his career (bringing the total to 714), he retired.

The last thirteen years of Ruth's life were financially comfortable—he had numerous corporate deals and even his own radio show—but Ruth missed being in baseball. At the new Baseball Hall of Fame in Cooperstown, New York, the sportswriters paid their respect by electing Ruth as one of the premier five members in 1936, but except for a brief stint as a coach with the Brooklyn Dodgers in 1938, his days on the field were over. Fans still gathered wherever he went, but there was little to do but play golf, visit ballparks, and sign autographs. He played in his last game, an old-timers' exhibition at Yankee Stadium, on 28 July 1943.

While undergoing minor surgery in January 1947, doctors confirmed that Ruth had throat cancer, although he was not told of the diagnosis. He acted as a spokesman for the Ford Motor Company, continued working on his autobiography, and was excited by a Hollywood project to film his life story. Baseball commissioner Happy Chandler proclaimed 27 April 1947 Babe Ruth Day with a Yankee Stadium celebration broadcast to every major league ballpark. On 13 June the Yankees celebrated the twenty-fifth anniversary of Yankee Stadium, where a visibly ailing Ruth made his final appearance. He died 16 August 1948 in Memorial Hospital in New York. His body was viewed at Yankee Stadium by from 75,000 to 200,000 people, while another 75,000 attended funeral services inside and outside at St. Patrick's Cathedral on a rainy 19 August. Still more lined the streets for the funeral cortege to Gate of Heaven Cemetery in Valhalla, New York, where a public ceremony was conducted. Ruth was buried in a private service on 24 October, more than two months later.

Ruth's importance to baseball and the nation cannot be overemphasized. His batting style marked the end of the scientific era of inside baseball and introduced new power and energy into the game, which translated into larger crowds and better salaries for the men who played in his shadow. Ruth and the long ball enhanced the commercialism of the game, which in turn fed the media boom of the 1920s. Many historians argue that Ruth saved the game of baseball after the Black Sox Scandal of 1919, when eight members of the Chicago White Sox team, including stars Shoeless Joe Jackson and pitcher Eddie Ciccotte, were discovered to have taken bribes to throw the World Series against the Chicago Redlegs. Awards and memorials were numerous during and after his lifetime. In 1969, the centennial year of professional baseball, the Baseball Writers of America voted Ruth the best player in the history of the game, and in 2000 ESPN named him the second most valuable athlete in the United States during the twentieth century.

Ruth's influence reached beyond the playing field. He exemplified the emergence of the sports hero as national celebrity, in part because he understood and used the power of the media. His name has entered the language as a synonym for achievement, and he is better remembered today than many of his contemporaries, including presidents, scientists, military heroes, or fellow sports figures. Writers are still apt to invoke Ruth in connection with athletes who reach the top of their fields: when Michael Jordan first retired in 1999, he was hailed as the Babe Ruth of basketball. And the advertising and product markets continue to benefit from the strategies initiated by Ruth and Christy Walsh, with Ruth's continuing appearance as a public figure who stirs the imagination and captures public affection.

★

Ruth's autobiography, *The Babe Ruth Story* (1948), written with Bob Considine; and earlier biographies such as Tom Meany, *Babe Ruth: The Big Moments of the Big Fellow* (1947); and Dan Daniel, *The Real Babe Ruth* (1948); tend to be quite anecdotal and clouded in the mythical quality of their subject. There have been over a hundred books written about Ruth, but the two most influential and thoroughly researched are Robert W. Creamer, *Babe: The Legend Comes to Life* (1974), and a psychological study, Marshall Smelser, *The Life That Ruth Built* (1975). Kal Wagenheim, *Babe Ruth: His Life and Legend* (1974) is also informative. There are also biographies by Claire Ruth, with Bill Slocum, *The Babe and I* (1959); by Dorothy Ruth Pirone, with Chris Martens, *My Dad, the Babe* (1988); and two by Julia Ruth Stevens: *Babe Ruth: A Daughter's Portrait,* with George Beim (1998), and *Major League Dad: A Daughter's Cherished Memories* (2001). Two books about Babe Ruth's place in American society are worth mentioning: Robert Smith, *Babe Ruth's America* (1974), and Ken Sobol, *Babe Ruth and the American Dream* (1974). An excellent source on Ruth's media influence is Lawrence Ritter and Mark Rucker, *The Babe: A Life in Pictures* (1988). An obituary is in the *New York Times* (18 Aug. 1948).

PATRICK A. TRIMBLE

RYAN, (Lynn) Nolan, Jr. (*b.* 31 January 1947 in Refugio, Texas), baseball player who holds the all-time major league record for strikeouts, pitched a record seven no-hit games, and was elected to the National Baseball Hall of Fame.

Ryan was the youngest of six children born to Lynn Nolan Ryan, Sr., and Martha Lee Hancock Ryan. An oil field supervisor, Ryan's father moved his family to Alvin, Texas, where his youngest son became an outstanding pitcher for Alvin High School. During his senior year, he drew the attention of major league scouts when he won twenty games. Ryan enrolled at Alvin Junior College in 1966, hoping to play baseball with the Houston Astros franchise, located only twenty miles from Alvin. The Astros failed to show much interest in Ryan, reportedly because the young pitcher was too slight and had sensitive skin, particularly on the fingertips of his pitching hand, which had been cut severely in a childhood accident. (Ryan would suffer from blisters on his pitching hand throughout his career.)

Passed over by Houston, Ryan was selected by the New York Mets in the eighth round of the 1965 free-agent draft. From 1965 to 1967 he pitched in the Mets farm system for Marion, Virginia (Appalachian League); Greenville, South Carolina (Western Carolinas League); Williamsport, Pennsylvania (Eastern League); Winter Haven, Florida (Florida State League); and Jacksonville, Florida (International League). Ryan missed a good portion of the 1967 season when he served for six months on active duty with the U.S. Army Reserve. On 26 June 1967 Ryan married his childhood sweetheart, Ruth Holdruff; they have three children.

In 1968 Ryan spent his first full season in the major leagues with the Mets, winning six games and losing nine while drawing attention with 133 strikeouts in 134 innings. Ryan saw little action during the 1969 season owing to a pulled groin muscle and another assignment on reserve duty with the army; however, he played a key role in the postseason success of the "Miracle Mets." His seven-inning relief stint in the third game of the National League East division playoffs with the Atlanta Braves propelled the Mets into the World Series. His relief appearance in the third game of the World Series preserved their victory. The Mets defeated the Baltimore Orioles four games to one, earning Ryan his only World Series ring. While Ryan established a reputation for a blazing fastball and dazzling curve, he experienced difficulty with his control. Following the 1971 season, in which he struck out 137 batters but walked 116, Ryan was traded to the California Angels for the shortstop Jim Fregosi. With the Angels, the power pitcher became one of the dominant hurlers in the American League. Ryan pitched four no-hit games in an Angels uniform (against the Kansas City Royals and Detroit Tigers in 1973, Minnesota Twins in 1974, and Baltimore Orioles in 1975). During his tenure with the Angels from 1972 to 1979, Ryan led the American League in strikeouts nine times and in walks six times. In 1973 he struck out a major league record 383 batters.

Nolan Ryan. Archive Photos, Inc.

In 1980 Ryan returned to his Texas roots, signing as a free agent with the Houston Astros. He pitched with Houston from 1980 through 1988. As an Astro, Ryan pitched a no-hit game against the Los Angeles Dodgers in 1981, led the National League in strikeouts in 1987 and 1988, and was the earned-run champion in 1981 and 1987. His victory total for nine years in Houston was only 106 wins against 94 losses. Before the 1989 season Ryan signed a new free-agent agreement with the Texas Rangers, with whom he pitched his final two no-hitters (against the Oakland A's in 1990 and the Toronto Blue Jays in 1991). Continuing to pitch effectively into his forties, Ryan established numerous career landmarks with the Rangers. On 22 August 1989 he was the first pitcher in major league history to strike out 5,000 batters in a career, fanning Rickey Henderson of the Oakland A's. On 31 July 1990 Ryan defeated the Milwaukee Brewers, becoming the twentieth pitcher in Major League Baseball history to win 300 games. Although he led the American League in strikeouts for the 1989 and 1990 seasons, by 1992 Ryan was able to register only five wins against nine losses. He retired after the season.

In his twenty-six major league seasons, Ryan won 324 games and lost 292 while striking out a record total of 5,714 batters. His career earned-run average was an outstanding 3.19. The pitcher was selected for the All-Star game eight times. Ryan earned his nickname the "Ryan Express" with a fastball clocked at more than 100 miles per hour. Ryan's pitching exploits were recognized by his 1999 election to the National Baseball Hall of Fame and Major League Baseball's All-Century team. Ryan's detractors, however, often point to his modest .526 win-loss percentage, 2,795 career walks allowed, and lack of world championships. Nonetheless, it is difficult to ignore Ryan's dominating fastball and curve, strikeouts, and seven no-hit games. A fan favorite, Ryan received numerous endorsement opportunities during and following his baseball career. A successful businessman, he owns four ranches and two banks. Ryan and his wife continue to live in Alvin, Texas. Beginning in 1999 he worked as assistant to the president of the Texas Rangers.

★

Background information on Ryan is available in his player file at the National Baseball Hall of Fame in Cooperstown, New York. Autobiographical accounts focusing on Ryan's baseball career include *Nolan Ryan: Fireball* (1975), written with Bill Libby; *Throwing Heat: The Autobiography of Nolan Ryan* (1988), written with Harvey Frommer; *Miracle Man: Nolan Ryan, the Autobiography* (1992), written with Jerry B. Jenkins; and *Nolan Ryan: Strikeout King* (1993), written with Howard Reiser. For an academic perspective on Ryan, see Nick Trujillo, *The Meaning of Nolan Ryan* (1994). See also William Leggett, "An Angel Who Makes Turnstiles Sing," *Sports Illustrated* (14 May 1973); Ron Fimrite, "Speed Trap for an Angel," *Sports Illustrated* (16 Sept. 1974), and "A Great Hand with the Old Cowhide," *Sports Illustrated* (29 Sept. 1986); and Richard Hoffer, "Armed and Still Dangerous," *Gentleman's Quarterly* (May 1988).

RON BRILEY

Jim Ryun, 1968. ASSOCIATED PRESS AP

RYUN, James Ronald ("Jim") (*b.* 29 April 1947 in Wichita, Kansas), the first high school runner to break four minutes in the mile, who became one of the greatest of All-American milers and a Republican representative from Kansas.

Ryun was the middle of three children of Gerald Ryun, a parts inspector for Boeing Aircraft Company, and Wilma Ryun, a department store clerk. He had an all-American childhood, but it would have been difficult to imagine him as an All-America athlete. As a child, Ryun was sickly and thin and suffered from partial deafness, nearsightedness, and allergies. Ryun tried out for sports like baseball, football, and basketball but was too frail and awkward. Then, in his freshman year at Wichita's East High School, he tried out for the track team but failed to make the cut after running a 5:38 mile. He persevered, however, and made the B squad on the cross-country team the following fall. In short order, he won a race and was elevated to the A squad. When Ryun improved his mile time to 4:26.4 during the track season, Coach Bob Timmons knew he had found a future star. "I took Jim aside and told him that eventually he would be a four-minute miler." At that time no high school runner had ever broken the four-minute barrier.

By the summer of 1963 Ryun, still just sixteen years old, had run a 4:08.2 mile and a 1:54.5 half-mile. Timmons encouraged his young runner to shoot for the 1964 Olympics, and Ryun accepted the challenge. He was a workout warrior, with an astonishing capacity to endure pain. Ryun sometimes ran 40 repetitions of 440 yards at three-fourths speed in a single workout. He supplemented these grueling sessions with calisthenics, weight lifting, and swimming. In the spring of 1964 Ryun began to race with collegians. The heightened competition pushed him to 4:01.7, 2 seconds faster than any high school athlete had ever run the mile. In June, only six weeks after his seventeenth birthday, Ryun ran against seven top collegiate milers. He finished last of eight, but his performance was the story of the meet. He had run the mile in 3:59. Dyrol Burleson, who won the race, commented: "There is simply no way to imagine how good Jim Ryun is or how far he will go. . . . What he did was more significant than Roger Bannister's first mile under four minutes."

Ryun continued to improve throughout the summer, peaking for the Olympic trials. On 13 September 1964 in Los Angeles, Ryun took third place in the 1500 meters, making the Olympic team before he had entered his senior year in high school. Unfortunately, when he arrived in Tokyo to compete, Ryun was hampered by a cold and finished 150 yards behind the winner of his semifinal. He failed to qualify for the final. After the bittersweet experience of his first Olympics, Ryun returned to Kansas. He had achieved international fame, but he seemed to remain the same nice, clean-cut boy his neighbors admired. He even kept his morning paper route.

Nevertheless, this down-home boy from Kansas struck fear into the hearts of his competitors. In 1965 at the Amateur Athletic Union (AAU) meet in San Diego—the American national championships of track and field—Ryun bested the field to win the mile in 3:55.3, a new U.S. record. This was also the best high school time ever, a record that stood for thirty-six years. Ryun shunned colleges from all over the country to attend the University of Kansas, where Bob Timmons was head track coach. In 1966 and 1967 Ryun was nearly untouchable in the middle-distance races, setting a flurry of U.S. and world records in the half-mile, mile, and two-mile races as well as their metric equivalents. Fans expected a record performance from Ryun every time he ran, and he was booed in 1966 at the AAU championships for winning the mile in 3:58.6.

During this time Ryun traveled internationally as a member of the U.S. track-and-field team. Of a trip to Kiev, in the Soviet Union, Ryun later remarked: "The stark differences between communism and democracy had a profound impact on my life." The stirrings of political ambition had begun, but Ryun's focus was still on the track, and he was looking ahead to 1968. He wanted a second chance to prove himself on the biggest stage of all, the Olympic Games. In the late spring of 1968, Ryun was stricken with a bad case of infectious mononucleosis. His training had to be curtailed sharply, and he was unable to compete until mid-August. At the Olympic trials in September, Ryun qualified for the 1500 meters but not the 800 meters. On 20 October in Mexico City, Ryun finished second in the 1500 meters, which was won by Kipchoge ("Kip") Keino of Kenya. Many track-and-field observers considered it a major disappointment for Ryun. Although an Olympic silver medal was a remarkable result for half a season's training, the aura of invincibility surrounding Ryun had evaporated. Even Ryun seemed to realize it. After the race, he said, "It's the first time that I've been beaten at 1500 meters or a mile since I was eighteen."

At about this time, Ryun shifted his attention to his private life. He became engaged to Anne Snider, a cheerleader at Kansas State University. They married in January 1969; the couple had four children. Ryun continued to race competitively in 1969 but retired after a disappointing season. He came back in 1972, qualifying again for the Olympics in the 1500 meters. In Munich he fell in a qualifying heat, missing the finals as he had in 1964. Ryun was the greatest U.S. miler ever, but his track career ended without an Olympic gold medal. Over the next twenty years, Ryun operated Jim Ryun Sports, a company that ran sports camps. He also worked as a motivational speaker and endorsed hearing aids. Ryun led largely a private life until May 1996, when the Kansas Republican senator Bob Dole stepped down from his seat to jump-start his campaign for the presidency. When Sam Brownback, the Republican representative from the Second Congressional District, ran for Dole's Senate seat, leaving his own seat vacant, Ryun decided to run for the House. Ryun won 62 percent of the vote in the Republican primary; in the general election he won 52 percent to 45 percent. Ryun has since been reelected twice with solid margins.

Ryun was thrust back into the public eye in 2001, not because of his work in Congress but when Alan Webb of Reston, Virginia, challenged and ultimately broke Ryun's high school record in the mile. Writing in *Time* in September 2001, Ryun congratulated Webb and shared his views on running: "Success in competitive running comes from pushing yourself hardest when your body is most exhausted and when the rewards are most distant. It comes from all those weekend and early-morning runs alone, without teammates to spur you on."

★

Ryun's autobiography, written with Mike Phillips, *In Quest of Gold: The Jim Ryun Story* (1984), follows his track career to its conclusion and discusses his conservative religious views. Ryun also is the subject of an insightful biography by Cordner Nelson, the cofounder and editor of *Track & Field News,* entitled *The Jim Ryun Story* (1967), which was published at the peak of Ryun's fame.

TIMOTHY KRINGEN

S

SAMPRAS, Peter ("Pete") (*b.* 12 August 1971 in Washington, D.C.), tennis player who, at age nineteen, was the youngest player to win the U.S. Open men's singles championship. After capturing his seventh Wimbledon singles title in 2000, Sampras became the first man to win thirteen Grand Slam championship titles.

Sampras was one of four children of Soterios ("Sam") Sampras, an aerospace engineer, and Georgia Vroustouris Sampras, a homemaker. When Sampras was seven years old, his family moved to Rancho Palos Verdes, California. Sampras's tennis career began in the warm southern California climate under the guidance of his father and his first coach, Pete Fisher, a pediatrician who was not a very good tennis player himself but knew how the game should be played. Under Fisher, Sampras not only developed his tennis skills but also began to envision his career as a professional player. From 1980 to 1984, Sampras rose rapidly in the junior rankings, becoming one of world's top players in his age group.

Despite the success of his protégé, Fisher believed that Sampras needed to change his two-handed backhand to a one-handed grip to compete at the next level. It was a long and painful process for the young Sampras. The unfamiliar new grip caused him great frustration and self-doubt. Sampras's ranking plummeted, but he stuck with his coach's advice, and eventually everything started to come together. As Sampras later stated, switching to the one-handed grip turned out to be the best thing that had ever happened to his game.

With the refinement of his skills and the growth of his body, Sampras's game improved dramatically. In 1987 he was selected to the U.S. Junior Davis Cup team. He also beat top-seeded Michael Chang at the U.S. Open Junior Championships. In 1988 Sampras left Palos Verdes High School and turned professional. He joined the Association of Tennis Professionals (ATP) Tour, and won half of his matches during the tour; at the end of the season he was ranked in the top 100. The transitional year in Sampras's career was 1989. With Jim Courier, he won his first international tournament doubles title at the Italian Open. At the U.S. Open, he deposed former champion Mats Wilander in the second round in five sets, and reached the fourth round himself before he was eliminated. He also made a major career decision at the end of the season—to break away from Fisher, who could no longer coach him at the game's highest level.

The first major milestone of Sampras's career came in 1990. Despite a disappointing first-round loss at Wimbledon, Sampras played brilliantly throughout the summer and entered the U.S. Open with confidence and maturity. Ranked as the twelfth seed at the championship, Sampras defeated all his opponents in the first four rounds to earn a showdown with Ivan Lendl, the top-ranked player in the world and three-time former U.S. Open champion. Sampras demonstrated not only his flawless serve-and-volley

Pete Sampras, 1988. AP/Wide World Photos

skills but also his maturity and composure under pressure. Serving twenty-six aces, Sampras toppled Lendl in five sets and eliminated the former champion, marking the first time that Lendl failed to reach the finals since 1981. Sampras seemed unstoppable. In the semifinals Sampras faced the legendary John McEnroe, a four-time former U.S. Open champion. McEnroe, unseeded for the first time since his U.S. Open debut thirteen years earlier, had captivated the Flushing Meadow, New York, crowds with the resurgence of his performance, but Sampras stemmed the comeback. With seventeen aces and youthful power, Sampras finished off McEnroe in four sets. The finals match was much easier. Against Andre Agassi, an old rival from his junior years, Sampras demolished his opponent in straight sets (6–4, 6–3, 6–2) in less than two hours. The competition, or lack of it, was best described by Agassi, who said: "It was a good old-fashioned street mugging." At nineteen years and twenty-eight days, Sampras became the youngest male champion in U.S. Open history.

A few months later, Sampras made a bigger financial splash by winning the inaugural Grand Slam Cup in Munich, Germany, collecting a $2 million first-place prize. By the end of the 1990 season, Sampras had established himself among the tennis elites, sharing the top ranking with Stefan Edberg of Sweden and Lendl of Czechoslovakia. He soon learned, however, that defending a title can be much harder than winning it.

For nearly three years after the 1990 season, Sampras failed to capture any major singles championship. His 1991 campaign to retain his U.S. Open title came up short when he was eliminated by Courier in three straight sets in the quarterfinals. In his 1992 attempt to regain the title, he lost the finals in four sets to Edberg. Despite the disappointing loss at the U.S. Open, Sampras did compile the best match record of his career, 70–18, while earning the number four spot in the year-end world rankings.

In 1993, with the ascendance of Sampras, a new era in tennis began. On 4 July Sampras defeated Courier in a thrilling "all-American" Wimbledon final. The victory at the All England Lawn Tennis Club was the beginning of Sampras's dominance. Two months later, Sampras recaptured his U.S. Open title by defeating the Frenchman Cedric Pioline in straight sets. By the end of 1993, Sampras had secured himself as the number one player and a new icon in the world of tennis. His thundering serves and crisp volleys, racing forehands, grit, determination, and fluid ground strokes signaled the Sampras era had arrived.

Sampras's most productive season was in 1994, when he won ten out of eighteen singles tournaments, including the Australian Open and a repeat of his Wimbledon title. He also set a single season financial record, bringing in over $5.4 million from his tour performances. Foot and hamstring injuries, however, hampered his performance in the second half of the year. Yet, at the conclusion of the season, Sampras did retain his number one ranking by winning the ATP Tour Championship in Frankfurt, Germany.

Sampras's successful career endured a tragic blow in early 1995. During the Australian Open, his mentor and close friend Tim Gullikson collapsed as a result of brain cancer (he died in 1996). Sampras was overcome with grief and lost control of his emotions in front of thousands of live spectators and millions of television viewers. The loss of Gullikson put everything into perspective. As Sampras put it: "Tennis is a great game, and I want to win every match I play, but it is not the most important thing in your life." In July 1995 Sampras successfully defended his Wimbledon title and became the first American man ever to win the world's most prestigious tournament three years in a row. Two months later in New York, Sampras also regained the U.S. Open title from Agassi and the number one ranking in the world.

Sampras continued his dominance in the remaining years of the twentieth century. Between 1996 and 2000 he captured his second Australian Open and fourth U.S. Open titles and won Wimbledon four times in a row. With a career record of thirteen Grand Slam singles titles, Sampras is one of the most celebrated players in the history of U.S. tennis.

The Sampras era concluded on a personal note. On 30 September 2000 Sampras married actress Bridgette Wilson, a former Miss Teen USA, in a sunset ceremony at his Beverly Hills, California, home. After winning at Wimbledon in 2000, Sampras failed to win any of the eighteen tournaments in which he competed, including the 2001 U.S. Open. Seeded tenth at the championship, his lowest since winning the first of his record thirteen Grand Slam championship titles in 1990, Sampras staged one of the most remarkable series of performances in the history of the U.S. Open. Defying media speculation of his decline and possible retirement, Sampras defeated three former champions in a row: the sixth seed, Patrick Rafter, in the fourth round; the second seed, Agassi, in the quarterfinals; and the third seed, Marat Safin, in the semifinals. However, Sampras's comeback soon ended when he was defeated in straight sets by a new tennis phenomenon, twenty-year-old Australian Lleyton Hewitt, in the finals.

There is no doubt that men's tennis in the last decade of the twentieth century belonged to Sampras. His performance at the 1990 U.S. Open displayed his power, speed, and dynamic youthfulness; his triumph in 2000 at Wimbledon (his seventh in eight years) reaffirmed that continued supremacy in the sport demands not only talent and skill, but most importantly, an unyielding will to win.

★

For information on Sampras, see Mark Stewart, *Pete Sampras: Strokes of Genius* (2000), and Bud Collins and Zander Hollander, eds., *Bud Collins' Tennis Encyclopedia* (1997). See also Alexander Wolff, "Upset Time," *Sports Illustrated* (17 Sept. 1990), and S. L. Price, "For the Ages: The Past and the Future Met in a Stirring Wimbledon Fortnight as Pete Sampras Won His Record 13th Grand Slam Title and Venus Her First," *Sports Illustrated* (17 July 2000).

YING WUSHANLEY

SANDE, Earl (*b.* 13 November 1898 in Groton, South Dakota; *d.* 19 August 1968 in Oregon), regarded as the most successful jockey of the 1920s, rode Gallant Fox to a Triple Crown series of victories in 1930 and won three Kentucky Derbies, five Belmont Stakes, and one Preakness Stakes.

Sande was one of six children of John C. Sande, a railroad worker, and Mrs. Sande, a homemaker. Sande's career as a jockey and horse trainer and breeder began during his youth on the rocky terrain of the American West. Born in the small town of Groton, Sande relocated with his family to American Falls, Idaho, during his childhood. At age twelve, Sande bought his first horse, which he raced at county fairs. Growing somewhat tall for a typical jockey at five feet, six inches, and struggling to maintain an ideal racing weight of 112 pounds, Sande nevertheless became determined to pursue a career in horse racing. As a teen-

Earl Sande, 1923. AP/WIDE WORLD PHOTOS

ager, Sande continued to race at county fairs for owner Doc Pardee in Phoenix, Arizona.

Although Sande attempted to enlist for military service in World War I, his slight stature disqualified him for duty. Carrying on with his training, Sande moved to New Orleans, where he became an apprentice rider to thoroughbred owner and trainer Joe Goodman. Under his contract with Goodman, Sande earned $20 a month; he was also promised a fee of $10 for every race he entered, with a bonus of an additional $15 if he won. More importantly, Sande's apprenticeship allowed him to qualify as a jockey after he won forty races. After his first victory on 21 January 1918 at the New Orleans fairgrounds, Sande completed his forty wins in just over three months, concluding with his 27 April 1918 win in Lexington, Kentucky.

Sande's graduation to jockey status in such a short time gained the young rider an impressive reputation, one that was enhanced by his four wins in six races in a single day in 1918 at Havre de Grace, Maryland. Sande claimed that his success resulted from understanding not only how his own horse performed, but how the other horses in the race would perform as well. Sande's almost preternatural ability to predict the habits of other horses in a race and adjust his own strategy accordingly would eventually give him a record of 968 wins, some 26.4 percent of all races he entered. At his peak in the 1920s, he won an average of ninety races each year and was regarded as the nation's leading rider in 1921, 1923, and 1927.

Sande married the former Marion Casey in 1923. His career continued to climb with his victory riding Zev in the Kentucky Derby at Churchill Downs in Louisville on 19 May. Sande and Zev took the one-and-a-quarter mile race by one-and-a-half lengths. The duo also won the Belmont Stakes in New York, but were prevented from earning a Triple Crown of victories when Zev was injured just before the Preakness Stakes in Baltimore. Sande himself suffered major injuries in August 1924 while racing in Saratoga, New York. When another horse cut across the field during the race, Sande was thrown from his mount and was trampled by three other horses. With multiple fractures in his right leg and a broken collarbone and rib, Sande was off the racetrack for several months.

Although some predicted that Sande would not regain his winning form, a second victory at the Kentucky Derby on 15 May 1925 on Flying Ebony put such doubts to rest. As in his 1923 run, Sande and Flying Ebony took the lead by one-and-a-half lengths; the win was especially impressive given the horse's lack of experience at such a distance. By now, Sande earned a salary that approached $50,000 a year and was regarded as the most popular jockey in the nation. However, as he approached his thirties, Sande was beset by a number of professional and personal setbacks. Marion Casey Sande died in September 1927. In addition to this loss, Sande faced a suspension by the Maryland Jockey Club in November of that year for cutting off another rider at Maryland's Pimlico track. Finally, Sande was beginning to have difficulty making the weight requirement of 112–115 pounds. Together, these factors contributed to Sande's decision to retire as a jockey in 1927 and take up a new career as a Thoroughbred trainer and owner.

Soon in debt for $75,000, Sande returned to the mount in 1930 on Gallant Fox; together, the team became one of horse racing's legendary pairings. In the first of the three races on the way to a Triple Crown, Sande rode Gallant Fox to a surprising victory at the Preakness Stakes on 9 May. With a poor start, Gallant Fox trailed the field for the greater part of the race, coming alive only in the final stretch to overtake Crack Brigade for the win. On 17 May 1930 at Churchill Downs, Sande and Gallant Fox duplicated their efforts at the Preakness; once again, a troubled start gave way to a powerful finish down the back stretch, and Gallant Fox took the Kentucky Derby by two lengths. Completing the Triple Crown, Sande and Gallant Fox rode to an easy victory by three lengths in the Belmont Stakes on 7 June. It was the first Triple Crown achievement in horse racing since 1919 and confirmed Sande's reputation as the best jockey of his generation; he even earned the sobriquet "the handy man" based on a Damon Runyon verse in tribute to his skills.

Retiring again from his career as a jockey in 1932, Sande became a successful trainer for a short period before becoming a horse breeder and owner. Unfortunately, Sande's talents as a rider did not translate into success as an owner, and he was soon in debt and out of business. While he was offered several lucrative endorsement and personal appearance deals, Sande's sense of pride refused to let him take the easy money. Instead, he reentered the race course as a jockey for one last race in 1953 at the age of fifty-five at the Jamaica Racetrack in New York. He won the race, although it was widely acknowledged that the other riders allowed him to win out of respect.

By the end of the 1950s, Sande was living in a small apartment without a bathroom above a bar on Long Island, New York. A second marriage had broken up; as in the first union, there were no children. Too poor to afford bus fare, Sande could not even take advantage of the season passes that were sent to him by area race tracks; despite the poverty, he continued to turn down offers to make personal appearances. In declining health, Sande returned west to live near his family and spent the last part of his life in an Oregon nursing home. He died on 19 August 1968 at the age of sixty-nine.

★

A survey of Sande's life by Gene Smith was published in *American Heritage* (Sept. 1996). A contemporary profile of Sande appears in Charles H. L. Johnston, *Famous American Athletes of Today, Second Series* (1930). Sande's famous races on Gallant Fox are recounted in Marvin Drager, *The Most Glorious Crown: The Story of America's Triple Crown Thoroughbreds, from Sir Barton to Secretariat* (1975). Additional information on Sande's career and horse racing in general is in Edward L. Bowen, *The Jockey Club's Illustrated History of Thoroughbred Racing in America* (1994), and Bill Doolittle, *The Kentucky Derby: Run for the Roses* (1998). An obituary appeared as an article by John S. Radosta, "Rode the Greats," in the *New York Times* (21 Aug. 1968).

TIMOTHY BORDEN

SANDERS, Barry (*b.* 16 July 1968 in Wichita, Kansas), premier college and professional football running back, winner of the Heisman Trophy, and one of the leading rushers in the history of the National Football League (NFL).

Sanders is one of the eleven children of William "Willie" Sanders, a construction worker and maintenance engineer, and Shirley Sanders, a homemaker. Barry Sanders had a troubled childhood. Something of a bully who frequently had fights, he also stole candy and threw rocks at cars. But the values of his parents finally prevailed. He also learned the virtues of hard work in the classroom and in sports at North High School in Wichita, Kansas.

Barry Sanders, 1996. AP/WIDE WORLD PHOTOS

As a youngster, Sanders began perfecting a running style for which he later became famous. Playing sandlot football, he learned to make lightning cuts, to run fast laterally, to stop suddenly, to accelerate rapidly, and above all to do whatever else it took to avoid a tackle. His high school coaches, however, were not impressed. They believed he was too small to play running back, so they turned him into a defensive back. Only in the last five games of his senior season in 1985 did he get a shot as a running back, and he averaged a phenomenal two hundred yards a game. Though not widely recruited as a college prospect upon his graduation in 1986, Sanders entered Oklahoma State University (OSU) that fall on an athletic scholarship. He chose OSU primarily because he wanted to major in business, and he had heard that school had a first-class business college.

At OSU, Sanders was still underrated, this time because two good running backs were ahead of him. One was Thurman Thomas, who won some All-America honors and became an all-pro running back for the Buffalo Bills. Used mainly as a kick returner, Sanders had a respectable freshman season and began a program that increased his leg strength and his weight from 175 pounds to 200 pounds.

For most of his sophomore season Sanders ran behind Thomas while continuing as a kick return specialist. Sanders increasingly rotated into games as a running back and had three 100-yard games out of the last four. The year was highlighted by a Sun Bowl victory over West Virginia University by a score of 35 to 33, and Sanders was named an All-American as a kick returner. The fast finish set the stage for a brilliant 1988 season. With Thomas now running for Buffalo, Sanders came into his own as a quality back who could handle the football. He set thirty-four National Collegiate Athletic Association (NCAA) records. He broke the rushing record by gaining 2,628 yards on only 344 carries, an astounding average of 7.6 yards per carry. In 4 games he went over 300 yards in rushing, an almost unheard of feat. Counting kickoffs and passes caught, he had 3,250 all-purpose yards for another NCAA record. His 39 touchdowns shattered yet another milestone. For the season he was the player most responsible for the OSU 9–2 record and a big win over Wyoming in the Holiday Bowl, a 62–14 blowout. Sanders's brilliant year virtually guaranteed him the Heisman Trophy as well as first-team All-America. The modest young man accepted the Heisman award but credited his offensive line and his blocking fullback for the honor.

Drafted by the Detroit Lions in 1989, after his junior year at OSU, Sanders made his mark in professional football his first year. Despite injuries that forced him to miss two complete games and parts of two others, he broke the Lions rushing record, gaining 1,470 yards, second in the

National Football League (NFL), and averaging more than 5 yards per carry. His fourteen touchdowns were another Lion record. For his feats Barry was named the NFL Rookie of the Year and was selected to the all-pro team. His second year was also stellar with 1,304 yards and more than a 5-yard average per rush. He won the rushing title in 1990 and came in second in 1991 by gaining 1,548 yards. In the latter year he was also chosen NFL Player of the Year.

One good season followed another. Sanders won the rushing title again in 1994, 1996, and 1997. He was the National Football Conference's Most Valuable Player in 1994. In 1997 he was again NFL Player of the Year, and that year he churned for 2,053 yards, which then ranked as the second-best rushing season ever.

When Sanders retired abruptly just before the 1999 season, his rushing total stood at 15,269 yards, then an all-time second to Walter Payton, who rushed for a record 16,726 yards during his career with the Chicago Bears. No one could explain Sanders's sudden retirement while still in the salad days of his career and making millions of dollars to boot. Rumors held that Sanders became dissatisfied with playing on a lackluster team, that he wanted to be traded to a team that could contend for a Super Bowl victory. Yet Sanders made no serious attempt either to return to the Lions or to join another team. Even his father could not convince him to return to professional football. Perhaps interested parties should have believed what Sanders said, that he wanted to do other things. Could that explanation be true? Most likely. Sanders had never cared for records, for he was always willing to share glory with his teammates. Apparently he played the game for as long as it was fun for him. When it was no longer fun, he walked away. He never showboated, he never spiked a ball, he never danced on the field, he never taunted other players, and he never argued with referees. In 2000 he married Lauren Campbell, a Detroit newscaster. Even though he cut his career short, Sanders will long be remembered as one of the best running backs of all time, perhaps even the best of all time.

★

Biographies of Sanders include Nathan Aaseng, *Barry Sanders: Star Running Back* (1994); and John F. Wukovitz, *Barry Sanders: 20* (1997). Also informative is Michael Wibon, "Barry Sanders: Beyond Compare," *Washington Post* (9 Nov. 1997). Sanders's seemingly abrupt decision to retire is discussed in Leonard Shapiro and Mark Maske, "Lions' Sanders Retires from NFL," *Washington Post* (29 July 1999). Also see Drew Sharp, "Sanders Says He's Happy and Enjoying Retirement," *Seattle Times* (20 Aug. 2000). Good websites are <http://barrysanders.hypermart.net> and <http://www.keyworlds.com/b/barry_sanders.htm>.

JAMES M. SMALLWOOD

SANDERS, Deion Luwynn (*b.* 9 August 1967 in Fort Myers, Florida), outstanding football cornerback and exciting kick returner who also achieved success in Major League Baseball; the first athlete to play in both the Super Bowl and the World Series.

Sanders's parents, Connie Sanders and Mims Sanders, divorced when Sanders was two years old, and he was raised by his mother and her new husband, Willie Knight. Sanders's football skills were first seen in the Pop Warner League when he was eight. He also began to excel at baseball and basketball. Sanders was a three-sport athlete with Fort Myers High School, and served as a ROTC commander. He played quarterback for his high school football team. As a player at Florida State University from 1985 to 1988, he switched from quarterback to defensive back. In his college career he scored six touchdowns on punt and interception returns, and he was named All-America twice as a defensive back. In addition, he earned the Jim Thorpe award as the best defensive back in the nation. Sanders also ran track and played for the college baseball team, the latter so well that the New York Yankee organization signed him in 1988.

In the 1989 National Football League (NFL) draft the Atlanta Falcons made Sanders the fifth pick in the first

Deion Sanders, 1998. AP/WIDE WORLD PHOTOS

round. Shortly thereafter, the American League (AL) New York Yankees brought him to Major League Baseball. There was some question about which sport he would choose, but the Falcons won him with a $4.4 million offer. He hit a home run for the Yankees against the Seattle Mariners, then packed his bags for Atlanta, where he scored on a punt return. No one had ever had a home run in Major League Baseball and a touchdown in Major League Football in the same week. Sanders went on to intercept five passes his rookie year in the NFL.

Sanders's return to baseball was not as impressive. In 1990 he batted a puny .158 for the Yankees, and the team said they would release him unless he gave up football. He refused, and they cut him loose. Back in football, Sanders prospered under Falcons coach Jerry Glanville's coaching. He returned two interceptions for touchdowns in 1990, and the following year he scored on two kickoffs and one interception return, intercepting six passes. The Falcons made it to the second round of the playoffs before losing to the eventual champion Washington Redskins.

Sanders still heard the call of baseball. He signed with the Atlanta Braves of the National League (NL), having a mediocre and truncated 1991 baseball season before returning to the gridiron. The next year, however, Sanders starred on the diamond, batting .304 with twenty-six stolen bases and an NL-leading fourteen triples. After the baseball season, he decided to have it both ways, playing in the World Series for the Braves and flying to Miami for a Falcons football game. Pundits such as sports broadcaster Tim McCarver (whom Sanders later doused with water in a locker-room confrontation) said that Sanders was being typically selfish, sacrificing his World Series play for a two-sport stunt. (Sanders batted .533 and scored four runs in the World Series.)

In 1993 Sanders batted a respectable .276 for the Braves, who won the NL West division, then returned to a Falcons team that had gone 0–5 without him. In a shortened season he found the time to lead the National Football Conference (NFC) in interceptions with seven, and get his first offensive score, catching a seventy-yard touchdown pass.

In 1994 Sanders was traded by the Braves to the Cincinnati Reds. When the baseball strike ended the season prematurely, Sanders was ready for a full season of football. A free agent, he signed with the San Francisco 49ers. He had six interceptions, returning three of them for touchdowns, and he was named the Associated Press Defensive Player of the Year. He intercepted passes in both the NFC Championship and the Super Bowl, as the 49ers became Super Bowl champions.

In 1995 Sanders again was a football free agent, and he signed with the Dallas Cowboys. Sanders favored their first playoff game with a remarkable all-around performance, scoring on a run from scrimmage, catching a pass, intercepting a pass, and returning two punts. In 1996 he began the season playing full-time at both cornerback and wide receiver, turning in good performances at both.

In 1997 Sanders announced that he had become a born-again Christian and returned to baseball with the Cincinnati Reds. He was on his way to his best season, with 126 hits and 56 stolen bases; but when the football season started the Reds were out of contention, so Sanders went back to the Cowboys. They, however, were on a decline, going 6–10 and missing the playoffs for the first time in years.

For the next two years Sanders concentrated on football with the Cowboys. The team was in disarray, and Sanders's skills were slipping. He was occasionally beaten deep by a fast receiver, his exciting returns were fewer and farther between, and he was a burden on the salary cap.

In 2000 the flamboyant Daniel Snyder took over as owner of the Washington Redskins. Snyder wanted to win and win fast, and he wanted to do it with stars. One step was to sign Sanders with an $8 million bonus, but the money did not buy Snyder success. After a disastrous 2000 season, veteran coach Marty Schottenheimer was hired with a mandate to clean house. Sanders was retained but objected that he had not been informed of the changes.

Sanders then decided to gave Major League Baseball one more shot, signing again with the Cincinnati Reds. In his first game of the 2001 season he had three hits, including a three-run homer. This was not a harbinger, however. By 22 June Sanders was hitting a dismal .173, and the Reds released him. Perhaps Sanders saw this as a more general handwriting on the wall. On 27 July Sanders and the Redskins negotiated his retirement from football, and he paid back a substantial portion of his bonus.

Sanders was always a controversial player. Many fans and sportswriters were put off by his ostentatious self-promotion, his excessive jewelry, and his showboating on the field. As a result, his actions were often painted in the most unflattering light possible, and his few relative weaknesses (such as tackling) were overemphasized. In his prime, however, Sanders may have been the best pass-coverage cornerback in the game, able to shut down the opposition's best receiver all by himself; and even at the end of his career, opposing teams kicked to him only with trepidation.

★

Sanders describes his own career and his turn to religion in *Power, Money and Sex: How Success Almost Ruined My Life* (1998), written with Jim Nelson Black and T. D. Jakes. Stew Thornley, *Deion Sanders: Prime Time Player* (1997), is a competent treatment of Sanders's career for children age nine to twelve.

ARTHUR D. HLAVATY

SANDERS, Summer Elisabeth (*b.* 13 October 1972 in Roseville, California), swimmer who captured worldwide attention in the 1992 Barcelona Olympics by winning four Olympic medals.

Born in a quiet northern California town, Sanders was one of two children of Bob Sanders, a dentist, and Barbara Sanders, a homemaker. Sanders's mother loved to swim, so by the time Sanders was two years old, her father had built a pool in their backyard. Her parents hired a swimming instructor for their children, and by age three Sanders could swim the width of the pool. Sanders said that her motivation came from wanting to do everything her older brother did. When her brother joined a swim team at the age of six, four-year-old Sanders wanted to join a team too. Soon she was swimming laps and competing in races against seven-year-olds.

Sanders joined a year-round swimming team when she was seven and immediately fell in love with the lifestyle. Other than competing, she loved the social aspects of the sport. She gloried in having a second life away from school and being able to travel. When Sanders was eight years old, her parents divorced, and she and her brother began moving between two different houses every six months. To the credit of her parents, their divorce did little to disrupt Sanders's swimming routine. Sanders quit swimming for short periods of time when she was ten and twelve, but apart from those brief hiatuses, she swam competitively from age seven. In 1988, at age fifteen, she went to the Olympic trials in Texas "just for the experience." It was there that her swimming aspirations caught fire. To everyone's surprise, including her own, in the 200-meter individual medley she came within .27 second of making the U.S. team that went to Seoul, Korea. Before this race Sanders had never qualified even for a national final. She was stunned but energized, realizing for the first time that the Olympics were within her reach. She came away with a new goal—to compete in the 1992 Olympics.

Summer Sanders, 1992.

Sanders rose to the occasion. Her morning practices while in high school required her to get up just after 4 A.M. every day except Sunday. She was an honors student throughout high school, motivated by her desire to be accepted by a good college with an excellent swim team. Her hard work paid off. She won a full athletic scholarship in 1990 to attend Stanford University, where she was coached by Richard Quick and swam with the team widely regarded as the best in the nation. Sanders won three gold medals at the 1990 Goodwill Games in Seattle and ended Janet Evans's four-year undefeated streak in the 400-meter individual medley. Sanders was named the National Collegiate Athletic Association (NCAA) Swimmer of the Year in both 1991 and 1992, and she was the world champion in the 200-meter butterfly in 1991. As the 1992 Olympics approached, Sanders gave up her NCAA eligibility to pursue endorsement opportunities. At the Olympic trials in Indianapolis, Indiana, in March 1992, Sanders established herself as the rising star of competitive swimming. She won the 200-meter and 400-meter individual medleys and the 200-meter butterfly and finished second in the 100-meter butterfly. She also qualified for the 400-meter medley relay. Sanders was only the third American woman in history to qualify for four individual swimming events.

At the Barcelona Olympics, Sanders was as popular with the U.S. viewing public as she was successful at swimming. At five feet, nine inches tall, Sanders was a pretty nineteen-year-old with long brown hair, brown eyes, and a beaming smile. Her personality was sweet, refreshing, and honest. Fans followed her through a roller-coaster week at the Olympics. Although Sanders started strong, winning a bronze in the 400-meter individual medley (IM), she won no medal in the 100-meter butterfly. Then she set a new U.S. record in the 200-meter IM but lost the gold by .26, placing second after China's Lin Li. Sanders was in tears after that loss but came back to win gold medals in her last two races—the 200-meter butterfly and 400-meter medley relay. She became the only U.S. swimmer to win four medals in Barcelona.

Sanders felt enormous relief after winning her final race and her first individual gold medal. After years of intense practice and an exhausting week at the Olympics, she gloried in realizing that no one expected her to do anything "great" the next day. However, making the transition from Olympic gold-medal swimmer to product spokesperson and motivational speaker was a jolt for Sanders. She immediately missed the camaraderie of team life and began to dread swimming for the first time in her life. In January 1994 she officially retired from swimming and began a broadcasting career, becoming a host on Music Television (MTV) and providing commentary at swim meets. Then, in April 1995, Sanders made a sudden about-face and returned to competitive swimming. She joined the U.S. Swimming Resident National Team training in Colorado Springs, newly motivated by the prospects of swimming in an Olympics in the United States. However, Sanders found that it was difficult to make up for her time away from training. Her rivals were new and younger, and Sanders could never match or surpass her earlier times. In March 1996 she failed to qualify for the Olympic Games at Atlanta.

With a second retirement imposed upon her, Sanders concentrated full-time on her television career. She was a swimming analyst at both the Atlanta Olympics and the 2000 Sydney Olympics, hosted a children's game show on Nickelodeon called *Figure It Out* (1997), appeared on *NBA Inside Stuff* (1998), and provided sideline analysis for broadcasts of the Women's National Basketball Association games on Lifetime (1997 to 1998). In 1999 Sanders wrote, *Champions Are Raised, Not Born: How My Parents Made Me a Success,* with Melinda Marshall. The book answers questions she received from parents and children striving for Olympic success, and is full of personal anecdotes. Sanders's private life took a very public turn during the closing ceremonies at the 1996 Atlanta Games, when Olympic gold medalist in swimming Mark Henderson proposed to Sanders on his knees in front of thousands of athletes and a national television audience. She readily accepted, and they were married on 4 July 1997.

Although swimming started as a family activity and Sanders felt that she did not take the sport seriously until she was fifteen, she came to embody an ideal blend of tireless effort, innate talent, and a strong mental attitude that made her the best in the world in 1992. When Sanders looked back at her successes, she gave much of the credit to her parents, who never pressured her to compete. She would be the first to say that she never could have done it if it had not been so much fun.

★

Frank Deford, "The Butterfly Queen," *Newsweek* (27 Jul. 1992), gives insights into how Americans pinned their hopes and ideals on Sanders at the 1992 Olympics. C. W. Nevius, "Emotions Churn Olympic Waters," *San Francisco Chronicle* (1 Aug. 1992), chronicles Sanders's reactions to winning a gold medal. Karen Rosen, "Swimming Medalist Sanders Seeks Swan Song at Olympics," *Atlanta Constitution* (8 Apr. 1995), describes Sanders's change of heart that led to training for the 1996 Olympics. For updates on Sanders's life, see Karen Allen, "Swimmers Wed on July 4," *USA Today* (2 Jul. 1997), and Oscar Dixon, "Sanders Thrives in 'Real World'," *USA Today* (29 Sept. 2000).

JANET INGRAM

SARAZEN, Gene (*b.* 27 February 1902 in Harrison, New York; *d.* 13 May 1999 in Naples, Florida), professional golfer who developed the sand wedge and was the first to win all four of the modern professional major golf championships.

It is surprising that Sarazen, born Eugenio Saraceni, became a professional golfer, not only because of his short stature of five feet, five inches, but also because his Italian immigrant parents knew nothing about the game and did

Gene Sarazen, 1985. ASSOCIATED PRESS AP

not live near a golf course. His father, Federico Saraceni, was a carpenter from Italy who had immigrated to New York with his wife, Adela, a homemaker. Sarazen had one sibling. To help support the family, Sarazen began caddying at Larchmont Country Club at age eight when his mother found out that a neighbor's son made good money caddying there. At Larchmont and later at Apawamis Country Club he started practicing golf, and learned from the amateurs on the course.

Federico Saraceni went into debt in the spring of 1917 when the United States entered World War I, the price of lumber soared, and he could not meet a contract. Sarazen left school to work with his father six days a week as a carpenter. In the summer the family moved to Bridgeport, Connecticut, to work in the war plants. Sarazen became a carpenter's helper at the Remington Arms, fulfilling his father's wish that he take up a career in carpentry rather than golf. In January 1918 Sarazen contracted pneumonia. He was unconscious for three days and long in recovering because he developed empyema, or pus in the pleural cavities between the lungs and the chest wall. He was finally released from the hospital in May, under doctor's orders to get an outdoor job. He determined to become a professional golfer at that time.

Sarazen turned to Al Ciuci, the professional at the local nine-hole course, Beardsley Park. Ciuci encouraged him and helped him to a career in golf. Sarazen hit the ball long with a draw. After learning at age eleven of Francis Ouimet's victory in the 1913 U.S. Open, Sarazen had adopted an interlocking grip, which is what Ouimet had, and it suited Sarazen's small hands perfectly. Sarazen also changed his name at age sixteen when he saw his name in a local newspaper and thought "Saraceni" sounded more like the name of a violin player than a golfer.

Success came early for Sarazen. In 1922 he started out by winning the Southern Open in New Orleans by eight shots. Then he won the U.S. Open at Skokie Country Club in Glencoe, Illinois, by a stroke with a final round of 68. He said, "All men are created equal, but I am one stroke better than the rest." Sarazen went on to win the Professional Golfers Association (PGA) Championship that year at Oakmont Country Club in Oakmont, Pennsylvania. He was late for his first round match because he was in Ohio playing an exhibition and forgot about the PGA Championship starting the next day. Under today's rules he would have been disqualified. He also won important exhibition matches against Jim Barnes for $1,500—three times his winnings in the U.S. Open, and Walter Hagen—over 72 holes and billed as the "World Championship of Golf"—for $2,000. In the latter match Sarazen had stomach pains but shrugged them off. He consulted doctors after the match who told him he had "nervous indigestion." Saying, "I don't get nervous when I play a match like this," he fortunately consulted another doctor who had him rushed to the hospital for an emergency appendectomy.

Sarazen was now on top of the golfing world, and in addition to playing in exhibitions, cashed in on his new fame with articles, an instruction manual on golf, and endorsements. In 1923 he became a member of the Wilson Sporting Goods Company advisory staff. That year Sarazen once again won the PGA Championship, playing a tight final match over thirty-eight holes against Hagen with another fantastic finish.

For the rest of the decade, Sarazen was regarded by many as being in a slump, winning no major championships except the Metropolitan Open in 1925, although he finished second or third in several majors and won other tournaments from 1926 on. His personal life took a positive turn in 1923, however, when he met Mary Catherine Henry. They married on 10 June 1924; the couple had two children.

Sarazen earned more money from the stock market than his golf in the 1920s, but when the stock market crashed in 1929, he lost most of his money and felt the need for a new reliance on his golf game. In January 1930 he won the Agua Caliente Open in Tijuana, Mexico and its $10,000 first prize; one of the eight PGA tour events he won that year. Sarazen also turned his thoughts to the shots he was losing trying to come out of bunkers with a lofted iron, which either bladed the ball or dug into the sand. While taking a flying lesson, he noticed how the plane rode up in the air as the flaps went down. Sarazen applied the same principle to the sole of a niblick, a lofted iron, by putting solder on the bottom and filing the sole at an angle down from the leading edge. He refined the angle of the flange so that it rode smoothly through the sand. By the winter of 1931 Sarazen had created the modern sand wedge.

Using the sand wedge and a refurbished grip, Sarazen won the British Open and the U.S. Open in 1932. At Prince's Golf Club in Sandwich, he also had the advantage of Hagen's old caddie, Skip Daniels. Daniels, who was then past sixty and in failing health, had promised Sarazen that they would win an Open together. Daniels carried Sarazen's clubs while using a cane and called his shots, and Sarazen led all four rounds for a record score of 283. At the U.S. Open at Fresh Meadow Country Club on Long Island, New York, Sarazen was 5 strokes behind after 36 holes. On the ninth hole of the third round he chipped in for a 2 and a 38 going out. Then he shot the back nine in 32 for a 70 and shot a 66 in the final round for a memorable streak of golf and a total of 286. Sarazen followed that win with another PGA Championship in 1933.

Sarazen's most famous shot—possibly the most famous shot in PGA history— was a double-eagle two at the par five fifteenth hole at the 1935 Augusta National Invitational Tournament (now the Masters). At the fifteenth hole, Sarazen needed to shoot three under par on the last four holes to tie Craig Wood. For his second shot Sarazen toed in a four-wood and hit a low shot that sent the ball 235 yards into the hole. The next day he defeated Wood in a thirty-six-hole playoff. Sarazen continued playing tournament golf long after that win. He won the PGA Seniors Championship in 1954 and 1958, and in 1963, at age sixty-one, he was the oldest player ever to make the cut in the Masters. In 1973, on the fiftieth anniversary of his first British Open, he scored a hole in one on the 126-yard eighth hole at Troon Golf Course. In 1967 Sarazen wrote an instructional book for seniors, *Better Golf After Fifty*. He won his last tournament, the New York State PGA Seniors Championship, in 1968.

In 1933 Sarazen bought a farm in Brookfield Center, Connecticut, and from that time on he became known as "the Squire." He sold the farm in 1944 and bought another in Germantown, New York, in 1945, where he stayed until 1969, when he moved to New London, New Hampshire. In 1961 Sarazen became the host of the television show *Shell's Wonderful World of Golf*, a series of golf matches played around the world that ran for nine seasons. Sarazen retired to Marco Island, Florida. He continued to be involved in golf and charities and was an honorary starter at the Masters from 1981 until the month before his death in 1999 from complications of pneumonia. He is buried in Marco Island Cemetery.

Sarazen played in all six Ryder Cup matches from 1927 to 1937 and holds the record for most PGA Championship matches won (fifty-one). The PGA Tour historical rankings from 1916 to 1988 rank Sarazen eleventh. He had thirty-seven official tour victories. As Bobby Jones wrote in his introduction to Sarazen's autobiography, "When he saw a chance at the bacon hanging over the last green, he could put as much fire and fury into a finishing round of golf as Jack Dempsey could into a fight."

★

Sarazen wrote his memoirs, *Thirty Years of Championship Golf: The Life and Times of Gene Sarazen* (1950), with Herbert Warren Wind. See also John M. Olman, *The Squire: The Legendary Golfing Life of Gene Sarazen* (1987). Al Barkow, *Gettin' to the Dance Floor: The Early Days of American Pro-Golf* (1986), includes an interview with Sarazen. An account of Sarazen's win at the Agua Caliente Open is in Peter F. Stevens, *Links Lore: Dramatic Moments and Forgotten Milestones from Golf's History* (1998). Sarazen wrote an article about his development of the sand wedge, "The Wedge and I," for *Golf* (May 1966). "A Conversation with Gene Sarazen," by Ira Berkow, appears in *Golfer's Digest*, 6th ed. (1974). See also Tim Rosaforte, "Sarazen's Last Interview," *Golf Digest* (Aug. 1999). Obituaries are in the *New York Times* and *Boston Globe* (both 14 May 1999).

ROBERT T. BRUNS

SAWCHUK, Terrance Gordon ("Terry") (*b.* 28 December 1929 in Winnipeg, Manitoba, Canada; *d.* 31 May 1970 in New York City), Hall of Fame hockey goaltender who set records for shutouts and victories.

Born and raised in East Kildonan, a working-class, Ukrainian section of Winnipeg, Sawchuk was the third of four sons and one adopted daughter of Louis Sawchuk, a tinsmith who had come to Canada as a boy from Austrian-controlled Ukraine, and his wife, Anne Maslak Sawchuk, a homemaker. Their second son died at a young age from scarlet fever and the oldest, an aspiring hockey goaltender whom Sawchuk idolized, died suddenly of a heart attack at age seventeen. At age twelve, Sawchuk injured his right elbow playing football and, not wanting to be punished, hid the injury, preventing the dislocation from properly healing. Thus, the arm was left with limited mobility and several inches shorter than the left, and bothered him for his entire athletic career.

After inheriting his brother's goalie equipment, Sawchuk began playing ice hockey in a local league and worked for a sheet-metal company installing vents over bakery ovens. His goaltending talent was so evident that at age fourteen a local scout for the Detroit Red Wings had him work out with the team, who later signed him to an amateur contract and sent him to play for their junior team in Galt,

Terry Sawchuk, 1950. ASSOCIATED PRESS AP

Ontario, in 1946, where he also finished the eleventh grade but most likely did not graduate from high school.

Glowing reports of Sawchuk's goaltending led the Red Wings to sign him to a professional contract in November 1947, and he quickly progressed through their developmental system, winning honors as the Rookie of the Year in both the U.S. and American Hockey Leagues. Sawchuk also capably filled in for seven games when the Detroit goalie Harry Lumley was injured in January 1950.

Although Lumley led the Red Wings to the 1949–1950 Stanley Cup, Detroit traded him to the Chicago Black Hawks to make room for the much-heralded Sawchuk. Some were skeptical of Sawchuk's unusual style; whereas most goalies would bend only their knees, the chubby youngster, who had lightning-fast reflexes and played with reckless abandon, bent over from the waist (described as a "gorilla crouch"), so that his face was forward and closer to the ice. This enabled him to see the puck more clearly, especially while being screened by opponents, but put tremendous strain on his lower back and, since goalies then did not wear masks, required tremendous courage.

Nicknamed "Ukey" or "The Uke" by his teammates, his first five years with the powerhouse Red Wings were phenomenal, as the team won three Stanley Cups. For his individual performance, Sawchuk won the Calder Trophy as the top rookie (the first to win such honors in all three professional hockey leagues) and three Vezina Trophies for the fewest goals allowed (he missed out the other two years by one goal). He was selected as an All-Star five times, had an astounding fifty-six shutouts, and his goals-against average (GAA) remained under 2.00. In the 1951–1952 playoffs the Red Wings swept both the Black Hawks and the Montreal Canadiens, with Sawchuk surrendering just five goals in eight games (for a minuscule 0.67 GAA), with four shutouts.

Sawchuk's personality seemed to change when the Detroit general manager Jack Adams ordered him to lose weight before the 1951–1952 season. After showing up at training camp weighing 219 pounds, he dropped more than forty pounds, became sullen and withdrawn, and struggled for years to regain the weight. Also contributing to his moodiness and self-doubt was the pressure of playing day in and day out despite repeated injuries—there were no backup goaltenders. During his career he had three operations on his right elbow, an appendectomy, countless cuts and bruises, a broken instep, a collapsed lung, ruptured discs in his back, and severed tendons in his hand. Years of crouching in the net caused Sawchuk to walk with a permanent stoop and resulted in lordosis (swayback), which prevented him from sleeping for more than two hours at a time. He also received approximately 400 stitches to his face before adopting a mask in 1962. He became increasingly surly with reporters and fans, and preferred doing crossword puzzles to giving interviews.

After a very brief courtship, Sawchuk married Patricia Ann Bowman Morey on 6 August 1953. They had seven children, and the family suffered for many years from Sawchuk's increasing alcoholism, philandering (a Toronto girlfriend became pregnant by him in 1967), and verbal and physical abuse. Morey threatened to divorce him numerous times, and finally did so in 1969.

Since the Red Wings had a capable younger goaltender in the minor leagues (Glenn Hall), Adams dealt Sawchuk to the Boston Bruins in June 1955, devastating the self-critical goalie. During his second season with Boston, he was diagnosed with mononucleosis, but returned to the team after only two weeks. Physically weak, playing poorly, and on the verge of a nervous breakdown, Sawchuk announced his retirement in early 1957 and was labeled a "quitter" by team executives and several newspapers. During his recuperation, however, Detroit soured on Hall's performance, and Adams reacquired Sawchuk for seven more seasons. The Red Wings, however, did not enjoy the same success as before, and when Detroit had another promising young goalie ready for promotion (Roger Crozier), Sawchuk was left unprotected in the intraleague waiver draft and was quickly claimed by the Toronto Maple Leafs. With Sawchuck sharing goaltending duties with the forty-year-old Johnny Bower, the veteran duo won the 1964–1965 Vezina Trophy and led Toronto to the 1966–1967 Stanley Cup. Left unprotected in the June 1967 expansion draft, Sawchuk played one season for the Los Angeles Kings before being traded back to Detroit. Sawchuk spent his final season with the New York Rangers, where he played sparingly but recorded the final shutout of his career.

After the 1969–1970 season ended, Sawchuk and his Rangers teammate Ron Stewart, both of whom had been drinking, argued over expenses for the house they rented together on Long Island, New York. During the scuffle, Sawchuk suffered internal injuries from falling on top of Stewart's bent knee. At Long Beach Memorial Hospital, Sawchuk's gallbladder was removed and he had a second operation on his damaged and bleeding liver. The press described the incident as "horseplay," and Sawchuk told the police that he accepted full responsibility for the events. At New York Hospital in Manhattan, another operation was performed on Sawchuk's bleeding liver, but he never recovered and died shortly thereafter from a pulmonary embolism at age forty. He is buried in Mount Hope Cemetery in Pontiac, Michigan. A Nassau County grand jury exonerated Stewart and ruled that Sawchuk's death was accidental.

In 1971 Sawchuk was posthumously named as the winner of the Lester Patrick Memorial Trophy for "outstanding service to hockey in the United States," and (with a waiver of the normal three-year waiting period) was inducted into the Hockey Hall of Fame. The Red Wings retired his number in 1994, and even though he had become a U.S. citizen in 1959, he was honored on a Canadian stamp in 2001. Sawchuk was a seven-time All-Star, and his record of 447 regular-season wins stood for thirty years, before being surpassed in 2000 by Patrick Roy. Upon his death, Sawchuk also held the record for regular-season games played by a goaltender (971) and shutouts (103). Sawchuk set the standard for measuring goaltenders, and was publicly hailed as the "best goalie ever" by a rival general manager in 1952, during only his second season.

★

Two excellent biographies of Sawchuk are Brian Kendall, *Shutout: The Legend of Terry Sawchuk* (1996), and David Dupuis, *Sawchuk: The Troubles and Triumphs of the World's Greatest Goalie* (1998). Sawchuk's crouching style is featured in "'Greatest Hockey Goalie Ever': In Second Year Up, Young Terry Sawchuk and His Gorilla Crouch Keep Detroit Red Wings Far in Lead," *Life* (18 Feb. 1952), and Marshall Dann, "How Sawchuk Stops 'Em," *Detroit Free Press* (16 Mar. 1952). Valuable early profiles are Al Silverman, "Hockey's New Mr. Zero," *Sport* (Apr. 1952), and Trent Frayne, "The Awful Ups and Downs of Terry Sawchuk," *Maclean's* (19 Dec. 1959). A professional makeup artist highlighted all the scars and injuries to his face for a photograph accompanying the article "The Goalie Is the Goat: Hockey's Reviled and Bludgeoned Fall-Guys," *Life* (4 Mar. 1966). The Red Wings of the early 1950s are covered in Stan Fischler, *Motor City Muscle* (1996). Obituaries are in the *Detroit Free Press, Detroit News, New York Times, New York Post, Long Island Press,* and *Newsday* (all 1 June 1970).

JOHN A. DROBNICKI

SAYERS, Gale Eugene (*b.* 30 May 1943 in Wichita, Kansas), running back for the Chicago Bears of the National Football League (NFL) who was the youngest player elected to the Pro Football Hall of Fame after a career that spanned just sixty-eight games and included only five full seasons.

Sayers was one of three boys born to Roger Winfield Sayers, a mechanic, and Bernice Ross Sayers, a homemaker. After living in Wichita for several years, the Sayers family moved to Speed, a small town in northwest Kansas. The life in rural Kansas, as Sayers remembered, was "big rains, putting up fences, killing snakes, and going to an outhouse." In 1957 after less than two years in Speed, the family moved to Omaha, Nebraska. About this time Sayers received his first sports award—marble champion of seventh grade of the Howard Kennedy Elementary School. Soon afterward Sayers moved to the football field, although at first he was

Gale Sayers, 1965. ASSOCIATED PRESS AP

miscast as a linebacker. As a sophomore at Omaha Central High School, Sayers finally got to do what would make him one of the game's immortals—run with the football. His brilliance earned him All-State honors as a halfback in both his junior and senior seasons. In addition to football, the speedy Sayers was something of a one-man track team, piling up points in the sprints and the jumps. Graduating from high school in 1961, Sayers caused quite a stir when he chose the University of Kansas over the University of Nebraska. He did so simply, he said, "because I liked the Jayhawks' coach Jack Mitchell."

The Chicago Bears, who eventually drafted and signed Sayers, had a glowing scouting report on Sayers before he even played a varsity game at Kansas. It said, "Sayers, halfback, great speed, great prospect. He should be graded in 1 Category. The "1 Category" translated into "a player who should become a starter as a rookie in the NFL."

When Sayers became eligible for varsity play as a sophomore, he proved all the ballyhoo was justified. Sayers gained 1,125 yards in a 10-game schedule, averaging a nation-leading 7.1 yards every time he carried the ball. One of his early games that season was a 283-yard effort against Oklahoma State. He became a marked man; defenses were geared specifically to stop Sayers. Despite a dwindling per-carry average—6.9 as a junior and 5.2 as a senior, he was a consensus All-American in both years. Inexplicably, Sayers finished out of the top ten in Heisman Trophy voting.

Professional scouts, however, were very much aware of his ability and unlimited potential. Both the Bears and the Kansas City Chiefs of the American Football League (AFL) tapped Sayers as their first draft choice for 1965. Even though the Chiefs oil millionaire owner Lamar Hunt offered more for his services, Sayers accepted an offer from the Bears George Halas.

Sayers exploded onto the NFL scene in 1965. He was NFL Rookie of the Year and set a still-standing rookie record of twenty-two touchdowns. He was the talk of the town in nearly every NFL franchise city. Nothing caused more of a buzz than his performance against the San Francisco 49ers on 12 December 1965. Sayers scored six touchdowns that day—no one has ever scored more in a single NFL game—on scrimmage runs of twenty-one yards, seven yards, fifty yards, and one yard; an eighty-yard pass reception; and an eighty-five-yard punt return. Someone asked the outspoken Ditka if he thought the muddy field that day hampered Sayers. Ditka said, "Yeah, on a dry field, the kid woulda scored ten touchdowns." There was no sophomore jinx for Sayers. He led the NFL in rushing in 1966 with 1,231 yards. He was well on his way to another 1,000-yard season (the benchmark for all great running backs) in 1968 when disaster struck. In the ninth game of the season (he had accumulated 862 yards at that point), he injured his knee—the worst injury a running back can sustain. He was still named to the All-Pro team, regardless of the truncated season.

Sayers was determined to come back. A grueling rehabilitation program prepared him for the 1969 season. He became the first NFL running back ever to gain 1,000 yards or more (1,032) in the first season back after a knee injury and the ensuing surgery. Again he was All-Pro and was voted the NFL's Most Courageous Player. Those who were not aware of Sayers's special relationship with his Bears teammate Brian Piccolo, who was suffering from what would prove to be fatal lung cancer, were aware after Sayers's acceptance speech. With all sincerity, he said, "I accept this award tonight, but tomorrow it is Brian Piccolo's. He has the heart of giant and a rare form of courage." Their friendship and Sayers's compassion for Piccolo during his illness inspired the best-selling book *A Short Season* (1971), by Jeannie Morris, and an enduring television movie *Brian's Song* (1972). The film was remade in 2001.

During the 1970 preseason, Sayers suffered an injury to "the other" knee that limited him to just two games. The next year, 1971, was no better, when he again played just two games. Sayers realized his glittering career was over and retired during the 1972 preseason. His name still dots the NFL record book: most touchdowns as a rookie (22), most touchdowns in a game (6), highest career kickoff return average (30.56 yards per return), second-best season kickoff return average (37.69 yards in 1967), third-best career per-carry average (5.0 yards—trailing only Jim Brown's 5.2 average).

Sayers made All-Pro in each of his five full seasons with the Bears. He played in the Pro Bowl four times (his first knee injury prevented him from playing in a fifth) and won Player of the Game honors in three of them. Fans were probably more upset about Sayers's shortened career than he was. He said, "It really wasn't as difficult as some people think. I was prepared to play and I was prepared to quit. I had something to turn to and that made it a great deal easier."

After his playing career, Sayers served as athletic director at the University of Southern Illinois and then settled into a career in his own computer supplies business in the Chicago suburb of Mt. Prospect, Illinois. Sayers married his high school sweetheart Linda Lou McNeil on 10 June 1962. The couple had two children, but their marriage ended in divorce. Sayers married Ardythe ("Ardie") Elaine Bullard on 1 December 1973. They live in Chicago.

In college Sayers was known as "the Kansas Comet." He truly had cometlike qualities—he blazed across the NFL sky briefly, and was gone. Steve Bisheff wrote of Sayers, "He was nonpareil, an artist with his own unique brushstrokes. Others may have been stronger and more durable, but nobody ran in the open field like Gale Sayers." It was an appropriate description in 1977, when at age thirty-three Sayers became the youngest player ever inducted into the Pro Football Hall of Fame. Sayers explained his ability, saying, "It was instinctive—God-given. I never planned those moves. All I needed was eighteen inches of daylight."

★

Sayers wrote an autobiography, *I Am Third* (1970), with Al Silverman. His life and career are also discussed in Hal Higdon, *Pro Football, USA* (1968); Murray Olderman, *The Running Backs* (1969); Berry Stainback, *How the Pros Play Football* (1970); Jeannie Morris, *A Short Season* (1971); and George Sullivan, *The Great Running Backs* (1972).

JIM CAMPBELL

SCHAYES, Adolph ("Dolph") (*b.* 19 May 1928 in New York City), one of the fifty greatest players in National Basketball Association (NBA) history.

Schayes was born into a lower middle class Jewish family in the Bronx. Although his parents, Carl Schayes and Tina Michel Schayes, were both born in Romania and came to the United States in 1920, they met in school on the Lower East Side of New York. They subsequently had three sons. Schayes's father was employed by Consolidated Laundries as a truck driver and later as a supervisor. He also moon-

Dolph Schayes *(right),* 1959. ASSOCIATED PRESS AP

lighted as a taxicab driver. Schayes's mother was a homemaker. Schayes's introduction to basketball occurred in the 1930s when he was eleven or twelve and a member of the Trylons, a group of ten friends who became one of the best basketball teams in the Bronx. They were in great demand to play in tournaments, and it was from this experience that Schayes developed his love of the game. Eventually reaching his full growth of six feet, eight inches, Schayes was already tall in junior high school, where he was a good basketball player. He was an excellent player at DeWitt Clinton High School in the Bronx, where he attended from 1941 to 1944. Schayes graduated from high school with an academic diploma at the age of sixteen.

Heavily recruited by such schools as Purdue, St. John's, Columbia, and New York University (NYU), he chose NYU because it was located not far from his home. He received a basketball scholarship in 1945 when NYU had one of the top teams in the country, and at age sixteen he was the youngest player on the team. Among Schayes's teammates at NYU were future NBA players Don Forman and Sid Tannenbaum, and their influence encouraged him to develop his outside shooting and rebounding. Schayes was named All-Metropolitan as a freshman in 1945 and helped lead the Violets to the National Collegiate Athletic Association (NCAA) championships, a contest they lost to Oklahoma A&M (now Oklahoma State University) 49–45. In 1948 Schayes was named All-American and won the Haggerty Trophy, awarded to the top player in the New York metropolitan area. During the same season, he set the single season scoring record at NYU with 356 points, as the Violets finished the season 20–3 but lost to St. Louis in the National Invitational Tournament (NIT) championship game 65–52. Schayes finished his NYU career with 815 points in 80 games.

Schayes graduated from NYU in 1948 as an honor student with a B.S. in aeronautical engineering. Following his graduation, Schayes was drafted by both the New York Knickerbockers (Knicks) of the Basketball Association of America (BAA) and the Tri-Cities Blackhawks of the National Basketball League (NBL). The rights to Schayes were obtained from the Blackhawks by the Syracuse Nationals (Nats), and because the Nats offered more money, Schayes signed with them. During his first year in the NBL in 1949 he was named Rookie of the Year after scoring 12.8 points per game. Schayes married Naomi Eva Gross in 1951. They had four children, one of whom (Danny) played professional basketball in the NBA.

The NBL folded in 1951, and the Nats moved to the newly named NBA, a product of the merger between the NBL and BAA. Playing the forward position, Schayes led his team in scoring with a 16.8 points per game average, as his team finished first in the league. The Nats, however, lost to the George Mikan–led Minneapolis Lakers in the NBA finals. During the following year, 1953–1954, Schayes led his team in scoring (17.1 points per game) and in rebounding (12.1 per game), but the Nats lost again to the Lakers in the finals. In the 1954–1955 season, the 24-second shot clock was introduced as Schayes continued to lead his team in scoring. In the NBA finals against the Fort Wayne Pistons, the Syracuse Nationals won their first championship game 92–91.

This was the last time that the Nats returned to the NBA finals, and the team became the Philadelphia 76ers in 1963. Nevertheless, between 1950 and 1961, Schayes remained one of the NBA's most dominant players. During these years, Schayes was named to the All-NBA First or Second Team every year and played in twelve consecutive All-Star games. He led the league in free throw shooting in 1958 (.904) and in 1962 (.897), and in rebounding in 1951 (16.4). Schayes was also a durable ballplayer, between 17 February 1952 and 26 December 1961 he played in a record 706 consecutive regular season games as well as in 103 playoff games. When he retired in 1964, Schayes was the NBA's all-time leading scorer (19,249 points), had played more games than anyone else thus far in NBA history (1,059), and was the NBA leader in free throws made (6,979) as well as free throw attempts (8,273). Schayes's lifetime NBA free throw percentage was .844 from the line. His lifetime scoring average was 18.2 points per game. He collected a career total of 11,256 rebounds and averaged 10.6 a game.

During the 1963–1964 season Schayes was the player-coach of the 76ers, playing in twenty-four games before becoming a full-time coach from 1964 to 1966. He was named the NBA Coach of the Year in 1966 when he led the 76ers to a 55–25 record, the best in the NBA. From 1966 to 1970 Schayes served as supervisor of NBA referees. He returned to coaching in 1970 for the Buffalo Braves, a new NBA franchise, but was dismissed after the opening game of his second season for not disciplining his players enough. Schayes's overall record as a professional coach was 151 wins and 172 losses.

In 1977 Schayes coached the U.S. Maccabiah team, with his son Danny playing, to an upset 92–91 victory over the Israeli team in the championship. Schayes was inducted into the Basketball Hall of Fame in 1973. He is also a member of the International Jewish Sports Hall of Fame, the New York Jewish Sports Hall of Fame, and the New York City Basketball Hall of Fame. Schayes and his wife live in Syracuse, New York.

Schayes was one of the great basketball players of his time. An excellent shooter and rebounder, Schayes was also an intelligent ballplayer and an athlete who always placed his team ahead of his own personal achievements.

There is no biography of Schayes, but several books about Jewish athletes include information about him, including Joseph Siegman, *Jewish Sports Legends: The International Jewish Hall of Fame* (1997); Robert Slater, *Great Jews in Sports* (1983); Peter Levine, *Ellis Island to Ebbets Field: Sport and the American Jewish Experience* (1992); and American Jewish Historical Society, ed., *American Jewish Desk Reference* (1999). The most important of the very few articles written about Schayes is William Simons, "Interview with Adolph Schayes," *American Jewish History* 74, no.3 (1985): 287–307. For further information see his profile at http://global.nba.com/.

JACK FISCHEL

SCHMIDT, Joseph Paul ("Joe") (*b.* 19 January 1932 in Pittsburgh, Pennsylvania), football player who was the first great middle linebacker in the National Football League (NFL) and the linchpin of the Detroit Lions defense that helped carry the team to several NFL championships in the 1950s.

Schmidt was one of two children of German immigrants Peter Schmidt, a brick mason who died when Schmidt was twelve, and Stella Bender Schmidt, a homemaker who went to work after her husband's death. Schmidt grew up in the Pittsburgh suburb of Brentwood when the Smokey City

Joe Schmidt, 1961. AP/WIDE WORLD PHOTOS

was a hotbed of collegiate football. His older brother played the game at Carnegie Tech (now Carnegie Mellon University). When he was about six years old, Schmidt remembers his brother's teammates visiting the Schmidt residence and "talking football." Schmidt was captivated by the sport, as were many young men in western Pennsylvania at the time. At age fourteen he played sandlot football against much older players, including battle-hardened veterans returning from World War II.

As a fullback at Brentwood High School, Schmidt earned an athletic scholarship to the University of Pittsburgh, where he enrolled in 1949 (he graduated in 1953 with a B.S. in education). Tough enough but not quite fast enough to continue playing fullback, Schmidt was converted to guard. Luckily for him it was the modern two-platoon era, when teams have 11 separate offensive players and 11 defensive players, and as a guard he was a linebacker on defense. His hard-nosed, intelligent approach to the game was quickly recognized by his coaches Len Casanova and Johnny Michelosen. However, injuries in each of his four seasons at Pittsburgh cut into his playing time. He broke two ribs as a freshman, broke his wrist and separated a shoulder as a sophomore, wrenched his knee as a junior, and tore knee cartilage and suffered a concussion as a senior. When he was on the field, though, Schmidt was the Panthers acknowledged leader.

He captained the team as a senior, and Schmidt's authoritarian leadership—coupled with his brilliant play—led to what was called "College Football's Upset of the Year" in 1952. On the train to South Bend, Indiana, to play Notre Dame, Schmidt challenged his teammates, "If you guys don't beat the Irish, I'll personally beat up each and every one of you." Schmidt, who was usually quiet and reserved, made his point. Pittsburgh played an inspired game and defeated Notre Dame 22–19. However, Schmidt did not put the onus entirely on his teammates, he personally sealed the upset victory with a sixty-yard interception return for the winning touchdown. Injuries cost him most postseason accolades, but he received All-America mention from the International News Service. Schmidt also was chosen to play in the Senior Bowl in January 1953. A Detroit Lions coach, Garrard ("Buster") Ramsey, scouted the Senior Bowl (a game that featured college seniors with professional potential) and was so impressed by Schmidt's stalwart play that the Lions drafted the stocky, blond Panther in the seventh round for the 1953 season. He signed a contract calling for $5,700 for the season.

Schmidt was joining a team that was defending NFL champion. He was not exactly welcomed with open arms by the veteran players—rookies seldom were. If he made the final roster, most likely he would be taking the place of a popular, established veteran. The roster limit in those days was just thirty-three men. Schmidt, who matured to six feet tall and 220 pounds, did make the team. In an era when teams did not have a middle linebacker, he played as an outside linebacker. The Lions repeated as NFL champions the year he joined the team. In 1954 the team switched to a 4–3 defense that featured a middle linebacker—Schmidt. It was akin to the defense he had played at Pittsburgh, and he adapted so well to the position that he was chosen to play in the Pro Bowl. He became a perennial Pro Bowl and All-Pro selection.

In 1957 Schmidt, who was by then the leader of the Lions defense, if not the team, issued another challenge to his teammates. The Lions and the San Francisco 49ers were tied for first place in the NFL's Western Division at the end of the regular season. In the playoff game San Francisco was ahead 24–7 at the half. During the intermission the Lions, through thin locker-room walls, could hear the 49ers celebrating what seemed to be a sure victory and a berth in the franchise's first NFL title game. Schmidt seethed in silence and right before the teams took the field for the second half said, "Listen to 'em. They're already spending their championship game checks. Let's do something about it." The Lions did. They roared back to win 31–27 in one of the NFL's biggest postseason comebacks ever. Almost to a man, the Lions credited Schmidt's leadership with pulling off the victory.

Schmidt married Marilyn Rotz on 29 December 1959; they had five children. Schmidt would appear in the Pro Bowl for nine consecutive years, from 1955 to 1963. He won All-Pro honors eight times during that period. In the late 1950s, television and much of the nation were awakening to the allure of professional football. Defensive players were gaining recognition previously reserved for quarterbacks, running backs, and receivers. In New York the Giants middle linebacker Sam Huff was the subject of a half-hour television special, "The Violent World of Sam Huff" (1961). Many thought Huff benefited greatly from being in the nation's media center and being overly touted by the powerful New York press. After watching the television special, one professional football observer said, "If they ever make 'The Violent World of Sam Huff' into a full-length feature film, they ought to have Joe Schmidt play the title role." The Minnesota Vikings center Mick Tingelhoff, who faced off with Schmidt twice a year, said, "He seemed to know exactly where the play was going—before it went." Vikings coach Norm Van Brocklin said, "If I were to start a team from scratch and pick out just one player, I'd select Joe Schmidt to form the core of my team." Coach George Allen, who faced Schmidt often as a Chicago Bears assistant coach, said, "He was a hard, ferocious—but clean—tackler. He played his position perfectly and called defensive signals brilliantly."

Schmidt, who was among the very best throughout his career, retired from play after the 1965 season. He had been team captain for nine seasons, had made twenty-four career interceptions, had been voted by his peers as NFL Defensive Player of the Year in 1960, and had recovered eight opponents' fumbles in his final season—still the second-best single-season mark in NFL history. At the behest of the Lions' owners, Schmidt stayed on as an assistant coach. In 1967, at age thirty-five, he became the Lions' head coach. Before retiring as coach in 1972, he compiled a 43–35–7 record—a .547 average that has not been matched by any of his successors. Upon his retirement he said simply, "It isn't fun anymore." Like many former Lions, Schmidt was involved in Detroit's auto industry as a manufacturer's sales representative. He resides with his family in suburban Bloomfield Hills, Michigan. Schmidt was elected to the Pro Football Hall of Fame in 1972, the same year he stepped down as Lions coach, and to the College Football Hall of Fame in 2001.

Professional football often is called a chess match played with 250-pound chessmen. Schmidt's contemporaries will vouch that no one strategized correctly more often or hit harder than Schmidt. He truly led the evolution of the middle linebacker to a glamour position.

★

There is no biography of Schmidt, but his life and career are discussed in Al Silverman, *The Specialist in Pro Football: Seventeen Top NFL Stars Tell How They Get Their Job Done* (1966); Jerry

Green, *Detroit Lions* (1973); Rick Korch, *The Truly Great: The 200 Best Pro Football Players of All Time* (1993); Stephen Majewski, *Great Linebackers: Football's Defensive Dynamos* (1997); and Bob Carroll and Joe Horrigan, *Football Legends of All Times* (1999).

JIM CAMPBELL

SCHMIDT, Michael Jack ("Mike") (*b.* 27 September 1949 in Dayton, Ohio), baseball's premier power hitter during the 1970s and 1980s and third baseman who won eight National League home run titles, ten Gold Glove awards, and selection to a dozen All-Star teams.

Schmidt is the son of Jack Schmidt, a restaurateur, and Lois Phillips, the proprietor of a swim club; he has one sibling, a sister. Sports became an integral part of Schmidt's life at age four, when his grandmother taught him how to hit a baseball. At age eight he was the starting third baseman on a neighborhood Little League team consisting mostly of twelve-year-olds. By his sophomore year at Fairview High School in Dayton, Ohio, Schmidt was the starting quarterback in football, a power forward on the basketball team, and a switch-hitting shortstop in baseball. While Jack Schmidt encouraged his son's love for sports, he was also sparing in his praise of Mike's athletic accomplishments. "My father has always been a very quiet man," said Schmidt. "I think he was proud of me and what I accomplished, but he always made it clear to me that I could do better."

Mike Schmidt, 1981. ASSOCIATED PRESS AP

Despite his early athletic success, Schmidt was not a "can't miss" prospect. High school football injuries to both of his knees prevented him from attracting much interest from either the minor leagues or a major Division I college program. Instead, upon his graduation from high school in June 1967, he decided to attend Ohio University, where he made the baseball squad as a walk-on. Through a grueling conditioning program designed to rehabilitate his knees and an exceptional on-the-field work ethic, Schmidt made himself into a two-time All-American shortstop, helping to lead the Bobcats to three straight Mid-American Conference championships and a fourth-place finish in the 1970 College World Series. The following year he graduated from Ohio with a B.A. degree in business administration.

Schmidt's play attracted major league scouts. The Philadelphia Phillies made him their second pick in the June 1971 draft and sent him to Double-A Reading, Pennsylvania. Schmidt, six feet, two inches and 190 pounds, struggled, batting .211 in 74 games with 8 home runs and 31 runs batted in (RBI). Nevertheless, in 1972 he was promoted to Eugene, Oregon, where he was named a Triple-A All-Star second baseman after hitting .291 with 26 home runs and 91 RBI in 131 games. Labeled a "late bloomer" by the scouts, Schmidt was converted to third base in the major leagues.

His rookie season with Philadelphia in 1973 was a nightmare. Schmidt's 18 home runs and 52 RBI were overshadowed by his .196 batting average and 136 strikeouts. The following season, however, he displayed the ability to become one of the most feared power hitters in the game, leading the major leagues with 36 homers, topping the National League with a .546 slugging percentage, and finishing second in the National League in RBI with 116. In the process Schmidt also raised his batting average 86 points to .282 and made the National League All-Star team as a write-in candidate. A brilliant career had taken off.

During the next three seasons Schmidt averaged 38 home runs and 100 RBI and hit around the .260 mark while winning his first two Gold Glove awards for fielding excellence at third base. His performance allowed the Phillies to clinch the National League's Eastern Division in 1976 and 1977, though the team eventually lost in the playoffs to stronger clubs from Cincinnati and Los Angeles, respectively. In February 1974 Schmidt married Donna Wightman; they had two children.

A succession of injuries led to a disappointing 1978 season for Schmidt. He hit just 21 home runs, drove in 78 runs, and batted .251. A perfectionist by nature, he became his own worst critic. The harder he pressed, the worse he performed. The "Boo-Birds," a vocal minority of Phillies fans, interpreted Schmidt's cool demeanor as "uncaring" and "egocentric." They wanted him to show his emotions and tried to provoke him with their jeers. On occasion Schmidt lashed back in the press, straining his relationships with both the media and the fans.

The adversity led him to join a growing Christian athlete movement in baseball. While he did not impose his religious beliefs on others, Schmidt let his faith speak for itself by sponsoring a host of charities, taking an active role in raising his own family, and embracing the responsibility of a role model for youngsters. Pete Rose's arrival in Philadelphia from Cincinnati in 1979 also had a positive influence on Schmidt's career. Rose's unparalleled enthusiasm and exceptional knowledge of the game inspired Schmidt to improve his own performance, and Rose's quick wit and magnetic personality took some of the media pressure off the younger third baseman. Schmidt learned to relax and to enjoy the game, especially in 1980 when the Phillies surprised the baseball world by capturing the first World Series championship in the history of the franchise.

Schmidt had a career year in 1980. He led the Phillies to the postseason games with his 48 home runs, 121 RBI, and .286 batting average, a performance that earned him the first of three Most Valuable Player (MVP) awards. He was even more impressive in the World Series against the Kansas City Royals, batting .381 and collecting 2 home runs and 7 RBI. His headfirst leap onto a pile of teammates after the final out of game six was a rare show of emotion for the normally serious-minded third baseman and is one of the most treasured images in Philadelphia sports history. At the end of the season the world champion Phillies rewarded Schmidt with a $10 million contract, making him the highest-paid player in the game at that time.

Schmidt improved his performance in 1981, collecting a .316 batting average with 31 home runs and 91 RBI in a season shortened by a strike. Though he fell short of the triple crown (leading the league in home runs, RBI, and batting average) by 9 RBI, he captured his second MVP award. Two years later he led the Phillies to the World Series again, only to lose to the Baltimore Orioles in five games. It was Schmidt's final postseason appearance.

The Phillies never finished higher than second during the next six years, but Schmidt gave the fans some memorable moments, including earning his third MVP award in 1986 and hitting his five hundredth home run in 1987. He also learned to joke about the city's negative media, surprising them with the memorable quip, "Philadelphia is the only place where you can experience the thrill of victory and the agony of reading about it the next day." On another occasion, after he criticized Phillies fans in the newspapers, Schmidt, in a psychological masterstroke, donned a long-haired wig and a pair of dark sunglasses and took the field incognito the next day. The fans, who had been waiting eagerly to boo him for his remarks, took to their feet and gave him a standing ovation instead.

When he retired on 29 May 1989, Schmidt did so with the same integrity that had come to characterize his seventeen-year major league career. He stated that he had always set high standards for himself and that he believed he could no longer play up to those standards, and admitted, "I could ask the Phillies to make me a part-time player in order to add to my statistical totals. However, my respect for the game, my teammates, and the fans won't allow me to do that." Fighting back tears, he continued: "I left Dayton, Ohio, with two very bad knees and a dream to become a major league baseball player. I thank God that the dream came true." Schmidt settled in Jupiter, Florida, where he became a golf pro. On 30 July 1995 he was inducted into the National Baseball Hall of Fame.

★

Schmidt wrote, with Barbara Walder, *Always on the Offense* (1982). His career is covered in William C. Kashatus, *Mike Schmidt: Philadelphia's Hall of Fame Third Baseman* (2000). See also Hal Bodley, *Philadelphia Phillies, World Champions 1980: The Team That Wouldn't Die* (1981).

WILLIAM C. KASHATUS

SCHMIDT, Milt(on) Conrad (*b.* 5 March 1918 in Kitchener, Ontario, Canada), hockey center and manager for the Boston Bruins who was elected to the Hockey Hall of Fame and won the Lester Patrick Trophy.

Schmidt, the youngest of six children, was born to Carl Schmidt, a leather worker, and Emma Schmidt, a homemaker. He began playing ice hockey almost as soon as he was able to walk. After attending King Edward Public School, he entered Kitchener Waterloo High School. It was young Schmidt's good fortune to meet the Montreal Canadiens' goalie George Hainsworth, who had grown up in Kitchener, at a school trophy presentation. Hainsworth gave Schmidt words of encouragement that remained with him throughout his lengthy career.

Schmidt and his boyhood pals Bobby Bauer and Woody Dumart originally gained recognition for their hockey skills on a local team known as the Greenshirts. In 1935 Bauer, the oldest, and Dumart were signed by the Boston Bruins and assigned to the Boston Cubs farm team. When Bauer and Dumart arrived at Boston Garden, they immediately made an appointment with the Bruins' general manager Art Ross and insisted that their center, Schmidt, was as good if not better than they were as professional prospects.

Milt Schmidt, 1950. AP/WIDE WORLD PHOTOS

Ross did not want a seventeen-year-old player and rebuffed the lads, but they persisted and the manager finally mailed a letter to Kitchener inviting Schmidt to the Bruins' training camp in autumn 1936. A week later, Ross received a letter from Schmidt, accepting the invitation and promising that he "would work all summer to save the money needed to report in Boston and would pay his train fare and board."

Schmidt made his National Hockey League (NHL) debut late in the 1936–1937 season, and even though he scored two goals, he nurtured doubts about his future. He mailed his first paycheck home to his mother with a note saying, "Better bank this for me, Mom; it may be the last I'll get." But once the Kitchener trio got the feel of big-league hockey, they provided a dominant forward line for the Bruins and became a hit with the fans. They were alternately known as the "Kraut Line," "Sauerkraut Line," and "Kitchener Kids." Schmidt won the Stanley Cup with the Bruins during the 1938–1939 season, and again during the 1940–1941 season.

The Krauts not only played together, traveled together, and relaxed together, they also presented a united front when it came to contract-signing time. "We felt if we went in together, asked for exactly the same salary for each, and took a stand in our dealings, we'd be better off," said Schmidt. So close were the Krauts that when Schmidt married Marie Peterson in 1946, Dumart and Bauer had to toss a coin to decide which one would be the best man. When Schmidt and his wife had a daughter in January 1948, he announced that Dumart and Bauer were both godfathers. Schmidt and his wife also had another child.

The trio's closeness was often reflected in their scoring statistics. During the 1939–1940 season, when the Bruins finished first, Schmidt led the league in scoring with fifty-two points while his linemates were tied for second with forty-three points apiece. It was Schmidt's fourth consecutive season finishing first with the Bruins. Not surprisingly, in early 1942, the Kraut Line enlisted as a unit in the Royal Canadian Air Force during World War II and played from time to time against other service teams. While stationed in England as a flying officer, Schmidt played hockey as often as possible and was as popular as ever.

After the fighting ended, it was feared that Schmidt, like so many other NHL stars returning from the war, might have lost his touch. But at age twenty-eight he regained his form, and in the 1946–1947 season he enjoyed the best productivity—27 goals, 35 assists, 62 points—of his entire career. Even Bauer's retirement in 1952 failed to put the brakes on Schmidt's performance, and in 1950–1951, still teaming with Dumart, he produced 22 goals and 39 assists for 61 points. It was enough to win him the 1951 Hart Trophy as the league's Most Valuable Player, and that year he was elected as First Team All-Star for the third time, having been previously elected in 1940 and 1947.

On 18 March 1952 the Bruins held a "Schmidt-Dumart Night" and talked Bauer out of retirement for one game. After elaborate pregame ceremonies, the Krauts got down to the business of winning a hockey game against the Chicago Blackhawks. Boston won the game 4–0, clinching a play-off berth in the process, and Bauer went back into retirement. Schmidt remained an active player until he was given the coaching reins of the then-struggling Boston hockey club on 25 December 1954. He stayed on through the 1965–1966 season, when Phil Watson was called in to take charge. Schmidt remained with the Bruins as general manager from 1967 until 1972 and enjoyed two Stanley

Cup triumphs in 1970 and 1972 with the help of trades he had engineered.

As the Bruins' manager, Schmidt's greatest accomplishment was a deal he made with the Chicago Blackhawks. He sent the Bruins' goalie Jack Norris, defenseman Gilles Marotte, and center Pit Martin to Chicago in return for the forwards Phil Esposito, Fred Stanfield, and Ken Hodge. In the view of some experts, it was the most one-sided deal in the NHL's annals and was directly responsible for Boston's cup victories in 1970 and 1972, along with the Schmidt-engineered drafting of the young blueliner Bobby Orr.

Schmidt left Boston in 1974 to become the first general manager of the new Washington (D.C.) Capitals franchise, but this move generated nothing but woe. The Caps, under Schmidt's administration, never became competitive, and he eventually left the club, returning to Boston to work for the Bruins in the ticket-selling department. He later ran the Boston Garden Club.

Inducted into the Hockey Hall of Fame in 1961, Schmidt was awarded the Lester Patrick Trophy in 1996 for contributions to U.S. hockey. Schmidt's hallmark as a player was his muted ruggedness. One longtime admirer called him "a gentleman's hockey player—until someone started pushing his teammates around." His adversaries swore by his creativity, endurance, and strength, but most of all by his soldierly fearlessness that somehow enabled him to accomplish more in the heat of battle than his contemporaries. Indeed, a case can be made that Schmidt was the greatest center in NHL history.

★

For further information on Schmidt see and Clark Booth, *Boston Bruins: Celebrating Seventy-five Years* (1998), and Stan Fischler, *Boston Bruins: Greatest Moments and Players* (1999). See also James Duplacey, Joseph Romain, Stan Fischler, Morgan Hughes, and Shirley Fischler, *Twentieth-Century Hockey Chronicle* (1999), and Dan Diamond, *Total Hockey: The Official Encyclopedia of the National Hockey League,* 2d ed. (2000).

STAN FISCHLER

SCHOLLANDER, Don(ald) Arthur (*b.* 30 April 1946 in Charlotte, North Carolina), U.S. Olympic swimming champion who was the first swimmer to win four gold medals in a single Olympics.

Schollander was the son of Wendell Leslie Schollander, a former all-state high school football player and an insurance company executive, and Martha Perry Schollander, an outstanding swimmer who appeared in a number of the *Tarzan* films with Johnny Weissmuller. Schollander's brother, Wendell Leslie, Jr., was an all-state football player in football and later played for the University of Pennsylvania team. While still quite young, Schollander moved with his family to Lake Oswego, Oregon, a suburb of Portland.

Don Schollander displays the four gold medals he won in the 1964 Olympic games. AP/WIDE WORLD PHOTOS

Schollander learned the basics of swimming as a child at Portland's Aero Club. By the age of ten, he set a national record in his age group for swimming the backstroke. High school presented the young athlete with a critical choice—to try out for the football or the swim team. Don's father suggested that his son try swimming, where he might have an opportunity to achieve quicker success. As a freshman, Don made the varsity, swimming against boys four years his senior. That first year, he won two events at the Oregon state finals, and by his sophomore year, he was beating all comers.

When Schollander and his family realized that he probably had progressed as far as he could as a swimmer in the local high school program, he left Lake Oswego at age 15 and moved to Santa Clara, California. There he joined the famed Santa Clara Swim Club, coached by George Haines. During his years in Santa Clara, he lived with local families and attended Santa Clara High School, graduating in June

1964. When training Schollander for the 1964 Olympic Trials, Haines expressed confidence that he could win any freestyle event for which he trained. Although the swimmer was particularly strong in the middle distances, Haines feared that it would be foolhardy to prepare Schollander for both the 100-meter sprint and the 1,500-meter race at the same time. He chose to focus Schollander's training on the 100-meter event, for which he felt Don had an almost perfect stroke, and Haines felt confident this good stroking would pay off in any come-from-behind challenge. The coach's strategy paid off. At the 1964 Olympics in Tokyo, Schollander handily won both the 100-meter freestyle, setting a new Olympic record, and the 400-meter freestyle, establishing a new world mark. In addition to his two gold medals for these personal events, Schollander took gold as a member of the winning U.S. relay teams in the 4 × 100-meter and 4 × 200-meter freestyle races.

Schollander's first event at the Tokyo Olympics was the 100-meter freestyle. The world record in the event was held by Alain Gottvalies of France, but he did not feature in the medals race. Schollander's main competition in the 100-meter race was Bobby McGregor of Scotland, whom he beat out by only one-tenth of a second, finishing in 53.4 seconds, a new Olympic mark. Next up for Schollander was the 400-meter freestyle, an event dominated in the two previous Olympics by Murray Rose of Australia. Swimming for Australia in 1964 were Alan Wood and Russell Phegan, but neither man could compete against the strength of Schollander, who took the gold medal with a new world record of 4 minutes, 12.2 seconds. In the 4 × 100-meter and 4 × 200-meter freestyle relays, Schollander anchored the U.S. teams to victory, setting a new world record in both events. When it was all over, Schollander had duplicated the feat of Jesse Owens at the memorable Olympics of 1936, winning four gold medals in four events.

As the first swimmer ever to win four gold medals in a single Olympics, Schollander was widely honored back in the United States. The Amateur Athletic Union (AAU) awarded him its James E. Sullivan Memorial Award for 1964. The Sullivan Trophy, which made its debut in 1930, is awarded annually to the athlete who "by his or her performance, example, and influence as an amateur, has done the most during the year to advance the cause of sportsmanship." The trophy is named for a former president of the AAU.

In 1965 Schollander was inducted into the International Swimming Hall of Fame as an Honor Swimmer. The program for the induction ceremony contained this tribute: "Nineteen-year-old Don Schollander is the world's most honored active swimmer. No swimmer in any year has received the honor that came to Schollander in 1964." Schollander in 1964 was selected as the top athlete at the Olympic Games and honored as both the U.S. and World Athlete of the Year.

After his victories in Tokyo, Schollander returned to the United States and enrolled at Yale University, where he also competed as a swimmer. Schollander graduated from Yale in 1968. At the 1968 Olympics in Mexico City he duplicated his winning ways in the 4 × 200-meter freestyle relays, taking the gold, and won a silver medal in the 200-meter freestyle race.

Shortly after his return from Mexico City, Schollander retired from competitive swimming. Deeply disillusioned by the new direction that he felt the Olympic movement was taking, the swimmer spoke out against the growing hypocrisy he saw in sports. In his autobiography Schollander offered this assessment of the state of sports and, more specifically, the Olympic movement: "The fault lies with nearly everyone—officials, national leaders, the athletes themselves who, too often, are concerned only with winning." In his view, a true sportsman plays for love of the game and not solely to win and that preoccupation with winning at any cost somehow perverts the goal of sporting events. In addition to winning five gold medals and one silver medal at the Olympics of 1964 and 1968, Schollander broke twenty-two world records and thirty-seven U.S. records during the course of his swimming career. Schollander was inducted into the U.S. Olympic Hall of Fame in 1983.

A true American hero, Schollander once offered these observations about how champions are defined by their ability to confront and conquer their pain in competition: "You learn pain in every practice, and you will know it in every race. As you approach the limit of your endurance, it begins coming on gradually, hitting your stomach first. Then your arms grow heavy and your legs tighten—thighs first, then the knees. You sink lower in the water as though someone was pushing down on your back. You experience perception changes. The sounds of the pool blend together and become a crashing roar in your ears. The water takes on a pinkish tinge. Your stomach feels as though it's going to fall out—every kick hurts like heck—and suddenly you hear a shrill internal scream. . . . It is right here, at the pain barrier, that the great competitors are separated from the rest."

★

Schollander provides an excellent profile of his early life and his Olympic victories in his autobiography, *Deep Water* (1971), written with Duke Savage. For a basic step-by-step guide to competitive swimming techniques from the Olympic champion himself, read Schollander, *Inside Swimming* (1974), in which he covers the various strokes as well as tips on water safety, training, and strategy. Other books that cover the accomplishments of U.S. swimmers in Olympic competition include Kelly A. Gonsalves, *First to the Wall: 100 Years of Olympic Swimming* (1999), and

P. H. Mullen, Jr., *Gold in the Water: The Extraordinary Pursuit of Olympic Glory* (2001).

DON AMERMAN

SCULLY, Vin(cent) Edward (*b.* 29 November 1927 in New York City), literate baseball announcer who, in more than fifty years with the Brooklyn and Los Angeles Dodgers, used evocative descriptions and an eye for detail to establish himself as perhaps the most outstanding and influential broadcaster in the game's history.

The son of Irish immigrants, Scully grew up in the Washington Heights area of northern Manhattan, just across the Harlem River from the Bronx. His family was poor but not destitute. Scully's father, Vincent Aloysius, was a traveling silk salesman who died when Scully was five. The boy was raised by his mother, Bridget Freehill, and her second husband, a man Scully liked. Scully frequently attended baseball games at the nearby Polo Grounds, and by the time the redhead was eight, he had formally declared his intention to become a sports broadcaster. He attended Fordham Prep School, graduating in 1945, and entered Fordham University on a partial scholarship that autumn. He earned spending money during his summers by delivering mail and milk, and by polishing silverware in the kitchen of an upscale hotel.

After his freshman year at Fordham, Scully joined the U.S. Navy, in which he served a year before returning to the Bronx campus. Scully was active on campus, where his activities included singing in a barbershop quartet, writing a sports column in the school newspaper, and covering Fordham football games for the *New York Times.* He also played center field on Fordham's baseball team. After graduating in 1949, Scully found work as a broadcaster with WTOP, a CBS affiliate in Washington, D.C. He was soon introduced to Red Barber, the famed Brooklyn Dodgers broadcaster and the sports director at CBS, who agreed to give Scully a tryout broadcasting a college football game. Barber was impressed by Scully's performance, and in 1950 he offered the twenty-two-year-old a $5,000 salary to join the Dodgers as an assistant broadcaster. Barber, known as the "Ol' Redhead," quickly took the young redhead under his wing. "Red was my teacher . . . and my father," Scully recalled. "I don't know—I might have been the son he never had. It wasn't so much that he taught me how to broadcast. It was an attitude. Get to the park early. Do your homework. Be prepared. Be accurate. He was a stickler for that."

Vin Scully *(left)* receiving an award for sports broadcasting, 1960. AP/ WIDE WORLD PHOTOS

The new position afforded Scully the opportunity to witness baseball's integration drama firsthand, as Brooklyn won four pennants during the 1950s behind the base-running exploits of Jackie Robinson. In 1955 Scully broadcast the clinching game in Brooklyn's only World Series triumph, a moment he always spoke of as his most cherished. In 1957 Barber, Scully's mentor, left for the New York Yankees, leaving the twenty-nine-year-old Scully as the Dodgers' head broadcaster. By then Scully had blended Barber's folksy style with his own talent for detailed description, creating the unique broadcasting style for which he became famous. The most intellectual of baseball announcers, Scully's broadcasts were marked by frequent literary references, as he aptly applied the words of William Shakespeare, Cole Porter, and Eugene O'Neill to explain different aspects of baseball. ("A humble thing, but thine own," he would say of a weak infield hit.)

Scully accompanied the Dodgers in 1958 when they left Brooklyn for Los Angeles. The team spent its first four seasons there playing in the Los Angeles Coliseum, a colossal football stadium ill-suited for baseball, which left many of its 90,000 occupants straining to see the distant action. To remedy this, fans soon began bringing transistor radios to games, and Scully's vivid descriptions of the action made him a cult figure of sorts. Even after the team moved into the more intimate Dodger Stadium in 1962, the practice of bringing radios to the ballpark continued, and it later spread to other major league stadiums. The Dodgers, meanwhile, won three pennants in the mid-1960s, with Scully artfully describing the exploits of Sandy Koufax, Don Drysdale, and Maury Wills. The most famous broadcast of his career came on 9 September 1965, when Koufax pitched a perfect game against the Chicago Cubs. "There are 29,000 people in the ballpark, and a million butterflies," Scully announced as the ninth inning began. "I would think that the mound at Dodger Stadium right now is the loneliest place in the world." Scully's work during that game was considered by many to be the best radio broadcast in baseball history.

By 1969 Scully was so popular that some mentioned him as a possible candidate to succeed the embattled William Eckert as the baseball commissioner. That never happened, but Scully's increasing fame enabled him to dabble in other areas of television broadcasting while simultaneously working for the Dodgers. He hosted the NBC game show *It Takes Two* (1969–1970), and the CBS variety program *The Vin Scully Show* (1973), which lasted only thirteen weeks. He also broadcast occasional football, golf, and tennis events on CBS from 1975 to 1982. In 1983 he left CBS to become the top baseball announcer for NBC, where for seven years he broadcast showcase events like the World Series and the All-Star game to a national audience.

In the 1980s and 1990s, as the baseball broadcasting industry changed to cater to viewers' shortening attention spans, Scully refused to budge. While most broadcasts featured teams of two or three announcers, Scully usually insisted on working alone, arguing that it made for better communication with the audience. "My approach to broadcasting has always been like I'm talking to a friend," he said. And although he was a loyal company man off the field, while on the air Scully steadfastly refrained from the home-team rooting engaged in by most broadcasters. "The fan is seeing things with his heart," he said, "but my responsibility is to see things with my eyes." In 2001 Scully broadcast his fifty-second season of Dodgers baseball and earned a reported $2 million annual salary.

Scully married Joan Crawford, a model, in 1958. They had three children before she died on 26 January 1972, at age thirty-five, from an apparently accidental overdose of prescription medication. The next year Scully married Sandra Schaefer, a secretary with the Los Angeles Rams, with whom he had one daughter and two stepchildren. Although he frequently complained of the loneliness of baseball road trips, Scully enjoyed filling his off-seasons with exotic vacations, including trips to Europe, China, Australia, and Egypt.

Scully received virtually every award presented to sportscasters. The most prestigious came in 1982, when he was given the Ford C. Frick Award, a lifetime achievement award for broadcasters presented annually by the Baseball Hall of Fame. Scully's other honors included four citations as the National Sportscaster of the Year, a Peabody Award, an Emmy Award for lifetime achievement, and an honorary doctoral degree from Fordham, where he delivered the commencement address in 2000. He won the California Sportscaster of the Year Award twenty-one times. In 1982 Scully earned the ultimate sign of acceptance in Los Angeles, a star on the Hollywood Walk of Fame.

Scully's fifty-two years with the Dodgers have established the longest term of service by any announcer with one team. Through 2001 Scully had broadcast twenty-five World Series, including twelve on network television, and twelve All-Star games. He also had called nineteen no-hitters, believed to be a record. On 3 and 4 June 1989 he set a record of another sort. To fulfill his dual duties with the Dodgers and NBC, Scully broadcast three extra-inning games, a total of forty-five innings, in a span of just twenty-seven hours. In addition, he was behind the microphone for many of the most significant moments in baseball history, including the first major league game played on the West Coast on 15 April 1958, Hank Aaron's record-breaking 715th home run in 1974, Bill Buckner's infamous error in the 1986 World Series, Kirk Gibson's dramatic World Series homer in 1988, and Barry Bonds's record-breaking 71st home run in 2001.

Scully's name has been revered by sportscasters nationwide, many of whom have imitated his style of broadcasting. Millions of baseball fans, although they have never met him, think of him as a treasured friend. In his half-century in baseball he has reported on many significant changes in the game, including the designated hitter, free agency, and corporate ownership, all while maintaining an impeccable sense of balance and perspective. His dual talents for observation and oratory, and his respect for his audience's intelligence, have won him nearly universal acclaim as the greatest broadcaster in baseball history.

★

The archives of the National Baseball Hall of Fame Library in Cooperstown, New York, contain an impressive collection of news clippings about Scully's career. Significant articles appear in *TV Guide* (28 Feb. 1970), *LA Weekly* (7 Aug. 1992), the *Newark Star-Ledger* (27 July 1995), and *Inside Sports* (Apr. 1998). In addition, the media guide published annually by the Los Angeles Dodgers contains a wealth of factual information.

ERIC ENDERS

SEAVER, George Thomas ("Tom") (*b.* 17 November 1944 in Fresno, California), one of the greatest pitchers in baseball history and the star of the 1969 world champion "Miracle Mets."

Seaver was the son of Charles H. Seaver, a Walker Cup golfer, and Betty Lee Cline Seaver. After graduating from high school, Seaver entered Fresno City College in 1964.

Tom Seaver, 1977. ASSOCIATED PRESS AP

In 1965 he left Fresno to attend the University of Southern California (USC). Seaver married Nancy Lynn McIntyre on 9 June 1966; they have two children.

The Braves offered Seaver $40,000 in 1966 to sign, but the National Collegiate Athletic Association (NCAA) and the baseball commissioner William Eckert voided the offer because the USC baseball season had begun. Instead, Eckert created a lottery for any team interested in Seaver who would match the Braves offer. The Phillies, Indians, and Mets submitted bids, and the commissioner picked the Mets out of a hat. Seaver became the ace of the Mets pitching staff from the very beginning. A hard-throwing right-hander, he won sixteen games for a hapless team that won only sixty-one games in 1967; he was selected as a National League (NL) All-Star and Rookie of the Year. Seaver would be an All-Star selection eleven times in his twenty-year career.

In 1969, the first year of division play, Seaver, nicknamed "Tom Terrific," led the Mets to the National League East title with the first of his Cy Young Award–winning seasons. He had a league-best 25–7 record, 208 strikeouts, and an earned run average (ERA) of 2.21. On 9 July Seaver barely missed tossing a perfect game against the Chicago Cubs, when Jimmy Qualls singled with one out in the ninth inning. The Mets won the game 4–0, however, and began to close in on the Cubs for the division lead. Seaver struggled in the first game of the NL championship series against the Atlanta Braves but was the winning pitcher when the Mets rallied for five runs after another player pinch-hit for Seaver in the eighth inning. In game one of the World Series, won by the Mets in five games against the favored Baltimore Orioles, Seaver surrendered a home run to the first batter he faced, Don Buford, and lost a 4–1 decision. Seaver rebounded with a great performance in game four, winning by 2–1 in ten innings.

Seaver continued his dominance in 1970. On 22 April 22 he struck out nineteen players in a game against the San Diego Padres, including a record ten in a row to end the game, and tied Steve Carlton's major league record for strikeouts in a game. Seaver finished the season with an 18–12 record and led the NL with 283 strikeouts and a 2.82 ERA. The year 1971 was even better, as Seaver finished 20–10 and led the league with 289 strikeouts and a 1.76 ERA. Seaver won twenty-one games in 1972 and then, in 1973, became the first pitcher to win the Cy Young Award with fewer than twenty wins. While leading the Mets to another division title, he went 19–10 with a league-best 251 strikeouts and a 2.08 ERA. In the first game of the NL championship series against the Cincinnati Reds, Seaver pitched brilliantly and drove in the Mets only run, but lost 2–1 when he gave up a home run to Pete Rose in the eighth inning and to Johnny Bench in the ninth. Seaver came back to win the deciding fifth game with a score of 7–2, sending the Mets to their second World Series. He pitched well against the defending world champion Oakland A's, but with little run support from his light-hitting team, he got a "no decision" in the Mets eleven-inning 3–2 loss in game three. He took the loss in game six after allowing two runs in seven innings.

Plagued by a sore hip for much of the season, Seaver struggled to an 11–11 record in 1974. He rebounded in 1975 with his last Cy Young Award season—highlighted by a NL-best 22 wins and 243 strikeouts. Over the next season, however, Seaver and the Mets general manager M. Donald Grant began to feud over Seaver's salary and the direction of the floundering team. On 15 June 1977 in the so-called "Midnight Massacre," Grant sent "the Franchise," as Seaver was dubbed, to the Reds for four players: pitcher Pat Zachary, infielder Doug Flynn, and outfielders Steve Henderson and Dan Norman. Mets fans were furious, and the team languished for years after the trade. Seaver, meanwhile, finished the 1977 season with a combined 21–6 record and led the league with seven shutouts. On 16 June 1978, a year after the trade from the Mets, Seaver pitched a no-hitter for the Reds after many near misses throughout his career, beating the Cardinals 4–0.

Seaver had four straight winning seasons with Cincinnati. In 1979 he led the Reds to the Western Division title with a 16–6 record and a league-best five shutouts. In game one of the NL championship series against the Pittsburgh Pirates, Seaver battled for eight innings against the Pirates' John Candelaria and left after eight innings with the game tied 2–2. The Pirates went on to win in the eleventh inning in what proved to be Seaver's last postseason appearance. After a mediocre 1980 season, Seaver went 14–2 in the strike-shortened 1981 season, leading the major league in victories, but he was narrowly edged out for the Cy Young Award by the Dodgers rookie sensation Fernando Valenzuela.

After a career-worst 1982 season in which he compiled a 5–13 record and 5.50 ERA, the Reds traded Seaver back to the Mets for three players. Seaver pitched reasonably well for the Mets in 1983, but poor run support led to a 9–14 record. After the season, however, the Mets angered their fans (and Seaver) once again when Seaver was left unprotected in the free-agent pool and was claimed by the Chicago White Sox. Seaver used his experience to compensate for a slower fastball and won thirty-one games for the White Sox over the next two years. On 4 August 1984 at Yankee Stadium in New York, Seaver won his 300th career game with a 4–1, six-hit complete game victory over the Yankees. Later that year Seaver passed Walter Johnson and took third place on the all-time strikeout list.

After a weak start in 1986, Seaver agreed to be traded to the Boston Red Sox, who needed another starter to help them stay ahead of the Yankees in their division. Unfortunately, Seaver suffered an ankle injury that kept him from playing against the Mets in the World Series. After the season, Seaver was released by Boston and signed a contract to pitch for the Mets for the third time. But at age forty-two, after a short time at the Mets training camp, Seaver said, "There are no pitches left in this arm," and retired to his home in Greenwich, Connecticut. He had won a career total of 311 games.

After his retirement Seaver remained active in the baseball world. In 1988 he began working as a broadcaster for the New York Yankees and on television with the National Broadcasting Company (NBC). Seaver became a color commentator for the New York Mets in 1999. In 1992 he was elected to the National Baseball Hall of Fame in his first year of eligibility with 98.84 percent of the vote—the highest percentage ever.

★

Seaver wrote *The Art of Pitching* (1984) with Lee Lowenfish. For details of his life and career, see Joel H. Cohen, *Inside Corner: Talks with Tom Seaver* (1974), and Marshall Burchard and S. H. Burchard, *Sports Star: Tom Seaver* (1974).

RICHARD L. DAVIDMAN

SELMON, Lee Roy (*b.* 20 October 1954 in Eufaula, Oklahoma), professional football player who was elected to the Pro Football Hall of Fame in 1995.

Selmon was the youngest of nine children born to Lucious and Jessie Selmon. His father was a farmer who worked a forty-acre plot ten miles south of Eufaula, and his mother was a homemaker. Selmon grew up on the farm and went to grade school in Eufaula. In 1967, when he was in the eighth grade, Selmon tried out for the junior-high football team and, with his advanced size and weight, easily made the team. Selmon's brother Dewey, who was eleven months older and in the same grade, joined his brother on the team.

When the two brothers reached the ninth grade, they both stood over six feet tall and weighed 230 pounds. On offense, the brothers were running backs because their size made it difficult for opposing teams to tackle them, and on defense they played linebacker. In his senior year Selmon averaged sixteen yards per carry for the Eufaula Ironheads. The brothers also excelled academically and were selected for membership in the National Honor Society in 1971, the year they graduated from high school.

The Selmon brothers were recruited by the University of Oklahoma in Norman to play football. Convincing them to play at Oklahoma was not difficult because their older brother Lucious was a member of the Sooners' offensive squad. In the fall of 1971, when Selmon entered the university as a special education major, he was six feet, two inches tall and weighed 256 pounds. He fulfilled the requirements for defensive tackle, while Dewey played middle guard.

In 1974 Selmon's outstanding defensive play, which included eighteen tackles for lost yardage, landed him an All-America team selection and led to a national championship win for the Sooners. The following year the Sooners repeated their accomplishment as national champions, and Selmon was again honored with an All-America selection, as was his brother Dewey. Honors for Selmon's senior season continued when he was awarded the Outland and Lombardi Trophies for outstanding play as a lineman. In his senior year Selmon posted 132 tackles, the most for his college career; he finished college play with a career total of 324 tackles.

Selmon's accomplishments on the field were well known, but he also excelled in the classroom. In 1975, his senior year at the University of Oklahoma, he was named as an Academic All-American, an honor also achieved by Dewey. He earned a B.A. degree in special education upon graduation in 1975.

It was no surprise that Selmon was the first college player selected in the 1976 draft by the Tampa Bay Buccaneers, a new National Football League (NFL) team in

Lee Roy Selmon accepting the Vince Lombardi Award for 1975. AP/WIDE WORLD PHOTOS

Florida. The Buccaneers also drafted Dewey, and the brothers played together on the team through 1980. Selmon played defensive end and Dewey played middle guard. Selmon displayed outstanding quickness for his size and defended the pass or run equally well. He consistently led his team in the number of sacks per season. Unfortunately, the Buccaneers lost all of their games in the team's inaugural season, and at the end of the season Selmon injured his leg. Before the start of the 1977 season he married Claybra Fields on 18 June 1977; the couple later had three children.

The Buccaneers' first franchise win came on 11 December 1977, when they defeated the New Orleans Saints. In that game Selmon recovered a fumble and posted twelve tackles, including three quarterback sacks. He finished the season with nineteen sacks, which earned him All-Conference honors. The 1978 season was a carbon copy for the Buccaneers and for Selmon. The Buccaneers won few games, but Selmon's performance again earned him All-Conference honors.

In 1979 Selmon and the Buccaneers had a breakthrough season. Selmon started the season by scoring his first defensive touchdown off a fumble recovery. The Buccaneers won ten games and entered the National Football Conference (NFC) divisional play-offs, but lost the championship game to the Los Angeles Raiders. Selmon posted 117 tackles and eleven sacks for the season, which earned him All-Pro honors, an honor he was granted every year through 1984. The Associated Press named him the NFL Defensive Player of the Year, and the *Sporting News* recognized him as the NFL Defensive Most Valuable Player for 1979.

In the 1980–1981 season the Buccaneers won only five games, but Selmon excelled on the field by leading the team in number of sacks. In 1980 he was voted by the NFL Players Association as both the NFC and NFL Defensive Lineman of the Year. He was the NFC Defensive Lineman of the Year again in 1981, and his performance on the field led the Buccaneers to the NFC divisional play-offs, where they were defeated by the Dallas Cowboys. From 1982 to 1985 Selmon spent the remainder of his professional playing years with the Buccaneers. A back injury forced him to miss the entire 1985 season, and he retired from the sport at the close of the season. In 1988 he was inducted into the College Football Hall of Fame, and in 1995 he was elected to the Pro Football Hall of Fame.

Selmon was prepared for retirement. During the off-season months, beginning in 1978, he had worked for the First National Bank of Miami as a marketing, promotion, and commercial credit executive. After his 1985 retirement from playing football he chaired the United Negro College Fund Sports Committee and supported the charitable efforts of the Ronald McDonald House and Special Olympics. In 1993 he accepted a position as the associate athletic director at the University of South Florida in Tampa, where he oversaw the department's marketing and corporate partnerships. In March 2001 he was named the director of intercollegiate athletics at the university.

Selmon, known as a premier defensive end for the Tampa Bay Buccaneers, was a feared opponent because of his quickness. He ended his professional career with a total of 78.5 sacks, 380 quarterback pressures, 28.5 forced fumbles, and 10 fumble recoveries. His unfortunate 1985 back injury brought a premature close to a professional career that no doubt would have brought more team victories to the Buccaneers as well as recognition to Selmon.

★

Don Pierson, *Lee Roy Selmon: The Giant from Oklahoma* (1982), covers Selmon's collegiate and professional career through 1982. Selmon's statistics as a player at the University of Oklahoma are in Cedric Jones and Jerald Moore, *1995 Oklahoma University Football Media Guide* (1995). Selmon's statistics as a Tampa Bay Buccaneer are in Matthew Silverman, ed., *Total Football II: The Official Encyclopedia of the NFL* (1999). An article in *JET* (11 June 2001) discusses Selmon's appointment as the athletic director at the University of South Florida.

JON E. TAYLOR

SHOEMAKER, William Lee ("Bill") (*b.* 19 August 1931 in Fabens, Texas), revered jockey who ranked as one of the all-time leaders in career victories, stakes victories, and purse earnings and who later became a trainer and novelist.

Shoemaker was one of two sons born to Bebe Shoemaker, a cotton mill worker, and Ruby Harris, a homemaker. He weighed only two and one-half pounds at birth and would not have survived without his grandmother's assistance. "She picked me off the bed, wrapped me up warm, turned the oven on low and put me on the stove door to keep me warm."

At age seven, following his parents' divorce, Shoemaker began living with his grandparents on a cattle and sheep ranch near Abilene, Texas. There he rode his grandfather's horse to get the daily mail. At age ten he moved to the San Gabriel Valley in California to live with his father and stepmother. Weighing only eighty pounds, he failed to make the football and basketball teams at El Monte Union High School. However, he made the wrestling team, competing in the 95- to 105-pound division and finishing undefeated. He also won a Golden Gloves boxing championship.

Shoemaker left school at age sixteen without his father's knowledge. Instead of studying, he began his first regular job with horses, cleaning out stalls at the Suzy Q Ranch in Puente, California. After a short time he advanced to breaking yearlings and exercising horses. Later, Shoemaker said of this time, "I knew I had found my niche in life." He earned $75 per month plus room and board.

The trainer George Reeves saw potential in the seventeen-year-old Shoemaker and signed him to an apprentice contract. Shoemaker rode his first race, finishing fifth, on 19 March 1949 at Golden Gate Fields in Albany, California, aboard the filly Waxahachie. On 20 April 1949 in only his third race, the four-foot, eleven-inch, 100-pound Shoemaker captured his first triumph aboard Shafter V. He won

Bill Shoemaker, 1985. ASSOCIATED PRESS

219 races that year and finished second to Gordon Glison in the jockey standings nationally. In 1950 Shoemaker battled the eastern rider Joe Culmone throughout the year for leading jockey honors. As the year came to a close, the two jockeys were tied. Shoemaker traveled to Caliente, Mexico, while Culmone rode in Cuba. Each won three races to tie with 388 wins, equaling a record set by Walter Miller in 1906. Shoemaker's mounts earned him $844,040 in 1950, making him second in the monies-won category, trailing Eddie Arcaro. During this year (1950) he married Ginny. They adopted two children and divorced in 1960.

The next year Shoemaker topped the nation's other jockeys in purse money with $1,329,890. He did not win that title in 1952 but regained it in 1953 and 1954, during which time Shoemaker was the best in total wins and winning percentage. In 1953 he rode a 29 percent winning mark. In 1954 he had a 30 percent victory record. In 1955 Shoemaker won his first Kentucky Derby by piloting Swaps to a one-and-a-half-length victory over the favored Nashua.

In 1956 Shoemaker became the first jockey to exceed the $2 million mark in purse money, but still was beaten that year by Bill Hartack for monies-won honors.

Shoemaker suffered his most humiliating defeat in the 1957 Kentucky Derby. As an apparent sure winner with Gallant Man, he mistook the sixteenth pole for the finish, stood up in the saddle, and allowed Iron Liege to win. The following month Shoemaker captured his first Belmont Stakes with Gallant Man. Shoemaker outpaced all other jockeys in monies won from 1958 through 1964 and led the nation's riders in victories in 1958 and 1959. In 1959 he won his second Kentucky Derby with Tomy Lee and the Belmont on Sword Dancer. Although his career was not yet half over, he was inducted into the National Thoroughbred Racing Hall of Fame in 1958 and the Jockey's Hall of Fame at Pimlico, near Baltimore, in 1959. In 1961 Shoemaker married his second wife, Babbs. He adopted her young son. The couple divorced in 1978, and Shoemaker later married Cindy Barnes, with whom he had a daughter. Shoemaker and Barnes divorced in 1994.

After winning the Belmont Stakes in 1962 aboard Jaipur, Shoemaker took the Preakness in 1963 on Candy Spots. In 1965 he piloted Lucky Debonair to victory in the Kentucky Derby. Two years later he took both the Preakness and Belmont Stakes aboard Damascus. Although sidelined for short periods several times, Shoemaker did not suffer serious injury until he broke a leg in a fall in January 1968 at Santa Anita in California and was sidelined for thirteen months. Only three months after returning to racing, he sustained a fractured pelvis and ruptured bladder in a paddock accident. On 5 September 1970, at age thirty-nine, Shoemaker equaled Johnny Longden's all-time winning record with 6,032 victories. Two days later aboard the filly Dares J. he broke the record. Longden took nearly forty years to set the record; Shoemaker broke it in his twenty-second season with 7,000 fewer mounts. In 1972 Shoemaker overtook the racing legend Arcaro's record of 554 stakes victories. In 1975 he won the Belmont Stakes riding Avatar.

On 3 March 1985 Shoemaker became the first jockey in history to earn more than $100 million in purses when he rode Lord at War to victory in the $500,000 Santa Anita Handicap. It was his 8,446th career victory and his 917th stakes triumph. In 1986 the fifty-four-year-old Shoemaker became the oldest jockey to ride a Kentucky Derby winner when he guided Ferdinand to victory in a 2:02.4 clocking. On 3 February 1990 Shoemaker rode Patchy Groundfog at Santa Anita in a $100,000 stakes that was run only once. Billed as the "Legend's Last Ride," the race marked Shoemaker's official retirement; the oldest rider and the oldest horse in the race lost by slightly more than a length and came in fourth. Shoemaker retired with a record 8,833 wins, a winning record of 22 percent, and $123 million in purses. His wins included ten Santa Anita Handicaps, eight Hollywood Gold Cups, five Belmonts and Woodwards, and four Kentucky Derbys.

Upon his retirement from riding, Shoemaker said he would work some of the horses he trained, but that he definitely had scaled a horse in the afternoon for the last time. He compared training to riding by saying, "When you're a trainer, you're stuck with a horse. When you're riding, you get off a bad horse." Shoemaker saddled his first winner as a trainer on 8 April 1990. Just over one year later Shoemaker's Ford Bronco tumbled down a steep embankment in San Dimas, California, leaving him a quadriplegic. After extensive physical therapy, he returned to training for several years before retiring in 1997 to his longtime home in San Marino, California. In 1990 and 1991 Shoemaker's horses won forty-six races and earned $2.4 million. His purse totals dropped after that, but his career total is 158 wins with purses of more than $7 million. In the mid-1990s he began appearing at fund-raisers for spinal cord research and launched a writing career. He published three mystery novels, *Stalking Horse* (1994), *Fire Horse* (1995), and *Dark Horse: A Coley Killebrew Novel* (1996).

Shoemaker's brilliant run as a jockey spanned more than four decades, beginning with his first win at Golden Gate in 1949 to his Kentucky Derby victory in 1986 through to his retirement in 1990. He personified grace under pressure, with the uncanny ability to extract every ounce of talent from his mounts. Even Shoemaker's rivals acknowledged his skills. Arcaro said, "Regardless of the particular sport, Bill Shoemaker by his accomplishments must be considered one of the outstanding athletes in the history of sports. I doubt we'll ever see another race rider having his special combination of talent. He has it all and has done it all." Longden said, "Both on and off the race track he's the greatest . . . a great rider and a great gentleman."

★

The best sources on Shoemaker's life and career are his autobiography, written with Barney Nagler, *Shoemaker* (1988), and the biography by Louis Phillips, *Willie Shoemaker,* ed. by Michael E. Goodman (1988). Additional information is available in "How Can Anybody Win 7,000 races?" *Blood Horse* (8 Mar. 1976); "Stepping Out," *Blood Horse* (14 July 1990); "Changing Shoes," *The Backstretch* (Apr. 1991), and "Shoemaker Retires as a Trainer," *Los Angeles Times* (1 Nov. 1997).

JOAN GOODBODY

SHORE, Edward William ("Eddie") (*b.* 25 November 1902 in Fort Qu'Appelle, Saskatchewan, Canada; *d.* 16 March 1985 in Springfield, Massachusetts), eight-time All-Star defenseman and four-time National Hockey League (NHL) Most Valuable Player (MVP) who was known for his skill and toughness and who led the Boston Bruins to two Stanley Cup Championships between 1926 and 1939.

Shore, one of seven children born to John T. Shore, a rancher, and Katherine Spanier Shore, a homemaker, never dreamed of becoming a hockey player while growing up in Saskatchewan. However, Shore's attitude changed abruptly when his skill and toughness were questioned by his brother Aubrey, who played for Manitoba Agricultural College in Winnipeg, where both were students. Embarrassed and angry, Shore responded by maneuvering his way onto the team and playing in the final three games of the college schedule. From such humble beginnings grew a legendary career.

Shore began his professional career as a forward with the Regina Capitals of the Western Canada Hockey League (WCHL), which became the Western Hockey League for the 1925–1926 season. Traded to the Edmonton Eskimos on 7 October 1925, Shore converted to defense but lost neither his aggressive instincts nor his scoring touch. When the Western Hockey League, unable to compete financially with the National Hockey League (NHL), suspended operations in 1926, league president Frank Patrick orchestrated what is probably the biggest transaction in the history of sports. He sold the entire Western Hockey League to the NHL. On 20 August 1926 Charles F. Adams, owner of the Boston Bruins, purchased Shore's contract over the objections of head coach Art Ross, who doubted Shore's ability. Shore wasted little time changing Ross's mind.

When Shore arrived in Boston in 1926, the Bruins were a mediocre club, having finished fourth in a seven-team league the previous season. He made an immediate impact, propelling Boston to second place in the NHL's new American Division. Between 1928 and 1931 the Bruins won four consecutive division titles, capturing the Stanley Cup in 1929. Shore also aided the franchise at the ticket window. Even after the team had lost in the 1927 Stanley Cup finals to the Ottawa Senators, fans submitted more than 29,000 applications for season tickets. Most wanted to see the acclaimed "Edmonton Express."

Eddie Shore. HOCKEY HALL OF FAME

Shore rarely, if ever, disappointed them. During a brilliant fourteen-year career, he was a First-Team All-Star seven times and a Second-Team All-Star once. In 1933 he became the first defenseman to win the Hart Memorial Trophy as most valuable player, having finished second in the balloting to Howie Morenz two years earlier. To prove the award justified, Shore won it three more times, in 1935, 1936, and 1938. No other defenseman, not even the incomparable Bobby Orr, has matched Shore's accomplishment.

With unwavering resolve, Shore also overcame virtually any injury or obstacle to play. In one contest against the Montreal Maroons, Shore broke his nose, lost three teeth, and suffered two black eyes, a two-inch cut over the left eye, and a deep gash along his cheekbone. He was in the lineup for the next game. Cracking two ribs when checked into the goal post, Shore fled while the Bruins team physician was arranging to have him admitted to the hospital. He played the next night, scoring two goals and collecting an assist. With an ear nearly severed, Shore refused anesthetic and asked only for a mirror so that he could observe the doctor reattach it. "I made him change the very last stitch," Shore remarked. "If I had not done that, he'd have left a scar."

When an accident in downtown Boston snarled traffic and prevented Shore from catching a train to Montreal for a game, he appropriated a wealthy friend's chauffeur and limousine. Inclement weather induced the chauffeur to abandon the journey; Shore took the wheel, driving all night in a blizzard across the White Mountains of New Hampshire. Arriving in Montreal, he played 58 of 60 minutes, his only respite coming while confined to the penalty box, and tallied the lone goal in a 1–0 Bruins victory.

These herculean labors notwithstanding, Shore's reputation was forever tarnished by a dreadful incident that almost cost Irvine ("Ace") Bailey his life. In a game against the Toronto Maple Leafs at Boston Garden on 12 December 1933, King Clancy and Red Horner checked Shore into the boards. Evidently mistaking Bailey for one of his assailants, Shore leveled him with a vicious check from behind. "I looked back," Clancy recalled, "saw Shore scrambling to his feet and then hit Bailey across the back of the legs. Eddie thought he was retaliating against me. I know he never meant it to be that bad." Bailey fractured his skull when his head struck the ice. He required two delicate brain operations to repair the damage, but his hockey career was at an end. The NHL suspended Shore for sixteen games.

Shore helped lead Boston to another Stanley Cup in 1939, but it was his Bruins finale. Traded to the New York Americans for rightwing Ed Wiseman and $5,000 on 24 January 1940, he retired after appearing in only ten games. Shore finished his NHL career with 105 goals, 179 assists, and 1,047 penalty minutes. Modest by contemporary standards, these numbers belie the extent to which Shore's exhilarating dashes and bone-jarring checks came to define the early years of the NHL. Anticipating retirement, Shore purchased the Springfield Indians of the American Hockey League (AHL) in 1939, where he also played for parts of three seasons between 1940 and 1942. He continued to operate the Springfield franchise until 1978, except during the 1943–1944 season, when he served as coach and general manager of the Buffalo Bisons, also of the AHL.

As an owner Shore was as domineering, combative, and antagonistic as he had been while a player. His personal life seemed tranquil by comparison. In 1929 Shore married Catherine Macrae, who gave birth to a son before dying in 1945. The following year Shore became a United States citizen. He married again in 1952 and remained with his second wife, Carol Ann Gaba, until her death in 1981. Four years later Shore died of natural causes at the age of eighty-two and is buried in Springfield, Massachusetts.

More than any player of his era, the five-foot, eleven-inch, 190-pound Shore embodied the rugged brand of hockey characteristic of the NHL during the 1920s and 1930s. An unrivaled talent on the blue line, he excelled at rushing the puck up the ice and flattening opponents who hindered his progress. Shore's style of play yielded high totals in both points and penalty minutes. Bruins trainer Hammy Moore said Shore was the only player he "ever saw who had the whole arena standing every time he rushed down the ice. When Shore carried the puck you were always sure something would happen. He would either end up bashing somebody, get into a fight or score a goal."

Shore's exploits on the ice and his fierce devotion to hockey have brought him a certain immortality. Inducted into the Hockey Hall of Fame in 1947, Shore also received the Lester Patrick Award in 1970 for outstanding service to hockey in the United States. In 1997 a panel of experts assembled by *The Hockey News* named Shore the tenth best player in the history of the NHL, according him one final honor twelve years after his death and nearly sixty years after he played his last game.

★

Biographical information on Shore is included in Stan Fischler, *Bad Boys: The Legends of Hockey's Toughest, Meanest, Most-Feared Players* (1991). Discussions of Shore's career with the Boston Bruins include Clark Booth, *The Boston Bruins: Celebrating 75 Years* (1998); Stan Fischler, *The Greatest Players and Moments of the Boston Bruins* (1999); and Brian McFarlane, *The Bruins* (2000). An obituary is in the *New York Times* (18 Mar. 1985).

MARK G. MALVASI

SHORTER, Frank Charles (*b.* 31 October 1947 in Munich, Germany), long-distance runner who won the gold medal in the Olympic marathon in the 1972 Munich Games and the silver medal in 1976 in Montreal, and who was credited with popularizing recreational running in the United States.

Shorter was one of eleven children of Samuel Sanford Shorter, a physician, and Katherine Chappell Shorter, an artist. Shorter was born in Munich while his father served as a doctor for the armed forces in postwar Germany. The family returned to the United States in 1948 and eventually settled in Middletown, New York, in 1951. Shorter was successful in athletics at an early age. The realization that he could excel at running led him to cross-country and track at the Mount Hermon School for boys (now known as Northfield Mount Hermon School), a preparatory school

Frank Shorter at the 1972 Munich Olympics. ASSOCIATED PRESS AP

in Mount Hermon, Massachusetts. In his senior year he was undefeated in cross-country, breaking records on every course he ran.

In autumn 1965 Shorter enrolled at Yale College in New Haven, Connecticut, where he trained under the guidance of Bob Giegengack, who had coached at the 1964 Olympics in Tokyo, Japan. Balancing running with academics, Shorter was a steady if not spectacular runner during his first three years at Yale, blossoming as a senior. In summer 1967 Shorter's father became a missionary doctor in Taos, New Mexico, and the family moved there from Middletown. The move was a boon to Shorter's running, permitting him to train at a 7,000-foot altitude during the summers away from Yale in 1967 and 1968, when the oxygen-thin air improved his conditioning.

In August 1968 Shorter traveled to Alamosa, Colorado, to take part in the Olympic marathon trials. Because he could not afford racing shoes, he borrowed a pair from Ambrose "Amby" Burfoot, a Wesleyan College runner against whom Shorter had competed, and the winner of the Boston Marathon four months before. Although Burfoot's generosity to a potential rival was large, his shoes were a half size too small, and while Shorter ran well in the heat and altitude, blistered and bleeding feet forced him to quit three-fifths of the way through. The experience was nevertheless valuable, since it revealed to Shorter that he was not far behind the country's elite runners, and could be even better with added training.

Shorter's summers of running at high altitude and his increased devotion to training resulted in All-America honors in his senior year at Yale. He improved from nineteenth place at the six-mile distance in the National Collegiate Athletic Association (NCAA) cross-country championship in November 1968 to first place at the same distance in the NCAA track championship the following June. Graduating with a B.A. in psychology from Yale in 1969, Shorter devoted himself completely to running. He trained winters in Florida and summers in Colorado. He entered medical school at the University of New Mexico in 1969 but dropped out after only six weeks for lack of funds and time. In the spring of 1971 he began attending law school at the University of Florida in Gainesville, but did so only when it did not interfere with training.

Although Shorter competed in the 10,000 meters, by the end of 1971 he determined that his best event was the marathon. In June 1971 he finished second in the Amateur Athletics Union (AAU) marathon championship in Eugene, Oregon, with a time of 2:17:45, and in August he won the event in 2:22:40 at the Pan-American Games in Cali, Colombia. Shorter's breakthrough came in December at the Fukuoka Marathon in Japan, a prestigious race limited by invitation to 100 elite world runners. Shorter won in 2:12:51, his best time by nearly five minutes, proving that he could prevail over a world-class field in the marathon. Shorter was determined to direct his training to peak during the following summer, with an eye on a possible medal in the Olympics. His efforts qualified him for both the 10,000 meters and the marathon.

At the 1972 Olympics in Munich, Germany, eleven Israeli athletes were murdered by Palestinian members of the Black September movement. However, the International Olympic Committee (IOC) determined that the games would go on. Shorter was devastated by the turn of events and felt genuine fear that there could be other attacks. Still, the tragedy put his own competition into perspective. The ultimate sacrifice made by the Israelis inspired him when the marathon race got tough. The result was a historic performance. No American had won the marathon since Johnny Hayes in 1908. Shorter's competition included the Australian world record holder Derek Clayton, the defending Olympic champion Mamo Wolde of Ethiopia, and the renowned British runner Ron Hill.

Shorter bided his time for the first nine miles of the race, choosing to run behind the leaders, but staying in close contact. At fifteen kilometers (9.3 miles), the pace slowed when the course took a 180-degree turn, and Shorter broke away from the lead pack. The aggressiveness of the move was risky, perhaps even reckless, since there were nearly seventeen miles left in the marathon. Nevertheless, he continued to press the lead, increasing it over the next three miles. With eight miles left, he had a sixty-second lead, which swelled to a minute and a half over the next three to four miles. His time of 2:12:19 was two minutes ahead of the silver medalist.

Shorter's victory had far-reaching effects. The 1972 marathon was the first to receive featured national television coverage, which included commentary by Erich Segal, the popular author of the popular novel *Love Story* (1970) and a marathon runner. As a professor at Yale, Segal knew Shorter, and provided the audience with a personal description of both the runner and the marathon as an event. The ruggedly handsome Shorter, with his thick dark hair and moustache, wore the attention well. The ensuing spotlight, including Shorter's picture on the cover of *Life* magazine, made him a pioneer in what became a boom in recreational running.

Shorter won the Fukuoka Marathon three more times (1972–1974), and the U.S. Olympic marathon trial in 1976. He was the national champion in the 10,000 meters five times (1971, 1973–1975, 1977). However, at the 1976 Olympics in Montreal, Canada, he was unable to repeat his Munich victory. When Shorter attempted a midrace surge as he had in Munich, he was followed by Waldemar Cierpinski of East Germany. Later, at twenty miles, Shorter could not match a similar surge by Cierpinski, who completed the race in a then-Olympic record of 2:09:55. Finishing second for the silver medal, Shorter realized that his independent method of training would no longer be sufficient against the scientific methods employed by the East Germans.

Years later, with the fall of communism in Eastern Europe and the opening of previously secret East German records, Cierpinski's name appeared on a list of athletes given illegal performance-enhancing substances. Although Shorter hoped to claim the 1976 marathon gold medal, an IOC rule set a three-year limitations period for revoking medals. Shorter became an advocate in the battle against illegal drug use in sports. In April 2000 he was appointed as the chairman of the U.S. Anti-Doping Agency, the organization in charge of Olympic drug testing in the United States.

Shorter popularized running in the United States, in part through his intense rivalry with Bill Rodgers, the four-time winner of the Boston and New York marathons. "Bill and I showed people that if you really focused on a goal and could withstand social pressure long enough, you could achieve something," Shorter reflected. "It was easy for people to identify with us. Then researchers began studying runners and showing how fitness reduced the risk of heart disease. This further validated what we did."

By age thirty-five Shorter realized that he could no longer compete at a world-class level. However, he continued to race in master's series events in his forties and fifties. After his career as an elite runner ended, he earned a law degree from the University of Florida in 1974. Admitted to the Colorado bar in 1975, he was briefly associated with the Boulder, Colorado, firm of French and Stone, but did not commence a career as an attorney. Rather, he remained active in the racing community and began a career as a television commentator for track and field events. His 1970 marriage to Louise Gilliland ended in divorce in 1985. On 23 May 1986 he married Patricia Walford, but the marriage ended in divorce in 2000. He fathered seven children. In 1991, while participating in a race to benefit victims of child abuse, Shorter revealed that he had suffered from such abuse.

Shorter was inducted into the U.S. Olympic Hall of Fame (1984), National Track and Field Hall of Fame (1989), and National Distance Running Hall of Fame (1998). With his Olympic success and his work as a television track and field commentator, Shorter has been the seminal figure in the American running boom.

★

Shorter's autobiography, written with Marc Bloom, is *Olympic Gold: A Runner's Life and Times* (1984). Useful articles include Shorter, "Through a Child's Eyes," *Runner's World* (Aug. 1996); John Meyer, "Run for the Ages: Shorter's Golden Moment in Munich Touched Millions," *Rocky Mountain News* (25 May 1997); and Marc Bloom, "Frankly Speaking," *Runner's World* (Sept. 1997).

DENNIS WATSON

SHULA, Don(ald) Francis (*b.* 4 January 1930 in Grand River, Ohio), professional football coach who won more games than any coach in the history of the National Football League (NFL) and molded the Miami Dolphins into one of the glamour teams of the 1970s and 1980s.

Shula, the third of six children, was born to Dan Shula and Mary Miller Shula. His father, an immigrant from Hungary, was a nurseryman and later an employee of a fishery; his mother was a homemaker. Shula played all sports at an early age and soon demonstrated a strong desire to win; throughout his life his competitiveness was legendary. At Harvey High School in Plantsville, Ohio, he played football, baseball, basketball, and was on the track team. He excelled at football, gaining All-League recognition and then a partial scholarship to John Carroll University, a Jesuit college in Cleveland, where he enrolled in the fall of 1947. He made a favorable impression as a freshman and

Don Shula after winning Super Bowl VII, 1973. ASSOCIATED PRESS AP

was offered a full football scholarship for his sophomore year. He became a starter at both defensive and offensive halfback in 1948; injuries kept him out of action in his junior year, but he returned as a five-foot, eleven-inch, 215-pound starter for his senior season, demonstrating his tenacity.

After graduating in 1951 with a B.S. in sociology, Shula was a ninth-round draft choice of the Cleveland Browns, where at age twenty-one he was the only rookie to make the team. He spent two years with the Browns and spent the off-season earning an M.A. at Cleveland's Case Western Reserve University. The degree was awarded in 1953, the same year Shula was traded to the Baltimore Colts, where he started at cornerback. Weeb Ewbank was hired to coach the Colts for the 1954 season and quickly recognized Shula's mind for football, asking him to call defensive plays on the field. Shula was released by the Colts just before the start of the 1957 season, whereupon he was picked up by the Washington Redskins for what would prove to be his last season as a player.

Shula returned to Plantsville after the 1957 NFL season and, having always seen his future in coaching, sought employment. On 19 July 1958 he married Dorothy Alice Bartish, with whom he raised five children, including two sons, David and Mike, who followed him into football coaching. He spent the 1958 season as an assistant football coach at the University of Virginia in Charlottesville. He moved in 1959 to Lexington, Kentucky, to become an assistant coach for the University of Kentucky. Shula took a job as defensive backfield coach with the Detroit Lions in 1960. In 1963, upon the recommendation of the departing coach, Shula succeeded Weeb Ewbank as head coach of the Baltimore Colts, where in seven seasons he went 71–23–4. However, Shula developed a reputation for being unable to win the big game, most notably Super Bowl III, the famous upset loss to the New York Jets on 12 January 1969, despite a 13–1 record that had led prognosticators to install the Colts as a seventeen-point favorite. An added insult was the fact that the Jets were the first former American Football League team to win a Super Bowl.

When the 1969 Colts finished 8–5–1, Shula found the timing right to accept owner Joe Robbie's offer ($70,000 a year with an option to buy into ownership) to coach the Miami Dolphins. The Dolphins had suffered a 15–39–2 record prior to the new coach's arrival on 18 February 1970 and had never had a winning streak longer than two games. While his overall record in Baltimore had been excellent, Shula came into his own at Miami, molding his own tradition while winning a few big games.

The turnaround in the hitherto unsuccessful south Florida franchise was immediate: the 1970 Dolphins won ten games, made the playoffs for the first time in their five-year history, and their formerly anemic rushing game went from worst to best thanks to the running of Larry Csonka and Jim Kiick. The 1971 Dolphins won the American Football Conference (AFC) title behind conference Most Valuable Player Bob Griese, a quarterback from Purdue University, and played in their first Super Bowl, losing 24–3 to the Dallas Cowboys. The stage was set for the historic 1972 season, featuring a record-shattering running game led by Csonka and Mercury Morris (each of whom ran for more than 1,000 yards as part of the team's NFL record 2,960 rushing yards, along with Jim Kiick, who scored the Super Bowl's winning touchdown), the dramatic success of thirty-eight-year-old fill-in quarterback Earl Morrall, who after Griese's injury in the season's eighth week led the team all the way to the Super Bowl without a loss, and the "No-Name" defense. Perhaps due to Shula's reputation, the 16–0 Dolphins were nevertheless two-point underdogs in Super Bowl VII, but they prevailed over the Washington Redskins 14–7 to complete their perfect 17–0 season on 14 January 1973 at the Los Angeles Memorial Coliseum, thus becoming the first undefeated NFL team.

The Dolphin's winning streak ended early in the fall 1973 season at nineteen (second longest in NFL history), but the team went on to play in their third straight championship game, defeating the Minnesota Vikings 24–7 in Super Bowl VIII. Between 1971 and 1974 the Dolphins set an NFL record by winning twenty-seven consecutive home games at the venerable Orange Bowl Stadium. The Dolphins remained a contender and played in Super Bowl XVII on 30 January 1983, losing to the Washington Redskins 27–17. But it was the arrival of quarterback Dan Marino, a late first-round draft choice and the sixth quarterback chosen in the fabled quarterback-rich draft of 1983, that marked the onset of the final era of Shula's career.

Marino had been a steal as the twenty-seventh overall choice. Shula demonstrated a willingness to reorient his offensive philosophy to accommodate his new quarterback's fantastic skills, and he was richly rewarded. Marino woke up the echoes of the Dolphins glorious recent past and made their present even more exciting with his long touchdown bombs and never-say-die comebacks. In Marino's third season, Shula coached the Dolphins in what was to be his last title game, Super Bowl XIX, a 38–16 loss to the San Francisco 49ers at the Bay Area's Stanford Stadium in Palo Alto, California. Shula resigned as Dolphins head coach on 6 January 1996, having compiled a record of 347–173–6 in 33 years as an NFL coach, a .665 winning percentage.

Following the death of Dorothy Shula of breast cancer on 25 February 1991, Shula founded the Don Shula Foundation to raise money for breast cancer research. He remarried on 15 October 1993 to Mary Anne Stephens.

During his reign with the Dolphins, Shula's teams were the least-penalized NFL team, and he suffered only two losing seasons out of twenty-six in Miami. His 2–4 record as a Super Bowl coach was thoroughly overshadowed by his 347 victories, making him the coach with the most wins in NFL history. Upon his retirement from coaching he was named vice chairman of the Dolphins. In many respects, Shula epitomized the older, more traditional NFL, with his background and traditionalism, which served him well, culminating in back-to-back Super Bowl wins and a unique undefeated season that a generation later remained unmatched. Yet he also saw the Dolphins into the Marino era, helping to develop the NFL's record-shattering quarterback of the 1980s and 1990s. Of himself, Shula remarked, "I'm about as subtle as a punch in the mouth. I'm just a guy who rolls up his sleeves and goes to work." He entered the Pro Football Hall of Fame in 1997.

★

Shula's *The Winning Edge* (1973), cowritten with Lou Sahadi, is a personal account of his values and career to that point, including the undefeated season. Shula's later book, cowritten with Ken Blanchard, *Everyone's a Coach* (1995), includes numerous discussions of his coaching career. Dan Marino's *Marino: On the Record* (1996), gives the perspective of Shula's greatest player. Austin Murphy's *The Super Bowl: Sport's Greatest Championship* (1998), chronicles Shula's greatest triumphs and frustrations.

LAWSON BOWLING

SIMMONS, Al(oysius) Harry (*b.* 22 May 1902 in Milwaukee, Wisconsin; *d.* 26 May 1956 in Milwaukee), professional baseball player made famous by his unique batting style and a lifetime batting average of .334. During a career that lasted 20 seasons, he batted in a total of 307 home runs.

Al Simmons, 1930. AP/WIDE WORLD PHOTOS

Born Aloysius Harry Szymanski, Simmons was the son of John Szymanski, foreman at a brush factory, and Agnes Czarniecki Szymanski, a homemaker. After his father died in 1912, Simmons became the primary breadwinner for the family. He worked a variety of after-school and weekend jobs, including newspaper delivery boy, messenger, and truck driver. Despite the heavy workload, Simmons managed to graduate from high school in June 1920. Involved in amateur baseball through most of his teens, Simmons played semiprofessional ball in Stevens Point and Juneau, Wisconsin, during the summer of 1921. In September of 1921 he began college at Stevens Point Normal School, which had recruited him for its football team. He suffered an injury in his first game for Stevens Point, quickly ending both his football and college career. In 1921 he changed his last name and signed with Aberdeen of the Dakota League. He was an overnight sensation, leading the league in total hits and batting .365 his first year out. He signed with Shreveport in the Texas League in 1923 and hit .360 for the season. At season's end he played a few games with the Milwaukee Brewers of the American Association. In 1924 the Brewers sold Simmons to the Philadelphia Athletics for $40,000.

A right-handed outfielder, Simmons was noted for his lightning speed and strong throwing arm. In 1925 he led all American League (AL) outfielders in total putouts. Switching from center field to left field in 1928, he continued to perform at high levels, leading AL outfielders in fielding percentage in 1929, 1930, and 1937. Although his batting style was unorthodox, it served Simmons very well. He was dubbed "Bucketfoot Al" for his habit of standing deep in the batter's box and then stepping toward third base as he swung the bat, a maneuver that ballplayers called "putting your foot in the bucket." For 13 full seasons, Simmons hit an average of .300 or better, earning a lifetime batting average of .334. He earned the AL's top batting honors in 1930 with an average of .381, and in 1931 with a .390. A particularly effective batter with teammates on base, Simmons drove in at least 100 runs in each of 12 seasons. His lifetime total of more than 1,800 runs batted in remains among the very best in baseball history.

Simmons's ability to deliver in desperate situations was perhaps best illustrated during the seventh inning of a World Series game the Athletics played against the Chicago Cubs on 12 October 1929. In that inning alone, Philadelphia scored 10 runs, eclipsing the Cubs earlier lead of 8–0. Simmons's contribution to the rally included a home run and a single. A player for the Philadelphia Athletics during that team's heyday in the late 1920s and early 1930s, Simmons earned a reputation as a slugger. The Philadelphia team, managed by the legendary Connie Mack and powered by such players as Mickey Cochrane, Jimmy Foxx, Lefty Grove, and Simmons, won three consecutive AL pennants in 1929, 1930, and 1931 and went on to win the World Series in 1929 and 1930. Simmons was named the AL's Most Valuable Player in 1929 and was selected by sportswriters to play outfield on the *Sporting News* All-Star Major League Team in 1927, 1929, 1930, 1931, 1933, and 1934.

Well aware of his popularity with fans and his value to the Athletics as both a hitter and an outfielder, Simmons was not above using this clout to win a handsome contract. In the depths of the Great Depression, he managed to pressure a very reluctant Philadelphia management into signing a three-year deal worth $100,000. That high salary eventually proved Simmons's undoing in Philadelphia. When the Athletics failed to win the AL pennant in 1932, the fans stopped flocking to games. This put pressure on Philadelphia's management to unload Simmons, whose hefty salary began to prove more and more of a burden. In the end, the Athletics traded Simmons and two other players to the Chicago White Sox in a deal worth $150,000 to Philadelphia. Simmons married Dorris Lynn Reader on 6 August 1934, but the marriage ended in divorce in 1941. The couple had one child.

Simmons served the White Sox well during the seasons of 1933 and 1934, but performed poorly in 1935, leading Chicago to sell him that winter to the Detroit Tigers for $75,000. He played well for Detroit in 1936, but when the Tigers did not win the pennant again that year, Simmons was sold to the Washington Senators for $15,000. After two lackluster seasons for the Senators, he was sold to the Boston Braves for the 1939 season. The Cincinnati Reds came shopping for Simmons in August 1939, hoping that he could help them clinch the pennant, which he did. Once that goal had been accomplished, however, it seemed that Cincinnati had no further need of his services. The Reds released Simmons, and he signed on with the Athletics as a player-coach. He held that position from 1940 through 1942, and again in the 1944 season. In 1943 he played for the Boston Red Sox. From 1945 through 1949, he remained with the Athletics as a nonplaying coach. Simmons's final season in professional baseball was spent as a coach for the Cleveland Indians in 1950.

As hard as he tried to make it a reality, Simmons never achieved one of his goals in baseball. Late in his career, he had announced his intention of attaining 3,000 base hits before he retired. Although he stayed in the game long beyond the point when he should have retired, he failed to make this mark by seventy-three hits. Disgusted with himself for the times that he had squandered his opportunities at bat or begged off playing altogether to nurse a hangover, Simmons offered this sage advice to the newcomer Stan Musial: "Never relax on any time at bat; never miss a game you can play."

Simmons may have had an unconventional batting stance, but it is doubtful whether the ball clubs for whom he played cared much how Simmons stood—not when he cranked out a career total of 307 home runs and a batting average of .334. Inducted into the National Baseball Hall of Fame in 1953, Simmons received 199 votes of the total 264 ballots cast by members of the Baseball Writers' Association of America. Perhaps the greatest tribute to Simmons came from his old coach at the Athletics, Connie Mack. Mack, who coached for more than fifty years, was asked who could provide the most value to a team. He puzzled over the question for a minute and then replied, "If I could only have nine players named Simmons." Simmons's reputation as a great hitter sometimes overshadows his talent as a fielder. After a few seasons as a center fielder, Simmons was shifted by Mack to left field, which turned out to be tailor-made for his talents. When Simmons left baseball in the early 1950s, he returned to his native Milwaukee, where he died of a heart attack just four days after his fifty-third birthday. He is buried at Saint Adalberts Cemetery in Saint Francis, Wisconsin.

★

Brief summaries and assessments of Simmons's career are in Thomas W. Meany, *Baseball's Greatest Hitters* (1950); Ira L. Smith, *Baseball's Famous Outfielders* (1954); Arthur Daley, *Kings of the Home Run* (1962); and Robert M. Broeg, *Super Stars of Baseball: Their Lives, Their Loves, Their Laughs, Their Laments* (1971). An obituary is in the *Milwaukee Journal* (26 May 1956).

DON AMERMAN

SIMPSON, Orenthal James ("O. J.") (*b.* 9 July 1947 in San Francisco, California), football player, sports commentator, and actor whose skill and speed in rushing made him one of the greatest running backs in history. His notorious 1995 murder trial revealed a darker side of his personality and exposed and intensified racial tensions many Americans believed had been resolved.

Simpson was the third of four children of Eunice Durden, a hospital worker, and James Lee Simpson, a bank custodian, who left the family when Simpson was five. Raised in the African-American area of Portero Hill, Simpson suffered from rickets when he was two years old; until age five he wore braces his mother made at home. As a teenager, he joined the Persian Warriors gang, ran afoul of the police, and was suspended from school several times. Nevertheless, he stayed on at Everett Junior High and Galileo High School for athletic opportunities in track, baseball, and football. He graduated in 1965.

Simpson's grades did not qualify him for a four-year college, and his high school team's mediocre record did not attract recruiters. He entered City College of San Francisco and broke records in junior college football with 26 touchdowns and average carries of 9.9 yards in his first year.

On 24 June 1967 Simpson married Marquerite Whitley, whom he had met in high school; they had three children. That fall Simpson entered the University of Southern California (USC) in Los Angeles. There he had to adjust to running the ball up the middle rather than considering every play a chance for a touchdown. In spring practice, according to coach John McKay, "he fumbled and was hesitant." But McKay recognized Simpson's potential. In his first season with the Trojans, Simpson led the team to the conference championship and a 14–3 victory over Indiana in the Rose Bowl. He also ran the 440-yard relay on the university's National Collegiate Athletic Association (NCAA) track team, establishing a new world record.

O. J. Simpson, 1979. AP/WIDE WORLD PHOTOS

Simpson performed even better in his second season at USC. In February 1969 *Sport* magazine named him Man of the Year, proclaiming, "most experts are rating O. J. Simpson as the greatest running back in the history of college football." In two years he gained 3,295 yards in 649 rushes and scored 36 touchdowns in 22 games. Named All-America for the second year, he also won both the Maxwell Award and the Heisman Trophy.

After the 1968–1969 football season, Simpson left USC and became the first draft pick of the Buffalo Bills, then the lowest-ranking team in professional football. Despite paying Simpson a large salary, the Bills used him so sparingly that Simpson ran less than 750 yards in each of his first three seasons. But when Lou Saban became the Buffalo coach in 1972, Simpson ran with the ball as many as thirty times a game. For five consecutive seasons starting in 1972, Simpson rushed for more than 1,000 yards; in four, he won National Football League (NFL) rushing titles. In 1973 he became the first player to run more than 2,000 yards in a season, with 2,003 yards, and he was named NFL Most Valuable Player. In 1975 he was the American Football Conference (AFC) Player of the Year.

While playing for the Buffalo Bills, Simpson acted in four Hollywood films, notably *Towering Inferno* (1974); made commercials for seven companies, memorably running through airports for Hertz Rent-a-Car; and worked as a commentator for American Broadcasting Companies (ABC) Sports.

After a knee injury in 1977, Simpson left the Buffalo Bills with a total of 9,626 yards gained. The same year he purchased a home in Brentwood, a wealthy area of Los Angeles, and in June met Nicole Brown, then eighteen years old. On 24 March 1978 Simpson signed with the San Francisco 49ers after being traded by the Bills, but retired after the 1979 season.

Simpson left the 49ers and football in 1979 with a remarkable lifetime record of 2,404 attempts, 11,236 yards gained, and 61 touchdowns. Six years later he was named to the Pro Football Hall of Fame.

During his final season, Simpson and Marquerite filed for divorce; five months later, on 18 August 1979, their youngest child, Aaren, drowned in the pool of Simpson's Brentwood home.

At six feet, one inch tall, and weighing just over 200 pounds, Simpson was an attractive man with considerable charm. He acted in six more films—the most popular were *Naked Gun* (1988) and *Naked Gun 2½* (1991)—and worked as a commentator for National Broadcasting Company (NBC) Sports from 1978 to 1986 and Home Box Office (HBO) *First and Ten* from 1986 to 1989. In March 1979

Simpson's divorce from Marquerite was granted, and on 2 February 1985 he married Nicole Brown. They had two children.

Although the Simpsons led a life of luxury and celebrity, there were reports of domestic abuse. On New Year's Eve 1989 and again in 1993, Nicole made emergency calls to police for protection. On the first occasion Simpson was brought to court and sentenced to community service.

On 6 January 1992 Nicole left Simpson, and on 25 February filed for divorce, which was granted on 15 October. But in May 1993 Simpson and Nicole began dating again. Thirteen months later, on 12 June 1994, Nicole Brown and Ronald Goldman were found brutally knifed outside her Brentwood condominium. After a widely televised low-speed car pursuit, Simpson was arrested for the double murder on 17 June.

The resulting trial riveted and divided the nation. Polls showed that two-thirds of whites thought Simpson guilty, while two-thirds of African Americans thought him innocent. The defense's revelations of an investigating officer's racist behavior proved to some a pattern of injustice to black citizens; to others it seemed like "playing the race card," a sham defense for a brutal act. Public opinion was vehement. Particularly damning to Simpson were blood samples of the victims found on materials in Simpson's home and automobile. The defense, however, successfully impugned the techniques whereby such samples were gathered, claiming they had been tainted by accident or by design. After more than eight months of proceedings, the jury took only three hours to find Simpson not guilty. The verdict was read 3 October 1995.

In February 1997, however, Simpson lost a civil suit brought by the families of Brown and Goldman. To pay damages of $33.5 million, authorities seized his house and goods, including his Heisman Trophy. In 2000 he moved with his children to the small community of Pinecrest, Florida, near Miami, where he played golf and socialized with supporters and friends. However, on 9 February 2001 he surrendered to police on an assault charge arising from a traffic dispute near his home; he was subsequently acquitted.

Of the two driving forces in Simpson's character, the more apparent was his desire to be well liked. He called Willie Mays, who at the request of a youth counselor in 1958 spent a day with Simpson, "the single biggest influence" on his life. The second and more powerful force in his nature was pure determination. As Pat Jordan observed, "It was Simpson's will, as much as his talent, that enabled him to become not only a great football player but also one of America's most beloved black athletes." Despite his popularity, the speed with which Simpson turned from hero to pariah was stunning. What he later described as his "ordeal" seemed to be the product of the immense but nebulous fame he had so determinedly sought.

★

Books about Simpson's football career are aimed at fans; they include Larry Fox, *The O. J. Simpson Story: Born to Run* (1974), and Jim Baker, *O. J. Simpson's Most Memorable Games* (1978). There are numerous accounts of the murder trial, many told by its principal participants; the best respected is journalist Jeffrey Toobin, *The Run of His Life: The People v. O. J. Simpson* (1996). Discussions of the trial's social implications can be found in Toni Morrison and Claudia B. Lacour, eds., *Birth of a Nation'hood: Gaze, Script, and Spectacle in the O. J. Simpson Case*; Jeffrey Abramson, ed., *Postmortem: The O. J. Simpson Case: Justice Confronts Race, Domestic Violence, Lawyers, Money and the Media* (1996); and Darnell M. Hunt, *O. J. Simpson Facts and Fictions: News Rituals in the Construction of Reality* (1999). Simpson's book, *I Want to Tell You* (1995), written largely by Lawrence Schiller, is based on letters sent to him during his imprisonment and contains a good chronology. Valuable reference materials are included in *Current Biography Yearbook* (1969); David L. Porter, ed., *Biographical Dictionary of American Sports: Football* (1987); and Bob Carroll and Joe Harrigan, *Football Legends of All Time* (1997). A vivid account of visiting Simpson in Florida is presented in Pat Jordan, "The Outcast: Conversations with O. J. Simpson," *New Yorker* (9 July 2001).

ALAN BUSTER

SISLER, George Harold (*b.* 24 March 1893 in Manchester, Ohio; *d.* 26 March 1973 in Richmond Heights, Missouri), professional baseball player who amassed a lifetime batting average of .340 and was a member of the National Baseball Hall of Fame.

Son of Cassius Sisler, a coal mine manager, and Mary Whipple Sisler, Sisler was an all-star athlete and ace pitcher at Akron Central High School in Ohio. At age seventeen he signed his first professional contract, making him the property of Akron's team in the Ohio-Pennsylvania League, a farm team of Columbus. Akron later sold Sisler to Columbus, which in turn sold the left-hander to the Pittsburgh Pirates. The Pirates demanded that Sisler join the team as soon as he graduated from high school, but Sisler refused. He had already set his heart on attending the University of Michigan and playing ball for the legendary Branch Rickey, who was then the university's baseball coach. The dispute was appealed to the National Commission, at that time responsible for overseeing the sport, which ruled that Sisler's contract was meaningless because he had signed it as a minor without his parents' consent.

Sisler entered the University of Michigan as a student in 1910. After graduating with a B.S. in mechanical engi-

George Sisler, 1920. ASSOCIATED PRESS AP

neering in 1915, he married Kathleen Holznagle, a fellow student, in 1916. They had four children, and all three sons had careers in baseball. George, Jr. was president of the International League, and both Dick and Dave had major league careers. After three successful seasons playing with the University of Michigan's baseball team, Sisler signed a contract with the St. Louis Browns, who had hired Rickey as their manager. The southpaw pitcher made his debut with the Browns in 1915, and in one of his earliest outings with the team he had the pleasure of striking out one of his boyhood idols, Walter Johnson of the Washington Senators.

Known by his teammates as "Gorgeous George," Sisler may have managed to beat Johnson, but overall his pitching skills were found wanting by Rickey. The manager soon gave Sisler a first baseman's mitt and suggested he familiarize himself with the position. To do so, Sisler shuttled between the pitcher's mound and first base and occasional service in the outfield. Final statistics for the 1915 season showed that Sisler played thirty-seven games at first base, twenty-nine in the outfield, and only fifteen on the pitcher's mound.

In 1916, his second full year in Major League Baseball, Sisler's brilliance as a hitter began to overshadow his contributions on the defensive side of the game. That year he hit an average of .305 and boasted a total of 34 stolen bases. The following year, Sisler's batting average climbed to .353, second only to Ty Cobb in the American League (AL). In 1918 Sisler took third place in the AL batting race, trailing Cobb and George Burns of the Philadelphia Athletics with a batting average of .341. But he did manage to take the crown for stolen bases that year with a total of 45. With a batting average of .352 in 1919, Sisler again found himself in third place, after Cobb and Bobby Veach.

Sisler blew away the competition in the batting derby of 1920, his batting average of .407 winning him his first batting crown. His overall performance that year was nothing short of remarkable: Sisler played every inning of all 154 games, amassing a league-high 631 at-bats, in which he managed to blast 257 hits, a record that still stands. Sisler's amazing performance in 1920 was unfortunately overshadowed by Babe Ruth's landmark 54-homer campaign, which grabbed most of the headlines in baseball that season.

Still batting a very respectable .371 in 1921, Sisler came in fourth that year in batting, trailing Detroit's Harry Heilmann, Cobb, and Ruth. For the second year in a row, he managed to accumulate more than 200 hits. He also won his second stolen-base title with a total of 35. Sisler bounced back in 1922, turning in an amazing batting average of .420. He led the AL with nearly 250 hits, the third season in a row in which he tallied more than 200 hits. Perhaps even more amazingly, Sisler struck out only 14 times in 586 at-bats. He also hit safely in 41 straight games, a record unsurpassed until Joe DiMaggio hit safely in 56 games in 1941.

From the heady successes of 1922, Sisler dropped to the lowest of low profiles in 1923. A severe case of sinusitis spread to his optic nerves, causing Sisler to see double. He had no choice but to sit out the entire season. Without Sisler's batting power, the Browns fell to fifth place and an overall record of 74 wins and 78 losses. When he returned to the game in 1924, he came back not only as a player but also as manager. Sadly, Sisler's performance as both a batter and first baseman began to suffer, and the team was unable to improve on its record of the previous year, again finishing with a total of 74 wins and 78 losses. Sisler finished the year with a batting average of only .305 and finished 29th among the batters of the AL.

In 1925 Sisler bounced back once again, finishing the year with a batting average of .345 and a total of 12 homers, the second highest total of his career. However, 1926 brought great disappointment and saw his batting average slip below .300 for the first time since 1915. He was back on his game in 1927, batting .327 and posting his fifth season with more than 200 hits. However, at the end of the season, the Browns sold Sisler to the Washington Senators for the paltry sum of $25,000. Then in 1928, after only twenty games, Washington sold him to the Boston Braves for $7,500.

Playing with Sisler on the Braves for the season of 1928 was Rogers Hornsby, who had made his first appearance for the St. Louis Browns along with Sisler in 1915. Both men turned in impressive performances for Boston in 1928, Hornsby winning his seventh batting title and Sisler leading all AL first basemen in assists.

Sisler proved he was still a formidable force at the plate in 1929, finishing the year with a batting average of .326, but his abilities on the defensive side of the game deteriorated sharply. He committed a career-high 28 errors at first base. In 1930, Sisler's final year in the majors, he turned in a very respectable batting average of .309. A few years after leaving baseball, Sisler published a slim booklet entitled *The Knack of Batting* (1934), outlining his thoughts about what it takes to be a good hitter.

After leaving the major leagues, Sisler drifted into the minors briefly, operated a St. Louis printing company and then a sporting goods store, and finally returned to the majors as a scout for Brooklyn and Pittsburgh. Looking back on his very impressive career, Sisler remained proudest of striking out Walter Johnson, his boyhood idol, in his very first year in the major leagues. He was inducted into the Baseball Hall of Fame in 1939 and became commissioner of the National Baseball Congress the same year.

After retirement, Sisler settled in St. Louis, home of his greatest baseball glories. He died there two days after his eightieth birthday, and is buried in the DesPeres Presbyterian Church Cemetery.

Ty Cobb, considered by many to be the greatest baseball player of all time, described Sisler as "the nearest thing to a perfect ballplayer." A sizzling hitter—his .420 average in 1922 was the third highest in baseball history—Sisler was also one of the greatest first basemen in baseball history.

★

Sisler shared some thoughts about his lengthy career in baseball in *Sisler on Baseball: A Manual for Players and Coaches* (1954). Other books that cover Sisler's life in baseball include Red Barber, *Walk in the Spirit* (1969); Bill Starr, *Clearing the Bases: Baseball Then and Now* (1989); and Roger A. Godin, *The 1922 St. Louis Browns: Best of the American League's Worst* (1991). Obituaries are in the *New York Times* and *St. Louis Post-Dispatch* (both 27 Mar. 1973).

DON AMERMAN

SLOAN, James Forman ("Tod") (*b.* 10 August 1874 in Bunker Hill, Indiana; *d.* 21 December 1933 in Los Angeles, California), jockey who became the most prominent in his sport in America and England at the close of the nineteenth century.

Sloan's mother died when he was five, and his father, a barber and realtor who abandoned him to the care of neighbors, left him with little more than the nickname "Tod," by which he became known. At age thirteen he was on his own, sweeping up in a saloon and traveling with sideshows. Everything he did was limited by the controlling fact of his life, his diminutive size. Fully grown, he was under five feet in height and, in his twenties, weighed only ninety pounds. While working in stables and caring for horses, Sloan gained a remarkable understanding of the animals' individual moods and temperaments. His guiding insight was that horses didn't want to be bullied and would not respond to whipping and digging into them with spurs. He came to have a sixth sense about horses; they responded to his touch, to the sound of his voice. Eventually, although he insisted that he had initially been terrified of being on horseback, he began a career as a professional jockey. In spite of a disappointing start, he did not give up, and in 1892 or 1893 he traveled to northern California to participate in the winter racing, which took place in the warmer climates of the country.

In the blatantly corrupt racing there, Sloan learned his craft, mastered the tricks of his trade, and created an unmistakable personal style, exhibiting bumptious independence and cocky self confidence. There, too, he evolved the

Tod Sloan. AP/WIDE WORLD PHOTOS

riding style that would be his enduring claim to fame, the forward seat: the rider perched on the withers of the horse, with short stirrups and short rein. In the memoirs he dictated many years later, he claimed that he had inadvertently and by himself stumbled on the advantages of riding this way, which included a clearer view of the field, better control of the horse, and less wind resistance. But Sloan did not invent this seat; it was an American variant of the traditional English style of riding: straight upright, long stirrups, and a long rein. This American style evolved gradually, shaped by the crude conditions of racing; it was the creation of innumerable stable boys, black and white, who had no formal training as jockeys and little equipment, and who rode in the small town and country race tracks. In the big city tracks, the traditional style still prevailed.

Wherever its origin, Sloan realized that the forward seat suited riders of his size and was adaptable to the growing emphasis in American racing on speed over endurance. This seat enabled him to win races, frequently and spectacularly, with all sorts of horses. After winning in San Francisco, Sloan then went east to the New York race tracks, the center of American racing; where he continued to win. Between 1896 and 1900 he dominated riding and achieved an astonishingly high percentage of winning mounts, often over 30 percent. Consequently, he became a favorite on the track and a celebrity off it.

In 1897 Sloan went to England to ride. The forward seat was greeted with incredulity and derision, mocked as a "monkey on a stick." Who was this upstart to defy two centuries of tradition? Nevertheless, Sloan won, and won again. His short visit to England was followed by a longer one in 1898, in which he repeated his success. Derision turned to admiration, and it was his triumphs in England that fixed him in the public mind as the originator of a new riding style. Soon, all English jockeys were riding in the same fashion.

Sloan's Yankee brashness gained him the affection of the British racing masses and adoption of his name into cockney rhyming slang, such that to be independent and to defer to no authority was "to be on your Tod": "on your own/Tod Sloan." The ultimate accolade came at the end of the 1900 season, when the Prince of Wales engaged him to ride for his stable the following year.

But ominous troubles were piling up. Some influential people considered Sloan more insolent than independent. Also, English racing was becoming inundated by a host of American gamblers and trainers who had followed in Sloan's wake and whose company he did not shun; trainers were widely believed to routinely use dope, though no one accused Sloan of this. Most troubling, Sloan wagered on horses heavily and openly, leading inevitably to suspicions of questionable riding. He was called to testify before the Jockey Club, which in December 1900 informed him that he "need not apply for a license to ride the following year." He could attend races and train horses; but he could not do the one thing he did supremely well. This crushing injunction, accepted by almost all American racetracks as well, was never lifted.

Although Sloan was just twenty-six, his career was over. The next three decades were ones of restless wandering, primarily throughout Europe and in the U.S. as well. He attempted a career in vaudeville, gambled incessantly, became a bookmaker, squandered all his money, and underwent two failed marriages: in 1907 he married Julia Sanderson and they divorced in 1913, without having any children; in 1920 he married Elizabeth Saxon Malone, with whom he had one child, a daughter, and whom he divorced in 1927. Sloan died of cirrhosis of the liver in Los Angeles, California, where he is buried.

The overworked term "legendary" can justly be applied to Sloan's life and career, for stories about him abounded in his day and after. In 1904 George M. Cohan composed a musical based on Sloan's life, *Little Johnny Jones,* containing some of Cohan's most memorable music (such as "Give My Regards to Broadway" and "Yankee Doodle Dandy"). In the 1920s, Ernest Hemingway wrote a moving short story, "My Old Man," sensitively exploring a life very like Sloan's. Over a career spectacular in its triumphs and failures, Sloan ironically helped bring about the modern, regulated form of American horse racing in which there was no place for him and his anarchic individualism.

★

Sloan's dictated memoirs, *Tod Sloan, by Himself,* edited by A. Dick Luckman (1988; reprint of 1915 edition), are bafflingly evasive. See also Roger Longrigg, *The History of Horse Racing* (1972); Wray Vamplew, *The Turf: A Social and Economic History of Horse Racing* (1976); and John Dizikes, *Yankee Doodle Dandy: The Life and Times of Tod Sloan* (2000).

JOHN DIZIKES

SMITH, Dean Edwards (*b.* 28 February 1931 in Emporia, Kansas), Hall of Fame basketball coach who guided the University of North Carolina (UNC) to 2 national championships and 879 wins in 36 years, breaking the collegiate record for coaching victories.

Smith was born to schoolteachers Alfred and Vesta Edwards Smith. His father, who was also a coach, challenged high school athletic administrators in Kansas by allowing a black student to join the basketball team. When Smith was sixteen, his family moved to Topeka, Kansas, where he played baseball, basketball, and football at Topeka High School. Upon graduation in 1949, Smith accepted an academic scholarship to the University of Kansas, where he

Dean Smith. AP/Wide World Photos

joined the Air Force ROTC and played basketball for legendary coach Phog Allen's national championship team in 1952 and runner-up team in 1953. However, Smith saw little court time, and aspired to follow in his parents' footsteps. "Teaching and coaching was all I ever thought about as a profession because it struck me that in addition to being very good people, my parents were also deeply happy ones," Smith would later write in *A Coach's Life*.

After graduating from Kansas in 1953, Smith served as an assistant coach at the school and played semiprofessional basketball until his U.S. Air Force orders came through in April 1954. Later that year Smith married Ann Cleavinger and was assigned to Germany, where he was a player and coach for Air Force basketball teams. That led to Smith becoming an assistant coach at the Air Force Academy in Colorado Springs, Colorado, in 1956. After two years there Smith left for a job as an assistant to coach Frank McGuire at UNC.

No one knew that this would be the beginning of a storied career at Chapel Hill. The early years were tough. As McGuire's only assistant, Smith's duties were numerous, and in 1960 the NCAA investigated UNC basketball for "excessive recruiting expenditures," leading to a one-year probation in 1961. McGuire left to become head coach of the National Basketball Association's (NBA) Philadelphia Warriors, and Smith was hired as his replacement.

Things got even tougher. Smith's first Tar Heel squad finished with eight wins and nine losses in the 1961–1962 season, and by early 1965 his teams had still not reached a postseason tournament. Those who had enjoyed McGuire's winning ways—including the 1957 national championship—were growing restless. Following a loss at Wake Forest on 6 January 1965, UNC students hanged Smith in effigy as the team returned to campus. At that point Tar Heels star forward Billy Cunningham challenged the crowd, and confiscated the replica of his coach in an emotional display of loyalty. In retrospect, many view this as the turning point of Smith's career.

UNC started winning more often at roughly the same time that Smith began to employ an offensive strategy he called the "four corners," a stalling tactic that frustrated opponents during the era when college basketball had no shot clock. In 1967 North Carolina advanced to the first of eleven "Final Fours" under Smith. The Tar Heels lost to the University of Dayton in the national semifinals, but advanced to the finals in 1968 with the help of Charlie Scott, the first African American to play at UNC. The team fell to UCLA, but after Smith led UNC back to the Final Four in 1969 and 1972, and added a National Invitation Tournament championship in 1971, his career was budding.

Smith coached the United States to Olympic basketball gold in 1976, aided by four of his own Tar Heel players. He guided UNC back to the national championship game in 1977 and 1981, but losses to Marquette and Indiana had supporters restless again. In six trips to the Final Four, Smith's teams had gone home empty. But on 29 March 1982, Smith broke through. A team featuring James Worthy, Sam Perkins, and a freshman named Michael Jordan defeated Georgetown University 63–62 in the title contest. After the game, a humble Smith said, "I don't think I'm a better coach now because we've won." However, a vindicated Smith also noted, "A great writer from Charlotte, North Carolina, once said that it was our system that kept us from winning the national championship. It's the most ridiculous comment ever made and I always wanted to say that."

The "system" included such innovations as the "four corners" offense and the "run and jump" defense, as well as players raising a fist to signify they needed a break, or pointing to a teammate to acknowledge an assist. On 5 April 1993 this system earned Smith another national championship, as UNC beat the University of Michigan 77–71 in the final. Coincidentally, a late-game mistake by the opponent played a role in both national titles. A bad pass by Georgetown's Fred Brown aided the Tar Heels in

1982, and a time-out called by Michigan's Chris Webber when his team had none remaining resulted in a crucial technical foul in 1993. "OK, call us lucky, but also call us national champions," said Smith after Webber's gaffe.

Under Smith, the Tar Heels developed a knack for erasing late deficits with amazing scoring spurts. On 2 March 1974 UNC scored eight points in the last seventeen seconds against Duke University to force overtime and eventually win, 96–92. On 10 February 1983 North Carolina outscored the University of Virginia 11–0 during the final 4:12 to cap a 64–63 victory. And on 27 January 1993 the Tar Heels went on a 28–4 run in the last 9 minutes to beat Florida State University 82–77.

Smith retired from coaching on 9 October 1997, but not before what may have been his best coaching job the previous winter. After a rocky 12–6 start, UNC reeled off sixteen straight wins to capture Smith's thirteenth Atlantic Coast Conference tournament title, and advance to the last of his eleven Final Fours. The Tar Heels lost to the University of Arizona in the national semifinals, but Smith finished the season with 879 career wins, breaking former University of Kentucky coach Adolph Rupp's previous record of 876, after years of saying he would never coach long enough to do it.

Along with the record 879 wins, Smith's 36-year résumé included 30 seasons of 20 or more wins, 27 NCAA tournament appearances, and 17 ACC regular-season titles. He was named ACC Coach of the Year 8 times, and over 96 percent of his varsity athletes graduated. In 1983 Smith was inducted into the Naismith Memorial Basketball Hall of Fame, and in 1986 UNC's new on-campus basketball arena was named the Dean E. Smith Center in his honor.

Dozens of Smith's players went on to NBA careers, including Cunningham, Scott, Worthy, Perkins, Jordan, Bobby Jones, Bob McAdoo, Walter Davis, Phil Ford, Brad Daugherty, Kenny Smith, Rasheed Wallace, Jerry Stackhouse, Antawn Jamison, and Vince Carter. Cunningham, Larry Brown, and George Karl also became outstanding NBA coaches, and Buzz Peterson and Matt Doherty succeeded as college coaches; the latter taking over at UNC in 2000. Legendary UCLA coach John Wooden called Smith "a better teacher of basketball than anyone else."

No one has higher praise for Smith than his former players. Jordan has said, "He's like a second father to me," both before and after his own father was murdered in 1993. Doherty has called UNC basketball alumni "a family like no other family," and many have admitted to taking Smith's personal advice on a regular basis. "Sometimes he'll give you an opinion and you'll go another way, but 90 percent of the time you'll do what he says," claimed Peterson just days before accepting the head coaching job at the University of Tennessee in 2001.

Smith and his first wife divorced in 1973, and Smith married Linnea Weblemoe in May 1976. He has five children: three from his first marriage and two from his second. Smith has spoken out on several social issues, but is most noted for his support of integration during his early years in Chapel Hill.

★

Smith chronicled his career in a book entitled *A Coach's Life* (1999), and he is also the author of *Basketball: Multiple Offense and Defense* (1982). More information about Smith's career can be found in Art Chansky, *The Dean's List* (1996). Further quotes and details are from *North Carolina National Championship 1982* (1982), and the UNC Sports Information office.

JACK STYCZYNSKI

SMITH, Emmitt James, III (*b.* 15 May 1969 in Pensacola, Florida), record-setting running back who won National Football League (NFL) and Super Bowl Most Valuable Player (MVP) awards with the Dallas Cowboys.

Smith was born to Emmitt Smith, Jr., and Mary Smith. He was the second child in a close-knit family, oldest of four sons. Smith's father was a bus driver, and also played semiprofessional football. As a baby Smith was captivated by football on television, and as a youngster his favorite team was the Dallas Cowboys. He began playing organized football when he was eight years old, and being big for his age, he usually played with older children. Later Smith helped his Escambia High School team become a two-time state champion after it had posted just one winning season in the previous eighteen years. Playing running back, Smith rushed for 8,804 yards at Escambia, and was *Parade* magazine's 1986 high school Player of the Year as a senior.

Smith graduated from Escambia in 1987. A good student who received scholarship offers from many colleges, Smith chose the University of Florida over Auburn and Nebraska. As a freshman at Florida, Smith broke the school's single game rushing record with 224 yards against the University of Alabama. He surpassed that mark when he ran for 316 yards against the University of New Mexico as a junior. In three years, Smith had set 58 school records and accumulated 3,928 yards on the ground when he decided to forgo his senior season to turn professional. Yet some experts thought the five-foot, nine-inch All-American was too small and slow to succeed in the NFL.

The Dallas Cowboys and head coach Jimmy Johnson disagreed. They recognized ability, and traded up to pick Smith seventeenth in the 1990 college draft. With quarterback Troy Aikman and wide receiver Michael Irvin already in Dallas, the selection paid handsome dividends. Although Smith missed training camp while his first contract was negotiated, the Cowboys improved their record by six

Emmitt Smith *(right)*, 2000. ASSOCIATED PRESS AP

games in 1990, and Smith earned a Pro Bowl invitation. He was also named 1990 NFL Offensive Rookie of the Year by the Associated Press. In 1991 Smith led the NFL with 1,563 rushing yards, and Dallas made the playoffs for the first time in 6 seasons. A year later, Smith's 1,713 yards again paced the league's runners, and the Cowboys advanced to Super Bowl XXVII, where they routed the Buffalo Bills 52–17 on 31 January 1993.

By this time, Aikman, Irvin, and Smith were nicknamed "The Triplets." Not only did each have exceptional football skills, but each also had a unique personality. The rugged, self-assured Smith balanced the cool, efficient Aikman and the fiery, inspirational Irvin. "Emmitt is the kind of guy you can yell at on the practice field without worrying that you're going to crush him," wrote Johnson in his book, *Turning the Thing Around* (1993). "He's too secure for that."

Smith was also secure enough to challenge Cowboys owner Jerry Jones at the beginning of the 1993 season. Dissatisfied with a new contract tendered by Jones, Smith sat out the first two games of the year. When Dallas lost both games, Jones raised his offer. Smith returned to the field and enjoyed his most spectacular season, capturing NFL MVP honors and a third consecutive league rushing title.

The first evidence of a special year came on 31 October 1993, when Smith ran for a single game team-record of 237 yards one rainy afternoon in Philadelphia. "I felt so hot and smooth, so natural and unforced, I believed that I could score on any play," wrote Smith in his autobiography, *The Emmitt Zone.* His 62-yard touchdown burst late in the contest sealed a 23–10 win over the Eagles.

Then on 2 January 1994 Smith totaled 168 yards rushing and 61 more yards on 10 catches in a division title showdown against the New York Giants, despite playing much of the game with a separated shoulder. In obvious discomfort, Smith somehow managed to gain 41 of his yards during the visiting Cowboys 52-yard game-winning drive in overtime. "I was off by myself somewhere, some private zone, feeling too much pain to focus on anything else but winning," recalled Smith in his book. A field goal gave Dallas a 16–13 victory, and Smith was hospitalized upon returning to Texas.

Finally, on 30 January 1994, after the Cowboys had won a second straight conference championship, Smith ran for 132 yards and 2 touchdowns on the way to being named Super Bowl XXVIII MVP, following a 30–13 win over Buffalo. With the victory, the Cowboys became the first 0–2 team to win a Super Bowl. Smith gained 61 of his 132 yards during a 64-yard third quarter drive that put Dallas ahead to stay, capping it with a 15-yard scoring run. "Normally, I don't watch myself in old games," penned Smith. "But I put that Super Bowl drive in my VCR a lot. I'll never forget it as long as I live."

In 1995 Smith gained a single season team-record 1,773 yards on the ground, caught a personal best 62 passes, and ran for 25 touchdowns, breaking the NFL mark previously set by the Washington Redskins John Riggins in 1983. Smith scored six more times in the postseason, and the

Cowboys won their third Super Bowl in four years, 27–17 over the Pittsburgh Steelers on 28 January 1996. After that, Dallas began a downward spiral, but Smith continued setting records. In 1998 he broke Marcus Allen's NFL career record for rushing touchdowns and Tony Dorsett's team record for rushing yardage. In 1999 he passed kicker Rafael Septien as the Cowboys all-time leading scorer. And in 2000 he notched a record-tying tenth consecutive season with at least 1,000 yards on the ground, and became the third back in NFL history to pass the 15,000-yard mark, following Walter Payton and Barry Sanders.

Off the field, Smith returned to the University of Florida and received a B.A. in public recreation in May 1996, fulfilling a promise he made to his mother. A professed Christian who has supported numerous charities, Smith married Patricia Southall Lawrence on 22 April 2000. The couple has two daughters.

★

Smith's autobiography, written with Steve Delsohn, is *The Emmitt Zone* (1994). More information about the Cowboys and Smith's career can be found in Jimmy Johnson with Ed Hinton, *Turning the Thing Around: My Life in Football* (1993); and Jeff Guinn, *Dallas Cowboys: The Authorized Pictorial History* (1996), a pictorial history book; and also on the official website of the Dallas Cowboys http://www.dallascowboys.com. A profile of Smith is "Emmitt Unplugged," *Sports Illustrated* (1 July 1996).

JACK STYCZYNSKI

SMITH, John William (*b.* 9 August 1965 in Del City, Oklahoma), wrestler who achieved international domination of the sport during a career that featured six consecutive world championships and two Olympic gold medals, and was also a successful coach at Oklahoma State University.

Smith is one of four brothers who have made significant marks in the world of amateur wrestling. Sons of Lee Roy Smith, director of data processing at the Oklahoma Department of Transportation, and Madalene Smith, an obstetrics nurse, they grew up in the town of Del City, not far from Oklahoma City, and each of them wrestled for Oklahoma State University (OSU) in Stillwater. Although Lee Roy, Pat, and Mark Smith each amassed considerable credentials in terms of victories and championships, their brother John—the second son in a family of twelve children—is clearly one of the greatest wrestlers ever to compete. For a period of six years, from 1986 to 1992, Smith dominated the sport at an international level to an unprecedented extent.

Smith's success began at the local high school, where he achieved 105 wins against only 5 losses and won individual state 4A championships in his last two seasons (1982–1983). Ten years later, at the end of his incredible athletic career, Del City High School named its gymnasium the John Smith Field House and honored its distinguished alumnus with the unveiling of a life-size sculpture.

Following in his older brother Lee Roy's footsteps, Smith went to OSU, where—wrestling at 126 and then 134 pounds—he achieved considerable success in his first two years of intercollegiate competition, attaining a second-place finish and All-America honors at the National Collegiate Athletic Association (NCAA) tournament in his sophomore season. That success notwithstanding, he sat out the 1985–1986 college season as a "redshirt," a college athlete who is kept out of varsity competition for a year in order to extend eligibility. Still, Smith was anything but inactive as a wrestler, and during this year achieved the first of many conspicuous successes in the freestyle wrestling community by winning his first national title in that competitive context and by taking home a gold medal from the Goodwill Games in Moscow. Not yet twenty-one years old, Smith defeated European champion Khazer Isaev, one of the Soviet Union's best wrestlers.

During his intercollegiate hiatus, Smith refined his skills and developed a "philosophy of motion" that featured an unorthodox style characterized by quickness down low. In the 1986–1987 season, Smith began a competitive run that remains unequaled. His season-opening collegiate bout that year was his last defeat at OSU; there followed over his two remaining seasons a string of ninety consecutive victories, two Big Eight Conference and NCAA individual championships, and his designation as Outstanding Wrestler at the 1987 national tournament. Graduating from Oklahoma State with a B.S. in education in 1988, he completed his intercollegiate career with an overall record of 154–7–2. Moreover, during those two years at Oklahoma State he won a gold medal at the Pan American Games; his first world freestyle championship, the second of what were to be five national freestyle championships; and—most significant of all—the gold medal in the 136.5-pound class at the Olympic Games in Seoul, Korea. And much more was yet to come.

The next four years brought Smith a staggering number of accomplishments and honors, culminating in his second Olympic gold medal at the Barcelona Games of 1992. He was the first wrestler from the United States in eighty years to win two Olympic championships. That 1992 triumph also represented an unprecedented sixth straight world title (the Olympic competition counts as the world-championship event for the years in which it is held) a truly remarkable demonstration of sustained competitive excellence. In addition to repeated national and Pan American freestyle championships, Smith earned several prestigious individual awards. In 1990 he was presented the "Master of Technique" award, which honors the best technical

John Smith *(right)* wrestling Asgari Mohammadian of Iran to win the featherweight freestyle gold medal at the 1992 Olympics in Barcelona. ASSOCIATED PRESS AP

wrestler in the world, by the Federation Internationale Des Luttes Associees (FILA), the organization that governs international wrestling. He also received the 1990 James E. Sullivan Award, given by the Amateur Athletic Union (AAU) to the nation's top amateur athlete, the first wrestler ever to win that award. Moreover, he was the 1991 FILA Outstanding Wrestler of the Year and won the 1992 Amateur Athletic Foundation World Trophy, an accolade given to the best athlete in a given geographical region, the first North American wrestler ever to receive that award.

The end of Smith's competitive career by no means signified the conclusion of his involvement in and contribution to the sport of amateur wrestling. Indeed, his accomplishments as a coach have been most impressive in their own right. In 1992, after a year as interim co-coach in a difficult period involving various NCAA regulatory violations during the tenure of the previous Oklahoma State coach, Smith became only the sixth true head coach in the long and proud history of the OSU wrestling program. When Smith took the team to a national championship in 1994, only his second season fully at the program's helm, one of his championship wrestlers was his younger brother Pat, who in his final season achieved an unprecedented fourth straight individual national championship. Throughout his coaching career at OSU, Smith has won numerous conference championships, achieved high place finishes in team standings at the NCAA tournament, and developed numerous All-America wrestlers, including some national individual champions. He has also been active and extremely successful in coaching freestyle wrestling at the national amateur level. Among other accomplishments, he coached the U.S. team to a gold medal in the 1999 Pan American Games; and he served as co-coach of the U.S. team in the 2000 Olympic Games at Sydney, Australia.

Smith married Toni Donaldson on 16 December 1995; they have three children.

It is no wonder that in 1996 Smith was honored at the Atlanta Olympic Games as one of the 100 Greatest Olympians, or that in 1997 he was inducted as a Distinguished Member of the National Wrestling Hall of Fame. Competing with the best in the world in a grueling sport that requires physical strength and skill, mental toughness and agility, and extraordinary self-discipline, Smith demonstrated a consistency of excellence that dominated international wrestling for a remarkable period of time. His numerous championships and his many awards and honors, some of them "firsts," remain eloquent testimony to the nature of his athletic achievement. Most significant of all might be his overall record as a wrestler. Beginning with his high school career in Del City, and concluding with his second Olympic gold medal in Barcelona, Smith competed in 458 wrestling matches. He won 436 of them: more than 95 percent of the total. In international freestyle competition, he won exactly 100 bouts—and lost only 5. That he has continued to enrich the sport in the years since his competitive career ended, only underscores his status as one of the world's greatest athletes.

★

For information concerning Smith's family background and wrestling career, see Bob and Doris Dellinger, *The Cowboys Ride Again!: The History of Wrestling's Dynasty* (1994), which discusses the impressive wrestling tradition at OSU. Shannon Brownlee, "How Low Can You Get?," *Sports Illustrated* (14 Mar. 1988), provides useful biographical information, some commentary on Smith's unusual wrestling style, and a hint of the international success that was to follow. The most complete and succinct account of Smith's achievements may be found at the National Wrestling Hall of Fame in Stillwater, Oklahoma, and in the annual wrestling media guide published by the Media Relations Office of the Athletic Department at Oklahoma State University.

JAMES R. KERIN, JR.

SMITH, Osborne Earl ("Ozzie") (*b.* 26 December 1954 in Mobile, Alabama), baseball player whose exceptional defensive skills at shortstop earned him thirteen consecutive Gold Glove awards and numerous fielding records while playing for the San Diego Padres and St. Louis Cardinals.

Ozzie Smith leaving the field for the last time in a regular-season game, 1996. ASSOCIATED PRESS AP

Born in Alabama, Smith spent most of his childhood in Los Angeles, California, and his father worked as a sandblaster at a California Air Force base. For college Smith chose California State Polytechnic in San Luis Obispo. As a college star, his defense and speed caught the eye of scouts, and after he graduated in 1977, the five-foot, ten-inch shortstop signed a minor-league contract with the San Diego Padres organization.

After only sixty-eight games as a minor leaguer, Smith cracked the Padres lineup as the starting shortstop in 1978. In his rookie season Smith made a play against the Atlanta Braves that still appears on highlight reels and was an announcement to the league that a new standard for defensive excellence would be set by the Padres young shortstop. On 20 April Smith dove to his left to field a ground ball off the bat of Atlanta's Jeff Burroughs. The ball took a bad hop, chopping well high of Smith's outstretched glove. Already prone, Smith reached up with his bare right hand, speared the ball above his head, and threw in one fluid motion to first base to retire Burroughs. Amazing as it was, the play was merely business as usual for Smith, who was runner-up in balloting for National League (NL) Rookie of the Year that season. During the next three years with the Padres, Smith established himself as baseball's preeminent shortstop, leading the NL in assists every year and winning his first two Gold Gloves in 1980 and 1981.

Smith's offensive production, however, was no match to his glove in his early years. He hit an anemic .232 cumulatively as a Padre. Although he hit for a low average and minimal power, Smith became a threat once he did reach base, stealing fifty-seven times in 1980.

After the 1982 season Smith was traded from the Padres, who did not want to meet his salary demands for so little offensive production, to the powerful St. Louis Cardinals for shortstop Gary Templeton. With St. Louis, Smith had an opportunity to play for a contender for the first time. Smith was an immediate hit in St. Louis, helping the Cardinals win the World Series and garnering another Gold Glove for himself. In 1983 Smith was named starting shortstop for the NL's All-Star squad, the first of a record twelve such awards. A new contract in 1985 with the Cardinals made Smith the highest paid player in the game, a position usually reserved for sluggers or star pitchers, netting $2.75 million a year over four years. Smith made good on the Cardinals investment. That year St. Louis again made the post-season, losing the series to cross-state rival Kansas City, and Smith was named Most Valuable Player (MVP) for the National League championship series.

Smith, a switch hitter, also began to come into his own behind the plate, becoming one of the most difficult batters to strike out in either league. Intelligence, speed, and grit made Smith a solid hitter over time, culminating in the 1987 campaign, during which he batted .303 with 75 RBI and 40 doubles. Smith also continued his defensive greatness, setting a Cardinal record and personal best with a fielding percentage of .987. He led the Cardinals to the World Series again, this time losing to the Minnesota Twins. That year Smith finished second in the balloting for MVP, the closest any National League shortstop had come to that award since 1962. Smith continued to excel, both on the bases and at shortstop, tying his personal record of fifty-seven steals in a season in 1988. Smith was named Shortstop of the Decade by *Sports Illustrated* magazine in 1989. His seemingly impossible playmaking and his trademark backflip when stepping on the field helped earn him the nickname "The Wizard of Oz."

On 1 November 1983 Smith married Denise Jackson, with whom he had three children. The couple divorced in 1996.

By the early 1990s the "Wizard" was an established baseball institution. He won his eleventh straight Gold Glove and started in the All-Star game for the ninth straight year. The following year he broke another record, setting an NL mark for fewest errors by a shortstop with a stingy eight.

Smith has made great contributions to St. Louis off the field as well. Since coming to the Cardinals in 1982, Smith made a point to support children's organizations. In 1983 the National Association for the Advancement of Colored People (NAACP) awarded him its Image Award for Sportsmanship, Humanitarianism, and Community Activities. In 1992 he was named St. Louis' Man of the Year, the first sports figure to garner the award. Baseball honored his humanitarian efforts in 1994 with the Branch Rickey Award, and in 1995 with the Roberto Clemente Award.

Smith retired in 1996, holding numerous defensive records including most assists (8,375) and most double plays (1,590). His 13 consecutive Gold Gloves are a record for shortstops. By the end, however, he had put up impressive offensive numbers as well, having amassed a substantial 2,460 hits and 580 stolen bases. Smith is eligible for induction into the Baseball Hall of Fame in 2002.

After his playing career Smith remained involved with baseball, working for the syndicated television show *This Week in Baseball* as well as continuing his connection to the Cardinals. Since 1998 Smith has served as a regular columnist and baseball analyst for Cable News Network-Sports Illustrated (CNN-SI). Smith and his family continue to have deep roots in St. Louis, where he owns a restaurant and remains involved in the philanthropic organizations he favored as a player, including the Ozzie Smith Foundation.

Arguably the greatest defensive shortstop ever, Smith brought a new level of acrobatic grace to his position. Over the course of a nineteen-year major league career with San Diego and St. Louis, Smith was a fifteen-time All-Star and holds more than a dozen fielding records. Smith's wizardry on the field and his poise and charitable work off the field made him one of the most respected players of his era.

★

Smith's autobiography is *Wizard* (1988), written with Rob Rains. Biographical essays appear in *Legends in Their Own Time* (1994), *Who's Who of Sports Champions* (1995), and *Current Biography* (1997). Smith has been the subject of countless articles in *Sports Illustrated* and the *Sporting News* throughout his career, including Michael Geffner, "Cardinal Singe," *Sporting News* (22 July 1996), an extended discussion of his career and retirement.

MATTHEW TAYLOR RAFFETY

SMITH, Walter Wellesley ("Red") (*b.* 25 September 1905 in Green Bay, Wisconsin; *d.* 15 January 1982 in Stamford, Connecticut), sports journalist esteemed for his unique blend of incisive commentary, technique, vitality, and humor.

Smith was the second of three children born to Walter Philip Smith, a third-generation wholesale produce and retail groceries salesman, and Ida Richardson, a homemaker. Both Smith and his brother Arthur Richardson were named after the Duke of Wellesley, whose Christian name was Arthur Wellesley. Smith's father gave him the nickname "Brick" because of his hair color. Later in life, "Brick" became "Red," a moniker that endured even after his hair receded and turned white. Smith graduated from East High School in Green Bay, Wisconsin, in 1922 with a "B" average and his first writing award, a free copy of the $3 yearbook, which he earned with a humorous essay about the school's debating team. After graduation, he was accepted to the University of Notre Dame in Indiana. He worked for a year as a clerk for a hardware company to save money for school.

Smith enrolled as a journalism major at Notre Dame in autumn 1923. During his freshman year, he worked for the school newspaper and by his junior year he was editing the university's annual, *The Dome*. When asked later to name the person on campus he most admired, Smith chose his journalism professor, who stressed factual accuracy, specific

Red Smith, 1970s. NEW YORK TIMES CO./HULTON|ARCHIVE

and straightforward language, and the importance of expanding one's areas of interest.

Smith graduated cum laude from Notre Dame with a B.A. on 5 June 1927, and he took his first newspaper job as a general assignment reporter for Wisconsin's *Milwaukee Sentinel.* Looking for a pay raise, he wrote to the *St. Louis Star* the following year and sold himself as a well-rounded veteran newspaperman. He was hired as a copyreader for $40 per week, a significant increase over the $24 he earned weekly from the *Sentinel.* Smith moved from copyreading to sportswriting after the paper fired half its sports staff for taking bribes from a wrestling promoter in exchange for favorable publicity.

In 1929, while covering the St. Louis Browns spring training camp, he earned his first byline—"W. W. Smith." He soon became a familiar sight in the Browns press box, typing with the same two-finger style he taught himself in high school. Later that year he met Catherine ("Kay") Cody, whom he married on 11 February 1933. The couple had two children, one of whom, Terence ("Terry") Fitzgerald, became a reporter for the *New York Times.* They faced hard times at first, because Smith's salary had increased only fifty cents per week since he joined the paper four years earlier. These financial struggles led him to become active in the newly formed American Newspaper Guild.

In June 1932 the *Star* merged with the *St. Louis Times* to form the *St. Louis Star-Times.* The merger forced substantial layoffs and job changes, and Smith became one of only two rewrite men employed by the paper. With the other rewrite man frequently on assignment, Smith often rewrote the entire paper by himself. Rewriting helped Smith's own writing, and he learned to use more concise language and precise images.

In 1936 Smith moved to Philadelphia and became a sportswriter for the *Philadelphia Record,* where he formed a friendship with the legendary sportswriter Grantland Rice. His first piece appeared on 20 June 1936 with the byline "Walt Smith." Influenced by his wife, Smith asked for another byline and received one both he and Kay agreed to, "Red." Smith never again published under a different name.

Although he never intended to have a career as a sportswriter, Smith ended up dedicating his life to sports, covering the Olympics, auto racing, baseball, basketball, fishing, boxing, and even dog shows. Baseball, however, was his focus. His quick wit, vibrant language, and close attention to rhythm and detail entertained millions of readers, as demonstrated in the following excerpt from a 4 October 1951 article written after Bobby Thomson's famous pennant-clinching home run: "Now it is done. Now the story ends. And there is no way to tell it. The art of fiction is dead. Reality has strangled invention. Only the utterly impossible, the inexpressibly fantastic, can ever be plausible again." Perhaps Smith's most famous baseball line was, "Baseball is dull only to those with dull minds." He also addressed other topics, particularly politics. In 1937 he interviewed Leon Trotsky, then in exile in Mexico. Later he covered the 1956 and 1968 national political conventions.

Smith's career reached its peak when he joined the staff of the *New York Herald Tribune* in August 1945. Within four months, Smith had his own column, which he wrote for the *Herald Tribune* until it closed in 1966. By 1954 he was the most widely syndicated sports columnist in the country. With his column distributed nationally by the Publishers-Hall Newspaper Syndicate, Smith kept working even after the *Herald Tribune* and its short-lived successor, the *World Journal Tribune,* ceased operation. The *New York Times* began running Smith's column three years later on 15 November 1971. Then age sixty-six, he began to expand the scope of his columns, writing more directly about how sporting events fit within a larger context of a politically turbulent world. He also endured changes in his personal life; his wife died of liver cancer in 1967, and he married the artist Phyllis Warner Weiss on 2 November 1968.

Smith's broader perspective won him a diverse readership and, in April 1976, the Pulitzer Prize for distinguished commentary.

Smith continued to work even after being diagnosed with cancer in the late 1970s. He refused to stop writing as long as the *Times* kept publishing his work and people kept reading it. Finally in 1981 he agreed to cut back from four to three columns per week. The first article he wrote under this revised schedule was published on 11 January 1982. Smith died four days later of heart failure. He is buried in Longridge Union Cemetery in Stamford, Connecticut.

Gifted with a startling memory and an uncanny knack for crafting incisive stories, Smith was, in Ernest Hemingway's words, "the most important force in American sportswriting." Smith's contemporary Shirley Povich of the *Washington Post* recalled, "Those, of all persuasions, who had an appreciation for the written word were attracted to him and his facility for using the language. He raised the sportswriting trade to a literacy and elegance it had not known before." With all of his success, however, Smith remained grounded, referring to his work merely as entertainment a reader might look forward to a few times a week. He admitted that his sympathies were always on the side he perceived as the underdog. It was no accident then that the targets of his quick wit were often the most powerful people in sports, such as the Major League Baseball commissioner Bowie Kuhn and the New York Yankees owner George Steinbrenner. Smith criticized historians and biographers who made politicians and celebrities in all fields into heroes. He took pride in not exaggerating the glory of athletes, preserving instead a sense of proportion and fairness. His unparalleled ability to do so, while at same time entertaining millions of readers with humor and acute insights, made Smith one of the most popular and respected sportswriters of the twentieth century.

★

Smith's papers are in the Notre Dame Archives, University of Notre Dame. His books include *Out of the Red* (1950); *The Best of Red Smith* (1963); *Red Smith on Fishing Around the World* (1963); *Strawberries in Wintertime: The Sporting World of Red Smith* (1974); *Press Box: Red Smith's Favorite Sports Stories* (1976); *To Absent Friends from Red Smith* (1982); *The Red Smith Reader* (1982), which offers 130 of his columns on a variety of topics; and *Red Smith on Baseball* (2000), a selection of 167 of Smith's most memorable columns. Ira Berkow, *Red: A Biography of Red Smith* (1986), is a full-scale biography that provides an insightful look at Smith's life and career. Helpful interviews include Jerome Holtzman, *No Cheering in the Press Box* (1974); James Grant, "Just a Newspaper Stiff," *The American Spectator* (Nov. 1977); and John L. Kern, "Red Smith in the Final Innings," *Writer's Digest* (June 1982). Other useful sources include Frank Deford, "It's a Quarter of a Century Overdue, But at Last Red Smith Has a Pulitzer," *Sports Illustrated* (7 June 1976), and Donald Hall, "First a Writer, Then a Sportsman," *New York Times Book Review* (18 July 1982). An obituary is in the *New York Times* (16 Jan. 1982).

DANIEL DONAGHY

SNEAD, Sam(uel) Jackson (*b.* 27 May 1912 in Ashwood, Virginia), considered the greatest natural player in the history of golf, who won eighty-one Professional Golfers' Association (PGA) tour titles and fifty-four other professional victories, including three PGA championships, three Masters, and one British Open, and who was known for his failure to win the U.S. Open.

Snead grew up on a farm in Ashwood, the youngest of five boys. He also had one sister. His father was a hotel maintenance engineer, and his mother ran the household. As a boy he learned to hit a golf ball by imitating his brother Homer's swing. "I'd cut a swamp maple limb with a knot on the end, carve a rough club-face with a penknife, leaving some bark for a grip, and swing by the hour." Beginning in 1919, at age seven, Snead and his friends would walk the two and one-half miles to Hot Springs, where they earned money by caddying at the Homestead Hotel golf club. Since shoes were only worn for school or church, he

Sam Snead, 1949. © BETTMANN/CORBIS

quit the long barefoot walk when the weather grew colder, but not before his toes were frostbitten.

As a teenager, the five-foot, eleven-inch, 175-pound Snead was considered a natural athlete. He played high-school football, baseball, basketball, and track, and appeared in three amateur golf tournaments. He avoided college, viewing it as time wasted from golf practice. Agile and double-jointed, Snead could kick to the top of an eight-foot-high doorjamb. At age seventy-six he could still stand on a curb and touch the road with his hands.

Snead played in his first professional event in 1936 in Hershey, Pennsylvania, with only eight clubs. When he missed a shot, the golfer George Fazio spoke encouragingly, "Hit another, son." In response, Snead shot 345 yards, arriving twenty feet from the pin. He learned to "expect good ones to follow bad ones." He carried his first putter in 1937 in the Ryder Cup tournament, playing on the team for nine years. Snead placed second in his first U.S. Open in 1937 at Oakland Hills Country Club in Detroit. With a complete set of clubs, he scored 284, one stroke over the record. Ralph Guldahl scored two shots better than Snead, and set a new U.S. Open record.

At the 1939 U.S. Open, Snead experienced the worst disappointment of his career. On the seventeenth hole of the final round at the Spring Mill Course in Philadelphia, Pennsylvania, he needed a par five to win, shot an eight, and lost to Byron Nelson and Craig Wood. Snead stumbled off the green, and Bobby Jones commented that he looked "like a fellow who has just been hit by Joe Louis." The next year Snead married his high-school girlfriend, Audrey. They traveled together until their first son was born in 1944. Snead admitted that he saw other women during lonely tournament nights, and that his wife tolerated his unfaithfulness. They also had a second son.

During World War II, Snead served for twenty-six months in the U.S. Navy as a physical-education specialist, before receiving a medical discharge for a back injury in September 1944. In November 1944 Snead won the Portland Open in Oregon with a one-over-par 289, taking home $2,675 in war bonds. Snead's military duty had meant missing income from tournament victories. Pleased with his Portland win, Snead said, "It's great to be back."

Snead played eight Masters tournaments in Augusta, Georgia, before winning in 1949, the first year that any Masters champion received the famous green jacket. Sports critics considered this the turning point in Snead's professional career, and he was named the 1949 Professional Golfers' Association (PGA) Player of the Year. In the 1952 Masters, Snead scored 286, four strokes ahead of Jack Burke, Jr. In the 1954 Masters he tied Ben Hogan, beating him seventy to seventy-one in the play-off. He was the top money winner in 1938, 1949, and 1950, his best year. In 1979 he remained a money winner on the regular professional tour. Fred Corcoran, the PGA organizer, said, "Walter Hagan is the first man to make a million dollars in golf and spend it. Snead is the first to make a million and save two."

In 1959 Snead was the first to break sixty at a tournament, with a fifty-nine at the Greenbrier in West Virginia, his home course. In 1965, at fifty-two years and ten months, he was the oldest winner of a U.S. tournament, once again at the Greenbrier. In 1963 Snead was admitted into the Hall of Fame. In 1965 he won his last tour event at the Greensboro Open in North Carolina. Nine years later, at age sixty-two, he tied third in the 1974 U.S. PGA championship. At the Quad Cities Open in 1979, he was the first man to beat his age on the U.S. tour, shooting sixty-six at age sixty-seven. Snead, who had putting difficulties, coined the golfing word "yips" for failures.

Snead's all-time eighty-one PGA wins included three PGA championships (1942, 1949, 1951), one British Open (1946), and three Masters (1949, 1952, 1954). "Slammin' Sam" Snead, along with Byron Nelson and Ben Hogan, dominated postwar golf. Snead credited his success to his sister. "She always told me I could do anything I put my mind to and, by golly, I tried to prove she was right." His tour victories spanned twenty-nine years (1936–1965). Snead's unparalleled record included more than one hundred victories.

Snead coauthored twelve books, including the 1975 best-seller *Sam Snead Teaches You His Simple "Key" Approach to Golf.* He established Sam Snead Enterprises, an equipment company, and Samuel Snead's Taverns. In retirement, he maintained a winter home in Boynton Beach, Florida, and a summer residence in Hot Springs. Always a bridesmaid at the U.S. Open, Snead's failure to win the fourth major golf title plagued him. Between 1937 and 1997 Snead appeared in thirty-seven U.S. Opens, finishing second four times, third once, and in the top ten seven other times. Following his 1939 loss, Snead reported, "I'll tell you this much, it hurt like hell. If I hadn't just let it go, it would have destroyed me." In 1997 Snead concluded, "I don't feel my career has not been fulfilled because I didn't win the U.S. Open."

★

Snead authored twelve books during his career. Snead with Don Wade, *The Lessons I've Learned: Better Golf the Sam Snead Way* (1989), includes memorable anecdotes and golfing tips, and Snead with Fran Pirozzolo, *The Game I Love* (1997), offers his words of wisdom on the game. Al Barkow, *Gettin' to the Dance Floor* (1986), provides an oral commentary by Snead about his golfing origins. Robert Sommers, *The U.S. Open: Golf's Ultimate Challenge* (1987), offers an in-depth study of the U.S. Open championship and Snead's frustration with the event. Dawson Taylor, *The Masters: Golf's Most Prestigious Tradition* (1986), gives an intimate review of Snead's tournament play. See also Robert Scharff, ed., *Golf Magazine Encyclopedia of Golf* (1973). Some of the best magazine articles on Snead are "Snead's Back," *Newsweek* (11 Dec. 1944); "Slammin' Sam," *Golf* (Dec. 1992); and "The Old Man and the Open," *Golf* (June 1994).

SANDRA REDMOND PETERS

SNIDER, Edwin Donald ("Duke") (*b.* 19 September 1926 in Los Angeles, California), All-Star professional baseball slugger who hit 407 home runs in eighteen seasons with the Brooklyn Dodgers.

Snider was the only child of Ward Snider, who worked in a naval shipyard and also played semiprofessional baseball, and Florence Johnson Snider, a homemaker. Snider grew up in Compton, California, and went to the public schools there, maintaining a "B" average at Compton High School.

Ward encouraged his son to play baseball and taught him to hit left-handed even though Snider was right-handed. The reason was simple: most major league parks favored southpaw pull hitters, and there were more right-handed than left-handed pitchers. In high school Snider usually played in the outfield and occasionally was a pitcher (he once tossed a perfect game). He also played basketball and football and ran track. By the time he graduated from Compton High in February 1944, he had won sixteen letters in sports. However, baseball was his best sport and his real love.

Snider's power hitting and speed attracted the attention of the Brooklyn Dodgers. A scout signed him to a contract when he was only one month out of high school. He played minor league baseball with Dodgers farm clubs in Montreal, Canada, and Newport News, Virginia, until he was drafted by the U.S. Navy in December 1944. On active duty until his release in May 1946, Snider served in the Pacific aboard the submarine tender *Sperry*.

Duke Snider, 1963. ASSOCIATED PRESS AP

Soon after he returned home to Compton, Snider married his high-school sweetheart, Beverly Null. The wedding took place on 25 October 1947, and the couple eventually had two children. The family later moved to Lynwood, California, where the Sniders became partners in developing an avocado farm near Oceanside.

After his military service, Snider played for a minor league team in Fort Worth, Texas. Then after a brief stint in the majors with the Brooklyn Dodgers, a team that had too many outfielders, he returned to playing minor league ball, this time with a club in Saint Paul, Minnesota. Gradually becoming a better hitter by not chasing bad balls out of the strike zone, he again played in Montreal before returning to Brooklyn in the last half of the 1949 season to hit .292 with twenty-three home runs. Snider also was an excellent center fielder.

In 1950 Snider struggled with frequent slumps at the plate; nevertheless he hit .321 and had thirty-one homers, followed in 1951 by .277 with twenty-nine home runs. The next year his batting average went back up to .303. He also had a great World Series in 1952, although the Dodgers lost it in seven games to their perennial rivals, the New York Yankees. Snider had 10 hits in 29 times at bat, while hitting 4 homers and driving in 8 runs. His four home runs tied the record held by Babe Ruth and Lou Gehrig.

Snider's 1953 season was grand. He hit .336 and had forty-two homers. He came into his own as a baseball slugger who also continued to be good with his glove. From the 1953 season to the end of the 1957 season, he hit forty or more home runs each year. In 1955 the Dodgers finally won the World Series against the Yankees. However, Snider's performance was not a big factor in the victory, with only three hits from twenty-one appearances at the plate. He played in several more World Series and averaged a respectable .286 with eleven total home runs. He was also named to the All-Star team seven times. He hit more home runs in the 1950s than any other major league player. His career totals were awesome: a .295 batting average, 407 homers, 1,259 runs scored, and 1,333 runs batted in. He also had more than 2,000 total hits.

Snider retired as a player in 1964, but he continued his baseball career. For one year he was a scout for the Los Angeles Dodgers, after which he became a minor league manager of a Dodgers farm club for three years. Then he was a broadcaster for the San Diego Padres for three more years before taking the manager's job with a minor league team affiliated with the Padres. In 1973 he was snubbed when he sought a major league coaching job with the Padres, after which he became an announcer for the Montreal Expos, a position he held until his final retirement in 1986. Along the way, Snider received many honors, including induction into the Baseball Hall of Fame in 1980.

The clean-cut Snider, who did not smoke and did not like alcohol, tarnished his image in 1995 when he admitted to cheating on his taxes. He received a $5,000 fine and a probated sentence. In part, Snider's trouble with the Internal Revenue Service (IRS) stemmed from his declining financial position. Million-dollar contracts were unknown in the 1950s, and Snider made less than $100,000 per season as a major league player. Also, he had bought a bowling alley in California that eventually bankrupted him. To recover, he earned money from signing autographs and making personal appearances that he did not report to the IRS.

Despite his tax problems, Snider will always be remembered as one of the "boys of summer" who entertained millions of people. When fans talk about the greatest players of the game, the "Duke of Flatbush" is usually on their short list, along with baseball superstars like Ty Cobb, Ted Williams, Mickey Mantle, and Pete Rose.

★

For a discussion of Snider's IRS problems, see Michael Berenbaum, "As a Boy of Summer, Snider Takes a Fall," *Washington Post* (31 July 1995). For an in-depth look at Snider's career, see his autobiography, *The Duke of Flatbush* (1988). For an evaluation of the autobiography and other details of Snider's life, see Barry Sussman, "Ebbets Field Lives on in Snider's Memories: The Duke's Book Spins Tales, Digs No Dirt," *Washington Post* (16 June 1988). Snider also receives much attention in Roger Kahn, *Boys of Summer* (1972). Snider's career achievements are mentioned in Joseph L. Reichler, ed., *The Baseball Encyclopedia: The Complete and Official Record of Major League Baseball* (1988), and Edward J. Reilly, *Baseball: An Encyclopedia of Popular Culture* (2000).

JAMES M. SMALLWOOD

SNYDER, James ("Jimmy the Greek") (*b.* 9 September 1919 in Steubenville, Ohio; *d.* 21 April 1996 in Las Vegas, Nevada), sports gambler, handicapper, oddsmaker, public relations director, and television personality who was the most famous sports gambling figure of the twentieth century.

Snyder, born Demetrios Georgos Synodinos, was one of three children of Greek immigrant parents, George and Sultania Synodinos, who operated a small neighborhood grocery store in the tough mill town of Steubenville, Ohio. As a teenager Snyder demonstrated a facility with mathematics and statistics that proved invaluable to his later gambling career. By age fourteen he had found employment as

"Jimmy the Greek" Snyder, 1979. ASSOCIATED PRESS AP

a runner for several of the town's bookmakers and also was working as a youthful professional card and craps dealer. He naturally gravitated toward sports wagering, demonstrating unusual skill at picking winning horses and college football teams. Speaking of his years in wide-open Steubenville, he once joked, "You had to bet to survive. I was twenty-five before I found out gambling was illegal."

Snyder dropped out of high school in 1935 at age sixteen to move to Florida, where he earned a living at the racetracks. On 28 March 1942 he married Pauline ("Sunny") Miles; they had one daughter and divorced after approximately five years of marriage. Snyder married Joan Specht in 1951; they remained married until his death and had four children, three of whom died of cystic fibrosis.

By 1950 he had relocated to New York City, where he was widely admired as an uncanny handicapper who routinely bet $10,000 on a race or game, sometimes increasing his wagers to six figures when he felt he had identified an exceptionally attractive opportunity. In 1951 he was identified as one of the nation's most prominent sports gamblers by witnesses before the Special Committee to Investigate Organized Crime in Interstate Commerce chaired by Senator Estes Kefauver. When the federal government launched an aggressive campaign against gambling in the wake of the hearings, Snyder relocated to Nevada, where gambling was legal.

In Las Vegas he pursued his craft free from worry about the authorities and honed his skills of self-promotion. Unlike most professional sports gamblers who shun the public spotlight, Snyder aggressively cast himself as a highly visible and popular character. His high-stakes bets were the talk of the Strip, and he caught on as a lines maker for the Las Vegas Turf and Sports Club. A 1961 laudatory article in *Sports Illustrated* identified him as "The Greek Who Makes the Odds."

That same year Snyder's luck turned sour when he was caught in a federal wiretap discussing an upcoming Utah–Utah State football game with a friend in Salt Lake City. Indicted by federal authorities for transmitting gambling information across state lines, he pleaded *nolo contendere* (accepting the conviction but denying guilt) and paid a $10,000 fine. Snyder believed that he had been singled out by Attorney General Robert Kennedy for a comment reported by the press in the wake of the passage of a harsh anti-gambling bill: "They lost in Laos, they lost in Cuba, they lost in East Berlin, but they sure are giving the gamblers a beating." President Gerald Ford pardoned him in 1974.

Snyder began in 1963 writing a column on sports betting for the *Las Vegas Sun.* Within a few years it was syndicated in more than 200 daily newspapers. For a time he worked as the publicist for the eccentric billionaire Howard Hughes, who had purchased several prominent hotel-casinos. Snyder's own public relations firm, Sports Unlimited, landed many prominent clients including Caesars Palace. Having forsworn the horses ("Never bet on anything that can't talk"), Synder continued to handicap football and basketball, selling his betting lines and personal evaluations of upcoming games to a select clientele.

He also set odds on major elections, a practice that was legal in Nevada until 1985. He won $100,000 on Harry Truman's 1948 upset presidential victory over Thomas E. Dewey after his sister advised him women were suspicious of men with mustaches; over the years several political pundits had openly praised his ability to handicap political races. In 1971 a Jim Berry cartoon showed a worried President Richard Nixon looking at polling data on the upcoming re-election campaign with an aide and commenting, "Frankly, John, I don't care about the Gallup Poll or the Harris Poll—What does Jimmy the Greek say?"

His national reputation as a superior handicapper was primarily the result of his own continuous self-promotion campaign. His standing among his professional gambling peers—the so-called Las Vegas wise guys—was that of someone who was greatly overrated. Even the *Las Vegas Sun,* for which he wrote, humorously acknowledged as much in a farewell editorial-obituary when it noted that among the wise guys "those in need of a big win would tune into CBS's Sunday football pre-game show, get Snyder's hottest pick, and then bet the other side."

In 1976 Snyder found himself in a position to greatly enhance the public's awareness about sports wagering when he joined the high-profile Sunday-afternoon program *The NFL Today* on CBS TV. Although he glibly interacted with cohosts Brent Musburger and Phyllis George, his primary role was presenting "The Greek's Board," a segment in which he released his predictions on the day's upcoming games. He exploited this opportunity to do what he had long done best—promote himself as the nation's Wizard of Odds. Although no record of all of his picks remains, it was mediocre at best.

After a twelve-year run on *The NFL Today,* Snyder's much-publicized public fistfight with Musburger over his on-camera time allocation, as well as his many disagreements with the show's producers, made him dispensable. Snyder was unceremoniously fired in January 1988 after a Washington, D.C., reporter published his off-the-cuff comments about the qualities of African-American athletes. Those comments were widely condemned as both historically inaccurate and even racist. One month later he suffered a serious heart attack. It proved to be the first of a series of major health problems that eroded his spirited outlook on life, including a painful case of shingles, diabetes, high blood pressure, and a broken hip. In late 1995 he suffered a major stroke; he died in April of the following year in the city he loved, Las Vegas. He is buried in Steubenville. One newspaper obituary aptly summarized his impact upon American society: "His gift for gab was responsible for helping make sports betting one of the most popular forms of mainstream entertainment."

★

Snyder is the subject of a warm but woefully sketchy biography by a family friend: Ginger Wadsworth, *Farewell Jimmy the Greek: Wizard of Odds* (1997). It draws heavily upon Snyder's own peripatetic autobiography, *Jimmy the Greek by Himself* (1975). Michael Rogin's "The Greek Who Makes the Odds," *Sports Illustrated* (18 Dec. 1961), introduced Snyder to a national audience. Art Manteris seeks to place Snyder in a Las Vegas insider's perspective in *Super Bookie: Inside Las Vegas Sports Gambling* (1991), and Mike Lupica provides a sound analysis of Snyder's comments about African-American athletes and his subsequent firing by CBS in "The Greek in Purgatory," *Esquire* (Jan. 1989). An obituary is in the *Las Vegas Sun* (23 Apr. 1996).

RICHARD O. DAVIES

SOSA, Samuel Peralta ("Sammy") (*b.* 12 November 1968 in Consuelo, Dominican Republic), baseball player who, in 1998, was one of two players to break the single-season home-run mark and was named the National League's Most Valuable Player (MVP).

Born on the outskirts of San Pedro de Macoris in the Dominican Republic, to Juan Bautista Montero, a tractor driver at a sugarcane plantation, and Lucrecia Montero Sosa, a housemaid, the future big league star was one of seven children who grew up in a loving home largely under the care of his mother. In 1975 his father passed away and left his mother to raise the family on her own. Mired in poverty, Sosa's mother took on all forms of employment, including housecleaning and cooking, to make ends meet. The six-year-old Sosa supplemented the family income by shining shoes and washing cars. In 1981 the family moved to San Pedro de Macoris. There Sosa attended school, but left following his eighth-grade year and took a $20 per week job at a shoe factory.

Apart from work, sports captured Sosa's attention. Ironically, although he was born into a country with a rich baseball tradition, Sosa did not adopt that sport until he was fourteen. Instead, he trained vigorously to pursue a career in boxing. However, his mother, concerned about the violence associated with prizefighting, convinced Sosa to try for a career in baseball. Sosa worked feverishly at the sport, and in fewer than two years he developed a reputation in the San Pedro de Macoris amateur leagues that attracted the professional scouts. Starstruck, the youngster signed what turned out to be a fabricated contract with a scout from the Philadelphia Phillies. The tenacious Sosa, however, did not quit, and he attended nearly every big league tryout session he could. Finally in 1985, after several frustrating episodes, the Texas Rangers organization penned Sosa to a legitimate contract that included a $3,500 signing bonus—a king's ransom to those on the island. In characteristic fashion, the future slugger bought a bicycle and then sent all but $200 to his mother.

Sammy Sosa. Archive Photos, Inc.

Sosa's path to the major leagues took four years. In 1989 he debuted with the Texas Rangers in Dallas and later that season was dealt to the Chicago White Sox. Shortly after he joined the White Sox, Sosa married Sonia; they had four children together. During his three-year stay with the White Sox, Sosa exhibited great power at times, but his paltry .240 batting average disappointed the American League club, and in 1992 they sent him to the Chicago Cubs of the National League. In the belief that he was at a crossroads in his career because of his undisciplined hitting, Sosa, who had learned the game much later in age than most professionals, decided to practice more patience at the plate. This decision soon paid great dividends.

Sosa, whom scouts had described as "malnourished" only seven years earlier, came alive with the Cubs and slammed thirty-three home runs in his first full year. Additionally, his runs batted in (RBI) total climbed, as did his average. With his increased production, in 1997 the Cubs rewarded Sosa with a whopping $42 million contract. The following year, he delivered as no Cub had done before.

Most baseball pundits did not consider Sosa a serious contender for the 1998 home-run title. Instead, Mark McGwire of the St. Louis Cardinals took center stage as the primary prospect, both to lead baseball in home runs and possibly to establish a new mark in that category. Shortly after the season began, McGwire had amassed twenty-seven home runs by the end of May and appeared to have no rivals. Between 25 May and 24 June, however, Sosa launched a furious assault to challenge the Cardinals giant. In that time, the Dominican blasted twenty-two home runs, which took his total from nine to thirty-one, three in back of McGwire. From mid-June through the end of the season, the two captured international attention with the greatest home-run race baseball had ever seen. Through it all, Sosa's fun-loving demeanor won him enormous support across the globe, and he became a source of inspiration for many Latinos in North America.

In August 1998 Hurricane Georges swept through Sosa's native Dominican Republic. Sosa offered to return to his homeland to assist in the rescue efforts, but Leonel Fernandez, the Dominican president, instead encouraged the national hero to remain in the United States and pursue the home-run title. Instead of making a personal appearance, Sosa spearheaded a relief drive that raised $700,000 for food and equipment for the storm-torn island. In addition to this relief work, he has also organized and supported several other charities, such as the Sammy Sosa Foundation, a program designed to help children in need that operates both in the Dominican Republic and in the United States.

On 8 September McGwire broke the single-season home-run record held by Roger Maris when he hit number sixty-two. Sosa, however, was close behind. Less than a week later, on 13 September, he also broke Maris's mark by hitting his sixty-second home run. Given a six-minute standing ovation at Chicago's Wrigley Field, the teary-eyed Sosa remembered, "I've never been so emotional. . . . It was something that I couldn't believe what I was doing." Sosa hit four more home runs before the end of the season and finished second to McGwire's seventy in what was one of the most memorable and exciting competitions ever seen in the history of sport.

Following the baseball season, in November 1998, the Baseball Writer's Association bestowed on Sosa that year's National League Most Valuable Player award. One month later, in a gesture of goodwill toward Latin America, President William J. Clinton invited the popular Sosa to help light the national Christmas tree. The next season, Sosa proved his 1998 home-run barrage was no fluke. In 1999 he launched sixty-three home runs and joined McGwire (who hit sixty-five) as the only other major leaguer to have hit sixty or more home runs twice in a career. From 1998 through 2000, Sosa hit 179 home runs and drove in an astonishing 437 runs. Then, in the 2001 campaign, he added sixty-four more home runs to his already impressive numbers. By doing so, he established himself as the only player in Major League Baseball history to have hit sixty or more home runs in three different seasons.

Sosa's baseball achievements transcended the diamond. Poor Dominicans were encouraged by his success, and Americans who knew of his humble origins viewed him as a classic Horatio Alger figure. Sosa's strong sense of nationalism and generosity also made him a national hero, and his propensity to exhibit his heritage galvanized America's Latino community. Finally, his enthusiasm and friendly nature on the ball field, graciousness as a competitor, and devotion to family endeared him to millions around the world.

★

Sosa's autobiography with Marcos Breton, *Sosa: An Autobiography* (2000), includes interesting insights into the slugger's thoughts, but the convoluted accounts from those who are close to Sosa sometimes mar its readability. Bill Gutman, *Sammy Sosa: A Biography* (1998), is one of the better general overviews, laced with heartwarming accounts of Sosa's Dominican roots. Samuel O. Regalado, "Sammy Sosa Meets Horatio Alger: Latin Ballplayers and the American Success Myth," in Robert Elias, *Baseball and the American Dream* (2001), places Sosa's emergence as a U.S. icon into historical perspective.

SAMUEL O. REGALADO

SPAHN, Warren Edward (*b.* 23 April 1921 in Buffalo, New York), pitcher for the Boston (later Milwaukee) Braves, who in the course of twenty-one seasons of major league play compiled one of the greatest records in baseball history, including 363 victories, the most ever by a left-handed pitcher.

Spahn was the eldest of six children and the first-born son of Edward Spahn, a wallpaper salesman and amateur baseball player, who taught his young son the basics of the game. Spahn was playing organized ball before the age of

Warren Spahn, 1964. ASSOCIATED PRESS AP

ten. A lanky boy who eventually grew to be six feet tall and 175 pounds, Spahn started out playing first base, but took up pitching on the advice that he had little chance of ousting the first baseman on his high school team. By his junior year at South Park High School, he was the ace of the pitching staff. He graduated from high school in 1940.

Spahn was first scouted by Billy Myers of the Boston Red Sox organization. When the Sox passed on the teenage southpaw, Myers sent a positive report to Boston's other team, the National League (NL) Braves, who signed Spahn in 1940. Moving quickly through the Braves farm system, he did stints at Bradford, Pennsylvania, of the Pony League; Evansville, Indiana, of the Three-I League; and Hartford, Connecticut, of the Eastern League. Spahn was called up to Boston at the tail of the 1942 season, but made just four appearances without a decision in an unspectacular major league debut.

That winter Spahn joined the U.S. Army and spent the next three years as a member of the 276th Combat Engineers. He saw ground action in the invasion of Europe, including frontline combat at the Battle of Remagen Bridge, where he earned a Bronze Star as well as a Purple Heart for a shrapnel wound. Exhibiting his trademark modesty, Spahn trivialized the injury, dismissing it as "only a scratch in the foot." In recognition of his leadership and bravery, Spahn was awarded a battlefield officer's commission as a second lieutenant, the only professional baseball player to be so honored during World War II.

Spahn settled down to civilian life in 1946, marrying Lorene Southard of Tulsa, and established his home in Oklahoma. The couple had one son and remained lifelong mates. Rejoining the Braves in midseason, the young pitcher compiled an undistinguished record of eight wins and five losses. However, he gained a spot in the starting rotation with an earned run average (ERA) of 2.93, a hopping fastball, and an unusual ability to go the distance. In 1947, his first full season in the majors, Spahn blossomed as a star. Emerging as the workhorse of the Boston staff, he amassed a 21–10 record. It was the first of thirteen seasons during which he would win twenty games or more.

In 1948 "Spahnie," as his teammates called him, helped the Boston Braves to their first NL pennant since 1914, only their second in the team's history. Considering the thinness of the Boston pitching staff, winning the pennant was little short of a miracle. The 1948 season included one of the rainiest summers on record, allowing Spahn and the team's only other top-ranked pitcher, right-hander Johnny Sain, an unusual number of starts. The formula for that winning season was encapsulated in a sing-song rhyme uttered by the long-suffering fans of the Boston Braves, "Spahn and Sain—and pray for rain." The Cleveland Indians defeated Boston 4–2 in the World Series, with Spahn taking a win and a loss.

Although the Braves quickly returned to their characteristic second-division ways, Spahn continued to reign as one of the most effective pitchers in the NL, chalking up his hundredth victory in 1951, only his fifth season. With rumors afoot of a franchise move, the demoralized 1952 Braves plummeted to a last-place finish, leaving Spahn with a record of 14–19, one of only two losing seasons he had with the team. Yet even under these conditions he managed to keep his season ERA under 3.00.

Now in his thirties, Spahn began to see his fastball lose its edge. Unlike many maturing fastballers, however, Spahn accepted the inevitable changes to his pitching and made adjustments that kept him at the top of the game for another decade. He developed a repertoire of breaking balls and change-ups, and used these pitches to set up fewer smokers. He also added a painfully unpredictable screwball and had an uncanny ability to deliver the difficult pitch without telegraphing it.

In 1953 the Boston Braves moved to Milwaukee in the first shift of a major league franchise since 1900. Although uncertainty prevailed among the players, glory days were ahead for the new Milwaukee Braves and their great pitching ace. Playing at a new stadium in front of large, adoring crowds, the Braves fielded great teams during the late 1950s, featuring such standouts as Hank Aaron, Eddie Matthews, and Lew Burdette.

Well-liked and as effective as ever on the mound, Spahn led Milwaukee to back-to-back pennants in 1957 and 1958, posting twenty-one and twenty-two wins in those championship seasons. The 1957 season was perhaps the height of Spahn's career. Following Milwaukee's victory over the New York Yankees in the World Series, he was named the winner of the Cy Young Award, baseball's highest pitching honor. The following year the Yankees got their revenge, but only after dropping two games to the Braves ace lefty.

Milwaukee's bubble burst during the 1960s, but Spahn, now reaching his forties, remained one of baseball's premier pitchers. He hurled his first no-hitter, against the Philadelphia Phillies, in 1960, and did an encore performance against the San Francisco Giants the following season. On the occasion of his 300th career win in 1961, a 2–1 complete-game six-hitter against the Chicago Cubs, he told the *New York Sunday News,* "The game was the kind I always wanted it to be. No fluke. No big scoring game where I would be sitting in the clubhouse at the end. It was low scoring and hard fought." A year later he chalked up his 327th victory, the most wins by any lefty in baseball history. One of his best seasons ever was 1963 when, at age 42, he finished the season 23–7.

By the mid-1960s Spahn was the highest-paid pitcher in baseball, earning a salary of about $80,000 per year. This turned out to be a mixed blessing. In 1965, with attendance falling in Milwaukee, the franchise's new management felt it could not afford to pay a forty-four-year-old pitcher that kind of money. After a quarter of a century in the Braves organization, Spahn left the team to play out an embarrassing big-league farewell summer split between the New York Mets (4–12) and San Francisco Giants (3–4). Whether it came out of an enduring innocent love for the game or an uncharacteristic crustiness he had developed as one of the game's oldest players, Spahn reacted angrily, telling the press, "I didn't quit; baseball retired me." Undaunted, he returned to the mound in the Mexican League and even pitched several minor league games before finally retiring as a player in 1967. He managed the minor-league Tulsa Oilers for the next three years, leading them to the 1968 Pacific Coast League pennant, and has served as a scout and minor league pitching instructor for several major league teams. In 1988 he retired from baseball to his Oklahoma cattle ranch, where he enjoyed fishing, swimming, riding, and other outdoor sports.

Spahn's exit from professional baseball was perhaps the only ungraceful performance of his career. He left the game with a lifetime record of 363–245, the "winningest" left-handed pitcher in major league history, posting a remarkable career ERA of just 3.09. His name is plastered all over the record books: league leader in victories eight times, in complete games nine times, and in strikeouts four times. He was a member of fifteen NL All-Star teams and held the record for the most career home runs hit by a pitcher (35). Spahn was elected to the National Baseball Hall of Fame in 1973, his first year of eligibility.

★

There are three biographies of Spahn. Two are fan books written at the height of his career: Milton J. Shapiro, *The Warren Spahn Story* (1958), and Al Silverman, *Warren Spahn: Immortal Southpaw* (1961). The third biography, Peter C. Bjarkman, *Warren Spahn* (1995), is part of a series of baseball biographies for teenagers.

DAVID MARC

SPALDING, Albert Goodwill ("A. G.") (*b.* 2 September 1850 in Byron, Illinois; *d.* 9 September 1915 in Point Loma, California), baseball player, promoter, and sporting goods executive who helped professionalize sports in the United States.

The son of James Lawrence Spalding and Harriet Irene Goodwill Wright Spalding, Spalding grew up in prosperity in a small village ninety miles west of Chicago. His sister was born in 1854, and his brother and future business partner James Walter in 1856. Spalding's mother brought an inheritance from a previous marriage, and his father farmed and managed rental property. When Spalding's father died in 1858, Spalding was sent to live with an aunt in Rockford, Illinois, where he attended public schools and eventually

A. G. Spalding. AP/WIDE WORLD PHOTOS

Rockford Commercial College. In Rockford, Spalding began watching local boys play baseball at the town commons. After catching a fly ball hit beyond center field during one game, Spalding threw the ball back to the participants with authority. His arm strength impressed the players, and they invited him to join their games.

Spalding's family joined him in Rockford in 1863, and city businessmen formed a new baseball club, the Forest Citys, in 1865. Spalding was recruited to pitch, and he led the club to a victory in 1867 over the Washington Nationals, considered one of the best teams in the country. Although rules during this era forbade salaries, teams often paid players "under the table" or provided additional employment. Urban boosters and businessmen were beginning to realize how effectively traveling baseball teams promoted individual cities, and Spalding received a position as a clerk in Rockford while playing for the Forest Citys.

Shortly after his successful pitching helped defeat the

Nationals, Spalding received competitive offers to play elsewhere. He elected to work in a wholesale grocery store and pitch for the Chicago Excelsiors in 1867. After financial disaster overtook this firm and other job prospects were poor, Spalding returned to Rockford and acted as a bookkeeper while again pitching for the Forest Citys. By 1870 Spalding was called "Big Al," in reference to his six-foot, one-inch, and 170-pound frame, and in 1871 he joined Harry Wright's newly created professional league, the National Association of Professional Base Ball Players (NAPBP). Spalding served as captain and pitcher for Wright's Boston Red Stockings, who won four NAPBP championships from 1872 to 1875. He compiled 207 wins during this period to become baseball's first 200-game winner. On 18 November 1875 Spalding married Sarah Josephine Keith; they had one son.

Spalding returned to Chicago in 1876 when local businessman and team president William Hulbert recruited him to pitch for and manage the Chicago White Stockings (later known as the Cubs). Spalding used his influence and fame in the Midwest to assist Hulbert in promoting the excitement of professional baseball. The National League of Professional Base Ball Clubs (eventually the National League) was established in 1876. Spalding acted as secretary and team manager of the Chicago club while working with Hulbert to draft a constitution for the new league. The bureaucratic nature of the venture appealed to Spalding, long a proponent of honorable play. National League bylaws forbade Sunday games, alcohol sales at baseball parks, and gambling.

Spalding's move to Chicago also led to business opportunities. In March 1876 Spalding and his brother James Walter launched a sporting goods business. They spent $800 to establish an emporium in Chicago that sold baseball equipment. In 1878 Spalding retired from pitching and concentrated full-time on team management and his sporting goods business. A. G. Spalding and Brothers became the exclusive provider of baseballs for league play and the publisher of *Spalding's Official Base Ball Guide*, an annual publication edited by Spalding himself from 1878 to 1880. Over time, the company manufactured footballs, basketballs, golf balls, and golf clubs in the United States and led marketing innovations such as sporting goods boutiques in department stores, celebrity endorsements, and team sponsorship. In 1885 the first store outside of Chicago opened in New York City, and in 1889 new stores opened in Denver and Philadelphia.

After Hulbert's death in 1882, Spalding served as president of the Chicago White Stockings until 1891. The squad won five pennants under his direction, and he continued to promote the game with passion. He organized professional baseball's first round-the-world tour in 1888, featuring the Chicago White Stockings and an All-Star squad. Contests were held before enthusiastic audiences in fourteen different countries of the world, spanning five continents. In 1900 Spalding's role as an international ambassador of sports competition was solidified when he was appointed United States Commissioner of the Olympic Games by President William McKinley.

Spalding was also a major contributor to the debate and intrigue surrounding baseball's heritage. The English game of rounders, which involved four bases laid out in diamond-shaped configuration, strikes, outs, and a "feeder" who tossed the ball to a "striker," preceded baseball. Yet Abraham G. Mills, then president of the National League, proclaimed during a New York baseball banquet at Delmonico's restaurant that baseball had evolved from U.S. origins. The men at the center of this debate were baseball writer Henry Chadwick and Albert Spalding. Chadwick believed baseball grew from English origins; Spalding felt U.S. ingenuity was the source. In Spalding's memoirs, *America's National Game* (1911), he argues that baseball was an adaptation of a New England game called town ball, itself inspired by the English game of cricket. However, Spalding also vigorously attempted to distinguish cultural differences. He claimed the English played cricket because it was easy and did not overtax their energy or their thought. Conversely, he believed baseball personified American courage, confidence, and combativeness. Mills chaired a commission assembled to research baseball's history from 1905 to 1907. The group's conclusion was that General Abner Doubleday had drawn the first known diagram of the baseball diamond in Cooperstown, New York, a finding drawn from the recollections of an elderly former Cooperstown resident. Since a great deal of evidence contradicts this explanation, baseball historians have never accepted the committee's conclusion.

Spalding's wife died suddenly in 1899 and he married Elizabeth Churchill Mayer, a widow and childhood friend from Rockford, nearly two years later. Historian Peter Levine contends that Mayer and Spalding shared a relationship for years and had a son. The newlyweds established a new life for themselves in Point Loma, California. Spalding was nominated to run in the Republican primary for the U.S. Senate in 1910, a race he lost by a slim margin.

Spalding died of heart failure in Point Loma in 1915; his remains were cremated. At the time of his death he was recognized nationally and internationally as the father of "America's game." He received further recognition in 1939 when the Committee on Baseball Veterans inducted him posthumously to the National Baseball Hall of Fame.

★

Spalding's papers are in the library at the National Baseball Hall of Fame in Cooperstown, New York, and in the Spalding Collection at the New York City Public Library. There also is a large selection of information and memorabilia available at the Byron Public Library in Byron, Illinois. In his memoirs, *America's*

National Game (1911), Spalding describes his version of the history of baseball and his involvement in the development of the sport. Harriet I. Spalding, *Reminiscences of Harriet I. Spalding* (1910), provides detailed information about Spalding's childhood and family background. Arthur Bartlett, *Baseball and Mr. Spalding; The History and Romance of Baseball* (1951), is a standard account of Spalding's life based primarily on Spalding's memoirs. Peter Levine, *A. G. Spalding and the Rise of Baseball: The Promise of American Sport* (1985), is the most comprehensive and helpful description available about Spalding's life and his impact on the growth of baseball. Harold Seymour, *Baseball* (1960), provides a good general history of baseball during Spalding's era. Warren Goldstein, *Playing for Keeps: A History of Early Baseball* (1989), delivers background information about mythology surrounding the history of baseball. Steven A. Riess, *City Games: The Evolution of American Urban Society and the Rise of Sports* (1989), is an insightful history of the connection between baseball teams and promoters like Spalding in urban America. Obituaries are in the New York Times (10 and 11 Sep. 1915).

R. JAKE SUDDERTH

SPEAKER, Tris(tram) E. (*b.* 4 April 1888 in Hubbard, Texas; *d.* 8 December 1958 in Lake Whitney, Texas), Hall of Fame baseball player who is considered one of the greatest centerfielders of all time; as a player-manager he led the Cleveland Indians to a World Series championship in 1920.

Tris Speaker, 1915. AP/WIDE WORLD PHOTOS

Speaker was one of eight children born to Archie Speaker, a carpenter, and Nancy Jane ("Jennie") Poer, a homemaker. Speaker's father died when he was ten and he was very close to his mother throughout his life. He broke his right arm as a youngster while breaking horses and so learned to throw and hit left-handed. He then broke his left arm playing football and doctors wanted to amputate. He refused and simply gave up football, instead concentrating on baseball. He pitched for two years for Fort Worth Polytechnic Institute (now Texas Wesleyan University), and in the summer following his sophomore year he played for a semiprofessional team in Corsicana, Texas.

Doak Roberts, owner of the Cleburne team in the North Texas League, discovered Speaker while scouting an outfielder on his team. Speaker was the winning pitcher and hit two home runs, so Roberts gave him a contract of $50 a month and $1 train fare to Waco, where Cleburne was playing. Speaker pocketed the $1 and hopped a freight, reporting to manager Benny Shelton at 6:30 A.M. Shelton started Speaker on the mound that day and he lost 3–2. He subsequently lost several more games, including one by a 22–4 score.

At this juncture, Speaker convinced Shelton to shift him to the outfield where he hit .263 and stole 33 bases in 87 games. The following year the North and South Texas Leagues merged and Roberts moved his franchise, along with Speaker, to Houston. There Speaker batted .318 and was purchased late in the season by the Boston Red Sox for $750 over the objections of his mother, who thought he was being "sold into slavery." He appeared in seven games for the Red Sox but only managed three hits in nineteen at-bats. The Red Sox did not think enough of Speaker to send him a contract over the winter, so in the spring of 1908 he traveled to nearby Marlin, Texas, where the New York Giants trained, and was twice rebuffed by legendary Giants manager John McGraw, who thought he had more outfielders than he could use.

Speaker then paid his own way to the Red Sox camp in Little Rock, Arkansas. The Red Sox did sign him again but left him with the Little Rock franchise of the Southern League at the end of spring training as partial payment for the stadium rent. The Red Sox retained the option to repurchase Speaker for $500 and did so in September after he hit .350 to lead the league. The Little Rock owner, Mickey Finn, had offers from the Giants, Pittsburgh Pirates, and Washington Senators, but felt honor bound to the Red Sox.

Speaker batted .309 in 1909, his first full major league

season and the first of eighteen seasons he would hit above .300. By 1910 he was a full-fledged star, batting .340, and in 1912 he hit .383 for the season and led the Red Sox to a World Series victory against the Giants, who had snubbed him only four years previously. With Boston he anchored what is often thought of as the greatest outfield in history with Duffy Lewis and Harry Hooper. That outfield also led the Red Sox to the 1915 American League pennant and another World Series victory in 1915, this time over the Philadelphia Phillies.

Even with the 1915 World Championship, Red Sox owner Joe Lannin tried to cut Speaker's salary because the war with the rival Federal League was over and Speaker had batted "only" .322 the previous year. The predictable salary impasse led to Speaker's trade to the Cleveland Indians on the eve of the 1916 season for $50,000, along with pitcher Sad Sam Jones and infielder Fred Thomas. Speaker responded by hitting .386 for his new team, ending Ty Cobb's extraordinary string of nine straight batting titles. He also led the league in hits, doubles, and slugging average.

The Indians named Speaker player-manager in July 1919, and he led the club to a long-awaited pennant and World Series victory in 1920. That year Speaker batted .388, second to George Sisler's .407, and he again led the league in doubles with fifty. As manager, he endured the August death of his shortstop Ray Chapman by a pitched ball. Chapman was his best friend on the team and the team's most popular player. Speaker was so upset by the tragedy that he left the club for several days.

The 1920 World Series against the Brooklyn Dodgers was a memorable one, involving Bill Wambsganss's unassisted triple play and the first grand-slam home run in Series history by Elmer Smith. When the Indians clinched the World Series against the Brooklyn Dodgers, Speaker raced from his position in centerfield and climbed into the stands behind the third-base line to embrace his mother.

On 15 January 1925 the thirty-seven-year-old Speaker married Frances Cudahy of Buffalo, New York, and celebrated by batting .389 for the season. In 1926 a gambling scandal broke involving Speaker and Ty Cobb, both of whom were accused by former pitcher Dutch Leonard of conspiring to fix a game in 1919. American League president Ban Johnson suspended both players, but commissioner Kenesaw Mountain Landis investigated and exonerated the two. In a strange twist, however, Landis insisted on placing both players with new teams, meaning both had to resign their managerial positions, Cobb with Detroit and Speaker after eight years as Cleveland's player-manager. Thus, Speaker played the 1927 season with the Washington Senators before joining old rival Cobb with the Philadelphia Athletics for both of their final years.

Speaker managed the Newark Bears of the International League in 1929 and 1930, where he batted .355 and .419 as a spot player. He then broadcast games in Chicago before becoming involved in the wholesale liquor business in Cleveland. He also served as chairman of the Cleveland Boxing Commission and later briefly became co-owner and manager of the Kansas City Blues of the American Association before returning to the broadcast booth, this time in Cleveland. The Indians later employed him as a scout, batting instructor, and advisor.

Speaker was one of the greatest all-round ballplayers of all time, although he was often overshadowed by his contemporary, Ty Cobb. He was a tremendous hitter with extra-base power to all fields and a fleet and skillful base runner with 433 lifetime stolen bases. He batted over .380 four times and over .360 eight times in his illustrious career. He had a lifetime batting average of .344 with 3,514 hits, placing him fourth all time. His 793 doubles are still a major league record. His "Gray Eagle" nickname bespoke both of his prematurely gray hair and his reputation as a heady ballplayer. Teammates commonly called him "Spoke," as in the key spoke in the wheel. He was the seventh player inducted into the Baseball Hall of Fame in 1937.

Speaker possessed one of the finest throwing arms of his day and is first in assists all time, throwing out thirty or more men in a season four times. His shallow play in centerfield allowed him to catch many short balls that would have otherwise fallen as hits. He would sometimes sneak in behind a runner on second for a pick-off play from the pitcher and several times completed unassisted double plays at second, once in the 1912 World Series and twice in one game in 1916. Once he even served as the pivot man on a routine ground ball double play: second baseman to center fielder to first baseman.

Speaker was also outstanding at going back for balls, a skill he attributed to legendary pitcher Cy Young, his teammate with Boston. Young was outstanding with a fungo bat and gave Speaker plenty of experience in racing for balls over his head during practice. Speaker once jumped over a fence in Washington to make a spectacular catch and is probably the first outfielder to test the wind by throwing grass in the air. He is second all time for putouts.

In December 1957 Speaker visited his hometown of Hubbard. While on a fishing trip to nearby Lake Whitney, he suffered a fatal heart attack at the age of seventy. His last words were, "I am Tris Speaker." He is buried in Hubbard.

★

The National Baseball Library in Cooperstown, New York, houses material on Speaker's career. The Ellery Clark, Jr., Red Sox Analytical Letter Collection in Annapolis, Maryland, contains interviews with Speaker and teammates under the title "A Closeup of Tris Speaker." For short biographical treatments see Ira Smith, *Baseball's Famous Outfielders* (1954); Bob Broeg, *Superstars of Baseball* (1971); and Lowell Reidenbaugh, *Cooperstown: Where Baseball's Legends Live Forever* (1983). Speaker's tenure with the Boston Red Sox is well covered in Frederick Lieb, *The Boston Red Sox* (1947); his career with the Cleveland Indians is covered in Franklin Lewis, *The Cleveland Indians* (1949). His role with the 1920 Cleveland Indians is chronicled in Tom Meany, *Baseball's Greatest Teams* (1949). Speaker's reaction to Ray Chapman's death in 1920 is detailed in Mike Sowell, *The Pitch That Killed* (1989). The 1926 gambling scandal involving Speaker and Ty Cobb is well developed in David Pietrusza, *Judge and Jury: The Life and Times of Judge Kenesaw Mountain Landis* (1998). An obituary is in the *New York Times* (9 Dec. 1958).

C. Paul Rogers III

SPITZ, Mark Andrew (*b.* 10 February 1950 in Modesto, California), swimmer who was the first athlete to win seven gold medals in a single Olympic Games, setting world records in all seven events.

The oldest of three children of Arnold Spitz, a steel executive, and Lenore Spitz, a homemaker, Spitz had been a "water baby" since age two when his father taught him to swim. After his father was transferred from Modesto to Honolulu, Hawaii, Spitz and his mother went to Waikiki Beach every day, and he would hurl himself into the ocean. The family moved to Sacramento, California, when Spitz was eight, and he received his first formal swimming instruction at the local Young Men's Christian Association. By age nine Spitz was being tutored by the noted swimming coach Sherman Chavoor at the Arden Hills Swim Club in Carmichael, California, and working out for an hour or more every Monday, Wednesday, and Friday. On Saturdays he had double workouts. At age ten Spitz held seventeen national age-group records and practiced ninety minutes a day, seven days a week.

Basic to Spitz's success as a swimmer was his parents' commitment to making their son a champion. Arnold Spitz stressed the importance of winning, telling his son, "Swimming isn't everything, winning is." Both parents pushed and sacrificed so that their son would have the best chance to win. Spitz's physique also contributed to his success. He was slim and had extraordinarily large, scoop-shaped palms that could push tremendous amounts of water. His knees flexed forward, giving him a thrust that went up to twelve inches deeper in the water than that of his competitors. This flexibility gave him an abnormally long stroke in the butterfly, the most difficult stroke in swimming. He could swim the length of a twenty-five-yard pool with only thirteen strokes; most swimmers require fifteen or sixteen. Taking advantage of Spitz's leg movements and kicking action, Chavoor worked with the swimmer, particularly on his butterfly and freestyle strokes.

When Spitz was fourteen, his father told him that he had reached a peak and could either stay in Sacramento and forget about competitive swimming or go to Santa Clara, California, to be coached by George Haines. The family moved to Walnut Creek, California, in order for

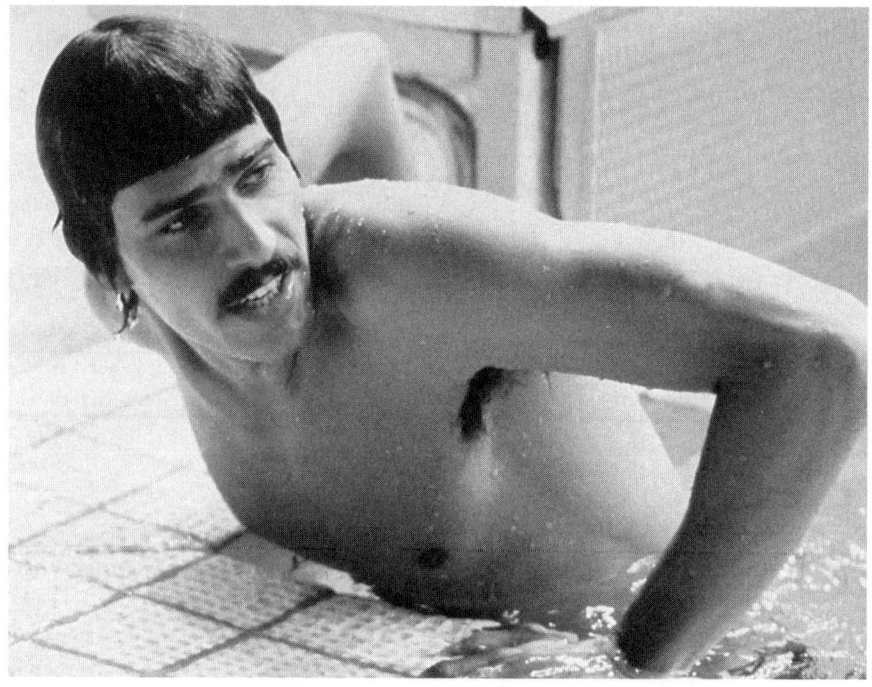

Mark Spitz at the 1972 Olympics in Munich. Associated Press AP

Spitz to work with Haines. Spitz and his mother had to get up at 5 A.M. to drive to the 6:30 A.M. practices, which were held forty miles away in Santa Clara. His father commuted 100 miles each day to work. Haines was the coach of the Olympic champion Don Schollander, and Spitz credited Haines with polishing his strokes and techniques, saying, "He gave me my foundation as a swimmer." Spitz did his part, swimming seven miles a day, two and a half hours in the morning and two hours in the evening.

Spitz showed the effects of Haines's coaching by qualifying for the 1964 national Amateur Athletic Union (AAU) championship competition. In August 1965 at the Maccabiah Games in Tel Aviv, Israel, he won four gold medals, three for individual events. In 1966 he won his first national AAU championship in what was to become his best event, the 100-meter butterfly. For Spitz 1967 was a record-breaking year. In June he set the first of his world records, in the 400-meter freestyle. The next month at the Santa Clara International Invitational, he set or tied five U.S. records, and that summer at the Pan-American Games in Winnipeg, Canada, he won five gold medals and set two more world records. September saw another world record in the 110-yard butterfly at a meet in London, England, and in October Spitz set two more world records in Berlin, Germany, in the 100-meter and 200-meter butterfly.

By early 1968 Spitz had become the media's darling, replacing Schollander as the dominant figure in U.S. swimming, and the pressure was building toward the 1968 Olympics in Mexico City, Mexico. Spitz qualified at the trials to swim in three individual events and three relays. Haines, the coach of the 1968 Olympic team, indicated that Spitz could win as many as six gold medals. Spitz, increasingly sure of himself because of his recent victories and imbued with his father's drive for him to be a winner, intimated that he would win six golds. However, Spitz failed to win any individual gold medals in Mexico. Haines thought Spitz choked from the pressure. Others blamed it on a cold that prevented Spitz from practicing at the team's high-altitude camp. Some said it was the attitude of his teammates who reportedly cheered for opposing swimmers. Although he did not dominate his three individual events, Spitz did win two gold medals in the relays, a silver in the 100-meter butterfly, and a bronze in the 100-meter freestyle. He came in dead last in the finals of the 200-meter butterfly, an event in which he held the world record.

Spitz graduated from Santa Clara High School in June 1968, but delayed entering college because of the Olympics. In January 1969 he enrolled as a predental student at Indiana University, a school noted for its championship swim team and the swimming coach James E. ("Doc") Counsilman. Spitz had a history of being a loner and uncooperative, but Counsilman made sure that members of the Indiana team judged Spitz on his behavior, not his reputation. Spitz's teammates gave him a chance, and Counsilman provided much-needed emotional support. Spitz fit in and eventually was elected as the team co-captain. Indiana was a powerhouse in swimming, and in March 1969 Spitz played a major role in securing the National Collegiate Athletic Association (NCAA) championship. He won three events, two in U.S. record time. For Spitz, it was like a comeback. In July he won three events at the Santa Clara International Invitational, tying records in each. Later in the month he won six gold medals at the Maccabiah Games.

Spitz continued to win and set records in the 1970s. In 1971 he set seven world and two U.S. records and won four national and two collegiate championships. In August 1971 at the AAU championships he won four events, setting two world records. This feat reestablished Spitz as "the cynosure of American swimming," according to William F. Reed in a September 1971 *Sports Illustrated* article. Once again Spitz was seen as a major contender for gold medals at the upcoming Olympics.

Spitz's accomplishments were recognized when he received the Sullivan Award as the outstanding amateur athlete of the year. In March 1972 he led Indiana to its fifth consecutive NCAA swimming title. At the Olympic trials in August, he set a world record in the 200-meter butterfly and qualified for participation in four individual events and three relay races. The specter of his failure at the 1968 Olympics was raised, but Spitz's former coach Sherm Chavoor, who now coached the women's Olympic team, stated that Spitz was physically stronger and emotionally more mature.

At six feet tall and weighing 170 pounds, Spitz was in shape. Resembling the actor Omar Sharif, he looked good. Unlike other swimmers who shaved their heads for competitions, Spitz kept his hair and his mustache for good luck. In Munich, Germany, Spitz was more careful with the press and comfortable with his teammates than he had been in Mexico City. His performance at the 1972 Olympics made history. Spitz's first event was the 200-meter butterfly; he knocked 2.6 seconds off his own world record to win the gold medal. Later that night he earned another gold medal in the 400-meter freestyle relay, swimming anchor. The next night he won the 200-meter freestyle. Two days later he won the 100-meter butterfly and earned a gold in the 800-meter freestyle relay. He made history in the 100-meter freestyle, becoming the first modern Olympic athlete to win six gold medals. Then he won a seventh in the 400-meter medley relay, swimming the butterfly. Unfortunately, Spitz could not stay in Munich to savor his victories. Just hours after his final race, Palestinian terrorists kidnapped and murdered members of the Israeli Olympic team. Spitz, who is Jewish, was flown home.

Spitz retired from competitive swimming immediately

following the 1972 Olympics. After fourteen years of effort, he was ready to try something different. He graduated from Indiana with a B.S. in 1972 and was accepted to dental school, but he put school on hold and signed with the William Morris Agency, which guided him into a number of lucrative product endorsements. The handsome athlete was highly marketable, and a poster of Spitz wearing nothing but his swimsuit, mustache, and seven gold Olympic medals was second in all-time popularity to the Betty Grable pinup of World War II. Over a two-year period, Spitz made more than $7 million. He married Susan Weiner, a college student and part-time model, on 6 May 1973; they had two sons. Spitz owned a surf-wear business and was involved in real estate. He wrote the *Mark Spitz Complete Book of Swimming* (1976), with Alan LeMond, and *Seven Golds: Mark Spitz' Own Story: The Growing Up of a Gold Medal Swimmer* (1981). Spitz was named the World Swimmer of the Year in 1969, 1971, and 1972.

In 1990 Spitz decided to train for the 1992 Olympics for the 100-meter butterfly, but did not qualify for the team. However, he continued to work out with the masters swim team at the University of California at Los Angeles. Spitz told *Sports Illustrated* in August 1997, "I squeak, rattle, and roll," but, "I enjoy the camaraderie."

Spitz was one of the greatest swimmers of all time. In his competitive career he set thirty-two world records and, in two Olympics, he won nine gold medals, one silver, and one bronze. He suffered the defeat and humiliation of the Mexico City Olympics and worked for the next four years to redeem himself. His victories in Munich became part of Olympic legend.

★

A principle source of information is Spitz's autobiography, *Seven Golds: Mark Spitz' Own Story: The Growing Up of a Gold Medal Swimmer* (1981). See also the essay in Bill Libby, *Stars of the Olympics* (1975). Helpful articles include "Water Baby to Beat," *Time* (12 Apr. 1968), for background on his life and physical strengths; "Kicking Up a Storm," *Newsweek* (16 Sept. 1968), for Coach Haines's comments; "Growing Up to the Legend," *Time* (25 July 1969), for reflections about the Mexico City Olympics. A lengthy article with good background is William F. Reed, "'Swimming Isn't Everything, Winning Is,'" *Sports Illustrated* (6 Mar. 1970). For information on the Munich Olympics, see Jerry Kirshenbaum, "Mexico to Munich: Mark Spitz and the Quest for Gold," *Sports Illustrated* (4 Sept. 1972); and the cover story, "Spitz uber Alles in Deutschland," *Time* (11 Sept. 1972). More recent articles are Kenny Moore, "Bionic Man: Olympic Champion Mark Spitz Plans Comeback at 39," *Sports Illustrated* (23 Oct. 1989), and Susan Reed, "Superswimmer Mark Spitz, 39, Aims for the '92 Olympics," *People Weekly* (15 Jan. 1990).

MARCIA B. DINNEEN

STAGG, Amos Alonzo, Sr. (*b.* 16 August 1862 in West Orange, New Jersey; *d.* 17 March 1965 in Stockton, California), revered as the "Grand Old Man of Football," he had such a profound effect on the game that fellow coaching immortal Knute Rockne said, "All football comes from Stagg."

Growing up the fifth of eight children, young "Lonnie" Stagg lived a typical—sometimes difficult—life of an average American boy in the middle of the nineteenth century. He pitched hay in the fields surrounding his family home in New Jersey but found enough time to earn the skills and reputation of a star baseball pitcher. It was this talent, plus a desire to be a minister, that led Stagg to Yale University in New Haven, Connecticut, in 1884, after graduating from Orange High School (in Orange, New Jersey) and Phillips Exeter Academy (in Andover, Massachusetts).

Stagg quickly became Yale's top athlete, excelling in baseball and football. A standout end, he was named to Walter Camp's inaugural All-America football team in 1889. Having defeated a major league team (the Boston Beaneaters) in an exhibition game, Stagg was offered a $4,200 contract at a time when the average U.S. worker made about $600 a year. But he declined the offer so that he could pursue his dream of being a minister. Shortly after

Amos Alonzo Stagg, 1888. AP/WIDE WORLD PHOTOS

entering Yale's graduate divinity school, however, he overheard a classmate remark critically of his speaking voice. The soft-spoken Stagg withdrew from Yale and became a faculty member at the International YMCA Training School (now Springfield College in Springfield, Massachusetts). Another faculty member was James Naismith. In fact, on 11 March 1892 Stagg was a member of the faculty team that played the students in the first game of Naismith's newly invented sport, basketball. Stagg scored the faculty's only point in a 5–1 loss.

Stagg's former divinity professor, Dr. William Rainey Harper, was by this time president of the newly formed University of Chicago. In 1892 he offered Stagg $2,500 and a professorship to coach track, baseball, and football. Stagg thus began a forty-one-year association with Chicago.

In the early days at Chicago, Stagg often suited up and played for the team he coached. On other occasions he refereed games in which his team played—his reputation for honesty, fairness, sportsmanship, and integrity was without peer. In the early days of the twentieth century Stagg's Chicago Maroons became known as a perennial powerhouse. His 1905 team, led by Walter Eckersall (who was called the "American Ideal"), was crowned mythical national champion. Stagg had many other teams that were close to being on par with the 1905 Maroons.

Stagg married Stella Robertson, a considerably younger Chicago student, on 10 September 1884. The couple had three children—sons, Amos Alonzo, Jr., and Paul, who both became coaches, and a daughter, Ruth.

By the 1920s all the knowledge and inventiveness of Stagg—he is credited with pioneering the huddle, the lateral pass, the reverse, the charging sled, the on-side kick, the Statue of Liberty play, the quick-kick, and many other innovations—were no match for the manpower of the big state universities of the Western Conference (later named Big Ten). The Maroons' glory was mostly in the past. Nevertheless, Stagg, in his sixties, was a venerated figure. By then he had already been known for some time as the "Grand Old Man of Football." He was involved in the Olympic movement and was a life-member of the College Football Rules Committee. Back in 1913 the Chicago trustees had changed the name of Marshall Field to Stagg Field. Later, the dormant athletic facility would be used in the development of the first atomic bomb.

Coinciding with the decline in Chicago's athletic fortunes was the arrival of the university's president Robert Maynard Hutchins, also known as the "Boy Wonder of Education." The thirty-year-old president was determined to do away with intercollegiate athletics—and the legendary Stagg, who had already had the mandatory retirement age of sixty-five waived. After the 1932 season, at the age of seventy, Stagg left Chicago. He did not go into retirement; he took another coaching position. Hutchins succeeded in getting rid of big-time football at Chicago in 1939.

The president of the College of the Pacific (COP), in Stockton, California, was Tully C. Knoles, who as a youngster rode his bicycle thirty-eight miles to see Stagg's Maroons play Stanford in 1894. Knoles offered Stagg a job and was rewarded as time after time Stagg worked miracles with his undermanned, underdog teams. Stagg's zenith at COP was 1943, when he was named Coach of the Year at age eighty-one. His squad defeated such Pacific Coast powers as California and UCLA and narrowly lost to Southern California. Two years later Stagg left COP, but not coaching—he joined his son, A. A., Jr., at Susquehanna University in Selinsgrove, Pennsylvania. Together the Staggs produced an unbeaten season in 1951.

Stagg always maintained that his wife was his best scout. Stella became immersed in her husband's coaching career. She understood the game. Nowhere was her scouting ability more needed than at Susquehanna, with its shoestring budget. Selinsgrove resident Bob Yerger, who would later play halfback for "young Stagg," recalled, "I would see A. A., Sr., put Stella on a Greyhound bus downtown on a Saturday morning. She was off to scout a team like Haverford, while Susquehanna was at home playing a team like Swarthmore. She was an effective scout, too. I remember Junior telling us how Stella thought Ursinus's defensive back committed early to the run and that she thought the Crusaders [Susquehanna] could pass behind him. When the two teams played, that was the first play—a deep pass, Rich Young to Mike Rising. It scored a touchdown."

From 1946 to 1952 the junior and senior Staggs were co-coaches at the tiny Lutheran school. Including the undefeated season of 1951, they compiled a 21–19–3 mark. As University of Alabama coach Paul "Bear" Bryant closed in on Stagg's all-time victory mark of 314 (Stagg's recognized career record at Springfield, Chicago, and the College of the Pacific is 314–199–35), Susquehanna petitioned the NCAA to count the twenty-one Susquehanna victories. Despite evidence of shared responsibilities, the NCAA declined to increase Stagg's victory total. It is irrelevant, though, since Stagg was much more than wins and losses. He devoted his life—an extremely long one at that—to developing youth. While not an ordained minister, Stagg used the gridiron as his bully pulpit. He truly encapsulated the ideal of Christian athleticism as taught at the YMCA school. He championed amateur sports and opposed professionalism vigorously.

Stagg declined to make a cross-country trip from Stockton to Selinsgrove in 1953 because of Stella's health. At ninety-one Stagg coached punters at Stockton Junior College. In 1960 at age ninety-eight, he finally retired from coaching, saying, "For the past seventy years I have been a coach. It is a good time to stop." Two years later Stagg joked about reaching the century mark, saying, "Actuarial tables show that very few men aged 100 die."

Stella Stagg died in 1964, and Stagg died eight months later of natural causes. He was born during the Civil War and died 102 years later while the United States was involved in the Vietnam War. Stagg is buried at Parkview Cemetery in Stockton, California.

More than a football coaching legend, Stagg was held up as an ideal of what a healthy, active, productive life could be. *Time* magazine did a cover story on aging in the 1960s, for which Stagg was the cover illustration. He is memorialized with many awards, trophies, a college bowl game, high schools, and buildings named for him. It is safe to say no one will duplicate his longevity as a coach, and perhaps no one will duplicate his positive influence on the game.

★

Stagg, with W. W. Stout, wrote the autobiography *Touchdown* (1927). An objective biography is Robin Lester, *Stagg's University* (1995). Stagg's life and career are discussed in Edwin Pope, *Football's Greatest Coaches* (1955); Ellis Lucia, *Mr. Football: Amos Alonzo Stagg* (1970); and Tim Cohane, *Great Football Coaches of the Twenties and Thirties* (1973). Stagg and H. L. Williams are credited with writing the first technical book on football, *A Treatise on American Football* (1893). A front-page obituary is in the *New York Times* (18 Mar. 1965).

JIM CAMPBELL

Dawn Staley, 1996. AP/WIDE WORLD PHOTOS

STALEY, Dawn (*b.* 4 May 1970 in Philadelphia, Pennsylvania), professional basketball point guard and two-time Olympic gold medalist; head coach of the Temple University women's basketball team.

Staley was one of five children born to Clarence Staley and Estelle Staley and grew up in the Raymond Rosen projects of Philadelphia. She began her career on a court "on the corner of Twenty-fifth and Diamond," often playing with her brothers. At Dobbins Vocational Technical High School, Staley led the Lady Mustangs and as a senior was awarded National Player of the Year. Her high school career scoring average was 33.1 points per game.

As a collegiate basketball star at University of Virginia, Staley led the Lady Cavaliers to four National Collegiate Athletic Association (NCAA) tournaments, three NCAA Final Four appearances, and three Atlantic Coast Conference (ACC) tournament titles. Standing at just five feet, five inches tall, she achieved a college-career scoring average of 18.5 points per game. She won the Naismith Award in 1991 and 1992, making her one of only three other women—Cheryl Miller, Clarissa Davis, and Chamique Holdsclaw—to win the award multiple times. She was named National Player of the Year in 1991 and 1992, and was a three-time Kodak All-American and a two-time All-American. She was also named most outstanding player of the 1991 Final Four. Staley's number 24 jersey was retired on 20 April 1993, making her one of just three Virginia Cavaliers who have had their numbers retired.

Prior to the WNBA and the ABL, Dawn began her professional career in Segovia, Spain, during the 1992–1993 season. She spent the 1993–1994 season playing with four different teams in Italy, France, Brazil, and Spain, then played in Tarbes, France, in the 1994–1995 season. During the 1997 and 1998 seasons, she played for the Richmond Rage of the American Basketball League (ABL) and was selected as an All-ABL player. After the ABL folded, Staley was signed by the Women's National Basketball Association (WNBA) on 31 August 1998 and joined the Charlotte (North Carolina) Sting in 1999. In 1999 she received the WNBA Sportsmanship Award. As a starting guard with the Sting, Staley averaged thirteen points per game during her first three seasons. At the end of the 2001 season, she ranked third in the WNBA in assists per game.

In 1994 Staley joined the U.S. Women's National Team to increase her strength and conditioning for the 1996 Olympics. She played on gold medal–winning U.S.

Women's National Teams during the 1994 Goodwill Games, the 1998 World Championship, the 1999 U.S. Olympic Cup, and the 1996 and 2000 Olympic games. The 1998 USA Women's World Championship Team was named the USA Basketball Team of the Year due in large part to Staley's all time World Championship assist record of fifty-two. Her travel and preparations for the 2000 Olympic games were chronicled in monthly installments of *Sports Illustrated for Women*.

On 12 April 2000 Staley replaced Kristen Foley as head coach of the Lady Owls at Temple University in Philadelphia. During her first season, the team posted their first winning season since 1989–1990 with eighteen wins and nine losses. The success of the Temple Owls under the leadership of Coach Staley earned them a third seed in the 2001 Atlantic Ten Conference championships.

Staley is a successful community activist in her hometown of Philadelphia, where she established the Dawn Staley Foundation. Her philanthropic activities with the foundation, which include after-school care and tutorials in academics and basketball, have garnered recognition from the American Red Cross, which in 1998 awarded Staley its Cross Spectrum Award, which celebrates women who have made outstanding contributions to their communities. She was also presented with the 1999 WNBA Entrepreneurial Spirit Award for the good work and community outreach sponsored through the Dawn Staley Foundation.

From her humble beginnings in the Philadelphia projects to basketball stardom, from collegiate coaching to inner-city activism, Staley has never stopped reaching for excellence. Her life is a testimony to her will to succeed. In 1996 a seven-story mural of Staley was painted on the side of a building at the corner of Eighth and Market Streets in Philadelphia overlooking her neighborhood to celebrate her accomplishments as the hometown favorite.

★

For more information on Staley, see Morgan G. Brenner, *College Basketball's National Championship: The Complete Record of Every Tournament Ever Played,* vol. 13 (1998), and Sara Corbett, *Venus to the Hoop: A Gold Medal Year in Women's Basketball* (1997). See also articles in *Sports Illustrated* (July 2000), *Hoop* (June 2001), and the *Orlando Sentinel* (16 July 2001). A profile of Staley is on the official WNBA website at <http://www.wnba.com>.

FAYE HALL JACKSON

STARR, Bryan Bartlett ("Bart") (*b.* 9 January 1934 in Montgomery, Alabama), outstanding Green Bay Packers quarterback (1961–1972) and coach (1975–1984); member of the Pro Football Hall of Fame.

Starr was one of two children of Benjamin Bryan Starr, a career noncommissioned U.S. Air Force master sergeant, and Lulu Inez Tucker, a homemaker. Starr was born knowing first-hand what stern discipline and unquestioning responsibility were all about, as his father ran the Starr household as he did his squadron. Starr attended Hurt Military Academy from 1940 through 1945. In the spring and summer he played baseball in a vacant lot, but in the fall he switched to football, playing a "championship" game without helmet or pads before an imaginary crowd. Starr became hooked on football after watching Harry Gilmer, the University of Alabama's spectacular tailback. He soon had a new hero and a new goal—to throw the football as well as Gilmer.

Starr played wingback at Baldwin Junior High in Montgomery using the Notre Dame "box formation" developed by Knute Rockne. He also played running back, blocker, and receiver. When Starr entered Sidney Lanier High School in 1949, his coach Bill Moseley said that Starr had no outstanding natural football ability but that his mind was focused totally on football. In the summer of 1951 arrangements were made for Starr to receive specialized training from Vito ("Babe") Parilli, Kentucky's All-America quarterback. Parilli taught Starr the fundamentals of the game and gave him confidence in himself. He also gave Starr a vision of becoming Coach Paul ("Bear") Bryant's

Bart Starr. ARCHIVE PHOTOS, INC.

star player for the University of Kentucky Wildcats. After Starr's senior year he was selected to the All-Star team and was recruited by every Southeastern Conference (SEC) school except Tennessee. Starr and his friends visited Bear Bryant at Kentucky, but his father wanted him to play for Alabama, and Tuscaloosa was much closer to the school Starr's girlfriend attended.

Starr received a scholarship to play for Alabama, securing a spot as the third quarterback. In 1953 during his freshman year, Alabama played Syracuse in the Orange Bowl and defeated them 61–6. During this game, Starr threw 29 passes and completed 17 for 170 yards. In his sophomore year, Starr became Alabama's starting quarterback. His punting average was 41.4, second only in the SEC to the University of Georgia's Zeke Bratkowski. He spent the 1954–1955 season sidelined with back problems while Alabama scored a disappointing 4–5–2. Starr married Cherry Louise Morton on 8 May 1954; the couple had two children. The next season, he severely sprained his ankle and sat on the bench while Alabama lost ten straight games, ending the year at 0–10. Alabama's basketball coach Johnny Dee spoke on Starr's behalf to the director of player personnel for the Green Bay Packers of the National Football League (NFL), who recommended Starr as a prospect. In January 1956 Starr was selected in the seventeenth round, the 200th player chosen overall. Starr graduated from Alabama in 1956 with a B.A. in history and prepared for his transition into professional football, embarking on a rigorous training program to improve his confidence in passing.

After seeing Starr in scrimmage, the Green Bay coach Lisle Blackburn chose Starr to back up Tobin Rote as quarterback in the preseason games. Starr made the team, and during his first season he had forty-four attempts and completed twenty-four, including two touchdowns and three interceptions. The Packers ended the year with a 4–8 record. Starr had been commissioned in the Reserve Officer Training Corps on college graduation. One month after the season ended he was called to active duty in the U.S. Air Force and assigned to Eglin Air Force Base near Panama City, Florida. After a physical revealed his back problems, he received a medical discharge and returned to Green Bay in early May. After Tobin Rote was traded to the Detroit Lions in 1957, Starr and Babe Parilli rotated quarterbacking, and the Packers finished with a 3–9 record. Then Coach Blackburn was released, and Ray ("Scooter") McLean, an assistant coach at Green Bay, was named his successor. Despite McLean's experience and friendly personality, the Packers won only one game and ended 1958 with discipline and morale at an all-time low. On 4 February 1959 Vince Lombardi became head coach and general manager of the Packers. Lombardi was a consistent and disciplined teacher, and his lessons extended far beyond the football field. During his first year as coach, the Packers finished the season with a record of 7–5.

Starr's first big game after Lombardi became coach was on 17 December 1960 against the Los Angeles Rams. With Starr as quarterback, the Packers beat the Rams 35–21, winning the Western Division title. They then lost the league title game to the Philadelphia Eagles. Starr had an opportunity to become the Packer's starting quarterback in 1961, when Lamar McHan was traded. On 31 December 1961 Green Bay hosted its first championship game against the New York Giants, which they won with a score of 37–0.

With the emergence of the American Football League (AFL) in 1965, there was increased competition for first-rate players. Green Bay, a provincial city in northeastern Wisconsin, was somewhat isolated from the turbulence that was shaking the foundations of professional football, where contracts were being negotiated for previously unheard-of salaries. Starr had become involved in a number of business ventures in Wisconsin that supplemented his football salary, including television commercials and ownership of several automobile dealerships, and he opted to stay with Green Bay. During the 1960s Starr led the team to six Western Division titles, five league championships, and two Super Bowl wins. He was named Most Valuable Player of Super Bowl I (1967) and Super Bowl II (1968). Starr led the NFL in passing in 1962, 1964, and 1966, and was named NFL Player of the Year in 1966.

On 31 December 1967, a bitterly cold afternoon, Starr climaxed his great football career by executing a quarterback sneak and scoring a touchdown from the Dallas Cowboys one-yard line with only thirteen seconds remaining in the game. The Packers won the NFL championship with a score of 21–17. It was their record third straight league win and their fifth in seven years.

Starr continued as the Packers top quarterback until 1972. He had undergone two major operations on both shoulders in 1971 and missed the first ten games of the season. Starr made the decision to retire in July 1972, remaining for the rest of the year as the Packers quarterback coach. He resigned in 1973 to pursue his business interests and to serve as a sports analyst for the Columbia Broadcasting System (CBS). In 1975 Starr accepted the position of head coach and general manager of the Packers with only one year of coaching experience; he stayed on as coach until 1984. Starr was elected to the Alabama Sports Hall of Fame in 1976, and the following year he was inducted into the Pro Football Hall of Fame. Starr and his wife retired to Birmingham, Alabama, in 1990, where Starr joined a real estate development company, Starr Sanders Properties, as chairman of the board, and an advertising firm, Barry, Huey, Bulek, and Cook, as a director.

Starr had the most wins of any quarterback in football, and holds the NFL record for the most passes without an interception, 294. His ability to listen, learn, and remain cool under pressure made him an outstanding player.

★

The Paul W. Bryant Museum Research Library contains books, player scrapbooks, photographs, and videos of football games featuring Starr. Starr wrote *A Perspective on Victory* (1972), with John Wiebusch. For highlights of Starr's career, see Tex Maule, *Bart Starr: Professional Quarterback* (1973). For more information, see Andrew Kilpatrick, "Bart Starr Comes Home to Bama," *Birmingham Post-Herald* (6 Mar. 1990).

BETTY B. VINSON

STAUBACH, Roger Thomas (*b.* 5 February 1942 in Cincinnati, Ohio), football player who won the Heisman Trophy at the United States Naval Academy and quarterbacked the Dallas Cowboys to two Super Bowl wins, gaining a reputation for leading his teams to thrilling come-from-behind victories.

Staubach was the only child of Robert Joseph Staubach, a sales manager, and Elizabeth Smyth. He attended Purcell High School in Cincinnati, and was an all-around athlete, playing football, basketball, and baseball. The popular Staubach was his senior class president at Purcell, and received numerous athletic scholarship offers from colleges and universities. Preferring football, he chose the United States Naval Academy over Notre Dame, which offered only a basketball scholarship. However, Staubach first had to attend a military preparatory school in New Mexico for a year in order to qualify academically for the Naval Academy.

At Annapolis, Staubach began playing football during his sophomore year. As a junior in the autumn of 1963, he quarterbacked Navy to a 9–1 regular-season record and a berth in the Cotton Bowl, where the Midshipmen lost to the University of Texas. Nonetheless, a nationwide panel of sportswriters and sportscasters voted Staubach the winner of the Heisman Trophy, given annually to college football's top player. Staubach was sidelined with an ankle injury for most of his senior season, but still had his number 12 football jersey retired at the Naval Academy when he graduated with a B.S. in June 1965. He had also starred in varsity baseball while there. Staubach married Marianne Jeanne Hoobler on 4 September 1965.

Despite the fact that Staubach was committed to a four-year tour of duty in the navy after graduation, the Dallas Cowboys of the National Football League (NFL) risked a tenth-round draft pick on the star quarterback in 1964. In December 1965 that risk paid off when the Cowboys signed Staubach to a contract assuring he would play in Dallas if and when he ever decided to enter professional football. While serving in Vietnam and Pensacola, Florida, Staubach continued to work out, and during the summer of 1968 he even participated in the Cowboys' training camp while on leave. "I had a fine camp," wrote Staubach in the foreword to *The Dallas Cowboys: An Illustrated History*. "I knew then I was going to play pro ball."

By 1969 Staubach was finished with his military commitment, and was officially a member of the Cowboys. However, he had to wait two more years before he was a contributor. Staubach spent most of his time on the sideline in 1969 and 1970 as Craig Morton quarterbacked the team. But in 1971 Dallas head coach Tom Landry began alternating Morton and Staubach at quarterback, and Staubach won the job outright midway through the season. On 16 January 1972 the Cowboys defeated the Miami Dolphins 24–3 in Super Bowl VI, and Staubach was named the game's Most Valuable Player.

That solidified Staubach as the brightest star of "America's Team" during the 1970s. Dallas returned to three more Super Bowls with Staubach at the helm, losing to the Pittsburgh Steelers in Super Bowls X and XIII, but beating Morton and the Denver Broncos 27–10 in Super Bowl XII on 15 January 1978. Nearly as dangerous running the ball as throwing it, Staubach was named to the Pro Bowl five times, and was the NFL's highest-rated passer four times.

Staubach had a reputation as a committed Christian and "straight arrow" off the field, but he was a fierce competitor on it. His never-say-die attitude resulted in twenty-three come-from-behind victories in the fourth quarter, fourteen of which were in the last two minutes or overtime. Three wins in particular sealed Staubach's nickname of "Captain Comeback." On 23 December 1972, after being sidelined during the regular season with a separated shoulder, Staubach replaced an ineffective Morton in the fourth quarter of a playoff game against the San Francisco 49ers and led the visiting Cowboys from a 28–13 deficit to a 30–28 victory. The unlikely turnaround featured Staubach touchdown passes to Billy Parks and Ron Sellers in the final two minutes. "It was the most unbelievable comeback, because we were totally out of it," said Staubach years later. "There wasn't even a pulse at one time during that game."

On 28 December 1975 Staubach engineered a ninety-one-yard drive late in another playoff contest against the Minnesota Vikings, which included the conversion of a fourth and sixteen play when he passed to Drew Pearson at midfield, and a subsequent fifty-yard "Hail Mary" touchdown pass to Pearson in the last seconds. "I've never been in a stadium that was so quiet," was how Staubach described Minnesota's Metropolitan Stadium after the touchdown that earned Dallas a 17–14 victory. "It was a weird moment, and I think that particular play was the biggest single play that I've ever been a part of."

Finally, on 16 December 1979, in what would turn out to be Staubach's last NFL win, he spearheaded two come-

Roger Staubach. AP/WIDE WORLD PHOTOS

backs in one game as the Cowboys turned a 17–0 deficit into a 21–17 lead, and a 34–21 deficit into a 35–34 victory over the Washington Redskins in the regular-season finale. Staubach threw touchdown passes to Ron Springs and Tony Hill in the closing minutes. "Up to that point I felt sure the high point had already been reached somewhere in my career," Staubach reflected later. "But that one was like no other game I've ever been a part of. It was, to put it simply, the most thrilling sixty minutes I ever spent on a football field."

A few months later, on 31 March 1980, the thirty-eight year-old Staubach fought back tears as he announced his retirement from football. He had taken his share of hard hits over the years, and decided to move on to the next part of his life, which included running a real estate company in Dallas and spending more time with his wife Marianne and their five children. In 1983 Staubach was inducted into the Cowboys Ring of Honor, and in 1985 he was voted into the Pro Football Hall of Fame.

★

Staubach's post-career memoir is *Time Enough to Win* (1980). More information about Staubach's career can be found in Richard Whittingham, *The Dallas Cowboys: An Illustrated History* (1981); Carlton Stowers, *Dallas Cowboys: The First Twenty-five Years* (1984); and Jeff Guinn, *Dallas Cowboys: The Authorized Pictorial History* (1996). Further quotes and highlights are available in the NFL Films video *The Greatest Moments in Dallas Cowboy History* (1987).

JACK STYCZYNSKI

STEINBRENNER, George Michael, III (*b.* 4 July 1930 in Rocky River, Ohio), shipbuilding executive best known as the controversial principal owner of the New York Yankees for the last quarter of the twentieth century.

Steinbrenner was one of three children, and the only son, of Rita Steinbrenner, a homemaker, and Henry Steinbrenner, the owner of the Kinsman Marine Transit Company, a Great Lakes shipping outfit based in Cleveland. He grew up in Bay Village, a suburb of Cleveland. Henry instilled in his son a competitive nature and a strong work ethic: "Always work as hard as, or harder than, anyone who works for you." To ensure that his children learned the value of work, Henry did not give them an allowance. Instead he gave his son chickens; by age nine, Steinbrenner had created a successful egg-delivery service. Henry was very demanding of his children, once publicly scolding his twelve-year-old son for finishing second at a track meet.

Steinbrenner attended Culver Military Academy in Indiana, graduating in 1948, and then Williams College in Williamstown, Massachusetts. Upon his college graduation in 1952, with a B.A. in English, Steinbrenner joined the U.S. Air Force, where he continued to exhibit an entrepreneurial spirit, setting up a successful sports program and food service on a base that served 16,000 military personnel. He was commissioned as a second lieutenant. Steinbrenner left the military in 1955 for a high-school football coaching position in Columbus, Ohio. He then spent one year as an assistant football coach for Northwestern University in Evanston, Illinois, followed by a year coaching at Purdue University in West Lafayette, Indiana. In 1957 he returned to Cleveland to work for his father's company. During this time he met Elizabeth Zieg; they were married on 12 May 1956 and had four children together.

While working for his father, Steinbrenner led a group of investors in purchasing an American Basketball Association charter franchise, the Cleveland Pipers. The team lasted only one season (1961–1962) and built a debt of $250,000, which nearly forced Steinbrenner to file for bankruptcy. In 1963 his father retired, and Steinbrenner took

George Steinbrenner. AP/WIDE WORLD PHOTOS

control of the family firm. He improved the company's finances, and in 1967 led a group of investors to purchase the American Ship Building Company. Steinbrenner was elected as the president and enjoyed the power and wealth that came with the position. He became a multimillionaire and was a leading fund-raiser for Democratic congressional candidates in 1968. In 1972 Steinbrenner switched parties and raised money for President Richard M. Nixon's reelection campaign. However, Steinbrenner was charged with making illegal campaign contributions under fictitious names; he eventually pleaded guilty to the charges and paid a $35,000 fine.

Although he had succeeded in business, Steinbrenner was desperate to return to his true love—sports. In 1972 he tried to purchase his hometown Cleveland Indians. In 1973 he led a group to buy the New York Yankees, the famous baseball team owned since the early 1960s by the Columbia Broadcasting System (CBS). The Yankees were in great disrepair and a bargain at $10 million. Steinbrenner insisted he would focus on building ships and allow his baseball people, led by the newly hired Gabe Paul, to run the team. Steinbrenner said, "We plan absentee ownership, as far as running the Yankees is concerned. We're not going to pretend we're something we aren't. I'll stick to building ships." His claim of a hands-off mode of managing became a reality in November 1974, when the baseball commissioner Bowie Kuhn suspended Steinbrenner for two years from the day-to-day operations of the club for his illegal campaign fund-raising. When Kuhn reinstated Steinbrenner in 1976, he began to micromanage the operation of the team, a practice that became his trademark. Paul made a number of good trades and brought the Yankees back to the World Series in 1976, although they were swept 4–0 by the Cincinnati Reds.

Steinbrenner's desire to win coincided with a fundamental change in the business of baseball. Starting in 1976, players could file for free agency, and owners with enough money could sign anyone. Steinbrenner dominated the early free-agent market. He signed the future Hall of Famers Catfish Hunter in the 1975 season and Reggie Jackson in 1977. Steinbrenner was rewarded with a World Series title in 1977 when the Yankees beat the Los Angeles Dodgers in six games. The Yankees followed suit the next year, but not before Steinbrenner fired manager Billy Martin, who had numerous conflicts with Jackson. The next manager, Bob Lemon, took the team from an improbable 14.5 games back in August 1978 to win the pennant and, eventually, the World Series.

Through the early 1980s the Yankees were always in contention for the pennant, but garnered "Boss" Steinbrenner's anger if they did not win it all. Lemon was replaced in 1979 with Martin in his second of five stints as the Yankees manager. Dick Howser, a highly respected baseball manager, was fired in 1980 after winning 103 games during the season because the team lost in the playoffs. All told, Steinbrenner went through seventeen managers during the first seventeen years of his ownership of the team. Steinbrenner's lack of patience was not only directed at managers—he routinely sent young players back to the minor leagues after bad performances, and frequently traded young prospects for established stars he believed would help the team.

In 1981 Steinbrenner approved the biggest contract in baseball history, a ten-year, $20 million contract with Dave Winfield, a multitalented athlete. Winfield had a great 1981 season with the Yankees, but batted miserably in the World Series loss to the Dodgers. Steinbrenner criticized Winfield, among others on the team, and ordered the publicity department to issue an apology to the people of New York City for the team's poor performance. Shortly afterward, Steinbrenner publicly questioned the way Winfield's foundation, established to aid poor children, was spending its money and hired Howard Spira, a known gambler, to unearth information that could be used against Winfield. Upon learning of this association, the commissioner Fay Vincent suspended Steinbrenner from day-to-day club operations indefinitely on 30 July 1990. Nothing ever was proven that the foundation did anything wrong.

In 1994 Steinbrenner was reinstated as the Yankees general partner and took over a team that had been rebuilt through its strong minor league system and astute trades. In four years the baseball operations stabilized and the team brought up young star players such as Derek Jeter, Andy Petite, Bernie Williams, and Mario Mendoza. Steinbrenner appeared to have mellowed during his four-year suspension, paving the way for greater stability in the Yankees organization. While the Yankees still traded for established stars like Roger Clemens and signed free agents, they no longer acted with disregard for the future. While Steinbrenner ensured that money was available for these players, for the first time he listened to his staff and took their advice on baseball moves. Steinbrenner, however, still had run-ins with fans and players, and he also fired manager Buck Showalter after the Yankees lost in the 1995 playoffs. He then hired Joe Torre, who served as the manager from 1996 through the 2001 season (the longest of any of Steinbrenner's managers). Under Torre, the Yankees saw unbelievable success, winning four World Series titles (1996, 1998–2000), compiling a 114–48 record in 1998, and winning fourteen straight World Series games.

Steinbrenner's contribution to baseball should be based on the success of the teams he fielded, his desire to win at any cost, and not his controversial management style. Since he became the owner of the Yankees after the 1973 season, only one team has won as many as half the six championships that the Yankees have won.

★

Information on Steinbrenner is available in an officials file at the National Baseball Hall of Fame Library in Cooperstown, New York. The primary books on Steinbrenner are Dick Schaap, *Steinbrenner!* (1981); Bill Madden and Moss Klein, *Damned Yankees: A No-Holds-Barred Account of Life with "Boss" Steinbrenner* (1990); and Maury Allen, *All Roads Lead to October: Boss Steinbrenner's Twenty-five-Year Reign over the New York Yankees* (2000). Information can also be found in Sparky Lyle and Peter Golenbock, *The Bronx Zoo* (1979), and Dave Winfield with Tom Parker, *Winfield: A Player's Life* (1988).

COREY SEEMAN

STENGEL, Charles Dillon ("Casey") (*b.* 30 July 1890 in Kansas City, Missouri; *d.* 29 September 1975 in Glendale, California), baseball player and one of the most popular and successful managers in baseball history.

Stengel was the youngest of three children of Louis E. Stengel, an insurance agent and owner of a street-sprinkling company, and Jennie Jordan Stengel, a homemaker and granddaughter of a federal judge. An outstanding high school athlete, Stengel signed a professional baseball contract in 1910 that paid him $135 a month. A left-handed outfielder, he played in such minor league outposts as Maysville, Kentucky, and Montgomery, Alabama, over the next two seasons. He attended the Western Dental School in Kansas City during the offseason, but he soon abandoned a prospective career in dentistry. As he explained, "I

Casey Stengel, 1934. AP/WIDE WORLD PHOTOS

didn't go back to school, because I had a different job I liked better." Stengel's baseball contract was sold to Brooklyn in September 1912.

Stengel spent part or all of the next fifteen seasons as an outfielder in the major leagues, all with National League (NL) teams in Brooklyn, Pittsburgh, Philadelphia, New York, and Boston. He was an above average player, batting .284 with 60 home runs in his career. His best seasons were 1914, when he batted .316, the fifth highest average in the NL; 1917, when he led the league in outfield assists with 30; and 1922, when he batted .368 for John McGraw's New York Giants. He was a .394 hitter in three World Series (1916 with Brooklyn; 1922 and 1923 with New York). Stengel was most famous as a player for his inside-the-park home run to win game one of the 1923 World Series for the Giants, the first home run hit in a World Series game at Yankee Stadium. With characteristic modesty, Stengel later downplayed his achievements as a player. As he explained, "I had many years that I was not so successful as a ballplayer, as it is a game of skill."

Stengel also earned a reputation as a clown. At a game in Brooklyn in May 1919, he released a sparrow from under his cap as he was about to bat. "The higher-ups complained I wasn't showing a serious attitude by hiding a sparrow in my hat," he remembered later, "but I said any day I got three hits, I figure I am showing a more serious attitude than a lot of players with no sparrows in their hats." He also began to speak to reporters in tortured syntax and fractured words woven around rambling digressions, a style of speech that came to be known as "Stengelese." Stengel's most famous outing as an orator was before the 1958 U.S. Senate committee investigating baseball's antitrust exemption. Senators and reporters alike found his forty-five minute patriotic address wildly funny and utterly baffling. According to Stengel, Ring Lardner, who featured Stengel as a character in several baseball stories for the *Saturday Evening Post* in 1932, once advised him, "'Just keep talking, and I'll get a story.' And that's what I did as a manager."

And it was as a manager that Stengel left his greatest mark on the game. He had spent six weeks in 1914 helping to coach the University of Mississippi (Ole Miss) team—hence his "Ol' Perfesser" nickname. He became a player-manager for Worcester in the Eastern League in 1925, moving to Toledo in the American Association (AA) from 1926 to 1931, before becoming a coach and then manager of the Brooklyn Dodgers from 1932 to 1936. Between 1938 and 1943 he managed the Boston Braves. When he left the Braves, he was fifty-three years old and had been a manager for sixteen seasons. After managing the Toledo Mud Hens to a pennant in 1927, however, he then led a team that finished higher than fifth only once. All of the nine major league teams he managed had finished in the second division. Or as Stengel put it: "After being in the minor leagues as a manager, I became a major-league manager in several cities and was discharged; we call it 'discharged,' because there is no question I had to leave."

After leading Milwaukee to the American Association pennant in 1944 and Oakland to the Pacific Coast League pennant in 1948, Stengel was the surprise choice to manage the New York Yankees. As Lee MacPhail, the Yankee farm director, later said, "The feeling around the Yankees in those days was that the Yankees had hired a clown." Stengel managed the New York Yankees for the next twelve seasons, from 1949 to 1960, and none of his teams finished with a losing record. In fact, during Stengel's tenure the Yankees were world champions seven times, including five straight years from 1949 to 1953; they also won ten AL championships. To be sure, he was surrounded by talent, including such future Hall of Famers as Joe DiMaggio, Mickey Mantle, Phil Rizzuto, Yogi Berra, Elston Howard, and Whitey Ford. Stengel was famous for his strategy of platooning, or freely substituting players to address changing circumstances on the field. "My platoon thinking started with the way McGraw handled me in my last years on the Giants," he once explained. "He had me in and out of the lineup, and he used me all around the outfield. He put me in when and where he thought I could do the most good." Stengel also founded a spring Instructional League for young players. However, he was not without his detractors, among them Rizzuto and sportscaster Howard Cosell, but he was generally credited with molding the Yankees into a dynasty.

Stengel was fired as manager of the Yankees after their loss to the Pittsburgh Pirates in the 1960 World Series. "I'll never make the mistake of turning seventy again," he said. He came out of retirement in 1962 to become the first manager of a NL expansion team, the New York Mets. Stengel promised before the Mets played a game that "if it ever gets to where I'm going to handicap this new machine, I'll be the first to know it, and I'll step out of the picture." In 1964, his last full season with the team, the last-place Mets attracted more spectators than the two-time world champion Yankees, 1.7 million to 1.3 million. The "Amazin' Mets" may not have been a competitive success on the field, but they were a commercial success largely as a result of Stengel's knack at promotion. After suffering a broken hip in late July 1965, he formally retired as Mets manager on 30 August 1965. He was inducted into the National Baseball Hall of Fame on 25 July 1966.

Although he was a comic figure with a craggy face and bandy legs, Stengel was also an astute investor in oil, and he retired to a bank vice presidency in Glendale, California, his home since his marriage to Edna Lawson on 18 August 1924. The Stengels, who had no children, lived in the same house in Glendale from 1924 until 1975. After his death from cancer in 1975, Stengel was buried in Forest Lawn Cemetery in Glendale.

★

Shortly after he left the Yankees, Stengel (with Harry T. Paxton) prepared an autobiography entitled *Casey at the Bat: The Story of My Life in Baseball* (1962), an indispensable anecdotal source about his life. The best of several biographies is Robert W. Creamer, *Stengel: His Life and Times* (1984). Richard Bak, *Casey Stengel: A Splendid Baseball Life* (1997), is lavishly illustrated. See also Joseph Durso, *Casey: The Life and Legend of Charles Dillon Stengel* (1967), and Maury Allen, *You Could Look It Up: The Life of Casey Stengel* (1979). An obituary is in the *New York Times* (1 Oct. 1975).

GARY SCHARNHORST

STEPHENS, Woodford Cefis ("Woody") (*b.* 1 September 1913, in Stanton, Kentucky; *d.* 22 August 1998 in Miami Lakes, Florida), Thoroughbred racehorse trainer and breeder who was named Trainer of the Decade (1980s), known for his knowledge of horses, quick wit, and great stories.

Stephens was the oldest of seven children of Lewis Stephens, a tenant farmer, and Helen Welsh Stephens, a homemaker. Stephens reminisced, "my mother and father raised five daughters, two sons, a bunch of chickens and somebody else's tobacco crops." "My father was a sharecropper," he said. "He'd sit me on the back of a mule and say, 'He's a born horseman.'" Stephens galloped his pony Bill to school in the 1920s and dreamed of being a jockey. When he was ten, his family moved to Midway, Kentucky.

Woody Stephens, 1978. © BETTMANN/CORBIS

At the age of sixteen Stephens dropped out of ninth grade to work for the stable of trainer John Ward at Everglade Stables. Stephens, in his autobiography, spoke about waking up "ahead of the roosters" and daydreaming about working with horses. He commented that he always had horses on his mind and that for more than fifty years "I've had my hands on horses, a few of them mine, most of them owned by other people bent on seeing them out on the racetrack creaming the competition."

In a very short time Stephens got his break and fulfilled his dream of becoming a jockey. He won his first race aboard Directly on 15 January 1931 at Hialeah Park in Florida, the horse paying $37.70 for a $2 wager. His career as a rider was short-lived, as he soon grew too big to be a jockey. He became a groom and then worked his way up to be Ward's assistant trainer. "I guess the luckiest thing that ever happened was for me to get fat." While working for Ward he earned his trainer's license on 18 June 1936 and saddled his first winner as the trainer of record of Deliberator at Latonia Park in Kentucky.

Stephens left Ward's stable in 1937; married Lucille Elizabeth Easley on 11 September the same year; and set out on his own. He became affiliated with Steve Judge in 1940 as assistant trainer for Woodford Farm. In 1940 he trained his first winner as an independent trainer, Bronze Bugle, at Keeneland in Kentucky.

Stephens got his first big break as a trainer in 1944 when he met a professional horseplayer named Jule Fink, who asked him to come to New York to train a string of horses for a salary of $1,000 a month and 15 percent of all winning purses. Stephens's first stakes winner was Sanguaro, who won the 1945 Excelsior Handicap at Aqueduct Race course in New York for Fink. Stephens stayed with Fink for about two and a half years before the two parted company. Stephens later hooked up with Royce Martin's Woodvale Farm and won his first major stake by sending out the farm's homebred mare Marta to win the 1951 Ladies Handicap.

Stephens's first classic race success came in 1952 when Blue Man won the Flamingo, finished third in the Kentucky Derby, and took the Preakness. Stephens had inherited Blue Man from one of his former mentors, Steve Judge. Judge owned Blue Man before selling the colt to Arthur Abbott, and Stephens took over the training at that time. Blue Man had been running in claiming races as a two-year-old, but as with many horses that others were willing to give up on, Stephens saw potential in the colt. When racing, "if you tried to take hold of him, he'd fight the bit, throw up his head and it was over for the day." But Stephens thought that Blue Man might be a pretty good horse if he was treated right. "I gave him a lot of time that fall to quiet down and get working. He was trained to the letter when I ran him in an allowance race at Belmont Park. I bet on him and he paid $41.00." Stephens felt that he was making progress with the colt and went on with him. Unlike trainers who tried to disassociate themselves from gambling, Stephens was no stranger to betting and that behavior made him a favorite of fans. He always relished scoring a big one.

Stephens's career progressed in a positive direction, and in 1956 he accepted a job with Captain Harry F. Guggenheim's Cain Hoy Stable at $50,000 a year and 20 percent of all profits. He worked for Cain Hoy for nine years and put the outfit at the top of the owner's list in 1959, with earnings of $742,081. Over one-third of this amount was earned by Bald Eagle, who won the first of his two Washington Internationals that year. Stephens left Cain Hoy when Captain Guggenheim refused to let him train horses owned by Stephen's wife, Lucille. It was a decision that Captain Guggenheim regretted many times. "It was my worst decision to let Woody get away."

In 1966 Stephens once again opened a public stable, which over the years attracted such prominent clients as John Gaines, Louis Lee Haggin, John Morris, John Okin, James Box Brady, August Belmont IV, Henryk de Kwiatkowski, Betty Moran's Brushwood Stables, Robert Kirkham, Claiborne Farm, Hickory Tree Farm, Newstead Farm, and Ryehill. Stephens's champions included Bold Bidder, Heavenly Body, Never Bend, and Sensational. His major winners included Iron Peg, Judger, Make Sail, Missile Belle, Smarten, Traffic Judge, White Star Line, Marta, Kittiwak, Number, Bless Bull, Mrs. Warren, Miss Oceana, and Forty Niner.

Stephens's two Kentucky Derby winners were Cannonade in 1974, and Swale in 1984, which gave Claiborne Farm its first Kentucky Derby victory. His five Belmont Stakes winners came in consecutive years: Conquistador Cielo (1982), Caveat (1983), Swale (1984), Crème Fraiche (1985), and Danzig Connection (1986). In the long history of Thoroughbred horse racing, no other trainer has come close to matching Stephens's record. He earned his first Eclipse Award in 1983 as Trainer of the Year.

Stephens officially retired on 22 September 1997 after sixty-seven years in the horse business, but kept in close touch with the racing industry up until his death. He was a champion in all ways. He trained horses that won over 200 stakes races in his career, more than 100 of them were Grade 1 stakes races. He trained eleven Eclipse Award winning horses. Stephens was inducted into the National Museum of Racing and Hall of Fame in 1976 and wrote his autobiography, *Guess I'm Lucky: My Life in Horseracing,* in 1976.

Stephens died at Heartland Health Care Center in Miami Lakes, Florida, of chronic emphysema and lung disease. He is buried at Hillcrest Cemetery in Lexington, Kentucky.

Stephens was a trainer that few who knew him will forget. His many friends and acquaintances and those whom he mentored will miss him for his enthusiasm, his zest for each and every day, his wit, wisdom, kindness, and humanity. Seth Hancock, longtime president of Claiborne Farm, said "He's the embodiment of what a real horseman is." Stephens was always upbeat, a trait for which his owners were grateful, and an unusual one in the racing game because of all the ups and downs of the business. A remarkable human being who always gave the best of himself, his time, his talent, and his wisdom, Stephens was also a raconteur of note who shared his great stories about his many horses.

★

Files on Stephens are at the National Museum of Racing and Thoroughbred Hall of Fame at Saratoga Springs, New York, and the New York Racing Association Public Relations office at Elmont, New York. His autobiography is *Guess I'm Lucky: My Life in Horseracing* (1976). Numerous books about the racing industry mention Stephens; Cliff Guilliams, *Final Calls to Absent Friends* (2001), is praised by his widow. Articles including Dan Farley, "Woody," *Thoroughbred Record* (11 Nov. 1981); David Schmitz, "A Handful of Belmonts," *Blood-Horse* (29 Aug. 1998); "Still Chipping Away," *Backstretch* (Feb. 1991); and Cliff Guilliams, "Love of the Horse Fueled Legend's Long Career," *Daily Racing Form*, (27 Sept. 1997); give insight into his career. An obituary is in the *New York Times* (23 Aug. 1998).

JOAN GOODBODY

STERN, David (*b.* 22 September 1942 in New York City), commissioner of the National Basketball Association (NBA) who presided over tremendous growth and financial success of the league during the 1980s and 1990s.

Stern was the son of William Stern and Anna Bronstein Stern. He spent his early years growing up in the Chelsea section of Manhattan, where his father owned a delicatessen. Chelsea was not far from Madison Square Garden, where Stern went to basketball games and developed an intense love for the game at a young age. In 1956 the family moved to northern New Jersey, where Stern attended Teaneck High School, graduating in 1959.

Stern entered Rutgers University later that year and earned a B.S. in history in 1963. On 27 November 1963 he married Dianne Bock; they had two children. After Rutgers, Stern went on to Columbia Law School, from which he received an LL.B. in 1966. After graduating from law school, Stern went to work for the law firm Proskauer, Rose, Goetz, and Mendelsohn in New York City, where he served as outside counsel to the National Basketball Association (NBA) beginning in 1968. In 1974, at age thirty-two, he became the firm's youngest partner ever. Stern worked on legal issues related to professional basketball for years. In 1978 he was offered the position of general counsel to the NBA and joined the league as a full-time employee. In 1980 he was elevated to the position of executive vice president.

During his long apprenticeship before being named commissioner, Stern was involved in virtually every business matter that shaped the NBA. Included in these activities was the landmark 1976 settlement between the league and its players leading to free agency. Stern also maintained a position of leadership when the NBA established a collective bargaining agreement, a salary cap, team revenue sharing, and professional sports' first antidrug agreement. While these alterations fortified the NFL's policies, they did not provide a solid economic foundation for the league. Professional basketball had not penetrated the American sporting public's psyche in the same way as football and baseball contests. The last games of the 1979 and 1980 NBA Finals were not even broadcast live on television. In the early 1980s the NBA was characterized as a league in near chaos, riddled by runaway salaries and widespread drug abuse. Critics cited quarrelsome owners and poor leadership. Television ratings, attendance, and corporate sponsorship were all in decline, and several franchises were on the verge of bankruptcy.

Stern was elected unanimously to succeed Larry O'Brien as the NBA's fourth commissioner on 1 February 1984. Over a sixteen-year period after Stern's ascendancy, the NBA grew from twenty-three to twenty-nine teams, enjoyed a fivefold increase in revenues, expanded television exposure dramatically, and launched the Women's National Basketball Association (WNBA). Marketing success led to the televising of NBA games in 205 countries and the opening of offices in eight cities outside North America by the year 2000. Beginning in 1984 Stern marketed the league as an entertainment company, and turned his focus to the fan base by incorporating special events subsidized by American corporations. These events, including slam dunk contests, three-point shooting contests, rookies on display in competitive games, festivals for kids, and all-star games played by teams that the fans selected, were lucrative for being both attended and televised. (A similar pattern also began to develop in the WNBA, where professional women players participated in the same type of festival atmosphere.) Stern also began employing the greatest athletes in the world. Aided by increasing revenues and the presence of popular players like Larry Bird, Earvin ("Magic") Johnson, and Michael Jordan, the NBA began to prosper. In a few short years the NBA was considered the most stable and successful sports league in the world, a model for successful merchandising. In 1990 Stern was named the best commissioner in organized sports by *Sport* magazine and recognized as the Sports Executive of the Decade by the Associated Press.

David Stern, 1986. © BETTMANN/CORBIS

Stern did not suffer significant public criticism until 1998 and 1999, when a labor struggle resulted in a 191-day lockout, canceling hundreds of games. While Stern insisted that the strike was a necessary correction to the system, a bevy of disillusioned fans and critics argued that the conflict was incited by greedy owners seeking to incorporate an adjusted salary cap and tighter rookie restrictions. As the league spokesman, Stern insisted that such new measures would guarantee team continuity. Players charged that they would lose bargaining power and would be forced to accept policies leading to the disintegration of free agency. Both sides in the conflict appeared greedy to a public not interested in hearing about the labor relations of rich athletes and managers. In 1998 the average player's salary was $2.5 million, and David Stern made $7 million a year.

Remarkably candid about league issues, Stern used this environment of struggle to suggest that NBA supporters needed to consider new philosophies. Speaking of personal creativity and the modern athlete, Stern said that professional basketball was an institution undergoing slow change. He cited the way that U.S. corporations treated employees in the 1940s and 1950s, when policy, procedure, and consistency were most valued, and argued that NBA teams in the 1990s were like jazz ensembles, needing freedom for personal creativity in order to sustain a pleasant environment for both players and management. When the lockout ended, Stern focused on new digital technologies to fuel the league's international marketing juggernaut. NBA Properties, the institution's marketing arm, joined NBA Entertainment, a television and multimedia production company, and www.nba.com TV, a twenty-four-hour digital network. By 2000 NBA websites received one-third of their traffic from users outside the United States. Stern advocated merging league websites, radio, television, satellite packages, and global programming into a coherent message stream.

Stern has a legacy of commitment to public service. He has contributed time and energy to the NBA's TeamUp program, which promotes community service and volunteerism. In the summers of 1993 and 1994, Stern led a group of NBA players and coaches that toured Africa to benefit the international relief agency CARE and to conduct coaching and children's clinics. He has also served on the boards of Columbia University, Beth Israel Medical Center, the Rutgers University Foundation, the National Association for the Advancement of Colored People, the Martin Luther King, Jr. Federal Holiday Commission, the Thurgood Marshall Scholarship Fund, and the Museum of Television and Radio and Jazz at Lincoln Center.

By the end of the twentieth century Stern was one of the most influential figures in sports. No other commissioner in professional sports appeared to have as much control over his organization as Stern. Instead of placing flamboyant owners or associates at the forefront, Stern acted as the spokesman for the NBA. Comfortable in both the boardroom and the arena, Stern has defined the direction of professional basketball. In 2001, he continued as commissioner and showed no signs of retiring.

★

"David J. Stern," NBA Media Ventures (2000), http://global.nba.com/Basics/00421436.html , is a short, standard biography highlighting Stern's background, business history, and social causes. The information is limited to his career with the league. David Halberstam, *Playing for Keeps: Michael Jordan and the World He Made* (1999), is perhaps the best source for information about Stern's early life and career. In "David Stern's Game Plan," *Industry Standard* (15 June 2001), Terry Lefton describes Stern's business philosophy.

R. Jake Sudderth

STERN, William ("Bill") (*b.* 1 July 1907 in Rochester, New York; *d.* 19 November 1971 in Rye, New York), popular sportscaster of the 1930s and 1940s, famous for his fictionalized sports vignettes and hyperbolic play-by-play style.

Stern was the second of two sons of Isaac Stern, head of Michaels-Stern, a large clothing firm, and Lena Reis Stern,

Bill Stern. AP/Wide World Photos

daughter of a wealthy Cincinnati family. Stern's father was generous with material possessions but not with his time. His mother was austere but kind. Stern's interests in sports, theater, and entertainment began in childhood. He announced mock sporting events from the shower and practiced his saxophone, confident of future fame. He formed an orchestra called "Bill Stern and his Bluegrass Music." When the band was underpaid for an engagement, Stern's father paid the deficit.

Stern attended Rochester public schools, was expelled from Hackley Preparatory School in Tarrytown, New York, and failed out of Cascadilla Preparatory School in Ithaca, New York. He finally graduated with a B.S. from the Pennsylvania Military College in Chester, Pennsylvania (PMC). At PMC, Stern learned about work for the first time. He advanced to captain adjutant, controlled his temper, got decent grades, acted in vaudeville, led the school orchestra, and participated in football, tennis, basketball, boxing, and rowing. After graduation in June 1930, he drove his new Pierce Arrow car, a gift from his father, to Hollywood to become a movie star. He failed interviews, squandered his father's funds at the Agua Caliente racetrack, and returned to Rochester after three days of digging postholes for $5 a day on the RKO parking lot.

Stern managed to land a job as a sports announcer at Rochester radio station WHAM in 1925. The job involved traveling around the country attending sporting events, and within a few years Stern had tired of it and quit to move to New York City. By 1931 he had advanced from usher to assistant stage manager at the immense Roxy Theater, and later became the first stage director of Radio City Music Hall in the Rockefeller Center. In October 1934 Stern shared two minutes with the National Broadcasting System's (NBC) Graham McNamee announcing the Navy–William and Mary football game in Baltimore. He worked part-time at NBC for the rest of the season. Stern quit Radio City in June 1935, and while on vacation met his cousin and future wife, Harriet May of Grand Rapids, Michigan. The couple married on 29 April 1937; they had three children.

Stern was hired at KWKH radio in Shreveport, Louisiana, and announced his first play-by-play football game on 12 October 1935. Eight days later, he lost a leg in a serious automobile accident while driving across Texas. In 1936 he worked as a full-time announcer for NBC. His first bowl assignment was the Sugar Bowl game in New Orleans on New Year's Day 1937, in which Army played Navy.

In October 1939 Stern announced his first *Colgate Sports Newsreel*, a weekly sports program. He reflected, "I decided on a show which would deal with stories with an O. Henry twist; stories set to music, and fableized and dramatized for appeal to the housewife as well as the sports-hungry husband." A male quartet opened the show with "Bill Stern the Colgate shave-cream man is on the air. Bill Stern the Colgate shave-cream man with stories rare. . . ."

Stern narrated fictional events of sports heroes and ordinary people, beginning "Portrait of an athlete!" or "Portrait of a man!" He earned the nickname "Aesop of the Airways" from anecdotes such as "And that little Italian boy with the baseball bat is now the Pope." Stern claimed that the inventor Thomas A. Edison's deafness resulted from being beaned by the pitcher Jesse James in a baseball game. In another fable Stern said Abraham Lincoln's dying words to Colonel Abner Doubleday inspired the game of baseball. Reporters disliked Stern's distortion of facts. Undaunted, Stern countered, "I was living the make-believe world of the theater and the license I took was basically harmless."

In 1939 Stern began interviewing entertainment and sports celebrities, including Babe Ruth, Leo Durocher, Joe DiMaggio, Judy Garland, Margaret Truman, Jack Benny, Ronald Reagan, and Frank Sinatra. Stern traveled to broadcast remote "on-the-scene" reports of football, tennis, golf, basketball, baseball, horse-racing, crew racing, hockey, track and field (including the 1936 Berlin Olympics and the 1948 London Olympics), bowling, skiing, rodeo, and boxing. He covered most of Joe Louis's title fights.

As a result of his accident in October 1935 in which he lost a leg, Stern took nighttime barbiturates and daytime Benzedrine along with morphine injections. By the end of 1941 he received weekly shots, and by 1943 these had increased to twice a week. By 1945 he was taking Demerol, Dilaudid, and morphine. He also experienced severe pain from kidney stones, a secondary factor that prolonged his dependence on morphine. In 1950 he tried a four-day cure, only to realize he was a "legal addict."

Stern was NBC's first sports director, from 1940 to 1952. During that span he was rated first place sportscaster in the *Radio Daily* poll every year, and he also received awards from *Motion Picture Daily*, *Radio and Television Mirror,* and *Scripps-Howard*. For fifteen years Stern made two MGM newsreels per week, filmed a sports short once a month for Columbia pictures, and appeared in movies: *Pride of the Yankees* (1942), *We've Never Been Licked* (1943), *Stage Door Canteen* (1943), *Here Come the Co-eds* (1945), and *The West Point Story* (1950). Stern earned nearly $5,000 a week for twelve years.

Stern began working for ABC-TV in September 1953. On 1 January 1956 in the ABC-TV box above the Sugar Bowl in New Orleans, Stern began announcing the starting lineup for the New Year's Game between the University of Pittsburgh Panthers and the Georgia Tech Yellow Jackets. His voice froze; morphine and sleeping pills stopped him cold. Stern entered the Institute of Living in Hartford, Connecticut, on 16 June 1956 for treatment and left clean on 22 December 1956.

On 6 March 1957 Stern returned to the airwaves with what critics described as the clearest commentary of his life. Later, with Oscar Fraley, Stern wrote *The Taste of Ashes* (1959), explaining his addiction. He also worked before his death as sports announcer for the Mutual Broadcasting Company. Stern suffered a fatal heart attack at his home in Rye, New York. His devoted fans remembered his sign-off in the 500th *Sports Newsreel* broadcast in 1949: "This is Bill Stern wishing you all a good, good night."

★

Stern's autobiography, written with Oscar Fraley, *The Taste of Ashes* (1959), presents a candid picture of Stern's life, balancing his career and his struggle with drug addiction. Frank Buxton and Bill Owen, *The Big Broadcast: 1920–1950* (1972), is a reference digest for the golden age of radio, with outstanding details about sports and sportscasters of the period, including Stern. John Dunning, *On the Air* (1998), describes the format of Stern's *Sports Newsreel*, quotes the quartet that accompanied the broadcasts, and explains Stern's legendary contribution to radio. Ron Lackmann's updated edition of *The Encyclopedia of American Radio: An A–Z Guide to Radio from Jack Benny to Howard Stern* (2000), provides the dates and times *Sports Newsreel* was aired and lists celebrities who were interviewed on the show. Stern's picturesque style is clearly demonstrated in "More Lateral than Literal," *Time* (6 June 1949). Obituaries are in the *New York Times* (21 Nov. 1971) and *Time* and *Newsweek* (both 29 Nov. 1971).

SANDRA REDMOND PETERS

STOCKTON, John Houston (*b.* 26 March 1962 in Spokane, Washington), professional basketball player who leads National Basketball Association (NBA) in career assists and steals.

Stockton was one of four children born to Jack Stockton, a tavern owner, and Clementine Stockton, a homemaker. He attended parochial schools and excelled academically and athletically. Stockton graduated from Gonzaga Preparatory School in Spokane in 1980 and continued his education at Gonzaga University, from which he earned a B. S. in 1984. He married Nada Stepovich on 16 August 1986; they have six children.

Although Stockton was relatively short and slight for a basketball player, at six feet, one inch tall and 175 pounds, he chose basketball over baseball as his sport in college. He averaged 20.9 points and 7.2 assists and shot .577 in 1984, his senior year, and was named Most Valuable Player (MVP) of the West Coast Conference and chosen for the United Press International All–West Coast First Team. For his college career, Stockton averaged 12.5 points and 5.2 assists. He was invited to the 1984 Olympic tryouts by the designated coach of the U.S. team, Bob Knight of Indiana. Although he was relatively unknown, Stockton competed against All Americans Michael Jordan, Patrick Ewing, and Sam Perkins. The coaching staff loved Stockton's knowledge of the game, his selflessness, and his fierce competitive nature. Although he remained until the final cut, he did not make the team. Nonetheless, the Olympic tryouts brought Stockton to the attention of NBA scouts, who saw him as a potential backup point guard.

John Stockton. AP/WIDE WORLD PHOTOS

In 1984 the Utah Jazz of the NBA drafted Stockton in the first round as the sixteenth overall pick. Stockton backed up the starter Rickey Green for most of three seasons before he became the floor leader of the Jazz. For the next fourteen years, he started every game in which he was in uniform. During his years in the NBA, John Stockton has achieved magnificent prominence. In 2000 Stockton and his Jazz teammate Karl Malone were named as two of the greatest players in the history of the league. Through the 2000–2001 season, he held the career record for the number of assists (14,503), as well as records for most assists in a season (1,164 in 1990–1991), and the highest average assists per game (14.5 in 1989–1990). Stockton led the NBA in assists for nine straight seasons between 1988 and 1996. A tenacious defender, he also led the league in steals for the 1988–1989 and 1991–1992 seasons. During 1996 he became the NBA's career leader in steals and garnered 2,976 through the 2000–2001 season.

Stockton has been named an NBA All-Star ten times and shared MVP honors with Karl Malone for the 1993 All-Star game, in which he dished out fifteen assists and had nine points and six rebounds. He has been named to the All-NBA First Team twice, the Second Team six times, and the Third Team three times. His defensive abilities were recognized by his selection to the NBA All-Defensive Second Team in five different years. He also played on the U.S. Olympic gold medal–winning "Dream Team" in 1992 and 1996. One of Stockton's career trademarks is durability. He played in all eighty-two games in each season fourteen times through 2000–2001, tying with A. C. Green for that record. He has played more games with one franchise (1,340) than any other player in history and is third in games played entering the 2001–2002 season, behind only Robert Parish (1,611) and Kareem Abdul-Jabbar (1,560). With Stockton on the team, the Jazz have been in the playoffs in seventeen consecutive years, an NBA record.

Although Stockton's career playoff statistics are impressive, he has been to the finals only twice (through the 2000–2001 season). In both 1997 and 1998 the Jazz played the Chicago Bulls for the conference title, but in both years the team was defeated in six games, although Stockton averaged nearly nine assists and more than twelve points per game. Stockton has gained the admiration of many basketball legends through his selfless play and determination. In the 2000–2001 season Stockton appeared in all 82 games and shot 50.4 percent from the field. He led all NBA guards in shooting percentage and shot 46 percent from the three-point range. With more than 17,000 points scored (through the 2000–2001 season), a fourth-best all-time career guard shooting percentage, league records in steals and assists, he has left his mark on the NBA. Stockton may be one of the toughest players to ever walk on the hardwood.

★

For details on Stockton's basketball career see Robert E. Schnakenberg, *Teammates: Karl Malone and John Stockton* (1998); Roland Lazenby, *Stockton to Malone: The Rise of the Utah Jazz* (1998); and Michael C. Lewis, *To the Brink: Stockton, Malone, and the Utah Jazz's Climb to the Edge of Glory* (1998).

F. ROSS PETERSON

STREET, Picabo (*b.* 3 April 1971 in Triumph, Idaho), two-time Olympic medalist in skiing and the first American to win the World Cup downhill race and to win it twice. Her success and personal appeal have helped raise the profile of U.S. skiers, especially women.

In addition to her Olympic achievements, Street is known for her distinctive name, personality, and speed. She was the second child of Ron ("Stubby") Street, a stonemason, and Dee Street, a music teacher. Picabo was known only as "Baby Girl" Street for several years until the Streets, including older brother Roland ("Baba"), traveled to Mexico. To meet U.S. passport requirements, the youngest Street needed a name. Picabo is based on a favorite children's game, but is spelled like a town in Idaho and is also a Native American term for "shining waters." Later, Street's hippie-like upbringing set her apart from wealthier teammates but also provided her with strong family ties.

The only girl in Triumph, a small town just eight miles from the Sun Valley ski area, Street thrived on competing with the boys. She took so many risks, her mother claimed, that while Roland just needed feeding, Picabo needed to be kept alive. When Street first skied at age five, she cried on the way up, then zoomed down. Speed and an outgoing manner have continued to be her most obvious characteristics. The freckle-faced, auburn-haired girl joined the Wood River Valley High School ski team, leaving after her junior year to finish school by correspondence. She won the Western Junior Championship at sixteen and the National Junior downhill and super-giant slalom (Super-G) at seventeen. In comparison with the speed required for the direct run of a downhill course, the Super-G involves more control and precision to maneuver through the gates at high speed on a somewhat shorter course.

In 1989, the year Street joined the U.S. Ski Team, she injured the anterior cruciate ligament (ACL) in her left knee during a World Cup race, but still competed in the World Junior Championship. Called brash and playful by some, Street was deemed undisciplined and out of shape by the officials, and she was suspended at the summer training camp in Park City, Utah. This marked a turning point for a chastened Street, who retreated to Hawaii, where with great determination and her parents' support, she added strength and technique to her natural speed. In the following two years, she won the North American overall championships despite further mishaps, including a knee injury and a compressed disk. In 1993 Street won the silver medal in the combined (downhill and slalom points) at the World Alpine Ski Championships at Morioka, Japan. She also took first in the Super-G, second in the combined, and third in the downhill at the U.S. Championship in Winter Park, Colorado.

At her first Olympics, in Lillehammer, Norway, in 1994,

Picabo Street. AP/WIDE WORLD PHOTOS

Street took the silver in the downhill with a time of 1:36:59. This, along with the three gold and silver medals won by Tommy Moe and Diane Roffe Steinrotter, gave the United States a name in Alpine skiing. In 1995 Street placed first in six downhill races and the following year took four first- and three second-place wins in prime ski areas around the world. Along with these achievements, she took first place in the U.S. Championship in Sugarloaf, Maine. Her international victories were notable as the first time an American had won a World Cup downhill race; they also marked the only time anyone had won the World Cup twice, as Street did in 1995 and 1996; in 1996 she took silver in downhill and bronze in super-G. The Europeans took notice, and Street recognized the importance of publicity for U.S. skiing. A vibrant personality, as well as an outstanding athlete, she has been able to raise the profile of American skiing.

In December 1996 Street crashed into a fence on Pepe's Face, a ski run at Vail, Colorado, breaking her left femur and tearing ligaments in her knee, an accident that required major surgery and significant emotional adjustment. It meant that the following March, when others skied the slopes of Nagano, Japan, in anticipation of the 1998 Olympics, Street had to be carried down the course on Coach Rickenbacker's back. However, on 11 February 1998, only fourteen months after ligament reconstruction, only twelve days after suffering a concussion in Are, Sweden, and on longer skis, Street took the first U.S. gold of the 1998 Winter Olympics when she won the Super-G. Street showed the world she was not only fast and fearless, but also superbly disciplined. A month later on Friday 13 March, she again crashed racing in Switzerland. This recovery took longer, but in March 2001 she won the International Federation of Skiing (FIS) Kandahar Downhill Cup, and was selected as a member of the U.S. Alpine team for the 2002 Winter Olympics in Salt Lake City, Utah.

Street is a five-feet, eight-inch, 160-pound speed demon who projects independence, strength, and optimism. Off the slopes, she maintains the same buoyancy. She is close to her family and owns a home in Park City, Utah, where she is Director of Skiing at Park City Mountain Resort. She appeared on *Sesame Street*, was welcomed at the White House in 1994, and created, with A. J. Kitt and Holly Flanders, two instructional *Let's Go Skiing* videos. She has signed lucrative contracts with Nike, Chap Stick, and Charles Schwab (supporters of NASTAR, the National Standard Race program) and has provided considerable resources to assist children. Street was on the *Sports Illustrated* 1995 list of the top fifty athletes of the twentieth century from each state. In 1995 and 1998 the U.S. Olympic Committee named her Sports Woman of the Year, and in 1998 *Good Housekeeping* acknowledged her as a Major American Female. Street uses her public image to support the American Federation of Skiing and the Olympic Committee.

★

The extensive coverage of Street's career in *Sports Illustrated* includes two articles by Michael Farber, "Double Exposure" (19 Dec. 1994), and "Playing Picabo" (18 Dec. 1995), in which Farber discusses Street's relationship with teammates. Chantal Knapp's interview with Street, "Picabo's Excellent Adventure" appears in *Women's Sports and Fitness* (July/Aug. 1994); Stephen Koep, "Street Smarts" in *Time* (9 Feb. 1998), discusses Street's preparation for the 1998 Olympics. Street features in two ESPN videos, *Let's Go Skiing,* as one of three instructors of beginning and intermediate/advanced technique.

RACHEL SHOR

SUGGS, (Mae) Louise (*b.* 7 September 1923 in Atlanta, Georgia), one of four players who dominated women's golf in the United States throughout the 1950s and one of the founding members of the Ladies Professional Golf Association (LPGA).

Suggs was a natural athlete for whom sports was a family passion. Her father, John, was a left-handed pitcher for the semiprofessional Atlanta Crackers of the old Southern Association. Her mother, Marguerite, was the daughter of the

Louise Suggs after winning the Women's National Open golf tournament, 1949. ASSOCIATED PRESS AP

Crackers team owner. After he retired from baseball, John Suggs managed a golf course in Lithia Springs, Georgia, and taught his daughter to play at an early age. Suggs took to the game and within a few years began winning important tournaments. Renowned for her smooth swing and remarkable club-head speed, she was occasionally called the female Ben Hogan, a view that the entertainer Bob Hope confirmed when he christened her "Miss Sluggs" after a sobering round.

In the 1940s Suggs quickly amassed a string of amateur victories. In 1940, at age sixteen, she won the Georgia State Amateur Championship, and repeated that feat in 1942. She won the Southern Amateur Championship twice (1941, 1947), the North and South Championship three times (1942, 1946, 1948), and the Western Open twice (1946, 1947). In 1946 she won the Titleholders, the women's equivalent of the Masters, played in March at the Augusta Country Club in Georgia. The next year she won the U.S. Amateur title, followed by the British Amateur in 1948. Also in 1948 she accepted an invitation to play on the U.S. Curtis Cup team.

In July 1948, as an amateur champion, Suggs decided to turn professional. She soon took a leading role in founding the LPGA in 1950, and served as its president three times. In the fourteen years she played professional golf (1948–1962), she became universally recognized as a member of the "big four" of women's golf, the others being Babe Didrikson Zaharias, Patricia Berg, and Betty Jameson. As a professional, Suggs compiled a record of fifty LPGA victories, including eight major championship titles. Since a professional women's golf tour on the level of the LPGA did not exist before 1950, the distinction between amateur and professional victories for women of Suggs's generation was neither clear nor, perhaps, even appropriate. This was especially true for major victories; Suggs won nine (combining her amateur and professional years), ranking third behind Berg and Mickey Wright.

After turning professional, Suggs, at five feet, five-and-a-half inches, and 120 pounds, won many of the same major tournaments she had won as an amateur. She added two more Western Open victories (1949, 1953) and three more Titleholders wins (1954, 1956, 1959). In her U.S. Open victory in 1949 (she also won in 1952), she shot a 291 total, winning by 14 strokes, an LPGA record until 1986. In 1957 she won the LPGA Championship, becoming the first player to achieve a career Grand Slam of four major championships.

In 1952 she won six tournaments. But her best year was 1953, when she won eight times and was the leading money winner with awards of almost $20,000, an unusually large sum for the women's tour in those days. In 1954 she won five tournaments. In 1958 she won the Babe Zaharias, Gatlinburg, and French Lick Opens and the Triangle Round Robin. In 1959 she won the Saint Petersburg and Dallas Civitan Opens. In 1960 she won the Dallas Civitan, Youngstown Kitchens, and San Antonio Civitan Opens and the Triangle Round Robin, and again was the tour's leading money winner. In 1961, the year before she retired from the tour, Suggs played in seventeen tournaments, won five (Sea Island Invitational, DeSoto Lakes, Dallas Civitan, Kansas City, and San Antonio Civitan Opens), finished second in four others, and tied for second twice. She won $15,339.80, only about $1,500 less than the previous year.

Suggs earned many awards for her career victories. In 1951 she was elected to the Women's Golf Hall of Fame. She won the Vare Trophy as the LPGA player with the lowest scoring average in 1957, and in 1959 she received the *Golf Digest* Performance Award. When the LPGA Hall of Fame was established in 1967, Suggs was in the first class of four inductees. Decades later, she was inducted into the Georgia Golf Hall of Fame (1989), and became the first woman elected to the Georgia Athletic Hall of Fame (1996). In 2000 she received the Patty Berg Award for her outstanding contributions to women's golf. Betsy Rawls, an LPGA Hall of Famer and a past president of the LPGA, remarked that while Zaharias was a better athlete, Suggs was a better golfer. Herbert Warren Wind, the great golf historian, observed a "modern technique" in Suggs's swing. Her athleticism gave her the ability to develop her club-head speed by delaying her release until the last moment, a technique later used by all male professionals. She was deadly accurate on the short approach with her six, seven, or eight irons, which Wind believed she played better than most of her contemporaries, female or male.

Suggs was not only a great golfer and an energetic promoter of the game; she was a feisty combatant who insisted that women's golf skills were equal to those of the best male players, whose only advantage was that they could hit the ball farther. In 1961 she had the opportunity to prove her point. At a par-three tournament at Palm Beach, Florida, she won in a field that included the men's champion Sam Snead. Along with her overpowering game, Suggs brought a strong personality to the golf course that resisted any attempts at intimidation, even by golfing great Ben Hogan. Teamed with Hogan in a two-day 1945 Victory Tournament in Chicago (which they won), Suggs outplayed him by a stroke for nine holes. When Hogan refused to speak to her on the following day, she called him on his behavior. "Mr. Hogan, I don't think you're a gentleman," she said. "I'm up here helping you win the tournament, and you won't even speak to me." Hogan relented, and it was not long before he was complimenting her game.

After her retirement from the LPGA tour in 1962, Suggs lived in Delray Beach, Florida, and Sea Island, Georgia, where she continued to play competitively through the 1980s and taught golf at the Cloisters Resort. In 2000, the

LPGA announced the creation of the Louise Suggs Trophy, to be presented annually to the Rolex Rookie of the Year. In 2001, in keeping with her commitment to support her sport, Suggs donated $500,000 to the LPGA to promote junior golf. As the LPGA celebrated its fiftieth anniversary at the turn of the century, a new generation of golfers learned about Suggs's many contributions to the modern women's game. "She was bound to be a winner," Ben Hogan once noted. "And, she was."

★

Biographical information about Suggs can be found in *Current Biography Yearbook* (1962); Len Elliott and Barbara Kelly, *Who's Who in Golf* (1976); Victoria Sherrow, *Encyclopedia of Women and Sports* (1996); and Ralph Hickok, *A Who's Who of Sports Champions* (1995).

MARTIN SHERWIN

SULLIVAN, John Lawrence (*b.* 15 October 1858 in Roxbury, Massachusetts; *d.* 2 February 1918 in Abington, Massachusetts), charismatic professional boxer who was the last bare-knuckle champion, the most popular fighter of the nineteenth century, and the United States' first national sports celebrity.

Sullivan was born into a congested working-class neighborhood of Boston to Michael and Catherine Kelly Sullivan, who were both Catholic immigrants from Ireland. His father carried hods for a living, while his mother tended the family, which also included Sullivan's younger sister and brother. Enrolled in local public schools, Sullivan favored baseball over academics, yet he completed grammar school and attended Comer's Commercial College. His claim to have enrolled in Boston College is not borne out by the school's records. Nevertheless, Sullivan got a good education by the standards of his day.

The Boston area was home to throngs of Irish immigrants and their descendants, but not hospitable to them. Domestic work for women was plentiful, as was the meanest, most dangerous labor for men; there was little opportunity to rise above that level. Sullivan tried a number of trades, though sports were his passion. An attractive teenager, he was tall and weighed almost 200 pounds. He worked at building his skill in fighting, gaining a reputation as the local "strong boy." Laws in Massachusetts against prizefighting (bare-knuckle battles for money) were rigorously enforced, so his early boxing contests were staged exhibitions of gloved sparring. Sullivan's first recognition in the press was for a trouncing he gave older fighter John Woods in a match set among the variety acts at the Alhambra Theater in 1879.

Success in the ring fostered in the young Sullivan an ambition to be a prizefighter, a calling so low—and illegal—that no one had actually made a living from it in the United States. There had been famed fighters—James Ambrose "Yankee" Sullivan, John Carmel "Benicia Boy" Heenan, and John Morrissey—all of whom had worked to support their ring careers. Most of them lived and died badly. Nevertheless, Sullivan envisioned boxing as his ticket to fame and fortune. Several factors made his timing excellent: the popular press was greedy for sensation, Americans were beginning to view sports as beneficial, and the Gilded Age spirit was one of masculine aggression and glitz.

Sullivan's courage and skill in the exhibition ring propelled the "Boston Strong Boy" to victories over Boston and New York toughs. His April 1880 defeat of the English heavyweight Joe Goss, who had lost the U.S. championship to Paddy Ryan, brought him greater celebrity. Issuing the following challenge, "My name is John L. Sullivan and I can lick any son-of-a-bitch alive," Sullivan barnstormed the country and took on anyone for fifty dollars, accumulating cash and notoriety. U.S. champion Paddy Ryan finally accepted the challenge. Although most of Sullivan's contests had been fought using gloves under the Queensberry rules, the match with Ryan was fought bare-knuckled under the old London Rules. On 7 February 1882, in Mississippi City, Mississippi, he knocked out Ryan in the ninth round for the heavyweight championship.

Sullivan's star had risen, and he became the idol of the sporting press and urban tabloids. For the next few years he toured the country and abroad, basking in glory, overindulging, and defending his championship in the ring and in the saloon, including in a bar he bought. The citizens of Boston officially recognized their native son as world champion, presenting Sullivan with a diamond-studded gold belt. Jake Kilrain, backed by *Police Gazette* owner Richard K. Fox, challenged the champion to what would be the last bare-knuckle championship in the United States. On 8 July 1889, in Richburg, Mississippi, Sullivan knocked out Kilrain after seventy-five rounds, a feat that made the front page of the *New York Times.* The world champion reigned for three more years, not only in the ring but also on vaudeville and lecture stages. In his only championship defense under the Queensberry rules, an aged, dissipated Sullivan was knocked out by the "scientific" fighter, James J. Corbett, in twenty-one rounds in New Orleans on 7 September 1892. This marked the end of a boxing career that totaled hundreds of exhibitions and nearly fifty prizefights, only one of which he lost.

Sullivan's personal life was scarred by ferocity, excess, and alcoholism. Although he earned fabulous sums—he was the first athlete in the United States to earn more than $1 million in his lifetime—little of it was saved. His marriage to Annie Bates Baily on 1 May 1883 ended in divorce

John L. Sullivan. THE LIBRARY OF CONGRESS

in 1908 after years of infidelity, violence, and over twenty years of separation. Their only child died at age two in 1886. A second, happier marriage to Katherine Harkins on 7 February 1910 lasted until her death in 1916.

In retirement the gifted showman returned to the stage and, after sobering up, gave lectures on the evils of drink. He hobnobbed with President Theodore Roosevelt and lived relatively quietly on his farm. On 2 February 1918 a heart attack killed him. His wake and funeral were massive affairs. He is buried in Boston's Old Calvary Cemetery.

Sullivan had his detractors, who dwelled upon the brutality of his sport, his drunkenness and adultery, and his refusal to fight a black man, yet these were far outnumbered by his admirers. Although he never regained his championship, to many Bostonians, boxing aficionados, Irish Americans, and others, "the Great John L." was still the greatest sports champion who ever lived. Sullivan changed the way the U.S. public perceived sports, injecting drama and personality into the fray, creating it forever as spectacle.

★

Sullivan wrote a creative autobiography, *Life and Reminiscences of a 19th Century Gladiator* (1892). An authoritative biography, Michael T. Isenberg, *John L Sullivan and His America* (1988), places the fighter in his milieu. Elliot J. Gorn, *The Manly Art: Bare-Knuckle Fighting in America* (1986), sets him in the history of his sport. Sullivan's gold championship belt (or possibly a replica) is in the collection of the Smithsonian National Museum of American History in Washington, D.C.

ELLEN RONEY HUGHES

SUMMITT, Pat(ricia) Head (*b.* 14 June 1952 in Clarksville, Tennessee), head basketball coach of the Lady Volunteers at the University of Tennessee at Knoxville who is considered one of the best college-level coaches.

Summitt, the daughter of James Richard Head, a self-employed businessman, and Hazel Albright Head, a homemaker, learned to play basketball in fourth grade, when she joined her three older brothers already competing against each other in their family's spacious barn loft. Considered a natural athlete, Summitt continued playing through her high school years at Cheatham County High School in Ashland City, Tennessee. After graduating from high school, Summitt attended the University of Tennessee at Martin, where she honed her skills and became an impressive all-around player known for nailing shots from the

Pat Head Summitt, 1999. AP/WIDE WORLD PHOTOS

perimeter. Summitt suffered a knee injury as a senior that almost ended her career, but she came back to the court and earned a spot on the 1976 U.S. Olympic team, which that year (the first games to include women's basketball) won a silver medal.

After graduating from the University of Tennessee at Martin in 1974 with a B.A. in physical education, Summitt accepted a position as head coach of the women's basketball team at the University of Tennessee in Knoxville; she was just twenty-two. She also studied full time as a graduate student and taught physical education classes. The Lady Volunteers finished their first two seasons under her direction with an impressive 32–19 record. During her first eight seasons, Summitt led the Lady Volunteers to the Final Four competitions four times. In 1980 Summitt married R. B. Summitt II; they had one child in 1990.

Under Summitt's leadership, the Lady Vols won National Collegiate Athletic Association (NCAA) championships in 1987, 1989, 1991, 1996, 1997, and 1998. Her 1997–1998 season, which was her twenty-fourth as head coach, ended with the Lady Vols racking up a 39–0 record and winning the NCAA championship for the third consecutive year. Summitt became the first female coach to appear on the cover of *Sports Illustrated* (1997), and her career was studied in a best-selling book, *Reach for the Summit* (1998), and an HBO special, "A Cinderella Season: The Lady Vols Fight Back" (1998). Summitt entered her twenty-fifth season with a record of 664–143, placing her among the top-ranked male and female coaches.

Summitt's other career achievements include winning nineteen Southeastern Conference (SEC) tournament and regular season championships, and producing eleven Olympians, sixteen Kodak All-Americans, and forty-five All-SEC performers. In 2000 Summitt was inducted into the Naismith Memorial Basketball Hall of Fame and named Naismith Coach of the Century. Five games into the 2000 season, she celebrated her 700th win as a collegiate basketball coach, and a resounding victory against Wisconsin merited her inclusion in the elite 700 Club. Summitt and University of Texas at Austin coach Jody Conradt are the only two female members of this prestigious organization. Also in 2000 was Summitt's twelfth NCAA Final Four appearance—a milestone she shares with former UCLA coaching legend John Wooden. Since 1985, the Lady Volunteers have always been in the Associated Press's top twenty-five teams.

Summitt is an inspiration both on and off the court. She sits on the boards of Fortune 500 companies and often delivers motivational speeches to the leaders of major corporations. She is a spokesperson for the United Way, Race for the Cure, and Juvenile Diabetes Foundation. Honoring her home state of Tennessee, Summitt works tirelessly with state affiliates of the American Heart Association and the Tennessee Lung Association. Former first lady Hillary Rodham Clinton named Summitt one of the "25 Most Influential Working Mothers," as well as being honored as one of *Glamour* magazine's "1998 Women of the Year."

The graduation rate of Summitt's student athletes is exceptional, every Lady Vol who has completed her eligibility at TN has received her degree or is in the process of completing her degree. Summitt encourages the Lady Vols to reach their full potential and to find success as students and athletes. "I love the challenges I get in this game," she said. "I love working with young women and helping them realize their potential, and I don't know that I could ever get tired of that."

★

The best source for material on Summitt's life is *Reach for the Summit* (1998). Additional information on her life and career can be found in David Porter, ed., *Biographical Dictionary of American Sports: Basketball and Other Indoor Sports* (1989); *Biographical Dictionary of American Sports* (1989); and *A Who's Who of Sports Champions—Their Stories and Records* (1995).

FAYE HALL JACKSON

SWOOPES, Sheryl Denise (*b.* 25 March 1971 in Brownfield, Texas), basketball player who became a one-of-a-kind superstar in collegiate, Olympic, and professional women's basketball.

Swoopes was born in a small Texas town about forty miles from Lubbock in West Texas. Her father left shortly after she was born, and Swoopes's mother, Louise, struggled to raise Sheryl and her three brothers on her own. Because Swoopes played basketball with her brothers and participated in neighborhood pickup games with boys, she developed an aggressive, physical playing style that would be her trademark throughout her career. Swoopes led her Brownfield High School team to a state championship and was an All-State and All-America athlete. While still a junior, she was chosen as Texas Player of the Year. Swoopes graduated from high school in 1989.

Having made her mark early, Swoopes was actively pursued by college recruiters. Her decision to accept a scholarship to the University of Texas at Austin (UT) proved to be a mistake. Only four days after arriving in September 1989, Swoopes was overwhelmed with homesickness and returned to Brownfield. Austin was 400 miles from her hometown, too far for a girl who had never been away. There were plenty of critics who felt she had thrown away her future, but Swoopes just went about her business. She left UT and enrolled in nearby South Plains Junior College, where she continued to play basketball. At South Plains, Swoopes became a junior college All-American and the 1991 Player of the Year. In her second season she averaged 21.5 points per game, 11.9 rebounds, 4.6 assists, and 4.7 steals.

Sheryl Swoopes. AP/Wide World Photos

In 1991 Swoopes transferred to Texas Tech University in Lubbock. A dangerous six-foot-tall shooting guard and forward known for her speed and shooting ability, Swoopes was nicknamed the "Texas Tornado" and compared to Michael Jordan. She led the Lady Red Raiders to a 58–8 record in two seasons, a 1993 National Collegiate Athletic Association (NCAA) title, and two Southwest Conference titles. She was named 1993 National Player of the Year and earned 1993 NCAA Final Four Most Valuable Player (MVP) honors when she set an NCAA Championship game record (for both men and women) with 47 points in Texas Tech's 84–82 win over Ohio State. Swoopes had five consecutive thirty-plus games in leading the Lady Raiders to victory. She won the prestigious Naismith Player of the Year Award (1993), along with many other awards. Swoopes was widely considered the best player in college basketball. In recognition of her unmatched achievements, Texas Tech retired her number 22 on 19 February 1994.

Despite Swoopes's incredible college career, the only place for a woman to play professional basketball in 1993 was overseas. She moved to Bari, Italy, and played for their team in the Italian women's league. But Swoopes's European stint lasted only ten games; she left when the team did not meet its contractual obligations. Once she was back in the United States there were few options available. She volunteered as a coach, played pickup basketball at the recreation center, and watched her skills deteriorate. She turned to other things, completing her B.A. in sports science in 1994 and marrying her high school sweetheart Eric Jackson on 17 June 1995.

Although in 1994 Swoopes played on a winning U.S. basketball team that competed against NCAA teams and toured Europe, Asia, and Australia, and earned a gold medal at the Goodwill Games in St. Petersburg, Russia, she was left with few opportunities to play with others at her level until the U.S. Women's National Team formed in 1995. This team remained undefeated as it played fifty-two games around the world in preparation for the Olympics. During this time Swoopes landed endorsement contracts, and Nike introduced the "Air Swoopes," making Swoopes the first woman athlete to have a Nike basketball shoe named after her. At the 1996 Olympics in Atlanta, Swoopes helped the U.S. team capture a gold medal.

With the formation of the Women's National Basketball Association (WNBA) in 1997, Swoopes was drafted to play for the Houston Comets. She became one of three WNBA stars to receive personal service contracts, which paid above and beyond the standard team rate of $50,000 in exchange for playing a central role in WNBA promotional campaigns. Swoopes's contract meant she received $150,000 in addition to her $50,000 salary from the Comets. Just as she was to start playing, Swoopes became pregnant and had to sit out most of the season. With all eyes on her as the new WNBA's performance standard-bearer, Swoopes gave birth to a son and amazed everyone by returning to the court within six weeks.

Swoopes and the Houston Comets dominated the WNBA. She was named to the All-WNBA First Team in 1998, 1999, and 2000. Under Swoopes's leadership, the Houston Comets were WNBA champions four years in a row—1997 through 2000. Swoopes was named the 2000 WNBA Defensive Player of the Year and voted the 2000 WNBA MVP. She was a fan favorite, charismatic and well spoken off the court. Swoopes and teammate Cynthia Cooper were a dynamic duo, drawing in large Houston crowds and a larger-than-predicted television audience, winning new fans everywhere for women's professional basketball. However, amidst all the successes in her professional life, Swoopes faced a new personal challenge in 2000, when she divorced her husband and became a single parent.

In May 2001 Swoopes tore the anterior cruciate ligament in her left knee during a preseason workout and was forced to sit out the season. This came on the heels of 2000, her best professional season yet. In 2000 she led the WNBA with 2.81 steals and scored her playoff high of 31 points in the Comets game that clinched their fourth title. Well aware that her age was becoming a factor, Swoopes was determined to make a slow and thorough recovery so she could come back strong the next year. She took the opportunity to practice her broadcasting skills, doing on-air sports analysis for the WNBA. Without Swoopes or Cooper, the Comets reign as WNBA Champions came to a close in 2001. As Swoopes neared the end of her recovery, she considered playing overseas during the off-season.

Swoopes's career heights remained unmatched at the close of the 2001 season. She had a mental toughness that allowed her to come back again and again, despite the lack of a playing venue, her divorce, the birth of her son, and a serious injury. She had entered a world that disproportionately rewarded male basketball players, but from the time she was young, Swoopes played the game as if this did not matter. In the process, she raised the rewards for women's basketball as well as for herself.

★

Several books for young readers have been written about Swoopes, including Sheryl Swoopes and Doug Keith, *Bounce Back* (1996), and Susan Kuklin and Sheryl Swoopes, *Hoops With Swoopes* (2001), a book full of vivid photos. For biographical essays about Swoopes's life and career, see *Contemporary Black Biography,* vol. 12. (1996), *Great Women in Sports* (1996), and *Newsmakers* (2000). Joe Drape, "Pro Basketball: Baby on Board; Swoopes Learns to Juggle Bouncing Ball and Bouncing Boy," *New York Times* (3 Aug. 1997), gives an account of the time Swoopes took off from basketball to have her baby. See also "Houston Comets Blaze with Third Straight WNBA Championship," *Jet* (27 Sept. 1999), which describes the Houston Comets third championship win; "Houston Comets Win Fourth Straight WNBA Championship," *Jet* (11 Sept. 2000), which reports on the Comets fourth WNBA championship win; and "Season-Ending Injury," *Jet* (14 May 2001), which announces Swoopes 2000 season-ending injury.

JANET INGRAM

T

TARKENTON, Fran(cis) Asbury (*b.* 3 February 1940 in Richmond, Virginia), professional football Hall of Fame quarterback who played eighteen seasons in the National Football League (NFL) and helped promote the passing style and a wide-open game that shocked traditionalists while attracting new fans.

Tarkenton was the son of Dallas Tarkenton, a Methodist minister, and Frances Tarkenton; Fran's middle name, Asbury, was that of a pioneer of American Methodism. At age five Tarkenton moved with his parents and brother to Washington, D.C., and at age ten he was playing end for the Merrick Boys Club football team. The Washington Redskins quarterback at the time, "Slingin'" Sammy Baugh, was a favorite of Tarkenton's. In 1951 the family moved to Athens, Georgia, home of the University of Georgia Bulldogs of the Southeastern Conference, who under Coach Wallace Butts had established a winning tradition in the 1940s with such greats as Frank Sinkwich, recipient of the Heisman Trophy in 1942, and Charley Trippi. Tarkenton quarterbacked the local Young Men's Christian Association (YMCA) team, moved on to lead the Athens High School Trojans, and was named All-State quarterback.

In the fall of 1957 Tarkenton enrolled at the University of Georgia, where he excelled at academics while playing three varsity seasons. In 1959, his sophomore year and first year on the varsity team, Georgia won its first Southeastern Conference championship since 1948 with Tarkenton, at six feet and 185 pounds, calling the signals in an 8–1 season capped by a 14–0 win over the University of Missouri in the Orange Bowl. He graduated in 1961 with a Bachelor's degree in business. He and his wife, Elaine Merrell, raised three children.

Tarkenton was a third-round draft choice, twenty-ninth selection overall, of the Minnesota Vikings, an NFL expansion team, under new coach Norm Van Brocklin. Tarkenton came into the Vikings first game, against the powerful Chicago Bears, and proceeded to have the best rookie game ever played by a quarterback. He threw for four touchdowns and ran for a fifth, going seventeen for thirty-three as the Vikings shocked Chicago, 37–13. However, the Vikings proceeded to lose their next seven games, finishing their first season in the league with a 3–11 record, but having found its field general.Tarkenton narrowly lost the voting for NFL Rookie of the Year to Mike Ditka of the Bears. The 1962 Vikings regressed to 2–11–1, but in 1963 they improved to 5–9. By that time Tarkenton was well on his way to establishing the image and reputation that gained him the nickname "Scrambler."

The Vikings lack of a strong offensive line to protect Tarkenton forced him to scramble out of the pocket to avoid getting sacked. But Van Brocklin soon expressed his unhappiness with the degree to which Tarkenton scrambled around, cracking that Tarkenton must think it was "pretty cute" to run around so much. In 1964 Van Brocklin opined that "with Tarkenton, you need to have an excep-

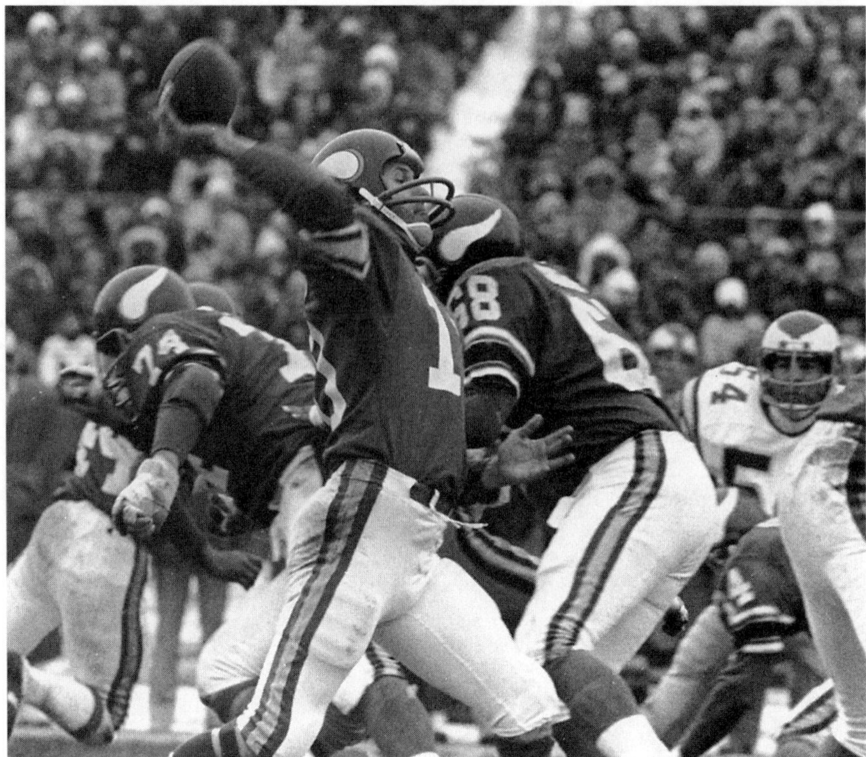

Fran Tarkenton, 1978. ASSOCIATED PRESS AP

tionally good third-and-forty offense." But the tradition-minded coach stuck with his quarterback, and that year the Vikings attained their first winning season, 8–5–1. Tarkenton had his best season yet, completing 171 of 306 attempts for 2,506 yards and 22 touchdowns, and was rated the second-best passer in the league behind the Green Bay Packers Bart Starr. Tarkenton was named the outstanding back in the 1965 Pro Bowl game. "Frantic Francis," who was allowed to call his own plays, was willing to go way, way back behind the line of scrimmage, weave around, and then make his way to the edge of the sideline, always looking for an open receiver. If the pass option was not there, Tarkenton would run. His mobility, fearlessness, and inventiveness made it work.

However, the Vikings declined to 7–7 in the 1965 season, and in 1966 Van Brocklin benched his established starter as Minnesota sunk further to a 4–9–1 record. On 10 February 1967 Tarkenton wrote Van Brocklin a letter of "resignation." The coach himself resigned the next day, and on 7 March Tarkenton was traded to the New York Giants, who had finished last in 1966, in return for some high draft choices. In six years with the Vikings, Tarkenton had thrown 113 touchdown passes and completed 53.9 percent of his passes; as a running quarterback he had averaged 6.5 yards per rush in 293 carries and had run for 15 touchdowns. Tarkenton piled up more yardage in his five seasons with the Giants, but the team was only 33–37 overall from 1967 through 1971. Returning to Minnesota for the 1972 season, Tarkenton proved that there were such things as second acts and that sequels could in fact be better.

In Tarkenton's seven remaining seasons with the Vikings, the Purple and Gold won six National Football Conference (NFC) titles and played in three Super Bowls in a four-year period under head coach Bud Grant. In 1975 Tarkenton was named NFL Player of the Year and won the Jim Thorpe Trophy for Most Valuable Player. He also led the NFC in passing, benefiting from the standout receivers Ahmad Rashad and Sammy White. Running back Chuck Foreman, who achieved the first of three consecutive 1,000-yard rushing seasons, was the third-option short receiver. The defense was led by a stellar front four known as the "Purple People Eaters." The Vikings were very good but not quite good enough; in their first appearance in the NFL's ultimate spectacle they lost Super Bowl VIII to the Miami Dolphins, 24–7, on 13 January 1974; on 1 January 1975 they lost their second consecutive Super Bowl, this time to the Pittsburgh Steelers, 16–6; their third and final Super Bowl loss of the twentieth century came on 9 January 1977 in Super Bowl XI to the Oakland Raiders, 32–14. Tarkenton excelled in none of these games. He played two more years, retiring after the 1978 season as the holder of every major passing record: 6,467 attempts, 3,686 completions, 342 passing touchdowns, and 47,003 yards gained in the air. In addition, his scrambling and mobility are attested in his 3,674 yards gained on the ground and his 32 rushing touchdowns.

Before retiring, Tarkenton began working in the off-season in various business capacities as a management consultant and motivational speaker, and while continuing this work he also was a television sports commentator and general program host. In his time Tarkenton was the greatest passing quarterback in the NFL. He opened up the game with his crowd-pleasing scrambling, a precursor to the West Coast offense. He was inducted into the Pro Football Hall of Fame in 1986 and the College Football Hall of Fame in 1987.

★

Tarkenton's books about his career are *No Time for Losing* (1967); *Broken Patterns: The Education of a Quarterback* (1971); and *Tarkenton* (1976), cowritten with Jim Klobucher. His career as a Viking is considered at length in Jim Klobucher, *Knights and Knaves of Autumn: 40 Years of Pro Football and the Minnesota Vikings* (2000).

LAWSON BOWLING

TATUM, Reece ("Goose") (*b.* 3 May 1921 in Calion, Arkansas; *d.* 18 January 1967 in El Paso, Texas), professional basketball and baseball player, and sports showman who played for the Harlem Globetrotters during the 1940s and 1950s, creating several of the stunts and routines associated with that basketball team.

A gifted athlete who grew up in El Dorado, Arkansas, Tatum used his massive hands and eighty-four-inch arm span to handle and pass basketballs with incredible finesse. He became the key architect of several of the Harlem Globetrotters' memorable routines after joining the team in 1942. The Globetrotters began their transformation toward combining entertainment and basketball three years before Tatum joined the squad when team members began experimenting with tricks and playful antics during games they were winning handily.

Wildly enthusiastic reactions from crowds led owner and founder Abe Saperstein to encourage his players to continue weaving their entertaining legerdemain within the traditional game. Globetrotter Inman Jackson initiated the original "Clown Prince" of basketball role. The "Floorman," usually an individual both nimble and artistic in respect to dribbling, worked directly with the "Prince" while the "Cornerman" often boosted both positions.

Tatum began his apprenticeship (focusing on the role of Clown Prince) in 1942. Only a brief period of service in the military with the U.S. Army Air Corps during World War II interrupted his early career. A quick study, Tatum became the new Clown Prince in the mid-1940s and developed several new routines. He refined his craft by attending circuses and studying clowns, which provided him with inspiration for on-court antics using referees and the crowd as foils. Tatum constantly practiced tricks like spinning a basketball on one finger, passing the ball behind his back, and effortlessly rolling basketballs on his arms. One of his favorite maneuvers involved manipulating a basketball fastened to the end of a huge rubber band, a trick that made opposing players and referees look foolish as they attempted to grab the ball. Once a game Tatum tossed shredded paper from a water bucket into the audience. From his position at the top of the key, he guided the Trotters' attack while performing a humorous nonstop monologue punctuated by animated facial expressions. Tatum was also able to score at will against most competition, relying on his patented hook shot. Some basketball historians credit Tatum with developing the "sky hook."

Reece "Goose" Tatum, 1944. AP/WIDE WORLD PHOTOS

Tatum's service with the team coincided with an era of Globetrotter pride when the squad proved their basketball skills were outstanding even against the toughest competition in the world. In 1939 the Globetrotters achieved a berth in the World's Professional Basketball Championship, an invitational tournament sponsored by the Chicago *Herald-American.* They lost to another all–African-American team, the New York Rens, in the final game, but they returned the following year and won the 1940 championship. Their competitive reputation was further enhanced when they won the International Cup Tournament in Mexico City in 1943. Worldwide acclaim followed. *Life* magazine featured the team prominently in the 2 December 1946 issue.

The Globetrotters, starring Tatum, continued their dominance over all competition when they beat the Minneapolis Lakers in 1948 and 1949. At the time the Lakers were considered world champions of the very segregated Basketball Association of America (BAA), a league that became the National Basketball Association (NBA) in 1949. The victories left no doubt that the Globetrotters were talented basketball players in addition to courtside showmen. The Lakers had a roster of stars, including forward Jim Pollard and center George Mikan, arguably the most famous basketball player of his era. Tatum and a team that included Globetrotter legend Marques Haynes defeated the world champion Lakers 61–59 before a crowd of 17,823 fans at Chicago Stadium on 19 February 1948.

A highly anticipated rematch occurred on 28 February 1949. Again, the Globetrotters won the contest (49–45) despite a tremendous height disadvantage. The Lakers had several players taller than Tatum, who guarded six-foot, ten-inch Mikan. Tatum and the Globetrotters basked in the applause of a crowd of over 20,000 at Chicago Stadium after proving they were the best basketball team in the world again. The team also competed in the World Series of Basketball (1950–1958 and 1961–1962) during this era. Tatum was named co-Most Valuable Player (MVP) in 1951 and MVP of the tournament in 1952.

Tatum's close association with the audience became even more intimate when theme music and new marketing techniques announced the presence of the Globetrotters in the 1950s. By then an entertainment conglomerate with an international reputation, the team entered arenas donned in garish uniforms. After their entrance, Tatum and his fellow players formed a circle at center court and tossed the basketball around as speakers blared artist Brother Bones singing "Sweet Georgia Brown." In 1950 and 1951 the team began to live up to its name, touring Europe, North Africa, and South America.

A multidimensional athlete, Tatum was a star baseball player for the Birmingham Black Barons before signing a basketball contract with the Globetrotters. He continued his participation in baseball intermittently throughout his career. Playing first base for the Indianapolis Clowns, Tatum proved that baseball fans appreciated entertaining antics as well. In 1952 the Clowns won the Negro American League championship with a young cross-handed slugger from Alabama named Hank Aaron.

Tatum's participation in Negro League baseball paralleled his professional basketball career. Segregation in both sports was pervasive during most of his playing days, and the Globetrotters were often the only professional avenue available for African-American basketball players.

In 1959 Tatum purchased the Detroit Stars and changed their name to the Detroit Clowns. He continued to play first base for his new acquisition. The Clowns were only one of Tatum's ventures. He formed his own basketball team, the Harlem Road Kings, after retiring from the Globetrotters in 1954. Known for their crowd-pleasing entertainment, the Road Kings traveled to Asia and Europe in addition to venues across North America. Tatum managed the team until his death, and he is buried in Fort Bliss National Cemetery in El Paso.

★

Stew Thornley, *Basketball's Original Dynasty: The History of the Lakers* (1989), provides rich detail about the rivalry between the Globetrotters and the Lakers. Rob Ruck, *Sandlot Seasons: Baseball in Pittsburgh* (1993), describes Negro League baseball during the era that Tatum and contemporaries like Aaron played. Robert W. Peterson, *Only the Ball Was White* (1999), delivers excellent background material about the era in which Tatum played. James A. Riley's reference volume, *The Biographical Encyclopedia of the Negro Baseball Leagues* (1994), offers data about Tatum's Indianapolis ball club. An obituary is in the *New York Times* (Jan. 1967).

R. JAKE SUDDERTH

TAYLOR, Lawrence Julius ("LT") (*b.* 4 February 1959 in Lightfoot, Virginia), professional football player whose pass-rushing ability revolutionized the role of outside linebacker.

Taylor was the middle son of Clarence Taylor, a truck driver at the shipyards in Newport News, Virginia, and Iris Taylor, a cashier and clerk who later ran a day-care center for preschool children. His parents worked hard, scrimped, and formed a God-fearing family in Williamsburg, Virginia, with their three boys, each born one year apart. As a child, Lawrence spent a great deal of time alone and was considered the wild one, a rebel. Other children called him "Candy Man" because he bought candy and resold it at school for a profit.

Clarence Taylor was a great fan of football, but his son loved baseball and dreamed of becoming a major league catcher. At age fifteen, while a sophomore at Lafayette High School, Lawrence, later called "LT," was practicing with the baseball team when he was spotted by Pete Bab-

Lawrence Taylor at his induction into the Pro Football Hall of Fame, 1999. AP/WIDE WORLD PHOTOS

cock, coach of the Williamsburg Jaycee football team, who asked the short, stocky youngster to come out for the team. Babcock made Taylor a linebacker. LT was hooked. He checked out books from the school library and read about famous linebackers, such as the New York Giant Sam Huff.

In his junior year in high school, the five-foot, seven-inch, 180-pound Taylor sat on the bench until the season's fifth game, when he won the game by blocking a punt. Coach Melvin Jones recognized his potential and made him a starter. By the end of his senior year in 1977, Taylor had grown to six feet, one inch and 205 pounds, and was named Male Athlete of the Year. Because he had started playing football relatively late, Taylor received few scholarship offers. He chose the University of North Carolina because he liked Mike Mansfield, its recruiter.

Taylor spent most of his first year at Chapel Hill sitting on the bench, playing occasionally as a member of the varsity special teams. Off the gridiron, he went crazy. His drinking, partying, and aggressive behavior gained him the nickname "Monster." He frequently was seen climbing the side of his dormitory building in a drunken stupor. In his sophomore year he got a new coach, Dick Crum, who started him as an inside linebacker. In the season opener, he broke a bone in his foot and missed several games. The team finished the season with a 5–6 record.

Taylor has admitted that in 1979, his junior year, he might have wound up in jail or dead if it had not been for two events. Halfway through the season, he had a great game against North Carolina State, which convinced him of his ability, and that evening, he met Deborah Belinda Cooley, with whom he fell in love and for whom he reformed his life. They were married on 19 June 1982 and had three children; they divorced in 1994. Taylor's team finished with an 8–3–1 record and won the Gator Bowl against Michigan, with Taylor making the play of the game, sacking Michigan's quarterback John Wangler. At the end of Taylor's senior year, North Carolina had lost only one game, to Oklahoma, and had an 11–1 record season, along with the number-one-ranked defense in the nation. In the Bluebonnet Bowl, they upset Texas. Taylor, now six feet, three inches and 230 pounds, was a consensus All-American and named Atlantic Coast Conference (ACC) Player of the Year.

In 1981 Taylor was drafted into the National Football League (NFL) by the New York Giants. The new linebacker, who had never even been to a professional football game before, signed a four-year contract starting at $125,000 a year and rising to $300,000 by the last year. In his first year, the Giants had their first winning season in ten years, and Taylor was named Rookie of the Year and Defensive Player of the Year. He was a unanimous Pro Bowl choice. The next season, Bill Parcells, former defensive coordinator for the Giants, replaced coach Ray Perkins, and Taylor was again named Defensive Player of the Year, going to the Pro Bowl for the second year in a row.

It was at this time that Taylor began using drugs. He was introduced to cocaine at a Halloween party and became hooked. Many attribute the Giants' terrible losing season of 1983 to Taylor's increased use of drugs. By 1985 he was using crack and staying out all night. Because of his wife's devotion and perseverance, he entered rehabilitation in March 1986, the season when the Giants won the Super Bowl, beating the Denver Broncos, the first championship season for New York since 1956. Taylor was named the NFL's Most Valuable Player.

Because of a players' strike and a hamstring injury, Taylor played in only nine games in 1987. Nevertheless, he was named to the Pro Bowl team and the All-NFL team for the seventh year in a row. In 1988 he received a four-game suspension for drug use. The following year, he seemed to have recovered and led the Giants to the playoffs. In 1990, after a season of eleven sacks, one interception, and ninety-three tackles, Taylor made NFL history as the only player ever to be named to the Pro Bowl ten times. The same year, Taylor had a lackluster game in the Giants' second Super Bowl victory, but the team beat the Buffalo Bills anyway.

Age and injuries, along with drugs and personal problems, took their toll, and Taylor retired in January 1994 with a career total of 132½ sacks, 1,088 tackles, 33 forced fumbles, 10 fumble recoveries, and 9 interceptions. His number 56 jersey was retired by the Giants in 1994, and in 1999 Taylor was inducted into the Pro Football Hall of Fame. As dominant as he was on the gridiron, Taylor's personal life was in shambles. After retirement, he was involved in a number of incidents involving traffic violations, non-payment of taxes and child support, and drug offenses in New Jersey, South Carolina, and Florida. With five children by three different women and paternity suits totaling $74,000 in 1998, Taylor found himself unable to pay the bills and was forced to declare bankruptcy. He lives in Florida and makes a living selling memorabilia on home shopping channels and making personal appearances.

Although his life after his football career ended has not been happy, during his career Taylor's combination of great intensity, speed, and muscle redefined the way the outside linebacker position was played. No longer would the linebacker read and react to quarterback moves; he would now charge past offensive linemen and attack the passer aggressively, looking not only to sack the quarterback but also to create fumbles. Taylor had an innate sense of the game. In his autobiography he wrote, "I was born for football the way some people are born to be engineers or musicians." Due in large part to Taylor's presence, the Giants had a ten-year winning streak in which they made the playoffs six times and won two Super Bowls. Since leaving the NFL, Taylor has also appeared in several movies, including *Any Given Sunday* (1999) and *Shaft* (2000).

★

Taylor's autobiography, *LT: Living on the Edge,* written with David Falkner (1987), gives an honest account of his personal problems along with his perceptions about his career. Dan Herschberg, *Lawrence Taylor* (1998), is also useful. In an article in *Sports Illustrated,* "LT on LT" (16 Sept. 1991), Taylor discusses racism, his relations with the press, and playing in New York. Several articles on Taylor and his exploits have appeared in the *New York Times* (21 Dec. 1981, 4 Jan. 1987, 23 Jan. 1994, 14 May 1998, and 25 Oct. 1998).

JOHN J. BYRNE

TAYLOR, Marshall Walter ("Major") (*b.* 26 November 1878 near Indianapolis, Indiana; *d.* 21 June 1932 in Chicago, Illinois), world's fastest bicycle racer and the first American-born African American to become a premier sports figure.

Taylor was born to Gilbert Taylor, a horseman, and Sophronia Kelter. He grew up in rural Indiana, close to the growing, industrial city of Indianapolis. Taylor's parents were poor farmers, descendants of slaves who had made their way to the free state of Indiana before or during the Civil War. Gilbert Taylor fought for the North in an African-American regiment during the war and later bought the small farm where he eked out a living for his wife and eight children. When Taylor was eight years old, his father took a job as a coachman for the Southards, a wealthy white family living in Indianapolis.

The small, bright, and charming Taylor became the

Major Taylor, c. 1900. HULTON | ARCHIVE

playmate and surrogate brother of Daniel Southard, a child his own age. Until about the age of twelve, Taylor was afforded all the privileges and luxuries the Southards provided for their own son—including his own bicycle. Taylor became a favorite among the well-off white children of the neighborhood, partially because of his trick riding skills. When Taylor's benefactors moved to Chicago, the budding cyclist landed a job at the Indianapolis bicycle repair shop of Hay and Wilits. He acquired the nickname "Major" because he wore a brassy soldier's uniform and a military cap while performing cycling tricks near the storefront.

In 1882 or 1883 Taylor met Louis "Birdie" Munger, a bicycle racing star and cycle manufacturer who was to become Taylor's employer, lifelong adviser, and friend. The experienced cyclist recognized Taylor's potential, telling people that the young boy would one day be a champion. In 1895 Taylor followed Munger to Worcester, Massachusetts, where Munger opened a factory and encouraged his protégé to become a professional rider. Taylor competed in a number of integrated amateur races in the Northeast, and at eighteen he registered as a professional racer, the first full-time African-American cyclist eligible to win cash prizes.

For the next eight years, Taylor raced on the national circuit. By the end of the 1897 season he had established a reputation marked by a series of wins against the reigning national champion, Eddie Bald, by many cash prizes, and by racism, which included death threats. As a result of his mother's death in 1897, Taylor committed himself to the Baptist faith, which prompted him to forgo Sunday races—a decision that cost him huge sums of money.

In spite of the racist climate in the South, which prohibited Taylor from training there, he established two world records in 1898. In August, Taylor defeated international Welsh star Jimmy Michael in the one-mile, paced, standing start race, setting a new world record of 41.4 seconds. He also set the coveted one-mile, paced, flying start record using a new chainless-gear bicycle. By the end of the year, Taylor held seven world records for races ranging from a quarter mile to two miles.

Taylor's amazing successes continued in 1899, when he won the world professional sprint championship at Queen's Park track in Montreal. He also won the U.S. national championship, and by the end of the year he held 22 first places and had defended his own 1-mile world record twice, reaching a speed of 45.56 miles per hour.

Following the purchase of a house in an affluent white neighborhood in Worcester, Taylor accepted a contract to compete in France. During his four-month European tour in 1901, Taylor rode in nearly every important European capital, beating champions from England, Italy, Belgium, Germany, and Denmark. Out of twenty-four races, he won eighteen. According to biographer Andrew Ritchie, Taylor became the unofficial "black American ambassador to Europe." Unfortunately, upon Taylor's return to the United States in July 1901, he was met with the same animosity and racism that marked his earlier days.

Taylor married the well-educated Daisy Victoria Morris on 21 March 1902; they had one child. Taylor returned to Europe shortly after the wedding, and for the next two years raced to the height of his international career. Everywhere he went Taylor was treated as a celebrity—especially in Australia, where he and his new wife were greeted by hundreds of boats honking and waving U.S. flags. Taylor miraculously crossed Australia's strict color line and was invited to speak from church pulpits. He and Daisy enjoyed the country so much that they named their only child Sydney after its capital city.

In 1902 Taylor began talking of retirement, but lucrative offers kept him riding until 1909, when he made his sixth and final European tour. The aging athlete lost several times, but the tour ended with a victory in France, where Taylor beat Victor Dupré, the reigning French and world champion.

Taylor retired at age thirty-two. Without a steady income the Taylors could not maintain the standard of living to which they had grown accustomed. Taylor and Daisy were forced to sell their house in Worcester. In 1928, while fading into anonymity, Taylor self-published his autobiography, *The Fastest Bicycle Rider in the World* (1928). Taylor found it difficult to remain in the city where he had once been known as a wealthy and successful athlete and moved to Chicago alone. He lived at the Young Men's Christian Association (YMCA) and sold copies of his book door-to-door—a practice he continued until his death. The Taylors divorced in 1930. Taylor died in the charity ward of a Chicago hospital due to a weak heart, and was buried in an unmarked grave in a cemetery thirty miles south of Chicago. In 1948, however, Schwinn Bicycle Company owner Frank Schwinn, along with other professional racers, moved Taylor's grave to a more prominent site, the Memorial Garden of the Good Shepherd, in Mount Glenwood Cemetery in Chicago. In 1982 Indianapolis opened a cycling track in Taylor's name—the Major Taylor Velodrome.

Taylor lived the life of an unsung hero. He has received little attention even though his career spanned three continents, earned him numerous world records, and proved him to be the fastest cyclist in the world.

★

Taylor's autobiography, *The Fastest Bicycle Rider in the World* (1928), sheds light on numerous aspects of the cyclist's life, personality, and career from an early age until his retirement in 1910. Andrew Ritchie's comprehensive and fascinating biography, *Major Taylor: The Extraordinary Career of a Champion Bicycle Racer*

(1988), includes information from hundreds of newspaper and magazine articles, scrapbooks, and interviews with Taylor's daughter. For a book with substantial references to Taylor, see Rebecca Chalmers Barton, *Witness for Freedom: Negro-Americans in Autobiography* (1948).

VALERIE LINET

TERRY, William Harold ("Bill") (*b.* 30 October 1898 in Atlanta, Georgia; *d.* 9 January 1989 in Jacksonville, Florida), Major League Baseball player and manager of the New York Giants who was the last National League player to hit over .400 in a single season.

The formative years of Terry, popularly known as "Memphis Bill," were somewhat marred by the unhappy marriage of his parents, William Thomas Terry and Bertha Blackman Terry. While his mother tended to the household, his father's efforts with the family grain business met with failure and finally led to divorce in 1915. By the age of twelve Terry had moved with his parents to seven different Atlanta homes, and he never attended high school. By 1912 he was working in an Atlanta railroad yard.

Terry's first baseball game was on 6 June 1912, playing for Grace Methodist in the Baraca Sunday School League in Atlanta. Three years later the left-handed thrower and hitter performed in his first professional game as a pitcher and first baseman for Dothan in the Georgia State League.

Bill Terry, 1936. ASSOCIATED PRESS AP

In 1916 Terry moved to Memphis, Tennessee. On 21 November that same year, Terry married Elvena Sneed from Memphis. They had four children.

Terry pitched in the All-Star game in the New Orleans winter league in 1917, but quit baseball the next year. He began working for Storage Battery Service and Sales Company in Memphis, but soon moved to Standard Oil of Louisiana as a salesman. On 15 June 1919 he established the company's semiprofessional team, the Polarines. Referring to his early professional career as a pitcher, Terry remarked: "I still think I would have made a first-class pitcher, but even for a left-hander, . . . I simply couldn't keep that ball away from the other fellows' bats, and right there I decided that if I ever hoped to get anywhere, it would have to be at the other end of the pitch."

Terry's reputation caught the attention of John McGraw, manager of the New York Giants, the best team of the period. While on tour during spring training, McGraw used local talent to improve the strength of his team for exhibition games. On 1 April 1922 McGraw offered Terry an opportunity to play in the majors, but Terry balked at McGraw's pay deal. McGraw finally gave in on 10 May, agreeing to pay Terry $800 per month, and the next day Terry was sent by the Giants to play for the Toledo Mud Hens of the American Association. Terry played for the Mud Hens through 1922 and 1923, until he played his first game for the Giants at first base in the Polo Grounds in New York City on 24 September 1923. At six feet, one inch, and 200 pounds, Terry's size, rather than his speed, was his greatest asset. Although he batted only .239 in his first full season, Terry did manage to hit a home run in his first World Series game in 1924. But in game seven of the series, McGraw decided to replace Terry with Irish Meusel, a right-hander better able to deal with the Washington Senators left-handed pitcher George Mogridge. However, as soon as Terry was removed, the Senators manager Bucky Harris brought in the right-handed Firpo Marberry, and the Senators came back to defeat the Giants and win the World Series. For the rest of his life Terry insisted that Harris won the series by conning McGraw into pulling him.

In the 1925 season Terry batted .319. During his distinguished career with the Giants, Terry hit over .350 in four different seasons: 1929, 1930, 1932, and 1934. In 1930 he batted .401, the last National League hitter to accomplish such a feat. He was one of only eight players to top the .400 mark in the twentieth century. The 1930 season was his most productive in terms of batting average, but it included a two-month period from 8 July to 3 September when he batted a sizzling .446. He also shared the National League record for hits in one season with 254.

In his fourteen-season career, Terry made an impressive .341 batting average. Starting in 1927 he drove in 100 or more runs for six consecutive seasons. In 1932 he hit six home runs in four games to tie a record held by Babe Ruth and Chuck Klein. On 6 July 1933 Terry became one of four players to get two hits in the first Major League All-Star game. From 1923 to 1936 Terry played in 1,721 games, collecting 2,193 hits, 373 doubles, 112 triples, 154 home runs, and 1,078 runs batted in (RBI). Terry led the league in doubles in 1931, a year after he was named first baseman on the *Sporting News* All-Star Major League team. In the three World Series he played in (1924, 1933, and 1936), Terry batted .295. In the 1924 Series he hit .429. When asked for his formula for successful hitting, Terry said: "If you want to accomplish something, you must have confidence in your method of doing it."

In spite of his successes, Terry's relationship with his manager and front office was acrimonious. He constantly challenged the club to "pay me or trade me." Although he had little formal education, Terry's intelligence and knowledge of the game led to his selection as player-manager of the Giants. Taking over from McGraw on 3 June 1932, Terry managed to pull the struggling team into a sixth place finish, and in 1933 they won the pennant. In the World Series that year, the Giants defeated the Washington Senators four games to one. In 1936 the Giants won the pennant but lost the World Series to the Yankees four games to two. The Giants repeated as National League champions in 1937 with a record of 95–57, but again lost the Series to the Yankees in five games. So began a slow decline. The next season the team finished third; in 1939 the Giants came in fifth; and in 1940 they landed in sixth place. In 1941 the team set a losing record and had a fifth-place finish. When the 1941 season ended, Terry was dismissed as manager. He finished his managerial career with 823 wins and 661 losses, a winning percentage of .555.

Terry officially quit the Giants organization on 30 November 1942, having served briefly as general manager. He accepted a position as a cotton trader in Memphis in 1944, and five years later moved permanently to Jacksonville, Florida, where he purchased a Buick car dealership. Terry was elected to the National Baseball Hall of Fame on 20 January 1954; his selection had been delayed because of his arrogance with the press. In the late 1950s Terry purchased the Jacksonville Braves in the Sally League and held on to them until 1964, when the team and league folded. His association with professional baseball came to an end that year. On 6 April 1983 the Giants, now in San Francisco, retired his uniform number (three).

Terry's car dealership thrived in the last years of his life. At the time of his death from natural causes, Terry's net worth was close to $30 million. Terry is buried at Evergreen Cemetery in Jacksonville. His career and life was best summed up by *New York Times* writer John Drebinger, "Among ball players Terry is regarded as a shrewd and calculating fellow who knows what he is worth and possesses the assurance and intelligence to get it."

★

Primary source material is in the William H. Terry File at the National Baseball Hall of Fame in Cooperstown, New York. Peter Williams, *When the Giants Were Giants: Bill Terry and the Golden Age of New York Baseball* (1994), is the most comprehensive study of Terry's life. Works discussing the Giants and Terry's career include two books by Frank Graham, *McGraw of the Giants: An Informal Biography* (1944), and *The New York Giants: An Informal History* (1952). Reference works that include entries on Terry are Joseph L. Reichler, *The Baseball Encyclopedia* (1969); Thomas Aylesworth and Benton Minks, *The Encyclopedia of Baseball Managers: 1901 to the Present* (1990); and Nicholas Acocella and Donald Dewey, *The Greatest Team of All Time: As Selected by Baseball's Immortals from Ty Cobb to Willie Mays* (1994). Articles on Terry include F. C. Lane, "The Terrible Terry," *Saturday Evening Post* (Apr. 1930); Frank Graham, "Baseball's Greatest First Baseman," *Baseball Magazine* (Nov. 1930); F. C. Lane, "John McGraw's Capable Successor," *Baseball Magazine* (Oct. 1933); Red Barber, "Bill Terry Recalls Days with John McGraw," *Baseball Digest* (Nov. 1971); and William B. Mead, "The Year of the Hitter," in John Thorn, *The National Pastime* (1981). Obituaries are in the *New York Times, Florida Times-Union,* and *Memphis Commercial-Appeal* (all 10 Jan. 1989).

CHARLES F. HOWLETT

THOMAS, Isiah Lord, III (*b.* 30 April 1961 in Chicago, Illinois), basketball player who spent thirteen seasons with the Detroit Pistons, becoming the franchise's all-time leader in points, assists, steals, and games played, and one of the best point guards in National Basketball Association (NBA) history.

Thomas was the youngest of nine children born to Isiah Lord Thomas II, a foreman at a manufacturing company, and Mary Thomas, a homemaker. Thomas's father was the first African-American foreman hired by International Harvester. After the plant closed, his father was only offered work as a janitor, and the stress from this job loss led to his parents' divorce. Thomas's father left the family when Thomas was three.

Mary Thomas took whatever jobs she could to make ends meet. She worked as a cook and found employment at a community center, a church, and with the housing authority. But providing for her two girls and seven boys was nearly impossible. The family of ten shared a three-bedroom home they could not afford to heat. Thomas remembered sleeping on the closet floor or on the ironing board in the hallway. He also remembered being hungry.

From his earliest days, Thomas tagged along with his

older brothers, playing basketball at a nearby pocket park. By the age of three he could already captivate a crowd with his basketball skills. His brothers played in a local youth league and the younger Thomas provided the halftime entertainment. The coach would slide a team jersey over Thomas's head—a jersey so big it drooped to his ankles—and he dribbled around the court, slinging in shot after shot.

Since Thomas was the youngest, his family called him "Junior," although his friends and later his fans called him "Zeke." After some of Thomas's brothers gave in to the street (two to heroin and one to pimping), the family kept a strict eye on Junior, hoping he would be the one to make it to the NBA. Thomas's mother feared so much for the future of her youngest son that she convinced the basketball coach Gene Pingatore to give Thomas financial aid so he could enroll at the Catholic, suburban Saint Joseph High School in Westchester, Illinois. Thomas had to get up in the predawn hours to catch a bus for school.

During his junior year Thomas provided the spark that led the Saint Joseph Chargers to a 32–1 record and a second-place finish in the state high-school basketball tournament. By his senior year of 1979, Thomas was recruited by college teams across the nation. He chose to attend Indiana University at Bloomington and was coached by Bobby Knight. During his first season (1979–1980) as a Hoosier, Thomas was named as a guard to the All–Big Ten team, the first freshman to receive the honor. During his sophomore year Thomas led Indiana to the 1981 National Collegiate Athletic Association championship title and stood at a crossroads—should he continue with the Hoosiers or turn professional? As a role model for underprivileged kids, Thomas wanted to complete college, but he also knew that entering the NBA would provide him with money to help his family.

In the end he decided to turn professional before completing college, and was the second pick in the June 1981 draft. The Detroit Pistons drafted Thomas, offering him a four-year contract worth $1.6 million. The first thing Thomas did was buy a house in the suburbs for his mother, who made him promise to finish school. Thomas spent the off-seasons working on his college degree and earned a B.A. in criminal justice from Indiana in 1987.

When Thomas joined the Pistons, they were one of the NBA's worst teams. But with Thomas the team won eight of its first thirteen games at the start of the 1981–1982 season. Home attendance nearly doubled and headlines in the local papers proclaimed, "Isiah the Savior." Thomas finished his rookie year with 1,225 points, an average of 17 per game, and 565 assists, earning a place on the All-Rookie and All-Star teams. In 1985 he married Lynn Kendall, and the couple later had two children.

During his career with the Pistons, Thomas was one of

Isiah Thomas, 2000. ASSOCIATED PRESS AP

the most dazzling NBA point guards. At six feet, one inch tall, and 182 pounds, Thomas was a runt by NBA standards. He gained fame, however, for his uncanny ability to get off shots against players who were several inches taller. Thomas was a crowd pleaser, a master of deception and change of pace. He was a pressure player who could pull through when time was running short. When the Pistons needed points, Thomas got the ball. He once scored sixteen points in the last ninety-four seconds of a 1984 playoff game. He also set an NBA record for the most points scored in a playoff quarter (twenty-five).

Thomas spent thirteen years in the NBA, all with the Detroit Pistons. He led the Pistons to the NBA finals three years in a row, helping them win the championship in 1989 and 1990. Thomas was named the Most Valuable Player of the 1990 finals. He was named to the NBA All-Star team twelve consecutive times and became the all-time Pistons leader in points (18,822), assists (9,061), steals (1,861), and games played (979). Thomas was one of only four players to amass more than 9,000 assists in a lifetime, along with Magic Johnson, Oscar Robertson, and John Stockton.

In 1994 Thomas retired from playing for the NBA after an Achilles tendon injury. He worked as an NBA analyst and television sportscaster for the National Broadcasting Company (NBC) starting in 1997 and became an executive with the Toronto (Canada) Raptors. Thomas also became a part owner of American Speedy Printing Centers and OmniBanc, a multistate bank holding company owned by African Americans that aims to revitalize inner-city neighborhoods. In 1999 Thomas purchased the nine-team Continental Basketball Association, with plans to develop it into a minor league with ties to NBA teams.

Thomas was named to the Naismith Memorial Basketball Hall of Fame in 2000, the same year he became head coach of the Indiana Pacers. During his first season, he coached his team to the finals. Although most people remember Thomas for his playing past, he is only at the start of his coaching career and will likely continue to make the record books—and headlines—for years to come.

★

Thomas and Matt Dobek chronicle Detroit's 1988–1989 championship season in *Bad Boys* (1989), which also includes Thomas's insights about his game and life. There are many short biographies on Thomas; one of the best is Ron Knapp, *Sports Great Isiah Thomas* (1992). Thomas also has been the subject of many magazine articles, including William Nack, "I Have Got to Do It Right," *Sports Illustrated* (19 Jan. 1987); Johnette Howard, "The Trials of Isiah," *Sport* (June 1992); and Dave Kindred, "He Made His Mama Proud," *Sporting News* (23 Oct. 2000).

LISA FRICK

David Thompson *(right)*. © BETTMANN/CORBIS

THOMPSON, David O'Neal (*b.* 13 July 1954 in Shelby, North Carolina), Hall of Fame basketball player known for his high-scoring seasons with North Carolina State University and the Denver Nuggets.

Thompson was the youngest of eleven children of Vellie Thompson, a textile worker, and Ida Gentry, a homemaker. He grew up in modest circumstances near Shelby and attended that town's Crest High School from 1968 to 1971, excelling in basketball and track. The heavily recruited Thompson picked North Carolina (NC) State University at Raleigh over its Atlantic Coast Conference (ACC) archrival the University of North Carolina. The National Collegiate Athletic Association (NCAA) assessed NC State a one-year probation for minor recruiting violations involving Thompson.

Thompson enrolled at NC State in autumn 1971. Freshmen were ineligible for varsity play at that time. Instead, he played for the freshman team, averaging more than thirty-five points per game. Thompson declined an invitation to try out for the 1972 U.S. Olympic team. NC State served its probation in 1972–1973, Thompson's first varsity season, so could not participate in the NCAA tournament. Despite the apparent lack of incentive, Thompson teamed with the seven-foot, four-inch junior Tommy Burleson to lead the Wolfpack to an undefeated 27–0 season. NC State defeated the highly regarded University of Maryland team three times, including a 76–74 win in the ACC tournament title game.

NC State overcame an early season loss to the perennial champion the University of California, Los Angeles (UCLA) early in the 1973–1974 season to again go undefeated in the ACC, finishing off its regular season with a 23–1 mark. Nonetheless, NC State needed to win the ACC tournament to receive the league's only bid to the NCAA tournament. It did so by the slimmest margin, edging Maryland in the finals 103–100 in a spectacular overtime contest frequently listed as one of the top college games ever played. NC State won the Eastern Regional despite enduring a scare when Thompson suffered a concussion in the finals against the University of Pittsburgh.

Thompson recovered in time for the Final Four, held the following week in nearby Greensboro, North Carolina. NC State opened against a powerhouse UCLA team hoping to capture its eighth consecutive NCAA title. NC State upset the Bruins and their peerless center Bill Walton 80–77 in two overtimes, with Thompson scoring 28 points. NC State followed up by defeating Marquette University 77–64 for the national title. Thompson scored 21 points in the title game as NC State finished the season 30–1.

Thompson clearly was the best player in the United States in 1975. Several of his teammates slumped, however, and NC State's season ended at 22–6 with an ACC tournament loss to the University of North Carolina. The team declined an invitation to play in the National Invitational Tournament.

Thompson was one of the most honored basketball players in NCAA history. In each of his three varsity seasons (1973, 1974, 1975), he was named the ACC Player of the Year, unanimous All-ACC, Associated Press (AP) and United Press International (UPI) All-American, and ACC leading scorer. He was named the AP National Player of the Year for 1974 and 1975, UPI National Player of the Year for 1975, and 1974 Final Four Most Outstanding Player. Thompson led the ACC in scoring three times, ending his varsity career with 2,309 points and a 26.8 points per game average. He scored 57 points against Buffalo in 1975, still a North Carolina State record. NC State went 79–7 during his varsity tenure. A soft-spoken and articulate man, Thompson was one of the first African Americans to become a genuine athletic hero at a major southern institution. He earned a B.S. in sociology from North Carolina State in 1975.

Thompson was the first selection in the National Basketball Association (NBA) and American Basketball Association (ABA) drafts following the 1975 season. He signed with the Denver Nuggets of the ABA after they acquired his draft rights from Virginia. For six seasons he was an outstanding professional player. In his sole ABA season, Thompson was named the Rookie of the Year and a second-team All-ABA. After the dissolution of the ABA, Denver joined the NBA for the 1977 season. Thompson was named a first-team All-NBA in 1977 and 1978. He finished second in the NBA in scoring in the 1978 season, averaging 27.15 points per game. Thompson was named the Most Valuable Player of the 1979 NBA All-Star game after scoring twenty-five points. His 73-point effort on 9 April 1978 against Detroit was the third-highest single-game scoring mark in NBA history, topped only by Wilt Chamberlain's 100-point and 78-point games. Thompson missed half of the 1980 season with injuries, but returned in 1981 to average 25.5 points per game and play in the NBA All-Star game for the fourth time.

Injuries and substance abuse shortened Thompson's professional career. He began using cocaine early in his career and also abused alcohol. Denver traded him to the Seattle SuperSonics in 1982. He entered drug rehabilitation after the 1983 season and again in 1986. On 10 March 1984 Thompson suffered a career-ending knee injury when he was knocked down a flight of stairs in a New York nightclub during an altercation. A domestic violence conviction in 1986 led to probation. When Thompson violated his probation he was sentenced to four months in a minimum-security prison in 1987.

Thompson finally overcame his drug habit in the late 1980s. He then became the director of community relations for the Charlotte (North Carolina) Hornets and a motivational speaker, frequently discussing the perils of drug addiction. He married Cathy Barrow on 31 January 1979; they had two daughters.

Thompson ended his NBA career with an average of 22.1 points per game in 509 games, and averaged 26 points per game in his single ABA season. He made 50.5 percent of his field-goal attempts as a professional and 88.1 percent of his foul shots. He was selected to the Naismith Memorial Basketball Hall of Fame in 1996. Thompson was a spectacular athlete, blessed with quickness, great leaping ability, and a silky grace. In college his vertical leap was measured at forty-four inches, and sportswriters joked that he could take a dollar bill off the top of the backboard and leave change. In a 2001 interview with the *Sporting News,* the famed player Bill Walton said, "David Thompson was the best college player I ever saw. By far. He was a terrific, terrific sportsman and what was so wonderful was that he played his best in the biggest of games." Thompson's natural athleticism, combined with refined basketball skills and a fierce competitive drive, made him one of the best basketball players of his generation.

★

Thompson's college career is covered in Ron Morris, *ACC Basketball: An Illustrated History* (1988); Norman Sloan, *Confessions of a Coach* (1991); Douglas Herakovich, *Pack Pride: The History of NC State Basketball* (1994); and Peter C. Bjarkman, *ACC: Atlantic Coast Conference Basketball* (1996). An excellent magazine article on Thompson is Mike Lupica, "David Thompson, Back to Earth," *Esquire* (Mar. 1990).

JIM SUMNER

THOMPSON, John Robert, Jr. (*b.* 2 September 1941 in Washington, D.C.), college basketball coach noted for being the first African-American coach whose team won the National Collegiate Athletic Association (NCAA) Division I men's basketball championship.

Thompson is the youngest of four children of John Robert Thompson, Sr., a tile-factory worker, and Anna L. Thompson, a teacher, domestic worker, and practical nurse. After struggling scholastically in elementary school because of poor eyesight, he did better in junior high, where he was also exposed to organized basketball. Growing quickly toward his eventual height of six feet, ten inches, he was recruited by Archbishop John Carroll High School to play basketball with several other fine players. In their three varsity years, the Lions won 103 games and lost only eight. They won their last fifty-five games and captured three league titles and two city championships. *Scholastic* maga-

John Thompson, 1999. AP/WIDE WORLD PHOTOS

zine named Thompson a high school All-American in his senior year, and he graduated in 1960, forty-eighth in a class of nearly three hundred.

During his junior season, Thompson met Father Thomas Aquinas Collins, a Dominican priest, basketball fan, and graduate of Providence College in Rhode Island. Collins arranged a campus visit, and Thompson decided to attend Providence. His freshman team had a record of 30–2, and he averaged 32 points a game. In his three varsity seasons, Providence went to the National Invitation Tournament twice and the NCAA tournament once. He graduated with a degree in economics and was picked by the Boston Celtics in the third round of the 1964 National Basketball Association (NBA) draft.

Thompson's professional career lasted only two seasons. Between them, in June 1965, he married his high school sweetheart, Gwendolyn Twitty. They had four children together, including John III, who became the head basketball coach at Princeton University, but divorced in 1999. For the Celtics, Thompson played center behind Bill Russell, saw limited playing time, and was bothered by injuries. Still, he became close friends with Russell and Arnold "Red" Auerbach, his coach and general manager. They showed him basketball at its highest level, taught him the importance of defense and a strong bench, and cautioned him to develop mental toughness and be wary of the media. Despite his selection by the Chicago Bulls in the NBA's 1966 expansion draft, he decided to retire as a player.

Instead, Thompson started working for an antipoverty program in Washington and taking graduate courses in guidance and counseling at Federal City College, later the University of the District of Columbia, earning an M.A. in 1971. He also began coaching at Saint Anthony's, a small high school with a mediocre basketball program. Over six seasons, he compiled a record of 128–22 while developing a style that stressed recruiting fast, rugged players, passing the ball to the big men on offense, and playing relentless defense. Moreover, he monitored his players' academic progress closely and insisted that they strive to get good grades.

In 1972 Georgetown University hired Thompson to reverse the fortunes of its basketball team, the Hoyas, that had finished 3–23 the previous season, and also to help the Jesuit school come to terms with the social changes of the 1960s. His first move was to hire Mary Fenlon, a Saint Anthony's teacher, to fill a new position, academic coordinator and administrative assistant. He also secured a promise from the admissions office to evaluate his intended recruits based not just on their test scores and grades but also on whether they possessed a reasonable chance to graduate.

Thompson's first team improved to 12–14, and his second bettered that by one game. In the 1974–1975 and 1975–1976 seasons, the Hoyas won the Eastern Collegiate Athletic Conference championship and earned berths in the NCAA tournament. He served as assistant coach to his friend, Dean Smith, for the 1976 U.S. Olympic team that won a gold medal in Montreal. In 1980 Georgetown, representing the new Big East Conference, nearly made the Final Four, losing the Eastern Regional final to Iowa 81–80.

The following season marked the start of the Ewing era, named for center Patrick Ewing, Thompson's best recruit.

In Ewing's freshman year, 1981–1982, the Hoyas advanced to the NCAA's final game, only to be defeated by Smith's North Carolina team, led by another outstanding freshman, Michael Jordan. After a disappointing season, the Hoyas rebounded in the 1983–1984 season to win their school's first national championship, beating the University of Houston 84–75 in the title game. In Ewing's senior year, Georgetown came close to repeating, losing to underdog Villanova by two points.

As his teams got better, Thompson became a national celebrity, and Georgetown was transformed from a nearly all-white bastion of Jesuit intellectualism to a multicultural university well known for its basketball team, composed mostly of African Americans. With his trademark, a folded, white towel draped over the shoulder of his suit, he evinced a distinctive coaching style that served as grist for many a journalist's mill. Thompson's teams played aggressive basketball that several times led to confrontations with the opposition. Moreover, he shielded his players from the press, staying at out-of-the-way hotels and refusing to let his freshmen submit to interviews. Openly slow to trust others, he nevertheless resented the phrase attached to his manner, "Hoya Paranoia." In 1988 he was sharply criticized when the Olympic team he coached won only a bronze medal.

A physically imposing man quite willing to offer his opinions, Thompson battled racism forthrightly, particularly when it was directed at Ewing and other prominent players, and he fought against charges that he was a racist himself. In 1989 he objected to Proposition 42, an NCAA regulation that denied financial aid to athletes whose high school grades and scores on standardized college entrance exams were below certain thresholds. Thompson called the regulation racially biased, and he boycotted two games to make his protest visible. Despite an intimidating manner that drove some players away from Georgetown and led to several difficult personal relationships, both with players who left and some who stayed, he maintained the primacy of education, keeping a deflated basketball in his office as a symbol of what his players would possess after their careers if they did not graduate.

On 8 January 1999 Thompson resigned as coach for personal reasons associated with his impending divorce. Subsequently, he hosted a radio talk show and did television analysis for professional basketball. His record at Georgetown, 596–239, included several coach-of-the-year awards, induction into the Basketball Hall of Fame, and a 97-percent graduation rate for those players who remained in school for four years.

★

The only biography of Thompson is Leonard Shapiro, *Big Man on Campus: John Thompson and the Georgetown Hoyas* (1991). Among the many newspaper and magazine stories on Thompson during his career, notable is William Gildea, "Georgetown's Thompson Resigns," *Washington Post* (9 Jan. 1999).

STEVEN P. GIETSCHIER

THORPE, James Francis ("Jim") (*b.* 22 May 1887 in Keokuk Falls, now Prague, Oklahoma; *d.* 28 March 1953 in Lomita, California), Native American who, as the winner of the decathlon and pentathlon at the 1912 Olympics and as an outstanding collegiate football and track and field star and professional baseball and football player, is considered one of the world's greatest all-around athletes.

Thorpe was the son of Hiram P. Thorp (the "e" was added later), a horse rancher, and Charlotte Vieux Thorp, a homemaker who raised Thorpe and his twin brother in the Roman Catholic faith. Thorpe's father, Hiram, was the son of Hiram G. Thorp, an Irishman, and No-ten-o-quah ("Wind Woman"), a Sac and Fox of the Woodland tribe that originated in the Wisconsin area. Thorpe's mother, Charlotte, was the daughter of a French father and an Indian mother of Potawatomi and Kickapoo descent; she belonged to the Thunder Clan of the great Sac and Fox chief Black Hawk. As a result, Thorpe was only partially Native American, although he was brought up as a member of the Sac and Fox tribe.

There was great personal sadness and tragedy in Thorpe's childhood. Hiram and Charlotte divorced, Hiram remarried, and then the couple reunited; Thorpe's twin brother died of pneumonia just short of their eighth birthday; Charlotte died when Thorpe was twelve; and Hiram

Jim Thorpe. AP/WIDE WORLD PHOTOS

died when he was sixteen. Prior to these events, the energetic, outgoing boy enjoyed a carefree existence in the fields and rivers near the Sac and Fox reservation east of Oklahoma City. Thorpe's father, according to his son and local reputation, was an unusually strong man as well as an outstanding athlete who taught Thorpe an instinctive method of all-over training—hunting, fishing, wrestling, swimming, high jump, broad jump, and horseback riding. Thorpe showed an early facility for long-distance running. He once ran away from the local Sac and Fox school after his father had dropped him off from a horse-drawn wagon. By the time Hiram arrived home, Thorpe had covered twenty miles, taking a shortcut, and was waiting for his father at the front door of the family's one-room home.

School was often a problematic exercise for Thorpe. Intelligent and highly observant, he resisted the regimentation and physical restriction of Indian education at the time. With hopes that a boarding school far away would help concentrate his son's study habits, Hiram decided in 1898 to send his difficult son to the Haskell Institute, an Indian school 300 miles away in Lawrence, Kansas. Thorpe lasted only one year at Haskell, after which he left home to work for a few months on a ranch in Texas. Throughout these difficult years, as Thorpe adjusted to family deaths and his father's growing exasperation, he picked up skills in the two sports that were to define major periods of his life—baseball and football.

In 1904, when Thorpe was sixteen, he was sent to the Carlisle Indian Industrial Training School in Carlisle, Pennsylvania, known as "Carlisle." Founded in 1879 by Richard Henry Pratt as a federal, coeducational institution to teach Native Americans the ways and skills of the white man, Carlisle was the showcase school of the post-frontier era. However misguided and paternalistic such a concept seems at the beginning of the twenty-first century, Pratt sincerely believed that Native Americans faced extinction if they did not learn how to stand up, through education, to the dominant white culture. To Pratt this meant erasing one's Native American ways and becoming white. Sports were a major part of the Carlisle experience. When Pratt hired Glenn Scobey ("Pop") Warner as the school's football and track and field coach, the Carlisle athletes, known as the Indians, became world-famous for their outstanding skill and power. At this time, the game of football was evolving and changing by the year, and Warner was one of the most prominent strategists and innovators in the game's history.

In spring 1907, in one of sports history's most legendary discovery stories, Thorpe was on his way across campus to an intramural football game when he casually cleared a Carlisle high-jump bar set at five feet, nine inches, setting a school record. Warner immediately put him on the track team, and Thorpe broke most of the Carlisle records. He also managed to squeeze in stints on the school's baseball and basketball teams. A year later, Thorpe won a gold medal for the high jump at the Penn Relays, then placed first in five events in a dual meet against Syracuse, and won every event he entered in both the Pennsylvania Intercollegiate and the Middle Atlantic Association meets. In 1909 at a remarkable dual meet against Lafayette, Thorpe won six gold medals and one bronze, in the 100-yard dash. Teammates noted that Thorpe was not usually interested in breaking records, but in winning.

Although Warner discouraged Thorpe from playing football because he did not want his star track athlete to get hurt, Thorpe insisted on trying out for the team in autumn 1907. He amazed the coach by running and tackling like a natural. Carlisle ended the season with a 10–1 record, including a 23–5 win over Harvard. Except for two games, Thorpe warmed the bench, but, as was his habit since boyhood, he watched the players' every move, visualizing the plays in his mind. By the end of the 1908 season, he was the most talked-about athlete in Pennsylvania and began attracting the national attention that marked his athletic career. With a team record of ten wins, two losses (one to Harvard), and one tie (with the University of Pennsylvania in the game Thorpe later called "the toughest game in my twenty-two years of college and professional football"), Thorpe made a series of brilliant plays that earned him recognition as a third-team All-American.

Off the field, Thorpe's behavior and attitude deteriorated as he enjoyed the privileges of being one of Warner's football boys, housed in a separate building and generally protected from the strict discipline that characterized the rest of the school. His excessive drinking, which plagued him the rest of his life, began at Carlisle. At the same time, school officials noted that Thorpe was a natural leader, generous, tolerant, and funny.

Age twenty-one and restive, Thorpe left Carlisle for two years to play baseball for a reported $15 per week in the East Carolina League for the Rocky Mount and the Fayetteville teams. He pitched and played first base and "circle[d] the bases like a deer." However, the league folded in 1911 and Thorpe was persuaded by Warner to return to school, not only to play football but also to train for the 1912 Olympics. Carlisle's 1911 football season was spectacular, with an 11–1 record. Thorpe stunned crowds by recovering his own punts, scoring multiple touchdowns, spearheading an 18–15 victory over the previously unbeaten Harvard, and kicking one punt of eighty-three yards against Brown University. Named as a first-team All-America halfback, his play showed an amazing blend of speed, stamina, and dexterity that captivated the nation.

At the fifth Olympiad in Stockholm, Sweden, in July 1912, Thorpe gained world acclaim by winning gold medals in the pentathlon and the decathlon, as well as placing in both the high jump and the long jump. For the pentathlon, he made four out of five (running broad jump, javelin throw, 200-meter dash, discus throw, and 1,500-meter race) first places and fourth in the javelin throw. In the ten events of the decathlon (100-meter dash, long jump, shot put, high jump, 400-meter race, discus throw, 110-meter hurdles, pole vault, javelin throw, and 1,500-meter race), Thorpe scored 8,412.95 out of a possible 10,000 points; this record stood for 36 years. Although stories circulated that, as a natural athlete, Thorpe never trained for the events, in fact he worked hard and consistently under the watchful eye of Warner. When King Gustav V presented the champion with his medals, as well as two lavish trophies, the king made the famous statement that immortalized Thorpe in sports history: "Sir, you are the greatest athlete in the world."

Returning to Carlisle in autumn 1912, Thorpe, as the team captain, led the Indians to the school's greatest football season with a 12–1–1 record. Dickinson, Villanova, Syracuse, Pittsburgh, Georgetown, Lehigh, West Point ("Thorpe went through the . . . line as if it were an open door"), and Brown—Thorpe thrilled audiences and sportswriters as a player "close to perfection." In an era when the evolving game of football was dominated by collegiate competition, Thorpe defined a new kind of aggressive play for a generation. For the second year in a row, he was named as a first-team All-American.

But all the glory quickly ended when it was reported in the *Worcester Telegram* (Massachusetts) in January 1913 that Thorpe was a professional athlete because he had received pay for playing baseball in North Carolina. In a decision that would roil sports fans and Native American sympathizers as an elitist sham for the rest of the century, the American Amateur Union (AAU) demanded that Thorpe return the medals and trophies and that his name be stricken from the Olympic records. Many would feel, passionately, that Thorpe had been abandoned by everyone, including Warner, in order to serve as a sacrificial symbol of the purity of amateurism. There would also always be a strong suspicion that a white athlete would have been treated differently. "I was not very wise in the ways of the world," Thorpe wrote in 1913 in a letter to the AAU, "and did not realize this was wrong."

The dramatic fall from grace was a major pivot in Thorpe's life—another huge disappointment in a life that was full of setbacks. He left Carlisle without graduating and switched to professional sports, signing in 1913 with the New York Giants baseball team. Until his last official game in Akron, Ohio, in 1928, he played with various teams, including the Cincinnati Reds and the Boston Braves. Baseball was not Thorpe's best sport (he was never really coached well) and a myth grew up that he could not hit a curveball. Nevertheless, playing for Boston in 1919, he hit .327 in 156 at bats and maintained good batting averages for the rest of the decade.

However, it was in professional football that Thorpe's enormous fame and skill brought a new level of respect, spectators, and money for what was then considered a stepchild to the collegiate gridiron. At a time when players stayed in for the entire sixty minutes and played without an armor of protective equipment, Thorpe's style continued to demonstrate a remarkable stamina and inventiveness—especially considering his age and the fact that he was playing both football and baseball throughout the 1920s. As the sportswriter Red Smith would comment after Thorpe's death, "Nobody who saw him . . . could ever forget the wild glory of that inexhaustible Indian."

Starting in 1915 Thorpe played and sometimes coached for the Canton (Ohio) Bulldogs, often before as many as 10,000 fans, as they won a couple of so-called world championships. In 1920 Thorpe was named the first president of the American Professional Football Association, the precursor to the National Football League (NFL). For two years, 1922 and 1923, he organized the almost circus-like football attraction of the Oorang Indians, a team sponsored by an Airedale dog kennel in Marion, Ohio. Native American dances and war whoops at halftime were big-ticket draws—attempts to use Thorpe's fame in the service of professional football. Before his last game (a brief, sad appearance) for the Chicago Cardinals in 1928, he also played for the Rock Island Independents and the New York Giants football team. Thorpe remained an amazing kicker, able to punt forty yards well into middle age.

Thorpe was married three times, with the first two unions ending in divorce. Drinking and a peripatetic lifestyle frustrated his sincere attempts at a stable married life. On 13 October 1913 he married his Carlisle classmate Iva Miller; they had a son who died in the influenza epidemic of 1918, and three daughters. They divorced in 1924. On 23 October 1925 he married Freeda Kirkpatrick, with whom he had four sons. They divorced in 1941. His third marriage, on 2 June 1945, was to Patricia Gladys Askew. With so many children to support and his athletic career finished, Thorpe moved to the Los Angeles area in the 1930s and appeared in more than sixty movies over the next twenty years, usually as an uncredited extra. There were also periodic—often exaggerated—newspaper reports that "Big Jim" was digging ditches, acting as an emcee for depression-era dance marathons, and otherwise on hard times. It is accurate to say that he was constantly in need of money. By the end of the 1930s Thorpe had become an outspoken critic of the U.S. Bureau of Indian Affairs and traveled around the country as a public speaker. One of the ironies of Thorpe's life was that his great talent and fame came too early in modern sports to yield him a secure, lucrative livelihood.

Although in his fifties when World War II broke out, Thorpe eagerly served his country, first as a security staff member at the Ford Motor Company plant in Dearborn, Michigan, and then in 1945 with the U.S. Merchant Marine. At the midcentury point, an Associated Press (AP) poll of sportswriters and broadcasters named "The Indian" as the greatest football player of the half-century; two weeks later, another AP poll named him the greatest athlete of the past fifty years. In 1951 Warner Brothers released the movie *Jim Thorpe—All-American,* starring Burt Lancaster as Thorpe (Thorpe had sold the rights to his life story to MGM during the Great Depression). After this brief echo of his former glory days, Thorpe suffered a massive heart attack and died in his trailer home in Lomita, California, on 28 March 1953.

In a bizarre series of mishaps, Thorpe's body remained without permanent burial until his widow arranged a deal with two adjacent Pennsylvania towns: If they would combine under a new town name, "Jim Thorpe," and build a proper memorial, they could have the honor of burying the athlete. The towns held an election and voted to become Jim Thorpe, Pennsylvania, and a red granite mausoleum was dedicated in 1957. Subsequent to Thorpe's death, other honors kept on coming. In 1955 the NFL announced the Jim Thorpe Trophy, an annual award for the Most Valuable Player. In 1963 he was inducted as a charter member of the Pro Football Hall of Fame, and a life-sized statue of him was erected in the lobby of the Hall of Fame headquarters in Canton, Ohio. After a long and difficult campaign by Thorpe's family members and supporters, in 1973 the AAU restored Thorpe's amateur status for 1912, paving the way for the restoration of his Olympic medals—and records—by the International Olympic Committee in 1982.

Thorpe was arguably the greatest all-around athlete of modern times. Certainly he was the first celebrity athlete in an era that would only increase its adulation of and financial rewards to sports heroes. His life and career formed a template that continues to define modern athletics: the outsider ethnic as athlete; the transition from collegiate to professional sports; the conflict between amateurism and professionalism; the exploitation of athletes by the media and commerce; the human toll superior talent plus fame exact from the athlete; and, most importantly, the insatiable hunger of fans and human beings in general to believe in a redemptive value in sports and the sacred place of the great athlete in our culture.

★

Significant archival materials regarding Thorpe's early life, family, and Sac and Fox background can be found at the Oklahoma Historical Society and the National Archives in Washington, D.C. Materials regarding the Carlisle Indian School are principally at the Cumberland Historical Society in Carlisle, Pennsylvania. The Pro Football Hall of Fame in Canton, Ohio, has materials covering Thorpe's professional football career. Reliable books written about Thorpe include Jack Newcombe, *The Best of the Athletic Boys* (1975); Robert Wheeler, *Jim Thorpe: World's Greatest Athlete,* rev. ed (1979); Bob Bernotas, *Jim Thorpe: Sac and Fox Athlete* (1992); and Robert Lipsyte, *Jim Thorpe: Twentieth-Century Jock* (1993). See also Jack McCallum, "The Regilding of a Legend," *Sports Illustrated* (25 Oct. 1982). An obituary is in the *New York Times* (29 Mar. 1953).

KATE BUFORD

TILDEN, William Tatem, Jr. ("Bill") (*b.* 10 February 1893 in Philadelphia, Pennsylvania; *d.* 5 June 1953 in Hollywood, California), champion tennis player and author who dominated the game during the 1920s, but whose career ended in disgrace.

Tilden was one of five children born to William Tatem Tilden, a successful businessman and local Republican political leader, and Selina Hey Tilden, a homemaker. Their

Bill Tilden, 1933. ASSOCIATED PRESS AP

first three children died from diphtheria in 1884; Tilden's idolized brother Herbert was born in 1887 and died in 1915. Herbert was his father's favorite; Tilden was very close to his mother. Because of the first children's deaths, Tilden's mother had him tutored at home. When she became ill in 1908 (she died three years later), he was sent to live with his spinster aunt Mary Elizabeth Hey and her niece, and he kept quarters with them for thirty years. Tilden began playing tennis at age seven at the Onteora (New York) Club in the Catskill Mountains where his family summered. He followed the serve-and-volley style of his brother, a successful competitor who introduced him to the game.

Tilden enrolled at Germantown Academy in 1908, and played on the Academy's tennis team for two years. He served as team captain in his senior year before graduating in 1910. Tilden then entered the Wharton School of the University of Pennsylvania, where he played for three years without distinction. Tilden left for a year after the death of his mother in 1911. His formal schooling ended during his senior year in 1915; he withdrew from the university after the deaths of his father and brother. Tilden was the only surviving member of his family. Although his father's fortune had suffered reverses, Tilden did inherit a fair sum. Around the time of his twenty-fifth birthday he legally changed his name, dropping the "Jr." to become William Tatem Tilden II.

After his father and brother died, tennis became Tilden's life, and he worked at competing with determination, studiously and efficiently. It was said that "nobody worked as hard at anything as Tilden did at tennis." Although only six feet, one-and-a-half inches, he seemed taller given his slim appearance, and early in his career he earned the nickname "Big Bill." Tilden's appearance splendidly complemented his energy, enthusiasm, and intelligence. As his many writings about tennis attest, he gave a great deal of thought to dealing with competitors. For Tilden, as he wrote in *The Art of Lawn Tennis*, "The primary object . . . is to break up the other man's game." Tilden was a formidable opponent.

In 1913 Tilden began coaching tennis without pay at the Germantown Academy. Not a completely natural player, he worked hard at improving himself and overcoming flaws in his playing. Unranked in 1914, he advanced to the group ranked between sixty-one and seventy in 1915, and to those ranked between eleven and twenty in 1916, the first year he competed unsuccessfully in the U.S. singles championship tournament. He was eliminated in the first round. Tilden enlisted in the U.S. Army in mid-1917, and while a private, played with some success in various tournaments.

In 1918 and 1919 Tilden did reach the final round of the U.S. singles championship, but lost in 1919 to William ("Little Bill") Johnston, who was among his most serious competitors in the 1920s. The defeat to Johnston led Tilden to modify his game, and he perfected a hard topspin backhand to accompany his awesome "cannonball" serve. Tilden mastered every kind of stroke and spin, using his canny ability to great effect. He became a super champion, and for much of the 1920s dominated the game as no one has ever since. Between 1916 and 1930, except for 1928 when he was suspended, Tilden played 80 matches in U.S. championship tournaments: he won 73, lost 7; he won 203 sets, lost 59; with 1,591 games won and 975 lost.

In 1920 Tilden was the first player from the United States to win the Wimbledon men's singles championship, winning again in 1921 and 1930. Between 1920 and 1925 he won the U.S. men's championship each year and led the U.S. Davis Cup team to victory, despite losing the middle finger of his racket hand to gangrene as the result of inefficient medical treatment. Other national titles won by Tilden during these years include: indoor (1920); doubles-U.S. (1921 to 1923), twice with Vinnie Richards and once with "Babe" Norton; and mixed doubles-U.S. (1922 and 1923), with Molla Bjurstedt Mallory. His biographer Frank Deford argues convincingly that "no man ever bestrode his sport as Tilden did for those years." But Tilden was more than just a great tennis player; like Babe Ruth and Jack Dempsey he was one of the American sports idols of the 1920s whose glory transcended their profession and captured the popular imagination.

After 1925, although still a master of the game, Tilden was no longer invincible. In 1926 he lost to Rene La Coste in the Davis Cup and to Henri Cochet in the U.S. final. In 1928 the U.S. Lawn Tennis Association, which governed the sport and with which Tilden was constantly at odds, barred him from Davis Cup play for flaunting a rule prohibiting amateurs from writing about tennis for pay. There was a huge outcry, especially from the French, who had just built a new stadium for the competition. Government officials, including the U.S. ambassador to France, intervened, and Tilden was allowed to play. Until 1929 he retained the top U.S. ranking. In 1930 he was beaten in the U.S. championship singles semifinal and turned professional.

Tilden was often testy on the courts with other players and officials and displayed a distinct apathy towards the tennis establishment. He was not much loved by his peers, but he was very popular and attracted large audiences. Tilden toured with expert players he recruited from the ranks of the amateurs such as Cochet, Ellsworth Vines, and Fred Perry. He continued to be a most vigorous and difficult opponent for men who were years younger; in his early forties Tilden beat former world champion Vines, aged twenty-two.

Tilden enjoyed writing, often listing "newspaperman" as his vocation, and had actually worked briefly as a reporter with a Philadelphia newspaper after leaving college. Unlike many celebrities whose only contribution to their byline was a name, Tilden actually wrote what was published in his name. Over the years Tilden authored plays, a novel, instructional books, magazine and newspaper articles, and short stories. His handling of tennis subjects was first-rate. *Match Play and the Spin of the Ball* (1925), and *How to Play Better Tennis* (1950), are classics. *The Art of Lawn Tennis* (1921), was reprinted a number of times. Other such books include *Singles and Doubles* (1923), and *The Common Sense of Lawn Tennis* (1924). Tilden's memoirs, *My Story* (1948), are mediocre.

Most of Tilden's fiction, such as the 1930 novel, *Glory's Net*, was indifferent pap, as was his boy's fiction collected in books such as *It's All in the Game* (1922). His plays, understandably, were brutally criticized. Tilden wasted much of his inheritance and earnings in backing stage productions of his plays and those of others, in which he acted with great lack of success. His appearances on stage and in the movies usually elicited much criticism.

A loner, in part because of his increasingly indiscreet homosexuality, Tilden, although maintaining a residence in Philadelphia until 1939, spent much of the year on tour both as an amateur and professional, hanging out at tennis clubs across the country. His status enabled him to stay on the cuff at leading hotels. He enjoyed playing bridge (he was an expert), and loved classical music, once declaring, "if I had to give up tennis or music, I would give up tennis."

Tilden moved to Los Angeles in 1939 and found work as a tennis instructor and support from personalities such as Charlie Chaplin and the actor Joseph Cotten. During World War II he organized and played in many exhibition tournaments for the benefit of the war effort. After the war he took the lead in organizing the Professional Tennis Players Association, and went on tour in 1946, playing well, and the assumption was that he would do well in the postwar boom.

However, in November 1946 Tilden was arrested for "contributing to the delinquency of a minor," after police found him engaged in sexual activity with a fourteen-year-old. Sentenced on 16 January 1947 to one year in prison, Tilden was released 30 August 1947 on probation with the stipulation that he "never associate with juveniles, as coach or friend." Seemingly unable to control his penchant for younger boys, he later told a judge, "I can't help myself," and was again arrested on 28 January 1949. The charge was reduced to violation of probation, and Tilden was again sentenced to one year in prison on 10 February 1949. He was released early for Christmas on 18 December 1949.

A virtual pariah as the result of his convictions, living in reduced circumstances because of his profligacy and inability to earn a living, Tilden was dependent on the charity of a few close friends. When he failed to turn up for a dinner his hosts went to check on him and found Tilden dead from a heart attack in his small, sparse Hollywood apartment. Few attended memorial services for him in Los Angeles and Philadelphia. His ashes were buried in the family plot in Philadelphia.

Since his death Tilden has been named in various polls of tennis writers as the best tennis player of the twentieth century. Certainly he was among the most charismatic, exciting, dramatic, and intelligent. Tilden has correctly been called "the finest all-around player in history." Whatever his flaws, he had an extraordinary impact on the sport.

★

There is material on Tilden at the University of Pennsylvania and at the International Tennis Hall of Fame in Newport, Rhode Island. In addition to his autobiography, *My Story: A Champion's Memoirs* (1948), Tilden wrote about his life in *Aces, Places, and Faults* (1938). An interesting biography is Frank Deford, *Big Bill Tilden: The Triumphs and the Tragedy* (1976). There are lengthy biographical profiles of Tilden in the *Dictionary of American Biography,* Supplement 5 (1977), and *American National Biography Online* at http://www.anb.org. Alison Danzig and Peter Schwed, eds., *The Fireside Book of Tennis* (1972), contains substantial excerpts from Tilden's writings. Arthur Voss, *Tilden and Tennis in the Twenties* (1985), splendidly places Tilden in context of the expansion of the sport in the 1920s, when it became a much more commercial operation. An obituary is in the *New York Times* (6 June 1953).

DANIEL J. LEAB

TITTLE, Y(elberton) A(braham), Jr. (*b.* 24 October 1926 in Marshall, Texas), outstanding quarterback in both college and professional football who was elected to the Pro Football Hall of Fame.

Tittle is the son of Abraham Tittle, Sr., a postal employee, and Alma Tittle. One of four children, Tittle received football instruction from his older brother Jack Tittle, who played at Tulane University. Tittle was an outstanding athlete at Marshall High School, where he played football, basketball, and baseball. Football was Tittle's best sport, and he received a number of scholarship offers during his senior year, 1943–1944. He decided to attend Louisiana State University (LSU) because it was a "civilian" school at a time when many colleges had armed service programs, which meant older intercollegiate players. "I'd be playing ball there with boys 17 and 18, boys my age," Tittle recalled.

During his freshman year Tittle was a reserve tailback, but he starred in the season-ending game by completing fifteen of seventeen passes in LSU's 25–6 victory over its archrival Tulane. The following year Coach Bernie Moore switched to the T-formation and named Tittle the starting

Y. A. Tittle, 1964. ASSOCIATED PRESS AP

quarterback. Tittle, six feet tall and 195 pounds, adjusted rapidly to the new formation and became one of the leading college passers of his era. In four seasons he passed for 2,576 yards and led the Tigers to a 23–11–2 record, including an appearance in the 1947 Cotton Bowl. Tittle was often overshadowed by other great passers of the period, such as Charlie Conerly, Harry Gilmer, Charlie Trippi, and Johnny Lujack. In 1945, however, Tittle outplayed Trippi in LSU's 32–0 upset victory over Georgia. The following year Tittle led the Tigers to an upset win over Gilmer and Alabama, 31–21. "Everybody said Gilmer would pass us dizzy," Tittle recalled. "He did, but I threw some strikes myself."

Tittle's most memorable college game was in 1947 against Mississippi and Charlie Conerly. Late in the last quarter, with Mississippi leading 20–18, Tittle intercepted a pass on the LSU thirty-yard line and headed up field. The last Mississippi player grabbed for Tittle and ripped off his belt before the would-be tackler tripped. Forty thousand fans, including Tittle's fiancée, watched as the LSU back's pants fell to his ankles thirty yards from the goal line. Tittle recalled: "[I] had to stop and hitch up my britches or I'd have stumbled. That's when the Rebels nailed me. Goodbye ball game!" Tittle married Minnette DeLoach in 1948; they had three children. He graduated from LSU with a B.S. in physical education.

In 1947 Tittle was the first-round draft choice of the Cleveland Browns of the All-America Football Conference (AAFC) and the Detroit Lions of the National Football League (NFL). He signed with the Browns, but the AAFC commissioner assigned his contract to the Baltimore Colts to balance play in the league. As a Colt, Tittle completed 55.7 percent of his passes for 2,522 yards and 16 touchdowns, and he won the AAFC Rookie of the Year award in 1948. Tittle's passing statistics were down in 1949 and again in 1950 after the AAFC disbanded and the Colts joined the National Football League (NFL). At the end of the 1950 season the Baltimore franchise folded, and Tittle was the first draft pick of the San Francisco 49ers. Tittle became the first player to be the first draft selection of three different teams.

During his first two seasons in San Francisco, Tittle competed with the popular Frankie Albert for the number one quarterback position. He won the job in 1952 and directed the 49ers offense for the next nine seasons, beating back challengers such as Earl Morrall and John Brodie. Tittle was a fierce competitor who set high standards for himself and his team. He was deeply disappointed that he was unable to lead San Francisco to an NFL championship despite the presence of talented players such as Joe Perry and Hugh McElhenny. The 49ers came close in 1957, when Detroit and San Francisco tied for the division title. Tittle kept the 49ers in contention for the division title in November, when he hit the end R. C. Owens with seconds to play on an alley-oop pass. San Francisco defeated Detroit 34–31 and the leaping, acrobatic alley-oop play became one of the most famous of the decade. In a special division playoff game at the end of the regular season, Detroit defeated the 49ers 31–27 despite trailing at halftime 27–7. "We just fell apart," Tittle recalled. The next three seasons Tittle had subpar years, and the team languished in third or fourth place in its division. In those years Tittle, nicknamed "Y. A." or "Bald Eagle" due to his baldness, was frequently booed at San Francisco's Kezar Stadium. Before the start of the 1961 season, he was traded to the New York Giants.

When he joined the Giants, Tittle shared quarterbacking duties with Conerly, his former college rival. But Tittle soon became number one quarterback and led New York to a 10–3–1 record and the Eastern Division title. After playing fourteen seasons without a division title, Tittle remembered the 1961 division-clinching 7–7 tie with Cleveland as his biggest thrill in football. In the 1961 NFL championship game in Green Bay, Wisconsin, the Giants were routed by the Packers 37–0. "They were a better team than we were, I admit that," Tittle said.

The following season Tittle led the Giants to another Eastern Division title with a record of 12–2. In a regular season 49–34 victory over Washington, he tied an NFL record by throwing seven touchdown passes. The Giants receiver Frank Gifford called it "the greatest passing performance I've ever seen." In the 1962 championship game, on a cold and windy day in New York City, Green Bay again defeated the Giants 16–7. "We lost," Tittle said, "but we were just as good as the Packers, in my opinion." Tittle may have had his best season in 1963, leading New York to another Eastern Division title. He threw thirty-six touchdown passes that year, an NFL record. The Giants lost their third straight championship game in a hard-fought battle with the Chicago Bears, 14–10. Tittle remarked, "Unfortunately, Lady Luck never did shine my way on championship day." After an injury-plagued season for both him and his team in 1964, during which New York finished with a record of 2–10–2, Tittle retired. He returned to his home in Atherton, California, where he continued to run the real estate and insurance business he had established in the 1950s. Tittle was selected as a member of the Pro Football Hall of Fame in 1971.

★

Materials relating to Tittle's career are in the Pro Football Hall of Fame in Canton, Ohio. Tittle wrote, with Tex Maule, "Y. A. Tittle: My Life in Pro Football," *Sports Illustrated* (Aug. 1965). Biographies of Tittle are Don Smith, *Y. A. Tittle* (1964); and Dianne Tittle De Laet, *Giants and Heroes* (1995). See also Fred Russell, "Just Call Him Y. A.," *Sport* (Dec. 1947); Steve Gelman, "The Twilight Crisis of Y. A. Tittle," *Sport* (Dec. 1962); and Rick Hines, "Y. A. Tittle: Champion Without a Ring," *Ragtyme Sports* (Mar. 1995).

JOHN M. CARROLL

TORRE, Joseph Paul ("Joe") (*b.* 18 July 1940 in Brooklyn, New York), professional baseball player and manager; considered one of the best hitters of the 1960s and 1970s, and later one of baseball's most successful managers as head of the New York Yankees.

Torre was the youngest of five children born to Joseph P. Torre, a New York City detective, and Margaret Rofrano, a homemaker. Raised in the Marine Park section of Brooklyn, he attended high school at Saint Francis Preparatory School, but did not play on the baseball team until his junior year. Instead, he was a standout for several seasons with a top-flight youth sandlot club called the Brooklyn Cadets, which played in several leagues. Playing for Saint Francis in his final two years of high school, he was an outstanding player with good hitting power, but at 245 pounds Torre did not impress major league scouts because of his lack of speed.

After graduating from Saint Francis in 1959, Torre went to work as a page at the American Stock Exchange and returned to playing with the Brooklyn Cadets. By late summer he had impressed scouts as a definite prospect as a catcher because of his hitting talent, and in August the Milwaukee Braves (with whom his brother Frank was playing) signed him to a contract for $22,500. Having pared his weight down to 220 pounds, that fall he was sent to the Instructional League, where he led the league in hitting with a .364 average.

He was assigned to Eau Claire, Wisconsin, of the Northern League (Class C) for the 1960 season, and there he led the league with a .344 average while hitting sixteen home runs, which earned him a late-season call-up by the Milwaukee Braves. Torre made his major league debut on 25 September 1960 against Pittsburgh. Opening the 1961 season with Louisville of the American Association, he hit .342 in twenty-seven games and was then called up in May to the major leagues—this time for good—by Milwaukee.

Torre played for the Braves through the 1968 season, and during that time he achieved a reputation as one of the game's best-hitting catchers. With quick hands at the plate, he could hit for both power and average. A very durable ballplayer, he was seldom injured. He was recognized as one of the top defensive catchers in the National League (NL); Torre also demonstrated his versatility by often playing first base and later becoming a regular third baseman.

The Milwaukee Braves of those years included such power hitters as Hank Aaron, Eddie Mathews, and Joe Adcock, and Torre chipped in several excellent seasons that included 1964 (.321 batting average, 20 home runs, and 109 RBI), 1965 (27 home runs and 80 RBI), and 1966 (.315 batting average, 36 home runs, and 101 RBI). For his efforts he was named to the NL All-Star team from 1963 to 1967, and also was selected to travel to Vietnam after the 1966 season as part of a tour of baseball personalities.

Torre was married on 21 October 1963 to Jacqueline Ann Reed, with whom he had one son. The marriage ended in divorce in late 1964. He then married Diane Romaine in January 1968, and the couple had one daughter.

Torre was traded to the St. Louis Cardinals in March 1969 in exchange for future Hall of Famer Orlando Cepeda. Playing first and third base, Torre went on a hitting spree through the next three seasons—1969 to 1971. After finishing second in batting in the NL for 1970 with an average of .325, he lost twenty pounds to get his weight down to 200 coming into the 1971 season. Torre opened the year with a 22-game hitting streak, closed it by hitting safely in 35 of the last 37 games, and finished as the league leader in batting average (.363), hits (230), and RBI (137). Torre was named the NL's Most Valuable Player, and the *Sporting News* Player of the Year for the major leagues in 1971.

Torre was named to the NL All-Star team from 1970 through 1973, but on 13 October 1974 he was traded to the New York Mets. He played two full seasons with the Mets (1975 to 1976), and was then named player-manager of the team on 31 May 1977, but retired as a player on 18 June 1977. Torre had appeared in eighteen seasons as a major league player; he finished with career marks that included a .297 batting average, 2,342 base hits, 344 doubles, 252 home runs, and 1,185 RBI. He managed the Mets through five seasons (1977 to 1981), during which they never finished higher than fifth place, and he was fired after the 1981 season.

Hired as manager of the Atlanta Braves for the 1982 season, his new club opened that year with a thirteen-game winning streak and then cruised to the NL West crown. Despite losing the NL playoff to St. Louis, Torre was named Manager of the Year by the Associated Press. However, he never got along well with team owner Ted Turner, and after leading the Braves to a pair of NL West second place finishes in 1983 and 1984, Torre was released. He then worked as a television broadcaster for the California Angels for six seasons (1985 to 1990), during which he was married for the third time, to Alice, on 23 August 1987; the couple has one daughter.

Late in the 1990 season Torre was hired by the St. Louis Cardinals, and managed the club until fired in June 1995, as the team had continued to struggle during his tenure as manager. He was then hired as manager of the New York Yankees for the 1996 season and led his new club to the American League championship that season. After losing the first two games of the World Series against the Atlanta Braves, the Yankees then swept four straight for the title. Torre was named American League Manager of the Year and the *Sporting News* Sportsman of the Year.

Always known for his positive attitude and ability to use his players effectively, Torre led the Yankees to another World Series title in 1998, compiling an American League record 114 wins in the regular season (125 overall), and he was again named Manager of the Year. During spring training in March 1999, Torre was diagnosed with prostate cancer and was operated on at Barnes-Jewish Hospital in St. Louis. He returned to the team on 18 May 1999 and went on to guide the Yankees to World Series titles in 1999

Joe Torre. ARCHIVE PHOTOS, INC.

and 2000, along with a seventh-game loss to the Arizona Diamondbacks in the 2001 Series. Through the 2001 season Torre had compiled an overall record of 1,476 wins and 1,390 losses during his twenty seasons as a major league manager.

As a manager Torre is considered to be a good communicator, a good strategist, and an excellent handler of players. His intensity and ability to get the most out of his teams, and the record he achieved in the 1990s, has made him one of the top managers in baseball at the end of the twentieth century. And, while he never garnered much support for induction to the Hall of Fame as a player, there is no question about the outstanding statistics he compiled as one of baseball's top hitters during his career.

★

Torre has coauthored an autobiography with Tom Verducci, *Chasing the Dream: My Lifelong Journey to the World Series* (1997), which is valuable for details of his early life and post–playing years. Many feature articles have also dealt with his life and days in baseball, and among the best are Neal Russo, "Swat King Torre—Player of the Year," *Sporting News* (23 Oct. 1971); Ken Shouler, "Grand Yankee," *Cigar Aficionado* (May-June 1997); and Colleen Roach, "Joe Torre—Touching All the Bases," *Westchester Wag* (Oct. 1999).

RAYMOND SCHMIDT

TRABERT, Marion Anthony ("Tony") (*b.* 16 August 1930 in Cincinnati, Ohio), tennis champion and television commentator known for his impeccable sportsmanship.

Trabert began playing tennis at age six, but never gave up his interest in other sports; he was especially good in basketball. At the University of Cincinnati, he was a member of both the tennis and basketball teams and was the president of the junior class. By 1950 he was already a standout for his All-America appearance and great serve.

Trabert entered amateur tennis in 1950 and came under the guidance of Bill Talbert. Also from Cincinnati, Talbert was a great doubles player who had overcome the handicap of juvenile diabetes to become the U.S. Davis Cup captain six years in a row. Talbert and Trabert won the doubles crown of the French championships at Roland Garros in 1950. Paris became the scene of some of Trabert's greatest victories; he won the French singles title in 1954 and 1955 and the doubles three times (once with Talbert and twice with Victor Seixas).

The U.S. Navy called Trabert to active duty in September 1951. Trabert put his navy stint to good use and returned as an even more effective player in June 1953. On 7 September 1953 he stunned the U.S. Open crowd at Forest Hills, New York, by routing Seixas 6–3, 6–2, 6–3. Observers called it one of the most striking turnarounds in tennis history, because until that point Seixas had been the senior member of the doubles duo.

At the peak of his skill, Trabert was known as a thinking player. The six footer possessed plenty of power, and his serves and volleys had a crispness that few could match. Trabert seldom simply overpowered opponents; he outguessed them and outfought them. If he had a single obvious weakness, it was in movement; he lacked Ken Rosewall's dexterity or Jack Kramer's speed to the net. Ultimately, Trabert overcame this weakness through his court sense, which he claimed was developed through years of playing basketball. He also had an uncanny ability to lift his game for the big matches; he won all five finals of the major championships he reached.

Tony Trabert, 1955. AP/Wide World Photos

Trabert's finest year was 1955. He won the singles titles at Roland Garros, Wimbledon, and Forest Hills, and did not concede a single set at the latter two. He surprised the fans by beating Lew Hoad in the U.S. Open semifinals and then by demolishing Rosewall in the finals. Over the course of the year, Trabert won 105 matches and lost only 6, one of the best records of any era. Only a semifinal loss to Rosewall at the Australian Open prevented Trabert from attaining the coveted Grand Slam. One of the finest compliments paid to Trabert came from the player Gardnar Mulloy, who in October 1955 in *World Tennis* wrote that Trabert was "sounder than Hoad and more dominating than Rosewall. He has had a completely astonishing record this year, losing only one big match and two lesser ones."

Trabert turned professional in December 1955. Until 1968, when the era of open tennis began, there was a marked separation between the amateur and professional tours. Trabert had accomplished all he could as an amateur; now the time had come to test the professional waters. He was thrown in against the hungry shark Pancho Gonzales, a Mexican-American player who had harmed his own career by turning professional too soon, in 1949. Gonzales ached for revenge on any player who came his way, and defeated Trabert 74–27 sets in the one-on-one matches of 1956. Playing against Trabert, Hoad, and other champions, Gonzales remained the king of the professional tour until about 1964.

Trabert lived in Paris from 1960 to 1963, and he helped Jack Kramer manage the European side of the professional tour. Trabert retired in 1963. He never achieved great success as a professional player, but he had already made his mark. Twice the champion at Forest Hills, twice the champion at Roland Garros, and once the Wimbledon champion, Trabert's fame lay in his clear attacking game and his sportsmanship. His successes at Roland Garros were particularly impressive. After Trabert's wins in 1954 and 1955, no other American took the French title until Michael Chang in 1989. U.S. greats like Stan Smith, Jimmy Connors, and John McEnroe were undone on the soft clay, where Trabert had thrived. In 1970 Trabert was named to the International Tennis Hall of Fame.

Trabert joined the Columbia Broadcasting System (CBS) as a sports commentator in 1972. Soon his voice (and that of Pat Summerall) became a regular part of tennis, especially as the sport's popularity boomed in the late 1970s. Trabert was a calm, methodical commentator. He rarely speculated about winners and losers, and unlike many other commentators, almost never chose to say that a ball was "in" or "out." Rather, he would note, "It's hard to say from the angle here." This measured judgment matched with his earlier reputation as a fine sportsman on the court. With CBS, Trabert assessed the careers of such tennis greats as Jimmy Connors, Bjorn Borg, John McEnroe, Ivan Lendl, and Andre Agassi. Although his comments were never explicit, one gathered that he approved most heartily of the attitude of Borg and Pete Sampras, both of whom were models of good on-court behavior.

Trabert found time to serve as the captain of the U.S. Davis Cup team between 1976 and 1980. His teams won two cups, and his win-loss record was the highest for any U.S. captain. Managing players like Connors and McEnroe was a difficult task, but one that brought Trabert pride.

Trabert outlived many of his former opponents and friends. Talbert, Gonzales, and others died in the 1990s, leaving Trabert as one of the last voices of the pre-Open era, in which tennis had been segregated between amateurs and professionals. Like other longtime survivors such as Kramer, Trabert probably was appalled at the size of the money awards granted, and at the lack of patriotism exhibited by many players. Trabert and his wife, Vicki, who had four children, retired to Ponte Vedra, Florida.

Trabert was a fine player with a keen eye for the court, and he understood the body mechanics of the game better than anyone else in his era. While he lacked Hoad's outstanding power or Rosewall's finesse, Trabert had a profound influence on the sport; he was one of the best representatives of U.S. tennis in the second half of the twentieth century.

★

For more information on Trabert's career see Jack Kramer with Frank Deford, *The Game: My Forty Years in Tennis* (1979); Bud Collins, *My Life with the Pros* (1989), and "Better than Ever," *Time* (19 Sept. 1955). Additional information can be found on the website of the Tennis Hall of Fame at http://www.tennisfame.org.

SAMUEL WILLARD CROMPTON

TRAYNOR, Harold Joseph ("Pie") (*b.* 11 November 1899 in Framingham, Massachusetts; *d.* 16 March 1972 in Pittsburgh, Pennsylvania), Hall of Fame third baseman who was manager for the Pittsburgh Pirates.

Traynor, the son of James H. Traynor, a newspaper compositor and baseball enthusiast, and Lydia Matthews, grew up in the Boston suburb of Somerville. The story of the origin of his nickname "Pie" has several versions, but according to Traynor it went back to when he was a foul ball retriever for a local baseball team at the age of eight. As a reward for doing a good job, the team captain would take him home and treat him to a piece of pie. Soon team members started calling him "Pie Face," which later was shortened to "Pie."

After graduating from Bingham High School in 1918, Traynor became a messenger and office boy in Boston. However, baseball was his true love. A shortstop, he had played high school and sandlot ball, and in 1919 he played semiprofessional ball on Cape Cod. Impressed by a tryout in the spring of 1920, the Boston Red Sox arranged for Traynor to play with their Portsmouth, Virginia, affiliate in the Virginia League. He performed so well that the Pittsburgh Pirates bought his contract in August 1920 for $10,000, then a record price for a player in the Virginia League. At the end of Portsmouth's season, Traynor joined the Pirates for the remainder of the 1920 major league season. He appeared in seventeen games and gave a glimpse of his further abilities by winning a game with a ninth-inning single in his first big league at bat.

The Pirates farmed out Traynor to the Birmingham Barons of the Southern League for the 1921 season, although he did appear in seven games for the Pirates at the end of the major league season. Traynor hit .336 at Birmingham, but he committed sixty-four errors. Moreover the Pirates already had a quality shortstop in Walter "Rabbit" Maranville. As a result, when he joined the Pirates permanently in 1922, Traynor was shifted to third base. Learning the position quickly, the six-foot, 170-pound Traynor became an outstanding defensive third baseman. He possessed quick hands and feet and a strong throwing arm and was equally adept at charging toward home plate for a bunt, ranging to his left to snag a ground ball, or stopping a hot smash directly over the third base bag to prevent a near certain two-base hit. To make it easier to field balls, Traynor used a glove with a felt interior rather than leather in the belief that if he did not field a hard-hit ball cleanly, the felt would cause the ball to drop at his feet, enabling him to pick it up quickly and throw out the runner. While Traynor led National League third basemen in fielding average only once, he led in putouts seven times and in assists three times.

Traynor's fielding prowess was matched by his success with the bat. In his first full season in the major leagues he batted a solid .282, but in 1923 he batted .338 and drove in 101 runs. A right-handed line-drive hitter, Traynor sprayed the ball to all fields rather than swinging for home runs and, while not exceptionally fast, knew how to stretch singles into extra-base hits. He struck out only 278 times in 7,559 at bats in his major league career. Usually batting fifth in the Pirates' order, Traynor had a career batting

Pie Traynor, 1932. ASSOCIATED PRESS AP

average of .320 and amassed 2,416 base hits. His best years were 1929 and 1930, when he hit .356 and .366, respectively. Traynor had seven seasons in which he drove in more than 100 runs and a lifetime total of 1,273 runs batted in. His World Series record was mixed. He hit .346 in 1925, when the Pirates defeated the Washington Senators four games to three. However, he hit only .200 in 1927, when the New York Yankees swept the Pirates four games to none. Traynor married Eva Helmer on 3 January 1931; they had no children.

In June 1934, with the Pirates in fourth place, Traynor replaced George Gibson as manager of the Pirates. The team, however, did not improve under his leadership and finished the season in fifth place. During that season Traynor injured his shoulder in a collision with another player at home plate. Thereafter he could not throw well, and his playing career virtually came to an end. He played in fifty-seven games in 1935, none in 1936, and only five in 1937.

Traynor continued to manage the Pirates but with limited success, for while the Pirates had several outstanding hitters, the pitching was mediocre. The team finished fourth in 1935, fourth in 1936, and third in 1937. For much of the 1938 season the Pirates were in first place; however, they faded in late September and finished in second place, two games behind the Chicago Cubs. The next year the Pirates finished in sixth place, and Traynor was fired. Given the limited talent on the Pirates roster, Traynor's overall record as a manager, 457 wins and 406 losses, was commendable, although some suggested that Traynor's gentle, outgoing personality and easygoing relationship with his players kept him from being more successful.

Following his managerial tenure, Traynor worked for the Pirates as an assistant to the farm director for several years, and later he was a part-time scout and instructor for the team. In 1944 he became a sports broadcaster for a Pittsburgh radio station, a post he held into the 1960s. During the 1950s and the 1960s he was a familiar local television personality with his commercials for a heating company on a wrestling show and late-night movies. Affable, always smiling, and a good storyteller, Traynor was one of Pittsburgh's most beloved residents, and he regularly spoke at banquets and business meetings. He died of heart failure in 1972 and is buried in Pittsburgh.

Traynor was highly regarded during and after his playing career. The *Sporting News* named him to its Major League All-Star team seven times between 1925 and 1933, and in the same period he finished in the top ten in voting for the National League Most Valuable Player award six times. In 1948 he was elected to the Baseball Hall of Fame, and in 1969 the Baseball Writer's Association named him the greatest third baseman over baseball's first one hundred years. Several post–World War II third basemen exceeded many of Traynor's fielding and hitting marks, but his finesse fielding, clutch hitting, overall consistency, competitive drive, and kindly spirit secure his place as one of the best-ever third basemen.

★

Material relating to Traynor's career is in Traynor's biographical file in the Carnegie Library in Pittsburgh and in Bob Smizik, *The Pittsburgh Pirates* (1990). Traynor's statistics are in *Total Baseball* (1999), edited by John Thorn, Pete Palmer, Michael Gershman, and David Pietrusza, with Matthew Silverman and Sean Lahman. Obituaries are in the *New York Times* (17 Mar. 1972), the *Pittsburgh Post-Gazette* (17 Mar. 1972), the *Pittsburgh Press* (17 Mar. 1972), and the *Sporting News* (1 Apr. 1972).

JOHN KENNEDY OHL

TREVINO, Lee Buck (*b.* 1 December 1939 in Dallas, Texas), Mexican-American golfer with an unorthodox style who became one of the best and most popular players on the Professional Golfers' Association (PGA) tour.

Trevino was born to Joseph Trevino and Juanita Barrett Trevino, a housecleaner. Trevino and his two sisters were raised by his mother and his grandfather, a gravedigger, in a four-room shack with dirt floors adjacent to the Glen Lakes Country Club in Dallas. Forced by economic circumstances to quit school at age fourteen, when he was in the eighth grade, Trevino got a job at a Dallas driving range in 1954. He hit range balls in his spare time and developed a short game at the nine-hole pitch-and-putt that he helped the owner, Hardy Greenwood, construct. Several years earlier, he had begun to play golf at Glen Lakes, where he worked retrieving balls, polishing clubs, and caddying.

Lee Trevino. AP/WIDE WORLD PHOTOS

By 1956, when he enlisted for a four-year tour of duty in the U.S. Marine Corps, Trevino estimated he was a four-handicap golfer. Stationed in Okinawa, Japan, he made the division golf team and with a lot of time to practice, began to build a strong game. His main problem was an unpredictable hook. But everything about Trevino's career was unpredictable, and he grew to cherish that aspect of his life. In many ways, it was the secret to his success.

In 1960, when Trevino mustered out of the service as a first sergeant, he had no particular ambitions; he just enjoyed hitting golf balls. He returned to his old job as a handyman at Greenwood's Dallas driving range/pitch-and-putt. Self-taught, and self-confident, Trevino realized that what he lacked in golfing finesse he made up for in bravado, and that many golfers who were more polished choked when playing for big stakes (an insight he carried into his professional career). Trevino supplemented his income by playing all comers, first conventionally, and later right-handed with left-handed clubs. When he had depleted the local supply of betting competitors, he switched to playing with a heavily taped twenty-six-ounce Dr. Pepper soda bottle, with which he had practiced diligently. In three years he never lost a bet playing with his bottle.

Trevino had a bad grip, an awkward swing, and strong, magnificent hands that a golfing friend once said worked like a computer. "He is not only one of the finest strikers of the ball in modern times but one of the best shotmakers in history," the golf historian Herbert Warren Wind wrote. Having learned to control a golf ball with both sides of an iron, and then with a taped soda bottle, and having hit tens of thousands of practice balls with regulation clubs, perhaps it is no surprise that Trevino even moved the golfing champion Ben Hogan to declare that he manipulated his club better than any other golfer.

On 24 August 1964 Trevino married Claudia Ann Fenley; they had four children. The next two years, Trevino entered and won the Texas State Open, prompting his wife to enter him in the 1966 U.S. Open at the Olympic Club in San Francisco. Staked by friends, he finished fifty-fourth, but was not too discouraged to enter the 1967 U.S. Open at Baltusrol Golf Course in New Jersey. Trevino had turned professional in 1960, but had never joined the Professional Golfers' Association, having had no idea he was good enough to compete. But at Baltusrol he won fifth place and $6,000, which gave him a pass into succeeding PGA events and, more importantly, the confidence that he could play successfully on the highest level. By the end of the season he had won another $20,000. Nevertheless, no one was more astonished than Trevino when he was named the 1967 PGA Rookie of the Year. "I never dreamed I could play with those guys on tour," Trevino recounted years later. "The longer I played, the easier it got. But I never dreamed I was going to be as good as I turned out to be."

Neither Trevino nor golfing fans had long to wait to discover just how good he was. In the first five months of the 1968 season he won more than $50,000. And then he won the U.S. Open at Oak Hill in Rochester, New York, with such convincing authority that he was catapulted to the front ranks of upcoming stars. He not only beat Jack Nicklaus down the stretch, but tied Nicklaus's earlier record score of 275, setting a U.S. Open record of his own by being the first to play all four rounds in the 60s: 69, 68, 69, 69.

In 1971 the five-foot, seven-inch, 190-pound Trevino became a superstar. In just twenty-three days he won a lifetime's worth of tournaments: his second U.S. Open, the Canadian Open, and the British Open. He was recognized as the PGA Player of the Year and became the *Sports Illustrated* Sportsman of the Year. He also was named the Hickok Professional Athlete of the Year and the Associated Press Athlete of the Year, joining only a handful of golfers so honored (Byron Nelson, Hogan, Arnold Palmer, Nicklaus, and Tiger Woods). During his career with the regular PGA tour Trevino won twenty-seven events, including six majors: two U.S. Opens (1968, 1971); two PGA championships (1974, 1984); and two British Opens (1971, 1972).

In 1975, playing in the Western Open at the Butler National Golf Club outside Chicago, Trevino and two other golfers, Jerry Heard and Bobby Nichols, were struck by lightning. Trevino was seriously hurt and remained in intensive care for several days. Within a year, he had developed a serious back problem he believed was caused by the lightning bolt, and underwent major surgery. The operation was a success, and Trevino won nine more PGA tour events while continuing on and off the course to entertain his fans, his colleagues, and the press. In 1980 Trevino won the Vardon Trophy for the fifth time. Trevino was inducted into the PGA/World Golf Hall of Fame in 1981. Two years later Trevino and Fenley were divorced. On 20 December 1983 he married Claudia Bove; they had two children together.

In addition to his autobiography, Trevino has written two golf how-to books, *I Can Help Your Game* (1971), with Oscar Fraley; and *Groove Your Golf Swing My Way* (1976), with Dick Aultman.

If Trevino had not succeeded at golf, his friends insisted he would have been a credible standup comedian. After winning the 1968 U.S. Open, he declared he would buy the Alamo and give it back to Mexico. But after a visit he recanted, explaining that it lacked indoor plumbing. "The older we get," he observed when he joined the PGA Senior Tour in 1989, "the better we played." Consistently irreverent to the golfing elite (to the extent that he stopped playing in the Masters tournament for a time over disagreements on how Augusta National was run), he said publicly on more than one occasion, "When I turn sixty, I'm going to get a blue sport coat, a can of dandruff, and run the USGA [the ruling body of amateur golf]." But as of 2001 Trevino remained an active player on the Senior Tour. He was named the Player of the Year in 1990, 1992, and 1994; and has won more tournaments as a senior than during his days on the regular PGA tour. And he still uses the unique style that Dick Aultman and Ken Bowden described in the *Masters of Golf* (1989), as "five wrongs [that] add up to an immaculate right."

★

Trevino's autobiography is *They Call Me Super Mex* (1983), written with Sam Blair. For additional information, see biographies in Len Elliott and Barbara Kelly, *Who's Who in Golf* (1976). See also Herbert Warren Wind, "The Sporting Scene: Mr. Trevino and Mr. Nicklaus," *New Yorker* (14 July 1980). Additional material on Trevino's career is on the official website of the PGA Tour at http://www.pgatour.com.

MARTIN SHERWIN

TRIPPI, Charles Louis ("Charley") (*b.* 14 December 1922 in Pittston, Pennsylvania), football halfback who earned fame at the University of Georgia and with the Chicago Cardinals, and who was named to both the College and Pro Football halls of fame.

Trippi was the son of Joseph Trippi, a coal miner, and Joanna Attardo Trippi, a homemaker. He grew up with his five brothers and sisters in the hard coal region of northeastern Pennsylvania, near Scranton; the area was famous for its rough-and-tumble style of football and was a fertile recruiting ground for college scouts. However, Trippi was small as a youngster and nothing about his early childhood foretold his future success on the gridiron.

Trippi's best childhood sport was baseball, and he continued to excel in the sport in high school and college. By the time he was a high-school junior he had grown to 155 pounds, and he decided to go out for football. Trippi was designated as a center, which he didn't mind, saying, "I really liked to back up the line on defense." Part of the team's early practice routine was to punt the ball back and forth. Trippi was an excellent kicker and caught the eye of the Pittston High School coach Paul Shebby, who moved him into the backfield. Trippi, who showed some speed and good passing ability, led the lackluster team to victory in his new position and earned a permanent spot in the

Charley Trippi. AP/WIDE WORLD PHOTOS

backfield. The next season Pittston was undefeated, with Trippi as the team's unquestioned leader.

Trippi wanted to go to college to continue his education and playing career, but the schools that regularly recruited in northeastern Pennsylvania all rejected him as too small for the college gridiron. Coach Shebby secured a scholarship for Trippi to LaSalle Military Academy, a preparatory school in upstate New York that Trippi entered in 1941. The training and diet at LaSalle added ten solid pounds to Trippi's six-foot frame—he weighed 175 pounds following his postgraduate year, 1942. This time the University of Georgia in Athens took a chance and awarded Trippi an athletic grant-in-aid.

The Georgia Bulldogs coach Wally Butts was so impressed by Trippi's running and all-around play that he shifted the All-America tailback Frank Sinkwich to fullback so that Trippi and Sinkwich could be on the field at the same time. In 1942 the duo led the Bulldogs to a 10–1 regular season record. On 1 January 1943 Trippi had the kind of day that defined his stellar career. In the Rose Bowl versus the University of California, Los Angeles (UCLA), he personally gained more yardage than UCLA did as a team. Georgia won, 9–0. By April 1943 Trippi was in the U.S. Army Air Corps, where he eventually earned the rank of sergeant. While in the service he played football for the Gremlins of the Third Air Force, stationed in Greensboro, North Carolina, and was rated as one of the service's best players.

After the end of World War II, Trippi returned to the University of Georgia, where in 1947 he would earn a B.S. degree. He continued to help the Bulldogs to great seasons and bowl victories after the regular seasons of 1945 and 1946. After earning All-America honors in 1945, Trippi made the All-America team a second time in 1946, this time unanimously; won the prestigious Maxwell Award; and was a runner-up in the Heisman Trophy balloting. After Georgia's Sugar Bowl victory (20–10 over North Carolina), Trippi was forced to choose between playing professional baseball or football. Baseball's New York Yankees offered him a four-year, $100,000 contract—big money at the time. But Trippi chose football.

In 1945, while he was still in the army, Trippi was taken by the Chicago (later Arizona) Cardinals as their number-one draft choice. The National Football League (NFL) and the All-America Football Conference (AAFC) were the two viable professional football leagues at the time. They entered a bidding war for Trippi's considerable talents. The AAFC team seeking Trippi's services was the New York Yankees, owned by Dan Topping of the baseball Yankees. Topping envisioned Trippi as a baseball and football Yankee, but because of a prior friendship with the Cardinals team owner Charlie Bidwill, Trippi signed with the NFL team. He was also permitted to play professional baseball, and before reporting to the Cardinals football camp he batted .334 for the Atlanta Crackers of the Southern Association.

As an NFL rookie in 1947, Trippi immediately became part of the "Dream Backfield" made up of the Cardinals quarterback Paul Christman, halfback Elmer Angsman, and fullback Pat Harder. With the halfback Trippi as their main man, the Cardinals backfield acted as a highly effective offensive unit. The famed Native American athlete Jim Thorpe once commented, "Charley Trippi is the greatest football player I ever saw."

The Cardinals won the NFL championship in Trippi's rookie season. On one of the first plays in the title game, Trippi burst for a forty-four-yard score. Halfway through the third quarter, Trippi, in a razzle-dazzle fashion, returned a punt for a seventy-five-yard touchdown. The Cardinals had one of their rare, and last, championships when the day was done, with a 28–21 victory over the Philadelphia Eagles.

The next season saw a rematch for the NFL title: the Cardinals, paced by Trippi, played the Eagles, led by Steve Van Buren. This time the game was played in a Philadelphia blizzard. Neither team could do much offensively, but the Eagles capitalized on a Cardinals fumble and scored after a short drive to win, 7–0. The game marked the end of the team's championship reign, although Trippi continued his brilliant career through 1954.

Trippi's main asset was his ability to run with the football, but he also was a versatile and unselfish player. When the Cardinals needed a quarterback after Christman's retirement, Trippi filled the bill, leading the team in passing in 1951. When the defensive backfield was depleted in 1953 and 1954, Trippi switched to the defensive unit, and played at such a high level that he was chosen for the annual NFL All-Star game, the Pro Bowl.

Throughout his career Trippi led more by actions than words. He never said much on the field, but he was a fierce competitor. The crosstown rivalry with the more successful Chicago Bears produced several tense moments during the season and in the annual preseason games. Ed Sprinkle, a noted roughneck defensive end for the Bears, earned his reputation by giving a little extra on each tackle—an elbow to the ribs or a face pushed in the dirt. During the last moments of one preseason game, Trippi put himself back in the game long after most established veterans were resting on the bench. He had one thought in mind—to get Sprinkle. Trippi calmly walked up to the rugged Bears player and uncorked a roundhouse right that caught Sprinkle flush on the chin. Knowing he would be ejected from the game, Trippi immediately walked off the field and said to his astonished teammates, "That should about even the score."

During his playing career Trippi frequently returned to Georgia to assist his old coach Butts with spring practice. Once, before the sessions started, Butts said, "Gentlemen, I want to introduce you boys to the greatest all-around football player I ever saw." An embarrassed Trippi simply looked at the ground, demonstrating his trademark modesty.

At the height of his playing career, Trippi wrote a how-to book on backfield technique aimed at youngsters, *Backfield Play* (1948). After retiring from the NFL, Trippi established a successful beverage distributorship and real-estate businesses in Athens, the home of his alma mater and the scene of his many collegiate football triumphs. Trippi had married his first wife in Athens in 1944. They eventually divorced, and he then married Peggy M. McNiven in 1977. Trippi and his second wife settled in Athens, where residents still revered Trippi for his performances "between the hedges" (a reference to the thick shrubbery surrounding the playing field at the Bulldogs' Sanford Stadium).

Trippi was one of football's most versatile and electrifying performers, playing in more All-Star games than any other college player. He was inducted into the College Football Hall of Fame in 1959. Nine years later, when Trippi was inducted into the Pro Football Hall of Fame, he chose his high school coach Paul Shebby to be his presenter. The Cardinals franchise has had relatively few points of light—only two NFL championships, and one of them (1925) was controversial. But the point that still shines brightest, in the estimation of many, is Trippi.

★

Trippi's life and career are discussed in George Sullivan, *Pro Football's All-Time Greats* (1968); Murray Olderman, *The Running Backs* (1969); and Joe Ziemba, *When Football Was Football* (1999).

JIM CAMPBELL

TUNNEY, James Joseph ("Gene") (*b.* 25 May 1897 in New York City; *d.* 7 November 1978 in Greenwich, Connecticut), one of the most skilled and intelligent boxers ever, usually ranked among the all-time top ten best heavyweight boxers by boxing historians, famed for defeating Jack Dempsey twice in championship matches.

Tunney was the son of John Joseph Tunney, a longshoreman, and Mary Lydon, a homemaker. He was born into a working-class Irish Catholic family in Greenwich Village, then a dismal place. Tunney acquired an early passion for boxing by looking at cartoons of boxers in the newspaper; he developed an early interest in reading because he wanted to read the stories that went with the pictures. When he was ten years old, his father gave him a pair of boxing gloves, which he wore out sparring with his brothers and friends.

Tunney attended St. Veronica's Parochial School. He loved to fight and did not pass up chances to brawl with youngsters in the street. In his mid-teens he started working out in a local gym, where he had the chance to spar with a local professional boxer. He was so beaten up after four rounds that he vowed never to box a professional again, but he had a passion for boxing that drew him back to spar again, and he focused on learning from the professional. Tunney attended La Salle Academy, graduating in 1915.

In 1918 Tunney joined the U.S. Marines and was sent to France during World War I. It was there that at Tunney's request a clerk taught him how to read Shakespeare's *Winter's Tale,* which gave him a thirst for more Shakespeare, and from Shakespeare, for more works of literature. But Tunney boxed when he could, eventually becoming Light Heavyweight Champion of the American Expeditionary Force. In 1919 he was released from duty and set about becoming a professional world champion.

Tunney's is a remarkable story. Even while he boxed, moving up the ladder of light heavyweight contenders, he educated himself; books were always with him, earning

Gene Tunney, 1924. AP/WIDE WORLD PHOTOS

him a reputation as a "sissy" and a "snob," neither of which was even remotely true. On the other hand, he was sometimes aloof. He took to studying boxing as if he were studying military tactics, and he was forever reassessing his own skills as they developed and matching them against the skills he saw in others. Further, he studied opponents, planning ahead how he would take advantage of the weaknesses of each. Tunney, while unpopular, had a modern boxing strategy.

He eventually had his chance to fight for the World Light Heavyweight championship and won a points victory over Battling Levinsky (born Barney Lebrowitz) on 13 Jan 1922 to earn the title. Then on 23 May 1922 Tunney fought Harry Greb, a great middleweight boxer who fought above his usual weight class, and Greb pounded Tunney. It was the only loss of Tunney's career. Tunney could have died, so savage was the beating, and he was hospitalized thereafter, but even in the hospital he planned a rematch with Greb, remarking that he had fought Greb all wrong. Tunney had lasted the full fourteen rounds of the fight without going down, proving that he had plenty of endurance. In their next match, a fast, furious match of great boxing skill, Tunney defeated Greb, regaining his world title. They met three more times, with Tunney winning once and the others ending in draws.

Tex Rickard, the boxing promoter who had shepherded heavyweight champion Jack Dempsey through a series of million-dollar fights, saw gold in a match-up between the fiery Dempsey and the cool Tunney, and brought them together in Philadelphia on 23 September 1926, with over 120,000 fans in attendance. Tunney was given little chance to win except by a few journalists, who were ridiculed for their views. Dempsey was expected to easily crush the book-reading sissy. Tunney had a very clear view of how he should fight; his skills were directed at avoiding being hit. He hoped that an overconfident Dempsey would begin to overswing after missing some punches. This Dempsey did, and in the first round Tunney stepped inside a wide left and hit Dempsey with a straight right, stunning him. Thereafter, Tunney dismantled Dempsey with slashing lefts and straight rights that left Dempsey with a swollen face and a closed eye. Tunney won the decision in the ten-round fight and became World Heavyweight Champion. He was touched by Dempsey's graciousness in defeat.

The two met again at Soldier Field in Chicago on 22 September 1927. Dempsey was in better condition than in their first fight, and a big crowd came to watch Dempsey beat the unpopular "snob" Tunney. Yet, from the start, Tunney dominated. He had observed that Dempsey's once fast footwork had slowed, and therefore he made Dempsey chase him. He would dart sharp lefts in Dempsey's face and dodge away. On the other hand, Dempsey was a very intelligent fighter, and he knew his opponent. In the seventh round he out-thought Tunney, worked him into a spot against the ropes, feinted right, let Tunney dodge back into the ropes and then come forward into a left hook. Tunney said that he never saw the punch. It almost leveled him, and Dempsey followed with seven more savage blows, sending Tunney senseless to the canvas.

Tunney recalled that he actually blacked out for a few seconds, hearing the referee calling out "two" while counting over him. He learned about the infamous long count later. Dempsey had failed to retreat to a neutral corner as he was supposed to, and the referee only started counting after Dempsey had retreated, adding five seconds to the time Tunney could stay down before getting up. Tunney always insisted that if the count had begun the moment he fell, he would still have gotten up on the count of "nine," as prizefighters are taught to do, and he would have done what he did, which was run away from Dempsey for the rest of the round. At the start of the next round, Tunney knocked Dempsey down, and Tunney eventually won the decision.

Tunney defended his title only one more time before yielding to his wife's urging that he retire; he was the first heavyweight champion to retire undefeated. He was a rich man from boxing and prospered all the rest of his life, becoming an executive of banks, manufacturing companies, insurance firms, and a newspaper, the *Toronto Globe and Mail*. He had married a rich woman, Josephine "Polly" Lauder, heiress to the Carnegie estate, on 3 October 1928. They had four children, one of whom, John V. Tunney, was a U.S. Senator from California from 1971–1977. During World War II, Tunney became a successful sports writer. He joined the U.S. Navy, became a commander, and supervised sports for the navy during the war years. By the 1950s, he had become a beloved national figure, along with the man who became one of his closest friends, Jack Dempsey. Tunney died at age eighty-one and is buried in Long Ridge Cemetery, near Stamford, Connecticut.

★

Perhaps the best book about Tunney is by Tunney himself: *A Man Must Fight* (1932) is a good read, full of colorful characters. Tunney, *Boxing and Training* (1928), offers insights into his strategic method of boxing. Bruce J. Eversen, *When Dempsey Fought Tunney: Heroes, Hokum, and Storytelling in the Jazz Age* (1996), reads a bit like an academic treatise, but places Tunney in the middle of the fascinating sports world of the 1920s. Mel Heimer, *The Long Count* (1969), is a sprightly account of the match between Tunney and Dempsey.

KIRK H. BEETZ

TURNER, Clyde Douglas ("Bulldog") (*b.* 10 March 1919 in Plains, Texas; *d.* 20 October 1998 in Gatesville, Texas), college and professional football player, considered to be the best center and linebacker of the 1940s.

Turner was the son of a traditional West Texas cowboy and a homemaker. In 1932 Turner and his family moved to Sweetwater, Texas, where he attended Newman High School and saw his first game of organized football. Turner took to the game immediately, especially since the alternative to football practice was picking cotton.

Sweetwater had a tradition of producing gridiron talent. The Pro Football Hall of Fame quarterback Sammy Baugh had played high-school ball there a few years before Turner, and his example encouraged Turner to further his career. After graduating from Newman High in 1936, Turner enrolled in Hardin-Simmons University in Abilene, Texas, where he received the nickname "Bulldog." Because he had graduated from high school at the age of sixteen, Turner was younger than most of the school's other players. To impress the coaching staff, Turner and another new recruit, A. J. Roy, decided to give each other menacing nicknames. They weren't needed; both players made the team on their own merits.

Clyde "Bulldog" Turner, 1945. AP/WIDE WORLD PHOTOS

Turner played center on offense and linebacker on defense at Hardin-Simmons. He won Little All-America honors his senior year. Hardin-Simmons played well enough to earn berths in the first two Sun Bowls, tying New Mexico State in 1936 and beating the University of Texas at El Paso in 1937. The coach Frank Kimbrough gave Turner a lot of credit for helping the Hardin-Simmons football team gain national attention.

Besides playing football, Turner spent his college years studying journalism. While still in school he married Gladys; they later had two daughters. After earning his B.A. in 1940, he became an immediate bone of contention in the National Football League (NFL) draft. George Richards, the owner of the Detroit Lions, wanted his coach to choose Turner in the first round of the draft. Richards fired the coach when he chose Doyle Nave instead, and then tried to convince Turner to tell the other league teams he was not interested in playing professional football. Richards planned to pay Turner to do nothing for a year, and then draft him in 1941. Hiding players in this way was against the NFL rules. Richards wound up losing his franchise, and the Chicago Bears wound up with Turner.

With the Bears, Turner immediately became a starter at center and a linebacker. At six feet, two inches tall and 235 pounds, he had ample size to play the line and the speed to cover receivers in pass defense. Bears fans considered

Turner to be one of the cornerstones of their football success in the 1940s. During his first four seasons, the Bears played in the championship game four times, winning three. Among their championship victories were a 73–0 defeat of the Washington Redskins in 1940, and a 37–9 victory over the New York Giants in 1941. For much of Turner's early career, the Bears dominated professional football.

Turner became noted for his pass interceptions. In 1942 he was one of the few linebackers ever to lead the league in that category, with eight interceptions. He used his speed in other ways, too. In one game, when a number of Bears were thrown out for fighting, Turner was shifted to halfback. On his only carry from scrimmage, he ran forty-eight yards for a touchdown.

Following the 1944 season Turner entered the U.S. Army Air Corps. In 1945 he played football for the Second Air Force team in Colorado Springs, Colorado. Because the pilots there had to log a certain number of hours of flying time each month, Turner was twice able to get flights to Bears games, where he played, despite being in the military. Following the end of World War II, Turner returned to the Bears. Esteemed for his blocking, he wrote the book *Playing the Line* (1948). Turner continued to play through 1952, spending his last year as a player-coach and taking most of the snaps as an offensive tackle.

Turner finished his career with sixteen pass interceptions and six years on the All-Pro team. He said his favorite play was a twisting, ninety-six-yard interception return of a Sammy Baugh pass, but he was better known for his clutch play in big games. Turner intercepted four passes in five championship games, and reportedly never made a bad snap from center.

Following his playing career, Turner went into football coaching. He was an assistant at Baylor University in Waco, Texas, in 1953, and also coached the Chicago Bears between 1954 and 1958. In 1962 Turner was named as the head coach of the New York Titans in the American Football League. His major achievement that year was keeping the team together. The Titans owner declared bankruptcy during the season, and the franchise had to be taken over by the league. Turner finished with a 5–9 record.

In addition to coaching, Turner owned a small ranch outside Gatesville, Texas. He raised cattle, sheep, and goats, and his wife was a noted dog breeder. By the end of his life, Turner grew to resent his nickname. While he once was proud to tell reporters that no one called him Clyde except his wife, and that was when she was mad, as a man in his seventies he found the name "Bulldog" inappropriate. He died in Gatesville from lung cancer and is buried in Greenbriar Cemetery, Coryell County, Texas.

Turner was inducted into the Pro Football Hall of Fame in 1966, and is remembered as one of the foremost offensive linemen and linebackers of the 1940s. He was a vital cog in the great Chicago Bears teams of that era, and one of the few offensive linemen skilled enough to escape that position's relative anonymity.

★

Extensive interviews with Turner appear in Myron Cope, *The Game That Was: An Illustrated Account of the Tumultuous Early Days of Pro Football* (1970). He is the subject of a brief biography in Richard Kaplan, *Great Linebackers of the NFL* (1970). See also Richard Whittingham, *The Chicago Bears: An Illustrated History* (1979). Obituaries are in the *Chicago Tribune* (31 Oct. 1998), and *New York Times* (2 Nov. 1998).

HAROLD W. AURAND, JR.

TYSON, Michael Gerard ("Mike"; "Iron Mike") (*b.* 30 June 1966 in Brooklyn, New York), professional boxer whose power, speed, and accuracy made him one of the most recognized athletes in the world and the most dominant figure in boxing.

Tyson, born at Cumberland Hospital in the Fort Greene section of Brooklyn, was the third child of Jimmy Kirkpatrick and his girlfriend, Lorna Smith Tyson. Lorna had used the Tyson name since her brief marriage to Percel Tyson and retained it until her death from cancer in 1982. The arrival of eight-pound, seven-ounce baby Michael forced Lorna, a single parent, to search for larger living quarters. Tyson's first years were nomadic; he moved often with his mother, older brother Rodney, and sister, Denise. When he was seven, the family settled at 178 Amboy Street in the Brownsville section of Brooklyn, an urban slum,

Mike Tyson. AP/WIDE WORLD PHOTOS

where Tyson was surrounded by awful living conditions, poverty, and crime.

Young Tyson was not tall, but he was unusually strong. As a child he never read a book or played games. He became a chronic truant, and by the time he was eight he was beating up anyone in the neighborhood who bothered his family. Stealing became a way of life. By age eleven he was drinking, smoking marijuana, mugging people, and shooting up the streets of Brooklyn. He was arrested over forty times before he was twelve. Since his mother could not control the boy, he was sent upstate to the Tryon Reform School in Johnstown, New York, in 1977.

Bobby Stewart, a prison counselor and its athletic coach, hoped that the five-foot, six-inch, 186-pound Tyson might be able to redirect his anger if he learned to box. Coached by Stewart, Tyson became a fanatic, shadow boxing in his cell until three or four each morning. In 1979 Stewart introduced Tyson to Constantine ("Cus") D'Amato, a fight trainer who had developed Floyd Patterson and Jose Torres, both former world champions. D'Amato immediately recognized the tough kid's potential and got him permission to stay at his training camp, a gym above the police station on Main Street in Catskill, New York. D'Amato became Tyson's legal guardian in 1981.

Under D'Amato's training, Tyson worked hard and began to fight in unofficial competitions. In his first match, when he was thirteen, he knocked out a boy four years his senior in the third round. His confidence and desire grew. He won the Junior Olympics in 1981, a program designed for children under sixteen. He lost only five of fifty-two amateur bouts. Tyson developed a reputation as a wild animal in the ring; his fame spread quickly throughout the boxing community. Because of his hammer-like punches, the only sparring partners willing to work with him cost D'Amato $1,000 a week.

Tyson made his professional debut on 6 March 1985, knocking out Hector Mercedes in the first round. He won his next fourteen fights by knockouts. The next year, on 22 November 1986, Tyson beat Trevor Berbick for the World Boxing Commission's (WBC) heavyweight title, becoming at age twenty-two the youngest heavyweight champion in the history of boxing. Within four months he gained his second title, the World Boxing Association (WBA) crown, by beating James "Bonecrusher" Smith. In August he beat Tony Tucker in his thirty-first consecutive victory, consolidating three world titles and becoming the undisputed heavyweight champion of the world. When he earned $21 million for knocking out Michael Spinks on 27 June 1988, Tyson became the biggest moneymaker in the history of boxing.

While in the ring Tyson seemed in total control, his personal life was anything but controlled. His promiscuous sex life led to frequent bouts of gonorrhea. He admitted to friends that he enjoyed hurting women. In March 1987 he began dating Robin Givens, an actress on ABC's sitcom *Head of the Class.* The couple was married in New York City on 9 February 1988. Soon newspaper articles appeared that alleged that Givens was afraid of her husband, that he hit her, and that he might even have caused her reported miscarriage. There seemed to be two Tysons: one who laughed, hugged, and spoke softly in a high-pitched voice, and another who enjoyed inflicting pain.

Eight months after their wedding, Givens filed for divorce. A few days later Tyson told reporters he was a manic-depressive. On 30 September 1988 Robin and her mother, Ruth Roper, who had taken formal control of Tyson's earnings, appeared on ABC's *20/20,* telling the country how Tyson was a sick man and life with him was hell. Shortly thereafter, in a rage, Tyson broke up the kitchen in his Bernardsville, New Jersey, mansion. The divorce became final on 14 February 1989.

A professional for five years, Tyson began 1990 with a 37–0 record with thirty-three wins by knockout. But on 11 February he suffered his first professional loss when James ("Buster") Douglas knocked him down in the tenth round. He won his next four bouts, trying to regain his title, before he was convicted in 1992 of raping eighteen-year-old Desiree Washington, a beauty pageant queen. Upon his release on 25 March 1995, after a forty-eight month break from boxing, he knocked out Peter McNeeley in round one of their 19 August 1995 match. In 1996 Tyson regained his WBA and WBC titles, then on 9 November 1996 he was knocked out in the eleventh round by Evander Holyfield.

In the famous 28 June 1997 rematch for the WBA title between Tyson and Holyfield, Tyson bit off part of Holyfield's ear, claiming later the cause was referee Mills Lane's ignoring Holyfield's constant head butting. When in the third round Tyson bit Holyfield's other ear, Tyson was disqualified, resulting in a one-year ban from boxing and a $3 million fine, the largest in sports history. His attempts to regain the boxing titles after his reinstatement were interrupted in 1999 when he served nine months at the Montgomery County Correction and Rehabilitation Center in Rockville, Maryland, convicted of assaulting two men in a road rage incident. After his release Tyson boxed both in and outside the United States.

Tyson lives in Bethseda, Maryland, with his wife, Monica Turner Tyson, a pediatrician, whom he married in 1997, her daughter, Gena, and their children, Rayna and Amir, along with Mickey, a daughter Tyson had from a previous relationship.

Tyson's powerful punching, swift movement, and ruthless aggression dominated professional heavyweight boxing throughout the late 1980s and early 1990s. Since the 1960s, when Muhammad Ali was king of the boxing ring, no other fighter but Tyson has been the undisputed heavyweight champion of the world. And no other boxer has gained such wealth and such notoriety.

★

Jose Torres, former light-heavyweight champion of the world and longtime friend of Tyson, relates numerous anecdotes in *Fire and Fear: The Inside Story of Mike Tyson* (1989). Richard Hoffer, *A Savage Business: The Comeback and Comedown of Mike Tyson* (1998), relates many comic details of Tyson's life, including the efforts of various promoters, such as Don King, to capitalize on Tyson's name. Former *New York Times* sports editor Phil Berger gives an impartial rendering of details from Tyson's life in and out of the ring in *Blood Season: Mike Tyson and the World of Boxing* (1996).

JOHN J. BYRNE

TYUS, Wyomia (*b.* 29 August 1945 in Griffin, Georgia), pioneering African-American track and field star who was the first athlete to win two consecutive Olympic gold medals for the 100-meter dash, and who was a civil rights activist and feminist.

Tyus was the fourth child and only daughter of Maria and Willie Tyus. Her mother was a laundress and her father worked in a dairy. Both parents encouraged her to play competitive sports at a young age. In high school Tyus gave up basketball in order to join the track team.

In 1961 the famous Tennessee State University (TSU) coach Ed Temple watched Tyus run in the Georgia High School State Track Championship. Temple, known for his coaching of the TSU Tigerbelles and for training Olympic champions, was impressed by Tyus's skills and asked her to join his summer track and field camp. Classmates raised money for Tyus's train ticket to Nashville, allowing her to work with Temple that summer. As a result the seventeen-year-old Tyus competed in the Girls Amateur Athletic Union (AAU) Championship in Los Angeles in 1962. She set a record for her age group and won the 100-yard dash. She graduated from Griffin High School in 1963.

Shortly before beginning college at TSU—the only university in 1963 that offered athletic work-exchange scholarships for women—Tyus competed in her first AAU senior women's meet, coming in second to the future gold-medal Olympian Edith McGuire. Ironically, the two competitors became instantaneous and lifelong friends who trained together under Temple. The 1960s provided female athletes with their share of rough times. Tyus recalled, "We practiced on a dirt track, so there were potholes when it rained. But we knew the quality of the track didn't make the athlete and that there were always obstacles." Tyus pushed her training to the limit, and in 1964—two weeks after defeating McGuire and winning the AAU 100-meter title—she gained a place on the U.S. Olympic team.

At the 1964 games in Tokyo, Japan, Tyus attracted global attention when she tied the world record of 11.2 seconds for the 100-meter dash. Many people, including nineteen-year-old Tyus, were shocked, because McGuire had dominated the 100-meter race over the previous few

Wyomia Tyus *(foreground)* during the 1968 Olympics in Mexico City. ASSOCIATED PRESS FILE

years. Tyus recounted the event in a *Runner's World* interview: "I had never beaten Edith. The gun went off and all the way down, I kept thinking, 'Gosh, Edith should be here. She should be close to me.' By the ninety-yard mark, I was thinking, 'God, where is she?' Of course, there she came. Afterward she was hugging me, and I said, 'Who won?' And she said, 'You did, you did!' " By the end of her first Olympics, Tyus had earned one gold medal and had been a pivotal member of the U.S. women's 4 x 100-meter relay team, which took home a silver medal.

Having tasted Olympic glory, Tyus returned to TSU determined to compete in the 1968 Games. In the few short years leading up to the Summer Olympics in Mexico City, Tyus earned a number of AAU titles, ran her way to the 200-meter crown at the 1967 Pan-American Games in Winnipeg, Canada, and was named—along with McGuire and Temple—as a Goodwill Ambassador to Africa. Tyus graduated from TSU in 1967.

In 1968, in the midst of a tense and troubled racial climate in the United States, many African-American athletes were faced with the difficult decision of whether to represent a country they believed was racist. Tyus decided to participate as a U.S. Olympian, but supported the boycott by wearing an article of black clothing in every event. Her greatest act of solidarity was to publicly dedicate her last gold medal, won in the 4 x 100-meter relay, to Tommie Smith and John Carlos, who had been expelled from the Olympic Village for raising their fists in a Black Power salute during the playing of the U.S. national anthem. "What I did was win a track event. What they did lasted a lifetime, and life is bigger than sport," Tyus told *People* magazine.

Tyus's performance at the Mexico City Games was unshaken by the pressure to defend her title at the age of twenty-three—an age considered to be too old to compete—or by the surrounding racial tensions. In an unprecedented eleven-second blaze, she was the first to win the 100-meter race in two consecutive Olympics. She set a second world record with her 4 x 100-meter relay team by running the last leg of the event and capturing another gold medal.

Following the 1968 Olympics, Tyus retired from amateur sports. She moved to Los Angeles, married Art Simburg (they eventually divorced), and had her first child. She spent five years away from competitive running, and in 1973 she agreed to participate in the Professional International Track Association's only women's event, the sixty-yard dash. In her second year as a professional trackster, Tyus won all twenty-two of the events she entered, impressing both competitors and fans with her agility.

Ultimately, Tyus's life proved to be "bigger than sport." In 1979 she had a child with her second husband, Duane Tillman. After her retirement from professional athletics, she worked as a community liaison for a Los Angeles councilman, as a career development coordinator for Job Corps, and as a naturalist at an outdoor education camp. In the 1980s she was inducted into the National Track and Field Hall of Fame (1980), Women's Sports Hall of Fame (1981), and U.S. Olympic Hall of Fame (1985). In 2000 she was chosen by the U.S. Olympic Committee (USOC) to be a participant in Project Gold, a program designed to further involve ethnic minority leaders in the USOC system.

Had she competed during another era, perhaps Tyus would have been given more recognition for being a world-record-breaking track star. Throughout her life, Tyus used her popularity and position as a respected athlete to help fulfill her lifelong goal of promoting and supporting women's participation in sports. As a founding member of the Women's Sports Foundation and a civil rights activist, she dedicated herself to overcoming the double barriers of racism and sexism in positive ways.

★

For information and anecdotes about Tyus's years at TSU, see the autobiography by her coach Ed Temple, *Only the Pure of Heart Survive* (1980). *Great Women in Sports* (1996), contains a thorough, yet concise, essay on Tyus's achievements and personal experiences. For a reflection on Tyus's life and career in her own words, see the compilation of interviews and photographic portraits by Brian Lanker, *I Dream a World* (1989). Valuable articles include those in *Runner's World* (June 1993), *People* (15 July 1996), and the *Los Angeles Times* (15 Sept. 2000).

VALERIE LINET

U

UNITAS, John Constantine ("Johnny") (*b.* 7 May 1933 in Pittsburgh, Pennsylvania), Hall of Fame quarterback who set many passing records and led the Baltimore Colts to victory in the 1958 National Football League (NFL) championship, perhaps the most famous professional football game ever played.

Unitas was the son of Lithuanian-American parents, Leon and Helen Unitas, the third of their four children. His father, who had a small coal-delivery business, died when Unitas was five, and Helen had to take over the business and do odd jobs to make ends meet.

Although he was the starting quarterback for St. Justin's High School, Unitas gained little recognition outside Pittsburgh, and he had to settle for a football scholarship at the University of Louisville (Kentucky), which he attended from 1951 to 1955. In 1955 he married his childhood sweetheart, Dorothy Jean Holle, with whom he had five children.

Unitas was the starting quarterback for the Louisville Cardinals, but his college career did little to advance his reputation. The Pittsburgh Steelers selected him in the ninth round of the 1955 National Football League (NFL) draft, perhaps mostly because he was a local talent. They were overstocked with quarterbacks, however, and released him without even giving him a chance to play in an exhibition game. Unitas moved to Bloomfield, New Jersey, where he worked in construction and played quarterback for a local team, the Bloomfield Rams, for $3 a game.

In February 1956 the Baltimore Colts offered Unitas a contract for $7,000. He was given more of a chance to play than the Steelers had offered and won the backup-quarterback spot behind George Shaw. In the fourth game of the 1956 season, Shaw suffered a broken leg, and Unitas stepped in. From then on he was the starter, and in the following season Unitas led the NFL in both touchdown passes and passing yardage.

On 28 December 1958 the Colts met the New York Giants for the NFL championship. There were only twelve teams in the NFL, and the Eastern Conference champion played the Western Conference champion for the title with no preliminary postseason games. The game was telecast to a then-remarkable audience of 50 million viewers.

Despite its later designation as "the greatest game ever played," in many ways it was an unremarkable contest until the end. With 1:56 remaining, the Colts trailed 17–14, and both their scores had followed Giants fumbles. Unitas, however, showed the leadership and quarterbacking skill for which he was already known and took the Colts far enough to set up the tying field goal. There had never before been an overtime game in the NFL. Indeed, the rule mandating a sudden-death overtime for the championship had been added only in 1955. The Colts lost the coin toss that determined first possession, but the Giants were unable to move the ball, and punted. The Colts took over at their twenty-yard line, and Unitas led them in another drive, this time without the time pressure. Masterfully mixing running plays with passes, Unitas moved the Colts downfield until they had the ball on the Giants one-yard line. Some thought they should go for the reasonably certain field goal, but Unitas handed off to Alan Ameche, and the big fullback scored to end the game 23–17.

The next season, Unitas was named the NFL's Most Valuable Player (MVP). The Colts again met the Giants for the championship, and this time they won 31–16. Through most of the 1960s Unitas was the league's dominant quarterback. In 1965 he set season records for touchdown passes and passing yardage, and almost every season he led in one or more major passing categories. He was MVP again in 1967.

After ten years of stardom, injuries began to take their toll on Unitas. He missed most of the 1968 season because of torn ligaments in his throwing arm. Nevertheless, the Colts went to that year's Super Bowl with Earl Morrall as quarterback. Unitas made a desperation appearance late in the game and led the team to its only score, but it was too late.

Unitas returned almost all the way to the top in 1969, when he was named NFL Man of the Year. In 1970 he led the Colts back to the Super Bowl, but he was knocked out of that game with bruised ribs, effectively ending his career; the team won without him in a game remembered as a comedy of errors. Unitas spent two more years with the Colts and one sad season as a backup with the San Diego Chargers. He also suffered upheaval in his private life, as he and his wife divorced in 1971. Unitas, known as the "Golden Arm," retired after the 1973 season, having established career records for passes thrown, completions, passing yards, touchdown passes, most 300-yard games, and most consecutive games throwing one or more touchdown passes.

Unitas moved to the broadcast booth at the Columbia Broadcasting System (CBS) in 1974, where his reporting added game color for the next five years. In contrast to his bland public image, he showed a sharp, self-deprecating wit in the booth. After a quarterback was buried under a pile of rushers in one play, Unitas was asked if that had ever happened to him. He replied, "Of course. You don't think I always looked like this?" In 1979 he was elected to the Pro Football Hall of Fame.

In addition to his broadcasting, Unitas re-created himself as an entrepreneur. Until 1988 he owned a Baltimore restaurant called the Golden Arm. Other enterprises include Unitas Management Corporation, which represents Unitas and other football greats such as Bart Starr; Johnny Unitas Realty; and Johnny Unitas Golden Arm Educational Foundation Inc., which provides financial assistance to deserving scholar-athletes.

In 2001 Unitas appeared in the news in two unusual ways. A punk rock group calling itself Unitas released an album entitled *Porch Life*. More dramatically, *Sports Illustrated* featured him on its cover again, this time to illustrate the bodily harm suffered by NFL athletes—Unitas had lost control of the right hand that threw 290 touchdown passes.

Johnny Unitas, 1960. ASSOCIATED PRESS AP

Unitas wrote two books (with George Dintiman): *The Athlete's Handbook: How to Be a Champion in Any Sport* (1979), and *Improving Health and Performance in the Athlete* (1979). He also wrote *Playing Pro Football to Win* (1968), with Harold Rosenthal.

Unitas's rise from $3-a-game sandlot football to stardom shows his heroic refusal to quit—and the folly of the NFL experts, all of whom had passed him by. He was the Most Valuable Player in the dramatic 1958 game that put professional football on the map. And most important, Unitas set a standard of continued quarterbacking excellence over a long career.

★

Unitas's autobiography, *Pro Quarterback: My Own Story* (1968), written with Ed Fitzgerald, gives basic information in a standard young-adult treatment, as does Lee Greene, *The Johnny Unitas Story* (1962). Art Donovan's autobiography, *Fatso* (1987), includes an irreverent, but respectful, teammate's view of Unitas. An in-depth discussion of Unitas's injury to his right arm is in *Sports Illustrated* (7 May 2001).

ARTHUR D. HLAVATY

UNSER, Al(fred), Sr. (*b.* 29 May 1939 in Albuquerque, New Mexico), race car driver who is one of only three four-time winners of the Indianapolis 500 and a three-time United States Auto Club (USAC) national champion.

The youngest of four sons of Jerry H. Craven, a race driver and garage owner, and Mary Craven Unser, a homemaker, Unser clearly had driving in his blood. The Unser family is a dynasty of sorts, with Unser a part of the driving clan including his father, two uncles (Louis and Joe), two brothers (Bobby and Jerry), and son, Al Unser, Jr. Six Unsers have started in the Indianapolis (Indy) 500, and older brother Bobby won the race three times.

Unser began his career driving modified stock cars on racing tracks near his home in Albuquerque, New Mexico, in the years 1957 to 1963. He also operated a junkyard with his brother Bobby. His first successful racing excursion was in the 1960 Pikes Peak International Hill Climb event in Colorado. Pikes Peak is a glorious setting for athletics, with a daunting mountain made accessible via a narrow, twisting road. Unser took second place and then, in 1964 and 1965, he won the race.

Al Unser, Sr., after winning the Indianapolis 500, 1978. ASSOCIATED PRESS AP

In 1965 Unser's racing apprenticeship gained momentum as he graduated from Pikes Peak to the venues of the USAC. He took part in thirteen USAC races in 1965, driving an Indianapolis-type race car, and, in subsequent years, had seven runner-up positions in races of 100 miles or more. Just before turning thirty, Unser had his first championship trail victory. It was the USAC's inaugural night race, which took place at Nazareth, Pennsylvania, on 13 July 1968. He had four more first-place finishes, and at season's end was in third place in the national (USAC) points standing.

The Unser name is synonymous with the Indy 500—his brother Jerry was killed at the Speedway in 1959—and Unser first qualified for the world's most famous car race in 1965 when he successfully completed the demanding rookie test. In his first Indy 500 outing, he finished in ninth place. A year later he dropped to twelfth, but in 1967 he drove well, his race car stayed intact, and he took second place.

In the 1965 race, Unser drove an eight-cylinder Ford with a Lotus chassis for the Ansted-Thompson racing team. He qualified with a speed of 154 miles per hour with racing colors of pearl, red, and blue. A year later Unser drove another eight-cylinder Ford, also with a Lotus chassis, but this time he was associated with the STP Division of Studebaker. In a red and white livery, Unser qualified with a speed of 162.372 miles per hour.

A critical aspect frequently ignored by histories of the Indianapolis 500 during the 1960s is the fact that the race was not a U.S. national championship, but the equivalent of a world championship. The Indianapolis 500 at the time was a magnet that brought the best racers to the heartland of America, so in the 1966 Indianapolis 500, although Unser only finished in twelfth place, he was in the same field as Formula One first-class drivers such as Graham Hill, Jim Clark, and Jackie Stewart.

Unser was able to race competitively even when the odds were stacked against him. For example, in early 1969 he had a nasty accident as a result of a recreational motorcycle spill. A broken leg sidelined him for two months, but later in 1969 he was back racing so successfully that he won five USAC races and very nearly bested rival Mario Andretti for the national championship. Because of his injury, however, he attended the 1969 Indianapolis as a spectator.

A year later Unser emerged from the wings to dominate U.S. auto racing. He easily took the USAC National Driving Championship with a series of stellar performances resulting in ten victories, and in five other races he placed second or third. The most famous of these wins was on the

Indianapolis Speedway circuit. The *Encyclopedia of Motor Sport* (1971) describes Unser's magical month of May 1970: "He turned the fastest practice laps consistently, earned the no. 2 starting position with a four-lap average speed of 170.221 miles per hour and led the field on Race Day for all but 10 of the required 200 laps. . . . He finished at an average speed of 155.749 miles per hour . . . collecting $271,697.72 as his share of auto racing's first million-dollar purse."

Unser won his second straight Indianapolis 500 in 1971, only the fourth competitor to be a consecutive winner. He very nearly managed to capture a hat trick (three consecutive victories) of Indianapolis 500 crowns. His second place, however, signaled the onset of a downturn in Unser's fortunes. He failed to notch one victory on the 1972 USAC circuit, and in the following three years, although qualifying for the Indianapolis 500 annually, he failed to finish. In 1976 and 1977 his Indianapolis placings were seventh and third, respectively. But Unser's performance in USAC races and in other racing formats indicated a return to his winning ways.

The *New York Times* account of the 1978 Indianapolis makes the point that Unser was "a great driver in search of the right car." His victory margin of 8.19 seconds over Tom Sneva should have been much greater, but for a pit stop mistake by Unser twenty-one laps from the finish. Unser drove an eight-cylinder Cosworth, which had been the premier engine for European-based Formula One grand prix racing during the 1970s. The Cosworth, with an English-built engine, was the first foreign-constructed engine to win the Indianapolis 500 since Wilbur Shaw's 1940 triumph in an Italian Maserati. After his victory in front of 300,000 spectators, Unser drank the traditional pint of milk and observed, "Everything just went lovely. It's a great feeling. Everybody always asks which one is the best, and let me say, this one is. It always is."

Following the excitement of 1978, Unser's career experienced a second decline, but he did enjoy three separate, but special, successes. In 1983 and 1985 he won the Indy series championship (in 1983 he became the first driver to race against his son at Indy). In 1987 he started in the Indianapolis 500 but was seen as no more than a forty-seven-year-old stand-in. Eleven days before race day, Unser had neither a sponsor nor a car. But then Danny Ongais experienced a concussion in a practice accident, which meant Roger Penske, the CEO of Penske Racing and one of the most influential figures in U.S. auto racing over the last three decades, needed to find a replacement. Ongais's bad luck became Unser's good fortune, and Unser, as the March-Cosworth driver, won at an average speed of 162.175 miles per hour. A year later, although not a winner at Indianapolis, Unser set what might be his most singular accomplishment. He surpassed the record for most laps led at the Indianapolis 500 and "established the new standard of 625 for future generations to pursue." Indeed, the Michigan Motor Sports Hall of Fame labels this accomplishment as a "Ruthian" feat, alluding to Babe Ruth's domination as a home-run slugger.

At the end of his career Unser had recorded thirty-nine first-place finishes in Indy-style racing, placing him third on the all-time list (1900–1998) with A. J. Foyt (sixty-seven) and Mario Andretti (fifty-two) in first and second place. He retired from racing on 17 May 1994. Unser now works as a driving consultant for the Indy Racing League.

Unser married Wanda Japperson on 22 April 1958. They had three children, but later divorced. He married Karen Barnes on 27 November 1977. He was inducted into the Indianapolis Hall of Fame in 1986.

★

G. N. Georgano, ed., *Encyclopedia of Motor Sport* (1971), is an invaluable source for the first half of Unser's career. Unser's career is ably covered in Terry Reed, *Indy: Race and Ritual* (1980). Shorter assessments of Unser as a racer can be found in Will Grimsley, ed., *A Century of Sports* (1971); and Jack C. Fox, *The Illustrated History of the Indianapolis 500, 1911–1994* (1994). Michael Katz's narrative on the 1978 Indianapolis race, which appeared in the *New York Times* (29 May 1978), is full of information and rich detail. Additional material on Unser's career can be found on the website of the Michigan Motor Sports Hall of Fame at http://www.mmshof.org.

SCOTT A. G. M. CRAWFORD

UNSER, Al(fred), Jr. (*b.* 16 April 1962 in Albuquerque, New Mexico), race car driver who won the Indianapolis 500 for the second time in three years in 1994 and had thirty-one Championship Auto Racing Teams wins in eighteen years.

Unser was one of three children born to the racing legend Al Unser, Sr., and Wanda Unser, and became the third race car driver from the Unser family. His uncle Bobby won the Indianapolis 500 three times and his father won the Indianapolis 500 four times. Continuing the family tradition of winning automobile races and racing at the Indianapolis 500 was important to Unser, known as "Little Al," who began racing minibikes at the age of six and climbed into a go-cart at age nine. Even after his parents divorced in 1971, Unser still had his father by his side patiently pointing out the boy's racing mistakes. After honing his skills in the go-cart series for seven years, Unser began to look toward bigger and better racing opportunities.

Unser's professional racing career began with his entrance into the World of Outlaws series at age sixteen. Moving from a limited-horsepower go-cart to the 700-horsepower sprint car represented a massive step forward

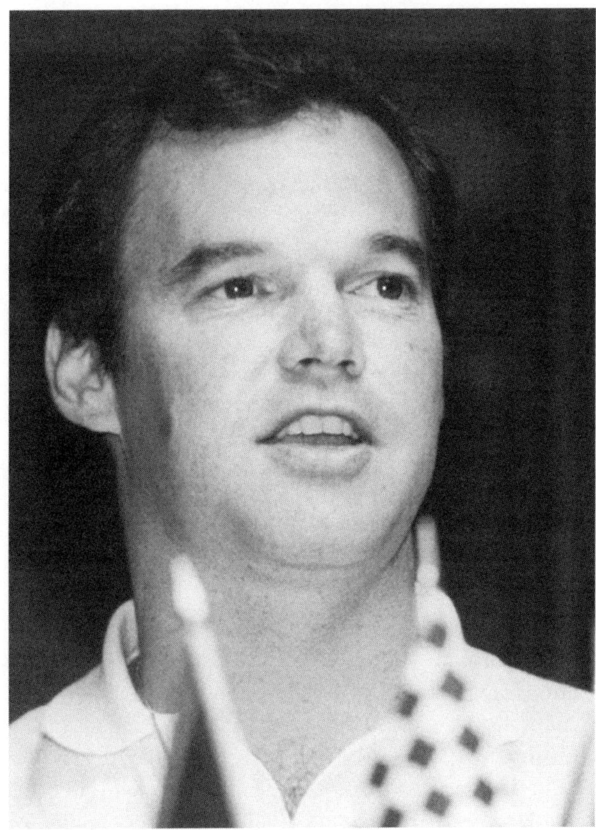

Al Unser, Jr. AP/WIDE WORLD PHOTOS

in Unser's racing career. While he was racing go-carts, Unser's age had not been much of an issue since most of the other drivers were about the same age. But his sixteen years sometimes betrayed him while racing the larger, more powerful sprint cars against drivers who were two and three times his age. In fact, Unser's small size was a challenge. At five feet, six inches tall and eighty-five pounds, Unser had to sit on two telephone books to see over the steering wheel. He used this opportunity to learn the ins and outs of racing wheel-to-wheel at top speed against other drivers who had the same dream of making it to the big time of Indianapolis.

Unser's path to success was not an easy one. Because racing was not a financial necessity for Unser, as it had been for his uncle and father, maintaining focus was a challenge for him. He had to make a commitment to becoming the best race-car driver possible. Once he made this commitment, Unser was well on his way to legendary status. After graduating from West Mesa High School in Albuquerque in 1980, Unser made steady progress in his career, from his 1981 Sports Car Club of America Rookie of the Year title to his 1983 record-setting win at Pikes Peak in Colorado, ensuring that the Unser family tradition of winning would continue. Unser married his wife, Shelley, in April 1981; they eventually had four children, including "Mini Al," a go-cart racer. The couple divorced in November 1998.

As a rookie driver in the Indianapolis 500 in 1983, the twenty-one-year-old Unser became the youngest driver to pass the 200-mile-per-hour barrier en route to a tenth-place finish. The next year Unser won his first Indy-car race at Oregon's Portland International Raceway. In 1990 he tied the single-season record after winning six Championship Auto Racing Teams (CART) races in a single season, and he set the record for consecutive wins at four by winning at Toronto, Michigan, Denver, and Vancouver. He finally tasted victory at Indianapolis with a .043-second victory (the closest finish in Indianapolis history) in 1992.

The 1994 racing season was a banner year for Unser. He had a score to settle with his teammate Emerson Fittipaldi, who had caused him to crash into the wall on lap 198 of 200 during the 1989 Indianapolis 500. On lap 185 of the 1994 Indianapolis 500 it appeared that Unser would once again lose the biggest race of the season to Fittipaldi, who had a 40-second lead—almost one full lap. Knowing that he had to make a fuel stop, Fittipaldi closed in on Unser to put him one lap down. Fittipaldi's car got caught in the turbulent air created by Unser's car and, as the two drivers entered turn four, Fittipaldi drove his car onto the apron of the track and lost control. His car disintegrated into a fiery mess as it crashed into the outside wall. Unser went on to win the race, his second at Indianapolis and the Unser family's eighth. Unser presented his winner's trophy to Unser, Sr., to commemorate his father's fiftieth birthday and retirement from driving.

Unser's win in the 1994 Indianapolis 500 was only one of his eight victories out of sixteen races that season. He also claimed four pole positions, the number-one starting position in the race. His success during the 1994 season made way for his second season championship. He was named the *ABC Wide World of Sports* Athlete of the Year, was given ESPN's ESPY Award for Auto Racing Performer of the Year, and was determined by the national media panel to be the driver of the year.

In June 1994 the governing body U.S. Auto Club (USAC) changed the racing rules, negatively affecting Unser's team along with many others. This caused a rift and the teams split into two factions, CART and the newly formed Indy Racing League (IRL). Because of this split, the teams that raced with CART would not race at the Indianapolis raceway starting in the 1996 season. It appeared that the Unser-Indianapolis tradition would come to an end. In 1999, after his contract with the Penske team expired, Unser signed a five-year contract with the Galles team of the IRL. He returned to Indianapolis during the 2000 season, starting in eighteenth position and finishing twenty-ninth due to an overheating engine.

Unser's popularity came only in part from his success on the racetrack. It also stemmed from the Unser family tradition, which provided fans with a connection to the past. Even with his many racing successes, Unser retained his image as a good, down-to-earth person.

★

For a history of the Unser family see Karen Bentley, *The Unsers* (1996). Brief biographies are in Patericia Pate Havlice, *Biography Index* (1990), and Coral Amende, *Legends in Their Own Time* (1994). Steve Herman "Al Unser Jr. Joins IRL and Will Drive for Galles Racing," *Detroit News* (1999), documents the split of CART from the IRL and Unser's return to the IRL.

JEROMY RUNION

UPSHAW, Eugene Thurman, Jr. ("Gene") (*b.* 15 August 1945 in Robstown, Texas), offensive guard for the Oakland Raiders, named National Football League (NFL) Lineman of the Year in 1977 and played in Super Bowls II, VI, and XV; executive director of the NFL Players' Association.

Upshaw never planned to become a professional football player. He grew up with his brother Marvin, who also had a successful NFL career, playing baseball and picking cotton. His father, Eugene Upshaw, Sr., who worked as a meter reader for an oil company but had played semi-professional baseball, made a deal with his two oldest boys: if they performed well on the baseball field, they would not have to pick cotton in the hot sun. When Upshaw's pitching was less than spectacular, his brother, the catcher, would walk out to the mound and remind him of the alternative. Their mother, Cora Riley Upshaw, was employed as a domestic worker. Upshaw had been a baseball star in high school, and he had the potential to play professional baseball after graduating from Robstown High School, but his family encouraged him to attend Texas A&I in Kingsville, Texas, instead.

Gene Upshaw, 1981. ASSOCIATED PRESS AP

Upshaw entered A&I without any real ambitions, although he had some idea he might become a schoolteacher. He also entered without a scholarship, but three days after trying out for the football team, he was awarded one. Upshaw was only five feet, ten inches tall, and 185 pounds. At A&I, however, he quickly grew to six feet, five inches, and filled out to 255 pounds. He tried a number of positions on the football team, including fullback and tight end, with no real success. When on defense, he sometimes played an entire game without completing one tackle. In his senior year, Upshaw's college record left him as a possible third-round pick as an NFL offensive lineman, but no more. His status changed quickly, though; he performed well in the Senior Bowl and was chosen as the team captain during the summer College All-Star Game. Upshaw received a B.S. from Texas A&I in 1968. He also attended California State University in 1969 and Golden Gate University Law School in 1982.

Al Davis drafted Upshaw for the Oakland Raiders (now the Los Angeles Raiders) in 1967, believing the rookie would make the perfect match for lineman Buck Buchanan of the Kansas City Chiefs, then Oakland's main rival. The reserved Upshaw had doubts about playing for Oakland; the team had a reputation for being rough and rowdy. Also, his first lineup against the tough Kansas City lineman proved disastrous, but even Buchanan realized that Upshaw had the potential to make a great offensive guard. He was large, allowing him to match up against defensive tackles, and he also had the speed to sweep out in front of running backs. Upshaw earned a starting position his first year and helped the Raiders win the American Football League (AFL) championship in 1967. The team lost Super Bowl II, however, to the Green Bay Packers, 33–14. Upshaw married Jimmye Hill 30 December 1967; they had one son but later divorced. He married Teresa Buich in 1986; they had two sons. Upshaw began a six-year period of service with the U.S. Army in 1967, but this did not interfere with his career.

The six-foot-five offensive guard, "was always a little hyper," wrote John Madden in *Hey, Wait a Minute (I Wrote a Book!)*. "Always up, always happy. If you were down and you talked to him, you soon were up." Madden also noted that "being a leader came naturally to Gene." Owner Davis often conferred with Upshaw and one or two of his teammates when considering a new player for the Raiders. The press also recognized his intelligence, encircling Upshaw in the locker room after a game as though he were the quarterback. Beginning in 1973, Upshaw became offensive team captain, a position he held for nine years. From 1976 to 1981 he also served on the Executive Committee of the National Football Leagues Players' Association, a collective bargaining organization.

Upshaw played for Oakland during many of their most successful years. In 1976 Oakland's 13–1 record placed them at the head of their division, and they defeated New England 24–21 in the first-round playoff game. Many expected a difficult challenge in the follow-up game against the defending champions, the Steelers, but the Raiders won a decisive 24–7 victory. The Raiders came out strong against the Vikings in Super Bowl XI, scoring on three successive drives and leading 16–0 at halftime. While the Vikings scored a touchdown in the third quarter, two fourth-quarter touchdowns by Oakland gave the team a 32–14 victory in their first Super Bowl title. It was four years before the Raiders returned to the Super Bowl. In 1980 the Raiders finished with a lackluster 11–5 season, but nonetheless defeated Houston 27–7 in the Wild Card Game. After winning the American Football Conference (AFC; the AFL changed names in 1970) title 34–27 against the Chargers, Oakland returned to the Super Bowl for the third time, facing the Philadelphia Eagles. The Raiders went up 14–0 early, and the Eagles never caught up. With a final score of 27–10, Oakland won Super Bowl XV and became the first Wild Card team to win the championship. Upshaw is the only player to appear in three Super Bowls in three different decades.

Upshaw retired in 1981 after sixteen seasons as a player. In 1983 however, he decided to combine his love of football with politics: he became executive director of the NFL Players' Association. His experience as a member of the association and as a player placed him in a good position to work with the complex issues of labor negotiations. Upshaw played an important role during the strike negotiations in 1982. He worked with Ed Garvey, the executive director of the Players' Association, to reach an agreement with the NFL. Although he received criticism for his heavy-handed methods, Upshaw remained trusted by the players, and this trust helped him secure the position of executive director when Garvey stepped down the following year. Long active in Democratic politics, Upshaw championed issues such as the right of free agency and the need for more minorities in coaching positions.

Upshaw played 217 games for the Raiders, missing only one league game during his entire career. He played in eleven playoff games, won eight division titles, and appeared in three Super Bowls. In 1973 and 1974 he was named AFC Lineman of the Year, and in 1977 was voted top lineman in the NFL. Along with his football career, Upshaw has been honored for humanitarian activities and his work with civic, community, and charitable organizations. Since 1983 he has served as the executive director of the Executive Committee of the NFL Players' Association, defending the rights of NFL players. He was inducted into the Pro Football Hall of Fame in 1987, his first year of eligibility.

★

A brief overview of Upshaw's career can be found in David L. Porter, ed., *Biographical Dictionary of American Sports: Football* (1987). Anecdotes about Upshaw are in John Madden, *Hey, Wait a Minute (I Wrote a Book!)* (1984). For a discussion of the offensive lineman's career, see Nathan Aaseng, *Football's Crushing Blockers* (1982). A lengthy portrait is in Frank Deford, "Bonus Piece: The Guard Who Would Be Quarterback," *Sports Illustrated* (14 Sept. 1987).

RONNIE D. LANKFORD, JR.

V

VAN BROCKLIN, Norm(an) Mack (*b.* 15 March 1926 in Eagle Butte, South Dakota; *d.* 2 May 1983 in Monroe, Georgia), football player and National Football League (NFL) coach considered one of the sport's greatest forward-passing quarterbacks.

Van Brocklin was the eighth of nine children born to farmers Mac Van Brocklin and Ethel Van Brocklin. Soon after Van Brocklin's birth the family moved to Walnut Creek, California, where he grew up. Attending Acalanes High School, he was a three-sport star in baseball, basketball, and football. After graduating from high school in 1943, Van Brocklin served in the U.S. Navy until he was discharged in early 1946.

Van Brocklin then enrolled at the University of Oregon and in the fall of 1946, since freshmen were eligible for varsity athletics, he joined the football team. The Oregon team was under the direction of Coach Tex Oliver, an advocate of the single-wing offense, and Van Brocklin ended up as fifth-string tailback because of his extremely slow running speed. But in 1947 Oregon hired a new football coach, Jim Aiken, who installed the T-formation offense and made Van Brocklin a quarterback.

By the third game of the 1947 season, Van Brocklin was the starting quarterback. His breakthrough game as a forward passer came against the University of California, Los Angeles (UCLA), when he completed 10 of 23 pass attempts for 197 yards, including two touchdown passes, in a victory over Stanford. Van Brocklin was the leading passer in the Pacific Coast Conference (PCC) for the season, finishing with 76 completions in 168 attempts for 939 yards, and he was named to the all-conference team.

Van Brocklin returned to quarterback for Oregon in his junior season in 1948, and again he was the leading passer in the PCC, completing 68 of 139 attempts for 1,010 yards. Highlights of the season included tossing a game-winning forty-seven-yard touchdown pass against Southern California and two scoring passes for a narrow win over Washington. Van Brocklin capped off the season by passing for 145 yards and one touchdown in a loss to Southern Methodist in the Cotton Bowl game.

For his offensive exploits in 1948, Van Brocklin finished sixth in the voting for the Heisman Trophy and received first team spots as an All-American from the International News Service (INS) and Deke Houlgate, a well-known Los Angeles sportswriter. The Los Angeles Rams, the only team aware that he would graduate early from Oregon, selected Van Brocklin in the fourth round of the 1949 National Football League (NFL) draft. That summer, after graduating with a B.S. degree in physical education and playing for the College All-Stars in Chicago, he reported to the Rams for the 1949 season. Later that fall Van Brocklin married Gloria Schiewe, his former biology teacher at Oregon, with whom he raised six children.

Van Brocklin, known as "the Dutchman," was six feet, one inch and 199 pounds, and had an exceptionally strong arm and large hands, which combined to give him the capability of lofting towering deep passes, rifling short "bullet" passes, or flicking short "touch" passes with remarkable accuracy. But Los Angeles already had a future member of the Hall of Fame at quarterback, Bob Waterfield, and Van Brocklin was initially relegated to the sidelines. Van Brocklin was soon discontented, and so began the controversy and feuding that typified most of his NFL career, both as a player and as a coach. His temper and lack of tact created confrontations with players, coaches, and sportswriters.

After playing minimally in 1949, Van Brocklin developed his capability as a passer to challenge Waterfield for playing time in the 1950 season. Coach Joe Stydahar began to rotate the two players, making neither happy. Sharing the playing time in 1950, Van Brocklin led the NFL in passing for the first of three times in his career (also in 1952 and 1954) with 127 complete of 233 attempts for 2,061 yards. Los Angeles reached the NFL championship game in 1950, the first of four times during Van Brocklin's years with the Rams. For the 1951 season opener Waterfield was out with an injury, and Van Brocklin proceeded to set an NFL record on 28 September 1951 as he passed for 554 yards against the New York Yanks. With the two quarterbacks sharing the playing time again, the Rams captured the 1951 NFL championship with a 24–17 win over the Cleveland Browns after Van Brocklin threw a seventy-three-yard touchdown pass in the fourth quarter.

Waterfield retired after the 1952 season, leaving the quarterback spot to Van Brocklin. In 1954 Van Brocklin compiled his best season statistically, as he completed 139 of 260 passes for 2,637 yards. But that same year the Rams drafted another quarterback, Bill Wade, and by 1955 Coach Sid Gillman was rotating the two players. Again unhappy, Van Brocklin announced his retirement at the close of the 1957 season, but the Rams traded him to the Philadelphia Eagles before the 1958 season. The deal paid off for Philadelphia in 1960, when Van Brocklin's passing and leadership carried the Eagles to the NFL championship, the second of Van Brocklin's career. He was named the league's Most Valuable Player. Announcing his retirement as a player after the title game, Van Brocklin believed he had been promised the Philadelphia head coach job for 1961, but no offer was made.

In early 1961 Van Brocklin was named head coach of the Minnesota Vikings expansion team. Coaching in Minnesota for six years (1961–1966), he posted an overall record of 29–51–4. His best season was in 1964, when the Vikings went 8–5–1. He was a strict disciplinarian both on and off the field, and his "gruff" approach toward the players and sportswriters created hard feelings. His long feud with the quarterback Fran Tarkenton culminated in Van Brocklin's sudden resignation in early 1967, just one year after signing a long-term contract.

Van Brocklin coached the College All-Stars in the summer of 1968. Three games into the season he was hired as head coach and general manager by the Atlanta Falcons. He compiled an overall record of 37–49–3 while at Atlanta, and his best season was in 1973 with a 9–5–0 mark. But his feuds with players and the media culminated in his dismissal midway through the 1974 season.

Norm Van Brocklin, 1950. © BETTMANN/CORBIS

After his NFL days Van Brocklin did occasional sports analyst work with Atlanta's WTBS television, and in 1979 he served as an assistant coach at Georgia Tech. But brain surgery that year ended his active football career, and Van Brocklin retired to his pecan farm near Social Circle, Georgia. He died near there at age fifty-seven after a heart attack.

As a head coach Van Brocklin's fiery personality invariably led to problems, no one disputes his place as one of the greatest forward passers in football history. An adept ball handler, he was the prototype drop-back passer. During his twelve seasons as an NFL player Van Brocklin passed for over 2,000 yards in seven different seasons, completed 53.6 percent of his career pass attempts, and was selected for the Pro Bowl game on nine occasions. He was elected to the College Football Hall of Fame in 1966 and the Pro Football Hall of Fame in 1971.

★

Material on the highlights of Van Brocklin's career is in many works on NFL history. Among the most useful are Phil Berger, *Great Moments in Pro Football* (1969); Steve Bisheff, *Los Angeles*

Rams (1973); and Mickey Herskowitz, *The Quarterbacks: The Uncensored Truth About the Men in the Pocket* (1990). A good summary of his coaching days is in "The Dutchman Is Half an Inch Away," *Sports Illustrated* (13 Sept. 1965). Obituaries are in the *New York Times* (3 May 1983) and the *Los Angeles Times* (3 May 1983).

RAYMOND SCHMIDT

VAN BUREN, Stephen Wood ("Steve") (*b.* 28 December 1920 in La Ceiba, Honduras), football running back known for his size, speed, power, and elusiveness, who was the first runner in the history of the National Football League to gain more than 1,000 yards in more than one season; led the Philadelphia Eagles to consecutive shutout championship victories in 1948 and 1949; and was inducted into the Pro Football Hall of Fame.

The son of an American fruit inspector, Wood Van Buren, and a Spanish woman, Lenare, Van Buren grew up in a Central American shipping port. At age ten he was orphaned, so in 1930 Van Buren, his brother, and his three sisters went to New Orleans to live with their grandparents. He recalled, "In Honduras, I was too young to play much of anything but running games. We'd never heard of football. But when I was about fifteen, my first year at Warren Easton High School in New Orleans, I used to watch the other boys play football. It seemed like a good game, so I went out for the team. But I only weighed a hundred twenty-five pounds, and all the coach would let me do was run up and down the field—not play or scrimmage. When it came to actually playing football, he told me to forget it. He was afraid I'd get hurt."

Steve Van Buren, 1950. AP/WIDE WORLD PHOTOS

Van Buren dropped out of high school, even though he was a good student, and worked in an iron foundry. "The foundry work was hard, but I liked it, and it built me up," he said. Two years and thirty pounds later Van Buren went back to high school. He played football as an end rather than as a running back. After graduation in 1940, Van Buren enrolled in the engineering program at Louisiana State University (LSU) in Baton Rouge, where he came close to his professional playing weight of 208 pounds. The six-foot Van Buren finally got to play in the backfield for the Bayou Tigers coached by Bernie Moore, but in his first two varsity seasons he rarely was given the chance to run with the ball. He was primarily a blocking fullback for the halfback Alvin Dark, who later gained notoriety as a Major League Baseball player and manager. When Dark went into military service—Van Buren was exempt because of a chronic eye ailment—Moore moved Van Buren to a halfback position, where he got to carry the ball frequently.

Van Buren responded positively to the change. He led the nation in scoring in 1943 with ninety-eight points and was second only to Notre Dame's Creighton Miller in rushing yardage. In 1944 Van Buren graduated from LSU with a B.S. in engineering.

On Moore's recommendation the Philadelphia Eagles picked Van Buren during the first round of the National Football League (NFL) college-player draft. Van Buren was unfamiliar with the Eagles, a perennial noncontender at the time, saying, "We didn't hear much about pro ball in the South. I only knew about the Washington Redskins and the Chicago Bears." As if to prove his point, Van Buren, on his first trip to Philadelphia, missed his stop at the North Philly station and ended up in New York. Still feeling the effects of an appendectomy, Van Buren missed some early games in his 1944 rookie season, carrying the ball only eighty times. However, his 5.5 yards-per-carry average earned him first team Associated Press All-Pro honors.

In 1945 he led the NFL in rushing with 832 yards and in scoring with 110 points. He also set a record by scoring eighteen touchdowns in a single season. In 1946 he slipped to third place in rushing (529 yards with a 4.6 average), but in 1947 Van Buren and the Eagles came back with a vengeance. In that year, Van Buren gained 1,008 yards—a feat previously achieved only by Beattie Feathers of the Chicago Bears, who in 1934 gained 1,004 yards. Also in 1947 the Eagles were in the championship game for the first time in their history. On the frozen turf of Chicago's Comiskey Park, they lost 28–21 to the Cardinals. In 1948 Van Buren fell below the 1,000-yard mark, but the Eagles were again in the title game—again facing the Chicago Cardinals. The game was played in a blizzard, but neither the snow nor the Cardinals could stop the "Movin' Van," as Van Buren was sometimes called. He scored the game's only touchdown.

In 1949 Van Buren and the Eagles broke new ground. Van Buren became the first NFL runner to have a second 1,000-yard season (1,146). The Eagles won another NFL championship, defeating the Los Angeles Rams, 14–0. This second consecutive shutout victory was unique in the history of football. Van Buren, referred to as "Supersonic Steve" as the jet age arrived, slogged through the Los Angeles Coliseum's quagmire for 196 yards—a mark that still stood in 2001 as an NFL/NFC championship game record. Van Buren married Grace Callahan during Philadelphia's championship era; they had three daughters.

By now Van Buren was a familiar sight in the NFL, both on and off the field. On the streets he looked like any other young professional, except he never wore socks. In postwar America, socklessness was a fashion statement. On the field, "Wham Bam" Van Buren was always seen with the ball tucked under his right arm (a shoulder injury prevented him from carrying the ball in his left arm or from switching the ball when a tackler approached), with his head down. One of his coaches, Earle "Greasy" Neale, told him he would be a better runner if he ran with his head up. Van Buren tried it and came to the bench with a puffy eye. "Greasy," he said, "now I know why I run with me head down." The Eagles end Jack Ferrante was once clipped by Van Buren when he cut more suddenly than Ferrante expected. As Ferrante lay on the ground, an unsympathetic opponent bent over him and said, "Hurts, doesn't it? Now you know how we feel when we try to tackle him."

Neale compared Van Buren to two football immortals, Red Grange and Bronko Nagurski, saying, "Steve is as fast and elusive as Grange, but he doesn't need to have the blocking Red did. He can, and does, run right over would-be tacklers like the Bronk did." The one thing Neale didn't like about Van Buren was his apparent disregard for punctuality. When his star runner was late for a meeting, Neale declared, "I've had enough! Either you or I go, Steve." With one voice, Van Buren's teammates chorused, "Good-bye, Greasy, good-bye."

As the winning Eagles nucleus aged in the 1950s, Van Buren suffered a broken toe and some fractured ribs. He still banged his way to a respectable 629 yards in the 1950 season, but his average fell to 3.3 yards per carry. The effects lingered in 1951, when the once unstoppable "Flying Dutchman" averaged just 2.9 yards to a total of 327 yards. He had also suffered a knee injury in the first scrimmage in training camp before the season. That year the Eagles—on name value alone, or perhaps in hope of recaptured glory—drafted Van Buren's younger brother, Ebert, during their first-round pick. Ebert's three-year career brought him a rushing total of sixty-one yards.

Determined to come back after two subpar seasons, Van Buren took countless whirlpool treatments and ran hundreds of sprints getting ready for 1952, but his ability to pivot, robbed by the knee injury, was gone. He tried so hard to regain it that he developed a bone spur on his once-broken toe. Van Buren retired with records for most career yards rushed (5,860), most career attempts (1,320), most yards rushed in a single season (1,146), and most touchdowns in a season (18). He was inducted into the Pro Football Hall of Fame with the class of 1965.

Although he was once named the Southeastern Conference scholar-athlete of the year, Van Buren, to whom money meant little, never put his engineering background to use. He was an Eagles assistant for a while and later worked as a head coach for the minor league Newark (New Jersey) Bears, owned a used-car lot and a dance hall, and indulged a lifelong passion for horse racing. In retirement, he lived in Bensalem, Pennsylvania, outside of Philadelphia.

Van Buren was a prototype for the NFL "franchise" running backs of the late twentieth century. At Eagles Alumni Day games, he is recognized as "Mr. Eagle," and the longest and loudest ovation is always for Van Buren. When former Eagles players reverently mention "Steve," there is no need to ask, "Steve who?" Without a trace of braggadocio, Van Buren once summarized his career by saying, "I set a record every year I wasn't hurt."

★

Van Buren's life and career are discussed in George Sullivan, *Pro Football's All-Time Greats* (1968); Murray Olderman, *The Running Backs* (1969); Myron Cope, *The Game That Was* (1970); and Lud Duroska, *Great Pro Running Backs* (1973).

JIM CAMPBELL

VARIPAPA, Andrew ("Andy") (*b.* 31 March 1891 in Carfizzi, Italy; *d.* 25 August 1984 in Hempstead, New York), top bowler of the twentieth century known for his trick-shot exhibitions and for popularizing the game.

The son of a wealthy farmer, Varipapa, along with his mother, Concetta, his brother, and his stepfather, immigrated to America when Varipapa was eleven and settled in Brooklyn, New York. As a young man he boxed, played semiprofessional baseball, and worked at a butcher shop and an insurance company. He also worked as a toolmaker and at one time owned a poolroom. In 1907 he began to bowl. On 17 June 1917 he married Alice (they would have three children), and from 1926 to 1931 he managed a bowling alley in Brooklyn. Averaging a score of 234 for forty-two games, Varipapa became prominent in 1930 when he joined world champion Joe Falcaro in a doubles match against American Bowling Congress champion Charles

Andy Varipapa, 1940. AP/WIDE WORLD PHOTOS

Riley and Philadelphia champion Jim Murgie in New York and Philadelphia.

The short and stocky Varipapa whipped his body into shape to become a champion bowler. He strengthened his legs by jogging back and forth across the Brooklyn Bridge. He developed sinewy arms and powerful wrists by playing catch with a sixteen-pound bowling ball, swinging the ball forward as if shooting for the head pin. At the moment of release he would flip the ball up and over his head. He also possessed a powerful chest and shoulders. Varipapa was often annoyed that his reputation as a trick-shot bowler overshadowed his championship feats. During his exhibitions he rolled strikes while blindfolded, while standing with his back to the pins, using his right hand, using his left hand, and using two hands. His greatest trick involved three lanes and fourteen pins knocked down by one ball.

Spectacular showmanship was a hallmark of Varipapa's career. After rolling a strike he would leap into the air. During a competition he would keep up such a constant stream of chatter that one writer nicknamed him "The Talking Machine." He would have liked to eliminate such antics but continued with them since he believed the fans expected them. He once remarked, "They think it's colorful. So I brag, put body English on the ball, and jump in the air when I make a big strike. But believe me when I say I'd like to cut it out."

Varipapa's spectacular career included many highlights, as well as a starring role in the first bowling film, *Strikes and Spares* (1934). In 1932 he played in his first bowling tournament, averaging 210 in 128 games in eight cities. From 1938 to 1947 he led the country with a 204.72 bowling average in ten consecutive American Bowling Congress tournaments. In 1946 and 1947 he became the first bowler to win the All-Star/United States Open Tournament in consecutive years. He and fellow American Bowling Congress Hall of Famer Lou Campi won the Bowling Proprietors Association of America doubles in 1947 and 1948. In 1948 Varipapa was named Bowler of the Year by the Bowling Writers Association.

Varipapa averaged 184 points for thirty-eight years in American Bowling Congress tournaments and racked up a Master 54-game, 190-point average. By appearing on television he made the public aware of bowling. He ran international bowling clinics and established successful nationwide tours.

At age seventy-eight Varipapa was plagued by painful wrist and arm problems. So he switched to left-handed bowling and averaged 180 points within eighteen months. The *That's Incredible* television program highlighted his bowling skills and clever badinage in 1981. He died in Hempstead, New York, of natural causes at the age of ninety-three.

In 1957 Varipapa was elected to the American Bowling Congress Hall of Fame, and in 1980 he was selected as the first bowler in the Italian-American Sports Hall of Fame. He was also a member of the New York State Bowling Association Hall of Fame, the New York City Bowling Association Hall of Fame (1951), and the Eastern Long Island Bowling Association Hall of Fame (1973). He received the Bowling Proprietors Association of America All-Star Award of Merit (1963), the Bowling Writers Association of America John O. Martino Award (1977), and the Brunswick Memorial World Open Award (1981).

Varipapa's greatness was reaffirmed in 1999 when he was named by *Bowling* magazine as one of the twenty greatest bowlers of the twentieth century. In June 2001 *Bowling Digest* placed him in third place on its list of the most influential bowlers. Even his name has become a bowling term. To bowl an "Andy Varipapa" means to roll twelve strikes in a row but spread over two games rather than in one. All of these honors capped a brilliant sports career that will be hard to surpass.

★

For primary sources on Varipapa's life, see the Andrew Varipapa file at the American Bowling Congress Hall of Fame in Glendale, Wisconsin. Biographical sketches appear in Frank Litsky, *Superstars* (1975), and David L. Porter, ed., *Biographical Dictionary of American Sports: 1992–1995 Supplement for Baseball, Football, Basketball, and Other Sports* (1995). Articles on Varipapa include "Bowling: Handy Andy," *Newsweek* (23 Dec. 1946); "The Greatest," *Time* (5 May 1947); "I'm a Man, Huh?" *Time* (22 Dec. 1947); " 'Andy the Great' Proves that He Is," *Life* (29 Dec. 1947); Bill Fay, "Bowling's Talking Machine," *Collier's* (10 Apr. 1948); and Larry Paladino, "Whatever It Takes," *Bowling Digest* (June 2001). An obituary is in the *New York Times* (27 Aug. 1984).

JOHN MORAN

VEECK, William L., Jr. ("Bill") (*b.* 1 September 1914 in Chicago, Illinois; *d.* 1 February 1986 in Chicago, Illinois), owner of three Major League Baseball teams and one racetrack, most noted for his innovations in the game of baseball and particularly for marketing to a broader spectrum of fans.

Veeck was the son of William Veeck, Sr., a sportswriter and president of the Chicago Cubs, and Grace De Forest Veeck, a homemaker. Veeck once stated that he was the only human being raised in a baseball stadium. He spent much of his youth with his father at Chicago's Wrigley Field. Following his father's death in 1933, Veeck took a position with the Cubs. While working with Cubs owner Philip Wrigley, Veeck was responsible for two notable facets of the aesthetically pleasing stadium. He planted the ivy growing on the outfield walls, which eventually became a hallmark of Wrigley Field, and he completed the work on the imposing center field scoreboard.

Veeck worked for the Cubs until 1941, when he, along with Charlie Grimm, a retired Cubs first baseman, purchased the minor league Milwaukee Brewers. They took a moribund franchise and converted it into a winning venture both on the field and at the box office. Innovations included scheduling games at 8:30 A.M. to accommodate war industry workers who were finishing work on the night shift.

Veeck joined the U.S. Marines in 1944. His leg was crushed while in combat in the Pacific theater, and after ten surgeries failed to fix the infected and damaged leg, it was amputated in 1946. Veeck purchased the Cleveland Indians from the owners of the team, the Bradley family, that same year, and by 1948 the Indians had won their first American League (AL) championship in twenty-eight years. Veeck moved all Indians games from the antiquated League Park into Cleveland Municipal Stadium, thus allowing the team to eventually draw over 2 million fans per year. Following Branch Rickey's hiring of Jackie Robinson in 1947, Veeck brought Larry Doby to the Indians as the American League's first African-American player. In the tight pennant race of 1948, Veeck added the legendary Satchel Paige to assist the team in winning both the pennant and the World Series championship, beating the Boston Braves. Veeck had become a hero to the fans of Cleveland, but at the expense of his marriage to Eleanor Raymond, whom he had wed on 8 December 1935. Their divorce in 1949 caused enough financial disruption that Veeck had to sell the Indians in order to facilitate a divorce settlement. He married Mary Frances Ackerman on 29 April 1950. They later had six children and together managed a Boston racetrack, Suffolk Downs.

Veeck disappeared from the active baseball scene until

Bill Veeck *(left)* with Larry Doby, the first African-American player in the American League, 1947. ASSOCIATED PRESS AP

1951, when he bought the St. Louis Browns, a team that had incurred great debt and lacked talent. In Veeck's first season as owner he increased attendance by 60 percent by using several gimmicks and promotions, the most famous of which was sending a midget, Eddie Gaedel, up to bat in a 1952 game. In 1953 he attempted to move the team to Milwaukee because he felt that St. Louis could not support two teams. However, Veeck had not done the appropriate planning and did not get the necessary approvals to make the move. The result was that he had to sell the team because of insufficient funding. Other league owners, who had come to despise Veeck because of his showmanship, allowed the new ownership to move the team to Baltimore the next season.

This move opened the door to more franchise shifting, which had not occurred since the advent of the modern structure of baseball in 1903. Unprofitable teams switched cities in order to find more lucrative sites, and the baseball industry eventually expanded the number of major league teams beyond the original sixteen.

By 1959 the Comiskey family wanted to sell the Chicago White Sox. Veeck bought the franchise and brought life to South Side Chicago fans by winning the first pennant in forty years. Although the White Sox lost the World Series to the recently moved Los Angeles Dodgers, baseball on the South Side had become vibrant again. Veeck eventually added a memorable scoreboard to Comiskey Park, complete with a fireworks system that discharged every time the team won or whenever a White Sox player hit a home run. Under Veeck's ownership, the names of players appeared for the first time on White Sox uniforms. Unfortunately, working extensive hours, smoking several packs of cigarettes a day, and drinking excessively for years led Veeck to suffer serious health problems, and he was forced to sell the White Sox in 1961.

During the early 1960s Veeck began writing books. His first, *Veeck as in Wreck* (1962), became a sports classic. His later works, *The Hustlers Handbook* (1965) and *Thirty Tons a Day* (1972), reflect the humor and unconventional wisdom that Veeck brought to baseball and to sports marketing.

When the White Sox were again up for sale in 1976, and threatened with the possibility of being moved to St. Petersburg, Florida, Veeck bought the team once again to keep it in his home city. His purchase of the White Sox for $7 million came a couple of weeks before free agency began. Veeck, short of money, kept the White Sox afloat during the late 1970s with his "rent-a-player" approach, bringing in well-known players for one year, knowing that he did not have the resources to offer them multiyear contracts. When his health problems resurfaced in 1980, Veeck sold the team for $20 million, this time pocketing a handsome profit.

During his final years Veeck was a regular fan, sitting in with the "bleacher bums" in the park of his youth. He died of congestive heart failure and is buried at Oakwoods Cemetery in Chicago. "Barnum Bill," as his fellow owners sometimes called him, was inducted into the National Baseball Hall of Fame in 1991.

★

The best sources of information about Veeck are his own books, *Veeck as in Wreck* (1962), *The Hustler's Handbook* (1965), and *Thirty Tons a Day* (1972). Also see Richard C. Lindberg, *The White Sox Encyclopedia* (1997). Articles include Thomas Boswell, "Always Leave 'em Laughing," *Inside Sports* (Mar. 1981), and Steven P. Geitschier, "Bill Veeck," *Timeline* (May 1990).

HARRY JEBSEN, JR.

VINES, Henry Ellsworth, Jr. ("Elly") (*b.* 28 September 1911 in Pasadena, California; *d.* 17 March 1994 in La Quinta, California), tennis player and golfer who was known as the hardest hitter in tennis history.

Vines grew up playing tennis on the hard courts that were a staple in California. His tennis heroes were "Big Bill" Tilden and "Little Bill" Johnston. Vines was lucky enough to have as his coach Mercer Beasley, one of the best in the sport. Beasley saw the talent and power of the fifteen-year-old, and he brought out Vines's best by having him aim for specific points on the court. Years of this type of practice

Elly Vines, 1933. AP/WIDE WORLD PHOTOS

helped Vines to develop shots that were more like rifle fire than tennis strokes. By the time he was eighteen, Vines had the game of a champion.

He burst onto the tennis scene in 1930. On his first trip to the East Coast, in his first play on grass courts, he beat Frank Hunter and Frank Shields. At once commentators began to describe him as the eventual successor to Big Bill Tilden. Not yet ready to concede his spot, Tilden came out and smothered Vines in their first match. Vines began to think of himself as a two-week wonder, a flash in the pan. However, he did win the U.S. Championship in 1931.

He further confirmed his status in 1932. The All-England Lawn Tennis Championships at Wimbledon were full of expectation that year; observers wanted to see a native son of England win the title. They were overjoyed when Henry "Bunny" Austin reached the finals, and took his place across the net from Vines. The match that followed was later described as one of the most devastating displays of power tennis ever witnessed; Vines crushed Austin 6–4, 6–2, 6–0. Austin later admitted he did not know whether Vines's last ace, the one that ended the match, went past on his left or right as it was too fast for him to see it.

Vines's 1932 win over Austin was all the more remarkable because it was the first Wimbledon of his career. Only Tilden and Gerald Patterson had accomplished the same feat, and no one would do it again until Boris Becker in 1985. The *New York Times* correspondent remarked, "No medieval torturer ever applied pressure upon a victim more unrelentingly than did this tall Californian youth, ranging the court like a terror and slyly throttling his opponent's game." He followed up his Wimbledon win in 1932 by winning his second straight U.S. Championship.

Vines had a sunny disposition, on court and off. Rather than dispute line calls with judges, he would either adjust his cap or turn slowly and grin at the linesman. These manners made Vines the most beloved man in lawn tennis. The crowds' affection could not keep Vines at the top of his form, however. While 1932 had been a year of stunning demonstrations and mastery for Vines, he was already slowing down by 1933. He lost that year's Wimbledon final to the Australian Jack Crawford, 4–6, 11–9, 6–2, 2–6, 6–4. Vines had been 9–1 in Davis Cup play in 1932, but fell to both Austin and Fred Perry in 1933. These comedowns were disappointing to tennis fans and very hard on Vines, who soon turned professional and joined Tilden's troupe.

Vines lost his opening match as a professional at Madison Square Garden to Tilden, 8–6, 6–3, 6–2, an amazing upset considering the difference in their ages (Tilden was then forty). Vines came back, however, and won the tour forty-seven matches to twenty-six. Together Vines and Tilden won the World Professional Champion Doubles in 1934 and 1935. Vines also won the Wembley World Pro title over Tilden in 1935, and over Hans Nusslein in 1936 and 1937.

Vines also defeated Lester Stoeffen in a U.S. tour in 1936. The following year he tied at thirty-seven matches apiece with Britain's Perry, a three-time Wimbledon champion who was considered a good bet to beat Vines. The American defeated him 49–35 in the Emblematic World Professional Title series in 1938. At his best in these years, Vines brought back the "rifle" shots that had been so convincing in 1932.

Vines remained the number-one professional on the tour until 1937, when his interest in tennis waned. During the last part of the decade, Vines was more important as a coach and inspiration than a player. His occasional workouts and practice play with the young Jack Kramer inspired Kramer to make his own game a combination of Vines's and Don Budge's styles. Years later, Kramer wrote, "Hell, when Elly was on, you'd be lucky to get your racket on the ball once you served it."

Keen for a new challenge, Vines took up professional golf, perhaps reasoning that his power and accuracy might be better served hitting on the tee. Vines never made a sensation in golf, but he was a solid player, reaching the semifinals of the Professional Golf Association Championship in 1951. He died in March 1994 at age eighty-two.

Vines is remembered as a hard-hitting tennis player who had a brief but spectacular career. Even the rise of "big hitters" like Boris Becker, Andre Agassi, and Pete Sampras did not dissuade those who had seen him play. At his peak, they maintained, he was simply the hardest hitter who ever stroked a tennis ball. Occasionally journalists would ask Vines whether he wished he had tempered his shots more and prolonged his tennis career. His answer invariably was, "If I had played it differently, it wouldn't have been my game." Vines was honored with other tennis champions at the Wimbledon Centenary in 1977.

★

Vines wrote four books on tennis. Three were solo efforts: *Tennis Simplified for Everybody, by Ellsworth Vines, Jr.: Basic Principles of the Game Explained in an Illustrated Series of Questions and Answers* (1933); *How to Play Better Tennis* (1938); and *Ellsworth Vines' Quick Way to Better Tennis: A Practical Book on Tennis for Men and Women* (1939). He also wrote, with Gene Vier, *Tennis: Myth and Method* (1978). Jack Kramer records his comments on Vines in his autobiography, written with Frank Deford, *The Game* (1979). A profile of Vines is in the *New York Times* (3 July 1932). An obituary is in the *New York Times* (20 Mar. 1994).

SAMUEL WILLARD CROMPTON

WADDELL, George Edward ("Rube") (*b.* 13 October 1876 in Bradford, Pennsylvania; *d.* 1 April 1914 in San Antonio, Texas), one of baseball's most famous left-handed pitchers, whose 1904 feat of 349 strikeouts in one season held the record for 61 years.

Waddell grew up on a family farm in Butler County, Pennsylvania, one of five children of John and Mary Waddell. He developed a muscular farmer's physique and learned how to throw by hurling rocks at the crows that plagued newly sown seeds during spring planting. Even as a young boy Waddell gained a reputation both as an athlete and as a braggart and eccentric. He always had a fascination with fire fighting and would run off, no matter the occasion at hand, if he heard about a fire in progress. He was also susceptible to other childlike temptations. On several occasions while pitching for local ball clubs, someone came by with fishing gear and easily lured Waddell off the ball field. Yet Waddell was, without any doubt, the best pitcher almost anyone had ever seen. He could hurl a fastball and spin curves like no other, and all with complete accuracy. Waddell was six feet, one-and-a-half inches tall, and generally weighed about 195 pounds. With his broad farm boy shoulders and equally broad grin, people readily came to refer to him as a "rube," and the nickname stuck. Waddell never actually liked the nickname; his friends and teammates always called him "Eddie." Waddell never finished high school, but was briefly in the Pennsylvania National Guard in 1897.

Waddell pitched well for some local clubs in western Pennsylvania, and in the late summer of 1897 he had gained enough of a reputation to be signed by the Louisville Colonels, then a team in the National League (NL). He pitched well for Louisville and was a hit with the fans, but his drinking and eccentric fun-loving ways irritated his manager, future Hall of Famer Fred Clarke. After the 1897 season, Clarke dropped Waddell from the club. In the next season, he pitched for several minor league teams, continuing to show incredible talent and outlandish behavior. Pitching for a team in Chatham, Ontario, Waddell several times called off his fielders and struck out the side with no defense behind him. He did this in several exhibition games and later tried, but was not allowed, to do it in the majors during regular season games (although he once had his outfielders sit down on the edge of the infield for an inning).

The Colonels took Waddell back toward the end of the 1899 season. With the Louisville club then merging with the Pittsburgh Pirates, Waddell, along with teammate Honus Wagner, found himself back in western Pennsylvania. Back home, Waddell married Florence Dunning on 21 October 1899 and opened the 1900 season with the Pirates. Fred Clarke was again his manager, and relations between the two remained strained. In July Waddell was tossed off the club. For a month, he pitched for the town

Rube Waddell, from an American Tobacco Co. baseball card, c. 1909–1911. BASEBALL CARDS FROM THE BENJAMIN K. EDWARDS COLLECTION/THE LIBRARY OF CONGRESS

of Punxsutawney, Pennsylvania, where, in late July, Connie Mack of the new American League (AL) Milwaukee Brewers came and signed him. An entourage of Punxsutawney citizens, including the mayor, turned out at the railroad station to make sure Waddell left town.

Waddell felt comfortable under Mack and pitched brilliantly. In one Sunday doubleheader against the Chicago Orphans, Waddell went the distance winning the first game, which stretched for seventeen innings. Then he came back out and pitched a shutout in the second game. Mack let him go fishing for three days as a reward. Waddell won ten games in four weeks for Milwaukee and received such notice that Pittsburgh reclaimed him on 2 September 1900. Back with the Pirates, Waddell and Clarke continued to clash. Despite his tense relations with Clarke, and being off the club for two full months that season, Waddell still led the NL in strikeouts. (In April he had promised people he would do that, and he was true to his word.) Waddell started the next season with the Pirates, but a few months into the schedule, an again fed-up Clarke traded him to Chicago (for a cigar).

Chicago's management did not know how to handle Waddell either. After three months, Waddell quit the team and ventured out to the West Coast on a barnstorming tour. A club in Los Angeles (the Loo-Loos) signed him for 1902. There he played to great acclaim, so much so that at the end of June, Mack, now the manager of the AL Philadelphia Athletics, enticed Waddell to come back East and play for him again. Comfortable under Mack's management, Waddell tore through the AL. From July to September, he compiled 24 wins and struck out 210, probably the greatest half season any pitcher ever had. With Waddell's fearsome pitching, Philadelphia won the AL pennant. That October, the NL refused to take part in a playoff, so Waddell and Philadelphia laid claim to the championship of baseball.

For the next several seasons, Waddell's pitching continued to terrorize the AL. Unlike the modern game, players then did not swing for the fences but just to make contact. Home runs and strikeouts were thus more rare. Despite this, Waddell struck out over 300 batters in several successive seasons. Before this, no one had ever topped 200. As a strikeout artist, Rube was in a class by himself. In nineteen months of pitching from July 1902 to September 1905, he struck out 1,149 batters, 349 in 1904 alone. The next highest strikeout total in the league in 1904 was 180. Waddell's 1904 record stood for decades. It was seldom even approached and was not broken until 1965 (by Sandy Koufax), with a longer season and with hitters swinging for the fences.

When he was on his game, Waddell was absolutely unhittable. The problem was that he was not always on form. As unfathomable as he was to opposing batters, Waddell was equally uncontrollable to his teammates and manager. After his first marriage ended in divorce, Waddell married May Wynne Skinner, but this second marriage on 2 June 1903 did anything but settle him down. Nothing did, and the lack of dependability inevitably led to problems. In September 1905 the A's were on the verge of winning the AL pennant, with Waddell set to lead them into the World Series against the New York Giants. Waddell injured his shoulder amid some silly horseplay with a teammate and had to sit out the series, which the Giants then won. Such undependability irritated teammates, and after narrowly losing the pennant to the Detroit Tigers in 1907 (with Waddell yielding a home run to Ty Cobb in a key game), several A's went to Mack demanding Waddell be traded. Mack yielded and sold Waddell to the St. Louis Browns.

Waddell pitched well for one season with St. Louis. He led the Browns in wins, and they nearly won the pennant. He also exacted revenge on Philadelphia that summer, striking out sixteen A's in one game, a single game mark that stood for thirty years.

By 1908 Waddell's drinking and generally undisciplined living had eroded his pitching skills. He continued to draw fans to games but was no longer the marvel he once was. Managers found him less useful and no less troublesome. After Waddell was hit on the elbow by a pitch (thrown by Eddie Cicotte) in May 1910, his major league career was over. He continued to pitch in the minors for several seasons. He married a third time (to Madge Maguire on 10 April 1910; they divorced in 1911), and clung to the false hope that a major league club would give him another chance.

Wintering at the Hickman, Kentucky, home of Joe Cantillon, his minor league manager, in 1912 and 1913, Waddell did several bouts of yeoman work, helping to save the town from flooding. He spent days in icy waters laying sandbags, an exposure to the cold that led to pneumonia and pleurisy. His health was never the same. Pitching for a lowly club in Virginia, Minnesota, in the summer of 1913, Waddell coughed incessantly and collapsed on the mound several times. That autumn he was picked up on the streets of St. Louis, a vagrant, now infected with tuberculosis. A sister in San Antonio took him in, hoping the warm climate would prove restorative. The disease was too strong, however, and Waddell died in the spring of 1914, on April Fools' Day. He is buried in San Antonio Mission Burial Park. Waddell left no children. His only legacy was that of one of the greatest and zaniest characters who ever played baseball. One of America's first baseball idols, he was celebrated as much for his off-field antics as for his greatness as a pitcher, and deservedly in both cases. Waddell was inducted into the National Baseball Hall of Fame in 1946.

★

Information about Waddell and his career can be found in Mike Shatzkin, ed., *The Ballplayers* (1990), and Alan Howard Levy, *The Zany, Brilliant Life of a Strikeout Artist* (2000). The website http://www.retroactive.com/july97/rube3.html, is a well-written but rather hard-hitting three-page article about Waddell. An obituary is in the *New York Times* (2 Apr. 1914).

Alan H. Levy

WAGNER, John Peter ("Honus") (*b.* 24 February 1874 in Mansfield [now Carnegie], Pennsylvania; *d.* 5 December 1955 in Carnegie, Pennsylvania), Hall of Fame shortstop for the Pittsburgh Pirates.

Wagner was one of six children of German immigrant parents, Peter Wagner, a coal miner, and Kathryn Wolf, a homemaker. Called "Honus," a mangled form of the German *Johannes,* Wagner attended a parochial school for six years until age twelve, when he followed his father and older brother into the coalfields in the Pittsburgh area, and earned $3.50 a week for loading coal.

Honus Wagner, 1909. AP/Wide World Photos

At an early age Wagner developed a love for baseball, playing catch and pickup games whenever he was not working and showing a natural talent for the sport. In 1893 Wagner quit working in the mines and began to play in a local semiprofessional league for $3 to $5 a game. The next year he played for a semiprofessional team in Dennison, Ohio. A fast base runner, a potent right-handed batter, and a strong thrower, Wagner became a professional player in 1895, signing a contract for $35 a month to play for the Steubenville, Ohio, team in the Inter-State League. Playing both shortstop and the outfield, he hit .369 in forty-four games before the team folded in June. For the remainder of the 1895 season Wagner played with Adrian, Michigan, in the Michigan State League and then with Warren, Pennsylvania, in the Iron and Oil League, hitting .365 with Adrian and .369 with Warren. During the 1895 season Wagner first made a concerted effort to improve his skills and to study baseball. Beginning a practice that continued throughout his career, he looked for ways to better his swing and base running techniques and carefully observed opposing pitchers to identify their pitching tendencies.

In February 1896 Wagner signed to play with the Paterson, New Jersey, team in the Atlantic League at $125 a month. He had a sensational season, batting .348, hitting for power, and stealing bases while playing mostly at first base. Wagner began the 1897 season with Paterson at third base, but in July his contract was sold to the Louisville Colonels of the National League (NL) for $2,100. Wagner immediately became the Colonels center fielder at a salary of $250 a month and usually batted in the third or fourth spot, hitting .338 in sixty-one games in his first major league season. During the next two years he hit .303 and .336 respectively while playing first and third bases and the outfield.

After the Louisville franchise was discontinued in early 1900, Wagner and several other outstanding players from the Colonels joined the Pittsburgh Pirates. Their addition enabled the Pirates to flourish during the next decade. The team finished in first place in 1901, 1902, 1903, and 1909 and had four second-place finishes. Wagner played various infield and outfield positions until 1903, when he became the regular shortstop. He played eighteen seasons in Pittsburgh, earning $2,400 in his first year, $5,000 a season for the next seven years, and $10,000 in 1908, then the top salary in baseball.

For most of his years in Pittsburgh, Wagner was the team's offensive leader. Counting his years with the Colonels, he hit over .300 for seventeen consecutive seasons and led the NL in batting for eight seasons. His best average was .381 in 1900, and his career average was .327 with 3,415 hits at a time when batters had to contend with the "dead" ball, trick pitches like the "spitball," and long outfields. A line-drive hitter who held his hands slightly apart on the bat, Wagner was a free swinger. He hit the ball with power to all fields, leading the NL in doubles for seven years and triples three times. Throughout his career Wagner was a consistent run producer, driving in 1,732 runs and leading the league in runs batted in five times. Wagner was also a speedster on the base paths. He stole 722 bases and five times was the NL's top base thief. His speed on the base paths led fans to dub him "the Flying Dutchman."

Wagner was an unlikely-looking shortstop. Standing six feet tall and weighing 200 pounds, he was barrel chested and bowlegged, which made him appear ungainly. But he had nimble feet, large hands, and long arms, and once he learned the shortstop position he became an outstanding fielder, scooping up everything hit even remotely near him and using his accurate, rifle arm to throw out runners with ease. He led NL shortstops in fielding average four times, and even after his batting average began to slip, his fielding kept him in the starting lineup.

The 1909 season was probably the high point of Wagner's career. He led the NL in batting average, doubles, and runs batted in, and the Pirates won the league pennant with 110 victories in 154 games. In the World Series the Pirates faced the Detroit Tigers, led by Ty Cobb, a twenty-two-year-old outfielder who led the American League in batting in 1909 with a .377 average. Wagner clearly outplayed his younger rival. Cobb batted .231, drove in 6 runs, and stole 2 bases, while Wagner batted .333, drove in 7 runs, and stole 6 bases, leading the Pirates to a 4 to 3 series victory over the Tigers.

The series, which was marked by widespread bench jockeying, hit batters, and the spiking of players, produced the most famous tale about Wagner. Cobb was a feared base runner who tried to intimidate opposing players by sliding into a base with his spikes up. He reached first base in the fifth inning of the first game and quickly stole second base, sliding into the bag underneath Wagner's sweeping tag. The mixture of the heated atmosphere of the series and the stature of Wagner and Cobb led to an exaggerated story about this incident that took on a life of its own. According to the story, when Cobb reached first base he yelled to Wagner, "I'm coming down on the next pitch, you big krauthead." Wagner was said to have yelled back, "I'll be ready." Cobb then took off for second base and slid into that base with his spikes flashing. Wagner applied a hard tag to Cobb's head and, depending on the source, either loosened three of Cobb's teeth, bloodied his lips, or nearly decapitated him. Other than Cobb stealing second base, the story has no truth. However, it has endured, perhaps for the way it epitomizes the two men in the public's eyes, the aggressive Cobb and the stalwart Wagner.

On the field Wagner was a tough competitor, but in person he was unpretentious, forthright, good natured, and simple in his ways. He was well liked by other players and beloved by fans. He was always willing to talk to them and reputedly signed as many as ten thousand autographs in a year.

In 1914 Wagner, now forty years of age, hit only .252, the first time in his major league career he did not hit .300. While his average slightly improved during the next two years, he did not again top .300 in those years. On 30 December 1916 Wagner married Bessie Bain Smith; they had two daughters. Saying his wife's "good home cooking" was taking its toll on him, he quickly gained weight, and whether because of a salary dispute or concern over his waning skills, he did not join the Pirates for the 1917 season until 7 June. The Pirates, who had lost forty out of their first sixty games, were atrocious. In late June the manager was fired, and Wagner reluctantly took his place. The team won its first game under Wagner, then lost the next four, prompting him to say that managing was not his type of job, and shortly thereafter he quit. No longer able to cover the ground at shortstop, Wagner alternated between first and third base, but he did hit over .300 into late July. He then injured his right foot, and when he returned to the lineup, he performed poorly. He finished the season batting .265, and with the Pirates mired in mediocrity, he retired.

During the following years Wagner played semiprofessional baseball in the Pittsburgh area, was physical education director at Carnegie Technical Institute from 1919 through 1921, served as commissioner of the National Semi-Pro Baseball Congress for six years, and became the unofficial patriarch of baseball in Pittsburgh. He also was involved in two sporting goods businesses, both of which failed. Anxious to get back into professional baseball after these failed ventures, Wagner became a coach with the Pirates in 1933, a post he held through the 1951 season. He died of heart failure and is buried in Pittsburgh.

At the time of his retirement in 1917, Wagner held virtually every NL batting record and was considered baseball's greatest player. In 1936 he was one of the first five players selected to the Baseball Hall of Fame, and in 1969 the Baseball Writers' Association named him the best shortstop in baseball's first one hundred years. Some argue that Cobb and Babe Ruth should be ranked ahead of Wagner as the greatest players of all time. But when baseball was establishing itself as the nation's pastime, Wagner was its premier player, and no other shortstop combined his excellence in the field and at the plate.

Wagner played more for the love of the game than for money. His salary never exceeded $10,000 a year, and he always refused to cash in on his fame. When a tobacco company put pictures of famous players in its cigarette packs, he made it stop distributing his because he did not want his celebrity status to be used to encourage young people to smoke. The few of these prints in circulation are among the most valuable baseball cards.

★

Material relating to Wagner's career is in his biographical file in the Carnegie Library in Pittsburgh. For full-length biographies of Wagner see Dennis de Valeria and Jeanne Burke de Valeria, *Honus Wagner: A Biography* (1995); William Hageman, *Honus: The Life and Times of a Baseball Hero* (1996); and Arthur D. Hittner, *Honus Wagner: The Life of Baseball's "Flying Dutchman"* (1996). See also Bob Smizik, *The Pittsburgh Pirates* (1990). Wagner's statistics are in *Total Baseball* (1999), edited by John Thorn, Pete Palmer, Michael Gershman, and David Pietrusza with Matthew Silverman and Sean Matthew. Obituaries are in the *New York Times* (6 Dec. 1955), the *Pittsburgh Post-Gazette* (6 Dec. 1955), the *Pittsburgh Press* (6 Dec. 1955), and the *Pittsburgh Sun-Telegraph* (6 Dec. 1955).

JOHN KENNEDY OHL

WALKER, (Ewell) Doak, Jr. (*b.* 1 January 1927 in Dallas, Texas; *d.* 27 September 1998 in Steamboat Springs, Colorado), college football legend who was one of the first players to earn consensus All-America honors three consecutive years, the first junior to win the Heisman Trophy, and a member of both the college (1959) and professional (1986) football Halls of Fame.

Always called "Doak," perhaps to distinguish him from his father, Ewell Doak Walker, Sr., Walker made football history at Highland Park High School in North Dallas and at Southern Methodist University (SMU)—both institutions were located within a few blocks of the Walker family's Stanford Avenue home. His father, a one-time teacher and coach who became the assistant superintendent of the Dallas Independent School District, and his mother, Emma, also a teacher, encouraged Walker to participate in sports even though he was of less-than-average size. Walker's parents, especially his father, taught family values long before the phrase became a buzzword. Walker explained that as a young adult, "My dad taught us to be competitive, but he was also very big on sportsmanship. . . . The values I have lived my life with, I got from my father a long time ago."

While Walker was at Highland Park High, another football immortal, Bobby Layne, was in the same backfield. Layne was a year ahead of Walker, and although they chose different colleges, they were reunited in the backfield of the Detroit Lions of the National Football League (NFL) in the franchise's championship days of the 1950s. After Walker graduated from high school in 1944, he and Layne joined the merchant marine together in January 1945. When World War II ended, it was assumed that Walker would join Layne on the University of Texas Longhorns.

Doak Walker, 1951. © BETTMANN/CORBIS

He almost did. The two buddies were discharged in New Orleans in October 1945 and decided to stay over and see the sights, also taking in the SMU-Tulane football game. Their old Highland Park coach Rusty Russell had become an assistant coach at SMU and offered Walker a ride back to Dallas on the team train. By the time the team arrived home, Walker was a member of the SMU Mustangs; a week later he faced Layne across a Dallas gridiron. A touchdown pass by Layne won the game for the Longhorns, 12–7. Although Walker only played five games in 1945, his performance with SMU was so stellar that he was voted to the All-Southwest Conference team.

Despite having served in the merchant marine, Walker was drafted by the U.S. Army in 1946. He returned to SMU as a sophomore in 1947 and again began leading the Mustangs to success. As a consensus All-American and a triple-threat tailback, Walker paced the SMU team to a 9–0–1 record. Only a 19–19 tie with Texas Christian University (TCU) marred a perfect record. In the postseason Cotton Bowl, SMU was tied again, 13–13, by Pennsylvania State University.

Although SMU lost to the University of Missouri, 20–14, and tied pesky TCU, 7–7, Walker was even better during the 1948 season. He was a unanimous All-American and became the first of only a handful of juniors to win the Heisman Trophy. The Mustangs were again in the Cotton Bowl after the regular season of 1948. They defeated the University of Oregon, 21–13, as Walker rushed for sixty-six yards and completed six of ten passes for seventy-nine yards. His only punt of the game traveled seventy-nine yards, and he kicked two extra points.

Walker's senior season was disappointing. Injuries caused him to miss several games, and the team slipped to a 5–4–1 record. Walker wrote to the All-America selection board and asked them not to consider him, since he had missed some important games. His request was ignored and he became a consensus All-American for the third consecutive year. During this time Dallas's Cotton Bowl became known as the "House That Doak Built." The on-campus 17,000-seat SMU stadium was too small to accommodate all those who wanted to see "the Doaker" play. Mustang games were moved to the 45,507-seat Cotton Bowl, which was further enlarged to 67,431 seats before Walker's illustrious career was over. Walker graduated from SMU in 1950, earning a B.S. degree.

In an era before mass communication, Walker was a legitimate national hero. He graced the covers of many magazines, including *Life*. He and his fiancée, Norma Peterson, were featured on the cover of *Collier's*. The couple married on 17 March 1950 and later had four children. As a professional player, Walker was the cover subject of an early issue of *Sports Illustrated* (3 October 1955). Walker left SMU as a bona fide Texas legend and with a bundle of records—3,582 total yards split almost evenly between running and passing, 38 touchdowns, 57 extra points, 288 points in 41 games, 27 receptions, 8 interceptions, a near-40-yard average on punts, a 15-yard average on punt returns, and a 29.4-yard average on kickoff returns—including a nation-leading 38.7-yard average in 1947. His coach Matty Bell added, "Doak could have been an All-America on his blocking alone."

Walker's size (five feet, eleven inches tall and 168 pounds) was on the low end of average for college backs in his era, but was decidedly small for a professional football halfback. Nevertheless, in 1950 he was reunited with his high-school buddy Layne on the Detroit Lions. His professional career was brief—only six years—but brilliant; he was inducted into the Pro Football Hall of Fame in 1986. Walker led the NFL in scoring as a rookie with 128 points and was named the Rookie of the Year. He was selected to five Pro Bowls and led the league in scoring in his final season (ninety-six points in 1955). When the Lions won championships in 1952 and 1953, Walker contributed mightily with a sixty-seven-yard touchdown in the 1952 title game, and the winning extra point in the 17–16 victory in 1953. When he retired after what was really a five-and-a-half-year career (he only played seven games in 1952), his career point total of 534 was incredibly the third all-time in NFL history.

After retiring as a player, Walker became a national sales representative in the construction business and eventually relocated to Denver. After he and his first wife divorced in 1965, Walker married Gladys "Skeeter" Werner, of the famous Olympic skiing Werner family, in 1969. He loved Colorado, skiing, and living in Steamboat Springs, despite once having been caught in an avalanche. On 30 January 1998 Walker was involved in a skiing accident that left him paralyzed from the neck down. He died of complications early that autumn and was cremated. His ashes were scattered at Longs Peak, Colorado.

Walker was one of football's all-time greats, and a modest, humble, and sincere celebrity for all of his adult life. He had a knack of doing whatever it took on the gridiron. His friend Bobby Layne said, "When the score was 20–0, we're ahead, Doak wasn't worth a damn. But tied 7–7 or down 13–14 and not much time left, he'd do the unbelievable." In Texas—where everything seems bigger, including legends—Walker's legend was bigger than most. His name continues to come before the public each year when college football presents the nation's top running back with the Doak Walker Award.

★

There are two biographies of Walker: Dorothy Kendall, *Doak Walker: Three-Time All-American* (1950), and Whit Canning, *Doak Walker: More Than a Hero* (1997). Walker's life and career are discussed in Kern Tips, *Texas Style* (1964), and Dan Jenkins, *I'll Tell You One Thing* (1999). An obituary is in the *New York Times* (28 Sept. 1998).

JIM CAMPBELL

WALKER, Edward Patrick ("Mickey") (*b.* 13 July 1901 in Elizabeth, New Jersey; *d.* 28 April 1981 in Freehold, New Jersey), middleweight and welterweight boxing champion during the 1920s, nicknamed the "Toy Bulldog" for his ferocity in the ring.

Walker was the son of Michael Walker, a bricklayer, and Elizabeth Higgins Walker. Walker's father wanted him to become an architect, but the boy's high-spirited tenacity led him to the career of boxing. Walker grew up in an Irish Catholic household in the Keighry Head neighborhood of Elizabeth, New Jersey, where he attended the Sacred Heart Grammar School for eight years before being expelled for misbehavior. He earned the nickname "Mickey" because he had a pug nose.

Walker went to work for the architectural firm George B. Post and Company during the day and attended the Mechanics Institute in the evenings. He was too young to enlist during World War I, so he became a riveter at the Elizabeth shipyard and later at the Staten Island shipyard. At the shipyard, the volatile young man got into a fight with Eddie McGill, who, unknown to Walker, was a professional boxer. Five thousand employees left their work sites to watch the twenty-five-minute bout, which Walker won. The fight, however, cost him his job. He spent a year out of work before deciding to become a boxer in 1919.

Mickey Walker, 1929. AP/WIDE WORLD PHOTOS

Walker fought his first professional match against Dominic "Young" Orsini on 10 February 1919 in Elizabeth. His mother watched the fight from a nearby rooftop (women were barred from attending fights) and became so wrapped up in the action that she broke a window and was arrested. Walker fought almost every three weeks during his first three years as a fighter for a record of 21–5, with 33 no decisions. ("No decisions" were often handed down during this era because anticorruption laws barred referees and judges from making decisions unless there was a knockout.) These successes won for Walker the opportunity to challenge the current world welterweight champion, Jack Britton, for the title. He had fought Britton the previous year in a twelve-round no-decision match. This time, the two men met at Madison Square Garden on 1 November 1922 and Walker won a decisive victory; at age twenty-one, he became the welterweight champion of the world.

After successfully defending his title against Pete Latzo in 1923, Walker was given the nickname "Toy Bulldog," a reference to his tenacity and persistence in the ring, by the publicist Francis Albertanti. He then recovered from a broken hand before defending his title in 1924 against Lew Tendler and Bobby Barrett. In 1925, after the manager Jack Bulger's death, Walker came under the guidance of Jack Kearns, the former manager of Jack Dempsy. "Kearns and Walker became great friends," wrote Luckett V. Davis in *American National Biography* (1999). "Always noted for high living, Walker picked up the pace, freely enjoying nightlife, gambling, and women." He married Maude Kelly in 1923 and they settled in suburban Rumson, New Jersey. The couple had two children, but Walker seldom saw his family.

In 1925 at the Polo Grounds in New York before 40,000 fans, Walker fought Harry Greb for the world middleweight championship. Walker came on strong, scoring well in the early rounds. Weakened by drinking an emetic fluid to lose weight, Greb seemed unprepared for the match. As the fight progressed, however, Greb began to use his speed to his advantage, closing Walker's right eye and winning a decisive victory in the final rounds. Later that night, when the two men were drinking at the Silver Slipper Saloon, Walker made a reference to Greb's illegal "thumbing" in the ring and the two stepped outside to fight once again. Walker always claimed that he won the second fight.

Walker began having trouble meeting the welterweight limit in 1926. He lost the title to Pete Latzo on 20 May

1926, and received a sound beating from Joe Dundee, who became the future champion. Many believed Walker's career as a boxer was over. After resting for several months, Walker returned on 3 December 1926 to fight Tiger Flowers for the middleweight championship in Chicago. Although Walker won the decision and the title, many believed Flowers had won the match; however, because he had knocked his opponent down, Walker maintained he had won fairly. He successfully defended his title against Tommy Milligan in London in 1927, and twice against Ace Hudkins in 1928 and 1929.

Kearns knew that the big money lay in a higher weight class, so in March 1929 in Chicago, Walker challenged the light heavyweight Tommy Loughran. Although Walker lost decisively, he successfully challenged the heavyweight Johnny Risko in 1930 and 1931. This led to a matchup with Jack Sharkey, who was five inches taller and twenty-nine pounds heavier than Walker. Living up to his reputation, the Toy Bulldog came out fighting and never let up. Although the fight was declared a draw, many felt Walker had won. Walker relinquished his middleweight title in 1931, and continued to win against heavyweights like Paolino Uzcudun, Salvatore Ruggirello, and King Levinsky. Walker had divorced his first wife Maude Kelly in 1930. He married Clara Hellmers in 1931; they had one son.

Walker suffered a brutal beating by Max Schmeling in September 1932, leading Kearns to stop the fight after eight rounds. After challenging Maxie Rosenbloom for the light heavyweight title and losing, Walker continued to box in a number of nontitled fights until he retired in 1935.

That same year Walker opened a saloon, the Toy Bulldog, in his hometown of Elizabeth, and in 1939, after years of heavy drinking, abruptly quit. He had separated from Hellmers and divorced in 1939. That same year he married Eleanor Marvil; they had one child. Walker and Marvil divorced in 1946, and he remarried Hellmers, who again divorced him in 1948. Walker remarried Maude Kelly that same year, but they divorced in 1955. In 1956 he married Martha Chudy Gallagher. Including the remarriages to his first and second wives, Walker was married six times and had four children.

In the early 1940s Walker began to paint, and in 1955 he held a one-man show at the Associated American Artists Galleries on Fifth Avenue in New York City. When comparing boxing to art, he noted they were both means of expression; physical expression was fine when he was a young man, but now art had taken its place. In 1955 he was elected to the Boxing Hall of Fame. Six years later he published his autobiography, *Mickey Walker: The Toy Bulldog and His Times.* Walker died of Parkinson's disease at the age of seventy-nine; his remains were cremated.

Walker's boxing career spanned 17 years, and over the course of 163 bouts he scored 60 knockouts and won 33 fights by decision. The sportswriter Jim Murray argued that the Toy Bulldog's love of the bottle kept him from becoming the only 155-pound heavyweight champion. Walker may not have won the heavyweight title, but he did win both the welterweight and middleweight titles, a rare enough feat. "Through it all," Bert Randolph Sugar wrote in *The 100 Greatest Boxers of All Time* (1984), "this man with the happy-go-lucky attitude . . . and the penchant for attempting seemingly impossible odds, will forever be known as boxing's version of 'The Happy Warrior.'" In 1990 Walker was elected to the International Boxing Hall of Fame.

★

Walker's autobiography, written with Joe Reichler, *Mickey Walker: The Toy Bulldog and His Times* (1961), provides a lively account of his boxing career. For a detailed biographical sketch see John A. Garraty and Mark C. Carnes, eds., *American National Biography* (1999). Highlights from Walker's career are included in Bert Randolph Sugar, *The 100 Greatest Boxers of All Time* (1984). An obituary is in the *New York Times* (29 Apr. 1981).

RONNIE D. LANKFORD, JR.

WALKER, Moses Fleetwood ("Fleet") (*b.* 7 October 1856 in Mount Pleasant, Ohio; *d.* 11 May 1924 in Cleveland, Ohio), baseball catcher, inventor, businessman, author, and anti-racism activist, who in 1884 was the first and last African American to play Major League Baseball until Jackie Robinson joined the Brooklyn Dodgers in 1947.

Walker and his four siblings were born in Mount Pleasant, a southeastern Ohio community with strong antislavery sentiments. Walker's father, Moses W. Walker, initially worked as a barrel maker, but by 1860 he had relocated the family to Steubenville, Ohio, making his livelihood as a physician and later as a Methodist Episcopal minister. Walker's mother, Caroline O'Harra, was a homemaker.

In 1877 the family moved to Oberlin, Ohio, where Walker, a graduate of Steubenville High School, enrolled in Oberlin College's preparatory program. In autumn 1878 Walker gained admission to Oberlin College, which was in the vanguard of racial and gender integration, and played catcher on a club team in 1880. He joined Oberlin's first intercollegiate baseball team in 1881. The slender, handsome Walker, with his affability and athletic prowess, was popular on campus. After completing his junior year in summer 1881, Walker enrolled at the University of Michigan in Ann Arbor in spring 1882 to play baseball and study law. Walker neither received a law degree nor practiced law. He ended his studies at Michigan in 1883.

During summer 1881 Walker played semiprofessional baseball for the White Sewing Machine Company in Cleve-

Fleet Walker *(middle row, far left)* and the Oberlin College baseball team. AP/WIDE WORLD PHOTOS

land. In August, Walker's team traveled south to play the Louisville (Kentucky) Eclipse, where racial discrimination kept him from eating breakfast with his team at a hotel and prevented him from playing. The following summer Walker played semiprofessional baseball in New Castle, Pennsylvania.

Walker joined professional baseball in 1883, playing for the Toledo (Ohio) Blue Stockings of the Northwestern League. In sixty games the right-handed batter hit a modest .251. Although he weighed only 160 pounds, his agility made him a decent catcher during an era when a wire mask and calfskin gloves were the catcher's only protection. Walker encountered the racial hostility of Adrian "Cap" Anson, the future Hall of Fame player and manager for the Chicago White Stockings, who announced before an exhibition game in Toledo that his team would not take the field against an African American. However, the White Stockings agreed to play after being informed they would forfeit their share of the gate receipts.

In 1884 Toledo joined the American Association, which was recognized by the National League as the other major league. On 1 May 1884 Walker became the first African American to play baseball at the major league level. Despite playing in only forty-two of the Blue Stockings' 104 games due to injuries and despite facing threats of violence and verbal taunts, especially in southern cities, Walker hit a respectable .263. (During 1884 Walker's younger brother Welday also played six games for Toledo, making him the second African American to play in the major leagues.) In retirement the Irish-born Tony Mullane, Toledo's talented pitcher, claimed that Walker was the best catcher he ever worked with, "but I disliked a Negro and whenever I had to pitch to him I used to pitch anything I wanted without looking at his signals." The gentlemanly, articulate Walker was a fan favorite in Toledo, but nonetheless was released by the club in October, making him the last African American to play for a major league team until Jackie Robinson joined the Brooklyn Dodgers in 1947.

Walker returned to minor league baseball in 1885, playing for Cleveland in the Western League and for Waterbury, Connecticut, in the Southern New England League. From 1887 through 1889 he played in the International League (Newark, New Jersey, in 1887 and Syracuse, New York, in 1888 and 1889). Syracuse released the nearly thirty-three-year-old Walker on 23 August 1889 due to injuries and diminished skills. Walker was the last African American to play in the International League, the highest level of the minors, until Jackie Robinson played for Montreal in 1946.

In 1890 Walker took a job as a railway mail clerk in Syracuse. Arrested for the stabbing death of a white man during a street fight on 9 April 1891, Walker was acquitted. Arabella Taylor, a former Oberlin classmate whom he had married on 9 July 1882, died on 12 June 1895. They had two sons and a daughter. Walker married Ednah Jane Mason, another former Oberlin classmate, on 14 May 1898. Arrested on federal charges of mail robbery on 19 September 1898, Walker served a one-year sentence, after which he moved back to Steubenville and purchased the Union Hotel. In 1902 he edited the *Equator,* a newspaper dedicated to African-American issues. In 1908 Walker wrote and published *Our Home Colony: A Treatise on the Past, Present, and Future of the Negro Race in America,* a book that expressed disillusionment with the United States and urged African Americans to return to Africa.

In 1904 he purchased the opera house in Cadiz, Ohio, which hosted opera, live drama, and motion pictures. In 1920 he registered three patents for equipment to expedite movie reel loading and changing. (In 1891 he had patented an artillery shell.) On 20 May 1920 his second wife died, and in 1922 he sold the opera house and retired to Cleveland, where he died from pneumonia. He is buried next to his first wife in Steubenville's Union Cemetery.

Walker, a journeyman catcher, competed with white players during a time when segregation eliminated most opportunities for African-American players. Baseball, believed to be a symbol for the American values of equality, fair play, and cooperation, was for Walker the American dream denied.

★

The Moses F. Walker file at the Oberlin College archives contains a range of documents, clippings, and secondary publications. The National Baseball Hall of Fame Library in Cooperstown, New York, has a clippings file on Walker. David W. Zang, *Fleet Walker's Divided Heart: The Life of Baseball's First Black Major Leaguer* (1995), is an excellent source of information. See also two pieces by Jerry Malloy, "Out at Home," in *The Armchair Book of Baseball II,* ed. John Thorn (1987), which focuses on race relations in professional baseball in 1887, and "Moses Fleetwood Walker," in *Nineteenth-Century Stars,* ed. Robert L. Tiemann and Mark Rucker (1989), which provides a career overview and statistical record. Donald Lankiewicz, "Fleet Walker in the Twilight Zone," *Queen City Heritage* (summer 1992): 2–11, places Walker's baseball career in the context of changing race relations in the late nineteenth century. Obituaries are in the *Steubenville Herald-Star* (13 May 1924) and the *Cleveland Gazette* (17 May 1924).

PAUL A. FRISCH

WALKER, Roberto Clemente. *See* Clemente (Walker), Roberto.

WALSH, Ed(ward) Augustine (*b.* 14 May 1881 in Plains, Pennsylvania; *d.* 26 May 1959 in Pompano Beach, Florida), Hall of Fame pitcher known for his remarkable physical strength and endurance and for his success with the Chicago White Sox in the early 1900s.

Walsh was the thirteenth child of the Irish immigrants Michael Walsh, a coal miner, and Mary Walsh, a homemaker. After a five-year education at a parochial grade school, he followed his father and brothers into the anthracite fields of eastern Pennsylvania, starting as a mule-team driver at the age of twelve. He developed into an exceptionally powerful six-foot, one-inch, 193-pound miner and enjoyed powering his fastball past batters in local semiprofessional baseball games.

In 1902, on a dare from friends, Walsh walked into a tryout camp, where he won a contract with Wilkes-Barre of the Pennsylvania State League. The Boston Red Sox showed interest in the muscular young right-hander, moving him the following season to their Meriden, Connecticut, club and then up the ladder to the Newark (New Jersey) Bears of the Eastern League. While in Meriden, Walsh met Rosemary Carney, an ice-cream vendor at the ballpark, whom he married in 1904. Charmed by the stark contrast between Meriden's middle-class propriety and the working-class poverty he had known as a child, Walsh gladly moved to his wife's hometown to start a family. The couple raised two sons and lived in the town for most of their lives.

Although Walsh won a total of twenty games during his split season at Meriden and Newark, scouting reports dismissed him as a kid from the boondocks with nothing to offer but a fastball. The Chicago White Sox owner Charles Comiskey had seen Walsh pitch at Newark, however, and drafted him for the bargain price of $750. Walsh reported to spring training in 1904 and won a spot on the White Sox pitching staff.

During his first two seasons in Chicago, "Big Ed" Walsh, as the sportswriters began to call him, was used only sparingly as an extra starter and bullpen short man. While his fastball indeed showed major league hop, he seemed unable to develop any effective breaking balls or off-speed deliveries. Complicating matters further, the brawny rookie did not at first believe that he needed any other pitching tools. The macho Walsh "could strut while sitting down," according to the baseball historians John Holway and Bob Carroll. To remedy the problem, the White Sox manager Fielder Jones brought Walsh under the tutelage of the spitballer Elmer Stricklett. Rooming with Stricklett and taking extra practices with him, Walsh gradually learned the intricacies of the pitch. Realizing that his future in the big leagues depended on it, Walsh put himself to the task until, as he recalled, "I had such control of my spitter that I could hit a tack on a wall with it." And because throwing a spitball required less exertion than his fastball, Walsh found pitching a game to be much less physically taxing.

Walsh was a changed player in 1906, starting 31 games for the White Sox, going the distance in 24 of them, and bringing home a 17–13 record with an earned run average (ERA) of 1.88. His ten shutouts were a major league record that stood until he broke it himself two years later. The White Sox won the American League (AL) pennant that

Ed Walsh, 1906. AP/WIDE WORLD PHOTOS

year, and in an all-Chicago World Series, Walsh struck out seventeen batters and collected two of the four victories in a successful effort against the arch-rival Cubs. They would be the only postseason opportunities of his career.

The White Sox's championship season marked the beginning of seven fat years for Walsh. His greatest season—arguably the greatest season ever enjoyed by any big league pitcher—was 1908. Walsh's numbers from that year are capable of dazzling even the most jaded of baseball fans: 40 wins and 15 losses, with a 1.42 ERA and 269 strikeouts, while leading both leagues in appearances (66), starts (49), innings pitched (464), complete games (42), and shutouts (11). He even chalked up 6 saves for Chicago in 17 relief appearances, and all this while on the mound for a team nicknamed "the Hitless Wonders." The 1908 White Sox had a team batting average of just .224, hitting only three home runs the entire season—one of them by Walsh. Despite the Sox's pathetic offense, their ace pitcher almost single-handedly won them the AL pennant.

On the last day of the 1908 season, with the Sox one game out of first place, Walsh went up against the Cleveland Indians, making his third start in as many days. He pitched a brilliant complete-game four-hitter, striking out fifteen and giving up just one (unearned) run. It was not good enough. His opponent, Addie Joss, pitched a perfect game against the Hitless Wonders, ending the White Sox season.

Walsh continued to be one of baseball's dominant pitchers for a succession of hapless Chicago teams in the years that followed. He was named the AL's Most Valuable Player in both 1911 and 1912, racking up 27 wins and almost 400 innings pitched in each campaign. However, the enormous burden of carrying an entire team was becoming too much for a man in his thirties. What seemed like a minor injury to his right arm at spring training in 1913 never fully healed, and after repeated comeback attempts, he was let go by the White Sox in 1916. A year later he joined the Boston Braves of the National League but was let go after just four appearances.

Walsh desperately hoped to remain a part of the game that had lifted him out the coal mines and made him a national celebrity. He played and managed in the minor leagues and even spent a season as an AL umpire before returning to Chicago as a pitching coach, a job for which the great spitballer was well suited. In 1926 he took a leave from the White Sox to coach the baseball team at Indiana's Notre Dame University, where his two sons were both starting pitchers. His older son Edward Arthur Walsh joined the White Sox pitching staff in 1928, but was struck with rheumatic fever after only four seasons and died shortly thereafter.

Walsh left baseball completely in 1930, following the banning of the spitball. He was easily elected to the National Baseball Hall of Fame in 1946. In his later years he suffered from chronic arthritis in his right arm and in 1957 was forced to leave Meriden for a warmer climate. He died of cancer in Pompano Beach, Florida, two years later, and is buried in that town's Forest Lawn Memorial Gardens.

Among Walsh's many accomplishments were his forty wins in the 1908 season, a total still unequaled in Major League Baseball in 2001; back-to-back complete-game victories in doubleheaders on two separate occasions; and the pitching of six shutouts in a single month, also done twice. One of the great masters of the spitball before the pitch was banned, Walsh had a career ERA of 1.82, which remains at the top of the all-time list in this most highly respected of pitching statistics.

★

Considering the wealth of biographies written about lesser baseball players, it is surprising that there has never been a detailed biography written about Walsh. The National Baseball Hall of

Fame contains a biographical sketch of Walsh and a statistical breakdown of his career, which can be accessed at the Cooperstown, New York, museum or on its website at www.baseballhalloffame.org. Virtually all baseball reference volumes include articles on Walsh; the most informative of these is by George Hilton in David L. Porter, ed., *The Biographical Dictionary of Sports: Baseball* (1987). Obituaries are in the *New York Times* (27 May 1959), and in *Sporting News* (3 June 1959).

DAVID MARC

WALSH, William ("Bill") (*b.* 30 November 1931 in Los Angeles, California) college and professional football coach who led the San Francisco 49ers to three Super Bowl victories and who is credited as the primary creator of the "West Coast offense."

Walsh, the son of a manual laborer and his homemaker wife, lived in Los Angeles until the family relocated to the East Bay area of San Francisco when he was fifteen. He was an outstanding multisport athlete at Hayward Union High School, from which he graduated in 1949. Walsh attended San Mateo Junior College for two years, then moved to San Jose State University; he graduated in 1954 with an M.A. in physical education. Walsh was a member of the football team at San Jose but played sparingly as quarterback and end due to a succession of injuries. He served a brief stint in the armed forces during the Korean War and married his wife, Geri, in 1955; they had three children.

Walsh's coaching career also began in 1955, when his college coach Bob Bronzan hired him as a graduate assistant. Bronzan later recommended Walsh to his next employer, Washington Union High School in Fremont, California, predicting that someday Walsh "will become the outstanding football coach in the United States." Walsh later identified Bronzan as the person who had most greatly influenced his own development as a coach.

In his two years at Washington Union, Walsh developed an innovative passing offense that enabled the team, which had won only once in the three previous seasons, to win a conference championship. In 1960 he became defensive coordinator at the University of California, Berkeley. Over the next seventeen years Walsh worked with some of the best college coaches of his era, including Marv Levy at California (1960 to 1962), and John Ralston at Stanford (1963 to 1965), where he was defensive and recruiting coordinator. Walsh moved to the professional ranks in 1966 as backfield coach for Al Davis and the Oakland Raiders in the National Football League (NFL). After working on his M.B.A. degree at Stanford for a year, which he earned in 1967, Walsh became quarterback coach and offensive coordinator for the legendary coach Paul Brown of an NFL expansion team, the Cincinnati Bengals.

Bill Walsh, 1996. ASSOCIATED PRESS AP

Walsh's eight seasons with the Bengals were among the most important in terms of his maturation as a professional coach, but also some of the most frustrating of his career. He developed two All-Pro quarterbacks, Greg Cook and Kenny Anderson, and installed a new offensive system for backup Virgil Carter when Cook was seriously injured. This system would eventually evolve into the "West Coast offense," a philosophy emphasizing quick reads of the defense by the quarterback, intricate crossing patterns involving three to five receivers, precision timing between quarterback and receiver, extensive use of running backs as receivers, and meticulous pregame planning, including the scripting of a game's first twenty-five plays. During Walsh's eight years in Cincinnati, the Bengals made the playoffs three times. By the early 1970s Walsh was widely hailed as a future head coach; at one point Brown even denied him an opportunity to interview with the Houston Oilers, apparently planning to make Walsh his own successor. But when Brown announced his resignation on 1 January 1976, he selected another assistant, Bill Johnson, as his replacement instead. Walsh has refused to speculate publicly about the snub that left him frustrated and embittered, but others have theorized that Brown feared being overshadowed by an innovative successor.

At age forty-five Walsh worried that his coaching career had reached a dead end. Some observers felt that Walsh's cerebral, innovative style intimidated owners; others speculated that owners hesitated to put him in charge because the legendary Brown had passed him over. Walsh joined the San Diego Chargers in 1976 as an assistant coach and helped Dan Fouts develop as a star quarterback while further refining his offensive concepts under head coach Don Coryell. He accepted the head coaching position at Stanford University in 1977, where in two seasons he produced a 17–7 record. At age forty-eight Walsh finally landed a head coaching position in the NFL in 1979, but with the San Francisco 49ers, the worst team in the league. He inherited a San Francisco team with a dismal 2–14 record. The franchise was in total disarray, having had six head coaches in five seasons.

Walsh, who was named head coach, general manager, and president by 49ers owner Eddie DeBartolo, immediately launched a long-term plan to revitalize the team, beginning with their porous defense. He demonstrated a superb talent for making astute player evaluations, successfully drafting Joe Montana, Dwight Clark, Ronnie Lott, Randy Cross, Roger Craig, and Jerry Rice. Bolstered by DeBartolo's willingness to spend vast sums for much-needed talent, Walsh also lured a number of high-profile free agents to San Francisco. In 1979 the 49ers record was once again 2–14, but the team had been revamped and Walsh's system installed. In 1980 the team's record improved to 6–10, even though a promising start was undercut by key injuries. In 1981 the 49ers shocked the sports world with a 13–3 regular season record, including a dramatic, last-minute 28–27 victory in the conference title game over the Dallas Cowboys. Finally, Walsh vindicated himself with a convincing win over the Bengals in the Super Bowl.

Under Walsh, the 49ers became the "Team of the 1980s," winning a second Super Bowl in 1984 by demolishing the Miami Dolphins 34–16, and a third in 1989, defeating the Bengals 20–16 with a dramatic last-minute touchdown drive. Walsh retired after the 1989 Super Bowl with an NFL coaching record of 102–63. Coaching, Walsh said, had become for him "a very stressful occupation." The team that he built, now coached by his longtime defensive assistant George Seifert, won two more Super Bowls in 1990 and 1995.

Walsh spent the 1990–1991 season garnering mixed reviews as an NBC game-day analyst, and in a surprising move, returned to Stanford for a two-year coaching stint in 1992. He rejoined the 49ers in an advisory capacity in 1994, and in 1999 once again became general manager, implementing a top-to-bottom rebuilding program for a team that had fallen on hard times in the era of free agency and salary caps. Walsh retired at the age of seventy in the spring of 2001.

Walsh's reputation as a head coach is often compared to that of Vince Lombardi. He will be remembered for his creation of the "West Coast Offense," his ability as an evaluator of talent, and his success as an administrator in building a solid organizational foundation for his teams.

★

For insight into Walsh's complex approach to coaching as well as building and managing a professional football team, see his intriguing manual, which he cowrote with Brian Billick and James A. Peterson, *Finding the Winning Edge* (1998). A biography of Walsh is in *Current Biography* (1990). Walsh is also the subject of countless articles, including Timothy Nolan, "Walsh's Urgent Creativity," *Scholastic Magazine* (Jan. 1997); "Back to School," *Sports Illustrated* (Nov. 1992); and an in-depth interview by Richard Rapaport in which Walsh discusses his ideas on professional football management, "To Build a Winning Team," *Harvard Business Review* (Jan./Feb. 1993).

RICHARD O. DAVIES

WALTON, William Theodore, III ("Bill") (*b.* 5 November 1952 in La Mesa, California), dominating basketball player who was named as one of the National Basketball Association's fifty greatest players and who also earned notoriety as an antiwar activist during the 1970s.

Walton was the second of four children of William Theodore "Ted" Walton II, a district chief for the San Diego Department of Public Welfare, and Gloria Anne Hickey Walton, a librarian. Walton grew up in La Mesa, California, where he learned to love the game of basketball. He entered Helix High School in September 1966 and soon rose to prominence on the basketball court. He helped the Helix Highlanders win the California Interscholastic Federation San Diego Section titles in 1969 and 1970. He was named a *Parade* All-American in his senior year, 1970, after leading his team to a 33–0 record by averaging 29.0 points and 22.4 rebounds per game. Walton also set a state record with 825 rebounds in a single season, and in 1970 became the first high-school player named to the U.S. team for the World Basketball Championships. He was recruited by nearly 150 colleges and universities, but decided to attend the University of California at Los Angeles (UCLA) and play for the coach John Wooden.

Walton joined the UCLA varsity team in 1971 after playing his freshman year on the junior varsity. By the time he joined the varsity players, Walton was a large man at six feet, eleven inches tall and 235 pounds. He quickly assumed a role as a team leader and demonstrated excellence in the college game, leading the Bruins to national cham-

Bill Walton *(right)*, 1974. ASSOCIATED PRESS AP

pionship victories in both 1972 and 1973. In the 1973 championship game against Memphis State (later the University of Memphis), Walton gave what many sports analysts consider the greatest single-game performance by a college player. He made twenty-one of twenty-two field-goal attempts for forty-four points, and his rebounding and outlet passing enabled UCLA to dominate from the beginning. Later that year he won the Sullivan Award as the nation's most outstanding amateur athlete. He also was a three-time member of the *Sporting News* All-America First Team and was named the National Collegiate Athletic Association (NCAA) Division I Tournament Most Outstanding Player in 1972 and 1973. In each of his three varsity seasons at UCLA, he won the James A. Naismith Award as the United Press International's Player of the Year.

During his college years Walton took a strong interest in political issues and became an outspoken critic of the U.S. government's involvement in Vietnam and of the Federal Bureau of Investigation (FBI). He participated in peace protests, marching through classrooms and lying down in the middle of Wilshire Boulevard in Los Angeles. He was arrested during a UCLA peace rally. He also was friends with the sports activists Jack and Micki Scott, and was questioned by the FBI regarding their possible involvement with Patty Hearst and other fugitives from justice. Walton also began his lifelong friendship with members of the musical group the Grateful Dead in the early 1970s. Walton graduated from UCLA in 1974, earning a B.A. in history.

Walton's professional athletic career began when he was drafted number one by the Portland (Oregon) Trail Blazers of the National Basketball Association (NBA) in 1974. He was a member of the Trail Blazers for the first five years of his career and achieved great success with the team. The Blazers won the NBA championship in 1977, and Walton was named the Most Valuable Player of the play-offs in 1977 and 1978. He was selected as the NBA's Most Valuable Player in 1978. However, injuries began to affect Walton early in his career, with the constant pounding of professional basketball taking its toll. He suffered from stress fractures and bone spurs in his feet, and he missed his first full season due to injury in 1978–1979, which was his last season with the Trail Blazers.

Walton was signed as a veteran free agent by the San Diego Clippers after the 1979 season. Although he was a member of the Clippers for six seasons (five in San Diego and, after the team moved, one in Los Angeles), he played in only 169 games and sat out the complete 1980–1981 and 1981–1982 seasons with foot injuries. Walton played the final two seasons of his professional career with the Boston Celtics in 1985–1986 and 1986–1987. He was the top man off the bench and helped propel the Celtics to the 1986 NBA title. He was named the NBA Most Valuable Player and received the NBA's Sixth Man Award in 1986. He played only ten regular-season games the following year, but again made contributions in the play-offs. Walton retired from playing basketball after the 1986–1987 season.

On 15 March 1990 Walton underwent surgery to fuse the bones in his ankles, thus ending his pain, but also eliminating any possibility of his playing basketball, professionally or recreationally, ever again. Walton then began a new career as a basketball commentator. As a child and young man, he had suffered from a stuttering problem, but he was able to overcome it in the early 1980s with the help of the longtime sports announcer Marty Glickman. Walton began his media career with XTRA radio in San Diego and later was employed by CBS-TV to cover the NCAA basketball finals (1991, 1992). He went to work for NBC during the 1994–1995 season as a game analyst. He began providing television commentary during the regular-season coverage, NBA play-offs and finals, and NBA All-Star games. He also covered basketball and indoor and beach volleyball during the 1996 Summer Olympics. Walton's four sons, all from his first marriage, all played basketball at the college level.

Walton excelled at every level of the game. He was inducted into the National High School Sports Hall of Fame (1997) and the Naismith Memorial Basketball Hall of Fame (1993), and in 1996 was selected as one of the NBA's fifty greatest players. In 1991 he received the NBA Players

Association Oscar Robertson Leadership Award. Plagued by injury, Walton made the most of a body that did not hold up for him during his professional career. Basketball fans and historians argue that, had Walton not been injured during such a large portion of his career, he would have been the game's most dominating big man ever.

★

Walton's autobiography, *Nothing but Net* (1994), gives a good overview of his life. *Sports Illustrated* has covered Walton's career better than any other magazine. Curry Kirkpatrick, "Who Are These Guys," *Sports Illustrated* (5 Feb. 1973), focuses on each member of the 1973 UCLA basketball team and captures the essence of Walton as a college student and athlete of the 1970s. Grant Wahl, "My Three Sons," *Sports Illustrated* (12 Mar. 2001), outlines Walton as a father and examines his career as a basketball commentator.

TODD TOBIAS

WARD, John Montgomery (*b.* 3 March 1860 in Bellefonte, Pennsylvania; *d.* 4 March 1925 in Augusta, Georgia), baseball player who excelled as both a pitcher and a shortstop, and who in 1890 led his fellow players in a mass revolt against the established major leagues.

Ward grew up in a small town in central Pennsylvania, the younger of two sons in a Presbyterian family. His childhood was not easy—he was an orphan by age fourteen. His father, James, a failed businessman whose debts once forced the family into bankruptcy, died of tuberculosis in 1871, and his mother, Ruth Hall, an assistant principal, passed away from pneumonia in 1874. In autumn 1873 Ward enrolled in the classics program at the nearby Pennsylvania State College. Although records indicate that he excelled in most of his courses, Ward spent much of his time playing baseball. In 1875 he and some fellow classmates formed the school's first organized baseball club, and Ward soon established himself as a formidable pitcher. Reputedly, he was the first in school history to throw a curveball. His tenure at the college came to an abrupt end in 1877, when he was caught stealing chickens from a neighboring farm and was expelled.

John Montgomery Ward, c. 1920s. © BETTMANN/CORBIS

Ward spent the next year traveling throughout the United States, playing baseball professionally in towns big and small—Williamsport and Philadelphia, Pennsylvania; Janesville, Wisconsin; and Buffalo and Binghamton, New York—before landing a contract in Rhode Island with the Providence Grays of the National League (NL) in July 1878. Against the country's best players, the eighteen-year-old Ward shined. In his first three major league seasons, the precocious pitcher notched 108 victories (including a record 47 in 1879), led his team to the 1879 pennant, and authored just the second perfect game in major league history when he blanked the Buffalo Bisons on 17 June 1880. That year the *New York Clipper* proclaimed that Ward ranked "second to none at his position," and attributed his instant success to his "puzzling" curveball and "thorough command" in the box.

When the Providence franchise hit hard financial times in 1882, Ward signed on to pitch with the New York Giants. He was no longer the same pitcher. In the course of throwing more than 2,000 innings in his first 5 seasons, the five-foot, nine-inch, 165-pound right-hander had overextended himself. Chronic arm fatigue limited his innings in 1883, and a shoulder injury he sustained the following season ended his pitching career—but not his baseball career. No longer capable of snapping off the curveball that had brought him fame, Ward moved to shortstop, where he soon transformed himself into one of the best at the position. In 1887 he enjoyed his finest season, batting .371 and leading the league with 111 stolen bases. Ward's superlative play helped form the nucleus of a powerful New York Giants team that featured six future Hall of Famers: Ward, Roger Connor, Buck Ewing, Jim O'Rourke, Tim Keefe, and Mickey Welch. They soon overwhelmed all competitors, winning back-to-back pennants in 1888 and 1889.

By the late 1880s Ward was the most famous baseball player on the country's most famous team—known as much for what he did off the field as for what he did on it. On 12 October 1887 he made headlines throughout New York City when he eloped with the stage actress Helen Dauvray. (The childless couple's divorce six years later attracted less attention.) He was also a rarity as an educated ballplayer. In 1885 he received an LL.B. from New York's Columbia College, where he attended classes from 1883 to 1885, and in 1888 he penned the instructional book *Base Ball: How to Become a Player* (1888), which included one of the first published histories of the game. In addition to writing *Base Ball: How to Become a Player*, Ward wrote numerous articles during his life. Two of the most illuminating are "Notes of a Base-Ballist," *Lippincott's* (August 1886), and "Is the Base-Ball Player a Chattel?" *Lippincott's* (August 1887). In an era when the profession held an unsavory reputation as a refuge for lowlifes and drunks, Ward was touted as the ideal ballplayer—talented, honest, and intelligent.

Major league owners, however, soon saw him as cunning and dangerous. Ever since the formation of the NL in 1876, the owners had used every means at their disposal to control players, from innocuous fines for drunkenness and poor play to the infamous "reserve clause," which effectively bound a player to his team for the duration of his career. Ward became the harshest critic of this system. In 1885 he formed the Brotherhood of Professional Base Ball Players, the first players' union in baseball history. In 1887 Ward wrote a controversial article for *Lippincott's* magazine in which he compared the reserve clause to slavery. "Like a fugitive slave law," he argued, "the reserve rule denies [the player] a harbor or a livelihood, and carries him back, bound and shackled, to the club from which he attempted to escape." These views made Ward his share of enemies, but also articulated the frustrations of his fellow players.

When the owners unilaterally imposed a salary classification system prior to the 1889 season, the press swirled with speculation over how the Brotherhood would respond. But no one expected what Ward and his followers had in store for baseball. In a series of secretive meetings held with select capitalists during the 1889 season, the Brotherhood established the foundations of a new major league, the Player's League (PL). The new league directly challenged the NL, placing seven of its eight franchises in NL cities. But the PL's strongest commodity was its labor force. After the 1889 season nearly every prominent baseball player jumped to the upstart league.

The new league lasted just one season. The baseball public, weary of labor talk, did not support the new circuit. After the 1890 season the PL's cash-strapped financial backers caved in at the negotiating table, and the league was dissolved. In the aftermath, the defeated players meekly returned to the established major leagues. The reserve clause remained in effect for another eighty-five years.

Despite the failure of his brainchild, Ward enjoyed a banner season in 1890, batting .335 and managing the PL's Brooklyn franchise to a second-place finish. After he returned to the NL, Ward remained in the player-manager role, piloting Brooklyn and New York to two second-place finishes. After leading the Giants to a postseason victory over the Baltimore Orioles in the 1894 Temple Cup Series (that era's version of the World Series), Ward retired from the game.

Ward remained active in baseball affairs for years to come. Through his Manhattan law practice, he occasionally represented players in their disputes with ownership. In 1910 he was nearly elected as the NL president, and in 1912 the former labor agitator briefly owned the Boston Braves. He also served as the business manager of the Brooklyn Tip-Tops of another upstart major league, the Federal League, until that circuit folded following the 1915 season.

On 17 September 1903 Ward married Katherine Waas, and in 1906 the couple settled on a 200-acre farm in North Babylon, New York. In retirement Ward became one of the top amateur golfers in the United States, winning several tournaments. He died in Augusta, Georgia, after having contracted pneumonia during a hunting trip, and is buried in Greenfield Cemetery in Hempstead, New York.

Recognition came late for Ward—he was not inducted into the Baseball Hall of Fame until 1964. This is curious, for Ward possessed one of the unique statistical résumés in baseball history. As a pitcher, he won 164 games in just 7 seasons, and his 2.10 lifetime earned run average ranked fourth all-time. As a batter Ward collected 2,136 hits in 17 seasons, and his 540 lifetime stolen bases ranked twenty-seventh on the all-time list. Ward may have been the most versatile player in baseball history, with the exception of Babe Ruth. Statistics aside, it was his bold stance against the abuses of baseball ownership that made him one of the most important figures of his era. Although baseball history is scarred with several contentious labor disputes, Ward's and the Brotherhood's shocking revolt was the most serious threat ever brought against the game's ruling class.

★

The library at the National Baseball Hall of Fame maintains a file of clippings on Ward. The definitive biography of Ward is Bryan Di Salvatore, *A Clever Base-Ballist: The Life and Times of John Montgomery Ward* (1999). See also David Stevens, *Baseball's Radical for All Seasons* (1998), for a good overview of Ward's life and career.

DAVID JONES

WARMERDAM, Cornelius Anthony ("Dutch") (*b.* 22 June 1915 in Long Beach, California; *d.* 13 November 2001 in Fresno, California), the first pole-vaulter in history to vault fifteen feet, he held the world's records for both indoor and outdoor pole vaulting for over fifteen years.

Warmerdam was one of four children born to Dutch immigrants Adrianous Dignam van Warmerdam and Gertrude Van der Klooster. The authorities at Ellis Island removed the "van" from van Warmerdam's name because they said his name was too long. Similarly, his mother adopted the name Gertrude in California, because Americans could not pronounce or spell her Dutch name. The couple met and married in California, where Adrianous worked in the oil fields in the San Joaquin Valley, then later in Long Beach.

Warmerdam, who came to be known as "Dutch," was born while the family lived in Long Beach. When he was three years old, they moved to Hardwick, California, and established a fruit farm. Warmerdam attended Hardwick Elementary School and Hanford High School. He began pole vaulting at age 12 but was not a standout in the sport; his greatest high school pole-vaulting accomplishment was a tie for third place in the 1932 California state high school meet. He attended Fresno State College, where he earned a degree in physical education, then attended Stanford University for one year, where he received a degree in general education. He met his future wife Juanita Anderson in January 1937 at a local dance; he was a college student and she was still in high school. They were married in 1940 and had five children.

After college Warmerdam taught and coached at a high school in Tuolumne, California. When World War II started, he decided to enlist rather than wait to be drafted, and joined the U.S. Navy, which was advertising for teachers and coaches. He served as an ensign (1943) and naval lieutenant (1944) on an aircraft carrier in the Pacific, and continued to jump while in the navy. After the war he returned to Fresno State as a physical education teacher and track and field coach. He became head track and field coach in 1960.

Dutch Warmerdam, 1942. AP/WIDE WORLD PHOTOS

During his competitive years Warmerdam dominated pole vaulting. At this time vaulters used bamboo poles and landed on their feet in a sawdust pit. Warmerdam changed the sport forever when he became the first vaulter in the world to clear fifteen feet on 13 April 1940 in Berkeley, California. Many attempts had been made to reach this mark, but all had ended in failure, and the height was widely thought to be unreachable.

Between 1938 and 1944 Warmerdam vaulted fifteen feet or higher forty-three times and was a seven-time Amateur Athletic Union pole-vaulting champion. The world indoor and outdoor pole-vaulting records he set stood for more than fifteen years. His highest indoor vault was 15 feet, 8½ inches, a record he set in Chicago on 20 March 1943. His highest outdoor vault was 15 feet, 7¾ inches, in Modesto, California, on 23 May 1942. Warmerdam amazed the world at the Millrose Games at Madison Square Garden in 1942, when he set an indoor record using a borrowed pole, which, unlike his own, was six inches shorter than the crossbar height. He was the last person to set world pole-vaulting records using a bamboo pole. Even after he was long retired—in 1975, at the age of 60—he vaulted a competitive 10 feet, 6 inches.

Warmerdam received many honors. In 1942 he won the prestigious Sullivan Award as the nation's best amateur athlete. In 1950 an American Press Institute poll named him "most outstanding athlete of the first half of the century." A United Press International poll in 1955 named him "the greatest athlete of all time." In January 2001 U.S.A. Track and Field named him "Bamboo Vaulter of the Century" and "American Pole-Vaulter of the Century." Warmerdam was elected to both the U.S. Track and Field Hall of Fame and the National Track and Field Hall of Fame. He was inducted into the Millrose Hall of Fame in 2001. That same year Fresno State named him "Greatest Athlete of the Century." The college also named its sports complex Warmerdam Field in his honor. Even his former high school honored him, electing him in 1992 to the Hanford Joint Union High School District Hall of Fame.

Warmerdam was a shy man and a devout Catholic who lived by the Ten Commandments. After his retirement, he and his wife lived in Fresno, California. He was later diagnosed with Alzheimer's disease and moved to a long-term-care facility in Fresno. He died in Fresno at the age of eighty-six.

Warmerdam dominated the sport of pole vaulting until

the advent of the aluminum pole. When asked for the secret of his success, he replied: "You have to be strong enough to do it in the first place," and added that after getting started, "I liked it very much and I kept at it all the time and that's why I think I got as far as I did."

★

There are no books about Dutch Warmerdam. For further information, see *Encyclopedia of World Biography* Supplement 21 (2001). Some online sources include "Vaulting into History," on Fresno State Online, Track and Field at <http://gobulldogs.fansonly.com/sports/c-track/spec-rel/030501aaa.html>; and "Pole Position for 'Dutch'," at <http://www.trans-world-sport.com/includes/cobranded_nav/nav_tws/260700dutch.htm>. An obituary is in the *New York Times* (15 Nov. 2001).

SUSAN E. CRAIG
ROBERT POLLOCK

WARNER, Glenn Scobey ("Pop") (*b.* 5 April 1871 in Springville, New York; *d.* 7 September 1954 in Palo Alto, California), premier American football coach and innovator who coached for forty-nine years, and who founded the Pop Warner Youth Football League.

Warner was the son of William Henry Warner, an independent businessman in sales, and Adeline Scobey Warner, a homemaker. Warner attended Springville's Griffith Institute, from which he graduated in 1889. Subsequently he attended Cornell University, graduating with an LL.B. in 1894. Warner was a solid guard on his college football team, the Rams (1892–1894), was team captain, and won the nickname "Pop" because he was a bit older than most of his teammates. He also ran track and became a heavyweight college boxing champion.

Warner had thoughts of a law career and was admitted to the New York bar in 1894, but he decided that he loved the football field more than a courtroom. After turning his back on the legal profession, Warner spent a year as football coach at Iowa State Agricultural College, and from 1895 to 1896 he was head coach at the University of Georgia. Originally hired for $340 on a ten-week contract, Warner was dismayed when he arrived at his new university to find that it had no athletic facilities. Out of the student body of 248, only thirteen men came out for football. His first team had a so-so 3–4 record, but his 1896 squad had an unbeaten, untied season, the first in the university's history. He accomplished the change by using iron discipline and by stressing the fundamentals of football. Warner left the University of Georgia to coach at Cornell during the seasons of 1897 and 1898 before he found the position that made him famous, the coaching job at the Carlisle Indian School (at first known as the Indian Industrial School) in Pennsylvania. He was there from 1899 to 1903 and again from 1907 to 1914 (coaching at Cornell again from 1904 to 1906). Warner married Tibb Loraine Smith in 1889. The couple had no children.

In his later stint at Carlisle, Warner turned Jim Thorpe into what some people called the "World's Greatest Athlete," coaching him in football, baseball, track, and several other college sports. In football, with Thorpe running wild, Warner and his Carlisle Indians won the national championship in the 1911–1912 season. Thorpe became a sensation at the 1912 Olympic Games, then went on to star in Major League Baseball and professional football. Meanwhile, from 1907 to 1914 Warner won seventy games in seven years, achieving national recognition.

Warner coached the University of Pittsburgh Panthers from 1915 to 1923. Three of his squads were undefeated from 1915 to 1917, capturing thirty-three straight victories. Two of those teams tied for the national championship, and one won it outright. Next, at Stanford from 1924 to 1932, Warner led the Cardinal to three Rose Bowls, where they won all three games. He went on to coach the Temple University Owls from 1933 to 1938. He coached the Owls to thirty-one victories. His 1934 team had the distinction of playing in the first Sugar Bowl in New Orleans. Warner finished his career in 1939 as an advisory coach for the San Jose State College (now San Jose State University) Spartans in California. When he retired, Warner had 319 career wins, which for a time was the all-time record in Division I-A football. He racked up 114 of those wins while coaching Native Americans at Carlisle. Warner also produced forty-seven All-Americans. His record was eventually broken by the legendary University of Alabama coach Bear Bryant.

In addition to his coaching career, Warner also became an author. In 1908 he wrote *Football for Players and Coaches*; the second edition was published in 1912. Fifteen years later he produced an updated version called *Football for Coaches and Players.* Warner also wrote *Pop Warner's Book for Boys* (1934), and updated it in 1942.

Warner is probably best known by most Americans for the "Pop Warner Youth Football League" he founded in 1929. In these "camps" for children from five to fifteen years of age, gender equality prevailed: boys and girls could all play football and/or become cheerleaders. Classroom instruction was mandatory, and the youngsters had to excel there before they took the field. Every year there was a "Pop Warner Little Scholars" program, with the best students being named as academic "All-Americans." Although the youth football league was having financial problems by 2001, thirty-nine American states and Mexico and Japan still had Pop Warner Football.

Throughout his career, Warner was known as an innovator. He introduced the practice of numbered plays and dummy scrimmaging, in which players practiced blocking

Pop Warner *(right)* receiving an award from Herb McCracken of the Touchdown Club of New York, 1947. ASSOCIATED PRESS AP

against a dummy rather than another player. Using dummies allowed coaches to better teach the fundamentals of blocking. Warner also developed the single-wing formation, which some still consider the most powerful formation for running the football. He then developed the double-wing formation, after other teams imitated the single-wing. In the double-wing, both the left half and the right half lined up just to the outside of the ends on their respective sides of the line. It was a good passing formation similar to the one-back offense many teams use today. Warner also introduced the spiral punt, the screen pass, the three-point stance, and the naked reverse, wherein blockers ran in one direction while the ball carrier ran in the opposite direction. Such a reverse often fooled the other team. Further, he inaugurated the use of numbered jerseys so individual players could be recognized, and the use of shoulder and thigh pads for players' safety. Warner is revered as a groundbreaker as well as one of the most successful coaches in the history of football.

After many years of enjoyable retirement, Warner died in Palo Alto, California, after a long bout with throat cancer.

★

To best understand Warner as a football coach, to understand all his innovations, and to understand how he felt about young people, one should read his books: *Football for Players and Coaches* (1908); *Football for Coaches and Players* (1927); and *Pop Warner's Book for Boys* (revised ed., 1942). Mike Bynum has written a recent biography of Warner, *Pop Warner: Football's Greatest Teacher* (1993). Warner is mentioned in Robert M. Ours, *College Football Encyclopedia: The Authoritative Guide to 124 Years of College Football* (1994). See also Scott Linnett, "Even in Death, 'Pop' Warner Tough to Beat," *San Diego Union-Tribune* (17 Nov. 1993). An obituary is in the *New York Times* (8 Sept. 1954).

JAMES M. SMALLWOOD

WATERFIELD, Robert Staton ("Bob") (*b.* 26 July 1920 in Elmira, New York; *d.* 25 March 1983 in Burbank, California), star quarterback, runner, punter, and kicker for the University of California, Los Angeles (UCLA) and the Cleveland and Los Angeles Rams.

Nothing in Waterfield's childhood would have led anyone to believe he would one day become a legendary quarterback in the National Football League (NFL). His father, Jack, moved the family to Van Nuys in Southern California when Waterfield was four. His father died five years later and Waterfield's mother, Frances, was left to raise and support her son on her own. At Van Nuys High School he played football and was on the gymnastics team, but he did not become starting quarterback until his senior year.

Bob Waterfield, 1946. ASSOCIATED PRESS AP

Waterfield graduated from high school in 1938 and worked at an aircraft factory before entering UCLA as a physical education major. He did not play football his freshman year, but became the starting quarterback in 1941, lettering that year and the next. In 1942 he was named an All-American and led the Bruins to their first Rose Bowl, although they lost 9–0 to the Georgia Bulldogs. He left UCLA for a stint in the U.S. Army, where he was commissioned a second lieutenant, but returned a few months later after being discharged for medical reasons (a knee injury from playing college football).

At this point in his career, it seemed that Waterfield's greatest claim to fame would be his marriage to his childhood sweetheart, screen star Jane Russell, on 24 April 1943. Unlike his high-profile wife, Waterfield was reserved and serious, and often resented the spotlight that Hollywood fame brought. His football career was far from over, however. In his graduating year of 1944–1945, he led UCLA to tenth place in offense; Waterfield himself ranked fourth in passing yardage and first in punting (he once kicked a ninety-one-yard punt). At the end of that season, he played in the East-West Shrine Game, and it was there on 1 January 1945, that Waterfield burst definitively onto the national stage as a star football player. Leading his team from behind in the fourth quarter, he threw two touchdown passes, helping the West to win the game 13–7. He also led the game in rushing (53 yards), made three impressive punts (80-, 74-, and 60-yards), and scored the winning touchdown himself on a 12-yard run. For his efforts, Waterfield was unanimously awarded the William M. Coffmann award for outstanding offensive player of the Shrine Bowl—the first player to receive the award. Waterfield graduated from UCLA with a bachelor's degree in physical education.

Waterfield was a third-round draft pick for the Cleveland Rams in 1944; the team offered him a $7,500 contract, more money than any NFL player had ever been offered. It was money well spent, however, as Waterfield led the Rams to a 15–14 championship win over the Washington Redskins, passing for three touchdowns and kicking two extra points. His cool leadership and pinpoint passing accuracy won him the league's Most Valuable Player (MVP) award, the first rookie to be so honored. Waterfield played both offense and defense during his first four years with the Rams, garnering twenty interceptions. When the team moved to Los Angeles in 1946, Waterfield, who had been popular in Southern California while at UCLA, enjoyed a resurgence. He led the league in passing against such seasoned star quarterbacks as Sid Luckman and Sammy Baugh. Despite this star performance, beginning in 1947 Waterfield started to share quarterbacking duties with Norm Van Brocklin, playing alternate quarters. In 1949 the duo led the Rams to the NFL western title. One of his star receivers, Elroy "Crazylegs" Hirsch, remarked that Waterfield was the best football player he had ever seen.

During Waterfield's eight-year NFL career, he was named to the All-NFL team three times. He led the Rams to three division championships, tied for another, and captured the NFL championships in 1945 and 1951. Waterfield was the league's passing leader twice during his career, and led the league a number of times in kicking extra points and field goals. He also ranked among the best in punting. In 1951 he appeared in his first movie, *Jungle Manhunt,* with Johnny Weissmuller.

Waterfield retired in 1952 at the height of his career, offering no reason for the move, though many assumed it was because of having to share the quarterback position. During his career he amassed 11,849 passing yards, 98 passing touchdowns, 13 rushing touchdowns, 615 extra points, 60 field goals, and had a 42.4-yard punting average. In 1965 he was the first Ram elected to the NFL Hall of Fame.

Shortly after retiring, Waterfield and his wife, Jane Russell, adopted three infants. In 1953 he starred in *Crazylegs, All-American,* a movie about Crazylegs Hirsch, in which he played himself. Waterfield and his wife also formed the production company Russ-Field Productions; Waterfield produced a film starring his wife entitled *The Fuzzy Pink Nightgown* in 1957.

In 1959, when Sid Gilman resigned as head coach of the Rams, Waterfield took the job. Although he had enjoyed great success as a player, his talents do not appear to have translated into coaching. Football writers began calling the Rams the "F-Troop" of the NFL—a reference to a popular television show of the time about a group of incompetent soldiers. Near the end of his third consecutive losing season, with a record of 9–25, Waterfield resigned. He remained as a scout for the Rams and, even though he later remarked that he did not enjoy scouting, drafted such future Rams stars as Roman Gabriel, Merlin Olsen, and Deacon Jones.

Waterfield's marriage had been rocky for some time, and Russell's drinking and infidelity finally led to a divorce in 1968. Waterfield later married Ann Mangus. After a long bout with a respiratory illness, Waterfield died at the age of sixty-two in Burbank, California.

While his coaching and film careers have quickly been forgotten, Waterfield's prowess on the football field remains legendary. His cool leadership, accuracy in passing, and skills at running, punting, and kicking make him one of the premiere athletes in professional football history.

★

Maxwell Stiles, *Football's Finest Hour: The Shrine East-West Game* (1950), summarizes the events of Waterfield's life in college and the NFL, focusing on his leap to stardom at the East-West Shrine Bowl in 1945. Jane Russell's autobiography, *Jane Russell: My Path and My Detours* (1985), relates much of Waterfield's career and life, as well as their marriage and divorce, from her point of view. Deacon Jones and John Klawitter, *Headslap: The Life and Times of Deacon Jones* (1996), describes Waterfield's coaching career from a player's perspective, and offers some personal observations about his marriage to Russell. Joe Horrigan and Bob Carroll, *Football Greats* (1998), details Waterfield's major accomplishments on the field and relates some anecdotes.

MARKUS H. MCDOWELL

WATSON, Thomas Sturges ("Tom") (*b.* 4 September 1949 in Kansas City, Missouri), professional golfer ranked among the best in the world during the 1970s and 1980s.

Watson's father, Raymond Watson, was an insurance broker and was once the champion at the Kansas City Country Club, where Watson learned to play golf. Watson's mother Sarah Elizabeth Ridge was a homemaker. Watson was a natural golfer, according to Stan Thirsk, the club professional, who first saw him swing a club at age six and who became his coach and friend. Watson quickly developed into an excellent golfer but stuck close to home, winning the Missouri Amateur title four times. In 1967, after graduating from Pembrook County Day School in Kansas City, where he played on the basketball and football teams, Watson attended Stanford University in California, where he

Tom Watson, 2001. ASSOCIATED PRESS AP

majored in psychology and played well enough on the golf team to turn professional upon graduating in 1971. Watson married his high-school sweetheart Linda Tova Rubin a year and a half after graduating from Stanford. They had two children.

Watson did not get off to a good start in his professional career. In 1972 he lost by a stroke in the Quad Cities Open. In 1973 he slipped twice on his way to the winner's circle, most dramatically at the Hawaiian Open, where he led by three stokes going into the fourth round. The U.S. Open at the Winged Foot Golf Club fell from his grasp in 1974 when, after leading for three rounds, he finished in second place with a score of seventy-nine. Finally he claimed his first victory at the Western Open, coming from six strokes behind. Watson's career took a turn for the better in 1975. He won the British Open at Carnoustie, Scotland, and finished every other major that year among the top ten players. The following year he finished in the top ten in eleven tournaments, winning a respectable $138,000.

Watson's string of successes began to threaten the status of Jack Nicklaus, who at that time was the greatest golfer of the twentieth century. In 1977 Watson won two majors, the Masters and the British Open. In each tournament he battled Nicklaus all the way to the seventy-second hole. At the British Open in Turnberry, Scotland, Watson won a victory that many consider the most dramatic head-to-head battle in modern golf history. With close scores in the first two rounds, Watson and Nicklaus were paired in the third round and again came up even. They were paired up for the final eighteen, with Watson leading by one stroke at the last tee. He drove to the middle of the fairway. Nicklaus drove into heavy rough, but his next shot put him just thirty feet from the cup. Then Nicklaus sunk his clutch putt for a score of sixty-six. But Watson had placed his second shot less than three feet from the flag and holed the putt for a winning sixty-five.

When the 1977 season ended Watson was the Professional Golfers' Association (PGA) Player of the Year and the Vardon Trophy winner with a stroke average of 70.32; his prize money topped the $300,000 mark; and he was hailed as the game's up-and-coming best player. Over the next seven years, Watson's triumphs and reputation for dramatic play grew steadily. In 1978 his earnings took him over the $1 million mark, he won five tournaments, and he again was named the PGA Player of the Year and the Vardon Trophy winner with a stroke average of 70.16, the best average in a decade. In 1979 he maintained this rising trajectory by winning five tournaments and, for an unprecedented third consecutive year, both the Player of the Year award and the Vardon Trophy with a 70.27 stroke average.

Although Watson had not won a major for several seasons, he was often in contention, and his play continued to be steady and impressive as he entered the 1980 season. He won six of the twenty-two events he entered in the United States, placed in the top ten of ten more, and earned money from all of them. Overseas, he edged out Lee Trevino to become the British Open champion for the third time. His stroke average was down to 69.95.

In 1981 Watson once again beat Nicklaus at the Masters and went on to win the Western Open, the Bing Crosby National Pro-Am, and the San Diego Open. At Pebble Beach, California, in 1982, he again snatched victory from Nicklaus, who appeared certain to win his fifth U.S. Open until Watson chipped in from deep rough for an unforgettable birdie-two on the seventeenth to take and hold the lead. Watson again won the British Open in 1982 and 1983, bringing his British victories to five, an achievement shared only with Peter Thomson. In the early 1980s he also won three more PGA Player of the Year awards.

During these years, Watson's magnificent play fascinated the golfing world. His driving, irons, and wedge techniques always were superior, and he had the "nerves of steel" that allowed him to become one of the best putters in the history of the game. His nerves frayed, however, in 1985, when even three- and four-foot putts became unsinkable. Byron Nelson, Watson's friend and mentor, said, "He's thinking too much. . . . But he'll come out of it. He's too good a golfer not to." In 1988 Watson was elected to the PGA World Golf Hall of Fame, but he did not recover his former dominance. From 1988 to 1999 he won only two events, the Memorial in 1996 and the Colonial in 1998.

Watson once said, "The game is important because it teaches you that there are rules that you have to live by." He put his principles into action in 1990, when the secret membership committee of the Kansas City Country Club rejected Henry Bloch, the cofounder and chairman of the tax-preparation firm H&R Block, who was Jewish. Watson resigned from the club to protest this clear-cut case of anti-Semitism, a wrenching decision for someone whose career and social life had revolved around the organization since he was old enough to swing a golf club. In *Sports Illustrated,* John Garrity wrote, "This single act of conscience will one day count for more than all the trophies he has won with his clubs."

The late 1990s were a time of transition for Watson. In 1998 he divorced his wife Linda, and soon married Hilary Watson, the former wife of professional golfer Denis Watson. In 1999, at age fifty, Watson joined the Senior PGA Tour. Golf fans eagerly anticipated his return to form. With new clubs and a new training regimen, Watson quickly made his mark as a senior player, and in 2001 won the Senior PGA Championship.

★

For biographical information about Watson, see David Porter, ed., *Biographical Dictionary of American Sports: Outdoor Sports* (1988), and Ralph Hickok, *A Who's Who of Sports Champions: Their Stories and Records* (1995). Watson has been featured in numerous magazine articles, including *Golf Digest* (Aug. 1999, Sep. 1999); *Golf Magazine* (June 1983, Sep. 1984, Aug. 1985, Oct. 1993); and *Sports Illustrated* (10 Dec. 1990, 17 July 1995, 10 June 1996, 20 Sep. 1999, 10 Apr. 2000). More biographical and career information is on the website of the PGA Tour at http://www.golfweb.com/players/bios/2256.html.

MARTIN SHERWIN

WEATHERSPOON, Teresa (*b.* 8 December 1965 in Pineland, Texas), two-time Olympic basketball guard known for playing on the 1988 Louisiana Tech University National Collegiate Athletic Association (NCAA) championship team and as an All-Star guard on the New York Liberty in the Women's National Basketball Association (WNBA).

Weatherspoon, the youngest of Charles and Rowena Weatherspoon's six children, was born in tiny Pineland, Texas, near the Louisiana border. Weatherspoon's mother encouraged her to be adventurous. Fascinated with sports, at the age of four Weatherspoon began playing basketball with her two brothers. Her father had played minor league baseball with the Minnesota Twins, and Weatherspoon also enjoyed the game. She declined the opportunity to play

Teresa Weatherspoon, c. 2000. © DUOMO/CORBIS

softball as a young girl, opting to play Little League baseball instead. Weatherspoon attended schools in the West Sabine Independent School District, where she excelled both athletically and academically, graduating in 1984 as the class valedictorian. Weatherspoon called her family the greatest influence in her success: "The most important thing that I had and that was given to each and every one of us," she said, "was love. My mother instilled morals in us that will forever be with us. It was hard, but I was told never to give up."

Weatherspoon attended Louisiana Tech University in Ruston, playing for the Louisiana Lady Techsters from 1985 to 1988. She led the Techsters to two NCAA finals; they won the championship in 1988 and Weatherspoon was named to the All-Final Four Team in both 1987 and 1988. As of 2001, she remained the team's career leader in assists (958) and steals (411), with 1,087 career points and 533 rebounds. During her college years, Weatherspoon won gold medals in the 1986 World Championship, 1986 Goodwill Games, and 1987 World University Games. She was named to the NCAA Women's Basketball Team of the Decade for the 1980s and won the 1988 Wade Trophy, an honor awarded to the country's top female college basketball player. That same year, she was named the Louisiana State Player of the Year and won the Broderick Cup. Additionally, Weatherspoon was a Kodak All-American in both 1987 and 1988.

In 1988 Weatherspoon played for Team USA in the Summer Olympics. While she was in Seoul, South Korea, her mother suffered a stroke. Weatherspoon wanted to return home, but her mother insisted that she remain in Seoul, and Weatherspoon helped her team win the gold medal. At the 1992 Olympics in Barcelona, Spain, Weatherspoon and her teammates captured the bronze. Her Olympic successes led to opportunities to play on women's basketball teams in Italy and Russia. She played for three Italian teams, Busto (1988–1989, 1990–1993), Magenta (1989–1990), and Como (1996–1997), as well as on the 1997 Italian League championship team and the Italian League All-Star team (1996–1997). From 1993 to 1995 she played for CSKA, becoming one of the first two U.S. women ever to play professional sports in Russia.

Weatherspoon returned to the United States in 1997 to take up an inaugural spot on the New York Liberty in the newly formed WNBA. In her first season with the Liberty, Weatherspoon led the league in assists (6.1 average) and steals (3.04); she also matched the WNBA season high with twelve assists in an August game against the Los Angeles Sparks. Named the Defensive Player of the Year in 1997 and 1998, she was also selected to the All-WNBA Second Team in 1997, 1998, and 2000. She led the New York Liberty in minutes played per game in the 1997 WNBA championships, and in 1998 led the WNBA in steals (3.33) for the second consecutive season. Mike Lupica of the *New York Daily News* noted her accomplishments by writing, "I'm now convinced that Teresa Weatherspoon is the best point guard we've got at the [Madison Square] Garden. Man or woman."

Weatherspoon had her best season to date in 1999, leading the Liberty in assists and steals and finishing second in the league in both categories. She was also voted the starting point guard for the first WNBA All-Star game. During her first four years with the New York Liberty, she led the team in both assists and steals; she also served as an All-Star starter on the 1999 and 2000 teams. On 4 September 1999 Weatherspoon made the videotape highlights on every television sports program. The New York Liberty trailed by fourteen points at halftime during a championship game against the Houston Comets. They closed the gap to two points, and with only 2.4 seconds on the clock, Weatherspoon sunk a fifty-foot shot. "When it left my hands, I knew it was good," she said. "I was just praying that it would go in. I've never done this before in a game."

In a sport where height is a condition for participation, Weatherspoon attained success despite her relatively small stature of five feet, eight inches, and 161 pounds. "Height is definitely not an issue," Weatherspoon once asserted. "It's the size of your heart. Not how big you are, how fast you are. It's the size of your heart and about having confidence in yourself." In an interview for the WNBA website, Weatherspoon revealed that she was a better base stealer than a ball stealer and dreamed of playing baseball for the Colorado Silver Bullets. She also has expressed an interest in coaching at the college or professional level after retiring as a player. However, she has pledged to help the Liberty win the WNBA championship before moving to the next stage of her career.

In the off-season, Weatherspoon has volunteered for Drug Crusades, giving talks to children in Texas about the dangers of drug use and sharing how athletes are role models for both boys and girls. When she was a child, Weatherspoon's athletic role model was the Olympic track and field star Jesse Owens. She wrote *Teresa Weatherspoon's Basketball for Girls* (1999), to encourage girls with athletic ability to pursue their dreams.

An aggressive point guard, Weatherspoon was a pioneer in U.S. professional women's basketball, setting records in both the offensive and defensive arenas. To honor her family's contributions toward her accomplishments, Weatherspoon has given back to the youth of her community while continuing to achieve goals in her professional development as an athlete.

★

Many newspaper and magazine articles chronicle Weatherspoon's career and give a sense of her personality and values. For the former, see Michael Wilbon, "U.S. Wins in Women's Basketball; Defeats Yugoslavia," *Washington Post* (22 Sept. 1988). For the latter see Philip Lerman, "Great Assist," *USA Today* (3 Oct. 1988), which recounts how Weatherspoon gave her Olympic basketball to an injured soldier in honor of his courage. See also David Fleming, "Sweet Liberty," *Sports Illustrated* (14 July 1997), and Jonathan Van Meter, "Tyra and Spoon," *Women's Sports and Fitness* (June 1998).

KELLY BOYER SAGERT

WEBER, Pete (*b.* 21 August 1962 in St. Louis, Missouri), one of professional bowling's most notorious and successful stars.

Weber, the youngest child of famed bowler Dick Weber, learned bowling secrets early by watching his father and other bowling greats in competition. Dick and Juanita, Weber's homemaker mother, raised an entire family of bowlers: older brothers Richard and John competed on the professional bowling circuit for a time, and his sister once rolled a perfect game.

As a toddler Weber was a regular bowler at his father's Florissant, Missouri, bowling alley. By the age of twelve he rolled his first perfect game and was spending three hours a day on the lanes. "I hated school," Weber later told *People Weekly*. "But trying to knock down ten pins every time, that fascinated me." At fifteen he began playing in American Bowling Congress (ABC) sanctioned competition, bowling another perfect game in his first game in the adult league in 1978.

In 1979 Weber quit McClure North Senior High School and joined the professional tour. In 1980 the Professional Bowling Association (PBA) named him Rookie of the Year. That year, he married his first wife DeeDee; they had two children.

Weber seemed destined for stardom. He had his father's skill and versatility but threw the ball with even more power. His style was much more flashy, with a dangerously high back swing combined with rapid footwork. At five feet, seven inches, and 135 pounds, Weber did not look athletic. He sported a mustache, had brooding eyes, and was quick-tempered.

Weber won his first two tournaments in 1982, finishing seventh in earnings on the tour. He was in the top ten in earnings the following year but did not win a title. Then, for the next ten seasons he won at least one tournament every year. No bowler in the history of the sport had ever accomplished so much at such a young age.

Weber almost threw it all away. A hard drinker and partyer even as a teenager, he soon acquired a cocaine habit. Over several years, Weber squandered an estimated $200,000 on the drug and began to act aggressively toward opponents. In 1984 he entered the White Deer Treatment Center in Lonedell, Missouri, for a four-week stay. He stopped using hard drugs but a year later began drinking again. When playing with his father, however, Weber was sober and restrained. "When I room with Dad, I don't party," Weber said. "He keeps me calm." Weber's marriage soon ended in divorce. His second wife, Tracy, brought a son into the marriage.

Weber continued to rub his rivals—and some fans—the wrong way. Cocky and flamboyant, he would taunt his opponents, kick ball racks, and scream obscenities during televised matches. "If you're emotionless, you're never going to be great," Weber said. "I let everyone know I'm bowling badly and I'm not happy about it. But that spirit and fire, that's what people want to see. That's what makes me fun to watch." Weber's gentlemanly father was bowling's most famous ambassador, and Weber struggled to emerge from his shadow. "Pete in his prime is definitely more talented than his father was," said PBA president Johnny Petraglia. "Dick was the complete package, though, and he was first; and that's what people use as the standard of comparison."

In 1987 Weber won bowling's most important competition—the Firestone Tournament of Champions—an event his father had never won. At twenty-five he became the youngest player in PBA history to win ten tournaments. Nevertheless, that year his peers voted his archrival Marshall Hollman PBA Player of the Year even though Hollman had not won a single tournament.

In 1988 Weber won the Bowling Proprietors' Association of America (BPAA) U.S. Open and the following year won the PBA National Championship, becoming only the fourth player to win the PBA Triple Crown. That same year, he was inducted into the PBA Hall of Fame in his first year of eligibility. Weber finished second in the ABC Masters in 1983 and 2000, just missing the chance to join Mike Aulby as the only player to win bowling's Grand Slam.

In the 1990s Weber added eleven more titles to his record, including the 1991 BPAA U.S. Open and the 1998 PBA National Championship. He never won Player of the Year; his discipline problems were still an embarrassment to his peers. Several of Weber's best seasons ended prematurely with a suspension.

In 1999 Weber, already on probation for verbal altercations with fans, was fined for "conduct unbecoming a professional" after getting into an argument with a fan and walking out of a PBA pro-am event (a tournament in which professional and amateur bowlers compete as pairs) in Bay City, Michigan. The PBA tour commissioner Mark Gerberich banned Weber from bowling for two years. Weber appealed the decision, and the parties ultimately agreed to a ten-month suspension, the longest in league history. At this point in his career, Weber trailed only Walter Ray Williams, Jr., on the PBA tour's all-time earnings list, with more than $2.2 million. His twenty-five career titles put him seventh all-time, one victory behind his father, who was tied for fourth.

The Grand Slam–winner Aulby was almost unanimously selected for inclusion into the 2001 American Bowling Congress Hall of Fame, but Weber received only 70 of 134 ballots cast—not nearly enough to be enshrined. However, Weber returned from his 2000 suspension with his usual confidence, vowing to become player of the year in 2001. "That's all I want to do—just go out there and beat them all," he told *Bowling Digest.* But he did not promise to turn a new leaf. "I'm going to be me," Weber said. "That's what they are going to get, whether they like it or not."

★

The magazine *Bowling Digest* (Feb. and Apr. 2001), is the best source for continuous information on Weber. See also *People Weekly* (22 Feb. 1988), and *Sports Illustrated* (15 July 1985 and 4 May 1987).

MICHAEL BETZOLD

WEISSMULLER, Peter John ("Johnny") (*b.* 2 June 1904 in Freidorf, Austro-Hungarian Empire [now Romania]; *d.* 20 January 1984 in Acapulco, Mexico), champion swimmer who won five Olympic gold medals and fifty-two national championships and established sixty-seven world swimming records; he also popularized the film character Tarzan.

Weissmuller's parents were Peter Weissmuller, a former soldier, and Elizabeth Kersch Weissmuller, a homemaker. The family came to the United States in 1905 and headed to Windber, Pennsylvania, the home of a relative. In 1908, three years after Weissmuller's younger brother was born, the family moved to Chicago. Weissmuller's father worked as a construction laborer and saloon proprietor, and then apparently left town and his family. Weissmuller attended St. Michael's parochial school in Chicago from 1908 to 1915, and then Menier Public School from 1915 to 1917, before dropping out so he could work and help support the family.

Weissmuller learned to swim around age twelve on the Chicago side of Lake Michigan at Fullerton Beach and at Stanton Park pool; in the winter he swam at the Young Mens Christian Association (YMCA). A swimming friend introduced him to William "Big Bill" Bachrach, a coach with the Illinois Athletic Club (IAC), who recognized Weissmuller's potential immediately and offered him an IAC membership.

Weissmuller's first competition was the National Amateur Athletic Union (AAU) Championships in Duluth, Minnesota on 6 August 1921, where he won the 50-yard freestyle. Thus began his streak of breaking world records. By early April 1922 Weissmuller had set seventeen new world records, and the *New York Times* wrote of this "remarkable" youth able "to propel himself through the water" so that "almost every time he plunges headlong an old record passes into oblivion." About the same time, Weissmuller helped the IAC establish four relay records. The press kept reporting on the IAC's "young aquatic marvel" and spoke of Weissmuller as one of the great "natators," "watermen," or "mermen" (other terms for "swimmers" found in the sports sections of the 1920s).

In one of his five races in Decatur, Illinois, on 4 July 1923, Weissmuller broke the world record for the 500-meter freestyle by 11 seconds at 6:55; his records then numbered over 50. In 1923 the Helms Athletic Foundation gave him its nonrepeated American Swimmer of the Year award, and the Helms World Trophy as Athlete of the Year, North America, in 1924.

There was no doubt that Weissmuller would qualify for the 1924 Olympics—except for a question about his citizenship. Despite some controversy, Weissmuller did go to Paris with the U.S. swimming team and won three gold

Johnny Weissmuller, 1936. ASSOCIATED PRESS

medals and one bronze. In the men's 100-meter freestyle, the handsome six foot, three inch Weissmuller, then at 195 pounds, achieved a new Olympic record of 59.0 by beating his teammates. Weissmuller set another Olympic record (5:04.2) in the 400-meter freestyle, and won the men's 4 x 200 meter freestyle relay. As part of the U.S. water polo team, Weissmuller and his teammates won bronze medals.

With his head and chest high in the water and a powerful kick (adjusting his basic pattern, when necessary, of six kicks for two arm strokes), Weissmuller continued to win indoor and outdoor national championships. In his second and final Olympics in 1928 in Amsterdam, Weissmuller won two more gold medals, one in the men's 100-meter freestyle with a new Olympic record of 58.6. As part of the men's 4 x 200 freestyle relay, he and his teammates took the gold, setting a world record time of 9:32.2. Weissmuller retired as an amateur athlete on 3 January 1929.

Weissmuller appeared in some swimming documentaries in 1929, earned $500 a week to promote swimwear, had a cameo role in Florenz Ziegfeld's film, *Glorifying the American Girl* (1929), and collaborated with his friend Clarence A. Bush to write *Swimming the American Crawl* (1930), which he dedicated to Coach Bachrach and the IAC members. In that book, Weissmuller discussed his success as a competitive swimmer and his perfection of the American crawl. Along with instructional photographs, he analyzed his "hydroplaning" of strokes and breathing techniques, timing, and "relaxation."

Beginning in 1931 Weissmuller began a series of four marriages and divorces: singer Bobbe Arnst (*m.* 28 February 1931; *d.* 4 October 1932); Mexican actress Guadalupe Villalobos ("Lupe") Velez (*m.* 20 June 1934; *d.* 15 August 1938); socialite Beryl Scott Ginter (*m.* 20 August 1939; *d.* 29 January 1948), mother of his three children; and golfer Allene Gates (*m.* 30 January 1948; *d.* 1962). On 23 April 1963 he married his fifth wife, Bavarian-born Gertrudis ("Trudi") Bauman Brock, with whom he remained until his death.

As the result of a successful screen test at MGM, Weissmuller, displaying his swimming ability and physical athletic presence, appeared in *Tarzan, the Ape Man* (1932), and became the first "talkie" Tarzan in more than a dozen popular box office features. Weissmuller appeared in other jungle, adventure, contemporary, and horror films off and on through the mid-1950s, and in 1948 he cofounded a motion picture production company that was responsible for all of his *Jungle Jim* films.

From May 1939 through October 1940 Weissmuller performed in Billy Rose's *Aquacade* with swimmer Eleanor Holm in the 275-foot outdoor pool at the New York's World Fair in Flushing Meadows. He raised war bonds during World War II and appeared in *Stage Door Canteen* (1943). Twice a week over a two-year period during the war, he trained Marines in San Pedro, California, by demonstrating how to make high-falling escape dives and how to swim in water enflamed with oil or gasoline.

Television was another successful medium for Weissmuller. He starred in twenty-six thirty-minute episodes of *Jungle Jim* in the 1950s. He was elected to the Helms Swimming Hall of Fame in 1949 and the following year was voted by the Associated Press as its "Greatest Swimmer of the First Half-Century." An honorary gold medal was presented to Weissmuller during the 1972 Summer Olympics in Munich. He was inducted into the Olympic Hall of Fame in 1983, among the first athletes to be so honored.

Weissmuller and his wife Trudi lived in Fort Lauderdale, Florida, from 1965 to 1973, where he played golf and assisted with the International Swimming Hall of Fame

(ISHOF), of which he was one of the first inductees. The couple then returned to the western United States, living in California and Nevada. On 27 August 1977 Weissmuller suffered a stroke that signaled a progressive decline in his health. In October 1979 he and his wife moved to Acapulco, Mexico, where Weissmuller died at home of pulmonary edema. He is buried at the Valle de la Luz Cemetery in Acapulco.

When the U.S. swimmer Mark Spitz won seven gold medals at the 1972 Summer Olympic Games in Munich, people debated which swimmer, Weissmuller or Spitz, was the best swimmer of all time; this debate continues. Weissmuller always convincingly asserted that his entire amateur swimming portfolio of records and wins, not just his gold medals, and his breakthrough leadership in swimming style and technique were unique in modern swimming history.

★

Biographical information is available in Weissmuller's *Swimming the American Crawl* (1930), with Clarence A. Bush. Biographies include Narda Onyx, *Water, World and Weissmuller, a Biography* (1964), and David A. Fury, *Johnny Weissmuller, Twice the Hero* (2000). For Weissmuller's film career, see Ray Narducy, *The International Dictionary of Films and Filmmakers: Vol. III: Actors and Actresses* (1986), James Vinson, ed.; and Ephraim Katz, *The Film Encyclopedia,* 2nd ed. (1994). Lengthy *New York Times* articles featuring Weissmuller include Bosley Crowther, "YAH-OOO-EE-OOO-EE!" (14 May 1939); Thomas Brady, "Toujours Tarzan" (5 Jan. 1947); Keith Monroe, "Johnny Weissmuller Was a Slow Swimmer" (18 Dec. 1966); Arthur Daley, "In Total Disagreement" (22 Dec. 1966); and Dave Anderson, "Tarzan Was 'Better Than Mark Spitz Is'" (4 Nov. 1972). An obituary is in the *New York Times* (22 Jan. 1984). Many of Weissmuller's films are readily available on videocassettes.

MADELINE SAPIENZA

WELLS, Willie James (*b.* 10 August 1906 in Austin, Texas; *d.* 22 January 1989 in Austin), scrappy, intelligent player in baseball's Negro Leagues for more than two decades, who was the first shortstop in baseball history to combine spectacular fielding with home run power.

Wells was the youngest of five children born to Lonnie Wells, a Pullman porter, and Cisco White, a homemaker who took in laundry to earn extra money. He grew up in Austin, at the time a dusty frontier town that had one paved street and a population of 22,000. As a youngster, Wells frequented Austin's Dobbs Field, where African-American baseball teams often played. The San Antonio Aces catcher, "Biz" Mackey (who many years later would become Wells's teammate), took the youngster under his wing, getting him into games for free and letting him sit on the bench with the team. Wells honed his own baseball skills at Anderson High School, Austin's segregated school for African Americans. He briefly attended Sam Huston College in Austin, but left school when the St. Louis Stars, a formidable team in the Negro National League, offered him $300 per month to play professional baseball.

As a rookie in 1924, Wells struggled to hit the curveball, but after working diligently he eventually became one of the best curveball hitters in the game. A contact hitter who seldom struck out, Wells was fussy about the bats he used, insisting on a heavy hickory model instead of the usual white ash. A right-handed batter, he enjoyed playing in the hitter-friendly Stars Park, and he frequently found himself among the league leaders in batting average, doubles, home runs, and stolen bases. Although Wells usually batted second in the lineup, he displayed a power stroke unprecedented for a shortstop. In 1929 Wells hit twenty-seven homers in eighty-eight league games, setting a single-season record that would never be broken. His closest friend on the Stars was speedy outfielder James ("Cool Papa") Bell, with whom he often played cards to pass the time on road trips. Led by Wells and Bell, St. Louis won championships in 1928, 1930, and 1931.

The bowlegged Wells displayed such impressive range at shortstop that, as opponent Judy Johnson noted, it "looked like he had roller skates on." While with St. Louis, Wells suffered an arm injury that hampered him for the rest of his career, but he compensated for the weak throwing arm by cutting a hole in the palm of his glove to enable him to get rid of the ball more quickly. "What he lacked in arm strength he made up for in wisdom," teammate Monte Irvin remembered. "He was very smart about playing hitters. Very rarely would anyone hit a ball that he couldn't get to." After the Great Depression forced the Stars to fold in 1931, Wells drifted from team to team, eventually landing in Chicago, where he played three years for the Chicago American Giants. With Wells's help, Chicago won the pennant in 1933. The next year, fans voted Wells as the starting shortstop in the inaugural East-West All-Star game, an annual contest in which he would eventually make eight appearances. In 1937 Wells left Chicago to join the Newark Eagles, a talented young team owned by gambler Abe Manley and his wife, Effa.

In 1940, after Newark refused to meet his salary demand, Wells joined the Veracruz Blues of the Mexican League. He was an immediate hit in Mexico, where affectionate fans nicknamed him "El Diablo" (The Devil). In 1942 he rejoined Newark as player-manager, but after only a year, he returned to Mexico. "One of the main reasons I came back to Mexico is because I've found freedom and democracy here, something I never found in the United States," Wells told the *Pittsburgh Courier.* "Not only do I get more money playing here, but I live like a king. . . . I

Willie Wells, Sr. *(center),* his son Willie Wells, Jr. *(right),* and Ira Wells, all players for the Negro League's Memphis Red Sox, 1948. ASSOCIATED PRESS AP

was branded a Negro in the States and had to act accordingly. Everything I did, including playing ball, was regulated by my color. They wouldn't even give me a chance in the big leagues because I was a Negro, yet they accepted every other nationality under the sun. Well, here in Mexico, I am a man. I can go as far in baseball as I am capable of going." Over his four summers in Mexico (1940, 1941, 1943, 1944), Wells batted .323 and posted a stellar .410 on-base percentage.

He had also spent many winters in Havana, where he became one of the best players in the history of the prestigious Cuban Winter League. Wells batted .320 over seven seasons in the league (1928–1930 and 1935–1940, inclusive), winning two home run titles. In the 1929–1930 season he was named Most Valuable Player (MVP) when he batted .322 to lead the underdog Cienfuegos team to its first-ever league title. Ten years later he won a second MVP trophy, batting .328 for pennant-winning Almendares.

Wells returned to Newark for a final season in 1945, again as player-manager. Wells studied opposing players meticulously to learn their tendencies, and he barked orders from his position at shortstop. He also received high marks for his teaching ability, and several of the young players he mentored later became major league stars, including Monte Irvin, Larry Doby, and Don Newcombe. Wells quit Newark in 1946 after a conflict with owner Abe Manley, and over the next several years he spent brief periods with teams in New York, Baltimore, and Memphis, where he and his son, Willie, Jr., were teammates. In 1950, along with his son, Wells went to Canada to join the Manitoba-Dakota League, an integrated independent league. In 1953, after two years managing the Winnipeg Buffaloes and two more with the Brandon (Manitoba) Greys, Wells retired from baseball.

Wells was married to Lorene Sampson and had two children. After he retired, Wells settled in New York City, where he worked for thirteen years in a delicatessen at Nassau and Liberty Streets in Lower Manhattan. He grew weary of the city's crime, however, and in 1973 he returned to his hometown of Austin to care for his ailing mother. He moved back into the modest home on Newton Street in which he had grown up and passed his later years watching baseball games on television and playing dominoes at the corner barbershop. Wells died of heart failure from complications of the diabetes that had left him legally blind, and is buried in Austin's Evergreen Cemetery. He was inducted posthumously into the Baseball Hall of Fame on 3 August 1997.

Wells seemed to save his best for exhibition games against white major leaguers, batting .392 in forty such games on record. In 1929, against a team of major league all-stars, Wells stole home on consecutive days to win both games. Although he stood just five feet, eight inches, and weighed 165 pounds, Wells was considered one of the toughest players in the game. He owned two sets of baseball shoes, one for regular play and one with longer, sharper spikes to intimidate infielders. His unrelenting style of play made him the target of frequent beanballs, or pitches thrown at a batter's head. After a hit by Baltimore's Bill Byrd in 1942, Wells pioneered a solution. In the next game, he appeared wearing a construction hard hat. It was said to be the first time a professional player had ever worn a protective batting helmet.

Wells was one of the most enduring and well-traveled players in baseball history, playing for thirty years in five countries and countless cities in the United States. His talent enabled him to make the entire Western Hemisphere his home. Wells was said to have a lifetime batting average of .332, and his slugging set the precedent for a bevy of power-hitting shortstops, including Ernie Banks and Cal Ripken. Wells determinedly overcame the racism that barred him from Major League Baseball, and his intelligence and teaching ability were admired by many. "He was always there when you needed help," one of his players, Len Pearson, remembered. "Willie Wells was a hell of a man."

★

A file of news clippings, correspondence, and other documents is in the archives of the National Baseball Hall of Fame Library in Cooperstown, New York. James Riley, *Dandy, Day, and the Devil* (1987), covers Wells's career and those of his teammates Ray Dandridge and Leon Day. Significant articles about Wells appeared in the *Austin American-Statesman* (12 May 1973, 2 Jan. 1977, 7 Aug. 1977), *Austin* magazine (June 1979), the *New York Times* (23 Mar. 1997), and the *Daily Texan* (9 Feb. 1998). An obituary is in the *New York Times* (25 Jan. 1989). A chapter on Wells is in the seminal work of the Negro Leagues oral history, John Holway, *Voices from the Great Black Baseball Leagues* (1975).

ERIC ENDERS

WEST, Jerry Alan (*b.* 28 May 1938 in Cabin Creek, West Virginia), basketball player who helped redefine the guard position in basketball; sucessful head coach; and general manager and executive vice president of the Los Angeles Lakers who built two of professional basketball's greatest dynasties during his tenure in the Lakers' front office.

West grew up in the West Virginia coalfields, where his father was an electrician in the mines and his mother was

Jerry West *(right)*, 1970. ASSOCIATED PRESS AP

a homemaker. Demonstrating the commitment that marked his career in athletics, he practiced basketball incessantly, becoming so frail that his physician ordered vitamin injections. West led the tiny East Bank High School to a state championship and became the first high school player in state history to score more than 900 points. He graduated from East Bank in 1956. Among scholarship offers from more than sixty colleges, West chose West Virginia University (WVU), where he followed in the tradition of All-Americans and professional players "Hot" Rod Hundley and Rod Thorn.

In 1956 West led his freshman team to an undefeated season, and each varsity year improved his personal accomplishments. As a sophomore, West averaged 17.8 points per game; as a junior, 26.6, leading the Mountaineers to the national championship in 1959. Scoring twenty-eight points in the championship game, he was named the tournament's Most Valuable Player (MVP). West increased his scoring average to 29.3 in 1960, leading the Mountaineers to a 26–5 season, then averaged thirty-five points per game in the National Collegiate Athletic Association (NCAA) tournament. A unanimous All-American in 1959 and 1960, West was subsequently voted to the NCAA Tournament 1950s All-Decade team. In 1958 he played in the Pan-American Games, and in 1960 West and Oscar Robertson led the United States team to an Olympic gold in Rome, Italy. He graduated from WVU with a B.A. in education in 1960.

West was the second player chosen in the 1960 draft by

the Lakers, who had just moved to Los Angeles. The team already boasted one outstanding player, Elgin Baylor. West at guard and Baylor at forward formed the nucleus of a squad that would dominate the National Basketball Association's (NBA) Western Division for the next decade. Unfortunately for the Lakers, the Boston Celtics dominated the Eastern Division, and the showdowns between these titans resulted six times in Boston victories. In 1969, despite a severe leg injury, West posted 42 points, 13 rebounds, and 12 assists in the championship's final game. Bill Russell, the future Hall of Fame center for the Celtics, commented on that performance. "Los Angeles has not won the championship, but Jerry West is still a champion." West won the tournament finals MVP award, the only time this distinction was given to a member of the losing team.

West was admired by teammate and foe alike as the quintessential pressure performer. He acquired the nickname "Mr. Clutch" after he sank a sixty-three-foot basket as the clock ran out, to send game three of the 1970 championship series into overtime.The nickname confirmed what everyone who followed professional basketball already knew: that West was a premier pressure player. He scored more than fifty points with a broken nose during a 1965 playoff game. West himself believes his best individual effort came in game three of the 1962 finals against the Celtics, when he sank two last-minute jumpers to tie the game, then intercepted an inbounds pass, drove the lane, and scored for a Lakers victory.

The legend of West as the player the Lakers wanted to handle the ball toward the end of a close game probably originated in a contest against the San Francisco Warriors. With the Lakers losing by one point, Coach Fred Schauss called a time-out to diagram a play. West told the huddle, "Throw me the damn ball and get away from me." The Lakers won on his fifteen-footer, and a sports legend was born. When the Lakers, tired of going to the playoffs without bringing home the championship, traded for legendary center Wilt Chamberlain in the 1968–1969 season, the question over lunch and in taverns across America was "Can they go undefeated?" With a dominating scorer and an intimidating rebounder in the lineup, West adapted his game to concentrate on assists and defense. The following year, Baylor and Chamberlain struggled with injuries, so West reemphasized scoring and led the NBA with 31.2 points per game.

The Lakers' dream came true in 1972. West, MVP in the All-Star game, led his team to its first league championship, leading the NBA with 9.7 assists per game and averaging more than twenty-five points. The team set records with thirty-three consecutive victories (the old one was twenty) and sixty-nine wins in a season, a record that stood until the 1995–1996 season. Even as the Lakers achieved the championship, however, the dynasty was crumbling. Baylor retired in 1971, and Chamberlain followed before the 1973–1974 season. West called it quits after thirty-one games that season, saying, "I'm not willing to sacrifice my standards. Perhaps I expect too much." For the first time since West joined the team in 1960, the Lakers failed to make the playoffs in 1974.

When he retired, West was the third player in NBA history to score more than 25,000 career points (25,192). He remains among the top five in career scoring average with twenty-seven points per game. The completeness of West's game is illustrated by his average of 5.8 rebounds and 6.7 assists per game over his career. He also stole the ball eighty-one times. West was elected to the Basketball Hall of Fame in 1979, and the Lakers retired his number (44) in 1983. In 1997 he was named among the fifty greatest players in league history. Bob Cousy of the Celtics recalled, "to the end of his career, Jerry wanted to take the last-second shot that meant the game. He wanted that responsibility."

West became head coach of the Lakers in 1976, and that year the team won the Pacific Coast Division with the NBA's best record, but were swept by the Portland Trailblazers in the West Coast finals. The next year, they were eliminated by the Seattle SuperSonics in the Western Division playoffs, then lost to the same team in the semifinal round the following year. A new owner purchased the team, and West resigned in 1979. As head coach, he presided over 145 wins, 101 losses, and 8 postseason victories.

After serving as a special consultant, West became general manager of the Lakers in 1982. Between 1982 and 1990, the Lakers played in seven championship finals, winning in 1982, 1985, 1987, and 1988. Through skillful negotiations and trades, West built the spectacular dynasty the press called "Showtime," which was structured around guard Earvin "Magic" Johnson. After Johnson's sudden retirement, the team struggled in the early 1990s, but West built another dynasty, "Showtime II," that went to playoffs in 1995, when West was named Executive of the Year. Sportswriter Alan Malamud wrote that there can be "no argument that [West] is among the most astute executives in any sport in America." Washington Bullets general manager Bob Frey agreed. "Jerry West, without a doubt, has done the best job of anyone in the NBA." Citing health reasons and forty consecutive years working for the team, West retired on 8 August 2000. The second dynasty he built won championships in both 2000 and 2001.

Following a first marriage that produced three sons but ended in divorce, West married Karen Bua in 1978. They had two sons.

West leaves an unparalleled legacy of dedication and excellence as a player, coach, and executive. During his forty years with the team, the Lakers experienced only seven losing seasons, won fifty or more games in twenty-three, and achieved seven championships. West's steely-eyed determination was captured perfectly when he described his role as team executive: "I take a personal responsibility when we don't win."

As a player, West helped redefine the guard position. Before the 1960s, the position was usually defined as one for smaller men, perhaps under six feet, who could either handle the ball like a wizard (Bob Cousy of the Celtics exemplified this skill) or shoot from the perimeter. Along with Oscar Robertson, West transformed the position into the model that shaped college and professional basketball for the remainder of the twentieth century. West and Robertson combined scoring that featured the modern jump shot and aggressive drives through the lane, with attacking defense and precision ball handling, resulting in many assists, as well as the ability to grab critical rebounds. Their achievements initiated the new guard tradition that has nurtured superstars like Michael Jordan, Isiah Thomas, and Magic Johnson.

Several professional players have brilliant careers, then move on to success in coaching or management. West uniquely combined all these talents, leading his team to the playoffs every year he played, then again in his three years as head coach, and finally rebuilding the team twice to form two distinct embodiments of one of professional basketball's greatest dynasties. The league's official logo features a player in silhouette; the model was West, whose career is a model of dedication to excellence and athletic discipline.

★

Print articles on West's life and career include Dave Anderson, "Sports of the Times: Cousy and the All-Time NBA Team," *New York Times* (2 Nov. 1980); Richard Hoffer, "Mister Clutch, Master Builder," *Sports Illustrated* (23 Apr. 1990); Allan Malamud, "NBA Finals: Lakers v. Bulls: West Is Still Scoring by Making Some Great Moves," *Los Angeles Times* (7 June 1991); Daniel Taub, "Lakers Legend," *Los Angeles Business Journal* (8 Feb. 1999); "Into the Sunset: Jerry West Retires as Lakers' Executive Vice President," *CNN-Sports Illustrated* (8 Aug. 2000); and Lyle Spencer, "Repeatedly Brilliant: West, Jackson, Shaq, Kobe," *Riverside California Press-Enterprise* (16 June 2001). The Lakers home page features extensive information on West's career. It can be found at http://www.nba.com/lakers.

DAVID C. DOUGHERTY

WHITE, Reginald Howard ("Reggie") (*b.* 19 December 1961 in Chattanooga, Tennessee), professional football player and Baptist minister who holds several records and who is often considered the game's best defensive end.

White, the son of Charles White and Thelma Dodds Collier, was raised by his mother and his grandparents. His

Reggie White. AP/WIDE WORLD PHOTOS

grandmother and a local minister, Bernard Ferguson, influenced his religious views. At thirteen, when White decided to "give his life to the Lord," he also decided that he wanted to become a professional football player. At Howard High School in Chattanooga he played tight end and nose tackle, lettering three times.

After high school, White attended the University of Tennessee, where he was a standout player for the Volunteers, setting school records for sacks in a season and in a career, and earning the nickname "Minister of Defense." In 1991 when the university celebrated its football program's 100th anniversary, White was named to the centennial team. In 1983 he was the South Eastern Conference player of the year and an All-American. He graduated with a B.A. in human services.

Instead of joining the National Football League (NFL), White signed with the Memphis Showboats of the upstart United States Football League (USFL), perhaps because he would have the chance to play in his home state. From 1984 to 1985 White played 34 games for the Showboats, recording 23.5 sacks and 193 tackles and forcing 7 fumbles, making him one of the league's best players during its short life.

In 1984 the NFL held a special draft of USFL players, and the Philadelphia Eagles selected White. He joined the team three games into the season and made an immediate impact, recording two sacks, as well as causing a fumble and tipping a pass to a teammate that was returned for a touchdown. He also began his career in public service, helping charitable organizations for the unemployed and for underprivileged youth. White's becoming an ordained minister made him the butt of numerous jokes, and he was ridiculed for his beliefs throughout the rest of his career. How, some wondered, could he be both a peacemaker and one of the most fearsome players in football? "I hit hard for the glory of God," White said.

White married Sara Copeland on 5 January 1985 and credits her with providing discipline to his finances, saying that she was "worth more to me than all the rubies in the world." They have two children.

White's play for the Eagles was outstanding; he recorded more sacks than games played. In 1991 the Eagle defense was ranked first in the NFL. During this period, White became an activist in a union, the NFL Players' Association. In 1992 he was one of the union's negotiators for talks that eventually led to free agency, and earned the union's Byron "Whizzer" White Humanitarian Award in recognition of the long hours he put in helping charitable organizations in Philadelphia and in his home state of Tennessee. Eventually, White and other players were conceded the right to become free agents, and, not unexpectedly, the Eagles made little effort to re-sign him.

At first White did not consider relocating to the town of Green Bay, Wisconsin, preferring to live in San Francisco or Chicago where he could minister to inner-city youth. But the Green Bay Packers pestered him until he agreed to meet with them. The Packers offered him $17 million a year and an important role in a team whose defense ranked twenty-third in the NFL the previous season. In 1993 White signed with the Packers, and was immediately criticized for being a greedy Christian.

White's signing with the Packers was one of the turning points in the history of U.S. football. White was the most sought-after player at the time, the one sure bet to join the Hall of Fame. Even so, his salary was ridiculously high. Teams began to change their outlooks on hiring and training players; no longer was investing in a good prospect who might need a year or two of seasoning the best way to spend money. Instead, a player who could fit in with a team's offensive or defensive scheme right away, despite questionable long-term prospects, was preferred over those who needed nurturing. This trend also influenced the college draft.

White's effect on the Packers was astonishing; the team ran essentially the same defense as the previous year but was ranked second in the NFL for 1993. White's teammates admired him, and his coaches were delighted. His leadership became legendary, and he was credited with encouraging and advising many players struggling to save their foundering careers. On defense, his ability to read offensive plays and set up appropriate defenses was extraordinary, and he became a valuable field general.

In 1995 White donated $1 million to Knoxville's Inner City Community Investment Corporation, which offers microloans to high-risk entrepreneurs. In 1996 he received the Jackie Robinson Humanitarian Award as well as the Tolerance Award from the Simon Wiesenthal Center. Also that year, the church in which he preached, Knoxville's Inner City Church, was burned down, possibly by anti-Christian aggressors. In Green Bay, White assisted small businesses through the Urban Hope Partnership organization.

White's crowning moment on the field may have been the 1997 Super Bowl. He kept his teammates focused during the chaotic week before the game, providing leadership when it was most needed, and he played a fine game. But the next season was difficult for him. He had played with injuries in the past, but a back injury hampered him to the point that after the season, he decided to retire. Remembering that he had promised the Packers at least one more year of play, he retracted his retirement and played the 1998 season, after which he again retired. After sitting out the 1999 season, he joined the Carolina Panthers, retiring again after a lackluster performance.

★

White wrote *Reggie White in the Trenches: The Autobiography* (1996), with James D. Denney; this book is the best resource for information about White's life and views. *God's Playbook: The Bible's Game Plan for Life* (1998), by White and Steve Hubbard shows how White incorporated his athletic life into his religious beliefs, and *Fighting the Good Fight: America's Minister of Defense Stands Firm on What It Takes to Win God's Way* (1999), by White and Andrew Peyton Thomas offers the fullest explanation of White's perspective on Christianity and American life.

KIRK H. BEETZ

WHITFIELD, Mal(vin) Greston (*b.* 11 October 1924 in Bay City, Texas), middle-distance runner who won five Olympic medals, three of them gold, and who devoted much of his life to promoting track and field in Africa.

Whitfield's family moved from Texas to Los Angeles when he was a toddler. By the time he was in elementary school, Whitfield was selling fruits and vegetables in Watts to help the family pay its bills. He began his education at the Forty-ninth Street School in Los Angeles, and progressed to the 111th Street School. In 1936, at age eleven, he snuck into the Los Angeles stadium to watch Jesse Owens—his idol—run. Not only did he get Owens's autograph, he also watched how Ohio State University (OSU) coach Larry Snyder instructed Owens, and was impressed. Whitfield dreamed of following the path of four great Ohio State

Mal Whitfield after winning a gold medal at the 1948 Olympics. AP/WIDE WORLD PHOTOS

runners—Jesse Owens, Mel Walker, Dave Albritton, and Charlie Beetham—as one of Snyder's protégés.

While attending Willowbrook Junior High School, George Washington Culver High School, and Jefferson High School in Los Angeles, Whitfield became a track star. After graduating from high school, he was offered scholarships at several colleges, but chose to enter OSU in autumn 1946 so he could train with Coach Snyder. He ran on the Ohio State varsity track team as a freshman, and in summer 1947 he joined the U.S. Air Force. Through the influence of his benefactor, the newspaper magnate Otis Chandler, Whitfield was stationed at Lockbourne Air Force Base, just outside Columbus, Ohio, as part of the 100th Fighter Squadron. While at Lockbourne, Whitfield married and competed in college track for the next two years. In 1948 he was one of three African Americans on the OSU track team.

At the 1948 National Collegiate Athletic Association (NCAA) championships held in Minneapolis, the six-foot, 165-pound Whitfield won the 800-meter event and placed fourth in the 400-meter run. Two weeks later at the Amateur Athletic Union (AAU) championships at Marquette University, Whitfield placed second in the 400-meter event. His performances earned him a place on the U.S. Olympic team headed for London, England.

Considered an outsider, Whitfield was not expected to make much of a splash in his first international competition. He proved, however, to be a strong contender. On the brick-red track at London's Wembley Stadium, he surprised everyone by winning the gold medal in the 800-meter run and 1,600-meter relay, and by taking a bronze in the 400-meter dash. He was the first Olympian in 28 years to win medals in both the 400- and 800-meter races.

After the Olympics, Whitfield returned to compete and study at Ohio State, while continuing to serve in the air force. From 1946 to 1949 he lettered in track four times and was elected as the cocaptain of the 1949 OSU outdoor track team, one of only two African Americans on the team. Following the 1949 school year, Sergeant Whitfield served a tour of duty in the Korean War (1950–1953) as a bombardier/tail gunner on a B-26. In 1950 he withdrew as a student from OSU without graduating. After Korea, he was reassigned to Lockbourne, where he continued his amateur track career.

In June 1951 Whitfield represented the United States at the Pan-American Games in Buenos Aires, Argentina, winning the 800-meter race. In late March 1952 at the sixteenth annual *Chicago Daily News* relays, Whitfield permanently retired the Frank Hill Trophy for the 600-yard run. The following month he helped the air force track team win the Mile Relay Championship of America at the Penn Relays. Finally, in June, he tied the U.S. record for the 800-meter run at the U.S. Olympic trials and won the AAU 400-meter title. In doing so, Whitfield qualified for his second Olympic team in both the 400- and 800-meter runs.

Whitfield was even more serious about his second Olympic chance than he was in 1948. He told reporters, "Sports can be a foundation for better social relations. We athletes have a common ground, not based on class or creed. I sincerely feel we can do a lot of good for America, not just in a sports way." As if to prove the truth of Whitfield's words, Mayor James Rhodes urged the citizens of Columbus to raise the $1,400 necessary to send "the flying sergeant" and his wife to the Helsinki Olympic Games.

On 22 July 1952 in Helsinki, Finland, Whitfield tied his own 800-meter Olympic record (1:49.2) in the finals, and won the race by two yards. He got off poorly in the finals of the 400-meter dash and placed sixth, but redeemed himself in the 4 x 400-meter relay to win his fifth Olympic medal, a silver. Although the U.S. team finished second to Jamaica by a yard, Whitfield ran a splendid race and the U.S. team, despite coming in second, broke the previous world record by more than four seconds.

Following the Helsinki Olympics, Whitfield left the air force, but continued to compete in track events. In 1954 he won both the 1,000-meter run at the eighteenth annual *Chicago Daily News* relays in record-setting time (2:10.5), and, for the fifth time, the AAU 880-yard championship.

As a result of these accomplishments, in 1954 Whitfield became the first African American to win the James E. Sullivan Memorial Award as the AAU athlete of the year. In 1955 Whitfield enrolled at Los Angeles State College, running for their track team and for the Los Angeles Athletic Club. He narrowly missed making the 1956 Olympic team, and soon retired from competitive running. In 1956 he graduated from Los Angeles State.

In 1957 "Marvelous Mal" Whitfield gave away twenty of his most prized trophies to the schools he had attended, former coaches, and those he believed had assisted him in achieving international fame, saying the gesture was inspired by what he had seen in the Belgian Congo while on a goodwill trip for the U.S. State Department: "I saw how badly the young athletes in those countries deep inside Africa needed equipment, facilities, and proper training. I saw these kids do so much with so little. . . . I always felt [that] without the interest people had in me, I never could have been successful."

Whitfield spent more than thirty years in Nigeria, Mali, and other African nations building physical education, academic, and sport programs, working as an employee of the U.S. State Department's Information and Foreign Services. In 1974 Whitfield was inducted as a member of the National Track and Field Hall of Fame. He also was inducted into the OSU Athletic Hall of Fame and the U.S. Olympic Hall of Fame (1988). As of 2001 he was a consultant in African affairs, living in Washington, D.C.

★

Reliable information on Whitfield is limited; in addition, he has been sparing with and, at times, inconsistent in reports about his personal life. The best sources of information are the *Ohio State University Directory Supplement* (winter 1947–1948 and 1948–1949); *Ohio State University Alumni Magazine* (June 1951, Apr. 1955, Oct. 1978, July 1983, Nov. 1992). Articles about Whitfield appear in the *Columbus Dispatch* (13 July 1948, 2 Aug. 1948, 5 Aug. 1948, 3 July 1952, 6 July 1952); *Atlanta Daily World* (3 Apr. 1952, 10 July 1952, 23 July 1952, 26 July 1952, 27 July 1952, 29 July 1952); *Bloomington Herald-Telephone* (22 Mar. 1954); and *New York Times* (19 Feb. 1956).

KEITH MCCLELLAN

WILKENS, Leonard Randolph ("Lenny") (*b.* 28 October 1937 in Brooklyn, New York), coach with most wins in National Basketball Association (NBA) history and one of only two men to be inducted into the Basketball Hall of Fame as both a player and a coach.

Lenny Wilkens. AP/WIDE WORLD PHOTOS

Wilkens was the oldest of four children of Leonard R. Wilkens, a chauffeur, and Henrietta Cross Wilkens, a factory worker. Growing up in the tough neighborhood of Bedford-Stuyvesant with a white mother and black father (who died when Wilkens was five years old), Wilkens struggled early in life with both poverty and bigotry. The young Wilkens learned his work ethic from his mother, a lesson he credits his Catholic education for reinforcing and honing. However it was learned, the lesson took, and the six-foot, one-inch Wilkens developed into an exceptional point guard on offense and defense.

Wilkens began as a street ball player, learning his game on the local blacktop rather than in organized leagues. He credits his playground education for his basketball acumen: "Back then, especially in the areas that I played, if you couldn't play, they wouldn't let you on the court. . . . It wasn't just slam dunk. It wasn't just three-point shots. We played, and we wanted to stay on the court."

Although Wilkens attended basketball powerhouse Boys High School in Brooklyn and made the squad as a freshman, he played only half a season of high school ball, believing he did not have the skills to start. In lieu of organized high school leagues, Wilkens opted for pickup games and a league run through the Catholic Youth Organization (CYO). His CYO coach Father Thomas Mannion convinced Providence College in Rhode Island to give Wilkens a try, and after his graduation from high school, he began his freshman year in 1956 on a scholarship. Mannion's eye for talent proved keen as Wilkens led the Providence freshman squad to an undefeated season. In three years with the varsity squad, Wilkens averaged 14.9 points per game, helped the Friars to a semifinal game in the National Invitational Tournament (NIT) in 1959, and was named Most Valuable Player (MVP) of the NIT final in a losing effort in 1960. He graduated with a B.A. in economics in 1960. Wilkens married Marilyn J. Reed on 28 July 1962; they had three children.

The NBA's St. Louis Hawks drafted Wilkens in the first

round in 1960, although Wilkens initially balked at a career as a professional athlete, in part because the $8,000 annual salary was not enough to live on. Once he saw he could hold his own with the level of competition in the NBA, however, Wilkens joined the Hawks, helping them to the NBA finals in his rookie season. All told, he played seven seasons for St. Louis and was named an All-Star five times. His career was interrupted for military service; he served in the U.S. Army from 1961 to 1962 and became a second lieutenant. His best year statistically came in the 1967–1968 season, when he averaged twenty points per game and was runner-up to Wilt Chamberlain for the league's MVP.

The following season, St. Louis dealt Wilkens to the expansion club Seattle SuperSonics, who were entering only their second season. Two seasons later, he was approached by Dick Vertlieb, the Sonics general manager, who asked if he would like to take over some of the team's coaching duties while remaining on the squad. From 1969 through 1972, Wilkens continued to excel on the court while learning the basics of coaching. At the beginning of the 1972–1973 season, the team management asked Wilkens to choose between his coaching and playing duties. Wilkens decided it was too soon to end his playing career and handed over the coaching reins. Tom Nissalke, the new coach, promptly traded Wilkens to the Cleveland Cavaliers, another expansion club.

Being dealt to yet another dreadful expansion team did not sit well with Wilkens, who initially refused to report. He relented, however, and ended up representing Cleveland in the 1973 All-Star Game. After two seasons in Cleveland, Wilkens returned to his role as player-coach, this time for the Portland Trail Blazers in 1974.

Although Wilkens retired as a player in 1975, an even more impressive phase of his career was only beginning. Wilkens remained in Portland as head coach after retiring for one season. He returned to Seattle in 1977 as head coach. The Sonics had started the year 5–17, but when Wilkens took over, he crafted what many believed was a talentless squad into a tight unselfish squad that worked well as a team. The Sonics turned their season around, and Wilkens led them as far as the NBA finals. The following season, Wilkens's squad won the championship. Says Wilkens of his so-called miracle in Seattle, "I heard general managers and other people say it was the worst team ever. And when I turned it around, all of a sudden everyone said, 'Well, we always knew they had talent.'"

Wilkens remained with the Sonics until 1987, when he took a job with the Cavaliers, another team from his playing days. Although he had considerable regular-season success with the Cavs, Wilkens could not get his squad past the powerhouse Chicago Bulls in the playoffs. He resigned after the season ended in 1993.

Other teams immediately began clamoring for his services, and Wilkens went back to the franchise he began his playing career with, the Hawks (who had by this time relocated to Atlanta). Wilkens continued his coaching success with the Hawks, posting a record of 310–232 over 7 seasons and being named NBA Coach of the Year in 1994. In 1995 he surpassed the Celtics' Red Auerbach as the coach with the most wins in NBA history (939 in 22 seasons). Wilkens became head coach for the Toronto Raptors in 2000. He lives in Seattle in the off-season with his wife, Marilyn.

As well as a fifteen-year Hall of Fame playing career and an equally luminous thirty-year coaching career, Wilkens is in his fifth decade in the NBA. The intelligence and unselfish play that made him a standout as a point guard formed the basis for an even more impressive coaching career that has seen Wilkens win the NBA championship, lead the United States to Olympic gold in 1996, and amass more victories than any other coach in basketball history.

Despite his low-key demeanor, Wilkens is an outspoken critic of what he sees as the systematic "blackout" of coaching opportunities for other African-American coaches. Although his own coaching career is an unparalleled success, Wilkens notes that even in recent years, the NBA seems to grant few coaching opportunities to African Americans. "If you're black and not successful right away, then it's tough." As one of the first African-American coaches in the league, Wilkens hopes to use his example to open up opportunities for others.

★

Wilkens wrote two autobiographies, *The Lenny Wilkens Story* (1974), with Paul S. Eriksson; and *Unguarded: My Forty Years Surviving the NBA* (2000), with Terry Pluto. He is also the subject of numerous articles, including a feature story in *Ebony* (Apr. 1999), and a piece in the "NBA Legends" section of http://www.nba.com.

MATTHEW TAYLOR RAFFETY

WILKINSON, Charles Burnham ("Bud") (*b.* 23 April 1915 in Minneapolis, Minnesota; *d.* 9 February 1994 in St. Louis, Missouri), football coach at the University of Oklahoma whose teams in the 1950s won three national championships and achieved a record winning streak of forty-seven games.

Wilkinson was one of two sons born to Charles Patton and Edith (Lindbloom) Wilkinson. His mother died in 1923 when he was eight years old and his father, a real estate developer and mortgage dealer in Minneapolis, later married Ethel Grace, who enjoyed a warm relationship with her stepson.

In 1928 Wilkinson entered Shattuck Military Academy in Faribault, Minnesota. He was an outstanding preparatory school athlete, earning varsity letters in football, baseball, hockey, and basketball. After graduating from Shattuck in 1933, Wilkinson pursued his education at the University of Minnesota at Minneapolis–Saint Paul, where he played football under the tutelage of the coach Bernie Bierman. In 1934 and 1935 Wilkinson performed as a guard, then switched to quarterback for his final two seasons. During Wilkinson's tenure at Minnesota, the football team won national championships in 1935 and 1937. In his final collegiate appearance as a player, Wilkinson quarterbacked the college All-Stars to a victory over Wisconsin's Green Bay Packers, the 1936 champions of the National Football League (NFL).

After earning his B.A. in English from Minnesota in 1937, Wilkinson worked briefly for his father in Minneapolis before pursuing a career in coaching football. In autumn 1937 he accepted an assistant coaching position at Syracuse University in New York, where he also earned an M.A. in English in 1940. At Syracuse, Wilkinson met Mary Shifflett, and they married in August 1938; they later had two sons. Wilkinson left Syracuse in 1941, returning to the University of Minnesota as an assistant coach.

Wilkinson remained at Minnesota until 1943, when he entered the U.S. Navy. Taking advantage of his football background, Wilkinson served as an assistant coach at the Iowa Pre-Flight School. Wilkinson saw action in the Pacific in 1944–1945 as a hangar deck officer on the aircraft carrier *Enterprise.* Commended for high performance of duty when his ship was under attack, he was discharged from the navy in 1945 with the rank of lieutenant commander.

After the end of World War II, Wilkinson again briefly worked for his father in Minneapolis, but the lure of football proved too strong. In 1946 Wilkinson accepted the post as the assistant football coach under Jim Tatum at the University of Oklahoma in Norman. When the 1946 team won eight of eleven games, the University of Maryland College Park hired Tatum. Oklahoma's officials filled the vacancy by appointing Wilkinson as the head football coach and athletic director.

Wilkinson's Oklahoma Sooners got off to a rocky start in 1947, winning only two of their first five contests, but after the coach went with younger players, the squad won six of the last seven games. Wilkinson began to create a college football dynasty in Norman. From 1948 to 1959 Oklahoma finished first in the Big Seven Conference. For eleven straight seasons (1948–1958) Oklahoma was selected to the Associated Press's list of top ten college teams. Wilkinson was tapped as the college coach of the year in 1949. Under his leadership the Sooners won three national championships (1950, 1955, 1956). Between 1948 and 1950 the team won 31 straight games, but later eclipsed this mark with a 47-game winning streak (1953–1957) that still stood in 2001 as a standard for college football excellence.

Bud Wilkinson, 1951. © BETTMANN/CORBIS

The modest Wilkinson credited much of his success to the split-T formation, pioneered by Don Faurot at the University of Missouri. However, he was responsible for innovations of his own and was a superb motivator. In addition to inventing the no-huddle offense, known in the 1950s as "Go-Go," Wilkinson emphasized teamwork, stating, "If a team is to reach its potential, each player must be willing to subordinate his personal goals to the good of the team." Wilkinson was a master at getting this type of effort from his players.

By the early 1960s Wilkinson's dynasty was in decline. In 1960 he suffered his first losing season at Oklahoma, but his national reputation for excellence was acknowledged when President John F. Kennedy asked the coach to serve part time as an unpaid special consultant on youth fitness. Wilkinson retired as the head football coach at the University of Oklahoma following the 1963 season. During his seventeen-year tenure at the university, Wilkinson's teams won 145 games, lost 29, and tied 4.

Wilkinson sought to capitalize on his football fame by moving into Oklahoma politics. In 1964 he gained the Republican nomination for the U.S. Senate, but the Democrat Fred Harris defeated him in a close election. Wilkinson spent less time in Oklahoma after this unexpected political setback, and pursued business interests in Minnesota and St. Louis, worked as a college football analyst for ABC television, and headed the President's Council on Physical Fitness under President Lyndon Johnson.

Wilkinson retired to St. Louis in the early 1970s. In August 1974 Wilkinson's first marriage ended in divorce, and on 18 November 1977 he married Donna O'Donnohue. Wilkinson surprised many of his friends by returning to the coaching ranks in 1978, accepting an offer to lead the professional St. Louis Cardinals of the NFL. He was unable to recapture his glory days at Oklahoma, and during two seasons with the Cardinals he compiled a record of eleven wins and twenty-one losses. Resigning after the 1979 season, Wilkinson pursued private business in St. Louis.

In late 1993 Wilkinson suffered a series of strokes that destroyed much of his vision. At age seventy-eight he died at his St. Louis home from congestive heart failure after surgery to repair a heart defect. Enshrined in the National College Football Hall of Fame in 1969, Wilkinson and his Oklahoma Sooner football teams of the 1950s attained a mark of excellence that remains unequaled in the history of college football.

★

A detailed account of the Oklahoma Sooners under Wilkinson's guidance is Harold Keith, *Forty-seven Straight* (1984). For insights into Wilkinson's successful coaching strategy and philosophy, see Bud Wilkinson, *Oklahoma Split-T Football* (1952), and Wilkinson with Gomer Thomas Jones, *Modern Defensive Football* (1957). Also see Jay Wilkinson with Gretchen Kirsch, *Bud Wilkinson: An Intimate Portrait of an American Legend* (1994), and Jim Dent, *The Undefeated: The Oklahoma Sooners and the Greatest Streak in College Football* (2001). Contemporary accounts of Wilkinson's glory days at Oklahoma include H. T. Paxton, "Visit with Bud Wilkinson," *Saturday Evening Post* (11 Oct. 1958); and W. B. Furlong, "Coach with Winning Ways," *New York Times Magazine* (9 Nov. 1958). For Wilkinson's views on physical fitness, see Wilkinson, "Quality Physical Education: A School Responsibility," *Education Digest* (Mar. 1968). On Wilkinson's return to coaching with the St. Louis Cardinals, see Bruce Newman, "Legend Returns to Turn Them On," *Sports Illustrated* (31 July 1978). An obituary is in the *New York Times* (11 Feb. 1994).

RON BRILEY

WILLIAMS, Theodore Samuel ("Ted") (*b.* 30 August 1918 in San Diego, California), powerful baseball hitter who had a lifetime batting average of .344 with 521 home runs and who hit a record-setting .406 in 1941.

Williams was the second son of Sam and May Venzer Williams. His father, who claimed to have served with

Ted Williams, 1950. © BETTMANN/CORBIS

Theodore Roosevelt's Rough Riders during the Spanish-American War, named his son "Teddy," after the president. Williams changed his name to "Theodore," but from an early age everyone called him "Ted." His father, who held a series of jobs including that of photographer, was rarely around after the boy's first years. His mother worked for the Salvation Army, and Williams was always a little ashamed that his mother was out on the streets collecting money and trying to convert the homeless.

San Diego was a navy town, and as a young teenager Williams and his friends played pickup baseball games with the sailors. He also played for Herbert Hoover High School, from which he graduated in 1936. At age sixteen he was six feet, three inches tall, weighed 148 pounds, and dreamed of being a pitcher. As a high-school junior he hit .583, which effectively ended his pitching career. He had a natural, fluid, left-handed swing, although he threw with his right hand.

Shortly before Williams was eighteen in 1936, he signed a contract with the San Diego Padres of the Pacific Coast League for $150 per month. One of his teammates was the second baseman Bobby Doerr, who later played for many years with him on the Boston Red Sox. Williams hit .271 the first year and .291 with twenty-three home runs the next. Eddie Collins of the Red Sox was impressed enough to buy Williams's contract, and he promised to pay him $3,000 the first year and $4,500 the second.

The Red Sox sent Williams to the Minneapolis Millers of the American Association in 1938, where he had a spectacular year and won the triple crown, leading the league in batting average, home runs, and runs batted in (RBI), but he was less than spectacular in the field. He dropped easy fly balls, turned singles into triples, and often seemed awkward and distracted. But when he stepped into the batter's box, Williams was completely focused. He had already learned to take many pitches and to wait for a pitch he could hit. He also had learned that his power came from his hips. When he turned his hips and whipped his bat through the strike zone with a slight uppercut, he usually drove the ball with power to right field.

In his rookie season with the Red Sox in 1939, Williams played right field; the next year he switched to left, where he remained for the rest of his career. Never a great fielder, he did learn to play the wall at Boston's Fenway Park expertly. In his first game for the Red Sox he hit a double off Red Ruffing of the Yankees, one of the best pitchers in the league. He went on to hit .327 in his rookie year, with 31 home runs and 145 RBI. One of his home runs cleared the right field roof in Briggs Stadium in Detroit, the first ball ever to be hit out of the park.

Before the 1940 season the Red Sox remodeled Fenway Park to make it easier for their prize player to hit home runs. They shortened right center field to 380 feet by placing the bull pens in front of the bleachers. Some began to call this section Williamsburg. In 1940 Williams had another good year, but his relationship with the Boston sportswriters deteriorated. He had a temper, and his mood swings caused him difficulties during his entire career. But especially during his first few years he often exploded in anger, and a reporter would inevitably describe the incident in his paper. Perhaps because there were seven newspapers in Boston in the early 1940s, all competing for readership, the sportswriters exaggerated. "Ted Williams is a grown man with the mind of a juvenile," one Boston writer decided.

The last year before the United States entered World War II, 1941, was one of the greatest baseball seasons ever. It was the year Williams hit .406 and Joe DiMaggio had a fifty-six-game hit streak. Williams and DiMaggio were often compared during their careers. Probably Williams was the better hitter and DiMaggio the better all-around player. Williams was hitting .405 when the All-Star game was held at Briggs Stadium in Detroit. The American League (AL) trailed 7–5 with two men on and two out in the ninth when Williams lined a pitch into the seats in right field to win the game. He leaped around the bases and was greeted by his joyous teammates. He later called it the most thrilling home run of his career. The Yankees won the pennant, but Williams entered the final doubleheader of the season in Philadelphia, Pennsylvania, hitting .3995. He would have been credited with .400, but he played both games, garnering four hits in five at bats in the first game with one home run and two for three in the second to finish at .406, the first player to finish above .400 since 1930. He had 37 home runs, 120 RBI, only 27 strikeouts, and 145 bases on balls, with an incredible on-base percentage of .551.

Williams played the 1942 season even though the United States was at war and many baseball players, including Hank Greenberg and Bob Feller, had enlisted. The Boston reporters, who thought Williams should be in the service, criticized him. He did sign up for the naval aviation program during the year and was activated after the season was over. He spent the war years training pilots in Florida and Hawaii. On 4 May 1944 Williams married Doris Soule, whom he had met in Minnesota in 1938. It was never a happy marriage and ended in a bitter divorce in 1954.

Williams, along with the other stars, returned to baseball in 1946, and he returned stronger at six feet, four inches tall and 185 pounds. He was surrounded by a supporting cast of Rudy York, Bobby Doerr, Johnny Pesky, and Dominic DiMaggio, among others, and the Red Sox ran away with the AL pennant. At the All-Star game played in Fenway Park he went four for four including two home runs. The second home run was hit off the Pirate Rip Sewell's high-arching "eephus" pitch. On 14 July at Fenway Park, Williams hit three home runs and a double in the first game of a doubleheader against Cleveland. In the second game, Lou Boudreau, Cleveland's player-manager, unveiled his "Williams shift." The second baseman played a shallow left field, but everyone else was on the right side of the diamond daring Williams to hit or bunt to left, which he stubbornly refused to do. Chicago had used a similar shift against him in 1941, and he had defeated it by hitting to left field. Even in 1946 he occasionally hit to left field including an inside-the-park home run that clinched the pennant for the Red Sox.

The 1946 season ended in disaster when Boston lost to the St. Louis Cardinals in the World Series, and Williams hit an anemic .200 with no home runs. His critics, over the years, charged that he never hit well in crucial situations, citing his World Series performance (the only series he ever played in), the single playoff game against Cleveland in 1948, and the two-game series against the Yankees at the end of the 1949 season. He hit well leading up to those crucial games, but the critics were never satisfied. They even criticized him for not being present when his daughter was born on 30 January 1948. He was fishing in Florida, his favorite activity away from the baseball field.

The fortunes of the Red Sox declined during the 1950s, but Williams continued to hit and to talk about hitting. His career was interrupted in 1952 when he was called back into the service during the Korean War. He flew thirty-nine combat missions in a jet fighter and had a narrow escape when he landed his badly damaged plane and barely escaped before it burst into flames. The Boston fans were often critical of Williams, but they greeted him warmly when he returned to the Red Sox in August 1953. He hit .407 with thirteen home runs in an abbreviated season. Even more remarkable, he hit .388 with thirty-eight home runs in 1957, the year he turned thirty-nine.

Williams finally retired in 1960. His last at bat at Fenway Park on Wednesday afternoon 28 September 1960 was immortalized by John Updike's famous *New Yorker* article, "Hub Fans Bid Kid Adieu." Williams barely missed a home run early in the game, but on his last at bat he drove a ball beyond the bull pen in deep right center field. "Williams ran around the square of bases at the center of our beseeching screaming," Updike wrote. "He ran as he always ran out home runs—hurriedly, unsmiling, head down, as if our praise were a storm of rain to get out of. He didn't tip his cap." Williams was inducted into the Baseball Hall of Fame on 25 January 1966, the first year he was eligible.

He married Lee Howard in 1961, but the couple quickly divorced. Later he married Dolores Wettach, with whom he had two children, but that marriage also ended in divorce. He returned to baseball briefly to manage the Washington (D.C.) Senators in 1969, but he always was known as a hitter not a manager.

In 1939 when Williams arrived in Boston as a brash twenty-year-old rookie, he announced, "All I want out of life is that when I walk down the street folks will say, 'There goes the greatest hitter who ever lived.' " At the end of the twentieth century, Williams was one of two or three contestants for the honor. Despite losing five seasons to military service and portions of two others to injuries in nineteen seasons, he had a career average of .344, the seventh-best all time and best of the modern era, with 2,654 hits, 521 home runs, and 2,019 bases on balls with only 709 strikeouts. He hit for both average and power. He won six batting titles, led the league in home runs four times, had two triple crowns, and two Most Valuable Player awards.

But Williams's success included more than statistics. He was a presence in the batter's box and away from the field. When he took batting practice, even opposing players stopped to watch. Red Sox fans often asked, "How did Williams do?" before they asked about the team. In the batter's box he had absolute concentration. Out of the box he was sometimes out of control, but that added to his persona and made him even more prominent on the sports pages. Between 1939 and 1960 baseball would have been a different and lesser game without him.

★

Williams with John Underwood, *My Turn at Bat: The Story of My Life* (1969), is a casually written autobiography filled with lively stories and portraits of teammates and opponents. Williams with John Underwood, *The Science of Hitting* (1971), is a fascinating book that spells out Williams's theory of hitting. Michael Seidel, *Ted Williams: A Baseball Life* (1991), is the best biography. Glenn Stout and Richard A. Johnson, *Red Sox Century: One Hundred Years of Red Sox Baseball* (2000), is organized year by year and includes a great deal about Williams. John Updike, "Hub Fans Bid Kid Adieu," *New Yorker* (22 Oct. 1960), is the classic article by a leading novelist, critic, and Red Sox fan.

ALLEN F. DAVIS

WILLIAMS, Venus Ebone Starr (*b.* 17 June 1980 in Los Angeles, California), U.S. Open and Wimbledon tennis champion dubbed "ghetto Cinderella" by her father, her coach and manager.

Williams began playing at age four, coached by her father Richard Williams on the public courts of inner-city Compton, California. Her father, the son of a Louisiana sharecropper and part owner of a security business, decided he would teach his children to play tennis after watching the winner of a tennis tournament receive $30,000. He taught himself and his wife, Oracene, a nurse, to play by reading books and watching videos. The couple had five daughters, but the two youngest, Venus and Serena, showed the most potential. Richard Williams immediately launched a marketing blitz, making sure the world knew of his two young tennis prodigies. Both his coaching and his marketing ef-

Venus Williams. AP/WIDE WORLD PHOTOS

forts bore results. By age ten Williams had won every junior tournament she entered, including the Southern California girl's title in the under-twelve division, and her sister was taking honors in the ten-and-under division.

Soon companies began to offer endorsement contracts to the family, and by 1991 they could afford to move to Florida, where Williams and her sister were taught by the famous coach Rich Macci. In a move hotly debated in the tennis world, Richard Williams pulled his daughters out of the junior competitive circuit. Their schedule for the next four years was to practice tennis six hours a day, six days a week. Williams's parents, who raised their children in the Jehovah's Witness faith, also made sure that their daughters were well educated. Oracene homeschooled them, and the girls later graduated from a small private high school with honors.

Richard Williams, seemingly something of a huckster and a marketing genius, managed to keep the family in the spotlight. He decreed that both girls would turn professional at fourteen. In 1994 Williams played her first professional tournament in Oakland, California. She won her first match, which was played against a woman ranked fifty-ninth in the world, and then came up against the second-ranked Arantxa Sanchez Vicario. Williams had Vicario down a set with a service break when her game seemed to fall apart, and she finally lost 2–6, 6–3, 6–0. What Williams lacked, the experts said, was experience in competitive play. Nevertheless, her father limited her schedule, but not her publicity. But the next year, with that one professional tournament under her belt, Williams signed a five-year, $12 million endorsement deal with Reebok.

Stunning to behold, Williams brought excitement and a new look to women's tennis, attracting a multitude of fans. She stood just over six feet tall and was slim and muscular. She dressed in eye-catching and unique outfits, and her cornrowed hair was festooned with beads. Flying about the court, Williams displayed great power, grace, and charisma as she overpowered her opponents. "I never thought anyone was better than me," she told a *New York Times* reporter in 1997, when she was still ranked 211. "Once you do that, you lose," she added. Pam Shriver, a former U.S. Open champion, played Williams in a training match and predicted greatness for her. Shriver noted that even though Williams lacked the tactical skills needed to win, she had a natural way of intimidating her opponents.

In 1997 the confident seventeen-year-old Williams entered Wimbledon with high expectations and a lot of media attention. She was defeated in the first round. At the U.S. Open only a few months later, she became the first unseeded player to reach the finals, losing to Martina Hingis 6–0, 6–4. In 1998 Williams finally won her first singles title in the IGA Tennis Classic and won a second singles title at the Lipton Championships. That year her serve was clocked at a new women's world record of 127 miles per hour. At the French Open in 1999 Williams and her sister, who was also moving up through the tennis rankings, won the doubles title.

In the 1999 U.S. Open, Williams made it to the semifinals before losing to Martina Hingis in an exhausting three-set match. Then she sat in stony silence, watching her sister defeat Hingis in the finals. Serena Williams became the first African-American woman to win a Grand Slam title (Wimbledon and the U.S., French, and Australian Opens) since Althea Gibson won the 1958 U.S. Open.

Williams would later say she had been miserable watching her sister win the U.S. Open and realized she had been expecting her opponents to bow down to her superior height, power, and speed. But before she was able to put a new attitude into practice, Williams developed tendinitis in both wrists. She could not play for several months, and rumors, sparked by her father, swirled about her impending retirement.

In 2000 Williams, after playing only nine matches all year, made it to the semifinals at Wimbledon, where she met and defeated her visibly nervous sister. Then on 8 July 2000 Williams dispatched defending champion Lindsay Davenport in straight sets to win Wimbledon, becoming the first African-American women's singles champion since Althea Gibson in 1957 and 1958. After winning the singles title, Williams teamed up with her sister to win the women's doubles title. In September, Williams won the U.S. Open after knocking off top-ranked Martina Hingis and second-ranked Lindsay Davenport. Winning the U.S. Open extended her winning streak to twenty-six consecutive matches. At the 2000 Sydney Olympic Games she won two gold medals—one in singles, the other in doubles with her sister. In December Williams was honored as the *Sports Illustrated for Women* Sportsman of the Year.

Richard Williams says he taught his daughters to be tough. They both have shown great maturity and strength of character in a tennis world sometimes fraught with racial tension and outright bigotry. Rumors and controversy have followed the Williams sisters, often ignited by their father. The sisters have always been each other's friend, and both flourished, with Williams leading the way. Their ascendancy in tennis and in corporate sponsorships has helped to changed the way Americans view African-American women, women athletes, and women in general. The sisters, young, spirited, intelligent, fun loving, confident, strong, and beautiful, were seen as ideal role models for women in the new century. Williams made history when she signed the largest endorsement deal in women's sports history, earning $40 million with Reebok. In 2001 the family's financial empire, fed by wins and endorsements, was estimated to be $150 million.

After winning Wimbledon, Williams said that tennis

was a part of her life, but not the only part. "Tennis was my father's dream, not mine," she said. "Winning, losing, money, riches, or fame don't make you happy," she added. Because of her many other interests, she started to limit her tournament schedule, but in 2001 she came roaring back to regain her Wimbledon title. In the final Williams pummeled Justine Henin 6–1, 3–6, 6–0. Later that year at the U.S. Open, Williams and her sister both advanced to the championship final, making them the first sisters since 1884 to meet in a grand slam final. In recognition of this achievement and because of the excitement this match generated, it was shown during prime time on national television—the first time a women's final was so covered. Williams struggled in the match, but in the end her power prevailed and she won 6–2, 6–4. Williams's display of power and strength showed that she has the potential for a long reign in tennis history. Gracious in her win, Venus thanked her family for their support and hinted at retirement. It seemed a confident Venus was telling the world she would manage her own place in history.

★

Carol Brennan, "Venus Williams," *Newsmakers* (1998), contains a biography of Venus up to age seventeen. For information on Williams's relationship with her father, see Pat Jordan, "Daddy's Big Test," *New York Times Magazine* (16 Mar. 1997). Other articles include Wayne Coffey, "Williams Sisters plus Father in Center of Another Controversy," *New York Daily News* (27 Mar. 2001), and Raquel Cepeda, "Courting Destiny, Venus and Serena Are Tennis's New Power Set. So Why Are They the Center of So Much Racket?," *Essence* (June 2001). Current information about Williams and her sister can be found on their website at www.venusserenafans.com.

JULIANNE CICARELLI

WILLS (MOODY), Helen Newington (*b.* 6 October 1906 in Centerville, California; *d.* 1 January 1998 in Carmel, California), dominant female tennis champion of the 1920s and 1930s, considered among the very best of all time.

Wills was born to Clarence Wills, a surgeon, and Catherine Wills, a teacher. She was not a strong child. In fact, her health was somewhat fragile. To counter this, her father tried to stimulate her interest in outdoor activities. First, Wills started swimming. When her father bought her a horse, she began riding. When Wills was eight, her father bought her a tennis racket and played with her every day. For her fourteenth birthday, her parents bought her a membership in the Berkeley Tennis Club. Practicing every day, Wills won the 1921 California State Women's Championship on her first try. Wills learned the game of tennis on the hard cement courts that would "make" her and so many

Helen Wills. © UNDERWOOD & UNDERWOOD/CORBIS

other champions from the West Coast, who could compete year-round on these courts. This gave them a distinct advantage over East Coast players who only had a six to eight month season of practice and play.

Wills was tutored at home by her mother until she was eight years old. She graduated from the top-ranked Anna Head School in Berkeley in 1923 and enrolled at the University of California. She became Phi Beta Kappa because of her academic excellence, graduating with a B.A. in fine arts. No longer in poor health, Wills now stood five feet, seven inches tall, and weighed 150 pounds.

Wills entered the tennis world in 1922. From the beginning, she had a concentration few other players could match. Wills's approach to tennis was simple: "Every shot, every shot, every shot." She played each point as hard as every other, and never gave in either to exuberance or desperation. Her opponents were flummoxed. Observers began to marvel at her sure shots and steady baseline game. Wills's strengths were in the power of her shots and in her demeanor; people began to call her "Little Miss Poker Face."

While her talent was unquestionable, Wills also enjoyed good fortune. She made her mark in the early 1920s, the very time when Americans, eager for what President Warren G. Harding had called "a return to normalcy," were flocking to sports events in record numbers. It was the era of Babe Ruth and Jack Dempsey, and Wills played her own part in the social kaleidoscope of the "Roaring Twenties."

The twenty-year-old Wills faced twenty-six-year old Suzanne Lenglen at Cannes, France, on 16 February 1926. Lenglen was the dominant figure in both French and European tennis, and a great deal of excitement preceded the match. King Gustav V of Sweden and many others scooped up tickets at the shockingly high rate of $50 each. Lenglen won the match 6–3, 8–6, with the points and games even closer than the final score suggests. Wills commented on the face-off: "Her balls were not particularly fast—not nearly as fast as some other women players whom I have met on the court—but they always came back." Considering that Wills was six years Lenglen's junior, and that her game could continue to develop, there was every reason to believe that a memorable rivalry had begun that day in Cannes. Yet the two players never played again.

However, the date of the match was fateful in another way. Just after it ended, financier Frederick Moody pushed through the crowd to introduce himself to Wills. The two married in 1929 but divorced in 1937. Two years later Wills married Irish polo player Aiden Roark. The couple divorced in the 1970s.

Wills dominated women's tennis between 1927 and 1937. During those years, she won eight singles titles at Wimbledon (a record only surpassed by Martina Navratilova in 1990), seven U.S. singles titles at Forest Hills (a record that has yet to be broken), and four French championships at Roland Garros. On top of all of this, Wills had perhaps the single greatest winning streak in the history of the game. Between 1927 and 1933 she won 180 consecutive matches, and in those matches did not lose a single set.

Wills's game was neither fast nor terribly well coordinated, but she made up for these deficiencies by striking the ball earlier and harder than her opponents. No less an authority than Don Budge—who is still regarded by many as the best men's player of all time—asserted that Wills hit the ball harder than any player he ever watched until Steffi Graff in the 1990s. Wills also had a striking profile, which her many admirers labeled "Grecian." She always wore the same stark white visor (which soon became a tennis classic), and cut a fashion statement in her simple but elegant skirts. She acted more in charge and in control than any other player of her era; only Alice Marble in the late 1930s could rival Wills in this respect. In addition, Wills cultivated an aura of invincibility. She was able to turn herself into a legend in the way that Babe Ruth and Charlie Chaplin did (the latter once remarked that the "movement of Helen Wills playing tennis" was the most beautiful sight he knew). Wills retired from tennis in 1938. She was inducted into the Tennis Hall of Fame in 1969.

Wills painted throughout her life and later helped to sponsor the work of Diego Rivera and Frieda Kahlo, the Mexican husband and wife who introduced Hispanic art to many American viewers. She wrote and illustrated two books on the game of tennis, including *Tennis* (1939). She also wrote a mystery novel, *Death Serves an Ace* (1939), and an autobiography (1937).

After her marriage to Roark in 1939, Wills moved first to the Los Angeles area, then to the Carmel Valley in central California in the 1950s. She died of natural causes at the Carmel Convalescent Hospital. Her remains were cremated and the ashes scattered at sea.

★

Wills's autobiography is *15–30: The Story of a Tennis Player* (1937). For biographical information, see Angela Lumpkin, *Women's Tennis: A Historical Documentary of the Players and Their Game* (1981). See also Larry Engelmann, *The Goddess and the American Girl: The Story of Suzanne Lenglen and Helen Wills* (1988). An obituary is in the *New York Times* (3 Jan. 1998).

SAMUEL WILLARD CROMPTON

WILSON, Lewis Robert ("Hack") (*b.* 26 April 1900 in Ellwood City, Pennsylvania; *d.* 23 November 1948 in Baltimore, Maryland), Major League Baseball player whose 1930 season runs batted in (RBI) record remains unbroken.

Wilson's father, Robert Wilson, a laborer, provided some financial support for his child but never married Jennie Kaughn Wilson, Wilson's mother. What little is known of Wilson's early life in Chester, Pennsylvania, indicates that he was neglected by his alcoholic father and his troubled and unstable mother, who died in 1907 at the age of twenty-three when Wilson was only seven years old. He left the sixth grade to work in a local print shop and later for a steel mill and shipyard. When Wilson was twenty-one, he stood five feet, six inches tall and weighed about 200 pounds.

Wilson started his professional career in the Blue Ridge League in 1921, playing for Martinsburg, West Virginia. When or why he acquired the nickname "Hack," which stuck with him throughout his baseball career, is not known, but it might have been derived from his resemblance to a wrestler named George Hackenschmidt or to former Chicago Cubs outfielder Hack Miller. In 1923 Wilson moved to the Virginia League and played for Portsmouth. Late in the season the New York Giants called him up, and he played three games for them. However, Giants manager John J. McGraw did not appreciate Wilson's talent and kept him on the bench for much of the 1924 season, which ended with the Giants winning the National League

Hack Wilson, 1931. ASSOCIATED PRESS AP

(NL) pennant but losing to the Washington Senators in the World Series. Wilson hit just 10 home runs and batted a .295 average that season. Halfway through the 1925 season the Giants decided to send Wilson to the Toledo Club, a minor league team in the American Association. Recognizing talent in the young outfielder, the Chicago Cubs purchased Wilson's contract for $5,000 before the start of the 1926 season in a deal protested by the Giants but approved by Commissioner Kenesaw Mountain Landis. Wilson married Virginia Riddleburger on 24 August 1923. They had one son.

The move to Chicago proved a turning point in Wilson's career. After batting a dismal .239 in his last season with New York, the squat, barrel-chested fielder came alive. In his first full season with the Cubs, Wilson led the NL with 21 home runs and 109 runs batted in (RBI). He led the NL in home runs for the next two years with a combined total of 61. In 1929 the Cubs, under manager Joe McCarthy, had one of their best seasons. A reliable if not particularly graceful outfielder, Wilson improved his offensive game by hitting .345 with a record 39 home runs and 159 RBI. Yet the season ended in frustration when the Cubs lost to the Philadelphia Athletics in the World Series. Wilson misjudged a fly ball and allowed three runs, helping the Athletics rally to win the crucial game and take the title. Wilson's uncharacteristic defensive failure overshadowed his remarkable .471 World Series batting average.

The 1930 season proved to be Wilson's crowning achievement. In just 150 games, he belted in 56 home runs and 191 RBI, smashing Lou Gehrig's 1927 record of 175. Wilson's NL home run record would last until both the Chicago Cubs Sammy Sosa and the St. Louis Cardinals Mark McGuire broke it in 1998. However, Wilson's major league RBI record still stands, with only Hank Greenberg, who hit 183, and Lou Gehrig, who hit 184, ever coming close.

After his phenomenal 1930 season, Wilson's fame and fortune proved to be his downfall. Always craving attention, he let his fame go to his head. After earning a remarkable $35,000 salary, Wilson was plagued by misfortune and was undermined by his personal vices. His temper and his fists had already gotten him in trouble. In a 1929 game against Cincinnati, Wilson tried to punch Reds pitcher Ray Kolp but was ejected from the game before inflicting any injury. That evening, however, he floored another Reds pitcher, Pete Donahue, at Chicago's Union Station while the two teams were waiting for trains. Wilson also reportedly had fights with reporters and neighbors. In 1930 Judge Kenesaw Mountain Landis banned baseball players from engaging in professional boxing during the off-season, purportedly following a pugilistic challenge made to Wilson by ballplayer Art "Whataman" Shires. Wilson's shortcomings suddenly became even more serious when the Cubs easygoing manager Joe McCarthy, who was patient with Wilson, left after the 1930 season. McCarthy had once tried to teach Wilson a lesson about the dangers associated with drinking by dropping a worm into a glass of gin. After the worm quickly died, McCarthy asked Wilson what the lesson was. "If you drink liquor, you won't have worms," Wilson replied.

The new Cubs manager in 1931 was Rogers Hornsby, a strict disciplinarian and, like Cubs owner William Wrigley, a devout prohibitionist. Another problem for Wilson was that the National League deadened the ball in 1931, making home runs harder to hit. But the greatest problem Wilson faced was himself. Working under a stern manager and always in the shadow of the American League slugger Babe Ruth, Wilson began to drink and carouse more than ever. He hit only a .261 with 13 home runs and 61 RBI. His attitude and poor performance angered Hornsby, and by the end of the season Wilson was benched and fined $6,500 for an off-field incident.

The Cubs traded Wilson to the St. Louis Cardinals for pitcher Burleigh Grimes at the end of the 1931 season. Wilson was outraged when the Cardinals offered a salary of just $7,500. During the winter, the Brooklyn Dodgers (then called the Robbins) acquired Wilson for the 1932 season. The new venue did not halt his descent into obscurity. In his three years with Brooklyn, Wilson never batted over .300, never came close to his RBI record, and hit only 48 home runs. In 1934 the Dodgers traded him to Philadelphia, who released him after just seven games. By now overweight (nearly 240 pounds), Wilson attempted a comeback in 1935 with the Albany, New York, team, but his heavy drinking and poor work habits ended his baseball career at age thirty-four.

Wilson drifted from job to job, ending up as a park swimming pool manager in Baltimore, Maryland. He and his wife, Virginia, divorced in 1938, and Wilson married Hazel Miller that same year. In 1948, three months after the nation buried Babe Ruth in what amounted to a state funeral, Wilson died of a respiratory infection. He had been broke, and his body lay unclaimed for three days until the NL president Ford Frick wired $350 to cover funeral expenses and the transport of Wilson's remains to Martinsburg, West Virginia, for burial.

Wilson was accepted into the National Baseball Hall of Fame in 1979 by a special veterans committee. His career covered twelve seasons, and included four NL home run titles and a lifetime batting average of .307. Moreover, in June 1999 Wilson's 1930 RBI record was increased to 191 after a baseball historian discovered that Wilson had been denied an RBI against the Cincinnati Reds in 1930.

★

For in-depth information about Wilson's life and career, see Robert Boone and Gerald Grunska, *Hack, The Meteoric Life of One of Baseball's First Superstars, Hack Wilson* (1978), and Clifton Blue Parker, *Fouled Away: The Baseball Tragedy of Hack Wilson* (2000). Articles about Wilson include "Lewis Robert (Hack) Wilson," *The Sporting News* (25 Aug. 1932). Other materials can be found in *The Sporting News* Archive, St. Louis, Missouri. An obituary is in the *New York Times* (24 Nov. 1948).

MICHAEL J. DEVINE

WINFIELD, David Mark ("Dave") (*b.* 3 October 1951 in St. Paul, Minnesota), Hall of Fame baseball player who starred as a major league outfielder between 1973 and 1995.

Winfield is one of two sons of Frank Winfield, a dining car waiter, and Arline Allison Winfield, a public school system employee. After his parents separated in 1954, Winfield grew up with his mother and grandmother. He graduated in 1969 from St. Paul Central High School, making the all-state baseball team as a senior. Winfield attended the University of Minnesota from 1970 to 1973, majoring in political science and black studies, and participating in basketball and baseball. In 1973 he compiled a 13–1 record as pitcher, batted .385, clouted 9 home runs, and was named Most Valuable Player (MVP) of the National Collegiate Athletic Association (NCAA) College World Series.

Dave Winfield, 1974. ASSOCIATED PRESS AP

The six-foot, six-inch, 220-pound Winfield was drafted by professional football, basketball, and baseball teams. The Minnesota Vikings selected him as an end even though he did not play college football. Since Winfield excelled as a basketball forward, the Atlanta Hawks of the National Basketball Association and the Utah Stars of the American Basketball Association also chose him. Though Winfield had not yet graduated from Minnesota, the San Diego Padres baseball club selected him in the first round of the June 1973 free agent draft.

Winfield, blessed with great speed and a powerful throwing arm, immediately joined San Diego as an outfielder and became the most prolific run producer in early franchise history, leading the Padres in runs batted in (RBI) six times (1974–1975, 1977–1980), home runs five times (1976–1980), runs scored five times (1974–1977, 1979), doubles and hits four times (1976–1979), stolen bases twice (1975–1976), batting average twice (1978–1979), and triples once (1979). He combined 20 home runs with 75 RBI in 1974 and knocked in 76 runs in 1975. In spite of missing the last month of 1976, Winfield hit .283 with 13 home runs and 69 RBI. In 1977 he set a Padres record by hitting in 16 consecutive games, clouted 25 home runs with 92 RBI, and made the first of 12 consecutive All-Star Game appearances.

After being named team captain, Winfield finished fifth in the National League with a .308 batting average in 1978 to help San Diego record its first winning season. He also paced the Padres with 181 hits, 24 home runs, and 97 RBI. His best San Diego season came in 1979, when he finished third in the National League Most Valuable Player balloting and became the first Padre voted to start an All-Star Game. Besides batting .308, Winfield led the National League with 118 RBI, 333 total bases, and 24 intentional walks and finished third with 34 home runs. He won National League Gold Glove awards in both 1979 and 1980 and made the *Sporting News* All-League team in 1979. In 1980 Winfield paced San Diego with 20 home runs. He ranks high on the all-time Padres lists in most offensive categories, ending his career in San Diego with a .284 average, 599 runs scored, 1,134 hits, 154 home runs, 626 RBI, and a .464 slugging percentage.

San Diego lost Winfield to free agency in December 1980. The Padres negotiated a contract renewal, but he demanded more money. When San Diego rejected his demands, Winfield left for the New York Yankees, who signed him to a ten-year contract worth nearly $25 million. Winfield played with the Yankees from 1981 through May 1990, increasing his regular season offensive production. However, he struggled in the 1981 playoffs against the Oakland Athletics and managed only one hit against the Los Angeles Dodgers in the World Series.

In 1982 Winfield hit a career-high 37 home runs and knocked in 106 runs, the first of 5 consecutive seasons over the 100 RBI mark. He was the first Yankee since Joe DiMaggio to accomplish that feat. In 1984 Winfield finished second to Don Mattingly for the American League batting championship with a .340 average. He scored over 100 runs in 1984 and 1985 and ranked third in the league with 114 RBI in 1985. Winfield often saved games with his excellent defense, winning Gold Glove awards in 1982, 1983, 1984, 1985, and 1987. Winfield was an American League All-Star from 1981 to 1988. Winfield married Tonya Turner on 18 February 1988. He had a daughter in a previous relationship.

In 1989 Winfield and the Yankee owner George Steinbrenner filed lawsuits against each other regarding payments to the Winfield Foundation, a fund that benefits underprivileged youth with free seats for baseball games, All-Star Game children's parties, and yearly scholarships. Winfield charged that Steinbrenner failed to make $450,000 in payments, while Steinbrenner claimed that his player failed to pay $300,000 in contractually committed donations. The controversy was settled out of court. Winfield agreed to pay $230,000 into the foundation and to reimburse it $30,000 for inappropriately expended funds.

A herniated disk sidelined Winfield for the entire 1989 season. In May 1990 the California Angels acquired him in a trade and agreed to extend his contract through 1991 at a $3.1 million salary. Winfield in 1990 led the Angels with 72 RBI, 63 runs scored, and a .466 slugging percentage. He was named Comeback Player of the Year by the *Sporting News*. On 24 June 1991 Winfield became the oldest player to hit for the cycle, that is, hitting a single, a double, a triple, and a home run in one game.

In December 1991 Winfield signed as a free agent with the Toronto Blue Jays. He batted .290 with 26 home runs and 108 RBI in 1992 and became the oldest player to record 100 or more RBI in a season, knocking in a record 32 runs in the month of August. Winfield clouted two home runs to help Toronto defeat the Oakland A's in the American League championship series. His two-run double in the eleventh inning of game six of the 1992 World Series gave the Blue Jays a 4–3 win over the Atlanta Braves and the world championship.

Winfield spent 1993 and 1994 with the Minnesota Twins. On 16 September 1993 he became the nineteenth major leaguer to attain 3,000 hits with a ninth-inning single off Dennis Eckersley of the Oakland A's. Winfield's major league career ended as a designated hitter with the Cleveland Indians in 1995. He settled in Fort Myers, Florida, where he and his brother Steve Winfield operate the Winfield Foundation.

During twenty-two major league seasons, Winfield batted .285 with 1,669 runs scored, 3,110 hits, and 223 stolen bases. His 1,093 extra-base hits included 540 doubles, 88 triples, and 465 home runs. He ranked among the top 20 in career games, at-bats, hits, home runs, total bases, and RBI. He was elected to the San Diego Padres Hall of Fame in 2000 and the National Baseball Hall of Fame in his first year of eligibility in 2001, becoming just the fourth Padre so honored.

★

The Winfield file is at the National Baseball Library in Cooperstown, New York. Dave Winfield with Tom Parker, *Winfield: A Player's Life* (1988), and Dave Winfield with Eric Swenson, *The Complete Baseball Player* (1990), recount most of his major league career. For biographical information see *Current Biography* (1984) and *Contemporary Black Biography,* vol. 5 (1994). For Winfield's role with the Yankees see Mark Gallagher, *The Yankee Encyclopedia,* vol. 3 (1997). Pertinent articles include Ron Fimrite, "Good Hit, Better Man," *Sports Illustrated* (9 July 1979); Fimrite, "Richest Kid on the Block," *Sports Illustrated* (5 Jan. 1981); William Oscar Johnson, "Al Gave It His All," *Sports Illustrated* (5 Jan. 1981);

David Whitford, "What Do You Think of Dave Winfield?," *Sport* (Oct. 1986); William Ladson, "The Sport Q & A: Dave Winfield," *Sport* (Aug. 1991); Rick Reilly, "I Feel a Whole Lot Better Now," *Sports Illustrated* (29 June 1992); and Tim Kurkjian, "Mr. Longevity," *Sports Illustrated* (27 Sept. 1993).

DAVID L. PORTER

WINSLOW, Kellen Boswell (*b.* 5 November 1957 in St. Louis, Missouri), football player who, because of his unique combination of size, speed, and agility, redefined the role of the tight end in professional football.

Winslow grew up in East St. Louis, Illinois, one of seven children. His father was a bus driver, and his mother worked as a clerical assistant in a number of offices. What the Winslows lacked in finances, they made up for with a loving, tightly bonded family. From an early age, Winslow planned to attend college on a scholarship, but he intended it to be an academic one rather than athletic. Winslow participated in few organized sports as a young man, preferring to spend his time playing chess. But his six-foot, four-inch, 184-pound body attracted notice from coaches at East St. Louis High School. Although the coaches tried to convince him to play football beginning in his freshman year, only in his senior year did they persuade him to play. Winslow immediately became the starting tight end.

Kellen Winslow, 1984. © BETTMANN/CORBIS

Winslow graduated from high school in 1975, and college recruiters from throughout the Midwest came calling. He received offers from Kansas State University, the University of Kansas, the University of Missouri-Columbia, and Northwestern University before he made the decision to attend Missouri. He played for the Missouri Tigers from 1975 to 1979, catching 71 passes for 1,089 yards and 10 touchdowns. Winslow was both Big Eight Player of the Year and a consensus All-American in 1978 (his senior year), and he played in the Liberty Bowl, the East-West Shrine Game, and the Senior Bowl. Winslow finally received a Bachelor of Educational Science degree in Counseling Psychology from Missouri in 1987, going back after he retired from professional football.

When the San Diego Chargers selected Winslow with the thirteenth pick of the 1979 National Football League (NFL) draft, he was six feet, five inches tall, and weighed 250 pounds. He blended this size with incredible agility and a sprinter's speed. Additionally, he was very intelligent and quickly adjusted to the Chargers offensive system. Winslow began his rookie year with success, but suffered a broken bone in his right leg during the seventh game, an injury that sidelined him for the remainder of the season.

Winslow recovered fully from his rookie-season injury and quickly became an integral piece of one of the greatest offensive strategies in professional football history, "Air Coryell." Coach Don Coryell took advantage of Winslow's raw talent and began to use his tight end more as an additional receiver than in the traditional role of a blocking tight end. Coryell had Winslow line up at the normal tight end position, but also out wide in the slot and occasionally in the backfield. The results were both immediate and long lasting. Winslow became, arguably, the greatest tight end in the history of the game.

Winslow returned to his second year of professional football with a vengeance, leading the NFL with 89 receptions for 1,290 yards and 9 touchdowns. He was equally dominating the following year and again led the league, this time with 88 receptions for 1,075 yards and 10 touchdowns. However, his phenomenal performances during those seasons paled in comparison to his 1981 postseason heroics.

The Chargers played the Dolphins in Miami in the 1981 American Football Conference (AFC) divisional playoff game, and Winslow was easily the most impressive player that day. Though heavily bruised and suffering from Miami's grueling heat and humidity, he still managed to haul in a playoff record of 13 receptions for 166 yards. With 4 seconds left in the game, Winslow leaped to block a potentially game-winning field goal by Miami's Uwe von Schamann to send the game into overtime. The Chargers finally won the game 41–38 on a Rolf Benirschke field goal, 13 minutes, 52 seconds into overtime. The exhausted Winslow had to be carried off the field by teammates Eric Sievers and Billy Shields.

The San Diego–Miami game is noted as one of the greatest games in football history. In the article, "Our Favorite Games," in the 25 October 1999 issue, *Sports Illustrated* called it their favorite game of the twentieth century, in all sports. Winslow's contribution has also been widely recognized as one of the top performances by a player in a single game. Unfortunately for the Chargers, their luck ran out in Miami, and they lost the following week to the Bengals in a game played in Cincinnati in temperatures well below freezing.

Winslow continued to play for the Chargers through the 1987 season. He reported to camp for the 1988 season, but a previously reconstructed knee caused him considerable difficulty, and he failed the team physical. Although he was later declared fit to play, Winslow realized that his playing days were over. A disagreement with team officials over the condition of the knee resulted in his suspension from the team, and he immediately retired.

Following his retirement from professional football, Winslow entered the University of San Diego School of Law and graduated in 1993 with a J.D. He left San Diego after graduation and practiced law for a firm in Kansas City, Missouri, specializing in representing athletes. Winslow returned to San Diego in 1996, performing commentary for Fox Sports and ESPN and giving motivational speeches throughout the United States. Winslow also established the Kellen Winslow Foundation, which is dedicated to funding community-based programs whose aim is to challenge, educate, and develop the talents of children living in underprivileged areas. He is the father of two sons, one of whom, Kellen II (Kellen Boswell Winslow, Jr.), started his college football career in 2001 as a wide receiver for the University of Miami Hurricanes.

Winslow is considered by many sports authorities to be the greatest tight end in the history of professional football. He retired with 541 receptions for 6,741 yards and 45 touchdowns. He twice led the NFL in receiving and led the Chargers receivers five times in nine seasons. In 1994, in conjunction with the seventy-fifth anniversary of the National Football League, Winslow was selected as one of two tight ends on the NFL All-Time team. In 1995 he was inducted into the San Diego Chargers Hall of Fame, the Breitbard Hall of Fame at the San Diego Hall of Champions, and the Pro Football Hall of Fame in Canton, Ohio.

★

The NFL-produced book *75 Seasons, 1920–1995* (1994), contains an entry focusing on Winslow and his contribution to football. It also outlines the NFL's All-Time team, of which Winslow is a member. For statistics and career achievements, the best resource is the 1988 San Diego Chargers Media Guide. *Sports Illustrated* dedicated multiple sections of the 25 October 1999 issue to the Chargers and Dolphins playoff game of 1982, and Winslow is featured throughout the issue.

TODD TOBIAS

WOODARD, Lynette (*b.* 12 August 1959 in Wichita, Kansas), pioneer in women's collegiate and professional basketball who set the record for the most career points in the history of women's collegiate basketball (3,649), and was the first woman to play for the Harlem Globetrotters.

Woodard grew up in Wichita, the third of four children of Lugene Woodard, a firefighter, and Dorothy Jenkins Woodard, a homemaker. At an early age she and her brother invented their own version of basketball called sockball, in which they practiced their basketball techniques by shooting a rolled-up pair of their father's socks over doorways. Their indoor games soon gave way to outdoor games on the public playground.

As a sophomore at Wichita North High School, Woodard played on the girls' basketball team. With her help the team won the 5A state championship in 1975 and 1977. Her playing also caught the eye of Marian Washington, the coach of the women's basketball team at the University of Kansas (KU). Her senior year Woodard was selected as a high-school All-American and was heavily recruited by college coaches. After graduating from high school in 1977, she decided to play for Coach Washington at KU.

In 1978, Woodard's first year at KU, she led the nation in rebounds with 14.8 and was second in scoring with 25.2 points per game. In her sophomore, junior, and senior years she led the nation in steals. During her four years at Kansas, the Lady Jayhawks won three Big Eight championships and had a four-year 108–32 win-loss record. Woodard was selected as the Big Eight Tournament Most Valuable Player (MVP) three times. She averaged 26.3 points per game and scored a record 3,649 points, an all-time scoring record for women's collegiate basketball. Her career record was especially spectacular because it was set in 1981, before the three-point rule. It is not listed as a National Collegiate Athletic Association (NCAA) record because it occurred one year before the NCAA took over the governance of women's college sports from the Association for Intercollegiate Athletics for Women (AIAW).

Woodard was a Kodak All-American all four years she played for Kansas (1978–1981). In her junior and senior years, she was also selected for Academic All-America honors. Her senior year she won both the Broderick Award and Wade Trophy as the women's college basketball player of the year. That same year she was selected as the Big Eight

Lynette Woodard, 1985. © BETTMANN/CORBIS

Conference Outstanding Female of the Year and the National Association for the Advancement of Colored People (NAACP) Wichita Chapter Woman of the Year. During her years at Kansas, playing forward and guard, she ranked first or second in the nation in steals, scoring, or rebounding. Woodard graduated from college in 1981 with a B.S. in speech communications and human relations. Her Lady Jayhawk retired jersey was hung next to those of Wilt Chamberlain and Danny Manning in the KU Allen Field House. In 1982, a year after graduating, the NCAA presented her with their Top V Award, naming her one of the top five collegiate athletes.

While at the University of Kansas, Woodard played on the U.S. national team that won a gold medal at the 1979 World University Games. She was selected for the 1980 U.S. Olympic women's basketball team, but due to the U.S. boycott of the Moscow Olympics the team never competed. In 1983 Woodard was a member of the U.S. national teams that won a gold medal at the Pan-American Games and a silver medal at the World Championships. In 1984 she captained the U.S. Olympic team that won a gold medal at the Los Angeles Olympics. Prior to the Los Angeles Olympics, the U.S. national team won a gold medal in international competition at the Jones Cup in Taipei, Taiwan, and Woodard was named to the All-Tournament team.

In 1985 Woodard made history when she became the first woman to play for the Harlem Globetrotters. Woodard had learned how to twirl a basketball years earlier from her cousin Hubert "Geese" Ausbie, a world-famous Harlem Globetrotter comedian whose twenty-four–year career ended in 1984. Woodard was presented with the Harlem Globetrotters prestigious "Legends" ring in 1996.

After playing with the Globetrotters for two years, Woodard played professionally in Italy for two seasons (1987–1989). In 1989 she helped her team win the Italian national championship. She then played three seasons (1990–1993) in Japan for Daiwa Securities. Her Japanese team won the divisional championship in 1992. While based overseas, she returned home to play for the U.S. national women's basketball teams that won a gold medal at the 1990 World Championships and a bronze medal at the 1991 Pan-American Games.

In 1992 Woodard became the athletic director for the Kansas City (Missouri) School District. She remained at this position for two years before moving to New York City to become a registered stockbroker with Magna Securities Corporation. But her playing days were not over, and in 1997 she was drafted to play for the Cleveland Rockers of the newly formed Women's National Basketball Association (WNBA). In 1997 she led the Cleveland Rockers in steals with forty-six. Woodard was selected for the WNBA Detroit Shock expansion team coached by Nancy Lieberman-Cline in 1998. She retired after the 1998 season to return to her alma mater, the University of Kansas, where she became the athletic department's special assistant for external relations and women's basketball, and put her extensive experience to work in her position as the assistant coach of the Lady Jayhawks.

At six feet tall, Lynette Woodard is considered one of the most outstanding women basketball players of all time.

She was a gifted complete player, who could play any position at the highest level. Her combined uncanny ability to anticipate and her exceptional quickness allowed her to dominate play. She received the Women's Sports Foundation Flo Hyman Award in 1993, and was inducted into the foundation's International Sports Hall of Fame. In 1996 she served as a member of the Olympic Committee Board of Directors, and was named the greatest female player in the history of the Big Eight Conference. *Sports Illustrated for Women* named her one of the one hundred greatest women athletes in 1999. The following year, Woodard became the first woman to be inducted into the Kansas City Sports Walk of Stars. Woodard will always be remembered as a trailblazer and one of the greatest players in women's basketball.

★

Useful sources include Kansas State Historical Society, "Biographies—Lynette Woodard" (1997), http://www.kshs.org/people/woodard.htm; Bert Rosenthal, *Lynette Woodard: The First Female Globetrotter* (1986); and Matthew Newman and Howard Schroeder, *Lynette Woodard* (1986). See also Gai I. Berlage, "Woodard, Lynette," in *The Encyclopedia of Ethnicity and Sports in the United States* (2000), George Kirsch, Othello Harris, and Claire E. Nolte eds. See also the magazine pullout "100 Greatest Female Athletes, 81. Lynette Woodard, Basketball," *Sports Illustrated for Women* (winter 1999–2000).

GAI INGHAM BERLAGE

WOODEN, John Robert (*b.* 14 October 1910 in Hall, Indiana), one of the most successful coaches in the history of college basketball, who was the first man to be named to the Naismith Memorial Basketball Hall of Fame as both a player and a coach.

Wooden was one of four sons of Joshua Wooden and Roxie Rothrock Wooden, rural Indiana farmers. His first home lacked both electricity and indoor plumbing, and his earliest attempts at basketball were made using a rag "ball" constructed by his mother and a tomato basket nailed to a barn wall. His father was a great moral influence, and Wooden wrote and spoke of him throughout his life, quoting his philosophical maxims, especially his saying, "Make each day your masterpiece." In 1924 the family moved to Martinsville, Indiana, where Wooden played on the Martinsville High School team for three years (with the nickname "Martinsville Rubberman"), earning All-State recognition each year; he also played baseball and ran track.

Wooden graduated from high school in 1928. He then traveled to West Lafayette, Indiana, and enrolled at Purdue University, where he played on the basketball team as a five-foot, ten-inch guard for Coach Ward "Piggy" Lambert. Noted for his hard drives to the basket, Wooden was named an All-American in each of his final three years as a Boilermaker. He was also named the national College Player of the Year as a senior and received the Big Ten Medal for excellence in athletics and scholarship that year. Wooden graduated in 1932 with a B.S. in engineering and married Nellie C. Riley, his high school sweetheart, on 8 August 1932. The marriage endured fifty-three years until her death in 1985; they raised a son and a daughter.

Offered $5,000 to play with the famous Boston Celtics, Wooden instead took a job teaching and coaching at Danville High School in Kentucky; in 1933–1934 he suffered his only losing record in a season as a coach. He returned to Indiana in 1934 to teach and coach at Central High School in South Bend while playing semiprofessional basketball with the Kautsky Grocers in Indianapolis. After the United States entered World War II, Wooden served as a fitness officer, lieutenant second grade, in the U.S. Navy from 1943 to 1946. After the war he took a job as the head basketball coach at Indiana State Teachers College in Terre Haute, where in two seasons he compiled a record of 47–14. Wooden declined an invitation to the National Association of Intercollegiate Athletics postseason tournament in Kansas City when he learned that his African-American reserve player Clarence Walker would not be permitted to play. Wooden earned his M.A. at Indiana in 1947.

Wooden's success at Indiana State made him marketable, and he hoped to land the vacant Big Ten head coaching position at the University of Minnesota. However, telephone transmission trouble meant that Minnesota lost out to the University of California, Los Angeles (UCLA), whose call got through first. In 1948 Wooden joined the historic midwestern migration to southern California, signing a three-year contract with the Bruins. Speaking to UCLA alumni upon his arrival, he told an audience, "The fast break is my system." Wooden's success was immediate. His first team in Westwood, the Los Angeles neighborhood housing the school, went 22–7, and his 1949–1950 team achieved a 24–7 record while winning the Pacific Coast League. After three seasons playing in the tiny campus gym, which seated only 1,000 people, the Bruins became nomadic for the next fourteen years, playing in various Los Angeles venues until the opening of Pauley Pavilion in the mid-1960s. The Bruins won league titles again in 1952 and 1956, but were overshadowed in California by the University of San Francisco teams of the mid-1950s, which won sixty consecutive games and back-to-back national titles under Coach Phil Woolpert, and the University of California Golden Bears under Coach Pete Newell, who won the 1959 National Collegiate Athletic Association (NCAA) tournament and then lost in the final game in 1960.

Wooden's competitiveness showed often as he yelled at both officials and opposing players, clutching a crucifix in one hand and a rolled-up program in the other. Wooden

John Wooden *(center)*, 1995. ASSOCIATED PRESS AP

never cared for recruiting, but his breakthrough came when Walt Hazzard of Philadelphia, Pennsylvania, came west to play for the Bruins. Wooden reached his first Final Four in 1962, losing to the eventual champion Cincinnati in the semifinals. In 1964 Wooden achieved his first national championship as the Bruins prevailed 98–83 over Duke University. With no player taller than six feet, five inches tall, UCLA won via its fast pace and constant pressure, made possible by superior conditioning that especially showed in the waning minutes of their games, the 2–2–1 zone press, and the leadership of Hazzard and his teammate Gail Goodrich. The Bruins successfully defended their title in an undefeated season in 1964–1965, beating the University of Michigan 91–80 in the final.

In autumn 1965 the seven-foot, one-inch recruit Lewis Alcindor (later Kareem Abdul-Jabbar) arrived on campus from New York City and led the freshman team to a 75–60 victory over the defending national champions. Wooden's 1966–1967 team started four sophomores from the previous year's unbeaten freshman team (freshmen were ineligible for varsity competition). He demonstrated his coaching flexibility in designing a low-post offense to take advantage of Alcindor's skills. Alcindor began his varsity career by scoring fifty-six points, a school record, against the crosstown rival Southern California. The Bruins won their third national title in four years, 79–64 over the University of Dayton, and finished 30–0. Dunking was outlawed after this season because of Alcindor. The Alcindor era concluded with two more NCAA championships, making an unprecedented three in a row. The rise in interest in college basketball was seen on 20 January 1968 when the University of Houston edged the Bruins 71–69 before an Astrodome audience of 52,693, an NCAA record, in the first regular-season college basketball game ever nationally televised. The Bruins went 88–2 during the Alcindor years.

But even with Alcindor's graduation in 1969, the beat went on in Westwood. With a mission to show there was more to UCLA basketball than one superstar, the 1969–1970 Bruins again won the national title, 80–69 over Jacksonville University, and made it five in a row in 1971. Some began to call the NCAA "The UCLA Invitational," Wooden was referred to as the "Wizard of Westwood," more and more people were becoming interested in his motivational system (dubbed the "Pyramid of Success"), and the UCLA mystique was at its height. The Bill Walton era began in 1971, freshmen now being eligible. The six-foot, eleven-inch center from San Diego helped stretch the Bruins winning steak to a new record of eighty-eight (ended at the University of Notre Dame but avenged a week later) and two more national titles, making that particular streak an unbelievable seven straight. The end finally came in the 1974 national semifinals against North Carolina State University, the eventual champions, in double overtime. Walton graduated, but Wooden's 1974–1975 team, with only one returning starter, again returned to the Final Four. After a narrow and difficult victory in overtime over the University of Louisville, coached by Wooden's former player and longtime assistant Denny Crum, at the press conference following that game, Wooden suddenly and shockingly announced that he had just decided his next game, the 1975 final, would be his last. The Bruins responded by defeating the University of Kentucky 92–85, to give Wooden a final NCAA title, his tenth.

Even in his nineties, Wooden remained active in retirement into the twenty-first century. He sometimes criticized showmanship and lack of team play, but coaches and players continued to seek out his opinions on all aspects of the game. He was a highly successful coach before his teams began their amazing streak of national championships. His many titles and impeccable integrity, founded on a strong and open Christian faith, aroused interest in his system and ideas, which were traditional. He was named to the Basketball Hall of Fame as a player in 1961 and as a coach in 1973, the first person so doubly honored. Wooden defined success as "peace of mind which is a direct result of self-satisfaction in knowing you did your best to become the best that you are capable of becoming."

★

Wooden's autobiography, *They Call Me Coach* (1972), written with Jack Tobin, appeared in a revised edition in 1988. A collection of the coach's thoughts appears in *Wooden: A Lifetime of Observations On and Off the Court* (1997), written with Steve Jamison. A long interview with Billy Packer is found in Packer with Roland Lazenby, *Fifty Years of the Final Four* (1987). Neville Johnson, *The John Wooden Pyramid of Success* (2000), includes an interview with Wooden. Arnold Hane, "Winning: With Nice Guys and a Pyramid of Principles," *New York Times Sunday Magazine* (2 Dec. 1973), is a cover story regarding Wooden's "Pyramid of Success."

LAWSON BOWLING

WOODS, Eldrick ("Tiger") (*b.* 30 December 1975 in Cypress, California), golfer who dominated the world golf circuit as soon as he turned professional.

Woods's father, Earl Woods, is a former career soldier who served two tours in Southeast Asia, including Thailand, where he met Kultilda Punsawad. They were married in New York City in 1969 and moved to California in 1975 where Woods was born. Earl called his son "Tiger" after his friend Nguyen Phong, a South Vietnamese soldier whose bravery had earned him that name.

Having learned to play golf late in life, Earl Woods was obsessed with practicing. He frequently hit balls into a net

Tiger Woods, 1997. AP/WIDE WORLD PHOTOS

in his garage while his son watched from his high chair. When Woods was old enough to walk, he began to swing a sawed-off golf club with remarkable effect and was soon putting with uncanny accuracy. Encouraged to develop his talent, Woods grew up with a clear goal—he would become the greatest golfer in history. Steadied by his mother's emphasis on education and spirituality, Woods worked hard under his father's tutelage, while the family spared no expense for coaches, trainers, and even sports psychologists to hone his skills.

Woods first entered the record books as an amateur. He is the only golfer to have won three consecutive Junior Amateur Championships (1991, 1992, 1993) followed by three consecutive U.S. Amateur victories (1994, 1995, 1996). Woods was a good student at Western High School in Anaheim, from which he graduated in 1994, and won a full scholarship to Stanford University. But in 1996, after completing his sophomore year, he left the university to turn professional. He earned two victories and three top tens in the eight tournaments he played during the remainder of that year, and was awarded the Professional Golf Association (PGA) Tour Rookie of the Year and the *Sports Illustrated* Sportsman of the Year Award. He prepared intensely for the 1997 season, which was among the most dramatic first full seasons in the history of sports. He won the year's first major, the 1997 Masters, by a record-shattering twelve strokes and finished with a record-breaking 270. By the end of the season, Woods had garnered five additional wins, prize money totaling over $2 million, the PGA money title (for the most money won in tournaments), and the Player of the Year Award.

However, in 1998 Woods failed to live up to the extraordinary expectations that his earlier performance had created. In defense of his Master's title, he lost by six strokes, and won just one PGA Tour for the season. Guided by Coach Butch Harmon, he began rebuilding his swing, seeking efficiency and simplicity. He began a vigorous aerobic and weight training regime that added 20 pounds of muscle to his six-foot, two-inch, 160-pound body. In 1999 Woods's winning ways returned; he won eight PGA events, the most victories in a season since Johnny Miller's eight in 1974.

Woods's 2000 season was nothing less than phenomenal. He won nine events (the most since Sam Snead's eleven in 1950). He won the three remaining majors—the U.S. Open, the British Open and the PGA Championship—equaling Ben Hogan's one-year, three-slam record. At twenty-four Woods was the youngest player to complete golf's professional Grand Slam, beating his only record-book rival, Jack Nicklaus, who had achieved that remarkable goal at twenty-six. Woods's victory at the U.S. Open at Pebble Beach was another performance that distanced him from his competitors. He won by fifteen, a rout reminiscent of his performance at the 1997 Masters. His season-scoring average was 68.17 (surpassing Byron Nelson's 68.33, set in 1945), his adjusted average was 67.79 (which give him the Vardon Trophy), and his earnings totaled a remarkable $9,188,321 (about double those of runner-up Phil Mickelson). Woods was first in greens in regulation (75.2 percent), first in consecutive cuts made (he had 59, the runner-up 18), and he finished in the top ten in 17 of 20 tournaments entered. "Tiger has raised the bar to a level that only he can jump over," golfing great Tom Watson observed.

By September 2001 Woods had won 29 times (about 30 percent of his matches) as a PGA professional. His game consists of the best qualities found in the games of his most distinguished predecessors. He has Hogan's work ethic, Nicklaus's concentration, Snead's grace, Palmer's daring, Nelson's ball control, and Jones's charisma. "If you were building the complete golfer," friend Mark O'Meara said, "you would build Tiger Woods."

Woods's long drives, his precise short game, and his remarkable putting, combined with his charisma, have dramatically increased golf's popularity. "The growth of golf is primarily due to Tiger Woods," former PGA official David Eger noted. "He is probably responsible for sixty cents of every dollar being played for on the men's tour today. Any time he plays in a tournament the television ratings skyrocket."

Golf in the post–World War II period has undergone a series of revolutions. Hogan changed how golfers practiced, Palmer changed how golfers were perceived, Nicklaus changed how golf was played, and now Woods is changing all of those things again. "Never before has one player affected so many people from so many walks of life," said Curtis Strange, two-time U.S. Open champion and American Broadcasting Companies (ABC) commentator. "People who never watched golf before are glued to the television set when Tiger is on."

But Woods's popularity has had a ripple effect beyond the world of professional golf. The enormous media attention he has received, his mixed heritage (his father is one-quarter Chinese, one-quarter Native American, and half African American; his mother is half Thai, one-quarter Chinese and one-quarter Caucasian), and Nike's effective "I am Tiger Woods" advertisements have made golf hip in the inner city. As PGA Tour commissioner Tim Finchem noted, "Tiger's impetus to all of golf and certainly to inner-city interest in golf was enormous, especially in the public sector." There Tiger is not compared to Ben Hogan or Jack Nicklaus, but with another (amateur) golfer, a sports icon named Michael Jordan.

★

A biography of Woods is David Owen, *The Chosen One: Tiger Woods and the Dilemma of Greatness* (2001). In Woods's own *Tiger Woods, How I Play Golf* (2001), he reveals the five secrets to his amazing success.

MARTIN SHERWIN

WORTHY, James Ager (*b.* 27 February 1961 in Gastonia, North Carolina), basketball player who helped his teams win championships at both the collegiate and professional levels, and was named one of the National Basketball Association's fifty greatest players.

Worthy was one of a large family born to Ervin Worthy, a minister, and Gladys Worthy, a registered nurse. He was raised in Gastonia, where he attended Ashbrook High School and became known as an outstanding basketball player. His ability was so pronounced that when he attended a University of North Carolina (UNC) summer basketball camp in eighth grade, he was pitted against older boys to even the competition. Worthy graduated from high school in 1979.

"James Worthy was one of a very few young men I ever looked at as a high schooler and felt certain was going to be a college star and pro player," wrote the legendary UNC basketball coach Dean Smith. "He had incredible quickness." The six-foot, nine-inch forward seriously considered offers from the University of Kentucky; University of California, Los Angeles (UCLA); and Michigan State University; but eventually chose to play for Smith at North Carolina. Worthy broke his right ankle in 1980, and was forced to sit out the second half of his freshman season; he returned to help his team advance to the National Collegiate Athletic Association (NCAA) championship games in his sophomore and junior years.

The Tar Heels lost the 1981 title contest to Indiana University, but came back with a vengeance the following year. On 29 March 1982 Worthy scored 28 points on 13-for-17 shooting, as UNC defeated the Georgetown University Hoyas 63–62 for the NCAA championship. Ironically, despite Worthy's excellent performance in this game, he was best remembered for intercepting an errant pass from the Georgetown guard Fred Brown in the closing seconds, sealing UNC's victory. Already a first-team All-American, Worthy was also named the Most Outstanding Player of the Final Four, an honor that put him on the cover of *Sports Illustrated,* and was named the National Player of the Year, along with the University of Virginia's Ralph Sampson. He also got a measure of revenge against a high school rival Eric "Sleepy" Floyd, one of the Hoyas star players whose team had beaten Worthy's Ashbrook High School squad in the state finals.

Worthy decided to forgo his senior year at UNC to enter the National Basketball Association (NBA) draft in 1982. He was selected first overall by the defending champion Los Angeles Lakers, which teamed him with the established professional stars Earvin "Magic" Johnson and Kareem Abdul-Jabbar. And with the widely respected Pat Riley taking over as his coach in place of Dean Smith, the transition could not have gone more smoothly. Worthy's fast-break style was perfectly suited for the "Showtime" Lakers, and he immediately became a big contributor for his new team.

As a rookie Worthy repeated history by breaking his left tibia just before the 1983 NBA playoffs, ending his first season as a professional just as he had finished his freshman year in college. Continuing the pattern, Worthy returned to help the Lakers advance to the championship series in his second and third seasons, winning his first NBA title in 1985, as Los Angeles beat the Boston Celtics in the finals, four games to two.

Although he was nearly traded to the Dallas Mavericks for Mark Aguirre following the Lakers 1986 playoff loss to the Houston Rockets, Worthy remained in Los Angeles and won two more NBA championships in 1987 and 1988. In game seven of the 1988 NBA finals against the Detroit Pistons, Worthy recorded his only career triple-double with thirty-six points, sixteen rebounds, and ten assists, propelling the Lakers to their fifth title in nine years and securing his nickname "Big Game James." He was named the Most Valuable Player of the series.

Los Angeles returned to the finals again in 1989 and 1991, but the Lakers era of dominance was over, and they were defeated by Detroit (4–0) and Chicago (4–1). Worthy

James Worthy, 1987. ASSOCIATED PRESS AP

retired from basketball on 10 November 1994, after playing his entire twelve-season professional career with the Lakers. He finished as a seven-time All-Star, with 16,320 points and three NBA championships. Worthy's number 42 jersey was retired by the Lakers on 10 December 1995, and his number 52 jersey was retired at UNC and at Ashbrook High School. Worthy was also inducted into the North Carolina Sports Hall of Fame.

Off the court, Worthy and his wife, Angela Wilder, whom he married in 1984, raised two daughters. After retiring from basketball, he founded the sports marketing firm Big Game James, and began work as a television basketball analyst. Actively involved in charitable endeavors, the only blemish on Worthy's career was a 1990 arrest for solicitation of prostitution in Houston. He pleaded no contest to a pair of misdemeanor charges, after he allegedly offered money to two plainclothes policewomen posing as prostitutes. Worthy was sentenced to one year's probation and forty hours of community service, and fined $1,000.

In 1996 one of Worthy's championship uniforms—complete with his trademark goggles—was placed in the

Smithsonian Institution in Washington, D.C. That same year he was also named one of the NBA's fifty greatest players as part of the league's fiftieth anniversary celebration. Of his basketball career, Worthy was quoted in the commemorative book the *NBA at Fifty* (1996) as saying, "I had my areas where I knew I could get to and what moves I was going to make when I got there. If you defended me three or four different ways, then I had three or four different moves. It was something I worked at, but I always believed I was quicker than most forwards I played against."

★

Information about Worthy's early career can be found in *North Carolina National Championship, 1982* (1982), and Dean Smith, *A Coach's Life: My Forty Years in College Basketball* (1999). Photos and quotations of the players honored at the NBA's fiftieth anniversary celebration, including Worthy, are in Mark Vancil, ed., *The NBA at Fifty* (1996). Details on his arrest and sentencing appear in the *Orange County Register* (15 Dec. 1990).

JACK STYCZYNSKI

WRIGHT, William Henry ("Harry") (*b.* 10 January 1835 in Sheffield, England; *d.* 3 October 1895 in Atlantic City, New Jersey), considered the father of professional baseball; he was the first to institute modern management practices and business philosophies and strategies into the game.

Wright was the eldest of five children of Samuel Wright and Ann Tone Wright, and immigrated to the United States with his parents around 1836 when he was two years old. He was educated in New York City grade schools. At fourteen he took a job working for a jewelry manufacturing firm, but Wright was drawn to cricket, the sport his father played professionally. In 1850 he became an assistant professional for the St. George Cricket Club on Staten Island, where he established himself as the best round arm bowler in the United States.

During his tenure with the St. George Club, Wright also began to play baseball, the fastest growing sport in New York. First he participated in the Fashion Course Games of 1857, the championship matches played between the best nines of New York and the best nines of Brooklyn. Then in 1858 Wright, who had played for the New York squad, joined the Knickerbocker Base Ball Club of New York. Unlike his status as a paid professional cricketeer, he was playing baseball as an amateur, because baseball, at least officially, was dominated by purists who believed the game should be played only for health and recreation.

In 1866 Wright left New York for Cincinnati to play cricket, joining the Union Cricket Club as its bowler and working as an instructor. That July, realizing baseball's immense popularity, Wright formed the Cincinnati Baseball Club, naming them the Red Stockings, with the idea of fashioning the club as a professional team like the cricket clubs he had played for. Wright, as captain, began to hire the best players with pay, and when his club defeated a rival team in Ohio, the Red Stockings became a force in the baseball world.

Wright continued to shine as a player despite his increased involvement as a manager. Wright, who had switched from pitcher to center fielder, had his finest game on 22 June 1867, at Newport, Kentucky, when he slugged seven home runs in a single game.

Under Wright's leadership, the Red Stockings were the first and only all-professional team in the United States by 1869 and embarked on a one-year national tour that featured an eighty-seven-game winning streak, which ended after a controversial loss to the Brooklyn Atlantics. During this tour Wright showed how prudent managerial skills both on and off the field could lead to a financially profitable club. Realizing the Red Stockings immense popularity, Wright demanded a third of the gate receipts when his club visited another city, wisely preferring to play clubs that only had strong drawing power.

With the formation of the National Association of Professional Base Ball Players in 1871, the Cincinnati Red Stockings disbanded and Wright went on to captain and play center field for the newly formed Boston Red Stockings. Joining him were his brother George, who played shortstop, and legendary pitcher Albert Goodwill Spalding. Under Wright's leadership, Boston won four of the five championships. In 1874 Wright led a baseball tour of all-stars to England. The players even participated in some cricket matches, astonishing the English with their skills honed by playing professional baseball.

Wright ended his playing days with Boston in 1876 but remained with the club for eleven years as its manager. It was also the first year of the owner-oriented National League of Professional Base Ball Clubs. By the winter of 1876, the National Association was experiencing problems. William Hulbert of the Chicago White Stockings took the opportunity to secretly sign the big star players from other teams to build his team. At the Grand Central Hotel in New York, on February 2, 1876, the National League of Professional Base Ball Clubs was formed by Hulbert and seven other club owners who wanted to split from the National Association. Wright cast his lot with Hulbert, joining the conspiracy because he thought the Association was a disciplinary failure. The new league and its new rules were controversial and unpopular. Players could not drink—on or off the field—and beer could not be sold at games. Gambling was not allowed at games, and games were not to be played on Sundays. Hulbert wanted the power to rest with the owners and not with the players, so revisions were made

Harry Wright, from a Goodwin & Co. baseball card, c. 1887–1890. BASEBALL CARDS FROM THE BENJAMIN K. EDWARDS COLLECTION/THE LIBRARY OF CONGRESS

to ensure that players were treated as no more than simple employees of the owners. Players who objected were fired and blacklisted.

In 1882 Wright left to manage the Providence Club, building a championship team that won after his premature departure in 1884. That year, he managed the Philadelphia club, eventually making them into a contender for the championship. When he left Philadelphia in 1893, he was finished with managing and was appointed chief of umpires of the National League.

Wright was married three times: first on 10 September 1868 to Mary Fraser of New York City, with whom he had four children, then to Rose Mulford, with whom he had four children. Wright later married his first wife's sister. In mid-September 1895, Wright was stricken with pneumonia and entered a sanatorium in Atlantic City, New Jersey. He died there three weeks later and is buried in the West Laurel Hill Cemetery outside Philadelphia.

In 1953 Wright and his brother George were inducted posthumously into the Baseball Hall of Fame by the Committee on Baseball Veterans.

★

For further information on Wright and his career, see Harry Ellard, *Base Ball in Cincinnati* (1907), and George Morland, *Balldom* (1926). Other general sources include Mike Shatzkin, ed., *The Ballplayers* (1990), and *Legends in Their Own Time* (1994). For a general overview of baseball's early years, including Wright's career, see the Major Leagues link of http://www.baseballhistory.com. An obituary is in the *New York Times* (4 Oct. 1895).

ANDREW SCHIFF

Y-Z

YAMAGUCHI, Kristi Tsuya (*b.* 12 July 1971 in Hayward, California), figure skater who was the only U.S. skater in the 1990s to win national, world, and Olympic championships in the same year, and the first U.S. female to accomplish this feat since 1976.

Born with a clubfoot so severe that she required corrective shoes, physical therapy, and a painful night brace, Yamaguchi didn't appear to be Olympic material. After watching Dorothy Hamill win the 1976 Olympic gold medal, however, Yamaguchi requested figure-skating lessons; her parents agreed. Jim, a dentist, and Carole, a medical secretary, hoped that those exercises, in addition to the ballet Yamaguchi had taken since age four, would strengthen her leg muscles. "I remember the first time she put on skates and was taking her first few lessons," her mother said in an interview. "She had a difficult time because she was very small and not very strong."

Over the next several years, Yamaguchi's parents juggled time spent raising their other two children, also athletes, with the many hours they dedicated to Yamaguchi's growing commitment to skating. By age eight her schedule was even more intense, as she awoke at four in the morning to practice with the coach Christy Kjarsgaard-Ness. She also continued her efforts in dance, foreshadowing the artistic style that would become her trademark.

A quick study, Yamaguchi skated both singles and pairs; she was one of the first U.S. females to attempt this dual level of competition. Teamed with Rudy Galindo, she won the junior pairs national competitions in 1986 and 1989. During this period, Yamaguchi received pairs coaching by Jim Hulick in addition to singles coaching by Kjarsgaard-Ness. In 1989 Yamaguchi also won the silver medal in the singles competition, the first woman to win a medal in two national events in the same year since Margaret Graham in 1954. Yamaguchi was only age seventeen, standing four feet, eleven inches and weighing just eighty-two pounds. In June 1989 Yamaguchi graduated from Mission San Jose High School.

In the 1989 World Championships in Paris, France, Yamaguchi finished sixth in singles and fifth in pairs, and the U.S. Olympic Committee named her the Athlete of the Year for figure skating. At the 1990 national competition, she and Galindo won pairs and Yamaguchi finished second in singles. While those accomplishments were astonishing, the dual training began to tire Yamaguchi, and in the 1990 World Championships she slipped in the rankings, placing fourth in singles and fifth in pairs.

Yamaguchi decided to concentrate solely on singles competition. "To improve in one or the other," Yamaguchi told the *New York Times* about her decision to stop skating with Galindo, "I had to choose. It was a difficult decision, but I knew something would have to change." While Yamaguchi later occasionally expressed doubts about that decision, her singles performances sparkled.

In 1990 she won the Goodwill Games, achieved gold-

Kristi Yamaguchi at the 1992 Olympics in Albertville, France. AP/WIDE WORLD PHOTOS

medal status at the Nations Cup, and won Skate America. The next year she placed second at the Goodwill Games and became the 1991 world champion in Munich, Germany. Tonya Harding earned the silver and Nancy Kerrigan the bronze, making the event the first where three women from the same country swept the competition.

Yamaguchi also won the 1992 nationals and competed in the 1992 Olympics in Albertville, France. She became the first U.S. female skater to win Olympic gold since her idol, Hamill. "There may be two or three performances in your life that are absolutely on, where all the planets are lined up for you, and you feel that you're invincible," Yamaguchi confided in a television interview, when asked about her Olympic performance.

One month after the Olympics, Yamaguchi captured the gold medal at the 1992 World Championships in Oakland, California, just miles from her hometown. After the triple victories in 1992, however, Yamaguchi had to make a choice: to train for the 1994 Olympics or to turn professional. She chose to focus her energy in the professional arena, joining Stars on Ice, a decision that startled many. Even when a change in the Olympic eligibility rules would have allowed her to reinstate her amateur status, she declined and did not compete in 1994. "I feel fortunate to be in this era of growth in professional figure skating, because I love what professional skating has to offer," Yamaguchi said.

Although she chose not to return to the Olympic arena, Yamaguchi's popularity did not fade. In 1996, 1997, and 1998 she was selected as the favorite female athlete by Nickelodeon's Kids' Choice Awards and was named the 1996 Skater of the Year by the American Skating World. She was inducted into the U.S. Figure Skating Hall of Fame in 1998 and the World Figure Skating Hall of Fame in 1999. She was also the World Professional Figure Skating Champion in 1992, 1994, 1996, and 1997.

After turning professional, Yamaguchi became actively involved in several charitable efforts. She served as a spokesperson for the American Lung Association and Christmas Seals. In 1996 she established the Always Dream Foundation to support organizations in California, Nevada, and Hawaii whose missions are to "encourage, support, and embrace the hopes and dreams of children." In 1999 she received the Make-a-Wish Grantor Recognition Award and was selected as the Goodwill Ambassador for the 2002 Winter Games to be held in Salt Lake City, Utah. On 8 July 2000 Yamaguchi married Bret Hedican, an ice-hockey defenseman for the Florida Panthers.

Yamaguchi overcame physical impairment to win national, world, and Olympic skating championships, the first time this feat was accomplished by a U.S. female during one year in nearly two decades. She enjoyed much public support, although she did suffer some criticism when she left Galindo to concentrate solely on singles competitions; when she shed her amateur status to become professional; and when she accepted numerous commercial endorsement offers. However, almost a decade after her Olympic triumph, Yamaguchi remained a popular athlete, lauded for her strength, grace, dedication, artistry, and charitable work.

★

Yamaguchi's autobiography, written with Greg Brown, is *Always Dream* (1998). For additional information about Yamaguchi, see the following books for young readers: Jeff Savage, *Kristi Yamaguchi: Pure Gold* (1993); Shiobhan Donohue, *Kristi Yamaguchi: Artist on Ice* (1994); and Richard Rambeck, *Kristi Yamaguchi* (1998).

KELLY BOYER SAGERT

YASTRZEMSKI, Carl Michael, Jr. (*b.* 22 August 1939 in Southampton, New York), Hall of Fame outfielder who played the entirety of his 23-season career with the Boston Red Sox; he was the first American League (AL) player to pass the 400 home run/3,000 hit combined mark and the last major league player to win batting's Triple Crown.

Yastrzemski grew up on a seventy-acre potato farm in a Polish-dominated community near Bridgehampton, New York, with his parents, Carl Michael, Sr. ("Mike") and Hedwig Skonieczny Yastrzemski, and his brother Joseph. He aspired to a big league baseball career from the time he could first remember. His father had been an outstanding player, good enough to attract the attention of scouts from the Dodgers and Cardinals, but he passed on the insecurity of pursuing a baseball career in order to start his family.

As a boy Yastrzemski played Little League baseball for his hometown team, but the real competition came from being the youngest member of his father's Bridgehampton White Eagles, who gained regional recognition for their hard-nosed style of play. Young Yastrzemski prided himself on practicing baseball every day of the year, swinging at a hanging ball in the family barn during winter months.

As a star pitcher and shortstop at Bridgehampton High School, he attracted the attention of major league scouts, hitting .650 his senior year and leading his team to its second consecutive county championship. When professional baseball teams failed to meet his father's demand for a $100,000 signing bonus, Yastrzemski entered the University of Notre Dame in 1957 on a combined baseball and basketball scholarship. After completing his freshman year in college, the Boston Red Sox finally satisfied his father's terms, making nineteen-year-old Yastrzemski a genuine bonus baby. He signed in 1958 for $108,000, a guaranteed two-year $5,000 per year minor league contract, and an agreement to fund the balance of the young slugger's college education expenses.

Carl Yastrzemski, 1968. ASSOCIATED PRESS AP

Despite his modest size (five feet, one inches, and 160 pounds when he signed), Yastrzemski's minor league performance measured up to Boston's high expectations. He hit .377 and became the Carolina League's Most Valuable Player (MVP) for Class A Raleigh in 1959. Then he hit .339 for AAA Minneapolis in 1960, when the Red Sox moved him from second base to left field, grooming him to replace Ted Williams for the 1961 season. Early comparisons with Williams proved troubling to the Red Sox rookie outfielder as he struggled during his first season, but a weekend meeting with baseball's "Splendid Splinter" caused Yastrzemski to regain his confidence. He hit over .300 during the last two months of the 1961 season and finished with 80 runs batted in (RBI) and a respectable .266 average.

Yastrzemski married Carolann Casper on 30 January 1960, and they eventually had four children. From 1962 to 1966 Yastrzemski proved to be a solid but unspectacular player, even winning the AL batting title (.321) in 1963, but his off-seasons were occupied with keeping the promise he made to his father of becoming the first member of the family to earn a college degree. Finally, in the spring of 1966, the young ballplayer received his B.S. from Merrimack College in Andover, Massachusetts, but then proceeded to have an underwhelming 1966 season, hitting .278 with eighty RBI.

With no college classes to fill his time during the 1966–1967 off-season, and recognizing that his strength and stamina were insufficient to withstand the rigors of a 162-game season, Yastrzemski committed himself to a rigorous conditioning program under the Hungarian Olympic coach Gene Berde. By the time spring training began in February 1967, Yastrzemski felt confident in his newly developed strength and quickness. He was ready to abandon his spray-hitter batting style and become a pull hitter with a power stroke.

The 1967 season became the most dramatic year ever for Boston Red Sox fans. The team overcame 100–1 odds, coming off its 72–90 ninth-place finish in 1966 and winning the AL pennant for the first time since 1946. Yastrzemski almost single-handedly made the difference. In his book on the 1967 Red Sox, *Lost Summer: The '67 Red Sox and the Impossible Dream* (1992), the Providence-based sportswriter Bill Reynolds encapsulates the essence of the Boston left fielder's Triple Crown (.326, 44 home runs, 121 RBI) season: "Who is more heroic than Yastrzemski? He seems to have stepped out of the pages of adolescent fiction. He gets the big hit. He makes the big play in the field. He says the right things afterward. Yaz always delivers."

As the 1967 AL pennant race went down to the wire, and the Twins, Tigers, White Sox, and Red Sox stayed within three games of each other, there were fifteen lead changes in the season's final twenty-seven games. In that span Yastrzemski hit .417 with 26 RBI and scored 24 runs. With Boston needing to win its last two games against Minnesota to stay in the hunt, Yastrzemski led the Bosox to both victories, going seven for eight, and giving the team the "Impossible Dream" pennant.

The pesky Red Sox extended the battle against the St. Louis Cardinals in the 1967 Fall Classic to seven games as Yastrzemski hit .400 with three home runs and five RBI, but Boston ultimately had no answer for either Bob Gibson (who won three games in the Series) or Lou Brock (who stole 7 bases and hit .414). After the 1967 season, honors poured in for the Red Sox hero: Yaz received the AL's MVP award, was named *Sports Illustrated*'s Sportsman of the Year, and was awarded the Hickok Belt as the best professional athlete of that year.

For the balance of his career from 1968 to 1983, Yastrzemski maintained a steady pace of greatness, playing Fenway Park's "Green Monster" in left field better than anyone before or since, winning the AL batting title (his third) in 1968, losing the batting title by .0003 to Alex Johnson in 1970, being a key member of the Red Sox 1975 pennant-winning team (which preserved the "Curse of the Bambino" by not being able to win a World Series since Babe Ruth's departure in 1914 by losing to the Cincinnati Cardinals in the seven-game World Series that year), being named to eighteen All-Star teams, winning seven Gold Glove awards, setting a league record for career games played (3,308), and ending his career as the first AL player to have over 3,000 hits and 400 home runs.

For all these career achievements, Yastrzemski became an easy first-ballot selection into the National Baseball Hall of Fame in 1989. He was the first veteran of Little League baseball to be inducted, receiving 94 percent support from the Baseball Writers of America, which, at that time, was the sixth highest total ever received. Since retiring, Yastrzemski has worked as a roving instructor for the Boston Red Sox during spring training, as well as being a regular at the Red Sox fantasy camps, where fans don the team uniform and play ball with their baseball heroes.

For almost a quarter of a century an average-sized baseball player put together an unusually great career through hard work and sheer determination. Yastrzemski endeared himself to an entire generation of baby boomer New Englanders as the game's hard-nosed working man, who gave baseball everything he had every day for twenty-three seasons. The *Boston Globe* sportswriter Peter Gammons put the perfect final touch on Yastrzemski's career in a column after the Red Sox (now retired) number 8's final game: "He was never Ted, only Yaz; never celluloid, only calloused flesh."

★

Yastrzemski's autobiography, *Yaz: Baseball, the Wall, and Me* (1990), written with Gerald Eskenazi, is the most complete account of his career, although he wrote an earlier book, *Yaz,* with Al Hirschberg (1968) after his Triple Crown year. Bill Reynolds, *Lost Summer: The '67 Red Sox and the Impossible Dream* (1992), is a vivid account of Yastrzemski's greatest season, and additional information can be found at Yastrzemski's website at http://www.yaz8.com.

TALMAGE BOSTON

YOUNG, Denton True ("Cy") (*b.* 29 March 1867 in Gilmore, Ohio; *d.* 4 November 1955 in Peoli, Ohio), pitcher who won 511 games, the most in baseball history.

The eldest of five children born to McKinzie Young, a farmer, and Nancy Miller, a homemaker, Young was raised on a farm in eastern Ohio, leaving school after sixth grade. A tall, strapping youth at six feet, two inches tall and 170 pounds, he broke into the majors in 1890 at the relatively advanced age of twenty-three, playing for the National League's (NL) Cleveland Spiders. Before long, he was nicknamed "Cyclone" because of the speed of his fastball,

Cy Young. ARCHIVE PHOTOS, INC.

and this was soon shortened to "Cy." Young quickly emerged as the Spiders' ace and helped the club to become, behind the Boston team and the Baltimore Orioles, the third-most successful franchise of the 1890s. He won more than thirty games three times during the decade and never failed to win at least twenty.

In 1892 Young led Cleveland into the postseason championship series against Boston. The opening game of that match-up, in which he dueled Jack Stivetts during eleven scoreless innings, is one of the most celebrated contests in baseball history. Three years later, when the Spiders met Baltimore in postseason play, Young led his team to a Temple Cup victory by winning three games against the powerful Orioles. In 1897, facing Cincinnati, Young threw his first no-hitter. His successes across the decade stamp him as one of a trio of outstanding pitchers—Kid Nichols and Amos Rusie are the other two—whose careers were not undone when the pitching distance was lengthened from fifty-five feet, six inches, to the current distance of sixty feet, six inches in 1893.

Prior to the 1899 season the Spiders' owner secured control of the NL's St. Louis franchise, and in an effort to escape Cleveland's revenue-damaging prohibition on Sunday baseball, shifted most of his squad to his new club. Young was unhappy in Missouri, however, and in 1900 the summer heat, combined with the first serious injury of his career, reduced his victory total to nineteen. (It is worth noting, though, that record-keeping was casual in those days and some historians credit him with twenty wins.)

In 1901 the American League (AL), aiming to break the NL's monopoly on major league status, persuaded various NL stars to jump to its franchises. Eager to improve upon an annual salary that cannot have exceeded $3,000 during the 1890s, Young left St. Louis and went to Boston. Although he was already the oldest regular pitcher in baseball, he quickly established himself as the dominant hurler in the new league. In each of his first two seasons he won more than thirty games.

Two years later in 1903, Young led his team to victory in the first World Series, defeating the Pittsburgh Pirates for the championship and making him the only pitcher to record postseason victories in both the nineteenth and twentieth centuries. An episode during this series underscores Young's celebrated commitment to honesty. In Pittsburgh, gamblers offered him a substantial sum of money to perform poorly. He spurned the offer, told them that they would be unwise to bet against him, and proceeded to compile the lowest earned run average of any pitcher in the series.

In the 1904 season, Young pitched a still-unequaled record of twenty-four consecutive hitless innings and against the Philadelphia Athletics hurled the first major-league perfect game at the longer pitching distance. The team won the AL pennant that year, with Young earning $6,000, the high-water mark for his career.

After this, age began to exact a visible toll on Young. Thirty-eight years old when the 1905 season began, visibly overweight, and pitching less frequently, he slipped below twenty wins that year, and fell to a lowly thirteen in 1906. He enjoyed a modest rebirth in 1907 and 1908, winning twenty-one games in each season and hurling his third career no-hitter against Washington in the latter year. Over the subsequent off-season in 1909 he was traded to the AL's Cleveland team, with whom, during the 1910 season, he recorded his 500th victory. In the middle of the 1911 season Cleveland concluded that Young's old mastery had permanently evaporated and released him. Young then rounded out his twenty-two-season career by winning four games for the NL's feeble Boston club.

Young married Robba Miller on 8 November 1892, but the couple's only child died in 1907 a few hours after birth. Caring little for city life, Young returned to Peoli, Ohio, as promptly as possible when each baseball season ended, where he spent his winters chopping wood, hiking, and hunting. After a stint at managing in the Federal League in 1913, Young retired permanently from baseball to become a full-time farmer. A few years after his wife's death in 1933 he moved in with a younger Peoli family, living the rest of his life on their farm. In 1939 Young was one of the charter inductees into the National Baseball Hall of Fame at Cooperstown. He died of heart failure and is buried in the Methodist churchyard in Peoli.

The ultimate craftsman, Young holds a variety of cumulative records that will never be eclipsed: the most career victories (511), the most losses (316), and the most innings pitched (7,356). His trademark pitch was a fastball, but unlike some of his contemporaries, he labored to hone his skills. Thus, as his career progressed, he expanded his repertoire with two curveballs, a change-up, and an occasional spitball. He studied hitters closely and, because he had exceptional control over all his offerings, he could exploit any weaknesses he detected. Although in only a few seasons was Young indisputably the "best" pitcher in baseball, he was among the best for almost two decades. Since he played in an era marked by brevity of pitching careers, frequency of pitching assignments, and imperfect attention to conditioning, this durability is remarkable. Young was, in short, a model athlete—gifted, smart, hard-working, and honest—and his name is therefore aptly affixed to the Cy Young Award, given annually to the best pitcher in each league.

★

The National Baseball Library at Cooperstown, New York, and the Temperance Tavern Museum in Newcomerstown, Ohio, contain files, scrapbooks, and physical artifacts related to Young. One biography is Ralph Romig, *Cy Young: Baseball's Legendary*

Giant (1964). The most recent biography is Reed Browning, *Cy Young: A Baseball Life* (2000). Issues of the *Sporting News* and *Sporting Life* from between 1890 and 1911 published many articles about Young. An obituary is in the *New York Times* (5 Nov. 1955)

REED BROWNING

YOUNG, Jon Steven ("Steve") (*b.* 11 October 1961 in Salt Lake City, Utah), Super Bowl champion and star quarterback for the San Francisco 49ers who was one of the best quarterbacks in NFL history.

Young was the oldest of five children of LeGrande Young, an attorney, and Sherry Steed Young, a homemaker. The family moved from Utah to Greenwich, Connecticut, in 1969. Young excelled in competitive sports in his elementary school years. He did not make the varsity football team as a tenth grader at Greenwich High School, but by his senior year, he was the first-string quarterback. Using the veer offense, which allows the quarterback maximum flexibility, Young won the first game of his senior season. Following the victory, Young was invited to a party, offered a beer, and politely refused. As a Mormon he does not use alcohol, caffeine, or tobacco. Young led his high school team to the Fairfield County Interscholastic Athletic Conference championship game, but lost the game to arch rival Darien. During his high school career, Young completed more than 40 percent of his passes for 1,220 yards and rushed for 1,928 yards, thus becoming the second best in high school history. He graduated from high school in 1979.

Cornell, Virginia, Syracuse, and North Carolina all offered Young athletic scholarships, but he decided to attend Brigham Young University (BYU) where his father had played fullback. His ancestor Brigham Young, a pioneer in U.S. history, helped lead a large group of Mormon settlers west to what later became the state of Utah and was one of the founders of the Church of Jesus Christ of Latter-Day Saints.

When Young arrived at the university in 1980, sportswriters were calling the school "Quarterback U" because Coach LaVell Edwards would call for fifty passes a game. It appeared that Young was not prepared for a passing offense, and he was listed as the team's eighth-string quarterback. However, halfway through the season, he was asked to run the "scout" team offense, the offensive formation used by the team's next opponent, against the varsity. His performance in practice that week got the attention of Coach Edwards.

With the arrival of Ted Tollner, a new quarterback coach, Young began his second season as the heir apparent to Jim McMahon. When McMahon was injured early in the season, sophomore quarterback Young helped the team defeat Colorado and became the star quarterback for the 1982 season. After a slow start, the team began winning big with Young's strong passing and running. BYU was selected to play in the 1982 Holiday Bowl game against Ohio State. Young scored two touchdowns, but the team still lost 40–17.

By his senior year Young was the starting quarterback and finished second to Mike Rozier of Nebraska in the voting for the 1983 Heisman Trophy. At the 1983 Holiday Bowl, Young used a trick play with thirty seconds left in

Steve Young after his San Francisco 49ers won Super Bowl XXIX, 1995. ASSOCIATED PRESS AP

the game against Missouri—he handed off to his halfback, then caught a return pass and ran for a touchdown to win the game 21–17. At the end of his college career, Young had the highest single-season passing percentage (71.3) in the National Collegiate Athletic Association (NCAA). Young received his B.S. in 1983.

The Cincinnati Bengals of the National Football League (NFL) were planning to draft Young in the first round, but he was also approached by the United States Football League (USFL) and signed in 1984 with the Los Angeles Express for $40 million, the largest contract in professional football history at that time. With a record of 2–3, the Los Angeles Express were ready for Young to play. After nine games the team was only 3–6. But Young led the team to win seven of their last eight regular season games and a slot in the playoffs. The Express ended the season with a 35–23 playoff game loss to the Arizona Wranglers.

By the end of Young's second season, the USFL was in deep financial trouble, and Young paid the league back over a million dollars in order to secure his release. He then signed a five-year $6 million contract with the NFL's Tampa Bay Buccaneers in September 1985.

The Buccaneers were one of the worst teams in the NFL, but Young was still only the backup quarterback to Leeman Bennett while he learned the offense. Young played in a few games, but the Buccaneers finished the season 2–14. In the next season, the Buccaneers struggled to another 2–14 season. At that point, the team drafted University of Miami quarterback Vinnie Testaverde in the first round, and Young felt his days at Tampa were numbered. Statistically he had one of the poorest records in the league. After four dismal seasons, Young was traded in April 1987 to the San Francisco 49ers.

Bill Walsh, the 49ers head coach, was a fan of Young's, and Walsh's quarterback coach Mike Holmgren had been one of Young's quarterback coaches at BYU. Young became the backup to Joe Montana, the top quarterback in the league. Walsh needed a quarterback who was familiar with the 49ers complicated offense to fill in when Montana was injured. Montana and Young's differences soon became apparent. Montana was methodical and precise, whereas Young was inventive and daring. San Francisco fans were not used to a quarterback who would put his head down and run over tacklers. In his first year with the 49ers, Young suffered his first concussion. Yet in the final exhibition game against the Los Angeles Raiders in 1997, he still was responsible for more offensive yardage than the Raiders entire team.

In the next season, Young played sparingly, splitting time with Montana. Late in the season Young stepped in for Montana, who was suffering from back problems. With two minutes to play in the game against the Minnesota Vikings, Young took the ball and ran downfield, escaping from eight Vikings to score the winning touchdown. Years later sportswriters characterized Young's run for a touchdown as the best run in NFL history.

In 1993 the 49ers coaches had to make a choice between an aging Montana and Young, who had still not proved himself in playoffs. Montana signed with the Kansas City Chiefs, and Young became the leader of the 49ers. Young had an exciting 1994 season and won his fourth consecutive ranking as the NFL's top quarterback. When the 49ers defeated the Dallas Cowboys for the championship, San Francisco fans seemed finally ready to support a new football star. In the Super Bowl against the San Diego Chargers, Young threw for six touchdowns, a Super Bowl record, and rushed for more yards than any of his teammates. The team beat San Diego 49–26, becoming world champions for the fifth time in San Francisco history. Young was named the Super Bowl's Most Valuable Player (MVP).

In the next few years, Young suffered numerous concussions and other injuries. Despite these problems, in 1996 he was the leading NFL quarterback for the fifth time, and the following year he reached the 3,000-yard mark for the fifth time in his career. Young was equally memorable in 1998 when he broke the single-season team record for most passing yards and touchdown passes.

Young married Barbara Graham on 14 March 1999, and their son was born the following year. After a seventeen-year career and two MVP awards, Young retired on 12 June 2000, saying, "For the record, I can still play." He was concerned that the numerous concussions he had suffered would make it dangerous for him to continue.

Young is the founder and president of the Forever Young Foundation that sponsors many charitable activities, including sports programs in the San Francisco schools and working to help Native Americans. He earned a law degree from Brigham Young University in 1993, and performs legal work for his foundation. Young took his passion for sports to the 2002 Olympic Winter Games as a Salt Lake Olympic Committee ambassador-at-large.

No one in the history of the NFL had ever played the quarterback position better. Young had perseverance, a strong passing arm on the run, and no fear. He was also the ideal height and weight for the position—six foot, two inches, and 205 pounds. His NFL rating was 112.8, an all-time single season record, and his career rating of 96.8 was the best in league history. His 35 touchdown passes and 70.2 percent completion mark set new records previously held by Montana. Young was named Player of the Week twice, Player of the Month once, and NFL Player of the Year.

★

Young wrote a children's book titled *Forever Young* (1996). See also Ron Knapp, *Steve Young: Star Quarterback* (1996) and Laura Livsey and Larry Livsey, *The Steve Young Story* (1995). Career statistics and articles reflecting on his retirement appear online at the *Sports Illustrated* website, <http://sportsillustrated.cnn.com>.

REED B. MARKHAM

ZAHARIAS, Mildred ("Babe") Didrikson. *See* Didrikson Zaharias, Mildred Ella ("Babe").

ZALE, Tony (*b.* 29 May 1913 in Gary, Indiana; *d.* 20 March 1997 in Portage, Indiana), two-time middleweight champion of the 1940s who is best remembered for his three fights against Rocky Graziano in 1946, 1947, and 1948.

Born Anthony Florian Zaleski, Zale was one of seven children of Joseph Zaleski, a steelworker, and Catherine Mazur Zaleski, a homemaker. Zale's early years were marked by hardship. His father died in a traffic accident when Zale was only two years old. Without her husband's income, Zale's mother struggled to raise their large family. Later Zale would refer to the prize money he could use to help support his mother as one of his primary motivations to become a boxer.

The sixth child in a close-knit and religious Polish immigrant family, Zale idolized his three older brothers and followed their interest in amateur boxing as he grew up. At fifteen, while completing his education at Gary's Froebel High School, Zale entered his first fight at the Chicago Arena. Zale took a pounding and lost the match, but his brothers encouraged him to continue training. Taking a job in one of Gary's steel mills, Zale won the welterweight title in the 1930 Golden Gloves tournament in Gary, a title he defended three more times. Zale also reached the welterweight finals of the 1932 Chicago Golden Gloves tournament, which he lost. Eventually, Zale held a 87–8 record as an amateur before making his professional debut on 11 June 1934 against Eddie Allen in Chicago, which he took in four rounds.

Tony Zale. © BETTMANN/CORBIS

However, Zale's debut as a professional was premature. His manager secured a heavy schedule of matches for Zale against experienced opponents that gave the young fighter little chance of honing his skills. Worse, Zale tore muscles in his side and continued to fight despite the pain. In July 1935 Zale took a break from boxing and returned to the steel mills in the hope that the strenuous work would toughen his body. The plan succeeded. Zale added muscle to his 160-pound, five-foot, eight-inch frame, but he still needed to improve his boxing style. Under new managers Art Winch and Sam Pian—who bought his contract for a paltry $200 in June 1938—Zale combined powerful and rapid punches with faster footwork and better defensive moves. Added to his capacity for absorbing almost any blow, Zale was now a formidable fighter. From his stint in the steel mills of Gary, he soon earned the nickname the "Man of Steel" in the ring.

Zale's comeback in 1939 gathered momentum after a draw and a loss in his first two fights after his return. By 29 January 1940 Zale had won a string of victories and challenged National Boxing Association middleweight champion Al Hostak in a nontitle fight. With the Chicago crowd behind the Gary native, Zale survived a knockdown in the first round and a series of blows in the fifth that allegedly broke Hostak's right hand. Zale's endurance eventually gave him the decision: he battered Hostak's midsection in the final rounds of the fight. On 19 July 1940 Zale met Hostak again—this time for the title—and sent the defending champion down three times with blows to his chest before winning on a technical knockout in the thirteenth round. Zale defended his title twice in 1941, and picked up the New York State middleweight crown by beating Georgie Abrams on 28 November that same year.

With the onset of World War II, Zale enlisted in the U.S. Navy and served as a physical education instructor at Chicago's Great Lakes Training Station and in Puerto Rico. Aside from one fight in February 1942, the defending middleweight champion did not fight for four years, although he still retained the title. In 1946 Zale returned to the ring for some tune-up matches for his first title defense since 1941 against Rocky Graziano, but a bout with pneumonia delayed the event.

Finally, on 27 September 1946 before a partisan crowd in Yankee Stadium, the heavily favored Graziano met Zale. Not only was Graziano nine years younger, but he had fought continually through the war after being declared unfit for military service. Graziano's troubled past and colorful personality also stood in sharp contrast to Zale's reputation as a devoted son and patriotic veteran. Making the odds worse for Zale, he had developed a sty in his eye just before the fight. After getting knocked down in the first round, Graziano paid Zale back in the next round and beat the defending champion until he was disoriented at the end of the fifth. Amazingly, Zale returned for the next round with renewed energy that demonstrated his staying power. Sending Graziano down with a combination of punches to the stomach and the chin, Zale won the fight by a knockout. When Zale returned home to Gary after the match, he was met at the train station by 30,000 people and given the key to the city.

A second Zale-Graziano match in Chicago on 16 July 1947 gave the champion the advantage of a hometown crowd. This time, however, it was Zale who failed to outlast his opponent. After leading Graziano for five rounds, Zale fell victim to the slugger's powerful arsenal of punches in the sixth. The referee stopped the fight on a technical knockout against Zale's wishes, and Graziano claimed the middleweight title. The event later became immortalized in the 1956 film *Somebody Up There Likes Me.* Zale was slated to portray himself in the movie, until his sparring rehearsals with actor Paul Newman, who played Graziano, raised fears that he might accidentally injure the star.

On 10 June 1948 Zale and Graziano met again in Newark for the final bout in their rivalry. Once again the underdog, Zale sent Graziano down twice before knocking him out for good in the third round with his classic combination of blows to Graziano's body and head. Zale retained the title for only three months, however, before losing it to French fighter Marcel Cerdan in an eleven-round fight that left Zale exhausted. The match was an anticlimax to one of the greatest boxing series in the sport's history—many said that Zale simply lost interest in fighting once his bouts with Graziano had ended—but the names Zale and Graziano would be forever linked.

After his defeat, Zale retired from boxing and made a comfortable living from his partnership in a Chicago automobile dealership. A bitter divorce in 1949—from the former Adeline Richwaski, with whom he had two daughters after their marriage on 10 April 1942—gave the dignified Zale some unwelcome attention. But the former fighter put his personal life back together with a 1970 marriage to Philomena Gianfrancisco. Zale also earned praise for his philanthropic work, particularly with Chicago-area Catholic Youth Organization activities. In 1990 Zale received the Presidential Citizen's Medal of Honor from President George H. W. Bush. In 1991 he was inducted into the International Boxing Hall of Fame. On 20 March 1997, after suffering from Parkinson's disease, Alzheimer's disease, and lymph node cancer, Zale died in a nursing home in Portage, Indiana, and is buried at the Calvary Cemetery there.

Best remembered for his series of fights with Graziano in the 1940s, Zale was a symbol of ethnic pride that made him a hero to his fellow Polish Americans. Active in philanthropic work in his retirement, Zale was also remembered at the time of his death as a man of unusual dignity outside the boxing ring.

★

James B. Lane recounted Zale's life and career in *"City of the Century": A History of Gary, Indiana* (1978). Zale's record as a fighter was compiled in James B. Roberts et al., *The Boxing Register: International Hall of Fame Official Record Book* (1999). A contemporary profile of Zale, Howard Roberts, "Hard-Luck Champion," appeared in the *Saturday Evening Post* (5 July 1947). Posthumous tributes to Zale included obituaries in the *New York Times* and *Chicago Tribune* (both 21 Mar. 1997), and a piece by sportswriter Shirley Povich in the *Washington Post* (30 Mar. 1997). The July 1947 Zale-Marciano fight was the climax of the film made from Marciano's autobiography, *Somebody Up There Likes Me* (1956).

TIMOTHY BORDEN

ZUPPKE, Robert Carl ("Bob") (*b.* 2 July 1879 in Berlin, Germany; *d.* 22 December 1957 in Champaign, Illinois), football coach at the University of Illinois known for his innovative strategies.

In 1881 Zuppke, his two siblings, and parents Franz Simon Zuppke, a jewelry designer, and Hermine Bocksbaum Zuppke, were among 210,485 emigrants who left Germany for a new life in the United States. The family settled in Milwaukee, Wisconsin, where his father was naturalized as a U.S. citizen. Zuppke walked to West Division High School, where he studied art and learned the newly popular game of football. At Milwaukee Normal School, Zuppke, known as "Contrary Rob," was the quarterback on a losing football team, a center fielder on the baseball team, and a yearbook illustrator. In 1900 he was a guard on a winning basketball team. After teaching in an elementary school, he went to the University of Wisconsin at Madison, where he played basketball and was a football substitute. He graduated in 1905.

In 1906, after a year in New York City, Zuppke moved to Muskegon, Michigan, where he taught and coached the state champion football team. He married Fanny T. Erwin on 27 June 1908; she died in 1936. From 1910 to 1912 he taught and coached football at Oak Park High School, located in a western suburb of Chicago. Oak Park had a strong sports tradition, and Zuppke developed a talented football team, which included future novelist Ernest Hem-

Bob Zuppke *(right)* and Lavere Astroth at Zuppke's last game as Illinois coach, 1941. © BETTMANN/CORBIS

ingway as a substitute player. In 1911 and 1912 the team won national interscholastic championships by defeating St. John's High School and Everett High School in Boston.

On 12 December 1912 the Athletic Board of Control at the University of Illinois at Urbana-Champaign offered Zuppke a three-year appointment as a full-time football coach at $2,700 a year. From 1913 to 1929 Zuppke's team won 70 percent of its games and claimed seven outright or shared Big Ten championships in 1914, 1915, 1918, 1919, 1923, 1927, and 1928. After a 4–2–1 season in 1913, Zuppke wrote that they did well, considering that they were slow and made "costly spiritless relaxations." He predicted that if the team members maintained their scholastic standing, increased their determination, and underwent "intelligent training and arduous preparation" throughout the year, they would be successful.

Zuppke was hailed as an energetic, dynamic, and conscientious coach who encouraged an open style, including forward and lateral passes that made good use of his faster and smaller players. Although others often credited Zuppke with the "invention" of the huddle, the center spiral snap, the screen pass, and trick plays like the "flea flicker" and "flying trapeze," he said, "A coach who thinks he has invented a new play generally forgets that a dozen others are crediting themselves the same way about the same play the same day." He was, however, adept and innovative in employing new formations to surprise the opposing teams.

Colleges realized the value of sports in attracting students and in promoting institutional recognition and alumni loyalty. Zuppke maintained that football taught sportsmanship to classes of 70,000 on autumn afternoons. In 1914 he began offering summer session football courses for high school and college teachers. During the next decade, 1,200 coaches from across the country came to Illinois for the course. In 1920 the College of Education approved a four-year athletic coaching and physical education course, which produced athletic directors and coaches until 1932. Zuppke's *Football Techniques and Tactics* (1922) consists of twenty-two of his lectures, in which he diagrammed plays and addressed the "moral obligation of the coach" to "further the principle of good sportsmanship" by respecting the rules.

Zuppke's coaching success caused him to be a "moving force behind the construction of the university's Memorial Stadium." The $1.7 million stadium was dedicated on 18 October 1924, when Illinois hosted Michigan, a team that had not lost a game since 1921. Illinois halfback Harold ("Red") Grange scored four touchdowns in the first twelve minutes, leading his team to a 39–14 victory. After a victory over Ohio State on 21 November 1925, Grange left for a tour with the Chicago Bears. A Seattle report described Grange as "collegiate to the soles of his gold-bringing feet." Zuppke failed to dissuade Grange from a professional career, but reflected public opinion when he confessed that he did not know when amateurism became professionalism.

The 1929 Carnegie Report on intercollegiate athletics, published at the request of the president of the Carnegie Foundation for the Advancement of Teaching with the cooperation of the National Collegiate Athletic Association (NCAA), was a direct challenge to athletic directors and coaches. The report alleged that sports had become an overrated by-product of educational institutions. Although Illinois did not subsidize athletes, it could not evade being charged with commercializing college football. Zuppke questioned the attack, claiming that football educated players and spectators and that it combined popular entertainment with valuable public relations events. Athletes capitalizing on their fame by becoming professionals also made higher education attractive.

From 1930 to 1941 Zuppke's teams were less successful. They won 44 percent of their games but only 32 percent in the Big Ten. The Great Depression caused the average game attendance to drop from 39,568 in 1929 to 18,535 in 1933, thus causing a decline in profits. The 1934 team won seven games, but the overall record from 1935 to 1939 was 16–20–4. On 30 October 1937, the Athletic Association celebrated Zuppke's twenty-fifth anniversary season with a tribute to him, but in November 1938, newspaper criticism and alumni pressure caused Zuppke to consider retirement. His "forced" resignation was rejected by the university Board of Trustees, and Zuppke continued to coach until his resignation in 1941.

During retirement he vacationed in Muskegon and Phoenix, Arizona, and devoted more time to painting impressionist landscapes. He was "a lover of untampered nature" and used skills acquired in school, at the Chicago Art Institute, visits to art galleries, and his lifelong use of sketchbooks. His 29-year coaching record was 131—81—12, and he was inducted into the National Football Hall of Fame in 1951.

Zuppke married his housekeeper, Leona Ray, in 1956, but the couple had only been married for a year when Zuppke died at the age of seventy-eight from the effects of a stroke. He is buried in Rose Lawn cemetery in Champaign, opposite Memorial Stadium.

★

The Robert C. Zuppke Papers, RS 28/3/20 in the University of Illinois Archives, contain primary sources. Archival records of the Division of Intercollegiate Athletics and university offices are valuable for their coverage of the years before 1937. Harold E. Grange, *Zuppke of Illinois* (1937), is the only biography. Frequent references related to contacts are included in George Halas, *Halas by Halas* (1979), and John M. Carroll, *Red Grange and the Rise of Modern Football* (1999). An obituary is in the Champaign-Urbana Courier (23 Dec. 1957).

MAYNARD BRICHFORD

DIRECTORY OF CONTRIBUTORS

ALEXANDER, CHARLES C.
Ohio University (Emeritus)
Hornsby, Rogers ("Rajah")

ALFONSO, BARRY
Journalist, Pittsburgh, Pa.
Corbett, James John
Graziano, Rocky
Jeffries, James Jackson

AMERMAN, DON
Freelance Writer, Saylorsburg, Pa.
Bradshaw, Terry Paxton
Carew, Rod(ney) Cline
Elway, John Albert
Gibson, Josh(ua)
Jansen, Dan
Johnson, William D. ("Bill")
Johnson, Earvin, Jr. ("Magic")
Leonard, Ray Charles ("Sugar Ray")
Miller, Marvin Julian
Parcells, Duane Charles ("Bill")
Riley, Pat(rick) James
Robinson, David Maurice
Schollander, Don(ald) Arthur
Simmons, Al(oysius) Harry
Sisler, George Harold

AURAND, HAROLD W., JR.
Pennsylvania State University, Schuylkill Campus
Blaik, Earl Henry ("Red")
Luckman, Sid(ney)
Marshall, George Preston
Paterno, Joseph Vincent ("Joe")
Turner, Clyde Douglas ("Bulldog")

BARBEAU, ART
West Liberty State College, West Virginia
Dorsett, Anthony Drew ("Tony")
Harris, Franco
Lambert, John Harold ("Jack")
Noll, Charles Henry ("Chuck")

BEETZ, KIRK H.
Author and Educator, Davis, Calif.
Campanella, Roy
Chesbro, John Dwight ("Jack")
Clemens, (William) Roger
Cochrane, Gordon Stanley ("Mickey")
Collins, Edward Trowbridge ("Eddie")
Dempsey, William Harrison ("Jack")
Ewbank, Wilbur Charles ("Weeb")
Feller, Robert William Andrew ("Bob")
Gifford, Frank Newton
Huggins, Miller James
Jackson, Philip Douglas ("Phil")
Keeler, William Henry
Landis, Kenesaw Mountain
Lanier, Willie E.
McGwire, Mark David
Parker, James Thomas ("Jim")
Payton, Walter Jerry
Tunney, James Joseph ("Gene")
White, Reginald Howard ("Reggie")

BELENKY, IRINA
Graduate Student in History, Rutgers University
Brooks, Herb(ert) P.
Jagr, Jaromir

BERLAGE, GAI INGHAM
Iona College, New Rochelle, N.Y.
Edwards, Teresa
Lieberman-Cline, Nancy
Woodard, Lynette

BETZOLD, MICHAEL
Freelance Journalist, Ann Arbor, Mich.
Cunningham, William John ("Billy")
Hearns, Thomas
Hull, Brett
Hull, Robert Marvin, Jr. ("Bobby")
Nagy, Steve
Weber, Pete

BORDEN, TIMOTHY
Toledo, Ohio
Armstrong, Henry Jackson, Jr.
Counsilman, James Edward ("Doc")
Kahanamoku, Duke
Kiraly, Karch

Moore, Archibald Lee ("Archie")
Murray, James Patrick ("Jim")
Owens, James Cleveland ("Jesse")
Pep, Willie
Sande, Earl
Zale, Tony

BOSTON, TALMAGE
Sports Historian, Dallas, Tex.
Barber, Walter Lanier ("Red")
Brock, Lou(is Clark)
Giamatti, A(ngelo) Bartlett ("Bart")
Yastrzemski, Carl Michael, Jr.

BOWLING, LAWSON
Manhattanville College
Davis, Al(len)
Gaines, Clarence Edward, Sr. ("Bighouse")
Knight, Robert Montgomery ("Bob")
Kurland, Robert ("Bob")
Marino, Daniel Constantine, Jr. ("Dan")
Shula, Don(ald) Francis
Tarkenton, Fran(cis) Asbury
Wooden, John Robert

BOYLE, MOLLY
Scituate, Mass.
Hagler, Marvin Nathaniel
Marciano, Rocky

BOYLES, MARY
University of North Carolina at Pembroke (Retired)
Rigby, Cathy

BRICHFORD, MAYNARD
University Archivist Emeritus, University of Illinois at Urbana-Champaign
Byers, Walter
Zuppke, Robert Carl ("Bob")

BRILEY, RON
Sandia Preparatory School, Albuquerque, N.Mex.
Alexander, Grover Cleveland
Alworth, Lance Dwight
Blanda, George Frederick
Drysdale, Don(ald) Scott
Killebrew, Harmon Clayton
Morgan, Joe Leonard
Ryan, (Lynn) Nolan, Jr.
Wilkinson, Charles Burnham ("Bud")

BRITTON, KATHARINE FISHER
Freelance Writer, Norwich, Vt.
Rudolph, Wilma Glodean

BROCK, TED
Freelance Writer, San Francisco, Calif.
Armour, Thomas Dickson ("Tommy")

BROWNING, REED
Kenyon College
Young, Denton True ("Cy")

BRUNS, ROBERT T.
Boston College
Sarazen, Gene

BUFORD, KATE
Author and Radio Commentator, Irvington, N.Y.
Thorpe, James Francis ("Jim")

BUSTER, ALAN
Harvard-Westlake School, Los Angeles
Simpson, Orenthal James ("O. J.")

BUTLER, J. MICHAEL
South Georgia College
Earnhardt, (Ralph) Dale
Robinson, Edward Gay ("Eddie")

BYRNE, JOHN J.
Bronx Community College
Abdul-Jabbar, Kareem
Bird, Larry Joe
Maravich, Peter Press ("Pete")
Taylor, Lawrence Julius ("LT")
Tyson, Michael Gerard ("Mike"; "Iron Mike")

CAMPBELL, JIM
Bucknell University (Retired)
Baugh, Samuel Adrian ("Sammy")
Bednarik, Charles Philip ("Chuck")
Berry, Raymond Emmett
Greene, Charles Edward ("Mean Joe")
Gregg, (Alvis) Forrest
Heisman, John William ("Johnny")
Jones, Jerral Wayne ("Jerry")
Lane, Richard ("Night Train")
Layne, Robert Lawrence, Sr. ("Bobby")
Leahy, Francis William ("Frank")
Lilly, Robert Lewis ("Bob")
Lott, Ronald Mandel ("Ronnie")
Louis, Joseph ("Joe")
McNally, John Victor ("Johnny Blood")
Marchetti, Gino John
Mathewson, Christopher ("Christy")
Mitchell, Robert Cornelius, Sr. ("Bobby")
Montana, Joseph Clifford, Jr. ("Joe")
Nevers, Ernest Alonzo ("Ernie")
Nitschke, Ray(mond) Ernest
Ringo, James Stephen ("Jim")
Rooney, Arthur Joseph ("Art"), Sr.
Sayers, Gale Eugene
Schmidt, Joseph Paul ("Joe")
Stagg, Amos Alonzo, Sr.
Trippi, Charles Louis ("Charley")
Van Buren, Stephen Wood ("Steve")
Walker, (Ewell) Doak, Jr.

CARDOSO, JACK J.
Professor Emeritus, State University of New York College at Buffalo

Johnson, Walter Perry ("The Big Train")
McCarthy, Joseph Vincent ("Joe")

Cardoso, Rosemarie S.
Art Educator and Independent Scholar, Clarence, N.Y.
Inkster, Juli Simpson
Karolyi, Béla

Carey, Robert B.
Empire State College, State University of New York
Graham, Otto Everett, Jr.
Groza, Lou

Carpenter, Brian B.
Texas A&M University Libraries
Andretti, (Gabriele) Mario
Garlits, Don(ald)
Muldowney, Shirley Roque

Carroll, John M.
Lamar University
Brown, Paul Eugene
Brown, James Nathaniel ("Jim")
Tittle, Y(elberton) A(braham), Jr.

Cayleff, Susan E.
San Diego State University
Didrikson Zaharias, Mildred Ella ("Babe")

Church, Gary Mason
Montgomery College Library
Bernstein, Kenneth Dale ("Kenny")
Matson, James Randel ("Randy")

Cicarelli, Julianne
Freelance Writer, Arlington Heights, Ill.
Marble, Alice
Williams, Venus Ebone Starr

Collar, Douglas E.
Heidelberg College
Marichal, Juan Antonio

Cooksey, Gloria
Freelance Writer, Sacramento, Calif.
Agassi, Andre Kirk
D'Amato, Constantine ("Cus")
Gibbs, Joe Jackson
King, Don(ald)
Lambeau, Earl Louis ("Curly")
Nagurski, Bronislau ("Bronko")

Craig, Susan E.
Freelance Writer, Westport, Conn.
Warmerdam, Cornelius Anthony ("Dutch")

Crawford, Scott A. G. M.
Eastern Illinois University
Arcaro, George Edward ("Eddie")
Cordero, Angel Tomas, Jr.
France, William Henry Getty, Sr. ("Bill")
Gordon, Jeff
Gurney, Dan(iel) Sexton
Pincay, Laffit Alegando, Jr.
Unser, Al(fred), Sr.

Crompton, Samuel Willard
Holyoke Community College, Holyoke, Mass.
Budge, (John) Donald ("Don")
Connors, James Scott ("Jimmy")
Davenport, Lindsay
Gibson, Althea
Gonzales, Richard Alonzo ("Pancho")
Kramer, John Albert ("Jack")
Riggs, Robert Larrimore ("Bobby")
Trabert, Marion Anthony ("Tony")
Vines, Henry Ellsworth, Jr. ("Elly")
Wills (Moody), Helen Newington

Davidman, Richard
Downtown Financial Network, New York City
Seaver, George Thomas ("Tom")

Davidson, Abraham A.
Tyler School of Art, Temple University
Auerbach, Arnold ("Red")
Cousy, Robert ("Bob")

Davies, Richard O.
University of Nevada, Reno
Hawkins, Cornelius L. ("Connie")
Motley, Marion
Rose, Peter Edward ("Pete")
Snyder, James ("Jimmy the Greek")
Walsh, William ("Bill")

Davis, Allen F.
Temple University
Williams, Theodore Samuel ("Ted")

Decker, Stefanie
Stillwater, Okla.
Betz, Pauline May

Devine, Michael J.
Director, Harry S. Truman Library
Gowdy, Curt(is)
Wilson, Lewis Robert ("Hack")

Dinneen, Marcia B.
Bridgewater State College
Albright, Tenley Emma
Button, Richard Totten ("Dick")
Mosbacher, Emil, Jr. ("Bus")
Spitz, Mark Andrew

Dizikes, John
Cowell College
University of California at Santa Cruz
Sloan, James Forman ("Tod")

Dolson, Frank
Former Sports Editor, Philadelphia Enquirer
Bunning, James Paul David ("Jim")

DONAGHY, DANIEL
Ph.D. candidate, University of Rochester
Smith, Walter Wellesley ("Red")
DORINSON, JOSEPH
Long Island University, Brooklyn Campus
Robinson, Jack Roosevelt ("Jackie")
DOUGHERTY, DAVID C.
Loyola College in Maryland
Banks, Ernest ("Ernie")
Gibson, Pack Robert ("Bob")
West, Jerry Alan
DROBNICKI, JOHN A.
York College Library, City University of New York
Sawchuk, Terrance Gordon ("Terry")
DYER, LEIGH
Charlotte Observer, N.C.
Hamm, Mariel Margaret ("Mia")
Kwan, Michelle Wing
EARLY, GERALD
Washington University, St. Louis
Ali, Muhammad
ENDERS, ERIC
Historian, Cooperstown, N.Y.
Foster, Andrew ("Rube")
Haskins, Donald Lee
Scully, Vin(cent) Edward
Wells, Willie James
ENNIS, LISA A.
Georgia College and State University
Blazejowski, Carol Ann
Donovan, Anne
Holdsclaw, Chamique Shaunta
Leslie, Lisa DeShaun
Meyers, Ann Elizabeth
EVENSEN, BRUCE J.
DePaul University
Caray, Harry Christopher
Halas, George Stanley
Lujack, John Christopher, Jr. ("Johnny")
Rickard, George Lewis ("Tex")
FAIR, JOHN D.
Georgia College and State University
Anderson, Paul Edward
Davis, John Henry
Kono, Tommy Tamio
FEEHAN, SARAH
Charles Scribner's Sons
Jacobs, Helen Hull
FIGONE, AL
Humboldt State University, Arcata, Calif.
Holman, Nathan ("Nat")
FISCHEL, JACK
Millersville University
Dickey, William Malcolm ("Bill")
Schayes, Adolph ("Dolph")
FISCHLER, STAN
Fischler Hockey Service, New York City
Bossy, Michael Dean ("Mike")
Brimsek, Francis Charles ("Frank")
Chelios, Chris ("Chel")
Clarke, Robert Earle ("Bobby")
Mullen, Joseph ("Joey")
Parent, Bernard Marcel ("Bernie")
Schmidt, Milt(on) Conrad
FITZPATRICK, JANE BRODSKY
Stephen B. Luce Library, State University of New York Maritime College
Cooper, Cynthia
FOUNTAIN, CHARLES
Northeastern University
Rice, Grantland
FRICK, LISA
Freelance Writer, Columbia, Mo.
Carter, Don(ald) James
Fraser, Gretchen Claudia
Garciaparra, (Anthony) Nomar
McCormick, Pat(ricia) Joan
Miller, Reginald Wayne ("Reggie")
Thomas, Isiah Lord, III
FRIED, RONALD K.
Television Producer and Writer, New York City
Dundee, Angelo
FRISCH, PAUL A.
Library, Our Lady of the Lake University, San Antonio, Tex.
Frisch, Frank Francis ("Frankie")
Leonard, Walter Fenner ("Buck")
Walker, Moses Fleetwood ("Fleet")
GEMS, GERALD R.
North Central College, Naperville, Ill.
Grange, Harold Edward ("Red")
GENTILE, RICHARD H.
Independent Scholar, South Easton, Mass.
Ouimet, Francis DeSales
GIETSCHIER, STEVEN P.
The Sporting News
Hayes, Wayne Woodrow ("Woody")
Mays, Willie Howard
Thompson, John Robert, Jr.
GIGLIO, JAMES N.
Southwest Missouri State University
Musial, Stanley Frank ("Stan the Man")
GINTHER, KRISTAN
Writer, Los Angeles, Calif.
Favre, Brett Lorenzo

Gmelch, George
Union College
Rodriguez, Alex Emmanuel
Goodbody, Joan
Sterling C. Evans Library, Texas A&M University
Fitzsimmons, James Edward ("Sunny Jim")
Hartack, William J. ("Bill")
Shoemaker, William Lee ("Bill")
Stephens, Woodford Cefis ("Woody")
Goodhand, Glen R.
Society for International Hockey Research
Hall, Glenn Henry
Howe, Gordon ("Gordie")
Gordon, Dan
Writer, Seekonk, Mass.
Martinez, Pedro Jaime
Goudsouzian, Aram
Purdue University
Russell, William Felton ("Bill")
Gould, Karen
Independent Scholar, Austin, Tex.
Connolly, Maureen Catherine ("Little Mo")
Evert, Christine Marie ("Chris")
King, Billie Jean Moffit
Gould, Lewis L.
University of Texas at Austin (Emeritus)
Campbell, Earl Christian
Gozick, Christopher T.
Brookdale Community College
LeMond, Greg(ory) James
Graff, Henry F.
Professor Emeritus, Columbia University
Hubbell, Carl Owen
Greenwald, Richard A.
U.S. Merchant Marine Academy
McEnroe, John Patrick, Jr.
Navratilova, Martina
Gruver, Ed
Sportswriter and Author, Lancaster, Pa.
Conn, William David, Jr. ("Billy")
Greb, Edward Henry ("Harry")
Hornung, Paul Vernon
Koufax, Sanford ("Sandy")
Lombardi, Vincent Thomas ("Vince")
Harmond, Richard P.
St. John's University, New York
Chamberlain, Wilt(on) Norman
Hawkins, Judith
New York City
Hamilton, Scott Scovell

Healy, John David
Drew University
Boucher, Frank Xavier
Mikita, Stan
Hlavaty, Arthur D.
Independent Scholar, Yonkers, N.Y.
Barkley, Charles Wade
Butkus, Richard Marvin ("Dick")
Deford, Frank
Namath, Joseph William ("Joe")
Sanders, Deion Luwynn
Unitas, John Constantine ("Johnny")
Hodges, Graham Russell
Colgate University
Bing, David ("Dave")
Malone, Moses Eugene
Patterson, Floyd
Robinson, Walker Smith, Jr. ("Sugar Ray")
Hoogenboom, Lynn
Copy Editor, New York Times News Service
Dean, Jay Hanna ("Dizzy")
Hornbuckle, Adam R.
Independent Scholar, Alexandria, Va.
Beamon, Robert Alfred ("Bob")
Oerter, Al(fred) Adolph, Jr.
Howell, Kenneth Wayne
Texas A&M University
Foyt, A(nthony) J(oseph), Jr.
Petty, Richard Lee
Howlett, Charles F.
Adelphi University
Amityville Public Schools
Rockne, Knute Kenneth
Terry, William Harold ("Bill")
Hughes, Ellen Roney
National Museum of American History, Smithsonian Institution
Sullivan, John Lawrence
Ingram, Janet
Freelance Writer, Pittsburgh, Pa.
Barry, Richard Francis, III ("Rick")
Sanders, Summer Elisabeth
Swoopes, Sheryl Denise
Jackson, Faye Hall
University of Houston
Staley, Dawn
Summitt, Pat(ricia) Head
Jebsen, Harry, Jr.
Capital University, Columbus, Ohio
Comiskey, Charles Albert
Fox, Jacob Nelson ("Nellie")
Jackson, Joseph Jefferson Wofford ("Shoeless Joe")
Veeck, William L., Jr. ("Bill")

Jolly, J. Christopher
Oregon State University
Naismith, James
Prefontaine, Steve Roland
Jones, David
Freelance Writer, West Patterson, N.J.
Ewing, William ("Buck")
Radbourn, Charles Gardner ("Charley"; "Old Hoss")
Ward, John Montgomery
Jones, Jeremy
Baseball Hall of Fame Library
Brown, Mordecai Peter Centennial
Klem, William Joseph ("Bill")
Kaplan, Jim
Writer, Northampton, Mass.
Grove, Robert Moses ("Lefty")
Kashatus, William C.
Philadelphia Daily News
Bench, Johnny Lee
Carlton, Steven Norman
Mack, Connie
Schmidt, Michael Jack ("Mike")
Kerin, James R., Jr.
United States Military Academy
Blanchard, Felix Anthony, Jr. ("Doc")
Smith, John William
Kevles, Daniel J.
Yale University
Kiphuth, Robert John Herman ("Bob")
King, Robert L.
Chancellor, State University of New York
Mantle, Mickey Charles
Kinyatti, Njoki-Wa-
York College Library, City University of New York
Ashe, Arthur Robert, Jr.
Jones, Marion Lois
Knight, Candice Mancini
Writer, Missoula, Mont.
Henderson, Rickey
Kringen, Timothy
Portland, Oreg.
Armstrong, Lance
Biondi, Matt(hew)
Ryun, James Ronald ("Jim")
Krueger, Ray
The New York Times
Gotch, Frank Alvin
Ladda, Shawn
Manhattan College
De Varona, Donna
Nyad, Diana
Laffaye, Horace A.
Norwalk Hospital, Yale University School of Medicine
Hitchcock, Thomas, Jr. ("Tommy")
Oldfield, Berna Eli ("Barney")
Langran, Robert W.
Villanova University
Arizin, Paul Joseph
Liquori, Martin William, Jr. ("Marty")
Lankevich, George J.
Professor of History Emeritus, City University of New York
Chandler, Albert Benjamin ("Happy")
Lardner, Ringgold Wilmer ("Ring")
Lankford, Ronnie D., Jr.
Freelance Writer, Appomattox, Va.
Kelly, John Brendan, Sr. ("Jack")
Kelly, Michael Joseph ("King")
Madden, John Earl
Maynard, Don(ald) Rogers
Upshaw, Eugene Thurman, Jr. ("Gene")
Walker, Edward Patrick ("Mickey")
Leab, Daniel J.
Seton Hall University
Cartwright, Alexander Joy, Jr.
Tilden, William Tatem, Jr. ("Bill")
Levy, Alan H.
Slippery Rock University
Lillard, Joseph ("Joe")
Waddell, George Edward ("Rube")
Liggett, Lucy A.
Eastern Michigan University (Emeritus)
Runyon, Damon
Linet, Valerie
Writer, Montreal, Quebec, Canada
Mahre, Phil(ip)
Taylor, Marshall Walter ("Major")
Tyus, Wyomia
Lizzio, Joan
Freelance Writer, Hawley, Pa.
Hamill, Dorothy Stuart
Louissaint, Sabine
Writer, New York City
Jenner, (William) Bruce
Moses, Edwin Corley
Pippen, Scottie
Rice, Jerry Lee
Love, Johnnieque B.
University of Maryland Libraries
Drexler, Clyde
Robertson, Oscar Palmer
Lowe, Stephen R.
Olivet Nazarene University
Hagen, Walter C.
Jones, Robert Tyre, Jr. ("Bobby")

McBride, Francis R.
Herrick Library, Alfred University
McLain, Dennis Dale ("Denny")
McClellan, Keith
Sport Historian and Author, Oak Park, Mich.
Calhoun, Lee Quency
Campbell, Milton Gray ("Milt")
Gable, Dan(iel)
Metcalfe, Ralph Horace
Whitfield, Mal(vin) Greston
McCurdy, Sheila
State University of New York, Maritime College
Conner, Dennis W.
Jobson, Gary
McDowell, Markus H.
Pepperdine University
Davis, Glenn Woodward ("Junior")
Dickerson, Eric Demetric
Fears, Thomas Jesse ("Tom")
Hirsch, Elroy Leon ("Crazylegs")
Jones, David ("Deacon")
Waterfield, Robert Staton ("Bob")
McKelvey, G. Richard
Deerfield Academy, Deerfield, Mass.
MacPhail, Leland Stanford, Sr. ("Larry")
McLean, Michael
Independent Scholar, New York City
Ketchel, Stanley
LaMotta, Jake
Liston, Charles ("Sonny")
Maltby, Marc S.
Owensboro Community College
Bell, DeBenneville ("Bert")
Malvasi, Mark G.
Randolph-Macon College, Ashland, Va.
Abel, Sid(ney) Gerald
Delvecchio, Alex Peter ("Fats")
Gehringer, Charles Leonard ("Charlie")
Griffith, Emile Alphonse
Lindsay, Robert Blake Theodore ("Ted")
Orr, Robert Gordon ("Bobby")
Potvin, Denis Charles
Shore, Edward William ("Eddie")
Marc, David
Freelance Writer, Syracuse, N.Y.
Arledge, Roone Pinckney, Jr.
Costas, Robert Quinlan ("Bob")
Glickman, Martin Irving ("Marty")
Lewis, Frederick Carlton ("Carl")
Lilly, Kristine Marie
Louganis, Greg(ory) Efthimios
McKay, James McManus ("Jim")
Spahn, Warren Edward
Walsh, Ed(ward) Augustine
Markham, Reed B.
California State Polytechnic University (Emeritus)
Bryant, Kobe
Ditka, Mike
O'Neal, Shaq(uille) Rashaun
Young, Jon Steven ("Steve")
Markoe, Karen
State University of New York, Maritime College
Ford, Edward Charles ("Whitey")
Markusen, Bruce
National Baseball Hall of Fame and Museum, Cooperstown, N.Y.
Clemente (Walker), Roberto
Hunter, James Augustus ("Catfish"; "Jim")
Mason, Daniel S.
University of Maryland
Gretzky, Wayne Douglas ("The Great One")
Patrick, (Curtis) Lester
Massey, Daniel
Freelance Writer, Bronx, New York
Erving, Julius Winfield, II ("Dr. J.")
Ewing, Patrick Aloysius
Frazier, Walt, II ("Clyde")
Leetch, Brian
Olajuwon, Hakeem Abdul
Piazza, Michael Joseph ("Mike")
Mayo, Louise A.
County College of Morris, Randolph, N.J.
Jackson, Reginald Martinez ("Reggie")
Merron, Myrna W.
Mount Dora, Fla.
Greenberg, Henry Benjamin ("Hank")
Miller, Jeannie P.
Texas A&M University Libraries
Evans, Janet
Miller, Shannon Lee
Pettit, Robert E. Lee, Jr. ("Bob")
Millikin, Mark R.
Author, Chesapeake Beach, Md.
Foxx, James Emory ("Jimmie")
Robinson, Brooks Calbert, Jr.
Moore, Jack B.
University of Southern Florida
DiMaggio, Joseph Paul ("Joe"; "The Yankee Clipper")
Moran, Dorothy L.
Freelance Writer, Brooklyn, N.Y.
Chadwick, Florence May
Moran, John
Queens Borough Public Library, New York
Varipapa, Andrew ("Andy")

MULLINS, WILLIAM H.
Oklahoma Baptist University
Iba, Henry Payne ("Hank")
NAPOLI, PHILIP
Brooklyn College
Griffey, (George) Ken(neth), Jr.
NELSON, KELLY
Arizona State University
Berenson Abbott, Senda
Miller, Cheryl DeAnn
NELSON, MURRY R.
Pennsylvania State University
Beckman, John
Fulks, Joseph Franklin ("Joe")
Lapchick, Joseph Bohomiel ("Joe")
Luisetti, Angelo Enrico ("Hank")
Mikan, George Lawrence, Jr.
NIELSEN, FRED
University of Nebraska at Omaha
Brett, George Howard
OHL, JOHN KENNEDY
Mesa Community College
Traynor, Harold Joseph ("Pie")
Wagner, John Peter ("Honus")
ORIARD, MICHAEL
Oregon State University
Buchanan, Junious ("Buck")
PARKER, JUDITH A.
Federal Government, Portland, Oreg.
Ashford, Evelyn
Johnson, Michael
PETERS, SANDRA REDMOND
Southwest Missouri State University
Hogan, (William) Ben
Snead, Sam(uel) Jackson
Stern, William ("Bill")
PETERSON, F. ROSS
Utah State University
Maddux, Greg(ory) Alan
Malone, Karl Anthony ("Mailman")
Olsen, Merlin Jay
Stockton, John Houston
PETERSON, ROBERT W.
Sports Historian and Author, Ramsey, N.J.
Bell, James Thomas ("Cool Papa")
Dandridge, Ray(mond) Emmitt
Doby, Lawrence Eugene ("Larry")
Johnson, William Julius ("Judy")
PIERCE, MATTHEW J.
Columbia University
Blatnick, Jeff(rey)
POLLEY, MICHAEL
Columbia College of Missouri
Gehrig, (Henry) Lou(is)
Paige, Leroy Robert ("Satchel")
POLLOCK, ROBERT
Author, Bridgeport, Conn.
Lalas, Alexi
Meola, Tony
Rote, Kyle, Jr.
Warmerdam, Cornelius Anthony ("Dutch")
PORTER, DAVID L.
William Penn University
Anson, Adrian Constantine ("Cap"; "Pop")
Gwynn, Anthony Keith ("Tony")
Winfield, David Mark ("Dave")
PRUTER, ROBERT
Lewis University, Romeoville, Ill.
Bleibtrey, Ethelda
Heffelfinger, William Walter ("Pudge")
Pollard, Frederick Douglas ("Fritz")
QUARATIELLO, ARLENE R.
Freelance Writer and Indexer, Atkinson, N.H.
Heiss Jenkins, Carol Elizabeth
RADER, BENJAMIN G.
University of Nebraska, Lincoln
Cobb, Ty(rus) Raymond
Rickey, Branch Wesley
RAFFETY, MATTHEW TAYLOR
Columbia University
Baylor, Elgin
Jones, K. C.
Smith, Osborne Earl ("Ozzie")
Wilkens, Leonard Randolph ("Lenny")
REGALADO, SAMUEL O.
California State University, Stanislaus
Sosa, Samuel Peralta ("Sammy")
RILEY, JAMES A.
Negro Leagues Baseball Museum, Canton, Ga., and Past President, Society for American Baseball Research
Charleston, Oscar McKinley ("Charlie")
Griffith, Clark Calvin
Lloyd, John Henry ("Pop")
ROGERS, C. PAUL
Southern Methodist School of Law
Gomez, Vernon Louis ("Lefty")
McGraw, John Joseph
Roberts, Robin Evan
Speaker, Tris(tram) E.
ROSEN, HY
Freelance Writer, New York City
Robustelli, Andrew ("Andy")

ROSEN, JEFFREY S.
Spotswood High School, New Jersey
Johnson, John Arthur ("Jack")
Ott, Mel(vin) Thomas

RUNION, JEROMY
University of Tennessee
Johnson, Robert Glenn, Jr. ("Junior")
Unser, Al(fred), Jr.

SAGERT, KELLY BOYER
Freelance Writer, Lorain, Ohio
Cunningham, Glenn
Weatherspoon, Teresa
Yamaguchi, Kristi Tsuya

SAPIENZA, MADELINE
Independent Scholar, Washington, D.C.
Crabbe, Clarence Linden ("Buster")
Henie, Sonja
Weissmuller, Peter John ("Johnny")

SAVAGE, STEVEN P.
Eastern Kentucky University
Jacobs, Hirsch
Longden, John Eric ("Johnny")

SCHAFFER, THOMAS
Texas A&M University
Gillman, Sid(ney)

SCHARNHORST, GARY
University of New Mexico
Berra, Lawrence Peter ("Yogi")
Maris, Roger Eugene
Stengel, Charles Dillon ("Casey")

SCHERER, JOHN L.
Minneapolis, Minn.
Carter, Cris D.
Page, Alan Cedric

SCHIFF, ANDREW J.
Brooklyn, N.Y.
Chadwick, Henry
Wright, William Henry ("Harry")

SCHMIDT, RAYMOND
Journalist and Author, Ventura, Calif.
Harmon, Thomas Dudley ("Tom")
Hubbard, (Robert) Cal
Hutson, Don(ald) Montgomery
McNamee, Graham
Torre, Joseph Paul ("Joe")
Van Brocklin, Norm(an) Mack

SCHUCK, RAYMOND I.
Chandler, Ariz..
Bonds, Barry Lamar
Johnson, Randall David ("Randy")
Ripken, Cal(vin) Edward, Jr.

SCRIBNER, CHARLES, IV
Charles Scribner's Sons
Baker, Hobart Amory Hare ("Hobey")

SEEMAN, COREY
University of Toledo
Aaron, Henry Louis ("Hank")
Anderson, George Lee ("Sparky")
Flood, Curt(is) Charles
McCovey, Willie Lee
Robinson, Frank
Steinbrenner, George Michael, III

SHERWIN, MARTIN J.
Tufts University
Berg, Patricia Jane ("Patty")
Nelson, (John) Byron, Jr.
Nicklaus, Jack William
Palmer, Arnold Daniel ("Arnie")
Suggs, (Mae) Louise
Trevino, Lee Buck
Watson, Thomas Sturges ("Tom")
Woods, Eldrick ("Tiger")

SHOR, RACHEL
Queens Borough Public Library, New York City
Kidd, William Winston ("Billy")
Street, Picabo

SMALLS, F. ROMALL
Journalist and Media Consultant, Westchester County, N.Y.
Reed, Willis, Jr.

SMALLWOOD, JAMES M.
Oklahoma State University
Bowden, Robert Cleckler ("Bobby")
Bryant, Paul William ("Bear")
Sanders, Barry
Snider, Edwin Donald ("Duke")

SMALLWOOD, JAMES M.
Oklahoma State University
Warner, Glenn Scobey ("Pop")

SMITH, JOHN KARES
State University of New York, Oswego
Povich, Shirley Lewis

SMITH, RONALD A.
Pennsylvania State University
Camp, Walter Chauncey

SOLON, LEONARD R.
Physicist and Educator, Fort Pierce, Fla.
Leonard, Benny

STARK, DOUGLAS A.
Librarian and Archivist, Naismith Memorial Basketball Hall of Fame
Havlicek, John Joseph
Murphy, Calvin Jerome

Newell, Peter ("Pete")
Pollard, James Clifford ("Jim")

STERTZ, STEPHEN A.
Dowling College
Brundage, Avery

STEVENSON, SANDRA
Skating Correspondent, The Daily Telegraph (United Kingdom)
Jenkins, David Wilkinson
Jenkins, Hayes Alan

STIMAGE, RACHENETTA V.
University of Texas Medical Branch
Hayes, Elvin Ernest

STOLL, SHARON KAY
University of Idaho, Center for Ethics (Director)
Heiden, Eric Arthur

STYCZYNSKI, JACK
Writer and Researcher, New York City
Aikman, Troy Kenneth
Carter, Vincent Lamar, Jr. ("Vince")
Jordan, Michael Jeffrey ("Air")
Landry, Thomas Wade ("Tom")
Penske, Roger S.
Smith, Dean Edwards
Smith, Emmitt James, III
Staubach, Roger Thomas
Worthy, James Ager

SU, DI
York College, City University of New York
Iverson, Allen Ezail
Lobo, Rebecca Rose
Mourning, Alonzo Harding, Jr.

SUDDERTH, R. JAKE
Columbia University
Frazier, Joe
Haynes, Marques Oreole
Hein, Mel(vin) John
Lemon, Meadow George ("Meadowlark")
Rozelle, Alvin Ray ("Pete")
Spalding, Albert Goodwill ("A.G.")
Stern, David
Tatum, Reece ("Goose")

SULLIVAN, JAMES J., III
State University of New York, Fashion Institute
Conner, Bart
Esposito, Phil(ip) Anthony
Jeter, Derek Sanderson
Lemieux, Mario

SUMNER, JIM L.
North Carolina Museum of History
Krzyzewski, Michael William ("Mike")
Thompson, David O'Neal

SUSSER, BENNET, ESQ.
Livinston, N.J.
Monroe, Earl Vernon, Jr.

SUSSER, MARGALIT
Queens Borough Public Library System
Boitano, Brian Anthony

TASSINARI, EDWARD J.
State University of New York, Maritime College
Heinz, Wilfred Charles ("Bill")
McElhenny, Hugh Edward, Jr.
Matson, Oliver Genoa, II ("Ollie")

TAYLOR, JON E.
Historian, Independence, Mo.
Allen, Marcus LeMarr
Allen, Forrest Clare ("Phog")
Archibald, Nathaniel ("Nate"; "Tiny")
Hunt, Lamar
Osborne, Thomas William ("Tom")
Selmon, Lee Roy

THORNTON, JOYCE K.
Texas A&M University Libraries
Duncan, Timothy Theodore
Griffith Joyner, Florence Delorez ("Flo Jo")

TOBIAS, TODD
San Diego Hall of Champions Sports Museum
Fingers, Roland Glen ("Rollie")
Walton, William Theodore, III ("Bill")
Winslow, Kellen Boswell

TOMASINO, ADRIANA C.
Ph.D. Candidate, City University of New York
Fleming, Peggy Gale
Joyner-Kersee, Jacqueline ("Jackie")
Krone, Julieanne Louise ("Julie")
Lopez, Nancy Marie
Retton, Mary Lou

TRIMBLE, PATRICK A.
Pennsylvania State University
Kaline, Al(bert) William
Palmer, James Alvin ("Jim")
Ruppert, Jacob
Ruth, George Herman ("Babe")

VINSON, BETTY B.
Freelance Writer, Mobile, Ala.
Hannah, John Allen
Starr, Bryan Bartlett ("Bart")

VORPERIAN, JOHN
Attorney, White Plains, N.Y.
Kiner, Ralph McPherran
Largent, Steve

WATSON, DENNIS
Attorney, Ann Arbor, Mich.
Rodgers, William Henry ("Bill")
Shorter, Frank Charles

WEDGE, ELEANOR F.
Freelance Writer and Editor, New York City
Frick, Ford Christopher
Lajoie, Nap(oleon)
WEISBLAT, TINKY "DAKOTA"
Museum of Television and Radio
Cosell, Howard
WHITMIRE, TIM
Charlotte Observer, N.C.
Durocher, Leo Ernest
Reese, Harold Henry ("Pee Wee")
Rupp, Adolph Frederick
WILES, TIMOTHY J.
National Baseball Hall of Fame and Museum, Cooperstown, N.Y.
Brickhouse, John Beasley ("Jack")
WINTERS, KELLY
Freelance Writer, Bayville, N.Y.
Boston, Ralph
Connolly, Harold V. ("Hal")
Dillard, Harrison
Ewell, Henry Norwood ("Barney")
Fosbury, Richard Douglas ("Dick")
Hayes, Robert ("Bob"; "Bullet")
O'Brien, (William) Parry, Jr.
WUSHANLEY, YING
Millersville University
Akers, Michelle Anne
Babashoff, Shirley
Blair, Bonnie
Ederle, Gertrude Caroline ("Trudy")
Sampras, Peter ("Pete")
ZARNOWSKI, FRANK
Mount St. Mary's College
Johnson, Rafer Lewis
Mathias, Robert Bruce ("Bob")
Richards, Robert Eugene ("Bob")

OCCUPATIONS INDEX, VOLUMES 1–2

See also the Alphabetical List of Subjects beginning on p. 553.

ALPHABETICAL LIST OF SUBJECTS, VOLUMES 1–2

See also the Occupations Index beginning on p. 545.